For Reference

Not to be taken from this room

Illustrated Dictionary
of
Place Names

Illustrated
Dictionary
of
Place **N**ames
United States and Canada

Edited by KELSIE B. HARDER

A HUDSON GROUP BOOK

VAN NOSTRAND REINHOLD COMPANY
NEW YORK   CINCINNATI   ATLANTA   DALLAS   SAN FRANCISCO
LONDON   TORONTO   MELBOURNE

Van Nostrand Reinhold Company Regional Offices:
New York Cincinnati Chicago Millbrae Dallas

Van Nostrand Reinhold Company International Offices:
London Toronto Melbourne

Copyright © 1976 by Kelsie B. Harder

Library of Congress Catalog Card Number: 75-26907
ISBN: 0-442-23069-9

Manufactured in the United States of America

Published by Van Nostrand Reinhold Company
450 West 33rd Street, New York, N.Y. 10001

Published simultaneously in Canada by Van Nostrand Reinhold Ltd.

15 14 13 12 11 10 9 8 7 6 5 4 3 2

Library of Congress Cataloging in Publication Data

Harder, Kelsie B.
  Illustrated dictionary of place names, United States
and Canada.

  "A Hudson group book."
  Includes bibliography,
  1. Names, Geographical—United States. 2. Unit-
ed States—History, Local. I. Title. II. Title:
Illustrated dictionary of place names, United States and
Canada.
E155.H37   917.3'003   75-26907
ISBN 0-442-23069-9

Book design—Martin Connell

TO LOUISE

Acknowledgements

A dictionary of place names could not have been compiled without the help of many persons and without reference to the vast amount of source material that is now available. Space does not allow naming the thousands of individuals who completed questionnaires and otherwise furnished material concerning names in their local areas. These generous people include local historians, overworked postmasters (both women and men), and librarians who probably had more important duties.

The greatest debt is owed to Robert O'Brien of Morningside Editorial Associates, who proposed and organized this dictionary, edited much of the material, and saw it through the press. Furthermore, he was responsible for all Canadian entries and wrote most of the entries for habitation places on the Eastern seaboard and in the South, all entries for names of states, and many of the headnotes. He was a true collaborator throughout the time of compiling this work.

The inspirational debt belongs to Professor George R. Stewart, whose *Names on the Land,* which I read for the first time in 1951 while studying with Professor Thomas Pyles, led me to an academic lifetime of devotion to the study of names in all their aspects. Professor Stewart's pervasive influence can be seen throughout the dictionary, as it can be seen throughout any modern dictionary of place names. All of us who have made a study of place names must follow in the wake of his encompassing and rigorous scholarship.

To Mr. Elsdon C. Smith, probably the world's foremost authority on personal names, I express my gratitude for his continuous insistence that I undertake and complete the project. Time and again over the years, I have turned to Mr. Smith for guidance in my work with the American Name Society. He and his wife Clare have always responded willingly.

Personal thanks are due to Edwin H. Bryan, Jr., Helen Carlson, Anthony O. Tyler, Barbara Yerdon, Ann LaShomb, Anne Sampson, Rose Ellers, Margaret M. Bryant, E. Wallace McMullen, Otto Whittaker, Israel Kaplan, Franklin R. Stern, and Conrad M. Rothrauff. Each contributed in some way, sometimes without knowing it. Also, the reference librarians at the Crumb Memorial Library, State University College, Potsdam, N. Y., helped me obtain obscure articles and long out-of-print books that I could not have consulted otherwise.

The editorial services of specialists at Morningside Editorial Associates have been of inestimable value. Mr. Gorton Carruth, president of Morningside, has a special knack for shoring up flagging spirits and correcting bad

ACKNOWLEDGEMENTS

prose. Diane Silberstein and Susan Quinn have done a heroic job of shepherding the manuscript through the editorial process, ably assisted by Lisa Silberstein, Ellen Gross, Elva Toutoundjian, and Lisa Goldman. I also owe a debt to the copy editors Mrs. Frances Halsey and Miss Mary Grace and the contributors Gene Brown, Richard Atkinson, Harriet Irgang, and Linda Skernick. The professional help of picture researcher Marion Urban was a major contribution to the book. Nor can I overlook the kindness and patience of the New York Public Library's Picture Collection and Print Division or Miss Claire Figley of the Canadian Consulate General in New York.

My wife Louise has patiently listened to my grumblings, put up with my frustrations, and chased down place names on maps, meanwhile keeping Frank, Thomas, and Ann from shifting piles of books, manuscript, and questionnaires. Two older sons, Gerald and Dennis, have assisted in one way or another, sometimes by merely mowing the lawn.

It is inevitable that errors in listing and in interpretation will appear, although I hope that they have been held to a minimum. They are my responsibility, and I welcome corrections and discussion.

The bibliography lists major printed sources and could have been extended to several hundred entries if articles and notes had been included. Their omission does not lessen their importance.

Kelsie B. Harder
Potsdam, N.Y.

Introduction

NATURE OF NAMING

The Europeans who came to the American areas covered here did not come to lands without languages and without names. At least 43 different Indian language families have been identified, meaning that several thousand dialects existed. The languages, however, were so different that only confusion has remained in regard to both the Indian languages and also the Indian names that have survived in much different shapes from their earlier forms, and all too often have been "folk etymologized" into the European language used in a particular area. In general, these languages are now French, Spanish, and English, the latter predominant in the United States, and French very important in Canada.

⋅What occurred is much what happened in other places where conquerors carried their languages into linguistic areas of the native inhabitants. In the Americas, wherever the European language came into contact with a local Indian language the latter was in many cases eradicated, or, worse, ignored. In fact, the Indians themselves were too often eradicated. Still, literally many thousands of names in the United States and Canada have their origin in Indian names. A phenomenon which can be called "onomastic interfacing" occurred; that is, the sometimes abrasive rubbing together of languages, in which aspects of two languages coalesce and different types of names — even languages — develop. For instance, *Bogalusa*, in Louisiana, has been rendered in Spanish, English, French, and American folk spellings: *Arroyo negro o Bos-holizà*; *Black Creek*, *Bogue Luca*, *Bogue Loosa*, and *Bogue Lusa*. In the Bogalusa area, each language has been dominant at certain times in relatively recent history. See *Bogulusa* in the glossary. Onomastic interfacing can be seen working also in such prosaic names as *Louisville* and *Lewisville*, *Mount Hope* and *Montaup*, or *Tickabum* and *Choctaw*.

The problem with naming, as is noted above, is that names seem to have little significance or meaning except as identifiers. Names tend to slip around, not stay in place, and change according to the whims of the public. The flood of public sympathy that changed Cape Canaveral to Cape Kennedy in November, 1963, is an example. (The name has now reverted back to Cape Canaveral.) This is not an isolated case, only a prominent and famous one, whereas every day, probably, a local board of some kind changes the name of a street, a school, a local landmark, to suit its sudden commemorative, ameliorative, or political purpose.

To anyone who has tried to study the vestiges of Indian names, it is obvious that they were abstracted from the lexicon or vocabulary of the particular language, and seldom, if ever, bestowed for commemorative purposes. The name was an identifier, "at the fishing place," "at the point," "at the falls," etc. In another sense, the names, as such, were directives, tracking names for others who needed to find the same place. Of course, the names and places changed from unit to unit, in some cases nation to nation, as each moved through the place, or places. It was a sensible method of naming, one that was practical and meaningful. The Europeans, on the other hand, with a sense of history, ancestral pride, and nostalgia, named with a vengeance and with not much meaning. Little practicality obtains in naming Chester, somewhere, after Chester, England, since no identification is achieved. It is a sound that fits the English wordstock, the intonation pattern, and the familiarity. It also reflects a lot of homesickness, although no stigma need be attached to that.

Names can be meaningful in the sense that they preserve vocabulary items that might otherwise have been lost. Remnants of Indian languages are being discovered in the names that appear now in Latinized form and in English spelling. Although exactness can never be achieved, an intimation of the form of the original language can be approximated. Names can also be meaningful outside the linguistic context. Europeans, with their sharpened sense of honor and nationalism, name for historical purposes, and have surrounded the earth — and what they know of outer space — with names from their classical and historical background. These are continuation names, the attempt to preserve the present for posterity. It no doubt is a noble projection, for the United States and Canada have thousands of such commemorative, continuation (genealogical), and historical names. They illustrate our self-esteem.

The names in the text illustrate the pride of these three countries, the aspirations, the hope, the desire for individual freedom, and their ideologies. On the other hand, the names also reflect darker sides of the human personality. This is no indictment, for this has occurred in the renaming of many places on this globe. Renaming occurs constantly, since names do not serve, as so often they did in our Indian cultures, as identifiers, but as meaningful sounds for national aspirations. Such is the naming process.

Most "European" names reflect their transatlantic roots as illustrated in name after name on the east coastal areas of Canada and the United States; *Nova Scotia*, *New England*, *New York*, etc. They also named for themselves such features as streams, lakes, mountains, and anything else that could get on a map. They named places for wives, husbands, daughters, sons, girl friends, and boyfriends. It was a democratic process, for no one can remember who they were nor what they did, except that they moved westward, or died in the obscure area that commemorates their name. It was a good naming process, although not necessarily memorable.

METHOD

George R. Stewart, "A Classification of Place Names," *Names*, II (1954), 1-12, has outlined naming methods that explorers and settlers used as they moved from east to west across the continent of North America. A name can be applied for almost any reason, according to the mind-set of the namer. Despite the reasons for application of a name, the categories of names are somewhat limited.

Descriptive names seem to be common in all languages. As Professor J. B. Rudnyckyj "Names in Contact. Canadian Pattern," *Place Names and Language Contact* (Quebec, 1972), 293-302, notes, a descriptive name often is translated through intervening languages, as from Indian to French to English. This simple translation, he calls "full assimilation: *Red River* from *Rivière Rouge* from a corresponding Indian name. Description, however, may be only partial, for the feature described may hold true in one part of the area named. *Falls River* may have only one "falls."

Possessive and personal names account for probably the majority of names in Canada and the United States. Such names as *Jones Creek*, *Grooms Hollow*, and *Governor Thomas E. Dewey Thruway* are ubiquitous. Incident names occur as the result of an event that took place on or near the area named. Names of battles, saints, and psychological conditions usually reflect incidents. Places such as *St. Augustine*, *St. Lawrence*, and *San Diego* were named by Spanish and French explorers for the Day of the Saint, or the day on which the place was sighted. Commemorative names usually honor a place or a person. In the United States, for instance, such names as Washington, Jefferson, Franklin, and Jackson honor persons of importance in the history of the country. These are always commemorative, as are a great many lesser known names.

The naming process continues, for such is the characteristic of humans. A place must be named, either with a number or a vocabulary item. It is almost a commonplace that a place with no name is not a place.

SCOPE

The study of place names in the United States and Canada can easily encompass a lifetime, indeed several lifetimes, and still remain incomplete. At some point such a study must halt, lest it continue endlessly. Such then is the scope of this dictionary, truncated, but intended for the generalist and for those who wish a ready reference to a place and a name, especially as to its location and origin.

The names of all provinces, states, provincial and state capitals, counties, and county seats are listed. An attempt is also made to include all cities with a population of 2,500 or more, based on census reports of 1970. The editor discovered early, however, that some habitation names in this category did not qualify, sometimes merely because a ZIP code number denoted only a postal facility and not a name. Occasionally, a local informant stated simply that the "city" did not exist. Many habitation places, listed as villages, or towns, or cities, with less than 2,500 persons are entered because of historical importance, or because a feature has taken its name from the place, or because of uniqueness.

Major features have been glossed. Coastal generics and their specifics, such as bays, capes, inlets, channels, gulfs, harbors, sounds, islands, reefs, and points, have been selected for entry generally on the basis of their historical importance, linguistic interest, or geographical location. Since so much of the United States and Canada is bordered by oceans, seas, and gulfs, these names have a significance that can easily be underestimated. History lives in such names as *Bering Sea*, *Hudson Bay*, *Long Island Sound*, *Gulf of Mexico*, *Pacific Ocean*, *Great Egg Harbor Inlet*, *Alexander Archipelago*, *Hecate Strait*, and *Santa Barbara Channel*, to mention some of the more obvious ones. Lesser known may be *Winyah Bay*, *Point No Point*, *Chandeleur Island*, *Buzzards Bay*, and *Cook Inlet*.

Internal features constitute a large number of geographical entries, probably more than do coastal names, partially because land features are not limited by a surrounding body of water, or the expanse of a large body of water. Entries are made for mountain ranges, peaks (mount, mountain), streams, lakes, bayous, ponds, and reservoirs. Both the specific and the generic appear in each feature listing, although the specific is listed first, as *Michigan, Lake*, unless the generic is an integral or specific part of the name, as *Lake City*.

Internal, or land, features have also been sometimes narrowly selected. For instance, *Driskill Mountain*, Louisiana, elevation 535 ft., is listed because in the context of the area it is important, whereas probably hundreds of peaks in the Rockies of the United States, in Western Canada, and in Alaska have been omitted because of their commonness, unless, such as *Mount McKinley*, there is a prominence about the peak that will cause it to be selected. Some features are entered because they reveal a pattern in naming; for instance, *Jeremy's River* illustrates the use of a personal name as well as a possessive one, as does *Watts Bar*, the latter having been extended to a dam and a reservoir. In some states, too, clusters of names exist because of legal boundaries. In New York, a village and a town will have the same name, although the village is incorporated into the town, the latter a legal boundary. The village, however, may have a larger population than would a city in other states. In general, when names occur in this manner, only one entry is made.

Headings for important names, such as states, presidents, historical figures, and the like, will have one entry, with places having the same name and derived from the heading being listed beneath. If, however, the same name has a different origin, it will be treated separately. *Marshall* occurs most often on places named for John Marshall, the statesman and Supreme Court Justice. But *Marshall* is also a name that occurs often throughout the land since there are other Marshalls who have achieved enough fame or property ownership to have places named for them.

Names derived from Indian languages appear often. Authorities seldom agree on the meaning of these names, sometimes not even on their linguistic origin. Although each such name has been checked against available sources, it must be understood that all too often only approximate meanings can be given.

Style

Main entries appear in boldface capital letters and are alphabetized letter by letter whether the entry is one or more words; **NORTHHAMPTON** is followed by **NORTH BEND,** for instance. When there is more than one entry for a particular name, the entries are arranged and alphabetized as follows: any main heading followed by a period appears first. Next come place names alphabetized by state (the full name, not the abbreviation), regardless of whether the entry is a town or county. Intermingled with these are natural features, alphabetized by specific and personal names, alphabetized by the forename. An example of this order is: CLARK, George; CLARK Co., Idaho; CLARK Co., Kan.; CLARK, Lake, Alaska; CLARK Co., Nev.; CLARK, N.J.; CLARK, Newton; CLARK, William.

Where there are several place names from a common source, subheadings appear below the boldface main entries. These are set in italics, except for the specific, which is in regular type, unless it is an integral part of the name. For example, under the entry **NIAGARA,** *Niagara* Falls, N.Y.-Ont., refers to the actual falls, whereas *Niagara Falls,* Ont., refers to the town in Ontario. The subheadings are listed according to the following priorities: state names appear first; followed by counties, listed alphabetically by state; towns, alphabetically by state; and finally features, alphabetically by specific. Following these are place names that combine the generic with another syllable or word; e.g., *West Pittsburg*, Calif. under the main entry **PITT.** However, if the generic is preceded by a word or syllable whose first letter alphabetically precedes that of the generic, then this place name is listed before the counties. For example, *East Pittsburg*, Pa., comes before *Pitt* Co., N.C., under the main head **PITT.**

Each town is followed by its county of location, and each county by its county seat. Natural features are followed by counties only when two or more identically named features occur in the same state.

Foreign and Indian words also appear in italics and are identified as to the language or dialect from which they are derived. Translations follow in quotes, in this style: from Choctaw *okkattahoola,* "beautiful white water."

A

ABAJO PEAK, Utah. From Spanish, "low."

ABBAYE, Point, Mich., on Huron Bay. For a local settler.

ABBEVILLE For the city of Abbeville, Somme, France.
Abbeville Co., S.C. (co. seat, *Abbeville*).
Abbeville, La. (parish seat of Vermilion., Parish). Named by settlers from Nova Scotia.
Abbeville, S.C. (co. seat of *Abbeville* Co.). Named by Huguenot settlers from France.

ABBEVILLE, Ala. (co. seat of Henry Co.). *Abbe-*, from an Indian name, variously translated as "panther," "grove," "dogwood," or "tree."

ABBEVILLE, Ga. (co. seat of Wilcox Co.). For Abbie McDuffie, wife of a prominent citizen.

ABBOTSFORD, B.C. For Harry B. Abbott, railwayman, brother of Sir John Abbott, prime minister of Canada (1891-92).

ABBOTT BUTTE, Ore. For Hiram Abbott, an early settler.

ABBOTTSFORD, Que. From the parish of St. Paul d'Abbottsford, for the Reverend Joseph Abbott, Anglican minister.

ABERDEEN For the county (Aberdeenshire) in Scotland, or for the city of Aberdeen. The name is popular in America in areas settled by Scottish immigrants or their descendants.
Aberdeen, Md. (Harford Co.).
Aberdeen, Miss. (co. seat of Monroe Co.).
Aberdeen, S.Dak. (co. seat of Brown Co.).
Aberdeen, Wash. (Grays Harbor Co.).

ABERNETHY, Sask. For a pioneer family.

ABERT Lake, Ore. Named by John C. Fremont for J. J. Abert, an officer of the United States Topographical Engineers.

ABIATHAR PEAK, Wyo. For Charles Abiathar White, of the United States Geological Survey of 1885.

ABILENE Biblical name (Luke 3:1), referring to a region of Syria.
Abilene, Kan. (co. seat of Dickinson Co.).
Abilene, Tex. (co. seat of Taylor Co.). For *Abilene*, Kan.

ABINGDON For Abingdon, Berkshire, England.
Abingdon, Ill. (Knox Co.).
Abingdon, Va. (co. seat of Washington Co.). Origin of name disputed: variously attributed to Mary Washington's home town; a Lord Abingdon; Daniel Boone's home, Abingdon, Pa.
Abingdon Creek, N.C.

ABINGTON For Great and Little Abington, Cambridgeshire, England.
Abington, Conn. (Windham Co.), town.

1

Abington, Mass. (Plymouth Co.), town. Or possibly for Lord Abington (1653-1699), a friend of Massachusetts Governor Dudley.

Abington, Pa. (Montgomery Co.).

ABITIBI For an Indian tribe of Algonquian linguistic stock that settled on the lake of the same name. The name, meaning "halfway water," derives from the lake's position halfway between the Ottawa River and Hudson Bay.

Abiti Co., Que. (co. seat, Amos).

Abiti Lake, Ont.

Abitibi River, Ont. Flows generally N to Moose R.

ABRAHAM Mount, Vt. For Abraham LINCOLN with Biblical overtones.

ABRAHAM MOUNT, Me. Origin of name not known, but probably Biblical.

ABRAM VILLAGE, P.E.I. For Abraham Arsenault, first settler.

ABSECON, N.J. (Atlantic Co.). From an Algonquian tribal name, *Absegami*, "place of swans."

ACADIA An early name (French *Acadie*) for the area that now includes Nova Scotia, New Brunswick, Prince Edward Island, and parts of Quebec and Maine. In 1755 the British displaced several thousand French settlers south to the present United States. Some continued southward to the territory later to become Louisiana, where their descendants are called Cajuns. Their journey is the subject of Longfellow's poem "Evangeline." Origin of the name is obscure, perhaps from Micmac *acada* (or *algatig* or *akade*), "camp," "village," or "place of abundance," or from Arcadia, a region in ancient Greece.

Acadia Parish, La. (parish seat, Crowley).

Acadia Natl. Park, Me.

ACCOMAC, Va. (co. seat of Accomack Co.). See ACCOMACK.

ACCOMACK Co., Va. (co. seat, Accomac). For a subtribe of the Powhatans living on the Eastern Shore of Virginia. The name is said to mean "the other side,"

since the tribe lived across Chesapeake Bay from their kinsmen. The county name retains the older spelling.

ACKERMAN, Miss. (co. seat of Choctaw Co.). For William K. Ackerman, president of the Illinois Central and Gulf railroad.

ACKIA BATTLEGROUND NATL. MONUMENT, Miss. For a Chickasaw village nearby; meaning unknown. It was established in 1938 to commemorate the 1736 battle between French forces and Chickasaws. The French were defeated, enabling English settlers to enter the area.

ACTON Probably for Acton, Middlesex, England, a center of Puritan activity during Cromwell's time.

Acton, Mass. (Middlesex Co.), town.

Acton, Ont.

Acton, Vale, Que.

ACUSHNET From Algonquian *acushena*, "at the cove" or "swimming place."

Acushnet, Mass. (Bristol Co.), town.

Acushnet River, Mass.

ACWORTH, Ga. (Cobb Co.). For an Acworth in New Hampshire.

ADA Co., Idaho (co. seat, Boise). For Ada Riggs, the first white child born in Boise.

ADA, Minn. (co. seat of Norman Co.). For the deceased six-year old daughter of William H. Fisher, an official of the St. Paul and Pacific railroad.

ADA, Okla. (co. seat of Pontotoc Co.). For Ada Reed, daughter of the first postmaster.

ADAIR, John (1757-1840), Kentucky soldier and statesman. He served as governor (1820-24).

Adair Co., Iowa (co. seat, Greenfield).

Adair Co., Ky. (co. seat, Columbia).

Adair Co., Mo. (co. seat, Kirksville).

ADAIR Co., Okla. (co. seat, Stillwell). For a prominent Cherokee family.

ADAMS Co., Colo. (co. seat, Brighton). For Alva Adams (1850-1922), Colorado statesman and governor (1887-89; 1897-99).

ADAMS, John (1735-1826), second President of the United States (1797-1801), from Massachusetts. One of the leaders of the American Revolution, he was a member of the Continental Congress (1774-77) and a signer of the Declaration of Independence (1776). Adams was a commissioner to France (1777-78), minister to the United Provinces of the Netherlands (1780), and one of three commissioners who negotiated the peace treaty with Great Britain (1778). He served as minister to Great Britain (1778) and as vice-president of the United States (1789-97). He was the father of John Quincy Adams.
Adams Co., Idaho (co. seat, Council).
Adams Co., Iowa (co. seat, Corning).
Adams Co., Miss. (co. seat, Natchez).
Adams Co., Neb. (co. seat, Hastings).
Adams Co., Ohio (co. seat, West Union).
Adams Co., Pa. (co. seat, Gettysburg).
Adams Co., Wash. (co. seat, Ritzville).
Adams Co., Wis. (co. seat, Friendship).
Adams, Mount, N.H., in the Presidential Range of the White Mtns.
Adams Head, Utah. Peak.

John Adams, the nation's second President, lived to see his son, John Quincy Adams, become America's sixth chief executive. [*New York Public Library*]

ADAMS, John Quincy (1767-1848), sixth President of the United States (1825-29), from Massachusetts. Adams was U.S. senator (1803-08), minister to Russia (1809-11), and an American negotiator of the Treaty of Ghent (1814), which ended the War of 1812. In 1815 he served as minister to Great Britain. Later he was secretary of state (1817-25) under Monroe and a U.S. representative (1831-48). He was the son of John Adams.
Adams Co., Ill. (co. seat, Quincy).
Adams Co., Ind. (co. seat, Decatur).

ADAMS Co., N.Dak. (co. seat, Hettinger). For a local citizen.

ADAMS, Samuel (1722-1803), Massachusetts statesman. Ardent patriot and leader of the "extreme" faction in the pre-Revolutionary period, he helped organize the Sons of Liberty, participated in the Boston Tea Party, signed the Declaration of Independence, and later served as governor of Massachusetts (1794-97).
Adams, Mass. (Berkshire Co.), town and village. Earlier, East Hoosuck.
Adams Natl. Historical Site, Mass.
North Adams, Mass. (Berkshire Co.).

ADDISON, Joseph (1672-1719), British essayist, poet, dramatist, and statesman, best known for his literary contributions to *The Tatler* (1709-11) and *The Spectator* (1711-12), which he co-founded with Sir Richard Steele. He was a commissioner for trade with the colonies (1716) and secretary of state for the southern department (1717-18).
Addison Co., Vt. (co. seat, Middlebury).
Addison, Ill. (Du Page Co.).

ADEL, Ga. (co. seat, Cook Co.). From Phil*adel*phia.

ADEL, Iowa (co. seat of Dallas Co.). From "a dell," for the valley in which the town is located.

ADIRONDACK For an Algonquian tribe. They were dubbed "tree-eaters" by their enemies, as first recorded by Roger Williams, who confused the tribe with the Mohawks. The meaning of the name has been lost but a semblance of the sound form

has been pepetuated in the present spelling.
Adirondack Mountains, N.Y. Highest peak, Mt. Marcy.
Adirondack Park, N.Y. Six million acres, the largest wilderness area east of the Mississippi.

ADMIRALTY ISLAND, Alaska, in the Alexander Archipelago. Named by George Vancouver in 1794 in honor of the British Admiralty.

ADOBE CREEK RESERVOIR, Colo. For a creek, in turn for the Indian dwellings. *Adobe* is from Spanish, "sun-dried brick."

ADRIAN, Mich. (co. seat of Lenawee Co.). For Hadrian, or Publius Aelius Hadrianus (76-138), emperor of Rome (117-138), noted scholar and orator, as well as militarist and administrator.

ADVOCATE HARBOUR, N.S. From French *avocat*, "lawyer."

AFOGNAK ISLAND, Alaska. Of Eskimo origin, meaning unknown.

AFFTON, Mo. (St. Louis Co.). For Johann George Aff, early settler and landowner.

AFTON, N.Y. (Chenango Co.). For the small river in Ayrshire, Scotland, immortalized by Robert Burns.

AGASSIZ, Jean Louis Rudolph (1807-1873), born in Switzerland, biologist and geologist, who travelled and surveyed in the western part of the United States.
Agassiz Glacier, Alaska.
Agassiz Lakes, Alaska.
Agassiz Mount, Utah.
Agassiz Mountain, Alaska.
Agassiz Peak, Alaska.
Agassiz Peak, Ariz.

AGASSIZ, Mount, B.C. For an early settler.

AGAWAM From Algonquian, possibly "low land," "overflowed land," or "crooked river." Several Indian river towns originally bore this name.
Agawam, Mass. (Hampden Co.), town.
Agawam River, Mass.

AGENCY For the presence of a nearby Indian agency.
Agency Lake, Ore., arm of Upper Klamath Lake. Near the Klamath Indian Agency.
Agency Valley Reservoir, Ore.

AGUA FRIA RIVER, Ariz. From Spanish, "cold water." It flows generally south into Gila River.

AHOSKIE, N.C. (Hertford Co.). Of Indian origin, meaning uncertain.

AIKEN, William (1806-1886), South Carolina statesman and governor (1844-46).
Aiken Co., S.C. (co. seat, *Aiken*).
Aiken, S.C. (co. seat of *Aiken* Co.).

AINSWORTH, Neb. (co. seat of Brown Co.). For Capt. James E. Ainsworth, a railroad engineer.

AITKIN, William A. (c.1787-1851), a local fur trader.
Aitkin Co., Minn. (co. seat, *Aitkin*).
Aitkin, Minn. (co. seat of *Aitkin* Co.).

AJAX, Ont. For one of the three British cruisers that cornered the German pocket battleship *Graf Spee* in 1939.

AJAX MOUNTAIN, Mont. Classical, for the Greek general.

AJO From Papago Indian *auauho*, "paint," for the red paint obtained from the ore in the area. The name was later confused with Mexican-Spanish *ajo*, "lily," for the wild plants that grew there.
Ajo, Ariz. (Pima Co.).
Ajo Range, Ariz.

AKAKOA POINT, Hawaii. From Hawaiian, "brave reflection."

AKLAVIK, N.W.T. From Eskimo, "where there are bears."

AKRON From Greek, "summit," used occasionally in the United States for places on ridges on high points.
Akron, Colo. (co. seat of Washington Co.).
Akron, N.Y. (Erie Co.).
Akron, Ohio (co. seat of Summit Co.).
Akron, Pa. (Lancaster Co.).

AKUTAN Of Aleut origin, meaning obscure, but may be from *hakuta,* "I made a mistake."
Akutan, Alaska.
Akutan Bay, Alaska.
Akutan Island, Alaska.
Akutan Peak, Alaska.

ALABAMA Possibly for an Indian tribe whose name derived from Choctaw *alba,* "thicket" or "plants," and *amo,* "cleaners" or "reapers"; thus *Alabama* means "thicket cleaners" or "plant reapers." The territory and state were named for the river.
Alabama, State of. 22nd state of the Union. settled: 1702. Territory: 1817 (part of Mississippi Territory, 1802-17). Admitted: 1819. Cap: Montgomery, first capital of the Confederate States of America. Motto: We Dare Defend Our Rights. Nickname: Yellowhammer State. Flower: Camellia. Bird: Yellowhammer. Tree: Southern (Longleaf) Pine. Song: "Alabama."

Alabama River, Ala. Flows generally W, then S, to the Tombigbee R.

ALABASTER, Ala. (Shelby Co.). For local alabaster quarries.

ALACHUA Co., Fla. (co. seat, Gainesville). For a Seminole Indian town settled by Creeks from Oconee, Ga., apparently from *luchuwa,* "jug," descriptive of a chasm, probably the Devil's Millhopper, near Gainesville.

ALALAKEIKI CHANNEL, Hawaii, passage between Maui and Kahoolawe Islands. From Hawaiian, "child's cry," which was believed to have been heard there.

ALAMANCE Co., N.C. (co. seat, Graham). From an Indian name of uncertain meaning, which has been interpreted as "noisy river."

ALAMEDA From Spanish, "grove of poplar trees," a popular place name in western states.

The "Old Plantation" is an American fact and myth of long standing. Here it is represented by an unknown 19th century artist. [*Metropolitan Museum of Art*]

Alameda Co., Calif. (co. seat, Oakland).
Alameda, Calif. (*Alameda* Co.).
Alameda, Idaho (Bannock Co.). Earlier,
  Fairview.

ALAMITO CREEK, Tex. From Spanish,
"little cottonwood." It flows generally south
into the Rio Grande.

ALAMO From Spanish, "poplar" or
"cottonwood." The name is popular in the
United States as a commemorative for the
Battle of the Alamo, Tex., March 6, 1836,
when General Santa Anna overran the
garrison (the Alamo Mission) and killed all
the defenders, including William Barret
Travis, James Bowie, and Davy Crockett.
Alamo, Ga. (co. seat of Wheeler Co.).
Alamo, Ind. (Montgomery Co.).
Alamo, Tenn. (co. seat of Crockett Co.).
Alamo, Tex. (Hidalgo Co.).
Alamo River, Calif.-Mex.
Alamo-Danville, Calif. (Contra Costa Co.).
  Danville for Danville, Ky.
Alamo Heights, Tex. (Bexar Co.).

ALAMOGORDO From Spanish *ojo de
alamo gordo*, "spring of the big cot-
tonwood."
Alamogordo, N.Mex. (co. seat of Otero
  Co.).
Alamogordo Reservoir, N.Mex.

ALAMOSA From Spanish, "cottonwood
trees."
Alamosa Co., Colo. (co. seat, *Alamosa*).
Alamosa, Colo. (co. seat of *Alamosa* Co.).
Alamosa Creek, Colo.
Alamosa River, N.Mex.

ALASKA From an Aleutian word, variously
spelled *Alaeksu, Alachschak, Alaschka*, and
Alaxa, meaning "mainland," used to
distinguish inhabitants of the mainland from
the many nearby islanders. An earlier name
for the region, during the Russian occupation, was Russian America. The
present name was suggested by Senator
Charles Sumner when the land was purchased (1867), by the United States apparently under the assumption that it meant
"great land." The form *Alaska*, sometimes

Alaskans can boast as Texans once did that their
state is the biggest. In fact, Juneau, their capital,
is America's largest city. [*New York Public
Library*]

spelled *Aliaska*, had already established
itself in popular usage by that time.
Alaska, State of. 49th state of the Union.
  Settled: 1784. Admitted: 1959. Cap:
  Juneau. Motto: North to the Future.
  Nickname: The Great Land. Flower:
  Forget-me-not. Bird: Willow ptarmigan.
  Tree: Sitka spruce. Song: "Alaska's
  Flag."
Alaska Creek, Alaska.
Alaska, Gulf of.
Alaska Peninsula, Alaska.
Alaska Range, Alaska.
Alaska Chief Falls, Alaska.

ALATNA RIVER, Alaska. From Koyukan
allakaket, "mouth of Ala," but other interpretations have been suggested, one
being that the form is derived from
Allenkakat, "mouth of Allen," to honor a
Lieutenant Allen.

ALAVA, Cape, Wash. For Jose Manuel de
Alava, a Spanish commissioner.

ALBANY For James, Duke of York and
Albany (1633-1701), later James II of
England.
Albany Co., N.Y. (co. seat, *Albany*).
Albany Co., Wyo. (co. seat, Laramie). For
  Albany, Ga.

6

Albany, Calif. (Alameda Co.). For *Albany*, N.Y., birthplace of the first mayor.
Albany, Ga. (co. seat of Dougherty Co.).
Albany, Ky. (co. seat of Clinton Co.).
Albany, Me. (Oxford Co.), town.
Albany, Mo. (co. seat of Gentry Co.). For *Albany*, N.Y.
Albany, N.H. (Carroll Co.), town.
Albany, N.Y. (co. seat of *Albany* Co.), state capital. Earlier, Beverwyck.
Albany, Ore. (co. seat of Linn Co.). For *Albany*, N.Y.
Albany, Tex. (co. seat of Shackelford Co.). For *Albany*, Ga.
Albany, Vt. (Orleans Co.), town.
Albany River, Ont. Flows generally NE into James Bay.
New Albany, Ind. (co. seat of Floyd Co.). Founded by three Scribner brothers, from New York.
New Albany, Miss. (co. seat of Union Co.).

ALBEMARLE, William Anne Keppel, 2nd Earl of (1702-1754), English soldier and statesman, governor of the colony of Virginia (1737-54), although he never visited America. He fought at the Battle of Culloden, Scotland (1746).
Albermarle Co., Va. (co. seat, Charlottesville).
Albemarle, N.C. (co. seat of Stanly Co.).
Albemarle Sound, N.C. Arm of the Atlantic.
Albemarle and Chesapeake Canal, Va.

ALBERT, Lake, S.Dak. For J. J. Abert, a colonel in the United States Army. A misspelling resulted in the present form.

ALBERTA For Princess Louise Caroline Alberta (1848-1939), daughter of Prince Albert and Queen Victoria, and wife of the Marquess of Lorne, governor general of Canada (1878-1883). He named the District of Alberta, from which the province takes its name.
Alberta, Canadian province. Settled: 1778. District: 1882. Entered confederation: 1905. Cap: Edmonton. Flower: Wild rose.

ALBERT LEA, Minn. (co. seat of Freeborn Co.). For Albert Miller Lea (1808-1891), member of expeditionary surveys in the upper Mississippi and Missouri River areas.

ALBIA, Iowa (co. seat of Monroe Co.). Believed locally to be from Celtic, "high flat plateau." Possibly it was taken from an Albia in New York, and thought to be a form of ALBION, an ancient name for England.

One of the great romantic organizations is the "Mounties," the Royal Canadian Mounted Police, shown here on parade. [*Canadian Consulate*]

ALBION An ancient name (from Latin *albus*, "white") for England and perhaps for the British Isles. The name appears in Pliny and also in the works of the Venerable Bede (c.672-735). Although probably applied only to southern England and the chalk cliffs of Dover, the word has become common as a mythological appellation for England. Francis Drake in 1579 claimed what is now California for the Crown and named his discovery New Albion because he happened to sail close to some white cliffs, which apparently reminded him of Dover.
Albion, Ill. (co. seat of Edwards Co.).
Albion, Ind. (co. seat of Noble Co.).
Albion, Me. (Kennebec Co.), town.
Albion, Mich. (Calhoun Co.). For *Albion*, Me.
Albion, Neb. (co. seat of Boone Co.). For *Albion*, Mich.
Albion, N.Y. (co. seat of Orleans Co.).
Albion, R.I. (Providence Co.), town.

ALBUQUERQUE, N.Mex. (co. seat of Bemalillo Co.). For Albuquerque, in

7

Pictured here is a street in the "Old Town" of Albuquerque, which is now in the center of the modern New Mexico city. [*Museum of Albuquerque Photo Collection*]

Badajoz province, Spain. Derivation is uncertain but has been given as *albus quercus*, "white oak." An oak tree appears on the seal of the Spanish town.

ALCOA, Tenn. (Blount Co.). For the Alcoa Aluminum Company, founder.

ALCONA Co., Mich. (co. seat, Harrisville). A local coinage, said to mean "beautiful plains." An earlier name was Neewaygo.

ALCORN Co., Miss. (co. seat, Corinth). For James Lusk Alcorn (1816-1894), Mississippi statesman and governor (1870-71).

ALCOVY RIVER, Ga. From Muskogean *ulcofauhatichie*, "river in the pawpaw trees." Flows south into Jackson Lake.

ALDEN, N.Y. (Erie Co.). For John and Prescilla Alden. John Alden (1599-1687) was one of the Mayflower pilgrims and deputy governor of Massachusetts (1664-65; 1677). The Aldens were immortalized in Longfellow's *Courtship of Miles Standish*

which tells the fictional story of how John married Prescilla after first wooing her for his friend Myles Standish.

ALEDO, Ill. (co. seat of Mercer Co.). For Aledo, Spain; named by an early settler. An earlier name was De Soto.

ALEGROS MOUNTAIN, N.Mex. From Spanish, "bright" or "pleasant."

ALENUIHAHA CHANNEL, Hawaii, passage between the islands of Hawaii and Maui. From Hawaiian, "waves smashing."

ALEUTIAN The adjective form of *Aleut*, for the natives of the chain of islands which separate the Bering Sea from the Pacific Ocean. The name was first used by Admiral von Krusenstern in 1827. Meaning of name is uncertain. Earlier names were Billy Mitchell Islands and Katerina Archipelago. *Aleutian* Islands, Alaska, extend WSW from Alaska Peninsula to Attu Island.
Aleutian Range, Alaska.

ALEXANDER Co., Ill. (co. seat, Cairo). For an early settler and legislator, William M. Alexander.

ALEXANDER Co., N.C. (co. seat, Taylorsville). For a North Carolina state legislator, William J. Alexander.

ALEXANDER ARCHIPELAGO, Alaska. Named in 1867 by United States Coast and Geological Survey in honor of Alexander (1777-1825), Czar of Russia.

ALEXANDER CITY, Ala. (Tallapoosa Co.). For Gen. E. P. Alexander, president of the Central of Georgia railroad.

ALEXANDRIA For Alexandria, Egypt, which was founded in 332 by Alexander the Great.
Alexandria, Ind. (Madison Co.).
Alexandria, Ky. (co. seat of Campbell Co.).
Alexandria, La. (parish seat of Rapides Parish).

ALEXANDRIA For John Alexander, a founder, or for his daughter.
Alexandria, N.H. (Grafton Co.), town. For *Alexandria*, Va.
Alexandria, Va. (independent city in Arlington Co.).

ALEXANDRIA, Minn. (co. seat of Douglas Co.). For Alexander Kincaid (1835-1868), an early settler.

ALEXANDRIA, S.Dak. (co. seat of Hanson Co.). For Alexander Mitchell, a railway official.

ALFALFA Co., Okla. (co. seat, Cherokee). For William Henry ("Alfalfa Bill") Murray (1869-1956), Oklahoma statesman. He was a U.S. representative (1913-17) and Oklahoma governor (1931-35).

ALFRED, Me. (co. seat of York Co.), town. For Alfred the Great (c.848-899), king of the West Saxons, England. His reign saw a rebirth of learning and a strengthened and centralized monarchy.

ALFRED, N.Y. (Allegany Co.), town and village. Possibly named by travelers who were reminded of King Alfred's seat near Winchester, Hampshire, England.

ALGER Co., Mich. (co. seat, Munising). For Russell Alexander Alger (1836-1907), Michigan soldier, statesman, and governor (1885-87).

ALGOMA Coined by Henry Rowe Schoolcraft, explorer and ethnologist, to describe the area surrounding Lake Superior. *Al*-stands for *Algonquin* and *goma* (or *gumee* or *gomee*) means "waters" in Ojibway; thus, "the Algonquin Sea."
Algoma Co., Ont. (co. seat, Sault Sainte Marie).
Algoma, Wis. (Kewaunee Co.).

ALGONA, Iowa (co. seat of Kossuth Co.). From *Algonquin*, with -*a* ending, common in place names; named by Asa C. Call, county judge. An earlier name was Call's Grove.

ALGONAC, Mich. (St. Clair Co.). Coined by H. R. Schoolcraft, explorer and ethnologist, from the first part of *Algonquin* plus -*ac*, which to him meant "place" or "land."

ALGONQUIN, Ill. (McHenry Co.). For a ship that one of the town trustees had sailed upon.

ALGONQUIN PEAK, N.Y. For the Algonkin Indian tribe, the easternmost division of the Chippewa group of Algonquian linguistic stock. Meaning of name is uncertain, possibly "at the place of spearing fish or eels (from the bow of a canoe.)"

ALHAMBRA, Calif. (Los Angeles Co.). For the Moorish palace in Spain; named by Benjamin D. Wilson, founder, who had read *The Alhambra* (1832) by Washington Irving.

ALIA POINT, Hawaii, on east coast of Hawaii Island. From Hawaiian, "salt."

ALICE, Tex. (co. seat of Jim Wells Co.). For Alice Kleberg, wife of Robert Kleberg, one of the founders and owners of the King Ranch.

ALIQUIPPA, Pa. (Beaver Co.). For an Indian queen who lived on the site of McKeesport, Pa., about 1775.

ALKALI Descriptive of mineral content in land or water.
Alkali Flats, Nev.
Alkali Lake, Nev.
Alkaline Lake, N.Dak.

ALKAWAI SWAMP, Hawaii. From Hawaiian, "lead."

ALLAGASH From Indian Abnaki, "bark cabin."
Allagash, Me. (Aroostook Co.).
Allagash Falls, Me.
Allagash Lake, Me.
Allagash River, Me. Flows generally NE from *Allagash* L. to the St. John R.

ALLAMAKEE Co., Iowa (co. seat, Waukon). Combined form of an Indian trader's name, Allan Makee.

ALL AMERICAN CANAL, Calif. So named because the canal lies wholly within the borders of the United States. It is the largest American canal, and irrigates the Imperial Valley with water supplied from the Colorado River.

ALLATOONA Probably for a Cherokee name with uncertain meaning and with spelling to reflect a romantic rhythm.
Allatoona, Ga. (Bartow Co.).
Allatoona Creek, Ga.
Allatoona Lake, Ga. For the creek.

ALLEGAN Probably suggested by ALLEGANY.
Allegan Co., Mich. (co. seat, *Allegan*).
Allegan, Mich. (co. seat of *Allegan* Co.).

ALLEGANY Variant of ALLEGHENY.
Allegany Co., Md. (co. seat, Cumberland).
Allegany Co., N.Y. (co. seat, Belmont).

ALLEGHANY Variant of ALLEGHENY
Alleghany Co., N.C. (co. seat, Sparta).
Alleghany Co., Va. (co. seat, Covington).

ALLEGHENY Probably from Delaware Indian, but the origin and meaning are uncertain. It has been derived from *welhik-hanna or oolik-hanne*, "fine river" or "beautiful river." Its stem *-aha[n]*, "lapping" or "alternate motion," may also refer to the river.

Allegheny Co., Pa. (co. seat, Pittsburgh).
Allegheny Mountains, Pa.-Va.-W.Va., part of the Appalachian Mtns.
Allegheny Natl. Forest, Pa.
Allegheny Plateau. Includes the mountains and sections of Pennsylvania, New York, and West Virginia.
Allegheny River, Pa.-N.Y. Flows generally NW into New York, then E to join the Monongahela R. to form the Ohio R.

ALLEMANDS, Lac des (Lake), La. From French, "lake of the Germans," for the German settlers living near it.

ALLEN, John, an army officer killed in Indiana territory.
Allen Co., Ind. (co. seat, Fort Wayne).
Allen Co., Ky. (co. seat, Scottsville).

ALLEN Co., Kan. (co. seat, Iola). For William Allen (1803-1879), Ohio statesman and governor (1874-76).

ALLEN Parish, La. (parish seat, Oberlin). For Henry Watkins Allen (1820-1866), Louisiana statesman, governor (1864-65), and general in the Confederate army.

ALLEN Co., Ohio (co. seat, Lima). For Ethan Allen (1738-1789), leader of the famous Green Mountain Boys of Vermont in the American Revolution.

ALLENDALE For a postmaster, Paul Allen.
Allendale Co., S.C. (co. seat, *Allendale*).
Allendale, S.C. (co. seat of *Allendale* Co.).

ALLEN PARK, Mich. (Wayne Co.). For Lewis Allen (1814-1894), attorney, land-owner, and prominent citizen.

ALLENSTOWN, N.H. (Merrimack Co.), town. For Gov. Samuel Allen of Massachusetts, who had an interest in land in the area.

ALLENTOWN, Pa. (co. seat of Lehigh Co.). For William Allen, landowner, founder, and jurist. An earlier name was North-ampton.

ALLERTON For Allerton, England.
Allerton, Mass. (Plymouth Co.), town.
Allerton, Point, Mass., in Boston Bay.

ALLIANCE, Neb. (Box Butte Co.). For a junction of railroads, and also for Alliance, Ohio, possibly chosen because it begins with *A*. Points along certain railroads were given names in alphabetical order as the line progressed westward.

ALLIANCE, Ohio (Stark Co.). For the grouping of small villages into a larger one, or for the junction of two railroads, or both; named by General Robinson, a railroad official.

ALLIGATOR For the amphibian.
Alligator Lake, Me. Its shape supposedly resembles an alligator.
Alligator Lake, N.C.
Alligator River, N.C. Rises in *Alligator* L. and becomes an inlet of Albemarle Sound.
Alligator Swamp, N.C.

ALLISON, Iowa (co. seat of Butler Co.). For William B. Allison (1829-1908), attorney and U.S. representative. He nominated Abraham Lincoln at the Republican National Convention of 1860 and served as U.S. senator from Iowa (1873-1908).

ALLOUEZ, Claude (1622-1689), French Catholic missionary who was active in the Wisconsin and Lake Superior area during the mid 1600s.
Allouez, Wis. (Brown Co.).
Allouez Bay, Wis. Also known as Superior Bay.

ALLOWAY For an Indian chief. *Alloway* means "fox."
Alloway, N.J. (Salem Co.).
Alloway Creek, N.J. Flows SW into Delaware R.

ALMA For the Alma River, Crimea, Russia, to commemorate the battle that took place there in 1854, when the French and Turkish troops defeated the Russians.
Alma, Que. (co. seat of East Lake St. John Co.).
Alma, Wis. (co. seat of Buffalo Co.).
Alma Island, Que.

ALMA, Ga. (co. seat of Bacon Co.). From the initials of the past and present Georgia capitals: Augusta, Louisville, Milledgeville, and Atlanta.

ALMA, Kan. (co. seat of Wabaunsee Co.). Named by German settlers for Alma, Germany; but there are claims for Alma, Crimea, and also for a place in Switzerland.

ALMA, Mich. (Gratiot Co.). Believed to be for Alma Gargett, daughter of an early settler.

ALMA, Neb. (co. seat of Harlan Co.). For Alma Cook, daughter of a founder.

ALMA HILL, N.Y. For the first name of a woman who lived in the area.

ALMANOR LAKE, Calif. For *Ali*ce, *Mart*ha, and *Eli*nore Earl, daughters of the president of the Great Western Power Company.

ALMOND, N.Y. (Allegany Co.), town. So named because a boy passed a plate of almonds to those assembled at a meeting to choose a name.

ALORTON, Ill. (Saint Clair Co.). Meaning of name not certain, but apparently a pseudoword.

ALPENA A local coinage meaning "partridge country."
Alpena Co., Mich. (co. seat, *Alpena*).
Alpena, Mich. (co. seat of *Alpena* Co.). Earlier, Anamickee.

ALPINE From the Alps, the great mountain system in central Europe. The name may also be influenced by the Alpines, a small range in France.
Alpine Co., Calif. (co. seat, Markleeville).
Alpine, Tex. (co. seat of Brewster Co.).

ALSEA RIVER, Ore. For a tribal name, listed by Lewis and Clark as *Ulseah*, meaning unknown. It flows west into the Pacific.

ALSEK RIVER, Yukon-Alaska. Of Indian Tlingit origin, meaning uncertain. Flows into the Gulf of Alaska.

ALSIP, Ill. (Cook Co.). For Frank Alsip (1827-1887?), founder of the Alsip Brick Company. The Alsip family did not reside in the area.

ALTADENA, Calif. (Los Angeles Co.). Combination of Spanish *alta*, "high," and *dena*, from nearby Pasa*dena*.

ALTAMAHA RIVER, Ga. Origin and meaning of this name are in dispute. It is obviously influenced by Spanish and seems to have been a combination of Spanish *Al*, "to the," and *tama*, probably a Creek name. It was named by Hernando DeSoto in 1540 and was applied to the inland province of what is now the state of Georgia. The river is formed by a juncture of Oconee and Ocomulgee rivers and flows into the Atlantic Ocean.

ALTAMONT Apparently a mixture of languages. *Alta*, from Spanish or Italian, "high"; *mount*, from French, "mount." Also spelled *Altamonte*.
Altamont, Tenn. (co. seat of Grundy Co.).
Altamonte Springs, Fla. (Seminole Co.).

ALTAMONT, Ore. (Klamath Co.). For a racehorse. The name means "high mount."

ALTAR RIVER, Ariz. From Spanish, "altar." Also called Altar Wash River. It flows south into Mexico.

ALTAVISTA, Va. (Campbell Co.). From Spanish, "high view." Probably promotional.

ALTICANE, Sask. Named by a Mr. McKye for his home town in Scotland.

ALTON For the Alton family, prominent in New Hampshire, where John, David, and Joseph Alton were early settlers. The name spread westward as settlers moved on.
Alton, Ill. (Madison Co.). For *Alton*, N.H.
Alton, Mo. (co. seat of Oregon Co.). For *Alton*, Ill.
Alton, N.H. (Belknap Co.).
Alton Bay, N.H. Arm of Lake Winnipesaukee.
East Alton, Ill. (Madison Co.). For the son of Rufus Easton, founder.

ALTONA For Altona, Germany.
Altona, Man. Named by Mennonite settlers.
Altona, N.Y. (Clinton Co.). Altona, Germany, was the birthplace of Count Charles Defredenburg, who was granted land in Clinton County.

ALTOONA Origin uncertain. Since Altoona, Pa., is known as the "Mountain City," the name may come from Latin *altus*, "elevated" or "lofty." It may also derive from Altona, Germany, or from *Allatoona*, a Cherokee name.
Altoona, Iowa (Polk Co.). For *Altoona*, Pa.
Altoona, Pa. (Blair Co.).
Altoona, Wis. (Eau Claire Co.). For *Altoona*, Pa.

ALTO PARK, Ga. (Chattooga Co.). *Alto-*, from Spanish, "high." Promotional.

ALTURAS, Calif. (co. seat of Modoc Co.). From Spanish, "heights."

ALTUS From Latin *altus*, "high." The original town with a different name was on low ground and was destroyed in a flood. The residents opted for higher land and a new name.
Altus, Okla. (co. seat of Jackson Co.).
Altus, Lake, Okla.

ALUM For the mineral.
Alum Creek, Ohio. Flows into Scioto R.
Alum Rock, Calif. (Santa Clara Co.).

ALVERSTONE, Mount, Alaska-Yukon. For Everard Webster Alverstone (1842-1915), a mediator on several commissions arbitrating Canadian and Alaskan disputes.

ALVIN, Tex. (Brazoria Co.). For Alvin Morgan (1842-1909), landowner, businessman, and promoter of the town.

ALVORD LAKE, Ore. For Benjamin Alvord (1813-1884), general officer in the United States Army, in command of troops in Oregon Territory in the 1860s.

AMADOR Co., Calif. (co. seat, Jackson). For Jose Maria Amador, an early landowner and a soldier in the Mexican army.

AMARGOSA From Spanish, "bitter water."
Amargosa Desert, Calif.
Amargosa Range, Calif. Forms E side of Death Valley.
Amargosa River, Calif. Flows across *Amargosa* Desert to a sink in Death Valley.

AMARILLO, Tex. (co. seat of Potter Co.). From Spanish, "yellow," for the color of the banks or the bottom of a nearby stream.

AMBERLEY, Ohio (Hamilton Co.). Promotional, from Amberley, England.

AMBLER, Pa. (Montgomery Co.). For Joseph Ambler, member of a prominent family of settlers who came to Pennsylvania in 1723.

AMBOY From Algonquin *omboge*, which was a changed form of *ambo*. *Omboge* possibly means "large level piece of ground" or "something hollowed out."
Perth Amboy, N.J. (Middlesex Co.). See
  PERTH.
South Amboy, N.J. (Middlesex Co.).

AMBRIDGE, Pa. (Beaver Co.). Abbreviated version of *American Bridge* Company, which purchased the community in 1901.

AMELIA For Amelia Sophia (1711-1786), second daughter of George II of England.
Amelia Co., Va. (co. seat, *Amelia*).
Amelia, Va. (co. seat of *Amelia* Co.).

AMENIA, N.Y. (Dutchess Co.). From Latin, "pleasant to the eye."

AMERICAN FALLS For an incident in which several American trappers were killed when their canoe was swept over the falls of the Snake River at this point.
American Falls, Idaho (co. seat of Power
  Co.).
American Falls Reservoir, Idaho.

AMERICAN FORK, Utah (Utah Co.). So named to complement Spanish Fork to the south.

AMERICUS, Ga. (co. seat of Sumter Co.). So named by lot, from a list of names placed in a hat. The slip of paper withdrawn by Isaac McCrary bore the word *Americus*. Thus, the new town was named for Amerigo (*Americus* in Latin) Vespucci (1451-1512), Italian explorer for whom America was named. Very soon the new settlers playfully called it "a merry cuss," for the difficulties in settling a new frontier area.

AMES, Iowa (Story Co.). For Oakes Ames

(1804-1873), U.S. representative from Massachusetts. He had railroad interests in the area.

AMESBURY, Mass. (Essex Co.), town and village. For Amesbury, Wiltshire, England. The English town is near Salisbury, as the Massachusetts town is near Salisbury, Mass.

AMETHYST MOUNTAIN, Wyo. For amethysts found there.

Lord Jeffrey Amherst, British Commander during the French and Indian War, is shown providing the Indians with humanitarian treatment. Actually Amherst was an innovator in biological warfare by sending smallpox infected blankets to the Indians. [*New York Public Library*]

AMHERST, Jeffrey Amherst, Baron (1717-1797), British general who achieved success in the French and Indian Wars, during the latter part of which he was named commander of British forces in North America. During the American Revolution he refused a North American command.
Amherst Co., Va. (co. seat, *Amherst*).
Amherst, Mass. (Hampshire Co.), town and
  village.
Amherst, N.H. (Hillsborough Co.), town.
Amherst, N.Y. (Erie Co.).

Amherst, N.S. (co. town of Cumberland Co.).
Amherst, Ohio (Lorain Co.).
Amherst, Va. (co. seat of *Amherst* Co.).
Amherst Island, Ont., in Lake Ontario.
Amherst Island, Que., in the Magdalen Islands (Isles des Madeleines), Gulf of St. Lawrence.
Amherstburg, Ont. (Essex Co.).
South Amherst, Ohio (Lorain Co.).

AMIDON, N.Dak. (co. seat of Slope Co.). For Charles F. Amidon, a jurist.

AMIENS, Sask. For Amiens, France, where Canadian troops fought in World War I.

AMITE From French, "friendship."
Amite Co., Miss. (co. seat, Liberty).
Amite, La. (parish seat of Tangipahoa Parish).
Amite River, La.

AMITYVILLE, N.Y. (Suffolk Co.). For the amicable settlement of an argument over what name the town should have.

AMMON, Idaho (Bonneville Co.). For a leader in the Book of Mormon.

AMNICON From Ojibway, "spawning ground."
Amnicon Lake, Wis.
Amnicon River, Wis. Flows NE into L. Superior.

AMORY, Miss. (Monroe Co.). For a Mr. Amory who was a railroad official.

AMOS, Que. (Abitibi Co.). For the maiden name of Lady Alice Gouin, wife of Sir Lomer Gouin (1861-1929), prime minister of Quebec when the town was named.

AMPHITHEATER PEAK, Wyo. Descriptive of shape.

AMSTERDAM For the Dutch city in the province of North Holland, Netherlands.
Amsterdam, N.Y. (Montgomery Co.). Earlier, Veddersburg, for Aaron Vedder, a miller.
Amsterdam, Sask.
New Amsterdam. Capital (1625-64) of the

Dutch colony of New Netherlands, now New York City.

AMUKTA Of Aleut origin, meaning unknown.
Amukta Island, Alaska. Westernmost island of the Islands of Four Mountains in the Aleutian Islands.
Amukta Pass, Alaska. Water passage between Andreanof Island and Fox Island, in the Aleutian Islands.

ANACAPA ISLANDS, Calif., in the Santa Barbara Islands. From Chumash *anyapah*, meaning unknown.

ANACONDA, Mont. (co. seat of Deer Lodge Co.). A boa constrictor found in South America (*Eunectus murinus*); used metaphorically to denote a constriction or encircling. Specifically, the giant copper mine in Montana received its name from a report that General Grant was encircling General Lee "like an anaconda." An earlier name was Copperopolis.

ANACORTES, Wash. (Skagit Co.). Named by the town planter, Amos Bowman, for his wife Anna Curtis. The spelling was purposefully changed to the Spanish form.

ANADARKO, Okla. (co. seat of Caddo Co.). For a tribe that belonged to the Hasinai Confederacy of Caddoan linguistic stock. The meaning of the name is uncertain.

ANAHEIM, Calif. (Orange Co.). Combination of *Ana*, from the Santa Ana River, and German *heim*, "home"; named by German settlers.

ANAHUAC, Tex. (co. seat of Chambers Co.). From Aztec, "waterland" or "near the water"; the name of a local chief may have influenced the spelling.

ANAKTUVUK RIVER, Alaska. From Eskimo, "excrement." It flows north into Colville River.

ANAMOSA, Iowa (co. seat of Jones Co.). Said to be the name of a little Indian girl who visited the area.

ANCHORAGE, Alaska. For Knik Anchorage, a settlement just offshore. This was named for a Tanaina Indian village, spelled *Kinik* and *Kinnick, which means "fire." Earlier names were Ship Creek and Woodrow.*

ANCHOR BAY, Mich. Descriptive for a harbor or anchorage.

ANCRAM, N.Y. (Columbia Co.), town. Named by early Scottish settlers for the Earl of Ancram, of Scotland.

ANDALUSIA, Ala. (co. seat of Covington Co.). For a region, consisting of eight provinces, in south and southwest Spain. An earlier name was New Site.

ANDERSON, Calif. (Shasta Co.). For Elias Anderson, landowner.

ANDERSON, Ind. (co. seat of Madison Co.). For William Anderson, a Delaware Indian chief, also known as Kikthawenund. An earlier name was Andersonville.

ANDERSON Co., Kan. (co. seat, Garnett). For Joseph C. Anderson, a legislator.
ANDERSON, Kenneth Lewis (1805-1845), Texas statesman.
Anderson Co., Tex. (co. seat, Palestine).
Anderson, Tex. (co. seat of Grimes Co.).

ANDERSON Co., Ky. (co. seat, Lawrenceburg). For Richard Clough Anderson (1788-1826), Kentucky statesman.

ANDERSON, Robert, a South Carolina officer in the American Revolution.
Anderson Co., S.C. (co. seat, *Anderson*).
Anderson, S.C. (co. seat of *Anderson* Co.).

ANDERSON Co., Tenn. (co. seat, Clinton). For Joseph Anderson (1757-1837), Tennessee statesman.

ANDOVER For Andover, Hampshire, England, from which several of the original settlers came.
Andover, Mass. (Essex Co.), town.
Andover, N.B. (co. seat of Victoria Co.). Earlier, Tobique.
North Andover, Mass. (Essex Co.), town.

ANDREAFSKY RIVER, Alaska. For the Andrea family, early settlers from Russia. It flows southwest into Yukon River.

ANDREW JOHNSON NATL. HISTORIC SITE, Tenn. Preserves Johnson's tailor shop, his home, and his grave. For Andrew Johnson (1808-1875), seventeenth president of the United States (1865-69). He was born in North Carolina but associated with Tennessee, where he moved (1826) and pursued the tailoring business. He was a U.S. representative (1843-53), governor of Tennessee (1853-57), and U.S. senator (1857-62; 1875). He served as brigadier general of the Union army during the Civil War. He was vice president (1865), and succeeded to the presidency on the death of Lincoln. Differences between Congress and Johnson with regard to reconstruction policies led to impeachment proceedings (1868); he was acquitted.

ANDREW Co., Mo. (co. seat, Savannah). For Andrew Jackson Davis, a distinguished lawyer from St. Louis.

ANDREWS, Richard, a soldier killed (1835) during the Texas Revolution.
Andrews Co., Tex. (co. seat, Andrews).
Andrews, Tex. (co. seat of *Andrews* Co.).

ANDREWS, S.C. (Georgetown Co.). For W. H. Andrews (1873-1935), first mayor.

ANDROSCOGGIN For the Indian tribe *Amasagunticook,* whose name means "fishing place for alewives" or "fish spearing."
Androscoggin Co., Me. (co. seat, *Auburn*).
Androscoggin Lake, Me.
Androscoggin River, N.H.-Me. Flows into Merrymeeting Bay.

ANGELES NATL. FOREST, Calif. For LOS ANGELES

ANGELICA, N.Y. (Allegany Co.). For Angelica Schuyler Church (?-1815), daughter of Philip Schuyler, a general in the American Revolution.

ANGELINA From Spanish diminutive for "angel."
Angelina Co., Tex. (co. seat, Lufkin).
Angelina Natl. Forest, Tex.
Angelina River, Tex.

ANGELS PEAK, N.Mex. From Spanish, "angel," with religious connotations.

ANGLETON, Tex. (co. seat of Brazoria Co.). For Mrs. George W. Angle, wife of a member of the Boston Syndicate, which was active in developing facilities at Velasco.

ANGOLA For a Portuguese colony in western Africa. The name was probably chosen for euphonic reasons.
Angola, Ind. (co. seat of Steuben Co.).
Angola, N.Y. (Erie Co.).

ANGOSTURA RESERVOIR, S.Dak., reservoir and dam on Cheyenne River. From Spanish, "narrows."

ANGWIN, Calif. (Napa Co.). For Edwin Angwin (?-1918), landowner.

ANKENY, Iowa (Polk Co.). For J. F. Ankeney, owner of the townsite, with a spelling change.

ANN, Cape, Mass. For Anne of Denmark (1574-1619), wife of King James I of England.

ANNA For Queen Anne of England.
North Anna River, Va. Flows to its junction with the *South Anna* R. to form the Pamunkey R.
South Anna River, Va. Flows to its junction with the *North Anna.*

ANNA, Ill. (Union Co.). For Anna ·Willard Davis, wife of a local landowner and farmer.

ANNAPOLIS The city of Anne, for ANNE ARUNDEL.
Annapolis Co., N.S. (co. town, *Annapolis Royal*).
Annapolis, Md. (co. seat of Anne Arundel Co.), state capital. Earlier, Providence and Anne Arundel Town.
Annapolis, N.S. (co. town of Bridgetown Co.).
Annapolis Basin, N.S. Arm of the Bay of Fundy.
Annapolis River, N.S. Flows into Annapolis Basin.
Annapolis Valley, N.S.
Annapolis Royal, N.S. (co. town of *Annapolis* Co.). Earlier, Port Royal.

ANN ARBOR, Mich. (co. seat of Washtenaw Co.). For the wives of John

Allen and Elisha Rumsey, settlers. Both women were named Ann.

ANNE ARUNDEL Co., Md. (co. seat, Annapolis). For Anne Arundell, daughter of Lord Thomas Arundell of Wardour and wife of Cecilius Calvert, Lord Baltimore.

ANNISTON, Ala. (co. seat of Calhoun Co.). For Annie Tyler (1838-1914), wife of Alfred Tyler, president of the South Carolina railroad and a founder of the city.

ANOKA From Siouan, "the other side" or "both sides."
Anoka Co., Minn. (co. seat, *Anoka*).
Anoka, Minn. (co. seat of *Anoka* Co.).

ANSON Co., N.C. (co. seat, Wadesboro). For George Anson, Baron Anson (1697-1742), British admiral assigned the duty of protecting the Carolina coast.

ANSON, Tex. (co. seat of Jones Co.). For Anson Jones (1798-1858), last president of Texas. The county was also named for him.

ANSONIA, Conn. (New Haven Co.). Latinized version of *Anson*, for Anson G. Phelps (1781-1853). Phelps, a merchant, manufacturer, and philanthropist, was the founder.

ANTELOPE For the animals.
Antelope Co., Neb. (co. seat, Neligh).
Antelope Hills, Okla.
Antelope Peak, Neb.
Antelope Reservoir, Ore.

ANTERO For a Ute chief.
Antero, Mount, Colo.
Antero Reservoir, Colo.

ANTHONY, Kan. (co. seat of Harper Co.). For George Toby Anthony (1824-1896), who recruited and organized the New York Volunteers in 1862. He was president of the state board of agriculture (1874-76) and governor of Kansas (1877-79).

ANTIETAM NATL. BATTLEFIELD SITE, Md. From Algonquian, meaning uncertain, but "flow" seems to be a part of the form. It was the site of a decisive battle (1862) between.the forces of Generals Lee and McClellan. The outcome is in dispute, but it gave President Lincoln the chance to publish his Emancipation Proclamation.

ANTIGO, Wis. (co. seat of Langlade Co.). From Ojibway, "place where evergreens grow."

ANTIGONISH From Micmac, "broken branches."
Antigonish Co., N.S. (co. town, *Antigonish*).
Antigonish, N.S. (co. town of *Antigonish* Co.).

ANTIOCH For an ancient city in Syria, often mentioned in the Bible.
Antioch, Calif. (Contra Costa Co.). Earlier, Smith's Landing.
Antioch, Ill. (Lake Co.).

ANTLERS, Okla. (co. seat of Pushmataha Co.). So named because deer antlers were fastened up at a spring to indicate a camp site.

ANTRIM Co., Mich. (co. seat, Bellaire). For county Antrim, Ireland. An earlier name was Meegisee.

ANVIK RIVER, Alaska. Of Ingalik Indian origin, meaning uncertain, possibly "going-out-place." It flows southeast into Yukon River.

APACHE For a tribe of Athapascan linguistic stock who inhabited southern New Mexico, Arizona, and other central United States areas. The name derives from the Zuni term for "enemy." During the westward expansion of the American colonies, Apaches were known for their fierce and tenacious defense of their territories.
Apache Co., Ariz. (co. seat, St. Johns).
Apache Mountain, N.Mex.
Apache Mountains, Tex.
Apache Natl. Forest, N.Mex.
Apache Pass, Ariz.
Apache Peak, Ariz., in the Whetstone Mtns.
Apache River, N.Mex.

APALACHEE For a tribe of Muskhogean linguistic stock who lived in northern Florida. The name may be Hitchiti for "on the other side," or derive from Choctaw *apelachi*, "helper." The Apalachee are first mentioned in the records of the Narvaez ex-

pedition in 1528 and are also prominent in the De Soto chronicles. The Appalachian Mountains are named for this tribe.
Apalachee Bay, Fla. Arm of the Gulf of Mexico.
Apalachee River, Ga. Flows generally SE into the Oconee R.

APALACHICOLA Believed to be a combination of Hitchiti *apalachi*, "on the other side," and *okli*, "people," possibly for a separate tribe of Muskhogean linguistic stock. Their earliest place of habitation was apparently along the river that bears their name. See also APALACHEE.
Apalachicola, Fla. (co. seat of Franklin Co.).
Apalachicola Bay, Fla. Arm of the Gulf of Mexico.
Apalachicola Natl. Forest, Fla.
Apalachicola River, Ga.-Fla. Flows generally S into *Apalachicola* Bay.

APISHAPA RIVER, Colo. From Ute, "standing water." It flows northeast into the Arkansas River.

APOPKA From Creek *aha*, "potato," and *papka*, "eating place."
Apopka, Fla. (Orange Co.).
Apopka, Lake, Fla.

APOSTLE ISLANDS, Wis., twenty-two islands in Lake Superior. Named by early Jesuit explorers, who thought there were only twelve islands, for the twelve apostles.

APPALACHIA, Va. (Wise Co.). For the Appalachian Mountains; named by officials of the Louisville and Nashville railroad. See APALACHEE.

APPALACHIAN MOUNTAINS Vast mountain system in eastern North America, extending from Alabama into Quebec. See APALACHEE.

APPANOOSE Co., Iowa (co. seat, Centerville). For a Sac chief prominent in Iowa and Kansas in the 1830s and 1840s. A respected chief, he was invited to Washington (1837) and gave addresses at Eastern institutions. In 1842 he signed a treaty to move his tribe to Kansas.

APPLE For the tree.
Apple Creek, Ill. Flows generally SW into the Illinois R.
Apple River, Ill. Flows into the Mississippi R.
Apple River, Wis. Flows SW into St. Croix R. For the crab apple.

APPLEGATE, Oliver Cromwell (1845-1938), an Indian agent.
Applegate Peak, Ore.
Applegate River, Ore.

APPLETON, Wis. (co. seat of Outagamie Co.). For Samuel Appleton, father-in-law of Amos A. Lawrence, founder of Lawrence University in Appleton.

APPLE VALLEY Descriptive.
Apple Valley, Calif. (San Bernardino Co.).
Apple Valley, Minn. (Dakota Co.).

APPLEWOOD, Colo. (Jefferson Co.). Promotional.

APPLING, Daniel (1787-1818), an officer in the War of 1812.
Appling Co., Ga. (co. seat, Baxley).
Appling, Ga. (co. seat of Columbia Co.).

APPOMATTOX For a subtribe (Appomattoc) of the Powhatan Indians of Algonquian linguistic stock and the village of Appamatuck on the site of Bermuda Hundred at the mouth of the Appomattox River. The origin of the name is obscure; "tobacco plant country" and "curving tidal estuary" have been suggested. Apumetec is mentioned as an Indian queen in John Smith's *History*.
Appomattox Co., Va. (co. seat, *Appomattox*).
Appomattox, Va. (co. seat of *Appomattox* Co.).
Appomattox River, Va. Flows E to the James R.
Appomattox Court House Natl. Historical Park, Va. Commemorates the surrender of Gen. Robert E. Lee, commander of the Confederate forces, to Gen. Ulysses S. Grant, commander of the Union forces, April 10, 1865.

APTOS, Calif. (Santa Cruz Co.). Probably from *Owatos*, an Indian village. The name means "meeting of the waters."

APUA POINT, Hawaii, on southeast coast of Hawaii Island. From Hawaiian, "fish basket."

AQUARIUS MOUNTAINS, Ariz. From Latin, "water carrier," for the many streams in the area.

AQUIDNECK ISLAND, R.I. From Narraganset, "at the island." It was the original name of Rhode Island and is the largest island in Narragansett Bay.

ARAB, Ala. (Marshall Co.). Biblical (Joshua; 15:52); a place in the Judah Mountains, in Hebron.

ARANSAS From the original name of the river, *Rio Nuestra Senora de Aranzazu*, in honor of the lady of a Spanish castle.
Aransas Co., Tex. (co. seat, Rockport).
Aransas Bay, Tex. Arm of the Gulf of Mexico.
Aransas Pass, Tex. A channel leading from the Gulf of Mexico to *Aransas* Bay and other inlets.
Aransas River, Tex. Flows into *Aransas* Bay.
Aransas Pass, Tex. (San Patricio and *Aransas* Cos.).

ARAPAHO For a tribe of Algonquian linguistic stock. They became identified with the northwestern Wyoming area after moving from the Red River Valley across the midwestern states. The name is probably a Pawnee word, *tirapihu*, "trader." "Blue-sky men," and "cloud men" have also been suggested, but these have no documentation.
Arapaho, Okla. (co. seat of Custer Co.).
Arapaho Natl. Forest, Colo.

ARAPAHOE Variant of ARAPAHO.
Arapahoe Co., Colo. (co. seat, Littleton).
Arapahoe Peak, Colo., in the Front Range of the Rocky Mtns.

ARBELA, Mo. (Scotland Co.). Biblical (I Macc. 9:2); now the ruin of Irbid, west of the Sea of Galilee.

ARBUCKLE, Lake, Fla. For a local community member.

ARBUCKLE, Matthew (1780?-1851), American soldier. Commissioned an ensign in the infantry in 1799, he rose to brigadier general with duty in the south and in the

Indian transfer to the Oklahoma territory.
Arbuckle Mountains, Okla.
Arbuckle Reservoir, Okla., on tributary of Washita R.

ARBUTUS LAKE, Wis. For the arbutus flower.

ARCADIA For a region in ancient Greece, noted, it is said, for its pastoral simplicity and contentment.
Arcadia, Calif. (Los Angeles Co.).
Arcadia, Fla. (co. seat of De Soto Co.).
Arcadia, La. (parish seat of Bienville Parish).

ARCATA, Calif. (Humboldt Co.). Believed to be from an Indian word, "place where the boats land." An earlier name was Uniontown.

ARCHBALD, Pa. (Lackawanna Co.). For James Archbald (1793-?), prominent civil and mining engineer employed by the Delaware and Hudson railroad and responsible for the line across Moosic Mountain, connecting Scranton and New York.

ARCHBOLD, Ohio (Fulton Co.). Naming in dispute: either for James ARCHBALD, or for two civil engineers, a Mr. Arch and Mr. Bold.

ARCHDALE, N.C. (Randolph Co.). For John Archdale (1642-1717), a Quaker who was colonial governor of North Carolina (1695-98).

ARCHDEACONS TOWER, Alaska, peak in Mount McKinley Natl. Park. For Hudson Stuck (1863-1920), Archdeacon of the Yukon, a member of the expedition which first climbed Mount McKinley (South Peak), June 7, 1913.

ARCHER, Branch Tanner (1790-1856), Texas statesman.
Archer Co., Tex. (co. seat, *Archer City*).
Archer City, Tex. (co. seat of *Archer* Co.).

ARCHES For the arches formed by erosion.
Arches Natl. Monument, Utah.
Arches Natl. Park, Utah.

ARCHULETA Co., Colo. (co.seat, Pagosa Springs). For Antonia D. Archuleta, a Colorado legislator.

ARCO, Idaho (co. seat of Butte Co.). Origin in dispute: for Arco Smith, a stage operator; Arco, Italy; a Count Arco, who supposedly visited the site; or from Spanish, "arch."

ARDEN, Calif. (Sacramento Co.). Promotional, possibly for the forest in Shakespeare's *As You Like It.*

ARDEN HILLS, Minn. (Ramsey Co.). For a developer.

ARDMORE For a small town in Ireland, on the Atlantic Coast.
Ardmore, Okla. (co. seat of Carter Co.). For Ardmore, Pa.
Ardmore, Pa. (Montgomery Co.).

ARENA, Point, Calif. For the cove, which was shaped like an arena.

ARENAC Co., Mich. (co. seat, Standish). A coined term, said to mean "sandy place."

ARGENTEUIL Co., Que. (co. seat, Lachute). For Pierre d'Ailleboust d'Argenteuil, seignoir of the Argenteuil concession.

ARGUELLO, Point, Calif. Named by Capt. George Vancouver in 1792 for Jose Dario Arguello, Spanish commander at Monterey.

ARICKAREE RIVER, Colo.-Neb. For the Indian tribe, also known as *Arikara*, of Caddoan linguistic stock. The name signifies "horns" or "elk," in reference to hair style. It flows northeast into North Fork Republican River.

ARIEL, Chitty, son of the first postmaster.
Ariel, Wash. (Cowlitz Co.).
Ariel Dam, Wash.

ARIZONA Probably from Pima or Papago *arizonac* or *aleh-zon*, variously translated as "little spring," "valley of the maiden," and "place of chastisement." It has also been suggested that the name derives from Spanish *arida*, "dry," and *zona*, "country or area." It is possible that the early Spaniards learned the Indian name and modified it.
Arizona, State of. 48th state of the Union. Settled: 1848. Territory: 1863. Admitted: 1912. Cap: Phoenix. Motto: *Ditat Deus*

(God Enriches). Nickname: Grand Canyon State. Flower: Saguaro Cactus. Bird: Cactus Wren. Tree: Paloverde. Song: "Arizona."

To the Navajos of Arizona sand paintings have therapeutic value; this one is designed to cure a sick child. [*American Museum of Natural History*]

ARKABUTLA RESERVOIR, Miss. For a creek, in turn said to have been named for a Chickasaw chief who lived on its bank. An earlier name was Skull Bone, for an incident in which two men were killed and their skulls displayed. *Arkabutla* sounded· better to village incorporators.

ARKADELPHIA, Ark. (co. seat of Clark Co.). A combination of *Arkansas* and *delphia*, pseudo-Greek for "brother." The name is probably modeled on other such names, especially PHILADELPHIA.

ARKANSAS For the Quapaw tribe of the Sioux. They called themselves *Ugakhpah*, "downstream people."
Arkansas, State of. 25th state of the Union. Settled: 1785. Territory: 1819. Admitted: 1836. Cap: Little Rock. Motto: *Regnat Popului* (The People Rule). Nickname: Wonder State. Flower: Apple Blossom. Bird: Mockingbird. Tree: Pine. Song: "The Arkansas Traveler."

Arkansas Co., Ark. (co. seat, DeWitt-Stuttgart).
Arkansas River, Colo.-Kan.-Okla.-Ark. Rising in the Rocky Mtns., flows generally SE to the Mississippi R.
Arkansas City, Kan. (Cowley Co.).
Arkansas Post, Ark. (*Arkansas* Co.). Oldest white settlement in the state.

ARLINGTON For the home of George Washington Parke Custis (1781-1857). He had named it for Henry Bennet, 1st Earl of Arlington (1618-1685), who shared with Lord Thomas Culpepper Charles II's grant of the colony of Virginia.
Arlington Co., Va. (co. seat, *Arlington*).
Arlington, Mass. (Middlesex Co.), town.
Arlington, N.Y. (Dutchess Co.).
Arlington, N.C. (Gaston Co.).
Arlington, Tex. (Tarrant Co.).
Arlington, Va. (co. seat of *Arlington* Co.).
Arlington Natl. Cemetery, Va.
Arlington Heights, Ill. (Cook Co.).
North Arlington, N.J. (Bergen Co.).

ARMOUR, S.Dak. (co. seat of Douglas Co.). For Philip D. Armour, a railway official.

ARMSTRONG Co., Pa. (co. seat, Kittanning). For John Armstrong (1758-1843), Pennsylvania soldier and statesman. He served in the American Revolution. A member of the Continental Congress (1778-80; 1787-88), Armstrong was later U.S. senator from New York (1800-02; 1803-04), minister to France (1804-10), and secretary of war (1813-14) under Madison.

ARMSTRONG Co., Tex. (co. seat, Claude). For the Armstrong family, pioneers.

ARMSTRONG MOUNTAIN, N.Y. For Thomas Armstrong (fl.1866-87), a lumberman with Adirondack real estate interests.

ARNETT, Okla. (co. seat of Ellis Co.). For A. S. Arnett, a minister.

ARNOLD, Pa. (Westmoreland Co.). For Andrew Arnold, owner of the townsite.

ARNOT PEAK, Calif. For Nathaniel D. Arnot, jurist.

ARNPRIOR, Ont. (Renfrew Co.). Named by early settlers who were descendants of John Buchanan, the first Laird of Arnpryor in Scotland.

AROOSTOOK From Algonquian, "clear river."
Aroostook Co., Me. (co. seat, Houlton).
Aroostook, N.B.
Aroostook River, Me. Flows generally E to the St. John R.

ARROWHEAD MOUNTAIN, Wyo. Descriptive of shape.

Indians on the prairie along the Arkansas River which flows 1450 miles through Oklahoma and Arkansas on its way to the Mississippi. [*New York Public Library*]

ARROYO From Spanish, "creek" or "canyon."
Arroyo del Macho River, N.Mex. Flows SE into Pecos R. *Del Macho*, from Spanish, "male."
Arroyo Chico River, N.Mex. Flows NE into Puerco R. *Chico*, from Spanish, "boy."
Arroyo Grande, Calif. (San Luis Obispo Co.). *Grande*, from Spanish, "great."

ARTESIA For artesian wells in the area.
Artesia, Calif. (Los Angeles Co.).
Artesia, N.Mex. (Eddy Co.).

ARTHABASKA Variant form of ATHABASKA.
Arthabaska Co., Que. (co. seat, *Arthabaska*).
Arthabaska, Que. (co. seat of *Arthabaska* Co.).

ARTHUR For a local settler.
Arthur, Lake, La.
Lake Arthur, La. (Jefferson Davis Parish).

ARTHUR, Chester Alan (1830-1886), twenty-first President of the United States (1881-85), from Vermont. For many years associated with Republican politics in New York State, he served as vice-president of the United States (1881) and, on the assassination of Garfield, became President.
Arthur Co., Neb. (co. seat, *Arthur*).
Arthur, Neb. (co. seat of *Arthur* Co.).
Arthur Peak, Wyo.

ARUNDEL, Anne. See ANNE ARUNDEL.

ARVADA, Colo. (Jefferson Co.). For Hiram Arvada Haskins, brother-in-law of Mrs. Benjamin F. Wadsworth, wife of a founder.

ARVIDA, Que. (Chicoutimi Co.). For *Ar*thur *Vi*ning *Da*vis, president of the Aluminum Company of Canada.

ARVIN, Calif. (Kern Co.). For Arvin Richardson, storekeeper and land developer.

ASBESTOS, Que. (Richmond Co.). For the local asbestos mines.

ASBURY PARK, N.J. (Monmouth Co.). For Francis Asbury (1745-1816), first bishop of the Methodist Episcopal Church consecrated in America. He organized scores of Methodist societies and ordained thousands of Methodist preachers, traveling throughout the United States.

ASCENSION Parish, La. (parish seat, Donaldsonville). For the ascension of Jesus Christ into heaven as decribed in the gospels of Mark and Luke and the Acts of the Apostles: "So then after the Lord had spoken unto them, he was received up into heaven, and sat on the right hand of God" (Mark 16:19). Ascension Day is celebrated on the fortieth day after Easter.

ASCUTNEY From Abnaki, probably "end of river fork."
Ascutney, Vt. (Windsor Co.), town.
Ascutney, Mount, Vt.

ASHBURN, Ga. (co. seat of Turner Co.). For W. W. Ashburn, landowner and speculator.

ASHBURNHAM, Mass. (Worcester Co.), town. For John Ashburnham, 2nd Earl of Sussex.

ASH CREEK, Utah. For the tree. It flows into Virgin River.

ASHDOWN, Ark. (co. seat of Little River Co.). For Lawrence Ashdown Byrne, a jurist.

ASHE, Samuel (1725-1813), North Carolina statesman and governor (1795-98).
Ashe Co., N.C. (co. seat, Jefferson).
Asheboro, N.C. (co. seat of Randolph Co.).
Asheville, N.C. (co. seat of Buncombe Co.).
　Earlier, Morristown.

ASHEPOO RIVER, S.C. From Muskogean, "river home," although "eel" has also been suggested. It flows southeast into the Atlantic.

ASHLAND For the home of Henry Clay in Kentucky and for the presence of ash trees.
Ashland Co., Ohio (co. seat, *Ashland*).
Ashland Co., Wis. (co. seat, *Ashland*).
Ashland, Ala. (co. seat of Clay Co.).
Ashland, Calif. (Alameda Co.). For *Ashland*, Ky.
Ashland, Kan. (co. seat of Clark Co.).
Ashland, Ky. (Boyd Co.).
Ashland, Me. (Aroostook Co.), town.
Ashland, Mass. (Middlesex Co.), town.
Ashland, Miss. (co. seat of Benton Co.).
Ashland, N.H. (Grafton Co.), town.
Ashland, Ohio (co. seat of *Ashland* Co.).
　Earlier, Uniontown.
Ashland, Ore. (Jackson Co.).
Ashland, Pa. (Columbia and Schuylkill Cos.).
Ashland, Va. (Hanover Co.).
Ashland, Wis. (co. seat of *Ashland* Co.).
Ashland, Mount, Ore.
Ashland City, Tenn. (co. seat of Cheatham Co.).

ASHLEY Co., Ark. (co. seat, Hamburg). For Chester Ashley (1790-1848), Arkansas statesman.

ASHLEY, N.Dak. (co. seat of McIntosh Co.). For Ashley E. Morrow, a railroad construction official.

ASHLEY, Pa. (Luzerne Co.). For Herbert Henry Ashley of Wilkes-Barre, a descendant of the English family of the same name.

ASHLEY, William H., a fur trader.
Ashley Creek, Utah. Flows generally SE into Green R.
Ashley Natl. Forest, Utah.

ASHLEY RIVER, S.C. For the Earl of Shaftsbury, Lord Anthony Ashley Cooper, a proprietor. It flows southeast into the Atlantic. See COOPER RIVER, S.C.

ASHOKAN From Algonquian "small mouth" or "outlet."
Ashokan, N.Y. (Ulster Co.).
Ashokan Reservoir, N.Y.

ASHTABULA From Algonquian, "fish river." It has also been translated "there are always enough moving," possibly with reference to fish.
Ashtabula Co., Ohio (co. seat, Jefferson).
Ashtabula, Ohio (*Ashtabula* Co.).
Ashtabula, Lake, N.Dak. Named by settlers from *Ashtabula*, Ohio.
Ashtabula River, Ohio. Flows generally N to Lake Erie.

ASHWAUBENON, Wis. (Brown Co.). From Ojibway, "a lookout," or perhaps for the Menominee chief Ashwaubamie.

ASOTIN From Nez Perce, "eel creek."
Asotin Co., Wash. (co. seat, *Asotin*).
Asotin, Wash. (co. seat of *Asotin* Co.).

ASPEN For aspen trees.
Aspen, Colo. (co. seat of Pitkin Co.).
Aspen Butte, Ore.
Aspen, Mount, Colo.
Aspen Hill, Md. (Montgomery Co.).

ASPERMONT, Tex. (co. seat of Stonewall Co.). From Latin *asper* plus *mont*, "rough mountain" or "a rough place."

ASPETUCK From Paugusett, "at the high place."
East Aspetuck River, Conn. Flows into Housatonic R.
West Aspetuck River, Conn. Flows into Housatonic R.

ASSABET RIVER, Mass. From Nipmuc, "miry place." It flows northeast to join Sudbury River to form Concord River.

ASSATEAGUE ISLAND, Va.-Md. From Algonquian, "beyond the island."

ASSAWOMPSET POND, Mass. From Wampanoag, meaning uncertain, but variously postulated as "bartering place," "place of the large rock," and others.

ASSINIBOIA A variant of ASSINIBOINE.
Assiniboia, District of (c.1812-1870). Established in the area near the present city of Winnipeg and more commonly known as the Red River Settlement, it formed the nucleus of the Province of Manitoba.
Assiniboia, District of (1882-1905). One of the four original divisions of the Canadian Northwest Territories, it was divided in 1905 into the southern quarter of Saskatchewan and a southeastern strip in Alberta.
Assiniboia, Sask. For the old district.

ASSINIBOINE Named for the Assiniboin Indians, a tribe of Siouan linguistic stock whose name comes from the Ojibway *usini*, "stone," and *upwana*, "he cooks by roasting," thus "one who cooks by the use of stones."
Assiniboine, Mount, Alta.-B.C.
Assiniboine Pass., Alta.-B.C., in the Rocky Mtns.
Assiniboine River. Flows into the Red R.

ASSISCUNK CREEK, N.J. From Delaware Indian, "the place for clay," used for paint. It flows west into Delaware River.

ASSUMPTION Parish, La. (parish seat, Napoleonville). For the Assumption, the taking of the Virgin Mary bodily to Heaven upon her death, according to the Bible. The festival is celebrated August 15.

ASSUNPINK CREEK, N.J. From Algonquian, meaning uncertain, but translated as "at the stony place." It flows northwest and southwest into Delaware River.

ASTORIA, Ore. (co. seat of Clatsop Co.). Latinized, for John Jacob Astor (1763-1848), owner of the Pacific Fur Company.

ATASCADERO, Calif. (San Luis Obispo Co.). From Spanish, "miry place."

ATASCOSA From Spanish, "wet" or "swampy."
Atascosa Co., Tex. (co. seat, Jourdanton). For the river.
Atascosa River, Tex. Flows into Nueces R.

ATCHAFALAYA From Choctaw, "long river."
Atchafalaya Bay, La. Arm of the Gulf of Mexico.
Atchafalaya River, La. Flows SSE into the bay.

ATCHISON, David Rice (1807-1886), Missouri statesman and U.S. senator (1843-55).
Atchison Co., Kan. (co. seat, Atchison).
Atchison Co., Mo. (co. seat, Rockport). Earlier, Allen.
Atchison, Kan. (co. seat of *Atchison* Co.).

ATHABASCA From Cree Indian, "where there are reeds," referring to the data area in the southwest part of Lake Athabasca. Also spelled *Athabaska*.
Athabasca, Lake, Alta.-Sask.
Athabasca River, Alta.
Athabaska, District of (1882-1905). One of the four original divisions of the Canadian Northwest Territories, it was divided in 1905 to form the northern halves of Alberta and Saskatchewan with a small eastern strip being added to Manitoba.

ATHENS For the Greek city famed in classical antiquity as the focal point of Greek learning and culture and thus a symbol of learning. Hence Boston, with its many colleges and universities, dubbed itself the "Athens of America." The name has been chosen frequently for college and university towns.
Athens Co., Ohio (co. seat, *Athens*).
Athens, Ala. (co. seat of Limestone Co.). Site of *Athens* College.
Athens, Ga. (co. seat of Clarke Co.). Site of the University of Georgia.

View of the public square. Atlanta was occupied by the 20th Army Corps, Major General Slocum commanding—and was afterwards strongly fortified by that Corps. [*New York Historical Society*]

Athens, Ohio (co. seat of *Athens* Co.). Site of Ohio University.

Athens, Pa. (Bradford Co.).

Athens, Tenn. (co. seat of McMinn Co.). Site of the Tennessee Wesleyan University.

Athens, Tex. (co. seat of Henderson Co.). Site of Henderson County Jr. College.

ATHERTON, Calif. (San Mateo Co.). For the father-in-law of the novelist Gertrude Atherton, Faxon D. Atherton, landowner and founder.

ATHOL, Mass. (Worcester Co.), town and village. For James Murray, 2nd Duke of Atholl (c.1690-1764), lord privy seal (1733-63). An earlier name was Pequoiag.

ATKINSON Co., Ga. (co. seat, Pearson). For William Yeats Atkinson (1854-1899), Georgia legislator and governor (1894-99).

ATKINS PEAK, Wyo., in the Yellowstone Natl. Park. For John D. Atkins, a commissioner for Indian affairs.

ATLANTA A coinage from ATLANTIC. The -*a* termination indicates that it was thought of as feminine and, therefore, appropriate as a place name.

Atlanta, Ga. (co. seat of Fulton Co.), state capital. Earlier, Terminus and Marthasville.

Atlanta, Mich. (co. seat of Montmorency Co.).

Atlanta, Tex. (Cass Co.).

North Atlanta, Ga. (De Kalb Co.). For *Atlanta*, Ga.

ATLANTIC For the great ocean named by the ancient Greeks "the sea beyond Mount Atlas." This mountain, in what is now Morocco, and the sea which lay to the west of it, were at the very edge of the world known to the Greeks.

Atlantic Co., N.J. (co. seat, Mays Landing).

Atlantic, Iowa (co. seat of Cass Co.).

Atlantic Peak, Wyo.

Atlantic City, N.J. (*Atlantic* Co.).

Atlantic Highlands, N.J. (Monmouth Co.).

ATOKA For a Choctaw athlete.

Atoka Co., Okla. (co. seat, *Atoka*).
Atoka, Okla. (co. seat of *Atoka* Co.).
Atoka Reservoir, Okla.

ATTAKAPAS, La., region comprising St. Mary's, St. Martin's, Vermilion, Iberia, and Lafayette parishes. From Choctaw, "man-eater," since the Atakapas sometimes ate their enemies.

ATTALA Co., Miss. (co. seat, Kosciusko). From Cherokee *otale*, "mountain."

ATTALLA, Ala. (Etowah Co.). Originally Atale, a corruption of Cherokee *otale*, "mountain."

ATTEAN For Etionno Orcon, an early settler. *Attean* is an Indian approximation of the pronunciation of Etienne.
Attean Lake, Me.
Attean Mountain, Me.

ATTICA For the region around Attica, Greece. The habit of giving classical names was common in the early 1800s.
Attica, Ind. (Fountain Co.). For *Attica*, N.Y.
Attica, N.Y. (Genesee and Wyoming Cos.).

ATTLEBORO For Attleborough, Norfolk, England.
Attleboro, Mass. (Bristol Co.).
North Attleboro, Mass. (Bristol Co.), town.

ATTU ISLAND, Alaska, in the Aleutian Islands. Of Aleut origin, meaning uncertain. It was the site of a 1943 battle between American and Japanese armed forces.

ATWATER, Calif. (Merced Co.). For Marshall D. Atwater, landowner and wheat rancher.

ATWOOD, Kan. (co. seat of Rawlins Co.). For Atwood Matheny, son of the town's founder.

ATWOOD LAKE, Ohio. For the post office stop on a narrow-gauge railroad, in turn for the first postmaster.

AUAU CHANNEL, Hawaii, water passage between Maui and Lanai Islands, the latter privately owned. From Hawaiian, "bathe."

AUBURN For Auburn, Yorkshire, England, especially through Oliver Goldsmith's poem "The Deserted Village," which begins, "Sweet Auburn, loveliest village of the plain."
Auburn, Ala. (Lee Co.).
Auburn, Calif. (co. seat of Placer Co.). For *Auburn*, N.Y. Earlier, Wood's Dry Diggings.
Auburn, Ill. (Sangamon Co.).
Auburn, Ind. (co. seat of De Kalb Co.).
Auburn, Me. (co. seat of Androscoggin Co.). Earlier, Bakerstown.
Auburn, Mass. (Worcester Co.), town. Earlier, Ward.
Auburn, Neb. (co. seat of Nemaha Co.).
Auburn, N.H. (Rockingham Co.), town.
Auburn, N.Y. (co. seat of Cayuga Co.). Earlier, Hardenburgh's Corners.
Auburn, Wash. (King Co.). Earlier, Slaughter.
Auburn, Lake, Me.
Auburndale, Fla. (Polk Co.).
Auburndale, Mass. (Middlesex Co.), town.

AUCILLA Of Timucuan origin, meaning unknown.
Aucilla, Fla. (Jefferson Co.).
Aucilla River, Fla.-Ga. Flows S into Apalachee Bay, Gulf of Mexico.

AUDRAIN Co., Mo. (co. seat, Mexico). For James H. Audrain (1782-1831), Missouri legislator.

AUDUBON, John James (1785-1851), ornithologist and artist, born in Santo Domingo (now Haiti). He emigrated to the United States in 1803. His famous work, *Birds of America* (1827-31), brought him recognition as America's foremost naturalist. He traveled widely in search of bird life, especially in the Eastern and Southern states.
Audubon Co., Iowa (co. seat, *Audubon*).
Audubon, Iowa (co. seat of *Audubon* Co.).
Audubon, N.J. (Camden Co.).
Audubon, Mount, Colo.
Audubon Mountain, Alaska.

AUGHWICK CREEK, Pa. Believed to have been derived from Delaware Indian, "bushy."

AUGLAIZE From French *au glaise*, "at the stream," or "at the lick," with possible reference to a salt lick.

Auglaize Co., Ohio (co. seat, Wapakoneta).
Auglaize River, Ohio. Flows into the Maumee R.

AU GRES From French, "gritty stone."
Au Gres, Mich. (Arenac Co.).
Au Gres Point, Mich., on Saginaw Bay.
Au Gres River, Mich. Flows generally SSE into Saginaw Bay.

AUGUSTA For Princess Augusta of Saxe-Gotha (1719?-1772), wife of Frederick Louis, Prince of Wales, and mother of George III of England.
Augusta Co., Va. (co. seat, Staunton).
Augusta, Ga. (co. seat of Richmond Co.).
Augusta, W.Va. (Hampshire Co.).
North Augusta, S.C. (Aiken Co.). For *Augusta*, Ga.

AUGUSTA, Ark. (co. seat of Woodruff Co.). Named by Thomas Hough for his niece, Augusta Cald.

AUGUSTA, Kan. (Butler Co.). For Augusta James, wife of a founder.

AUGUSTA, Me. (co. seat of Kennebec Co.), state capital. Probably for Pamela Augusta Dearborn, daughter of Gen. Henry Dearborn (1751-1829), officer in the American Revolution and secretary of war (1801-09) under Jefferson.

AUGUSTINE ISLAND, Alaska, in Kamishak Bay. For Saint Augustine. Earlier, it was named Saint Augustine Island by Capt. John Cook (1778).

AUGUTIKADO, Alaska, a bluff on Saligvik Ridge. From Eskimo, "little food bag," or "seal's stomach," which the bluff was said to resemble.

AURORA For the Roman goddess of dawn. The name, being classical, and having pleasant connotations, has had great appeal in the United States.
Aurora Co., S.Dak. (co. seat, Plankinton).
Aurora, Colo. (Adams and Arapahoe Cos.).
Aurora, Ill. (Kane Co.). Translated from Iroquoian *deawendote*, "constant dawn."
Aurora, Ind. (Dearborn Co.).
Aurora, Me. (Hancock Co.), town.
Aurora, Minn. (St. Louis Co.).
Aurora, Mo. (Lawrence Co.).
Aurora, Neb. (co. seat of Hamilton Co.).

Aurora, Ohio (Portage Co.).
Aurora, Ont. (York Co.).
East Aurora, N.Y. (Erie Co.). Earlier, Willink.
North Aurora, Ill. (Kane Co.).

AU SABLE From French, "sandy place." Also spelled *Ausable*.
Au Sable, Mich. (Iosco Co.).
Ausable Chasm, N.Y.
Au Sable Point, Mich., on L. Huron.
Au Sable River, Mich. Flows E into L. Huron.
Ausable River, N.Y. Flows NE into L. Champlain.
Ausable Forks, N.Y. (Essex and Clinton Cos.).

AUSTERLITZ, N.Y. (Columbia Co.). Named by Martin Van Buren, who was then a state senator, in honor of Napoleon, his hero. Napoleon's defeat at Waterloo had already been commemorated in the naming of a Seneca County town. Van Buren therefore proposed that this locale be named for the emperor's 1805 victory over the Russian and Austrian armies.

AUSTIN, Minn. (co. seat of Mower Co.). For Austin R. Nichols (1814-1914), first settler.

AUSTIN, Nev. (co. seat of Lander Co.). For Leander ("Kelse") Austin, uncle of a mine owner.

AUSTIN, Stephen Fuller (1793-1836), pioneer settler in Texas and statesman. With his father, Austin helped colonize Texas. Active in the organization of the state, he served in the legislature (1831-32) and was president of the Texas convention. Chosen commander (1834) to resist General Santa Anna, he was also a member of the commission to seek aid from the United States for Texas forces. A candidate for the presidency of the Republic of Texas, he was defeated by Sam Houston. He served as secretary of state of the Republic and died in office.
Austin Co., Tex. (co. seat, Bellville).
Austin, Ind. (Scott Co.).
Austin, Tex. (co. seat of Travis Co.), state capital.

AUSTIN STREAM, Me. For the Austin family, landholders in the area. It flows generally southwest into Kennebec River.

AUSTINTOWN, Ohio (Mahoning Co.). For Eliphalet Austin, early landowner and jurist.

AUTAUGA For an ancient Alabama Indian town; from Creek Indian, probably "border."
Autauga Co., Ala. (co. seat, Prattville).
Autauga Creek, Ala.

AU TRAIN From French *trainerant*, "at the dragging place," where canoes or boats had to be pulled over the area.
Au Train, Mich. (Alger Co.).
Au Train Bay, Mich. Inlet of L. Superior.

AUX BARQUES, Point, Mich. From French, "at the ships," connoting "where the ships pass."

AUXVASSE CREEK, Mo. From French *aux vases*, "at the swamps." It flows southeast and south into the Missouri River.

AVA, Mo. (co. seat of Douglas Co.). For a Biblical place name (2 Kings 17:24).

AVALON, Pa. (Allegheny Co.). From Celtic, "orchard" or "land of apples."

AVENAL, Calif. (Kings Co.). From Spanish, "oat field."

AVERILL For a local community member.
Averill, Vt. (Essex Co.), town.
Great *Averill* Lake, Vt.

AVERY Co., N.C. (co. seat, Newland). For Waightstill Avery (1745-1821), legislator, officer in the American Revolution, and state official.

AVERY, Ore. (Benton Co.). For Joseph C. Avery (1817-1876), legislator and landowner. See also CORVALLIS.

AVOCADO HEIGHTS, Calif. (Los Angeles Co.). For the tropical fruit.

AVON For a river in England, probably the Upper Avon, on which stands Stratford-on-Avon, home of Shakespeare.
Avon, Conn. (Hartford Co.), town.
Avon, Mass. (Norfolk Co.), town.
Avon, N.Y. (Livingston Co.).
Avon, Ohio (Lorain Co.). For *Avon*, N.Y.

Avondale, Ariz. (Maricopa Co.). For the Avondale Ranch, possibly for *Avondale*, Ohio.
Avondale, Ohio (Belmont Co.).
Avon Park. Fla. (Highlands Co.).

AVOYELLES Parish, La. (parish seat, Marksville). For an Indian tribe. The name probably means "flint people."

AWUMA RIVER, Alaska. From Eskimo, possibly "westward." It flows into Colville River.

AYER, Mass. (Middlesex Co.), town. For Dr. James Cook Ayer (?-1876), the manufacturer of patent medicines.

AYLMER, Que. (Gatineau Co.). For Lord Aylmer, governor-in-chief of Canada (1831-35).

AZISCOOS LAKE, Me. From Abnaki, "young pine tree." Also spelled *Aziscohos*.

AZLE Tex. (Tarrant Co.). For Dr. Azle Stewart, an early settler.

AZTEC The Aztecs, known also as Nahuatls, were the major tribe of Indians during the period of the Spanish conquest of the area that is now Mexico. They belonged to the Uto-Aztecan linguistic stock and lived mainly in the region that is now Mexico City, although tribes were scattered throughout Mexico.
Aztec, N.Mex. (co. seat of San Juan Co.). Named because it was believed that the ruins of a nearby pueblo had once been inhabited by a tribe of the Aztecs.
Aztec Ruins Natl. Monument, N.Mex.

AZURE MOUNTAIN, N.Y. Poetically descriptive for its blue appearance.

AZUSA, Calif. (Los Angeles Co.). From Gabrielino Indian *azuncsbit*, "skunk hill." Locally it is said to be the name of a beautiful maiden, daughter of an Indian chief. Columnists' folklore read it as "A to Z in the U.S.A." The Indian derivation is correct.

AZUSA, Wyo. (Sweetwater Co.). Said to be for the manager of a Chinee store in Rock Springs, Wyo.

BABBITT, Minn. (Saint Louis Co.). For Francis E. Babbitt, a schoolteacher who discovered evidence of man living in the Minnesota area during the Ice Age.

BABYLON, N.Y. (Suffolk Co.). Biblical, for the city in Mesopotamia where the Hanging Gardens, one of the Seven Wonders of the World, were built.

BACA Co., Colo. (co. seat, Springfield). For an early pioneer family.

BACHELOR BUTTE, Ore. So named because it is separate from the nearby Three Sisters peaks.

BACHELOR RIVER, Mass. For a bachelor who lived in the area. It flows west southwest into Connecticut River.

BACK BAY, Mass. (section of Boston). Descriptive; it is in back of the city, if Boston is conceived as facing the ocean or the main bay.

BACK BAY, Va. Descriptive of a bay extending back of the beach.

BACKBONE MOUNTAIN, Md. Descriptive.

BACK RIVER, N.W.T. For Sir George Back, who explored it in 1834. It flows generally northeast into Chantrey Inlet. An earlier name was Great Fish River.

BACON Co., Ga. (co. seat, Alma). For Augustus Octavius Bacon (1839-1914), Confederate army officer and Georgia statesman.

BACON RIDGE, Wyo. So named because its appearance supposedly resembled bacon, a common item in the frontier diet.

BAD AXE, Mich. (co. seat of Huron Co.). So named because a surveyor, after finding a dull axe in a hunter's cabin, recorded the name Bad Axe Camp on his maps.

BADEN, Pa. (Beaver Co.). For Baden-Baden, Germany.

BADGER CREEK, Colo. For the animal. It flows generally north into South Platte River.

BADLANDS Descriptive of rough terrain. It is a translation from French *mauvaises terres,* "bad lands in which to travel."
Badlands, N.Dak.
Badlands, Wyo.-S.Dak.
Badlands Natl. Monument, S.Dak.

BAD RIVER, S.Dak. Translation from Siouan word; so named because a cloudburst drowned some Indians camped on the shore of the river. It flows east into Missouri River.

BAD RIVER, Wis. From a Chippewa word, *maski,* "swamp," which was mistaken for *matchi,* "bad." It flows north into Lake Superior.

BAD WATER LAKE, Wis.-Mich. Descriptive.

BAFFIN, William (1584-1622), an English explorer and navigator.
Baffin Bay, inlet on the Atlantic Ocean between Greenland and *Baffin* Island. Discovered by William Baffin.
Baffin Bay, Tex., inlet of Laguna Madre. For *Baffin* Bay, off the coast of Greenland.
Baffin Island, .N.W.T., largest island of Canadian Arctic Archipelago. Earlier, Baffin Land.

BAGLEY, Minn. (co. seat of Clearwater Co.). For Sumner C. Bagley (?-1915), early pioneer and businessman.

BAGOT, Sir Charles (1781-1843), British diplomat and administrator who served in the foreign ministry and in many ambassadorial posts. In 1817 he negotiated the Rush-Bagot agreement with the United States. Although in ill-health, he served ably as governor general of British North America (1841-43).
Bagot Co., Que. (co. seat, Saint Liboire).
Bagotville, Que. (Chicoutimi Co.).

BAIE-COMEAU, Que. (Saguenay Co.). *Baie*, from French, "bay," for its location on the Baie des Anglais. *Comeau*, for Napoleon Alexandre Comeau, personality and author of *La Vie et la Sport sur la Cote Nord.*

BAILEY, Mount, Ore. Origin unknown, but possibly a clerical error for *Baldy*, descriptive of the mountaintop.

BAILEY Co., Tex. (co. seat, Muleshoe). For a soldier killed (1836) at the Battle of the Alamo.

BAILEY BROOK, Me. For a Bailey in the area. It flows generally northwest into the St. John River.

BAINBRIDGE, Ga. (co. seat of Decatur Co.). For Commodore William Bainbridge (1774-1833), commander of the *Constitution* in the War of 1812.

BAIRD, Tex. (co. seat of Callahan Co.). For Matthew Baird, a director of the Texas and Pacific railroad.

BAIRD MOUNTAINS, Alaska. For Spencer Fullerton Baird (1823-1887), American naturalist and ornithologist. He was secretary of the Smithsonian Institution

(1850-87) and U.S. commissioner of fish and fisheries (1871-87).

BAKER, Edward Dickinson (1811-1861), Illinois and later Oregon statesman and officer in the Union army, killed in battle.
Baker Co., Ore. (co. seat, *Baker*).
Baker, Ore. (co. seat of *Baker* Co.). Earlier, Baker City.

BAKER Co., Fla. (co. seat, Macclenny). For James McNair Baker (1821-1892), Florida statesman and jurist.

BAKER Co., Ga. (co. seat, Newton). For an army officer, John Baker.

BAKER, Joseph, an officer in an expedition with Captain George Vancouver. Vancouver named the Mount for him, from which the lake takes its name.
Baker Lake, Wash.
Baker, Mount, Wash., in Cascade Range.

BAKER, Mont. (Fallon Co.). For A. G. Baker, superintendent of construction for the Chicago, Milwaukee, St. Paul and Pacific railroad.

BAKER BROOK, Me. For the Baker family. It flows north into the St. John River.

BAKERSFIELD, Calif. (co. seat of Kern Co.). For Col. Thomas Baker (1810-1872), U.S. senator and one of the founders of the town.

BAKERSVILLE, N.C. (co. seat of Mitchell Co.). For David Baker, an early settler.

BALA-CYNWYD, Pa. (Montgomery Co.). For Bala and Cynwyd, two towns in Merionethshire, Wales.

BALCH POND, Me.-N.H. For a local community member.

BALCH SPRINGS, Tex. (Dallas Co.). For John Balch, a blacksmith, who settled in eastern Dallas County in 1877. His farm contained springs that were the only source of water in the area.

BALCONES HEIGHTS, Tex. (Bexar Co.). From Spanish, "balconies," to give the impression of a balcony-like overview on the heights. Promotional.

BALD Descriptive, for mountain peaks bare of trees at the time of naming.
Bald Mountain, Colo.
Bald Mountain, Me.
Bald Mountain, Vt. (Bennington Co.).
Bald Mountain, Vt. (Orleans Co.).
Bald Mountain, Wyo.
Bald Hill Creek, N.Dak. Flows SE into Sheyenne R. For the nearby hill.
Bald Knob Peak, Va. (Amherst Co.).
Bald Knob Peak, Va. (Augusta Co.).
Bald Knob Peak, Va. (Bath Co.).
Bald Mountain Pond, Me.
Bald Peak, N.Y.
Baldy Mountain, Mont.
Baldy Peak, Ariz.
Big Baldy, Idaho.

BALD EAGLE For a Wapalanne Indian chief, whose name was so translated.
Bald Eagle Mountain, Pa.
Bald Eagle Creek, Pa. Flows NE into Susquehanna R.

BALDWIN, Abraham (1754-1807), American clergyman and statesman, born in Connecticut but associated with Georgia. He was a member of the Continental Congress (1785), the Constitutional Convention (1787), the House of Representatives (1789-99), and U.S. Senate (1799-1807). He founded Franklin College (now the University of Georgia).
Baldwin Co., Ala. (co. seat, Bay Minette).
Baldwin Co., Ga. (co. seat, Milledgeville).

BALDWIN, Mich. (co. seat of Lake Co.). For Henry P. Baldwin (1814-1892), legislator and banker. He was state senator (1861-62), governor of Michigan (1869-73), U.S. senator (1879-81), and president of the Detroit National Bank (1883-87).

BALDWIN, N.Y. (Nassau Co.). For F. W. Baldwin, an early settler.

BALDWIN, Pa. (Allegheny Co.). For Henry Baldwin, a justice of the Pennsylvania Supreme Court (1830-44).

BALDWIN CITY, Kan. (Douglas Co.). For James Baldwin, sawmill operator.

BALDWIN PARK, Calif. (Los Angeles Co.). For Elias J. ("Lucky") Baldwin (1825-1910), financier and landowner.

BALDWINSVILLE, N.Y. (Onondaga Co.). For Dr. James Baldwin, founder.

BALFOUR, N.C. (Henderson Co.). For the Balfour family, early residents.

BALLARD Co., Ky. (co. seat, Wickliffe). For Bland W. Ballard (1761-1853), professional guide and army officer.

BALLINGER, Tex. (co. seat of Runnels Co.). For William Pitt Ballinger, attorney for the Santa Fe railroad. In 1850 he was also U.S. attorney for the District of Texas and in 1875 a member of the constitutional convention of Texas.

BALL MOUNTAIN BROOK, Vt. Origin uncertain; may have been a shift from *Bald*, or may be from a personal name. It flows generally northeast into the West River.

BALLSTON SPA, N.Y. (co. seat of Saratoga Co.). For Eliphalet Ball, a clergyman, third cousin of George Washington.

BALLWIN, Mo. (St. Louis Co.). For John Ball, purchaser of the Spanish land grant on which the town is located.

BALSAM LAKE, Wis. (co. seat of Polk Co.). Origin uncertain; probably for the tree.

BALTIMORE For the Lords Baltimore, the hereditary title of the Calvert family, proprietors of the colony of Maryland, whose seat was the barony of Baltimore in Ireland. See George CALVERT.
Baltimore Co., Md. (co. seat, Towson).
Baltimore, Md. (independent city in *Baltimore* Co.).
New Baltimore, Mich. (Macomb Co.). For *Baltimore*, Md.

BAMBERG For a local family, especially for Gen. William Seborn Bamberg, a farmer and Confederate general during the Civil War.
Bamberg Co., S.C. (co. seat, *Bamberg*).
Bamberg, S.C. (co. seat of *Bamberg* Co.).

BANDED PEAK, Colo. So named because it has a band of rock formation around the sides.

BANDELIER NATL. MONUMENT, N.Mex. For Adolph F. Bandelier, archeologist. Site of Indian ruins.

Cecilius Calvert, 2nd Baron Baltimore and proprietor of the Colony of Maryland, covered the landscape with places named after his family, his friends, and himself. [*New York Public Library*]

BANDERA From Spanish, "flag," probably for some feature of the nearby mountains.
Bandera Co., Tex. (co. seat, *Bandera*).
Bandera, Tex. (co. seat of *Bandera* Co.).

BANGOR, Me. (co. seat of Penobscot Co.). Possibly for a church hymn of the same name, a lugubrious song of death and resurrection. It is said that a Reverend Seth Noble was whistling it when he was asked the name of his new town at a Massachusetts legislature session. He misunderstood the question and answered, "Bangor," and the name was accepted. The name may also be for Bangor, Wales, or Bangor, Ulster, Ireland. See BANGOR, Pa. An earlier name was Kenduskeag Plantation.

BANGOR, Pa. (Northampton Co.). For the Welsh seaport town of Bangor, in Caernarvonshire.

BANGS, Mount, Ariz. For James E. Bangs, a member of the Clarence King survey party.

BANISTER RIVER, Va. For Richard B. Bannister, with a slight change in spelling. It flows generally south and southeast into the Dan River.

BANKS For a local physician.
Banks Co., Ga. (co. seat, Homer).
Banks Lake, Ga.

BANKS LAKE, Wash. For a local citizen.

BANNER Co., Neb. (co. seat, Harrisburg). Named by citizens who wanted the county "to be the brightest star in the constellation of Nebraska counties."

BANNING, Calif. (Riverside Co.). For Phineas Banning (?-1885), instrumental in improving transportation facilities in southern California.

BANNOCK An Indian tribe, whose name, in Shoshonean, means "hair in backward motion," for their habit of wearing a lock of hair tossed back over their heads.
Bannock Co., Idaho (co. seat, Pocatello).
Bannock Peak, Wyo.

BANTAM From Mahican, "he prays," with English folk spelling causing the name to be frequently misinterpreted as descriptive for size.
Bantam Lake, Conn.
Bantam River, Conn. Flows SE then SW through *Bantam* L. into Shepaug R.

BARABOO An Americanized spelling of Baribeau, the name of brothers who lived in the area. The river was named first.
Baraboo, Wis. (co. seat of Sauk Co.).
Baraboo River, Wis. Flows generally SE to the Wisconsin R.

BARAGA Co., Mich. (co. seat, L'Anse). For Frederic Baraga (1797-1868), Catholic missionary to the Ojibways.

BARANOF ISLAND, Alaska. Named in 1805 for Alexander Andreievich Baranof, first governor of the Russian American colonies.

BARATARIA BAY, La. Inlet of Gulf of Mexico. From Spanish, "deception."

BARBER Co., Kan. (co. seat, Medicine Lodge). For Thomas W. Barber, a Free State settler, later murdered.

BARBERS POINT, Hawaii. SW point of Oahu Is., Honolulu Co. For Capt. Henry Barber, shipwrecked near the point on Oct. 31, 1796.

BARBERTON, Ohio (Summit Co.). For Ohio Columbus Barber (1841-1919), president of the Diamond Match Company.

BARBOUR Co., Ala. (co. seat, Clayton). For James Barbour (1775-1842), Virginia statesman, brother of Philip Pendleton Barbour. He was governor of Virginia (1812-14), U.S. senator (1815-25), secretary of war (1825-28) under John Quincy Adams, and minister to England (1828-29).

BARBOUR Co., W.Va. (co. seat, Philippi). For Philip Pendleton Barbour (1783-1841), West Virginia statesman, brother of James Barbour. He was a jurist and U.S. Supreme Court justice (1836-41).

BARBOURVILLE, Ky. (co. seat of Knox Co.). For James Barbour, who in 1801 gave thirty-eight acres of land for the townsite.

BARDON LAKE, Wis. For a Bardon who lived in the area.

BARDSTOWN, Ky. (co. seat of Nelson Co.). For David Baird, an early settler and landowner.

BARDWELL, Ky. (co. seat of Carlisle Co.). So named because a boarded (or barred) well was in the area.

BARGE CANAL, N.Y. Waterway between Oneida Lake and Mohawk River, leading into the Hudson River. Part of the New York State Barge Canal System. Descriptive.

BAR HARBOR, Me. (Hancock Co.), town. For a narrow strip, or bar, of land (covered by high tide) that connects Mount Desert Island with another island.

BARKLEY, Lake, Ky., dam and lake on Cumberland River. For Alben William Barkley (1877-1956), attorney, statesman, and jurist. He was a U.S. representative (1913-27), senator (1927-49; 1955-56), and vice president (1949-53) under Truman.

BARLOW PEAK, Wyo., in Yellowstone Natl. Park. For J. W. Barlow, army commander of expedition of 1871.

BARNEGAT From Dutch, "breaker's inlet."
Barnegat Bay, N.J. Inlet of the Atlantic Ocean.

Barnegat Inlet, N.J. Water passage between Island Beach and Long Beach island reefs.

BARNES Co., N.Dak. (co. seat, Valley City). For a local jurist.

BARNESVILLE, Ga. (co. seat of Lamar Co.). For Gideon Barnes (1791-1871), landowner and storekeeper. He was a popular civic leader.

BARNESVILLE, Ohio (Belmont Co.). For a family of early settlers.

BARNEY TOP, Utah, peak. For a personal name, but it is uncertain whose.

BARNSTABLE For Barnstaple, Devonshire, England. Original meaning: "Bearda's staple or post," or "post to which a warship was moored." Folk etymology changed *-staple* to *-stable*.
Barnstable Co., Mass. (co. seat, *Barnstable*).
Barnstable, Mass. (co. seat of Barnstable).

BARNWELL For a local family.
Barnwell Co., S.C. (co. seat, *Barnwell*).
Barnwell, S.C. (co. seat of *Barnwell* Co.).

BARONETT PEAK, Wyo., in Yellowstone Natl. Park. For C. J. Baronett, a scout who built the first bridge across Yellowstone River in 1871.

BARRE, Col. Isaac (1726-1802), British soldier and politician. He was wounded while fighting under General Wolfe at Quebec in the French and Indian Wars, and later served as a member of Parliament (1761-90), during which time he defended the rights of the American colonists against the policies of Lord North.
Barre, Mass. (Worcester Co.), town.
Barre, Vt. (Washington Co.), town and village. For *Barre*, Mass. The naming caused a dispute between two former inhabitants of Massachusetts towns. After a town meeting they went out behind a barn and settled the issue with their fists.
East Barre Reservoir, Vt.

BARREN Descriptive of the area.
Barren Co., Ky. (co. seat, Glasgow).
Barren Island, Alaska. Named by Capt. James Cook for the "naked appearance."
Barren River, Ky.

BARRETT, Tex. (Harris Co.). For a local citizen.

BARRIE, Ont. (co. town of Simcoe Co.). For either Captain Barry of York or for Commodore Barrie, who commanded the squadron at Kingston.

BARRINGTON For GREAT BARRINGTON, Mass.
Barrington, Ill. (Cook Co.).
Barrington, N.J. (Camden Co.).
Barrington Hills, Ill. (Cook Co.).

BARRINGTON, R.I. (Bristol Co.), town. For John Shute, Viscount Barrington (1678-1734), prominent theologian, lawyer, and friend of John Locke. His brother, Samuel Shute, was governor of Massachusetts.

BARRON For a local jurist. An earlier name was Dallas, for George Dallas, vice-president of the United States (1845-49) under Polk.
Barron Co., Wis. (co. seat, *Barron*).
Barron, Wis. (co. seat of *Barron* Co.).

BARROW Co., Ga. (co. seat, Winder). For David Crenshaw Barrow (1852-1929), a teacher and later chancellor at the University of Georgia.

BARROW, Point, Alaska, northernmost point of the United States. Named in 1826 for Sir John Barrow, member of the British naval administration.

BARRY, William Taylor (1784-1835), Kentucky statesman and soldier, U.S. representative (1810-11), U.S. senator (1815-16), and postmaster general (1829-35) under Jackson.
Barry Co., Mich. (co. seat, Hastings).
Barry Co., Mo. (co. seat, Cassville).

BARSTOW, Calif. (San Bernardino Co.). For William Barstow Strong, a railroad president.

BARTHOLOMEW Co., Ind. (co. seat, Columbus). For Joseph Bartholomew (?-1840), Indiana pioneer and patriot, who rose to the rank of general and was severely wounded while commanding a battalion at the Battle of Tippecanoe. He served as a state senator (1821-24).

BARTHOLOMEW BAYOU, Ark-La., river. Origin uncertain; *Bartholomew* may be either for a local dweller or for the saint. *Bayou* means "sluggish stream." It flows south into Ouachita River.

BARTLESVILLE, Okla. (co. seat of Washington Co.). For Jacob Bartles (1842-1908), U.S. Army officer, merchant, rancher, and founder. He supervised the building of the Santa Fe railroad from Caney, Kan., to Collinsville, Okla. (1898-99).

BARTLETT, Ill. (Cook and Du Page Cos.). For Luther Bartlett, who granted a right of way through his forty acres of land and a station site for the Chicago and Pacific railroad.

BARTLETT, Neb. (co. seat of Wheeler Co.). For Ezra Bartlett Mitchell, founder.

BARTLETT PEAK, Nev. For a local community member.

BARTLETTS FERRY LAKE, Ga.-Ala., on Chattahoochee River. For the operator of the ferry once there.

BARTON Co., Kan. (co. seat, Great Bend). For Clara Barton (1821-1912), nurse and humanitarian. She achieved fame as a Civil War nurse and later was instrumental in founding the American Red Cross, becoming its first president.

BARTON, William (1748-1831), an early settler who held a land grant in the area. A general in the American Revolution, he captured the British General Prescott. Barton was later imprisoned for fourteen years for the nonpayment of a judgment on his land.
Barton, Vt. (Orleans Co.), town.
Barton River, Vt.

BARTONVILLE, Ill. (Peoria Co.). For William Coatsworth Harrison Barton (1818-1896), farmer and distiller.

BARTOW, Francis S., Confederate general killed at the Battle of Manassas Plains, first officer of such rank to be killed in action during the Civil War.
Bartow Co., Ga. (co. seat, Cartersville).
Bartow, Fla. (co. seat of Polk Co.).

BASIN, Wyo. (co. seat of Big Horn Co.). For BIG HORN Basin.

BASIN MOUNTAIN, N.Y. So named because it dominates a valley forming an almost perfect basin.

BASKAHEGAN Of Abnaki origin, but meaning unclear; believed to mean "stream divides downstream."
Baskahegan Lake, Me.
Baskahegan Stream, Me.

BASS For the fresh-water game fish.
Bass Islands, Ohio. Group of three main islands (North, Middle, and South). The islands are also known as the Wine Islands, for the wine industry developed on them by German settlers.
Bass Lakes, Wis.

BASSETT, Neb. (co. seat of Rock Co.). For J. W. Bassett, first cattleman in the area and an agricultural experimenter.

BASSWOOD For the tree, possibly translated from Ojibway.
Basswood Island, Wis., in Apostle Islands.
Basswood Lake, Minn.-Ont.

BASTROP, Felipe Enrique Neri, Baron de, an early Texas colonizer.
Bastrop Co., Tex. (co. seat, *Bastrop*).
Bastrop, Tex. (co. seat of *Bastrop* Co.).

BASTROP, La. (parish seat of Morehouse Parish).

BATAVIA For ancient Batavia, between the Rhine River and the North Sea, now the Netherlands. The names in the United States derive from Batavia, N.Y.
Batavia, Ill. (Kane Co.).
Batavia, Iowa (Jefferson Co.).
Batavia, N.Y. (co. seat of Genesee Co.). Named by Joseph Ellicott, who founded it as capital of the Holland Purchase.
Batavia, Ohio (co. seat of Clermont Co.).

BATES Co., Mo. (co. seat, Butler). For Frederick Bates, Missouri jurist and statesman, territorial governor of Missouri several times, and governor of the state of Missouri (1824-25).

BATESBURG, S.C. (Lexington Co.). For Andrew David Bates (1823-1891), a local plantation owner.

BATESVILLE, Ark. (co. seat of Independence Co.). For James Woodson Bates (1778-1846), territorial judge, congressman, member of the state constitutional convention, registrar of public lands, and prominent citizen.

BATESVILLE, Ind. (Ripley Co.). For Joshua Bates, a surveyor.

BATESVILLE, Miss. (a co. seat of Panola Co.). For James W. Bates (1821-1900), a much-esteemed Methodist minister. He was also a conductor on the Mississippi-Tennessee railroad, which he helped bring through the town then named Panola, later changed to Batesville in his honor.

BATH Descriptive of a place where one bathes in medicinal waters, usually warm sulfur springs.
Bath Co., Ky. (co. seat, Owingsville).
Bath Co., Va. (co. seat, Warm Springs).

BATH, Me. (co. seat of Sagadahoc Co.). For Bath, Somersetshire, England.

BATH, N.Y. (co. seat of Steuben Co.). For Henrietta, Countess of Bath, the only child and heiress of Sir. William Pulteney of Bath, England, who at one time owned in a "blind trust" more than a million acres of land in western New York.

BATHHURST, N.B. (co. seat of Gloucester Co.). For Earl Bathurst, Britain's colonial secretary in 1826 when the town was named.

BATON ROUGE From French, "red stick," translated from Choctaw *istrouma,* "red pole," probably a boundary mark between two Indian tribes.
Baton Rouge, La. (parish seat of *East Baton Rouge* Parish), state capital.
East Baton Rouge Parish, La. (parish seat, *Baton Rouge*).
West Baton Rouge Parish, La. (parish seat, Port Allen).

BATSTO RIVER, N.J. From Dutch, "bath house," for a bathing place on the river. It flows generally southeast into Mullica River.

BATTEN KILL RIVER, Vt.-N.Y. From the personal name *Batten* plus Dutch *kill,* "stream." It rises in Vermont and flows west and southwest into the Hudson River in New York.

BATTLE AX MOUNTAIN, Ore. Either for its shape or for a brand of tobacco.

BATTLE CREEK, Mich. (Calhoun Co.). For a stream on which a small battle took place (1824) between two Indians and two surveyors.

BATTLEFIELDS MEMORIAL NATL. MILITARY PARK, Va. For Civil War battle areas.

BATTLEMENT Descriptive of shape.
Battlement Mesa, Colo. Named by members of the Hayden expedition.
Battlement Mountain, Wyo.

BAUDETTE, Minn. (co. seat of Lake of the Woods Co.). For Joe Beaudette, a trapper in the area in the 1800s. The first *e* was dropped by clerical error.

BAXLEY, Ga. (Appling Co.). For Wilson Baxley (1802-1892), a cattleman.

BAXTER Co., Ark. (co. seat, Mountain Home). For Elisha Baxter (1827-1899), Arkansas statesman, jurist, and governor (1872-74).

BAXTER PEAK, Colo. For A. S. Baxter (1861-?), rancher.

BAXTER SPRINGS, Kan. (Cherokee Co.). For an early settler, either A. or J. Baxter, who seems to have been a missionary, a tavern keeper, and a sawmill operator. He was also called an infidel.

BAXTER STATE PARK, Me. For Percival P. Baxter, governor of Maine.

BAY For location on or near a bay.
Bay Co., Fla. (co. seat, Panama City). For bay of the Gulf of Mexico.
Bay Co., Mich. (co. seat, *Bay City*). For Saginaw Bay, Lake Huron.
Bay City, Mich. (co. seat of *Bay* Co.).
Bay City, Tex. (co. seat of Matagorda Co.). Near the Gulf of Mexico.

BAY For bay trees.
Bay River, N.C. Flows generally NE to the Neuse R.
Bayboro, N.C. (co. seat of Pamlico Co.). For *Bay* River.

BAYARD, N.Mex. (Grant Co.). For a nearby fort, which was named for G. D. Bayard, Civil War general.

BAYFIELD Co., Wis. (co. seat, Washburn). For Henry W. Bayfield, an admiral in the British navy. An earlier name was La Pointe.

BAYLOR Co., Tex. (co. seat, Seymour). For Henry Weidner Baylor, a physician in the army during the Mexican War.

BAY MINETTE, Ala. (co. seat of Baldwin Co.). For Minette Bay, an estuary near the eastern shore of Mobile Bay. The bay itself was named for a French surveyor, Minet, associated with the founding of Mobile.

BAYONNE, N.J. (Hudson Co.), on Newark Bay. For the port city of Bayonne, France, on the Bay of Biscay.

BAYPORT, Minn. (Washington Co.). Descriptive; on a bay of the St. Croix River.

BAY ST. LOUIS, Miss. (co. seat of Hancock Co.). For the bay on which it is located, which was named for King Louis IX of France. See ST. LOUIS.

BAYSIDE, Wis. (Milwaukee Co.). Descriptive; on Lake Michigan.

BAY SPRINGS, Miss. (co. seat of Jasper Co.). For a bay tree near fresh springs.

BAYTOWN, Tex. (Harris Co.). Descriptive; on Galveston Bay.

BAY VILLAGE, Ohio (Cuyahoga Co.). Descriptive; on Lake Erie.

BAYWOOD-LOS OSOS, Calif. (San Luis Obispo Co.). Combination of *Baywood*, "woods on the bay," probably promotional, and *Los Osos*, from Spanish, "the bears," which were abundant here at the time of settlement.

BEACH, N.Dak. (co. seat of Golden Valley Co.). For Warren Beach of the Eleventh Infantry, who accompanied the Stanley Railroad Survey in 1873. The city was established and named by Northern Pacific railroad officials.

BEACH HAVEN Descriptive and promotional.
Beach Haven, N.J. (Ocean Co.).

Beach Haven Crest, N.J. (Ocean Co.).
Beach Haven Park, N.J. (Ocean Co.).
North Beach Haven, N.J. (Ocean Co.).

BEACH POND, Conn.-R.I. For a local citizen.

BEACHWOOD, Ohio (Cuyahoga Co.). Promotional.

BEACON, N.Y. (Dutchess Co.). For the adjacent Mount Beacon, where signal fires were lit during the American Revolution to warn of approaching British ships.

BEACON FALLS, Conn. (New Haven Co.), town. For the use of signal fires on a nearby hill.

BEADLE Co., S.Dak. (co. seat, Huron). For William Henry Harrison Beadle (1838-1915), soldier, officer, and educator.

BEALE EAST, Calif. (Yuba Co.). For Beale Air Force Base, which was named for Brig. Gen. Edward Fitzgerald Beale (1822-1893), career officer and diplomat. He served as a naval officer in the Mexican War. In 1852 he accepted the post of commissioner of Indian affairs for the California-Nevada territories. In the Civil War he served under the Union flag and was appointed surveyor general of California and Nevada. During the 1870s he was U.S. minister to Austria.

BEAR For the animal, either for the animal's presence or for an incident involving a bear.
Bear Creek, Ill.
Bear Hill, Neb.
Bear Island, N.H., in L. Winnipesaukee.
Bear Island, Wis., in L. Superior.
Bear Lake, Idaho-Utah.
Bear Lake, Wis.
Bear, Mount, Alaska.
Bear Mountain, Conn.
Bear Mountain, Me.
Bear Mountain, S.Dak.
Bear River, Idaho-Utah-Wyo.
Bearfort Mountain, N.J.
Bear Lake Co., Idaho (co. seat, Paris).

BEARDSTOWN, Ill. (Cass Co.). For Thomas Beard, founder.

BEAR EARS. Descriptive of the shape of peaks.

Bear Ears, Utah. From Spanish *arejas del oso*, "ears of the bear."
Bears Ears Peaks, Colo.

BEATRICE, Neb. (co. seat of Gage Co.). For Julia Beatrice Kinney, daughter of J. F. Kinney, a jurist and U.S. representative.

BEATTYVILLE, Ky. (co. seat of Lee Co.). For Samuel Beatty, early settler.

BEAUCE Named by early settlers for the province in France because they felt that the soil in the North American namesake was comparably fertile to the European counterpart.
Beauce Co., Que. (co. seat, *Beauceville-Est*).
Beauceville, Que. (*Beauce* Co.).
Beauceville-Est (Beauceville East), Que. (co. seat of *Beauce* Co.).

BEAUCOUP CREEK, Ill. From French, "too much." Reason for naming is not known. It flows south into Big Muddy River.

BEAUFORT, Henry Somerset, Duke of (1684-1714), a proprietor of the colony of South Carolina.
Beaufort Co., N.C. (co. seat, Washington).
Beaufort Co., S.C. (co. seat, *Beaufort*).
Beaufort, N.C. (co. seat of Carteret Co.). Earlier, Archdale, for Gov. John Archdale.
Beaufort, S.C. (co. seat of *Beaufort* Co.).

BEAUFORT SEA, Alaska. For Sir Francis Beaufort (1774-1857), hydrographer to the British Admiralty.

BEAUHARNOIS, Charles de la Boische, Marquis de (1670-1749), French naval officer and diplomat who served as governor of New France (1726-47). He was granted a tract of land in this area in 1729.
Beauharnois Co., Que. (co. seat, *Beauharnois*).
Beauharnois, Que. (co. seat of *Beauharnois* Co.).

BEAU LAKE, Me.-Que., on international line. From French, "beautiful."

BEAUMONT Calif. (Riverside Co.). From French, "beautiful mountain."

BEAUMONT, Tex. (co. seat of Jefferson Co.). For the Beaumont family, early settlers. The particular family member is not certain, but it seems probable it was Jefferson.

BEAUPORT, Que. (Quebec Co.). For the bay in Brittany, France.

BEAUREGARD Parish, La. (parish seat, De Ridder). For Pierre Gustave Toutant de Beauregard (1818-1893), Confederate general. He directed the bombardment of Fort Sumter, fought at First Bull Run, Shiloh, and Corinth, and conducted the defense of Petersburg.

General P. T. Beauregard was Superintendent of West Point when the Civil War broke out; he resigned to fight for the South. [*New York Public Library*].

BEAUSEJOUR, Man. From French, "good stopping-place."

BEAVER Descriptive; where beavers are found.
Beaver Co., Okla. (co. seat, *Beaver*). For the *Beaver* R., Okla.
Beaver Co., Pa. (co. seat, *Beaver*). For the *Beaver* R., Pa.
Beaver Co., Utah (co. seat, *Beaver*).
Beaver, Okla. (co. seat of *Beaver* Co.).
Beaver, Pa. (co. seat of *Beaver* Co.).
Beaver, Utah (co. seat of *Beaver* Co.).
Beaver Brook, Me.

Beaver Brook, Mass.
Beaver Brook, N.H.
Beaver Creek, Alaska.
Beaver Creek, Kan.-Neb.
Beaver Creek, Mo.
Beaver Creek, Mont.
Beaver Creek, Okla.
Beaver Island, Mich., in L. Michigan.
Beaver Mountains, Alaska.
Beaver Reservoir, Ark.
Beaver River, N.Y.
Beaver River, Okla.
Beaver River, Pa.
Beaver River Flow (reservoir), N.Y.
Beaver City, Neb. (co. seat of Furnas Co.).
Beaver Falls, Pa. (*Beaver* Co.). For falls on *Beaver* R., Pa. Earlier, Brighton.
Beaver Run Reservoir, Pa.
Beaverton, Ore. (Washington Co.). For the beaver dam area, a rich soil much in demand.

BEAVER DAM For beaver dams found on streams or lakes.
Beaver Dam, Ky. (Ohio Co.).
Beaver Dam, Wis. (Dodge Co.).
Beaver Dam Lake, Wis. (Barron Co.).
Beaver Dam Lake, Wis. (Dodge Co.).

BEAVERHEAD For a rock formation in the shape of a beaver's head.
Beaverhead Co., Mont. (co. seat, Dillon).
Beaverhead Natl. Forest, Mont.
Beaverhead River, Mont.

BECANCOUR, Que. (co. seat of Nicolet Co.). For Rene Robineau de Becancourt, 1st Baron de Portneuf, who was granted this land by the company of one-hundred associates (Companie des Cent Associes) in 1657. He was knighted by the king (1681) and commanded the Canadian militia during Frontenac's expedition against the Iroquois (1696).

BECHAROF LAKE, Alaska. For an Imperial Russian Navy navigator, Bocharov.

BECKER Co., Minn. (co. seat, Detroit Lakes). For George Loomis Becker (1904-1928), civic official and legislator.

BECKHAM Co., Okla. (co. seat, Sayre). For John Crepps Wickliffe Beckham (1869-1940), Kentucky governor (1900-07) and U.S. senator (1915-21).

The beaver hat of this Canadian voyageur explains why men of his kind braved hostile Indians and harsh winters—the fur trade with Europe was vast and lucrative. [*New York Public Library*]

BECKLEY, W.Va. (co. seat of Raleigh Co.). For Gen. Alfred Beckley (?-1888), an army officer who resigned his commission (1836) to serve as clerk of the U.S. House of Representatives and who founded the town.

BECKWITH CREEK, La. For a local citizen. It flows south into Houston River.

BEDFORD   For Bedford, Bedfordshire, England.
Bedford, Mass. (Middlesex Co.), town.
Bedford, N.Y. (Westchester Co.), town.
Bedford, Ohio (Cuyahoga Co.).
Bedford Heights, Ohio (Cuyahoga Co.).
Bedford Hills, N.Y. (Westchester Co.).
New Bedford, Mass. (Bristol Co.).

BEDFORD, Iowa (co. seat of Taylor Co.). Origin in dispute. The original spelling was Beadforde, which could point to a namesake

in Bedford, England; other suggestions are Bedford, Pa., home of the government engineer; Bedford, Ind., home of the original surveyor; or Thomas J. Bedford, a trading-post owner who claimed to be the first postmaster.

BEDFORD, John Russell, 4th Duke of (1710-1771), British statesman and Whig leader who negotiated the peace treaty that ended the French and Indian Wars (1757-62),
Bedford Co., Pa. (co. seat, *Bedford*).
Bedford Co., Va. (co. seat, *Bedford*).
Bedford, N.H. (Hillsborough Co.), town. The Duke of Bedford was a close friend of Gov. Benning Wentworth, who named the town.
Bedford, Pa. (co. seat of *Bedford* Co.). Earlier, Ray's Town and Fort Bedford.
Bedford, Va. (co. seat of *Bedford* Co.). Earlier, Liberty.

BEDFORD, Thomas, an army officer.
Bedford Co., Tenn. (co. seat, Shelbyville).
Bedford,   Ind.   (co.   seat   of Lawrence Co.). For *Bedford* Co., Tenn.
Bedford, Tex. (Tarrant Co.). For *Bedford* Co., Tenn.

BEE, Barnard E. (1787-1853), Texas soldier and statesman.
Bee Co., Tex. (co. seat, *Beeville*).
Beeville, Tex. (co. seat of *Bee* Co.).

BEEBE, Ark. (White Co.). For Roswell Beebe, a surveyor.

BEECH For the tree.
Beech Creek, Pa. Flows E and N into Bald Eagle Creek.
Beech Hill Pond, Me.
Beechwood, Mich. (Iron Co.).

BEECH FORK CHAPLIN RIVER, Ky. For the tree and for a local citizen named Chaplin. It flows generally northwest into Rolling Fork River.

BEECH GROVE, Ind. (Marion Co.). Descriptive and promotional; derived from the Beech Grove Improvement Company, a real-estate firm.

BEL AIR, Md. (co. seat of Hartford Co.). From French, "good air."

BELCHERTOWN, Mass. (Hampshire Co.), town and village. For Jonathan Belcher (1681/2-1757), merchant and governor (1729-41). He was a founder of Princeton College.

BELDING, Mich. (Ionia Co.). For Hiram Belding (1805-?), silk merchant.

BELEN, N.Mex. (Valencia Co.). From Spanish, "Bethlehem."

BELFAST, Me. (co. seat of Waldo Co.). Named by a settler from Belfast, Northern Ireland.

BELKNAP, Jeremy (1744-1798), New Hampshire clergyman and historian, author of *History of New Hampshire* (1784-92) and *American Biography* (1794-98).
Belknap Co., N.H. (co. seat, Laconia).
Belknap Mountains, N.H., in the White Mtns.

BELKNAP, Mount, Utah, on Tushar Plateau. For William Worth Belknap, secretary of war (1869-76) under Grant.

BELKNAP CRATER, Ore. For R. S. Belknap, early settler.

BELL, Calif. (Los Angeles Co.). For J. G. Bell and Alphonso Bell, founders.

BELL Co., Ky. (co. seat, Pineville). For Joshua Fry Bell (1811-1870), Kentucky legislator. He was a U.S. representative (1845-47).

BELL Co., Tex. (co. seat, Belton). For Peter Hansborough Bell (1812-1898), Texas soldier, statesman, and governor (1849-53).

BELLAIRE Probably of Old French origin, meaning "beautiful air." The usage is by American adoption.
Bellaire, Mich. (co. seat of Antrim Co.).
Bellaire, Ohio (Belmont Co.).
Bellaire, Tex. (Harris Co.). For *Bellaire,* Ohio.
Bellaire, Lake, Mich.

BELLECHASSE From French, "beautiful hunt." The island was originally named Isle de la Chasse, "island of the hunt," by Samuel Champlain in 1629. The present name is probably a contraction of some intermediate name, Belle Isle de la Chasse.

Bellechasse Co., Que. (co. seat, St. Raphael).
Bellechasse Island, Que.
Bellechasse Stream, Que.

BELLEFONTAINE From French, "beautiful spring."
Bellefontaine, Ohio (co. seat of Logan Co.).
Bellefontaine Neighbors, Mo. (St. Louis Co.). *Neighbors* was added to indicate a friendly community.

BELLEFONTE, Pa. (co. seat of Centre Co.). From French, "beautiful spring," for a large spring at the site. It is believed that Count Talleyrand suggested the name.

BELLE FOURCHE Probably a French translation from an Indian name for "beautiful fork."
Belle Fourche, S.Dak. (co. seat of Butte Co.).
Belle Fourche Dam, S.Dak., also known as *Belle Fourche* Reservoir.
Belle Fourche River, Wyo.-S.Dak. Flows generally NE to the Cheyenne R.

BELLE RIVER, Mich. From French, "beautiful." It flows southeast into St. Clair River.

BELLEVILLE, Ill. (co. seat of St. Clair Co.). From French, "beautiful city"; named by George Blair, who wanted to form a settlement that might become one of the most beautiful cities of America. An earlier name was Compton Hill.

BELLEVILLE, Kan. (co. seat of Republic Co.). For Ara*belle* Tutton, wife of an early settler.

BELLEVILLE, Ont. (co. town of Hastings Co.). For Ara*belle,* wife of Lieutenant Governor Gore of Upper Canada (1816).

BELLEVUE From French *belle vue,* "beautiful view."
Bellevue, Ky. (Campbell Co.). For a view of the Ohio R. from this point.
Bellevue, Neb. (Sarpy Co.). Named by the trapper and trader Manuel de Lisa (1772-1820), first white settler in Nebraska.
Bellevue, Ohio (Huron and Sandusky Cos.). Named by James Bell, early settler.
Bellevue, Pa. (Allegheny Co.).
Bellevue, Wash. (King Co.).

BELLFLOWER, Calif. (Los Angeles Co.). For the abundance of bellflower apple trees.

BELL GARDENS, Calif. (Los Angeles Co.). Promotional; suburb of BELL. Calif.

BELLINGHAM, Mass. (Norfolk Co.), town. For Richard Bellingham (c.1592-1672), colonial governor of Massachusetts (1641; 1654; 1665-72).

BELLINGHAM, Wash. (co. seat of Whatcom Co.). Probably for Sir William Bellingham, an official who supervised the voyage of George Vancouver; named by Joseph Whidbey, in Vancouver's command.

BELLMAWR, N.J. (Camden Co.). For the old Bell Farm, on which the town was founded by Quakers. *Mawr* is Welsh for "hill."

BELLMEAD, Tex. (McLennan Co.). Named by an official of the Missouri, Kansas and Texas railroad for a farm in Tennessee; probably a spelling variant of *Belle Meade,* formerly a large plantation, now a residential suburb of Nashville, Tenn.

BELLOWS FALLS, Vt. (Windham Co.). For Col. Benjamin Bellows. An earlier name was Great Falls.

BELLVILLE, Tex. (co. seat of Austin Co.). For Thomas Bell, who donated land for the site.

BELLWOOD, III. (Cook Co.). Origin uncertain, but possibly Bell's woods, from a surname.

BELMAR, N.J. (Monmouth Co.). From French *belle mer*, "beautiful sea"; the town borders the Atlantic Ocean.

BELMONT From French, "beautiful mountain."
Belmont Co., Ohio (co. seat, St. Clairsville).
Belmont, Calif. (San Mateo Co.).
Belmont, Mass. (Middlesex Co.), town.
Belmont, N.Y. (co. seat of Allegany Co.). Earlier, Phillipsville.
Belmont, N.C. (Gaston Co.).

BELOEIL From French, "beautiful eye," connoting "beautiful view."
Beloeil, Que. (Vercheres Co.). For the mount.

Beloeil, Mount, Que. One of the Monteregian Hills.

BELOIT Said to be an analogy with *Detroit*, a name fancied by an early settler and founder. *Bel* probably suggested "beautiful," with *-oit* borrowed from the Michigan city name.
Beloit, Kan. (co. seat of Mitchell Co.). For *Beloit* Wis.; named by a former resident of that city.
Beloit, Wis. (Rock Co.).
South Beloit, III. (Winnebago Co.). Adjoins *Beloit*, Wis.

BELPRE, Ohio (Washington Co.). From French, "beautiful prairie."

BEL-RIDGE, Mo. (independent city in St. Louis Co.). Promotional.

BELTON Contraction of Bell Town.
Belton, Tex. (co. seat of Bell Co.). Earlier, Nolanville.
Belton Reservoir, Tex.

BELTON, Mo. (Cass Co.). For Marcus Lindsey Belt (?-1921), a friend of the founder.

BELTRAMI Co., Minn. (co. seat, Bemidji). For Giacomo Constantino Beltrami (1779-1855), an Italian who, under the name James Constantine, explored the sources of the Mississippi River. His most celebrated account of his travels is *A Pilgrimage in Europe and America, Leading to the Discovery of the Sources of the Mississippi and Bloody River.*

BELTSVILLE, Md. (Prince Georges Co.). For Truman Belt, from whom the Baltimore and Ohio railroad purchased land.

BELVEDERE, Calif. (Marin Co.). From Italian, "beautiful to see."

BELVIDERE From Italian, "beautiful view."
Belvidere Mountain, Vt.
Belvidere Center, Vt. (Lamoille Co.).
Belvidere Corners, Vt. (Lamoille Co.).

BELVIDERE, III. (co. seat of Boone Co.). Perhaps named by one of the founders for his birthplace in Canada, or possibly for Belvedere, Italy.

BELVIDERE, N.J. (co. seat of Warren Co.). From French, "terrace," "fine view," or "place of beauty."

BELZONI, Miss. (co. seat of Humphreys Co.). For Count Giovanni Battista Belzoni, Italian explorer and engineer, a friend of the founder, Alvirez Fiske.

BEMIDJI For an Ojibway chief. The meaning of the name is uncertain; it has been translated as "river crossing lake," in reference to the Mississippi River flowing through the lake.
Bemidji, Minn. (co. seat of Beltrami Co.). For the lake.
Bemidji Lake, Minn.

BENBROOK, Tex. (Tarrant Co.). For J. M. Benbrook, early settler.

BEND, Ore. (co. seat of Deschutes Co.). For a double bend in the Deschutes River.

BEN DAVIS POINT, N.J., on Delaware Bay. For Benjamin Davis.

BENDELEBEN, Baron Otto von, leader of the Western Union Telegraph exploring expedition in 1866.
Bendeleben, Mount, Alaska, in *Bendeleben* Mtns.
Bendeleben Mountains, Alaska.

BEND, SOUTH See SOUTH BEND.

BENEWAH Co., Idaho (co. seat, St. Maries). For a chief of the Coeur d'Alene tribe.

BEN HILL Co., Ga. (co. seat, Fitzgerald). For Benjamin Harvey Hill (1823-1882), Georgia statesman and U.S. senator.

BENICIA, Calif. (Solano Co.). For Mariano G. Vallejo, landowner. One of his first names was Benicia.

BENKELMAN, Neb. (co. seat of Dundy Co.). For J. G. Benkelman, early settler.

BEN LOMOND, Calif. (Santa Cruz Co.). For Ben Lomond, a mountain in Stirlingshire, Scotland. *Ben* means "mount" or "mountain."

BENNETT Co., S.Dak. (co. seat, Martin). For either John E. Bennett or Granville G. Bennett, South Dakota jurists and legislators.

BENNETT BRANCH, Pa. For Titus Bennett, who founded Minersville, in Schuykill County. It flows northeast into Sinnemahoning Creek.

BENNETT PEAK, N.Mex. For F. T. Bennett, an Indian agent.

BENNETTSVILLE, S.C. (co. seat of Marlboro Co.). For Thomas Bennett, governor (1820-22).

BENNINGTON For Benning Wentworth (1696-1770), colonial governor of New Hampshire (1741-67), who encouraged settlement west of the Connecticut River in what is now Vermont. He was a founder of Dartmouth College. Another theory is that the name came from Bennington, Hertfordshire, England. See also WENTWORTH.
Bennington Co., Vt. (co. seat, *Bennington*).
Bennington, Vt. (co. seat of *Bennington* Co.), town and village.

BENSON, Ariz. (Cochise Co.). For William B. Benson, a judge and friend of the president of the Southern Pacific railroad.

BENSON, Minn. (Co. seat of Swift Co.). For Ben H. Benson (1846-?), local merchant and landowner, or for Jared Benson (1821-1894), a rancher and legislator.

BENSON Co., N.Dak. (co. seat, Minnewaukan). For a Dakota Territory legislator.

BENT Co., Colo. (co. seat, Las Animas). For William Bent, early settler and fur trader.

BENTON, Thomas Hart (1782-1858), journalist, lawyer, and statesman, great-uncle of the artist named for him. He served in the War of 1812 and was a U.S. senator from Missouri for thirty years and then a congressman. His lifelong championing of sound money (gold and silver instead of paper) earned him the nickname "Old Bullion." Benton was also known for his political biography, *Thirty Years View* (1854-56).
Benton Co., Ark. (co. seat, *Bentonville*).
Benton Co., Ind. (co. seat, Fowler).
Benton Co., Iowa (co. seat, Vinton).
Benton Co., Minn. (co. seat, Foley).

Benton Co., Miss. (co. seat, Ashland).
Benton Co., Mo. (co. seat, Warsaw).
Benton Co., Ore. (co. seat, Corvallis).
Benton Co., Tenn. (co. seat, Camden).
Benton Co., Wash. (co. seat, Prosser).
Benton, Ark. (co. seat of Saline Co.).
Benton, Ill. (co. seat of Franklin Co.).
Benton, Ky. (co. seat of Marshall Co.).
Benton, La. (parish seat of Bossier Parish).
Benton, Mo. (co. seat of Scott Co.).
Benton, N.H. (Grafton Co.), town.
Benton, Tenn. (co. seat of Polk Co.).
Benton Central, Mich. (Berrien Co.). For
    Benton Harbor.
Benton Harbor, Mich. (Berrien Co.).
Benton South, Mich. (Berrien Co.).
Bentonville, Ark. (co. seat of *Benton* Co.).
Fort Benton, Mont. (co. seat of Chouteau
    Co.).

BENWOOD, W.Va. For a man named
Benjamin, landowner of the site. Known also
as Ben's Woods.

BENZIE Co., Mich. (co. seat, Beulah).
Origin uncertain; perhaps a variant of the
name of the Betsie River, a French transliteration of Ojibway, "duck."

BEREA For the Biblical city in ancient
Syria.
Berea, Ky. (Madison Co.).
Berea, Ohio (Cuyahoga Co.).

BERGEN For the town of Bergen-op-zoom,
Noord (North) Brabant, Netherlands; named
by early Dutch settlers.
Bergen Co., N.J. (co. seat, Hackensack).
North Bergen, N.J. (Hudson Co.).

BERING, Iran Ivanovitch (1681-1741), also
known as Vitus Bering, a Danish navigator.
He had served in the British East India
Company, and was selected by Peter the
Great to command a Russian expedition to
ascertain whether Asia and North America
were joined. The first expedition (1728) was
unsuccessful. The second expedition (1741)
resulted in Bering discovering the sea and
strait which now bear his name, reaching
what is now probably Kayak Island off the
southeast coast of Alaska, where he
remained only ten hours, on July 20, 1741.
On the return trip to Russia, Bering died of
scurvy on an island which now bears his
name in the Pacific Ocean.

Bering Glacier, Alaska.
Bering Sea, north part of the Pacific Ocean
    between Siberia and Alaska.
Bering Strait, water passage separating Asia
    (U.S.S.R.) and North America (Alaska)
    and connecting the Bering Sea and the
    Arctic Ocean.

BERKELEY, Calif. (Alameda Co.). For the
brilliant Irish philosopher George Berkeley
(1685-1753), who wrote verses regarding
the founding of a college. His major work
was *Principles of Human Knowledge.*

BERKELEY, Ill. (Du Page Co.). Op-
timistically named for BERKELEY, Calif.,
when it was incorporated in 1924.

BERKELEY, Mo. (St. Louis Co.). For the
person who planned the subdivision.

BERKELEY Co., S.C. (co. seat, Moncks
Corner). Apparently for John Berkeley
(1607-1678), proprietor of South Carolina
during the reign of Charles II.

BERKELEY Co., W.Va. (co. seat, Martinsburg). For Norborne Berkeley, Lord
Botetourt (1718-1770), a colonial governor
of Virginia (1768-70). See also BOTETOURT
Co.

BERKELEY HEIGHTS, N.J. (Union Co.).
For Lord John Berkeley, landowner. He
shared with Sir George Carteret a royal
grant of the lands that are now much of New
England and New York and all of New
Jersey. Earlier names were Turkey, for the
fowl, and Providence Township.

BERKELEY SPRINGS, W.Va. (co. seat of
Morgan Co.). Origin uncertain, since many
Berkeleys held offices of importance during
colonial days. It may have been named for
Norborne Berkeley, Baron de Botetourt,
(see BERKELEY Co., W. Va.), or for William
Berkeley or his brother John (see
BERKELEY Co., S.C.), both active in
colonial affairs, the former a governor of
Virginia. An earlier name was Bath, for the
English spa, because there are springs in
the area.

BERKLEY, Mich. (Oakland Co.). For a local
farm or a school that had been so named,
possibly for the English-sounding quality.

Although Berlin was once a common name in North America, anti-German sentiment during World War I caused many communities to change names. Berlin, N.H. resisted this pressure, as did Moscow, Idaho, during the Cold War. [*German Information Service*]

BERKS Co., Pa. (co. seat, Reading). In the shortened form, for Berkshire, England, which also has a Reading as its county seat. *Berk* is a British (and Welsh) term meaning "top" or "summit."

BERKSHIRE For Berkshire county in England. See also BERKS.
Berkshire Co., Mass. (co. seat, Pittsfield).
Berkshire Hills, Mass.

BERLIN For Berlin, Germany, formerly the capital of Prussia.
Berlin, Conn. (Hartford Co.), town.
Berlin, N.H. (Coos Co.).
Berlin, Wis. (Green Lake Co.).

BERNALILLO From Spanish, "little Bernal." A family name, its origin is in dispute. Records indicate that the name Gonzales-Bernal occurs in the area as early as 1680. It may also have been named for Fray Juan Bernal, a friend of one of the community leaders in the same period. The use of the masculine diminutive ending has not been explained satisfactorily.
Bernalillo Co., N.Mex. (co. seat, Albuquerque).
Bernalillo, N.Mex. (co. seat of Sandoval Co.).

BERNARD PEAK, Wyo. Origin of name unknown.

BERNARDSVILLE, N.J. (Somerset Co.). For Sir Francis Bernard (1712-1779), colonial governor of New Jersey (1758-60) and Massachusetts (1760-69).

BERNE, Ind. (Adams Co.). For Berne (or Bern), Switzerland.

BERRIEN, John Macpherson (1781-1856), Georgia soldier, jurist, statesman, United States senator (1825-29; 1841-45; 1845-52), and attorney general (1829-31) under Jackson.
Berrien Co., Ga. (co. seat, Nashville).
Berrien Co., Mich. (co. seat, St. Joseph).

BERRYESSA, Jose Jesus and Sisto, soldiers and land grantees.
Berryessa, Calif. (Santa Clara Co.).
Berryessa Reservoir, Calif., on Putah R.

BERRYVILLE, Ark. (co. seat of Carroll Co.). For Henderson Blackburn Berry (1814-1893), founder.

BERRYVILLE, Va. (co. seat of Clarke Co.). For Benjamin Berry, founder. An earlier name was Battletown.

BERTHIER, Capt. Isaac Alexandre (1638-1708), French soldier who arrived in Canada in 1665. In 1672, as a reward for services, he received the seigniory of Bellechase.
Berthier Co., Que. (co. seat, *Berthierville*).
Berthier en Bas (Lower Berthier), Que. (Montmagny Co.).
Berthierville, Que. (co. seat of *Berthier* Co.). Earlier, Berthier en Haut (Upper Berthier).

BERTIE Co., N.C. (co. seat, Windsor). Said to be named for two brothers, James Bertie (1673-1735) and Henry Bertie (1675-1735), both of whom held proprietary shares in the colony of North Carolina.

BERWICK For Berwick, Dorsetshire, England.
Berwick, Me. (York Co.), town.
South Berwick, Me. (York Co.), town.

BERWICK, Pa. (Columbia Co.). For the town of Berwick-on-Tweed, Berwick county, Scotland.

BERWYN, Ill. (Cook Co.). For a Berwyn in Pennsylvania.

BERWYN HEIGHTS, Md. (Prince Georges Co.). For a chapel of a new Presbyterian church in the area, which was presumably named for a family.

BESSEMER, Sir Henry (1813-1898), English inventor who discovered the iron-smelting process that bears his name.
Bessemer, Ala. (Jefferson Co.). The steel industry was vital in the economic development of this town.
Bessemer, Mich. (co. seat of Gogebic Co.).
Bessemer, Pa. (Lawrence Co.).
Bessemer City, N.C. (Guilford Co.).

BETE GRISE BAY, Mich., inlet on Lake Superior. From French, "gray beast," for an animal seen in area. Also claimed to be named for the color and shape of the shore line.

BETHALTO, Ill. (Madison Co.). Combination of the Biblical place *Bethel* and *alto:* "higher Bethel," to distinguish it from another post office named Bethel. From Hebrew, "house of God."

BETHANY For the village in the New Testament. From Hebrew, "house of dates."
Bethany, Conn. (New Haven Co.), town.
Bethany, Mo. (co. seat of Harrison Co.).
Bethany, Okla. (Oklahoma Co.).

BETHEL, Conn. (Fairfield Co.), town. For the Old Testament place. From Hebrew, "house of God."

BETHESDA, Md. (Montgomery Co.). For a pool in Jerusalem mentioned in the Bible. From Hebrew, "house of mercy."

BETHLEHEM, Pa. (Northampton and Lehigh Cos.). For the birthplace of Christ. From Hebrew, "house of bread."

BETHPAGE, N.Y. (Nassau Co.). For the Biblical village of Bethpage (halfway between Bethany and the top of the Mount of Olives), because the American village lay between settlements then known as Jericho and Jerusalem. From Hebrew, "house of figs."

BETSIE From French *bec scies*, "sawbill duck." Also spelled *Betsy*.

Betsie River, Mich. Flows SW then NW into L. Michigan.

Betsy Lake, Mich.

Betsy River, Mich. Flows E into Whitefish Bay.

BETTENDORF, Iowa (Scott Co.). For the Bettendorf family, industrialists, and especially for W. P. Bettendorf and J. W. Bettendorf, president and secretary-treasurer, respectively, of the company, which manufactured railroad equipment.

BEULAH Biblical; a name prophesied (Isaiah 62:4) for Israel, "for the Lord delighteth in thee." The Hebrew word means "married," used as a woman's name.

Beulah, Mich. (co. seat of Benzie Co.).

Beulah, Lake, Wis.

BEVERLEY, Lake, Alaska, one of the Wood River Lakes. For Beverley N. Polley, a prospector.

BEVERLY For Beverley, county seat of the East Riding of Yorkshire, England. Recent development of the name is promotional and is applied to subdivisions and residential areas because of its English sound.

Beverly, Alta.

Beverly, Mass. (Essex Co.).

Beverly, N.J. (Burlington Co.).

Beverly Hills, Calif. (Los Angeles Co.).

Beverly Hills, Mich. (Oakland Co.).

BEXAR Co., Tex. (co. seat, San Antonio). For the Spanish family of the Duke of Bexar.

BEXLEY, Ohio (Franklin Co.). Probably named for Bexley, England.

BIBB, William Wyatt (1781-1820), a physician who became a U.S. representative from Georgia (1807-13), senator (1813-1816), and first governor of Alabama (1817-20).

Bibb Co., Ala. (co. seat, Centerville).

Bibb Co., Ga. (co. seat, Macon).

BICKNELL, Ind. (Knox Co.). For a John Bicknell, probably an early settler.

BIDDEFORD, Me. (York Co.). Probably for Bideford, Devonshire, England, named by English settlers. An earlier name was Winter Harbour, for a winter spent there by Capt. Richard Vines.

BIENVILLE Parish, La. (parish seat, Arcadia). For Jean Baptiste Le Moyne, Sieur de Bienville (1680-1765), governor of the French colony of Louisiana (1701-13; 1718-26; 1733-43) and a founder of New Orleans.

BIG Descriptive of size.

Big Falls, Vt., in Missisquoi R.

Big Lake, Me.

Big Pond, Mass.

Big River, Alaska. Flows NW to join Middle Fork Kuskokwim R. Translation of Eskimo *kwikpak*, "big river."

Big River, Mo. Flows generally N into Meramee R.

Big Baldy, Idaho. See BALD.

Big Cabin Creek. See CABIN CREEK, Okla.

Big Colly Bay, N.C. See COLLY.

Big Cypress Swamp, Fla.

Big Dry Creek, Mont. Flows NE into Fort Peck Reservoir. Named by Lewis and Clark in 1805 for the dry bed of what looked like a large river.

Big Flat Brook, N.J. Flows SW into Delaware R.

Big Fork River, Minn. Flows N into Rainy R.

Big Graham Creek, Ind. Flows SW into Muscatatuck R. *Graham* is from a personal name.

Big Indian Creek, Ga. Flows SE into Oconee R. For an Indian chief noted for his physical attributes.

Big Indian Lake, Me. For its size and for Indians who lived nearby.

Big Lake, Tex. (co. seat of Reagan Co.).

Big Lost River, Idaho. Flows NE and SE into a depression, where it gets "lost," disappearing from sight.

Big Machias Lake, Me. See MACHIAS.

Big Muddy Creek, Colo. Flows SE into Colorado R.

Big Muddy River, Ill. Flows S and S into Mississippi R.

Big Pine Mountain, Calif. See PINE.

Big Rapids, Mich. (co. seat of Mecosta Co.). For rapids on the Muskegon R.

Big Rib River, Wis. See RIB.

Big Round Lake, Wis.

Big Sand Lake, Wis.

Big Shiney Mountain, Pa.

Big Spring, Tex. (co. seat of Howard Co.).

Big Star Lake, Mich. For its shape.

Big Stone Co., Minn. (co. seat, Ortonville). A translation of either a Dakota or Siouan word.

Big Swamp River, N.C. Flows into Lumber R.

Big Timber, Mont. (co. seat of Sweet Grass Co.).

Big Wood Lake, Me.

BIG BAY Descriptive.

Big Bay, Mich. (Marquette Co.).

Big Bay, Mich., inlet of L. Superior.

Big Bay Point, Mich., on L. Superior.

Big Bay de Noc, Mich., inlet on Green Bay. *De*, from French, "of." *Noc*, from Ojibway *noke*, "bear totem."

BIG BEAR, Calif. (San Bernardino Co.). Probably for a large bear or for some feature thought to resemble one.

BIG BELT MOUNTAINS, Mont. Name transferred from BELT BUTTE. An earlier name was Girdle Mountains.

BIG BEND For location near a bend in a river.

Big Bend Dam., S.Dak., on Missouri R.

Big Bend Natl. Park, Tex. Near the Rio Grande R.

BIG BLACK Descriptive of size and darkness.

Big Black Creek, Va. Flows SSE into Jackson R.

Big Black Mountain, Ky.

Big Black River, Me. Flows NE into St. John R. Translation from an Indian name.

Big Black River, Miss. Flows SW into Mississippi R.

BIG BLUE Descriptive of size and color.

Big Blue River, Ind. Flows SW into E. Fork White R. Translated from French *Riviere de l'Eau Bleue*, itself a translation from an Indian name.

Big Blue River, Neb.-Kan. Flows S into Kansas R.

BIG BUSHKILL CREEK, Pa. From Dutch, "wood," plus *kill*, "creek." It flows southeast and southwest into Big Flat Brook.

BIG CHINO WASH RIVER, Ariz. *Chino*, from Spanish, "China grass," or "grama grass," curly in appearance, descriptive of the way the river meanders. It flows generally southeast.

BIG EAU PLEINE RESERVOIR, Wis., on Wisconsin River. From French, "full water."

BIGELOW BROOK, Conn. For a local citizen. It flows generally south into Natchaug River.

BIGELOW MOUNTAIN, Me. Believed to have been named for a Maj. Timothy Bigelow, an officer in Benedict Arnold's unsuccessful Quebec campaign (1775), who climbed the mountain en route to Quebec.

BIG FLATS, N.Y. (Chemung Co.), town. So named because it is on a big flat along the Chemung River.

BIG FOOT PASS, S.Dak. For Big Foot, a Sioux chief who used this pass to escape white troops. He was killed at the Battle of Wounded Knee.

BIG HOLE Descriptive. Hole frequently refers to a basin or valley.

Bighole Butte, Colo.

Big Hole River, Mont. Flows N and SE into Jefferson R.

Big Hole Battlefield Natl. Monument, Mont., near Big Hole R. Established in 1910 to commemorate the battle fought August 9-10, 1877 between the command of Col. John Gibbon and five bands of Nez Perce Indians. The battle was a stand-off but the Indians were weakened and later forced to surrender.

BIG HORN For the American bighorn sheep. The river was named first.

Big Horn Co., Mont. (co. seat, Hardin).

Big Horn Co., Wyo. (co. seat, Basin).

Big Horn, Wyo. (Sheridan Co.). For the Mountains.

Big Horn Basin, Wyo.

Big Horn Canyon, Wyo.

Big Horn Mountains, Wyo. For the river.

Big Horn Natl. Forest, Wyo.

Big Horn River, Mont.-Wyo. Named (1803) by Lewis and Clark.

Little Big Horn River, Mont.-Wyo.

BIGHORN See BIG HORN.

Bighorn Natl. Forest, Wyo.

Bighorn Peak, Wyo., in Yellowstone Natl. Park.

BIG KONIUJI ISLAND, Alaska. From Aleut, "big crested auk."

BIG MAMUELLE LAKE, Ark. From French, "breast" or "hill."

BIG SABLE From French *sable*, "sandy." *Big Sable* Point, Mich., on L. Michigan. *Big Sable* River, Mich. Flows W into L. Michigan.

BIG SAGE RESERVOIR, Calif. For the sagebrush.

BIG SANDY Possibly translation of an Indian name, descriptive of the sandy nature of parts of the river.
Big Sandy Creek, Colo. Flows NE and SE into Rush Creek.
Big Sandy Creek, Neb. Flows SE into Little Blue R.
Big Sandy River, Ariz.
Big Sandy River, Ky. W.Va. Flows into Ohio R.

BIG SATILLA CREEK, Ga. See SATILLA.

BIG THOMPSON RIVER, Colo. Origin not certain, but may have been named for David Thompson, an English engineer in the employ of the Northwest Fur Company in the 1810s. It flows east into South Platte River.

BIJOU CREEK, Colo. For Joseph Bijeau, guide. The name of the creek is spelled like the French word, "jewel." It flows north and east into South Platte River.

BILLERICA, Mass. (Middlesex Co.), town. From an alternate spelling of Billericay, Essex, England.

BILLINGS, Frederick K. (1823-1890), president of the Northern Pacific railroad (1879-81).
Billings Co., N.Dak. (co. seat, Medora).
Billings, Mont. (co. seat of Yellowstone Co.).

BILLINGTON SEA, Mass., a pond. For Billington, England.

BILOXI, Miss. (Harrison Co.). For an Indian tribe, the Biloxis. The name means "broken pot."

BINGHAM, Cape, Alaska, on north coast of Yakobi Island. Named in July 1794 by Capt.

George Vancouver for Margaret Bingham, Countess of Lucan.

BINGHAM Co., Idaho (co. seat, Blackfoot). For Henry Harrison Bingham (1841-1912), Union officer and U.S. representative (1879-1912) from Pennsylvania, a close personal friend of Governor Bunn of Idaho. He was awarded the Congressional Medal of Honor for gallantry in the Battle of the Wilderness (1864).

BINGHAM, William (1752-1804), Philadelphia merchant and founder of Binghamton, N.Y.
Binghamton, N.Y. (co. seat of Broome Co.).
Binghamton, Ill. (Lee Co.). For *Binghamton,* N.Y.

BIRCH For the tree.
Birch Creek, Alaska. Flows N to join McKinley R. to form Kantishna R.
Birch Creek, Alaska. Flows N into Yukon R.
Birch Island, Me.
Birch Lake, Minn.
Birch Lake, Wis.
Birch Mountain, Me.
Birch Stream, Me.

BIRD CREEK, Okla. For a settler who lived near the creek. It flows southeast into Verdigris River.

BIRD ROCK, Que., island in St. Lawrence River. For gannets that nest there in large numbers.

BIRMINGHAM For Birmingham, a large industrial and metal-manufacturing city and county borough in Warwickshire, England.
Birmingham, Ala. (co. seat of Jefferson Co.).
Birmingham, Iowa (Van Buren Co.).
Birmingham, Mich. (Oakland Co.).
Birmingham, Mo. (Clay Co.).
Birmingham, Ohio (Erie Co.).
Birmingham, Pa. (Huntingdon Co.).

BIRTHDAY CAKE PEAK, Wyo. Descriptive of the shape, which supposedly resembles a cake with candles.

BISBEE, Ariz. (co. seat of Cochise Co.). For DeWitt Bisbee, investor in the Copper Queen Consolidated Mining Company.

BISCAYNE BAY, Fla. Named by early Spanish explorers for a man known as El

Birmingham, England, shown here in 1852, is to Britain's midlands what Birmingham, Alabama, is to the South—a major industrial center. [*New York Public Library*]

Biscaino because he came from the province of Viscaya (Biscaya).

BISHOP, Calif. (Inyo Co.). For Samuel A. Bishop, cattleman from Virginia, who served in the Mariposa Battalion and became supervisor of Kern County, Calif.

BISHOP, Tex. (Nueces Co.). For Francis Zion Bishop (1880-1950), early promoter of the town.

BISHOPVILLE, S.C. (co. seat of Lee Co.). For Dr. Jacques Bishop (1760-1840), a native of Pennsylvania who was an early landowner and postmaster.

BISMARCK, N.Dak. (co. seat of Burleigh Co.), state capital. For Otto von Bismarck (1815-1898), chancellor of Germany (1871-90), in recognition of financial aid given by Germans to the Northern Pacific railroad. An earlier name was Edwinton.

BISON, S.Dak. (co. seat of Perkins Co.). For the bison, or buffalo; so named because a pile of bison bones was found near the site.

BISTINEAU, Lake, La. Origin and meaning of name unknown.

BITTER LAKE, S.Dak. For the taste of the water.

BITTERROOT For the bitterroot plant, sometimes in translation from Indian names for the plant. Also spelled *Bitter Root*.
Bitterroot Natl. Forest, Idaho-Mont.
Bitterroot Range, Idaho-Mont., in the Rocky Mtns.
Bitterroot River, Mont. Flows N into Clark Fork.

BIXBY, Okla. (Tulsa Co.). For Tams Bixby, chairman of the Dawes Commission, which was appointed (1893) by President Cleveland to negotiate with the Seminoles, Chertokees, Chickasaws, Choctaws, and Creeks over an act of Congress that permitted Indian landowners to become American citizens.

BIVOUAC PEAK, Wyo. So named because climbers had to remain overnight on the mountain.

BLACK Descriptive of dark color, sometimes translated from Indian descriptive names.

Black Brook, Me. Flows W into Kennebec R.

Black Butte, Ore.

Black Canyon, Colo. Part of the Gunnison Natl. Monument.

Black Crater, Ore.

Black Creek, Ariz.

Black Creek, Miss. Flows SE into Pascagoula R.

Black Creek, N.Mex.-Ariz. Flows SSW into Puerco R.

Black Creek, S.C. Flows ESE into Pee Dee R.

Black Creek, Vt. Flows S, then NNW into Missisquoi R.

Black Hills, S.Dak.-Wyo. Translated from Sioux *paha sapa.*

Black Lake, La.

Black Lake, Mich.

Black Lake, N.Y.

Black Lake, Que., wide stretch in Becancour R. Also called St. Desire-du-Lac-Noir.

Black Mesa, Ariz. Translation from Navajo.

Black Mesa, Okla. For the color of the volcanic ash and for the mesa, or flat top.

Black Mountain, Me.

Black Mountain, N.Y.

Black Mountain, Wyo.

Black Mountains, Ariz.

Black Mountains, N.C.

Black Mountains, Tex.

Black Pond, Me.

Black River, Alaska. Flows NW into Bering Sea.

Black River, Alaska. Flows NE into Kuskokwim R.

Black River, Alaska. Flows NW into Porcupine R.

Black River, Ariz. Flows into White R.

Black River, La. Flows generally S into Red R.

Black River, Mich. Flows N into *Black* L.

Black River, Mich. Flows SSE into St. Clair R.

Black River, Mich. Flows N into L. Superior.

Black River, Mo.-Ark. Flows S into White River.

Black River, N.C. Flows into Cape Fear R.

Black River, N.Y. Flows NW and W into L. Ontario.

Black River, S.C. Flows SE into Pee Dee R.

Black River, Vt. Flows NNE into Lac Memphremagog.

Black River, Vt. Flows generally SE into Connecticut R.

Black River, Wis. Flows SW to the Mississippi R.

Black Stream, Me. Flows SE into Penobscot R.

Black Hills, Natl. Forest, S.Dak.-Wyo.

Blackledge River, Conn. Flows S into Salmon R.

Black Mountain, N.C. (Buncombe Co.). For the dark firs and balsams on surrounding mountains.

Black Oak, Ind. (Lake Co.).

Black River Falls, Wis. (co. seat of Jackson Co.). For falls on the *Black* R., Wis.

Black Tooth Peak, Wyo.

BLACK BEAR CREEK, Okla. For the animal. It flows east into Arkansas River.

BLACKBEARD ISLAND, Ga. For Edward Teach (?-1718), a pirate nicknamed "Blackbeard."

BLACKBERRY RIVER, Conn. For the blackberry shrub. Flows south and west into Schenob Brook.

BLACKBURN, Mount, Alaska. For Joseph Clay Stiles Blackburn (1838-1918), lawyer, Confederate soldier and officer, U.S. representative (1875-85) and senator (1885-97; 1901-07) from Kentucky, and governor of the Canal Zone (1907-09).

BLACKFOOT, Idaho (co. seat of Bingham Co.). For the Indian tribe.

BLACKFORD Co., Ind. (co. seat, Hartford City). For Isaac Newton Blackford (1786-1859), Indiana legislator and jurist.

BLACK HAWK Co., Iowa (co. seat, Waterloo). For Black Hawk (1767-1838), famous Indian warrior and chief of the Sac and Fox tribes.

BLACKLICK Translation from Indian, "the salt lick with dark water."

Blacklick Creek, Pa. Flows S then W into Loyalhanna R.

Blacklick Creek, Ohio. Flows generally N.
Blacklick Estates, Ohio (Franklin Co.).

BLACK MOUNTAIN, Ariz. For George
Black, early settler and rancher.

BLACK ROCK Descriptive.
Black Rock Desert, Nev.
Black Rock Desert, Utah.
Black Rock Range, Nev.

BLACKSHEAR, Ga. (co. seat of Pierce
Co.). For Gen. David Blackshear (1764-
1837), soldier and legislator. He fought in
the American Revolution (at age 12), was an
officer in the War of 1812 and in Indian wars
of the period, and became a state senator.

BLACKSTONE, Va. (Nottoway Co.).
Originally Blacks and Whites, for two rival
tavern owners, the name was changed
(1885) to that of the famous English jurist,
William Blackstone (1723-1780).

BLACKSTONE, William (1595-1675), the
first settler in the area.
Blackstone, Mass. (Worcester Co.), town.
  For the river.
Blackstone River, Mass.

BLACK WARRIOR RIVER, Ala. A
translation of *Tuscaloosa*. The river flows
generally southwest to the Tombigbee River.

BLACKWATER Descriptive, frequently
translated from Indian names.
Blackwater, Va. (Lee Co.). So named
  because the sawmill dust turned the
  nearby water to a dark color.
Blackwater River, Fla.-Ala. Flows S and SW
  into the Gulf of Mexico.
Blackwater River, Mo. Flows generally NE
  into Lamine R.
Blackwater River, N.H. Flows E and SSE
  into Contoocook R.
Blackwater River, Va. Flows into Nottoway
  R. The black color is caused by juniper
  berries falling into the river. Earlier,
  Indian River.

BLACKWELL, Okla. (Kay Co.). For Andrew
J. Blackwell, founder.

BLACKWELL BROOK, Conn. For a local
citizen. Flows southeast into Quinebaug
River.

BLAINE, James Gillespie (1830-1893),
legislator and statesman. He was a Maine
state legislator, U.S. representative (1863-
76), speaker of the House of Representatives, and U.S. senator (1876-81). He
served as secretary of state (1881) under
Garfield and Arthur and was Republican
candidate for President (1884), secretary of
state (1889-92) under Benjamin Harrison,
and first president of the Pan-American
Congress.
Blaine Co., Idaho (co. seat, Halley).
Blaine Co., Mont. (co. seat, Chinook).
Blaine Co., Neb. (co. seat, Brewster).
Blaine Co., Okla. (co. seat, Watonga).
Blaine, Minn. (Anoka Co.).
Blaine, Mount, Alaska.

BLAIR, Neb. (co. seat of Washington Co.).
For John I. Blair (1802-1899), president of
the Sioux City and Pacific railroad.

BLAIR Co., Pa. (co. seat, Hollidaysburg).
For a local legislator, John Blair.

BLAKELY, Capt. Johnston (1781-1814),
naval hero. He was commander of the U.S.
sloop *Wasp* during the War of 1812. In 1814
the *Wasp* entered the English Channel and
harassed merchant ships and seaport
towns. From there Blakely went on to win
three sea battles with the British before he,
the ship, and the crew were lost at sea.
Blakely, Ga. (co. seat of Early Co.).
Blakely, Pa. (Lackawanna Co.).

BLANCA PEAK, Colo. From Spanish,
"white," descriptive.

BLANCHARD RIVER, Ohio. For Jean
Jacques Blanchard (?-1802), a tailor and
French adventurer who married a Shawnee
in the 1770s, and it is said became the
father of twelve sons. He was supposedly a
well-educated man. The river flows north
and west into Auglaize River.

BLANCHESTER, Ohio (Clinton Co.). Origin
uncertain, although possibly an English
from, *blan* plus *chester*, "town." It could
also be from French *blanche*, "white," with
the addition to indicate "town."

BLANCO From Spanish, "white," or
perhaps for a local resident.
Blanco Co., Tex. (Co. seat, Johnson City).
Blanco, Cape, Ore., on the Pacific Ocean.

Blanco Creek, Tex.-N.Mex.
Blanco River, Tex. Flows E and SE into San
  Marcus R.

BLAND, Richard (1710-1776), Virginia
statesman, a member of the Continental
Congress (1774-75). He was the first to
publish a statement of the colonies' position
on taxation, *An Inquiry into the Rights of the
British Colonies* (1776).
Bland Co., Va. (co. seat, *Bland*).
Bland, Va. (co. seat of *Bland* Co.).

BLECKLEY Co., Ga. (co. seat, Cochran).
For Logan Edwin Bleckley (1827-1907),
Confederate soldier, jurist, and state of-
ficial.

BLEDSOE Co., Tenn. (co. seat, Pikeville).
Probably for Anthony Bledsoe (1733-1788),
American Revolutionary officer in Virginia
and member of the Virginia legislature,
active in establishing Tennessee as a state,
or it may be named for Abraham Bledsoe,
also a Revolutionary soldier.

BLEWETT FALLS For William Bluit
(1719-1810), landowner in the area in the
18th century.
Blewett Falls, N.C.
Blewett Falls Lake, N.C. For the falls.

BLIGH ISLAND, Alaska. For William Bligh
(1754-1816), master of the HMS *Resolution*
on Capt. James Cook's third voyage.
Captain Bligh was later to command the
HMS *Bounty*, famous for the mutiny in 1789.

BLISSFIELD, Mich. (Lenawee Co.). For
Hervey Bliss (1789-1841), landowner,
founder, and first postmaster.

BLOCK ISLAND. For an island discovered
and named by Adrian Block, Dutch
navigator.
Block Island, R.I., in the Atlantic Ocean.
Block Island, R.I. (Washington Co.), town
  and village.
Block Island Sound, body of water connecting Long Island Sound and Atlantic
  Ocean.

BLOODROOT MOUNTAIN, Vt. For the
poppy plant and American wildflower,
Sanguinaria canadensis, which grows on the
mountain.

BLOODS BROOK, N.H. For a local citizen
named Blood. It flows northwest into
Connecticut River.

BLOOMER, Wis. (Chippewa Co.). For a
land developer of this name, which was
originally applied to the prairie.

BLOOMFIELD Descriptive.
Bloomfield, Conn. (Hartford Co.), town.
Bloomfield, Iowa (co. saet of Davis Co.).
  For "a blooming field of prairie flowers."
Bloomfield, Mo. (co. seat of Stoddard Co.).
Bloomfield Hills, Mich. (Oakland Co.).

BLOOMFIELD, N.J. (Essex Co.). For Gen.
Joseph Bloomfield, governor of New Jersey.

BLOOMINGDALE For flowers in a valley.
Bloomingdale, Ill. (Du Page Co.).
Bloomingdale, N.J. (Passaic Co.). For
  Bloemendaal, Netherlands; Dutch,
  "valley of flowers."

BLOOMINGTON Descriptive.
Bloomington, Calif. (San Bernardino Co.).
Bloomington, Ill. (co. seat of McLean Co.).
  Earlier, Keg Grove and Blooming Grove.
Bloomington, Ind. (co. seat of Monroe Co.).
  Probably for wild roses that grew on the
  original site. Another version is that an
  early settler said that he was trying to get
  to the "bloomin' town."
Bloomington, Minn. (Hennepin Co.).

BLOOMSBURG, Pa. (co. seat of Columbia
Co.). Apparently for Samuel Bloom, a
county commissioner. However, there is a
theory that the name came from
"bloomeries," iron-making furnaces in
which the iron is formed into a bar and kept
at a constant heat until it is ready to be
formed in the final process; hence,
blooming mills. A Bloom Street, on which
the furnaces were located, still exists and
was named prior to the time of Samuel
Bloom.

BLOUNT, William (1749-1800), North
Carolina legislator and delegate to the
Continental Congress and Constitutional
Convention (1787). Later he was territorial
governor of Tennessee (1790-96) and U.S.
senator from Tennessee (1796-97).

Blount Co., Ala. (co. seat, Oneonta).
Blount Co., Tenn. (co. seat, Maryville).
Blountville, Tenn. (co. seat of Sullivan Co.).

BLOUNTSTOWN, Fla. (co. seat of Calhoun Co.). For John Blount, a Seminole chief, whose name was given him because he supposedly had the attributes of William Blount, superintendent of Indian affairs in 1790.

BLUE Descriptive of color, frequently in reference to haze on mountain peaks or to the color of water.
Blue Creek, Neb. Flows SE and S.
Blue Mesa, Colo.
Blue, Mount, Me.
Blue, Mount, N.H.
Blue Mountain, Ariz.
Blue Mountain, Ark.
Blue Mountains, Me.
Blue Mountains, Ore.-Wash.
Blue Mountains, Wash.
Blue River, Colo. Flows NW into Colorado R.
Blue River, Ind. Flows SSW into the Ohio R.
Blue River, N.Mex.-Ariz. (Greenlee Co.). Flows into San Francisco R. Translation from Spanish *Rio Azul*.
Blue River, Okla. Flows SE into Red R.
Blue Cypress Lake, Fla. For the cypress trees, which look blue, as well as white.
Bluefield, W.Va. (Mercer Co.) and Va. (Tazewell Co.). For blue flowers (the plant has not been definitely identified) and bluegrass.
Blue Hill Bay, Me.
Blue Island, Ill. (Cook Co.). For the resemblance of a hill in the area to an island covered with blue flowers or by a blue haze.
Blue Knob Mountain, Pa.
Blue Mountain Lake, N.Y. For the mountain.
Blue Mountain Pass, Ore.
Blue Mountain Range, Pa., in the Appalachian Mtns.
Blue Nose, Idaho. Peak, named for color of rocks and for shape.
Blue Ridge, Ga. (co. seat of Fannin Co.). For the mountains.
Blue Ridge, N.Y., mountain (Essex Co.).
Blue Ridge, N.Y., mountain (Hamilton Co.).
Blue Ridge or *Blue Ridge* Mountains, Va.-N.C.-Ga., part of the Appalachian Mtns.
Blue Ridge Lake, Ga.

Bluestone Reservoir, W.Va., on New R. Descriptive of the color of the stone in the river.

BLUE ASH, Ohio (Hamilton Co.). For a species of ash tree, *Fraxinus quadrangulata.*

BLUE EARTH A translation of the Nankato name for the color of the earth in the river, and also probably for pigment taken from it.
Blue Earth Co., Minn. (co. seat, Mankato). For the river.
Blue Earth, Minn. (co. seat of Faribault Co.).
Blue Earth River, Iowa-Minn. Flows generally N to the Minnesota R.

BLUEJOINT LAKE, Ore. For bluejoint grass.

BLUFFTON For high bluffs along a stream.
Bluffton, Ind. (co. seat of Wells Co.). On the Wabash R.
Bluffton, Ohio (Allen and Hancock Cos.).

BLYTHE, Calif. (Riverside Co.). For Thomas H. Blythe (1823-1883), landowner.

BLYTHEVILLE, Ark. (co. seat of Mississippi Co.). For Henry T. Blythe, a minister and farmer who settled in the area in the 1880s. Earlier names were Blythesville and Chickasawba, for an Indian tribe.

BOARDMAN, Ohio (Mahoning Co.). For Frederick Boardman, the original proprietor.

BOARDMAN RIVER, Mich. For William Boardman, landowner. It flows southwest then north into Traverse Bay.

BOAZ, Ala. (Marshall Co.). For Boaz, a Biblical character (Ruth 4:18-22), a rich Bethlehemite of Judah who married Ruth the Moabite woman, Mahlon's widow.

BOBS CREEK, Pa. For an early settler named Bob. It flows south into Dunning Creek.

BOCA RATON, Fla. (Palm Beach Co.). From Spanish *Boca des Ratones,* "mouth (bay) of pointed rocks."

BODCAU RIVER, Ark. Probably from Caddo Indian, origin and meaning unknown. It flows into Red River.

BOEUF From French, "ox" or "beef," for the animal.
Boeuf Bayou, La. Flows SE to form Bayou Techne.
Boeuf River, Ark.-La. Flows SE into Ouachita R.

BOERNE, Tex. (co. seat of Kendall Co.). For Louis Boerne, German poet; settled by German immigrants.

BOGACHIEL RIVER, Wash. From Indian, "muddy waters." It flows northwest into Soleduck River.

BOGALUSA, La. (Washington Parish). From Choctaw, "stream-black."

BOGGY CREEK, Okla. See CLEAR Boggy Creek.

BOGOTA, N.J. (Bergen Co.). From the name of a Dutch family of early settlers, Bogert.

BOGUE CHITTO RIVER, Miss.-La. From Choctaw, "large stream." It flows southeast into Pearl River.

BOGUE HOMA CREEK, Miss. From Choctaw, "red stream." Flows S into Pascagoula R.

BOIS BLANC From French, "white wood" or "birch."
Blois Blanc Island, Mich. Translation from an Indian name.
Bois Blanc Island, Ont.

BOIS BRULE RIVER, Wis. From French, "burnt wood," for a nearby burned forest area. It flows northeast and north into Lake Superior.

BOIS BUBERT ISLAND, Me. Probably French personal name plus *bois*, "wooded area," possibly "Bubert's Wooded Island."

BOIS DE SIOUX RIVER, Minn.-N.Dak. From French, "woods of the Sioux."

BOISE From French *bois*, "wooded area"
Boise Co., Idaho (co. seat, Idaho City).
Boise, Idaho (co. seat of Ada Co.), state capital.
Boise Natl. Forest, Idaho.

Boise River, Idaho.
Boise City, Okla. (co. seat of Cimmarron Co.).
For *Boise*, Idaho.

BOLINGBROOK, Ill. (Will Co.). For Bolingbroke, Lincolnshire, England, and for the Bolingbroke family. The change in spelling may result from the way the English name is pronounced.

BOLIVAR, Simon (1783-1830), soldier-adventurer who led South Americans in their revolts against Spanish rule. Acclaimed both "the Liberator" and "George Washington to South America," he is commemorated with the country name Bolivia.
Bolivar Co., Miss. (co. seats, Cleveland and Rosedale).
Bolivar, Mo. (co. seat of Polk Co.).
Bolivar, N.Y. (Allegany Co.).
Bolivar, Tenn. (co. seat of Hardeman Co.).
Bolivar Peninsula, Tex.

BOLLINGER Co., Mo. (co. seat, Marble Hill). For an early settler.

BOLLINGER PEAK, Wyo. For Karl Bollinger, mountaineer.

BOLTON, Conn. (Tolland Co.), town. Probably for Bolton, Lancashire, England.

BOMBER MOUNTAIN, Wyo. Commemorative, for a B-17 bomber crash in 1943.

BOMOSEEN, Lake, Vt. From Abnaki, "keeper of ritual fire." The last Abnaki, William Simon (*Obum Sawin* in the native language) reflects the form of the name as it developed through folk etymology.

BONA, Mount, Alaska. Named by Prince Luigi Amedeo di Savoia, Duke of the Abruzzi, for the racing yacht *Bona*.

BONANZA PEAK, Wash. From Spanish, "prosperity."

BONAVENTURE From French *bonne*, "good," plus *aventure*, "fortune." The island was named first, called Bonne Aventure by Jacques Cartier.
Bonaventure Co., Que. (co. seat, New Carlisle).
Bonaventure, Que. (*Bonaventure* Co.).
Bonaventure Island, Que.

Bonaventure River, Que. Flows S into Chaleur Bay.

BOND Co., Ill. (co. seat, Greenville). For Shadrach Bond (1773-1832), first governor (1818-22).

BONDVILLE, Vt. For a Mr. Bond, who gave land for the town.

BONE LAKE, Wis. Probably for bones found there.

BONHAM, Tex. (co. seat of Fannin Co.). For Col. James Butler Bonham (1807-1836), Texas patriot who died at the Battle of the Alamo. An earlier name was Bois D'Arc.

BON HOMME Co., S.Dak. (co. seat, Tyndall). From French, "good man"; name taken from a village, which was named for a large island in the Missouri River mentioned in Lewis and Clark's journals.

BONIFAY, Fla. (co. seat of Holmes Co.). For F. B. Bonifay, an official of the Pensacola and Atlantic railroad, built across western Florida in 1881-82.

BONNER, Edwin L., an early settler of northern Idaho, and ferry operator on the Kootenai River.
Bonner Co., Idaho (co. seat, Sandpoint).
Bonners Ferry, Idaho (co. seat of Boundary Co.).

BONNER SPRINGS, Kan. (Wyandotte Co.). For Robert Bonner, editor and horseman.

BONNEVILLE, Benjamin Louis Eulalie de (1796-1878), French-born soldier who explored areas of the Northwest. He was immortalized in Washington Irving's *Adventures of Captain Bonneville* (1837).
Bonneville Co., Idaho (co. seat, Idaho Falls).
Bonneville, Ore. (Multnomah Co.).
Bonneville Dam, Ore., on Columbia R.
Bonneville's Folly, or Fort Nonsense, Wyo. (Lincoln Co.). Cabins were built here by Captain Bonneville in 1832.

BONNEY, Orrin H., mountaineer and author.
Bonney Pass, Wyo.
Bonney Pinnacle, Wyo.

BONNYVIEW, Calif. (Shasta Co.). Promotional.

BONPAS CREEK, Ill. From French, "good walk." It flows south into Wabash River.

BOOM LAKE, Wis. Probably for logging operations there.

Men like Daniel Boone pushed America's frontiers westward with a blend of courage and resourcefulness. [*New York Public Library*]

BOONE, Daniel (1734-1820), frontiersman, one of the best known and most influential settlers of the area west of the Appalachians, especially in Kentucky. Boone became famous when, with the help of John Filson (c.1747-1788), he published *Discovery. Settlement and Present State of Kentucky* (1784). He has become the archetype of the resourceful, raw-boned backwoodsman with coonskin cap and long rifle.
Boone Co., Ark. (co. seat, Harrison).
Boone Co., Ill. (co. seat, Belvidere).
Boone Co., Ind. (co. seat, Lebanon).
Boone Co., Iowa (co. seat, Boone).
Boone Co., Ky. (co. seat, Burlington).
Boone Co., Mo. (co. seat, Columbia).
Boone Co., Neb. (co. seat, Albion).

Boone Co., W.Va. (co. seat, Madison).
Boone, N.C. (co. seat of Watauga Co.).
Boone Lake, Tenn.
Boone River, Iowa.
Booneville, Ark. (co. seat of Logan Co.). For
    Booneville, Ky.
Booneville, Ky. (co. seat of Owsley Co.).
Booneville, Miss. (co. seat of Prentiss Co.).
Boonville, Mo. (co. seat of Cooper Co.). For
    Booneville, Ky.
Daniel Boone Natl. Forest, Ky.

BOONE, Iowa (co. seat of Boone Co.).
Probably for Nathan Boone, son of Daniel
Boone. Nathan (1782-1863) was a captain
of Company H, First Regiment, U.S.
Dragoons, which marched through the area
on June 23, 1835. One of his relatives, W.
M. Boone, moved there in the 1850s, at the
time of the founding of Boonesboro, now
part of Boone.

BOONEVILLE (or Boonville). See also
Daniel BOONE.

BOONVILLE, Ind. (co. seat of Warrick
Co.). For Ratliff Boon (1780-1846) or his
father, Jesse Boon (1754-1838). Ratliff
Boon was first representative from Warrick
County in the state legislature (1816). Jesse
Boon offered acreage for the city but was
refused by the commissioners at the time.

BORAH, Mount, Idaho. For William Edgar
Borah (1865-1940), attorney, U.S. senator
from Idaho (1907-40).

BORDEN Co., Tex. (co. seat, Gail). For
Gail Borden (1801-1874), publisher and
inventor of food products, including con-
densed milk.

BORDEN MOUNTAIN, Mass. Probably for
Borden, Kent, England.

BOREAS For the mythological god of the
north wind.
Boreas Mountains, N.Y.
Boreas River, N.Y. Flows SW into the
    Hudson R.

BORGER, Tex. (Hutchinson Co.). For A. P.
Borger (?-1934), promoter and co-founder.

BORGNE, Lake, La. Bay of Mississippi
Sound, Gulf of Mexico. Origin of the name is
in some doubt. It could be for Borgne River,
Switzerland; or from French, "one-eyed,"

which could mean "defective," for a lake
that is not a lake but resembles one; or for a
one-eyed Indian.

BOSCAWEN, N.H. (Merrimack Co.), town.
For Admiral Sir Edward Boscawen (1711-
1761), who led the British fleet in the
capture of Fort Louisbourg, relieving the
French threat to the New England fishing
industry.

BOSCOBEL, Wis. (Grant Co.). Origin
uncertain; it may mean "wood-beautiful."
Other interpretations exist, such as the
facetious "Co Bos, co Bell," a call for a
cow.

BOSQUE From Spanish, "woody."
Bosque Co., Tex. (co. seat, Meridian).
Bosque River, Tex.

BOSSIER Parish, La. (parish seat, Benton).
For Pierre Bossier (1797-1844), Louisiana
statesman, member of the U.S. House of
Representatives (1843-44).

BOSSIER CITY, La. (Bossier Parish). For
John Baptiste Bossier, a congressman from
the area.

BOSTON For Boston, Lincolnshire,
England, a center of Puritan activity. Many
of the settlers came from there.
Boston, Mass. (co. seat of Suffolk Co.),
    state capital.
Boston, N.Y. (Erie Co.), town. Presumably
    for Boston, Mass.
Boston Bay, Mass.
Boston Mountains, Ark.-Okla. For Boston,
    Mass.
Boston Peak, Wash. For Boston, Mass.
New Boston, Ohio (Scioto Co.). For Boston,
    Mass.

BOSTON, W. J., first store owner.
Boston, Tex. (co. seat of Bowie Co.).
New Boston, Tex. (Bowie Co.).

BOTETOURT Co., Va. (co. seat, Fincastle). For Norbone Berkeley, Baron de
Botetourt. See BERKELEY Co., W.Va.

BOTTINEAU, Pierre, an early settler of the
Red River Valley.
Bottineau, Co., N.Dak. (co. seat, Bot-
    tineau).
Bottineau, N.Dak. (co. seat of Bot-
    tineau Co.).

A view of the Boston Commons in 1768. [*New York Historical Society*]

BOUCHER, Pierre (1622-1717), French pioneer who came to Canada in 1635. He studied the Huron language and customs with the Jesuits of Huronia, and was governor at Trois-Rivieres (1653-1667). His history of Canada was published in 1664.
Boucher Lake, Que.
Boucher River, Que.
Boucherville, Que. (Chambly Co.).
Boucherville Islands, Que.

BOULDER For huge rock formations.
Boulder Co., Colo. (co. seat, *Boulder*). For *Boulder* and *Boulder* Creek.
Boulder, Colo. (co. seat of *Boulder* Co.).
Boulder, Mont. (co. seat of Jefferson Co.). On *Boulder* R.
Boulder Creek, Colo.
Boulder Dam, Ariz.-Nev., on the Colorado R.; former name of Hoover Dam.
Boulder River, Mont. Flows generally SE to the Jefferson R.
Boulder City, Nev. (Clark Co.).

Boulder Rock Creek, Idaho-Ore. Flows NW and W into Owyhee R.

BOUNDARY For position on or near the Canadian border.
Boundary Co., Idaho (co. seat, Bonners Ferry).
Boundary Mountains, Me.-Que.

BOUNDARY PEAK, Nev. So named because it was formerly on the California-Nevada border; later surveying parties placed it in Nevada.

BOUNTIFUL, Utah (Davis Co.). From "Land of Bountiful," in the Book of Mormon.

BOURBEUSE RIVER, Mo. From French, "muddy." It flows northeast into Meramec River.

BOURBON The French royal family that ruled in France, Spain, and Naples from the latter part of the 1500s until, in Spain, the 1900s.

Paul Revere engraved, printed, and sold this view of the so-called "Boston Massacre" in which British troops attacked a group of American protesters. Two were killed and four wounded. [*The Metropolitan Museum of Art, Gift of Mrs. Russell Sage, 1910*]

Bourbon Co., Kan. (co. seat, Fort Scott). For *Bourbon* Co., Ky.
Bourbon Co., Ky. (co. seat, Paris).

BOURBONNAIS, Ill. (Kankakee Co.). For Francois Bourbonnais, Jr., French-Indian landowner and signer of the Council Bluffs Treaty (1846). See also MANTENO.

BOURQUIM HILL, Neb. For William E. Bourquim, homesteader.

BOW Descriptive of bowed shape.
Bow Lake, N.H.
Bow Lake, Alta.
Bow River, Alta.

BOWBELLS, N.Dak. (co. seat of Burke Co.). For the Bow bells in St. Mary-le-Bow Church, London; named by an English stockholder of the Soo railroad.

BOWIE, Col. James A. (1795-1836), pioneer and soldier in the Texas Revolution, killed at the Alamo. The bowie knife is named for him.

Bowie Co., Tex. (co. seat, Boston).
Bowie, Tex. (Montague Co.).

BOWIE, Md. (Prince Georges Co.). For Governor Bowie of Maryland; named after he obtained railroad service between Bowie and Washington, D.C.

BOWIE CREEK, Miss. For a local citizen. It flows southeast into Leaf River.

BOWLDER MOUNTAIN, Mont. Variant of BOULDER.

BOWLING GREEN A place for playing the game of bowls.
Bowling Green, Ky. (co. seat of Warren Co.). Earlier, Bolin Green.
Bowling Green, Mo. (co. seat of Pike Co.). For *Bowling Green*, Ky.
Bowling Green, Ohio (co. seat of Wood Co.). For *Bowling Green*, Ky.
Bowling Green, Va. (co. seat of Caroline Co.). Named by Thomas Hoomes for his family estate in England.

BOWMAN For a Dakota Territory assemblyman.
Bowman Co., N.Dak. (co. seat, *Bowman*).
Bowman, N.Dak. (co. seat of *Bowman* Co.).

BOWMAN CREEK, Pa. For a local settler. It flows northeast into Susquehanna River.

BOWMANVILLE, Ont. (Durham Co.). For Charles Bowman, proprietor of a general store there in 1824.

BOW MOUNTAIN, Wyo. Descriptive of shape of glacier at base.

BOWYER'S BLUFF, Wis. (Door Co.). For Col. John Bowyer, Indian agent.

BOX BUTTE Descriptive of the rectangular-shaped butte.
Box Butte Co., Neb. (co. seat, Alliance).
Box Butte, Neb.
Box Butte Creek, Neb. Flows into Niobrara R.
Box Butte Reservoir, Neb., on Niobrara R.

BOX ELDER Co., Utah (co. seat, Brigham City).

BOXFORD, Mass. (Essex Co.), town. For Boxford, Suffolk, England.

BOYD Co., Ky. (co. seat,.Catlettsburg). For Lynn Boyd (1800-1859), Kentucky statesman. He was a member of the U.S. House of Representatives (1835; 1839-55; speaker, 1852-55).

BOYD Co., Neb. (co. seat, Butte). For James E. Boyd (1834-1906), governor of Nebraska (1891; 1892-93).

BOYDEN LAKE, Me. For the Boyden family, early settlers.

BOYD LAKE, Me. For J. P. Boyd, early settler.

BOYDTON, Va. (co. seat of Mecklenburg Co.). For Alexander Boyd (?-1801), merchant and "Gentleman Justice" of the county court.

BOYER RIVER, Iowa. For the Boyer family from Pennsylvania. It flows southwest into Missouri River.

BOYES HOT SPRINGS, Calif. (Sonoma Co.). For H. E. Boyes, owner and developer of the springs.

BOYLE Co., Ky. (co. seat, Danville). For John Boyle (1774-1835), Kentucky legislator and jurist.

BOYNE For the Boyne River in Ireland.
Boyne, Mich. (Charlevoix Co.). For the river. Known also as *Boyne City.*
Boyne River, Mich. A small river that flows into L. Charlevoix.

BOYSEN RESERVOIR, Wyo., on Big Horn River. For Asmus Boysen, rancher.

BOZEMAN, Mont. (co. seat of Gallatin Co.). For John Marion Bozeman (1835-1867), guide to emigrants moving west, leader of settlers into the Montana area, land promoter, and proprietor. He was killed by Indians.

BRACKEN Co., Ky. (co. seat, Brooksville). For an early settler.

BRACKETTVILLE, Tex. (co. seat of Kinney Co.). For Oscar B. Brackett, pioneer and prominent resident.

BRADDOCK, Maj. Gen. Edward (1695-1755), British general, known for his incompetent leadership in the French and Indian Wars. He was defeated here and died of his wounds.
Braddock, Pa. (Allegheny Co.).
North Braddock, Pa. (Allegheny Co.).

BRADENTON, Fla. (co. seat of Manatee Co.). For Joseph Braden, pioneer sugar planter.

BRADFORD Co., Fla. (co. seat, Starke). For the first Florida officer killed in the Civil War. An earlier name was New River.

BRADFORD Co., Pa. (co. seat, Towanda). For William Bradford (1755-1795), Pennsylvania statesman and jurist, second attorney general of the United States (1794-95), under Washington.

BRADFORD MOUNTAIN, Conn. For a surveyor.

BRADLEY Co., Ark. (co. seat, Warren). For a local settler, William L. Bradley.

BRADLEY, Ill. (Kankakee Co.). For the Bradley Manufacturing Company.

BRADLEY Co., Tenn. (co. seat, Cleveland). For a Tennessee officer in the War of 1812 and the Southern Indian wars.

BRADY, Peter, member of the first party to survey the county.
Brady, Tex. (co. seat of McCulloch Co.).
Brady Creek, Tex.

BRAINERD, Minn. (co. seat of Crow Wing Co.). For the family of the wife of John Gregory Smith, first president of the Northern Pacific railroad.

BRAINTREE, Mass. (Norfolk Co.), town. For Braintree, Norfolk, England.

BRANCH Co., Mich. (co. seat, Coldwater). For John Branch (1782-1863), governor of North Carolina (1817-20), U.S. senator (1823-29), territorial governor of Florida (1844-45), and secretary of the navy (1829-31) under Jackson.

BRANCH LAKE, Me. Descriptive.

BRANDENBURG, Ky. (co. seat of Meade Co.). For Solomon Brandenburg, who donated the land for the site.

BRANDON, Man. For Brandon House, a Hudson's Bay Post. The head of the house of Douglas, a shareholder in the Hudson Bay company, was named Duke of Brandon in 1782.

BRANDON, Miss. (co. seat of Rankin Co.). For Gerard C. Brandon, governor.

BRANDON, Vt. (Rutland Co.), town. Probably for one of the Dukes of Brandon. There may also be some allusion to a "burnt town" because of an Indian attack.

BRANDY POND, Me. Descriptive of the color of the water.

BRANDYWINE Origin of name in question, but probably from Dutch *branntwein*, "brandy," with added folk meaning from the name of Andrew Braindwine, a landowner. General Howe defeated General Washington (Sept. 11, 1777) near the banks of the creek.
Brandywine Creek, Pa.-Del. Flows SSE into White Clay R.
Brandywine Summit, Pa.

BRANFORD From a variant spelling of Brentford and Chiswick, Middlesex, England.
Branford, Conn. (New Haven Co.), town.
North Branford, Conn. (New Haven Co.), town.

BRANTFORD, Ont. (co. town of Brant Co.). For Joseph Brant, Mohawk chief.

BRANT LAKE, N.Y. For a local community member.

BRANTLEY Co., Ga. (co. seat, Nahunta). For William Gordon Brantley (1860-1934), state legislator.

BRASSTOWN BALD, Ga. Highest mountain in Georgia. Folk etymologized form of a Cherokee name, "green valley place."

BRASSUA LAKE, Me. From Abnaki pronunciation of Frank, name of a chief, folk-etymologized to *Brassway.*

BRATTLEBORO, Vt. (Windham Co.), town and village. For Col. William Brattle, a land speculator and grantee of the town land.

BRAWLEY, Calif. (Imperial Co.). Originally this way to be named for J. H. Braly, landowner. For fear of failure of the settlement,

he refused, and as a compromise the similar name of a manager's friend in Chicago was chosen.

BRAWLEY PEAKS, Nev. For James M. Braley, miner.

BRAWLEY WASH RIVER, Ariz. Derived from Bawley Ranch, in turn probably named for an early settler named Bowley. It flows generally north into Santa Cruz River.

BRAXTON Co., W.Va. (co. seat, Sutton). For Carter Braxton, Virginia statesman, a leader in the American Revolution, and a signer of the Declaration of Independence.

BRAZIL, Ind. (co. seat of Clay Co.). For Brazil, South America; named at the time of that country's rebellion against Portuguese rule.

BRAZORIA Latinized form of BRAZOS.
Brazoria Co., Tex. (co. seat, Angleton).
Brazoria, Tex. (*Brazoria* Co.).

BRAZOS From Spanish, "arms" or "forks," as the forks of a river.
Brazos Co., Tex. (co. seat, Bryan). For the river.
Brazos Island, Tex.
Brazos Peak, N.Mex.
Brazos River, Tex. Flows generally SE to the Gulf of Mexico.

BREA, Calif. (Orange Co.). From a Spanish word for a bed of asphalt. Fossils of extinct animals are often found in such beds.

BREAD LOAF MOUNTAIN, Vt. Probably descriptive to the namer, who thought it looked like a loaf of bread.

BREATHITT Co., Ky. (co. seat, Jackson). For John Breathitt (1786-1834), Kentucky legislator and governor (1832-34).

BREAUX BRIDGE, La. (St. Martin Parish). For Agricole Breaux, a local settler who ferried people on his raft across Bayou Teche before a bridge was built.

BRECKENRIDGE, John Cabell (1821-1875), major of the Third Kentucky Volunteers (1847-48) during the Mexican War, member of the state house of representatives (1849), U.S. representative (1851-55), and vice-president of the United States (1856) under Buchanan (youngest vice-president ever in office until that time). He was defeated (1860) for the Presidency by Lincoln, served in the U.S. Senate from March to December, 1861, and then joined the Confederate army. He was Confederate secretary of war from January until April, 1865.

Breckenridge, Minn. (co. seat of Wilkin Co.).

Breckenridge, Tex. (co. seat of Stephens Co.).

BRECKINRIDGE, Colo. (co. seat of Summit Co.). For John Cabell Breckinridge, early settler.

BRECKINRIDGE Co., Ky. (co. seat, Hardinsburg). For John Breckinridge (1760-1806), Kentucky statesman, U.S. senator (1801-05), and attorney general (1805-06) under Jefferson.

BRECKINRIDGE HILLS, Mo. (Saint Louis Co.). For the developer.

BRECKSVILLE, Ohio (Cuyahoga Co.). Named for John Breck in 1814.

BREESE, Ill. (Clinton Co.). For Sidney Breese, a jurist on the state supreme court.

BREMEN, Ind. (Marshall Co.). For Bremen, Germany.

BREMER Co., Iowa (co. seat, Waverly). For Frederika Bremer (1801-1865), a Swedish author and early feminist.

BREMERTON, Wash. (Kitsap Co.). For William Bremer, founder of the town.

BRENHAM, Tex. (co. seat of Washington Co.). For Dr. Richard Fox Brenham (1810-1843), Texas patriot who died in Mexico while helping fellow Texans escape.

BRENTON POINT, R.I., extends into Rhode Island Sound. For a local citizen.

BRENTWOOD, Calif. (Contra Costa Co.). Named by first settlers for their home, Brentwood, Essex, England.

BRENTWOOD, Md. (Prince Georges Co.). For Giles Brent, an early settler.

BRETON For Breton, France. The island seems to have been named first.

Breton Island, La., in Breton Sound.

Breton Sound, La., on the Gulf of Mexico.

BREVARD Co., Fla. (co. seat, Titusville). Probably for Theodore Washington Brevard (1804-1877), a Florida state official. An earlier name was St. Lucie. See also BREVARD, N.C.

BREVARD, N.C. (co. seat of Transylvania Co.). For Ephraim Brevard (1744-1781), a North Carolina teacher, secretary of the convention that proposed the Mecklenburg Resolves of 1775. He was a surgeon in the American Revolution. Some believe that BREVARD Co., Fla., was named for him.

BREVORT, Henry, a surveyor. Also spelled Brevoort.

Brevort, Mich. (Mackinac Co.).

Brevoort Lake, Mich.

BREWER, Col. John, an early settler.

Brewer, Me. (Penobscot Co.).

Brewer Pond, Me.

BREWSTER, Neb. (co. seat of Blaine Co.). For Elder William Brewster, a member of the *Mayflower* party; named by a direct descendant, George Washington Brewster (1837-1928), founder of the town and publisher of the *Brewster News.*

BREWSTER Co., Tex. (co. seat, Alpine). For Henry Percy Brewster (1816-1884), Texas soldier and patriot who served in the Civil War and in administrative posts for both the Republic and state of Texas.

BREWTON, Ala. (co. seat of Escambia Co.). For E. T. Brewton, railroad station agent.

BRIAN HEAD, Utah. Mountain named for a member of the U.S. Geological Survey.

BRIARCLIFF MANOR, N.Y. (Westchester Co.). Descriptive and promotional.

BRIAR CREEK, Ga. From a translation of an Indian name referring to the briars on the banks of the stream. It flows southeast into Savannah River. Also spelled *Brier.*

BRIDAL VEIL FALLS, Calif., in Yosemite Natl. Park on Merced River. Descriptively named in 1850.

BRIDGE Descriptive.

Bridge City, Tex. (Orange Co.).

Bridgeport, Calif. (co. seat of Mono Co.).

Bridgeport, Conn. (co. seat of Fairfield Co.). On Long Island Sound.

Bridgeport, Neb. (co. seat of Morrill Co.). On the North Platte R.

Bridgeport, Ohio (Belmont Co.).

Bridgeport, Pa. (Montgomery Co.). On the Schuylkill R.

Bridgeport, Tex. (Wise Co.). On the Trinity R.

Bridgeport, W.Va. For a bridge across a creek.

Bridgeton, Mo. (St. Louis Co.). On Coldwater R. Earlier, Marais des Liards and Bridgetown.

Bridgeton, N.J. (co. seat of Cumberland Co.). On the Cohansey R. Earlier, Cohansey Bridge.

Bridgetown, Ohio (Hamilton Co.).

Bridge View, Ill. (Cook Co.). Also *Bridgeview*.

Bridgeville, Pa. (Allegheny Co.).

BRIDGER NATL. FOREST, Wyo. For Jim Bridger, early explorer.

BRIDGEWATER For Bridgewater, Somersetshire, England.

Bridgewater, Mass. (Plymouth Co.), town and village.

East Bridgewater, Mass. (Plymouth Co.), town.

West Bridgewater, Mass. (Plymouth Co.), town.

BRIDGTON, Me. (Cumberland Co.), town. For Moody Bridges, one of the original proprietors.

BRIER MOUNTAIN, Pa. Descriptive of the vegetation.

BRIGHAM CITY, Utah (co. seat of Box Elder Co.). For Brigham Young (1801-1877), Mormon leader. An earlier name was Box Elder.

BRIGHTON For the great English seaside resort fifty miles south of London, in Sussex.

Brighton, Colo. (co. seat of Adams Co.). Probably for *New Brighton*, Pa.

New Brighton, Pa. (Beaver Co.).

BRIGHTWATERS, N.Y. (Suffolk Co.). For the artificial lakes and marina in the area.

BRILLION, Wis. (Calumet Co.). Named by the U.S. Post Office Department, reason unknown, though possibly for Brilon, Germany.

BRIMSTONE MOUNTAIN, Wyo. For the sulphuric odor in the area.

BRINKLEY, Ark. (Monroe Co.). For R. C. Brinkley, a railroad official.

BRISBANE, Calif. (San Mateo Co.). Either for the city in Australia or for Arthur Brisbane (1864-1936), journalist, editor of leading newspapers in New York City and Chicago, columnist, and author.

BRISCOE Co., Tex. (co. seat, Silverton). For Andrew Briscoe (1810-1849), Republic of Texas patriot.

BRISTOL For Bristol, Gloucestershire and Somerset, England, long an important seaport and trade center.

Bristol Co., Mass. (co. seat, Taunton).

Bristol Co., R.I. (co. seat, *Bristol*).

Bristol, Conn. (Hartford Co.).

Bristol, Fla. (co. seat of Liberty Co.).

Bristol, Pa. (Bucks Co.).

Bristol, R.I. (co. seat of *Bristol* Co.), town.

Bristol, Tenn. (Sullivan Co.). So named in the hope that it would be a manufacturing city.

Bristol, Va. (independent city in Washington Co.).

Bristol Bay, Alaska, in Bering Sea.

Bristol, Vt. (Addison Co.), town. For *Bristol*, Conn.

Bristol Lake, Calif.

BRISTOL BAY, Alaska. Named by Capt. James Cook in 1778 for the Admiral Earl of Bristol.

BRISTOW, Okla. (Creek Co.). For Joseph Little Bristow (1861-1944), publisher, and U.S. senator from Kansas (1909-15). He held many positions at both state and national levels.

BRITTON, S.Dak. (co. seat of Marshall Co.). For Isaac Britton, railroad official and a founder.

BRITISH COLUMBIA Originally intended to be named New Caledonia, from the Roman name *Caledonia*, "Scotland," when the Crown Colony was formed in 1858, when Vancouver Island and New Caledonia, mainland British Columbia, were united. At

From the forests of British Columbia comes a steady stream of timber; this mill in Powell River turns some of it into newsprint. [*National Film Bureau*]

the suggestion of Queen Victoria, the name was changed to British Columbia to avoid confusion with the French island of New Caledonia and to honor Columbus.

British Columbia, Canadian province. Settled: 1778. Colony: 1858. Entered confederation: 1871. Cap: Victoria. Flower: Dogwood.

BROAD Descriptive of width of a river.
Broad River, Ga. Flows SE into Savannah R.
Broad River, N.C.-S.C. Flows SE to join Saluda R.
Broad River, S.C. A broad tidal channel.

BROADHEAD, Wis. (Green Co.). For Edward H. Broadhead, a railroad official.

BROADUS, Mont. (co. seat of Powder River Co.). For the Broaddus family, early settlers, headed by Oscar Broaddus.

BROADVIEW Descriptive and probably promotional.
Broadview, Ill. (Cook Co.).
Broadview Heights, Ohio (Cuyahoga Co.).

BROADWATER Co., Mont. (co. seat, Townsend). For Charles Broadwater, president of the Montana Central railroad and local resort proprietor.

BROCKPORT, N.Y. (Monroe Co.), town. For Hiel Brockway (1775-1842), a local landowner. The town is a port on the Erie Canal (part of the New York State Barge Canal System).

BROCKTON, Mass. (Plymouth Co.). For a town in Ontario, Canada, which was named for Sir Isaac Brock (1769-1812), lieutenant governor of Canada. An earlier name was North Bridgewater.

BROCKVILLE, Ont. (co. town of Leeds Co.). For Sir Isaac Brock (1769-1812). British soldier and later lieutenant governor of Canada. He was named major general (1811) and forced the surrender of Gen. William Hull's forces at Detroit (1812).

BRODERICK-BRYTE, Calif. (Yolo Co.). Combination of *Broderick*, possibly for Sen. David C. Broderick (?-1859), and *Bryte*, for George Bryte, a local farmer.

BRODHEAD CREEK, Pa. For a local dweller. It flows south into Delaware River.

BRODIE MOUNTAIN, Mass. For a local citizen.

BROKEN ARROW, Okla. (Tulsa Co.). From a Creek Indian ceremony to symbolize the return of peace to the country after the Civil War.

BROKEN BOW So named because the person who suggested this name had found a broken bow.
Broken Bow, Neb. (co. seat of Custer Co.).
Broken Bow, Okla. (McCurtain Co.). For *Broken Bow*, Neb.

BROKENSTRAW CREEK, N.Y.-Pa. Believed to be a translation of Algonquian *cushandauga*, "place of broken straw," for the flats on which prairie grass was found. It flows generally southeast into Allegheny River.

BROKEN TOP, Ore. For the peak's jagged shape.

BROME For the manor at Barham in Kent County, England.
Brome Co., Que. (co. seat, Knowlton).
Brome Lake, Que.

BROMLEY MOUNTAIN, Vt. For a local citizen.

BRONSON, Fla. (co. seat of Levy Co.). For an early settler.

BRONTOSAURUS MOUNTAIN, Alaska. For the dinosaur, which the mountain is supposed to resemble in shape.

BRONX Ultimately for Jonas Bronck, or Bronk (?-1643), the first European settler to arrive on the mainland north of Manhattan, building his home there in 1641. His origin is obscure, but he was a Dane who had married into a Dutch family. Bronck's farm was called "Broncksland," but the name fell into disuse, although the river was called "the Broncks River," with various other spellings. The Borough of The Bronx took its name from the river. The county is conterminous with the borough. Traditionally, the area is called The Bronx.
Bronx Co., N.Y. (co. seat, *Bronx*).
Bronx, N.Y. (co. seat of *Bronx* Co.).
Bronx River, N.Y.
Bronxville, N.Y. (Westchester Co.). For the river.

BROOKE Co., W.Va. (co. seat, Wellsburg). For Robert Brooke (1751-1791), Virginia soldier and statesman, who served in the American Revolution. He was governor (1794-96).

BROOKFIELD Descriptive of an area near a stream or streams.
Brookfield, Ill. (Cook Co.).
Brookfield, Wis. (Waukesha Co.).

BROOKFIELD, Conn. (Fairfield Co.), town. For Rev. Thomas Brooks (?-1799), pastor of the First Congregational Church (1757-99).

BROOKHAVEN. Descriptive.
Brookhaven, Miss. (co. seat of Lincoln Co.). For *Brookhaven*, N.Y.
Brookhaven, N.Y. (Suffolk Co.), town.

BROOKINGS, Ore. (Curry Co.). For Robert S. Brookings, a timberland stockholder.

BROOKINGS, Wilmot W. (1833-?), immigrant from Maine to the Dakota Territory as legal representative of land companies. He became a prominent legislator, promoter, and jurist. "Judge Brookings" was the name of the first locomotive to enter what is now South Dakota.
Brookings Co., S.Dak. (co. seat, *Brookings*).
Brookings, S.Dak. (co. seat of *Brookings* Co.).

BROOKLINE, Mass. (Norfolk Co.), town. So named because the boundary of the estate of Samuel Sewall (1652-1730) touched on two brooks at this location.

BROOKLYN Probably transferred from Brooklyn, N.Y.

Brooklyn, Minn. (Hennepin Co.). For a *Brooklyn* in Mich.

Brooklyn Center, Minn. (Hennepin Co.). For *Brooklyn*, Minn.

Brooklyn Park, Minn. (Hennepin Co.).

BROOKLYN, N.Y. (co. seat of Kings Co.), borough of New York City. Anglicized form of Dutch *Breuckelyn*, for a village in Holland.

BROOKLYN, Ohio (Cuyahoga Co.) Named for reasons of euphony, not for Brooklyn, N.Y.

BROOK PARK, Ohio (Cuyahoga Co.). Descriptive and promotional; near a branch of the Rocky River.

BROOKS Co., Ga. (co. seat, Quitman). For a local citizen.

BROOKS Co., Tex. (co. seat, Falfurrias). For James Abijah Brooks (1855-1944), Texas rancher, legislator, and jurist.

BROOKS RANGE, Alaska. Named by U.S. Geological Survey for Alfred Hulse Brooks (1871-1924), chief Alaskan geologist of the survey.

BROOKSVILLE, Fla. (co. seat of Hernando Co.). For Preston Smith Brooks (1819-1857), lawyer and U.S. representative from South Carolina (1853-56). He resigned after violently assaulting Charles Sumner for a speech attacking his uncle, Sen. Andrew Pickens Butler. Re-elected, he served in Congress (1856-57) until his death.

BROOKSVILLE, Ky. (co. seat of Bracken Co.). For David Brooks, an early settler.

BROOKVILLE For a stream or streams at the townsite.

Brookville, Ind. (co. seat of Franklin Co.).

Brookville, Ohio (Montgomery Co.).

Brookville, Pa. (co. seat of Jefferson Co.).

BROOME Co., N.Y. (co. seat, Binghamton). For John Broome (1700-

Manhattan was linked with Brooklyn in 1883 with the inauguration of the Brooklyn Bridge. [*The Metropolitan Museum of Art, The Edward W. C. Arnold Collection of New York Prints, Maps and Pictures. Bequest of W. C. Arnold, 1954*]

1810), New York statesman and businessman, active in the American Revolution. He was lieutenant governor (1804-11).

BROOMFIELD, Colo. (Boulder Co.). For a field of broomcorn.

BROWARD Co., Fla. (co. seat, Fort Lauderdale). For Napoleon Bonaparte Broward (1857-1910), Florida lawyer, legislator, and governor (1905-09).

BROWN, Gen. Jacob Jennings (1775-1828), Pennsylvania soldier, associated with New York. He fought in the War of 1812 and was victorious at the Battle of Niagara (1814). He commanded the United States Army (1821-28).
Brown Co., Ill. (co. seat, Mt. Sterling).
Brown Co., Ind. (co. seat, Nashville).
Brown Co., Ohio (co. seat, Georgetown).
Brown Co., Wis. (co. seat, Green Bay).
Brownstown, Ind. (co. seat of Jackson Co.).
Brownsville, Ky. (co. seat of Edmonson Co.).
Brownsville, Tenn. (co. seat of Haywood Co.).

BROWN, Joseph Renshaw (1805-1870), a leading pioneer citizen, publisher, legislator, and trader.
Brown Co., Minn. (co. seat, New Ulm).
Brown's Valley, Minn.
Brown's Valley, Minn. (Traverse Co.).

BROWN Co., Kan. (co. seat, Hiawatha). For Albert Gallatin Browne (1813-1880), associated with Mississippi as legislator, jurist, Confederate army officer, and governor (1844-48). The e was dropped in naming the county.

BROWN Co., Neb. (co. seat, Ainsworth). For two legislators named Brown who sponsored the bill for organization of the county.

BROWN Co., S.Dak. (co. seat, Aberdeen). For Alfred Brown (1836-?), member of the Dakota Territory legislature instrumental in consolidating the then existing counties, thereby earning the nickname of "Consolidation Brown." One area was left over, and his associates suggested he name it for himself, which he did although he never set foot in the county.

BROWN Co., Tex. (co. seat, Brownwood). For Henry Stevenson Brown (1793-1834), Republic of Texas patriot, trader, and soldier.

BROWN DEER, Wis. (Milwaukee Co.). For the animals.

BROWNFIELD, Tex. (co. seat of Terry Co.). For A. M. ("Dick") Brownfield (1877-1967), pioneer rancher and cattleman.

BROWNLEE PARK, Mich. (Calhoun Co.). For the realtor.

BROWNSBURG, Ind. (Hendricks Co.). For James B. Brown, who in 1824 became the first settler in the township.

BROWNS MILLS, N.J. (Burlington Co.). For grist mills owned by the Brown brothers.

BROWNS MOUNTAIN, Ore. For an early settler.

BROWNS RIVER, Vt. For a local community member. It flows west and north into the Lamoille River.

BROWNSTOWN, Ind. For Jacob Jennings BROWN.

BROWN'S VALLEY, Minn. For Joseph Renshaw BROWN.

BROWNSVILLE, Ky. and Tenn. For Jacob Jennings BROWN.

BROWNSVILLE, Pa. (Fayette Co.). For Thomas and Basil Brown, who had an Indian trading post there.

BROWNSVILLE, Tex. (co. seat of Cameron Co.). For Fort Brown, which was named for Maj. Jacob Brown, killed (1846) in a bombardment of the fort by Mexican forces.

BROWNWOOD For Capt. Henry S. Brown (1783-1834), soldier in the War of 1812 and prominent member of Austin's Colony (1824).
Brownwood, Tex. (co. seat of Brown Co.).
Brownwood, Lake, Tex.

BRULE From French *brule*, "burned," partial translation of *sicangu*, "burned thighs," from the Indian tribal name. The Brule Indians were a tribe of the Sioux.
Brule Co., S.Dak. (co. seat, Chamberlain).
Brule Lake, Minn.

Brule River, Mich.-Wis. Flows SE into Michigamme R. For a burned forest area nearby.

Lower Brule Indian Reservation Area, S.Dak.

BRUNEAU RIVER, Nev.-Idaho. Origin of name uncertain; may be for a French-Canadian trapper or from French, for the brownish color of the water. Formed by two forks: West Fork flows north into Snake River; East Fork flows into West Fork.

BRUNSWICK City and duchy in central Germany. Duke of Brunswick was one of the titles of the British house of Hanover, which included Georges I to IV, William IV, and Victoria. The name Hanover was changed to Windsor during World War I.

Brunswick Co., N.C. (co. seat, Southport).

Brunswick Co., Va. (co. seat, Lawrenceville).

Brunswick, Ga. (co. seat of Glynn Co.). For George III.

Brunswick, Me. (Cumberland Co.), town and village. Probably for George II.

East Brunswick, N.J. (Middlesex Co.).

New Brunswick, Canadian province. For George III of the House of Brunswick, Britain's reigning house when the Canadian province was named (1784). Settled: 1604. Province: 1784. Entered confederation: 1867, one of the four original provinces. Cap: Fredericton. Flower: Purple violet.

New Brunswick, N.J. (co. seat of Middlesex Co.). For George I.

North Brunswick, N.J. (Middlesex Co.).

BRUNSWICK, Ohio (Medina Co.). Local tradition has it that the name was chosen simply because it was pleasing.

BRUSH, Colo. (Morgan Co.). For Jared L. Brush, cattleman and sheepman.

BRYAN Co., Ga. (co. seat, Pembroke). For Jonathan Bryan, early settler.

BRYAN, Ohio (co. seat of Williams Co.). For John A. Bryan, auditor of the state in 1839.

BRYAN Co., Okla. (co. seat, Durant). For William Jennings Bryan (1860-1925), lawyer and statesman. He was a candidate for President in 1896, 1900, and 1908, defeated each time. He served as secretary of state (1913-15) under Wilson and was a prosecutor in the trial of John Scopes for teaching the theory of evolution (1925).

BRYAN, Tex. (co. seat of Brazos Co.). For Henry Joel Bryan, an uncle of Stephen F. Austin. Bryan donated land for the railroad

BRYANT CREEK, Mo. For a Bryant who lived in the area. It flows southeast into Norfolk Lake.

BRYCE CANYON NATL. PARK, Utah. For Ebenezer Bryce, early settler.

BRYN MAWR, Pa. (Montgomery Co.). From Welsh, "great hill."

BRYSON CITY, N.C. (co. seat of Swain Co.). For Thaddeus Dillard Bryson (1829-1890), a founder.

BUCHANAN, James (1791-1868), fifteenth President of the United States (1857-61), from Pennsylvania. His administration saw the start of the Civil War with the secession of South Carolina (1860). He was a member of the House of Representatives (1821-31), minister to Russia (1832-34), U.S. senator (1834-45), secretary of state (1845-49) under Polk, and minister to Great Britain (1853-56).

Buchanan Co., Iowa (co. seat, Independence).

Buchanan Co., Mo. (co. seat, St. Joseph).

Buchanan Co., Va. (co. seat, Grundy).

Buchanan, Ga. (co. seat of Haralson Co.).

Buchanan, Mich. (Berrien Co.).

BUCHANAN, Lake, Tex. For a creek, in turn for a local settler.

BUCHANAN, Va. (Botetourt Co.). For John Buchanan, a surveyor and son-in-law of the town's founder.

BUCKEYE, Ariz. (Maricopa Co.). For Ohio, the "Buckeye State."

BUCKEYE LAKE, Ohio (Licking Co.). Probably for the horse chestnuts that grow in the area. (The nut resembles the eye of a buck). Another source states that Ohioans are also known as Buckeyes, a term at first applied to any backwoodsmen, which might refer to Ohio's pioneers.

BUCKHANNON Probably for Buckannon, an early settler, but possibly for a Delaware Indian chief, Buckongahelas.
Buckhannon, W.Va. (co. seat of Upshur Co.). For the river.
Buckhannon River, W.Va. Flows generally N to the Tygart R.

BUCKINGHAM A dukedom held by George Villiers, 1st Duke, and his son, George Villiers, 2nd Duke. The name is taken from Buckingham, county town of Buckinghamshire, England. In North America the names may derive from the duke or from the town.
Buckingham Co., Va. (co. seat, *Buckingham*).
Buckingham, Va. (co. seat of *Buckingham* Co.).

BUCKINGHAM, Que. (Papineau Co.). For Buckingham County, England; the first settlers came from there in 1827.

BUCK MOUNTAIN, Wyo. For George A. Buck, topographer.

BUCKNECK MOUNTAIN, Ore. Probably descriptive.

BUCKS Co., Pa. (co. seat, Doylestown). From the short form of Buckinghamshire, a county in England.

BUCKSKIN Possibly for an incident involving a buckskin.
Buckskin Mountains, Ariz.
Buckskin Gulch River, Utah.

BUCKSPORT, Me. (Hancock Co.), town. For Col. Jonathan Buck (?-1795), an original settler and prominent citizen.

BUCYRUS, Ohio (co. seat of Crawford Co.). The origin is in debate, although certainly named by a surveyor named Kilbourne. One theory is that he named it for Cyrus, the Persian general, with the prefix, *bu* for "beautiful." Others state that it was named for Busiris, Egyptian city on the Nile and place of worship of Osiris.

BUECHEL, Ky. (Jefferson Co.). For John Buechel, owner of the White Cottage tavern in the 1870's and first postmaster (c.1883).

BUENA PARK, Calif. (Orange Co.). *Buena*, from Spanish, "beautiful"; probably promotional.

BUENA VISTA (Spanish, "beautiful view"). For the Mexican town in Coahuila, where, during the Mexican War, Gen. Zachary Taylor won a battle (February 22-23, 1847) from the Mexican General Santa Anna, giving Taylor control of northern Mexico.
Buena Vista Co., Iowa (co. seat, Storm Lake).
Buena Vista, Ga. (co. seat of Marion Co.).
Buena Vista, Va. (independent city in Rockbridge Co.).

BUFFALO For the presence of bison, or American buffalo.
Buffalo Co., Neb. (co. seat, Kearney).
Buffalo Co., S.Dak. (co. seat Gann Valley).
Buffalo Co., Wis. (co. seat, Alma).
Buffalo, Okla. (co. seat of Harper Co.). For *Buffalo* Creek.
Buffalo, Wyo. (co. seat of Johnson Co.).
Buffalo Creek, Okla.
Buffalo Creek, Pa.-W.Va.
Buffalo Creek, Wyo.
Buffalo Lake, Tex.
Buffalo Lake, Wis.
Buffalo River, Ark.
Buffalo River, Tenn.
Buffalo Grove, Ill. (Ogle Co.). For bones found here.

BUFFALO For a creek that flows into Lake Erie. The origin of the name for Buffalo Creek is in dispute, for it was not a place inhabited by buffalo, or bison. The Indians named the stream Beaver Creek and the place *te-osah-way*, "basswood," for the trees. Bones of large animals found along the banks of the stream may have led to the name *Buffalo*, although the bones probably came from elk, moose, or "wild cattle." Other theories are that the name derives from French *beau fleuve*, "beautiful river," or from Buffalo, an Indian who lived there.
Buffalo, Mo. (co. seat of Dallas Co.). For *Buffalo*, N.Y.
Buffalo, N.Y. (co. seat of Erie Co.).
New Buffalo, Mich. (Berrien Co.). For *Buffalo*, N.Y.

Buffalo herds, like this one in Kansas in 1871, may have disappeared but the animal's name dots the map of the West. [*Santa Fe Railway*]

BUFFALO, Minn. (co. seat of Wright Co.). For Buffalo Lake nearby, named because of its buffalo fish.

BUFFALO BILL RESERVOIR, Wyo., on Shoshone River. For William Frederick ("Buffalo Bill") CODY.

BUFORD, Ga. (Gwinnet Co.). For A. S. Buford, president of the railroad that served the area.

BUGGS For a prominent family in the area.
Buggs Island, Va. in the Roanoke R.
Buggs Island Lake, N.C.-Va. For the island.
   See KERR RESERVOIR.

BUHL, Idaho (Twin Falls Co.). For Frank H. Buhl, a founder of an irrigation project in the county.

BULL For either Steven Bull or his descendant John Bull.
Bull Bay, S.C.
Bull Island, S.C.

BULLION BUTTE, N.Dak. For a mining camp.

BULLITT Co., Ky. (co. seat, Shepherdsville). For Alexander Scott Bullitt (1761-1816), Kentucky legislator.

BULLOCH Co., Ga. (co. seat, Statesboro). For Archibald Bulloch (1730-1777), attorney, patriot, legislator, officer in the American Revolution, first man in Georgia to read the Declaration of Independence, and first governor of Georgia (1776-77).

BULLOCK Co., Ala. (co. seat, Union Springs). For a local citizen.

BULL RUN, Va., from Loudoun Co. to Occuquan Creek. Probably descriptive; named as early as 1730. Site of two battles of the Civil War fought near Manassas, Va., the first on July 21, 1861 (known as First Manassas or First Bull Run), the second on August 29-30, 1862 (known as Second Manassas or Second Bull Run). In both battles the Union forces were repulsed.

BULLRUN ROCK, Ore. Reason for naming is unknown.

BULL SHOALS LAKE, Ark.-Mo., on White River. For the animal and for shoals on the river.

BULLY CREEK, Ore. Supposedly for an incident in the 1850s in which a man fell into the river and the onlookers cried, "Bully, bully!" It flows east into Malheur River.

BUNCOMBE, Edward (1742-1778), a North Carolina officer in the American Revolution who died while a prisoner of the British.
Buncombe Co., N.C. (co. seat, Asheville).
Buncombe Horse Range Ridge, N.C.

BUNDICKS CREEK, La. For a local community member. It flows southeast into Calcasieu River.

BUNKER HILL The hill was presumably for George Bunker, early settler in Charlestown, Boston. It was the site of a Revolutionary War battle, June 17, 1775. The other place names were named for this battle site.
Bunker Hill, Mass.
Bunker Hill, III. (Macoupin Co.).
Bunker Hill, Ind. (Miami Co.).
Bunker Hill, Tex. (Harris Co.).
Bunker Hill Peak, Nev.

BUNNELL, Fla. (co. seat of Flagler Co.). For Alva A. Bunnell, founder.

BURBANK, Calif. (Los Angeles Co.). For Dr. David Burbank (c.1821-?), New Hampshire-born dentist who practiced in Los Angeles.

BURBANK, III. (Cook Co.). For Luther Burbank (1849-1926), experimental horticulturist.

BUREAU An Anglicization of the name of Pierre de Buero, a trader.
Bureau Co., III. (co. seat, Princeton).
Bureau Creek, III. Flows generally E to the Illinois R.

BURGAW, N.C. (co. seat of Pender Co.). Probably an Anglicized form of an Indian name, meaning unknown.

BURKBURNETT, Tex. (Wichita Co.). For Capt. S. Burk Burnett, a cowhand who won his boss's ranch in a card game. Oil was discovered on the property, and he became one of the richest men in Texas.

BURKE, Edmund (1729-1797), British statesman, philosopher, and orator, who defended the American colonies.
Burke Co., Ga. (co. seat, Waynesboro).
Burke Mountain, Vt.

BURKE Co., N.C. (co. seat, Morganton). For Thomas Burke (1747-1783), North Carolina physician, member of the Continental Congress (1776-81) and governor (1781-82). He was kidnapped by Tories in 1781, but escaped.

BURKE Co., N.Dak. (co. seat, Bowbells). For John Burke (1859-1937), legislator and governor (1907-13).

BURKE, S.Dak. (co. seat of Gregory Co.). Charles H. Burke (1861), legislator, U.S.

representative (1899-1907; 1909-15); and commissioner of Indian affairs (1921-29).

BURKESVILLE, Ky. (co. seat of Cumberland Co.). For Samuel Burk, owner of the townsite and a founder. Burksville was the original spelling.

BURLEIGH Co., N.Dak. (co. seat, Bismarck). For Walter Atwood Burleigh (1820-1896), attorney, physician, state legislator, and Dakota Territory delegate to Congress.

BURLESON, Edward (1798-1851), soldier in the War of 1812, Republic of Texas patriot and army officer, and Texas legislator. He was elected vice-president of the Republic (1841) and ran for president of the Republic (1844) but was defeated by Anson Jones.
Burleson Co., Tex. (co. seat, Caldwell).
Burleson, Tex. (Johnson Co.).

BURLEY, Idaho (co. seat of Cassia Co.). For David E. Burley, an official of the Union Pacific railroad.

BURLINGAME, Calif. (San Mateo Co.). For Anson Burlingame (1822-1870), U.S. ambassador to China and well-known orator. He became envoy extraordinary of the Chinese government, in which capacity he negotiated a number of important treaties and contributed much to Chinese-American relations.

BURLINGTON For the Burling family of Westchester, N.Y., landholders in Colchester and Huntington, Vt., or for an alternate spelling of Bridlington, Yorkshire, England, influenced by the way it is pronounced in England.
Burlington Co., N.J. (co. seat, Mount Holly).
Burlington, Colo. (co. seat of Kit Carson Co.). For *Burlington*, Iowa.
Burlington, Iowa (co. seat of Des Moines Co.). For *Burlington*, Vt. Earlier, Flint Hills.
Burlington, Kan. (co. seat of Coffey Co.). For *Burlington*, Vt.
Burlington, Ky. (co. seat of Boone Co.). Probably for *Burlington*, N.J. ·
Burlington, Mass. (Middlesex Co.), town.
Burlington, N.J. (*Burlington* Co.). Earlier, New Beverly, Bridlington.

Burlington, N.C. (Alamanée Co.). Name taken from a postal guide.

Burlington, Vt. (co. seat of Chittenden Co.).

Burlington, Wis. (Racine Co.). For *Burlington*, Vt.

BURNABY, Robert (1828-1878), English businessman who spent the years 1858 to 1874 in British Columbia. He was briefly associated with the surveys of Col. Richard Moody. The lake was named first.

Burnaby, B.C., unincorporated municipality.

Burnaby Island, B.C.

Burnaby Lake, B.C.

Burnaby, Mount, B.C.

BURNET, David Gouverneur (1778-1870), Republic of Texas statesman. He was a delegate to the second convention of Texas (1833), president *ad interim* of the Republic, (1836), and its vice-president (1838) and secretary of state (1846).

Burnet Co., Tex. (co. seat, *Burnet*).

Burnet, Tex. (co. seat of *Burnet* Co.).

BURNETT Co., Wis. (co. seat, Grantsburg). For Thomas P. Burnett (?-1846), Wisconsin lawyer and legislator.

BURNHAM, Ill. (Cook Co.). For a local citizen or for Burnham-on-Sea, Somersetshire, England.

BURNHAM, Pa. (Mifflin Co.). For William Burnham (?-1918), who had been president and chairman of the board of Standard Steel Division, the major local industry.

BURNS, Ore. (co. seat of Harney Co.). For Robert Burns (1759-1796), the Scottish poet.

BURNSHIRT RIVER, Mass. For an incident; the details have been lost. It flows generally southwest to join Moose Brook to form Ware River.

BURNSVILLE, Minn. (Dakota Co.). For William Burns and his family, first settlers.

BURNSVILLE, N.C. (co. seat of Yancey Co.). For Otway Burns (1775-1850), a privateersman in the War of 1812, shipbuilder, and legislator. He was active in the formation of the western counties in North Carolina.

BURNT RIVER, Ore. For the burned area along the banks of the stream. It flows generally east into Snake River.

BURNTSIDE LAKE, Minn. From Ojibway, "burned forest side of lake."

BURRILLVILLE, R.I. (Providence Co.), town. For James Burrill, Jr. (1772-1820), state attorney general, speaker of the Rhode Island General Assembly, chief justice of the state superior court, and U.S. senator (1817-20).

BURT Co., Neb. (co. seat, Tekamah). For Francis Burt (1807-1854), publisher and first territorial governor (1854).

BURT LAKE, Mich. For William A. Burt (1792-1858), surveyor.

BURTON ISLAND, Vt., in Lake Champlain. For a local citizen.

BURTON LAKE, Ga. For the Burton family.

BURWELL, Neb. (co. seat of Garfield Co.). For Miss Ada Burwell, fiancee of Fred Webster, brother of the founder. Mr. Webster was killed by a falling tree two weeks before the intended marriage.

BUSHNELL, Fla. (co. seat of Sumter Co.). For a railroad engineer who surveyed the right of way for a railroad through the area.

BUSHNELL, Ill. (McDonough Co.). For Nehemiah Bushnell, a railroad official.

BUSSERON CREEK, Ind. For Capt. Francois Riday Busseron (1748-1791), an officer in the command of George Rogers Clark. He lowered the British flag at Fort Sackville, and commanded the fort under its new name of Fort Patrick Henry. It flows generally southwest into Wabash River.

BUTLER, Hugh, Lake. See HUGH BUTLER Lake.

BUTLER Co., Kan. (co. seat, El Dorado). For Andrew Pickens Butler (1796-1857), South Carolina legislator, attorney, jurist, and U.S. senator (1846-57). See also BROOKSVILLE, Fla.

BUTLER Co., Neb. (co. seat, David City). For David Butler (1829-1891), first governor of Nebraska (1867-71).

BUTLER, Maj. Gen. Richard (1743-1791), Irish-born Pennsylvania soldier and Indian fighter who served in the American Revolution and later as Indian commissioner. He was killed by Indians while with Arthur St. Clair's expedition into what is now Ohio.
Butler Co., Ky. (co. seat, Morgantown).
Butler Co., Ohio (co. seat, Hamilton).
Butler Co., Pa. (co. seat, *Butler*).
Butler, Pa. (co. seat of *Butler* Co.).

BUTLER, William (?-1818), a Georgia legislator and soldier killed by Indians.
Butler Co., Ala. (co. seat, Greenville).
Butler, Ala. (co. seat of Choctaw Co.).

BUTLER, William Orlando (1791-1880), Kentucky soldier, member of the U.S. House of Representatives, and Democratic candidate for vice-president (1848).
Butler Co., Iowa (co. seat, Allison).
Butler Co., Mo. (co. seat, Poplar Bluff).
Butler, Ga. (co. seat of Taylor Co.).
Butler, Mo. (co. seat of Bates Co.).

BUTLERS POINT, Mass., on Buzzards Bay. For a local citizen named Butler.

BUTNER, N.C. (Granville Co.). For Maj. Gen. Henry W. Butner, a North Carolina native.

BUTTE For a nearby butte (a flat-topped, isolated mountain).
Butte Co., Calif. (co. seat, Oroville).
Butte Co., Idaho (co. seat, Arco).
Butte Co., S.Dak. (co. seat, Belle Fourche).
Butte, Mont. (co. seat of Silver Bow Co.).
Butte Mountains, Nev.

BUTTER CREEK, Ore. So named because soldiers in the area took butter from the stores for use in enlisted men's mess. It flows north into Umatilla River.

BUTTERNUT For the tree.
Butternut Lake, Wis. (Ashland and Price Cos.).
Butternut Lake, Wis. (Forest Co.).

BUTTS Co., Ga. (co. seat, Jackson). For Sam Butts (1777-1815), army officer killed in action.

BUXTON, Me. (York Co.), town. For Buxton, Norfolk, England.

BUZZARDS BAY, Mass., inlet on Atlantic Ocean. For the bird.

BYRAM For a Byram who settled in the area.
Byram, Conn. (Fairfield Co.).
Byram Lake, N.Y.
Byram River, N.Y.-Conn. Flows generally S into Long Island Sound.

C

CABALLO From Spanish, "horse," for the wild horses in the mountains.
Caballo, N.Mex. (Sierra Co.).
Caballo Reservoir, N.Mex. On the Rio Grande.

CABARRUS Co., N.C. (co. seat, Concord). For Stephen Cabarrus (1754-1808), legislator.

CABELL Co., W.Va. (co. seat, Huntington). For William H. Cabell (1772-1853), Virginia statesman, jurist, and governor (1805-08).

CABIN CREEK, Okla. For a cabin in the vicinity. It flows south into Grand River. Also known as Big Cabin Creek.

CABOT, Mount, N.H. For Sebastian Cabot, son of John Cabot, Italian sailing commanders employed by England, whose claim to North America was based on their voyages in 1497 and 1498.

CACAPON RIVER, W.Va. From Algonquian, possibly "rising river." It flows northeast to Potomac River.

CACHE From French, "hiding place," because early trappers or hunters stored furs or other things there.
Cache Co., Utah (co. seat, Logan).
Cache Creek, Okla.
Cache Mountain, Wyo. For an incident in which mules had to be hidden there.
Cache Natl. Forest, Idaho-Utah.
Cache Peak, Idaho.
Cache River, Ark.

Cache River, Ill.
Cache la Poudre River, Colo. Where gunpowder was hidden.

CACHUMA, Lake, Calif. Of Indian origin, meaning unknown.

CADDO Name applied to a group of tribes of a common (Caddoan) linguistic stock. It is derived from one of the tribal groups, the Kadohadacho Confederacy. In Caddoan, *kadohadacho* means "real chiefs." Caddoan tribes were found in Louisiana and Texas and many later settled in what is now Oklahoma.
Caddo Parish, La. (parish seat, Shreveport).
Caddo Co., Okla. (co. seat, Anadarko).
Caddo Creek, Okla. Flows into the Washita R.
Caddo Lake, Tex.-La. border.
Caddo River, Ark. Flows into the Ouachita R.

CADILLAC, Sieur Antoine de la Mothe (c. 1658-1730), French founder of Detroit.
Cadillac, Mich. (co. seat of Wexford Co.). Earlier, Clam Lake.
Cadillac Mountain, Me. Cadillac received the land as a grant from the king of France.

CADIZ For the city in Spain, whose name occurs in America because Cadiz was mentioned often in newspapers during the War of the Spanish Peninsula (1808-14).
Cadiz, Ky. (co. seat of Trigg Co.).
Cadiz, Ohio (co. seat of Harrison Co.).
Cadiz Lake, Calif.

CAHABA RIVER, Ala. From Choctaw *oka,* "water," plus *aba,* "above." The name was first applied to a village. It flows generally southwest into Alabama River.

CAHILL MOUNTAIN, Pa. For a local community member.

CAHOKIA, Ill. (Saint Clair Co.). For an Indian tribe of the Illinois Confederacy; meaning uncertain. Indian mounds near here have the same name, though now believed to have been built by another tribe.

CAIN CREEK, S.Dak. For John Cain, early settler. It flows southeast into James River.

CAIRN PEAK, Wyo. Descriptive of its shape which resembles a cairn, a heap of stones piled up as a memorial or as a landmark.

CAIRO For the Egyptian city.
Cairo, Ga. (co. seat of Grady Co.). Named during a time when it was popular to choose exotic or foreign names.
Cairo, Ill. (co. seat of Alexander Co.). So named because the town was situated at the mouth of the Ohio R., similar to the Egyptian city which is on the Nile delta.

CALAIS, Me. (Washington Co.). For Calais, a seaport in France, probably because Calais, Me. is across the St. Croix River from Dover Hill in New Brunswick, Canada, which would suggest the relative positions of Dover, England, and Calais, France. An earlier name was Township No. 5.

CALAMUS RIVER, Neb. For the plant, sweet flag, which grows along the river. It flows southeast into North Loup River.

CALAPOOYA For the Indian tribal name, meaning unknown.
Calapooya Mountains, Ore.
Calapooya River, Ore. Flows NW into Willamette R.

CALAVERAS From Spanish, "skulls." The river was named first, for skulls found there in the 1830s.
Calaveras Co., Calif. (co. seat, San Andreas).
Calaveras Reservoir, Calif.
Calaveras River, Calif. Flows SW into San Joaquin R.

CALCASIEU Said to be from Atakapan, "crying eagle."
Calcasieu Parish, La. (parish seat, Lake Charles). For the river.
Calcasieu Lake, La.
Calcasieu River, La.

CALDRON FALLS RESERVOIR, Wis. On Peshtigo River. For the falls which resembled boiling water in a caldron.

CALDWELL, Idaho (co. seat of Canyon Co.). For Alexander Caldwell (1830-1917), U.S. senator from Kansas and official of a promotional company in the area.

CALDWELL Co., Ky. (co. seat, Princeton). For John Caldwell, an early Kentucky legislator.

CALDWELL Parish, La. (parish seat, Columbia). For Matthew Caldwell, a pioneer from North Carolina.

CALDWELL, Matthew, Republic of Texas patriot and soldier.
Caldwell Co., Tex. (co. seat, Lockhart).
Caldwell, Tex. (co. seat of Burleson Co.).

CALDWELL Co., Mo. (co. seat, Kingston). For Matthew Caldwell, an officer of the Kentucky Volunteers in the War of 1812.

CALDWELL Co., N.C. (co. seat, Lenoir). For Joseph Caldwell, first president of the University of North Carolina.

CALDWELL, Ohio (co. seat of Noble Co.). For Joe Caldwell, who drilled the first oil well in Ohio in 1814.

CALEDONIA The ancient name of Scotland.
Caledonia Co., Vt. (co. seat, Saint Johnsbury).
Caledonia, Minn. (co. seat of Houston Co.).

CALEXICO, Calif. (Imperial Co.). A border town whose name is coined from *Cali*fornia and Me*xico.*

CALGARY, Alta. For the fort built in 1875, which was named by Col. James F. Macleod (1836-1894) of the Royal Canadian Mounted Police, for the village on the Isle of Mull in Scotland where some of his kinsmen lived.

CALHOUN, John Caldwell (1782-1850), statesman, who achieved lasting fame,

From Alberta's sprawling rangeland come the bucking broncs for Calgary's week-long stampede.
[*Canadian Government Travel Bureau*]

particularly in the South, for his articulate championship of Southern causes, notably states' rights and slavery. He was a U.S. representative (1811-17) and senator (1832-43; 1845-50) from South Carolina, secretary of war (1817-25) under Monroe, and vice-president (1825-32) under John Quincy Adams and Andrew Jackson.
Calhoun Co., Ala. (co. seat, Anniston).
Calhoun Co., Ark. (co. seat, Hampton).
Calhoun Co., Fla. (co. seat, Blountstown).
Calhoun Co., Ga. (co. seat, Morgan).
Calhoun Co., Ill. (co. seat, Hardin).
Calhoun Co., Iowa (co. seat, Rockwell City). Earlier, Fox Co.
Calhoun Co., Mich. (co. seat, Marshall).
Calhoun Co., Miss. (co. seat, Pittsboro).
Calhoun Co., S.C. (co. seat, St. Matthews).
Calhoun Co., Tex. (co. seat, Port Lavaca).
Calhoun Co., W.Va. (co. seat, Grantsville).
Calhoun, Ga. (co. seat of Gordon Co.).
Calhoun, Ky. (co. seat of McLean Co.).

CALIFORNIA From the Mexican peninsula to the south. The peninsula, Baja (lower) *California*, was discovered by Hernando Cortes in 1535. As explorers moved north along the Pacific coast they continued to use the name *California*, with the area above the peninsula (roughly that of the present state) referred to as Alta (upper) *California*. Whether the name was first used in America by Cortes, Diaz del Castillo, or some other explorer, it seems to have been drawn originally from a Spanish romance, *Las sergas de Esplandian* (The Exploits of Esplandian, 1510) by Ordonez de Montalvo, which states that "on the right hand of the Indies, there is an island called California, very near to the Terrestrial Paradise . . . " The roots of the word have been variously described as being Spanish *califa*, "succession," or *calif*, "sovereign," or a combination of Latin words, *calida* and *forno*, "hot furnace".

California, originally a part of the Spanish dominions, attracted large numbers of American prospectors in the great gold rush of 1849. The center of this feverish activity was the Sacramento Valley, focused on Sutter's Mill, a sawmill belonging to Gen. John Augustus Sutter, who became so disgusted with the gold rush that he returned to the East. (*New York Public Library*]

California, State of. 31st state of the Union. Settled: 1769. Independent Republic: 1846-50 (after secession from Mexico). Admitted: 1850. Cap: Sacramento. Motto: *Eureka* (I Have Found It). Nickname: Golden State. Flower: Golden Poppy. Bird: California Valley Quail. Tree: Redwood. Song: "I Love You, California."

California, Pa. (Washington Co.). For the state.

CALIFORNIA, Mo. (co. seat of Moniteau Co.). For California Wilson, who offered a jug of whiskey to have the place named for him.

CALISPELL PEAK, Wash. From the tribal name *kalispel*, probably "camas root people." The tribe was also called Pend d'

Oreilles, "pendants hanging from ears." See also PEND OREILLE.

CALLAHAN, Mount, Nev. For a local settler.

CALLAHAN Co., Tex. (co. seat, Baird). For James Hughes Callahan (?-1856), a soldier and Texas Ranger, killed by Indians.

CALLAWAY Co., Mo. (co. seat, Fulton). For James Callaway (?-1815), an officer killed by Indians.

CALLOWAY Co., Ky. (co. seat, Murray). For Col. Richard Calloway, who migrated to Kentucky (1776) to survey the town site of Boonesborough.

CALOOSAHATCHEE RIVER, Fla. For the Calusa Indian tribe, of Muskhogean linguistic stock. The meaning of the name is uncertain, although the tribe was known as "the fierce people," but the name may also be associated with Spanish *Carlos*, for Emperor Charles V. *Hatchee* means "stream." The river flows southwest into the Gulf of Mexico.

CALUMET From French *chalemel*, "straw" or "little reed," later in Amerindian French extended to "pipe," hence, "peace pipe."
Calumet Co., Wis. (co. seat, Chilton). Area at one time or another was the home of six Indian tribes.
Calumet City, Ill. (Cook Co.). Earlier, West Hammond.
Calumet Park, Ill. (Cook Co.). Promotional. Earlier, Burr Oak.

CALVERT, Cecilius, 2nd Baron Baltimore (1605-1675), first proprietor of the colony of Maryland. His other interests kept him in England and he never visited the colony. See ANNE ARUNDEL Co. and CECIL Co., Md.

CALVERT, Charles, 3rd Baron Baltimore (1637-1715), second proprietor of the colony of Maryland. He was the son of Cecilius Calvert and Anne Arundell. See CHARLES Co., Md.

CALVERT, Frederick, 6th Baron Baltimore (1731-1771), fifth and last proprietor of the colony of Maryland. He tried to name his illegitimate son, Henry Harford, as his heir but without success. See HARFORD Co., Md. and FREDERICK. Md.

CALVERT Co., Md. (co. seat, Prince Frederick). For George Calvert, 1st Baron Baltimore, (c.1580-1632), father of Cecilius Calvert. Interested in the colonization of America, he negotiated the grant of a colonial charter from Charles I but died before he could receive it. The charter then passed to his son.

CALWA, Calif. (Fresno Co.). Coined from *California Wine Association.*

CAMANCHE, Iowa (Clinton Co.). Believed to have been named (1836) by the founder for a famous race horse in the East.

CAMARILLO, Juan (?-1880), landowner.
Camarillo, Calif. (Ventura Co.).
Camarillo Heights, Calif. (Ventura Co.).

CAMAS From the Chinook name for the camass; an edible root of the lily family.
Camas Co., Idaho (co. seat, Fairfield).
Camas, Wash. (Clark Co.).

CAMBRIA An ancient name of Wales, from Welsh *cymy*, or *cumbri*, "brotherhood" or "fraternity," for those who band together in a common cause.
Cambria Co., Pa. (co. seat, Ebensburg).
Cambrian Park, Calif. (Santa Clara Co.).
  Promotional.

CAMBRIDGE For Cambridge, Cambridgeshire, England.
Cambridge, Ill. (co. seat of Henry Co.). For *Cambridge*, Mass.
Cambridge, Md. (co. seat of Dorchester Co.).
Cambridge, Mass. (co. seat of Middlesex Co.). Earlier, New Town.
Cambridge, Minn. (co. seat of Isanti Co.)
Cambridge, Ohio (co. seat of Guernsey Co.). For *Cambridge*, Mass.
Cambridge Reservoir, Mass.

CAMDEN, Sir Charles Pratt, 1st Earl of (1714-1794), English statesman and jurist. He led the opposition, in the House of Lords, to taxation of the American colonies and was vigorous in his denunciation of the Stamp Act.
Camden Co., Ga. (co. seat, Woodbine).
Camden Co., Mo. (co. seat, *Camdenton*).
  Earlier, Kinderhook Co.

Camden Co., N.J. (co. seat, *Camden*).
Camden, N.Y. (Oneida Co.).
Camden Co., N.C. (co. seat, *Camden*).
Camden, Ala. (co. seat of Wilcox Co.). For *Camden*, S.C.
Camden, Ark. (co. seat of Ouachita Co.).
Camden, Me. (Knox Co.), town and village.
Camden, N.J. (co. seat of *Camden* Co.).
Camden, N.C. (co. seat of *Camden* Co.).
Camden, S.C. (co. seat of Kershaw Co.). Earlier, Pine Tree Hill.
Camden, Tenn. (co. seat of Benton Co.).
Camdenton, Mo. (co. seat of *Camden* Co.).

CAMDEN BAY, Alaska. For Sir John Jeffreys Pratt (1759-1840), 2nd Earl and 1st Marquis of Camden, son of Sir Charles Pratt. He was lord of the British Admiralty and lord lieutenant of Ireland in the ministry of William Pitt.

CAMEL HUMP Descriptive of a mountain which supposedly resembles a camel's hump. Also spelled *Camels Hump.*
Camels Hump, Vt.
Camel Hump Butte, N.Dak.

CAMERON, Capt. Ewen (1811-1843), a member of the Mier expedition executed by the Mexicans.
Cameron Co., Tex. (co. seat, Brownsville).
Cameron, Tex. (co. seat of Milam Co.).

CAMERON Co., Pa. (co. seat, Emporium). For Simon Cameron (1799-1889), statesman, publisher, and railroad president. He was adjutant general of Pennsylvania, U.S. senator (1845-49; 1857-61; 1867-77), secretary of war (1861-62) under Lincoln, and minister to Russia (1862).

CAMERON, Robert Alexander, a soldier of the Confederate army in the Red River campaign. He was active in Louisiana politics immediately after the Civil War.
Cameron Parish, La. (parish seat, *Cameron*).
Cameron, La. (parish seat of *Cameron* Parish).

CAMILLA, Ga. (co. seat of Mitchell Co.). For Camilla Mitchell, granddaughter of Gen. Henry Mitchell, for whom the county was named.

CAMP Co., Tex. (co. seat, Pittsburg). For John Lafayette Camp (1828-1891), Texas legislator and judge.

CAMPBELL, Calif. (Santa Clara Co.). For Benjamin Campbell (1826-?) landowner and postmaster (1885-92).

CAMPBELL, Ohio (Mahoning Co.). For James A. Campbell, a former president of the Youngstown Sheet and Tube Company, now Youngstown Steel Company. An earlier name was East Youngstown.

CAMPBELL Co., S.Dak. (co. seat, Mound City). For Norman B. Campbell, Dakota Territory legislator.

CAMPBELL Co., Tenn. (co. seat, Jacksboro). Either for Arthur Campbell, a negotiator with the Indians, or for George Washington Campbell (1769-1848), attorney, U.S. representative (1803-09) and U.S. senator (1811-14; 1815-18) from Tennessee, secretary of treasury under President Madison (1814) and ambassador to Russia (1818-20).

CAMPBELL Co., Va. (co. seat, Rustburg) For Gen. William Campbell (1745-1781), Virginia soldier who saw action in several major battles of the American Revolution, including King's Mountain, Guilford Court House, and Yorktown.

CAMPBELL Co., Wyo. (co. seat, Gillette). Probably for John Allen Campbell (1835-1880), Civil War general and first governor of Wyoming (1869-75), or possibly for Robert Campbell, member of an expedition into the Missouri River area in 1822.

CAMPBELL HILL, Ohio. State's highest point. For Edward Campbell, who owned the land.

CAMPBELLSVILLE, Ky. (co. seat of Taylor Co.). For Adam Campbell, first settler.

CAMP FORSYTH, Kan. (Wyandotte Co.). For George A. Forsyth. See FORSYTH. Mont.

CAMP FUNSTON, Kan. (Riley Co.). For Gen. Frederick Funston, known as "the Fighting Bantam," who served in Cuba, the Philippines, and with Pershing in Mexico.

CAMP HILL, Pa. (Cumberland Co.). For a hill where camp meetings for the Church of God were held.

CAMPTON, Ky. (co. seat of Wolfe Co.). A shortened form of Camptown, an earlier name. Another earlier name was Swiftville.

CAMROSE, Alta. For the Welsh town Camrose. An earlier name was Sparling, but it was changed to avoid confusion with the towns Sperling and Stirling.

CANAAN For the Biblical Promised Land. The Hebrew word means "lowland."
Canaan, N.Y. (Columbia Co.), town. Named by settlers from a Canaan in Connecticut.
New Canaan, Conn. (Fairfield Co.), town.
North Canaan, Conn. (Litchfield Co.), town.

CANADA Apparently derived from Huron-Iroquoian *kanata*, "village" or "community." The name first appeared in 1534 in the narrative of Jacques Càrtier, in reference to the Indian community of Stadacona. It was then applied to the St. Lawrence River (1638), "that famous river of Canada" on Robert Merchant's Map of Canada, and so to the whole country. The name continued in popular usage, although after the British conquest (1763) the official description of the colony was "the province of Quebec." The name *Canada* became official with the Canada Act (or Constitutional Act) of 1791, which divided the province into Lower and Upper Canada. With the passage of the British North America Act (1867), the term was made to apply to the Dominion of Canada, a federation of Upper Canada, Lower Canada, New Brunswick, and Nova Scotia. Canada remained a British dominion until 1931, when the British Parliament passed a statute declaring that all British dominions had legal status, and Canada became one of the voluntary partners of the British Commonwealth of Nations. The national capital is Ottawa.
Canada Falls Deadwater, Me. A lake near the Canadian border.

CANADIAN The river, known to the Osage as *Ne-sout-che-bra-ra*, was probably named in honor of their homeland by French-Canadian explorers or traders.
Canadian Co., Okla. (co. seat, El Reno).

Canadian, Tex. (co. seat of Hemphill Co.). For the *Canadian* River, on which it is located.

Canadian River, N.Mex.-Tex.-Okla. Flows generally E to the Arkansas R.

CANAJOHARIE, N.Y. (Montgomery Co.). From an Indian word meaning "pot that washes itself," for a pothole in the creek bed.

CANANDAIGUA From Iroquoian *Gandundagwa*, perhaps "townsite."
Canandaigua, N.Y. (co. seat of Ontario Co.).
Canandaigua Lake, N.Y. One of the Finger Lakes.

CANASTOTA, N.Y. (Madison Co.). From an Indian term, *kniste*, "cluster of pines," and *stota*, "still," "silent," or "motionless."

CANDLER Co., Ga. (co. seat, Metter). For Allen Daniel Candler (1834-1910), Confederate officer, state legislator, U.S. representative (1883-91), and Georgia governor (1899-1902).

CANDLEWOOD For the wood of the pitch pine, splinters of which could be burned as candles.
Candlewood, N.J. (Ocean Co.).
Candlewood Lake, Conn. For the pines on the nearby hill.

CANDO, N.Dak. (co. seat of Towner Co.). Named by commissioners who said they could name the county seat as they wished when others said they could not. The name reflected their authority: *can* plus *do*.

CANE For canebrakes or the growth of cane, often along the banks of a river.
Cane Creek, Utah. Flows generally NW into Colorado R.
Cane River, N.C. Flows N to join Toe R. to form the Nolichucky R.
Caney River, Kan. Flows S and SE into Verdigris R.
Caney Fork River, Tenn. Flows W and NW into Cumberland R.

CANEADEA, N.Y. (Allegany Co.). From an Indian word meaning "where the heavens kiss the earth" or "heavenly rest."

CANFIELD, Ohio (Mahoning Co.). For Jonathan Canfield, one of the original proprietors.

CANISTEO From Seneca *kanestie*, "head of navigation" or possibly "board on water."
Canisteo, N.Y. (Steuben Co.).
Canisteo River, N.Y.

CANNELTON, Ind. (co. seat of Perry Co.). For a deposit of cannel coal in the area.

CANNING, Stratford. 1st Viscount Stratford de Redcliffe (1786-1880), British diplomat. He negotiated the Treaty of Bucharest between Russia and Turkey (1812). In 1830 he drew up the statement of British claims in the America boundary question, which was approved by the arbitrator, the king of the Netherlands, and the claim awarded.

CANNING RIVER, Alaska. For George Canning (1770-1827), British statesman. He was foreign secretary (1807-09; 1822-27) and prime minister (1827). A great orator, he acknowledged the independence of the Spanish-American colonies (1823) by calling "the new world into existence to redress the balance of the old."

CANNON Co., Tenn. (co. seat, Woodbury). For Newton Cannon (1781-1841), War of 1812 veteran, U.S. representative from Tennessee (1814-17; 1819-23), Indian treaty negotiator, and Tennessee governor (1836-39).

CANNONBALL RIVER, N.Dak. So named because stones in the stream resembled cannon balls. It flows generally southeast into the Missouri River.

CANNON RIVER, Minn. From French *Riviere aux Canots*, "Canoe River," which was misunderstood by early English-speaking explorers to be Cannon River. It flows northeast into the Mississippi River.

CANOE RIVER, Mass. Probably named for an incident involving a canoe. It flows southeast into Taunto River.

CANON CITY, Colo. (co. seat of Fremont Co.). A variant form of *canyon* for nearby Royal Gorge.

CANTERBURY, Conn. (Windham Co.). Probably for Canterbury, Kent, England.

CANOOCHEE From Creek *canosi*, meaning unknown.
Canoochee, Ga. (Emanuel Co.).
Canoochee River, Ga. Flows SE into Ogeechee R.

CANTON For Canton, China, or possibly from French, "district" or "subdivision."
Canton, Conn. (Hartford Co.), town.
Canton, Ga. (co. seat of Cherokee Co.). It is said that the terrain surrounding this city resembled that of the Chinese city. Also, the early inhabitants wished to enter the silk-production field, which they associated with Canton, China.
Canton, Ill. (Fulton Co.).
Canton, Mass. (Norfolk Co.), town. Canton, China was a port of call for Boston ships.
Canton, Miss. (co. seat of Madison Co.).
Canton, Mo. (Lewis Co.). For *Canton*, Ohio.
Canton, N.Y. (co. seat of St. Lawrence Co.). In an area where several villages were given names of famous cities of the world.
Canton, Ohio (co. seat of Stark Co.). Named by Bezaleel Wells for Canton, the Baltimore estate of his friend Capt. John O'Donnell, who had named it for Canton, China. See also KENTON, Okla.
Canton, S.Dak. (Lincoln Co.). The settlers believed that they were situated diametrically opposite the Chinese city.
Canton Reservoir, Okla.
North Canton, Ohio (Stark Co.).

CANTON, Tex. (co. seat of Van Zandt Co.). Origin is in dispute. One source gives French *canton*, "division" or "subdivision." Another states that it was named for Canter, a horse that won a race; another that it is derived from Canton, China. The first explanation seems probable, since Van Zandt County had been a subdivision of Nacogdoches Territory.

CANTONMENT, Fla. (Escambia Co.). For an army encampment.

CANYON Descriptive.
Canyon Co., Idaho (co. seat, Caldwell).
Canyon, Tex. (co. seat of Randall Co.). For Palo Duro Canyon.
Canyon City, Ore. (co. seat of Grant Co.). Situated in a canyon where important gold discoveries were made.
Canyonlands Natl. Park, Utah.

CANYON DE CHELLY De Chelly, from Navajo *tseyi*, "among the cliffs," transmitted through a Spanish form and further changed to resemble a French form by Americans, who assumed it was of French origin.
Canyon de Chelly, Ariz. (Apache Co.).
Canyon de Chelly Natl. Monument, Ariz.

CANYON FERRY RESERVOIR, Mont. On the Missouri River. For the canyon ferry and village formerly there.

CAPE. Names that do not appear in this part of the book may be found under the basic name. For example, for Cape May and Cape May County, N.J., see MAY.

CAPE CANAVERAL. From Spanish, "canebrake." It was named by an early Spanish voyager for its appearance as seen from the sea.
Cape Canaveral, Fla. (Brevard Co.).
Cape Canaveral, Fla., cape extending into the Atlantic Ocean.

CAPE CORAL, Fla. (Lee Co.). Descriptive.

CAP-DE-LA-MADELEINE, Que. (Champlain Co.). For Abbe of Ste. Marie Madeleine, to whom the seigniory was granted in 1636.

CAPE ELIZABETH, Me. (Cumberland Co.), town. For Princess Elizabeth (1596-1662), daughter of James I of England. She was known as the "Queen of Hearts" because of her beauty.

CAPE GIRARDEAU For Jean Girardot, a French naval officer and trading-post operator.
Cape Girardeau Co., Mo. (co. seat, Jackson).
Cape Girardeau, Mo. (*Cape Girardeau* Co.).

CAPISTRANO BEACH, Calif. (Orange Co.). For San Juan Capistrano. See SAN JUAN

CAPITOLA, Calif. (Santa Cruz Co.). Coined from *capitol*; probably promotional.

CAPITOL HILL, Wyo. So named because a cupola was built on it for an administrative building for Yellowstone National Park.

CAPITOL PEAK, Colo., in Elk Mountains. For its shape, which supposedly resembles a capitol.

CAPITOL REEF Sandstone dome area, so named because of its resemblance to the U.S. Capitol building in Washington, D.C.
Capitol Reef Natl. Monument, Utah.
Capitol Reef Natl. Park, Utah.

CAP SANTE, Que. (co. seat of Portneuf Co.). From French, "cape of health."

CAPULIN From Spanish, "chokeberry," for the wild cherries on the mountain.
Capulin, N.Mex. (Union Co.).
Capulin Mountain, N.Mex.
Capulin Mountain Natl. Monument, N.Mex.

CARBON Usually for large coal deposits underneath the place or nearby.
Carbon Co., Mont. (co. seat, Red Lodge).
Carbon Co., Pa. (co. seat, Jim Thorpe).
Carbon Co., Utah (co. seat, Price).
Carbon Co., Wyo. (co. seat, Rawlins).
Carbon Peak, Colo. See CASTLE.
Carbonate Mountain, Colo.
Carbondale, Ill. (Jackson Co.).
Carbondale, Pa. (Lackawanna Co.).

CARDIFF-BY-THE-SEA, Calif. (San Diego Co.). For Cardiff, county seat of Glamorganshire, Wales.

CARDIGAN, Mount, N.H. For a local settler.

CARDOZO, Mount, Alaska. In Chugach Mountains. For Benjamin Nathan Cardozo (1870-1938), U.S. Supreme Court associate justice.

CAREY, Ohio (Wyandot Co.). For Judge John Carey, president of the Indiana, Bloomington and Western railroad, owner of the land on which the town was founded.

CARIBOU The origin is in dispute because of transliteration through several languages: From Algonquian, through French, "reindeer" (the name survives as *caribou*, a species of deer); or for an Indian sub-group of the Tutchone tribe from what is now

British Columbia, where the regional name *The Cariboo* still exists. This name means "grabber" or "scratcher." Names in the United States usually mean "reindeer."
Caribou Co., Idaho (co. seat, Soda Springs). For "Caribou" or "Cariboo" Fairchild, who acquired his nickname in the Cariboo mine fields of British Columbia. He was active in the mining of silver in Idaho.
Caribou, Me. (Aroostook Co.). Many caribou once inhabited the area.
Caribou Mountain, Me.
Caribou Natl. Forest, Idaho.
Caribou Pond, Me.

CARL BLACKWELL, Lake, Okla. For Carl Blackwell.

CARLETON, Sir Guy, 1st Baron Dorchester (1724-1808), British soldier, statesman and administrator and the dominant Canadian figure during the first half-century of British rule. An intelligent, able autocrat, he helped save Canada from the Americans (1775-76) and skillfully handled the problems subsequent to the American Revolution. He was governor-in-chief of British North America (1768-78; 1786-96), served as commander-in-chief of the British North American forces (1782-83), and, althugh absent in England (1770-74), was chiefly responsible for the Quebec Act (1774). He was the brother of Thomas Carleton. See also DORCHESTER and GUYSBOROUGH.
Carleton, Mount, N.B.
Ottawa-Carleton Co., Ont. (co. seat, Ottawa).

CARLETON, Thomas (1735-1817), British soldier and administrator. He served during the American Revolution under his brother, Sir Guy Carleton, and was promoted to lieutenant-general (1798). He was the first governor, later called lieutenant-governor, of New Brunswick (1784-1817), although he was in England after 1803.
Carleton Co., N.B. (co. seat, Woodstock).
Carleton Mountain, N.B.

CARLETON PLACE, Ont. (Lanark Co.). For Carlton, Scotland. An earlier name was Murphy's Falls. Also spelled *Carlton Place*.

CARLINVILLE, Ill. (co. seat of Macoupin Co.). For Thomas Carlin, governor (1838-42).

CARLISLE For Carlisle, Cumberland, England.
Carlisle, Ky. (co. seat of Nicholas Co.). Probably for *Carlisle*, Pa.
Carlisle, .Mass. (Middlesex Co.), town.
Carlisle, Pa. (co. seat of Cumberland Co.).
Carlisle Barracks, Pa. (Cumberland Co.).

CARLISLE Co., Ky. (co. seat, Bardwell). For John Griffin Carlisle (1835-1910), Kentucky statesman. He was lieutenant governor, member (1877-90) and speaker (1883-89) of the U.S. House of Representatives, U.S. senator (1890-93), and secretary of the treasury (1893-97) under Cleveland.

CARLISLE, Ohio (Warren Co.). For George B. Carlisle, an agent of the Cincinnati railroad who platted the town.

CARLOS, Lake, Minn. For a friend of Glendy King, early settler and landowner.

CARLSBAD For resemblance to the springs in Karlsbad, Bohemia.
Carlsbad, Calif. (San Diego Co.).
Carlsbad, N.Mex. (co. seat of Eddy Co.). Earlier, Eddy.

CARLSTADT, N.J. (Bergen Co.). For Dr. Carl Klein, the leader of a group of German exiles who cooperatively bought the land for the town from the original American owners. It means "Carl's town." An earlier name was Tailor Town, for settlers who worked for tailors in New York.

CARLTON, Reuben B. (1812-1863), a settler from New York State. He migrated to the Minnesota Territory as a farmer and blacksmith and became a trustee of the city of Fond du Lac and a state legislator.
Carlton Co., Minn. (co. seat, *Carlton*).
Carlton, Minn. (co. seat of *Carlton* Co.).

CARLYLE, Ill. (co. seat of Clinton Co.). For Thomas Carlyle (1795-1881), Scottish author of *Sartor Resartus, Past and Present,* and many biographies and books of essays.

CARMAN, Man. For Rev. Albert Carman (1833-1917), bishop of the Methodist Episcopal Church in Canada (1874-83) and general superintendent of the Methodist Church in Canada (1883-1917).

CARMEL Biblical, for Mount Carmel, in northwest Israel, famous for its caves, which housed Christian anchorites, and for its association with Elijah and Elisha. The name of the Carmelite order is also derived from that of the mount.
Carmel, Ind. (Hamilton Co.).
Carmel, N.Y. (co. seat of Putnam Co.).
Carmel-by-the-Sea, Calif. (Monterey Co.). Named by three friars of the Carmelite order, who in turn probably named the land for their patron, Our Lady of Carmel.
Carmel Valley, Calif. (Monterey Co.).

CARMI Biblical, for the son of Reuben, first-born of Jacob (Genesis 46:89).
Carmi, Ill. (co. seat of White Co.).
Carmi, Lake, Vt.

CARMICHAEL, Calif. (Sacramento Co.). For Daniel Carmichael, landowner and early developer.

CARNEGIE, Pa. (Allegheny Co.). For Andrew Carnegie (1835-1919), steel manufacturer and philanthropist.

CARNESVILLE, Ga. (co. seat of Franklin Co.). For Thomas Petter Carnes (1762-1822), attorney, U.S. representative from Georgia (1793-95), state legislator, and agriculturist.

CARO, Mich. (co. seat of Tuscola Co.). A shortened form of *Cairo*, Egypt, adopted because it was easy to spell.

CAROLINA For Charles I of England, who called the territory occupied by the states of North and South Carolina "Carolana" in his grant (1629) to Sir Robert Heath. At this time, however, the area was already known as "Carolina," having been so named in 1562 by Jean Ribaut (c.1520-1565) in honor of his patron, Charles IX (1550-1574), king of France. The name was officially changed from Carolana to Carolina in 1663.
North Carolina, State of. 12th state of the Union. Settled: 1650. One of the original 13 colonies. Ratified Constitution: 1789. Cap: Raleigh. Motto: *Esse Quam Videri* (To Be Rather Than to Seem). Nickname:

The scene: A North Carolina beach at Kitty Hawk. The event: The Wright Brothers' first manned flight in 1903. [*New York Public Library*]

Tarheel State. Flower: Dogwood. Bird: Cardinal. Tree: Pine. Song: "The Old North State."

South Carolina, State of. Eighth state of the Union. Settled: 1670. One of the original **13 colonies. Ratified Constitution: 1788.** Cap: Columbia. Motto: *Animis Opibusque Parati* (Prepared in Mind and Resources). Nickname: Palmetto State. Flower: Carolina (Yellow) Jessamine. Bird: Carolina Wren. Tree: Palmetto. Song: "Carolina."

Carolina Sandhill Natl. Wildlife Refuge, S.C.

CAROLINE Co., Md. (co. seat, Denton). For Caroline Calvert, sister of Frederick Calvert, 6th Baron Baltimore and the last proprietor of Maryland.

CAROLINE Co., Va. (co. seat, Bowling Green). For Princess Wilhelmina Carolina of Anspach (1683-1737), wife of George II of England.

CAROLINE ISLANDS , part of the U.S. Trust Terr. of the Pacific Islands, under supervision of the United Nations. For Charles II, king of Spain (1665-1700). During his reign the islands were annexed (1686) by Spain.

CAROL STREAM, Ill. (Du Page Co.). For Carol Stream, daughter of the developer.

CARP A fish of the family *Cyprinidae*, plentiful in many fresh-water streams in the United States and Canada.

Carp Lake, Mich. (Emmet and Cheboygan Cos.).

Carp Lake, Mich. (Chippewa Co.).

Carp River, Mich. Flows SE into L Huron.

CARPENTER MOUNTAIN, Ore. For a local settler.

CARPENTERSVILLE, Ill. (Kane Co.). For D. G. Carpenter, an early settler.

CARPINTERIA, Calif. (Santa Barbara Co.). From Spanish *la carpinteria*, "the carpenter shop"; named by settlers for an Indian village where they had witnessed the building of a canoe.

CARRABASSETT Of Abnaki origin, meaning uncertain, but believed to mean either "small moose place" or "sturgeon place."

Carrabassett, Me. (Franklin Co.).

Carrabassett River, Me. Flows NE and then SE into the Kennebec R.

CARRBORO, N.C. (Orange Co.). For Julian S. Carr (1854-1924), owner of cotton mills around which the town grew.

CARRIGAIN, Mount, N.H. Presumably for a local resident.

CARRINGTON, N.Dak. (co. seat of Foster Co.). For M. D. Carrington, official of a land promotion company.

CARRIZO From an Indian word meaning "reed" or "cane." Loosely translated, it means "river cane."
Carrizo Creek, N.Mex.
Carrizo Springs, Tex. (co. seat of Dimmit Co.).
Carrizozo, N.Mex. (co. seat of Lincoln Co.). Supposedly with zo added to indicate abundance.

CARR MOUNTAIN, N.H. For a local citizen.

CARROLL, Charles (1737-1832), Maryland patriot and statesman known as "Charles Carroll of Carrollton." Active in the American cause during the American Revolution, he was a member of the Continental Congress (1776-78), a signer of the Declaration of Independence, a U.S. senator (1789-92), and a founder of the Baltimore and Ohio railroad.
Carroll Co., Ark. (co. seats, Berryville and Eureka Springs).
Carroll Co., Ga. (co. seat, Carrollton).
Carroll Co., Ga. (co. seat, Mount Carroll).
Carroll Co., Ind. (co. seat, Delphi).
Carroll Co., Iowa (co. seat, Carroll).
Carroll Co., Ky. (co. seat, Carrollton).
Carroll Co., Md. (co. seat, Westminster).
Carroll Co., Miss. (co. seats, Carrollton and Vaiden).
Carroll Co., Mo. (co. seat, Carrollton).
Carroll Co., N.H. (co. seat, Ossipee).
Carroll Co., Ohio (co. seat, Carrollton).
Carroll Co., Va. (co. seat, Hillsville).
Carroll, Iowa (co. seat of Carroll Co.).
Carrollton, Ala. (co. seat of Pickens Co.).
Carrollton, Ga. (co. seat of Carroll Co.).
Carrollton, Ill. (co. seat of Greene Co.).
Carrollton, Ky. (co. seat of Carroll Co.).
Carrollton, Miss. (a co. seat of Carroll Co.).
Carrollton, Mo. (co. seat of Carroll Co.).
Carrollton, Ohio (co. seat of Carroll Co.).

East Carroll Parish, La. (parish seat, Lake Providence).
Mount Carroll, Ill. (co. seat of Carroll Co.).
New Carrollton, Md. (Prince Georges Co.). Changed from Carrollton to distinguish it from other places of the same name in Maryland.
West Carroll Parish, La. (parish seat, Oak Grove).

CARROLL Co., Tenn. (co. seat, Huntingdon). For William Carroll, a general in the War of 1812 and governor of Tennessee (1821-27; 1829-35).

CARROLLTON, Mich. (Macomb Co.). For a Dr. Carroll, a landowner.

CARROLLTON, Tex. (Dallas Co.). There are a number of versions as to how this town received its name: early settlers may have named it for their home, Carrollton, Ill. or for Carroll County, Ill.; or it may have been named for George Carroll, a pioneer from Carrollton, Md.

CARRY FALLS RESERVOIR, N.Y. For falls in the Raquette River, in turn for a portage or place where canoes had to be carried around the falls.

CARSON, Calif. (Los Angeles Co.). For George Henry Carson (1829-1901), landowner and successful businessman.

CARSON, Christopher, known as "Kit" (1809-1868), famous frontiersman. He was a trapper (1831-42), a guide for the Fremont expeditions of 1842, 1843, and 1845, and an Indian agent (1853-61).
Carson Lake, Nev.
Carson Natl. Forest, N.Mex.
Carson Pass, Calif. Discovered by Capt. John Fremont and Kit Carson (1834).
Carson River, Nev.
Carson Sink, Nev.
Carson City, Nev. (independent city in Lyon Co.), state capital.

CARSON, N.Dak. (co. seat of Grant Co.). For Frank Carter and David and Simon Pederson, local businessmen.

CARSON Co., Tex. (co. seat, Panhandle). For Samuel Price Carson (1798-1838), state legislator, U.S. representative from North Carolina (1825-33), secretary of state of the

Republic of Texas (1836-38), and Texas patriot who served in many official capacities.

CARTER Co., Ky. (co. seat, Grayson). For a local citizen.

CARTER Co., Mo. (co. seat, Van Buren). For an early settler.

CARTER Co., Mont. (co. seat, Ekalaka). For Thomas Henry Carter (1854-1911), Montana legislator and U.S. senator (1895-1901; 1905-11).

CARTER Co., Okla. (co. seat, Ardmore). For Charles David Carter (1868-1929), U.S. representative from Oklahoma (1907-1927).

CARTER Co., Tenn. (co. seat, Elizabethton). For Landon Carter (1760-1800), who held many offices in North Carolina, in the territories, and in Tennessee, whose statehood he advocated.

CARTER DOME, N.H., in the Presidential Range. For a local dweller.

Kit Carson joined the ranks of American folk heroes during his lifetime. [*New York Public Library*]

CARTERET, N.J. (Middlesex Co.). For Sir George Carteret (c.1610-1680), who in 1650 was granted what is now the state of New Jersey by King Charles II. He was soon forced to surrender this claim, but he received East Jersey when the province was divided into two sections. An earlier name was Roosevelt.

CARTERET Co., N.C. (co. seat, Beaufort). For John Carteret, Earl Granville (1690-1763), a lord proprietor of the Carolinas.

CARTER LAKE, Iowa. (Pottawattamie Co.). Probably for the popular book *Colonel Carter of Cartersville*, by Francis Hopkinson Smith, published in 1891.

CARTER MOUNTAIN, Wyo. For the foster brother of William ("Buffalo Bill") Cody.

CARTERSVILLE, Ga. (co. seat of Bartow Co.). For Col. Farish Carter (1780-1861), landowner.

CARTERVILLE, Ill. (Williamson Co.). For Laban Carter, first settler.

CARTHAGE. For the ancient city of northern Africa (in what is now Tunisia), perennial enemy of the Roman Empire. When classical names were in vogue, many American localities adopted this name.
Carthage, Ill. (co. seat of Hancock Co.).
Carthage, Miss. (co. seat of Lake Co.).
Carthage, Mo. (co. seat of Jasper Co.).
Carthage, N.Y. (Jefferson Co.).
Carthage, N.C. (co. seat of Moore Co.).
Carthage, Tenn. (co. seat of Smith Co.).
Carthage, Tex. (co. seat of Panola Co.).

CARUTHERSVILLE, Mo. (co. seat of Pemiscot Co.). For Samuel Caruthers (1820-1860), attorney and U.S. representative from Missouri (1853-59).

CARVER, Jonathan (1732-1780), explorer and officer in the French and Indian Wars, author of *Travels Through the Interior Parts of North America* (1778), in which the name *Oregon* appeared in print for the first time. He died in London, England, leaving lands ceded to him by the Sioux that were not acknowledged by the U.S. Congress.
Carver Co., Minn. (co. seat, Chaska).
Carver Glacier, Ore., on South Sister Peak.
Carver Lake, Minn.

CARY, Ill. (McHenry Co.). For W. D. Cary, landowner.

CARY, N.C. (Wake Co.). For Samuel Fenton Cary (1814-1900), a prominent Ohio temperance leader who frequently visited the area in the 1850s.

CASA GRANDE From Spanish, "great house," probably for the vast Indian ruins in the area.
Casa Grande, Ariz. (Pinal Co.).
Casa Grande Natl. Monument, Ariz.

CASCADE Descriptive.
Cascade Co., Mont. (co. seat, Great Falls). For rapids and cascades in the Missouri R.
Cascade, Idaho (co. seat of Valley Co.). For falls in the Payette River.
Cascade Range, Calif.-Ore.-Wash.-Bc. For the narrows of the Columbia R., known as the Cascades.
Cascade Reservoir, Idaho.

CASCO From Micmac, "mud" or "muddy."
Casco, Me. (Cumberland Co.).
Casco Bay, Me.

CASEY Co., Ky. (co. seat, Liberty). For a local citizen.

CASEY, Zadoc, lieutenant governor of Illinois (1830-33), U.S. representative (1833-43), and state legislator.
Casey, Ill. (Clark Co.).
Caseyville, Ill. (St. Clair Co.).

CASHION, Ariz. (Maricopa Co.). For James Cashion, a landowner and railroad employee.

CASPER, Wyo. (co. seat of Natrona Co.). For Caspar W. Collins, lieutenant of the Eleventh Ohio Cavalry, killed by Indians.

CASPIAN LAKE, Vt. For the Caspian Sea, between Europe and Asia, because the lake was thought to resemble the sea in shape, though not in size.

CASS, Lewis (1782-1866), Ohio lawyer, state legislator, army officer, and Indian negotiator. He was governor of Michigan Territory (1813-31), secretary of war under Jackson, secretary of state under Buchanan, and three times unsuccessful Democratic candidate for President.
Cass Co., Ill. (co. seat, Virginia).
Cass Co., Ind. (co. seat, Logansport).
Cass Co., Iowa (co. seat, Atlantic).
Cass Co., Mich. (co. seat, Cassopolis).
Cass Co., Minn. (co. seat, Walker). Earlier, Van Buren.
Cass Co., Mo. (co. seat, Harrisonville).
Cass Co., Neb. (co. seat, Plattsmouth).
Cass Co., Tex. (co. seat, Linden).
Cass Lake, Mich.
Cass Lake, Minn.
Cass River, Mich.
Cass City, Mich. (Tuscola Co.).
Cassopolis, Mich. (co. seat of *Cass* Co.). Pseudo-Greek; *Cass* plus *opolis*, "city."
Cassville, Mo. (co. seat of Barry Co.).
Cassville, Pa. (Huntingdon Co.).

CASS Co., N.Dak. (co. seat, Fargo). For a Northern Pacific railroad president.

CASSADAGA CREEK, N.Y. From Algonquian, "under the rocks." It flows southeast into Conewango River.

CASSELMAN For a local settler.
Casselman, Pa. (Somerset Co.).
Casselman River, Md.-Pa. Flows into Youghiogheny R.

CASSIA Co., Idaho (co. seat, Burley). For cassia plants, trees and shrubs of the pea family.

CASTILLO DE SAN MARCOS NATL. MONUMENT. Fla. The northernmost point of the Spanish empire in the New World. For Saint Mark, the Evangelist.

CASTLE For rock formations resembling castles or towers.
Castle Peak, Alaska.
Castle Peak, Colo. Also called Carbon Peak.
Castle Peak, Wash.
Castle Dale, Utah (co. seat of Emery Co.).
Castle Gate, Utah (Carbon. Co.). For two sandstone pinnacles at the end of Prince R. Canyon.
Castle Hills, Tex. (Bexar Co.).
Castle Rock, Colo. (co. seat of Douglas Co.).
Castle Rock, Ore.
Castle Rock Flowage, Wis.

Castle Rock Table, S.Dak.
Castleton, Vt. (Rutland Co.).

CASTLE DOME PEAK, Ariz. Originally called Capital Dome because it was the highest peak in the mountains; the name was changed to the present form through error and possibly also because of resemblance to a castle.

CASTOR From French, "beaver," for the animal.
Castor Bayou, La. Flows SE and SW to join Dugdemona R. to form Little R.
Castor River, Mo. Flows SE and S into Little R.

CASTOR PEAK, Wyo. Mythological; for one of the twin sons of Leda, brothers of Helen of Troy.

CASTRO Co., Tex. (co. seat, Dimmitt). For Henri Castro (1786-1865), Republic of Texas colonizer, later consul to France.

CASTRO VALLEY, Calif. (Alameda Co.). For Guillermo Castro, a landowner.

CASTROVILLE, Calif. (Monterey Co.). For Juan Battista Castro, landowner and founder.

CASWELL Co., N.C. (co. seat, Yanceyville). For Richard Caswell (1729-1789), American Revolutionary general, North Carolina statesman, and its first and fifth governor (1775-79; 1784-87).

CATAHOULA From an Indian name of uncertain origin. At least three derivations have been suggested: for the river Etacoulow, "River of the Great Spirit," now named Little River, which runs through the parish; or from Choctaw *okkattahoola*, "beautiful white water"; or a Choctaw and French combination, "lake people."
Catahoula Parish, La. (parish seat, Harrisonburg).
Catahoula Lake, La.

CATAMOUNT MOUNTAIN, N.Y. For a species of wildcat, or perhaps because someone saw a large animal on the mountain.

CATARACT CREEK, Ariz. Descriptive, for the many falls in the stream. It flows north into the Colorado River.

CATASAUQUA, Pa. (Lehigh Co.). From the Indian phrase *gotto shacki*, "burnt ground," "parched land," or "the earth thirsts."

CATAWBA From an Indian tribe; origin of name unknown. A member of the Siouan linguistic stock, the tribe lived in what are now North Carolina and Tennessee and was recognized as the most powerful in the area.
Catawba Co., N.C. (co. seat, Newton).
Catawba Lake, N.C.-S.C.
Catawba River, N.C.

CATAWISSA From Algonquian *gattawisi*, "fattish." Reason for the name unknown, but probably for an incident that occurred along the creek.
Catawissa, Pa. (Columbia Co.).
Catawissa Creek, Pa.

CATERPILLAR MOUNTAIN, Me. Descriptive of shape.

CATHANCE LAKE, Me. From Abnaki, "the main fork," in reference to the small stream that leads into Cobscook Bay.

CATHEDRAL For a resemblance in shape to a cathedral.
Cathedral Bluffs, Colo.
Cathedral Mountain, Tex.

CATHEDRAL, Calif. (Riverside Co.). For a rock formation resembling a cathedral.

CATHLAMET, Wash. (co. seat of Wahkiakum Co.). For a tribe of Chinookan linguistic stock. Although the origin of the name is uncertain, it may have come from *calamet*, "stone."

CAT ISLAND, Miss. For an incident involving the killing of some raccoons.

CAT ISLAND, Wis., one of the Apostle Islands. So named because it is supposedly shaped like a cat.

CATO, N.Y. (Cayuga Co.). For Marcus Porcius Cato, called Uticensis (95-46 B.C.), great-grandson of Cato the Censor, leader of the Senate nobility who tried to preserve the Roman republic against Caesar.

CATOCTIN NATL. PARK, Md. From Algonquian, "speckled rock," for the color of stone in the area.

CATONSVILLE, Md. (Baltimore Co.). For Richard Caton, who owned an estate that included the townsite. The estate was a wedding present to him and his bride from his father-in-law, Charles Carroll of Carrollton, Md. An earlier name was Johnnycake.

CATOOSA Co., Ga. (co. seat, Ringgold). Probably for a Cherokee chief.

CATRON Co., N.Mex. (co. seat, Reserve). For Thomas Benton Catron (1840-1921), soldier in the Confederate army, lawyer, legislator, and U.S. senator 1912-17).

CATSKILL From a Dutch name, "Kat's stream," probably from a personal name respelled into English and folk-etymologized so that it would appear to be named because of a wildcat seen in the area.
Catskill, N.Y.(co. seat of Greene Co.). For the creek.
Catskill Creek, N.Y. Flows into the Hudson R.
Catskill Mountains, N.Y., an Appalachian range of the Mtns.

CATTARAUGUS Probably from Seneca, "bad smelling shore."
Cattaraugus Co., N.Y. (co. seat, Little Valley). For the creek.
Cattaraugus Creek, N.Y.

CAUCOMGOMOC LAKE, Me. From Abnaki, "lake with many gulls."

CAVALIER For Charles T. Cavileer, an early settler and public official; spelling changed to seem French.
Cavalier Co., N.Dak. (co. seat, Langdon).
Cavalier, N.Dak. (co. seat of Pembina Co.).

CAVANAL MOUNTAIN, Okla. From French, "cavernous."

CAYCE, S.C. (Lexington Co.). For William J. Cayce, a local resident.

CAYUGA One of the "Five Nations" of the Iroquois, located near Cayuga Lake, N.Y.
Cayuga Co., N.Y. (co. seat, Auburn).
Cayuga, Ont. (co. seat of Haldimand Co.).
Cayuga Lake, N.Y. One of the Finger Lakes.
Cayuga Heights, N.Y. (Tompkins Co.).

CAYUTA From Onandaga, meaning uncertain, possibly "log in water," "river," "lake," or "mosquito."
Cayuta Lake, N.Y.
Cayuta River, N.Y.-Pa. Rises in *Cayuta* L., flows SE into Susquehanna R.

CAZENOVIA, N.Y. (Madison Co.). For Theophilus de Cazenove, an agent of the Holland Land Company, a syndicate of Dutch financial houses.

CEBOLLETA MOUNTAINS, N.Mex. From Spanish, "little onions," for the flowers of the plants which grew on the slopes.

CECIL Co., Md. (co. seat, Elkton). For Cecilius CALVERT

CEDAR For the coniferous tree. These place names are sometimes influenced by Biblical allusion to the cedars of Lebanon.
Cedar Co., Iowa (co. seat, Tipton).
Cedar Co., Mo. (co. seat, Stockton).
Cedar Co., Neb. (co. seat, Hartington).
Cedar Bayou, Tex.
Cedar Creek, Colo.
Cedar Creek, N.J.
Cedar Hills, N.Dak.
Cedar Lake, Ill.
Cedar Lake, Mich.
Cedar Lake, Minn.
Cedar Lake, Wis.
Cedar Mountain, N.Mex.
Cedar Mountains, Utah.
Cedar River, Iowa-Minn.
Cedar River, Mich.
Cedar River, Neb.
Cedar River, N.Dak.
Cedar River, Wash.
Cedar Bluff Reservoir, Kan.
Cedar Breaks Natl. Monument, Utah. *Breaks* is a geographical term for "a disruption," as in a line of cedars or cliffs.
Cedarburg, Wis. (Ozaukee Co.).
Cedar City, Utah (Iron Co.).
Cedar Falls, Iowa (Black Hawk Co.). For rapids in the *Cedar* R.
Cedar Grove, N.J. (Essex Co.).
Cedar Hill, Tex. (Dallas Co.).
Cedarhurst, N.Y. (Nassau Co.).
Cedar Lake, Ind. (Lake Co.).
Cedar Rapids, Iowa (co. seat of Linn Co.). For the swift rapids in the *Cedar* R. Earlier, Rapids City.
Cedartown, Ga. (co. seat of Polk Co.).

CEDAR CREEK, S.Dak. For Cedar Boy, an Indian policeman. It flows into Grand River.

CELINA, Ohio (co. seat of Mercer Co.). For a Salina in New York.

CENTENNIAL WASH RIVER, Ariz. So named because it is supposed to be about 100 miles long. It flows generally southeast into Gila River.

CENTER For its central position, usually in the center of the county. See also LE CENTER. Minn.
Center, Neb. (co. seat of Knox Co.).
Center, N.Dak. (co. seat of Oliver Co.).
Center, Tex. (co. seat of Shelby Co.).
Center Pond, Mass.
Center City, Minn. (co. seat of Chisago Co.). Between Chisago City and Taylor's Falls.
Centereach, N.Y. (Suffolk Co.)
Center Hill Lake, Tenn.
Center Line, Mich. (Macomb Co.). For the middle trail to a trading post from Detroit.
Center Point, N.Y. (Jefferson Co.).
Centerville, Mass. (Barnstable Co.).
Centerville, Mo. (co. seat of Reynolds Co.).
Centerville, Ohio (Montgomery Co.).
Centerville, Pa. (Crawford Co.).
Centerville, Tenn. (co. seat of Hickman Co.) Earlier, Centreville.
Centerville, Tex. (co. seat of Leon Co.).
Centerville, Utah (Davis Co.).

CENTER MORICHES, N.Y. (Suffolk Co.). From an Indian word *meritche*, meaning not known.

CENTERVILLE, Iowa (co. seat of Appanoose Co.). For William Tandy Senter (1801-1848), U.S. representative from Tennessee, who visited the area. The spelling was changed later, by design or through clerical error.

CENTRAL For a central location.
Central City, Colo. (co. seat of Gilpin Co.). It was the center of supplies and mail for the Gregory Gulch mining area.
Central City, Neb. (co. seat of Merrick Co.). Centrally located in a farming region.
Central Falls, R.I. (Providence Co.). Between Valley Falls and Pawtucket

Falls. Earlier, Chocolate Mill, for an early chocolate factory.

CENTRAL CITY, Ky. (Muhlenberg Co.). For the Central Coal and Iron Company. An earlier name was Morehead's Horse Mill.

CENTRALIA For central location, with the Latinized ending popular in the 1800s.
Centralia, Ill. (Clinton and Marion Cos.).
Centralia, Mo. (Boone Co.).
Centralia, Wash. (Lewis Co.).

CENTRAL POINT, Ore. For a junction of two wagon trails in the center of Rogue River Valley.

CENTRE Variant spelling of CENTER.
Centre Co., Pa. (co. seat, Bellefonte). In the center of the state.
Centre, Ala. (co. seat of Cherokee Co.).
Centreville, Ill. (Saint Clair Co.).
Centreville, Md. (co. seat of Queen Anne's Co.). Earlier spellings, Centre Ville, Centerville.
Centreville, Mich. (co. seat of St. Joseph Co.).

CENTREVILLE, Ala. (co. seat of Bibb Co.). For a town in France; named by a Mrs. Chautard, who had lived in France.

CERES, Calif. (Stanislaus Co.). For the Greek goddess of grain.

CERRITOS, Calif. (Los Angeles Co.). From Spanish *cerrito*, "hillock."

CERRO DIABLO, Tex. From Spanish, "devil's hill."

CERRO GORDO Co., Iowa. (co. seat, Mason City). For Cerro Gordo, Mexico, site of a battle during the Mexican War.

CHACO From Spanish, "desert," but may have been influenced by an Indian word.
Chaco Canyon Natl. Monument, N.Mex. Ruins of Pre-Columbian pueblos.
Chaco River, N.Mex. Flows NW and N into San Juan R. So named because the river bed is intermittently dry.

CHACUACO CREEK, Colo. Of Indian origin, meaning uncertain. It flows generally north.

CHADDS FORD, Pa. (Delaware Co.). For John Chadds, landowner and ferry operator. It was the site of the battle of Brandywine.

CHADRON, Neb. (co. seat of Dawes Co.). For Pierre Chadron, a French-Indian trapper who lived in the area.

CHAFFEE Co., Colo. (co. seat, Salida). For Jerome Bounty Chaffee (1825-1886), legislator, financier, and U.S. senator (1876-79). An earlier name was Lake County.

CHAGRIN FALLS, Ohio (Cuyahoga Co.). Named for the river, whose name has a variety of explanations, one being that a party of early surveyors under Harvey Rice named the river because of their disappointment at finding they were not following the course of the Cuyahoga R. A second source says that it comes from the Indian word *shaguin*, or *shagrin*, "clear water."

CHAIN LAKES, Me. Descriptive of a series of lakes.

CHAKACHAMNA LAKE, Alaska. Of Tanaina origin, meaning unknown.

CHALFONT Pa. (Bucks Co.). For Chalfont St. Giles, Buckinghamshire, England, burial place of William Penn.

CHALK DRAW RIVER, Tex. For the chalk-like color and texture of the stream bed. It flows southeast into the Rio Grande.

CHALLIS For A. P. Challis, the founder of the town.
Challis, Idaho (co. seat of Custer Co.).
Challis Natl. Forest, Idaho.

CHALMETTE For the Chalmette family, which owned much of the land in the area; perhaps specifically for Ignace Martin de Lino de Chalmette (1775-1815), on whose plantation the Battle of New Orleans was fought.
Chalmette, La. (parish seat of St. Bernard Parish).
Chalmette Natl. Historical Park, La.

CHAMBERLAIN, S.Dak. (co. seat of Brule Co.). For Selah Chamberlain, a railroad official.

CHAMBERLAIN LAKE, Me. For the Chamberlain family, early settlers.

CHAMBERS Co., Ala. (co. seat, Lafayette). For Henry H. Chambers (1790-1826), physician, legislator, and U.S. senator (1825-26).

CHAMBERS Co., Tex. (co. seat, Anahuac). For Thomas Jefferson Chambers (1802-1865), Republic of Texas official and soldier, who was assassinated.

CHAMBERSBURG, Pa. (co. seat of Franklin Co.). For Benjamin Chambers (1708-1788), landowner, founder, and local leader.

CHAMBERS ISLAND, Wis. (Door Co.). For Col. Talbot Chambers, a member of an expedition here (1816) on the ship *George Washington.*

CHAMBLY, Jacques de (?-1687), French administrator and soldier. He was governor of Acadia (1673-77), governor of Grenada (1679), and governor of Martinique (1680). He was granted the seigniory of Chambly in 1672.
Chambly Co., Que. (co. seat, Longueuil).
Chambly, Que. (*Chambly* Co.).
Chambly Basin, Que.
Chambly Canal, Que.

CHAMPAIGN Variation or old spelling of French *campagne*, "field" or "plain."
Champaign Co., Ill. (co. seat, Urbana). For *Champaign* Co., Ohio.
Champaign Co., Ohio (co. seat, Urbana).
Champaign, Ill. (*Champaign* Co.). Earlier, The Depot (on Illinois Central railroad), New Town, West Urbana.

CHAMPLAIN, Samuel de (1567-1635), French explorer who founded Quebec. His expeditionary force fought a battle with Indians on the shore of a lake, which he named for himself, although disclaiming that he did so. His modesty was real and becoming.
Champlain Co., Que. (co. seat, Sainte Genevieve).
Champlain, Lake, Vt.-N.Y. Discovered by Champlain in 1609.

CHANCELLORSVILLE, Va. (Spotsylvania Co.). For the local Chancellor family. Site of a bloody battle of the Civil War, after which Union troops were forced to withdraw.

CHANDELEUR From French the day of blessing of candles, February 2, which was

the day the islands were discovered by the French.
Chandeleur Islands, La.
Chandeleur Sound, La.

CHANDLAR RIVER, Alaska. Folk etymologized from French *gens de large*, "nomadic people," into present English form. It flows southeast into the Yukon River.

CHANDLER, Ariz. (Maricopa Co.). For Alexander John Chandler (1859-1950), veterinary surgeon.

CHANDLER, Okla. (co. seat of Lincoln Co.). For George Chandler, the first assistant secretary of the interior, under Benjamin Harrison.

CHANDLER RIVER, Alaska. For a lake, which was named for William E. Chandler (1835-1917), secretary of the navy under Arthur. It flows northeast into Colville River.

CHANEY LAKE, Mich. Probably from French, *chaine*, "chain," folk etymologized into its present form and pronunciation.

CHANHASSEN, Minn. (Carver Co.). From Siouan, "sugar maple." The combination of *chan* and *hasan* or *haza* literally means "tree with sweet juice."

CHANNEL-PORT AUX BASQUES, Nfld. From French, reason for naming uncertain.

CHANNEL ISLANDS NATL. MONUMENT, Calif. Established in 1938, on Santa Barbara Island and Anacapa Islands. So named because the area is in the Santa Barbara Channel.

CHANNING, Tex. (co. seat of Hartley Co.). For Channing Rivers, a railroad official.

CHANUTE, Kan. (Neosho Co.). For Octave Chanute (1832-1910), civil engineer for the Santa Fe railroad (1863-67) and a pioneer exponent of heavier-than-air flight. His ideas preceded the invention of the airplane by more than fifty years, and he has been called the "Father of Aviation."

CHAPEL HILL, N.C. (Orange Co.). For a chapel of the Church of England that was in the town.

Although he founded Quebec City, it is a lake that bears Samuel de Champlain's name. [*New York Public Library*]

CHAPPAQUIDDICK ISLAND, Mass. Off Martha's Vineyard. From Wampanoag, "place of the separated island."

CHAPPELL, Neb. (co. seat of Deuel Co.). For John Chappell, founder and president of the Union Pacific railroad.

CHAPPELL POND, Mich., on Cedar River. For a local settler.

CHARDON, Ohio (co. seat of Geauga Co.). For Peter Chardon Brooks, who donated the land for the site of the county seat.

CHARITON For a French fur trader, probably Jean Chariton, who established a trading post on the north bank of the Missouri River, in what is now Iowa, during the 1700s.
Chariton Co., Mo. (co. seat, Keytesville).
Chariton, Iowa (co. seat of Lucas Co.).
Chariton River, Iowa-Mo.

CHARLEROI, Pa. (Washington Co.). For the Belgian city of Charleroi, which is known for its glass factories. The Belgian town, originally Charnoe, was captured by the Spanish in 1666 and renamed Charleroi in honor of Charles II of Spain. The Pennsylvania town also has glass factories.

CHARLES I (1600-1649), king of Great Britain (1625-49). Though his intentions were on the whole benevolent, his mismanagement of money and dubious, often harsh, expedients for raising it, plus his support of the persecution of Puritans by Archbishop Laud, led to great resentment, growing emigration to the New World, and finally the English Civil War. Defeated, and refusing to plea in what he considered an illegal trial, he was beheaded.

Charles, Cape. Southern tip of the Eastern Shore of Virginia, at the mouth of Chesapeake Bay. It was so named (1608) by Capt. John Smith because it lay across from Cape Henry, which was named for Charles's elder brother.

Charles River, Mass. Flows generally NE into Boston Bay.

Charles City Co., Va. (co. seat, *Charles City*).

Charles City, Va. (co. seat of *Charles City* Co.).

Charlestown, Mass. Formerly a separate town, now part of Boston.

CHARLES II (1630-1685), king of Great Britain (1660-85), eldest son of Charles I and Henrietta Maria. The "Merry Monarch" (so called because of his extravagant lifestyle and many mistresses) ascended the British throne with the Restoration of the monarchy in 1660, the third of the Stuart line. During his reign, the American colonies, which had suffered during the uncertainties of the Commonwealth, moved vigorously forward with help from the crown. Connecticut (1662) and Rhode Island (1663) were granted charters. Carolina, named for Charles himself, was granted to eight proprietors in 1663. The Dutch lost their territory in America (1664), and their domains were granted to the King's brother, James, Duke of York and Albany (later James II). The bulk of these lands was soon divided into New York and New Jersey. New Hampshire was chartered in 1679, and the great middle Atlantic region was opened with the Pennsylvania charter in 1681. Charles II also made the first enduring British impact upon what is now Canada with

the chartering of the Hudson's Bay Company (1670). When Charles ascended the throne, there were seven colonies: two (Connecticut and Rhode Island) without charters and two (Plymouth and New Haven) that would later be absorbed into others. When he died, the thirteen original colonies were complete, except for Delaware (still part of Pennsylvania) and Georgia (yet to be founded).

Charleston Co., S.C. (co. seat, *Charleston*).

Charleston, Miss. (co. seat of Tallahatchie Co.). For *Charleston*, S.C.

Charleston, S.C. (co. seat of *Charleston* Co.). Earlier, Charles Town.

CHARLES Co., Md. (co. seat, La Plata). For Charles CALVERT.

CHARLES CITY, Iowa (co. seat of Floyd Co.). For Charles FLOYD, for whom the county was also named.

CHARLES MIX Co., S.Dak. (co. seat, Lake Andes). For either Charles E. Mix, a commissioner of Indian affairs, or Charles E. Mix, a scout during the Civil War.

CHARLES MOUND, Ill. Highest point in the state. For Elijah Charles, who settled in a log house at the base of the mound.

CHARLES M. RUSSELL NATL. WILDLIFE RANGE, Mont. For Charles M. Russell, artist of Western life.

CHARLESTON For Charles Clendenin, the father of George Clendenin, founder. An earlier name was Charles Town.

Charleston, W.Va. (co. seat of Kanawha Co.), state capital.

South Charleston, W.Va. (Kanawha Co.). Actually W of Charleston, on the S bank of the Kanawha R.

CHARLESTON, Ark. (a co. seat of Franklin Co.). For Charles Kellum (?-c.1865), a clergyman.

CHARLESTON, Ill. (co. seat of Coles Co.). For Charles Morton, a founder.

CHARLESTON PEAK, Nev. Probably for CHARLESTON, S.C., but a claim is also made for CHARLES TOWN, W.Va.

CHARLESTOWN, Ind. (Clark Co.). For Charles Beggs, one of the surveyors who platted the town.

Charles II, shown landing at Dover to assume English throne, is perhaps best remembered for his liaison with Nell Gwyn. [*New York Public Library*]

CHARLESTOWN, N.H. (Sullivan Co.), town. For Admiral Sir Charles Knowles (?-1777), a friend of Gov. Benning Wentworth, who named the town. Knowles was then governor of Jamaica.

CHARLES TOWN, W.Va. (co. seat of Jefferson Co.). For Charles Washington, who owned the site and founded the town. He was a brother of George Washington.

CHARLEVOIX, Pierre Francois Xavier de (1682-1761), French explorer and writer who traveled in the area.
Charlevoix Co., Mich. (co. seat, *Charlevoix*).
Charlevoix Co., Que. (co. seats, La Malbaie and Baie Saint Paul).
Charlevoix, Mich. (co. seat of *Charlevoix* Co.).
Charlevoix Lake, Mich.

CHARLEY KANDIK RIVER, Alaska. *Charley* is for a Chief Charley. *Kandik* is of Indian origin, meaning unknown. It is also known as Kandik River, Charley Creek, and Charlie Creek. It flows southwest into the Yukon River.

CHARLOTTE For Charlotte Sophia, Princess of Mecklenburg-Strelitz (1744-1818), wife of George III of England.
Charlotte Co., N.B. (co. town, St. Andrews).
Charlotte Co., Va. (co. seat, *Charlotte Court House*).
Charlotte, N.C. (co. seat of Mecklenburg Co.).
Charlotte Court House, Va. (co. seat of *Charlotte* Co.).
Charlottesville, Va. (co. seat of Albemarle Co.).

Charleston, S.C., once called Charles Town in honor of Charles II, was the center of early Southern wealth and culture. [*New York Historical Society*]

Charlottetown, P.E.I. (co. seat of Queens Co.), provincial capital. Earlier, Port La Joie; renamed by the British when they captured it (1758).

CHARLOTTE For the Calusa tribe of southwestern Florida, who, under the influence of the Spaniards, changed their name to "Carlos" to conform to that of the Emperor Carlos (Charles) V. The name was later Anglicized.
Charlotte Co., Fla. (co. seat, Punta Gorda).
Charlotte Harbor, Fla.

CHARLOTTE, Mich. (co. seat of Eaton Co.). For the wife of Edmond Bostwick, an early landowner and developer.

CHARLOTTE, Tenn. (co. seat of Dickson Co.). For Charlotte Robertson, wife of James ROBERTSON. "Father of Tennessee.

CHARLOTTE CREEK, N.Y. For the first name of a woman who lived in the area. It flows southwest into Susquehanna River. Also known as Charlotte River.

CHARLTON Co., Ga. (co. seat, Folkston). For Robert Milledge Charlton (1807-1854), legislator, jurist and U.S. senator (1852-53).

CHARLTON, Mass. (Worcester Co.). For Sir Francis Charlton, member of the Privy Council at the time of naming.

CHARTIERS CREEK, Pa. For Peter Chartier, trader. It flows northeast into the Ohio River.

CHASE Origin unknown, possibly from a personal name, but the cluster of names in the area indicates that the origin is probably from "chase," a hollow through which a stream flows.
Chase Lake, Me.
Chase Mountain, Me. For the Chase family.
Chase Pond, Me.

CHASE Co., Neb. (co. seat, Imperial). For Champion S. Chase (?-1898), first attorney general of Nebraska, mayor of Omaha, and army officer.

CHASE, Salmon P. (1808-1873), Ohio statesman. He was a U.S. senator (1849-

52), governor (1855-59), secretary of the treasury (1861-64) under Lincoln, and chief justice of the U.S. Supreme Court (1864-73).
Chase Co., Kan. (co. seat, Cottonwood Falls).
Chase City, Va. (Mecklenburg Co.).

CHASKA, Minn. (co. seat of Carver Co.). From Siouan "first-born son."

CHATEAUGAY Probably of Iroquoian origin with overlays of French spelling, meaning uncertain.
Chateaugay, N.Y. (Franklin Co.).
Chateaugay Lakes, N.Y.
Chateaugay River, N.Y.-Que. Flows N into St. Lawrence R.

CHATEAUGUAY For Chateaugai, a town in France.
Chateauguay Co., (co. seat, Sainte Martine).
Chateauguay, Que. (*Chateauguay* Co.).
Chateauguay Centre, Que. (*Chateauguay* Co.).

CHATHAM For Chatham, Kent, England.
Chatham, Mass. (Barnstable Co.), town.
Chatham, Ont. (co. seat of Kent Co.).

CHATHAM, William PITT (the Elder) 1st Earl of (1708-1778), member of Parliament and prime minister. See also CHATOM.
Chatham Co., Ga. (co. seat, Savannah).
Chatham Co., N.C. (co. seat, Pittsboro).
Chatham, Ill. (Sangamon Co.).
Chatham, N.B. (Northumberland Co.).
Chatham, N.J. (Morris Co.).
Chatham, N.Y. (Columbia Co.), town.
Chatham, Va. (co. seat of Pittsylvania Co.).
Chatham Strait, Alaska. Named in 1794 by Capt. George Vancouver.

CHATOM, Ala. (co. seat of Washington Co.). For William PITT, 1st Earl of Chatham. The spelling was changed so as not to conflict with other places named CHATHAM.

CHATSWORTH, Ga. (co. seat of Murray Co.). For Chatsworth Castle, in northern England. The name was suggested by Indian fortifications on Fort Mountain two miles east.

CHATTAHOOCHEE From an Indian word, probably "marked rocks," for painted stones found in the river.
Chattahoochee Co., Ga. (co. seat, Cusseta).
Chattahoochee, Fla. (Gadsden Co.).
Chattahoochee Natl. Forest, Ga.
Chattahoochee River. Part of boundary between Georgia and Alabama. Flows SW and S to join the Flint R. and form the Apalachicola R.

CHATTANOOGA, Tenn. (co. seat of Hamilton Co.). Probably from the Creek name for what is now Lookout Mountain, "rock rising to a point." It is also stated that the name was first applied to a Cherokee village, which had once been a Creek village. An earlier name was Ross's Landing, for John Ross, founder. Chattanooga was the site of a major Civil War battle. Confederate forces under Bragg occupied Lookout Mountain and Missionary Ridge but were repulsed by Union Generals G. H. Thomas and Joseph Hooker under Grant's direction.

Charlotte of Mechlanburg gave her name to both Mechlanburg County, N.C., and its county seat, Charlotte. Such naming practice was typical in Colonial times. [*New York Public Library*]

CHATTOOGA From Cherokee, probably someone "has crossed the river," or possibly someone "drank by sips." The county was named for the river.
Chattooga Co., Ga. (co. seat, Summerville).
Chattooga River, Ga.-Ala.

CHATUGE LAKE, Ga.-N.C. Apparently of Cherokee derivation, *tsatugi*, "he sips," or "he has crossed the stream."

CHAUEKUKTULI, Lake Alaska. From Eskimo, meaning unknown.

CHAUTAUQUA From an Indian name, of uncertain origin, applied to the lake. Some suggested translations are "where the fish was taken out," "foggy place," "bag tied in the middle," "place where a child was washed away," "place of easy death," and "place where one was lost."
Chautauqua Co., Kan. (co. seat, Sedan). For *Chautauqua* Co., N.Y.
Chautauqua Co., N.Y. (co. seat, Mayville).
Chautauqua, Lake, N.Y.

CHAUVENET MOUNTAIN, Wyo. For Louis Chauvenet, topographer.

CHAVES Co., N.Mex. (co. seat, Roswell). For Jose Francisco Chaves (1833-1904), physician, colonel in the Union army, U.S. representative (1865-67; 1869-71), and state official. He was assassinated in 1904.

CHAZY For a Lieutenant de Chazy, a French officer killed while fighting Indians in the area in 1666.
Chazy, N.Y. (Clinton Co.), town.
Chazy Lake, N.Y.
Great Chazy River, N.Y. Flows NE and E into L. Champlain.
Little Chazy River, N.Y. Flows E into L. Champlain.

CHEAHA MOUNTAIN, Ala. Probably from Choctaw *chaha*, "high." It may also be for an Indian tribe.

CHEATHAM Co., Tenn. (co. seat, Ashland City). Apparently for Edwin S. Cheatham, legislator, although possibly for others named Cheatham.

CHEAT RIVER, W.Va.-Pa. Origin of name uncertain. At least four theories exist: for a kind of grain, from an Indian word, for the deceitful nature of the river's depth, or from a nickname or shortening of a name such as Cheatham. It flows northwest into Monongahela River.

CHEBOYGAN From an obscure Algonquian word, probably "pipe" or "funnel."
Cheboygan Co., Mich. (co. seat, *Cheboygan*).
Cheboygan, Mich. (co. seat of *Cheboygan* Co.).

CHECOTAH, Okla. (McIntosh Co.). For Samuel Checote, a Creek chief.

CHEHALIS From a local Indian language, "sand." The river was named first, for the deposit of sand at its mouth.
Chehalis, Wash. (co. seat of Lewis Co.). Earlier, Saundersville.
Chehalis, Point, Wash.
Chehalis River, Wash. Flows NW into Grays Harbor.

CHELAN From a Salishan tribal name, said to mean either "deep water" or "land of bubbling water." The county was named for the lake.
Chelan Co., Wash. (co. seat, Wenatchee).
Chelan, Wash. (*Chelan* Co.).
Chelan Lake, Wash.

CHELLY, CANYON DE, Ariz. See CANYON DE CHELLY.

CHELMSFORD, Mass. (Middlesex Co.), town. For Chelmsford, Essex, England.

CHELSEA For the residential section of London on the north bank of the Thames. It is associated with many famous cultural figures of England's past, including Sir Thomas More, Oscar Wilde, George Eliot, Charles Dickens, as well as artists and humanists from other countries, such as Holbein and Erasmus. In recent years it has become a center for youth culture.
Chelsea, Me. (Kennebec Co.), town.
Chelsea, Mass. (Suffolk Co.). Earlier, Winnisimmet.
Chelsea, Mich. (Washtenaw Co.).
Chelsea, Vt. (co. seat of Orange Co.).

CHEMO POND, Me. From Abnaki, "large bog," probably for the nearby bog of the same name.

CHEMQUASABAMTICOOK LAKE, Me. From Abnaki, "place where a large lake and a river are combined." Also spelled *Chequam Sabamticook.*

CHEMUNG For a former Seneca village near the townsite. The name means "big horn."
Chemung Co., N.Y. (co. seat, Elmira).
Chemung, N.Y. (*Chemung* Co.), town.
Chemung River, N.Y.

CHENANGO From Onondaga, "bull thistle."
Chenango Co., N.Y. (co. seat, Norwich).
Chenango River, N.Y.

CHENEY, Wash. (Spokane Co.). For Benjamin Pierce Cheney (1815-1895), a founder of the Northern Pacific railroad. In 1836 he established the Cheney and Company Express between Boston and Montreal, which merged with the American Express Company.

CHEPACHET From Narraganset, "river-fork."
Chepachet, R.I. (Providence Co.).
Chepachet River, R.I. Flows NE to join Pascoag R. to form Branch R.

CHEQUAMEGON From a French spelling of an Ojibway word. Meaning uncertain, but probably referring to a piece of land extending into water. The point was named first.
Chequamegon Bay, Wis.
Chequamegon Natl. Forest, Wis.
Chequamegon Point, Wis.

CHERAW, S.C. (Chesterfield Co.). For a local Indian tribe.

CHEROKEE For Indians of Iroquoian linguistic stock, mostly in southern Appalachian Mountains from southern Virginia down into Tennessee, North Carolina, Alabama, and Georgia. The name may derive from Creek *tciloki,* "people of a different speech." They were moved to what is now Oklahoma (1838-39)—a forced march in which some twenty-five per cent died. Under treaties of 1828 and 1833 they established the Cherokee Nation with its capital at Tahlequah. The nation was disbanded in 1906.

Cherokee Co., Ala. (co. seat, Centre).
Cherokee Co., Ga. (co. seat, Canton).
Cherokee Co., Iowa (co. seat, *Cherokee*).
Cherokee Co., Kan. (co. seat, Columbus).
Cherokee Co., N.C. (co. seat, Murphy).
Cherokee Co., Okla. (co. seat, Tahlequah).
Cherokee Co., S.C. (co. seat, Gaffney).
Cherokee Co., Tex. (co. seat, Rusk).
Cherokee, Iowa (co. seat of *Cherokee* Co.).
Cherokee, Okla. (Alfalfa Co.).
Cherokee Dam and Lake, Tenn., on the Holston R.
Cherokee Natl. Forest, N.C.
Cherokee Outlet or *Cherokee Strip,* Okla. Former Cherokee territory (12,000 sq. mi.), opened for settlement in 1893.
Cherokees, Lake o' the, Okla. Formed by the Pensacola Dam on the Grand (Neosho) R. Other names: Grand Lake, Pensacola Reservoir.

CHERRY For cherry trees or orchards.
Cherry Creek, Ariz. (Gila Co.).
Cherry Creek, Ariz. (Yavapai Co.).
Cherry Creek, Colo. Flows N into South Platte R.
Cherry Creek, N.Dak. Flows NE and SE into Little Missouri R.
Cherry Creek, S.Dak. Flows ESE into Cheyenne R. Translation from Sioux, "chokeberry."
Cherry Creek, N.Y. (Chautauqua Co.), town. For a nearby stream, which was probably named for wild cherry trees.
Cherry Hill, N.J. (Camden Co.). For an old farm that was on a hill with a path lined by cherry trees leading to it.
Cherry Hills Village, Colo. (Arapaho Co.).
Cherryland, Calif. (Alameda Co.).
Cherryvale, Kan. (Montgomery Co.).
Cherry Valley, Calif. (Riverside Co.).
Cherryville, N.C. (Gaston Co.).

CHERRY Co., Neb. (co. seat, Valentine). For Samuel A. Cherry, an army officer killed in 1881. It claims to be the largest county in the United States.

CHESANING, Mich. (Saginaw Co.). From Algonquian, "big rock."

CHESAPEAKE From Algonquian, possibly "on the big bay," but the meaning is in dispute.
Chesapeake, Va. (Independent city).

Forced by the Treaty of New Echota to leave their tribal lands, the Cherokee tribe endured the "March of Tears," depicted here in an oil mural by Elizabeth James. [*Oklahoma Historical Society Museum*]

Chesapeake, W.Va. (Kanawha Co.).
Chesapeake Bay, Va.-Md. Atlantic Ocean inlet, extending into Virginia and Maryland. with bulk in Maryland.

CHESHIRE. For Cheshire, county in England.
Cheshire Co., N.H. (co. seat, Keene).
Cheshire, Conn. (New Haven Co.), town.
Cheshire, Mass. (Berkshire Co.).
Cheshire Reservoir, Mass.

CHEST CREEK, Pa. Reason for name unknown, but probably an indication of depth at a specific place. It flows north into Susquehanna River.

CHESTER. For Chester, Cheshire, England, home town of many settlers brought to America by William Penn.
Chester Co., Pa. (co. seat, *West Chester*).
Chester Co., S.C. (co. seat, *Chester*). For *Chester* Co., Pa.
Chester, Conn. (Middlesex Co.), town.
Chester, Ill. (co. seat of Randolph Co.).
Chester, Mont. (co. seat of Liberty Co.). For *Chester*, Pa.
Chester, Pa. (*Chester* Co.). Earlier, Uppland; named by Swedish and Finnish settlers (earliest settlement in the state).
Chester, S.C. (co. seat of *Chester* Co.).
Chester, Vt. (Windsor Co.).
Chester, W.Va. (Hancock Co.). Probably

for Chester, England; another theory is that the founder simply used a short name he liked.
Chester River, Md. Flows S into Chesapeake Bay.
Chestertown, Md. (co. seat of Kent Co.).
West Chester, Pa. (co. seat of *Chester* Co.).

CHESTER Co., Tenn. (co. seat, Henderson). For Robert I. Chester (1793-c.1860), a quartermaster in the War of 1812, postmaster of Jackson, Tenn., U.S. marshal, and a colonel in the Republic of Texas army. He practiced law and served as a representative to the Tennessee state legislature.

CHESTERFIELD, Philip Dormer Stanhope, 4th Earl of (1694-1773), English statesman and writer. During a long and varied public career, he held many high positions including lord lieutenant of Ireland (1745-46) and one of the principal secretaryships of state (1746-48). He is best remembered, however, for his brilliant and sophisticated *Letters to His Son* (1774).
Chesterfield Co., S.C. (co. seat, *Chesterfield*).
Chesterfield Co., Va. (co. seat, *Chesterfield*).
Chesterfield, S.C. (co. seat of *Chesterfield* Co.).

Chesterfield, Va. (co. seat of *Chesterfield* Co.).

CHESTERTON, Ind. (Porter Co.). From the name of the township, Westchester, Ind. Earlier names were Coffee Creek, for a wagon-load of coffee that overturned, and Calumet.

CHESUNCOOK LAKE, Me. From Abnaki, "place of main outlet."

CHETAC LAKE, Wis. Probably for an Ojibway chief. The name has been translated as "pelican."

CHETCO RIVER, Ore. From an Indian tribal name. It flows into the Pacific Ocean.

CHEVELON. For a trapper named Chevelon who died on the bank of the creek.
Chevelon Butte, Ariz. For the creek.
Chevelon Creek, Ariz. Flows NE into Little Colorado R.

CHEVIOT, Ohio (Hamilton Co.). For a tavern, which was named for the Cheviot Hills on the boundary between England and Scotland.

CHEVREUIL, Point, La. Extends into Atchafalaya Bay. From French, "deer."

CHEYENNE From Dakota Indian, "red talkers." The tribe, of Algonquian linguistic stock, lived west of the Mississippi, north of Texas, east of the Rocky Mountains, and also for a time in Montana and Wyoming. Originally a farming tribe, they became nomadic and perhaps the most famous of the Plains Indians.
Cheyenne Co., Colo. (co. seat, *Cheyenne Wells*).
Cheyenne Co., Kan. (co. seat, St. Francis).
Cheyenne Co., Neb. (co. seat, Sidney).
Cheyenne, Okla. (co. seat of Roger Mills Co.).
Cheyenne, Wyo. (co. seat of Laramie Co.), state capital.
Cheyenne River, S.Dak.-Wyo.
Cheyenne River Indian Reservation Area, S. Dak.
Cheyenne Wells, Colo. (co. seat of *Cheyenne* Co.).
Northern Cheyenne Indian Reservation, Mont.

CHIBOUGAMAU From an Indian term, "the water is stopped," in reference to the lake's narrow outlet.
Chibougamau, Que. (Abitibi Co.).
Chibougamau Lake, Que.
Chibougamau River, Que.

CHICAGO From Algonquian, "garlic field."
Chicago, Ill. (co. seat of Cook Co.).
Chicago River, Ill. On site of *Chicago*, formerly flowed into L. Michigan, but is now part of the Chicago Drainage Canal, also known as the Sanitary and Ship Canal.
Chicago Heights, Ill. (Cook Co.). Promotional.
Chicago Ridge, Ill. (Cook Co.).
East Chicago, Ind. (Lake Co.).
East Chicago Heights, Ill. (Cook Co.).
North Chicago, Ill. (Lake Co.).
South Chicago Heights, Ill. (Cook Co.).
West Chicago, Ill. (Du Page Co.).

CHICHAGOF ISLAND, Alaska. Named in 1805 for Admiral Vasili Yakov Chichagov, of the Imperial Russian Navy, who explored the area (1765-66).

CHICKAHOMINY RIVER, Va. Probably from Algonquian, "land of grain," but this is speculation. The latter part certainly refers to grain, the famous boiled Indian maize *rokahamen*. Civil War battles, including the Seven Days Battle, were fought along its banks.

CHICKAMAUGA For a Cherokee tribal sub-group, meaning of name uncertain, possibly "sluggish or dead water," or "boiling pot," for a whirlpool.
Chickamauga, Ga. (Walker Co.).
Chickamauga Lake, Tenn.
Chickamauga and Chattanooga Natl. Military Park, Ga.-Tenn. Established to commemorate Civil War battles for the control of CHATTANOOGA, Tenn.

CHICKASAW For an Indian tribe; meaning unknown, but probably a place name. The tribe, closely connected with the Choctaw and of Muskhogean linguistic stock, lived in the mid-central and southern states. They migrated to Oklahoma between 1837 and 1847.

Chickasaw Co., Iowa (co. seat, New Hampton).

Chicasaw Co., Miss. (co. seats, Houston and Okolona).

Chickasaw, Ala. (Mobile Co.).

CHICKASAWHAY RIVER, Miss. From a Choctaw town name plus *hay* or *ahe*, "potato." The spelling follows a French form and is often confused with CHICKASAW. It flows south to join Leaf River to form Pascagoula River.

CHICKASHA, Okla. (co. seat of Grady Co.). Variant of CHICKASAW.

CHICKLEY RIVER, Mass. Of Algonquian origin, meaning uncertain. It flows north into Deerfield River.

CHICKWOLNEPY STREAM, N.H. From Algonquian *chigual*, "frog," plus a suffix, probably "place." It flows west into Androscoggin River.

CHICO From Spanish *arroyo chico*, "little stream."

Chico, Calif. (Butte Co.).

Chico North, Calif. (Butte Co.).

Chico West, Calif. (Butte Co.).

CHICOPEE From Algonquian, possibly "swift" or "violent water."

Chicopee, Mass. (Hampden Co.).

Chicopee River, Mass.

CHICOT Co., Ark. (co. seat, Lake Village). For Point Chicot on the Mississippi River, from French, "stumpy," descriptive of navigational difficulties at the point.

CHICOUTIMI From Montagnais Indian, *shkoutimeou*, "end of the deep water," since the site of the town is at the fall line of the Saguenay River.

Chicoutimi Co., Que. (co. seat, Chicoutimi).

Chicoutimi, Que. (co. seat of Chicoutimi Co.).

The devastation of Chicago's Great Fire of 1871 was almost total; 300 died, 90,000 were left homeless and 17,450 buildings worth $200,000,000 were destroyed.

Chicoutimi-Nord, Que. (*Chicoutimi* Co.).
Chicoutimi River, Que. Flows N to Saguenay R.

CHIKASKIA   RIVER, Kan.-Okla. From Osage, "salt," for part of name; rest not known, although it has been interpreted as "white spotted deer." It flows south and southeast into Salt Fork of the Arkansas River.

CHILI Variant spelling of *Chile*, South America.
Chili, N.Y. (Monroe Co.).
North Chili, N.Y. (Monroe Co.).

CHILKOOT PASS, Alaska. From the Indian tribal name.

CHILLICOTHE Possibly from Shawnee, "village".
Chillicothe, Ill. (Woodford Co.). For *Chillicothe*, Ohio.
Chillicothe, Mo. (co. seat of Livingston Co.). For *Chillicothe*, Ohio.
Chillicothe, Ohio (co. seat of Ross Co.). The first capital of Ohio, laid out (1796) as "first settlement made in peace west of the mountains."

CHILTON Co., Ala. (co. seat, Clanton). For William Parish Chilton (1810-1871), legislator, jurist, and member of the Confederate Congress. An earlier name was Baker County.

CHILTON, Wis. (co. seat of Calumet Co.). Probably for Chillington, England, from which one of the settlers came.

CHIMMENTICOOK STREAM, Me. From Abnaki, "main islands in river."

CHIMNEY ROCK NATL. HISTORICAL SITE, Neb. Historic landmark on the Oregon Trail. So named for the shape of the rock.

CHINA So named because of the importance and abundance of Chinese laborers during the days of the gold rush.
China Lake, Calif.
China Lake, Calif. (Kern Co.).

CHINA For a sad hymn, "China."
China, Me. (Kennebec Co.).
China Lake, Me.

CHINATI PEAK, Tex. From Spanish, "blackbird," but also possibly for Indian chief.

CHINCOTEAGUE BAY, Va.-Md. Probably from Abnaki, "large stream."

CHINLE WASH RIVER, Ariz. From Navajo, "mouth of canyon." Flows north from the mouth of Canyon de Chelly into San Juan River.

CHINO, Calif. (San Bernardino Co.). From a land grant called Santa Ana del Chino. *Chino* is Spanish for a person with mixed blood; probably the landowner was a *chino*.

CHINOOK, Mont. (co. seat of Blaine Co.). For the chinook wind, a warm breeze that melts winter snow on the eastern slopes of the Rocky Mountains. The wind was named for the Chinook Indians.

CHINOOK PASS, Wash., in the Cascade Mountains. For the Indian tribe, *Tsinuk*, also known as Flatheads, for a custom of deforming the head. Meaning of name unknown.

CHIPLEY, Fla. (co. seat of Washington Co.). For William Dudley Chipley (?-1897), soldier in the Confederate army who rose to the rank of lieutenant colonel. Wounded at both Shiloh and Chickamauga, he was captured and held prisoner until the end of the war. A railroad director, he was instrumental in building the Pensacola railroad, which, through his efforts, became a part of the Louisville and Nashville system. The city that now bears his name was a popular siding for one of the branches. He served as a state senator.

CHIPOLA Probably from Creek *hachapala*, "on the other side of the stream."
Chipola, Fla. (Calhoun Co.).
Chipola River, Ala.-Fla. Flows generally S to join the Apalachicola R.

CHIPPEWA (more properly Ojibway). For a large Indian tribe of Algonquian linguistic stock, which occupied much of southwestern Ontario and southern Manitoba in Canada and, in the United States, lived principally in Minnesota, northern Wisconsin and eastern North Dakota,—also in parts of Illinois, Indiana, Iowa, Kansas, Michigan,

and Ohio. Many of their legends are incorporated in Longfellow's "Hiawatha" (1855). Their name, in Ojibway, means "puckered" and refers to the puckered seam in their moccasins.
Chippewa Co., Mich. (co. seat, Sault Sainte Marie).
Chippewa Co., Minn. (co. seat, Montevideo).
Chippewa Co., Wis. (co. seat, *Chippewa Falls*).
Chippewa Lake, Mich.
Chippewa Lake, Wis.
Chippewa Natl. Forest, Minn.
Chippewa River, Mich.
Chippewa River, Minn. Flows generally S to the Minnesota R.
Chippewa River, Wis. Flows into the Mississippi R.
Chippewa Falls, Wis. (co. seat of *Chippewa* Co.).

CHIPUTNETICOOK LAKES, Me.-N.B. Chain of lakes (North, Grand, Spednik, and Palfrey) bordering Canada and the United States. From Abnaki, "the place of the large hill stream."

CHIRICAHUA From Apache *tsil,* "mountain," and *kawa,* "great."
Chiricahua Mountains, Ariz.
Chiricahua Natl. Monument, Ariz.
Chiricahua Peak, Ariz.

CHIRIKOF ISLAND, Alaska. Named by Capt. George Vancouver for Capt. Alexi Cherikov, Imperial Russian Navy commander of the *St. Paul* in Bering's expedition in 1741.

CHISAGO From Ojibway *kichisaga,* "fair" or "beautiful." The first syllable was omitted, and a clerical error changed *a* to *o.*
Chisago Co., Minn. (co. seat, Center City). For the lake.
Chisago Lake, Minn.

CHISANA RIVER, Alaska. From Indian, "red river." It flows generally north to Tanana River.

CHISHOLM For Jesse Chisholm, a guide and trader, said to be part Cherokee.
Chisholm, Minn. (St. Louis Co.).
Chisholm Trail. Famous early cattle trail from Texas to Kansas.

CHITINA RIVER, Alaska. From Indian, "copper river." It flows generally northwest into Copper River.

CHITTENANGO, N.Y.(Madison Co.).From an Indian word meaning "waters divide and run north"; a stream flowed through the village.

CHITTENDEN, Thomas(1730-1797),one of the founding fathers of Vermont. He was governor of the republic of Vermont (1778-89) and governor of the state (1791-97).
Chittenden Co., Vt. (co. seat, Burlington).
Chittenden Reservoir, Vt.

CHITTENDEN MOUNTAIN, Wyo. For George B. Chittenden, of the Rayden Survey of 1878.

CHOCOLATE MOUNTAINS, Ariz. For their color.

CHOCORUA, Mount, N.H. Of Pennacook origin, meaning uncertain, possibly for the name of chief or from *tsikweres,* "frog."

CHOCTAW For an Indian tribe of Muskhogean linguistic stock who lived in southeastern Mississippi and southwestern Alabama. They moved (c.1822-40) to what is now Oklahoma. The meaning of the name is unknown.
Choctaw Co., Ala. (co. seat, Butler).
Choctaw Co., Miss. (co. seat, Ackerman).
Choctaw Co., Okla. (co. seat, Hugo).
Choctaw, Okla. (Oklahoma Co.).

CHOCTAWHATCHEE Of Indian origin; *Choctaw* or *Chatot,* Muskogean tribal names, plus *hatchee,* "stream."
Choctawhatchee Bay, Fla.
Choctawhatchee River, Ala.-Fla. Flows generally S into the Gulf of Mexico.

CHOPTANK RIVER, Del.-Md. From an Algonquian tribal name of the Nanticoke tribe. It possibly refers to "tidal change," or "tidal creek." The spelling is folk etymologized. It flows southwest into Chesapeake Bay.

CHOTEAU, Mont. (co. seat of Teton Co.). For Auguste and Pierre CHOUTEAU. The spelling was changed to distinguish the city from the county.

CHOUTEAU Co., Mont. (co. seat, Fort Benton). For Auguste (1749-1829) and Pierre (1758-1849) Chouteau, pioneers, fur traders, and founders of St. Louis, Mo.

CHOWAN For the Chowanoc, an Algonquian Indian tribe, "those in the south," in the 1500s the leading tribe in northeastern North Carolina. They declined in importance and disappeared in the 1700s.
Chowan Co., N.C. (co. seat, Edenton).
Chowan River, N.C.

CHOWCHILLA, Calif. (Madera Co.). For a nearby ranch, river, mountain, and canal. Probably from the Chauciles Indian group, who were aggressive and referred to as "killers."

CHRISTIAN, William (1743-1786), attorney and officer in the French and Indian Wars, brother-in-law of Patrick Henry. He was a legislator, colonel of the militia, and land-owner in Virginia, and was killed (1786) while in pursuit of raiding Indians.
Christian Co., Ill. (co. seat, Taylorville). For Christian Co., Ky.
Christian Co., Ky. (co. seat, Hopkinsville).
Christian Co., Mo. (co. seat, Ozark).
Christiansburg, Va. (co. seat of Montgomery Co.).

CHRISTOPHER, Ill. (Franklin Co.). For Christopher Harrison, an early settler.

CHUBBUCK, Idaho (Bannock Co.). For Earl Chubbuck, a train conductor. An earlier name was Beet Dump, probably a point to which farmers brought sugar beets to await processing.

CHUGACH From the Eskimo tribal name.
Chugach Islands, Alaska.
Chugach Mountains, Alaska.

CHUGINADAK ISLAND, Alaska, in the Aleutian Islands. From Aleut, with con-notation of "roasting" or "frying," but exact meaning uncertain.

CHULA VISTA, Calif. (San Diego Co.). From Spanish chula, "graceful" or "at-tractive," and vista, "view."

CHULITNA Of Tanaina Indian origin, meaning not known.
Chulitna River, Alaska. Flows E into Turner Bay.

Chulitna River, Alaska. Flows SW into Susitna R.

CHURCHILL, John (1650-1722), 1st Duke of Marlborough, governor of Hudson's Bay Company (1685-91).
Churchill, Man.
Churchill, Cape, Man., on Hudson Bay.
Churchill Lake, Sask.
Churchill River, Alta.-Sask.-Man. Flows E and NE into the Hudson Bay. Earlier, English River, because it was the route into the interior of Canada used by the "English," or Hudson's Bay Company traders.

CHURCHILL Co., Nev. (co. seat, Fallon). For Fort Churchill, which was named for Charles C. Churchill, an officer of the Third U.S. Artillery Regiment.

CHURCHILL, Winston (1874-1965). British prime minister during World War II. The mountain peaks in Alaska were named in 1965 after his death.
Churchill, Mount, Alaska.
Churchill Peaks, Alaska.

CHURCH POINT, La. (Acadia Parish). For a church that was at the point of Bayou Plaquemine Brulee.

CHUSKA MOUNTAINS, Ariz.-N.Mex. From Navajo, "white spruce."

CHUTE POND, Wis. From French, "waterfall."

CIBOLA From Spanish, "buffalo," probably a translation from an Indian word.
Cibola Natl. Forest, N.Mex.
Cibola Cone, N.Mex.
Cibola Draw, N.Mex. Draw is a term for a gully.

CICERO, Ill. (Cook Co.). For the Roman orator, Marcus Tullius Cicero.

CIMARRON Meaning and specific ap-plication of the term are uncertain. The river may have been called in Spanish El Rio de los Carneros Cimarron, "River of the Wild Sheep," although some suggest that cimarron means "wild" in the sense of "wilderness." Still other translations are "outcast" and "tawny," the color of the elk seen in the area.
Cimarron Co., Okla. (co. seat, Boise City).

Cimarron, Kan. (co. seat of Gray Co.). For the river. A folk belief is that it is taken from a cook's frustrating cry "Simmer on," because his beans did not turn out in gourmet fashion.

Cimarron River, N.Mex.-Okla.-Kan. Flows E, NE, then SE to the Arkansas R.

CINCINNATI, Ohio (co. seat of Hamilton Co.). For the Society of the Cincinnati; said to have been named by Gen. Arthur St. Clair, governor of the Northwest Territory. The society was named for Cincinnatus, farmer-soldier of the Roman Empire.

CINNAMINSON, N.J. (Burlington Co.). From Algonquian, possibly "stone-tree," as for the sugar maple.

CIRCLE, Mont. (co. seat of McCone Co.). For the Circle Ranch; named by Peter Rorvik, rancher.

CIRCLE PINES, Minn. (Anoka Co.). Descriptive.

CIRCLEVILLE, Ohio (co. seat of Pickaway Co.). For the circular Mound Builders' earthworks at the site. The mounds contain prehistoric bones and artifacts.

CISCOE, Tex. (Eastland Co.). For John J. Cisco, New York financier and an officer and stockholder of the Texas and Pacific railroad.

CISPUS RIVER, Wash. Of Indian origin, meaning unknown. It flows west into Cowlitz River.

CITADEL MOUNTAIN, Wyo. Descriptive of shape.

CITRUS For groves of citrus trees.
Citrus Co., Fla. (co. seat, Inverness).
Citrus, Calif. (Sacramento Co.).
Citrus Heights, Calif. (Sacramento Co.). Promotional.

CITY OF REFUGE NATL. HISTORICAL PARK, Hawaii. So named because it served as a sanctuary for those who sought asylum or wished to escape taboo punishment.

CLACKAMAS For the tribe, of Chinookan linguistic stock; meaning unknown.

Cincinnatus, for whom Cincinnati was named, dictator of Rome, defeated the Aequians and then resigned his post — all within sixteen days. [*New York Public Library*]

Clackamas Co., Ore. (co. seat, Oregon City).
Clackamas River, Ore.

CLAIBORNE, William Charles Cole (1775-1817), statesman, U.S. representative from Tennessee (1797-1801). He was governor of the Mississippi Territory (1801-05), governor of the Orleans Territory (1804-12), and governor of Louisiana (1812-16). In 1817 he was elected U.S. senator from Louisiana but died before taking office.
Claiborne Parish, La. (parish seat, Homer).
Claiborne Co., Miss. (co. seat, Port Gibson).
Claiborne Co., Tenn. (co. seat, Tazewell).

CLAIREMONT, Tex. (Kent Co.). For Claire Rohmberg, daughter of R. L. Rohmberg, owner of the townsite.

CLAIRTON, Pa. (Allegheny Co.). Origin uncertain; thought to be derived from the last syllable of the last name of Samuel Sinclair, a Pennsylvania landowner.

CLALLAM For an Indian tribe, of Salishan linguistic stock, "big brave nation."
Clallam Co., Wash. (co. seeeat, Port Angeles).
Clallam Bay, Wash.
Clallam River, Wash.

CLAM For the mollusk or shellfish.
Clam Lake, Wis. On *Clam* R., Wis.
Clam River, Mass. Flows generally SE.
Clam River, Mich. Flows E and SE into Muskegon R.
Clam River, Wis. Flows NNW into St. Croix R
Clam Falls, Wis. (Polk Co.).

CLANTON, Ala. (co. seat of Clinton Co.). For General Clanton, a Confederate officer.

CLARE For county Clare, Ireland.
Clare Co., Mich. (co. seat, Harrison).
Clare, Mich. (*Clare* Co.). Earlier, Kaykakee.

CLAREMONT For John Holles, 1st Earl of Clare (1564-1637), an ancestor by marriage of Gov. Benning Wentworth of New Hampshire. Holles's home was known as Claremont Castle.
Claremont, Calif. (Los Angeles Co.). For *Claremont*, N.H.
Claremont, N.H. (Sullivan Co.).

CLAREMORE, Okla. (co. seat of Rogers Co.). For Clermont, an Osage chief. The name was folk etymologized to its present form.

CLARENDON Co., S.C. (co. seat, Manning). For Edward Hyde, 3rd Earl of Clarendon (1661-1723), colonial governor of New York and New Jersey. He held other positions in the colonies.

CLARENDON, Tex. (co. seat of Donley Co.). For a Lord Clarendon of England; named by early settlers from there.

CLARENDON HILLS, Ill. (DuPage Co.). For Clarendon, near Salisbury, England.

CLARENDON RIVER, Vt. For a member of the Clarendon family, English nobility. It flows generally north into Castleton River.

CLARINDA, Iowa (co. seat of Page Co.). For Clarinda Buck, niece of Alexander M. Tice, a pioneer.

CLARION For the sound of the ripples in the river, "like the notes of a distant clarion."
Clarion Co., Pa. (co. seat, *Clarion*).
Clarion, Iowa (co. seat of Wright Co.). Probably for *Clarion*, Pa.
Clarion, Pa. (co. seat of *Clarion* Co.). For the river.
Clarion River, Pa. Flows generally SW to the Allegheny R.

CLARK, George Rogers (1752-1818), frontiersman in the Northwest Territory, now the north central states, brother of William Clark. He fought against the Indians and was a general in the American Revolution. The name is sometimes spelled *Clarke*.
Clark Co., Ill. (co. seat, Marshall).
Clark Co., Ind. (co. seat, Jeffersonville).
Clark Co., Ky. (co. seat, Winchester).
Clark Co., Ohio (co. seat, Springfield).
Clark Co., Wis. (co. seat, Neillsville). Possibly for an early settler.
Clarksburg, W.Va. (co. seat of Harrison Co.).
Clarksville, Ind. (Hamilton Co.).
Clarksville, Tenn. (co. seat of Montgomery Co.). Named by John MONTGOMERY.

CLARK Co., Idaho (co. seat, Dubois). For Sam Clark, an early settler. The name may have been chosen because it also honors the explorer, George Rogers Clark.

CLARK Co., Kan. (co. seat, Ashland). For Charles F. Clarke, a Union officer in the Civil War who died while on duty in 1862.

CLARK LAKE, Alaska. For John W. Clark, a trading post operator in 1891.

CLARK Co., Nev. (co. seat, Las Vegas). For William Andrews Clark (1839-1925), U.S. senator from Montana (1899-1900); 1901-07).

CLARK N.J. (Union Co.). For Abraham Clark (1726-1794), a signer of the Declaration of Independence, member of the Continental Congress (1776-78; 1779-83; 1787-89), U.S. representative from New Jersey (1791-94).

CLARK, Newton, pioneer schoolteacher and legislator.
Clark Co., S.Dak. (co. seat, *Clark*).
Clark, S.Dak. (co. seat of *Clark* Co.).

CLARK, William (1770-1838), explorer, soldier, and Indian agent, brother of George Rogers Clark. He served under Wayne at the Battle of Fallen Timbers and in 1794 was co-leader of the Lewis and Clark Expedition. He was appointed (1807) brigadier general of the Louisiana territorial militia and was governor of Missouri Territory (1813-21). During the War of 1812 he protected the frontiers from Indian invasion. U.S. superintendent of Indian affairs in St. Louis (1813-38), he was also surveyor general for Illinois (1824-25). In 1825 he attempted to effect permanent peace with the Indians in the Treaty of Prairie du Chien. He was also a mapmaker and a wildlife artist.
Clark Co., Ark. (co. seat, Arkadelphia).
Clark Co., Mo. (co. seat, Kahoka).
Clark Co., Wash. (co. seat, Vancouver). Also spelled *Clarke*.
Clark Fork (river), Mont.-Idaho.
Clark Fork (river), Mont.-Wyo.
Clark Natl. Forest, Mo.
Clarks River, Ky. Flows into Tennessee R.

CLARKE Co., Ala. (co. seat, Grove Hill). For a local Indian fighter.

CLARKE, Elijah (1733-1799), Georgia soldier and general in the American Revolution.
Clarke Co., Ga. (co. seat, Athens).
Clark Hill Reservoir, Ga.-S.C.

CLARKE Co., Iowa (co. seat, Osceola). For James Clarke (1811-1850), a publisher and governor of Iowa Territory.

CLARKE Co., Miss. (co. seat, Quitman). For Joshua G. Clarke, a Mississippi official.

CLARKE Co., Va. (co. seat, Berryville). For George Rogers CLARK.

CLARKE (officially *Clark*) Co., Wash. For William CLARK.

CLARKESVILLE, Ga. (co. seat of Habersham Co.). For John C. Clarke (1776-1832), son of Elijah Clarke, and governor of Georgia (1819-23).

CLARK LAKE, Mich. For a local settler.

CLARKSDALE, Miss.(co. seat of Coahoma Co.). For John Clark (1823-1893), a planter.

CLARKS SUMMIT, Pa. (Lackawanna Co.). For Deacon William Clark, who, in 1799, cleared the land in the area.

CLARKSTON, Ga. (DeKalb Co.). For Col. W. W. Clark, a director of the Georgia Railroad and Banking Company.

CLARKSVILLE See also CLARK. George Rogers.

CLARKSVILLE, Tex. (co. seat of Red River Co.). For James Clark, early settler from Tennessee and founder.

CLATSOP For an Indian tribe of Chinookan linguistic stock, whose name means "dried salmon." They lived along the banks at the mouth of the Columbia River, and south along the Pacific Coast.
Clatsop Co., Ore. (co. seat, Astoria).
Clatsop Spit, Ore. A land area at the mouth of the Columbia R.
Fort Clatsop Natl. Memorial, Ore.

CLAUDE, Tex. (co. seat of Armstrong Co.). For Claude Ayers, the first engineer to run a train through the village.

CLAWSON, Mich. (Oakland Co.). For John Lawson, a storekeeper, but a clerical error occurred and the name as approved was Clawson.

CLAXTON, Ga. (co. seat of Evans Co.). For Philander Priestly Claxton (1862-1957), a native of Tennessee. He was a great crusader for public education and was given the position of U.S. commissioner of education (1911). Also claimed for Kate Claxton (1878-1924), a popular actress.

CLAY, Henry (1777-1852), Kentucky statesman, known as the "Great Pacificator" because he frequently advocated compromise to avert national crises. When the question of slavery became an explosive issue, Clay helped initiate the Missouri Compromise (1820) and the Compromise of 1850, thus postponing the Civil War. He was twice defeated as the Whig candidate for president (1832; 1844). He was four times a U.S. senator (1806-07;

Henry Clay was called "The Great Pacificator" for his ability to find compromise where none seemed to exist. Had he lived, the Civil War might never have been fought. [*New York Public Library*]

1810-11; 1831-42; 1849-52), three times a U.S. representative (1811-14; 1815-21; 1823-25), and served a long term as speaker of the House. From 1825 to 1829 he was secretary of state under John Quincy Adams.
Clay Co., Ala. (co. seat, Ashland).
Clay Co., Ark. (co. seats, Piggott and Corning). Earlier, Clayton Co., for John Middleton Clayton ´ (see CLAYTON Co., Iowa). His brother, Powell Clayton, was Reconstruction governor of Arkansas and outraged the people, who forced a change (1875) in the name.
Clay Co., Fla. (co. seat, Green Cove Springs).
Clay Co., Ga. (co. seat, Fort Gaines).
Clay Co., Ill. (co. seat, Louisville).
Clay Co., Ind. (co. seat, Brazil).
Clay Co., Kan. (co. seat, *Clay Center*).
Clay Co., Minn. (co. seat, Moorhead). Earlier, Breckinridge Co.
Clay Co., Miss. (co. seat, West Point). Earlier, Colfax Co.

Clay Co., Mo. (co. seat, Liberty).
Clay Co., Neb. (co. seat, *Clay Center*).
Clay Co., N.C. (co. seat, Hayesville).
Clay Co., S.Dak. (co. seat, Vermillion).
Clay Co., Tenn. (co. seat, Celina).
Clay Co., Tex. (co. seat, Henrietta).
Clay Co., W.Va. (co. seat, *Clay*).
Clay, W.Va. (co. seat of *Clay* Co.).
Clay Center, Kan. (co. seat of *Clay* Co.).
Clay Center, Neb. (co. seat of *Clay* Co.).

CLAY Co., Iowa (co. seat, Spencer). For Henry Clay, Jr. (1807-1847), an officer killed during the Mexican War.

CLAY Co., Ky. (co. seat, Manchester). For Gen. Green Clay (1757-1826), Kentucky soldier and legislator who raised the siege of Fort Meigs (1813).

CLAYTON, Ala. (a co. seat of Barbour Co.). For the Clayton family, who owned a large estate in the area.

CLAYTON, Augustin Smith (1783-1839), attorney, Georgia legislator, jurist, and U.S. representative (1832-35).
Clayton Co., Ga. (co. seat, Jonesboro).
Clayton, Ga. (co. seat of Rabun Co.).

CLAYTON Co., Iowa (co. seat, Elkader). For John Middleton Clayton (1796-1856), Delaware legislator, secretary of state (1849-50) under Taylor, and U.S. senator from Delaware (1829-36; 1845-49; 1853-56).

CLAYTON, Mo. (co. seat of St. Louis Co.). For Ralph Clayton, a local landowner.

CLAYTON, N.Mex. (co. seat of Union Co.). For Clayton C. Dorsey, son of Sen. Stephen W. Dorsey (Arkansas), landowner.

CLAYTOR LAKE, Va. For Graham Claytor, a power company executive.

CLEAR For a stream or body of clear water.
Clear, Cape, Alaska.
Clear Creek, Ariz.
Clear Creek, Colo.
Clear Creek, Okla. Flows NE and N into Beaver R.
Clear Lake, Calif.
Clear Lake, La.
Clear Lake, Utah.

Clear Stream, N.H. Flows E into Androscoggin R.

Clear Boggy Creek, Okla. Flows SE into Red R. Also called Boggy Creek.

Clear Creek Co., Colo. (co. seat Georgetown).

CLEARFIELD Translated from an Indian word meaning "cleared field."
Clearfield Co., Pa. (co. seat, Clearfield).
Clearfield, Pa. (co. seat of *Clearfield* Co.).
Clearfield Creek, Pa.

CLEARFIELD, Utah (Davis Co.). So named because there was almost nothing there—a clear field.

CLEAR LAKE Descriptive.
Clear Lake, S.Dak. (co. seat of Deuel Co.).
Clear Lake Reservoir, Calif.
Clear Lake City, Iowa (Cerro Gordo Co.).
Clearlake Highlands, Calif. (Lake Co.).

CLEARWATER Descriptive.
Clearwater Co., Idaho (co. seat, Orofino). For the river.
Clearwater Co., Minn. (co. seat, Bagley). For the nearby river and lake; translation of Ojibway *Gawakomitigweia*.
Clearwater, Fla. (co. seat of Pinellas Co.). For the waters of the Gulf of Mexico off the beaches at the site.
Clearwater Lake, Mo.
Clearwater Mountains, Idaho.
Clearwater Natl. Forest, Idaho.
Clearwater River, Idaho.
Clearwater River, Minn.

CLEBURNE, Patrick R. (1828-1865), Confederate soldier and general killed in battle at Franklin, Tenn.
Cleburne Co., Ala. (co. seat, Heflin).
Cleburne Co., Ark. (co. seat, Heber Springs).
Cleburne, Tex. (co. seat of Johnson Co.).

CLE ELUM From Indian, "swift water."
Cle Elum Dam, Wash., on the river.
Cle Elum Lake, Wash.
Cle Elum River, Wash.

CLEMSON, S.C. (Pickens Co.). For Thomas Green Clemson (1807-1888), a planter, engineer, agronomist, and founder of Clemson Agricultural College.

CLENDENING LAKE, Ohio. Perhaps for David Clendenin, U.S. representative from Ohio (1814-17), also active in the early formation of the steel industry.

CLERMONT Co., Ohio (co. seat, Batavia). From French, "clear mountain."

CLEVELAND For Moses Cleaveland (1754-1806), officer in George Washington's army, attorney, and surveyor of the Western Reserve.
Cleveland, Ohio (co. seat of Cuyahoga Co.). Earlier, Cleaveland.
Cleveland Heights, Ohio (Cuyahoga Co.).
East Cleveland, Ohio (Cuyahoga Co.).

CLEVELAND, Benjamin (1738-1806), North Carolina legislator and soldier. He was an American Revolutionary hero at the Battle of Kings Mountain, where he commanded "Cleveland's Bull Dogs."
Cleveland Co., N.C. (co. seat, Shelby).
Cleveland, Ga. (co. seat of White Co.).

CLEVELAND, Stephen Grover (1837-1908), twenty-second and twenty-fourth President of the United States (1885-89; 1893-97), born in New Jersey but associated with New York. Governor of New York (1883-85), he subsequently served his first term as President. Defeated by Benjamin Harrison in 1888, he was again elected in 1892.
Cleveland Co., Ark. (co. seat, Rison). Earlier, Dorsey County.
Cleveland Co., Okla. (co. seat, Norman).
Cleveland, Miss. (a co. seat of Bolivar Co.).
Cleveland, Okla. (Pawnee Co.).
Cleveland, Mount, Mont., in Glacier Natl. Park.
Cleveland Natl. Forest, Calif.

CLEVELAND, Tenn. (co. seat of Bradley Co.). For John Cleveland, an early settler from North Carolina and founder.

CLEVELAND, Tex. (Liberty Co.). For Charles Lander Cleveland, cotton broker, landowner, and land promoter.

CLIFF Descriptive.
Cliffside Park, N.J. (Bergen Co.).
Cliffwood Beach, N.J. (Middlesex Co.).

CLIFFORD LAKE, Me. For a local community member.

CLIFTON For cliffs in the area.
Clifton, Ariz. (co. seat of Greenlee Co.).
Clifton, N.J. (Passaic Co.).
Clifton, Tenn. (Hardin Co.).
Clifton, Tex. (Bosque Co.). Earlier, Cliff Town.
Clifton Forge, Va. (Alleghany Co.).
Clifton Heights, Pa. (Delaware Co.).

CLINCH Apparently from a personal name, although folk stories also exist as to the origin of the name.
Clinch Mountains, Va.-Tenn. For the river.
Clinch River, Va.-Tenn. Flows SW into Tennessee R.

CLINCH Co., Ga. (co. seat, Homerville). For Duncan Lamont Clinch (1787-1849), general in the Indian wars and U.S. representative.

CLINGMANS DOME, N.C.-Tenn. Peak on state line, named for Thomas Lanier Clingman (1812-1897), attorney and state legislator. He was a U.S. representative (1843-45; 1847-58), U.S. senator from North Carolina (1858-61), then resigned to become (1862) a general officer in the Confederate service. His interest in measuring and exploring peaks led to this spectacular landmark being named for him.

CLINTON, De Witt (1769-1828), New York legislator, U.S. senator (1802-03), mayor of New York City, governor of New York (1818-23; 1824-26), and projector of the Erie Canal. He was an unsuccessful candidate for President in 1812. See also DE WITT.
Clinton Co., Ill. (co. seat, Carlyle).
Clinton Co., Ind. (co. seat, Frankfort).
Clinton Co., Iowa (co. seat, Clinton).
Clinton Co., Ky. (co. seat, Albany).
Clinton Co., Mich. (co. seat, St. Johns).
Clinton Co., Pa. (co. seat, Lock Haven).
Clinton, Ark. (co. seat of Van Buren Co.).
Clinton, Conn. (Middlesex Co.), town and village.
Clinton, Ill. (co. seat of De Witt Co.).
Clinton, Ind. (Vermillion Co.).
Clinton, Iowa (co. seat of *Clinton* Co.). Earlier, New York.
Clinton, Ky. (co. seat of Hickman Co.).
Clinton, La. (parish seat of East Feliciana Parish).
Clinton, Me. (Kennebec Co.), town.
Clinton, Mass. (Worcester Co.), town.
Clinton, Miss. (Hinds Co.).

Cleveland, Ohio, shown here in 1834, owed much of its early growth to the opening in 1827 of the Ohio and Erie Canal. [*New York Historical Society*]

In 1809 DeWitt Clinton proposed the Erie Canal; by the time it was finished in 1825 he was Governor of New York. Public Library)

Clinton, Mo. (co. seat of Henry Co.).
Clinton, S.C. (Laurens Co.).
Clinton, Tenn. (co. seat of Anderson Co.).
Clinton Reservoir, N.J.
Clinton River, Mich. Flows generally E to L. St. Clair.

CLINTON, George (1739-1812), New York attorney, legislator, first governor (1777-95), again governor (1801-04), and vice-president of the United States (1805-12) under Madison. He was an uncle of De Witt Clinton.
Clinton Co., Mo. (co. seat, Plattsburg).
Clinton Co., N.Y. (co. seat, Plattsburgh).
Clinton Co., Ohio (co. seat, Wilmington).

CLINTON, Ky. (co. seat of Hickman Co.). For a Captain Clinton who was stationed in the area in 1826.

CLINTON, N.C. (co. seat of Sampson Co.). For Richard Clinton (1721-1796), a captain of militia during the American Revolution and a state senator.

CLINTON, Okla. (Custer Co.). For Clinton Irwin, jurist.

CLINTONVILLE, Wis. (Waupaca Co.). For Norman Clinton, the first permanent settler.

CLINTWOOD, Va. (co. seat of Dickenson Co.). For Henry Clinton Wood (1836-1909), a major in the Confederate army. He served two terms in the Virginia Senate, two years as speaker (1881-82), and was the first president of the South Atlantic and Ohio railroad.

CLIVE, Iowa (Polk Co.). For a local resident.

CLOQUET For a fur trader, whose first name has been lost.
Cloquet, Minn. (Carlton Co.). For the river. Earlier, Knife Falls.
Cloquet River, Minn.

CLOUD Co., Kan. (co. seat, Concordia). For William F. Cloud, an officer in the Kansas Volunteers. An earlier name was Shirley County.

CLOUD PEAK, Wyo. For the clouds that usually surround the peak.

CLOUDY MOUNTAIN, Alaska. For cloudy skies.

CLOVER For the plant.
Clover, S.C. (York Co.).
Clover Creek, Utah-Nev. Flows generally W into Meadow Valley Creek.
Cloverdale, Calif. (Sonoma Co.).

CLOVIS, Calif. (Fresno Co.). For Clovis Cole, landowner and wheat farmer.

CLOVIS, N.Mex. (co. seat of Curry Co.). Named by the daughter of a town official for Clovis (c.466-511), king of a German tribe, the Salian Franks.

CLUTE, Tex. (Brazoria Co.). For S. J. Chute, whose wife donated land for the site.

CLYDE Possibly for the river in Scotland.
Clyde, N.Y. (Wayne Co.).
Clyde, Ohio (Sandusky Co.). For *Clyde*, N.Y. Earlier, Hamer's Corners, Centerville.

CLYDE RIVER, Vt. Named by a Scottish surveyor for the Clyde River in Scotland. It flows northwest into Lake Memphremagog.

CLYMER, George E. (1739-1813), promi-
nent Philadelphia merchant, member of the
Continental and U.S. Congresses, U.S.
representative (1789-91), and a signer of
the Declaration of Independence and the
Constitution.
Clymer, N.Y. (Chautauqua Co.).
Clymer, Pa. (Indiana Co.).

COACHELLA, Calif. (Riverside Co.).
Probably for a division of the Shoshoni living
in this area, whose name is variously spelled
Caguilla, *Coahuillas*, *Coahuila*, and
Cahuilla. Another version is that the name is
derived from Spanish *conchilla*, "shell,"
supposedly for shell deposits in the valley.

COAHOMA Co., Miss. (co. seat,
Clarksdale). For Sweet Coahoma, known
also as Coahoma Sheriff, daughter of the
last Choctaw in the area. The name, in
Choctaw, means "red panther."

COAL For a region where coal is found or
mined.
Coal Co., Okla. (co. seat, *Coalgate*).
Coal Creek, N.Mex. Flows W into Chaco R.
Coal Creek, Okla.
Coal Mountain, Colo.
Coal River, W.Va.
Coal City, Ill. (Grundy Co.).
Coaldale, Pa. (Schuylkill Co.).
Coalgate, Okla. (co. seat of *Coal* Co.).
Coal Grove, Ohio (Lawrence Co.).
Coal Valley, Ill. (Rock Island Co.).
Coalville, Utah (co. seat of Summit Co.).
Little Coal River, W.Va.

COALINGA, Calif. (Fresno Co.). Originally
known as Coaling Station on the railroad, it
was transformed into a town name by the
addition of the letter *a*.

COANQUANNOCK Indian name, probably
tribal, for the site of what is now
Philadelphia. It was translated as "the grove
of tall pines."

COAST Descriptive of location.
Coast Mountains, Alaska.
Coast Ranges, Alaska-Mex., along the
   Pacific coast.

COATESVILLE, Pa. (Chester Co.). Named
by the planner and first postmaster, Moses
Coates, for either himself or his grandfather,
Moses Coates, an Irish Quaker who settled
in Pennsylvania in 1717.

COATICOOK From Iroquoian *kivaktakwak*,
"something crooked which straightens
itself," used by the Indians in designating
the Coaticook River. According to others,
the name comes from two Abnaki words,
koa, "pine," and *tegu*, "a river," thus "river
of the pines."
Coaticook, Que. (Stanstead Co.).
Coaticook River, Que.

COATUE POINT, Mass., on Nantucket Island. From Wampanoag, "place of the pine
tree."

COBB Co., Ga. (co. seat, Marietta) For
Thomas Cobb (1784-1830), jurist, U.S.
representative (1817-21; 1823-24) and U.S.
senator (1824-28).

COBB, Howell (1815-1868), attorney and
statesman. He was a U.S. representative
from Georgia (1843-51; 1855-57), speaker
of the house in the 31st Congress, governor
of Georgia (1851-53), secretary of the
treasury (1857-60) under Buchanan, and
major general in the Confederate Army.
Cobb Creek, Okla. Flows SE into Washita R.
Fort Cobb, Okla. (Caddo Co.).
Fort Cobb Reservoir, Okla., in *Cobb* Creek.

COBBLE MOUNTAIN RESERVOIR, Mass.
Descriptive of the rounded stones found on
the nearby mountain.

COBBOSSEECONTEE LAKE, Me. From
Abnaki, "place of sturgeon." Also spelled
Cobeskonte and *Cobossecontee*.

COBLESKILL, N.Y. (Schoharie Co.). For a
creek (Dutch *kill*), which had been named
after a local miller, Jacob Cobel.

COBOURG, Ont. (co. seat of Northumberland and Durham Cos.). In honour of the
marriage (1819) of Princess Charlotte to
Prince Leopold of Saxe-Coburg.

COBSCOOK BAY, Me. From Malecite,
"rocks under water."

COBURN MOUNTAIN, Me. For Abner and
Philander Coburn, surveyors.

COCHECO RIVER, N.H. From Abnaki,
"rapid current place." It flows southeast
into Piscataqua River.

COCHICHEWICK, Lake, Mass. From Pennacook, "swift current place."

COCHISE Co., Ariz. (co. seat, Bisbee). For the Apache chief Cochise (c.1825-1874), who conducted raids in Mexican territory and later, after brutal treatment by U.S. Army officers, against the United States.

COCHRAN, Ga. (co. seat of Bleckley Co.). For Arthur E. Cochran (1820-1865), lawyer, jurist, state legislator, and president of the Macon and Brunswick railroad.

COCHRAN Co., Tex. (co. seat, Morton). For Robert Cochran (?-1836), a soldier killed at the Alamo.

COCHRANE For Hon. Francis Cochrane, a minister of lands, forests, and mines for Ontario.
Cochrane District, Ont. (district seat. Cochrane).
Cochrane, Ont. (district seat of Cochrane district.

COCKE Co., Tenn. (co. seat, Newport). For William Cocke (1747-1828), companion of Daniel Boone. He was U.S. senator from Tennessee (1796-97; 1799-1805), a jurist in Mississippi, and a veteran of the War of 1812.

COCKRELL HILL, Tex. (Dallas Co.). For Alexander Cockrell, a ferryboat operator on the Trinity River.

COCOA For the coconut palm limited to southern Florida.
Cocoa, Fla. (Brevard Co.).
Cocoa Beach, Fla. (Brevard Co.).
Cocoa West, Fla. (Brevard Co.).

COCONIMO For an Indian tribe, now surviving in their descendants, the Havasupai, "blue, or green, water dwellers." Coconimo is a Zuni name borrowed from the Hopi, meaning "pinon people." It is also a Havasupai word meaning "little water."
Coconimo Co., Ariz. (co. seat, Flagstaff).
Coconimo Natl. Forest, Ariz.
Coconino Plateau, Ariz.

COD, CAPE. For the fish. The Massachusetts peninsula was named first, in 1602 by Bartholomew Gosnold.
Cape Cod, Mass. Peninsula.

Cape Cod Bay, Mass. Arm of Massachusetts Bay.
Cape Cod Canal, Mass. Connects Cape Cod Bay with Buzzards Bay.
Cape Cod Natl. Seashore, Mass. Recreational area, arm of Cape Cod.

CODINGTON Co., S.Dak. (co. seat, Watertown). For G. S. S. Codington, a clergyman and Dakota Territory legislator.

CODORUS From Algonquian, "rapid water."
Codorus, Pa. (York Co.).
Codorus Creek, Pa.

CODY, William Frederick ("Buffalo Bill") (1846-1917), founder of the town. He was an army scout, Indian fighter, buffalo hunter, and showman, who took "Buffalo Bill's Wild West Show" on many tours. See also BUFFALO BILL RESERVOIR.
Cody, Wyo. (co. seat of Park Co.).
Cody Peak, Wyo.

COEUR D'ALENE From French, "heart of awl," said to have been used by a chief to describe the size of a trader's heart. It is a French name for the Skitswish tribe.
Coeur d' Alene, Idaho (co. seat of Kootenai Co.).
Coeur d'Alene Lake, Idaho.
Coeur d'Alene Mountains, Idaho-Mont.
Coeur d'Alene Natl. Forest, Idaho.
Coeur d'Alene River, Idaho. Flows generally S to Coeur d'Alene Lake.

COEYMANS, N.Y. (Albany Co.). For Barent Pieterse Coeymans (c.1625-1710), who was given this area as a land grant by Governor Lovelace of New York in 1673.

COFFEE Co., Ga. (co. seat, Douglas). For John Coffee (1782-1836), a relative of John Coffee (1772-1833). He was a general in the Indian wars and a legislator.

COFFEE, John (1772-1833), Tennessee surveyor and soldier, a general in the War of 1812 and the Indian wars, associate of Andrew Jackson. He came to the Mississippi area after the Treaty of Dancing Rabbit Creek and the Treaty of Pontotoc to ensure orderly removal of the Choctaws and Chickasaws to Oklahoma Territory.
Coffee Co., Ala. (co. seat, Elba).
Coffee Co., Tenn. (co. seat, Manchester).

Coffeeville, Miss. (a co. seat of Yalobusha Co.).

COFFEY Co., Kan. (co. seat, Burlington). For Col. A. M. Coffey, a settler from Missouri, first known white man in Kansas. He served as a member of the Bogus Legislature in 1855.

COFFEYVILLE, Kan. (Montgomery Co.). For James A. Coffey, first settler.

COHANSEY RIVER N.J. For an Indian chief. It flows south and west into Delaware River.

COHASSET, Mass. (Norfolk Co.), town. From Algonquian, "fishing promontory."

COHOCTON From Iroquoian, "trees in the water." Also spelled *Conhocton.*
Cohocton, N.Y. (Steuben Co.), town.
Cohocton River N.Y. Flows SE to join Tioga R. to form Chemung R.

COHOES, N.Y. (Albany Co.). From Algonquian, "pine tree."

COKE Co., Tex. (co. seat, Robert Lee). For Richard Coke (1829-1897), jurist, Texas governor (1873-77) and U.S. senator (1877-95).

COLBERT Co., Ala. (co. seat, Tuscumbia). For two Cherokee brothers, George and Levi Colbert.

COLBY, Kan. (co. seat of Thomas Co.). For J. R. Colby, early settler and postmaster.

COLCHESTER For Colchester, Essex, England.
Colchester, Conn. (New London Co.), town.
Colchester Borough, Conn. (New London Co.).

COLCHESTER, Vt. (Chittenden Co.). For Viscount Tunbridge, Baron Enfield and Colchester, a political figure under George II.

COLD Descriptive of the water.
Cold River, Mass. Flows SE and E into Deerfield R.
Cold River, N.H. Flows into Bearcamp R.
Cold River, N.H. Flows SW into Connecticut R.
Cold Stream Pond, Me.

COLDBAR MOUNTAIN, Alaska. Punning name reported in 1898 for a "dead bear found near top."

COLDEN, N.Y. (Erie Co.), town. For Cadwalader Colden, a local political leader.

COLD SPRING For a spring or springs in the environs. Also known as *Cold Springs, Coldsprings,* and *Coldspring.*
Coldspring, Tex. (co. seat of San Jacinto Co.).
Cold Spring Harbor, N.Y. (Suffolk Co.).

COLDWATER Descriptive.
Coldwater, Kan. (co. seat of Comanche Co.). For *Coldwater*, Mich.
Coldwater, Mich. (co. seat of Branch Co.). For the river. Earlier, Lyons.
Coldwater, Miss. (Tate Co.). For the river.
Coldwater, Ohio (Mercer Co.).
Coldwater Creek, Okla.-Tex.
Coldwater River, Mich. Flows generally NW to the St. Joseph R.
Coldwater River, Miss. Flows to the Tallahatchie R.

COLE Co., Mo. (co. seat, Jefferson City). For Stephan Cole, an Indian fighter.

COLEEN RIVER, Alaska. Origin of name unknown. It flows southeast into Porcupine River.

COLEMAN, Col. Robert M. (1799-1837), Texas pioneer who was one of the signers of the Texas Declaration of Independence and a member of Sam Houston's staff.
Coleman Co., Tex. (co. seat, *Coleman*).
Coleman, Tex. (co. seat of *Coleman* Co.).

COLES Co., Ill. (co. seat, Charleston). For Edward Coles (1768-1868), humanitarian, confidant of President Madison, emissary to Moscow, and governor (1822-26).

COLFAX, Schuyler (1823-1885), New York (later Indiana) statesman, a collateral descendant of Gen. Philip Schuyler. He was a U.S. representative (1855-69; speaker, 1863-69) from Indiana and vice-president of the United States (1869-73) under Grant.
Colfax Co., Neb. (co. seat, Schuyler).
Colfax Co., N.Mex. (co. seat, Raton).
Colfax, La. (parish seat of Grant Co.).
Colfax, Wash. (co. seat of Whitman Co.).

COLLEGE For a college or university in or near the town.
College, Alaska. Site of the University of Alaska.
Collegedale, Tenn. (Hamilton Co.).
College Park, Ga. (Fulton and Clayton Cos.). Site of Georgia Military Academy. Earlier, Manchester.
College Park, Md. (Prince Georges Co.). Site of the University of Maryland.
College Place, Wash. (Walla Walla Co.).
College Station, Tex. (Brazos Co.). Site of Texas Agricultural and Mechanical College.
Collegeville, Pa. (Montgomery Co.).

COLLETON Co., S.C. (co. seat, Walterboro). For Landgrave James Colleton, colonial proprietor of the area that is now South Carolina. He served as governor of the colony (1686-90).

COLLEYVILLE, Tex. (Tarrant Co.). For Dr. Lilburn Colley, who served the community along with his son, Dr. Thaddeus C. Colley.

COLLIER Co., Fla. (co. seat, Everglades). For Barron Gift Collier (1873-1939), promoter active in the development of the southwest coast of Florida.

COLLIN Co., Tex. (co. seat, McKinney). For Collin McKinney, Republic of Texas patriot and legislator.

COLLINGSWORTH Co., Tex. (co. seat, Wellington). For James T. Collingsworth (1806-1838), Republic of Texas patriot and jurist.

COLLINGWOOD, Ont. (Simcoe Co.). For a township formerly in Simcoe County, which in turn was named for Admiral Collingwood Nelson, second-in-command at Trafalgar.

COLLINS,Miss. (co. seat of Covington Co.). For a Mr. Collins, a prominent Republican in a largely Democratic area. In return for securing a postmastership for a friend, he allowed the town to be named for him.

COLLINSVILLE, Ill. (Madison Co.). For the Collins family, founders, specifically William Collins.

COLLINSVILLE, Okla. (Tulsa Co.). For D. H. Collins, a prominent resident.

COLONIAL Descriptive. It suggests an admired style of architecture and also ancient ancestry.
Colonial Natl. Historical Park, Va. Established (1930) to include historic areas in Virginia, including Jamestown Island, Williamsburg, Yorktown, and surrounding areas.
Colonial Heights, Va. (Chesterfield Co.).

COLONIE, N.Y. (Albany Co.). *Colonie*, meaning "the little settlement outside the Fort or City," was part of the patronship of Kiliaen Van Rensselaer. It was so named because of its proximity to Ft. Orange, later Albany.

COLORADO From Spanish *colorado*, "reddish-brown," for the river; named by unknown Spanish explorers to describe the color of its waters. It was originally called *Rio de Tison*, "firebrand river," by the Spanish explorer Bernal Diaz del Castillo (c.1492-1581). In 1540 the area that was to be the territory and state was named for the river.
Colorado, State of. 38th state of the Union. Settled: 1858. Territory: 1861. Admitted: 1876. Cap: Denver. Motto: *Nil Sine Numine* (Nothing Without Providence). Nickname: Centennial State. Flower: Columbine. Bird: Lark Bunting. Tree: Colorado Blue Spruce. Animal: Bighorn Sheep. Song: "Where the Columbines Grow."
Colorado Co., Tex. (co. seat, Columbus).
Colorado Desert, Calif. See IMPERIAL VALLEY.
Colorado Natl. Monument, Colo.
Colorado River, Colo.-Utah-Ariz. Forms part of the Arizona-Nevada border and all of the Arizona-California border; flows into the Gulf of California, in Mexico.
Colorado River, Tex.
Colorado City, Tex. (co. seat of Mitchell Co.). For the river, on which it is located.
Colorado River Aqueduct, Calif.
Colorado Springs, Colo. (co. seat of El Paso Co.). Mineral springs.

COLLY Origin uncertain, but possibly meaning "coal-black," descriptive of water color.
Big Colly Bay, N.C.

Colly Creek, N.C. Rises in *Big Colly* Bay, flows SE into Black R.

COLQUITT, Walter Terry (1799-1855), attorney, jurist, and Methodist minister. He served as a state legislator, U.S. representative (1839-40; 1842-43), and U.S. senator (1843-48).
Colquitt Co., Ga. (co. seat, Moultrie).
Colquitt, Ga. (co. seat of Miller Co.).

COLTON, Calif. (San Bernardino Co.). For David D. Colton, financial director of the Central Pacific railroad.

COLUMBIA Feminine form of COLUMBUS, used as a poetical and patriotic name for America and as a symbol of liberty. The name dates from 1775 and seems to have occurred independently in different places, indicating that it was part of the revolutionary movement against British rule.
Columbia Co., Ark. (co. seat, Magnolia).
Columbia Co., Fla. (co. seat, Lake City).
Columbia Co., Ga. (co. seat, Appling).
Columbia Co., N.Y. (co. seat, Hudson).
Columbia Co., Oro. (co. seat, St. Helens). For the *Columbia* River.
Columbia Co., Pa. (co. seat, Bloomsburg).
Columbia Co., Wash. (co. seat, Dayton). For the river.
Columbia Co., Wis. (co. seat, Portago).
Columbia, Conn. (Tolland Co.), town.
Columbia, Ill. (Monroe Co.).
Columbia, Ky. (co. seat of Adair Co.).
Columbia, La. (parish seat of Caldwell Parish).
Columbia, Me. (Washington Co.), town.
Columbia, Md. (Howard Co.).
Columbia, Miss. (co. seat of Marion Co.). For *Columbia,* S.C. Earlier, Lott's Bluff.
Columbia, Mo. (co. seat of Boone Co.).
Columbia, N.C. (co. seat of Tyrell Co.).
Columbia, N.H. (Coos Co.), town.
Columbia, Pa. (Lancaster Co.). Earlier, Wright's Ferry.
Columbia, S.C. (co. seat of Richland Co.), state capital.
Columbia, Tenn. (co. seat of Maury Co.).
Columbia Glacier, Alaska.
Columbia, Mount, on Alta.-B.C. border.
Columbia, Mount, Colo.
Columbia Mountains, B.C.
Columbia River, B.C.-Wash.-Ore. Named (1792) by Robert Gray, who explored the river in his ship *Columbia.* It forms most of the Oregon-Washington boundary and flows into the Pacific Ocean.
Columbia City, Ind. (co. seat of Whitley Co.).
Columbia Falls, Me. (Washington Co.), town.
Columbia Falls, Mont. (Flathead Co.). For falls in the Flathead R., a tributary of the *Columbia* R.
Columbia Heights, Minn. (Anoka Co.). Promotional.
District of Columbia. Capital district (formed 1791) of the United States.
West Columbia, S.C. (Lexington Co.). For *Columbia,* S.C.
West Columbia, Tex. (Brazoria Co.). Comprises the former *Columbia* and *East Columbia.*

COLUMBIANA A variant of COLUMBUS or COLUMBIA The endings -a and *iana* were considered feminine and therefore appropriate for place names.
Columbiana Co., Ohio (co. seat, Lisbon).
Columbiana, Ala. (co. seat of Shelby Co.).
Columbiana, Ohio (*Columbiana* Co.).

COLUMBUS, Christopher. Part Latinized, part Anglicized name of Cristoforo Colombo (1451-1506), Italian navigator in the service of Spain. He was long credited with discovering the Americas, though evidence has been found of earlier visits by Vikings about 1000 A.D. and possibly even by Carthaginians about 550 B.C. Attempting to find a passage to India, Columbus landed on the island now called San Salvador in 1492, the date accepted until recently as the white man's first landing in the Western Hemisphere. The people he met were subsequently called Indians through the error of his believing he had landed on the coast of India. During the American Revolution *Columbus* was often feminized to *Columbia* as a symbolic name for the new nation and for liberty.
Columbus Co., N.C. (co. seat, Whiteville).
Columbus, Ga. (co. seat of Muscogee Co.). Or possibly for John Christopher Columbus Hill, the first white child born there.
Columbus, Ind. (co. seat of Bartholomew Co.).

Columbus, Kan. (co. seat of Cherokee Co.). For *Columbus*, Ohio.

Columbus, Miss. (co. seat of Lowndes Co.).

Columbus, Mont. (co. seat of Stillwater Co.).

Columbus, Neb. (co. seat of Platte Co.). For *Columbus*, Ohio.

Columbus, N.C. (co. seat of Polk Co.).

Columbus, Ohio (co. seat of Franklin Co.), state capital.

Columbus, Tex. (co. seat of Colorado Co.).

Columbus, Wis. (Columbia Co.).

Columbus Salt Marsh, Nev.

COLUSA The name, of unknown meaning, probably originated in the Patwin Indian territory and has many and various spellings. The town and county were both previously called Colusi.

Colusa Co., Calif. (co. seat, *Colusa*).

Colusa, Calif. (co. seat of *Colusa* Co.).

COLVILLE, Andrew, London governor of the Hudson's Bay Company, which held fur-

trading interests in the northwest area. Several place and feature names derive from Fort Colville, a trading post established in 1826.

Colville, Wash. (co. seat of Stevens Co.).

Colville Indian Reservation, Wash.

Colville Lake, Wash.

Colville Natl. Forest, Wash.

Colville River, Alaska. Flows NE into Harrison Bay.

Colville River, Wash. Flows generally NW to the Columbia R.

COMAL Co., Tex. (co. seat, New Braunfels). From Spanish, "basin," for an area drained by a stream.

COMANCHE For an Indian tribe of Shoshonean linguistic stock occupying northwestern Texas and most of central Oklahoma. The Texas Rangers were organized to protect against the tribe's raids. They were eventually settled in southwestern Oklahoma. The meaning of the name is unknown.

Though depicted here under divine guidance, Christopher Columbus died in poverty and neglect, still believing he had discovered the Asian coast. [*New York Public Library*]

Comanche Co., Kan. (co. seat, Coldwater).
Comanche Co., Okla. (co. seat, Lawton).
Comanche Co., Tex. (co. seat, *Comanche*).
Comanche, Tex. (co. seat of *Comanche* Co.).
Comanche Creek, Tex. Flows into the Pecos R.
Comanche Natl. Grassland, Colo.
Comanche Peak, Tex.

COMBAHEE RIVER, S.C. Probably of Muskogean origin, meaning uncertain, although *kom-* is the first element in words that express wish, desire, think, and wonder. Formed by a juncture of Salkehatchie and Little Salkehatchie Rivers, it flows southeast into Coosaw River.

COMBINED LOCKS, Wis. (Outagamie Co.). For the locks at the dam on the Fox River.

COMMACK, N.Y. (Suffolk Co.). From Algonquian *winne-comac*, "pleasant land, field, or house."

COMMERCE Promotional, in hope that the town would develop into a thriving business community.
Commerce, Calif. (Los Angeles Co.).
Commerce, Ga. (Jackson Co.). For *Commerce*, Tex. Earlier, Harmony Grove; the town was searching for a more "prosperous-sounding" name.
Commerce, Okla. (Ottawa Co.).
Commerce, Tex. (Hunt Co.).
Commerce City, Colo. (Adams Co.).

COMPTON, Griffith Dickenson (1820-1905), an early settler and one of the founders of the University of Southern California.
Compton, Calif. (Los Angeles Co.).
East Compton, Calif. (Los Angeles Co.).

COMPTON Co., Que. (co. seat, Cookshire). For Compton, Surrey, England.

COMSTOCK, Mich. (Kalamazoo Co.). For Horace H. Comstock, an early settler.

COMSTOCK PARK, Mich. (Kent Co.). For Charles C. Comstock, U.S., representative (1885-86).

CONANICUT ISLAND, R.I., in Narragansett Bay. From Narraganset, "very long place"; also possibly for Chief Canonicus (?-1647).

CONASAUGA RIVER, Ga.-Tenn. Of Cherokee origin, meaning uncertain, possibly "grass." It flows northwest and south into Oostanaula River.

CONCEPTION, Point, Calif., entrance to Santa Barbara Channel. Named by Sebastian Vizcaino, Spanish explorer, for the day of the Immaculate Conception.

CONCHAS. From Spanish, "shells," for shells of river mollusks.
Conchas Dam and Reservoir, N.Mex., on Canadian R.
Conchas River, N.Mex. Flows S and E into *Conchas* Reservoir.

CONCHO From Spanish, "shell."
Concho Co., Tex. (co. seat, Paint Rock). For the river.
Concho River, Tex.

CONCORD For agreement or harmony.
Concord, Calif. (Contra Costa Co.). For a town in New England.
Concord, Mass. (Middlesex Co.), town. Indicative of the peaceful circumstances under which the town was settled.
Concord, N.H. (co. seat of Merrimack Co.), state capital. For the peaceful settlement of a boundary dispute.
Concord, N.C. (co. seat of Cabarrus Co.). Factions agreed "in harmony" over selection of a place for the county seat.
Concord River, Mass.

CONCORDIA For Concordia, Roman goddess of peace and harmony, or a Latinized form of *concord*, "harmony."
Concordia, Kan. (co. seat of Cloud Co.). For the harmony and goodwill prevailing at the organizational meeting of the town.

CONDON, Ore. (co. seat of Gilliam Co.). For Harvey C. Condon (?-1831), a lawyer and member of a prominent family.

CONECUH Probably from Creek Indian *kono ika*, "ploecat's head."
Conecuh Co., Ala. (co. seat, Evergreen). For the river.
Conecuh Natl. Forest, Ala.
Conecuh River, Ala.-Fla.

CONEJOS From Spanish, "rabbits."
Conejos Co., Colo. (co. seat, *Conejos*). Earlier, Guadalupe.

Conejos, Colo. (co. seat of *Conejos* Co.).
Conejos River, Colo.

CONEMAUGH From Algonquian, "otter creek."
Conemaugh, Pa. (Cambria Co.).
Conemaugh River, Pa.

CONE MOUNTAIN, Colo. Descriptive of its shape.

CONESTOGA From Susquehanna *Kanastoge*, "at the place of the immersed pole," for the sub-group of the Susquehanna Indian tribe.
Conestoga, Pa. (Lancaster Co.).
Conestoga Creek, Pa.

CONESUS From Iroquoian, "place where berries are abundant." The name has many variations and some dispute as to the meaning.
Conesus, N.Y. (Livingston Co.), town.
Conesus Lake, N.Y.

CONEWANGO From Indian, "walking slowly" or "the place of the rapids."
Conewango, N.Y. (Cattaraugas Co.).
Conewango Creek, N.Y.-Pa. Flows S into Allegheny R.

CONFUSION RANGE, Utah. So named because of the frustrating terrain with many valleys.

CONGAMOND LAKES, Conn.-Mass. From Nipmuc, "long fishing place."

CONGAREE RIVER, S.C. From Siouan tribal name, meaning unknown. Formed by a juncture of Broad and Saluda Rivers, it flows southeast to join Wateree River to form Santee River.

CONGERS, N.Y. (Rockland Co.). For Abraham B. Conger, a local politican.

CONNEAUT Derivation is disputed: it may be a corruption of Indian *gunniate*, "it is a long time since he is (or they are) gone," or from Seneca, "many fish." A third explanation is "snowy place," and a fourth source may be Iroquoian, "mud," descriptive of the creek.
Conneaut, Ohio (Ashtabula Co.). For the creek.
Conneaut Creek, Pa.-Ohio.

CONNECTICUT From Mohican *Quonehtacut* or *Quinnehtukguet* or *Connittecock*, "the long river." The colony and state were named for the river.
Connecticut, State of. Fifth state of the Union. Settled: 1635. One of the original 13 colonies. Ratified Constitution: 1788. Motto: *Qui Transtulit Sustinet* (He Who Transplanted Continues to Sustain). Nicknames: Constitution State; Nutmeg State. Flower: Mountain Laurel. Bird: Robin. Tree: White Oak.
Connecticut River, N.H.-Vt. boundary-Mass.-Conn. Flows generally S to Long Island Sound.

CONNELLSVILLE, Pa. (Fayette Co.). For Zachariah Connell, an early settler.

CONNERSVILLE, Ind. (co. seat of Fayette Co.). For John Conner (1775-1826), Indian trader, enterpreneur, state senator, and member of the commission that selected Indianapolis as the state capital. He was a negotiator of Indian treaties and founder of the city that bears his name.

CONOCOCHEAGUE CREEK, Pa.-Md. From Algonquian, meaning uncertain, but first part has the connotation of "long" or "length." It flows west and south into the Potomac River.

CONODOGUINET CREEK, Pa. Of Algonquian origin, meaning unknown. It flows east northeast into Susquehanna River.

CONOLAWAYS CREEK, Pa. See TONOLOWAY.

CONOQUENESSING CREEK, Pa. From Algonquian, "for a long time straight." It flows into Beaver River.

CONRAD, Mont. (co. seat of Pondera Co.). For William G. Conrad (1848-1914), who owned or controlled some 200,000 acres of land in the area.

CONROE, Tex. (co. seat of Montgomery Co.). For Capt. Isaac Conroe, sawmill owner who was responsible for making *Conroe* a stop on the railroad.

CONSHOHOCKEN,Pa. (Montgomery Co.). From an Indian word, "pleasant valley."

CONSTANTINE,Cape, Alaska. Probably for the Russian American Company ship *Constantine.*

CONTINENTAL DIVIDE The "Backbone of the Nation," the high ridge of the Rocky Mountain Region and the watershed between rivers that flow into the Atlantic Ocean and Gulf of Mexico and those that flow into the Pacific. The highest point is Gannett Peak, in Wyoming, named for Henry Gannett of the U.S. Geological Survey, author of *Origin of Certain Place Names in the United States.*

CONTOOCOOK Of Indian origin, either from Pennacook, "place of the river near the pines," or from Abnaki, "nut-trees river."
Contoocook Lake, N.H.
Contoocook River, N.H. Rises in *Contoocook* L., flows NE into Merrimack R.

CONTRA COSTA Co., Calif. (co. seat, Martinez). From Spanish, "opposite coast," designating the coast of San Francisco Bay opposite San Francisco.

CONVENT, La. (parish seat of St. James Parish). For the Convent du Sacre Coeur (Convent of the Sacred Heart), founded in 1825 by French nuns.

CONVERSE Co., Wyo. (co. seat, Douglas). For Amasa R. Converse, prominent Cheyenne businessman who established the Converse Cattle Company.

CONWAY An early, politically prominent family. Henry W. Conway (1793-1827) was a general. His daughter Nellie was the mother of James Madison, fourth President of the United States. His son Moncure was a brother-in-law of George Washington. The family was also connected with that of John Sevier, governor of Tennessee. James S. Conway was the first governor (1836-40) of Arkansas. His brother Elias served two terms (1852-60) as governor.
Conway Co., Ark. (co. seat, Morrilton).
Conway, Ark. (co. seat of Faulkner Co.).
Conway, Lake, Ark.

CONWAY, Henry Seymour (1721-1795), member of Parliament and soldier. He opposed the Stamp Act and fought British policies harmful to the colonies.

Conway, N.H. (Carroll Co.), town.
Conway Lake, N.H.

CONWAY, S.C. (co. seat of Horry Co.). For Robert Conway (1753?-1823), landowner and a general in Marion's Brigade in the American Revolution, succeeding Peter Horry. Later he was a county official. Earlier names were Kingston, for George II, and Conwayborough.

COOK Co., Ga. (co. seat, Adel). For Philip Cook (1817-1894), Confederate general, legislator, and U.S. representative.

COOK Co., Ill. (co. seat, Chicago). For Daniel Pope Cook (1794-1827), attorney and U.S. representative.

COOK Co., Minn. (co. seat, Grand Marais). For Michael Cook (1828-1864), Minnesota soldier and statesman killed in the Civil War at the Battle of Nashville, or for John Cook, killed (1872) by Ojibway Indians.

COOKE Co., Tex. (co. seat, Gainesville). For William G. Cooke (1808-1847), officer in the Texas War for Independence.

COOKEVILLE, Tenn. (co. seat of Putnam Co.). For Maj. Richard F. Cooke, hero of the Mexican War and founder of the town.

COOK INLET, Alaska. For Capt. James Cook (1728-1779), who explored the region in 1778.

COOKSHIRE, Que. (co. seat of Compton Co.). For John Cook, one of the founders.

COOLIDGE, Ariz. (Pinal Co.). For the Coolidge Dam, which was named for Calvin Coolidge (1872-1933), thirtieth President of the United States.

COON. For the raccoon.
Coon Creek, Pa. Flows into Tionesia Creek.
Coon Rapids, Minn. (Anoka Co.). For rapids resulting from a dam built on a small nearby creek, which was named for the animal.

COOPER Co., Mo. (co. seat, Boonville). For an early settler.

COOPER, Tex. (co. seat of Delta Co.). For state senator L. W. Cooper of Houston, sponsor of a bill in the Texas legislature to organize Delta County.

COOPER RIVER, S.C. For the Earl, of Shaftesbury, Lord Anthony Ashley Cooper, a proprietor. See also ASHLEY. It flows south into the Atlantic Ocean.

COOPERSTOWN, N.Y. (co. seat of Otsego Co.). Settled and named by William Cooper, father of James Fenimore Cooper, the novelist.

COOPERSTOWN, N.Dak. (co. seat of Griggs Co.). For R. C. Cooper (1845-1938), farmer who owned or controlled 20,000 acres. He donated the site for the county seat.

COOS For an Indian tribe of Kusan linguistic stock, whose habitat is known to have been in what is now the Coos Bay area. First mentioned as *cook-koo-oose* in the Lewis and Clark Expedition journals, the name has been interpreted as either "lake" or "place of pines." For a place name the latter is more probable.
Coos Co., Ore. (co. seat, Coquille).
Coos Bay, Ore. (Coos Co.). For the bay itself. Earlier, Marshfield.
Coos Bay, Ore., on the Pacific Coast.
Coos River, South Fork, Ore.

COOS Co., N.H. (co. seat, Lancaster). From Pennacook, "pine tree" or "place where pines grow."

COOSA Probably from Choctaw *kusha*, "cane," as in a canebrake. The county was named for the river.
Coosa Co., Ala. (co. seat, Rockford).
Coosa River, Ala.-Ga. Flows generally SW to join the Tallapoosa R. to form the Alabama R.

COOSAWATTEE From Cherokee, meaning uncertain, possibly "Creek-old-place."
Coosawattee, Ga. (Murray Co.).
Coosawattee River, Ga. Flows SW into Oostanaula R.

COOSAWHATCHIE RIVER, S.C. From Muskogean, "Coosa stream." (See COOSA.) It flows southeast into Broad River.

COOSAW RIVER, S.C. From a tribal name, possibly Creek, meaning "reed."

COPANO BAY, Tex. From Spanish, but reason for naming is uncertain.

COPIAH Co., Miss. (co. seat, Hazelhurst). From an Indian word, said to mean "panther," but uncertain. It is believed locally to mean "clear water."

COPLAY, Pa. (Lehigh Co.). From the name of a local Indian, recorded as Kolapecki.

COPPER For the presence of the metal.
Copper Butte, Wash., in Kettle R. Range.
Copper River, Alaska. Flows S into Gulf of Alaska. Translated from Indian *atna*, "copper."

COPPERAS COVE, Tex. (Coryell Co.). For the high mineral content in the nearby creek. Supposedly these deposits cause the creek to glow at night. An earlier name was Cove.

COPTER PEAK, Alaska. Named in 1956 by Dr. Donald J. Orth, of the U.S. Geological Survey, for a difficult helicopter landing on the peak.

COQUILLE The French word means "shell," but the name almost certainly has an Indian origin not satisfactorily explained. The tribes Miluk and Mishikhwutmetunne both inhabited what is now the Coquille River area, and both were known by the French as Coquilles, although they belonged to different tribal stocks.
Coquille, Ore. (co. seat of Coos Co.).
Coquille River, Ore.

COQUITLAM For the Indian tribe. The name means "a small red salmon."
Coquitlam Lake, B.C.
Coquitlam Mountain, B.C.
Coquitlam River, B.C. Flows N through *Coquitlam* L. into Disappointment L.
Port Coquitlam, B.C.

CORAL GABLES, Fla. (Dade Co.). So named because the first house to be built had gables decorated with coral rock.

CORALVILLE, Iowa (Johnson Co.). So named (1866) after Louis Agassiz, naturalist and geologist, who lectured about the coral that is found in abundance along the banks of the Iowa River, which flows through the town.

CORAOPOLIS, Pa. (Allegheny Co.). For Cora Watson, daughter of Thomas F.

Watson, who was responsible for laying out an important addition to the town.

CORBIN, Ky. (Knox and Whitley Cos.). For James Corbin Floyd, a circuit-riding minister.

CORCORAN, Calif. (Kings Co.). For William Corcoran, civil engineer and division superintendent of the Santa Fe railroad.

CORDELE, Ga. (co. seat of Crisp Co.). For Cordelia, daughter of Col. Samuel H. Hawkins, president of the Savannah, Americus and Montgomery railroad.

CORDELL, Okla. (co. seat of Washita Co.). For Wayne W. Cordell, acting postmaster general (1892) when Cordell was named. Also called New Cordell.

CORDOVA, Ala. (Walker Co.). For the city in Spain, probably with little reason except the liking for a romantic name.

CORINTH For the city in Greece which has both classical and Biblical connotations. It is now the chief city and port of the northeastern Peloponnesus. In the United States, the name is probably taken from the New Testament, though possibly with some classical influence.
Corinth, Me. (Penobscot Co.), town.
Corinth, Miss. (co. seat of Alcorn Co.). Site of a Civil War battle.
Corinth, N.Y. (Saratoga Co.).
Corinth, Vt. (Orange Co.), town.

CORNING, Calif. (Tehama Co.). For John Corning (?-1878), a railroad official.

CORNING, Erastus (1794-1867), iron manufacturer, mayor of Albany, N.Y. (1834-37), New York State legislator, and U.S. representative (1857-59; 1861-63).
Corning, Ark. (a co. seat of Clay Co.). For Corning, N.Y.
Corning, Iowa (co. seat of Adams Co.).
Corning, N.Y. (Steuben Co.).

CORNPLANTER, Pa. (Warren Co.). Site of the Cornplanter Indian Reservation. Named Garganwahgah, Seneca Indian chief, "the cornplanter."

CORNWALL, Ont. (co. seat of Stormont, Dundas, and Glengary Cos.). For Prince George, Duke of Cornwall, eldest son of George III.

CORONA, Calif. (Riverside Co.). From Spanish, "crown," or from Latin, "wreath" or "circle." The city has a circular drive around it.

CORONADO, Calif. (San Diego Co.). For nearby islands, which were named for four brothers (known as the *Cuatro Coronados*), who were martyred and were canonized by the church.

CORONADO NATL. FOREST, Ariz.-N.Mex. For Francisco Vasquez de Coronado (1510-1554?), Spanish explorer.

CORPUS CHRISTI From Latin, "body of Christ."
Corpus Christi, Tex. (co. seat of Nueces Co.).
Corpus Christi Bay, Tex.
Corpus Christi, Lake, Tex.

CORRY, Pa. (Erie Co.). For Hirma Corry; named when he sold his farm to the Atlantic and Great Western railroad.

CORSICANA, Tex. (co. seat of Navarro Co.). For the island of Corsica; named by Jose Antonio Navarro in honor of the birthplace of his father. See also NAVARRO Co.

CORSON Co., S.Dak. (co. seat, McIntosh). For Dighton Corson (1827-1915), a native of Maine, later a lawyer and jurist in South Dakota.

CORSONS INLET, N.J., water passage into Ludlam Bay. For a family that lived nearby.

CORTE MADERA, Calif. (Marin Co.). From Spanish *corte de madera*, "a place where wood (or lumber) is cut." An abundance of wood and a sawmill supplied most of the lumber for early buildings.

CORTEZ, Hernando (1485-1547), Spanish leader of the forces that conquered Mexico and killed Montezuma, famed Aztec leader. Ironically, place names often connect the two leaders.
Cortez, Colo. (co. seat of Montezuma Co.).
Cortez Mountains, Nev.

CORTLAND For Pierre van Cortland, Jr. (1762-1848), New York statesman and businessman. He was a U.S. representative (1811-13).

Cortland Co., N.Y. (co. seat, *Cortland*).
Cortland, N.Y. (co. seat of *Cortland* Co.).
Cortland, Ohio (Trumbull Co.). Named by
the Erie Railroad Company for *Cortland*,
N.Y.

CORUNNA, Mich. (co. seat of Shiawassee
Co.). For Corunna (La Coruna), Spain;
named by Andrew Mack, who took a
shipload of sheep to Spain when he was
twenty-four.

CORVALLIS Ore. (co. seat of Benton Co.).
Coined by Joseph C. AVERY. pioneer and
landowner, from Latin *cor* and *vallis*, which
he intended to mean "heart of the valley."

CORYDON Named by William Henry
Harrison (seventh President of the United
States) for a name he found in a poem, "The
Pastoral Elegy." He was the principal
landowner and founder of Corydon, Ind.
Corydon, Ind. (co. seat of Harrison Co.).
Corydon, Iowa (co. seat of Wayne
Co.). For *Corydon*, Ind.

CORYELL Co., Tex. (co. seat, Gatesville).
For a Texas Ranger killed (1873) by Indians.

COSHOCTON From Delaware Indian
goschachgunk, "black bear town," or
possibly "crossing" or "ford."
Coshocton Co., Ohio (co. seat, *Coshocton*).
Coshocton, Ohio (co. seat of *Coshocton*
Co.). Earlier, Tuscarawas.

COSSATOT RIVER, Ark. From French
cassetete, "tomahawk." It flows south into
Little River.

COSTA MESA, Calif. (Orange Co.). From
Spanish *costa*, "coast," and *mesa*,
"tableland."

COSTILLA Co., Colo. (co. seat, San Luis).
For a river, which was named for a Spanish
family that settled in the area.

COSUMNES RIVER, Calif. For an Indian
village, in turn probably for a tribe; possibly
from Miwok *kosum*, "salmon," and *-umne*,
"tribe." It flows southwest into Mokelumne
River.

COTEAU LANDING, Que. (co. seat of
Soulanges Co.). From French, "hillock." So
named because there used to be a landing

place on the lakeshore at the foot of a
hillock.

COTTAGE GROVE, Minn. (Washington
Co.). Promotional and descriptive.

COTTAGE GROVE, Ore. (Lake Co.). So
named because the first postmaster lived in
a house in an oak grove.

COTTLE Co., Tex. (co. seat, Paducah). For
George Washington Cottle (1798-1836),
killed at the Alamo.

COTTON Co., Okla. (co. seat, Walters).
For cotton grown in the area.

COTTONWOOD For the trees.
Cottonwood Co., Minn. (co. seat, Windom).
  For the river; translated from Dakota or
  Siouan *waraju*, "cottonwood."
Cottonwood, Ariz. (Yavapai Co.).
Cottonwood, Utah (Salt Lake Co.).
Cottonwood Butte, Idaho.
Cottonwood Creek, Tex. Flows E and SE into
  Toyah L.
Cottonwood Creek, Utah.
Cottonwood River, Kan. Flows generally E to
  the Neosha R.
Cottonwood River, Minn.
Cottonwood Falls, Kan. (co. seat of Chase
  Co.). For the falls on *Cottonwood* River.

COUDERSPORT, Pa. (co. seat of Potter
Co.). For Jean Samuel Couderc, official in
an Amsterdam banking company, Couderc,
Brants, and Changuion, which invested in
land in the area and donated part of the
townsite to Potter County.

COTULLA, Tex. (co. seat of La Salle Co.).
For Joseph Cotulla, a landowner who was a
native of Poland. He contributed 120 acres
to the development of the townsite with the
hope of the International-Great Northern
railroad building a depot on this land.

COULEE DAM Origin of the name is not
definitely known, although *Coulee* is
believed to have a connotation of "stream
course," or place where a stream runs
during wet weather.
Coulee Dam, Wash. (Douglas Co.).
Coulee Dam Natl. Recreation Area, Wash.
Grand Coulee Dam, Wash.

COUNCIL, Idaho (co. seat of Adams Co.).
For a meeting place between the Shahaptin
and Shoshoni Indians.

COUNCIL BLUFFS, Iowa (co. seat of Pottawattamie Co.). For the meeting held there (1804) between leaders of the Lewis and Clark Expedition and the Otoe Indians. An earlier name was Kanesville.

COUNCIL GROVE, Kan. (co. seat of Morris Co.). For the site on which a treaty was signed with the Osage tribe to assure safe travel to the West.

COUNTER IMAGE PEAK, Wyo. So named because its reflection can be seen in the adjacent lake.

COUNTRY CLUB HILLS, Ill. (Cook Co.). Promotional.

COUNTRYSIDE, Ill. (Cook Co.). Promotional and descriptive of the rural, or "countryside," air.

COURTLAND, Va. (co. seat of Southampton Co.). Probably so named as a place where "court" was held, a function of a county seat.

COURT OREILLES, Lake, Wis. From French, "short ears," for a tribe of Ottawa Indians.

COUSHATTA, La. (parish seat of Red River Parish). From Choctaw, "white reed brake"; the Coushatta, or *Koasati*, a small tribe, acquired the name because they lived near the brake.

COVEDALE, Ohio (Hamilton Co.). Descriptive and promotional.

COVE MOUNTAIN, Pa.-Md. For a nearby cove.

COVENTRY For Coventry, Warwickshire, England.
Coventry, Conn. (Tolland Co.), town.
Coventry, R.I. (Kent Co.), town.
South Coventry, Conn. (Tolland Co.).

COVINA The name is said to mean "place of vines"; probably descriptive.
Covina, Calif. (Los Angeles Co.).
West Covina, Calif. (Los Angeles Co.).

COVINGTON, Ind. (co. seat of Fountain Co.). For Isaac Covington, a veteran of the War of 1812 and brother-in-law of Isaac Coleman, the founder.

COVINGTON, Leonard Wales (1768-1813), general in the War of 1812. He died of wounds received in battle.
Covington Co., Ala. (co. seat, Andalusia Co.).
Covington Co., Miss (co. seat, Collins).
Covington, Ga. (co. seat of Newton Co.).
Covington, Ky. (a co. seat of Kenton Co.).
Covington, La. (parish seat of St. Tammany Parish).
Covington, Ohio (Miami Co.).
Covington, Tenn. (co. seat of Tipton Co.).
Covington, Va. (co. seat of Alleghany Co.).
May have been named for Prince Edward Covington by his relative James Merry, founder.

COVODE, Pa. (Indiana Co.). For John Covode (1808-1871), U.S. representative from Pennsylvania (1855-63; 1867-70).

COWAN, Mount, Mont. For a local settler.

COWANSVILLE, Que. (Missisquoi Co.). For Peter Cowan, first postmaster and storekeeper.

COW CREEK, Wash. Probably for an incident involving a cow, but not certain. It flows south into Palouse River.

COWETA Co., Ga. (co. seat, Newnan). So named in honor of William McIntosh, Coweta Indian of the Creek nation. *Coweta* may mean "falls."

COWHORN MOUNTAIN, Ore. For its resemblance to a cow's horn.

COWIKEE CREEK, Ala. Probably from Hitchiti *oki*, "water," and *awaiki*, "carrying," thus "a place for water-carrying." The resulting form *kawaiki* was folk-etymologized into the present form. It is a tributary of the Chattahoochee River.

COWLEY Co., Kan. (co. seat, Winfield). For a Civil War officer who died on duty in 1864.

COWLITZ From an Indian tribal name of Salishan linguistic stock; meaning uncertain, but said to be "power" or "catching the spirit."
Cowlitz Co., Wash. (co. seat, Kelso).
Cowlitz River, Wash. Flows W and S into Columbia R.

COWPASTURE RIVER, Va. The Indian name was Wallawhatoola, meaning uncertain; settlers renamed it for the bordering grazing areas, cow pastures. It flows southwest to join the Jackson River to form the James River.

COXCOMB MOUNTAIN, Wyo. Metaphorically descriptive, a cock's comb.

COYOTE For the animal.
Coyote Lake, Calif. Reservoir formed by a dam on Coyote Creek.
Coyote Creek, Calif. Flows generally SE.
Coyote Wash, N.Mex. Flows N into Chaco R.

COZAD, Neb. (Dawson Co.). For John J. Cozad, founder.

CRAB ORCHARD LAKE, Ill. For the small creek on which it is formed, in turn for the crab apple tree.

CRAFTON, Pa. (Allegheny Co.). For James S. Craft, a prominent Pittsburgh lawyer, on whose land the town was built by his son, Charles C. Craft.

CRAG MOUNTAIN, Mass. Descriptive.

CRAIG, Colo. (co. seat of Moffat Co.). For Rev. Bayard Craig, minister of the First Christian Church.

CRAIG Co., Okla. (co. seat, Vinita). For Granville Craig, a prominent Cherokee citizen.

CRAIG Co., Va. (co. seat, New Castle). For Robert Craig (1792-1852), Virginia statesman and U.S. representative (1829-33; 1835-41.

CRAIGHEAD Co., Ark. (co. seats, Jonesboro and Lake City). For Thomas B. Craigshead, Mississippi legislator.

CRAIG LAKE, Mich. Probably for George Craig, early settler.

CRANBERRY For cranberry bushes.
Cranberry Lake, N.Y.
Cranberry River, W.Va. Flows generally W into Gauley R.

CRANBROOK, B.C. For Cranbrook Farm owned by Col. James Bufer, an early settler who named the farm for Cranbrook, Kent, England.

CRANDON, Wis. (co. seat of Forest Co.). For Frank P. Crandon, a railroad official.

CRANE, William Carey, clergyman and educator.
Crane Co., Tex. (co. seat, Crane).
Crane, Tex. (co. seat of Crane Co.).

CRANE MOUNTAIN, N.Y. For the legendary Ichabod Crane, of Sleepy Hollow fame.

CRANE PRAIRIE RESERVOIR, Ore. For the cranes that feed on fish in the streams on the marshy prairie.

CRANFORD, N.J. (Union Co.). For the Crane family, descendants of Stephen Crane, one of the first Elizabethtown Associates. Earlier names were Craneville and Cranesford.

CRANSTON, R.I. (Providence Co.). For Samuel Cranston, (1659-1727), governor of Rhode Island from 1698 until his death. While in office he fought off British attempts to stifle smuggling and piracy in Rhode Island's waters. He also helped his state win boundary disputes with Massachusetts and Connecticut.

CRATER For the crater of an extinct volcano.
Crater Lake, Ore. The crater is found on Mt. Mazarna, of the Cascade Range, which contains the lake.
Crater Mountain, Wyo. The crater is found at the top.
Crater Lake Natl. Park, Ore.

CRAVEN Co., N.C. (co. seat, New Bern). Probably for William Craven (1668-1711), 2nd Earl of Craven, or possibly for the 1st Earl (1606-1697), a proprietor of Carolina, or for the 3rd Earl.

CRAWFORD Co., Kan. (co. seat, Girard). For Samuel J. Crawford (1835-1913), Kansas legislator, general in both the Civil War and the Indian wars, and governor of Kansas (1865-68).

CRAWFORD, William (1732-1782), Virginia Indian fighter active in many campaigns in what became the Northwest Territory. He was killed by Indians near the site of the village of Crawfordsville, Ohio.
Crawford Co., Mich. (co. seat, Grayling).

Crawford Co., Ohio (co. seat, Bucyrus).
Crawford Co., Pa. (co. seat, Meadville).

CRAWFORD, William Harris (1772-1834), Virginia statesman associated with Georgia. He was U.S. senator from Georgia (1807-13; president pro tempore, 1812), minister to France (1813-15), secretary of war (1815-16) under Madison, secretary of the treasury under Madison and Monroe (1816-25), and unsuccessful Democratic candidate for President (1824).

Crawford Co., Ark. (co. seat, Van Buren).
Crawford Co., Ga. (co. seat, Knoxville).
Crawford Co., Ill. (co. seat, Robinson).
Crawford Co., Ind. (co. seat, English).
Crawford Co., Iowa (co. seat, Denison).
Crawford Co., Mo. (co. seat, Steelville).
Crawford Co., Wis. (co. seat, Prairie du Chien).
Crawford, Lake, Me.
Crawfordsville, Ind. (co. seat of Montgomery Co.).
Crawfordville, Ga. (co. seat of Taliaferro Co.).

CRAWFORDVILLE, Fla. (co. seat of Wakulla Co.). For John L. Crawford (1816-1902), doctor, planter, and member of the Florida legislature. He was Florida secretary of state for twenty four years.

CRAZY Translation from Indian name, for a unique or "weird" appearance.
Crazy Mountains, Alaska. Reason for name not certain.
Crazy Mountains, Mont.
Crazy Peak, Mont.

CREDIT So named because in former times it was a center for fur trade, where the traders met the Indians and gave them, on credit, the supplies they needed for the winter's hunt.
Credit River, Ont. (Peel Co.).
Port Credit, Ont. (Peel Co.).

CREEDE, Colo. (co. seat of Mineral Co.). For Nicholas C. Creede (1842-1897), miner and prospector.

CREEK Co., Okla. (co. seat, Sapulpa). For the Creek Indians, a loose confederation of southeastern tribes of Muskhogean linguistic stock, dominated by the Muskogees. The name Creek was applied to them by settlers in what is now Tennessee. They were probably the Yuchi, who lived on Ocheese Creek (now the Ocmulgee River). They were resettled (1836-41) in what is now Oklahoma.

CRENSHAW Co., Ala. (co. seat, Luverne). For Anderson Crenshaw (1776-?), lawyer, statesman, and jurist.

CRESCENT Originally of Latin derivation, meaning "half moon."
Crescent Pond, Me. Descriptive of shape.
Crescent Lake, Fla.
Crescent Lake, Neb.
Crescent Lake, Wash.
Crescent City, Calif. (co. seat of Del Norte Co.) For the crescent-shaped bay nearby.
Crescent North, Calif. (Del Norte Co.).

CRESCO, Iowa (Howard Co.). From Latin cresco, "I grow"; promotional.

CRESSKILL, N.J. (Bergen Co.). Probably from Dutch kers-kil, "cherry-stream," though kers can also mean "watercress."

CRESSON, Pa. (Cambria Co.). For Elliott Cresson, a Philadelphia merchant.

CRESSONA, Pa. (Schuylkill Co.). For John Chapman Cresson, founder. He was also president of the Mine Hill and Schuylkill Haven railroad.

CREST HILL, Ill. (Cook Co.). Promotional.

CRESTLINE Descriptive of the location.
Crestline, Calif. (San Bernardino Co.).
Crestline, Ohio (Crawford Co.). On the crest line of the middle elevation of the state.

CRESTON, Iowa (co. seat of Union Co.). Chosen by officials of the Burlington railroad as "The Summit," the highest point between the Missouri and Mississippi rivers, for a division point and for housing the second largest roundhouse in the world.

CRESTVIEW, Fla. (co. seat of Okaloosa Co.). Descriptive.

CRESTWOOD Descriptive and promotional.
Crestwood, Ill. (Cook Co.).
Crestwood, Mo. (St. Louis Co.).

CRETE For the island of Crete, in the Mediterranean.

Crete, Ill. (Will Co.).
Crete, Neb. (Saline Co.). For *Crete*, Ill.

CREVE COEUR From French, "break heart" or "heartbreak," probably for Fort Creve Coeur, established (1680) near what is now the city in Illinois by the French explorer La Salle.
Creve Coeur, Ill. (Tazewell Co.).
Creve Coeur, Mo. (St. Louis Co.). For *Creve Coeur*, Ill.

CRIPPLE CREEK, Colo. (co. seat of Teller Co.). For a stream, which was named by cowhands who found the banks were so steep that the cows often broke their legs going down after water.

CRISFIELD, Md. (Somerset Co.). For John Woodland Crisfield (1808-1897), a lawyer and U.S. representative (1847-49; 1861-63) from Maryland, responsible for bringing the railroad to the town.

CRISP Co., Ga. (co. seat, Cordele). For Charles Frederick Crisp (1845-1896), Confederate army officer, jurist, and U.S. representative.

CRITTENDEN Co., Ark. (co. seat, Marion). For Robert Crittenden, a veteran of the War of 1812 and Arkansas Territory official.

CRITTENDEN Co., Ky. (co. seat, Marion). For John Jordan Crittenden (1787-1863), officer in the War of 1812, legislator, U.S. senator (1817-19; 1842-48; 1855-61), U.S. representative (1861-63), attorney general under Harrison and Fillmore, and governor of Kentucky (1848-50).

CROATAN Variant of CROATOAN.
Croatan Natl. Forest, N.C.
Croatan Sound, N.C.

CROATOAN ISLAND, N.C. Named in 1585 by an English explorer, probably of Algonquian origin; meaning uncertain, but possibly "talk town" for a chief's residence. See also CROATAN.

CROCKER MOUNTAIN, Me. For the Crocker family.

CROCKETT, David ("Davy") (1786-1836), frontiersman. He was a scout under Andrew Jackson in the Creek War of 1813-14, justice of the peace, colonel of militia,

Tennessee legislator, and U.S. representative (1827-31; 1833-35). Having joined the fight for Texan independence, he was killed at the Alamo. Crockett was famous as a brave soldier, able scout, and expert rifleman.
Crockett Co., Tenn. (co. seat, Alamo).
Crockett Co., Tex. (co. seat, Ozona).
Crockett, Tex. (co. seat of Houston Co.).
Davy Crockett Natl. Forest, Tex.

CROMWELL, Conn. (Middlesex Co.), town. For Oliver Cromwell (1599-1658), Puritan general and self-styled Lord Protector of England. He organized the Model Army against Charles I and declared the Protectorate in 1653. His rule was marked by high ideals but mixed practical results. Toleration, highly valued by Cromwell, was unevenly applied. His son Richard succeeded him in 1658, but without the elder Cromwell the Protectorate was not viable and the country reverted to a commonwealth the following year.

CROOK, George (1829-1890), official and general in the Oregon Territory.
Crook Co., Ore. (co. seat, Prineville).
Crook Co., Wyo. (co. seat, Sundance).
Crooks Tower (peak), S.Dak.

CROOKED Descriptive of shape.
Crooked Creek, Ore. Flows generally NE into Owyhee R.
Crooked Creek, Pa. Flows generally E into Tioga R.
Crooked Creek, Pa. Flows E into Indiana County.
Crooked Lake, Fla.
Crooked River, Me. Flows generally SE into Sebago L.
Crooked River, Ore. Flows generally NW into Deschutes R.

CROOKSTON, Minn. (co. seat of Polk Co.). For William Crooks (1832-1907), a Union officer in the Civil War. He was a prominent official of the St. Paul and Pacific railroad.

CROOKSVILLE, Ohio (Perry Co.). For Joseph E. Crooks, store owner and first postmaster.

CROSBY, N.Dak. (co. seat of Divide Co.). For S. A. Crosby, a founder. He built up a merchandising business, established a post office, and promoted development of the area.

CROSBY, Stephen F. (1800-1869), chief clerk of the land office and land commissioner (1853-55).
Crosby Co., Tex. (co. seat, *Crosbyton*).
Crosbyton, Tex. (co. seat of *Crosby* Co.). For the county.

CROSS For a crossing of pathways.
Cross Lake, La.
Cross Lake, Me. So named because it was a crossing place of two other lakes, Mud and Square.
Cross Lake, N.Y.
Cross City, Fla. (co. seat of Dixie Co.). For a crossing of two public roads.
Crossville, Tenn. (co. seat of Cumberland Co.). For a crossing of roads. Earlier, Scotts Cross Roads.

CROSS Co., Ark. (co. seat, Wynne). For Edward Cross (1798-1887), jurist and U.S. representative.

CROSSETT, Ark. (Ashley Co.). For E. S. Crossett, of the Crossett Lumber Company.

CROSS ISLAND, Me. Origin of name uncertain. It may have been named because a cross was erected there by an early French explorer; or it may be a translation of an Indian term for "crossing" or "portage," a passage over which Indians and later white settlers carried their canoes.

CROSS SOUND, Alaska, water passage extending from Icy Strait to Gulf of Alaska. Named by Capt. James Cook on May 3, 1778, noted on his calendar as Holy Cross Day.

CROSSWICK CREEK, N.J. A folk-etymologized form of an Algonquian word, meaning uncertain, but with a root, "separation." It flows north and west into Delaware River.

CROTCHED MOUNTAIN, N.H. For its shape.

CROTCH ISLAND, Me. So named because it is between islands.

CROTON-ON-HUDSON, N.Y. (Westchester Co.). *Croton*, from the name of an early Indian chief, recorded as Cnoten. *On-Hudson*, because it borders on the Hudson River.

CROW For the bird; translated from Ojibway.
Crow Lake, Minn.
Crow River, Minn. Formed by N. Fork and S. Fork, flows NE into the Mississippi R.

CROW For the Indian tribe, of Siouan linguistic stock.
Crow Buttes, S.Dak. A battle between the Sioux and Crow Indians took place in the area.
Crow Creek, Wyo.-Colo. Flows E then S.
Crow's Nest Butte, S.Dak. The Crow tribe escaped from this peak during a battle with the Sioux.

CROWELL, Tex. (co. seat of Foard Co.). For George T. Crowell, landowner.

CROWLEY Co., Colo. (co. seat, Ordway). For John H. Crowley (1849-?), horticulturist. He was state senator from Otero County when Crowley County was formed.

CROWLEY, Lake, Calif. For John J. Crowley, a priest.

CROWLEY, La. (parish seat of Acadia Parish). For Patrick C. Crowley (1850-1909), roadmaster for the Louisiana and Western railroad at the time of construction through this area. A site near the present town was known as Crowley's Switch.

CROWLEY, Tex. (Tarrant Co.). For S. H. Crowley, master of transportation for the Gulf, Colorado and Santa Fe railroad.

CROWN POINT, Ind. (co. seat of Lake Co.). So named because it is the highest point in the county, and also because it is on the watershed of waters draining north to the Great Lakes and the St. Lawrence and south to the Ohio and Mississippi rivers. An earlier name was Liverpool.

CROW WING A translation of Ojibway *kagiwigwan* or *gagagiwigwuni*, "raven-feather river." The exact meaning has been obscured by confusion of "crow" and "raven," as well as "feather" and "wing."
Crow Wing Co., Minn. (co. seat, Brainerd).
Crow Wing River, Minn.

CROYDON PEAK, N.H. For Croydon, Surrey, England.

CRUM HILL, Mass. For a local dweller.

CRYSTAL Descriptive, usually of water, and often promotional.
Crystal, Minn. (Hennepin Co.).
Crystal Lake, Mich.
Crystal Lake, N.H.
Crystal Lake, Vt.
Crystal River, Colo. Flows into Roaring Fork R.
Crystal City, Mo. (Jefferson Co.).
Crystal City, Tex. (co. seat of Zavala Co.).
Crystal Falls, Mich. (co. seat of Iron Co.). For the falls on the Paint R.
Crystal Lake, Ill. (McHenry Co.).
Crystal Lakes, Ohio (Clark Co.).
Crystal Springs, Miss. (Copiah Co.). For nearby springs.

CRYSTAL PEAK, Wyo. For crystals found in the area.

CUCAMONGA, Calif. (San Bernardino Co.). From Shoshonean, "sandy place."

CUCHARAS RIVER, Colo. From Spanish, "spoons." It flows northeast into Huerfano River.

CUDAHY, Patrick, merchant and meat-packing industrialist.
Cudahy, Calif. (Los Angeles Co.). For *Cudahy*, Wis.
Cudahy, Wis. (Milwaukee Co.).

CUDDEBACK LAKE, Calif. For John Cuddeback, miner.

CUDJO KEY, Fla. From a West African personal day name, *Cudjo*, "born on Monday."

CUERO, Tex. (co. seat of De Witt Co.). From Spanish, (animal) "hide."

CUIVRE RIVER, Mo. From French, "copper," possibly for color of river, although the source of the name is uncertain. Formed by North Fork and West Fork, it flows into the Mississippi River.

CULBERSON Co., Tex. (co. seat, Van Horn). For David Browning Culberson (1830-1900), Texas soldier and statesman. He served as a Confederate officer in the Civil War and was a U.S. representative (1875-97).

CULEBRA PEAK, Colo. From Spanish, "snake."

CULLMAN, Johann Gottfried (1823-1895), Bavarian revolutionary who fought against Bismarck in the Revolution of 1840. He established a colony in the present county and purchased thousands of acres of land from the Louisville and Nashville railroad. Under his energetic and wise leadership, the colony, settled (1874) by German immigrants, thrived as a successful business community. The city was founded first.
Cullman Co., Ala. (co. seat, *Cullman*).
Cullman, Ala. (co. seat of *Cullman* Co.).

CULPEPER, Sir Thomas (1635-1689), colonial governor. He was commissioned (1675) to be governor of Virginia for life. Beginning his duties in 1680, he pardoned all surviving participants in Bacon's Rebellion. He returned to England during a time of much turmoil and unrest and was removed from his position in 1683. His name is also spelled *Culpepper* or *Colepeper*.
Culpeper Co., Va. (co. seat, *Culpeper*).
Culpeper, Va. (co. seat of *Culpeper* Co.).

CULVER CITY, Calif. (Los Angeles Co.). For Harry H. Culver, real-estate developer.

CULVER LAKE, N.J. For a local community member.

CUMBERLAND, William Augustus, Duke of (1721-1765), second son of George II. He defeated the Scottish forces under Charles Stuart, the "Young Pretender" (1720-1788), at Culloden (1746). His title is taken from the county of Cumberland, England, which may be the source of some of these names.
Cumberland Co., Ill. (co. seat, Toledo). For the *Cumberland* Road, which was to pass through the area.
Cumberland Co., Ky. (co. seat, Burkesville).
Cumberland Co., Me. (co. seat, Portland).
Cumberland Co., N.J. (co. seat, Bridgeton).
Cumberland Co., N.C. (co. seat, Fayetteville).
Cumberland Co., Pa. (co. seat, Carlisle).
Cumberland Co., Tenn. (co. seat, Crossville).
Cumberland Co., Va. (co. seat, *Cumberland*).
Cumberland, Ky. (Harlan Co.).
Cumberland, Me. (*Cumberland* Co.), town.
Cumberland, Md. (co. seat of Allegany Co.).

By 1872 the Cumberland Gap had ceased to be the gateway to the West. [*New York Public Library*]

Cumberland, R.I. (Providence Co.). Earlier, Attleboro Gore.

Cumberland, Va. (co. seat of *Cumberland Co.*).

Cumberland Gap, Ky.-Tenn.

Cumberland Island, Ga.

Cumberland Lake, Ky.

Cumberland Mountains, Ky.-Tenn.-Va.-Ala. Also called *Cumberland* Plateau.

Cumberland River, Ky.-Tenn. Flows into the Ohio R.

Cumberland Road, Md.-Pa.-Ohio. From Cumberland, Md. to Vandalia, Ohio, crossing the Appalachian Mtns. at first to the head of navigation on the Monongahela R. and later extended. Also called the National Turnpike, it is now U.S. Route 40.

Cumberland Gap Natl. Historical Park, Ky.-Va.-Tenn.

New Cumberland, Pa. (*Cumberland* Co.).

New Cumberland, W.Va. (co. seat of Hancock Co.).

CUMING Co., Neb. (co. seat, West Point).

For Thomas B. Cuming, a Nebraska Territory official.

CUMMING, Ga. (co. seat of Forsyth Co.). For Col. William C. Cumming (1788-1863), attorney, a hero in the War of 1812, and a controversial figure in the argument between those who believed in states' rights and those who believed in a strong central Federal government.

CUMMINS PEAK, Ore. For F. L. Cummins, early settler.

CUPERTINO, Calif. (Santa Clara Co.). For San Giuseppe (St. Joseph) de Cupertino, patron saint of students and flight.

CUPSUPTIC RIVER, Me. From Abnaki, "a closed stream." It flows generally south into Mooselookmeguntic Lake.

CURRENT RIVER, Mo.-Ark. Descriptive. Flows southeast into Black River.

CURRITUCK From an obscure Indian name, said to mean "wild geese."

Currituck Co., N.C. (co. seat, *Currituck*).

Currituck, N.C. (co. seat of *Currituck* Co.).
Currituck Sound, N.C.

CURRY Co., N.Mex. (co. seat, Clovis). For
George Curry (1863-1947), Spanish-
American War veteran, county official,
governor in the Philippines, and U.S.
representative.

CURRY Co., Ore. (co. seat, Gold Beach).
For George Law Curry (1820-1878), a
publisher and governor of Oregon Territory.

CUSHING, Okla. (Payne Co.). For Marshall
Cushing, an assistant to John Wanamaker,
postmaster general (1889-93) under
Benjamin Harrison.

CUSHMAN, Lake Reservoir, Wash., on
Skokomish River. For Orrington Cushman,
frontiersman and guide.

CUSP PEAK, Wyo. Descriptive of shape.

CUSSETA, Ga. (co. seat of Chattahoochee
Co.). A variant of *Kashita*, name of a Creek
tribe. The meaning is unknown, although the
Creeks connected the name with *hasihta*,
"born of the sun."

CUSSEWAGO CREEK, Pa. From
Iroquoian, possibly·"in-basswood-country"
or "the snake with a big belly." It flows
south into French Creek.

CUSTER, George Armstrong (1839-1876),
Ohio soldier and Indian fighter, a controversial figure who has been variously
labeled as a "valiant hero" and a "cruel and
insubordinate fool." He was active during
the Civil War and, after 1867, saw duty in
the West. Cavalry forces under his im-
mediate command were annihilated in the
Battle of the Little Big Horn (June 25, 1876)
by the Sioux and Cheyenne under Sitting Bull
and Crazy Horse. The battle is also known
as "Custer's Last Stand."
Custer Co., Colo. (co. seat, Westcliffe).
Custer Co., Idaho (co. seat, Challis).
Custer Co., Mont. (co. seat, Miles City).
Custer Co., Neb. (co. seat, Broken Bow).
Custer Co., Okla. (co. seat, Arapaho).
Custer Co., S.Dak. (co. seat, *Custer*).
Custer, S.Dak. (co. seat, *Custer* Co.).
Custer Mountain, S.Dak.
Custer Natl. Forest, Mont.-S.Dak.
Custer Peak, S.Dak.
Custer Battlefield Natl. Monument, Mont.

Little Big Horn was not George Armstrong
Custer's only defeat; he was last in his class at
West Point. [*National Archives*]

CUT BANK For the gorge made by Cut
Bank Creek. The creek was named first.
Cut Bank, Mont. (co. seat of Glacier Co.).
Cut Bank Creek, Mont.
Cut Bank Creek, N.Dak. Flows SE and NNE
    into Souris R.

CUTHBERT, Ga. (co. seat of Randolph
Co.). For John A. Cuthbert (1788-1881),
attorney, state legislator, officer during the
War of 1812, Indian commissioner, U.S.
representative (1819-21), and jurist.

CUTLER, Calif. (Tulare Co.). For John
Cutler, pioneer who later became a judge in
the area.

CUTLERVILLE, Mich. (Kent Co.). For John
Cutler, head of the family.

CUTTYHUNK ISLAND, Mass. From a
distorted spelling of an Indian name,
meaning uncertain; possibly from Wampanoag, "a thing that lies out in the great
water," as an island, or "broken land."

CUYAHOGA From an Indian word, but the
exact origin is uncertain. Some attribute it to
Cayahaga, "crooked," others to
Cuyahoganuk, "lake river," or to the
Iroquoian word for "river," usually applied
to an important river.

Cuyahoga Co., Ohio (co. seat, Cleveland).
Cuyahoga River, Ohio.
Cuyahoga Falls, Ohio (Summit Co.). For the
  river.

CUYAMA RIVER, Calif. From Chumash
Indian, "clams." It flows generally south
into Santa Maria River.

CUYLER, N.Y. (Cortland Co.), town. For
John M. Cuyler, soldier in the Indian wars
and the Mexican War.

C. W. McCONAUGHY, Lake, Neb. Named
for C. W. McConaughy, a pioneer of central
Nebraska irrigation. He organized and
directed the Tri-County Power and Irrigation
District, a company that constructed the
dam north of Ogallala, Neb.

CYNTHIANA, Ky. (co. seat of Harrison
Co.). For Cynthia and Anna, daughters of
Robert Harris, founder.

CYPRESS For cypress trees.
Cypress, Calif. (Orange Co.).
Cypress Gardens, Fla. (Polk Co.).

DADE, Francis Langhorne (1793-1835), officer and Indian fighter killed in the Seminole War, sometimes called the Florida Indian War (1835-42), in which the Seminoles were led by Osceola.
Dade Co., Fla. (co. seat, Miami).
Dade Co., Ga. (co. seat, Trenton).
Dade Co., Mo. (co. seat, Greenfield).
Dade City, Fla. (co. seat of Pasco Co.).
Dadeville, Ala. (co. seat of Tallapoosa Co.).

DAGGETT Co., Utah (co. seat, Manila). For a surveyor, Ellsworth Daggett.

DAHLONEGA, Ga. (co. seat of Lumpkin Co.). From Cherokee *talonega*, "place of yellow money," the site where gold was first discovered in the United States (c.1818). A mint was later established there.

DAKOTA For the Dakota Indians, a major tribal grouping of Siouan linguistic stock. The name, in their language, means "friend" or "ally." The Dakotas are more popularly known as the Sioux, a French version of Ojibway *Nadouessioux*, "adder" or "enemy." Other tribes attribute names according to their reaction toward the Dakotas: "roasters," because of their torturing enemies, "long arrows," "cutthroats," "birds," and others.
North Dakota, State of. 39th or 40th state of the Union. Settled: 1766. Territory: 1861 (part of *Dakota* Territory). Admitted: (with *South Dakota*) 1889. Cap: Bismarck. Motto: Liberty and Union, Now and Forever, One and Inseparable. Nickname: Flickertail State. Flower: Wild Prairie Rose. Bird: Western Meadowlark. Tree: American Elm. Song: "North Dakota Hymn."
South Dakota, State of. 39th or 40th state of the Union. Settled: 1856. Territory: 1861 (part of *Dakota* Territory). Admitted: (with *North Dakota*) 1889. Cap: Pierre. Motto: Under God, the People Rule. Nickname: Coyote State. Flower: Pasque Flower. Bird: Ring-necked Pheasant. Tree: Black Hills Spruce. Song: "Hail, South Dakota."
Dakota Co., Minn. (co. seat, Hastings).
Dakota Co., Neb. (co. seat, *Dakota City*).
Dakota City, Iowa (co. seat of Humboldt Co.).
Dakota City, Neb. (co. seat of *Dakota* Co.).

DALE Co., Ala. (co. seat, Ozark). For Sam Dale (1772-1841), officer in the Indian wars, scout, and legislator in both Alabama and Mississippi.

DALE HOLLOW RESERVOIR, Ky.-Tenn. For a town, in turn a personal name.

DALEVILLE, Ala. (Dale Co.). So named because it is at the geographical center of Dale County.

DALHART, Tex. (co. seat of Dallam Co.). Located on the boundary between Dallam and Hartley Counties, the city takes its name from the first syllable of each name.

They came to the Dakotas in search of land and freedom and peace; they built their sod houses and turned the plains into America's bread basket. [*Santa Fe Railway*]

DALHOUSIE, N.B. (co. seat of Restigouche Co.). For the Earl of Dalhousie, governor general of Canada when the town was named (1826).

DALL, William Healy (1845-1927), active for many years with the United States Geological Survey. He was a member of the Harriman Alaska Expedition in 1899.
Dall Lake, Alaska.
Dall Mountain, Alaska.
Dall Point, Alaska.
Dall Ridge, Alaska.
Dall River, Alaska. Flows SE into Yukon R.

DALLAM Co., Tex. (co. seat, Dalhart). For James Wilmer Dallam (1818-1847), Texas legal writer.

DALLAS Co., Ala. (co. seat, Selma). For Alexander James Dallas (1759-1817), Pennsylvania attorney and statesman. He was secretary of the treasury (1814-16) and acting secretary of war (1815) under Madison. He was the father of George Mifflin Dallas.

DALLAS, George Mifflin (1792-1864), Pennsylvania statesman and jurist. He was U.S. senator (1831-33), minister to Russia (1837-39), vice-president of the United States (1845-49) under Polk, and minister to Great Britain (1856-61).
Dallas Co., Ark. (co. seat, Fordyce).
Dallas Co., Iowa (co. seat, Adel).
Dallas Co., Mo. (co. seat, Buffalo).
Dallas Co., Tex. (co. seat, *Dallas*).
Dallas, Ga. (co. seat of Paulding Co.).
Dallas, N.C. (Gaston Co.).
Dallas, Ore. (co. seat of Polk Co.).
Dallas, Tex. (co. seat of *Dallas* Co.). Earlier, Peter's Colony.

DALLES, The. See THE DALLES.

DALTON, Ga. (co. seat of Whitfield Co.). Either for the maiden name of the wife or mother of Edward White, a founder, or for John Dalton, engineer who platted the town.

DALTON, Mass. (Berkshire Co.), town. For Tristram Dalton (1738-1817), speaker of the Massachusetts House of Representatives when the town was incorporated.

DALY CITY, Calif. (San Mateo Co.). For John Daly, owner of a ranch where people found refuge after the San Francisco earthquake.

DAMARISCOTTA LAKE, Me. From Abnaki, "place of alewives," which are herring-like fish.

DAMARISCOVE ISLAND, Me. Origin uncertain, but probably an English name, Damarill, plus *cove*, with influence from *Damariscotta.*

DAN River named by Col. William Byrd while exploring the south central part of Virginia (1728). While he recorded no reason for the name, it may be Biblical, from the tribe and city of Dan. The name became synonymous with the concept of remoteness: ". . . from Dan even to Beersheba . . ." (I Kings 4:25).
Dan River, Va.-N.C.-Va. Flows into Buggs Island Lake.
Danville, Va. (independent city in Pittsylvania Co.). For the river. Earlier, Wynne's Falls, for an early settler.

DANA POINT, Calif. (Orange Co.). For Richard H. Dana, author of *Two Years Before the Mast.* He is said to have rescued people stranded on the cliff.

DANBURY For Danbury, Essex, England.
Danbury, Conn. (Fairfield Co.), town.
Danbury, N.C. (co. seat of Stokes Co.).

DANBY LAKE, Calif., in the Mojave Desert. One of the alphabetical names given by officials of the Atlantic and Pacific railroad, now the Santa Fe Railroad. Others in the area are Amboy, Bristol, Cadiz, Edson, Fenner, and Goffa. Danby probably was suggested by Danby, Vt.

DANCING RABBIT CREEK, Miss. Site of a treaty (1833), at which the Choctaw Indians ceded their lands east of the Mississippi and agreed to move to new lands in the west. From Choctaw, *chook fa ahihla*

bogue, "place or creek where the rabbit dances."

DANDRIDGE, Tenn. (co. seat of Jefferson Co.). For Martha Dandridge Curtiss Washington, wife of George Washington.

DANE Co., Wis. (co. seat, Madison). For Nathan Dane (1752-1835), Massachusetts legislator and jurist. He proposed the Ordnance of 1787 to govern the Northwest Territory.

DANIEL, Mount, Wash., in Cascade Range. Reason for naming unknown.

DANIELS Co., Mont. (co. seat, Scobey). For an early settler.

DANIELSON, Conn. (Windham Co.). For Gen. James Danielson, grandson of the first James Danielson to enter the area in the late 17th century.

DANIELSVILLE, Ga. (co. seat of Madison Co.). For Gen. Allen Daniel.

DANNEMORA, N.Y. (Clinton Co.). Named for Dannemora, Sweden, by General St. John Skinner. He had been studying mining in Sweden and noticed the similarity of the mountains and ore beds.

DANSVILLE, N.Y. (Livingston Co.). For Daniel Faulkner (?-1802), one of the original settlers.

DANVERS, Mass. (Essex Co.), town. For the Danvers Osborn family of New York. An earlier name was Salem Village.

DANVILLE, Ill. (co. seat of Vermilion Co.). For Dan Beckwith, landowner and founder.

DANVILLE, Ind. (co. seat of Hendricks Co.). For Dan Wick, brother of Judge William Watson Wick, the man responsible for naming the county seat.

DANVILLE, Ky. (co. seat of Boyle Co.). For Walker Daniel, founder.

DANVILLE, Pa. (co. seat of Montour Co.). For Daniel Montgomery, Jr. (1765-1831), founder and storekeeper. He was a state legislator, U.S. representative (1807-09), major general of the Ninth Division of Militia, and canal commissioner. An earlier name was Dan's Town.

DANVILLE, Va. See DAN.

D'ARBONNE For the d'Arbonne family, early settlers.
D'Arbonne, Lake, La.
D'Arbonne, Bayou, La. Flows SE into Ouachita R.

DARBY For Derby, Derbyshire, England.
Darby, Pa. (Delaware Co.).
Upper Darby, Pa. (Delaware Co.).

DARDANELLE, Ark. (a co. seat of Yell Co.). Probably for the Dardanelles, straits off the coast of Turkey, site of a battle in the Crimean War. An earlier name was Dardanelle Rock, for the promontory commanding a view of the river and surrounding area. A local legend has it that a young Cherokee of the name jumped from the rock to his death because of unrequited love for a Choctaw maiden.

DARE Co., N.C. (co. seat, Nanteo). For Virginia Dare, born (1587) on Roanoke Island, the first child of English parents to be born in the Americas.

DARIEN Named by Scottish Highlanders for an ill-fated Scottish settlement or expedition to the Isthmus of Darien (Panama) in 1697.
Darien, Conn. (Fairfield Co.), town.
Darien, Ga. (co. seat of McIntosh Co.).

DARKE Co., Ohio (co. seat, Greenville). For William Darke (1736-1801), veteran of the Indian wars and officer in the American Revolution.

DARLING, Lake, N.Dak. For a local settler.

DARLINGTON For Darlington, in the county of Durham, England.
Darlington Co., S.C. (co. seat, *Darlington*).
Darlington, S.C. (co. seat of *Darlington* Co.).

DARLINGTON, Wis. (co. seat of Lafayette Co.). For Joshua Darling, a land investor.

DARTMOUTH, Mass. (Bristol Co.), town. For the port of Dartmouth, Devonshire, England.

DARWIN PEAK, Wyo. For Charles Darwin (1809-1892), scientist and naturalist, famous for his theory of evolution by natural selection.

DAUPHIN For the Dauphin of France. The name was given to a post on the Mossy River, built by Pierre la Verendrye in 1741, and to several posts in later years built by the Hudson's Bay and Northwest companies in the Lake Dauphin area.
Dauphin, Man.
Dauphin Lake, Man.

DAUPHIN Co., Pa. (co. seat, Harrisburg). From the title of the heir apparent to the French throne. The Dauphin at the time the county was established was Louis Joseph (1781-1789), eldest son of Louis XVI and Marie Antoinette.

DAVENPORT, Iowa (co. seat of Scott Co.). For Col. George Davenport (1785-1845), who served in Indian campaigns and in the War of 1812. He became postmaster (1825) at Rock Island and later (1832) took an active part in the Black Hawk War. He had great influence with the Sac and Fox tribes.

DAVENPORT, N.Y. (Delaware Co.). Probably named for John Davenport, the first town supervisor.

DAVID CITY, Neb. (co. seat of Butler Co.). For the maiden name of a Mrs. Miles who donated the land for the town, or possibly either for David Butler, first state governor, for whom the county was named, or for a Mr. Davids, friend of William Miles, the owner of the site.

DAVIDSON, William Lee (1746-1781), Brigadier general of the Western Militia of North Carolina during the American Revolution. He was killed at the Battle of Cowan's Ford trying to prevent Lord Cornwallis from crossing the Catawba River.
Davidson Co., N.C. (co. seat, Lexington).
Davidson Co., Tenn. (co. seat, Nashville).
Davidson, N.C. (Mecklenburg Co.).

DAVIDSON MOUNTAINS, Alaska. For George Davidson (1825-1911), member of the U.S. Coast and Geodetic Survey, who made several exploratory and surveying expeditions into Alaska, one before the purchase of the area from Russia.

DAVIE Co., N.C. (co. seat, Mocksville). For William Richardson Davie (1756-1820), American Revolutionary soldier and officer, governor of North Carolina, minister to

France, and a founder of the University of North Carolina.

DAVIES, Joseph Hamilton (1774-1811), Virginia soldier and jurist, also associated with Kentucky, who was unsuccessful in his attempt to indict Aaron Burr for treason (1806). He was killed at the battle of Tippecanoe.
Daviess Co., Ind. (co. seat, Washington).
Daviess Co., Ky. (co. seat, Owensboro).
Daviess Co., Mo. (co. seat, Gallatin).
Jo Daviess Co., Ill. (co. seat, Galena).

DAVIS, Calif. (Yolo Co.). For Jerome C. Davis (1822-1881), who owned the Jerome C. Davis Stock Farm in the 1850s. A portion of this land eventually became the site for the town.

DAVIS Co., Iowa (co. seat, Bloomfield). For Garrett Davis (1801-1872), U.S. representative (1839-47) and U.S. senator (1861-72) from Kentucky.

DAVIS MOUNTAINS, Tex. For Jefferson Davis (1808-1889), president of the Confederate States (1862-65). Previously he had served as U.S. representative and senator from Mississippi, and as secretary of war (1853-57), under Pierce. See also. FORT DAVIS, JEFF DAVIS, and JEFFERSON DAVIS

DAVIS, Mount, Pa. For a local settler.

DAVIS Co., Utah (co. seat, Framington). For Daniel C. Davis (1804-1850), commander of "The Mormon Volunteers," killed near Fort Kearney, Neb.

DAVISON, Mich. (Genesee Co.). For Norman Davison, early settler and first postmaster.

DAVISON Co., S.Dak. (co. seat, Mitchell). For an early settler.

DAWES Co., Neb. (co. seat, Chadron). For James William Dawes, governor (1883-87).

DAWSON, George Mercer (1849-1901), geologist and head of the Geological Survey of Canada. He surveyed much of British Columbia.
Dawson Creek, B.C. Earlier, Dawson's Brook, named by Dawson himself (1879).
Dawson, Mount, B.C., in Glacier Natl. Park.

DAWSON Co., Mont. (co. seat, Glendive). For Andrew Dawson, commander of Fort Benton for the American Fur Company.

DAWSON Co., Neb. (co. seat, Lexington). For a local postmaster, Jacob Dawson.

DAWSON Co., Tex. (co. seat, Lamesa). For Nicholas Mosby Dawson (1808-1842), Republic of Texas army officer killed in action.

DAWSON, William Crosby (1798-1856), attorney, U.S. representative (1836-41), circuit court judge, and U.S. senator (1849-55). He presided over the Southern convention at Memphis (1853).
Dawson Co., Ga. (co. seat, *Dawsonville*).
Dawson, Ga. (co. seat of Terrell Co.).
Dawsonville, Ga. (co. seat of *Dawson* Co.).

DAWSON SPRINGS, Ky. (Hopkins Co.). For a Dawson prominent in the area. Formerly a famous health resort.

DAY Co., S.Dak. (co. seat, Webster). For Merritt H. Day (1844-1900), early settler and Dakota Territory legislator.

DAYTON, Jonathan (1760-1824), soldier and statesman. He entered the Continental Army (1776) and rose to the rank of general. After serving in the New Jersey legislature, he was a delegate to the Constitutional Convention (1787), the youngest member. He later served in the House of Representatives (1771-99), the last four years as speaker, and as U.S. senator (1799-1805), during which time he was arrested in connection with the conspiracy of Aaron Burr, his distant relative. He was also one of four proprietors of lands in the Ohio territorial area.
Dayton, Ky. (Campbell Co.). Earlier, Jamestown.
Dayton, Ohio (co. seat of Montgomery Co.).
Dayton, Tenn. (co. seat of Rhea Co.). For *Dayton*, Ohio.

DAYTON, Tex. (Liberty Co.). For I. C. Day, a native of Tennessee who moved to Texas in 1830. An earlier name was Daystown.

DEAD Descriptive of the sluggishness of the flow of a river.
Dead Creek, Vt. Flows N into Otter Creek.

Dead Lake, Fla. For the flow of water of the Chipola R., which flows through the lake.

Dead River, Me. Flows into Flagstaff Lake.

Dead Stream, Me. Flows SE into Penobscot R.

Dead Diamond River, N.H. Flows S into Swift Diamond R. *Dead* was used to contrast with swift.

DEAD INDIAN Probably from the fact that a dead Indian was found there, although stories differ as to reason.

Dead Indian Creek, Wyo.

Dead Indian Pass, Wyo.

Dead Indian Peak, Wyo.

DEAD RIVER Translated from French *riviere de mort*, "river of the dead," in turn from Indian, "river of the spirits."

Dead River, Mich. Flows SE into L. Superior.

Dead River Storage Basin, Mich. Reservoir in the basin.

DEADWOOD, S.Dak. (co. seat of Lawrence Co.). Descriptive of an area where dead trees are conspicuous, usually because of a fire.

DEAF SMITH Co., Tex. (co. seat, Hereford). For Erastus ("Deaf") Smith (1787-1837), Republic of Texas patriot and soldier.

DEARBORN, Henry (1751-1829), American Revolutionary hero and general. He was U.S. representative from Massachusetts, secretary of war (1801-09), under Jefferson, and minister to Portugal.

Dearborn Co., Ind. (co. seat, Lawrenceburg).

Dearborn, Mich. (Wayne Co.).

Dearborn Heights, Mich. (Wayne Co.).

DEASE INLET, Alaska. For Peter Warren Dease (1783-1837?), officer of the Hudson's Bay Company, partner in an expedition in 1837.

DEATH VALLEY Named in 1849 by a party of gold seekers, for its forbidding appearance and desolation and also possibly for the deaths of some of the members who died while trying to cross the valley.

Death Valley, Nev.-Calif., desert basin extending NW from Mojave Desert

between Panamint Mtns. and Amaragosa Range.

Death Valley Natl. Monument, Nev.-Calif. Established in 1933.

DE BACA Co., N.Mex. (co. seat, Fort Sumner). For Ezequiel Cabeza de Baca (1864-1917), publisher and governor (1917), who died in office.

DECATUR, Stephen F. (1779-1820), distinguished commodore of the U.S. Navy during the War of 1812 and against the Barbary pirates, killed in a duel with another officer. He was the source of the often cited patriotic tribute to his country, "May she always be in the right; but our country, right or wrong."

Decatur Co., Ga. (co. seat, Bainbridge).

Decatur Co., Ind. (co. seat, Greensburg).

Decatur Co., Iowa (co. seat, Leon).

Decatur Co., Kan. (co. seat, Oberlin).

Decatur Co., Tenn. (co. seat, *Decaturville*).

Decatur, Ala. (co. seat of Morgan Co.).

Decatur, Ga. (co. seat of De Kalb Co.).

Decatur, Ill. (co. seat of Macon Co.).

Decatur, Ind. (co. seat of Adams Co.).

Decatur, Miss. (co. seat of Newton Co.).

Decatur, Tenn. (co. seat of Meigs Co.).

Decatur, Tex. (co. seat of Wise Co.).

Decatur Lake, Ill.

Decaturville, Tenn. (co. seat of *Decatur* Co.).

DECORAH, Iowa (co. seat of Winneshiek Co.). For Waukon-Decorah, a chief of the Winnebago tribe, and descendant of Sabrevoir de Carrie, an officer in the French colonial army who married a Winnebago maiden.

DEDHAM, Mass. (co. seat of Norfolk Co.), town. For Dedham, Essex, England.

DEEP Descriptive.

Deep Creek, Md.

Deep River, N.C. Flows SE and E to unite with Haw R. to form Cape Fear R.

Deep Creek Lake, Md.

Deep Creek Range, Utah. For the nearby creek.

Deephaven, Minn. (Hennepin Co.). For the harbor on L. Minnetanka.

Deep River, Conn. (Middlesex Co.), town. For the Connecticut R.

Aptly named, Death Valley is the lowest point in the continental United States. This wasteland is less than 80 miles from Mount Whitney, the highest point south of Alaska. [*New York Public Library*]

Deep River, Ont. (Renfrew Co.). For the Ottawa R.

DEER For the animal.
Deer Butte, Ore.
Deer Creek, Ind. Flows NW and W into Wabash R.
Deer Creek, Neb. Flows E into Old Logan R.
Deer Creek, Ohio. Flows SE into Scioto R.
Deer Creek, Okla. Flows SE into Salt Fork of Arkansas R.
Deer Island, Me., on Penobscot Bay.
Deer Isle, Me., adjacent to *Deer* Island.
Deer Lake, Mich.
Deer Mountain, Me.
Deer Peak, Colo.
Deer River, Me. Flows S into inlet in Atlantic.
Deer River, N.Y. Flows NW into St. Regis R.
Deer Isle, Me. (Hancock Co.), town.

Deers Ears Butte, S.Dak. For the resemblance of two peaks on the butte to the ears of a deer.
Forked Deer River, Tenn. Formed by S. Fork, Middle Fork and N. Fork, flows W into Mississippi R.

DEERFIELD For deer In the area.
Deerfield, Ill. (Lake Co.).
Deerfield, Mass. (Franklin Co.), town.
Deerfield River, Mass.-Vt.

DEERING RESERVOIR, N.H. For a local settler.

DEER LODGE Descriptive of an area in which deer came to the salt licks.
Deer Lodge Co., Mont. (co. seat, Anaconda).
Deer Lodge, Mont. (co. seat of Powell Co.).

DEER PARK Descriptive, sometimes promotional; possibly in some cases for a private park containing deer.
Deer Park, N.Y. (Suffolk Co.).
Deer Park, Ohio (Hamilton Co.).
Deer Park, Tex. (Harris Co.).

DEFIANCE For Fort Defiance, the strongest post built by Anthony Wayne during the campaign of 1794. It was situated at the junction of the Auglaize and Maumee rivers within what is now Defiance, Ohio. Wayne repeatedly exclaimed, "I defy the English, Indians, and all the devils in hell to take it," and Gen. Charles Scott replied, "Then call it Fort Defiance." From it, Wayne moved down the Maumee valley to the victory of Fallen Timbers (large numbers of fallen trees in the vicinity), a decisive battle in the Indian wars.
Defiance Co., Ohio (co. seat, *Defiance*).
Defiance, Ohio (co. seat of *Defiance* Co.).

DE FUCA, Juan, part of the history of the search for a passage between the Pacific and Atlantic. In *Purchas his Pilgrimmes* (1625) the story was published of Juan de Fuca, a Greek mariner whose real name was Apostolos Valerianos, who claimed to have discovered the passage in 1592 and to have sailed in it more than twenty days. Although this was a fabrication, the strait south of Vancouver Island, sometimes called the "Strait of Anian," was given his name. See JUAN DE FUCA STRAIT.

DE FUNIAK SPRINGS, Fla. (co. seat of Walton Co.). For Fred De Funiak, an official of the Louisville and Nashville railroad.

DE KALB For Johann Kalb, known as Baron de Kalb (1721-1780), German-born French soldier who served ably with the Americans during the American Revolution. He was killed at the Battle of Camden.
De Kalb Co., Ala. (co. seat, Fort Payne).
De Kalb Co., Ga. (co. seat, Decatur).
De Kalb Co., Ill. (co. seat, Sycamore).
De Kalb Co., Ind. (co. seat, Auburn).
De Kalb Co., Mo. (co. seat, Maysville).
De Kalb, Ill. (*De Kalb* Co.). Earlier, Buena Vista.
De Kalb, Miss. (co. seat of Kemper Co.). Earlier, Choctaw, *olitassa* or *holihtasaha*, translated as Fort Town.

DELAFIELD, Wis. (Waukesha Co.). For Charles Delafield, a landowner.

DE LAND, Fla. (co. seat of Volusia Co.). For Henry A. De Land, baking-powder manufacturer, owner of the townsite.

DELANO, Columbus (1809-1896), statesman. He served as U.S. representative from Ohio (1845-47; 1865-69) and as secretary of the interior (1870-75) under Grant.
Delano, Calif. (Kern Co.).
Delano Peak, Utah, on the Tushar Plateau.

DELAVAN, Edward Cornelius, temperance leader.
Delavan, Wis. (Walworth Co.).
Delavan Lake, Wis.

DELAWARE (or De La Warr), Thomas West, Lord (1577-1618), first British governor of the colony of Virginia. Delaware Bay was named for him by Capt. Samuel Argall, who discovered it while en route from England to Virginia in 1610. The river, the Indian tribe (also Leni or Leni-Lenape), the colony, and the state are named for the bay. The tribe originally occupied the central Atlantic states, but they had been pushed to Kansas by 1835. In 1867 they settled in what is now eastern Oklahoma.
Delaware, State of. First state of the Union. Settled: 1683. One of the original 13 colonies. Ratified Constitution: 1787. Cap: Dover. Motto: Liberty and Independence. Nicknames: Diamond State, First State. Flower: Peach Blossom. Bird: Blue Hen Chicken. Tree: American Holly. Song: "Our Delaware."
Delaware Co., Ind. (co. seat, Muncie).
Delaware Co., Iowa (co. seat, Manchester). For the state.
Delaware Co., N.Y. (co. seat, Delhi).
Delaware Co., Ohio (co. seat, *Delaware*).
Delaware Co., Okla. (co. seat, Jay).
Delaware Co., Pa. (co. seat, Media).
Delaware, Ohio (co. seat of *Delaware* Co.).
Delaware Bay, Del.-N.J.
Delaware Creek, Tex.-N.Mex. Flows ENE into Pecos R. For the tribe.
Delaware Mountains, Tex.
Delaware Reservoir, Ohio.
Delaware River, N.Y.-Pa.-N.J.-Del. Flows into *Delaware* Bay.
Delaware Water Gap, Del.-N.J.

The capes of the Delaware, shown here in 1890, were named for Lord De La Warr, the first Governor of the Colony of Virginia. Delaware, originally an extension of Pennsylvania, was separated in 1704 and, in 1787, became the first state to ratify the Constitution. [*New York Public Library*]

DEL CITY, Okla. (Oklahoma Co.). For Delphine Campbell, daughter of George Epperly, founder.

DELHI For the city in India; named during a time when it was the fashion to give names of famous foreign capitals and cities.
Delhi, La. (Richland Parish). Said locally to be taken from the name "Delhi" carved on a tree.
Delhi, N.Y. (co. seat of Delaware Co.), town.

DEL MAR, Calif. (Monterey Co.). The name was chosen for its proximity to the scene of Bayard Taylor's poem "The Fight of Paso del Mar."

DEL NORTE Shortened form of Spanish *Rio Grande Del Norte*, "great river of the North."
Del Norte Co., Calif. (co. seat, Crescent City).
Del Norte, Colo. (co. seat of Rio Grande Co.).

DE LONG MOUNTAINS, Alaska. Named in 1887 for George Washington De Long

(1841-1881), lieutenant commander in the U.S. Navy and an explorer. He died in the Lena Delta, Alaska.

DELPHI, Ind. (co. seat of Carroll Co.). For the ancient city of Delphi, Phocis, Greece, seat of the oracle of Apollo.

DELPHOS, Ohio (Allen and Van Wert Cos.). From the classical name DELPHI.

DEL RIO, Tex. (co. seat of Val Verde Co.). From Spanish, "of the river," from *San Felipe Del Rio*, former name of a place on the Rio Grande, named by early Spanish missionaries for King Philip of Spain.

DELSON, Que. (Laprarie Co.). So named because it was an important stop on the *Del*aware and Hud*son* railway.

DELTA For a river delta, or for triangular shape.
Delta Co., Colo. (co. seat, *Delta*). On the Uncompahgre R.
Delta Co., Mich. (co. seat, Escanaba).
Delta Co., Tex. (co. seat, Cooper).
Delta, B.C.

Delta, Colo. (co. seat of *Delta* Co.).

Delta, Ohio (Fulton Co.).

Delta Lake, N.Y.

Delta Natl. Forest, Miss. For the alluvial deposits.

Delta River, Alaska. Flows N into Tanana R.

DEMARCATION POINT, Alaska, cape extending into Beaufort Sea. So named in 1826 because it was on the boundary between British and Russian areas.

DEMING, N.Mex. (co. seat of Luna Co.). For Mary Ann Deming, wife of Charles Crocker, one of the early builders of the railroad.

DEMOPOLIS Probably named in the wave of enthusiasm for things pertaining to the classical period of Greece. It means "people-city."

Demopolis, Ala. (Marengo Co.).

Demopolis Dam, Ala.

DENAY CREEK, Nev. For a local dweller. It flows north into Humboldt River.

DENISON, Iowa (co. seat of Crawford Co.). For J. W. Denison, surveyor who platted the townsite.

DENISON, Tex. (Grayson Co.). For George Denison, vice-president of the Missouri-Kansas-Texas railroad, founder.

DENMARK, S.C. (Bamberg Co.). For Captain Denmark of Savannah, Ga., an official of the Seaboard railroad.

DENNIS, Mass. (Barnstable Co.), town. For the Reverend Josiah Dennis, first pastor of the church in the east precinct of Yarmouth (1727-63).

DENNISON, Ohio (Tuscarawas Co.). For William Dennison (1815-1882), banker, railroad president, governor of Ohio (1860-62), and postmaster general (1864-66) under Lincoln and Andrew Johnson.

DENT Co., Mo. (co. seat, Salem). For Lewis Dent (1808-1880), landowner and legislator.

DENTON, John B. (1806-1841), an officer killed by Indians.

Denton Co., Tex. (co. seat, *Denton*).

Denton, Tex. (co. seat of *Denton* Co.).

Denton Creek, Tex.

DENTON, Md. (co. seat of Caroline Co.). For Sir Robert Eden, provincial governor (1769-76). First named Eden Town, the name was shortened and fused to the present form.

DENVER, James William (1817-1892), a governor of Kansas Territory; named by settlers from Kansas.

Denver Co., Colo. (co. seat, *Denver*).

Denver, Colo. (co. seat of *Denver* Co.), state capital. Earlier, Denver City.

DENVER CITY, Tex. (Yoakum Co.). For the Denver Producing Company, one of the main oil-producing companies in the area at the time of its establishment.

DE PERE, Wis. (Brown Co.). Named by Father Claude Allouez as *Rapides des Peres*, "Rapids of the Fathers," for the site on the Fox River.

DEPEW, N.Y. (Erie Co.). For Chauncey M. Depew (1834-1928) railroad executive and Republican party leader. He was president of the New York Central and Hudson River railroad (1885-98) and served on the boards of directors of many other railroads. He was a U.S. senator from New York (1898-1911).

DEPOT For the supply camps, or "depots," for lumbermen.

Depot Lake, Me.

Depot Mountain, Me.

DE QUEEN, Ark. (co. seat of Sevier Co.). An Anglicized pronunciation of De Goeijen, the name of a Dutch railway investor. See also DE RIDDER.

DERBY For Derby, Derbyshire, England.

Derby, Colo. (Adams Co.).

Derby, Conn. (New Haven Co.).

Derby, Kan. (Sedgwick Co.).

Derby, Vt. (Orleans Co.), town.

DE RIDDER, La. (parish seat of Beauregard Parish). For Ella De Ridder, maiden name of the sister-in-law of Jan De Goeijen, Dutch investor in the Kansas City Southern Railroad.

DERMOTT, Ark. (Chicot Co.). From the family name McDermott, for an early group of settlers.

In 1866, five years after its incorporation, Denver was known as the "City of the Plains"; today it is called the "Mile High City," being 5,280 feet above sea level. [*New York Historical Society*]

DERBY For Londonderry (also called Derry), county seat of county Derry, Northern Ireland; named by a group of Scottish immigrants who had settled there before crossing the Atlantic to make their homes in New Hampshire.
Derry, N.H. (Rockingham Co.), town and village.
Derry, Pa. (Westmoreland Co.). Believed to be named for county Derry, Ireland, or for Londonderry.

DES ARC, Ark. (a co. seat of Prairie Co.). From French, "of the bend," for a curve in the White River.

DESCHUTES From French, "of the falls," used by men of the Hudson's Bay fur-trading company.
Deschutes Co., Ore. (co. seat, Bend).
Deschutes River, Ore. Flows N into the Columbia R.
Deschutes River, Wash. Flows into Puget Sound near Olympia.

DESERET From the Book of Mormon, "honeybee."
Deseret. Former name of UTAH and parts of several other states; a provisional Mormon state (1849-50) that became Utah Territory.
Deseret Peak, Utah.

DESERT Descriptive.
Desert Island, Mount, Me.
Desert Peak, Utah.

DESERT HOT SPRINGS, Calif. (Riverside Co.). Descriptive.

DESHA Co., Ark. (co. seat, Arkansas City). For either Joseph Desha or Robert Desha, U.S. representatives and officers in the War of 1812.

DES LACS From French, "the lakes."
Des Lacs Lakes, Sask.-N.Dak.
Des Lacs River, N.Dak. Rises in *Des Lacs* Lake, flows SE into Souris R.

DE SMET, S.Dak. (co. seat of Kingsbury Co.). For Peter John (or Pierre Jean) De Smet (1801-1873), Belgian Jesuit missionary and explorer, known as the "Apostle to the Indians."

DES MOINES From French *des*, "of the," and *moines*, a form of the Indian tribal name *Moingona*, "river of the mounds." The French name became *Riviere des Moines*, "river of the monks," because the area was explored by Catholic missionaries. Variations of the name are De Moin, De Moyen (for the middle or principal river between the Missouri and Mississippi rivers), and Demoine.

Des Moines Co., Iowa (co. seat, Burlington).

Des Moines, Iowa (co. seat of Polk Co.), state capital.

Des Moines River, Iowa. Flows generally SE to the Mississippi R.

West Des Moines, Iowa (Polk Co.).

DESOLATION PEAK, Wyo. Descriptive of the area.

DE SOTO, Hernando or Fernando (1496-1542), Spanish explorer, who led an expedition through what is now the southern part of the United States. He fell sick and died on the eastern bank of the Mississippi River, near the present site of Memphis, Tenn.

De Soto Co., Fla. (co. seat, Arcadia).

De Soto Parish, La. (parish seat, Mansfield).

De Soto Co., Miss. (co. seat, Hernando).

De Soto, Mo. (Jefferson Co.).

De Soto, Tex. (Dallas Co.).

De Soto Natl. Memorial, Fla.

De Soto Natl. Forest, Miss.

DES PLAINES From French, "the maples," for the maples along the river.

Des Plaines, Ill. (cook Co.). For the river.

Des Plaines River, Wis.-Ill. Flows to join the Kankakee R. to form the Illinois R.

DE TOUR From French, "go around."

De Tour Passage, Mich., water passage between Michigan and Drummond Island.

Detour, Point, in L. Michigan.

DETROIT From French, "strait." So named because the settlement lay between Lake Erie and St. Clair Lake; founded by Antoine Cadillac, French explorer.

Detroit, Mich. (co. seat of Wayne Co.).

Detroit Lake, Ore. For *Detroit*, Mich.

Detroit River, Mich.-Ont.

Detroit Lakes, Minn. (co. seat of Becker Co.). For the lakes.

East Detroit, Mich. (Macomb Co.). Earlier, Halfway; midway between Detroit and Mt. Clemens.

DEUEL Co., Neb. (co. seat, Chappell). For Henry Porter Deuel (1836-1914), an early settler of Omaha, later a local railroad official.

DEUEL Co., S.Dak. (co. seat, Clear Lake). For Jacob S. Deuel, a sawmill operator and legislator.

DEUX MONTAGNES From French, "two mountains," for two prominent mountains near the shore of the lake.

Deux Montagnes Co., Que. (co. seat, Sainte Schloastique).

Deux Montagnes, Que. (*Deux Montagnes* Co.).

Deux Montagnes Lake, Que.

DEVILS Possibly translated from Indian, "spirits," for a belief in the presence of spirits or in an incident involving spirits, or for forbidding terrain.

Devils Lake, Mich. According to legend, it was named by an Indian chief whose daughter had drowned in the lake. He believed that spirits or devils had taken her.

Devils Lake, Tex. For the river.

Devils River, Tex. For the forbidding terrain. Flows SW and S into the Rio Grande.

Devils Hole Mountain, Colo. It was believed that spirits resided in a cave or hole in the mountain.

Devils Postpile Natl. Monument, Calif. Contains several basalt columns of strange shape and arrangement. The resulting landscape was thought to resemble hell.

Devils Tower Natl. Monument, Wyo. For the monolith, claimed by Indians to have been inhabited by "bad spirits."

Devils Track Lake, Wis. From Ojibway, possibly "place where spirits walk."

DEVILS LAKE From Siouan *miniwaukan*, "lake hole one," which was misunderstood by white settlers as "devil's lake."

Devils Lake, N.Dak. (co. seat of Ramsey Co.).

Devils Lake (lake), N.Dak.

DEVINE, Tex. (Medina Co.). For Judge Thomas J. Devine (1812-1890), from San Antonio, Tex.

DEWEY, George (1837-1917), naval officer under Farragut during the Civil War. As commander of the Asiatic Squadron, he executed the capture of Manila during the Spanish-American War and was given the rank of Admiral of the Navy.

Detroit has become synonomous with the automobile industry, although many of the assembly plants are in neighboring cities. This Ford plant in Dearborn is shown turning out a stream of cars in the depression year of 1932. [*Courtesy of the Ford Archives, Dearborn, Michigan*]

Dewey Co., Okla. (co. seat, Taloga).

Dewey, Okla. (Washington Co.).

Dewey Dam, Ky. For the post office, in turn for George Dewey.

DEWEY Co., S.Dak. (co. seat, Timber Lake). For William P. Dewey, a surveyor general in the Dakota Territory. An earlier name was Rusk County.

DE WITT For De Witt CLINTON.

De Witt Co., Ill. (co. seat, Clinton).

De Witt, Ark. (a co. seat of Arkansas Co.).

De Witt, Iowa (Clinton Co.).

DE WITT, N.Y. (Onondaga Co.). For Maj. Moses De Witt, a local mayor, surveyor, and judge.

DE WITT Co., Tex. (co. seat, Cuero). For Green C. De Witt (1787-1835), an early colonizer in Mexican Texas.

DEXTER, Me. (Penobscot Co.), town and village. For Samuel D. Dexter (1761-1816), secretary of war (1800) under John Adams and of the treasury (1801) under Jefferson. He ran, unsuccessfully, for governor of Massachusetts (1816).

DIABLO From Spanish, "devil." See also DEVILS.

Diablo Canyon, Ore. Apparently for the forbidding terrain.

Diablo Creek, Calif.

Diablo, Mount, Calif. Earlier, Monte Diavolo, from Italian, "devil's wood."
Diablo Mountain, Ore. For the canyon.
Diablo Range, Calif.
Diablo Valley, Calif.

DIAMOND BAR, Calif. (Los Angeles Co.). Either for the former mineral deposits (probably diamond or quartz) or for the shape of a natural feature.

DIAMOND HEAD, Hawaii. Cape and landmark on south shore of Oahu Island. For quartz, resembling diamonds, found there. An earlier name was Laeahi, "brow of the ahi-fish."

DIAMOND PEAK, Ore. For John Diamond, an early settler.

D'IBERVILLE, Miss. (Harrison and Jackson Cos.). For the French-Canadian explorer Pierre, Sieur d'IBERVILLE.

DIBOLL, Tex. (Angelina Co.). For C. C. Diboll, owner of the land on which the town was established.

DICKENS, J., killed at the Alamo.
Dickens Co., Tex. (co. seat, *Dickens*).
Dickens, Tex. (co. seat of *Dickens* Co.).

DICKENSON Co., Va. (co. seat, Clintwood). For William J. Dickenson (1828-1907), lawyer and legislator. He served as the Commonwealth's attorney and as a representative of Russell County for two terms, but did not favor secession. He was twice elected to the legislature in later years.

DICKEY Co., N.Dak. (co. seat, Ellendale). For Alfred M. Dickey, a North Dakota state official.

DICKINSON, Daniel Stevens (1800-1866), New York State public official, legislator, and U.S. senator (1844-51).
Dickinson Co., Iowa (co. seat, Spirit Lake).
Dickinson Co., Kan. (co. seat, Abilene).

DICKINSON Co., Mich. (co. seat, Iron Mountain). For Donald McDonald Dickinson (1846-1917), postmaster general (1888-89) under Cleveland.

DICKINSON, N.Dak. (co. seat of Stark Co.). For Wells S. Dickinson, a railroad land agent who owned the site and founded the town.

DICKINSON, Tex. (Galveston Co.). For Dickinson Bayou, formerly Dickinson Creek, which was named for John Dickinson, probably the first white man in the area during the 1820s. One of Stephen Austin's "Old Three Hundred," he received a Mexican land grant in 1824, but not the actual townsite of present Dickinson.

DICKSON, William (1770-1816), Tennessee legislator and U.S. representative.
Dickson Co., Tenn. (co. seat, Charlotte).
Dickson, Tenn. (*Dickson* Co.).

DICKSON CITY, Pa. (Lackawanna Co.). For Thomas Dickson, president of the Delaware and Hudson Canal Company (1869-84). He served as an officer or director in twenty or more industrial companies and became a man of great wealth and influence.

DIGBY, Robert, an admiral who convoyed settlers to Nova Scotia in 1784.
Digby Co., N.S. (co. seat, *Digby*).
Digby, N.S. (co. seat of *Digby* Co.).

DIGHTON, Kan. (co. seat of Lane Co.). For Richard Deighton, town platter, with a change in spelling.

DIGHTON, Mass. (Bristol Co.), town. Possibly for Deighton, Yorkshire, England.

DILLON, James W. (1826-1913), merchant, landowner, and prominent citizen.
Dillon Co., S.C. (co. seat, *Dillon*).
Dillon, S.C. (co. seat of *Dillon* Co.).

DILLON, Mont. (co. seat of Beaverhead Co.). For Sidney Dillon, president of the Union Pacific railroad.

DILLON RESERVOIR, Ohio. For a local community member.

DIMMITT, W. C., a circuit-riding minister.
Dimmitt Co., Tex. (co. seat, Carrizo Springs).
Dimmitt, Tex. (co. seat of Castro Co.).

DINNEBITO WASH RIVER, Ariz. From Navajo *dine*, "people," and *bito*, "spring." It flows southwest into Little Colorado River.

DINOSAUR NATL. MONUMENT, Colo.-Utah. Established to commemorate the area where remains of dinosaurs were found.

DINUBA, Calif. (Tulare Co.). For a famous Greek battleground; supposedly named because of reports of a battle between factions of Greek and Austrian laborers in this vicinity.

DINWIDDIE, Robert (1693-1770), lieutenant governor of Virginia (1751-58), responsible for the defense of the colony during the French and Indian Wars (1754-63).
Dinwiddie Co., Va. (co. seat, *Dinwiddie*).
Dinwiddie, Va. (co. seat of *Dinwiddie* Co.).

DIRTY DEVIL RIVER, Utah. Named by an explorer who found the water muddy and foul smelling. Formed by a juncture of Muddy Creek and Fremont River, it flows generally southwest into Colorado River.

DISAPPOINTMENT Descriptive.
Disappointment, Cape, Wash., on Pacific Coast. So named because John Meares, English explorer in 1788, could not find a river that had been mistakenly entered on the maps of earlier Spanish explorers.
Disappointment Peak, Wyo. Named by a climbing party which was disappointed.

DISHNA RIVER, Alaska. Of Ingalik origin, meaning unknown. It flows north into Innoko River.

DISMAL Descriptive of a dismal or swampy area.
Dismal River, Neb. Flows E into Middle Loup R.
Dismal Swamp Canal, Va.-N.C. Connects Chesapeake Bay with Albemarle Sound.

DITCH RIVER, Ind. A stretch of Kankakee River. Descriptive.

DIVERSION CHANNEL, Mo. So named because the channel was to divert water from the Mississippi River. It extends west southwest to Castor River.

DIVIDE Co., N.Dak. (co. seat, Crosby). Descriptive; the county is divided by a mountain range.

DIVISION PEAK, Nev. For its position near the dividing lines of Washoe and Humboldt Counties.

DIX, John Adams (1798-1879), legislator and army officer, serving in the War of 1812 and the Civil War. He was U.S. senator (1845-49), secretary of the treasury (1861), minister to France (1866-69), and governor of New York (1873-75).
Dix Mountain, N.Y.
East Dix Mountain, N.Y.
South Dix Mountain, N.Y.

DIX HILLS, N.Y. (Suffolk Co.). For Dick Pechegan, a local Indian.

DIXIE Co., Fla. (co. seat, Cross City). For the name applied to the Confederate States and the song composed by Daniel Decatur Emmett (1859), said to be derived from a Creole pronunciation of the second name in Mason and Dixon Line.

DIXON See also MASON AND DIXON LINE.

DIXON, Calif. (Solano Co.). For Thomas Dickson, donator of land for the townsite. (The error in spelling was supposedly made by the Post Office.)

DIXON, Ill. (co. seat of Lee Co.). For Father John Dixon, founder.

DIXON, Ky. (co. seat of Webster Co.). For Archibald Dixon (1802-1876), legislator and diplomat. He was a state legislator (1830-41) and lieutenant governor of Kentucky (1843), U.S. senator (1852-55), and a delegate to the Frankfort peace convention (1863). He also was the author of the bill to repeal the Missouri Compromise.

DIXON Co., Neb. (co. seat, Ponca). For an early settler.

DIXON ENTRANCE, Alaska, water passage between Queen Charlotte Island and Alexander Archipelago. For Capt. George Dixon (1755-1800), commander of the *Queen Charlotte*. He explored the south coast of Alaska with Capt. Nathaniel Portlock in 1786 and 1787.

DIX RIVER, Ky. For a local citizen. It flows northwest into Kentucky River.

Dixie, immortalized and romanticized in the song by Dan Emmett, has become the "national anthem" of the South. In this French print we see the happy slaves and benevolent masters who figured so largely in the myth of the Old South. [*New York Public Library*]

DOANE, Gustavus C., an army officer in the Washburn party of 1870.
Doane Mountain, Wyo.
Doane Peak, Wyo.

DOBBS FERRY, N.Y. (Westchester Co.). For Jeremiah Dobbs, who operated a ferry across the Hudson River.

DOBSON, N.C. (co. seat of Surry Co.). Either for William Dobson, a local officeholder, or for William P. Dobson, a legislator.

DODDRIDGE Co., W.Va. (co. seat, West Union). For Philip Doddridge (1773-1832), Virginia legislator and U.S. representative.

DODGE Co., Ga. (co. seat, Eastman). For William Earle Dodge (1805-1883), businessman, active in the attempt to avoid Civil War (1861). He was a U.S. representative from New York.

DODGE, Henry (1782-1867), general in the Black Hawk War (1832). As first governor of Wisconsin Territory, he made treaties with the Ojibways and Sioux. He served as a U.S. senator (1848-57) from Wisconsin. See also FORT DODGE and HENRY Co.
Dodge Co., Minn. (co. seat, Mantorville).
Dodge Co., Wis. (co. seat, Juneau).
Dodgeville, Wis. (co. seat of Iowa Co.).

DODGE Co., Neb. (co. seat, Fremont). For Augustus Caesar Dodge (1812-1883), Iowa statesman, son of Henry Dodge. He was the first U.S. senator (1848-55) from Iowa and a minister (1855-59) to Spain.

DODGE CITY, Kan. (co. seat of Ford Co.). For Richard I. Dodge (1827-1895), commander of Fort Dodge when the city was established. An earlier name was Buffalo City.

DODGEVILLE, Wis. See Henry DODGE.

DOG Probably for an incident involving a dog.
Dog Island, Fla., in Gulf of Mexico.
Dog River, Vt. Flows generally NE into Winooski R. Different versions of incidents exist; an early settler lost his dog in or by the river; or a dog belonging to Jonathan Richardson was chasing a moose across the river and both fell through the ice and drowned.

DOLBEAU, Que. (West Lake St. John Co.). For the Recollet father, Jean Dolbeau, first missionary to the Montagnais Indians in 1615.

DOLGOI ISLAND, Alaska. Transliteration of the Russian descriptive name *Ostroy Dolgoy,* "long island."

DOLLARD-DES-ORMEAU, Que. (Montreal and Jesus Island Co.). For Adam Dollard des Ormeaux (1635-1660), a French-Canadian soldier. He was killed at the foot of the Long Sault, in a gallant stand against hostile Indians, which probably saved New France from an invasion planned by the Five Nations.

DOLORES From Spanish *Rio de Neustra Senora de los Dolores,* "River of Our Lady of Sorrows."
Dolores Co., Colo. (co. seat, Dove Creek).
Dolores River, Colo.-Utah.

DOLTON, Ill. (Cook Co.). For Andrew H. Dolton, founder.

DOME Descriptive of shape.
Dome Peak, N.W.T.
Dome Rock Mountains, Ariz.
Dome Shaped Mountain, Mont.
Dome, The (mountain), Vt.

DOMINGUEZ, Calif. (Los Angeles Co.). For Juan Jose Dominguez and his family, among the first settlers and landowners.

DONA ANA Co., N.Mex. (co. seat, Las Cruces). According to legends, either for Dono Ana Robledo, a woman famous for charity in the 1600s, or for Dona Ana Maria Nina de Cordova, a girl captured during an Apache raid and not seen again.

DONALDSVILLE, La. (parish seat of Ascension Parish). For William Donaldson.

DONALSONVILLE, Ga. (co. seat of Seminole Co.). For John E. Donalson (1846-1920), founder. He was a veteran of the Civil War who became an outstanding lawyer in Georgia and also a large landowner in the area.

DONIPHAN, Alexander William (1808-1887), Missouri legislator and officer in the Mexican War.
Doniphan Co., Kan. (co. seat, Troy).
Doniphan, Mo. (co. seat of Ripley Co.).

DONLEY Co., Tex. (co. seat, Clarendon). For Stockton P. Donley (1821-1871), Confederate army officer and Texas jurist.

DONNA, Tex. (Hidalgo Co.). For Donna Hooks Fletcher (1879-1969), daughter of Thomas J. Hooks, early pioneer and settler. She built the first hotel, owned a store, and became the first postmistress.

DONNER For the Donner Party, a group of eighty-one immigrants who wintered near Donner Lake. Thirty-six members died (1846).
Donner Lake, Calif.
Donner Pass, Calif., in the Sierra Nevada Mtns.

DONNER UND BLITZEN RIVER, Ore. From German, "thunder and lightning," so named because troops crossed the river during a thunderstorm in 1864. It flows north into Malheur Lake.

DONORA, Pa. (Washington Co.). For the president of the Union Improvement Company, William H. Donner, and for the wife of Andrew W. Mellon of Pittsburgh, stockholder in the company. Donora was derived by combining the first syllable of Donner with Nora, the baptismal name of Mrs. Mellon.

DOOLY Co., Ga. (co. seat, Vienna). For John Dooly, American Revolutionary officer in Georgia, killed by British sympathizers.

DOONERAK, Mount, Alaska, in Brooks Range. From Eskimo, "a devil" or "a spirit."

149

DOOR Co., Wis. (co. seat, Sturgeon Bay). Origin uncertain. A legend exists that an incident involving Indians caused the channel between Washington Island and the mainland to be named in French *La Porte des Morts*, "Door of the Dead." The county later took the name Door from the strait.

DORCHEAT BAYOU RIVER, Ark.-La. Ultimately from Indian, probably a tribal name in the Caddo family, folk etymologized into present form.

DORCHESTER For Sir Guy CARLETON, 1st baron Dorchester.
Dorchester Co., Que. (co. seat, Ste. Henedine).
Dorchester, N.B. (co. seat of Westmorland Co.).
Dorchester, Cape, N.W.T., on Baffin Island.

DORCHESTER For Dorchester, Dorsetshire, England.
Dorchester Co., S.C. (co. seat, St. George. For *Dorchester*, Mass.; named by settlers from there.
Dorchester, Mass. (Norfolk Co.). Now part of Boston.

DORCHESTER Co., Md. (co. seat, Cambridge). For Richard Sackville II, 5th Earl of Dorset (1622-1677), a friend of the Calvert family.

DORION, Que. (Vandreuil Co.). For Sir Antoine Aime Dorion (1818-91), attorney, politician, and judge. He was a Montreal representative in the legislative assembly of Canada (1854-61), joint premier of United Canada (1858; 1863-64), and chief justice of the Quebec Court of Queen's Bench (1874-91).

DORMONT, Pa. (Allegheny Co.). From French *mont d'or*, "mount of gold," to describe beautiful hills and the opportunities offered by them.

DORSET PEAK, Vt. For Dorset County in England.

DORVAL, Que. (Montreal and Jesus Islands Co.). For Jean-Baptiste Bouchard, surnamed Dorval, who held a large area of land during the French regime.

DOT, B.C. Nickname of Dalton P. Marpole, Canadian Pacific railroad general superintendent for British Columbia in the 1880s.

DOTHAN, Ala. (co. seat of Houston Co.). Biblical: "For I heard them say, let us go to Dothan" (Gen. 37:17).

DOUBLE Descriptive.
Double Springs, Ala. (co. seat of Winston Co.).
Doubletop Mountain, N.Y.
Doublet Peak, Wyo.

DOUGHERTY Co., Ga. (co. seat, Albany). For Charles Dougherty (?-1853), jurist.

DOUGLAS For a local settler of that name.
Douglas Lake, Mich.
Douglas Lake, Tenn.

DOUGLAS, Ariz. (Cochise Co.). For James Stewart Douglas (1837-1918), mining engineer, inventor of the revolving furnace for roasting ores and also of the Hunt and Douglas process of copper extraction. Originally trained as a physician, he was in the vanguard of cancer research. For his work in both medicine and mining, he received many honors and was twice president of the American Institute of Mining Engineers.

DOUGLAS, Dr. John, canon of Windsor. He later became Bishop of Salisbury.
Douglas, Cape, Alaska. Named by Capt. James Cook.
Douglas, Island, Alaska. Named by Capt. George Vancouver.
Douglas, Mount, Alaska. For the cape.

DOUGLAS, Stephen Arnold (1813-1861), known as the "Little Giant," a statesman of great ability during the two decades before the Civil War. As a U.S. senator from Illinois (1847-61), he was the opponent of Abraham Lincoln in the famous Lincoln-Douglas debates. He was Democratic candidate for the Presidency (1860), defeated by Lincoln.
Douglas Co., Colo. (co. seat, Castle Rock).
Douglas Co., Ga. (co. seat, *Douglasville*).
Douglas Co., Ill. (co. seat, Tuscola).
Douglas Co., Kan. (co. seat, Lawrence).
Douglas Co., Minn. (co. seat, Alexandria).
Douglas Co., Mo. (co. seat, Ava).
Douglas Co., Neb. (co. seat, Omaha).
Douglas Co., Nev. (co. seat, Minden).
Douglas Co., Ore. (co. seat, Roseburg).

Although Stephen Douglas was a prominent United States Senator, he is best remembered as a man who bested Abraham Lincoln in debate and lost to him in the race for the presidency.

Douglas Co., S.Dak. (co. seat, Armour).
Douglas Co., Wash. (co. seat, Waterville).
Douglas Co., Wis. (co. seat, Superior).
Douglas, Ga. (co. seat of Coffee Co.).
Douglas, Wyo. (co. seat of Converse Co.).
Douglas, Mount, Mont.
Douglasville, Ga. (co. seat of *Douglas* Co.).

DOVE CREEK, Colo. (co. seat of Dolores Co.). For the large flocks of doves ("wild pigeons") that flocked around a spring in a nearby arroyo.

DOVER For the channel port of Dover, Kent, England. See also DOVER, N.H. and DOVER, Tenn.
Dover, Del. (co. seat of Kent Co.), state capital. Named (1683) by William Penn.
Dover, Mass. (Norfolk Co.), town.
Dover, N.Y. (Dutchess Co.).
Dover, Ohio (Tuscarawas Co.).
Dover-Foxcroft, Me. (Piscataquis Co.), town and village. *Foxcroft*, for J. E. Foxcroft, landowner and developer.

DOVER Probably for Robert Dover (1575-1641), an English lawyer who protested the severe laws of the Puritans. Also said to take its name from Dover, England.
Dover, N.H. (co. seat of Strafford Co.). Earlier, Bristol, Northam.
Dover, N.J. (Morris Co.). For *Dover*, N.H.

DOVER, Tenn. (co. seat of Stewart Co.). General belief is that the town's name was adopted from the trade name of the iron produced in the area. The name ultimately derives from Dover, Kent, England.

DOWAGIAC From Pottawattomi *ndowagayuk*, "subsistence area," where food, clothing, and shelter could be found.
Dowagiac, Mich. (Cass Co.).
Dowagiac River, Mich.

DOWNERS GROVE, Ill. (Du Page Co.). For Pierce Downer, early settler.

DOWNEY, Calif. (Los Angeles Co.). For John Gately Downey (1827-1894), governor of California (1860-62), and divider of the land on which the town was built.

DOWNINGTOWN, Pa. (Chester Co.). For Thomas Downing, a miller who, in 1786, strongly resisted the plan of making Downingtown the county seat.

DOWNS MOUNTAIN, Wyo. For John Downs, a hunter.

DOWNSVILLE DAM, N.Y. For Abel Downs, a tanner.

DOYLESTOWN, Pa. (co. seat of Bucks Co.). For William Doyle, early settler and tavern keeper as early as 1735.

DRACUT, Mass. (Middlesex Co.), town. Named and spelled from the pronunciation of Draycott, Derbyshire, England.

DRAKE PEAK, Ore. For John M. Drake, an officer who fought in several campaigns against the Snake Indians.

DRAYTON PLAINS, Mich. (Oakland Co.). Named by an early settler who had owned a Drayton Mill in England. The name ultimately derives from Drayton, England.

DRESDEN, Tenn. (co. seat of Weakley Co.). For Dresden, Germany.

DREW Co., Ark. (co. seat, Monticello). For Thomas Stevenson Drew (1802-1879), businessman and governor of Arkansas (1844-49).

DREWS RESERVOIR, Ore. For Lt.-Col. C. S. Drew, cavalry commander in 1864.

DRIFTWOOD For the large amount of driftwood found in the creek.
Driftwood, Pa. (Cameron Co.).
Drfitwood Creek, Pa. Flows into Sinnemahoning R.

DRIGGS, Idaho (co. seat of Teton Co.). For the members of a Mormon settlement, all with the surname Driggs.

DRISKILL MOUNTAIN, La. For a local settler.

DRUM INLET, N.C., between Core Banks and Portsmouth Island. For the drum fish (*Sciaenidae* family).

DRUMMOND, Sir Gordon (1771-1854), soldier in the British army who served in the Netherlands, Egypt, and the West Indies. He became administrator of Upper Canada (1813-15), and of Canada (1815-16).
Drummond Co., Que. (co. seat, *Drummondville*).
Drummondville, Que. (co. seat of *Drummond* Co.).
Drummond Island, Mich.

DRUMMOND LAKE, Va. Reason for name uncertain, but claimed for William Drummond, a governor of North Carolina.

DRUMRIGHT, Okla. (Creek Co.). For Aaron Drumright, who owned the farm on which the first oil well in the area was drilled.

DRY Descriptive.
Dry Brook, Mass. Flows SSE into Connecticut R.
Dry Creek, Ga. Flows S into Spring Creek.
Dry Lake, N.Dak.
Dry River, N.H. Flows S into Saco R.
Dry Creek Butte, Ore.
Dry Falls Dam, Wash. Prehistoric dry falls of the Columbia R.

DUARTE, Calif. (Los Angeles Co.). For Andres Duarte, landowner.

DUBLIN For Dublin, Ireland.
Dublin, Calif. (Alameda Co.), supposedly because of the abundance of Irishmen in the area.
Dublin, Ga. (co. seat of Laurens Co.).
Dublin, Tex. (Erath Co.). Probably for Dublin, Ireland, since the civil engineer who laid out the streets was named O'Neil and most of the street names are Irish. A less plausible theory is that it came from "double in," a practice of citizens who moved in together to protect themselves against marauding Indians.

DUBOIS, Idaho (co. seat of Clark Co.). For Fred Thomas Dubois, U.S. senator from Idaho (1890-97; 1901-07).

DUBOIS Co., Ind. (co. seat, Jasper). For an early settler.

DU BOIS, Pa. (Clearfield Co.). For John Du Bois, an early settler who came to the Sandy Creek area on the western slope of the Allegheny Mountains in 1772 and began extensive lumbering operations that brought much prosperity to the town.

DU BOULLIE MOUNTAIN, Me. From a French personal name.

DUBUQUE, Julien (1762-1810), French-Canadian settler at the site of the city in 1785. He was the first permanent white settler in Iowa. A miner, he erected his first village about two miles south of the present city and called it Les Mines d'Espagne. He died in Dubuque.
Dubuque Co., Iowa (co. seat, *Dubuque*).
Dubuque, Iowa (co. seat of *Dubuque* Co.).

DUCHESNE Origin in dispute: for Sister Duchesne, a Catholic mother; for a fur trapper, Du Chesne; or for Fort Duquesne, Pa.
Duchesne Co., Utah (co. seat, *Duchesne*).
Duchesne, Utah (co. seat of *Duchesne* Co.).
Duchesne River, Utah.

DUCK For the fowl, often for the occurrence of wild duck.
Duck Creek, Nev.
Duck Island, Me., in the Atlantic Ocean.
Duck Lake, Me.
Duck Lake, Mich. (Gogebic Co.).
Duck Lake, Mich. (Grand Traverse Co.).

Duck River, Tenn. Flows WNW into Kentucky L.

DUDLEY, Mass. (Worcester Co.), town. For two descendants of Gov. Thomas Dudley (1576-1653): Paul Dudley (1675-1751), attorney general and chief justice of the Massachusetts Supreme Court; and William Dudley.

DUFFERIN Co., Ont. (co. seat, Orangeville). For Frederick Temple Blackwood, 1st Marquess of Dufferin and Ava, governor general of Canada (1872-78).

DUKES Co., Mass. (co. seat, Edgartown). County that includes the island of Martha's Vineyard and smaller islands; named when it was under the administration of James II, Duke of YORK.

DULUTH, Minn. (co. seat of St. Louis Co.). For Daniel Greysolan, Du Luth or Du Lhut (1649-1710), French explorer in the area in 1070.

DUMAS, Ark. (Desha Co.). For William B. Dumas (1841-?), landowner, proprietor of the first store and first freight office, surveyor, constable, and school director. He owned the land on which the city was located.

DUMAS, Tex. (co. seat of Moore Co.). For Louis Dumas (1856-1923), early farmer and president of the townsite company that founded the town.

DUMONT, N.J. (Bergen Co.). For Dumont Clarke (1846-1909), former mayor and banker.

DUNBAR, W.Va. For Dunbar Baines, a businessman.

DUNCAN, Okla. (co. seat of Stephens Co.). For William Duncan, early settler and owner of a store where the post office was located.

DUNCANVILLE, Tex. (Dallas Co.). For John Duncan, who helped in the building of the railroad later taken over by the Santa Fe. Earlier names were Duncan Switch and Duncan.

DUNDAS, Hon. Henry, later Lord Melville.
Dundas Co., Ont. (co. seat, Cornwall).
Dundas, Ont. (Wentworth Co.).

Dundas Island, B.C., largest of the Dundas Islands. Named by Capt. George Vancouver in 1793.
Dundas Islands, B.C.

DUNDY Co., Neb. (co. seat, Benkelman). For Elmer S. Dundy (1830-1896), jurist.

DUNELLEN, N.J. (Middlesex Co.). Origin uncertain. It is believed that the president of the Central railroad of New Jersey, which was responsible for the establishment of the town, took the first name of his friend Ellen Betts and added the prefix *dun* because he liked the combination.

DUNKIRK Anglicized form of *Dunquerque*, France. In Indiana the name was first applied to the local Masonic lodge.
Dunkirk, Ind. (Jay Co.).
Dunkirk, N.Y. (Chautauqua Co.).
Dunkirk, Ohio (Hardin Co.).

DUNKLIN Co., Mo. (co. seat, Kennett). For Daniel Dunklin (1790-1844), governor of Missouri (1833-36).

DUNMORE, Lake, Vt. Named for and by John Murray, Earl of Dunmore, who practically baptized himself in the water.

DUNN, N.C. (Harnett Co.). Named by the Atlantic Coastline railroad for a chief engineer.

DUNN Co., N.Dak. (co. seat, Manning). For John P. Dunn, a city official of Bismarck.

DUNN Co., Wis. (co. seat, Menomonie). For Charles Dunn, a legislator and jurist.

DUNNING CREEK, Pa. For a local settler. It flows southeast into Raystown Brook.

DUNNVILLE, Ont. (Haldimand Co.). Probably for the Hon. John Henry Dunn, receiver-general of Upper Canada.

DU PAGE From the French name of a local Indian chief.
Du Page Co., Ill. (co. seat, Wheaton). For the river.
Du Page River, Ill. Flows generally SW to the Des Plaines R.

DUPLIN Co., N.C. (co. seat, Kenansville). For Thomas Hay, Lord Duplin (1710-1787).

DUPO, Ill. (St. Clair Co.). A shortened form of French *Prairie Du Pont*, "Field of the Bridge" or, in this case, "the common fields of the area connected by a bridge." The spelling is influenced by the French pronunciation of *Du Pont*.

DUPREE, S.Dak. (co. seat of Ziebach Co.). For Fred Dupris, one of the first white settlers in the area. The spelling reflects the pronunciation.

DU QUOIN, Ill. (Perry Co.). For Jean-Baptiste Ducoigne, French name for a Kaskaskia chief.

DURAND, Mich. (Shiawassee Co.). For George H. Durand, U.S. representative (1875-76).

DURAND, Wis. (co. seat of Pepin Co.). For Miles Durand Prindle, an early settler and landowner.

DURANGO, Colo. (co. seat of La Plata Co.). For Durango, Mexico.

DURANT, Okla. (co. seat of Bryan Co.). For Dixon Durant (1809-1906), Choctaw minister, businessman, and town founder.

DURHAM For Durham, county of Durham, England.
Durham Co., Ont. (co. seat, Cobourg). Earlier, Bentinck.
Durham, Conn. (Middlesex Co.), town.

DURHAM, Bartlett S. (1822-1858), land donor.
Durham Co., N.C. (co. seat, *Durham*).
Durham, N.C. (co. seat of *Durham* Co.).

DURHAM, N.H. (Strafford Co.), town and village. For Richard Barnes (1532-1587), Bishop of Durham, England. He was known as the "Puritan Bishop."

DURYEA, Pa. (Luzerne Co.). For Abram Duryea, first settler.

DUTCHESS Co., N.Y. (co. seat, Poughkeepsie). For Mary of Modena (1658-1718), wife of James, Duke of York and Albany, later James II of England.

DUTCH MOUNTAIN, Utah. For a settler's nickname.

DUTTON, Mount, Utah. For Clarence E. Dutton, geologist.

DUVAL Co., Fla. (co. seat, Jacksonville). For William Pope Duval (1784-1854), U.S. representative from Kentucky (1813-15) and governor of the Florida Territory (1822-34).

DUVAL Co., Tex. (co. seat, San Diego). For Burr H. Duval (1809-1836), an officer killed during the Texas Revolution.

DUXBURY For Duxbury Hall, the Standish family seat in England, in honor of Miles Standish (c.1584-1656). A soldier who accompanied the Pilgrims and helped secure and govern their colony, Standish, with John Alden, founded the town of Duxbury. Although much of his fame is attributable to Longfellow's poem "The Courtship of Miles Standish," the story of Standish, Alden, and Priscilla, is without factual basis.
Duxbury, Mass. (Plymouth Co.), town.
Duxbury Bay, Mass.

DWIGHT, Ill. (Livingston Co.). For Henry A. Dwight, a founder.

DYBERRY CREEK, Pa. Origin uncertain, but probably a translation from an Indian descriptive name for berries used for dyeing. It flows generally southeast into Lake Wallenpaupack.

DYER, Ind. (Lake Co.). For Martha Dyer Hart, wife of the town founder, Aaron N. Hart.

DYER, Robert H., a prominent fighter in the Indian wars.
Dyer Co., Tenn. (co. seat, *Dyersburg*).
Dyer, Tenn. (Gibson Co.).
Dyersburg, Tenn. (co. seat of *Dyer* Co.).

DYERSVILLE, Iowa (Dubuque Co.). For James J. Dyer, Jr. (1820-1864), leader of English settlers in the area as organizer, developer, builder, merchant, and adviser.

E

EADS, Colo. (co. seat of Kiowa Co.). Named by S. H. Mallory, town founder, for an engineer, Eads, who directed the construction of a bridge across the Mississippi River.

EAGLE For the birds. The bald eagle is the national bird and symbol of power of the United States; the golden eagle is the more common species. Places have for the most part been named for the presence of an eagle or eagles, of whichever kind, rather than for patriotic reasons.
Eagle Co., Colo. (co. seat, *Eagle*).
Eagle, Colo. (co. seat of *Eagle* Co.).
Eagle Creek, Ariz.
Eagle Creek, Ky.
Eagle Lake, Calif.
Eagle Lake, Me. (Aroostook Co.).
Eagle Lake, Me. (Piscataquis Co.).
Eagle Lake, Ont.
Eagle Lake, Tex.
Eagle Lake, Wis.
Eagle Mountain, Minn.
Eagle Mountain, Tex.
Eagle Peak, N.Mex., in the Tularosa Mtns.
Eagle River, Colo.
Eagle Cap, Ore., in the Wallowa Mtns. Once thought to be the highest in, or cap of, the range, then called *Eagle* Mtns.
Eagle Grove, Iowa (Wright Co.).
Eagle Lake, Tex. (Colorado Co.).
Eagle Mountain Lake, Tex.
Eagle Nest Butte, S.Dak.
Eagle Pass, Tex. (co. seat of Maverick Co.).

From Spanish *paso del aguila*, for flights of eagles to and from their nests.
Eagle Point Lake, Minn.
Eagle River, Mich. (co. seat of Keweenaw Co.). For a small stream that flows into L. Superior; probably a translation from an Indian name.
Eagle River, Wis. (co. seat of Vilas Co.). A translation of Indian *misgisiwisibi*, "eagle," or "eagle place."
Eagles Rest Peak, Wyo.
Eagleton, Tenn. (Blount Co.).

EARLIMART, Calif. (Tulare Co.). Named by real-estate promoters to indicate early maturation of crops.

EARLY Co., Ga. (co. seat, Blakely). For Peter Early (1773-1817), U.S. representative (1803-07), jurist, and governor (1813-15).

EARTHQUAKE LAKE, Mont. For the occurrence of earthquakes in the area.

EASLEY, S.C. (Pickens Co.). For William King Easley, attorney and state legislator. He was a signer of the South Carolina ordinance of secession and first adjutant general of South Carolina.

EAST Descriptive, directional. Names that do not appear in this part of the book may be found under the basic name. For example, for East Aurora, N.Y., see AURORA.

Congress selected the bald eagle as the American national emblem in 1782 over the objections of Benjamin Franklin, who strongly favored the American wild turkey. Since that time both birds have become endangered. [*New York Public Library*]

East Bay, La.

East Butte, Idaho.

East Creek, Vt. Flows into L. Champlain.

East Lake, Me. Lies east of North L.

East Pass, Fla., waterway between St. George Island and Dog Island.

East Point, Mass., extends into Boston Bay.

East Bay River, Vt.-N.Y. Flows into L. Champlain.

Eastern Point, Mass., on Cape Ann Island.

Eastern River, Me. Flows SW into Kennebec R.

East Grand Lake, Me.-N.B. One of the Chiputneticook Lakes.

East Long Pond, Me.

East Long Pond, Vt.

East Spring Creek, Colo. Flows NE to join Hell Creek to form S. Fork Republican R.

Eastview, Ont. (Carleton Co.). It is located east of Ottawa on Highway 17. Now called VANIER.

EASTCHESTER, N.Y. (Westchester Co.). *East*, directional; -*Chester*, for the town and county in England.

EAST DOUGLAS, Mass. (Worcester Co.). For William Douglas, an eminent Boston physician.

EAST DUNDEE, Ill. (Kane Co.). On the eastern shore of the Fox River, opposite West Dundee.

EASTERN SHORE Name applied to the great peninsula including parts of Maryland, Delaware, and Virginia, which lies east of the Chesapeake Bay. A later, promotional term, Delmarva Peninsula, is also used.

EAST FAXON, Pa. (Lycoming Co.). For a man named Faxon who was secretary of industrial development for Albuquerque, N.Mex. He also assisted the industrial development organization for this part of Pennsylvania.

EAST FLAT ROCK, N.C. (Henderson Co.). Northeast of Flat Rock, now the smaller place.

EAST GRAND FORKS, Minn. (Polk Co.). For its location east of the Red River, across from GRAND FORKS N.Dak.

EAST GREENWICH, R.I. (co. seat of Kent Co.). For a district of London, England.

EAST HAMPTON, Conn. (Middlesex Co.). Named by the first settlers for their native town of Eastham, Mass.

EASTHAMPTON, Mass. (Hampshire Co.), town. East with regard to NORTHAMPTON and SOUTHAMPTON.

EASTLAKE, Ohio (Lake Co.). For its location, northeast of Cleveland, on Lake Erie.

EASTLAND, William Mosby (1806-1843). Texas Revolutionary officer, member of the Mier Expedition, executed by General Santa Anna.
Eastland Co., Tex. (co. seat, *Eastland*).
Eastland, Tex. (co. seat of *Eastland* Co.).

EASTMAN, Ga. (co. seat of Dodge Co.). For William Pitt Eastman, pioneer settler and landowner.

EAST MILLCREEK, Utah (Salt Lake Co.). For its location on Mill Creek, which was so named because of grist mills and sawmills on the stream.

EASTON, Conn. (Fairfield Co.), town. So named because of its incorporation from the eastern part of WESTON.

EASTON, Md. (co. seat of Talbot Co.). For the Talbot County Court House, which had become known as the "East Capital of Maryland." Earlier names were Talbot County Courthouse and Talbot Town.

EASTON, Mass. (Bristol Co.), town. Probably descriptive, but may have been named for Gov. John Easton (1625-1705) or for Nichols Easton (1593-1675) of Rhode Island.

EASTON, Pa. (co. seat of Northampton Co.). For Eastern Neston, Northamptonshire, England, the country seat of the Earl of Pomfret, whose daughter was the wife of Thomas Penn, William Penn's son.

EAST RAINY BUTTE, N.Dak. Named by haulers who were often stuck in the sticky mud on the road near the butte.

EAST SETAUKET, N.Y. (Suffolk Co.). For the Secatogue Indians.

EAST TAVAPUTS PLATEAU, Utah. Meaning and origin uncertain, *Tava* is possibly from Ute, "sun."

EAST TOHOPEKALIGA LAKE, Fla. From Seminole-Creek, "place of a fort."

EASTVILLE, Va. (co. seat of Northampton Co.). Said to be so named because it was east of other settled places.

EASTWOOD, Mich. (Saginaw Co.). For Edward A. Eastwood, farmer and first postmaster.

EASY DAY PEAK, Wyo. So named because a climbing party had an easy day before a difficult climb.

EATON, John Henry (1790-1856), Tennessee statesman and governor of Florida Territory. He was also a U.S. senator (1818-29), secretary of war (1829-31) under Jackson, and minister to Spain.
Eaton Co., Mich. (co. seat, Charlotte).
Eaton Rapids, Mich. (*Eaton* Co.).

EATON, William (1764-1811), officer in the American Revolution and in campaigns against hostile Indians until 1798, at which time he was sent to Tunis as American consul. In 1801 he was commander at the Battle of Tripoli, returning to America in 1803, when he was appointed U.S. naval agent to the Barbary States.
Eaton, Ohio (co. seat of Preble Co.).
Eatonton, Ga. (co. seat of Putnam Co.).

EAU CLAIRE From French, "clear water."
Eau Claire Co., Wis. (co. seat, *Eau Claire*).
Eau Claire, Wis. (co. seat of *Eau Claire* Co.).
Eau Claire Lake, Wis.
Eau Claire River, Wis.

EAU GALLE, Lake, Wis. From French, "gravel water," probably connoting "gravel spring."

EAU PLEINE. See BIG EAU PLEINE.

EBENSBURG, Pa. (co. seat of Cambria Co.). For Ebenezer, deceased infant son of Rev. Reese Lloyd, who had been ordained as a minister in Ebenezer, Pontypool, Monmouthshire, Wales. An earlier spelling was Ebensburgh.

ECHECONNEE CREEK, Ga. From Creek, "place where deer are trapped." It flows southeast to join Big Indian Creek to form Altamaha River.

ECHOLS Co., Ga. (co. seat, Statenville). For Robert M. Echols, a Georgia officer killed (1847) in Mexico during the Mexican War.

ECONFINA RIVER, Fla. From Creek, "natural bridge." It flows southwest into Apalachee Bay.

ECONOMY, Pa. (Beaver Co.). Descriptive of industry, thrift, and adept business management.

ECORSE, Mich. (Wayne Co.). From French, *Riviere aux Ecorces,* "Bark River"; probably translated from an Indian term. An earlier name was Grand Port, for its situation on the Detroit River.

ECTOR Co., Tex. (co. seat, Odessa). For Matthew D. Ector (1822-1879), Texas legislator, general, and jurist.

EDCOUCH, Tex. (Hidalgo Co.). For County Judge Ed C. Couch, landowner and promoter of the town.

EDDY Co., N.Mex. (co. seat, Carlsbad). For Charles B. Eddy, promoter and railroad builder.

EDDY Co., N.Dak. (co. seat, New Rockford). For E. B. Eddy, banker and developer.

EDDYVILLE, Ky. (co. seat of Lyon Co.). For Thomas Eddy, a friend of Matthew LYON.

EDEN For the Garden of Eden, because of location in an area of fertile soil.
Eden, N.Y. (Erie Co.).
Eden, N.C. (Rockingham Co.). William Byrd in his survey of the North Carolina-Virginia state line called this area the "wonderful land of Eden."

Eden, Vt. (Lamoille Co.), town.
Eden Prairie, Minn. (Hennepin Co.).

EDENTON, N.C. (co. seat of Chowan Co.). For Charles Eden (1673-1722), colonial governor (1714-22).

EDGAR Co., Ill. (co. seat, Paris). For John Edgar, an early prominent citizen.

EDGARD, La. (parish seat of St. John the Baptist Parish). For Edgar Perret, postmaster; the *d* was added to distinguish the post office from one named Edgar.

EDGARTOWN For Edgar, son of the Duke of York, later James II of England.
Edgartown, Mass. (Dukes Co.). Earlier, Great Harbor.
Edgartown Great Pond, Mass.

EDGECOMBE Co., N.C. (co. seat, Tarboro). For Richard Edgecumbe, 1st Baron Edgecumbe (1680-1758), English statesman. Spelling is now accepted as Edgecombe.

EDGEFIELD Said to be so named because it was situated near an Indian battlefield, and partly for Edgewood, a plantation.
Edgefield Co., S.C. (co. seat, *Edgefield*).
Edgefield, S.C. (co. seat of *Edgefield* Co.).

EDGERTON, Wis. (Rock Co.). For Benjamin Edgerton, a railway official.

EDGEWATER, Colo. (Denver Co.). Descriptive; it borders on a lake.

EDGEWOOD Descriptive.
Edgewood, Ky. (Kenton Co.).
Edgewood, Md. (Harford Co.).
Edgewood, Ohio (Ashtabula Co.).
Edgewood, Pa. (Northumberland).

EDINA A name derived from Edinburgh, a Scottish city from which the settlers came.
Edina, Minn. (Hennepin Co.). For the Edina flour mill, in turn for the Scottish city.
Edina, Mo. (co. seat of Knox Co.).

EDINBORO, Pa. (Erie Co.). For Edinburgh, Scotland.

EDINBURG For Edinburgh, Scotland.
Edinburg, Ind. (Johnson Co.).
Edinburg, Tex. (co. seat of Hidalgo Co.). For the birthplace of an early settler.

EDISON, Thomas Alva (1847-1931), electrical engineer and inventor. He sold an electrical engineering consultation business (1870) and with the profits set up his own shop with assistants to devote themselves to improvements in telegraphy. Among his many inventions are a resonator for analyzing sound waves (1875), the carbon telephone transmitter (1876), and the phonograph (1877). In 1883 he demonstrated that the incandescent lamp could be used as a valve admitting negative but not positive electricity, the "Edison effect," a discovery that made possible the vacuum tube. The "kinetoscope," an apparatus for exhibiting photographs of moving objects, was patented by Edison in 1891. He also devised a dictating machine and a mimeograph. In 1887 he moved his lab from Menlo Park to West Orange, N.J. and put in motion many commercial companies for manufacturing and selling his inventions.

These companies were consolidated as the Edison General Electric Company, later General Electric.
Edison, N.J. (Middlesex Co.).
Edison Natl. Historical Site, N.J.

EDISTO From a tribal name, meaning unknown.
Edisto Island, S.C.
Edisto River, S.C. Formed by N and S Branches, flows SE, dividing into N and S Rivers just before emptying into the Atlantic Ocean.
Edisto Island, S.C. (Charleston Co.).

EDMOND, Okla. (Oklahoma Co.). For a Santa Fe railroad engineer who maintained a fueling station, or for a rancher, Eddy B. Townsend.

EDMONSON Co., Ky. (co. seat, Brownsville). For John Edmonson, an officer killed (1813) at River Basin, Mich. in an

Edinburgh, also fondly known as Dunedin, is the historic capital of Scotland. Possibly its most famous landmark is ancient Edinburgh Castle. [*Courtesy of Marion Urban*]

engagement between Americans and a body of British and Indians.

EDMONTON, Alta., provincial capital. For Fort Edmonton, built in 1795 by George Sutherland of the Hudson's Bay Company, whose clerk, John Prudens, was from Edmonton, England (now a part of Greater London). The original fort, on the North Saskatchewan River, twenty miles downstream of the present city, was destroyed in 1807. A new fort was built in 1808 on the site of the present city.

EDMONTON, Ky. (co. seat of Metcalfe Co.). For Edmund Rogers, a governor of Kentucky Territory.

EDMUNDS Co., S.Dak. (co. seat, Ipswich). For Newton Edmunds (1819-1908), governor of Dakota Territory (1863-66).

EDMUNDSTON, N.B. (co. seat of Madawaska Co.). For Sir Edmund Head, governor of New Brunswick at the time the town was named.

EDNA, Tex. (co. seat of Jackson Co.). For Edna H. Telferner, daughter of Count Joseph Telferner, a native of Italy who helped built the Texas-New Orleans railroad, which served this section.

EDWARD For Prince Edward Augustus, Duke of Kent (1767-1820), fourth son of George III of England and father of Queen Victoria. Because he had displayed an interest in Charlottetown's fortifications, the province was named for him in 1799. An earlier name was Ile St. Jean.
Prince Edward Island, Canadian province. Settled: 1719. British colony: 1758. Entered confederation: 1873. Cap: Charlottetown. Flower: Lady's slipper.
Prince Edward Co., Ont. (co. seat, Picton).

EDWARDS Co., Kan. (co. seat, Kinsley). For W. C. and R. E. Edwards, prominent early settlers.

EDWARDS, Ninian (1775-1833), Illinois statesman, governor (1826-30) of Illinois Territory.
Edwards Co., Ill. (co. seat, Albion).
Edwards River, Ill.
Edwardsville, Ill. (co. seat of Madison Co.).

EDWARDSVILLE, Pa. (Luzerne Co.). For Daniel Edwards (?-1901), a Welshman who was superintendent of the Kingston Coal Company from 1868 until his death. He was responsible for much of the industrial growth in the area.

EEK RIVER, Alaska. From Eskimo, meaning unknown. It flows northwest to join Eenayarak River to form Kuskokwim River.

EEL For the fish.
Eel Point, Mass., on Nantucket Island.
Eel River, Calif. Flows SW and NW into the Pacific Ocean. For the many eels obtained by explorers from the Indians.
Eel River, Ind. Flows into W. Fork of White R.

EFFIGY MOUNDS NATL. MONUMENT, Iowa. For the Indian burial mounds, which date back at least 1,000 years and contain bear and bird effigies in alignment.

EFFINGHAM Probably for Effingham Nichols, a railroad promoter, or possibly for Thomas Howard, Earl of Effingham, an English officer who was pro-colonist.
Effingham Co., Ill. (co. seat, *Effingham*).
Effingham, Ill. (co. seat of *Effingham* Co.).

EFFINGHAM Co., Ga. (co. seat, Springfield). Probably for Thomas Howard, Earl of Effingham, an English officer who was pro-colonist.

EGAN RANGE, Nev. For Howard E. Egan, mail service agent.

EGG From Dutch, usually related to the finding of eggs or the nesting of seagulls and other sea fowl.
Egg Harbor City, N.J. (Atlantic Co.).
Egg Island Point, N.J., extends into Delaware Bay. No island is there.
Great Egg Harbor, N.J.
Great Egg Harbor Inlet, N.J., water passage from Atlantic Ocean into Great Egg Harbor.
Great Egg Harbor River, N.J. Flows SE into Great Egg Harbor.
Little Egg Harbor, N.J.
Little Egg Inlet, N.J., water passage into Great Bay.

EGYPT, Lake of, Ill. The rich delta area of southern Illinois is known as Egypt and a major city is named CAIRO. The reason for the naming is not known, but it is certainly through analogy with the Arabic country and the Nile River.

EIGHT MILE BROOK, Conn. Descriptive. Flows south into Housatonic River.

EKALAKA, Mont. (co. seat of Carter Co.). For Ijkalaka, a Sioux woman who lived on the site. She married a local settler, David Harrison Russell, and is said to have been a niece of Chief Sitting Bull.

ELBA, Ala. (a co. seat of Coffee Co.). For the island of Elba, the place of imprisonment of Napoleon Bonaparte. The name was drawn from a hat after being submitted by John B. Simmons. An earlier name was Bridgeville.

ELBERT, Samuel, American Revolutionary hero.
Elbert Co., Ga. (co. seat, *Elberton*).
Elberton, Ga. (co. seat of Elbert Co.).

ELBERT, Samuel H. (1833-1907), Colorado jurist and territorial governor (1873-74).
Elbert Co., Colo. (co. seat, Kiowa).
Elbert, Mount, Colo.

ELBOW LAKE, Minn. (co. seat of Grant Co.). For a nearby lake; descriptive of its shape.

EL CAJON, Calif. (San Diego Co.). From Spanish, "the box," for a city in a valley.

EL CAMPO, Tex. (Wharton Co.). From Spanish, "the camp."

EL CENTRO, Calif. (co. seat of Imperial Co.). From Spanish, "the center," for its central location in the county.

EL CERRITO, Calif. (Contra Costa Co.). From Spanish, "the little hill," located at the south end of the city.

EL CUERVO BUTTE, N.Mex. From Spanish, "the crow."

EL DIENTE, Colo. From Spanish, "the tooth," descriptive of the shape of the peak.

ELDORA, Iowa (co. seat of Hardin Co.). For Eldora Edgington, deceased infant of Mrs. Samuel Edgington. An earlier name was Eldorado, for the discovery (1851) of gold along the Iowa River.

EL DORADO From Spanish, "the gilded" or "the golden," originally a legendary chief and city thought to be in South America. The name may refer to gold, rich soil, or other attributes, some noted below.
El Dorado Co., Calif. (co. seat, Placerville). Here the name took on real significance when gold was discovered in 1848.
El Dorado, Ark. (co. seat of Union Co.). The first settler, Matthew F. Rainey, may have so named it for his good fortune in finding an end to his journey from New Orleans. Another version is that settlers from the East had a favorite expression, "Are you looking for your El Dorado?"
Eldorado, Ill. (Saline Co.). Earlier, Elderreed, for Elder and Reed, founders.
El Dorado, Kan. (co. seat of Butler Co.).
Eldorado, Tex. (co. seat of Schleicher Co.).
Eldorado Natl. Forest, Calif.
Eldorado Pass., Ore. Named in the 1860s during the gold rush.

ELECTRA, Tex. (Wichita Co.). For Electra Waggoner, daughter of W. T. Waggoner, landowner.

ELECTRIC PEAK, Mont. So named because of an incident in which a climbing party "felt electricity" during a storm in 1872.

EL ENCANTO HEIGHTS, Calif. (San Diego Co.). Probably promotional, from Spanish *encanto*, "charm" or "fascination."

ELENORE, Mount, Utah. From a woman's first name.

ELEPHANT For a resemblance to the animal, usually in reference to mountains.
Elephant Butte, N.Mex.
Elephant Mountain, Me.
Elephant Back (peak), Wyo., in Yellowstone Natl. Park.
Elephant Butte Reservoir and Dam, N.Mex. On the Rio Grande.

ELEVEN POINT RIVER, Mo.-Ark. Named by riverboat pilots or river travelers for a measure of distance, as indicated by points of land. It flows east and south into Spring River.

ELGIN For a Scots hymn tune, "Elgin"; named by James T. Gifford, a founder, a devout Congregationalist; or it may be for Elgin, Scotland, or for a Lord Elgin, a title in Scotland.
Elgin, Ill. (Kane and Cook Cos.).
South Elgin, Ill. (Kane Co.).

ELGIN, James Bruce, 8th Earl of Elgin, governor general of Canada (1847-54).
Elgin Co., Ont. (co. seat, St. Thomas).
Elgin, N.B. (Albert Co.).
Elgin, Ont. (Leeds Co.).

ELGIN, Tex. (Bastrop Co.). For Robert M. Elgin, civil engineer who surveyed the route for the Southern Pacific railroad through the town. Another source says his name was James W. Elgin.

ELIOT, Me. (York Co.), town. For Robert Eliot, son of a member of the Provincial Council of New Hampshire.

ELIZABETH I (1533-1603), queen of England (1558-1603), daughter of Henry VIII and Anne Boleyn.
Elizabethtown, Ill. (co. seat of Hardin Co.).
Elizabethtown, N.C. (co. seat of Bladen Co.). Or for the fiancee of the owner of the land.

ELIZABETH, N.J. (co. seat of Union Co.). For Lady Elizabeth, wife of Sir George Carteret, who shared a royal grant that gave him much of New England and New York and all of what is now New Jersey.

ELIZABETH, W.Va. (co. seat of Wirt Co.). For Elizabeth W. Beauchamp, wife of the founder.

ELIZABETH CITY, N.C. (co. seat of Pasquotank Co.). For Elizabeth Tooley, wife of the owner of the land.

ELIZABETH ISLANDS, Mass., between Buzzards Bay and Vineyard Sound, named for Princess Elizabeth (1596-1662), daughter of James I of England.

ELIZABETH MOUNTAIN, Utah. For Elizabeth Emily Williams, a member of the Fuelling family, landowners in the area.

ELIZABETHTON, Tenn. (co. seat of Carter Co.). For Elizabeth Carter (1765-1784), wife of Landon CARTER.

ELIZABETHTOWN see also ELIZABETH I.

ELIZABETHTOWN, Ky. (co. seat of Hardin Co.). For Elizabeth Hynes, wife of Col. Andrew Hynes, one of the founders.

ELIZABETHTOWN, N.Y. (co. seat of Essex Co.). For two women with the same name, Elizabeth Gilliland, wife and daughter of William Gilliland (1734-1796), pioneer settler in the Champlain Valley.

ELIZABETHTOWN, Pa. (Lancaster Co.). Origin uncertain: probably for Elizabeth Reeby, wife of Michael Reeby, who sold the first building lots in 1795.

ELK For the large North American deer, the elk or wapiti.
Elk Co., Kan. (co. seat, Howard). For the river.
Elk Co., Pa. (co. seat, Ridgeway).
Elk Creek, Pa.
Elk Creek, S.Dak.
Elk Hill, Pa.
Elk Lake, Mich.
Elk Mountain, Okla.
Elk Mountain, Wyo.
Elk River, Colo.
Elk River, Kan.
Elk River, Mich.
Elk River, Minn. Flows generally SE to the Mississippi R.
Elk River, Tenn.-Ala. Flows generally SW into the Tennessee R.
Elk River, W.Va.
Elk City, Okla. (Beckham Co.).
Elk Grove, Calif. (Sacramento Co.). Probably promotional.
Elk Grove, Ill. (Cook Co.). Probably promotional.
Elk Point, S.Dak. (co. seat of Union Co.). For a point on the Missouri R.; named (1804) by members of the Lewis and Clark Expedition for elk "sign" found there.
Elk River, Minn. (co. seat of Sherburne Co.). For the river.

ELKADER, Iowa (co. seat of Clayton Co.). For Abd-el-kader, an Algerian revolutionary leader against the French. The name reflects the tendency of Americans in the early and mid 1800s to honor revolutionary leaders in other countries.

ELKHART Probably a translation of either a Potawatomi or a Kickapoo term for "elk's heart." The French used the nàme *Coeur de Cerf*," "heart of stag," while the early English spelling was *Elksheart*.

Elkhart Co., Ind. (co. seat, Goshen).

Elkhart, Ind. (*Elkhart* Co.).

Elkhart, Kan. (co. seat of Morton Co.). For *Elkhart*, Ind.

ELKHORN For elk horns found in the area.

Elkhorn, Wis. (co. seat of Walworth Co.).

Elkhorn Creek, Ill. Flows S and SW into Rock R.

Elkhorn Creek, Ky. Flows NNW into Kentucky R.

Elkhorn River, Neb. Flows SE into Platte R. Translated from French *corne de cerf*, "horn of an elk," descriptive of the shape of the two upper branches of the river.

Elkhorn Ranch Site, N.Dak. Site of the ranch owned by President Theodore Roosevelt, who ranched there (1883-1887).

ELKIN, N.C. (Surry Co.). For a creek that flows through the town, in turn for an early settler.

ELKINS, W.Va. (co. seat of Randolph Co.). For Stephen Benton Elkins (1841-1911), Civil War veteran, attorney general of the Territory of New Mexico, and U.S. representative (1873-77). He was secretary of war (1891-93) under Benjamin Harrison and U.S. senator from West Virginia (1895-1911).

ELKO From *elk* plus *-o*; so named by Charles Crocker, a railway official.

Elko Co., Nev. (co. seat, *Elko*).

Elko, Nev. (co. seat of *Elko* Co.).

ELK MOUNTAIN, Wyo. For Chief Standing Elk, Sioux warrior. Also claimed for the animal.

ELKTON, Ky. (co. seat of Todd Co.). For Elk Fork Creek, a prong of the Red River, which runs through the county.

ELKTON, Md. (co. seat of Cecil Co.). For an Elk River, so named (1608) by John Smith, either because of the shape of the river, like antlers, or because he saw what he thought to be elk on the river banks. An earlier name was Head of Elk.

ELLAVILLE, Ga. (co. seat of Schley Co.). For Ella, eldest daughter of Robert Burton, founder.

ELLEN, Mount, Utah. For Ellen Powell, wife of Leslie Powell.

ELLEN, Mount, Vt. For an Ellen, a popular forename in the nineteenth century.

ELLENBURG, N.Y. (Clinton Co.). For Ellen Murray, in gratitude for the kindness of the Murray family to early settlers.

ELLENDALE, N.Dak. (co. seat of Dickey Co.). For Ellen Dale Merrill, wife of a railway official.

ELLENSBURG, Wash. (co. seat of Kittitas Co.). For Mary Ellen Shoudy, wife of the town founder.

ELLICOTT CITY, Md. (co. seat of Howard Co.). For the Ellicott brothers, Andrew and John, who settled the area in 1772 and built grist mills. An earlier name was Ellicott's Mills.

ELLICOTTVILLE, N.Y. (Cattaraugas Co.). For Joseph Ellicott (1760-1826), surveyor and agent for the Holland Land Company, which had large holdings in the area.

ELLIJAY, Ga. (co. seat of Gilmer Co.). From Cherokee *elatsayyi*, "earth is green here" or "narrow valley." The Cherokee village dates back to 1540.

ELLINGWOOD PEAK, Wyo. For Albert R. Ellingwood, a mountain climber who was the first to ascend the peak.

ELLIOT KEY, Fla. Barrier Island in Atlantic Ocean. From a personal name.

ELLIOTT Co., Ky. (co. seat, Sandy Hook). For John Milton Elliott (1820-1879), Kentucky legislator and jurist.

ELLIS For the Ellis family, prominent in Oxford Co., Me.

Ellis Pond, Me.

Ellis River, Me. Rises in *Ellis* Pond, flows generally S into Androscoggin R.

ELLIS Co., Kan. (co. seat, Hays). For George Ellis, an officer killed (1864) during the Civil War at Jenkins Ferry, Ark.

ELLIS Co., Okla. (co. seat, Arnett). For Albert H. Ellis, an Oklahoma constitutional convention delegate in 1907.

ELLIS Co., Tex. (co. seat, Waxahachie). For Richard Ellis (1781-1846), Alabama jurist and legislator.

ELLIS RIVER, N.H. For a local settler. It flows south into Saco River.

ELLISVILLE, Miss. (co. seat of Jones Co.). For Powhaten Ellis (1790-1863), attorney, jurist, U.S. senator (1825-26; 1827-32), and minister to Mexico (1839-42).

ELLISVILLE, Mo. (Ballwin Co.). For an Ellis plus -*ville.*

ELLSWORTH For Fort Ellsworth, which was named for Allen Ellsworth, an officer in the Iowa Cavalry.
Ellsworth Co., Kan. (co. seat, *Ellsworth*).
Ellsworth, Kan. (co. seat of *Ellsworth* Co.).

ELLSWORTH, Lake, Okla. For a local dweller.

ELLSWORTH, Me. (co. seat of Hancock Co.). For Oliver Ellsworth, Connecticut delegate to the Constitutional Convention in Philadelphia.

ELLSWORTH, Wis. (co. seat of Pierce Co.). For Elmer Ephraim Ellsworth (1837-1861), one of the first officers killed during the Civil War. He commanded a regiment trained in French Zouave tactics and wearing the Zouave uniform.

ELLWOOD CITY, Pa. (Beaver Co.). For Col. I. L. Ellwood, one of the earliest manufacturers of wire fencing. He was a chief stockholder in the Pittsburgh Company.

ELMA, N.Y. (Erie Co.). For a large elm tree in the town.

ELM For the tree.
Elm Lake, S.Dak.
Elm River, S.Dak.
Elm Grove, Wis. (Waukesha Co.).

ELMHURST, Ill. (Du Page Co.). From *elm* plus *hurst,* "elm grove"; named by an early settler.

ELMIRA For Elmira Teall, daughter of a friend of Assemblyman Emmanuel Coryell.
Elmira, N.Y. (co. seat of Chemung Co.). Earlier, Newtown.
Elmira Heights (Chemung Co.).
Elmira Heights North (Chemung Co.).
West Elmira (Chemung Co.).

EL MIRAGE, Ariz. (Maricopa Co.). From Spanish, "the illusion," for the desert area.

EL MONTE From Spanish, "the thicket" or "the mountain"; descriptive.
El Monte, Calif. (Los Angeles Co.). An earlier name was Lexington.
South El Monte, Calif. (Los Angeles Co.).

ELMORE Co., Ala. (co. seat, Wetumpka). For John Archer Elmore, a pioneer.

ELMORE Co., Idaho (co. seat, Mountain Home). For the Ida Elmore Quartz Mine, which throve during the gold rush of the 1860s.

EL MORRO NATL. MONUMENT, N.Mex. From Spanish, "bluff." Established in 1906 to preserve "Inscription Rock," on which more than 500 separate carvings appear.

ELMWOOD Descriptive and probably promotional.
Elmwood Park, Ill. (Cook Co.).
Elmwood Place, Ohio (Hamilton Co.).

ELOY, Ariz. (Pinal Co.). Origin uncertain, but said to be the Biblical *eloi,* "my God" (Mark 15:34).

EL PASO From Spanish, "the pass" when applied to a mountainous place, "the ford" when applied to a place on a river.
El Paso Co., Colo. (co. seat, Colorado Springs).
El Paso Co., Tex. (co. seat, *El Paso*).
El Paso, Tex. (co. seat of *El Paso* Co.). For a major ford of the Rio Grande. Also said to be named because early discoverers found the valley by going through a pass in the mountains.

EL PASO DE ROBLES, Calif. (San Luis Obispo Co.). From Spanish, "the passage through the oaks."

EL RENO, Okla. (co. seat of Canadian Co.). For Jesse L. Reno (1823-1862), Union general killed at the Battle of Antietam.

EL RIO, Calif. (Ventura Co.). From Spanish, "the river."

ELSA, Tex. (Hidalgo Co.). For Mrs. Elsa George, an early settler.

EL SEGUNDO, Calif. (Los Angeles Co.). Named by Colonel Rheem of the Standard Oil Company from Spanish, "the second," that is, the company's second California refinery.

ELSINORE, Calif. (Riverside Co.). Named by Donald Graham for the Danish castle in Shakespeare's *Hamlet.*

ELSMERE, Ky. (Kenton Co.). Reason for name unknown, either promotional or for a New York town.

EL TORO From Spanish, "the bull."
El Toro, Calif. (Orange Co.).
El Toro`Station,* Calif. (Orange Co.).

ELWHA RIVER, Wash. From Indian, possibly "elk." It flows north into Juan de Fuca Strait.

ELWOOD, Ind. (Madison Co.). For Elwood Frazier, son of Jesse B. Frazier, one of the founders. Earlier names were Duck Creek and Quincy.

ELWOOD, Neb. (co. seat of Gosper Co.). For Elwood Thomas, a local farmer.

ELY, Minn. (St. Louis Co.). For Arthur Ely, who helped finance the construction of the Duluth and Iron Range railroad, completed in 1888, or possibly for Edmund Franklin Ely (1809-1882), a missionary to the Ojibways.

ELY, Nev. (co. seat of White Pine Co.). For either John H. Ely or Smith Ely, both local mine owners and developers.

ELYRIA, Ohio (Lorain Co.). For Herman Ely (1775-1852), merchant, landowner, and founder.

EMANUEL Co., Ga. (co. seat, Swainsboro). For David Emanuel (c.1742-1803), American Revolutionary soldier, legislator, and governor (1801).

EMBARRASS From French, "obstacle." The name has taken on derogatory and humorous connotations in English.
Embarrass, Wis. (Waupaca Co.).

Embarrass River, Ill. Flows generally S into Wabash R.
Embarrass River, Wis.

EMBDEN LAKE, Me. For Emden, Germany. The *b* was inserted by an early scribe.

EMERY Co., Utah (co. seat, Castle Dale). For George Emery, a territorial governor (1875-80).

EMERYVILLE, Calif. (Alameda Co.). For Joseph S. Emery, a settler from New Hampshire, landowner, and stonemason.

EMINENCE, Mo. (co. seat of Shannon Co.). Although the present town does not stand on a hill or high point, the original Eminence, from which the name was transferred, was situated on a bluff.

EMMAUS, Pa. (Lehigh Co.). For Emmaus in Palestine. The Hebrew word means "hot springs."

EMMET, Robert W. (1778-1803), Irish patriot executed by the English for his revolutionary activities. Places were named for him during a time when leaders of rebellions were honored by Americans.
Emmet Co., Iowa (co. seat, Estherville).
Emmet Co., Mich. (co. seat, Petoskey).
Emmetsburg, Iowa (co. seat of Palo Alto Co.).

EMMETT, Idaho (co. seat of Gem Co.). For the son of Thomas D. Cahalan, first postmaster, or possibly for a nearby mine.

EMMONS, Mount, N.Y. For Ebenezer Emmons (1799-1863), professor at Williams College and geologist in charge of the exploration of the Adirondack region. He led the first expedition (1837) up to Mt. MARCY, which he named. He also contributed the name ADIRONDACK to the area mountain range.

EMMONS, Mount, Utah, in the Uinta Mtns. For S. F. Emmons, a geologist.

EMMONS Co., N.Dak. (co. seat, Linton). For James A. Emmons, steamboat captain, businessman, and promoter.

EMORY For Emory RAINS.
Emory, Tex. (co. seat of Rains Co.).
Emory Peak, Tex.

EMORY RIVER, Tenn. For a local citizen. It flows southeast into Watts Bar Lake.

EMPORIA From Latin, "center of trade," either the feminine or plural form of *Emporium.*
Emporia, Kan. (co. seat of Lyon Co.).
Emporia, Va. (co. seat of Greensville Co.).

EMPORIUM, Pa. (co. seat of Cameron Co.). From Latin, "center of trade."

ENCINITAS, Calif. (San Diego Co.). From Spanish, "little oaks."

ENDERS RESERVOIR, Neb. For a rancher.

ENDICOTT, N.Y. (Broome Co.). For Henry B. Endicott, a partner in the Endicott-Johnson leather business.

ENDICOTT MOUNTAINS, Alaska. For William Crowninshield Endicott (1826-1900), secretary of war (1885-89) under Cleveland.

ENDLESS LAKE, Me. So named because crossing it seemed to take forever.

ENDWELL, N.Y. (Broome Co.). For a shoe manufactured by the Endicott-Johnson corporation.

ENFIELD, Conn. (Hartford Co.), town. For Enfield, Middlesex, England.

ENGLAND, Ark. (Lonoke Co.). For John C. and J. E. England, prominent businessmen in Arkansas.

ENGLAND See NEW ENGLAND.

ENGLEWOOD Promotional, although it exists as a name in England. For an *Englewood* in Illinois.
Englewood, Colo. (Arapahoe Co.).
Englewood, N.J. (Bergen Co.).
Englewood Cliffs, N.J. (Bergen Co.).
Englewood Park, Mich. (Calhoun Co.).

ENGLEWOOD, Ohio (Montgomery Co.). Possibly named by an early settler for a place mentioned in a novel he was reading at the time, or for an Engle family prominent in the community.

ENGLISH, Ind. (co. seat of Crawford Co.). For William Hayden English (1822-1896), jurist, banker, legislator, U.S. representative (1853-61), and a candidate for vice-president in 1886.

ENGLISHMAN BAY, Me. Probably named for an Englishman who lived in the area.

ENID, Okla. (co. seat of Garfield Co.). For a character in *Idylls of the King*, by Lord Tennyson.

ENID LAKE, Miss. From a woman's first name.

ENNIS, Tex. (Ellis Co.). For Cornelius Ennis, an officer of the Houston and Texas Central railroad and also a newspaper publisher.

ENOREE For an Indian tribe that lived along the banks of the river.
Enoree, S.C. (Spartanburg Co.).
Enoree River, S.C. Flows SE into Broad R.

ENO RIVER, N.C. Believed to be for an Indian tribe of the Siouan linguistic stock; meaning of name uncertain. It flows southeast to join Flat River to form Neuse River.

ENTERPRISE For the enterprising spirit of the people.
Enterprise, Ala. (a co. seat of Coffee Co.).
Enterprise, Calif. (Shasta Co.).
Enterprise, Ore. (co. seat of Wallowa Co.).

ENTIAT RIVER, Wash. From Indian, "rapid water." It flows southeast into Columbia River.

EPHRATA From the Old Testament, mentioned as a second name or epithet for Bethlehem. From Hebrew, "fruitful."
Ephrata, Pa. (Lancaster Co.).
Ephrata, Wash. (co. seat of Grant Co.).

EQUINOX MOUNTAIN, Vt. Origin uncertain, but may be a folk etymologized Indian name.

ERATH Co., Tex. (co. seat, Stephenville). For George Bernard Erath (1813-1891), Texas officer, Ranger, and legislator.

ERIE For an Indian tribe of Iroquoian linguistic stock, located along the southern shore of Lake Erie from western New York to

The earliest major American engineering achievement was the building of the Erie Canal connecting the Mohawk River with Lake Erie. Completed in 1825, the canal is shown in the process of excavation near Lockport, New York. [*Lithograph by Anthony Imbert. Metropolitan Museum of Art*]

northern Ohio. Their name, *erie, erike,* or *eriga,* is usually interpreted as "long tail," in reference to the wildcat or panther, which has resulted in the tribe being called the Cat Nation. After a bloody war with the Iroquois, who had access to firearms, the tribe was assimilated into the conquerors, except for some members who escaped to what is now Oklahoma.

Erie Co., N.Y. (co. seat, Buffalo).

Erie Co., Ohio (co. seat, Sandusky).

Erie Co., Pa. (co. seat, *Erie*).

Erie, Kan. (co. seat of Neosho Co.). Either for a lake nearby or for *Erie,* Pa.

Erie, Pa. (co. seat of *Erie* Co.).

Erie Canal, N.Y., from Lake *Erie* to the Hudson R. Officially, New York State Barge Canal.

Erie, Lake, N.Y.-Ont.-Pa.-Ohio. Largest of the Great Lakes.

Erieville, N.Y. (Madison Co.), town.

Fort Erie, Ont. (Welland Co.). For the lake.

ERIN For Ireland.

Erin, N.Y. (Chemung Co.), town. Named by an Irish settler.

Erin, Tenn. (co. seat of Houston Co.).

ERLANGER, Ky. (Kenton Co.). For Baron Frederic d'Erlanger, a land speculator, head of a London land syndicate that invested in southern Kentucky.

ERLING, Lake, Ark. For a local settler.

ERWIN, N.C. (Harnett Co.). For the Erwin Cotton Mills.

ESCALANTE For Fray Francisco Silvestre de Escalante, leader of a Spanish expedition in 1776.

Escalante, Utah (Garfield Co.).

Escalante Desert, Utah.

Escalante River, Utah. Rises from several tributaries, flows SE into Colorado R.

ESCAMBIA A Spanish transliteration of an Indian word, either Choctaw or Chickasaw, possibly meaning "killer," "rain maker," "matricide," or others. (Spanish *cambiar*, "to exchange," "trade," or "barter," has only a similarity in sound.) Other meanings are also noted: "a cane-cutting place," or "to be (hide?) in the cane." See also TUSCUMBIA.

Escambia Co., Ala. (co. seat, Brewton).

Escambia Co., Fla. (co. seat, Pensacola).

Escambia River, Ala.-Fla.

ESCANABA From Ojibway, "flat rock," descriptive of the river bed.

Escanaba, Mich. (co. seat of Delta Co.).

Escanaba River, Mich. Flows into Green Bay.

ESCATAWPA RIVER, Miss.-Ala. From Choctaw, "cane-there-cut." It flows into Piscagoula Bay.

ESCONDIDO, Calif. (San Diego Co.). From Spanish, "hidden"; named for a nearby creek.

ESCUDILLA MOUNT, Ariz. From Spanish, "bowl," for the shape of the top of the mountain.

ESMERALDA Co., Nev. (co. seat, Goldfield). From Spanish "emerald," for the stones found there.

ESOPUS, N.Y. (Ulster Co.), town. For the Esopus Indians.

ESPANOLA From Spanish, "Spanish lady," or a variation of *Hispaniola*, "New Spain."

Espanola, N.Mex. (Rio Arriba Co.).

Espanola, Ont. (Sudbury Co.).

ESPENBERG, Cape. Alaska, on Seward Peninsula. Named in 1816 for Karl Espenberg, a surgeon.

ESSEX For the county of Essex, England.

Essex Co., Mass. (co. seat, Salem).

Essex Co., N.J. (co. seat, Newark).

Essex Co., N.Y. (co. seat, Elizabethtown).

Essex Co., Ont. (co. seat, Windsor).

Essex Co., Vt. (co. seat, Guildhall).

Essex Co., Va. (co. seat, Tappahannock).

Essex, Conn. (Middlesex Co.), town.

Essex, Md. (Baltimore Co.).

Essex, Mass. (*Essex* Co.).

Essex, N.Y. (*Essex* Co.).

Essex, Vt. (Chittenden Co.), town.

Essex Junction, Vt. (Chittenden Co.).

ESSEXVILLE, Mich. (Bay Co.). For Ransom P. Essex, founder.

ESTANCIA, N.Mex. (co. seat of Torrance Co.). From Spanish, "large estate," "cattle ranch," or a "resting place," in this case for a stopping place near a spring.

ESTERO BAY, Calif., on Pacific Coast. From Spanish, "estuary" or "inlet."

ESTEVAN, Sask. For George *Ste*phan and Sir William *Van* Horne of the Canadian Pacific railway.

ESTES PARK, Colo. (Larimer Co.). For Joel Estes, founder.

ESTHERVILLE, Iowa (co. seat of Emmet Co.). For Esther A. Ridley, wife of one of the founders.

ESTILL Co., Ky. (co. seat, Irvine). For James Estill (1750-1792), killed fighting Indians. An early pioneer, he established Fort Estill in 1781.

ETHEL, Mount, Colo. From a woman's forename.

ETNA, Pa. (Allegheny Co.). For the volcano Etna (or Aetna) in Sicily. Earlier names were Stewartsville and Centerville.

ETOLIN STRAIT, Alaska. Water passage between Nunivak Island and Yukon-Kuskokwim Delta. For Capt. Adolph Karlovich Etolin, of the Imperial Russian Navy. He was governor of the Russian American colonies (1841-45).

ETOWAH For the Etowah Indian mound in Georgia; origin not clear, either Cherokee or Creek Indian, meaning "high tower," or possibly Creek, "village" or "tribe."

Etowah Co., Ala. (co. seat, Gadsden).

Etowah, Tenn. (McMinn Co.).

ETOWAH Co., Ala. (co. seat, Gadsden). For the Etowah Indian mound in Georgia;

origin not clear, either Cherokee or Creek Indian, meaning "high tower," or possibly Creek, "village" or "tribe."

ETOWA RIVER, Ga. Variant form of ETOWAH. It flows west to join Oostanaula River to form the Coosa River.

ETTA, Lake, N.Dak. From a woman's first name.

EUCLID Named by surveyors for the celebrated geometrician of Alexandria.
Euclid, Ohio (Cuyahoga Co.).
South Euclid, Ohio (Cuyahoga Co.).

EUDORA, Ark. (Chicot Co.). For Eudora James, deceased young daughter of E. C. James.

EUFAULA A Creek name transferred from a village on the banks of the Chattahooche River in Alabama; meaning unknown. In Oklahoma the name is believed to mean "they split up here and went to other places," but this may be purely fanciful.
Eufaula, Ala. (co. seat of Barbour Co.). Earlier, Irvington.
Eufaula, Okla. (co. seat of McIntosh Co.).
Eufaula Reservoir, Okla.

EUGENE, Ore. (co. seat of Lane Co.). For Eugene F. Skinner (1809-1864), pioneer and postmaster.

EULESS, Tex. (Tarrant Co.). For Elisha Adam Euless (1848-1911), first cotton-gin owner and county sheriff (1892-96).

EUNICE, N.Mex. (Lea Co.). For Eunice Carson (1889-1959), daughter of J. N. Carson, an early settler.

EUREKA From Greek, "I have found it," in reference here to having found an ideal place to settle. The name was popular among early settlers.
Eurkea Co., Nev. (co. seat, *Eureka*).
Eureka, Calif. (co. saet of Humboldt Co.). *Eureka* also became the motto used on the state seal of California.
Eureka, Ill. (co. seat of Woodford Co.).
Eureka, Kan. (co. seat of Greenwood Co.).
Eureka, Nev. (co. seat of *Eureka* Co.).
Eureka Springs, Ark. (a co. seat of Carroll Co.).

EUTAW, Ala. (co. seat of Greene Co.). For the Battle of Eutaw Springs, S.C., in the American Revolution, in which Gen. Nathanael Greene participated. See also UTAH.

EVANGELINE Parish, La. (parish seat, Ville Platte). For the heroine of Henry W. Longfellow's poem of the same name. See also ACADIA.

EVANS, Colo. (Weld Co.). For John Evans, a governor of Colorado Territory.

EVANS Co., Ga. (co. seat, Claxton). For Clement Anselm Evans, (c.1833-1911), prominent Georgia citizen, jurist, and general.

EVANS, Mount, Mont. Probably for an early explorer.

EVANS CREEK, Nev. For a local settler. It flows intermittently southwest into Humboldt River,

EVANSDALE, Iowa (Blackhawk Co.). For William T. *Evans* and *Dale* van Eman.

EVANS NOTCH NATL. FOREST, Me. Either for a family or an individual who lived in the area.

EVANSTON, Ill. (Cook Co.). For John Evans, a founder of Northwestern University. An earlier name was Ridgeville.

EVANSTON, Wyo. (co. seat of Uinta Co.). For James A. Evans, a railroad surveyor for the Union Pacific.

EVANSVILLE, Ind. (co. seat of Vanderburgh Co.). For Robert Evans, who platted the townsite.

EVANSVILLE, Wis. (Rock Co.). For a local doctor named Evans.

EVELETH, Minn. (St. Louis Co.). For a woodsman, Eveleth, but no information is available other than that he was commissioned to buy pinelands for a lumber company.

EVENING SHADE, Ark. (a co. seat of Sharp Co.). So named by William Thompson, a relative of President Polk, when he filled out an application for a post office name during the early evening hours.

Florida Everglades are sometimes described as a vast "grassy river" of marshy wetlands, laced by streams and dotted with hummocks, little hills of firm ground.

EVERTS MOUNTAIN, Wyo., in Yellowstone Natl. Park. For Truman C. Everts, member of the Washburn party of 1870.

EVERETT, Edward (1794-1865), Harvard classicist, U.S. representative (1825-35), governor of Massachusetts (1836-39), and U.S. senator (1853-54).
Everett, Mass. (Middlesex Co.).
Everett, Mount, Mass.

EVERETT, Wash. (co. seat of Snohomish Co.). For Everett Colby, son of Charles Colby, a landowner and promoter of the area.

EVERGLADES From *ever* plus *glades.* The mass of swampy land and rivers in southern Florida that comprises an area of about 1,500,000 acres.
Everglades, Fla. (co. seat of Collier Co.). For the swamp.
Everglades Natl. Park, Fla.

EVERGREEN For pine or other evergreen trees.
Evergreen, Ala. (co. seat of Conecuh Co.). The chief industry was the shipment of evergreens to Northern markets.
Evergreen Park, Ill. (Cook Co.). Promotional.

EVERMAN, Tex. (Tarrant Co.). For John W. Everman, an official of the Texas and Pacific railroad.

EVITTS Probably for an early explorer or settler.
Evitts Creek, Pa.-Md. Flows SSW into N Branch of the Potomac R.
Evitts Mountain Range, Pa.

EXCELSIOR From Latin, "ever higher."
Excelsior, Minn. (Hennepin Co.). For the Excelsior Pioneer Association, which was named for "Excelsior", a poem by Longfellow.
Excelsior Springs, Mo. (Ray and Clay Cos.).

EXCELSIOR, Minn. (Hennepin Co.). For the Excelsior Pioneer Association, which was named for "Excelsior," a poem by Longfellow. *Excelsior* in Latin means "ever higher."

EXETER For Exeter, Devonshire, England.
Exeter, Calif. (Tulare Co.). Named by D. W. Parkhurst of the Pacific Land and Improvement Company, for his home town in England.
Exeter, N.H. (co. seat of Rockingham Co.), town and village. Named by Rev. John Wheelwright, a member of the Exeter Combination, English colonizers, in 1838.
Exeter, R.I. (Washington Co.), town.
Exeter River, N.H.

ℱ

FABENS, Tex. (El Paso Co.). For George Fabens, assistant land commissioner on the Southern Pacific lines in Texas and Louisiana when the station was established.

FABIUS RIVER, Mo. Probably for a trapper. Formed by three branches, *North Fabius,* which rises in Iowa, *Middle Fabius,* and *South Fabius.* They flow generally southeast and join to form Fabius River, which then flows one mile into the Mississippi River. Earlier names were Fabiane and Ferbein.

FACTORY HILL, Wyo., in Yellowstone Natl. Park. So named because the mists around the peak were thought to resemble a factory.

FAIRBANKS, Alaska. For Charles Warren Fairbanks (1852-1918), senator from Indiana who headed a commission to settle the Alaska boundary dispute. He was vice-president (1905-09) under Theodore Roosevelt.

FAIRBORN, Ohio (Greene Co.). A combination of two neighboring villages, *Fair*field and *Osborn.*

FAIRBURN, Ga. (Fulton Co.). Said to have been named by an early postmaster, William McBride, for his home in Scotland.

FAIRBURY Another way of saying "fair city."
Fairbury, Ill. (Livingston Co.). Named by Caleb Patton, who donated half of his farm toward the site.

Fairbury, Neb. (co. seat of Jefferson Co.). For *Fairbury,* Ill.

FAIRFAX, Ala. (Chambers Co.). For the euphony of the name.

FAIRFAX, Calif. (Marin Co.). Believed to have been named for a Baron Fairfax of Cameron, Scotland (which one has not been ascertained) by Charles Snowden Fairfax (1829-1869), attorney, clerk of the state supreme court, and speaker of the California Assembly.

FAIRFAX, Ohio (Hamilton Co.). From a personal name, with the added promotional connotation.

FAIRFAX, Thomas, 6th Baron Fairfax of Cameron (1692-1780), English nobleman who inherited from his maternal grandfather, Lord Thomas Culpeper, the "Fairfax Proprietary," vast estates between the Rapahannock and Potomac rivers in northern Virginia. After a brief visit (1735-37), he settled permanently in Virginia (1747), the colonies' only resident peer. Although a friend of George Washington, he remained loyal to England during the American Revolution.
Fairfax Co., Va. (co. seat, *Fairfax*).
Fairfax, Va. (co. seat of *Fairfax* Co.). Earlier, Providence.

FAIRCHILD, Wis. (co. seat of Eau Clair Co.). For Lucius Fairchild, governor (1866-72).

FAIRFIELD Descriptive of a beautiful or clear place.

Fairfield Co., Conn. (co. seat, Bridgeport).
Fairfield Co., Ohio (co. seat, Lancaster).
Fairfield Co., S.C. (co. seat, Winnsboro).
Fairfield, Ala. (Jefferson Co.).
Fairfield, Calif. (co. seat of Solano Co.).
Named by Captain Robert H. Waterman
(1808-1884), for *Fairfield*, Conn., his
former home.
Fairfield, Conn. (Fairfield Co.), town.
Earlier, Uncoway or Unquowa.
Fairfield, Idaho (co. seat of Camas Co.).
Fairfield, Ill. (co. seat of Wayne Co.).
Fairfield, Iowa (co. seat of Jefferson Co.).
The name was chosen by a Mrs. Bon-
nifield, whose name also means "fair
field."
Fairfield, Me. (Somerset Co.), town and
village.
Fairfield, Ohio (Butler Co.).
Fairfield, Tex. (co. seat of Freestone Co.).

FAIRHAVEN Descriptive.
Fairhaven, Mass. (Bristol Co.). For its
harbor, on Buzzard's Bay at the mouth of
the Acushnet R.
Fair Haven, Vt. (Rutland Co.), town.

FAIRHOPE, Ala. (Baldwin Co.). Named by
single-tax colonists for the "fair hopes" of
their new idea.

FAIRLAWN Descriptive and promotional.
Fair Lawn, N.J. (Bergen Co.).
Fairlawn, Ohio (Summit Co.).

FAIRMONT Descriptive and promotional.
Fairmont, Minn. (co. seat of Martin Co.).
Earlier, Fair Mount, for the elevated area
above the nearby lakes.
Fairmont, N.C. (Robeson Co.).
Fairmont, W.Va. (co. seat of Marion Co.).
Probably a contraction of *Fair Mountain.*
The two parts of the city (*East Fairmont*
and *West Fairmont*) were originally
Palatine and Middletown.
Fairmont City, Ill. (Vermilion Co.).

FAIRMOUNT, Ind. (Grant Co.). For
Fairmount Park, in Philadelphia, Pa. The
community's first settlers were Quakers,
and it was believed that Fairmount Park,
which contains a number of colonial houses,
had been a Quaker community.

FAIR OAKS Named by Gen. O. O.
Howard, whose brother, Gen. C. H.

Howard, a land promoter of the Howard
Wilson Company had lost an arm during one
of the Civil War battles at Fair Oaks, Va.
Fair Oaks, Calif. (Sacramento Co.).
North Fair Oaks, Calif. (Sacramento Co.).

FAIR PLAIN, Mich. (Berrien Co.).
Descriptive. Also spelled *Fairplain.*

FAIRPLAY, Colo. (co. seat of Park Co.).
For an honest citizenship in contrast to
reputedly dishonest neighbors in other
villages.

FAIRPORT Descriptive.
Fairport, N.Y. (Monroe Co.). On the New
York State Barge Canal, or Erie Canal.
Fairport, Ohio (Lake Co.). Has a harbor on
Lake Erie.

FAIRVIEW Descriptive.
Fairview, N.J. (Bergen Co.).
Fairview, N.Y. (Dutchess Co.).
Fairview, Okla. (co. seat of Major Co.).
Named by Henry Bower, merchant, for
the approach to the city, "It's a fair view
to Fairview."
Fairview Mountain, Colo.
Fairview-Ferndale, Pa. (Northumberland
Co.). For the view from a hillside and for
the presence of ferns.
Fairview Heights, Ill. (St. Clair Co.).
Promotional.
Fairview Park, Ohio (Cuyahoga Co.).
Promotional.

FAIRWEATHER Named by Capt. James
Cook in 1778, presumably because of the
good weather encountered at the time.
Fairweather, Cape, Alaska.
Fairweather, Mount, Alaska.

FALCON HEIGHTS, Minn. (Ramsey Co.).
Promotional.

FALCON LAKE, Tex.-Mexico. For the
bird.

FALFURRIAS, Tex. (co. seat of Brooks
Co.). There are a variety of explanations for
the origin of this name, one being that the
name means "mouth of the furies," so
called because of the town's location.
Another is that the name is a variation of
Falduras, used to describe a man who once
lived in the area and wore a type of skirt
known as a *falduras*. A third version, perhaps

"Falls" is commonly used as a name on the American landscape — Falls Co., Texas; Fall River, Massachusetts; or Falls Village, Connecticut. Above are the Kettle Falls on the Columbia River in Washington; Niagara Falls (right); and Ribbon Falls in Yosemite Park, California. [*New York Public Library*]

best substantiated, is that the word is derived from French *fanfarron*, "fanfare," which apparently also means "a swaggerer or blusterer," or "showy." The name *Falfurrias* was evidently given to an early settler who was "full of fury."

FALLBROOK, Calif. (San Diego Co.). For a village in Pennsylvania.

FALLON Co., Mont. (co. seat, Baker). For Benjamin O'Fallon, an Indian agent and army officer, and a relative of the explorer William Clark.

FALLON, Nev. (co. seat of Churchill Co.). For Michael Fallon, a rancher.

FALL RIVER Probably translated from the Indian name.
Fall River Co., S.Dak. For the river.
Fall River, Mass. (a co. seat of Bristol Co.). For the river.
Fall River, Kan. Flows generally SE to the Verdigris R.
Fall River, Mass. Flows through *Fall River*, Mass.; called *quequechan*, "falling water," by the Indians.
Fall River, S.Dak. Flows into the Cheyenne R. A warm stream throughout the year, it has become a tourist attraction.
Fall River Reservoir, Kan.

FALLS Co., Tex. (co. seat, Marlin). For the rapids on the Brazos River.

FALLS CITY, Neb. (co. seat of Richardson Co.). For falls in the Great Nemaha River.

FALLS RIVER, Vt.-Mass. For falls on the river. Flows south into the Connecticut River.

FALMOUTH For Falmouth, Cornwall, England.
East Falmouth, Mass. (Barnstable Co.).
Falmouth, Ky. (co. seat of Pendleton Co.). For a Falmouth in Virginia.
Falmouth, Me. (Cumberland Co.), town.
Falmouth, Mass. (Barnstable Co.), town and village.

FALSE DE TOUR CHANNEL, Mich.-Ont. So named because this channel is the wrong one to follow to enter Lake Superior from Lake Huron. *De Tour* is from French, "go around."

FANNIN, James Walker (1809-1836), a Georgia soldier killed in action in the Texas War of Independence.
Fannin Co., Ga. (co. seat, Blue Ridge).
Fannin Co., Tex. (co. seat, Bonham).

FANWOOD, N.J. (Union Co.). For Fanny, wife of a railroad president.

FARGO For William George Fargo (1818-1881), a director of the Northern Pacific railroad and founder of the Wells-Fargo Express.
Fargo, N.Dak. (co. seat of Cass Co.).
West Fargo, N.Dak. (Cass Co.).

FARIBAULT, Jean Baptiste (1774-1860), a fur trader in the Northwest Territory who had great influence with the Sioux.
Faribault Co., Minn. (co. seat, Blue Earth).
Faribault, Minn. (co. seat of Rice Co.). Named by Alexander Faribault (1806-1882), founder, for his father.

FARMERS BRANCH, Tex. (Dallas Co.). Apparently for a branch of the Trinity River. The early settlers were all farmers.

FARMERSVILLE For a surrounding farming community.
Farmersville, Calif. (Tulare Co.).
Farmersville, N.Y. (Cattaraugus Co.).

FARMERVILLE, La. (parish seat of Union Parish). For the Farmer family, particularly W. W. Farmer. They were one of the most prominent families in the area.

FARMINGDALE, N.Y. (Nassau Co.). Descriptive of an agricultural area.

FARMINGTON Descriptive of a town or city in a good farming area, or one that it is hoped will be.
Farmington, Conn. (Hartford Co.), town.
Farmington, Ill. (Fulton Co.). For Farmington in Tennessee.
Farmington, Me. (co. seat of Franklin Co.), town and village.
Farmington, Mich. (Oakland Co.).
Farmington, Minn. (Dakota Co.).
Farmington, Mo. (co. seat of St. Francois Co.).
Farmington, N.H. (Strafford Co.), town and village. Earlier, Farmington Dock, for its location on the Cocheco R. Named by Gen. Richard Furber.

Farmington, N.Mex. (San Juan Co.).
Farmington, Utah (co. seat of Davis Co.).
Farmington Reservoir, Conn.
Farmington River, Conn.

FARM RIVER, Conn. Said to have been named for the settlement of farmers along its banks. It flows generally southwest into Long Island Sound.

FARMVILLE So named because it is in a farming area, or for "Village of Farmers."
Farmville, N.C. (Pitt Co.).
Farmville, Va. (co. seat of Prince Edward Co.).

FARNHAM, Que. (Missisquoi Co.). For the community in Surrey, England.

FARRAGUT, David Glasgow (1801-1870), naval officer who commanded the *Erie* on a mission (1838) to protect Americans and property in Mexico during the Franco-Mexican War. In 1862 he captured New Orleans, a victory that earned him the rank of rear admiral, the Navy's leading officer. By the end of 1862 he held the whole of the Gulf Coast within the limits of his command, with the exception of Mobile. On August 5, 1864, he forced his way through the mines in Mobile Bay, leading his fleet to victory with the cry, "Damn the torpedoes! Full speed ahead!" On July 26, 1866, he was commissioned admiral, a grade created especially for him.
Farragut, Iowa (Fremont Co.).
Farragut, N.Y. (Brooklyn Co.).
Farragut, Tenn. (Knox Co.).

FARRELL, Pa. (Mercer Co.). For James A. Farrell, president of United States Steel when the town was incorporated. An earlier name was South Sharon.

FARWELL, Tex. (co. seat of Parmer Co.). For the Farwell brothers, John Villiers and Charles Benjamin. C. B. Farwell (1823-1903) was a businessman, banker, U.S. representative (1871-76), and U.S. senator (1887-91). The brothers helped finance the building of the Texas capitol building in Austin in exchange for three million acres of land in the Texas Panhandle, on which they established and developed the famous XIT Ranch.

FAULK, Andrew Jackson (1814-1898), Dakota Territory official and governor.
Faulk Co., S.Dak. (co. seat, *Faulkton*).
Faulkton, S.Dak. (co. seat of *Faulk* Co.).

FAULKNER Co., Ark. (co. seat, Conway). Said to be for Sandford C. Faulkner, who wrote "The Arkansas Traveler," the state song. Other Faulkner family names occur in the area.

FAUQUIER Co., Va. (co. seat, Warrenton). For Francis Fauquier (1704?-1768), English statesman, lieutenant governor of the colony of Virginia (1758-68), who assumed the duties of the absent nominal governors, the Earl of Loudon (1756-63) and Lord Jeffrey Amherst (1763-68). In general, he was considered a fair and able man and a friend of the colonists.

FAUSSE From French, "false."
Fausse Riviere, La. From French, "false river."
Fausse Pointe, Lake, La. From French, "false point."

FAYETTE American shortened version of the name (sometimes spelled La Fayette) of the Marquis de LAFAYETTE.
Fayette Co., Ala. (co. seat, *Fayette*).
Fayette Co., Ga. (co. seat, *Fayetteville*).
Fayette Co., Ill. (co. seat, Vandalia).
Fayette Co., Ind. (co. seat, Connersville).
Fayette Co., Iowa (co. seat, West Union).
Fayette Co., Ky. (co. seat, Lexington).
Fayette Co., Ohio (co. seat, Washington Court House).
Fayette Co., Pa. (co. seat, Uniontown).
Fayette Co., Tenn. (co. seat, Somerville).
Fayette Co., Tex. (co. seat, La Grange).
Fayette Co., W.Va. (co. seat, *Fayetteville*).
Fayette, Ala. (co. seat of *Fayette* Co.).
Fayette, Me. (Kennebec Co.).
Fayette, Miss. (co. seat of Jefferson Co.).
Fayette, Mo. (co. seat of Howard Co.).
Fayette, N.Y. (Seneca Co.).
Fayetteville, Ark. (co. seat of Washington Co.).
Fayetteville, Ga. (co. seat of *Fayette* Co.).
Fayetteville, N.Y. (Onandaga Co.).
Fayetteville, N.C. (co. seat of Cumberland Co.).
Fayetteville, Tenn. (co. seat of Lincoln Co.).
Fayetteville, W.Va. (co. seat of *Fayette* Co.). Earlier, Vandalia.

FEAR So named because a shipwreck nearly occurred off the point of the cape.
Cape Fear River, N.C. For the cape. Flows S and SE into the Atlantic.
Fear, Cape, N.C., on Smith Island.

FEATHER RIVER, Calif. Flows generally southwest to the Sacramento River. It was also known by its Spanish name, *Rio de las Plumas*; both names refer to the many feathers used by the local Indians for decoration.

FELICIANA From Spanish; said to be named for Felicite, the wife of a colonial governor, or from Spanish, "happiness."
East Feliciana Parish, La. (parish seat, Clinton).
West Feliciana Parish, La. (parish seat, Saint Francisville).

FENCE Probably a translation from Indian, "trap," for the catching of animals or fish.
Fence Lake, Mich.
Fence Lake, Wis.
Fence River, Mich. Flows S into Michigamme Reservoir.

FENHOLLOWAY RIVER, Fla. From Seminole-Creek, "high footlog" or "high bridge." It flows southwest into Apalachee Bay.

FENTON, Mich. (Genesee Co.). For William M. Fenton, attorney, lieutenant governor, and a founder of the town.

FENTRESS Co., Tenn. (co. seat, Jamestown). For James Fentress, statesman.

FERGUS, James (1813-1897), legislator. Born in Lanarkshire, Scotland, he emigrated to the United States in 1835. He became a rancher and jurist and was active in the Montana legislature.
Fergus Co., Mont. (co. seat, Lewistown).
Fergus Falls, Minn. (co. seat of Otter Tail Co.).

FERNANDINA Either for King Ferdinand of Spain or for Don Domingo Fernandez, who in 1785 obtained a land grant. Evidence seems to favor the latter.
Fernandina, Fla. (co. seat of Nassau Co.).
Fernandina Bay, Fla.
Fernandina Beach, Fla. (Nassau Co.).

FERNDALE, Mich. (Oakland Co.). For ferns in a valley.

FERRON CREEK, Utah. For A. D. Ferron, surveyor. It flows east into San Rafael River.

FERRY Co., Wash. (co. seat, Republic). For Elisha Peyre Ferry (1825-1895), first governor (1889-93) of the state.

FESSENDEN, N.Dak. (co. seat of Wells Co.). For Cortez Fessenden, surveyor for the Dakota Territory.

FIFTEEN MILE FALLS RESERVOIR, Vt.-N.H., dam and reservoir in Connecticut River. For the length of the rapids in the river.

FILLMORE, Calif. (Ventura Co.). For J. A. Fillmore, general superintendent of the Southern Pacific railroad.

FILLMORE, Millard (1800-1874), 13th President of the United States (1850-53), from New York. A member of the House of Representatives (1833-35; 1837-43), he was also vice-president of the United States (1849-50) and, on the death of Zachary Taylor (1850), became President.
Fillmore Co., Minn. (co. seat, Preston).
Fillmore Co., Neb. (co. seat, Geneva).
Fillmore, Utah (co. seat of Millard Co.).

FINCASTLE, Va. (co. seat of Botetourt Co.). For George, Lord Fincastle.

FINDLAY, Ohio (co. seat of Hancock Co.). For James Findlay (1770-1838), from the fort he erected while a regimental commander during the War of 1812. A territorial legislator, he was later mayor of Cincinnati (1805-06; 1810-11) and a brigadier general of the state militia. He served as U.S. representative (1825-33) and was an unsuccessful candidate for governor of Ohio (1834).

FINGER Descriptive of features long and thin like a finger.
Finger Buttes, S.Dak.
Finger Lakes, N.Y.

FINLEY, N.Dak. (co. seat of Steele Co.). For J. B. Finley, an official of the Great Northern railroad.

FINNEY Co., Kan. (co. seat, Garden City). For David W. Finney, Kansas state official. An earlier name was Sequoyoh.

176

FIREBAUGH, Calif. (Fresno Co.). For A. D. Fierbaugh, who established a trading post and a ferry.

FIRESTEEL RIVER, Mich. Reason for the name uncertain, but probably for the mining operations near the head of the river. It flows northwest into Lake Superior.

FIRST CONNECTICUT LAKE, N.H. Apparently named by someone traveling north from Connecticut. See also SECOND CONNECTICUT LAKE and CONNECTICUT.

FISH For a place where fish and fishing are abundant. Also, *Fishing*.
Fish Creek, N.Y. Formed by E. Branch and W. Branch, flows into Oneida L.
Fish Lake, Utah.
Fish Point, Mich. Extends into Saginaw Bay.
Fishing Creek, Pa. Flows into Bald Eagle Creek. Probably translated from Indian.
Fishing Creek, Pa. Flows into Susquehanna R. The nearby town was famous for the Fishing Creek Confederacy, a small group of men who at first refused to serve during the Civil War.
Fishlake Natl. Forest, Utah.

FISH, Ira, early explorer of the area.
Fish River, Me. Flows SE then N through *Fish River* Lakes and into the St. John R.
Fish River Lakes, Me. One of the *Fish River* Lakes.
Fish River Lakes, Me. Chain of lakes, including Fish River, Portage, St. Froid, Eagle, Square, Cross, and Long lakes.

FISHEATING CREEK, Fla. From Seminole *lalo-papka-hachi, "fish-eating place-creek."* It flows south and east into Lake Okeechobee.

FISHER Co., Tex. (co. seat, Roby). For Samuel Rhoads Fisher (1794-1839), Texas patriot and state official.

FISHERS ISLAND, N.Y., in Long Island Sound. For an early settler.

FISHKILL From Dutch *Vis Kill,* "a stream full of fish."
Fishkill, N.Y. (Dutchess Co.).
Fishkill Creek, N.Y. Flows SW into the Hudson R.

FITCHBURG, Mass. (a co. seat of Worcester Co.). For John Fitch (1707/08-1795), an early settler.

FITZGERALD, Ga. (co. seat of Ben Hill Co.). For Philander H. Fitzgerald, attorney, publisher, and humanitarian, who proposed that a colony of Union soldiers be allowed to settle in Georgia. The plan was approved and approximately twenty-seven hundred Union veterans moved to the area.

FIVE MILE RIVER, Conn. Descriptive of supposed length of stream. It flows south and southwest into Quinebaug River.

FLAGLER Co., Fla. (co. seat, Bunnell). For Henry Morrison Flagler (1830-1913), New York industrialist and financier who was a partner with John D. Rockefeller in the establishment of the Standard Oil Company (1865). He founded the Florida East Coast railroad (1886) and was a leader in developing Florida as a resort area.

FLAGSTAFF From a plantation name, in turn named for a flagstaff raised by Gen. Benedict Arnold on his return from Quebec in 1775.
Flagstaff Lake, Me.
Flagstaff Mountain, Me.

FLAGSTAFF, Ariz. (co. seat of Coconino Co.). Although exact circumstances are in debate, the name resulted from a flag that was flown from a lone pine tree.

FLAGSTAFF LAKE, Ore. For the place where the flag was flown.

FLAGSTONE PEAK, Wyo. For the flagstones found on the summit.

FLAMBEAU From French, "flames," for the torches used by Indians while fishing at night.
Flambeau Flowage, Wis.
Flambeau River, Wis. Formed by North and South Forks, flows SW from *Flambeau* Flowage into Chippewa R.
Lac du Flambeau, Wis. (Vivas Co.).
Lac du Flambeau (lake), Wis.

FLAMING GORGE For the red cliffs in the river gorge.
Flaming Gorge Dam and Reservoir, Utah-Wyo.
Flaming Gorge Natl. Recreation Area, Utah.

FLANDREAU, S.Dak. (co. seat of Moody Co.). For Charles E. Flandrau, a jurist. The Frenchified *e* was added later.

FLANNAGAN RESERVOIR, Va. For John William Flannagan, Jr. (1885-1955), attorney, banker, and U.S. representative from Virginia (1831-49).

FLAT Descriptive.
Flat River, Mich. Flows SSW into Grand River.
Flat Top Butte, S.Dak.

FLATHEAD A name shared by several Indian tribes (Choctaw, Chinook, Salish, Waxhaw, and others of the Catawba group), some of whom flattened the heads of their infants, while others had naturally flat heads.
Flathead Co., Mont. (co. seat, Kalispell).
Flathead Indian Reservation, Mont.
Flathead Lake, Mont.
Flathead Natl. Forest, Mont.
Flathead River, Mont.-B.C.

FLAT RIVER, N.C. Descriptive, of depth and terrain. Flows southeast to join Eno River to form Neuse River.

FLAT ROCK Descriptive.
Flat Rock, Mich. (Wayne Co.). For the rock bed of the Huron R.
Flat Rock Butte, N.Dak.
Flat Rock River, Ind. Flows SSW into E. Fork of White R.

FLATTERY, Cape, Wash. Extends into the Pacific Ocean. So named in 1778 by Capt. James Cook because he "was flattered . . . with hopes of finding a harbour there."

FLATWOODS Descriptive.
Flatwoods, Ky. (Greenup Co.).
Flatwoods, Tenn. (Perry Co.).

FLEMING, John (?-1794), early settler, army officer, and member of a prominent family.
Fleming Co., Ky. (co. seat, *Flemingsburg*).
Flemingsburg, Ky. (co. seat of *Fleming* Co.).

FLEMINGTON, N.J. (Hunterdon Co.). For Samuel Flemming or Fleming, a local resident.

FLETCHER POND, Mich. For a local settler.

FLIN FLON, Man.-Sask. For Josiah Flintabbetey Flonatin, hero of *The Sunless City* (1905), a novel by the English writer J. E. Preston-Muddock.

FLINT Usually descriptive of the stones in the area; also for arrowheads used by Indians.
Flint, Mass. (Fall River Co.).
Flint, Mich. (co. seat of Genesee Co.). For the river.
Flint River, Ga. Flows S to join the Chattahoochee R. to form the Apalachicola R.
Flint River, Mich. Flows SW to the Shiawassee R.
Flint River, Tenn.-Ala. Flows S to the Tennessee R.

FLOOK LAKE, Ore. Probably for a member of the party of Capt. William Horace Warner in 1849.

FLORA, Ill. (Clay Co.). For Flora Whittleby, the founder's daughter.

FLORALA, Ala. (Covington Co.). From the first four letters of *Flor*ida and the first three letters of *Ala*bama. The town is on the border of the two states.

FLORAL PARK Promotional.
Floral Park, Mont. (Silver Bow Co.).
Floral Park, N.Y. (Nassau Co.).

FLORENCE For Florence Harllee, whose father, W. W. Harllee, was an official in a railroad company that extended tracks through the farmland area. The county was named for the city.
Florence Co., S.C. (co. seat, *Florence*).
Florence, S.C. (co. seat of *Florence* Co.).

FLORENCE For Florence Hulst, wife of an early developer.
Florence Co., Wis. (co. seat, *Florence*).
Florence, Wis. (co. seat of *Florence* Co.).

FLORENCE, Ala. (co. seat of Lauderdale Co.). For Florence, Italy; named by Ferdinand Sannoner, engineer who planned the city.

FLORENCE, Ariz. (co. seat of Pinal Co.). For the sister of Richard McCormick, governor when the city was established.

FLORENCE, Colo. (Fremont Co.). Named by James A. McCandless, founder, for his sister, Florence McCandless.

FLORENCE LAKE and PASS, Wyo. For Florence, daughter of an early settler.

FLORESVILLE, Tex. (co. seat of Wilson Co.). Supposedly first settled by Don Francisco Flores de Abryo, who donated the land for the townsite. It is also said that the name comes from Spanish, "village of flowers."

FLORIDA Named by Juan Ponce de Leon, who discovered it on Easter Sunday (*Pascua Florida*) in 1512. *Florida* means "flowering" in Spanish.
Florida, State of. 27th state of the Union. Settled: 1565. Territory: 1822 (after being ceded by Spain in 1819). Admitted: 1845. Cap: Tallahassee. Motto: In God We Trust. Nickname: Sunshine State. Flower: Orange Blossom. Bird: Mockingbird. Tree: Sabal Palm. Song: "Swanee River."
Florida Bay, Fla.

FLORIN, Calif. (Sacramento Co.). Possibly for silver coins used in Europe, still minted in Great Britain.

FLOSSMOOR Named by a contest of the Illinois Central railroad in the late 1890s. The name selected was Floss-Moor, from Scots, "dew on the flowers" or "gently rolling countryside," so local residents believe.
Flossmoor, Ill. (Cook Co.).
Flossmoor Highlands, Ill. (Cook Co.). Promotional.

FLOYD, Charles (?-1804), a member of the Lewis and Clark Expedition.
Floyd Co., Iowa (co. seat, Charles City).
Floyd River, Iowa.

FLOYD Co., Ga. (co. seat, Rome). For John Floyd (1769-1839), a general in the Indian wars and later a U.S. representative (1827-29).

FLOYD, John (1783-1837), Virginia statesman. He was a U.S. representative (1817-29). As governor (1830-34), he was a leading exponent of states' rights.
Floyd Co., Ind. (co. seat, New Albany).
Floyd Co., Ky. (co. seat, Prestonsburg).

Floyd Co., Va. (co. seat, *Floyd*).
Floyd, Va. (co. seat of *Floyd* Co.).

FLOYD Co., Tex. (co. seat, Floydada). For Dolfin Ward Floyd (?-1836), killed at the Alamo.

FLOYDADA, Tex. (co. seat of Floyd Co.). The origin of the name is uncertain. One version is that the name was derived from *Floydalia*, combination of *Floyd* and the name of one of the heroes of the Alamo. The name may also have been combined from *Floyd* and Mrs. *Ada* Price, mother of T. W. Price, a large landowner.

FLUSHING Anglicized form of Dutch *Vlissingen*, for the city in Holland.
Flushing, Mich. (Genesee Co.).
Flushing, N.Y. (Queens Co.). A section of the borough of Queens.

FLUVANNA Co., Va. (co. seat, Palmyra). A combination of Latin *fluvius*, "river," and *anna*, for Queen Anne of England.

FOARD Co., Tex. (co. seat, Crowell). For Robert J. Foard (1831-1898), a Confederate army officer and prominent local citizen.

FOLEY, Ala. (Baldwin Co.). For John Burton Foley (1857-1925), Chicago businessman and Republican party leader who headed the Magnolia Land Company.

FOLEY, Minn. (co. seat of Benton Co.). For John Foley (?-1908), founder and landowner.

FOLKSTON, Ga. (co. seat of Charlton Co.). For Dr. William Brandon Folks (1830-1886), a prominent physician and surgeon.

FOLLANSBEE, W.Va. (Brooke Co.). For the Follansbee brothers, who owned a mill there. The business still exists.

FOLSOM, Capt. Joseph (?-1855), commander of the Presidio of San Francisco during a period of military government.
Folsom, Calif. (Sacramento Co.).
Folsom Lake, Calif.

FOLSOM PEAK, Wyo., in Yellowstone Natl. Park. For David E. Folsom, of the United States Geological Survey.

FONDA, N.Y. (co. seat of Montgomery Co.). For Duow Fonda (fl.1750), an early Dutch settler.

179

FOND DU LAC From French, literally, "end of the lake," translated from Wanikamiu, an Indian village, with the similar meaning "farthest point of the lake."
Fond du Lac Co., Wis. (co. seat, *Fond du Lac*).
Fond du Lac, Minn. (now part of Duluth, Minn.).
Fond du Lac, Wis. (co. seat of *Fond du Lac* Co.).
Fond du Lac Indian Reservation, Minn.
North Fond du Lac, Wis. (*Fond du Lac* Co.).

FONTANA, Calif. (San Bernardino Co.). Either for a family name or poetical Spanish for "fountain."

FONTANA LAKE, N.C. For the town whose site is now covered by the Tennessee Valley Authority lake; the town was named for falls in the river that resembled fountains.

FORAKER, Mount, Alaska, in Mt. McKinley Natl. Park. For Joseph Benson Foraker (1846-1917), Union Army officer in the Civil War, lawyer, jurist, and U.S. senator from Ohio (1897-1909).

FORD, Thomas (1800-1850), Illinois jurist and governor (1842-46).
Ford Co., Ill. (co. seat, Paxton).
Ford River, Mich. Flows SE into Green Bay. Thomas Ford explored the area (1842-46).

FORD Co., Ill. (co. seat, Paxton). For Thomas Ford (1800-1850), Illinois jurist and governor (1842-46).

FORD Co., Kan. (co. seat, Dodge City). For James H. Ford, an officer in the Colorado cavalry during the Civil War.

FORD CITY, Calif. (Kern Co.). For the famous Model "T" Fords.

FORD CITY, Pa. (Armstrong Co.). For J. B. Ford, founder and builder of the town's first glass works.

FORDYCE, Ark. (co. seat of Dallas Co.). For Samuel W. Fordyce, president of the St. Louis and Southwestern railroad.

FOREST Usually for large forests in the area.
Forest Co., Pa. (co. seat, Tionesta).

Forest Co., Wis. (co. seat, Crandon).
Forest, Miss. (co. seat of Scott Co.).
Forest River, N.Dak. Flows SE and E into Red R.
Forest Acres, S.C. (Richland Co.).
Forest City, Iowa (co. seat of Winnebago Co.).
Forest City, N.C. (Rutherford Co.).
Forest Grove, Ore. (Washington Co.). Earlier, West Tualatin Plain; the change was made when proposed by a local citizen who had given the name to his own claim in the territory.
Forest Hill, Tex. (Tarrant Co.).
Forest Lake, Minn. (Washington Co.).
Forest Park, Ga. (Clayton Co.). For many park areas deeded to Atlanta, of which this is a suburb, by the Central of Georgia railroad.
Forest Park, Ill. (Cook Co.). Promotional. Earlier, Harlem.
Forest Park, Ohio (Montgomery Co.).

FORMAN, N.Dak. (co. seat of Sargent Co.). For Cornelius Hageman Forman (1833-1923), founder, township supervisor, justice of the peace, and clerk of the public school.

FORREST, Nathan Bedford (1821-1877), famous Confederate army general and tactician, often quoted as saying, "Get there fustest with the mostest."
Forrest Co., Miss. (co. seat, Hattiesburg).
Forrest City, Ark. (co. seat of St. Francis Co.).

FORSYTH, John (1780-1841), attorney, U.S. representative (1813-18), U.S. senator (1819; 1829-34), governor of Georgia (1827-29), and secretary of state (1834-41) under Jackson and Van Buren.
Forsyth Co., Ga. (co. seat, Cumming).
Forsyth, Ga. (co. seat of Monroe Co.).
Forsyth, Mo. (co. seat of Taney Co.).

FORSYTH, Mont. (co. seat of Rosebud Co.). For George A. Forsyth, who entered the Civil War as a private and rose to rank of brigadier general in the Union Army. He was cited for meritorious service in a battle (1868) with hostile Indians on the Arickaree Fork of the Republican River. See also CAMP FORSYTH.

FORSYTH Co., N.C. (co. seat, Winston-Salem). For Benjamin Forsyth (c.1760-1814), an army officer killed during the War of 1812.

FORT ARBUCKLE, Okla. For Matthew ARBUCKLE

FORT ATKINSON, Wis. (Jefferson Co.). For Henry Atkinson, leader of Federal forces during the Black Hawk War of 1832.

FORT BELVOIR, Va. (Fairfax Co.). For the Belvoir plantation, which occupied the site and was owned by Col. William Fairfax. The name means "beautiful to see."

FORT BEND Co., Tex. (co. seat, Richmond). For a fort built on the Brazos River.

FORT BENTON, Mont. For Thomas Hart BENTON.

FORT BRAGG For Gen. Braxton Bragg (1817-1876), Mexican War and Civil War hero.
Fort Bragg, Calif. (Mendocino Co.).
Fort Bragg, N.C. (Cumberland Co.).

FORT BRANCH, Ind. (Gibson Co.). For the fort established (1811) to protect pioneers against Indian raids, and for the branch of water that flowed nearby.

FORT COBB RESERVOIR, Okla. For Howell COBB.

FORT COLLINS, Colo. (co. seat of Larimer Co.). For Col. W. O. Collins (1809-1880), commander of the Eleventh Ohio Cavalry at Fort Laramie, Wyo.

FORT DAVIS, Tex. For Jefferson DAVIS.

FORT DODGE, Iowa. For Gen. Henry DODGE.

FORT DONELSON NATL. MILITARY PARK, Tenn. For Andrew J. Donelson (?-1859), career army officer. Commemorates Gen. Ulysses S. Grant's first decisive victory, when the Confederate post surrendered to his forces on Feb. 16, 1862. It gave the Union forces a clear way through the heart of the Confederacy.

FORT ERIE, Ont. For Lake ERIE.

FORT FAIRFIELD, Me. (Aroostook Co.), town. For John Fairfield (1797-1847), governor of Maine (1838-39; 1841-42).

FORT FRANCES, Ont. (co. seat of Rainy River Co.). For the wife of Sir George Simpson, a member of the Hudson's Bay Company which occupied the village in 1821. An earlier name was St. Pierre.

FORT FREDERICA NATL. MONUMENT, Ga. For Frederick Louis (1707-1751), father of George III of England.

FORT GAINES, Ga. For Gen. Edmund Pendleton GAINES.

FORT GIBSON For George Gibson (1785?-1851), quartermaster general of the U.S. Army in 1816, commissary general of subsistence in 1818, cited for meritorious conduct during the war with Mexico, retired as major general. The fort was established in 1824 and named before the town.
Fort Gibson, Okla. (Muskogee Co.).
Fort Gibson Dam and Reservoir, Okla. In Neosho R.

FORT GORDON, Ga. (Richmond Co.). For Lt. Gen. John Brown Gordon (1832-1904), an active and heroic soldier in the Civil War, Georgia governor (1887 90), and U.S. senator (1873-80; 1891-97).

FORT HAMILTON, N.Y. A residential section of Brooklyn; named for Alexander HAMILTON.

FORT HUACHUCA, Ariz. (Cochise Co.). For a Pima Indian village on the site; meaning unknown.

FORT KENT, Me. (Aroostook Co.), town and village. For Edward Kent (1802-1877), governor of Maine (1838-39; 1840-41).

FORT LAUDERDALE, Fla. (co. seat of Broward Co.). For Maj. William Lauderdale, leader of an expedition against the Seminole Indians in 1838, or possibly for the Scottish home of a Capt. William S. Maitland.

FORT LEAVENWORTH, Kan. For Gen. Henry LEAVENWORTH.

FORT LOUDON For John Campbell LOUDON.
Fort Loudon Historic Site, Tenn. Commemorates the fort built by the British at the request of the Cherokee Indians. The

fort, which was occupied until 1760, is now restored.
Fort Loudon Lake, Tenn.

FORT MADISON, Iowa (a co. seat of Lee Co.). For a fort, which was named for James Madison, then secretary of state.

FORT MATANZAS NATL. MONUMENT, Fla. See MATANZAS.

FORT McKINLEY, Ohio (Montgomery Co.). For President McKINLEY.

FORT MITCHELL, Ky. (Kenton Co.). For Ormsby M. Mitchell (?-1862), Union Army general during the Civil War.

FORT MORGAN, Colo. For Christopher Anthony MORGAN.

FORT MYERS For Gen. Abraham Charles Myers (1811-1889), career soldier. He was the first quartermaster general (1861-63) of the Confederate army.
Fort Myers, Fla. (co. seat of Lee Co.).
Fort Myers Beach, Fla. (Lee Co.).
Fort Myers Southeast, Fla. (Lee Co.).
Fort Myers Southwest, Fla. (Lee Co.).
Fort Myers Villas-Pine Manor, Fla. (Lee Co.).

FORT NECESSITY NATL. BATTLEFIELD SITE, Pa. Commemorates the site of the first battle of the French and Indian War, which took place on July 3, 1754, when George Washington surrendered to the French forces. The fort was so named by George Washington as a needed military facility.

FORT PAYNE, Ala. (co. seat of De Kalb Co.). For Capt. John Howard Payne, author of the song "Home Sweet Home."

FORT PECK For the fort, a trading post, in turn named for Campbell K. Peck, trader.
Fort Peck, Mont. (Valley Co.).
Fort Peck Reservoir, Mont. On Missouri R.

FORT PIERCE For Benjamin Kendrick Pierce, brother of President Franklin Pierce.
Fort Pierce, Fla. (co. seat of St. Lucie Co.).
Fort Pierce Northwest, Fla. (St. Lucie Co.).

FORT PIERRE, S.Dak. (co. seat of Stanley Co.). For a nearby fort established by Pierre Chouteau, a French fur trader. See also PIERRE.

FORT POLK For the Rt. Rev. Leonidas Polk (1806-1864), bishop of the Diocese of Louisiana, owner of a large sugar plantation that failed, founder of the University of the South at Sewanee, Tenn., and a major-general in the Confederate army. He was killed at Pine Mountain, Ga.
North Fort Polk, La. (Vernon Parish).
South Fort Polk, La. (Vernon Parish).

FORT PULASKI NATL. MONUMENT, Ga. Established in 1924 in honor of Count Casimir PULASKI.

FORT RALEIGH NATL. HISTORICAL SITE, N.C. Established to commemorate the place of Sir Walter Raleigh's attempt (1585-1591) to build an English colony in America. Virginia Dare was born here in 1587. See also RALEIGH.

FORTRESS MOUNTAIN, Wyo. Descriptive of the shape of the peak.

FORT RIVER, Mass. For the fort built on the bank of the river. It flows south and southwest into Connecticut River.

FORT ST. JOHN, B.C. For ST. JOHN.

FORT SCOTT, Kan. For Gen. Winfield SCOTT.

FORT SHAWNEE, Ohio (Allen Co.). For the Shawnee Indians.

FORT SHERIDAN, Ill. For Gen. Philip H. SHERIDAN.

FORT SMITH, Ark. (co. seat of Sebastian Co.). For Thomas A. Smith, commanding general of Western frontier forces when the original fort was established.

FORT STOCKTON, Tex. For Commodore Robert Field STOCKTON.

FORT SUMNER, N.Mex. (co. seat of De Baca Co.). For Gen. Edwin Vose Sumner (1797-1863), Ninth Military District commander.

FORT SUMTER NATL. MONUMENT, S.C. For Thomas SUMTER. Commemorates the beginning of the Civil War when South Carolina artillery fired on Union forces, April 12, 1861, and took the fort. Two years later Union forces laid siege to the fort for twenty months and finally took it.

FORT THOMAS, Ky. For George Henry
THOMAS.

FORT TILDEN, N.Y. For Samuel Jones
TILDEN.

FORTUNA, Calif. (Humboldt Co.). So named for good fortune; believed to be an ideal place to live.

FORT UNION NATL. MONUMENT, N.Mex. Reason for the name unknown, but probably commendatory and patriotic during pre-Civil War times. Built in 1851 as a trading post and military center, it was abandoned in 1890, and established as a monument in 1956.

FORT VALLEY, Ga. (co. seat of Peach Co.). Believed to have been a postal clerk's misreading of *Fox Valley.*

FORT WAYNE, Ind. For Anthony WAYNE.

FORT WILLIAM, Ont. (Thunder Bay Co.). For William McGillivray, principal director of the North West Company.

FORT WOLTERS, Tex. (Palo Pinto Co.). For Gen. Jacob F. Wolters (1871-1935), attorney who served in the Texas National Guard, commanding and organizing the Fifty-sixth Cavalry Brigade.

FORT WORTH, Tex. For William Jenkins
WORTH.

FORT WRIGHT-LOOKOUT HEIGHTS, Ky. (Kenton Co.). Combination of *Fort Wright,* named for Maj. Gen. Horatio Gouverneur Wright (1820-1899), Civil War officer who was appointed chief engineer for the completion of construction of the Washington Monument, and *Lookout Heights,* descriptive.

FORT YATES, N.Dak. (co. seat of Sioux Co.). For a military post, which was named for George W. Yates (?-1876), an army officer killed at the Little Big Horn.

FORTY FORT, Pa. (Luzerne Co.). For the first forty Connecticut settlers in the Wyoming Valley, Pa.

FORTYMILE RIVER, Alaska. So named because the mouth of the river is forty miles below a former Hudson's Bay Company post. It flows northeast into Yukon River.

FOSSIL, Ore. (co. seat of Wheeler Co.). For fossils that the postmaster found on his land.

FOSS RESERVOIR, Okla., on Washita River. For J. M. Foss, prominent resident of the area.

FOSTER Co., N.Dak. (co. seat, Carrington). For James Foster, an immigration officer.

FOSTER, R.I. (Providence Co.), town. For Theodore Foster (1752-1828), U.S. senator (1790-1803).

FOSTER LAKE, Ore. For a local settler.

FOSTORIA, Ohio (Seneca and Hancock Cos.). A Latinized derivation of the personal name *Foster,* for Charles Foster, Ohio congressman and governor (1880-84), and secretary of the treasury (1891-93) under Benjamin Harrison.

FOUNTAIN, Colo. (El Paso Co.). For a creek, which had been named by French trappers.

FOUNTAIN Co., Ind. (co. seat, Covington). For James Fountain (originally Fontaine), an army officer killed in action against the Indians on the Maumee River near Fort Wayne (1790).

FOUNTAIN HILL, Pa. (Lehigh Co.). For the estate of August Fiot in Fontainebleau, France. This area reminded him of his home.

FOUNTAIN INN, S.C. (Greenville Co.). For a well-known inn once located near the site of the town.

FOUNTAIN CREEK, Colo. For the mineral spring. It flows northeast and southeast into Arkansas River.

FOUNTAIN VALLEY, Calif. (Orange Co.). Descriptive.

FOUR Descriptive.
Four Peaks, Ariz.
Four Corners, Ore. (Marion Co.). For an intersection of two heavily travelled roads.
Four Mountains, Islands of the, Alaska. For four volcanoes on the islands.

FOURCHE LA FAVE RIVER, Ark. From French *fourche la fauve*, "wild fork." It flows generally northeast into Arkansas River.

FOWLER, Ind. (Benton Co.). For a local community member.

FOX For the Indian tribe, of Algonquian linguistic stock.
Fox Islands, Mich. in L. Michigan.
Fox River, Mich. Flows SE into Manistique R.

FOX Translated from Indian, "fox," either for the animal or the tribe.
Fox Lake, Wis.
Fox River, Wis. Flows generally NE into Green Bay.
Fox River, Wis. Flows S and SW into Illinois R.

FOXBOROUGH, Mass. (Norfolk Co.), town and village. For Charles James Fox (1749-1806), English politician and opponent of the policies of Lord North. Fox called for better treatment of the rebellious colonies.

FOX LAKE, Ill. (Lake Co.). For a lake, which was named for the animal, or possibly for the Fox Indians.

FOX ISLANDS, Alaska. Translated from Russian *ostrova lisyy*, "fox islands."

FOX POINT, Wis. (Milwaukee Co.). Named by early surveyors, but the reason is unknown.

FRACKVILLE, Pa. (Schuylkill Co.). For Daniel Frack, founder.

FRAMINGHAM, Mass. (Middlesex Co.), town. Probably for Framingham, Suffolk, England.

FRANC, Otto, a settler and hunter from Germany.
Franc's Peak, Wyo.
Franks Peak, Wyo.

FRANCIS CASE, Lake, S.Dak. For Francis Higbee Case (1896-1966), marine corps officer, publisher, and U.S. representative (1937-51) and senator (1951-62) from South Dakota.

FRANCIS, Lake, N.H. For a local settler.

FRANCONIA Named by Sir Francis Bernard, who was granted land there in 1764, for Franconia, a duchy in Germany.
Franconia, N.H. (Grafton Co.), town.
Franconia Notch, N.H. Pass in White Mtns.

FRANKENMUTH, Mich. (Saginaw Co.). A compound name, from German *Franken*, adjective for *Franconia*, a Bavarian community, and *muth*, "courage."

FRANKFORT, Ind. (co. seat of Clinton Co.). For Frankfurt am Main (or Frankfort on the Main), Germany, home of the landowners' ancestors.

FRANKFORT, Ky. (co. seat of Franklin Co.), state capital. From the earlier name, Frank's Ford, for Stephen Frank, an early settler killed by Indians.

FRANKFORT, N.Y. (Herkimer Co.). For a local fort in command of a General Frank.

FRANKLIN For President Franklin PIERCE.
Franklin Lake, Nev.
Franklin Pierce Lake, N.H.

FRANKLIN, Benjamin (1706-1790), one of the most popular and versatile of American Revolutionary patriots, born in Boston but

Some consider Benjamin Franklin as the equal of George Washington as a contender for the title "Father of His Country." A Bostonian by birth, he spent most of his life in Philadelphia. [*New York Public Library*]

A man of many talents, Franklin was a philosopher, writer, inventor, printer, and diplomat. Here he is shown making his famous electrical experiment with the kite. [*New York Public Library*]

associated with Pennsylvania, where he spent his adult years. A printer by trade, he published *The Pennsylvania Gazette* (1730-48) and was pseudonymous author of *Poor Richard's Almanack* (1732-57). He was a founder of the American Philosophical Society and the Philadelphia Library, a developer in the areas of municipal lighting and postal service, inventor of the Franklin stove, and a scientist who experimented in various fields, including electricity. He spent the years 1766 to 1775 in England pleading the cause of the colonies and was a member of the Second Continental Congress (1775) and a signer of the Declaration of Independence (1776). As an American agent in France (1776-81), he raised money and secured French support for the American cause. He was one of the three commissioners who negotiated peace with England (1781), a member of the Pennsylvania Executive Council (1785-87), and a delegate to the Constitutional Convention (1787). His *Autobiography* is a classic of American literature.

Franklin Co., Ala. (co. seat, Russellville).
Franklin Co., Ark. (co. seats, Charleston and Ozark).
Franklin Co., Fla. (co. seat, Apalachicola).
Franklin Co., Ga. (co. seat, Carnesville).
Franklin Co., Ill. (co. seat, Benton).
Franklin Co., Ind. (co. seat, Brookville).
Franklin Co., Iowa (co. seat, Hampton).
Franklin Co., Kan. (co. seat, Ottawa).
Franklin Co., Ky. (co. seat, Frankfort).
Franklin Parish, La. (parish seat, Winnsboro).
Franklin Co., Me. (co. seat, Farmington).
Franklin Co., Mass. (co. seat, Greenfield).
Franklin Co., Miss. (co. seat, Meadville).
Franklin Co., Mo. (co. seat, Union).
Franklin Co., Neb. (co. seat, *Franklin*).
Franklin Co., N.Y. (co. seat, Malone).
Franklin Co., N.C. (co. seat, Louisburg).
Franklin Co., Ohio (co. seat, Columbus).
Franklin Co., Pa. (co. seat, Chambersburg).
Franklin Co., Tenn. (co. seat, Winchester).
Franklin Co., Vt. (co. seat, St. Albans).
Franklin Co., Va. (co. seat, Rocky Mount).
Franklin Co., Wash. (co. seat, Pasco).

Franklin, Ga. (co. seat of Heard Co.).
Franklin, Ind. (co. seat of Johnson Co.).
Franklin, Ky. (co. seat of Simpson Co.).
Franklin, La. (parish seat of St. Mary Parish).
Franklin, Mass. (Norfolk Co.).
Franklin, Mich. (Oakland Co.).
Franklin, Neb. (co. seat of *Franklin* Co.).
Franklin, N.H. (Merrimack Co.).
Franklin, N.J. (Sussex Co.).
Franklin, N.C. (co. seat of Macon Co.).
Franklin, Ohio (Warren Co.).
Franklin, Pa. (co. seat of Venango Co.).
Franklin, Tenn. (co. seat of Williamson Co.). So named by Hugh Williamson for his friend Benjamin Franklin, whom he met in Paris.
Franklin, , Va. (independent city in Southampton Co.).
Franklin, W.Va. (co. seat of Pendleton Co.). Earlier, Frankfort, probably from Frank's Ford, for Francis ("Frank") Evick, an early settler.
Franklin, Wis. (Milwaukee Co.).
Franklin Lake, Wis.
Franklin, Mount, N.H.
Franklin Park, Ill. (Cook Co.). Promotional.
Franklin Square, N.Y. (Nassau Co.).
Franklinton, La. (parish seat of Washington Parish).
Franklinville, N.Y. (Cattaraugus Co.).

FRANKLIN Co., Idaho (co. seat, Preston). For Franklin D. Richards, a Mormon who established the first permanent settlement in Idaho.

FRANKLIN, Point, Alaska. For Sir John Franklin (1786-1847), of the British Royal Navy, commander of an Arctic exploration in 1826. On a later expedition (1847), he and his crew disappeared in northern Canada.

FRANKLIN Co., Tex. (co. seat, Mount Vernon). For Benjamin Cromwell Franklin (1805-1873), an officer in the Republic of Texas army and later a Texas jurist.

FRANKLIN, Tex. (co. seat of Robertson Co.). For an early settler, W. G. Franklin. An earlier name was Morgan.

FRANKLIN LAKES, N.J. (Bergen Co.). For William Franklin (1731-1816), son of Benjamin Franklin and the last royal governor of New Jersey. A loyalist, he was

arrested by the revolutionary forces during the American Revolution.

FRANKS PEAK See FRANC.

FRASER, Mich. (Macomb Co.). For Alexander J. Frazer (?-1871), attorney and landowner.

FREDERICK For Frederick CALVERT.
Frederick Co., Md. (co. seat, *Frederick*).
Frederick, Md. (co. seat of *Frederick* Co.).

FREDERICK For Frederick Louis, Prince of Wales (1707-1751), son of George II and father of George III of England.
Frederick Co., Va. (co. seat, Winchester).
Fredericksburg, Va. (independent city in Spotsylvania Co.).

FREDERICK, Okla. (co. seat of Tillman Co.). For Frederick Van Blarcom, son of J. C. Van Blarcom, an executive of the Frisco railroad, who offered the town an iron flagpole if the people would name it after his son.

FREDERICKSBURG, Tex. (co. seat of Gillespie Co.). For Prince Frederick of Prussia, a member of the group that sponsored the German settlers' migration to Texas.

FREDERICK SOUND, Alaska. Water passage between Chatham and Dry Straits. Named by Capt. George Vancouver in 1794 for Frederick, Duke of York, son of King George III of England.

FREDONIA A pseudo-Latin word coined by Samuel Latham Mitchell to mean "place of freedom," seriously proposed as the name for the United States.
Fredonia, Kan. (co. seat of Wilson Co.). For *Fredonia*, N.Y.
Fredonia, N.Y. (Chautauqua Co.).

FREEBORN Co., Minn. (co. seat, Albert Lea). For William Freeborn (1817-1900) born in Ohio, who moved to St. Paul and held large business interests in the area. He was a territorial legislator (1854-57).

FREEDOM, Calif. (Santa Cruz Co.). For a saloon—characteristic of the late 1800s.

FREEHOLD, N.J. (co. seat of Monmouth Co.). For the freeholders, or landowners, who established the county. The term is still used for supervisors of the county administration.

FREEPORT, III. (co. seat of Stephenson Co.). Named by Mrs. William Baker, wife of the first settler, in disgust at too much hospitality on the part of her husband, who maintained a "free port," as a house was called where all comers were welcome.

FREEPORT, Me. (Cumberland Co.), town. Probably for the expansive appearance of the harbor. It has also been suggested that Sir Andrew Freeport, a character in a Joseph Addison play, was the source.

FREEPORT, N.Y. (Nassau Co.). So named because in colonial day cargo ships used the small, unwatched port to avoid British taxes. An earlier name was Raynortown, for Edward Raynor, a local farmer.

FREEPORT, Tex. (Brazoria Co.). Descriptive and promotional; situated at the mouth of the Brazos River.

FREER, Tex. (Duvall Co.). For O. J. Freer, an early settler.

FREETOWN, Mass. (Bristol Co.), town. Named by the twenty-six "Free Men" who purchased the town from the Indians.

FREMONT, John Charles (1813-1890), explorer, politician, and soldier. He was a protege of Sen. Thomas Hart Benton of Missouri and married his daughter, Jessie. He led five different expeditions to the West, the first to survey the Oregon Trail, with Kit Carson as guide. His written report of this trip gave him a wide popular reputation. The second expedition reached the Columbia River, later crossing the Sierra Nevada into California, where he refitted at Sutter's Fort. A third expedition blazed a new trail across

Fremont and his party are shown being surprised by an old squaw left to die by her tribe. [*New York Public Library*]

Nevada and then to Monterey and San Jose, Calif. Fremont inspired American settlers in the Sacramento valley to the "Bear Flag revolt," gave them armed support and, with his "California Battalion," took part in the capture of Los Angeles. He was briefly the civil governor of California but was convicted of mutiny and insubordination in a court-martial. President Polk remitted his penalty, but Fremont resigned. He served as a senator from California (1850-51) and was nominated as Republican candidate for President in 1856. During the Civil War he was a major general.

Fremont Co., Colo. (co. seat, Canon City).
Fremont Co., Idaho (co. seat, Saint Anthony).
Fremont Co., Iowa (co. seat, Sidney).
Fremont Co., Wyo. (co. seat, Lander).
Fremont, Calif. (Alameda Co.).
Fremont, Mich. (Newaygo Co.).
Fremont, Neb. (co. seat of Dodge Co.).
Fremont, Ohio (co. seat of Sandusky Co.).
Fremont Peak, Wyo.
Fremont River, Utah.

FRENCH BROAD RIVER, N.C.-Tenn. For its width and for eighteenth century French ownership. It flows generally northwest to join Holston River to form the Tennessee River.

FRENCHBURG, Ky. (co. seat of Menifee Co.). For Richard French (1792-1854), attorney, state legislator, jurist, and U.S. representative (1835-37; 1843-45; 1847-49).

FRENCH CREEK, N.Y.-Pa. So named because the French used the stream as a supply route to their forts along the Ohio River. It flows generally south into Allegheny River.

FRENCHMAN For a Frenchman who lived in the area or for an incident involving one.
Frenchman Bay, Me. Or so named because it was a grouping point for French ships.
Frenchman Creek, Sask.-Mont. Flows SE into Milk R.
Frenchman River, Colo. Flows ESE into Republican R.

FRENCH RIVER, Conn.-Mass. Reason for name unknown, but probably for presence of a Frenchman at some time in history. It flows south into Quinebaug River.

FRESNO From Spanish, "ash," for the tree, *Fraxinus oregona*, native to the area.
Fresno Co., Calif. (co. seat, *Fresno*).
Fresno, Calif. (co. seat of *Fresno* Co.).
Fresno Reservoir, Mont.
Fresno River, Calif.

FRIDAY HARBOR, Wash. (co. seat of San Juan Co.). Possibly for the day on which some ship and its crew arrived in the harbor, or for a shepherd in the area who called himself "Friday."

FRIDLEY, Minn. (Anoka Co.). For Abram McCormick Fridley (1817-1888), Indian agent, farmer, and legislator.

FRIENDSHIP Promotional.
Friendship, N.Y. (Allegany Co.).
Friendship, Wis. (co. seat of Adams Co.). For *Friendship*, N.Y.

FRIENDSWOOD, Tex. (Galveston Co.). So named because it was a Quaker settlement surrounded by woods.

FRIO From Spanish, "cold," descriptive of weather or water.
Frio Co., Tex. (co. seat, Pearsall). For the river.
Frio River, Tex.

FRIONA, Tex. (Parmer Co.). For a small river, Frio Draw, which runs nearby. The *-na* was added to distinguish the town from another called FRIO.

FRONTENAC, Louis de Buade, Count of Palluau and Frontenac (c.1620-1698), governor of New France (1672-82).
Frontenac Co., Ont. (co. seat, Kingston).
Frontenac Co., Que. (co. seat, Magantic).
Frontenac, Mo. (independent city in St. Louis Co.).

FRONTIER Co., Neb. (co. seat, Stockville). So named because it was on the Nebraska frontier at the time of naming.

FRONT ROYAL, Va. (co. seat of Warren Co.). The origin of the name is uncertain. One account, locally accepted, is that a drill sergeant was having trouble making his orders understood by the troops and, being unable to make them execute an about-face, finally ordered them to "Front the Royal Oak," the huge oak that stood in the village square. The name supposedly became a joke and then the town's name. The oak is the "royal" tree of England. Another version is that the name derives from a password used by soldiers to challenge those who wished to enter the village. A simpler explanation is that the name is derived from French *le front royal,* or the English frontier, since the town is on the southern boundary of what was then Frederick County.

FROSTBURG, Md. (Allegheny Co.). For Mesach Frost, who in 1812 established a tavern in the area. Earlier names were Mount Pleasant and Frost's Town.

FRUITDALE, Ore. (Josephine Co.). Descriptive and promotional. The place is an area near Grants Pass where much fruit is grown.

FRYXELL, Fritiot, a mountain climber.
Fryxell, Mount, Wyo. Earlier, Nameless Peak.
Fryxell Mountain, Wyo.

FUCA, Juan de. See JUAN DE FUCA STRAIT.

FUEGO MOUNTAIN, Ore. From Spanish, "fire," probably for forest fires that occurred in the area.

FULLERTON, Calif. (Orange Co.). For George H. Fullerton, land-company president and a promoter of the California Central railroad.

FULLERTON, Neb. (co. seat of Nance Co.). For Randall Fuller (1823-1901), founder and leading citizen.

FULLERTON, Pa. (Allegheny Co.). For James W. Fuller, owner of the Fuller Lehigh Company, a large ironworks.

FULTON Co., Ark. (co. seat, Salem). For William Savin Fulton (1795-1844), Arkansas Territory governor and U.S. senator (1836-44).

FULTON, Robert (1765-1815), inventor, artist, and civil engineer. In 1786 he journeyed to London for his health. He lived there for twenty years, during which time he patented machines for sawing marble, spinning flax, and twisting hemp rope, and a "doubly inclined plane" for raising and lowering canal boats; he also invented a dredge for cutting channels and designed cast-iron low-cost aqueducts and bridges. He built a diving boat for Napoleon and was authorized to proceed against British ships, but after a summer's unsuccessful reconnoitering the French lost interest and gave him no money for expenses. He then negotiated with the British and blew up a brig but failed against the French fleet, and his invention was not adopted. He entered into an agreement with Robert R. Livingston to construct a steamboat to navigate between New York and Albany. The *Clermont,* built in New York by Charles Brown with a Watt engine, successfully navigated the Hudson to Albany and back in five days (August 17-22, 1807). He also designed a steam warship, and experimented with firing guns under water.
Fulton Co., Ga. (co. seat, Atlanta).
Fulton Co., Ill. (co. seat, Lewistown).
Fulton Co., Ind. (co. seat, Rochester).
Fulton Co., Ky. (co. seat, Hickman).
Fulton Co., N.Y. (co. seat, Johnstown).
Fulton Co., Ohio (co. seat, Wauseon).
Fulton Co., Pa. (co. seat, McConnellsburg).
Fulton, Ill. (Whiteside Co.).
Fulton, Ky. (*Fulton* Co.).
Fulton, Miss. (co. seat of Itawamba Co.).
Fulton, Mo. (co. seat of Callaway Co.).
Fulton, N.Y. (Oswego Co.).
Fulton Chain of Lakes, N.Y.
Fultondale, Ala. (Jefferson Co.).

FUNSTON, Camp. Kan. See CAMP FUNSTON.

FUQUAY SPRINGS, N.C. (Wake Co.). For settlers of French descent.

FURNACE BROOK, Vt. For a furnace near the river. It flows southwest into Clarendon River.

FURNAS Co., Neb. (co. seat, Beaver City). For Robert W. Furnas (1824-1905), educator and governor (1873-75).

English sovereigns of the House of Hanover played a crucial role in the movement for American independence. George I (bottom) neglected the colonies; George II (right) encouraged them; and George III (left) drove them into rebellion. [*New York Public Library*]

GADSDEN, James (1788-1858), South Carolina soldier and politician who settled in Florida (1822-39). In 1818 he participated in the Seminole War. President Monroe appointed him (1823) commissioner to effect the removal of the Seminoles to reservations in the southern part of the territory. This was accomplished with the Treaty of Fort Moultrie. Gadsden made a survey of the reservations and built the first roads of the U.S. government in Florida. He was a member of the first territorial legislative council. As minister to Mexico under Pierce, Gadsden was authorized to buy as much border land as possible for $50 million—the Gadsden Purchase, an area comprising the southern part of Arizona and New Mexico.
Gadsden Co., Fla. (co. seat, Quincy).
Gadsden, Ala. (co. seat of Etowah Co.).

GAFFNEY, S.C. (co. seat of Cherokee Co.). For Michael Gaffney, founder. An earlier name was Gaffney's Old Field.

GAGE Co., Neb. (co. seat, Beatrice). For William D. Gage (1803-1885), a local official.

GAGES LAKE-WILDWOOD, Ill. (Lake Co.). For the Gage family, early settlers. The addition is promotional.

GAGETOWN, N.B. (co. seat of Queens Co.). For Gen. Thomas Gage (1721-1787), commander-in-chief of the British forces at Bunker Hill, who received a grant of the township in 1765. An earlier name was Grimross.

GAHANNA, Ohio (Franklin Co.). Originally a stream name, believed to be of Algonquian origin, from *hanna*, "stream."

GAIL, Tex. (co. seat of Borden Co.). For Gail BORDEN

GAILLARD, Lake, Conn. For G. Y. Gaillard, president of the New Haven Water Company (1929-52).

GAINES, Edmund Pendleton (1777-1849), a commander during the War of 1812, the Seminole Indian War, and the Mexican War. In command of Fort Erie in the War of 1812, he defended it against a superior force (1814). He is remembered also as a captor of Aaron Burr, who was brought to trial (1807) for treason but acquitted.
Fort Gaines, Ga. (co. seat of Clay Co.).
Gainesboro, Tenn. (co. seat of Jackson Co.).
Gainesville, Fla. (co. seat of Alachua Co.).
Gainesville, Ga. (co. seat of Hall Co.).
Gainesville, Mo. (co. seat of Ozark Co.). For *Gainesville*, Ga.
Gainesville, Tex. (co. seat of Cooke Co.).

GAINES Co., Tex. (co. seat, Seminole). For James Gaines (1776-1850), Texas patriot, jurist, and legislator.

GAITHERSBURG, Md. (Montgomery Co.). For Benjamin Gaither, who built the first house in the town.

GALENA For *galena*, the lead sulfide mined nearby; the ore is also known as *galenite*. *Galena*, Ill. (co. seat of Jo Daviess Co.). *Galena*, Kan. (Cherokee Co.). For *Galena*, Ill. *Galena*, Mo. (co. seat of Stone Co.). *Galena* River, Wis.-Ill. Flows SW into the Mississippi R.

GALENA PARK, Tex. (Harris Co.). For the Galena-Signal Oil Company, leading industry of the town at the time of incorporation. An earlier name was Clinton.

GALE RIVER, N.H. For a local settler. It flows northwest into Ammonoosuc River.

GALESBURG, Ill. (co. seat of Knox Co.). For George W. Gale, founder.

GALION, Ohio (Crawford Co.). Previously known as Goshen, at the time of obtaining a post office it was found there was already a town by that name, and the postmaster general suggested this name, for reasons unknown.

GALIURO MOUNTAINS, Ariz. Originally named Salitre. From Spanish, "salt peter" or "nitrate," for the mineral found there. The name, through spelling changes and misconceptions, became Calitre, Calitro, Caliuro, and finally Galiuro.

GALLATIN, Albert (1761-1849), statesman and diplomat. He was born in Switzerland, emigrated to America in 1780, and served in the Revolutionary Army. He began his political career as a radical member of the 1788 Harrisburg Conference, called to consider revision of the U.S. Constitution. After election to the U.S. Senate from Pennsylvania (1793), he was ousted by the Federalists, who challenged him for political reasons on the inadequate length of time he had been a citizen. He helped to subdue the "Whiskey Rebellion" (1794) in western Pennsylvania. He was a Democratic congressman from Pennsylvania (1795-1801) and leader of the minority. His insistence on the strict accountability of the Treasury Department to Congress caused the creation of the Ways and Means Committee. Jefferson made him secretary of the treasury in 1801, and he held the post until 1814. He worked to conclude a favorable British-American commercial treaty (1815) and was U.S. minister to France (1816-23), during which time he assisted the American minister in London in negotiating the Treaty of 1818 with Great Britain. He was U.S. minister to London (1826-27), and helped arrange the arbitration of the northeast U.S.-Canadian boundary by the King of the Netherlands. *Gallatin* Co., Ill. (co. seat, Shawneetown). *Gallatin* Co., Ky. (co. seat, Warsaw). *Gallatin* Co., Mont. (co. seat, Bozeman). *Gallatin*, Mo. (co. seat of Daviess Co.). *Gallatin*, Tenn. (co. seat of Sumner Co.). *Gallatin* Natl. Forest, Mont. *Gallatin* Peak, Mont. *Gallatin* Range, Mont., in the Rocky Mtns.

GALLIA Co., Ohio (co. seat, Gallipolis). The Latin name for "Gaul" (France), chosen by French colonists.

GALLINA From Spanish, "hen," but probably connotes "turkey." Also, *Gallinas*, "hens." *Gallina*, N.Mex. (Rio Arriba Co.). *Gallinas*, N.Mex. (Lincoln Co.). *Gallinas* Mountains, N.Mex. *Gallina* Peak, N.Mex. *Gallinas* Peak, N.Mex. *Gallinas* River, N.Mex. Flows SE into Pecos R.

GALLIPOLIS, Ohio (co. seat of Gallia Co.). Original French settlers combined *Gallia*, the Latin name for France, with Greek *polis*, "city."

GALLOO ISLAND, N.Y. Either for an early resident, or from French *galet*, "gravel."

GALLUP, N.Mex. (co. seat of McKinley Co.). Named by railroad workers for David L. Gallup, paymaster (hence the phrase "going to the Gallups to collect wages").

GALT, Calif. (Sacramento Co.). For a town in Ontario, Canada, which was named for John Galt, Scottish novelist.

GALT, Ont. (Waterloo Co.). For John Galt, a commissioner of the Canada Company and a friend of Hon. William Dickson, town founder.

GALVA, Ill. (Henry Co.). For Gelfe, Sweden, in an Americanized form.

GALVESTON For Bernardo de Galvez (1746-1786), Spanish colonial leader and statesman, active especially in Spanish possessions in the southern part of what is now the United States and along the Gulf of Mexico. The form of the name is Anglicized. Earlier names were Galvez and Campeche.
Galveston Co., Tex. (co. seat, *Galveston*).
Galveston, Tex. (co. seat of *Galveston* Co.).
Galveston Bay, Tex.
Galveston Island, Tex.

GANANOQUE From Indian, "rocks rising out of the water."
Gananoque, Ont. (Leeds Co.).
Gananoque River, Ont.

GANNETT HILL, N.Y. For an early settler or explorer.

GANNETT PEAK, Wyo. For Henry Gannett (1846-1914), geographer and a member of U.S. Geological Survey explorations. He is also the author of *Origin of Certain Place Names in the United States.*

GANNVALLEY, S.Dak. (co. seat of Buffalo Co.). For Herst Gann, an early settler.

GARDEN Descriptive and usually promotional.
Garden Co., Neb. (co. seat, Oshkosh). Citizens thought it the "garden spot of the West."
Gardena, Calif. (Los Angeles Co.). For fertile lands.
Garden Island, Mich.
Garden Acres, Calif. (Orange Co.).
Garden City, Kan. (co. seat of Finney Co.).
Garden City, Mich. (Wayne Co.). Lots were large enough for the owners to cultivate gardens.
Garden City, N.Y. (Nassau Co.).
Garden Grove, Calif. (Orange Co.).

GARDEN CITY, Tex. (co. seat of Glasscock Co.). A misspelling of *Gardner City*, for William Gardner, an early store owner.

GARDINER, Me. (Kennebec Co.). For Dr. Sylvester Gardiner, founder.

GARDINERS For Lyon Gardiner, a Scotsman.
Gardiners Bay, N.Y.
Gardiners Island, N.Y. In the bay.

GARDNER, Mass. (Worcester Co.). For Col. Thomas Gardner (1724-1775), killed at Bunker Hill.

GARDNER LAKE, Conn. For Stephen Gardner, who bought a parcel of land including the lake, about 1700. Earlier names were Obtintksok, meaning unknown, and Marsataug, from Algonquian, "great pond."

GARDNER LAKE, Me. For Laban Gardner, an early settler.

GARFIELD, James Abram (1831-1881), twentieth President of the United States (1881), from Ohio. He was a general during the Civil War and a member of the House of Representatives (1863-80). After less than four months in office, he was shot (July 2, 1881) by Charles J. Guiteau in Washington. He died on September 19 and was succeeded by his vice-president, Chester A. Arthur.
Garfield Co., Colo. (co. seat, Glenwood Springs.
Garfield Co., Mont. (co. seat, Jordan).
Garfield Co., Neb. (co. seat, Burwell).
Garfield Co., Okla. (co. seat, Enid).
Garfield Co., Utah (co. seat, Panquitch).
Garfield Co., Wash. (co. seat, Pomeroy).
Garfield, N.J. (Bergen Co.). Earlier, Cadmus Melon Patch.
Garfield, Lake, Mass. The President once visited the area. Named shortly after his assassination.

GARFIELD Peak, Ore. For James R. Garfield (1865-1950), son of President Garfield. He was secretary of the interior (1907-09) under Theodore Roosevelt.

GARLAND, Augustus Hill (1832-1899), lawyer. He was Union delegate to the Arkansas state convention that passed the ordinance of secession in 1861, governor of Arkansas (1874-76), U.S. senator (1877-85), and attorney general (1885-89) under Cleveland.
Garland Co., Ark. (co. seat, Hot Springs).
Garland, Tex. (Dallas Co.).

GARNER, Iowa (co. seat of Hancock Co.). For an official of the Chicago, Milwaukee and St. Paul railroad.

GARNETT, Kan. (co. seat of Anderson Co.). For William Garnett, a founder.

GARNICKS NEEDLES (peak), Wyo. For Notsie and Frank Garnick, early explorers.

GARRARD Co., Ky. (co. seat, Lancaster). For James Garrard (1749-1822), Kentucky legislator and governor (1796-1804).

GARRET Co., Md. (co. seat, Oakland). For John Work Garrett (1820-1884), Maryland industrialist, president of the Baltimore and Ohio railroad (1858-84).

GARRISON RESERVOIR, N.Dak. For an early settler.

GARVIN Co., Okla. (co. seat, Pauls Valley). For Samuel J. Garvin, a Chickasaw leader.

GARWOOD, N.J. (Union Co.). For the president of a development company.

GARY, Elbert H., Lawyer and chairman of the board of directors of the U.S. Steel Corporation, which founded the city.
East Gary, Ind. (lake Co.).
Gary, Ind. (Lake Co.).

GARZA, Geronimo, a colonizer who founded San Antonio.
Garza Co., Tex. (co. seat, Post).
Garza-Little Elm Reservoir, Tex.

GAS CITY, Ind. (Grant Co.). For the natural gas wells in the area.

GASCONADE Origin uncertain, but seems to allude to a Gascon (someone from Gascony, France), or perhaps an incident characterized by bravado.
Gasconade Co., Mo. (co. seat, Hermann).
Gasconade River, Mo.

GASPE Probably for Gaspar Corte-Real who landed in Quebec in 1500; or it may be from Indian *gespeg*, "end of the world."
Gaspe Co., Que. (co. seats, Perce and Sainte Anne des Monts).
Gaspe, Que. (*Gaspe* Co.).
Gaspe Bay, Que.
Gaspe, Cape, Que.
Gaspe Peninsula, Que., extends into Gulf of St. Lawrence.

GASTON, William (1778-1844), North Carolina legislator and jurist.
Gaston Co., N.C. (co. seat, *Gastonia*).
Gaston Dam, N.C.
Gaston Lake, N.C.
Gastonia, N.C. (co. seat of *Gaston* Co.). Pseudo-Latin form of *Gaston*.
Gastonia South, N.C. (*Gaston* Co.).

GATE CITY, Va. (co. seat of Scott Co.). For a gap or pass to coal mines to the west.

GATES, Horatio (1728?-1806), colonial army officer who became a general in the Continental Army, defeating the British under Burgoyne at the Battle of Saratoga (1777).
Gates Co., N.C. (co. seat, *Gatesville*).
Gatesville, N.C. (co. seat of *Gates* Co.).

GATESVILLE, Tex. (co. seat of Coryell Co.). For nearby Fort Gates, which was for Maj. G. R. Gates of the Fourth U.S. infantry.

GATINEAU, Nicholas, a fur trader who came to Canada in 1649 and reputedly drowned (co.1683) in the river which now bears his name.
Gatineau Co., Que. (co. seat, Maniwaki).
Gatineau, Que. (Hull Co.).
Gatineau River, Que.

GAULEY Origin uncertain; either from a personal name or from French, "river of the Gauls."
Gauley River, W.Va.
Gauley Reservoir, W.Va. On the river.

GAYLORD, Mich. (co. seat of Otsego Co.). For A. S. Gaylord, attorney for the Jackson, Lansing and Saginaw railroad.

GAYLORD, Minn. (co. seat of Sibley Co.). For Edward W. Gaylord, a railway official.

GAYLOR MOUNTAIN, Ark. In Boston Mountains. Probably for an explorer.

GEARY Co., Kan. (co. seat, Junction City). For John White Geary (1819-1873), a governor of Pennsylvania, officer in the Mexican and Civil Wars, and territorial governor of Kansas.

GEAUGA Co., Ohio (co. seat, Chardon). Possibly from Iroquoian *sheauga*, "raccoon," but the name is in dispute. It may be a form of *Cuyahoga*, for the river of that name, in translation "raccoon river," or of *Cageauga*, "dogs around the fire." It may also have been named for an Indian chief.

GEERS POINT, Wyo. For William C. Geers, geologist from Cornell University.

GEIKIE MOUNTAIN, Wyo. For Archibald Geikie, geologist from Scotland.

GEIST RESERVOIR, Ind. For Clarence H. Geist (?-1938), president of the Indianapolis Water Company.

GEM Co., Idaho (co. seat, Emmett). From the supposed Indian meaning for *Idaho*, "Gem of the Mountain."

GENESEE From Iroquoian, "beautiful valley."

Genesee Co., Mich. (co. seat, Flint).
Genesee Co., N.Y. (co. seat, Batavia).
Genesee River, Pa.-N.Y.

GENESEO Variant of GENESEE.
Geneseo, Ill. (Henry Co.). For the Genesee R., N.Y.
Geneseo, N.Y. (co. seat of Livingston Co.).

GENEVA Name for Geneva, Switzerland, by Swiss settlers. See also LAKE GENEVA.
Geneva Co., Ala. (co. seat, *Geneva*).
Geneva, Ala. (co. seat of *Geneva* Co.).
Geneva, Ill. (co. seat of Kane Co.). For *Geneva*, N.Y.
Geneva, Neb. (co. seat of Fillmore Co.). For *Geneva*, N.Y.
Geneva, N.Y. (Ontario Co.).
Geneva, Ohio (Ashtabula Co.).

Quebec's famed Gaspe Peninsula runs alongside the St. Lawrence River. Shown here are flocks of gannets on craggy Bonaventure Island off the peninsula's tip. [*Canadian National Railways*]

GENOA For the city in Italy.
Genoa, Ill. (De Kalb Co.). For *Genoa*, N.Y.
Genoa, N.Y. (Cayuga Co.).

GENTRY Co., Mo. (co. seat, Albany). For Richard Gentry (1788-1837), officer in the Indian Wars, killed by the Seminoles in Florida.

GEORGE Co., Miss. (co. seat, Lucedale). For James Zachariah George (1826-1897), Confederate army general and U.S. senator (1881-97).

GEORGES For ST. GEORGE.
Georges Harbor, Me.
Georges Island, Me.

GEORGETOWN For George Augustus of Hanover (1683-1760), crowned (1727) king of England as George II. See also GEORGIA and LAKE GEORGE.
Georgetown Co., S.C. (co. seat, *Georgetown*).
Georgetown, Ga. (co. seat of Quitman Co.).
Georgetown, S.C. (co. seat of *Georgetown* Co.).

GEORGETOWN For George WASHINGTON.
Georgetown, Ky. (co. seat of Scott Co.). Earlier, McClelland's Station.
Georgetown, Ohio (co. seat of Brown Co.). For *Georgetown*, Ky.

GEORGETOWN For George William Frederick (1738-1820), crowned (1760) king of England as George III.
Georgetown, Ont. (Halton Co.).
Georgetown, P.E.I. (co. seat of Kings Co.). Named by Capt. Samuel Hall.

GEORGETOWN, Colo. (co. seat of Clear Creek Co.). For George Griffith, a local official.

GEORGETOWN, Del. (co. seat of Sussex Co.). For George Mitchell, a commissioner and prominent citizen.

GEORGETOWN, Ill. (Vermilion Co.). For George Haworth, a founder's son.

GEORGETOWN, Tex. (co. seat of Williamson Co.). For George Washington Glasscock (1810-1879), representative of the area at the time of naming, who donated

Rural Georgia during the 1800s. This peaceful scene shows a Georgia railroad train against the backdrop of Stone Mountain in DeKalb County. [*New York Public Library*]

"Going into action" during the bloody skirmish at Cemetery Ridge at the crucial battle of Gettysburg in 1863. [*Etching by Edwin Forbes. New York Public Library*]

land for the county seat after commissioners promised to name the city for him. See also GLASSCOCK Co.

GEORGE WASHINGTON CARVER NATL. MONUMENT, Mo. Commemorates the birthplace of George Washington Carver (1864-1943), teacher botanist, black leader, and pioneer conservationist.

GEORGE WEST, Tex. (co. seat of Live Oak Co.). For George W. West, a rancher who gave $75,000 toward building a county courthouse.

GEORGIA For George II of England; named by James Oglethorpe, who received a royal charter to settle the land in 1732. See also GEORGETOWN.
Georgia, State of. Fourth state of the Union. Settled: 1733. One of the original 13 colonies. Ratified Constitution: 1788. Cap: Atlanta. Motto: Wisdom, Justice, Moderation. Nicknames: Empire State of the South; also Peach State, Buzzard State, Cracker State, Goober State. Flower: Cherokee Rose. Bird: Brown

Thrasher. Tree: Live Oak, Song: "Georgia."

GERBER RESERVOIR, Ore. For Louis C. Gerber, early settler.

GERDINE, Mount, Alaska, in Tordrillo Mountains. For Thomas Golding Gerdine (1872-1930), U.S. Geological Survey engineer.

GERING, Neb. (co. seat of Scotts Bluff Co.). For Martin Gering, a prominent citizen and businessman.

GERMANTOWN Settled by German immigrants.
Germantown, N.Y. (Columbia Co.). Settlers from the Rhineland.
Germantown, Ohio (Montgomery Co.).
Germantown, Pa. Section of Philadelphia.
Germantown, Tenn. (Shelby Co.).
Germantown, Wis. (Washington Co.).

GERO ISLAND, Me. Meaning of name unknown.

GETTYSBURG For Gen. James Gettys, founder. Gettysburg, Pa. has become famous for the Civil War battles fought there between June 3 and August 1, 1863. The Confederate forces were defeated in the major battle of July 1 through 4.

Gettysburg, Pa. (co. seat of Adams Co.). Earlier, Marsh Creek Settlement.

Gettysburg, S.Dak. (co. seat of Potter Co.). Named for the Battle of *Gettysburg* by Civil War veterans.

Gettysburg Natl. Military Park and Natl. Cemetery, Pa.

GIANT Subjectively descriptive of size.

Giant Hill, Neb.

Giant Mountain, N.Y. Short for *Giant of the Valley*, since it dominates the valley.

GIBBSBORO, N.J. (Camden Co.). Probably for a local citizen.

GIBRALTAR, Mich. (Wayne Co.). For the Gibralter and Flat Rock Company. The spelling was apparently changed to conform with the name of the famous rock off the coast of Spain.

GIBSON, Ga. (co. seat of Glascock Co.). For Judge William Gibson (1822-1893), who donated $500 toward the building of a county courthouse.

GIBSON Co., Ind. (co. seat, Princeton). For John Gibson (1740-1822), general in the American Revolution and jurist. He was active in the Indian wars and in Indian affairs.

GIBSON Co., Tenn. (co. seat, Trenton). For John Gibson, an officer under Andrew Jackson's command in 1812.

GIBSON CITY, Ill. (Ford Co.). For the Gibson family, the founder's in-laws.

GIDDINGS, Tex. (co. seat of Lee Co.). For J. D. Giddings, an early settler.

GIFFARD, Que. (Quebec Co.). For Robert Giffard (1587-1668), a surgeon and apothecary who served on ships engaged in the Canadian fur trade (1627). He was granted the seigniory of Notre Dame de Beauport near Quebec (1634) and was an active colonizer and member of the council of Quebec.

GIHON RIVER, Vt. Biblical; for the river that flows out of the Garden of Eden. It flows southwest into Lamoille River.

GILA Probably from an Indian tribal name of obscure meaning now, transliterated through Spanish.

Gila Co., Ariz. (co. seat, Globe). For the river.

Gila Mtns., Ariz.

Gila Natl. Forest, N.Mex.

Gila River, N.Mex.-Ariz. Flows into the Colorado R.

Gila Cliff Dwellings Natl. Monument.

GILBERT PEAK, Utah, in the Uinta Mtns. For Grove K. Gilbert, a member of the U.S. Geological Survey.

GILCHRIST Co., Fla. (co. seat, Trenton). For Albert Waller Gilchrist (1858-1926), Florida soldier, statesman, and businessman. He was governor (1909-13).

GILE FLOWAGE, Wis. For the nearby village, in turn for Gordon H. Gile, a mine owner.

GILES, William Branch (1762-1830), Virginia statesman, U.S. representative (1790-98; 1801-03), U.S. senator (1804-15), and governor (1827-30).

Giles Co., Tenn. (co. seat, Pulaski).

Giles Co., Va. (co. seat, Pearisburg).

GILFORD, N.H. (Belknap Co.), town. For the Battle of Guilford Court House (1781) in North Carolina. Although not an immediate American victory, this engagement decimated the forces of Lord Cornwallis and led indirectly to his surrender at Yorktown. Lemuel B. Mason, a New Hampshire officer who served under Gen. Nathanael Greene at Guilford Court House, suggested the name.

GILLESPIE, Ill. (Macoupin Co.). For Joseph Gillespie, jurist and legislator.

GILLESPIE Co., Tex. (co. seat, Fredericksburg). For Robert Addison Gillespie, killed (1846) during the Mexican War.

GILLETTE, Wyo. (co. seat of Campbell Co.). For Weston E. Gillette, surveyor for the Burlington railroad. An earlier name was Donkey Town.

GILLIAM Co., Ore. (co. seat, Condon). For Cornelius Gilliam (1798-1848), veteran of the Indian wars, former county official in Montana, and local citizen.

While not common in North America, except in Alaska and northwestern Canada, there are many prominent continental glacial features, including the famous Columbia Glacier in Alberta and the Canadian-American Glacier National Park. [*New York Public Library*]

GILMER Co., Ga. (co. seat, Ellijay). For George Rockingham Gilmer (1790-1859), veteran of the Indian wars, U.S. representative (1827-29; 1857-61), and twice governor of Georgia (1829-31; 1837-39).

GILMER, Thomas Walker (1802-1844), lawyer, member of the Virginia House of Delegates (1829-36; 1839-40), serving as speaker the last two years, governor of Virginia (1840-41), and U.S. representative (1841-44). He was killed by the bursting of a gun on the U.S.S. *Princeton*. Before his death he had served as secretary of the navy (1844) under Tyler for a total of thirteen days.
Gilmer Co., W.Va. (co. seat, Glenville).
Gilmer, Tex. (co. seat of Upshur Co.).

GILMORE LAKE, Wis. For a local dweller.

GILPIN Co., Colo. (co. seat, Central City).

For William Gilpin (1822-1894), U.S. Army officer and first territorial governor of Colorado.

GILROY, Calif. (Santa Clara Co.). For John Cameron Gilroy (1794-1869), Scottish sailor and landowner and influential man in the town.

GIMLI, Man. For "the great hall of heaven" in Norse mythology. From Old Icelandic, *gim*, "fire," plus *li*, "shelter," presumably describing a place safe from fire.

GIRARD, Ohio (Trumbull Co.). For Stephen Girard (1750-1831), merchant, banker, and philanthropist. He founded Girard College for poor white orphan boys in Philadelphia.
Girard, Kan. (co. seat of Crawford Co.). For
   Girard, Pa.
Girard, Ohio (Trumbull Co.).
Girard, Pa. (Erie Co.).

GLACIER For glaciers on high mountains.

Glacier Co., Mont. (co. seat, Cut Bank).
Glacier Bay, Alaska.
Glacier Natl. Park, Mont., on the Continental Divide.
Glacier Peak, Wash. (Snohomish Co.).
Glacier Peak, Wash. (Whatcom Co.).
Glacier Bay Natl. Monument, Alaska.
Glacier Park, Mont. (*Glacier* Co.).
Glacier Peak, ·Wilderness, Wash.

GLADES Co., Fla. (co. seat, Moore Haven). A popular shortened form of EVERGLADES.

GLADEWATER, Tex. (Gregg Co.). For the abundance of trees and the water in a nearby creek.

GLADSTONE, William Ewart (1809-1898), British statesman and several times prime minister.
Gladstone, Mich. (Delta Co.). British money was provided for the railway built through the community.
Gladstone, Mo. (Jackson Co.).
Gladstone, Ore. A local citizen much admired the statesman.

GLADWIN, Henry (1729-1791), British soldier in command of the post at Detroit (1763) when Pontiac's War broke out, in an Indian effort to hold back English expansion. Gladwin successfully defended Detroit, one of two major ports that managed to escape the destruction and slaughter. This defense is the central theme of *History of the Conspiracy of Pontiac* (1851) by Francis Parkman. After the defense of Detroit, Gladwin was carried on the army lists as "Deputy Adjutant General in America" until 1780, although he never returned to America after 1764. He declined to serve in the American Revolution.
Gladwin Co., Mich. (co. seat, *Gladwin*).
Gladwin, Mich. (co. seat of *Gladwin* Co.).

GLASCOCK Co., Ga. (co. seat, Gibson). For Thomas Glascock (1790-1841), Georgia legislator and member of the U.S. House of Representatives (1835-39).

GLASGOW For Glasgow, Scotland.
Glasgow, Ky. (co. seat of Barren Co.).
Glasgow, Mont. (co. seat of Valley Co.).
New Glasgow, N.S. (Picore Co.).

GLASS For the presence of the obsidian mineral, volcanic glass, or another glass-like mineral.
Glass Mountain, Calif.
Glass Mountains, Tex.

GLASSCOCK Co., Tex. (co. seat, Garden City). For George Washington Glasscock (1810-1879), an associate of Abraham Lincoln, later an emigrant to Texas, where he was a businessman and legislator. See also GEORGETOWN, Tex.

GLASTENBURY Possibly a variant of GLASTONBURY.
Glastenbury, Vt. (Bennington Co.), town.
Glastenbury Mountain, Vt.

GLASTONBURY, Conn. (Hartford Co.), town. For Glastonbury, Somersetshire, England.

GLEN Descriptive, for a glen or valley.
Glen Canyon, Utah-Ariz.
Glen Lake, Mich.
Glen Canyon Natl. Recreation Area, Utah.

GLEN AVON, Calif. (Riverside Co.). From *glen* and Celtic *avon*, "river."

GLEN BURNIE, Md. (Anne Arundel Co.). Developed by and named for John Glen, who acquired an estate in the area in the 1880s. The second part of the name was taken from Scottish, and means "brook."

GLENCOE, Ill. (Cook Co.). From *glen* plus *coe*, the latter the maiden name of the founder.

GLENCOE For the Glencoe valley, Scotland.
Glencoe, Minn. (co. seat of McLeod Co.). Named by Martin McLEOD , in memory of the MacDonalds killed there in the Glencoe Massacre (1692).
Glencoe Spire (peak), Wyo.

GLENDALE Descriptive and often promotional.
Glendale, Ariz. (Maricopa Co.).
Glendale, Calif. (Los Angeles Co.).
Glendale, Mo. (St. Louis Co.).
Glendale, Ohio (Hamilton Co.).
Glendale, Wis. (Milwaukee Co.). Chiefly because the voters liked the name.
Glendale Heights, Ill. (Du Page Co.).

GLENDIVE, Mont. (co. seat of Dawson Co.). From Gaelic, "valley of the deer"; named by Sir George Gore, an Irish sportsman who hunted along the Yellowstone River (1855-56).

GLENDORA, Calif. (Los Angeles Co.). Named by George Whitcomb, from *glen* and his wife's name, Le*dora.*

GLENDO RESERVOIR, Wyo., on N. Platte River. From *glen* plus *-do.*

GLENELLYN, Ill. (Du Page Co.). *Ellyn* was added onto *glen,* a nearby feature, probably for euphonic reasons.

GLENGARRY Co., Ont. (co. seat, Cornwall). For Glengarry, Inverness, Scotland.

GLENN Co., Calif. (co. seat, Willows). For Hugh J. Glenn, an influential citizen and wheat farmer.

GLEN RIDGE, N.Y. (Essex Co.). Descriptive.

GLEN ROCK, N.J. (Bergen Co.). For a rock that was an Indian landmark and was so used in property deeds.

GLEN ROSE, Tex. (co. seat of Somervell Co.). Named by Mrs. T. C. Jordan, wife of a prominent businessman during the early days of the town, for the wild roses that grew in profusion in the area.

GLENVIEW, Ill. (Cook Co.). Promotional.

GLENVILLE, W.Va. (co. seat of Gilmer Co.). For the glen, a narrow valley, there.

GLENWOOD Descriptive and sometimes promotional.
Glenwood, Ill. (Cook Co.).
Glenwood, Iowa (co. seat of Mills Co.). For the glens and vales in the area.
Glenwood, Minn. (co. seat of Pope Co.). For a large glen in the Lake Minnewaska valley.
Glenwood Springs, Colo. (co. seat of Garfield Co.). For *Glenwood,* Iowa, and for hot springs.

GLOBE, Ariz. (co. seat of Gila Co.). Either for the Globe Mine, which may have been named for its size, or for a globe-shaped boulder.

GLOCESTER, R.I. (Providence Co.), town. A variant spelling of Gloucester, Gloucestershire, England.

GLORY MOUNTAIN, Wyo. So named because it was liked.

GLOUCESTER For Gloucester, Gloucestershire, England.
Gloucester, Mass. (Essex Co.).
New Gloucester, Me. (Cumberland Co.), town. For *Gloucester,* Mass.

GLOUCESTER, Henry, Duke of (1639-1660), third son of Charles I of England and brother of Charles II and James II.
Gloucester Co., N.J. (co. seat, Woodbury).
Gloucester Co., Va. (co. seat, *Gloucester*).
Gloucester, Va. (co. seat of *Gloucester* Co.).

GLOUCESTER Co., N.B. (co. town, Bathurst). For Mary, Duchess of Gloucester (1776-1857), daughter of George III of England.

GLOVER CREEK, Okla. For a local settler. It flows south into Little River.

GLOVER PEAK, Wyo. For George M. Glover, ranger and warden.

GLOVERSVILLE, N.Y. (Fulton Co.). For the glove industry, founded by the first settlers, the dominant industry in the area and one of the most important of this kind in the world. An earlier name was Stump City.

GLYNN Co., Ga. (co. seat, Brunswick). For John Glynn (1722-1779), a member of the British Parliament who sympathized with the colonists in their struggle for independence.

GOAT ROCKS For the presence of mountain goats.
Goat Rocks, Wash. Peak in Cascade Mtns.
Goat Rocks Wilderness, Wash.

GOBACK MOUNTAIN, N.H. Origin uncertain, but perhaps a warning, "Go back."

GODERICH, Ont. (co. seat of Huron Co.). For Viscount Goderich, chancellor of the exchequer when the British Government sold the land in the Huron Tract to the Canada Company.

GOFF CREEK, Okla. For a local dweller. It flows southeast into Beaver River.

GOFFSTOWN, N.H. (Hillsborough Co.), town. For Col. John Goffe, leader of the original group of settlers.

GOGEBIC From the Ojibway name of uncertain origin, although *bic* translates as "lake."
Gegebic Co., Mich. (co. seat, Bessemer).
Gegebic, Lake, Mich.

GOLCONDA, III. (co. seat of Pope Co.). For Golconda, in Hyderabad, India. The city in India is known for its trading in precious stones, and hence the name may refer to mines in the area.

GOLD BEACH, Ore. (co. seat of Curry Co.). For gold discovered there in the 1850s.

GOLDEN, Colo. (co. seat of Jefferson Co.). For Thomas L. Golden, an early settler; gold was also discovered there in 1859.

GOLDENDALE, Wash. (co. seat of Klickitat Co.). Probably descriptive and promotional.

GOLDEN GATE, Wyo. Descriptive of a pass into Yellowstone Natl. Park.

GOLDEN ISLES, Ga. So named by Sir Robert Montgomery in 1717, in hope that the islands would provide abundance for colonizers.

GOLDEN MEADOW, La. (Lafourche Parish). For the meadows of goldenrod in the area.

GOLDEN SPIKE NATL. HISTORICAL SITE, Utah. Commemorates the site where the last spike was driven (May 10, 1869) to complete the first transcontinental railway. It joined the Union Pacific from the east and the Central Pacific from the west.

GOLDEN VALLEY Descriptive and sometimes promotional.
Golden Valley Co., Mont. (co. seat, Ryegate).
Golden Valley Co., N.Dak. (co. seat, Beach). For the "valley," actually a plateau, which looked golden with ripe grass and wheat in the fall.
Golden Valley, Minn. (Hennepin Co.).

GOLDFIELD, Nev. (co. seat of Esmeralda Co.). For the gold fields discovered there in 1902.

GOLDSBORO, N.C. (co. seat of Wayne Co.). For Maj. Matthew T. Goldsborough, a civil engineer for the Wilmington and Weldon railroad.

GOLDTHWAITE, Tex. (co. seat of Mills Co.). For J. G. Goldthwaite, a railroad official.

GOLD MANOR, Ohio (Hamilton Co.). Descriptive and promotional.

GOLIAD Probably originally of Biblical origin from *Goliath*; some also believe it to be a form of *Hidalgo*, an expression for freedom accepted by the 1829 Texas Congress.
Goliad Co., Tex. (co. seat, *Goliad*).
Goliad, Tex. (co. seat of *Goliad*, Tex.).

GOLOVNIN From the ship *Golovnin*, in turn for Capt. Vasili Mikhailovich Golovnin, of the Imperial Russian Navy.
Golovnin Bay, Alaska. Extends from the lagoon to Norton Sound.
Golovnin Lagoon, Alaska.

GONZALES, Calif. (Monterey Co.). Possibly for Alfredo and Mariano Gonzales, both associated with the Monterey and Salinas railroad.

GONZALES, Don Rafael (1789-1857), provisional governor of Coahuila and of Texas when the town was established.
Gonzales Co., Tex. (co. seat, *Gonzales*).
Gonzales, Tex. (co. seat of *Gonzales* Co.). Site of the first battle of the Texas Revolution.

GOOCH, Sir William (1681-1751), English statesman, governor of the colony of Virginia (1727-49). He was popular with the colonists and ably defended their interests.
Goochland Co., Va. (co. seat, *Goochland*).
Goochland, Va. (co. seat of *Goochland* Co.).

GOODHUE Co., Minn. (co. seat, Red Wing). For James Madison Goodhue (1810-1852), lawyer and prominent editor in the Minnesota Territory.

GOODING, Frank Robert (1859-1928), governor of Idaho (1905-08), U.S. representative (1921), and U.S. senator (1921-28).
Gooding Co., Idaho (co. seat, *Gooding*).
Gooding, Idaho (co. seat of *Gooding* Co.).

GOODLAND, Kan. (co. seat of Sherman Co.). Descriptive of the richness of the land, or possibly from a personal name; also perhaps for a Goodland, Indiana, former home of the developer.

GOOSE For the fowl, usually for the presence of wild geese.
Goose Creek, Neb. Flows SE into Middle Loup R.
Goose Lake, Calif.-Ore.
Goose Pond, N.H.
Goose River, N.Dak. Flows SE into Red R.
Goose Creek, S.C. (Berkeley Co.). For a creek in the area, which was named either for the large number of Canadian geese that rest there during their migrations or for the resemblance of part of the creek to the neck of a goose.
Goose Eye Mountain, Me. Reason for naming unknown.

GORDON Co., Ga. (co. seat, Calhoun). For William Washington Gordon (1796-1842), prominent Georgia railroad official.

GORDON CREEK, Neb. For a local settler. It flows east and northeast into Niobrara R.

GORE Either from a personal name or descriptive, for a triangular-shaped piece of land.
Gore Mountain, N.Y.
Gore Mountain, Vt.
Gore Pass, Colo.
Gore Range, Colo. For either a Denver gunsmith or for Sir George Gore, leader of an expedition (1854-56).

GORHAM, Capt. John, early settler and soldier. He fought in King Philip's War and was one of the original grantees of the town.
Gorham, Me. (Cumberland Co.), town and village.
Gorham, N.H. (Coos Co.), town. Name suggested by a Sylvester Davis, from *Gorham*, Me., which had been founded by his ancestors.

GOSHEN Biblical. Goshen was the Egyptian home of the Israelites before the Exodus. Although there is no solid evidence, the meaning is usually interpreted as "land of plenty or abundance." ("And Israel dwelt in the land of Egypt, in the country of Goshen; and they had possessions therein, and grew, and multiplied exceedingly." Genesis 47:27). For this hopeful reason, many places in the United States have been so named.
Goshen Co., Wyo. (co. seat, Torrington).
Goshen, Conn. (Litchfield Co.).
Goshen, Ind. (co. seat of Elkhart Co.).
Goshen, Mass. (Hampshire Co.).
Goshen, N.H. (Sullivan Co.).
Goshen, N.Y. (co. seat of Orange Co.).
Goshen, Vt. (Addison Co.).

GOSHUTE, Utah (Juag Co.). For the subtribe of Utes, "dust people."

GOSHUTE LAKE, Nev. From *Gossip*, an Indian chief, plus *Ute*, the tribal name.

GOSPER Co., Neb. (co. seat, Elwood). For John J. Gosper, a popular state official.

GOTHAM Village near Nottingham, England, noted in legend for the foolishness of its inhabitants. The authors of the *Salmagundi Papers* (among them Washington Irving) applied the nickname to New York City.

GOTHENBURG, Neb. (Dawson Co.). For Gothenburg (Anglicized form of Goteburg), Sweden.

GOTHICS (Mountains), N.Y. Descriptive, for cathedral-like "gothic" peaks.

GOUVERNEUR, N.Y. (St. Lawrence Co.). For Gouverneur Morris or his mother, Sara Gouverneur.

GOVE, Grenville L. (?-1864), Union army officer.
Gove Co., Kan. (co. seat, *Gove*).
Gove, Kan. (co. seat of *Gove* Co.).

GOWANDA, N.Y. (Erie and Cattaraugus Cos.). From an Indian phrase which meant "valley among the hills."

GRACE, Mount, Mass. From a woman's forename.

GRADY, Henry Woodfin (1850-1889), Georgia orator and journalist, who helped found the *Atlanta Herald* in 1872 but went broke. Cyrus V. Field lent him $20,000, and he bought a quarter interest in the *Atlanta Constitution* and became its editor. He helped alleviate the postbellum despair of the South through his writings, by encouraging the development of local resources, crop diversification, manufacturing, and a logical adjustment of the Negro problem.
Grady Co., Ga. (co. seat, Cairo).
Grady Co., Okla. (co. seat, Chickasha).

GRAFTON, Augustus Henry Fitzroy, 3rd Duke of (1735-1811), English statesman, secretary of state for the northern department (1765-66) and prime minister (1768-70).
Grafton Co., N.H. (co. seat, Woodsville).
Grafton, N.Dak. (co. seat of Walsh Co.). For *Grafton* Co., N.H.
Grafton Pond, N.H.

GRAFTON, Mass. (Worcester Co.), town. For Charles Fitzroy, 2nd Duke of Grafton (1683-1722), member of the Privy Council.

GRAFTON, W.Va. (co. seat of Taylor Co.). Probably from the surname of a local family.

GRAFTON, Wis. (Ozaukee Co.). Original reason for naming is not known, but probably for a *Grafton* in the Eastern states.

GRAHAM Origin uncertain; may have been named for William A. Graham, a cabinet member of the time, or for Lawrence Pike Graham, an army officer.
Graham Co., Ariz. (co. seat, Safford).
Graham, Mount, Ariz.

GRAHAM Co., Kan. (co. seat, Hill City). For John L. Graham (?-1863), a Kansas infantry officer killed at Chickamauga.

GRAHAM, Tex. (co. seat of Young Co.). For the families of the two developers, E. S. and G. Graham, first settlers.

GRAHAM, William Alexander (1804-1875), North Carolina statesman, secretary of the navy (1850-52) under Fillmore, Confederate senator, and governor (1845-49).
Graham Co., N.C. co. seat, Robbinsville).
Graham, N.C. (co. seat of Alamance Co.).

GRAHAM LAKE, Me. For John R. Graham (1847-1915), founder of the Bangor-Hydro-Electric Company.

GRAINGER Co., Tenn. (co. seat, Rutledge). For Mary Grainger, maiden name of the wife of William Blount, governor of Tennessee.

GRANBURY, Tex. (co. seat of Hood Co.). For Gen. H. B. Granbury.

GRANBY, John Manners, Marquis of (1721-1770), member of Parliament from Cambridge, England, and holder of various offices in the British government.
East Granby, Conn. (Hartford Co.).
Granby, Conn. (Hartford Co.), town.
Granby, Mass. (Hampshire Co.), town.

GRANBY, Que. (Shefford Co.). For the village in Nottinghamshire, England.

GRANBY, Lake, Colo. For a local settler.

GRAND Usually from French, "great," "magnificent," or just "large." The adjective occurs in areas once visited or occupied by the French, or occasionally, by the Spanish.
Grand Co., Colo. (co. seat, Hot Sulphur Springs).
Grand Co., Utah (co. seat, Moab). From the river, now the Colorado R.
Grand Canyon, Ariz. Canyon of the Colorado R., ranging down more than 6,000 feet in places, one of the great geological, and spectacular, sights of the world. Earlier, Big Canyon.
Grand Falls, Ariz.
Grand Island, Mich.
Grand Island, N.Y., in the Niagara R.
Grand Isle, Vt.
Grand Lame, La. (Cameron Parish).
Grand Lake, La. (St. Martin Parish).
Grand Lake, Me. (Piscataquis Co.).
Grand Lake, Me. (Washington Co.).
Grand Lake, Mich.
Grand Lake, Ohio.
Grand River, Mich. Flows generally W into L. Michigan.
Grand River, Iowa-Mo.
Grand River, Ohio.
Grand River, Okla.
Grand River, S.Dak.
Grand Canyon Natl. Monument, Ariz.

Grand Canyon Natl. Park, Ariz.
Grand Falls, N.B. (Victoria Co.).
Grand Falls, Nfld.
Grand Falls Lake, Me.
Grand Island, N.Y. (Erie Co.), town.
Grand Isle Co., Vt. (co. seat, North Hero).
Grand Mesa Natl. Forest, Colo.
Grand Wash Cliffs, Ariz.

GRAND BLANC, Mich. (Genesee Co.). From a nickname, "Big White," given to a French trader by the Indians.

GRAND COULEE DAM, Wash. See COULEE DAM.

GRANDE, La. See LA GRANDE.

GRANDE RONDE VALLEY, Ore., also spelled locally *Grand Ronde.* From French, "great round," descriptive of its appearance. See also LA GRANDE.

GRAND FALLS See GRAND.

GRAND FORKS A translation from French *La Grand Fourche*, at the forks of the Red River of the North and Red Lake River.
Grand Forks Co., N.Dak. (co. seat, *Grand Forks*).
Grand Forks, N.Dak. (co. seat of *Grand Forks* Co.).

GRAND HAVEN, Mich. (co. seat of Ottawa Co.). For both the New Haven Company, a land-developing agency, and the Grand River, on which the company's headquarters stood.

GRAND ISLAND, Neb. (co. seat of Hall Co.). For a large island in the Platte River at this point.

GRAND JUNCTION, Colo. (co. seat of Mesa Co.). For its location at the junction of the Grand (now Colorado) River and the Gunnison River.

GRAND LEDGE, Mich. (Eaton Co.). For the ledges on the Grand River nearby.

GRAND MANAN Descriptive; from Abnaki, "island." The island was named first.
Grand Manan Channel, Me. Water passage between S coast of Maine and the island.
Grand Manan Island, N.B.

GRAND MARAIS, Minn. (co. seat of Cook Co.). From French, "great marsh."

GRAND'MERE, Que. (Champlain Co.). For a rock in which the Indians saw the likeness of an elderly woman's profile.

GRAND PORTAGE NATL. MONUMENT, Minn. Commemorates the "great carrying place," the nine-mile trail from a trading post on Lake Superior to a log post above the rapids on Pigeon River.

GRAND PRAIRIE, Tex. (Dallas Co.). Promotional and descriptive of the surrounding terrain.

GRAND RAPIDS, Mich. (co. seat of Kent Co.). For the great number of rapids in the Grand River. The city is often called "The Rapids" locally.

GRAND RAPIDS, Minn. (co. seat of Itasca Co.). For the rapids in the Mississippi River.

GRAND TERRACE, Calif. (San Bernardino Co.). Descriptive.

GRAND TETON For the highest peak in the Teton Range.
Grand Teton, Wyo.
Grand Teton Natl. Park, Wyo.

GRAND TRAVERSE From French, *Le Grand Traverse*, "the long crossing," for the trail across the foot of Grand Traverse Bay.
Grand Traverse Co., Mich. (co. seat, *Traverse* City).
Grand Traverse Bay, Mich., on L. Mich.

GRANDVIEW, Mo. (Jackson Co.). Descriptive.

GRANDVIEW HEIGHTS, Ohio (Franklin Co.). Descriptive and locational.

GRANDVILLE, Mich. (Kent Co.). For the Grand River.

GRANGER-HUNTER, Utah (Salt Lake Co.). From surnames, but early documents have been lost. *Hunter* was for either Jacob Hunter, first settler, or his brother, Edward Hunter, Mormon bishop in the area.

GRANGEVILLE, Idaho (co. seat of Idaho Co.). For the local Grange, a farmers' organization.

GRANITE For the rock used in building.

Granite Co., Mont. (co. seat, Philipsburg). For the massive rock formations in the area.

Granite Pass, Wyo.

Granite Peak, Mont.

Granite Mountain, Utah.

Granite Peak, Utah.

Granite Range, Alaska.

Granite Range, Nev.

Granite Falls, Minn. (Chippewa and Yellow Medicine Cos; co. seat of Yellow Medicine Co.). For rock outcropping at the falls on the Minnesota R.

Granite Park, Utah (Salt Lake Co.). So named because it was a night stop in the hauling of granite for the building of the Salt Lake Temple walls.

GRANITE CITY, Ill. (Madison Co.). For graniteware manufactured here.

GRANNYS CAP (peak), Me. Descriptive, by witty analogy.

GRANT For a trapper and Indian trader named Grant.

Grant Co., Wis. (co. seat, Lancaster). For the river.

Grant River, Wis.

GRANT Co., Ind. (co. seat, Marion). For Samuel and Moses Grant, killed by Indians in 1790.

GRANT Co., Ky. (co. seat, Williamstown). For Samuel Grant, an early settler.

GRANT, Ulysses Simpson (1822-1885), eighteenth President of the United States (1869-77), from Ohio. Although Grant's administration was marred by a series of scandals, his reputation was untouched. While his early military career was similarly marred, by charges that he drank too much, he was clearly the most resourceful and tenacious of Union commanders during the Civil War.

Grant Co., Ark. (co. seat, Sheridan).

Grant Co., Kan. (co. seat, Ulysses).

Grant Parish, La. (parish seat, Colfax).

Grant Co., Minn. (co. seat, Elbow Lake).

Grant Co., Neb. (co. seat, Hyannis).

Grant Co., N.Mex. (co. seat, Silver City).

Grant Co., N.Dak. (co. seat, Carson).

Grant Co., Okla (co. seat, Medford).

Grant Co., Ore. (co. seat, Canyon City).

Grant Co., S.Dak. (co seat, Millbank).

Grant Co., Wash. (co. seat, Ephrata).

Grant Co., W.Va. (co. seat, Petersburg).

Grant, Neb. (co. seat of Perkins Co.).

Grant Range, Nev.

Grant City, Mo. (co. seat of Worth Co.).

Grantsburg, Wis. (co. seat of Burnett Co.).

Grants Pass, Ore. (co. seat of Josephine Co.). Probably for Ulysses S. Grant, but disputed, since the surname existed there before and at the time of naming.

Grants Pass Southwest (Josephine Co.). Ore.

Grantsville, Utah (Tooele Co.).

Grantsville, W.Va. (co. seat of Calhoun Co.).

GRANTS, N.Mex. (Valencia Co.). For Grant brothers, Angus A., John R., and Lewis A., who set up a camp for railroad workers. An earlier name was Grant's Camp.

GRANVILLE, John Carteret, Earl of (1690-1763), a landowner in North Carolina. He

After his great success during the Civil War, Ulysses S. Grant moved from the battlefield into the White House where he was less successful. This cartoon shows him being accused by Uncle Sam of complicity in the scandals which surrounded his administration, charges which never were proved. [*New York Public Library*]

was active in English political affairs.
Granville Co., N.C. (co. seat, Oxford).
Granville, Mass. (Hampden Co.).
Granville, Ohio (Licking Co.). For *Granville*,
  Mass.

GRAPEVINE, Tex. (Tarrant Co.). For a
nearby stream with its banks covered with
grapevines.

GRASS RIVER, N.Y. From French *la
grasse riviere*, "the fertile river." It flows
northeast into St. Lawrence River.

GRASS VALLEY, Calif. (Nevada Co.).
Descriptive.

GRATIOT, Charles (1786-1855), U.S.
regular army officer active in the Michigan
area during the early 1800s.
Gratiot Co., Mich. (co. seat, Ithaca).
Gratiot Lake, Mich.

GRAVES Co., Ky. (co. seat, Mayfield). For
Benjamin Graves (? 1813), an officer killed
by Indians.

GRAY, Ga. (co. seat of Jones Co.) For
James Madison Gray, a plantation owner.

GRAY Co., Kan. (co. seat, Cimarron). For
Alfred Gray, a Kansas state official.

GRAY, Me. (Cumberland Co.), town. For
Thomas Gray, one of the proprietors of the
town.

GRAY, Robert (1755-1806), discoverer of
Grays Harbor, who named it Bulfinch for an
owner of his ship. George Vancouver, in his
exploration of the area, established the
present name, although occasionally on
maps it appears as Whidbey or Whitbey
Harbor, for an officer of Vancouver's
command.
Grays Harbor, Wash. Inlet on Pacific
  Ocean.
Grays Harbor Co., Wash. (co. seat,
  Montesano).

GRAY Co., Tex. (co. seat, Pampa). For
Peter W. Gray (1819-1874), Texas legislator
and jurist.

GRAYBACK MOUNTAIN, Ore. Descriptive of color.

GRAYLING, Mich. (co. seat of Crawford
Co.). For the grayling trout in the Au Sable
River.

GRAY PEAK, N.Y. For Asa Gray (1810-
1888), New York botanist, recognized as
one of the foremost botanists and natural
historians of the 19th century. It was to Gray
that Charles Darwin wrote his famous letter
(1857) outlining his theory of evolution.

GRAYS HARBOR For Robert GRAY.

GRAYS LAKE, Idaho. Possibly for John
Gray, a Hudson's Bay Company trapper. An
earlier name was John Day's Lake.

GRAYSLAKE, Ill. (Lake Co.). For William
Gray, an early settler.

GRAYSON, Ky. (co. seat of Carter Co.).
For Col. Robert Grayson.

GRAYSON Co., Tex. (co. seat, Sherman).
For Peter William Grayson (1788-1838),
Texas patriot and state official.

GRAYSON, William (1736/40-1790),
Virginia soldier and statesman, an aide to
George Washington during the American
Revolution. He was a member of the
Continental Congress (1785-87), where he
opposed the Constitution, and U.S. senator
(1789-90).
Grayson Co., Ky. (co. seat, Leitchfield).
Grayson Co., Va. (co. seat, Independence).

GREAT Descriptive.
Great Bay, N.H.
Great Bay, N.J.
Great Brook, Mass. Flows N into Westfield
  R.
Great Point, Mass. On Nantucket Island.
Great Pond, Me.
Great Sound, N.J.
Great Bend, Kan. (co. seat of Barton Co.).
  For a sharp bend in the Arkansas R.

Great Chazy River, N.Y. See CHAZY.
Great Coharie River, N.C. See COHARIE.
Great East Lake, Me.-N.H.
Great Egg. See EGG.
Great Pond, Me. (Hancock Co.).
Great Salt Plains Reservoir, Okla.
Great Sand Dunes Natl. Monument, Colo.

GREAT AVERILL LAKE, Vt. See
AVERILL.

GREAT BARRINGTON, Mass. (Berkshire Co.), town and village. Probably for William Wildman, 2nd Viscount Barrington (1717-1793), a member of Parliament and holder of several offices in the British government. He was a nephew of Massachusetts Governor Samuel Shute, who named the town. The appellation *great* may have been used to distinguish it from a similarly named town in Rhode Island.

GREAT BASIN, Nev.-Utah-Idaho-Ore.-Ariz.-Calif. Named descriptively by J. C. Fremont when he explored the plateau (1843-45). This elevated area lies between the Sierra Nevada Range and the Wasatch Range of the Rocky Mountains.

GREAT FALLS For nearby large waterfalls.
Great Falls, Mont. (co. seat of Cascade Co.). On the Missouri R.
Great Falls, S.C. (Chester Co.). On the Catawba R.
Great Falls Lake, Tenn. In Caney Fork R.

GREAT NECK For an isthmus or peninsula, a narrow strip of land between two bodies of water.
Great Neck, N.Y. (Nassau Co.).
Great Neck Estates, N.Y. (Nassau Co.).
Great Neck Plaza, N.Y. (Nassau Co.).

GREAT QUITTACAS POND, Mass. From Wampanoag, meaning uncertain, possibly "red rocks" or "long brook."

GREAT SALT LAKE For its size and its salt content (20 to 27 percent).
Great Salt Lake (roughly 1,500 sq. mi.), Utah. The largest American lake west of the Mississippi, it is fed by the Weber, Jordan, and Bear rivers but has no outlet, which accounts for its heavy concentration of salt.
Great Salt Lake Desert, Utah.

GREAT SMOKY For the haze that resembles smoke.
Great Smoky Mountains, N.C.-Tenn. In the Appalachian Mtn. Range.
Great Smoky Mountains Natl. Park, N.C.-Tenn.

GREAT WASS ISLAND, Me. For Wilmot Wass, early settler.

GREAT WORKS STREAM, Me. So named for the extensive mill operations in the area in the 1800s. It flows generally west into Penobscot River.

GREELEY, Horace (1811-1872), editor of the New York *Tribune*. He championed westward expansion and is credited with the famous admonition, "Go west, young man." He was active in politics and was candidate for the Presidency of the United States on the Democratic ticket in 1872, losing to the incumbent, U. S. Grant.
Greeley Co., Kan. (co. seat, Tribune).
Greeley Co., Neb. (co. seat, *Greeley Center*).
Greeley, Colo. (co. seat of Weld Co.).
Greeley Center, Neb. (co. seat of *Greeley* Co.).

GREEN For Gen. Nathanael GREENE.
Green Co., Ky. (co. seat, Greensburg).
Green Co., Wis. (co. seat, Monroe).

GREEN A color name applied to many features. It occurs in every state; some important examples are noted.
Green Bay, Mich.-Wis. An arm of L. Michigan; from French *La Baie Verte*, for the color of the water.
Green Lake, Me.
Green Lake, Mich.
Green Lake, Minn.
Green Mountain, Colo.
Green Mountain, Mont.
Green Mountains, Vt.
Green Mountains, Wyo.
Green Pond, N.J.
Green River, Colo.-Utah.
Green River, Ill.
Green River, Ky.
Green River, Mass.-Vt.
Green River, Wash. (King Co.).
Green River, Wash. (Cowlitz Co.).
Green River, Wyo. Earlier, Spanish River and Indian *Seeds-ke-dee*, "sage hen."
Green Bay, Wis. (co. seat of Brown Co.). For the bay.
Green Cove Springs, Fla. (co. seat of Clay Co.). For trees and springs.
Green Lake Co., Wis. (co. seat, *Green Lake*). Translation from French, in turn from Winnebago Indian.
Green Lake, Wis. (co. seat of *Green Lake* Co.).

Greenland. Danish province off coast of North America. First American example of promotional naming. Named by Eric the Red.

Green Mountain Natl. Forest, Vt.

Green Mountain Reservoir, Colo.

Green Pond Mountain, N.J.

Green River, Wyo. (co. seat of Sweetwater Co.). For the river, in turn descriptive of the color, though some believe it to have been named for a person so named.

Green River Desert, Utah.

Green River Reservoir, Vt.

Green Rock, Ill. (Henry Co.). So named because it lies between *Green* River and Rock River.

GREENBELT, Md. (Prince Georges Co.). A planned community with a greenbelt surrounding the city.

GREENBO LAKE, Ky. A compound name formed from *Green*up and *Boyd* Counties.

GREENBRIER For the thorny vine, *Smilax rotundifolia.*

Greenbrier Co., W.Va. (co. seat, Lewisburg).

Greenbrier River, W.Va.

GREENCASTLE, Ind. (co. seat of Putnam Co.). For a Greencastle in Pennsylvania.

GREENDALE, Wis. (Milwaukee Co.). Descriptive of the layout of the city. It originated in the 1936 Resettlement Administration program, which constructed the greenbelt towns in the area.

GREENE, Gen. Nathanael (1742-1786), Rhode Island soldier, quartermaster general (1778-80) during the American Revolution. He participated in the Battle of Trenton (1776) and after 1780 was commander of the Continental Army of the South, which he used to great effect against the British in Georgia and the Carolinas. (In many place names honoring him the *e* has been dropped; these are entered elsewhere.)

Greene Co., Ala. (co. seat, Eutaw).

Greene Co., Ark. (co. seat, Paragould).

Greene Co., Ga. (co. seat, Greensboro).

Greene Co., Ill. (co. seat, Carrollton).

Greene Co., Ind. (co. seat, Bloomfield).

Greene Co., Iowa (co. seat, Jefferson).

Greene Co., Miss. (co. seat, Leakesville).

Greene Co., Mo. (co. seat, Springfield).

Greene Co., N.Y. (co. seat, Catskill).

The icebound island of Greenland, as typified by the great Humbolt Glacier, was named by the Norse explorer Eric the Red. His choice was probably influenced by his desire to attract settlers. [*New York Public Library*]

Greene Co., N.C. (co. seat, Snow Hill).
Greene Co., Ohio (co. seat, Xenia).
Greene Co., Pa. (co. seat, Waynesburg).
Greene Co., Tenn. (co. seat, *Greeneville*).
Greene Co., Va. (co. seat, Stanardsville).
Greene, N.Y. (Chenango Co.).
Greeneville, Tenn. (co. seat of *Greene* Co.).

GREENFIELD Descriptive.
Greenfield, Calif. (Monterey Co.).
Greenfield, Ind. (co. seat of Hancock Co.).
Greenfield, Iowa (co. seat of Adair Co.).
Greenfield, Mass. (co. seat of Franklin Co.), town and village. For Green R.
Greenfield, Mo. (co. seat of Dade Co.).
Greenfield, Ohio (Highland Co.).
Greenfield, Wis. (Sauk Co.). For *Greenfield*, Mass.

GREENFIELD PARK, Que. (Chambly Co.). Translated from French.

GREENHILLS, Ohio (Hamilton Co.). Descriptive and probably promotional; a Federal Resettlement Administration model community.

GREENLAWN, N.Y. (Suffolk Co.). Descriptive and promotional.

GREENLEE Co., Ariz. (co. seat, Clifton). For Mason Greenlee (1835-1903), an early settler.

GREENSBORO For Gen. Nathanael GREENE.
Greensboro, Ala. (co. seat of Hale Co.).
Greensboro, Ga. (co. seat of Greene Co.).
Greensboro, N.C. (co. seat of Guilford Co.).

GREENSBURG For Gen. Nathanael GREENE.
Greensburg, Ind. (co. seat of Decatur Co.). For *Greensburg*, Pa.
Greensburg, Ky. (co. seat of Green Co.).
Greensburg, Pa. (co. seat of Westmoreland Co.).

GREENSBURG, Kan. (co. seat of Kiowa Co.). For D. R. Green, a stagecoach driver nicknamed ''Cannonball'' because he was a fast driver.

GREENS PEAK, Ariz. For Col. John Green, commander of Fort Apache.

GREENSVILLE Co., Va. (co. seat, Emporia). For Gen. Nathanael GREENE.

GREENUP, Christopher (c.1750-1818), Virginia-born Kentucky statesman active in the American Revolution. He was a U.S. representative (1792-97) and Kentucky governor (1804-08).
Greenup Co., Ky. (co. seat, *Greenup*).
Greenup, Ky. (co. seat of *Greenup* Co.).

GREENVILLE Probably for Isaac Green (1762-1831), pioneer and mill owner. Some maintain that the name is descriptive; some that it was named for Nathanael GREENE.
Greenville Co., S.C. (co. seat, *Greenville*).
Greenville, Ala. (co. seat of Butler Co.). For *Greenville*, S.C.
Greenville, S.C. (co. seat of *Greenville* Co.).

GREENVILLE For Gen. Nathanael GREENE.
Greenville, Ga. (co. seat of Meriwether Co.).
Greenville, Ill. (co. seat of Bond Co.).
Greenville, Ky. (co. seat of Muhlenberg Co.).
Greenville, Miss. (co. seat of Washington Co.).

Nathanael Greene, who distinguished himself in both the quartermaster corps and as the commander of the Revolutionary troops in the southern campaigns, is shown here in the traditional pose of a major-general. [*New York Public Library*]

Greenville, Mo. (co. seat of Wayne Co.).
For *Greenville*, Ohio.
Greenville, N.C. (co. seat of Pitt Co.).
Greenville, Ohio (co. seat of Darke Co.).
Greenville, Pa. (Mercer Co.).

GREENVILLE, Mich. (Montcalm Co.). For John Green, founder.

GREENVILLE, Tex. (co. seat of Hunt Co.). For Gen. Thomas J. Green (1801-1863), soldier in the Texas Revolution. He was congressman for the Texas Republic and, after moving to California, introduced the first bill for the creation of the University of California. He later returned to Texas and laid out the town of Velasco.

GREENWICH, Conn. (Fairfield Co.), town. For Greenwich, a metropolitan borough of London, England. An earlier name was Elizabeth's Neck.

GREENWOOD Descriptive
Greenwood Co., S.C. (co. seat, *Greenwood*).
Greenwood, S.C. (co. seat of *Greenwood* Co.). Earlier, Green Wood.
Greenwood Lake, N.J.-N.Y.
Greenwood Lake, S.C.
Greenwood Village, Colo. (Arapahoe Co.).

GREENWOOD, Alfred Burton (1811-1889), jurist and authority on Indian affairs. He also served as U.S. representative from Arkansas (1835-59).
Greenwood Co., Kan. (co. seat, Eureka).
Greenwood, Ark. (a co. seat of Sebastian Co.).

GREENWOOD, Miss. (co. seat of Leflore Co.). For Greenwood Le Flore. See LEFLORE Co.

GREER Co., Okla. (co. seat, Mangum). For John A. Greer, a state official.

GREER, S.C. (Greenville and Spartanburg Cos.). For Manning Greer, original owner of the townsite.

GREESON, Lake, Ark. For a local settler.

GREGG Co., Tex. (co. seat, Longview). For John Gregg (1828-1864), Texas general killed during the Civil War.

GREGORY Co., S.Dak. (co. seat, Burke). For John Shaw Gregory (1831-?), active as an Indian agent and legislator in the Dakota Territory.

GREGORY BALD (Mountain), N.C.-Tenn. For a Gregory, plus *bald*, descriptive of the sparse vegetation. Also known as Bald Spot Mountain.

GRENADA Believed to have been named for the island in the West Indies. The name was chosen when the towns of Pittsburg and Tullohoma united after some years of rivalry. There is also a theory that it is a form of Granada, Spain.
Gronada Co., Miss. (co. seat, *Gronada*).
Grenada, Miss. (co. seat of *Grenada* Co.).
Grenada Lake, Miss.

GRENVILLE Co., Ont. (co. seat, Brockville). For Baron Grenville, British secretary of state for foreign affairs (1791-1801).

GRESHAM, Ore. (Multnomah Co.). For Walter Quinton Gresham (1832-1895), a general in the Union army during the Civil War, attorney, postmaster general (1883-84) and secretary of the treasury (1884) under Arthur, and a candidate for President in both 1884 and 1888. Changing parties, he served as secretary of state (1893-95) under Cleveland.

GRETNA, La. (parish seat of Jefferson Parish). For Gretna Green, Scotland. Earlier names were Mechanickham, Gouldsboro, and Mcdonoghville.

GREY Co., Ont. (co. seat, Owen Sound). For Earl Grey, British colonial secretary (1846-52).

GREYLOCK, Mount, Mass. For a Waranoke Indian chief.

GRIDLEY, Calif. (Butte Co.). For George W. Gridley, landowner.

GRIFFIN, Ga. (co. seat of Spalding Co.). For Gen. Lewis Lawrence Griffin, founder, banker, and president of the Macon and Western railroad.

GRIFFIN POINT (peak), Utah. For a local explorer or settler.

GRIFFITH, Ind. (Lake Co.). For a contractor associated with the Grand Trunk railroad.

GRIGGS Co., N.Dak. (co. seat, Cooperstown). For Alexander Griggs, closely identified with the earliest navigation on the Red River of the North. A river pilot, he was known as "Captain."

GRIMES Co., Tex. (co. seat, Anderson). For Jesse Grimes (1788-1866), Tex. patriot and legislator.

GRINNELL, Iowa (Poweshiek Co.). For Josiah B. Grinnell (1821-1891), founder.

GRISWOLD, Conn. (New London Co.), town. For Roger Griswold (1762-1812), governor (1811-12).

GROESBECK, Tex. (co. seat of Limestone Co.). For Abraham Groesbeeck, a director of the Houston and Texas Central railroad, with a change in spelling.

GROSSE From French, "large," or "big."
Grosse Isle, Mich. (Wayne Co.).
Grosse Point, Mich. (Wayne Co.).
Grosse Pointe Farms, Mich. (Wayne Co.).
Grosse Pointe Park, Mich. (Wayne Co.).
Grosse Pointe Shores, Mich. (Wayne and Macombe Cos.).
Grosse Pointe Woods, Mich. (Wayne Co.).

GROSSMONT-MOUNT HELIX, Calif. (San Diego Co.). Combination of Grossmont, for William B. Gross, realtor, and Mount Helix, so named "because the trail ascends it in a spiral."

GROTON, Mass. (Middlesex Co.), town. For Groton, Suffolk, England, a location near the birthplace of Gov. John Winthrop.
Groton Borough, Conn. (New London Co.).
Groton, Conn. (New London Co.), town.

GROVE Descriptive.
Grove, Okla. (co. seat of Delaware Co.).
Grove Hill, Ala. (co. seat of Clarke Co.). For oaks on a plateau.
Groveton, Tex. (co. seat of Trinity Co.). For a grove of pine trees.

GROVER CITY, Calif. (San Luis Obispo Co.). For Henry Grover.

GROVES, Tex. (Jefferson Co.). For Asa B. Groves, representative of a Madison, Wis., development company.

GRUNDY, Felix (1777-1840), lawyer, jurist, and politician. Born in Virginia, he grew up in Kentucky and served there as a legislator and appeals judge. He moved to Tennessee, where he was a Democratic congressman (1811-15). Serving on the Committee of Foreign Affairs, he played a leading part bringing on and sustaining the War of 1812 with Great Britain. He was a U.S. senator from Tennessee (1829-38; 1839-40) and attorney general (1838-39) under Van Buren and took an active part in the nullification controversy of 1832.

Grundy Center, Iowa (co. seat of Grundy Co.).
Grundy Co., Ill. (co. seat, Morris).
Grundy Co., Iowa (co. seat, Grundy Center).
Grundy Co., Mo. (co. seat, Trenton).
Grundy Co., Tenn. (co. seat, Altamont).
Grundy, Va. (co. seat of Buchanan Co.).

GUADALUPE For Our Lady of Guadalupe, the patron saint of Mexico. The name occurs often in areas formerly belonging to Spain or Mexico.
Guadalupe, Calif. (Santa Barbara Co.).
Guadalupe Co., N.Mex. (co. seat, Santa Rosa).
Guadalupe Co., Tex. (co. seat, Seguin).
Guadalupe Peak, Tex.
Guadalupe River, Calif.
Guadalupe River, Tex.

GUERNSEY Co., Ohio (co. seat, Cambridge). For Guernsey, an island in the English Channel; it is also the name of a breed of cattle from that island.

GUILDERLAND, N.Y. (Albany Co.). For Guelderland (or Gelderland), the hereditary province of the Van Rensselaers in Holland.

GUILDHALL, Vt. (Essex Co.). Probably for the Guildhall which is in the center of London, England.

GUILFORD, Conn. (New Haven Co.), town and village. For Guildford, Surrey, England. An earlier name was Menunkatucket.

GUILFORD Co., N.C. (co. seat, Greensboro). For Francis North, 1st Earl of Guilford (1637-1685).

GULF In these cases, for the Gulf of Mexico.
Gulf Co., Fla. (co. seat, Wewahitchka).
Gulfport, Fla. (Pinellas Co.).
Gulfport, Miss. (co. seat of Harrison Co.).

West Gulfport, Miss. (Harrison Co.).

GUNNISON, John William (1812-1853), Indian fighter. He was a surveyor for a proposed transcontinental railroad when he was killed by Indians. See also Black Canyon of the Gunnison Natl. Monument.
Gunnison Co., Colo. (co. seat, Gunnison).
Gunnison, Colo. (co. seat of Gunnison Co.)
Gunnison Natl. Forest, Colo.
Gunnison River, Colo.

GUNTER, John, an early settler in Alabama. From Scotland, he had been adopted by a Cherokee tribe.
Guntersville, Ala. (co. seat of Marshall Co.). Earlier, Marshall. Previous to that, it was a Cherokee Indian town.
Guntersville Reservoir, Ala.

GURNEE, Ill. (Lake Co.). For either Louis J. Gurnee, a railroad surveyor, or Walter S. Gurnee, a political leader and a mayor of Chicago, who had extensive landholdings along the Chicago, Milwaukee and St. Paul railroad. It is possible that the names were confused, with priority belonging to the surveyor.

GUSTINE, Calif. (Merced Co.). Named by Henry Miller for his daughter Augustine.

GUTHRIE, Edwin, an army officer killed during the Mexican War.
Guthrie Co., Iowa. (co. seat, Guthrie Center).
Guthrie Center, Iowa (co. seat of Guthrie Co.).

Traditionally "groves" are areas in villages or towns which are somewhat more woodsy than parks. Frequently they have gazebos or bandstands. This one, in Lakeville, Conn., features a marina on the shores of Lake Wononscopomuc. [*Photo by Mary Lou Estabrook. Courtesy of The Lakeville Journal*]

GUTHRIE, Okla. (co. seat of Logan Co.). For John Guthrie, a jurist of Topeka, Kansas.

GUTTENBERG, N.J. (Hudson Co.). For Johann Gutenberg (c.1397-1468), inventor of printing from movable type.

GUYANDOT RIVER, W.Va. Probably a variant of the Indian tribal name WYANDOT, influenced by the French spelling of a personal name.

GUYMON, Okla. (co. seat of Texas Co.). For E. T. Guymon, founder. He was the first president of the Beaver County Bank.

GUYOT, Mount, N.C.-Tenn. In Great Smoky Mountains. For A. H. Guyot, geologist.

GUYSBOROUGH For Sir Guy Carleton, Lord Dorchester.
Guysborough Co., N.S. (co. seat, *Guysborough*).
Guysborough, N.S. (co. seat of *Guysborough* Co.).

GWINNETT Co., Ga. (co. seat, Lawrenceville). For Button Gwinnett (1735-1777), a signer of the Declaration of Independence. He died from an injury suffered in a duel. His autograph is one of the most valuable in the world.

GYPSY PEAK, Wash. Possibly for the presence of a gypsy camp at one time.

Named by Norwegian immigrants for
Haakon VII (1872 1067), king of Norway.

HABERSHAM Co., Ga. (co. seat,
Clarkesville). For Joseph Habersham (1751-
1815), officer in the American Revolution,
member of the Continental Congress, and
postmaster general (1795-1801) under
Washington and John Adams.

HACIENDA HEIGHTS, Calif. (Los Angeles
Co.). Promotional; *Hacienda* from Spanish,
"estate" or "farm."

HACKENSACK, N.J. (co. seat of Bergen
Co.). From *Ackinchesacky* or *Ackenack*, an
Indian, tribal name of uncertain meaning,
variously interpreted as "hook mouth," "the
confluence of streams," "big snake land,"
and "low ground."

HACKETTSTOWN, N.J. (Warren Co.). For
Samuel Hackett (fl. mid 1700s), the largest
landowner in the area. He became popular
when he set up free drinks at the opening of
a new hotel.

HADDAM For Much Hadham and Little
Hadham, Hertfordshire, England.
East Haddam, Conn. (Middlesex Co.).
Haddam, Conn. (Middlesex Co.), town.

HADLEY For one of several towns with this
name in England.
Hadley, Mass. (Hampshire Co.), town.

South Hadley, Mass. (Hampshire Co.),
town.
HADLEY LAKE, Me. For the Hadley family.

HAGEMEISTER For Leonti Andreanovich
Hagemeister, of the Imperial Russian Navy.
He commanded voyages to the Russian
American colony and was governor of the
colony (1818).
Hagemeister Island, Alaska. In Bristol Bay.
Hagemeister Strait, Alaska. Water passage
between *Hagemeister* Island and the
mainland.

HAGERSTOWN, Md. (co. seat of
Washington Co.). For the founder, Jonathan
Hager (1714-1775), land developer and
Indian trader. An earlier name was
Elizabethtown, for his wife, Elizabeth Hager.

HAHNVILLE, La. (parish seat of St.
Charles Parish). For Michael Hahn (1830-
1886), attorney, U.S. representative (1862-
63), publisher, governor (1864-65), jurist,
and farmer.

HAILEY, Idaho (Blaine Co.). For John
Hailey, landowner and a founder.

HAILEYBURY, Ont. (co. seat of
Timiskaming Co.). Named by C. C. Farr,
town founder, for the school he attended in
England.

HAILEY PASS, Wyo. For Ora Hailey,
sheepherder and later a Wyoming state
senator.

HAIWEE RIVER, Calif. From Indian, "dove." It is actually a reservoir in the Owens River complex.

HALALII LAKE, Hawaii, on Nihau Island. For the owner of the area on which the lake exists.

HALAWA For Polynesian, "curve," apparently for the shape of the line of the bay.
Halawa Bay, Hawaii. On Molokai Island.
Halawa, Cape, Hawaii. Off Molokai Island.

HALDIMAND Co., Ont. (co. seat, Cayuga). For Sir Frederick Haldimand (1718-1791), British soldier and governor-in-chief of Canada (1778-86).

HALE Co., Ala. (co. seat, Greensboro). For an early settler, Stephen F. Hale.

HALE Co., Tex.(co. seat, Plainview). For a Texas patriot, John C. Hale (?-1836), killed in battle.

HALEDON Probably for Haledon, a historic spot near Brunswick, England on the Scottish border.
Haledon, N.J. (Passaic Co.).
North Haledon, N.J. (Passaic Co.).

HALES BAR LAKE, Tenn. In Tennessee River. From a personal name plus *bar*, a sandy or rocky area that obstructs navigation in a river.

HALES CORNERS, Wis. (Milwaukee Co.). For William Hale, early settler, proprietor, and postmaster.

HALEY MOUNTAIN, Wash. Probably for an Indian trader.

HALF HOLLOW HILLS Descriptive and promotional.
East Half Hollow Hills, N.Y. (Suffolk Co.).
Half Hollow Hills, N.Y. (Suffolk Co.).

HALF MOON LAKE, Wis. Descriptive of shape.

HALIBURTON Co., Ont. (co. seat, Minden). For Thomas Chandler Haliburton (1796-1865), Nova Scotian writer and judge, and first chairman of the Canadian Land and Emigration Company.

HALIFAX, Charles Montagu Dunk, 2nd Earl of (1716-1771), English statesman, president of the Board of Trade (1748-61), and a strong exponent of trade with the American colonies. He was one of the founders of the colony of Nova Scotia. His nephew, Lord North, was prime minister during the American Revolution.
Halifax Co., N.C. (co. seat, *Halifax*).
Halifax Co., N.S. (co. seat, *Halifax*).
Halifax Co., Va. (co. seat, *Halifax*).
Halifax, N.C. (co. seat of *Halifax* Co.).
Halifax N.S. (co. seat of *Halifax* Co.), provincial capital.
Halifax, Va. (co. seat of *Halifax* Co.).

HALIFAX, Mass. (Plymouth Co.), town. For Halifax, Yorkshire, England.

HALKETT, Cape, Alaska. For a director of the Hudson's Bay Company.

HALL Co., Ga. (co. seat, Gainesville). For Lyman Hall (1731-1790), a governor of Georgia (1783-84) and a signer of the Declaration of Independence.

HALL Co., Neb. (co. seat, Grand Island). For Augustus Hall (1814-1861), U.S. representative and jurist.

HALL Co., Tex. (co. seat, Memphis). For Warren D. C. Hall (1788-1867), Texas Republic patriot and official.

HALLELUJAH PEAK, Wyo. Named by W. B. and A. W. Willcox, for the awe-inspiring peak.

HALLETTSVILLE, Tex. (co. seat of Lavaca Co.). For the Hallett family: John Hallett, a colonist who in 1833 erected a log cabin overlooking the Lavaca River, and his wife, who donated the land for the townsite.

HALLOCK, Minn. (co. seat of Kittson Co.). For Charles Hallock (1834-?). entrepreneur, naturalist, publisher, and sportsman.

HALLOWELL, Me. (Kennebec Co.). For Benjamin Hallowell, a prosperous Boston merchant and a proprietor of a tract of land that included the town.

HALLS MOUNTAIN, Wyo. For Harry Hall.

HALLS STREAM, N.H.-Que. For a local settler.

HALSEY LAKE, Wis. For a local settler.

HALTON Co., Ont. (co. seat, Milton). For Maj. William Halton, secretary to Francis Gore, lieutenant-governor of Upper Canada.

HAMBLEN Co., Tenn. (co. seat, Morristown). For Hezekiah Hamblen (1775-1854?), a member of the county court of Hawkins County; named by his grandson, William Green, a state sentator.

HAMBURG, Ark. (co. seat of Ashley Co.). Said to be so named because a deer killed by a commissioner had a remarkable pair of hams.

HAMBURG For Hamburg, Germany, a seaport in the state of Schleswig-Holstein.
Hamburg, N.Y. (Erie Co.).
Hamburg Mountain, N.J.-N.Y.

HAMDEN For John HAMPDEN.
Hamden, Conn. (New Haven Co.), town.
Hamden, N.Y. (Delaware Co.). For Hampden Co., Mass.

HAMILTON, Alexander (1757-1804), statesman. He was aide-de-camp to George Washington in the American Revolution and the first U.S. secretary of the treasury. He was killed in a duel with Aaron Burr. See also FORT HAMILTON.

Hamilton, Ala. (co. seat of Marion Co.).

West Indian born Alexander Hamilton left an indelible mark on American political and financial philosophy. He was co-author of the Federalist Papers and Secretary of the Treasury. [*New York Public Library*]

Hamilton Co., Fla. (co. seat, Jasper).
Hamilton Co., Ill. (co. seat, McLeansboro).
Hamilton Co., Ind. (co. seat, Noblesville).
Hamilton Co., Kan. (co. seat, Syracuse).
Hamilton Co., Neb. (co. seat, Aurora).
Hamilton Co., N.Y. (co. seat, Lake Pleasant).
Hamilton Co., Ohio (co. seat, Cincinnati).
Hamilton Co., Tenn. (co. seat, Chattanooga).
Hamilton, Ga. (co. seat of Harris Co.).
Hamilton Mountain, N.Y. For the county.
Hamilton, N.Y. (Madison Co.).
Hamilton, Ohio (co. seat of Butler Co.).
Hamilton, W.Va. (co. seat of Lincoln Co.).

HAMILTON, Ill. (Hancock Co.). For Artois Hamilton, an early settler.

HAMILTON Co., Iowa (co. seat, Webster City). For William H. Hamilton, an Iowa legislator.

HAMILTON, James (1786-1857), South Carolina governor and legislator. He championed the cause of Texas independence and later (1855) settled there.
Hamilton Co., Tex. (co. seat, *Hamilton*).
Hamilton, Tex. (co. seat of *Hamilton* Co.).

HAMILTON, Lake, Ark. For an early settler.

HAMILTON, Mont. (co. seat of Ravalli Co.). For James Hamilton, an engineer and land agent employed by Marcus Daly, copper magnate, to plat the town.

HAMILTON, Mount, Nev. For W. A. Hamilton, surveyor.

HAMILTON, Ont. (co. seat of Wentworth Co.). For George Hamilton (1787-1835), founder and landowner, who began developing the townsite in 1813.

HAMILTON RESERVOIR, Mass. For a local dweller.

HAMLIN Co., S.Dak. (co. seat, Hayti). For Hannibal Hamlin (1809-1891), Maine statesman and vice-president (1861-65) under Lincoln.

HAMLIN, Tex. (Jones Co.). For a vice-president of the Kansas City, Missouri and Orient railroad. He surveyed the right of way for the railway.

HAMLIN, W.Va. (co. seat of Lincoln Co.). Probably originally for Leonidas Lent Hamline, a Methodist preacher. The spelling indicates also that a claim can be made for the citizens' having decided to honor Hannibal Hamlin (1809-1891), vice-president under Lincoln, for whom the county is named.

HAMMONASSET For the Hammonasett dialect of Algonquian, with meaning uncertain, possibly "the place of small islands or harbors."
Hammonasset Point, Conn. Extends into Long Island Sound.
Hammonasset River, Conn. Flows into Long Island Sound.

HAMMOND, Ind. (Lake Co.). For George H. Hammond (1838-1886), founder of the Hammond meat-packing house and, with Marcus M. Towle, of the city. It is said that the two tossed a coin for the name.

HAMMOND BAY, Mich. Inlet on Lake Huron. For a local settler.

HAMMONTON, N.J. (Atlantic Co.). For John Hammond Coffin, the owner of a glassworks in the area during the early to mid 1800s.

HAMPDEN, John (1594-1643), English statesman and member of Parliament, a leading opponent of Charles I. He was killed in the early fighting of the English Civil War. Hampden was influential in the establishment of Puritan colonies in North America. See also HAMDEN.
Hampden Co., Mass. (co. seat, Springfield).
Hampden, Mass. (*Hampden* Co.).
Hampden, Me. (Penobscot Co.), town.

HAMPSHIRE For the county of Hampshire, England; named by Capt. John Mason (1586-1635), who received a grant to a portion of the territory later occupied by the

New Englanders were fond of naming their villages, towns and counties for fondly remembered places in England. Ironically, New Hampshire is the only New England state so named.
[*New York Public Library*]

colony and state of New Hampshire. He had been governor of Portsmouth in Hampshire, England.

New Hampshire, **State of. Ninth state** of the Union. Settled: 1623. One of the original 13 colonies. Ratified Constitution: 1788. Cap: Concord. Motto: Live Free or Die. Nickname: Granite State. Flower: Purple Lilac. Bird: Purple Finch. Tree: Paper (White) Birch. Song: "Old New Hampshire."

Hampshire Co., Mass. (co. seat, Northampton).

Hampshire Co., W.Va. (co. seat, Romney).

HAMPTON Named by Rev. Stephen Bachiler, who had preached in Hampton, Middlesex, England.

Hampton, N.H. (Rockingham Co.), town and village.

New Hampton, Iowa (co. seat of Chickasaw Co.). New Hampshire was the former home of Osgood Gowan, the first postmaster.

North Hampton, N.H. (Rockingham Co.), town.

HAMPTON, Iowa (co. seat of Franklin Co.). For Hampton Roads, Va., a channel which was named for the Earl of Southampton. See SOUTHAMPTON. Co., Va.

HAMPTON, N.B. (co. seat of Kings Co.). For Hampton, Middlesex, England. An earlier name was Ossekeag.

HAMPTON, Wade (1818-1902), legislator and soldier. He was U.S. senator from South Carolina (1858-62), Confederate general in the Civil War, a distinguished leader during the Reconstruction era, and governor of South Carolina (1876-79). Re-elected to the Senate in 1878, he served until 1891, and later was U.S. railroad commissioner (1893-97).

Hampton Co., S.C. (co. seat, *Hampton*).

Hampton, S.C. (co. seat of *Hampton* Co.).

HAM SOUTH, Que. (co. seat of Wolfe Co.). For Ham, Essex, England.

HAMTRAMCK, Mich. (Wayne Co.). For Col. John Francis Hamtramck, commander of troops that occupied Detroit after the British left (1796).

HANALEI From Polynesian, "crescent," for the shape of the bay's shore line.

Hanalei Bay, Hawaii, on Kauai Island.

Hanalei River, Hawaii. Flows N into the bay.

HANAPEPE From Polynesian, "crushed bay," for landslides.

Hanapepe, Hawaii (Kauai Co.).

Hanapepe Bay, Hawaii. Inlet off S coast of Kauai Island.

Hanapepe River, Hawaii. Flows S into the bay.

John Hancock's signature is the first and largest signature on the Declaration of Independence. He wished to make sure that "fat German George could read it without his spectacles." [*New York Public Library*]

HANCOCK, John (1737-1793), Massachusetts merchant and statesman, one of the leaders of the American Revolution. As president of the Continental Congress (1775-77), he was the first to sign the Declaration of Independence. So bold and large was his signature (so that George III could "read it without his spectacles") that "John Hancock" has passed into the language as a slang term for a signature. He was a member of the Continental Congress (1775-80; 1785-86) and governor (1780-85; 1787-93).

Hancock Co., Ga. (co. seat, Sparta).
Hancock Co., Ill. (co. seat, Carthage).
Hancock Co., Ind. (co. seat, Greenfield).
Hancock Co., Iowa (co. seat, Garner).
Hancock Co., Ky. (co. seat, Hawesville).
Hancock Co., Me. (co. seat, Ellsworth).
Hancock Co., Miss. (co. seat, Bay St. Louis).
Hancock Co., Ohio (co. seat, Findlay).
Hancock Co., Tenn. (co. seat, Sneedville).
Hancock Co., W.Va. (co. seat, New Cumberland).
Hancock, Mich. (Houghton Co.).
Hancock, N.Y. (Delaware Co.), town.

HANCOCK   MOUNTAIN, Wyo., in Yellowstone Natl. Park. For W. S. Hancock, a general officer who explored the park.

HAND Co., S.Dak. (co. seat, Miller). For George H. Hand (1837-1891), Dakota Territory official.

HANFORD, Calif. (co. seat of Kings Co.). For James Hanford, treasurer of the Southern Pacific railroad, which founded the city.

HANLEY HILLS, Mo. (independent city in St. Louis Co.). For a Hanley who lived in the area.

HANNIBAL, Mo. (Marion Co.). Classical; for the famous Carthaginian general (247-183 B.C.), who invaded Roman territory by crossing the Alps.

HANOVER British royal house. The line began with George I (1660-1727), Duke of Hannover, Anglicized to Hanover.
Hanover Co., Va. (co. seat, Hanover).
Hanover, Conn. (New London Co.).
Hanover, Ind. (Jefferson Co.). For Hanover, N.H.
Hanover, Me. (Oxford Co.).
Hanover, Mass. (Plymouth Co.), town. For George I.
Hanover, N.H. (Grafton Co.), town and village. For Hanover, Conn.
Hanover, N.J. (Morris Co. For George I
Hanover, Pa. (York Co.).
Hanover, Va. (co. seat of Hanover Co.).
Hanover Park, Ill. (Cook and Du Page Cos.).
New Hanover Co., N.C. (co. seat, Wilmington).

HANSFORD Co., Tex. (co. seat, Spearman). For John M. Hansford, attorney and jurist, who was killed in 1844.

In the grand tradition of naming places for ancient or classical heroes, Hannibal, shown here crossing the Rhone River, gave his name to the famous hometown of Mark Twain in Missouri. [New York Public Library]

HANSON, Mass. (Plymouth Co.), town. For Alexander C. Hanson (1786-1819), who in 1808 founded at Baltimore the *Federal Republican*, which represented extreme Federalist opinion. His paper was a virulent opponent of President Madison and of the war with England, and his newspaper office was twice attacked by a mob in the summer of 1812. Public indignation was aroused by the attacks, and Hanson was elected to Congress in 1813 and later served as a U.S. senator until his death.

HANSON Co., S.Dak. (co. seat, Alexandria). For Joseph R. Hanson (1837-1917), early settler of Yankton, Dakota Territory legislator, and Indian affairs official.

HANTS Co., N.S. (co. seat, Windsor). Abbreviation of Hampshire, England. Most of the early settlers came from New Hampshire.

HARAHAN, La. (Jefferson Parish). For James T. Harahan, former president of the Illinois Central and Gulf railroad.

HARALSON Co., Ga. (co. seat, Buchanan). For Hugh Anderson Haralson (1805-1854), Georgia legislator and U.S. representative.

HARCUVAR MOUNTAINS, Ariz. From Mohave, probably "a little water."

HARDEE Co., Fla. (co. seat, Wauchula). For Cary Augustus Hardee (1876-1957), governor of Florida (1921-25).

HARDEMAN Co., Tenn. (co. seat, Bolivar). For Thomas Jones Hardeman (1788-1854), Tennessee officer in the War of 1812, later Texas patriot and justice.

HARDEMAN Co., Tex. (co. seat, Quanah). For Bailey Hardeman (1795-1836), Republic of Texas patriot and official, brother of T. J. Hardeman (see HARDEMAN Co., Tenn.).

HARDIN, Mont. (co. seat of Big Horn Co.). For Samuel Hardin, an early settler and rancher.

HARDIN Co., Tenn. (co. seat, Savannah). For Joseph Hardin, an officer in the American Revolution and a Tennessee legislator.

HARDIN Co., Tex. (co. seat, Kountze). For William Hardin (1801-1839), a local official.

HARDING Co., N.Mex. (co. seat, Mosquero). For Warren Gamaliel Harding (1865-1923), twenty-ninth President of the United States (1921-23), from Ohio. Editor of the *Marion Star*, he was also a U.S. senator (1915-21). His administration was marked by scandal, including the notorious Teapot Dome Affair. He died in office and was succeeded by his vice-president, Calvin Coolidge.

HARDING Co., S.Dak. (co. seat, Buffalo). For J. A. Harding, a Dakota Territory legislator.

HARDINSBURG, Ky. (co. seat of Breckenridge Co.). For Capt. William Hardin, an early settler.

Few men looked more presidential than Warren Gamaliel Harding; few were less successful in that position. But Harding has the distinction of being the last American president to have a county named for him. [*New York Public Library*]

HARDIN, John (1753-1792), Virginia soldier and Indian fighter, associated with Kentucky. He served during the American Revolution and was killed by Indians in what is now Hardin Co., Ohio.
Hardin Co., Ill. (co. seat, Elizabethtown). For *Hardin* Co., Ky.
Hardin Co., Ky. (co. seat, Elizabethtown).
Hardin Co., Ohio (co. seat, Kenton).

HARDIN, John J. (?-1847), Illinois legislator and an officer in the Mexican War. In command of the First Regiment of Illinois Volunteers at the Battle of Buena Vista, he was killed in action.
Hardin Co., Ill. (co. seat, Elizabethtown). Also possibly for Hardin Co., Ky. (see John HARDIN.)
Hardin Co., Iowa (co. seat, Eldora).
Hardin, Ill. (co. seat of Calhoun Co.).

HARD LUCK MOUNTAIN, Wyo. Metaphoric.

HARDWOOD MOUNTAIN, Me. For the hardwood trees that grow on it.

HARDY, Ark. (co. seat of Sharp Co.). For a railroad contractor for the Kansas City, Fort Scott and Memphis railroad.

HARDY Co., W.Va. (co. seat, Moorefield). For Samuel Hardy (1758-1785), Virginia statesman and a member of the Continental Congress (1783-85).

HARDY DAM POND, Mich. Reservoir and dam on Muskegon River. For a local settler or explorer.

HARFORD Co., Md. (co. seat, Bel Air). For Henry Harford, an illegitimate son of Frederick Calvert, 6th Lord Baltimore and last proprietor of the colony of Maryland.

HARLAN, Iowa (co. seat of Shelby Co.). For James Harlan (1820-1899), U.S. senator traveling in the area at the time of naming. A claim is also made that it was named for Harlan, Ky.

HARLAN Co., Neb. (co. seat, Alma). For Thomas Harlan, a local official and a nephew of Sen. James Harlan of Iowa.

HARLAN, Maj. Silas (?-1782), a young officer killed at the Battle of Blue Licks.

Harlan Co., Ky. (co. seat, *Harlan*).
Harlan, Ky. (co. seat of *Harlan* Co.).
Harlan Co., Neb. (co. seat, Alma).
Harlan County Reservoir, Neb. On Republican R.

HARLAN, Thomas, a local official and a nephew of Sen. James Harlan of Iowa.

HARLINGEN, Tex. (Cameron Co.). For Van Harlingen, Netherlands, a city, like the Texas town, located on a barge canal. The place was also known as "Six Shooter Junction," for the aggressive manner in which law and order were enforced.

HARLOWTON, Mont. (co. seat of Wheatland Co.). For Richard Harlow, a construction engineer for the Milwaukee railroad.

HARMON Co., Okla. (co. seat, Hollis). For Judson C. Harmon (1846-1927), governor of Ohio (1908-13). He served as mayor of Wyoming, Ohio (1857-76) and was one of the judges who served in the Court of Common Pleas (1876-78). He was president of the Ohio Bar Association (1897-98) and a candidate for the Democratic nomination for the Presidency (1912).

HARNETT Co., N.C. (co. seat, Lillington). For Cornelius Harnett (1723-1781), American Revolutionary patriot who died while an English prisoner.

HARNEY, William Selby (1800-1889), a leader in operations against the Indians in the first half of the 1800s. He later became a general in the Oregon area.
Harney Co., Ore. (co. seat, Burns).
Harney Lake, Ore.
Harney Peak, S.Dak. Highest peak east of the Rocky Mtns.

HARO STRAIT, Wash.-B.C. Channel between San Juan Islands, Wash., and Vancouver Island, B.C. For Lopez Gonzales de Haro, Spanish explorer who probably discovered the strait.

HARPER Co., Kan. (co. seat, Anthony). For Marion Harper (?-1863), a soldier in the Kansas Cavalry killed in the Civil War.

HARPER, Mount, Alaska. Probably for Arthur Harper (1835-1897), Yukon pioneer.

Harper's Ferry, formerly in Virginia and now in West Virginia, became a landmark in American history when a band led by John Brown attacked the United States arsenal there on Oct. 16, 1859. [New York Public Library]

HARPER Co., Okla. (co. seat, Buffalo). For Oscar G. Harper, an official at the Oklahoma constitutional convention.

HARPER LAKE, Calif. For J. D. Harper, early settler.

HARPERS FERRY NATL. HISTORICAL PARK, W.Va.-Md. For Robert Harper, who settled in the area in 1734. The U.S. arsenal established there in 1796 was seized in 1859 by John Brown in his historic raid.

HARPERSFIELD, N.Y. (Delaware Co.). For Col. John Harper, an American Revolutionary soldier who held numerous town offices.

HARPER WOODS, Mich. (Wayne Co.). For Walter Harper, for whom a street had been named earlier. He was the founder of the Harper Hospital.

HARPETH RIVER, Tenn. For an early settler. It flows northwest into Cumberland River.

HARPSWELL, Me. (Cumberland Co.), town. Probably for Harpswell, Lincolnshire, England.

HARRINGTON LAKE, Me. For a local settler.

HARRINGTON PARK, N.J. (Bergen Co.). Probably either for the Harring family, early settlers, or for James Harrington (1611-1677), English philosopher.

HARRIS Co., Ga. (co. seat, Hamilton). For Charles Harris (1772-1827), a city official in Savannah.

HARRIS, John (1727-1791), eldest son of the first settler and first white child born in Pennsylvania west of the Conewego Hills. He owned a large plantation, including most of the land that the early Harrisburg encompassed.
Harrisburg, Neb. (co. seat of Banner Co.). For *Harrisburg*, Pa.
Harrisburg, Pa. (co. seat of Dauphin Co.), state capital.

HARRIS Co., Tex. (co. seat, Houston). For John Richardson Harris (1790-1829), Texas businessman and steamboat owner.

HARRISBURG, Ark. (co. seat of Poinsett Co.). For William C. Harris (?-1843), farmer and founder.

HARRISBURG, Ill. (co. seat of Saline Co.). For the Harris family, first settlers.

HARRISON, Ark. (co. seat of Boone Co.). For M. LaRue Harrison (1839-1890), Union general commanding the Thirty-sixth Illinois Volunteers and surveyor of the townsite in 1870.

HARRISON Co., Ky. (co. seat, Cynthiana). For Col. Benjamin Harrison, a representative from Bourbon County in the Kentucky legislature when the county was formed in 1793.

HARRISON Co., Mo. (co. seat, Bethany). For Albert Galliton Harrison (1800-1839), U.S. representative.

HARRISON, N.Y. (Westchester Co.). For John Harrison, a Quaker leader from Long Island.

HARRISON Co., Tex. (co. seat, Marshall). For Jonas Haralson (1777-1836), co-founder of Buffalo, N.Y., master of chancery of New York State, and U.S. collector of customs and internal revenue at Niagara Falls, New York. He moved to Texas (1828) and was a member of the Texas convention of 1832, and the lawyer for Sam Houston's divorce suit. His San Augustine resolutions (1835) advocated immediate declaration of independence from Mexico and earned him the title "Patrick Henry of Texas." The name was entered as *Harrison* because of a clerical error.

HARRISON, Benjamin (1726?-1791), Virginia statesman and father of President William Henry Harrison. Active during the American Revolution, he was a member of the Continental Congress (1774-78), a signer of the Declaration of Independence (1776), and governor (1782-84).
Harrison Co., W.Va. (co. seat, Clarksburg).
Harrison, Neb. (co. seat of Sioux Co.).

HARRISON, William Henry (1773-1841), ninth President of the United States (1841), from Virginia., secretary of the Northwest Territory (1798) and governor of Indiana Territory (1801-13), he won acclaim by defeating the Shawnees at the Battle of Tippecanoe (Nov. 7, 1811). He was a U.S. representative from Ohio (1816-19) and U.S. senator (1825-28). Defeated as the Whig candidate for President in 1836, he was elected in 1840. "Tippecanoe" had become his nickname, and the Whigs' slogan in that election was "Tippecanoe and Tyler too." He died after a month in office and was succeeded by his vice-president, John Tyler. He was the grandfather of President Benjamin Harrison.
Harrison Co., Ind. (co. seat, Corydon).
Harrison Co., Iowa (co. seat, Logan).
Harrison Co., Miss. (co. seat, Gulfport).
Harrison Co., .Ohio (co. seat, Cadiz).
Harrison, Mich. (co. seat of Clare Co.).
Harrison, N.J. (Hudson Co.).
Harrison, Ohio (Hamilton Co.).

HARRISONBURG, La. (parish seat of Catahoula Parish). For the Harrison family of Virginia.

HARRISONBURG, Va. (co. seat of Rockingham Co.). For Thomas Harrison, early settler and landowner of the site.

HARRISON LAKE, Mich. For Bazel Harrison (1774-1874), first settler.

HARRISVILLE, Mich. (co. seat of Alcona Co.). For the Harris family, including Benjamin Harris and his sons, Levi and Henry, early landowners and settlers. Levi was the first postmaster.

HARRISVILLE, W.Va. (co. seat of Ritchie Co.). Obviously from a surname, but there is local dispute as to whose: either for John Maley Harris, an early resident, or for Thomas Harris, a general and hero in the Union army during the Civil War.

HARRODSBURG, Ky. (co. seat of Mercer Co.). For James Harrod (1742-1792), soldier, surveyor, and founder.

HARRY STRUNK LAKE, Neb. For Harry D. Strunk, editor of the *McCook Gazette*. He helped obtain the dam now built on Medicine Creek after the 1947 flood.

HART Name taken from a ranch brand shaped like a heart, with a change in spelling.
Hart Lake, Ore.
Hart Mountain, Ore.
HART Co., Ky. (co. seat, Munfordville). For Nathaniel Hart (?-1813), killed in battle by Indians.
HART, Mich. (co. seat of Oceana Co.). For Wellington Hart, operator of a trading post. Formerly the county seat was at Whiskey Creek.
HART, Nancy (1735?-1830?). A grave marker near Henderson, Ky., shows these dates. A native of North Carolina whose maiden name was Morgan, she married Benjamin Hart of Kentucky and moved to Georgia. She exhibited much courage and heroism in the American Revolution.
Hart Co., Ga. (co. seat, *Hartwell*).
Hartwell, Ga. (co. seat of *Hart* Co.).
Hartwell Reservoir, Ga.-S.C.
HARTFORD For Hertford and Hertfordshire, England. The spelling may have been influenced by the pronunciation of the English names.
Hartford Co., Conn. (co. seat, *Hartford*).
East Hartford, Conn. (*Hartford* Co.), town.
Hartford, Conn. (co. seat of *Hartford* Co.) state capital.
Hartford, Vt. (Windsor Co.), town.
Hartford, Wis. (Washington Co.). Probably for *Hartford*, Conn., although a nearby lake is heart-shaped and may have influenced the name.
New Hartford, Conn. (Litchfield Co.), town. For *Hartford*, Conn.
West Hartford, Conn. (*Hartford* Co.), town.
HARTFORD, Ky. (co. seat of Ohio Co.). The origin of this name is uncertain, but several hypotheses have been presented, one being that there was a ford adjacent to the home of a settler by the name of Hart. Another is that the name is derived from the English word for a male animal, especially deer, and that these animals crossed at the ford in the river. And a third explanation is simply that it was named for *Hartford*, Conn.
HARTFORD, Mich. (Van Buren Co.). Originally Hartland, for a Hartland in New York, but changed because of another Hartland in Michigan.

HARTFORD CITY, Ind. (co. seat of Blackford Co.). For David Hart, a farmer who controlled a ford across Little Lick Creek, known as Hart's Ford.
HARTINGTON, Neb. (co. seat of Cedar Co.). For a Lord Hartington of England, who had visited the United States when the site was named.
HARTLAND, Wis. (Waukesha Co.). Origin uncertain; may have been either for a surname or for "heart land."
HARTLEY Co., Tex. (co. seat, Channing). For Oliver Cromwell Hartley (1823-1859), Texas attorney, legislator, and legal scholar.
HARTSDALE, N.Y. (Westchester Co.). For John Hart, a leaseholder of a Philipse Manor farm who purchased his land from the state after the American Revolution.
HARTSELLE, Ala. (Morgan Co.). For a George Hartselle.
HARTSVILLE, Tenn. (co. seat of Trousdale Co.). For James Hart, an early settler. He was an ancestor of Thomas Hart Benton.
HARTVILLE, Mo. (co. seat of Wright Co.). For Isaac Hart, an early settler.
HARTWELL, Ga. For Nancy HART.
HARVARD, John (1607-1638), a teaching elder of the Congregational Church in Charlestown, Mass., and a benefactor of Harvard College (later University), which was named for him.
Harvard, Mass. (Worcester Co.), town.
Harvard, Ill. (McHenry Co.). For Harvard University.
Harvard, Mount, Colo.
HARVEY, Ill. (Cook Co.). For Turlington W. Harvey, founder.
HARVEY Co., Kan. (co. seat, Newton). For James Madison Harvey (1833-1894), a veteran of the Civil War and governor of Kansas (1869-73).
HARVEYS LAKE, Pa. For Benjamin Harvey, who settled there in 1775.
HARWICH, Mass. (Barnstable Co.), town and village. For Harwich, Essex, England.

HARWINTON, Conn. (Litchfield Co.), town. Coined from *Hart*ford, *Wind*sor, and Farming*ton*, indicating the origin of the town lands.

HARWOOD HEIGHTS, Ill. (Cook Co.). From the first syllable of *Har*lem Avenue, plus *wood*. Harlem Avenue is the street that bisects the village.

HASBROUCK HEIGHTS, N.J. (Bergen Co.). For a Dutch colonist who settled in the area in 1685.

HASH ROCK (peak), Ore. For Allan Hash, early settler.

HASKELL, Charles Ready (1817-1836), Republic of Texas soldier killed in battle. *Haskell* Co., Tex. (co. seat, *Haskell*). *Haskell*, Tex. (co. seat of *Haskell* Co.).

HASKELL Co., Kan. (co. seat, Sublette). For Dudley Chase Haskell (1842-1883), businessman, Kansas legislator, and U.S. representative.

HASKELL Co., Okla. (co. seat, Stigler). For Charles Nathaniel Haskell (1860-1933), the first governor (1907-11).

HASKELL HILL, Mass. For a local settler.

HASSAYAMPA RIVER, Ariz. From Mohave, probably, "watering place at big rocks." It flows south into Gila River.

HASTINGS, Mich. (co. seat of Barry Co.). For Eurotas P. Hastings, bank president and landowner who sold his holdings to promoters on the condition that his name would be perpetuated.

HASTINGS, Minn. (co. seat of Dakota Co.). For Henry Hastings Sibley, a fur trader and the first governor of the state (1858-60).

HASTINGS, Neb. (co. seat of Adams Co.). For Thomas Del Monte Hastings (1836-1897), an official and construction engineer of the St. Joseph and Denver City railroad.

HASTINGS Co., Ont. (co. seat, Belleville). For Francis Rawdon-Hastings, Earl of Moira and aide-de-camp to General Clinton during the American Revolution.

HATBORO For the labors of John Dawson, a hatter who lived in what is now Hatboro, Pa.

Hatboro, Pa. (Montgomery Co.). *West Hatboro*, Pa. (Montgomery Co.).

HATCHIE RIVER, Miss.-Tenn. From Choctaw, "stream" or "river," illustrating a case where a tautology across languages would make it "river river." It flows north then northwest into the Mississippi River.

HATCHINEHA, Lake, Fla. From Seminole-Creek, "cypress tree," descriptive.

HAT CREEK, Neb.-S.Dak. Translated from Siouan, "War Bonnet Creek." Settlers simply called it *Hat Creek*, although a General Custer report lists it as Hot Creek. It flows north into Cheyenne River.

HATTERAS For an Indian tribe of Algonquian linguistic stock. Meaning of the name is unknown, but was first recorded by English explorers in the 16th century. *Hatteras*, N.C. (Dare Co.). On the island. *Hatteras*, Cape, N.C. *Hatteras* Inlet, N.C. Connects Pamlico Sound and Atlantic Ocean. *Hatteras* Island, N.C. In Pamlico Sound.

HATTIESBURG, Miss. (co. seat of Forrest Co.). For Hattie, the wife of W. H. Hardy, founder.

HAUPPAUGE, N.Y. (Suffolk Co.). From Algonquian, "overflowed-land," to describe a swampy area.

HAVASU LAKE, Calif. From Mojave, "blue."

HAVEN Descriptive. See also NEW HAVEN. *East Haven*, Conn. (New Haven Co.). *North Haven*, Conn. (New Haven Co.). *West Haven*, Conn. (New Haven Co.).

HAVERHILL For Haverhill, Essex, England, which was the birthplace of the first minister of Haverhill, Mass. An earlier (Indian) name was Pentucket. *Haverhill*, Mass. (Essex Co.). *Haverhill*, N.H. (Grafton Co.), town.

HAVERSTRAW, N.Y. (Rockland Co.). Recorded (1640) as *Averstroo*, from Dutch, "oat-straw," but probably from a Dutch personal name.

HAVRE, Mont. (co. seat of Hill Co.). For Le Havre, France; named by early settlers from the French city.

HAVRE DE GRACE, Md. (Harford Co.). Named (1785) while under French protection, from French, "haven of grace." It may refer to the French seaport of Le Havre, which is on the English Channel. The Maryland town lies on the Susquehanna River at the point where it meets Chesapeake Bay. Earlier names were Susquehanna and Lower Ferry.

HAWAII Possibly from the name of Polynesian settlers' original home. Discovered by Capt. James Cook in 1778, the 132 islands in the Hawaiian chain were once called the Sandwich Islands for the Earl of Sandwich.

Hawaii, State of. 50th state of the Union. Settled: 1778. Admitted: 1959. Cap: Honolulu. Motto: The Life of the Land is Perpetuated in Righteousness. Nickname: Aloha State. Flower: Red Hibiscus. Bird: Hawaiian Goose. Tree: Kukui. Song: "Hawaii Ponoi."
Hawaii Co., Hawaii (co. seat, Hilo).
Hawaii Islands, Hawaii.
Hawaii Volcanoes Natl. Park, Hawaii. Volcanic area on *Hawaii* Island.

HAWAIIAN GARDENS, Calif. (Los Angeles Co.). Promotional.

HAWARDEN, Iowa. (Sioux Co.). For Hawarden, Wales, in honor of the English prime minister, William Ewart Gladstone, whose home was in the Welsh hamlet. An earlier name was Calliope.

Hawaii, America's great tropical island chain (and its fiftieth state), was created by volcanic activity. Shown here is Haleakala Crater in Hawaii Volcanos National Park on the island of Maui. [*Photo by Irving Rosen. Courtesy of Frederic Lewis*]

HAWESVILLE, Ky. (co. seat of Hancock Co.). For Richard Hawes, a prominent landholder in early western Kentucky.

HAWKESBURY, Ont. (Prescott Co.). For Charles Jenkinson, Baron Hawksbury and Earl of Liverpool (1727-1808).

HAWKINS, Benjamin (1754-1816), staff interpreter for George Washington during the American Revolution and a member of the Continental Contress (1781-84; 1786; 1787). He was also an Indian negotiator, U.S. senator from North Carolina (1789-95), and Indian agent for tribes south of the Ohio River (1796-1816).
Hawkins Co., Tenn. (co. seat, Rogersville). *Hawkinsville*, Ga. (co. seat of Pulaski Co.).

HAWKINS PEAK, Utah. For a local settler.

HAWK'S NEST (peak), N.Dak. For the hawks nesting on it.

HAWORTH, N.J. (Bergen Co.). Believed to be for Haworth, Yorkshire, England.

HAW RIVER, N.C. A shortened form of *Sissipahaw*, for the Indian tribe of Siouan linguistic stock. It flows northeast and southeast to join Deep River to form Cape Fear River.

HAWTHORNE, Calif. (Los Angeles Co.). For Nathaniel Hawthorne (1804-1864), famed American novelist.

HAWTHORNE, Nev. (co. seat of Mineral Co.). For William Hawthorne, a rancher and prominent citizen.

HAVANA, Ill. (co. seat of Mason Co.). For Havana, Cuba.

HAY, Mount, Alaska. For John Milton Hay (1838-1905), private secretary to President Lincoln, ambassador to Great Britain, and secretary of state (1897-1905) under Presidents McKinley and Theodore Roosevelt. He helped negotiate the treaty with England for the Alaskan Boundary Tribunal.

HAY CANYON BUTTE, S.Dak. For hay harvested in the canyon.

HAYDEN PEAK, Utah, in the Uinta Mtns. Probably for Ferdinand Vandiver Hayden (1829-1887), an eminent geologist of the West.

HAYES, Mount, Alaska, in Alaska Range. For Charles Willard Hayes (1858-1916), geologist.

HAYES, Rutherford Birchard (1822-1893), nineteenth President of the United States (1877-81), from Ohio. He was a general in the Civil War, U.S. representative (1865-67), and governor (1868-72); 1876-77). He was elected President over Samuel Tilden in a contested election in which there were charges of fraud.
Hayes Co., Neb. (co. seat, *Hayes Center*). *Hayes Center*, Neb. (co. seat of *Hayes* Co.).

HAYESVILLE, N.C. (co. seat of Clay Co.). For George W. Hayes (1804-1864), a legislator who helped form the county.

HAYESVILLE, Ore. (Marion Co.). For a local citizen named Hayes.

HAYNES MOUNTAIN, Wyo., in Yellowstone Natl. Park. For Frank J. Haynes, pioneer photographer.

HAYNESVILLE, La. (Claiborne Parish). For Samuel Haynes, a local farmer.

HAYNEVILLE, Ala. (co. seat of Lowndes Co.). For Robert Young Hayne (1791-1839), a veteran of the War of 1812, lawyer, and U.S. senator from South Carolina. He was governor of South Carolina (1832-34). It has also been said to be named for Arthur P. Hayne, who was with Jackson in the War of 1812 and lived for a while in Autauga County.

HAY PASS, Wyo. For John Hay, a sheep raiser and banker.

HAY RIVER, Wis. For the wild grass that grew along its banks that could be used for hay. It flows southeast into Red Cedar River.

HAYS, Kan. (co. seat of Ellis Co.). For Fort Hays, now abandoned, in turn named for Gen. Alexander Hays (?-1864), killed at the Battle of the Wilderness.

HAYS Co., Tex. (co. seat, San Marcos). For John Coffee Hays (1817-1883), an officer in the Mexican War.

HAYSTACK Descriptive of shape.
Haystack, Mount, N.Y.
Haystack Mountain, Vt. (Orleans Co.).
Haystack Mountain, Vt. (Windham Co.).
Haystack Peak, Utah.

HAYSVILLE, Kan. (Sedgwick Co.). For W. W. Hays, farmer and local official.

HAYTI, Mo. (Pemiscot Co.). Variant spelling of *Haiti*, West Indies.

HAYTI, S.Dak. (co. seat of Hamlin Co.). Said to have been named "hay-tie" at a meeting of pioneers who twisted hay for fuel. Later it was believed to be named for a hay dealer named Tie. It was probably also influenced by *Haiti*, West Indies.

HAYWARD, Calif. (Alameda Co.). For William Hayward, postmaster and hotel owner.

HAYWARD, Wis. (Sawyer Co.). For Anthony Judson Hayward, a local sawmill owner.

HAYWOOD, John (1755-1826), Tennessee jurist.
Haywood Co., N.C. (co. seat, Waynesville).
Haywood Co., Tenn. (co. seat, Brownsville).

HAZARD, Ky. (co. seat of Perry Co.). For Oliver Hazard PERRY.

HAZEL For hazelnut bushes.
Hazel Crest, Ill. (Cook Co.).
Hazel Park, Mich. (Oakland Co.). Earlier, Hazel Slump.
Hazelwood, Mo. (St. Louis Co.).

HAZELTON PEAK, Wyo. For Hazel, daughter of Thomas J. Smith, rancher.

HAZLEHURST, Miss. (co. seat of Copiah Co.). For George H. Hazlehurst, engineer for the Illinois Central railroad, who surveyed the townsite.

HAZEN BAY, Alaska, on Bering Sea. For Gen. William Babcock Hazen, a chief signal officer in the United States Army.

HAZLET, N.J. (Monmouth Co.). For a doctor or minister from the area.

HEAD HARBOR ISLAND, Me. Descriptive of its location.

HEALDSBURG, Calif. (Sonoma Co.). For Harmon G. Heald (1821-1858), store owner, county supervisor, and state assemblyman.

HEARD Co., Ga. (co. seat, Franklin). For Stephen Heard, governor of Georgia (1780-81) and jurist.

HEARNE, Tex. (Robertson Co.). For C. C. Hearne, a pioneer who donated the land for the townsite. Another source states it was named for H. R. Hearne, also an early settler.

HEART Translated from an Indian name, meaning that the stream flowed from "the heart of the land." The river was named first.
Heart Butte, N.Dak.
Heart River, N.Dak. Flows E and NE into Missouri R.
Heart Butte Dam, N.Dak.

HEART MOUNTAIN, Wyo. Descriptive of shape.

HEATH, Ohio (Licking Co.). For a Mr. Heath, a Pure Oil Company official who negotiated land for the industry.

HEATHSVILLE, Va. (co. seat of Northumberland Co.). For John Heath (1758-1810), a founder of Phi Beta Kappa at the College of William and Mary (1776), soldier in the American Revolution, attorney for the Commonwealth of Virginia, state legislator, U.S. representative (1793-97), and a member of the Virginia Privy Council (1803-10).

HEAVENER, Okla. (Le Flore Co.). For Joseph Heavener, a local merchant.

HEBBRONVILLE, Tex. (co. seat of Jim Hogg Co.). For W. R. Hebbron, founder.

HEBER, Utah (co. seat of Wasatch Co.). For Heber C. Kimball, an aide to Brigham Young, the Mormon leader.

HEBGEN LAKE, Mont., dam and reservoir in Madison River. For a local settler or explorer.

HEBRON For Hebron, a city in Palestine, which figured in Biblical history. The Hebrew word means "enclosure."
Hebron, Conn. (Tolland Co.), town.
Hebron, Neb. (co. seat of Thayer Co.).

HEDGES PEAK, Wyo., in Yellowstone Natl. Park. For Cornelius Hedges, of the United States Geological Survey. He was a member of Washburn's party in 1870.

HEDWIG VILLAGE, Tex. (Harris Co.). For Hedwig Road, which was for Mrs. Hedwig Janokoski Schroeder, born (1887) in Grenhagen, Germany. She came to the area in 1906 and farmed there for fifty-one years, after which time she deeded her land over to the town.

HEFLIN, Ala. (co. seat of Cleburne Co.). For Dr. William L. Heflin, a prominent East Alabama citizen.

HELEN, Mount, Nev. From a woman's forename.

HELENA For Helena Phillips, daughter of Sylvanus PHILLIPS.
Helena, Ark. (co. seat of Phillips Co.).
West Helena, Ark. (Phillips Co.).

HELENA For a Helena in Minnesota.
Helena, Mont. (co. seat of Lewis and Clark Co.), state capital.
Helena Natl. Forest, Mont.

HELENA, Tex. (Karnes Co.). For Helen, wife of Dr. Lewis S. Owings, a founder; formerly the county seat.

HELL For forbidding terrain.
Hell Creek, Colo. Flows E to join E Spring Creek to form S Fork Republican R.
Hells Canyon, Ore.-Idaho. Extends N-S between Wallowa Mtns., Ore., and Seven Devils Mtns., Idaho.

HELLERTOWN, Pa. (Northampton Co.). For Christopher and Simon Heller, early settlers who emmigrated from Germany about 1740.

HEMET Possibly the Shoshonean name of the valley, or from Swedish *hemmet*, "in the home."
Hemet, Calif. (Riverside Co.).
Hemet East, Calif. (Riverside Co.).

HEMLOCK LAKE, N.Y. Translated from Indian, for the tree.

HEMPHILL, John (1803-1862), Texas jurist and U.S. senator.
Hemphill Co., Tex. (co. seat, Canadian).
Hemphill, Tex. (co. seat of Sabine Co.).

HEMPSTEAD For the settlers' native home in England, Hemel Hempstead, Hertfordshire.
Hempstead, N.Y. (Nassau Co.).
West Hempstead-Lakeview, N.Y. (Nassau Co.). *Lakeview*, descriptive.

HEMPSTEAD Co., Ark. (co. seat, Hope). For Edward Hempstead, an early settler.

HEMPSTEAD, Tex. (co. seat of Waller Co.). For G. S. B. Hempstead, a physician; named by his brother-in-law, R. R. Peebles, also a physician.

HENDERSON, James, an officer under the command of Andrew Jackson in the War of 1812.
Henderson Co., Tenn. (co. seat, Lexington).
Henderson. Tenn. (co. seat of Chester Co.).

HENDERSON, James Pinckney (1808-1858), attorney and Texas patriot. Commissioned brigadier general and sent to the United States to recruit help, he returned to Texas (1836) with a company. He was Republic of Texas attorney general (1836), its secretary of state (1836-37), and minister to France and to England, and first governor (1846-47) of the state of Texas. In the Mexican War he led the Second Texas Regiment at the Battle of Moneterrey. He served one term as a U.S. senator (1857-58).
Henderson Co., Tex. (co. seat, Athens).
Henderson, Tex. (co. seat of Rusk Co.).

HENDERSON, Leonard (1772-1833), North Carolina jurist, a chief justice of the North Carolina Supreme Court.
Henderson Co., N.C. (co. seat, *Hendersonville*).
Henderson, N.C. (co. seat of Vance Co.).
Hendersonville, N.C. (co. seat of *Henderson* Co.).

HENDERSON, Nev. (Clark Co.). For Charles Belknap Henderson (1873-1954), a member of the Nevada house of representatives (1905-07). He served in Torrey's Rough Riders during the Spanish-American War, was U.S. senator (1918-21), was appointed to the board of directors of the Reconstruction Finance Corporation (1934) and served as its chairman (1941-

47). He was also president and director of Elko Telephone Company and a director of the Western Pacific railroad.

HENDERSON, Richard (1734-1785), an early settler in the Kentucky area, where Henderson River was named for him. He participated in the ventures of the Transylvania Land Company (later the Richard Henderson Company), which founded Henderson, Ky.
Henderson Co., Ill. (co. seat, Oquawak). For *Henderson* Co., Ky.
Henderson Co., Ky. (co seat, *Henderson*). For the river.
Henderson, Ky. (co. seat of *Henderson* Co.). Earlier, Red Banks.
Henderson River, Ky.

HENDERSON PEAK, Wyo. For Kenneth A. Henderson, mountaineer and author.

HENDERSONVILLE, N.C. For Leonard HENDERSON.

HENDRICKS Co., Ind. (co. seat, Danville). For William Hendricks (1782-1850), Indiana statesman and governor (1822-25).

HENDRY Co., Fla. (co. seat, La Belle). For Francis Asbury Hendry.

HENLOPEN CAPE, Del. Probably of Dutch origin, either for Hindelopen, a town in Friesland, or for Tymen Jacobsen Hinlopen of Amsterdam.

HENNEPIN, Louis (1640-1701), Franciscan missionary known as Father Hennepin, a member of La Salle's expedition, and explorer of the upper Mississippi River and the Illinois River. He later published an account of his travels and of his capture by a band of Sioux Indians.
Hennepin Co., Minn. (co. seat, Minneapolis).
Hennepin, Ill. (co. seat of Putnam Co.).

HENRICO Co., Va. (co. seat, Richmond). For Prince Henry Frederick (1594-1612), Prince of Wales and son of James I. Originally the name was applied to a settlement which was called Henricopolis (with the addition of the ancient Greek suffix *-polis* meaning "city of Henry"). The shortened form prevailed.

HENRIETTA, Tex. (co. seat of Clay Co.). For Henry and Etta Parrish, early settlers. Another source states that the town was named for Henry Clay's wife, Henrietta.

HENRY, Cape, Va. Extends into Atlantic Ocean. For Henry, Prince of Wales, son of King James I of England. See also HENRICO Co.

HENRY Co., Iowa (co. seat, Mount Pleasant). For Henry DODGE.

HENRY, Ill. (Marshall Co.). For James D. Henry, a general in the Black Hawk War (1832).

Patrick Henry, shown here in an uncharacteristic docile pose, was the fiery Virginia orator known for such famous phrases as "Give me liberty or give me death!" [*New York Public Library*]

HENRY, Patrick (1736-1799), Virginia patriot and statesman, one of the most dynamic and eloquent spokesmen for American independence. Two of his famous statements are: "Caesar had his Brutus; Charles the First his Cromwell; and George the Third—may profit by their example. If this be treason, make the most of it!" (1765) and "Give me liberty or give me death!"

(1775). He was a member of the Continental Congress (1774-76) and governor (1776-79; 1784-86).
Henry Co., Ala. (co. seat, Abbeville).
Henry Co., Ga. (co. seat, McDonough).
Henry Co., Ill. (co. seat, Cambridge).
Henry Co., Ind. (co. seat, New Castle).
Henry Co., Ky. (co. seat, New Castle).
Henry Co., Mo. (co. seat, Clinton).
Henry Co., Ohio (co. seat, Napoleon).
Henry Co., Tenn. (co. seat, Paris).
Henry Co., Va. (co. seat, Martinsville).

HENRYETTA, Okla. (Okmulgee Co.). For Henry G. and Etta Ray Beard.

HENRY MOUNTAINS, Utah. For Joseph Henry, secretary of the Smithsonian Institution.

HENRYS For a partner in the Northwest Fur Company.
Henrys Lake, Idaho.
Henrys Fork River, Idaho. Rises in the lake, flows S and SW into Snake R.

HENSHAW, Lake, Calif. Man-made reservoir on San Luis Rey River. For William G. Henshaw, a rancher.

HEPPNER, Ore. (co. seat of Morrow Co.). For Henry Heppner (1829-1905), a local merchant, born in Zerkow, Prussia. He was a traveling salesman and a town founder.

HERBERT ISLAND, Alaska. One of the Islands of Four Mountains. For Hilary Abner Herbert (1834-1919), lawyer, officer in the Confederate Army, U.S. representative (1877-93) from Alabama, and secretary of the navy (1893-97) under Cleveland.

HEREFORD, Tex. (co. seat of Deaf Smith Co.). For the Hereford breed of cattle, which an early settler brought to the site of the town.

HERINGTON, Kan. (Dickinson Co.). For Monroe D. Herington, town founder.

HERKIMER, Nicholas (1728-1777), New York soldier and patriot, known for his part in the Battle of Oriskany. In August, 1777, while marching to relieve Fort Schuyler, he was ambushed by British and Indian forces and seriously wounded. He nevertheless directed his men to victory. An earlier name was German Flats, for German settlers.

Herkimer Co., N.Y. (co. seat, *Herkimer*).
Herkimer, N.Y. (co. seat of *Herkimer* Co.).

HERLONG, Calif. (Lassen Co.). For Henry W. Herlong (1911-1941), first U.S. Army ordnance officer to be killed in World War II.

HERMANN, Mo. (co. seat of Gasconade Co.). Germanized form of Arminius (17 *B.C.*-21 *A.D.*), leader of the Germans against the Romans in the battle of Teutoberg Forest (9 *A.D.*), in which the Romans were defeated.

HERMISTON, Ore. (Umatilla Co.). For *The Weir of Hermiston*, by Robert Louis Stevenson, because a founder liked the name.

HERMITAGE, Mo. (co. seat of Hickory Co.). For the home of Andrew Jackson at Nashville, Tenn.

HERMOSA BEACH, Calif. (Los Angeles Co.). From Spanish *hermosa*, "beautiful." The city has a two-mile sandy beach.

HERNANDO For Hernando DE SOTO.
Hernando Co., Fla. (co. seat, Brooksville).
Hernando, Miss. (co. seat of De Soto Co.).

HERRICK MOUNTAIN, Vt. For Amos Herrick, early settler.

HERRIN, Ill. (Williamson Co.). For Isaac Herrin, first settler.

HERSHEY, Pa. (Dauphin Co.). For Milton S. Hershey (1857-1945), manufacturer and philanthropist, who developed a model town around his chocolate factory here.

HERTFORD Co., N.C. (co. seat, Winton). For Francis Seymour Conway (1719-1794), Earl of Hertford.

HERTFORD, N.C. (co. seat of Perquimans Co.). For Hertford, England; the word means "stag ford."

HESPELER, Ont. (Waterloo Co.). Named in 1857 for Jacob Hespeler from Wurttemberg, Germany, who opened a business here in 1844.

HESPERIA, Calif. (San Bernadino Co.). From Greek and Latin, "the Western Land," used by Greek and Roman poets, or possibly for a Hesperia in Michigan.

HETTINGER, Mathias, of Illinois. The county was named for him by his son-in-law, a legislator and county founder.
Hettinger Co., N.Dak. (co. seat, Mott).
Hettinger, N.Dak. (co. seat of Adams Co.).

HEYBURN RESERVOIR, Okla. On Polecat Creek. For the nearby village, in turn for Clay Heyburn, a prominent resident.

HIAWASSEE, Ga. (co. seat of Towns Co.). From Cherokee *ayuhwasi*, "meadow."

HIAWATHA For an Algonquin deity. Besides the mythological attributes given him by Longfellow, he is said to have organized the Five Nations, which later became Six, of the Iroquois Confederacy. The name means "river maker."
Hiawatha, Kan. (co. seat of Brown Co.).
Hiawatha Lake, N.J.
Hiawatha Natl. Forest, Mich.

HIBBING, Minn. (St. Louis Co.). For Frank Hibbing (1857-1897), founder and a miner.

HICKMAN, Ky. (co. seat of Fulton Co.). For a Miss Hickman who became the wife of the founder. An earlier name was Mills Point.

HICKMAN Co., Tenn. (co. seat, Centerville). For Edwin Hickman (?-1791), killed by Indians.

HICKORY Co., Mo. (co. seat, Hermitage). From the nickname, "Old Hickory," of Andrew Jackson.

HICKORY HILLS, Ill. (Cook Co.). For the hilly terrain and large stands of hickory trees.

HICKSVILLE, Ohio (Defiance Co.). For Henry W. Hicks, member of a New York City timber investment company that purchased large landholdings in the area.

HIDALGO From Spanish, "nobleman." As a place name it may come from Guadalupe Hidalgo, D.F., Mexico, or may be in honor of Miguel Hidalgo y Costilla (1753-1811), Mexican priest and patriot, a hero of the Mexican war for independence from Spain.
Hidalgo Co., N.Mex. (co. seat, Lordsburg).
Hidalgo Co., Tex. (co. seat, Edinburg).

HIGGINS LAKE, Mich. For Sylvester Higgins, topographer.

HIGGINSVILLE, Mo. (Lafayette Co.). For Harvey J. Higgins, landowner.

HIGH Descriptive.
High Island, Mich. In L. Michigan.
High Falls Reservoir, Wis. On Peshtigo R.
High Point (peak), N.J.
High Rock (peak), N.J.
High Rock (peak), Wash.
High Rock Lake, N.C. On Yadkin R.

HIGHLAND Descriptive. See also HIGHLANDS.
Highland Co., Ohio (co. seat, Hillsboro).
Highland Co., Va. (co. seat, Monterey).
Highland, Calif. (San Bernardino Co.).
Highland Lake, Conn.
Highland Lake, N.H.

HIGHLAND, Ill. (Madison Co.). For the Scottish Highlands.

HIGHLAND, Ind. (Lake Co.). So named by railroad surveyors because it was the first high land they had reached for miles.

HIGHLAND FALLS, N.Y. (Orange Co.). Thought to be for nearby Buttermilk Falls. The village itself is on a hill.

HIGHLAND HEIGHTS, Ky. (Campbell Co.). From "Highland Baby Farms," a land-development and promotional company.

HIGHLAND HEIGHTS, Ohio (Cuyahoga Co.). Descriptive and promotional.

HIGHLAND PARK Descriptive and promotional.
Highland Park, Ill. (Lake Co.).
Highland Park, Mich. (Wayne Co.).
Highland Park, Tex. (Dallas Co.).
Highland Park, N.J. (Middlesex Co.). Earlier, Raritan Falls.

HIGHLANDS Descriptive.
Highlands Co., Fla. (co. seat, Sebring).
Highlands, Tex. (Harris Co.).
North Highlands, Calif. (San Bernardino Co.). For Highland, Calif.

HIGHMORE, S.Dak. (co. seat of Hyde Co.). Probably descriptive, but three possibilities are suggested: for high land; from the name of a surveyor in the area; and from a foreigner's attempt to describe the place as "higher."

HIGH POINT, N.C. (Guilford Co.). From a remark by Captain Gregg, chief engineer of the surveyors of the North Carolina railroad from Goldsboro to Charlotte: "This is the highest point along the whole survey, so we will mark it High Point."

HILGARD PEAK, Mont. For a local settler or explorer.

HILL, George Washington (1814-1860), Republic of Texas statesman.
Hill Co., Tex. (co. seat, *Hillsboro*).
Hillsboro, Tex. (co. seat of *Hill* Co.).

HILL Co., Mont. (co. seat, Havre). For James Jerome Hill (1838-1916), president and developer of the Great Northern railroad.

HILL CITY, Kan. (co. seat of Graham Co.). For W. R. Hill, a founder.

HILL CREEK, Utah. Descriptive. Flows north into Willow Creek.

HILLERS, Mount, Utah. For a local settler.

HILLIARD, Ohio (Franklin Co.). For a local citizen.

HILLMAN PEAK, Ore. For John W. Hillman, explorer and discoverer of Crater Lake.

HILLS For John H. Hill, rancher.
Hills Creek, Ore.
Hills Creek Reservoir, Ore.

HILLSBORO Descriptive.
Hillsboro, Ill. (co. seat of Montgomery Co.).
Hillsboro, N.C. (co. seat of Orange Co.).

HILLSBORO, Kan. (Marion Co.). For John G. Hill, early settler and local official.

HILLSBORO, N.Dak. (co. seat of Traill Co.). Originally descriptive, the town being built on a hill; later in honor of James J. Hill (1838-1916), founder of the Great Northern railroad.

HILLSBORO, Ohio (co. seat of Highland Co.). For Lord Hillsborough, member of the British Board of Trade and plantation commissioner who administered the King's Domain in western areas.

HILLSBORO, Ore. (co. seat of Washington Co.). For David Hill (1809-1850), early settler and legislator.

HILLSBORO CANAL, Fla. Extends from Lake Okeechobee to Atlantic Ocean. Probably a respelling of Hillsborough, for Viscount Hillsborough (1718-1793), who held a land grant during the English occupation of Florida.

HILLSBOROUGH, Wills Hill, 1st Earl of (1718-1793), English statesman who was secretary of state for the colonies (1768-72) and for the northern department (1779-82). He was generally unsympathetic to the demands of the American colonists.
Hillsborough, Calif. (San Mateo Co.). For a Hillsboro, N.H., home of W. D. M. Howard, landowner.
Hillsborough Co., Fla. (co. seat, Tampa).
Hillsborough Co., N.H. (co. seat, Nashua).
Hillsborough River, Fla.

HILLSDALE Descriptive.
Hillsdale Co., Mich. (co. seat, *Hillsdale*).
Hillsdale, Mich. (co. seat of *Hillsdale* Co.).
Hillsdale, Mo. (independent city in St. Louis Co.).
Hillsdale, N.J. (Bergen Co.).

HILLSIDE Descriptive of hilly terrain.
Hillside, Ill. (Cook Co.).
Hillside, N.J. (Union Co.).

HILLSVILLE, Va. (co. seat of Carroll Co.). For the Hill family, farmers who settled the area.

HILLTOWN, Pa. (Bucks Co.). Descriptive.

HILO Of Hawaiian origin, meaning uncertain, possibly from a personal name.
Hilo, Hawaii (co. seat of Hawaii Co.).
Hilo Bay, Hawaii. Inlet on E coast of Hawaii Island.

HILTON HEAD ISLAND, S.C., in Atlantic Ocean. For William Hilton, English sea captain and adventurer who explored the island in 1663.

HINCHINBROOK ISLAND, Alaska, in William Sound. Named by Capt. James Cook in 1778 for Viscount Hinchinbrook.

HINDMAN, Ky. (co. seat of Knott Co.). For James Hindman, a lieutenant governor of Kentucky.

HINDS Co., Miss. (co. seats, Jackson and Raymond). For Thomas Hinds (1780-1840), Mississippi statesman and U.S. representative.

HINESVILLE, Ga. (co. seat of Liberty Co.). For Charlton Hines, a prominent citizen.

HINGHAM For Hingham, Norfolk, England. Many of the first settlers came from this town.
Hingham, Mass. (Plymouth Co.), town. Earlier, Barecove Common.
Hingham Bay, Mass.

HINSDALE Co., Colo. (co. seat, Lake City). For George A. Hinsdale, a state official.

HINSDALE, Ebenezer, missionary, soldier, and prosperous trader.
Hinsdale, N.H. (Cheshire Co.).
Hinsdale, N.Y. (Cattaraugus Co.), town. For *Hinsdale*, N.H., the birthplace of Assemblyman E. T. Foot's mother, who was a member of the standing committee on the erection of towns and counties.

HINSDALE, Ill. (Du Page Co.). For H. W. Hinsdale, a director of the Burlington railroad.

HINTON, W.Va. (co. seat of Summers Co.). For Evan Hinton (1821-1897).

HITCHCOCK Co., Neb. (co. seat, Trenton). For Phineas Warrener Hitchcock (1831-1881), U.S. senator (1871-77).

HITCHCOCK, Tex. (Galveston Co.). For L. M. Hitchcock, a land developer.

HIWASSEE From Cherokee, "meadow."
Hiwassee Dam, N.C. On *Hiwassee* R.
Hiwassee Lake, N.C.
Hiwassee River, Ga.-N.C.-Tenn. Flows N through *Hiwassee* L., then NW into the Tennessee R.
Hiwassee Dam, N.C. (Cherokee Co.).

HIXSON, Tenn. (Hamilton Co.). Named by the Southern Railway Company for E. F. Hixson (1862-1932), station agent, postmaster, and owner of the general store.

HOBACK PEAK, Wyo. For John Hoback, trapper.

HOBART, Ind. (Lake Co.). Named by George Earle, who platted the town in 1848, for his brother, Hobart, who had gone to Australia.

HOBART, Okla. (co. seat of Kiowa Co.). For Garrett Augustus Hobart (1844-1899), twenty-fourth vice-president of the United States (1897-99) under McKinley, lawyer, and New Jersey legislator.

HOBBS, N.Mex. (Lea Co.). For J. B. James Isaac, and "Grandma" Hobbs, first settlers.

HOBBS PEAK, Wyo. For William Hobbs, explorer.

HOBOKEN, N.J. (Hudson Co.). From the Delaware Indian territory of *Hobocan Hackingh*, "land of the tobacco pipe." Hoboken is also the name of a village in northern Belgium, near the Dutch border.

HOCKANUM RIVER, Conn. From Podunk, "a hook." It flows southwest into Connecticut River.

HOCKING From Algonquian, in an Anglicized form, meaning uncertain, perhaps referring to cleared fields.
Hocking Co., Ohio (co. seat, Logan).
Hocking River, Ohio.

HOCKLEY Co., Tex. (co. seat, Levelland). For Gen. G. W. Hockley (1802-1854), chief of staff for Sam Houston and later secretary of war for the Republic of Texas.

HODGEMAN Co., Kan. (co. seat, Jetmore). For Amos Hodgman, Kansas Civil War officer who was killed in Mississippi (1863). The insertion of *e* was made by mistake when the county was named.

HODGENVILLE, Ky. (co. seat of La Rue Co.). For Robert Hodgen (1742-1810), a pioneer settler who operated Hodgen's Mill and owned thousands of acres in the area. His second wife was Sara La Rue.

HODGES PEAK, Wyo. For a member of a survey party in 1905.

HOFFMAN MOUNTAIN, N.Y. For a local settler.

HOFMANN FOREST, N.C. For Julius V. Hofmann (1882-1965), a professor of forestry at North Carolina State College.

HOGBACK Descriptive of a ridge of land with steeply sloping sides and a sharp summit.

Hogback Mountain, N.Mex.

Hogup Mountain, Utah. Probably a shortened form of *Hogback*.

HOG ISLAND, Mich. In Sturgeon Bay. For the swine, which were turned loose there.

HOHENWALD, Tenn. (co. seat of Lewis Co.). From German, "high woods." Meriwether Lewis was said to have been murdered nearby (1809) on his way to Washington along the Natchez Trace.

HOHOLITNA RIVER, Alaska. Of Eskimo origin, meaning unknown. It flows northwest into Holitna River.

HOH RIVER, Wash. From an Indian tribal name. It flows west into the Pacific Ocean.

HOISINGTON, Kan. (Barton Co.). For A. J. Hoisington, early settler and newspaperman.

HOKE Co., N.C. (co. seat, Raeford). For Robert F. Hoke (1837-1912), a general in the Confederate army.

HOLBROOK, Ariz. (co. seat of Navajo Co.). For H. R. Holbrook.

HOLBROOK, Mass. (Norfolk Co.), town. For Elisha Niles Holbrook, a boot and shoe manufacturer and banker.

HOLDEN, Mass. (Worcester Co.), town. For Samuel Holden, philanthropist and a director of the Bank of England.

HOLDENVILLE, Okla. (co. seat of Hughes Co.). For J. F. Holden, a railroad official. Earlier names were Echo and Fentress.

HOLDREGE, Neb. (co. seat of Phelps Co.). For George Ward Holdrege (1847-1926), master builder of the Burlington railroad west of the Missouri River and western general manager of its lines (1885-1921).

HOLE IN THE MOUNTAIN PEAK, Nev. So named because it has a natural stone window near its top. Also called Lizzie's Window.

HOLITNA RIVER, Alaska. Of Eskimo origin, meaning unknown. It flows northeast into Kuskokwim River.

HOLLADAY, Utah (Salt Lake Co.). For John Holladay, an early settler.

HOLLAND, Mich. (Ottawa Co.). For the country, from which the first settlers came.

HOLLAND, N.Y. (Erie Co.). For the Holland Land Company, a group of Dutch land speculators active in this area at the beginning of the nineteenth century.

HOLLANDALE, Miss. (Washington Co.). For the Holland family, who gave the railroad a right of way.

HOLLAND POND, Vt. Possibly for Charles James Fox, Lord Holland.

HOLLIDAYSBURG, Pa. (co. seat of Blair Co.). For the Holliday family and in particular for Adam Holliday (c.1728-1799), who, with his cousin William, founded the town.

HOLLIS, N.H. (Hillsborough Co.), town. For John Holles, Earl of Clare. See CLAREMONT.

HOLLIS, Okla. (co. seat of Harmon Co.). For George W. Hollis, a general-store operator and local developer.

HOLLISTER, Calif. (co. seat of San Benito Co.). For Col. W. W. Hollister, a sheep rancher who first acquired the land on which the community was founded.

HOLLISTON, Mass. (Middlesex Co.), town. For Thomas Hollis, a London merchant and patron of Harvard College.

HOLLY For holly shrubs or trees.

Holly, Mich. (Oakland Co.).

Holly Springs, Miss. (co. seat of Marshall Co.). For a large spring surrounded by holly trees.

Holly Springs Natl. Forest, Miss.

Hollywood, Calif., section of Los Angeles. Named by the wife of Horace A. Wilcox, the developer.

Hollywood, Ga. Named by Tom Bramblet, an early settler, for a beautiful holly tree that stood on the site of the first store.

West Hollywood, Calif. (Los Angeles Co.).

HOLMES Co., Fla. (co. seat, Bonifay). For a Creek Indian chief, killed (1818) by troops under the command of Andrew Jackson, or possibly for Thomas J. Holmes, also an Indian chief.

HOLMES Co., Miss. (co. seat, Lexington). For David Holmes (1769-1832), Mississippi statesman, governor, and U.S. senator (1820-25).

HOLMES Co., Ohio (co. seat, Millersburg). For Andrew Hunter Holmes, an army officer killed (1814) at Fort Mackinac, Mich., during the War of 1812.

HOLMES MOUNTAIN, Wyo., in Yellowstone Natl. Park. For W. H. Holmes, geologist and illustrator for the Hayden party.

HOLSTON RIVER, Va.-Tenn. For Stephen Holston, early settler. Rising from several forks, it flows southwest to join French Broad River to form Tennessee River.

HOLT, Mich. (Ingham Co.). For Joseph Holt, postmaster general (1859-61).

HOLT Co., Mo. (co. seat, Oregon). For David Rice Holt (1803-1840), Missouri legislator. An earlier name was Nodaway County.

HOLT Co., Neb. (co. seat, O'Neill). For Joseph Holt (1807-1894), appointed postmaster general (1859) and secretary of war (1860) by Buchanan and judge advocate general (1862) by Lincoln.

HOLTON, Kan. (co. seat of Jackson Co.). For Edward D. Holton, wealthy philanthropist who financed the first settlers.

HOLY CROSS, Mount of the, Colo. For the shape, a "cross of pure white, a mile high."

HOLYOKE, Colo. (co. seat of Phillips Co.). For a railroad official.

HOLYOKE, Mass. (Hampden Co.). Either for Rev. Edward Holyoke, president of Harvard (1737-1769), or for Eliezur Holyoke, an early settler and explorer of the Connecticut River. An earlier name was Springfield.

HOME GARDENS, Calif. (Riverside Co.). Promotional.

Hollywood Boulevard, the main thoroughfare of the movie capital of America, at its zenith in 1936. On the left is the famous Grauman's Chinese Theater. [*Paramount Productions. New York Public Library*]

HOMER (fl. ?850 *B.C.*), Greek poet, author of the *Iliad* and the *Odyssey*.

Homer, Ga. (co. seat of Banks Co.). Believed to be named for the famous Greek poet. The story also goes, however, that at the meeting for deciding the name, one man said, "Name it what you want to; I am going home." Another said, "That is a good name, Homer, let's go home."

Homer, La. (parish seat of Claiborne Parish).

Homer, N.Y. (Cortland Co.).

HOMERVILLE, Ga. (co. seat of Clinch Co.). For Dr. John Homer Mattox (1827-1896), resident physician, farmer, and founder.

HOMESTEAD, Pa. (Allegheny Co.). Either for the Homestead and Life Insurance Company, which laid out the town, or for "the McClure Homestead" in the area.

HOMESTEAD NATL. MONUMENT, Neb. Commemorates the homestead movement in American history. The monument occupies the site of the claim of Daniel Freeman, one of the first to apply for the one-quarter section (160 acres) under the Homestead Act of 1862.

HOMETOWN, Ill. (Cook Co.). Promotional.

HOMEWOOD, Ill. (Cook Co.). For Homewood in Pennsylvania.

HOMINY Although known as a dish made of corn, the name may have been derived from Harmony, the name of a mission.

Hominy, Okla. (Osage Co.).

Hominy Creek, Okla. Flows SE into Bird Creek.

HOMOCHITTO From Choctaw, "red-big" or "big red," descriptive.

Homochitto Natl. Forest, Miss.

Homochitto River, Miss. Flows SW and W into the Mississippi R.

HONDO, Tex. (co. seat of Medina Co.). From Spanish, "deep," for the deep valley of the Medina River; named (1689) by Alonzo de Leon.

HONEA PATH, S.C. (Anderson Co.). For a family of early settlers named Honea, or

for an Indian word *honea*, "path", or for an Indian path that was known as their "Honey Path."

HONEOYE LAKE, N.Y. From Iroquoian *hayeayeh*, "a finger lying," apparently from a legend of a snake having bitten off a finger of an Indian.

HONESDALE, Pa. (co. seat of Wayne Co.). For Philip Hone, mayor of New York and first president of the Delaware and Hudson Canal.

HONEY LAKE, Calif. So named because a sweet substance was found on oats growing in the area.

HONOLULU From Hawaiian, "protected bay."

Honolulu Co., Hawaii (co. seat, *Honolulu*).

Honolulu, Hawaii (co. seat of *Honolulu* Co.), state capital.

HOOD, Samuel (1724-1816), English seaman and admiral in the British Navy. He saw extensive service during the American Revolution and was awarded a baronet for his leadership. As a member of the Board of Admiralty, he was responsible for the Vancouver Expedition in the 1790s. The mountain peak and canal were named by Capt. George Vancouver in 1792.

Hood Bay, Alaska.

Hood Canal, Wash.

Hood, Mount, Ore.

Hood River, Ore. Flows into Columbia R.

Hood River Co., Ore. (co. seat, *Hood River*). Or possibly for Arthur William Acland Hood (1824-1901), British naval admiral.

Hood River, Ore. (co. seat of *Hood River* Co.).

HOOD Co., Tex. (co. seat, Granbury). For John Bell Hood (1831-1879), commander of troops from Texas in the Confederate army and later commander of the Confederate Army of Tennessee.

HOODOO For the goblin-like appearance of the place.

Hoodoo Basin, Wyo.

Hoodoo Peak, Wyo.

HOOKER Co., Neb. (co. seat, Mullen). For Joseph Hooker (1814-1879), a famous Union general during the Civil War.

HOOKER MOUNTAIN, Wyo. For Sir Joseph Dalton Hooker, English author and explorer.

HOOKS, Tex. (Bowie Co.). For Warren Hooks, a large landowner.

HOOKSETT, N.H. (Merrimack Co.), town. For an island in the Merrimack River shaped like a hook. Another factor was its popularity as a fishing spot.

HOOPESTON, Ill. (Vermilion Co.). For Thomas E. Hoopes, founder.

HOOSAC Probably from Mahican, "earthen kettle rim" or "stone place." Also spelled *Hoosic* and *Hoosick*.
Hoosac Range, Vt.-Mass.
Hoosic River, Mass.-N.Y.-Vt. Flows N and NW into Hudson R.
Hoosick Falls, N.Y. (Rensselaer Co.).

HOOVER RESERVOIR, Ohio. For Herbert Clark Hoover (1874-1964), thirty-first President of the United States (1929-33), from Iowa. He was United States food administrator (1917-18), secretary of commerce (1921-28) under Harding and Coolidge, chairman of Famine Emergency Commission (1947), and chairman of the Hoover Commission on Organization of the Executive Branch of the Government (1947).

HOP For the hop plant, *Humulus lupulus*, whose extract is used in malt liquor.
Hop Brook, Mass. Flows NW into Housatonic R.
Hop River, Conn. Flows SE into Natchaug R.
Hop River, Conn. (Tolland Co.).

HOPATCONG From an Indian word, literally "hill above a body of still water having an outlet."
Hopatcong, N.J. (Sussex Co.). For Lake Hopatcong.
Hopatcong, Lake, N.J. Largest inland body of water in the state.

HOPE, Ark. (co. seat of Hempstead Co.). For Hope Loughborough, daughter of James Loughborough, a director of the Cairo and Fulton railroad.

HOPKINS, Minn. (Hennepin Co.). For Harley H. Hopkins (1824-1882), postmaster.

HOPKINS, Samuel (1756?-1819), a general in the American Revolution.
Hopkins Co., Ky. (co. seat, Madisonville).
Hopkinsville, Ky. (co. seat of Christian Co.).

HOPKINS Co., Tex. (co. seat, Sulphur Springs). For the David Hopkins family, early settlers.

HOPKINTON. For Edward Hopkins (1600-1657), wealthy merchant and governor of Connecticut for several nonconsecutive terms beginning in 1641. He later retired to England and in his will left a bequest with which Harvard College purchased a township and named it for him.
Hopkinton, Mass. (Middlesex Co.), town.
Hopkinton, N.H. (Merrimack Co.), town.

HOPKINTON, R.I. (Washington Co.), town. For Stephen Hopkins (1707-1785), governor of Rhode Island (1775-57). He was a justice of the Rhode Island Superior Court and a signer of the Declaration of Independence. Hopkins served as the first chancellor of Rhode Island College (later Brown University) and was active in the colony's literary and scientific life.

HORICON, Wis. (Dodge Co.). For Lake Horicon, N.Y., now Lake George. The name was used by James Fenimore Cooper in *The Last of the Mohicans*. An Indian tribe of the name appears on early maps; the meaning has been given as "silver water," but this not known for certain.

HORNADAY, Mount, Wyo., in Yellowstone Natl. Park. For William T. Hornaday, zoologist.

HORN ISLAND, Miss. In Gulf of Mexico. Descriptive of shape.

HORRY Co., S.C. (co. seat, Conway). For Peter Horry (1743-1815), prominent citizen and holder of official positions including state senator, justice of the peace, and commissioner of public accounts. He served in the American Revolution in Francis Marion's brigade, rising to the rank of brigadier general, and later wrote a biography of Marion.

HORSE For the animal.
Horse Creek, Mo. Flows NW and NE into Sac R. For the horses which grazed along the banks.

Horse Mountain, N.Mex.

Horsehead Lake, N.Dak. So named because its shape supposedly resembled a horse's head.

Horseheads, N.Y. (Chemung Co.). Different stories exist as to the origin of the name: either because of horse skulls discovered in the area by early settlers that were thought to be remains of pack horses destroyed in an expedition against the Iroquois; or for an incident in the American Revolution when some soldiers killed their horses for food, and left the heads piled up.

Horseshoe Hill, Wyo., in Yellowstone Natl. Park. Descriptive of shape.

HORTONIA, Lake, Vt. From a personal name plus the pseudo-Latin ending *-ia.*

HOT Descriptive of water temperature.
Hot Brook Lake, Me.
Hot Creek Range, Nev.
Hot Sulphur Springs, Colo. (co. seat of Grand Co.).

HOT SPRING Co., Ark. (co. seat, Malvern). Descriptive. See also HOT SPRINGS.

HOT SPRINGS Descriptive. See also HOT SPRINGS.

Hot Springs Co., Wyo. (co. seat, Thermopolis).

Hot Springs, Ark. (co. seat of Garland Co.).

Hot Springs, S.Dak. (co. seat of Fall River Co.). Translated from the ane of an Indian camping spot, *Minnekahta*, "warm waters."

Hot Springs Natl. Park, Ark.

HOUGH PEAK, N.Y. For Franklin Benjamin Hough (1822-1875), New York forester, regional historian and director of the United States census of 1870.

HOUGHTON, Douglas (1809-1845), geologist.

Houghton Co., Mich. (co. seat, *Houghton*).

Houghton, Mich. (co. seat of *Houghton* Co.).

Houghton Lake, Mich.

Among the more famous Hot Springs which dot the North American are those in Arkansas. Here gentlemen bathe their feet in the medicinal waters of a "corn-hole." [*From a photograph by J. F. KennedyNew York Public Library*]

HOULTON, Me. (co. seat of Aroostook Co.), town and village. For Joseph Houlton, founder. He was a farmer, surveyor, justice of the peace, and mill owner.

HOUMA, La. (parish seat of Terrebonne Parish). From Choctaw *humma*, "red," but the significance is in dispute: for body paint, for color of moccasins, or for red crawfish, a tribal war symbol.

HOUSATONIC RIVER, Mass.-Conn. From Mahican, "at the place beyond the mountain." It flows south into Long Island Sound.

HOUSE Descriptive, for the peaks which supposedly resembled houses or housetops.
House Range, Utah.
Housetop Mountain, Wyo.

HOUSTON Co., Ala. (co. seat, Dothan). For George Smith Houston (1808-1879), U.S. representative and senator from Alabama. He was also governor (1874-78).

HOUSTON Co., Ga. (co. seat, Perry). For John Houston (1744-1796), American Revolutionary patriot and Georgia governor

HOUSTON, Samuel (1793-1863), Texas patriot and statesman. Born in Virginia, he moved to Tennessee and lived with the Cherokee Indians for several years. He served under Andrew Jackson in the war with the Creek Indians (1813-14), where he was seriously wounded. After becoming an attorney, he was U.S. representative from Tennessee and then governor (1827-29). He moved to Texas and took part in the Texas War for Independence, becoming commander in chief and president of the Republic of Texas before that state's annexation by the United States. He served as U.S. senator from the state of Texas and as governor (1859-61), later forced to leave office because of his opposition to the Confederacy.
Houston Co., Minn. (co. seat, Caledonia).
Houston Co., Tenn. (co. seat, Erin).
Houston Co., Tex. (co. seat, Crockett).
Houston, Miss. (a co. seat of Chickasaw Co.).
Houston, Mo. (co. seat of Texas Co.).
Houston, Tex. (co. seat of Harris Co.).
Houston, Lake, Tex.

Houston River, La. Flows S and E into Calcasieu R.
South Houston, Tex. (Harris Co.).

Sam Houston, soldier, settler, statesman and founder of Texas, was a man of action. Perhaps it was the boredom of endless debate that caused him to whittle in the United States Senate. [*New York Public Library*]

HOVENWEEP NATL. MONUMENT, Colo.-Utah. Preservation of Anasazi ruins dating from 400 A.D. *Hovenweep* is from Ute, possibly "deserted valley."

HOWARD For the fore- or surname of a local explorer or settler.
Howard, Mount, Wash.
Howard Mountain, Colo.

HOWARD Co., Ark. (co. seat, Nashville). Said to be named for James Howard, a local citizen.

HOWARD Co., Md. (co. seat, Ellicott City). For John Eager Howard (1752-1827), Maryland soldier and statesman who fought in the American Revolution. He was a member of the Continental Congress (1784-88), governor (1788-91), and U.S. senator (1796-1803).

HOWARD Co., Mo. (co. seat, Fayette). For Benjamin Howard (1760-1814), Kentucky legislator and U.S. representative and, later, governor of Louisiana Territory.

HOWARD, Oliver Otis (1830-1909), general during the Civil War, army educator, and president of Howard University, which is also named for him.
Howard Co., Neb. (co. seat, St. Paul).
Howard, Kan. (co. seat of Elk Co.).

HOWARD, S. Dak. (co. seat of Miner Co.). For the deceased son of J. D. Farmer, a judge and landowner.

HOWARD Co., Tex. (co. seat, Big Spring). For Volney E. Howard (1809-1889), Mississippi legislator and U.S. representative from Texas.

HOWARD, Tilghman Ashurst (1797-1844), Tennessee legislator, U.S. representative from Indiana, and Texas patriot.
Howard Co., Ind. (co. seat, Kokomo).
  Earlier, **Richardville**.
Howard Co., Iowa (co. seat, Cresco).

HOWARD, Wis. (Brown Co.). For Benjamin Howard, a general in the War of 1812.

HOWE BROOK MOUNTAIN, Me. For the nearby stream, which was probably named for an early settler.

HOWELL, Mich. (co. seat of Livingston Co.). For Thomas Howell, a friend of the first postmaster.

HOWELL Co., Mo. (co. seat, West Plains). For James Howell, a local citizen.

HOWELL MOUNTAIN, Wyo. For Billy Howell, a rancher.

HOWELL PEAK, Utah. For a local settler.

HOWLOCK MOUNTAIN, Ore. For a Paiute chief.

HOXIE, Kan. (co. seat of Sheridan Co.). For M. M. Hoxie, Missouri Pacific railroad official.

HOYT LAKES, Minn. (St. Louis Co.). For Eldon S. Hoyt, vice-president of the Pickands Mather Company, Cleveland, Ohio.

HOYT PEAK, Wyo. For John W. Hoyt, a territorial governor.

HUALAPAI For the Indian sub-tribe, of Yuman linguistic stock.
Hualapai Mountains, Ariz.
Hualapai Peak, Ariz.

HUBBARD Co., Minn. (co. seat, Park Rapids). For Lucius Frederick Hubbard (1836-1913), publisher, general in both the Civil War and Spanish-American War, businessman, and governor (1882-87).

HUBBARD, Ohio (Trumbull Co.). For Nehemiah Hubbard, Jr., an original member of the Connecticut Land Company, which owned a portion of the land on which the town was built.

HUBBARD LAKE, Mich. For Bela Hubbard, surveyor.

HUBBARD RIVER, Mass.-Conn. For a local settler or explorer. It flows generally southeast into Barkhamsted Reservoir.

HUBBARDTON For Thomas Hubbard, founder of the town.
Hubbardton, Vt. (Rutland Co.), town.
Hubbardton River, Vt. Flows SSW to join
  Poultney R. to form East Bay R.

HUBER HEIGHTS, Ohio (Montgomery Co.). For Charles Huber, the builder and developer.

HUCKLEBERRY MOUNTAIN, Wyo. For the growth of huckleberry bushes on the mountain.

HUDSON, Henry (?-1611), English navigator and explorer who made four major voyages of exploration, all of them in search of a water route to the East Indies by routes suggesting a "Northwest Passage," the most famous being along the northeastern coast of North America, including what is now the Hudson River, and, in 1610, northward through what is now Hudson Strait into Hudson Bay. His men mutinied and he was cast adrift on June 23, 1611. Names derived from his name occur rather often in the eastern part of North America, and some appear in the West through the trading enterprise of the Hudson's Bay Company, named for the bay. Although *Hudson* appears often elsewhere in the United States, it is usually in honor of a local citizen.
Hudson Co., N.J. (co. seat, Jersey City).
Hudson, N.Y. (co. seat of Columbia Co.).
  Earlier, **Claverack Landing**.
Hudson, Wis. (co. seat of St. Croix Co.).
  The St. Croix R. was thought to resemble
  the *Hudson* R., N.Y.

Hudson Bay, NE Canada. Large inland sea.

Hudson River, N.Y. Flows generally S into New York Bay.

Hudson Strait, NE Canada, between the Atlantic and Hudson Bay.

Hudson Falls, N.Y. (co. seat of Washington Co.).

HUDSON, Mass. (Middlesex Co.), town and village. For Charles Hudson (1795-1881), minister, philanthropist, newspaper editor and U.S. representative (1841-49). Earlier names were Howes Mills and Feltonville.

HUDSON, Mich. (Lenawee Co.). For Daniel Hudson, a landowner.

HUDSON, N.H. (Hillsborough Co.), town. The Merrimack River was at one time thought to flow east from the Hudson River. It was near this point in New Hampshire that the Merrimack's source was finally discovered to be to the north. An earlier name was Nottingham.

HUDSON, N.C. (Caldwell Co.). For the Hudson brothers, who ran a sawmill camp.

HUDSON, Ohio (Summit Co.). For David Hudson (1760-1836), founder. He also started the First Congregational Church and was the founder of Western Reserve College.

HUDSONVILLE, Mich. (Ottawa Co.). For Horace A. Hudson, a storekeeper.

HUDSPETH Co., Tex. (co. seat, Sierra Blanca). For Claude Benton Hudspeth (1877-1941), Texas statesman and U.S. representative (1919-31).

HUECO MOUNTAINS, Tex. From Mexican-Indian, "notched," descriptive of the range. The name is also influenced by the French *houechas*, for the Indian tribe.

HUERFANO From Spanish, "orphan" or "alone," in reference to a butte in the Huerfano River.

Huerfano Co., Colo. (co. seat, Walsenburg).

Huerfano Butte, Colo.

Huerfano River, Colo.

HUGH BUTLER LAKE, Neb. On Red Willow River. For Hugh Alfred Butler (1878-1954), a civic leader, businessman, construction engineer for Chicago, Burlington and Quincy railroad, and U.S. senator from Nebraska (1941-54).

HUGHES Co., Okla. (co. seat, Holdenville). For William C. Hughes, a delegate to the Oklahoma constitutional convention in 1907.

HUGHES Co., S.Dak. (co. seat, Pierre). For Alexander Hughes, a Dakota Territory legislator and area promoter. He was a member of the commission that located the state capital at Bismarck.

HUGO, Colo. (co. seat of Lincoln Co.). Probably for Hugo Richards (c.1838-1911), pioneer and special agent for the mail express to Denver.

HUGO, Victor-Marie (1802-1885), French poet and novelist, most famous in the United States for his novels *Notre-Dame de Paris* (The Hunchback of Notre Dame) and *Les Miserables* (The Wretched Ones).

Hugo, Okla. (co. seat of Choctaw Co.)

Hugoton, Kan. (co. seat of Stevens Co.).

Hugo died the year the town was founded.

HULAH From Osage, "eagle."

Hulah, Okla. (Osage Co.).

Hulah Dam and Reservoir, Okla. In Caney R.

HULAHULA RIVER, Alaska. Named by whalers; from Hawaiian, "a dance." It flows west and north into Camden Bay.

HULL For Hull (or Kingston upon Hull), East Riding, Yorkshire, England.

Hull Co., Que. (co. seat, Hull).

Hull, Que. (co. seat of Hull Co.). Named by Philemon Wright, founder, whose parents emigrated from Hull, England.

HULL, Mass. (Plymouth Co.), town. For Hull, Yorkshire, England.

HUMBLE, Tex. (Harris Co.). For Pleasant Humble, first postmaster and judge. The Humble Oil and Refining Company was named for the city.

HUMBOLDT, (Friedrich Heinrich) Alexander von (1769-1859), German explorer, naturalist, and statesman noted for his many researches into the fields of meteorology, oceanography, vulcanology, and botany. He also participated in several major expeditions to Central and South America. The Humboldt Current, off the west coast of South America, is named for him.

Humboldt Co., Calif. (co. seat, Eureka).
Humboldt Co., Iowa (co. seat, Dakota City).
Humboldt Co., Nev. (co. seat, Winnemucca).
Humboldt, Ill. (Coles Co.).
Humboldt, Iowa (*Humboldt* Co.).
Humboldt, Kan. (Allen Co.).
Humboldt, Minn. (Kittson Co.).
Humboldt, Neb. (Richardson Co.).
Humboldt, Sask.
Humboldt, Tenn. (Gibson Co.).
Humboldt Bay, Calif., on the Pacific.
Humboldt Natl. Forest, Nev.
Humboldt Peak, Colo.
Humboldt Range, Nev.
Humboldt River, Nev. Flows into *Humboldt* Sink.
Humboldt Salt Marsh, Nev.
Humboldt Sink, Nev. Fed by *Humboldt* R.

HUMMOCK POND, Mass. On Nantucket Island. For Nana Humacke, a Nantucket chief.

HUMPHREYS, Andrew A. (1812?-1883), officer in the U.S. Army, who rose to the rank of Brigadier General during the Civil War and was decorated for gallantry. He also directed surveying parties in the West, and was chief of the Corps of Engineers in 1871.
Humphreys, Mount, Calif.
Humphreys Mountain, Wyo. In Yellowstone Natl. Park.
Humphreys Peak, Ariz. General Humphreys had been an officer in the Ives expedition there in 1851.

HUMPHREYS Co., Miss. (co. seat, Belzoni). For Benjamin Grubb Humphreys (1808-1882), Confederate general in the Civil War, legislator, and governor of Mississippi (1865-66).

HUMPHREYS Co., Tenn. (co. seat, Waverly). For Parry Wayne Humphreys (?-1839), jurist and U.S. representative from Tennessee (1813-15).

HUMPTULIPS RIVER, Wash. A humorous and confused folk etymologizing of an Indian word or name whose exact meaning and form are now unknown, although two versions of the meaning have survived: "chilly region" and "hard to pole." It flows southwest into Grays Harbor.

HUNDRED AND TWO RIVER, Iowa-Mo. From an English rendering of French *Cent Deux*, the name of an Indian village near the head of the river, itself probably the French version of an Indian name with quite different meaning. It flows south into Little Platte River.

HUNGER, Mount, Vt. Reason for naming uncertain.

HUNGRY HORSE RESERVOIR, Mont. On S. Fork Flathead River. Probably for an incident.

HUNT, Co., Tex. (co. seat, Greenville). For Memucan Hunt (1807-1856), Republic of Texas general and statesman.

HUNTERDON Co., N.J. (co. seat, Flemington). For Robert Hunter (?-1734), a colonial governor of Virginia, New York, and Jamaica.

HUNTER MOUNTAIN, N.Y. For the nearby town, which was named for John Hunter, a landowner.

HUNTINGBURG, Ind. (Dubois Co.). Named by Col. Jacob Geiger (1779-1867) for an early hunting expedition he enjoyed.

HUNTINGDON For Huntingdon, Huntingdonshire, England.
Huntingdon Co., Que. (co. seat, *Huntingdon*).
Huntingdon, Que. (co. seat of *Huntingdon* Co.). Earlier, Bowron.

HUNTINGDON, Selina Shirley Hastings, Countess of (1707-1791), religious reformer who led a Calvinist sect within the Methodist Church, famed for her missionary zeal. She was the wife of Theophilus Hastings, 9th Earl of Huntingdon (1695-1746).
Huntingdon Co., Pa. (co. seat, *Huntingdon*).
Huntingdon, Pa. (co. seat of *Huntingdon* Co.).

HUNTINGDON, Tenn. (co. seat of Carroll Co.). For Memucan HUNT, who donated land for the site. Two folk stories also exist concerning the origin of the name. One is that when the white men came to the area, the Indians said, "Hunting is done." Another is that the place was named for "Huntingdon", a popular song of the time.

HUNTING ISLAND, S.C. In Atlantic Ocean. So named because it was once the private hunting ground of a group of antebellum plantation owners.

HUNTINGTON For a local settler or explorer.
Huntington, Vt. (Chittenden Co.), town.
Huntington River, Vt. Flows N and NE into Winooski R.

HUNTINGTON Possibly for Huntingdon, England, the birthplace of Oliver Cromwell, or to mean "Hunting Town," because of the abundance of game.
Huntington, N.Y. (Suffolk Co.).
Huntington Bay, N.Y. (Suffolk Co.).
Huntington Station, N.Y. (Suffolk Co.).
South Huntington, N.Y. (Suffolk Co.).

HUNTINGTON, Henry E., influential in the promotion of electric railroads.
Huntington Beach, Calif. (Orange Co.).
Huntington Park, Calif. (Los Angeles Co.).

HUNTINGTON, Samuel (1731-1796), Continental Congressman and presiding officer and governor of Connecticut.
Huntington Co., Ind. (co. seat, *Huntington*).
Huntington, Ind. (co. seat of *Huntington* Co.).
Huntington Creek, Pa. Flows SW into Susquehanna R.
Huntington Mills, Pa. (Luzerne Co.).

HUNTINGTON, W.Va. (co. seat of Cabell Co.). For Collis P. Huntington, founder.

HUNTINGTON CREEK, Nev. For Lott Huntington, member of an exploration party in 1859. It flows generally north into South Fork Humboldt River.

HUNTINGTON CREEK, Utah. For a local settler. It flows generally southeast to join Ferron Creek to form San Rafael River.

HUNTINGTON WOODS, Mich. (Oakland Co.). For the excellent hunting early settlers found there.

HUNT MOUNTAIN, Wyo. For Wilson Price Hunt, a fur trader.

HUNTSVILLE For John Hunt, first settler of Huntsville, Ala., merchant, and county coroner.
Huntsville, Ala. (co. seat of Madison Co.).
Huntsville, Ark. (co. seat of Madison Co.).
    For *Huntsville*, Ala.
Huntsville, Tex. (co. seat of Walker Co.).
    For *Huntsville*, Ala.

HUNTSVILLE, Mo. (co. seat of Randolph Co.). For Daniel Hunt, an early settler.

HUNTSVILLE, Tenn. (co. seat of Scott Co.). For a hunter named Hunt, who became the first settler. His first name has been lost.

HURLEY, N.Y. (Ulster Co.). For the English estate on the Thames of Governor Lovelace.

HURLEY, Wis. (co. seat of Iron Co.). For M. A. Hurley, a mining official.

HURON For a tribe of Iroquoian linguistic stock, later known as the Wyandot; from a French word for "rough," with a derogatory suffix, -on, probably indicating that the Hurons were formidable opponents. When European explorers arrived, the Hurons primarily inhabited the St. Lawrence River area. Various nicknames applied to the tribe are "cave dwellers," "islanders," "ruffians" (from the French), "wild boars," and "base ones." The Hurons contributed many names to the North American continent, a tribute to their tenacious defense of their territories and to their integrity as a tribe. See also CANADA and WYANDOT.
Huron Co., Mich. (co. seat, Bad Axe).
Huron Co., Ohio (co. seat, Norwalk).
Huron Co., Ont. (co. seat, Goderich).
Huron, Ohio (Erie Co.). For the lake.
Huron, S.Dak. (co. seat of Beadle Co.).
Huron Bay, Mich.
Huron, Lake, Mich.-Ont. One of the Great Lakes.
Huron River, Mich.

HURRICANE For high winds or their effects.
Hurricane, W.Va. (Putnam Co.). For the creek.
Hurricane Creek, W.Va. Flows into the Kanawha R. It was so named because of evidence of a hurricane, seen in the area by surveyors. The name *Kanawha* is said to mean "hurricane."
Hurricane Creek, Ark.
Hurricane Mesa, Wyo. For the strong winds that prevail there.

HURST, Tex. (Tarrant Co.). For William Letchworth Hurst (?-1922), an early settler.

HUSLIA RIVER, Alaska. Of Koyukan origin, meaning unknown. It flows southeast into Koyukuk River.

HUTCHINSON, Kan. (co. seat of Reno Co.). For C. C. Hutchinson, founder.

HUTCHINSON, Minn. (McLeod Co.). For the Hutchinson brothers, Asa (1823-1884), John (1821-?), and Adoniram (1817-1859), founders. The Hutchinson family was well known as a singing group during the mid 1850s.

HUTCHINSON Co., S.Dak. (co. seat, Olivet). For John Hutchinson, Dakota Territory official and acting governor. He was a member of a famous singing group (see HUTCHINSON, Minn.).

HUTCHINSON Co., Tex. (co. seat, Stinnett). For Anderson Hutchinson (1798-1853), a district judge and Republic of Texas patriot.

HYANNIS For an Indian chief, Hianna.
Hyannis, Mass. (Barnstable Co.).
Hyannis, Neb. (co. seat of Grant Co.). For *Hyannis*, Mass.

HYATTSVILLE, Md. (Prince Georges Co.). For Christopher Clarke Hyatt, a local businessman who purchased the townsite.

HYDE Co., N.C. (co. seat, Swan Quarter). For Edward Hyde (1661-1723), Earl of Clarendon, a controversial colonial governor of New Jersey and New York. He refused to allow assemblies to meet. Some names in the United States, however, derive from Hyde Park, London, England, and not from the Earl of Clarendon. An earlier name was Wickham County.

HYDE, Co., S.Dak. (co. seat, Highmore). For James Hyde (1842-1902), Civil War veteran, prisoner of war at Andersonville, Dakota legislator, and prominent businessman.

HYDEN, Ky. (co. seat of Leslie Co.). For John Hyden (1814-1883), state senator and one of the commissioners who supervised the formation of the county.

HYDE PARK For Hyde Park, London, England. The original meaning of *hyde* is "household," or "enough land to support one family." An earlier name was Stoutenburgh, for the founder, Jacobus Stoutenburg.
Hyde Park, N.Y. (Dutchess Co.), town and village. Home of Franklin D. Roosevelt.
New Hyde Park, N.Y. (Nassau Co.).

HYDE PARK, Vt. (co. seat of Lamoille Co.). For Jedediah Hyde, an early settler.

HYNDMAN PEAK, Idaho. For an early settler.

HYSHAM, Mont. (co. seat of Treasure Co.). For Charles Hysham, a rancher.

I

IATT, Lake, La. From a variant form of *Hietan*, for the Indian tribe of the southern Camanches.

IBERIA For the European peninsula that includes the countries of Spain and Portugal.
Iberia Parish, La. (parish seat, *New Iberia*).
New Iberia, La. (parish seat of *Iberia* Parish).

IBERVILLE, Pierre le Moyne, Sieur d' (1661-1706), French-Canadian explorer and naval officer who, continuing La Salle's exploration of the lower Mississippi, was the first to explore the Mississippi delta. He established the first French colonies along the American coast of the Gulf of Mexico, at Biloxi and Mobile (1698), literally the founder of the Louisiana Territory. He was successful in a number of naval engagements with the British (1686-1706), defeating them in naval combat in the Hudson Bay area and along the Hudson River. See also D'IBERVILLE, Miss.
Iberville Parish, La. (parish seat, Plaquemine).
Iberville Co., Que. (co. seat, *Iberville*).
Iberville, Que. (co. seat of *Iberville* Co.).

ICHAWAYNOCHAWAY CREEK, Ga. Of Muskogee origin, meaning uncertain, possibly "the place where deer sleep." It flows south into Flint River.

ICY Descriptive.
Icy Bay, Alaska. On Gulf of Alaska. Named by Capt. George Vancouver.

Icy Cape, Alaska. Extends into the bay.
Icy Strait, Alaska. Translated from Russian *proliu ledyanoy*.

IDA Probably classical, for Mount Ida, in Asia Minor, southeast of ancient Troy; but some evidence points to its being named for Ida, the first white child born in the community (July 19, 1856), daughter of Edwin Smith, a trapper. The grove was the only natural stand of timber in Ida County.
Ida Co., Iowa (co. seat, *Ida Grove*).
Ida Grove, Iowa (co. seat of *Ida* Co.).

IDABEL, Okla. (co. seat of McCurtain Co.). For Ida and Belle Purnell, daughters of a railroad official.

IDAHO From Shoshonean *Ee*, "coming down," *dah*, a stem word denoting both "sun" and "mountain," and *how*, an exclamatory phrase. The sense of the combined words has been variously given as "Sunup!," "Behold! the sun coming down the mountain," "Light on the mountains!," and "Gem of the mountains." The name was first applied (1859) to a village, Idaho Springs, then to Idaho County, which for a time was part of Washington state. When the Idaho Territory was organized (1863), Sen. Harry Wilson of Massachusetts led the fight for the name *Idaho* over *Montana*.
Idaho, State of. 43rd state of the Union. Settled: 1842. Territory: 1863. Admitted: 1890. Cap: Boise. Motto: *Esto Perpetua* (May You Endure Forever). Nickname: Gem State. Flower: Syringa. Bird: Moun-

tain Bluebird. Tree: Western White Pine. Song: "Here We Have Idaho."

Idaho Co., Idaho (co. seat, Grangeville).

Idaho City, Idaho (co. seat of Boise Co.).

Idaho Falls, Idaho (co. seat of Bonneville Co.). Promotional, for a settlement on the Snake R., leading settlers to believe that water power was available from the river. Although this was untrue, a prosperous city developed. Earlier, Eagle Rock.

IDITAROD RIVER, Alaska. Of Ingalik origin, meaning unknown. It flows northeast and west into Innoko River.

IKPIKPUK RIVER, Alaska. From Eskimo, *ikpikpak*, "big cliff or bank." It flows north into Smith Bay.

ILIAMNA Lake, Alaska. From Eskimo, supposedly for the name of a mythical great

blackfish which inhabited the lake.

ILIO POINT, Hawaii. On Molakai Island. From Hawaiian, "dog."

ILION, N.Y. (Herkimer Co.). For Ilion (Troy), the ancient city in Asia Minor.

ILLINOIS From an Indian tribe who called themselves the *Inini*, "perfect and accomplished men." The French called them *Illini* and added the suffix -*ois* to denote the tribe.

Illinois, State of. 21st state of the Union. Settled: 1720. Territory: 1809. Admitted: 1818. Cap: Springfield. Motto: State Sovereignty-National Union. Nickname: Prairie State. Flower: Native Violet. Bird: Cardinal. Tree: Bur Oak. Song: "Illinois."

Illinois Pass, Wyo., In the Rocky Mtns. Named by climbers from *Illinois*.

Once log cabins, such as this one in Illinois, marked the westward progress of the American people. Abraham Lincoln was raised in a cabin very little different from this one. [*New York Public Library*]

Illinois River, Ark.-Okla. Flows into the Arkansas R.

Illinois River, Calif.-Ore. Flows generally N into Rogue R. Named by early settlers from Peoria.

Illinois River, Ill. Flows W and SW into the Mississippi R.

Illinois and Michigan Canal, Ill.

Illinois and Mississippi Canal, Ill.

IMAGE, Wyo. (Teton Co.). For the reflection of mountains in a nearby lake.

IMMOKALEE, Fla. (Collier Co.). From Cherokee, "water-tumbling."

IMPERIAL For the Imperial Land Company, a subsidiary of the California Development Company, an enterprise established to obtain land in the early 1900s.

Imperial Co., Calif. (co. seat, El Centro).

Imperial, Calif. (*Imperial* Co.).

Imperial Dam, Calif.-Ariz.

Imperial Valley, Calif.-Mexico. The former Colorado Desert, formed by the Colorado R. delta cutting off the N part of the Gulf of California; now irrigated and one of the greatest producers of vegetables in the United States.

Imperial Beach, Calif. (San Diego Co.).

IMPERIAL, Neb. (co. seat of Chase Co.). For the Imperial City of Rome, the seat of the Catholic religion; named by Thomas Mercier, founder and first postmaster.

IMURUK Of Eskimo origin, meaning unknown.

Imuruk Basin, Alaska.

Imuruk Lake, Alaska.

INDEPENDENCE Locally believed to have been so named in recognition of Andrew Jackson's independence of character. Another plausible story is that the Jackson Countians noted that their rival county, Clay, had a county seat named Liberty. Clay was a statesman; Jackson was a statesman; there can be no liberty without independence; thus the reasoning and hence the name.

Independence, Mo. (co. seat of Jackson Co.).

Independence, Ore. (Polk Co.). For *Independence*, Mo.

INDEPENDENCE Commemorative of the signing of the Declaration of Independence.

Independence Co., Ark. (co. seat, Batesville).

Independence, Calif. (co. seat of Inyo Co.).

Independence, Iowa (co. seat of Buchanan Co.). The town was established on a date near the Fourth of July.

Independence, Kan. (co. seat of Montgomery Co.). For *Independence*, Iowa.

Independence, Ohio (Cuyahoga Co.).

Independence, Lake, Mich.

Independence Mountains, Nev. For the adjacent valley, which was supposedly discovered by U.S. soldiers on a Fourth of July.

Independence River, N.Y. Flows W into Black R.

INDEPENDENCE, Ky. (co. seat of Kenton Co.). For the new county's independence from Campbell County. The site was in "dead center" of the new county, as required by law for county seats.

INDEPENDENCE, Va. (co. seat of Grayson Co.). So named because two rival groups could not agree on the site for a county seat. A third group claimed that they were independent. The county seat was then located where this group lived.

INDEX PEAK, Wyo. Descriptive of its shape, which supposedly resembled that of an index finger.

INDIALANTIC, Fla. (Brevard Co.). So named because of its location on the Atlantic Ocean near the Indian River.

INDIAN For the Indians who inhabited the area.

Indian Creek, S.Dak. Flows SE into Belle Fourche R.

Indian Creek, Utah. Flows NNW into Colorado R.

Indian Hill, Neb.

Indian Lake, Mich.

Indian Lake, N.Y.

Indian Lake, Ohio. Formerly a Chippewa Indian area.

Indian Mountain, Wyo.

Indian Peak, Utah.

Indian Pond, Me.

Indian River, Fla. A long lagoon parallel to the Atlantic.

Indian River, Mich. Flows SE into L. Michigan.

Indian River, N.Y.

The Hoosier state of Indiana is noted for many things but none are more celebrated than the famous Indianapolis "500," America's most famous automobile race and one of the top sporting events of the late spring. [*Frederic Lewis*]

Indian Stream, N.H. Flows SSW into Connecticut R.

Indian Prairie Canal, Fla.

Indian River Co., Fla. (co. seat, Vero Beach). For the river.

INDIANA Latinized form of *Indian* meaning "land of the Indians." The name appears as early as 1768 in reference to a territory ceded to the Philadelphis Trading Company by the Iroquois and was later applied to areas in what is now West Virginia and elsewhere. When the Northwest Territory was divided in 1800, the Indiana Territory was created.

Indiana, State of. 19th state of the Union. Settled: 1733. Territory: 1800. Admitted: 1816. Cap: Indianapolis. Motto: The Crossroads of America. Nickname: Hoosier State. Flower: Peony. Bird: Cardinal. Tree: Tulip (yellow poplar). Song: "On the Banks of the Wabash."

Indiana Co., Pa. (co. seat, *Indiana*). For the Indiana Territory.

Indiana, Pa. (co. seat of *Indiana* Co.).

INDIANAPOLIS, Ind. (co. seat of Marion Co.), state capital. From *Indiana* plus Greek *polis*, "city."

INDIAN HILL, Ohio (Hamilton Co.). So named because at one time a band of Indians stole a horse from a nearby village, and in the process one of the Indians was shot and was buried on the top of a hill.

INDIANOLA From *Indian* plus either a pseudo-Latin ending or Choctaw *olah*, "this side of." It was a popular name for places during the 1700s and 1800s, especially the latter.

Indianola, Iowa (co. seat of Warren Co.).

Indianola, Miss. (co. seat of Sunflower Co.).

INDIAN PASS, Wyo., in the Rocky Mtns. For an Indian trail.

INDIO, Calif. (Riverside Co.). From Spanish "Indian."

INEZ, Ky. (co. seat of Martin Co.). For Inez Frank, daughter of the postmaster of Louisa, Ky.

INGALLS, Mount, Calif. For the Ingalls family, early settlers.

INGHAM Co., Mich. (co. seat, Mason). For Samuel Delucenna Ingham (1779-1860), Pennsylvanian statesman and secretary of the treasury (1829-31) under Jackson.

INGLESIDE, Tex. (San Patricio Co.). From Gaelic, "fireside"; probably promotional.

INGELWOOD, Calif. (Los Angeles Co.). Possibly for the Canada home of the sister-in-law of one of the promoters.

INGERSOLL, Ont. (Oxford Co.). For Maj. Thomas Ingersoll, the father of Laura Secord, who arrived from Massachusetts in 1793. During the War of 1812 she walked twenty miles through American lines to warn Lt. James Fitzgibbon of a surprise American attack.

INKSTER, Mich. (Wayne Co.). For Robert Inkster, an early settler and sawmill operator.

INLAND Descriptive of location.
Inland Lake, Alaska.
Inland Lake, Ala.

INNOKO RIVER, Alaska. Probably of Ingalik origin, meaning unknown. It flows northeast and southwest into Yukon River.

INNOMINATE, THE, Wyo. A mountain, named by mountaineers for Innominate Crack in England.

INSCRIPTION ROCK, Mount, N.Mex. For the rock on which carvings, signatures, and messages have been left by explorers dating back to 1600. See also EL MORRO NATL. MONUMENT.

INSULA LAKE, Minn. From French, "island," for the island in it.

INTERNATIONAL FALLS, Minn. (co. seat of Koochiching Co.). Founded as Koochiching village at the falls of the river of the same name, now translated as Rainy River; the town is located on the boundary between the United States and Canada.

INVER GROVE HEIGHTS, Minn. (Ramsey Co.). From a township in Dakota County, in turn named for an Inver in Ireland, former home of the early settlers.

INVERNESS For Inverness, Scotland.
Inverness Co., N.S. (co. seat, Port Hood).
Inverness, Fla. (co. seat of Citrus Co.).
Inverness, Que. (co. seat of Megantic Co.).

INWOOD, N.Y. (Nassau Co.). Descriptive.

INYO From an Indian name for mountains in the area, said to mean "where the great spirit dwells."
Inyo Co., Calif. (co. seat, Independence).
Inyo Mountains, Calif.
Inyo Natl. Forest, Calif.

IOLA, Kan. (co. seat of Allen Co.). For Iola Colburn, wife of an early settler.

IONIA Classical, for Ionia, Greece.
Ionia Co., Mich. (co. seat, *Ionia*).
Ionia, Mich. (co. seat of *Ionia* Co.).

IOSCO Co., Mich. (co. seat, Tawas City). Coined name from a book by H. R. Schoolcraft *The Myth of Hiawatha and Other Oral Legends* (1856). He intended it to mean "shining water." An earlier name was Kanotin County.

IOWA For the Iowa tribe of Siouan linguistic stock. The name is a French version of the Dakota name for the tribe; variously given as *Ayuhwa*, *Ouaouia*, *Aiouez*, and *Ioways*, it is believed to mean "the sleepy ones." Names given by other tribes include "snakes," "dusty heads," "dusty noses," and "snow heads." The river was named for the tribe, and the territory and state names derive from the river.
Iowa, State of. 29th State of the Union. Settled: 1788. Territory: 1838. Admitted: 1846. Cap: Des Moines. Motto: Our Liberties We Prize and Our Rights We Will Maintain. Nickname: Hawkeye State. Flower: Wild Rose. Bird: Eastern Goldfinch. Tree: Oak. Song: "The Song of Iowa."
Iowa Co., Iowa (co. seat, Marengo).
Iowa Co., Wis. (co. seat, Dodgeville).
Iowa River, Iowa. Flows SE into the Mississippi R.
Iowa City, Iowa (co. seat of Johnson Co.). The first capital of Iowa (1846-57).
Iowa Column, Wyo. For climbers from the state of *Iowa*.

Iowa Falls, Iowa (Hardin Co.). For rapids in the *Iowa* R. before a power dam was built. Falls are there now.

Iowa Park, Tex. (Wichita Co.). For the state of *Iowa* and for the many parks planned in the original plat.

IPSWICH For Ipswich, Suffolk, England. Colonists bound for Massachusetts Bay were treated well there.

Ipswich, Mass. (Essex Co.), town and village. Earlier, Agawam.

Ipswich Bay, Mass.

Ipswich River, Mass.

Ipswich, S.Dak. (co. seat of Edmunds Co.). For either *Ipswich*, Mass., or Ipswich, England.

IREDELL Co., N.C. (co. seat, Statesville). For James Iredell (1751-1799), a delegate to the Constitutional Convention of 1788.

IRELAND MOUNTAIN, Ore., in the Blue Mtns. For Henry Ireland, Forest Service official.

IRION Co., Tex. (co. seat, Mertzon). For Robert Anderson Irion (1806-1861), Texas statesman.

IRISH, Mount, Nev. For O. H. Irish, an Indian agent.

IRISH MOUNTAIN, Ore. For Irish settlers.

IRON Descriptive; where iron deposits are found.

Iron Co., Mich. (co. seat, Crystal Falls).

Iron Co., Mo. (co. seat, *Ironton*).

Iron Co., Utah (co. seat, Parowan).

Iron Co., Wis. (co. seat, Hurley).

Iron River, Mich. Flows SE into Brule R.

Iron River, Wis.

Iron Mountain, Mich. (co. seat of Dickinson Co.).

Iron River, Mich. (*Iron* Co.). For the river.

Ironton, Mo. (co. seat of *Iron* Co.).

IRONTON, Ohio (co. seat of Lawrence Co.). So named because the town was originated to get rid of a "ton of iron," since it was a port on the Ohio River for the Iron railroad, which led to the pig-iron furnaces in the hills of Lawrence County.

IRONWOOD, Mich. (Gogebic Co.). For James R. ("Iron") Wood, a prominent citizen and mining engineer who discovered a large iron deposit.

The fertile, corn-bearing plains of Iowa lie between two great rivers, the Missouri and the Mississippi. Here, at Dubuque in 1872, there were already substantial bridges linking the city to Illinois across the Mississippi. [*New York Public Library*]

IROQUOIS For the Indian tribe; from Algonquian, "real adders," with French transliteration. When the Europeans invaded the continent, the Iroquois inhabited what is now called the Mohawk Valley and central New York. The Five Nations, subdivisions of the tribe, were Cayuga, Mohawk, Onondaga, Oneida, and Seneca.
Iroquois Co., Ill. (co. seat, Watseka).
Iroquois Peak, N.Y.
Iroquois River, Ill.-Ind.
Iroquois Point, Hawaii.

IRVINE, Ky. (co. seat of Estill Co.). For the Irvine brothers, Indian fighters with James Estill. One of the brothers, Christopher Irvine, was later a member of the Virginia legislature and was active in the admittance of Kentucky to statehood.

IRVING, Tex. (Dallas Co.). Named by one of the founders, simply because "he liked the name."

IRVING, Washington (1783-1859), American writer, known for *The Sketch Book*, *Diedrich Knickerbocker's History of New York*, and the short stories "The Legend of Sleepy Hollow" and "Rip Van Winkle." Irving also served as minister to Spain (1842-46).
Irvington, N.J. (Essex Co.). Earlier, Camptown.
Irvington, N.Y. (Westchester Co.). Irving lived here at "Sunnyside." Earlier, Dearman.

IRWIN, Jared (1750-1818), Georgia legislator and governor.
Irwin Co., Ga. (co. seat, Ocilla).
Irwinton, Ga. (co. seat of Wilkinson Co.).

ISABELLA For Queen Isabella (1451-1504), of Spain, who provided financial backing for Christopher Columbus.
Isabella Co., Mich. (co. seat, Mount Pleasant).
Isabella Reservoir, Calif. Named in 1893 during the Columbian exposition.

ISABELLE, Point, Mich. Extends into Bete Grise Bay. From a woman's name, reason for naming not known.

ISANTI Co., Minn. (co. seat, Cambridge). For the Indian tribe which inhabited the area. The name means "knife," or perhaps "ones who make knives."

ISCHUA CREEK, N.Y. From Iroquian, "floating nettles." It flows south into Allegheny River.

ISHPEMING, Mich. (Marquette Co.). From Ojibway, "high place."

ISLAND Descriptive.
Island Co., Wash. (co. seat, Coupeville). So named because the county is wholly composed of islands in Puget Sound.
Island Lake, Minn. For the island in it.
Island Lake, Wis. So named because it is a lake surrounded by land, and "island of water."
Island Pond, N.H. For the island in it.
Island Park, N.Y. (Nassau Co.). For its location on an island.
Island Park Reservoir, Idaho. For a Mormon settlement on Teton Island.

ISLA VISTA, Calif. (Santa Barbara Co.). From Spanish, "island view"; probably promotional.

ISLE OF PALMS, S.C. (Charleston Co.). For the numerous palm and palmetto trees on the island.

ISLE OF WIGHT For the island off the southern coast of England.
Isle of Wight Co., Va (co. seat, *Isle of Wight*).
Isle of Wight, Va. (co. seat of *Isle of Wight* Co.)

ISLIP Town. For Islip, Oxfordshire, England, the home of the town's first settler.
Central Islip, N.Y. (Suffolk Co.).
East Islip, N.Y. (Suffolk Co.).
Islip, N.Y. (Suffolk Co.).
Islip Terrace, N.Y. (Suffolk Co.).

ISRAEL RIVER, N.H. For Israel Glines, a trapper. It flows northwest into Connecticut River.

ISSAQUAH, Wash. (King Co.). Of Indian origin, meaning uncertain.

ISSAQUENA Co., Miss. (co. seat, Mayersville). From Choctaw, "deer's head."

ISTOKPOGA, Lake, Fla. From Creek, "lake where someone was killed in the water."

ITASCA Coined by H. R. Schoolcraft, who discovered the lake and thought it to be the "true source" of the Mississippi; from Latin *veritas*, "truth," and *caput*, "head." *Itasca* is formed from the last part of *veritas* plus the first part of *caput*.

Itasca Co., Minn. (co. seat, Grand Rapids). For the lake.

Itasca, Ill. (Du Page Co.).

Itasca, Tex. (Hill Co.). From Ill. For *Itasca*, Ill.

Itasca, Lake, Minn., popularly considered the source of the Mississippi R.

ITAWAMBA Co., Miss. (co. seat, Fulton). From an Indian personal name, of uncertain meaning.

ITHACA For the island of the Ionian group off the coast of Greece, known as the homeland of Ulysses (Odysseus). In the United States, the name has often been given to places that are rocky. Such names occurred during a time in the 1800s when classical names were in vogue.

Ithaca, Mich. (co. seat of Gratiot Co.).

Ithaca, Neb. For *Ithaca*, N.Y.

Ithaca, N.Y. (co. seat of Tompkins Co.). So named because it was formerly the center of the township of Ulysses.

ITKILLIK RIVER, Alaska. From Eskimo *itkillik*, "Indian." It flows northeast and northwest into Colville River.

IUKA, Miss. (co. seat of Tishomingo Co.). For a Chickasaw chief, who was one of the lesser chiefs of the tribe and a friend of Tishomingo. He supposedly died around 1836 while camping at the springs near what is now Iuka. The name is probably a contraction of the longer *Ish-ta-ki-yu-ka-tubbe*, a name that appears as an endorser on the Treaty of Pontitock Creek, and which probably is a corruption of Choctaw *isht iki yukpo*, "a hater," and *tabi*, which is apparently a termination common in the names of men.

IVANHOE For *Ivanhoe*, a novel by Sir Walter Scott.

Ivanhoe Co., Minn. (co. seat, *Ivanhoe*).

Ivanhoe, Minn. (co. seat of *Ivanhoe* Co.).

IVISHAK RIVER, Alaska. From Eskimo *ivishaq*, "red paint," for iron oxide. It flows northwest into Sagavanirktok River.

IZARD Co., Ark (co. seat, Melbourne). For George Izard (1777-1828), general in the War of 1812 and later governor of Arkansas Territory.

J

JABISH BROOK, Mass. Probably from Algonquian, meaning uncertain. Also claimed from Mahican, "swarm of flies." It flows south to join Ware and Quaboag rivers to form Chicopee River.

JACINTO CITY, Tex. (Harris Co.). From Spanish, "hyacinth."

JACK For the Jack brothers, William Houston (1806-1844) and Patrick Churchill (1808-1844), who were both Texas statesmen and legislators.
Jack Co., Tex. (co. seat, *Jacksboro).*
Jacksboro, Tex. (co. seat of *Jack* Co.)

JACK MOUNTAIN, Wash. Either for a local settler or for the jackass, the pack animal.

JACKS For a Captain Jack who lived in the area as early as 1750 and is buried in an unmarked grave at the base of Jacks Mountain.
Jacks Creek, Pa. Flows SW into Juniata R.
Jacks Mountain, Pa.

JACKSBORO, Tenn. (co. seat of Campbell Co.). For John Finley Jack (1766-1829), lawyer, political leader, state legislator, and judge.

JACKS FORK RIVER, Mo. From the forename of a local settler. It flows east into Current River.

JACKSMITH BAY, Alaska. For a local citizen.

JACKSON, Andrew (1767-1845), seventh President of the United States (1829-37), born in South Carolina but associated with Tennessee. He was a U.S. representative (1796-97) and senator (1797-98; 1823-25). He led a campaign against the Creeks (1814) and attained fame as the hero of the battle of New Orleans (1815), where he soundly defeated the British forces unaware of the fact that the Treaty of Ghent had been signed two weeks earlier, ending the war. Jackson also campaigned against the Seminoles (1818) and became governor of Florida (1821). The unsuccessful Democratic candidate for president in 1824, he was elected four years later. He is popularly known as a founder of the modern Democratic party; he introduced the political "spoils system," eliminated the Bank of the United States, and countered South Carolina's attempt to "nullify" the collection of uniform federal tariffs. See also IN-DEPENDENCE and JACKSONVILLE.

Jackson Co., Ala. (co. seat, Scottsboro).
Jackson Co. Ark. (co. seat, Newport).
Jackson Co., Colo. (co. seat, Walden).
Jackson Co., Fla. (co. seat, Marianna).
Jackson Co., Ill. (co. seat, Murphysboro).
Jackson Co., Ind. (co. seat, Brownstown).
Jackson Co., Iowa (co. seat, Maquoketa).
Jackson Co., Kan. (co. seat, Holton).
Jackson Co., Ky. (co. seat, McKee).

Jackson Parish, La. (parish seat, Jonesboro).
Jackson Co., Mich. (co. seat, Jackson).
Jackson Co., Miss. (co. seat, Pascagoula).
Jackson Co., Mo. (co. seat, Independence).
Jackson Co., N.C. (co. seat, Sylva).
Jackson Co., Ohio (co. seat, Jackson).
Jackson Co., Okla. (co. seat, Altus).
Jackson Co., Ore. (co. seat, Medford).
Jackson Co., Tenn. (co. seat, Gainsboro).
Jackson Co., Tex. (co. seat, Edna).
Jackson Co., W.Va. (co. seat, Ripley).
Jackson Co., Wis. (co. seat, Black River Falls).
Jackson, Ala. (Clark Co.).
Jackson, Ga. (co. seat of Butts Co.).
Jackson, Ky. (co. seat of Breathitt Co.).
Jackson, La. (East Feliciana Parish). Earlier, Bear Corners.
Jackson, Mich. (co. seat of Jackson Co.).
Jackson, Miss. (co. seat of Hinds Co.), state capital.
Jackson, Mo. (co. seat of Cape Girardean Co.).
Jackson, N.C. (co. seat of Northampton Co.).
Jackson, Ohio (co. seat of Jackson Co.).
Jackson, Tenn. (co. seat of Madison Co.). Named by William Edward Butler, founder, whose wife was the niece of Jackson's wife.
Jackson Lake, Ga.

JACKSON, Calif. (co. seat of Amador Co.). For "Colonel" Alden M. Jackson, a lawyer who helped to settle quarrels out of court.

JACKSON, David E., an early trapper. The town was named first, by Jackson's partner, William Sublette.
Jackson, Wyo. (co. seat of Teton Co.).
Jackson Lake, Wyo.

JACKSON Co., Ga. (co. seat, Jefferson). For James Jackson (1757-1806), statesman, general officer in the American Revolution, and governor of Georgia (1798-1801).

JACKSON, Henry (1811-1857), Minnesota official, merchant and territorial legislator. There is also a debatable claim that the county was named for Andrew JACKSON.
Jackson Co., Minn. (co. seat, Jackson).
Jackson, Minn. (co. seat of Jackson Co.).

JACKSON Co., S. Dak. (co. seat, Kadoka). For John R. Jackson, Dakota Territory legis-

James II, brother of Charles II and formerly Duke of York and Albany, named the following for himself or his brother: Albany, Kingston, Dutchess Co., Kings Co., Queens Co., Richmond Co., all in New York (also named for him). For good measure he threw in Dukes Co., Mass. [New York Public Library]

lator when the county was formed. A claim has also been made for Andrew JACKSON, but seems to be unjustified.

JACKSON MOUNTAIN, Me. For the Jackson family, early settlers.

JACKSON MOUNTAINS, Nev. Probably for a local settler.

JACKSON RIVER, Va. For an early settler. It flows generally southwest to join Cowpasture River to form James River.

JACKSONVILLE For Andrew JACKSON.

Jacksonville, Ala. (Calhoun Co.). The name was changed from Dayton (1834) in honor of Andrew JACKSON, for his refusing to remove the white settlers from the Indian lands as called for in the treaty of Cussetta.

Jacksonville, Fla. (co. seat of Duval Co.).

Jacksonville, Ill. (Morgan Co.). Also claimed for A. W. Jackson, a black minister.

Jacksonville, N.C. (co. seat of Onslow Co.).

South Jacksonville, Ill. (Morgan Co.).

JACKSONVILLE, Ark. (Pulaski Co.). For Nicolas Jackson (?-1916), local landowner and first postmaster.

JACKSONVILLE, Tex. (Cherokee Co.). For both William Jackson, first physician for the town, and Jackson Smith, donator of the land for the town.

JAFFREY, N.H. (Cheshire Co.). For George Jaffrey, scion of a prominent Portsmouth family and a landowner in the area.

JAGGER PEAK, Wyo. Origin of name uncertain, but may be descriptive for its ruggedness.

JAL, N.Mex. (Lea Co.). From the initial of *John A. Lynch*, of east Texas, who sold cattle branded with his initials to the Cowden Land and Cattle Company.

JAMAICA, N.Y. (co seat of Queens Co.). For the small tribe of Algonquian linguistic stock, *jameco*, "beaver people." The present spelling and pronunciation were probably influenced by Jamaica, the Island in the West Indies.

JAMES. For James I (1566-1625), king of England as James I (1603-25) and of Scotland as James VI (1567-1625). As king of England he sought to assert divine right of

kings, favored a foreign policy of peace at any price, and aspired to literary fame, publishing works of both verse and prose, including his famous *Counterblaste to Tobacco* (1604). He was the son of Mary, Qeen of Scots.

James River, Va. Formed by confluence of Jackson and Cowpasture rivers, flows into Hampton Roads. Earlier, King's River and Powhatan's River.

James City Co., Va. (co. seat, Williamsburg).

Jamesburg, N.J. Middlesex Co.).

Jamestown, Va. (*James City* Co.). Named by the colonists on Mary 14, 1607, "in honor of the King's most excellent majesty." It was the capital of the colony of Virginia (1607-99).

Jamestown Island, Va. In the James R.

Jamestown Natl. Historic Site, Va. Includes *Jamestown* and *Jamestown* Island. Commemorates the site of the first permanent English settlement in North America (1607).

JAMES From French *Riviere aux Jacques*, "River of James."

James River, N.Dak.-S. Dak. Flows SSE into the Missouri R. Also called Jim River.

Jamestown, N.Dak. (co. seat of Stutsman Co.). For the river.

JAMES, Lake, Ind. For a local settler.

JAMES, Lake, N.C. On Catawba River. For James B. Duke (1856-1925), official of the Duke Power Company.

JAMES PEAK, Colo. For Edwin James (1797-1861), botanist and geologist. He was the first man to climb Pikes Peak.

JAMES RIVER, Mo. For ST. JAMES. It flows into Table Rock Reservoir.

JAMESTOWN, Ky. (co. seat of Russell Co.). For James Wooldridge, who donated land for the site.

JAMESTOWN, R.I. (Newport Co.). For James II (1633-1701), king of England, Scotland and Ireland (1685-88). His Catholicism and autocratic ways brought him into conflict with Parliament, which forced him to abdicate. The crown was then offered to his daughter and her husband, William of Orange.

JANESVILLE, Wis. (co. seat of Rock Co.). For Henry Janes, first postmaster.

Jamestown, Va., shown here as it might have appeared in 1619, is the oldest permanent English settlement in North America. It was named for James I, the first of the Stuart kings of England. Eastern Virginia is littered with names honoring English royalty. *(From the original painting by Sidney King)*

JASPER, Sgt. William (1750-1779), South Carolina soldier who fought with great distinction during the American Revolution. He was a hero of the battle at Fort Sullivan (Fort Moultrie) and Savannah, where he was killed.
Jasper Co., Ga. (co. seat, Monticello).
Jasper Co., Ill. (co. seat, Newton).
Jasper Co., Ind. (co. seat, Rensselaer).
Jasper Co., Iowa (co. seat, Newton).
Jasper Co., Miss. (co. seats, Bay Springs and Paulding).
Jasper Co., Mo. (co. seat, Carthage).
Jasper Co., S.C. (co. seat, Ridgeland).
Jasper Co., Tex. (co. seat, *Jasper*).
Jasper, Ala. (co. seat of Walker Co.).
Jasper, Ark. (co. seat of Newton Co.).
Jasper, Fla. (co. seat of Hamilton Co.).
Jasper, Ga. (co. seat of Pickens Co.).
Jasper, Ind. (co. seat of Du Bois Co.).
Jasper, Tenn. (co. seat of Marion Co.).
Jasper, Tex. (co. seat of *Jasper* Co.).

JAY, John (1745-1829), American jurist and statesman. He was a member of the Continental Congress (1774-77) and its president (1778-79), minister to Spain (1779), secretary of foreign affairs (1784-89), first chief justice of the U.S. Supreme Court (1789-95), and governor of New York (1795-1801). He was the author of several of the *Federalist Papers*, and negotiated the 1874 treaty with Great Britain that bears his name.
Jay Co., Ind. (co. seat, Portland).
Jay, Me. (Franklin Co.).
Jay, N.Y. (Essex Co.).
Jay Peak, Vt.

JAYTON, Tex. (co. seat of Kent Co.). For James B. Jay, a cattleman, and R. A. Jay, a banker and real estate man. Both helped to organize the county.

JEANNETTE, Pa. (Westmoreland Co.). For Jeannette McKee, wife of H. Sellers McKee, who helped to establish (1889) a glass works in the area which transformed a farm site into an industrial city.

JEDEDIAH SMITH MOUNTAIN, Wyo. For Jedediah S. Smith, trapper, a companion of William Sublette.

JEFF DAVIS For Jefferson DAVIS.
Jeff Davis Co., Ga. (co. seat, Hazelhurst).
Jeff Davis Co., Tex. (co. seat, Fort Davis).

JEFFERSON Co., Tex. (co. seat, Beaumont). For Jefferson·Beaumont, who was named for Thomas Jefferson. See BEAUMONT, Tex.

JEFFERSON, Thomas (1743-1826), third President of the United States (1801-09), from Virginia. One of the most popular and respected figures in American history, he was a principal framer of the Declaration of Independence and an important contributor to the Constitution. As President, he was responsible for the Louisiana Purchase. He had been governor of Virginia (1779-81), minister to France (1785-89), secretary of state (1790-93) and vice-president (1797-1801). A talented architect, he designed his own home, Monticello, and several buildings of the University of Virginia, which he founded.
Jefferson Co., Ala. (co. seat, Birmingham).
Jefferson Co., Ark. (co. seat, Pine Bluff).
Jefferson Co., Colo. (co. seat, Golden).
Jefferson Co., Fla. (co. seat, Monticello)
Jefferson Co., Ga. (co. seat, Louisville).
Jefferson Co., Idaho (co. seat, Rigby).
Jefferson Co., Ill. (co. seat, Mount Vernon).
Jefferson Co., Ind. (co. seat, Madison).
Jefferson Co., Iowa (co. seat, Fairfield).
Jefferson Co., Kan. (co. seat, Oskaloosa).
Jefferson Co., Ky. (co. seat, Louisville).
Jefferson Parish, La. (parish seat, Gretna).
Jefferson Co., Miss. (co. seat, Fayette).
Jefferson Co., Mo. (co. seat, Hillsboro).
Jefferson Co., Mont. (co. seat, Boulder).
Jefferson Co., Neb. (co. seat, Fairbury).
Jefferson Co., N.Y. (co. seat, Watertown).
Jefferson Co., Ohio (co. seat, Steubenville).
Jefferson Co., Okla. (co. seat, Waurika).
Jefferson Co., Ore. (co. seat, Madras).
Jefferson Co., Pa. (co. seat, Brookville).
Jefferson Co., Tenn. (co. seat, Dandridge).
Jefferson Co., Wash. (co. seat, Port Townsend).
Jefferson Co., W.Va. (co. seat, Charlestown).
Jefferson Co., Wis. (co. seat, *Jefferson*).
Jefferson, Ga. (co. seat of Jackson Co.).
Jefferson, Iowa (co. seat of Greene Co.).
Jefferson, Ohio (co. seat of Ashtabula Co.).
Jefferson, Tex. (co. seat of Marion Co.).

Jefferson, Wis. (co. seat of *Jefferson* Co.).
Jefferson, Mount, N.H. In the Presidential Range of the White Mtns.
Jefferson, Mount, Nev.
Jefferson Mount, Ore. Named by Lewis and Clark.
Jefferson Natl. Forest, Ky.-Va.
Jefferson River, Mont. Flows N and NE to join Madison and Gallatin rivers to form the Missouri R.
Jefferson City, Mo. (co. seat of Cole Co.), state capital.
Jefferson City, Tenn. (*Jefferson* Co.).
Jefferstown, Ky. (*Jefferson* Co.).
Jeffersonville, Ga. (co. seat of Twiggs Co.).
Jeffersonville, Ind. (co. seat of Clark Co.).
JEFFERSON DAVIS For Jefferson DAVIS.
Jefferson Davis Parish, La. (parish seat, Jennings).
Jefferson Davis Co., Miss. (co. seat, Prentiss).

JEKYLL ISLAND, Ga. For Sir Joseph Jekyll (1663-1738), who helped finance the venture of James E. Oglethorpe.

JELM MOUNTAIN, Wyo. For E. C. Gillem, timberman, with a change in spelling.

Thomas Jefferson, one of our most honored presidents, was not always so revered. The first president from what has become the Democratic Party, he was villified by a hostile press and shown tearing down the pillars of Federal Government which Washington and Adams had erected. [*New York Public Library*]

JEMEZ From Tanoan *hay mish*, "people," for the Indian tribe, rendered in Spanish as *jemez*.
Jemex Mountains, N.Mex.
Jemez River, N.Mex.

JENA, La. (parish seat of La Salle Parish). Named for a Jena in Illinois, which was named for Jena, Germany. An earlier name was Hemp's Creek.

JENISON, Mich. (Ottawa Co.). For Lumah (1813-1899) and Lucius (1813-1893?) Jenison, twin sons of Lemuel Jenison, Founder.

JENKINS Co., Ga. (co. seat, Millen). For Charles Jones Jenkins (1805-1883), Georgia legislator and jurist. He was governor of Georgia (1865-67).

JENKINS, Ky. (Letcher Co.). For a local community member.

JENNINGS Co. Inc. (co. seat, Vernon). For Jonathan Jennings (1784-1834), Indiana territorial legislator and later first governor of the state (1816-22).

JENNINGS, La. (parish seat of Jefferson Davis Parish). For Jennings McComb, contractor in charge of building a section of the Southern Pacific railroad from Orange, Tex., to Lafayette, La. It is claimed to be a dual namesake with McCOMB, Miss.

JENNINGS, Mo. (St. Louis Co.). For James Jennings (?-1855), a landowner and prominent citizen.

JENNY JUMP MOUNTAIN, N.J. Reason for naming uncertain.

JERALEE PEAK, Wyo. So named by an ascending party from the forenames of members, Jerry and Lee.

JERAULD Co., S.Dak. (co. seat, Wessington Springs). For H. A. Jerauld, a Dakota Territory legislator when the county was formed.

JEREMY POINT, Mass. Extends into Cape Cod Bay. For a local settler.

JEREMY'S RIVER, Conn. For a local settler. This is one of the few place names to retain the apostrophe to indicate possession. It flows generally southwest to join Blackledge River to form Salmon River.

JERICHO, N.Y. (Nassau Co.). Probably for the Biblical city.

JERIMOTH HILL, R.I. Biblical: from Hebrew, "elevation."

JEROME For Jerome Kuhn, a principal figure in the Twin Falls North Side Irrigation Project.
Jerome Co., Idaho (co. seat, *Jerome*).
Jerome, Idaho (co. seat of *Jerome* Co.).

Jersey, one of the Channel Islands off the coast of France, remained loyal to the crown during the Commonwealth due to the efforts of Sir George Carteret who was rewarded with the proprietorship of the colony of New Jersey. It is also the source of the famous breed of cow. [*New York Public Library*]

JERSEY For the island of Jersey, a British possession in the English Channel. When the British acquired the Dutch territories in America (1664), the territories that later comprised the colonies of New York and New Jersey were granted by Charles II of England to his brother James, Duke of York and Albany. The territory west of the Hudson River was briefly called "Albania" after the second of James's titles. James, however, granted the territory to Lord Berkeley (?-1678) and Sir George Carteret (1609/17-1680), the latter a native of the isle of Jersey and its principal royal defender during the Commonwealth.
New Jersey, State of. Third state of the Union. Settled: 1664. One of the 13 original colonies. Ratified Constitution: 1787. Cap: Trenton, Motto: Liberty and Pros-

perity. Nickname: Garden State. Flower: Purple Violet. Bird: Eastern Goldfinch.

Jersey Co., Ill. (co. seat, *Jerseyville*).

Jersey Island, Calif., in the San Joaquin R.

Jersey City, N.J. (co. seat of Hudson Co.). For the state. Earlier, Jersey.

Jersey Shore, Pa. (Lycoming Co.). For the state.

Jerseyville, Ill. (co. seat of *Jersey* Co.).

JESSAMINE Co., Ky. (co. seat, Nicholasville). Either for Jessamine Creek, descriptive of the flowers on the bank, or for Jessamine Douglass, daughter of an early settler and supposedly scalped by Indians as she sat "in maidenly contemplation." Evidence points to both the creek and the town as having been named for Jessamine Douglass.

JESSE, Mount, N.H. For a family who lived at its top.

JETMORE, Kan. (co. seat of Hodgeman Co.). For Abraham Bucker Jetmore, a director of the Kansas Freeman's Relief Association, an attorney for the Santa Fe railroad, and governor of Kentucky. An earlier name was Buckner.

JEWELL Co., Kan. (co. seat, Mankato). For Lewis R. Jewell (?-1862), an officer in the Kansas Cavalry during the Civil War, who died of wounds received in action.

JEWELL CAVE NATL. MONUMENT, S.Dak. For the cave, whose walls looked like they had jewels on them.

JIM HOGG Co. Tex. (co. seat, Hebbronville). For James Stephen Hogg (1851-1906), Texas governor (1891-95) and legislator.

JIM THORPE, Pa. (co. seat of Carbon Co.). For James Francis Thorpe (1888-1953), winner of the pentathlon and decathlon events in the 1912 Olympics and a college and professional football player of distinction. An earlier name was Mauch Chunk, "narrow valley."

JIM WELLS Co., Tex. (co. seat, Alice). For James B. Wells, a jurist.

JO DAVIESS Co., Ill. (co. seat, Galena). For Joseph Hamilton DAVIESS.

JOES Probably for an early settler.

Joes Brook, Vt. Flows S through *Joes* Pond, then SE into Passumpsic R.

Joes Pond, Vt.

JOHN DAY RIVER, Ore. For John Day (1771-1819), a member of the Astor-Hunt overland party in the 1810s. It flows generally northwest into the Colorado River.

JOHN MARTIN RESERVOIR, Colo. On Arkansas River. For John Andrew Martin (1868-1939), locomotive fireman, city administrator, attorney, state legislator, and U.S. representative from Colorado (1909-13; 1933-39).

JOHN RIVER, Alaska. For John Bremmer, prospector. It flows south into Koyukuk River.

JOHNSON, Andrew. See ANDREW JOHNSON NATL. HISTORIC SITE.

JOHNSON Co., Ark. (co. seat, Clarksville). For Benjamin Johnson, a jurist.

JOHNSON Co., Ga. (co. seat, Wrightsville). For Herschel Vespasian Johnson (1812-1880), jurist, U.S. senator, and governor (1853-57).

JOHNSON Co., Ind. (co. seat, Franklin). For John Johnson, one of the judges of the first supreme court of the state.

JOHNSON Co., Kan. (co. seat, Olathe). For Thomas Johnson (1802-1865), a missionary to the Shawnee Indians and legislator, who was murdered.

JOHNSON, Kan. (co. seat of Stanton Co.). For A. S. Johnson, a Union officer in the Civil War. He was a leader in a group of veterans who founded the town.

JOHNSON, Richard Mentor (1780-1850), Kentucky statesman. He was a U.S. representative (1807-19; 1829-37), U.S. senator (1819-29), and vice-president of the United States (1837-41) under Van Buren.

Johnson Co., Ill. (co. seat, Vienna).

Johnson Co., Iowa (co. seat, Iowa City).

Johnson Co., Ky. (co. seat, Paintsville).

Johnson Co., Mo. (co. seat, Warrensburg).

Johnson Co., Neb. (co. seat, Techumseh).

Johnson Reservoir, Neb.

JOHNSON Co. Tenn. (co. seat, Mountain City). For Cave Johnson (1793-1866), banker, jurist, and postmaster general (1845-49) under Polk.

JOHNSON Co., Tex. (co. seat, Cleburne). For Middleton Tate Johnson (1810-1866),

Alabama legislator who later became a Texas patriot and soldier and a Texas legislator.

JOHNSON Co., Wyo. (co. seat, Buffalo). For E. P. Johnson, a lawyer. An earlier name was Pease County.

JOHNSON CITY, N.Y. (Broome Co.). For George F. Johnson and the Endicott-Johnson Corporation. The town was built up by the corporation.

JOHNSON CITY, Tenn. (a co. seat of Washington Co.). For Henry Johnson (1809-1874), who came to the area in 1834 and established a store next to the railroad right of way.

JOHNSON CITY, Tex. (co. seat of Blanco Co.). For James Johnson, uncle of Lyndon B. Johnson, who together with Jesse, John, Sam Ealy, Sr., and Tom Johnson, began cattle drives and initated the settlement of the land. The land for the townsite was donated by James Johnson.

JOHNSON CREEK, Utah-Ariz. For W. D. Johnson, photographer in an expedition (1871-72) into the Grand Canyon. It flows into Kanab Creek.

JOHNS RIVER, N.H. For a local settler. It flows northwest into the Connecticut River.

JOHNSTON Co., N.C. (co. seat, Smithfield). For Gabriel Johnston (1699-1752), colonial governor.

JOHNSTON Co., Okla. (co. seat, Tishomingo). For Douglas H. Johnston (1856-1939), last Chickasaw governor, who remained in office until his death. (As of 1971, the Chickasaws have the right to elect their own governors by popular vote of tribal members.)

JOHNSTON, R.I. (Providence Co.), town. For Augustus Johnston (c.1730-1790). He achieved early reknown as attorney general of Rhode Island (1757-1766), but his later actions as an administrator of the Stamp Act and his Loyalist sympathies during the American Revolution led to his downfall. His property was confiscated, and he died in poverty in New York City.

JOHNSTON CITY, Ill. (Williamson Co.). For a railway contractor named Johnston.

JOHNSTON ISLAND Possession of the United States, 700 miles southwest of Honolulu, Hawaii, in the Pacific Ocean, not included in the Hawaii statehood bill. For Charles James Johnston, an English sea captain who discovered and explored the island in 1807.

JOHNSTOWN For John, the son of Sir William Johnson (1715-1774). Sir William has been called "Builder of an Empire." He was superintendent of Indian Affairs of North America and a general in the British Army.
Johnstown, N.Y. (co. seat of Fulton Co.).
Johnstown, Ohio (Licking Co.). Probably for *Johnstown*, N.Y.

JOHNSTOWN, Pa. (Cambria Co.). For Joseph Johns, Jahns, or Yahns, who owned land in the area. Born in Switzerland, he came to America in 1769.

JOHN THE BAPTIST See ST. JOHN (The Baptist).

JO JO MOUNTAIN, Wyo. For two early settlers named Joseph.

JOLIET, Ill. (co. seat of Will Co.). For Louis Jolliet or Joliet (1645-1700), French-Canadian explorer of the Mississippi River area.

JOLIETTE, Barthelemy, establisher of a saw mill at the site of the present town in 1823.
Joliette Co., Que. (co. seat, *Joliette*).
Joliette, Que. (co. seat of *Joliette* Co.).

JO-MARY LAKES, Me. For Jo-Mary, an Indian chief.

JONES Co., Ga. (co. seat, Gray). For James Jones, Georgia legislator and U.S. representative.

JONES, George Wallace (1804-1896), territorial official and U.S. senator (1848-59) from the state of Iowa.
Jones Co., Iowa (co. seat, Anamosa).
Jones Co., S.Dak. (co. seat, Murdo). Named by settlers from *Jones* Co. Iowa.

JONES Co., Miss. (co. seats, Ellisville and Laurel). For John Paul Jones (1747-1792), commander of the *Bonhomme Richard* in its victory over the British ship *Serapis* during the American Revolution. He later served as an officer in the Russian Navy.

JONES Co., N.C. (co. seat, Trenton). For William Jones (1740-1801), American Revolutionary leader. He later opposed the adoption of the Constitution. See also JONESBORO, Tenn.

JONES Co., Tex. (co. seat, Anson). For Anson Jones (1798-1858), medical officer and Texas statesman. He was president of the Republic of Texas (1844-46).

JONESBORO, Ark. (co. seat of Craighead Co.). For William A. Jones, state senator at the time of naming Craighead County. An opponent of Sen. Thomas B. Craighead, he managed to establish another county while Senator Craighead was absent from the chamber. He recommended that the county be named for his opponent, and his colleagues then recommended Jones's name for the county seat.

JONESBORO, Ga. (co. seat of Clayton Co.). For Samuel Goode Jones, a civil engineer who revived a bankrupt railroad, the Macon and Western. An earlier name was Leakesville.

JONESBORO, Ill. (co. seat of Union Co.). For the surname of a prominent family.

JONESBORO, La. (parish seat of Jackson Parish). Believed to be named for Stella Blanch Jones, the first baby girl born (1900) in the community, daughter of Dr. William Samuel Jones and granddaughter of Joseph F. Jones, one of the original settlers.

JONESBORO, Tenn. (a co. seat of Washington Co.). For William Jones. See JONES Co., N.C.

JONES PASS, Wyo., in Yellowstone Natl. Park. For W. A. Jones, an officer in command of an expedition in 1873.

JONESVILLE, La. (Catahoula Parish). For the Jones family, large plantation owners, who gave the land for the town.

JONQUIERE, Que. (Chicoutimi Co.). For the Marquis de Jonquiere.

Louis Joliet (or Jolliet), a French Canadian explorer, and Pere Jacques Marquette, a French Jesuit, discover the Mississippi at its confluence with the Wisconsin River in 1673. [*New York Public Library*]

JOPLIN, Mo. (Jasper and Newton Cos.). For Harris G. Joplin, a Methodist minister.

JOPPA, Md. (Harford Co.). For the Biblical seaport, which is probably from Hebrew, "beauty."

JORDAN, Mont. (co. seat of Garfield Co.). Locally said to have been named by one Arthur Jordan for a friend also named Jordan.

JOSEPH. For Chief Joseph (1837-1904), a Nez Perce Indian chief.
Joseph Creek, Ore.-Wash. Flows N into Grande Ronde R.
Joseph Peak, Wyo. In Yellowstone Natl. Park.

JOSEPHINE Co., Ore. (co. seat, Grants Pass). For Josephine Creek, which was named for Virginia Josephine Rollins (1835-c.1911), daughter of Lloyd Rollins, a miner and leader of a wagon train bound for California.

JOSHUA TREE NATL. MONUMENT, Calif. For the desert tree *Yucca brevifolia*, called Joshua tree by the Mormons as a symbol of their being led out of the wilderness.

JOURDANTOWN, Tex. (co. seat of Atascosa Co.). For Jourdan Campbell, a pioneer settler. Earlier names were Jourdanton and Jourdanville.

JUAB Co., Utah (co. seat, Nephi). From a Gosiut Indian word, probably "plain"; interpretations differ on the exact meaning.

JUAN DE FUCA STRAIT, Wash.-B.C. According to the story told in *Purchas his Pilgrimmes* (1625) (originally *Purchas his Pilgrimage*), a Greek navigator in Spanish service, Juan de Fuca, claimed to have found a passage between the Pacific and Atlantic oceans. His real name is said to have been Apostolos Valerianos. Although the story has no basis in truth, it has become a popular myth and may have some connection with the name San Juan of various nearby features.

JUDITH For Judith Hancock (?-1820), cousin of Meriwether Lewis and later the wife of William Clark, of the Lewis and Clark expedition.

Judith River, Mont.
Judith Basin Co., Mont. (co. seat, Stanford). For the basin of the *Judith* R.

JULESBURG, Colo. (co. seat of Sedgwick Co.). For Jules Beni (?-1861), a trading-post operator, killed by Jack Slade in a dispute over the superintendency of the Overland Stage. The place is a landmark of historic distinction, since it was on the line of travel toward the West.

JUMP RIVER, Wis. So named because the upper streams were narrow enough to be jumped. Formed by North and South Forks, it flows southwest into Holcombe Flowage.

JUNCTION Descriptive.
Junction, Tex. (co. seat of Kimble Co.). Lies at the junction of the North and South Llano rivers.
Junction, Utah (co. seat of Piute Co.). For the joining of two branches of the Sevier River.
Junction City, Kan. (co. seat of Geary Co.). For the confluence of the Republican and Smoky Hill Rivers.

JUNEAU, Alaska, state capital. Named in 1881 for Joseph Juneau, one of the original discoverers of gold there.

JUNEAU, Solomon (1793-1856), a Canadian fur trader on the site of what is now Milwaukee, said to be "the father of the city," becoming its first mayor.
Juneau Co. Wis. (co. seat, Mauston).
Juneau, Wis. (co. seat of Dodge Co.).

JUNIATA From an Indian word of uncertain origin. Various definitions have been suggested, including "they stay long" and "beyond the great bend."
Juniata Co., Pa. (co. seat, Mifflintown).
Juniata River, Pa. Flows generally E into Susquehanna R.

JUNIOR LAKE, Me. Origin of name uncertain, but may have been named for its size.

JUNIPER MOUNTAINS, Ariz. For the tree.

JUNIPERO SERRA PEAK, Calif. For Padre Junipero Serra (1713-1784), a mission founder.

JUSTICE, Ill (Cook Co.). For "righteous treatment" of the citizens.

K

KAALA, Mount, Hawaii. On Oahu Island. Of Hawaiian origin, meaning unknown.

KABETOGAMA LAKE, Minn. From Ojibway, "the lake that lies parallel," for its comparative position to Rainy Lake.

KABITO PLATEAU, Ariz. From Navajo, "willow spring."

KADOKA, S.Dak. (co. seat of Jackson Co.). From Siouan, "opening" or "hole in wall," descriptive of a feature in the Badlands.

KAELAKEKUA Of Hawaiian origin, meaning unknown.
Kaelakekua, Hawaii (Hawaii Co.).
Kaelakekua Bay, Hawaii. On W coast of Hawaii Island.

KAENA From Hawaiian, "the heat," but also a name of the companion of the legendary Pele.
Kaena Point, Hawaii. On Lanai Island.
Kaena Point, Hawaii. On Oahu Island.

KAHOKA, Mo. (co. seat of Clark Co.). A variant form of *Cahokia*, for the Indian tribe. See CAHOKIA, Ill.

KAHUKU POINT, Hawaii. On Oahu Island. From Hawaiian, "point."

KAHULUI From Hawaiian, "the winning," probably because of the surfing sport there.
Kahului, Hawaii (Maui Co.).
Kahului Bay, Hawaii. On Maui Island.

KAIBAB From Paiute, "a mountain lying down," descriptive of the plateau.
Kaibab Natl. Forest, Ariz.
Kaibab Plateau, Ariz.

KAILIO POINT, Hawaii. On southwest shore of Maui Island. From Hawaiian, meaning uncertain.

KAIPAROWITS PLATEAU, Utah. From the Indian tribal name, "mountain home of these people."

KAIWI CHANNEL, Hawaii. Water passage between Oahu and Molokai Islands. From Hawaiian, "the bone," apparently descriptive, but also translated as "sea of lingering."

KAIYUH MOUNTAINS, Alaska. From the Ingalik sub-tribal name, "lowland people."

KAKA POINT, Hawaii. On Kohoolawe Island. From Hawaiian, "fake," reason for naming uncertain.

KA LAE, Hawaii. South point on Hawaii Island. From Hawaiian, "point."

KALAMAZOO From Algonquian, *Ke-Kalamazoo*, of uncertain meaning, interpreted as connected with "smoke," "beautiful water," "otters," or "boiling water."
Kalamazoo Co., Mich. (co. seat, *Kalamazoo*).
Kalamazoo, Mich. (co. seat of *Kalamazoo* Co.). Earlier, Bronson.
Kalamazoo River, Mich.

KALAWAO From Hawaiian, "mountain area."
Kalawao, Hawaii. Area on Molokai Island consisting of the Kalaupapa leper colony, which was made famous by James Michener's novel, *Hawaii*.
Kalawao, Hawaii (Maui Co.). Site of original leper settlement, where Father Damien began his work (1873).

KALIHIWAI BAY, Hawaii. On north shore of Kauai Island. From Hawaii, "water's edge."

KALISPELL, Mont. (co. seat of Flathead Co.). For the Kalispel Indian tribe, of Salishan linguistic stock. The name is said to mean "camas," a genus of the lily family with edible roots. See also CAMAS.

KALKASKA From an Indian word of uncertain origin and meaning.
Kalkaska Co., Mich. (co. seat, *Kalkaska*). Earlier name, Wabassee Co.
Kalkaska, Mich. (co. seat of *Kalkaska* Co.).

KALOHI CHANNEL, Hawaii. Water passage between Molokai and Lanai Islands. From Hawaiian: "the slowness," probably descriptive of the flow of the water.

KALOLI POINT, Hawaii. On east shore of Hawaii Island. From Hawaiian, meaning uncertain.

KALOPA GULCH, Hawaii. From Hawaiian, "the tenant farmer." It flows northeast into the Pacific Ocean.

KAMAIKI POINT, Hawaii. On southeast shore of Lanai Island. From Hawaiian, "small person."

KAMAKOA GULCH, Hawaii. On Hawaii Island. Of Hawaiian origin, meaning uncertain, possibly "the fearless." It flows west into the Pacific Ocean.

KAMAKOU (peak), Hawaii. On Molokai Island. From Hawaiian, for an herb.

KAMLOOPS, B.C. From Indian *Kahm-o-loops*, either "the meeting of the waters" or "the meeting place."

KAMOHIO BAY, Hawaii. Inlet on Kahoolawe Island. From Hawaiian, "the blow of the wind."

KAMOURASKA Co., Que. (co. seat, Saint Pascal). From Indian, "where there are rushes on the side of the river."

KAMPESKA, Lake, S.Dak. From Sioux, "shining," for the water's reflection.

KANAB From Paiute, "willows."
Kanab, Utah (co. seat of Kane Co.). For the creek.
Kanab Creek, Utah-Ariz. Flows S into Colorado R.

KANABEC Co., Minn. (co. seat, Mora). So named at the suggestion of William H. C. Folsom, from Ojibway, "snake," suggested by the presence of the Snake River and descriptive of the meandering of the stream.

KANAPOU BAY, Hawaii. Inlet on Kahoolawe Island. Of Hawaiian origin, meaning unknown.

KANAWHA For an Indian tribe probably located at one time along the river that bears their name. They may be the same tribe as the Conoy, of Algonquian linguistic stock, which were later located in Maryland and southern Pennsylvania. *Kanawha* has been said to mean "hurricane."
Kanawha Co., W.Va. (co. seat, Charleston).
Kanawha River, W.Va. Flows into the Ohio R.
Little Kanawha River, W.Va. Flows (separately) into the Ohio R.

KANDIK RIVER, Alaska. See CHARLEY KANDIK RIVER.

KANDIYOHI Co., Minn. (co. seat, Willmar). From Siouan, "place where the buffalo fish arrive," probably the Indian name for several lakes at the source of the Crow River.

KANE Co., Ill. (co. seat, Geneva). For Elisha Kent Kane (1796-1835), jurist, legislator, and U.S. senator (1825-35).

KANE, Thomas Leiper (1822-1883), an army officer who was active in negotiations during the "Mormon War" of 1858 and later served with distinction as a general in the Union army during the Civil War.
Kane Co., Utah (co. seat, Kanab).
Kane, Pa. (McKean Co.). Thomas Kane led an expedition to the area and founded the borough in 1859.

KANKAKEE From Mohegan, "wolf" or "wolf-place," probably from the river, since the Mohegans were also called "river Indians"; but the meaning is disputed.
Kankakee Co., Ill. (co. seat, *Kankakee*).
Kankakee, Ill. (co. seat of *Kankakee* Co.).
Kankakee River, Ill.-Ind.

KANNAPOLIS, N.C. (Cabarrus Co.). The name is made up of two Greek words and means "city of looms." It is the site of Cannon Mills Company.

KANSAS From the old Siouan language, *Kansa*, "people of the south wind."
Kansas, State of. 34th state of the Union. Settled: 1827. Territory: 1854. Admitted: 1861. Cap: Topeka. Motto: *Ad Astra per Aspera* (To the Stars through Difficulties). Nickname: Sunflower State. Flower: Sunflower. Bird: Western Meadow Lark. Tree: Cottonwood. Animal: Buffalo. Song: "Home on the Range."
Kansas River, Kan. Flows E into the Missouri R.

Kansas City, Kan. (co. seat of Wyandotte Co.). Earlier, Wyandotte, for the Wyandot Indians, original owners of the land.
Kansas City, Mo. (Jackson Co.).
North Kansas City, Mo. (Clay Co.).

KANTISHNA RIVER, Alaska. Of Indian origin, meaning unknown. It flows north into Tanana River.

KANUTI RIVER, Alaska. From Koyukan *konootena*, "old man river." It flows west into Koyukuk River.

KAPUSKASING From Indian, "divided waters," for the confluence of two rivers to form Kapuskasing River.
Kapuskasing, Ont. (Cochrane Co.).
Kapuskasing River, Ont. Flows N into James Bay.

KARNES, Henry Wax (1812-1840), Texas Republic military scout and captain.
Karnes Co., Tex. (co. seat, *Karnes City*).
Karnes City, Tex. (co. seat of *Karnes* Co.).

Kansas was the scene of some of the bloodiest civilian slaughters of the Civil War. On August 21, 1863, William Clarke Quantrill and a band of Confederate guerillas attacked Lawrence, Kansas, leaving 150 dead and the city in ruins. [*New York Public Library*]

KASHUNK RIVER, Alaska. Of Eskimo origin, meaning unknown. It flows southwest into the Yukon-Kuskokwim Delta.

KASKASKIA From the Indian tribal name, meaning uncertain.
Kaskaskia, Ill. (Randolph Co.). Capital of Illinois Territory (1809) and of the State of Illinois (1818-20).
Kaskaskia River, Ill. Flows SSW into Mississippi R.

KATAHDIN, Mount, Me. From Abnaki, "main mountain."

KATECHAY ISLAND, Mich. In Saginaw Bay. From Indian, origin and meaning unknown.

KATMAI Of Eskimo origin, meaning unknown.
Katmai, Mount, Alaska. Volcano.
Katmai Natl. Monument, Alaska. Includes Mt. *Katmai* and surrounding area.

KATY, Tex. (Harris Co.). So named because "Katy" is the nickname for the Missouri, Kansas and Texas railroad, on whose route the town is located.

KAUAI From Hawaiian, possibly "desert."
Kauai Co., Hawaii (co. seat, Lihue).
Kauai Channel, Hawaii. Water passage between *Kauai* and Honolulu Islands.
Kauai Island, Hawaii.

KAU DESERT, Hawaii. On Hawaii Island. From an old poetic name with cognates in Samoan and Mortlock, "windy back."

KAUFMAN, David Spangler (1813-1851), Republic of Texas legislator and later U.S. representative.
Kaufman Co., Tex. (co. seat, *Kaufman*).
Kaufman, Tex. (co. seat of *Kaufman* Co.).

KAUKAUNA, Wis. (Outagamie Co.). From Ojibway *okakaning*, probably designating a place for fishing. The meaning is not certain and has been variously translated also as "long portage" and "crows' roost," among others.

KAULAKAHI CHANNEL, Hawaii. Water passage between Kauai and Niihau Islands. From Hawaiian, "the single flame."

KAUNA POINT, Hawaii. On southwest coast of Hawaii Island. From Hawaiian, "beach."

KAWAIHAE From Hawaiian, "the water of wrath," descriptive of a place where people fought to obtain water from a pool. The town was apparently named first.
Kawaihae, Hawaii (Hawaii Co.).
Kawaihae Bay, Hawaii. Inlet on NW coast of Hawaii Island.

KAWAIHOA POINT, Hawaii. On south coast of Niihau Island. From Hawaiian, "the friend's water" or "stream which belongs to a friend."

KAWAIKINI PEAK, Hawaii. On Kauai Island. From Hawaiian, "the many waters."

KAWEONUI POINT, Hawaii. On north shore of Kauai Island. From Hawaiian, "the large redness."

KAWICH From Shoshone, "mountain," for a chief's name.
Kawich Peak, Nev.
Kawich Range, Nev.

KAY Co., Okla. (co. seat, Newkirk). For the letter "K." The first seven counties of Oklahoma were originally numbered. The next fifteen were lettered (A-Q, except I and J). All later received names except "K" County, which became Kay County.

KAYAK ISLAND, Alaska. In Gulf of Alaska. From Aleut *quayaq*, "hill."

KAYSVILLE, Utah (Davis Co.). For William Kay, first Mormon bishop of the district.

KEAHOLE POINT, Hawaii. On west coast of Hawaii Island. From Hawaiian *ahole*, for the name of a fish.

KEALAIKAHIKI From Hawaiian, "passage to other places," descriptive of the channel.
Kealaikahiki Channel, Hawaii. Waterway between Kahoolawe and Lanai Islands.
Kealaikahiki Point, Hawaii. On W coast of Kahoolawe Island.

KEALAKEKUA From Hawaiian, "pathway of the god."
Kealakekua, Hawaii (Hawaii Co.).
Kealakekua Bay, Hawaii. Inlet on W coast of Hawaii Island.

KEARNEY See KEARNY, Stephen Watts.

KEARNS, Utah (Salt Lake Co.). For Thomas Kearns (1862-1918), mine operator, member of the Utah state constitutional convention in 1895, and U.S. senator (1901-05).

KEARNY, Philip (1814-1862), hero of the Mexican and Civil Wars. He also fought with the French against the Prussians in 1859 and was the first American awarded the Cross of the Legion of Honor. He led the first New Jersey troops into the Civil War and was killed at the Battle of Chantilly.
Kearny Co., Kan. (co. seat, Lakin).
Kearny, Ariz. (Pinal Co.). Kearny led an expedition into the area in 1849-50.
Kearny, N.J. (Hudson Co.)

KEARNY, Stephen Watts (1794-1848), professional soldier and general in the War of 1812 and Mexican War.
Kearney Co., Neb. (co. seat, Minden).
Kearney, Neb. (co. seat of Buffalo Co.).

KEARSAGE, Mount, N.H. Origin disputed: some authorities claim that the name is not from Indian; others claim that it is from Abnaki or Pennacook, possibly "pointed mountain." The name was also applied to the Civil War Union ship Kearsage.

KEAWANUI BAY, Hawaii. Inlet on northwest coast of Niihau Island. From Hawaiian, "large channel."

KEECH POND, R.I. For a local settler.

KEEGO HARBOR, Mich. (Oakland Co.). From Ojibway "small fish."

KEENE, N.H. (co. seat of Chesire Co.). Named by Gov. Benning Wentworth for Sir Benjamin Keene (1697-1757), who was appointed British consul to Madrid in 1724. He arranged the Treaty of Seville in 1729 (which was a defensive alliance between England, Spain, and France), and was recalled to England in 1739 when war broke out between England and Spain. In 1746 he was sent as envoy extraordinary and plenipotentiary to Portugal, to bring about peace with Spain, and in 1754 he was knighted by the king of Spain.

KEEWATIN From Cree Indian, "the north wind" or "home of the northwest wind."
Keewatin, District of. One of the three districts of the present Northwest Territories. It was established in 1876, but has undergone many territorial changes since its creation.

Keewatin, Ont. (Kenora District).
Keewatin River, Man.

KEG CREEK, Iowa. Probably for an incident involving a keg. It flows southwest into Missouri River.

KEGONSA, Lake, Wis. From Ojibway, "small fish."

KEITH Co., Neb. (co. seat, Ogallala). For either M. C. Keith or John Keith, prominent citizens of North Platte.

KEIZER, Ore. (Marion Co.). For the Keizer family, early settlers.

KELLEYS ISLAND, Ohio. In Lake Erie. For two Kelley brothers who owned the island in the 19th century.

KELLOGG, Idaho (Shoshone Co.). For Noah Kellogg, discoverer of a mine in the vicinity. A spiritualist, he believed that his dead brother had led him to it.

KELLY LAKE, Wis. For a local settler.

KELOWNA, B.C. From Indian, "grizzly bear."

KELSEY, Mount, N.H. For a local settler or explorer.

KELSO, Wash. (co. seat of Cowitz Co.). Named by a Scottish settler for Kelso, Roxburgh, Scotland.

KEMMERER, Wyo. (co. seat of Lincoln Co.). For M. S. Kemmerer, president of a local coal company.

KEMP, Lake, Tex. In Wichita River. For a nearby town, in turn believed to have been named for a woman.

KEMPER Co., Miss. (co seat, De Kalb). For Reuben Kemper, a Virginian and a hero of the Florida and Mexican Wars.

KENAI For a local Indian tribe. The meaning of the name is unknown.
Kenai, Alaska.
Kenai Mountains, Alaska.
Kenai Peninsula, Alaska.

KENANSVILLE, N.C. (co. seat of Duplin Co.). For James Kenan (1740-1810), a member of the provincial congress and a general during the American Revolution.

KENDALL, Amos (1789-1869), publisher, national official, and postmaster general

(1835-40) under Jackson and Van Buren.
Kendall Co., Ill. (co. seat, Yorkville).
Kendallville, Ind. (Noble Co.).

KENDALL Co., Tex. (co. seat, Boerne). For George Wilkins Kendall (1809-1867), journalist, publisher, and Republic of Texas army officer.

KENDUSKEAG STREAM, Me. From Malecite, "eel weir place" or "place where eels are caught in fishing pens." It flows southeast into Penobscot River.

KENEDY Capt. Mifflin (1818-1895), merchant, rancher, and commercial navigator of the Rio Grande.
Kenedy Co., Tex. (co. seat, Sarita).
Kenedy, Tex. (Karnes Co.).

KENHORST, Pa. (Berks Co.). For two prominent local families, the Horsts, who owned a large estate, and the Kendalls, who owned a large farm.

KENILWORTH Name of a novel by Sir Walter Scott, which takes its title from a castle at Kenilworth, Warwickshire, England.
Kenilworth, Ill. (Cook Co.).
Kenilworth, N.J. (Union Co.).

KENNADAY PEAK, Wyo. For Jack Kennaday, ranger.

KENNEBAGO From Abnaki, "large lake."
Kennebago Lake, Me.
Kennebago Mountain, Me. For the lake.

KENNEBEC From Algonquian, "long lake."
Kennebec Co., Me. (co. seat, Augusta). For the quiet stretch of the *Kennebec* R.
Kennebec River, Me.
Kennebec, S. Dak (co. seat of Lyman Co.).

KENNEBUNK From an Indian word, "the long cut bank." Kennebunk is located between the Kennebunk and Mousam rivers.
Kennebunk, Me. (York Co.), town and village.
Kennebunk River, Me.
Kennebunkport, Me. (York Co.).

KENNEDALE, Tex. (Tarrant Co.). For O. S. Kennedy, who surveyed this section in 1880.

KENNEDY, Cape, Fla. For John Fitzgerald Kennedy (1917-1963), thirty-fifth President of the United States (1961-63), from Massachusetts. He was a U.S. representative (1947-53) and senator (1953-60). He was assassinated on November 22, 1963. Much controversy followed the subsequent proclamation of President Lyndon B. Johnson which changed name of the cape, formerly *Canaveral*, to *Kennedy*. The name has since been changed back to CAPE CANAVERAL.

KENNER, La. (Jefferson Co.). For William Kenner (?-1825), a large plantation owner and merchant.

KENNESAW For an Indian settlement.
Kennesaw, Ga. (Cobb Co.).
Kennesaw Mountain, Ga.
Kennesaw Mountain Natl. Battlefield Park, Ga. For the Civil War Battle of *Kennesaw* Mtn.

KENNETT, Mo. (co. seat of Dunklin Co.). For Luther Martin Kennett (1807-1873), St. Louis alderman (1843-46), vice-president of the Pacific railroad company, mayor of St. Louis (1850-53), president of the St. Louis and Iron Mountain railroad (1853), and U.S. representative (1855-57). Earlier names were Chilletecaux and Butler.

KENNEWICK, Wash. (Benton Co.). Meaning uncertain; locally thought to be from Indian, "grassy place."

KENOGAMI From Indian, "long lake."
Kenogami, Que. (Chicoutimi Co.).
Kenogami Lake, Que.
Kenogami River, Ont. Rises in Long Lake, flows NE and N to Albany R.

KENORA An acronym, formed in 1905 from the first two letters of *Keewatin*, a former nearby territory, *Norman*, an adjoining village, and *Rat* Portage, an earlier name for the town, so named because it was on a route frequented by migrating muskrats.
Kenora District, Ont. (district seat, *Kenora*).
Kenora, Ont. (district seat of *Kenora* District).

KENOSHA From a Potawatomi (Algonquian) word, "pike" or "pickerel," both of which were plentiful in the area.
Kenosha Co., Wis. (co. seat, *Kenosha*). For the village, now county seat.
Kenosha, Wis. (co. seat of *Kenosha* Co.). Earlier names were Pike Creek and Southport.

KENOVA, W.Va. (Wayne Co.). From a combination of abbreviations for *Kentucky, Ohio* and *West Virginia*, the site being at the meeting of the three states.

KEN ROCK, Ill. (Winnebago Co.). A combined form taken from the names of the Morris Kennedy and Rock River school districts. A contest was held to determine the name. The area is a part of Rockford, Ill.

KENSINGTON For the London district of Kensington.
Kensington, Calif. (Contra Costa Co.).
New Kensington, Pa. (Westmoreland Co.).

KENT, Edward Augustus, Duke of (1767-1820), fourth son of George III and father of Queen Victoria of England; or United States names may be for the county in England from which the title is taken. See also EDWARD.
Kent Co., Del. (co. seat, Dover).
Kent Co., Md. (co. seat, Chestertown).
Kent Co., N.B. (shire town, Richibucto).
Kent Co., R.I. (co. seat, East Greenwich).

Kentville, N.S. (co. seat of Kings Co.). Earlier, Horton Corners.
New Kent Co., Va. (co. seat, *New Kent*).
New Kent, Va. (co. seat of *New Kent* Co.).

KENT, James (1763-1847), a New York jurist.
Kent Co., Mich. (co. seat, Grand Rapids).
Kentwood, Mich. (*Kent* Co.). Probably from the county, plus promotional *wood*.

KENT, Ohio (Portage Co.). For Marvin Kent, a railway investor. An earlier name was Franklin Mills.

KENT Co., Tex. (co. seat, Clairemont). For Andrew Kent (1798-1836), Texas soldier killed at the Alamo.

KENT, Wash. (King Co.). For the county of Kent, England. This region in Washington cultivated hops, as did the county in England.

KENTLAND, Ind. (co. seat of Newton). For Alexander J. Kent, a farmer and landowner.

KENTON, Okla. (co. seat of Cimarron Co.). A spelling variant of CANTON, Ohio.

Kentucky is famed for its blue grass and its magnificent thoroughbred horses. One of the best known of its racing stables is Calumet Farms near Lexington. [*Photo by Lawrence D. Thornton. Frederic Lewis*]

KENTON, Simon (1755-1836), Kentucky scout and Indian fighter who fought in the Battle of the Thames, Canada (1813) in which Tecumseh, the famous Indian leader, was killed.
Kenton Co., Ky. (co. seats, Covington and Independence).
Kenton, Ohio (co. seat of Hardin Co.).

KENTUCKY From Wyandot *ken-tah-teh*, "land of tomorrow." The name was first used for the Virginia county organized in 1776 and was well established by the time of statehood (1792).
Kentucky, Commonwealth of. 15th state of the Union. Settled: 1774. Admitted: 1792. Cap: Frankfort. Motto: United We Stand, Divided We Fall. Nickname: Bluegrass State. Flower: Goldenrod. Bird: Cardinal. Tree: Tulip Poplar. Song: "My Old Kentucky Home."
Kentucky Lake, Ky.-Tenn.
Kentucky River, Ky. Flows NW into Ohio R.
Kentucky Red River, Ky. Flows into *Kentucky* R.

KENTVILLE, N.S. (co. seat of Kings Co.). Named in 1826 for the Duke of KENT.

KENTWOOD, Mich. For James KENT.

KENWOOD, Ohio (Lucas Co.). Promotional.

KEOKUK For Keokuk (c.1780-1848), chief of the Sac and Fox Indians at the time the first settlers arrived. His name, originally *Kiyokaga*, means "he who moves around alert."
Keokuk Co., Iowa (co. seat, Sigourney).
Keokuk, Iowa (a co. seat of Lee Co.).

KEOSAUQUA, Iowa (co. seat of Van Buren Co.). From an Algonquian word of uncertain meaning, interpreted as a name for the Des Moines River and particularly for the bend in the river at this point.

KEOWEE RIVER, S.C. From Indian, possibly "place of mulberries." It flows south into Hartwell Reservoir.

KERMAN, Calif. (Fresno Co.). For two promoters, from the first three letters of each name.

KERN, Edward M., a topographer and artist for J. C. Fremont.

Chief Keokuk of the Sac and Fox Indians distinguished himself for bravery during the Black Hawk war. He later negotiated peace with the White Man. [*New York Public Library*]

Kern Co., Calif. (co. seat, Bakersfield). For the river.
Kern River, Calif.

KERR, James, a Texas statesman.
Kerr Co., Tex. (co. seat, *Kerrville*).
Kerrville, Tex. (co. seat of *Kerr* Co.).

KERR RESERVOIR, N.C.-Va. For John Hosea Kerr (1873-1958), attorney, jurist, solicitor, University of North Carolina trustee, and U.S. representative from North Carolina (1923-53). Also called Buggs Island Lake.

KERSHAW Co., S.C. (co. seat, Camden). For Joseph Kershaw, South Carolina army officer during the American Revolution.

KESHENA, Wis. (co. seat of Menominee Co.). From Indian, origin and meaning unknown.

KETCHIKAN, Alaska. For a nearby creek. This, in turn, is believed to be derived from the Tlingit Indian word *kitschkhin*, meaning either "eagle wing river," due to a resemblance to an eagle's wing at some point on the river, or "city under the eagle."

KETIK RIVER, Alaska. Of Eskimo origin, meaning unknown. It flows north into Avalik River.

KETTERING, Ohio (Montgomery Co.). For Charles Franklin Kettering (1876-1958), an engineer who developed the automobile self-starting ignition system. He was also a founder of DELCO (Dayton Engineering Laboratories Company).

KETTLE CREEK, Pa. Locally believed to have been named for an incident when a party of Indians with kettles in their canoe tipped over into the water and lost all of their kettles and other implements. It flows southwest into Susquehanna River.

KETTLE RIVER, Minn. Translated from Ojibway, for the shape and copper color of the rocks at the rapids. It flows south into St. Croix River.

KETTLE From a Salish Indian term for a tightly woven basket, somewhat resembling a kettle, used for catching fish at what is now Kettle Falls. The French name was *La Chaudière*, "kettle," which they believed to be descriptive for the frothing of the water below the falls which resembled boiling water in a kettle.
Kettle River, Wash.
Kettle Falls, Wash (Stevens Co.).
Kettle River Range, Wash.

KEUKA From Iroquoian, "place for landing canoes."
Keuka, N.Y. (Steuben Co.), town.
Keuka Lake, N.Y.

KEWANEE, Ill. (Henry Co.). From Potawatomi, "prairie hen," probably here derived from an Indian personal name. Compare KEWAUNEE.

KEWAUNEE From Ojibway, variously translated as "to cross a point" or "prairie hen" or "wild duck." The name has also been said to be Potawatomi.
Kewaunee Co., Wis. (co. seat, *Kewaunee*).. For the river.
Kewaunee, Wis. (co. seat of *Kewaunee* Co.).
Kewaunee River, Wis.

KEWEENAW A spelling variant of KEWAUNEE.
Keweenaw Co., Mich. (co. seat, Eagle River).

Keweenaw Bay, Mich.
Keweenaw Peninsula, Mich.
Keweenaw Point, Mich.

KEYA PAHA From Dakota Indian, "turtle" and "hill," for turtle-shaped hills.
Keya Paha Co., Neb. (co. seat, Springview). For the river.
Keya Paha River, Neb.
Keya Paha River, S.Dak.

KEY LARGO, Fla. One of the larger of the Florida Keys. *Largo* is from Spanish, "long," descriptive.

KEYSER, W.Va. (co. seat of Mineral Co.). For William Keyser, a railway official. An earlier name was Paddy's Town, for Patrick McCarthy, the founder.

KEYSTONE RESERVOIR, Okla. For the village, now inundated, which was so named because of its "key" position at the junction of the Arkansas and Cimarron rivers.

KEYTESVILLE, Mo. (co. seat of Chariton Co.). For James Keyte, a Methodist minister who donated fifty acres of land for a county seat.

KEY WEST From Spanish *Cayo Hueso*, "island of bones," for human bones found there. The island is the farthest west of any of the Florida Keys, and through folk etymology and Anglicization the name acquired its present form and pronunciation.
Key West, Fla. (co. seat of Monroe Co.).
Key West Island, Fla.

KEZAR, George, a hunter in the late 1800s.
Kezar Lake, Me.
Kezar Pond, Me.
Kezar River, Me.

KGUN LAKE, Alaska. From Eskimo, "source."

KIALEGAK, Cape, Alaska. Of Eskimo origin, meaning unknown.

KIAMICHI RIVER, Okla. From French, "horned screamer," for a kind of bird found near the stream. It flows southeast and south into Red River.

KIBBY MOUNTAIN, Me. For a local settler.

KICKAPOO For the Indian tribe, of Algonquian stock, whose name means "he moves about."

Kickapoo Creek, Ill. Flows SW into Salt Creek.

Kickapoo Creek, Ill. Flows SE into Illinois R.

Kickapoo River, Wis. Flows SSW into Wisconsin R.

KIDDER Co., N.Dak. (co. seat, Steele). For Jefferson Parish Kidder (1815-1883), Vermont legislator who later became a jurist in the Dakota Territory.

KIEL, Wis. (Manitowoc Co.). For Kiel, Germany, former home of an early settler.

KIKEPA POINT, Hawaii. On Niihau Island. From Hawaiian, "sarong," for the garment worn by women.

KILAUEA POINT, Hawaii. On north coast of Kauai Island. From Hawaiian, "spewing."

KILBUCK MOUNTAINS, Alaska. For Rev. John H. Kilbuck, a Moravian missionary in Alaska.

KILDONAN For Kildonan, Sutherlandshire, Scotland, from which most of the earliest settlers emigrated.

East Kildonan, Man.

North Kildonan, Man.

Old Kildonan, Man.

West Kildonan, Man.

KILGORE Tex. (Gregg Co.). For Constantine Buckley Kilgore (1835-1897), Civil War veteran, member of the state constitutional convention of 1875 and of the state senate (1884-88), serving as president of the latter (1885-87). He was a U.S. representative (1887-95), and was appointed by President Cleveland southern district judge of the Indian Territory, serving from 1895 to 1897.

KILLARNEY Man. For Killarney, Kerry, Ireland.

KILLBUCK CREEK, Ohio. For a Delaware Indian chief. It flows generally south into Walhonding River.

KILLDEER MOUNTAINS, N.Dak. Translated from Sioux, "the place where deer are killed."

KILLEEN, Tex. (Bell Co.). For the Killeen family, early settlers.

KILLIK RIVER, Alaska. Of Eskimo origin, probably from a tribal name. It flows north into Colville River.

KILLINGLY, Conn. (Windham Co.), town. For Kellingley (or Killansie) Manor, Yorkshire, England, ancestral home of Gov. Gurdon Saltonstall.

KILLINGTON PEAK, Vt. For an early settler.

KIMBALL, Thomas Lord (1831-1899), an official of the Union Pacific railroad.

Kimball Co., Neb. (co. seat, *Kimball*).

Kimball, Neb. (co. seat of *Kimball* Co.).

KIMBERLY, Wis. (Outagamie Co.). For Kimberly Clark, a land developer and proprietor.

KIMBLE Co., Tex. (co. seat, Junction). For George C. Kimble (1810-1836), a Texas officer killed at the Alamo.

KINCHAFOONEE From Creek, "mortar nutshells" or, literally, "nutcracker."

Kinchafoonee Creek, Ga. Flows SE into Flint R.

Kinchafoonee Lake, Ga.

KING Co., Tex. (co. seat, Guthrie). For William King (1812-1836), a soldier killed at the Alamo.

KING Co., Wash. (co. seat, Seattle). For Vice-President William Rufus King (1786-1853), who died within two months after assuming his office.

KING AND QUEEN For William and Mary, king and queen of England.

King and Queen Co., Va. (co. seat, *King and Queen*).

King and Queen, Va. (co. seat of *King and Queen* Co.).

KING CITY, Calif. (Monterey Co.). For C. H. King (c.1860-c.1930), landowner and planner of the town.

KINGFISHER Probably for King David Fisher (1819-1863), who camped and ranched along the stream that bears his name and from which the town and then the county took their names. Other theories, less plausible, are that the creek was named either for the kingfisher bird or for a John King Fisher (1854-1881).

Kingfisher Co., Okla. (co. seat, *Kingfisher*).

Kingfisher, Okla. (co. seat of *Kingfisher* Co.). Earlier, Lisbon.

KING GEORGE For King George I of England.
King George Co., Va. (co. seat, *King George*).
King George, Va. (co. seat of *King George* Co.).

KINGMAN, Ariz. (co. seat of Mohave Co.). Named for himself by Lewis Kingman, a railroad surveyor.

KINGMAN, Samuel Austin, Kansas jurist.
Kingman Co., Kan. (co. seat, *Kingman*).
Kingman, Kan. (co. seat of *Kingman* Co.).

KINGMAN CANYON PASS, Wyo., in Yellowstone Natl. Park. For D. C. Kingman, an army officer who supervised the building of a road here in 1884.

KING MOUNTAIN, Ore. For E. H. King, a sawmill operator.

KINGS Translated and shortened form of Spanish *Rio de los Santos Reyes*, "River of the Holy Kings," for the "kings" more commonly referred to in English as the Magi or Three Wise Men. The river is believed to have been discovered on January 6, 1806 (their feast day) by a party of Spanish explorers.
Kings Co., Calif. (co. seat, Hanford). For the river.
Kings River, Calif.
Kingsburg, Calif. (Fresno Co.).

KINGS Often from the name of an early settler or explorer.
Kings River, Ark. Flows N into White R.
Kings River, Ore.-Nev. Flows S into Quinn R.

KINGS Co., N.Y. (co. seat, Brooklyn). Conterminous with the Borough of Brooklyn, New York City. For King Charles II of England; named by the Duke of York. See also YORK.

KINGS Co., P.E.I. (co. seat, Georgetown). For King George III of England.

KINGSBURY Co., N.Dak. (co. seat, De Smet). For two brothers, George Washington and T. A. Kingsbury, prominent in territorial affairs. George W. Kingsbury, a native of New York, was an author, publisher, and legislator in the Dakota area.

KINGSBURY, Sanford, a jurist.
Kingsbury, Me. (Piscataquis Co.).
Kingsbury Stream, Me. Flows NE into Piscataquis R.

KINGSFORD, Mich. (Dickinson Co.). For Edward G. Kingsford, a Ford Motor Company executive.

KINGSLEY LAKE, Neb. For George P. Kingsley, a businessman and active promoter of the Tri-County Power and Irrigation District.

KINGS MOUNTAIN, Alaska. For Al King, prospector.

KINGS PEAK, Utah, in the Uinta Mtns. For Clarence King, geologist.

KINGSPORT, Tenn. (Sullivan Co.). Probably for Col. James King who established a mill there. *-Port* was added because it was a shipping point on the Holston River.

KINGSTON In colonial times, a name given in honor of the reigning king of England. See also KINGSTOWN.

KINGSTON For Charles II (1630-1685), King of England (1660-1685). His reign, known as the Restoration, was marked by relative prosperity, an increase in England's naval strength, and the growth of the power of Parliament. Having sired no legitimate heir, he was succeeded by his brother, James II.
Kingston, N.Y. (co. seat of Ulster Co.). Earlier, Wiltwyck and King's Town.
Kingston, Pa. (Luzerne Co.). For *Kingston*, R.I.
Kingston, R.I. (Washington Co.).
North Kingston, R.I. (Washington Co.).
South Kingston, R.I. (Washington Co.).
West Kingston, R.I. (co. seat of Washington Co.).

KINGSTON Probably for Evelyn Pierrepont, Duke of Kingston (1655-1726), member of Parliament and privy councillor. Another possibility is that it is in honor of King William III of England.
Kingston, Mass. (Plymouth Co.), town and village.
Kingston, N.H. (Rockingham Co.), town. For *Kingston*, Mass.

KINGSTON, Mo. (co. seat of Caldwell Co.). For Austin A. King, governor (1842).

KINGSTON, Ont. (co. seat of Frontenac Co.). Named by English Loyalists who had fled to Canada for George III. See GEORGETOWN. The original name was Kingstown.

KINGSTON, Tenn. (co. seat of Roane Co.). For Maj. Robert King, trader, tavern keeper, and officer in the American Revolution.

KINGSTOWN For the reigning king of England.
North Kingstown, R.I. (Washington Co.), town.
South Kingstown, R.I. (Washington Co.), town. For George I.

KINGSTREE, S.C. (co. seat of Williamsburg Co.). For the majestic pine tree standing on the bank of the Black River.

KINGSVILLE, Tex. (co. seat of Kleberg Co.). For Richard King, founder of the King Ranch.

KING WILLIAM For King William III of England.
King William Co., Va. (co. seat, *King William*).
King William, Va. (co. seat of *King William* Co.).

KINGWOOD, W.Va. (co. seat of Preston Co.). Two explanations of the name's origin exist: that it was named for a wooded area on land belonging to the British Crown and was therefore called at first King's Wood; or for some especially tall trees in the wooded area.

KINLOCH, Mo. (St. Louis Co.). For the Virginia estate of the Hunter family, early settlers and landowners, in turn taken from a Scots name.

KINNEY Co., Tex. (co. seat, Brackettville). For H. L. Kinney, a Texas legislator.

KINNICKINNIC RIVER, Wis. From Algonquian, "smoking material," which was made of tobacco or other plants or bark of trees. It flows southwest into St. Croix River.

KINSLEY, Kan. (co. seat of Edwards Co.). For Edward W. Kinsley of Boston, Mass., who donated funds for building in the town.

KINSTON, N.C. (co. seat of Lenoir Co.). Named Kingstown or Kingston in honor of King George III of England, but changed to Kinston after the American Revolution to eliminate any reference to a king. For a time Atkins Bank for Robert Atkins and later Caswell for Richard Caswell, the first governor, the name was changed back to Kinston.

KINZUA CREEK, Pa. From Algonquian, "turkey stream," so named because turkeys could be found there. It flows west into Allegheny River.

KIOWA For the Indian tribe, of Tanoan linguistic stock, from the area including parts of Oklahoma, Kansas, Colorado, New Mexico, and Texas. In 1868 they were resettled in what is now southwestern Oklahoma. Their name means "principal people."
Kiowa Co., Colo. (co. seat, Eads).
Kiowa Co., Kan. (co. seat, Greensburg).
Kiowa Co., Okla. (co. seat, Pittsburg).
Kiowa, Colo. (co. seat of Elbert Co.).
Kiowa Creek, Colo. Flows N into South Platte R.
Kiowa Creek, Tex.-Okla. Flows into Beaver R.

KIRBY, Tex. (Bexar Co.). Origin uncertain, but probably for an employee of the Southern Pacific railroad.

KIRKSVILLE, Mo. (co. seat of Adair Co.). For Jesse Kirk, a local businessman.

KIRKWOOD, Mo. (St. Louis Co.). For James P. Kirkwood, one of the founders.

KIRTLAND, Ohio (Lake Co.). For Turhand Kirtland, an agent of the Connecticut Land Company, which owned portions of this land. He was elected state senator from Trumbull County (1814) and served more than twenty years as a justice of the peace in that area.

KIRWIN RESERVOIR, Kan. For a nearby town, which was named for a local community member.

KISATCHIE From Choctaw, "reed river." *Kisatchie,* La. (Natchitoches Parish). *Kisatchie* Natl. Forest, La.

KISHWAUKEE RIVER, Ill. From Sauk, "sycamore," for the tree. It flows south and southwest into Rock River.

KISKIMINETAS RIVER, Pa. From Algonquian, "place of walnuts." It flows northwest into Allegheny River.

KISSIMMEE Origin unknown, but may be from Seminole-Creek *ki*, "mulberry," and *asima*, "yonder." *Kissimee*, Fla. (co. seat of Osceola Co.). *Kissimee*, Lake, Fla. *Kissimee* River, Fla.

KIT CARSON Co., Colo. (co. seat, Burlington). For Christopher ("Kit") CARSON.

KITCHENER, Ont. (co. seat of Waterloo Co.). For Herbert Horatio Kitchener (1850-1916), a field-marshall lord. Earlier names were Sand Hills, Mt. Pleasant, and, most recently, Berlin as named by German settlers. The name was changed during World War I.

KITSAP Co., Wash. (co. seat, Port Orchard). For an Indian chief and medicine man who was active against the whites in the war on Puget Sound in 1856. Originally named Slaughter in honor of Lt. W. A. Slaughter, killed in 1855 the choice, in a popular election, of a hostile Indian chief's name has not been explained, although it is said that he warned early settlers in the area of an impending massacre and was thereby remembered more kindly. His name means "brave."

KITTANNING, Pa. (co. seat of Armstrong Co.). From Delaware Indian *kithannink*, "town on the great river," from *kithanne*, "great river," for its position on the Allegheny River. It was founded by Colonel John Armstrong, for whom the county was named.

KITTATINNY MOUNTAINS, N.J.-N.Y. From Delaware Indian, "place of big mountains."

KITTERY, Me. (York Co.), town and village. For the manor of Kittery Court in Kingsweare, Devonshire, England.

KITTITAS Co., Wash. (co. seat, Ellensburg). Probably from a subtribal name of the Yakima Indian tribe. The meaning is uncertain, with "shoal people" as most appropriate, although "land of bread" and "clay gravel valley" have also been suggested.

KITT PEAK, Ariz. Either for an Indian, Kit the cook, a member of surveying party led by George Roskruge; or for a member of the Kitt family, relatives of Roskruge.

KITTSON Co., Minn. (co. seat, Hallock). For Norman Wolfred Kittson (1814-1888), a leading pioneer from Canada, fur trader, merchant, mayor of St. Paul, and legislator. An earlier name was Pambina.

KITTY HAWK, N.C. (Dare Co.). Of Indian origin, possibly Algonquian, meaning uncertain. It is near the site of the first airplane flight made by the Wright brothers.

KLAMATH Probably from Chinook *tlamatl*, their name for the sister tribe of the Modocs, who called themselves *maklaks*, "people" or "community." Other names were bestowed by rival tribes, including "people of the chipmunks," "those above the lakes," and "people of the lakes." The name has also been spelled *Claminitt* and *Clammitte*. The meaning is unknown. *Klamath* Co., Ore. (co. seat, *Klamath Falls*). *Klamath* Mountains, Ore.-Calif. *Klamath* Natl. Forest, Calif. *Klamath* River, Ore.-Calif. Flows generally SW into the Pacific. *Klamath Falls*, Ore. (co. seat of *Klamath* Co.). *Lower Klamath* Lake, Calif. *Upper Klamath* Lake, Ore.

KLEBERG Co., Tex. (co. seat, Kingsville). For Robert Justus Kleberg (1803-1888), lawyer and soldier. A native of Germany, he settled in the Texas area, fought in the War for Texas Independence, and took part in the Battle of San Jacinto.

KLEBERG, Tex. (Dallas Co.). For Richard Mifflin Kleberg, Sr. (1887-1955), a lawyer. He was president of the board of Tex. College of Arts and Industry (1929-31), U.S. representative (1931-45), and a member of the State Game and Fish Commission (1951-55).

KLICKITAT For an Indian tribal name meaning "beyond," or those who live "beyond the mountains," the name apparently given by the Chinooks to those who lived at the falls called *hladachut*, a variant of *klickitat*. Other names given them by different tribes include "scalpers," "inland people," and "prairie people."
Klickitat Co., Wash. (co. seat, Goldendale).
Klickitat River, Wash.

KLONDIKE An English corruption of an Indian name for the river, which was derived from its use as a salmon stream. The Klondike Region refers to the gold-bearing area in Alaska and Canada, site of the Klondike gold rush of 1896.
Klondike River, Yukon. Flows W to Yukon R.
Klondike (peak), Wyo. For the Klondike Region.

KLUTINA From Ahtena Indian, "glacier river."
Klutina Lake, Alaska.
Klutina River, Alaska. Flows NE into Cooper R.

KNIFE POINT MOUNTAIN, Wyo. Descriptive.

KNIFE RIVER, N. Dak. So named because flintstone is found there, from which the Indians made knives. It flows generally east into Missouri River.

KNIGHTVILLE RESERVOIR, Mass. For the nearby town, which was named from a personal name plus *-ville*.

KNOLLWOOD, Ohio (Montgomery Co.). Descriptive.

KNOTT Co., Ky. (co. seat, Hindman). For James Proctor Knott (1830-1911), Kentucky educator, legislator, and governor (1883-87).

KNOWLTON, Que. (co. seat of Brome Co.). For Col. Paul Holland Knowlton founder, who opened the first store and grist mill there.

KNOX, Gen. Henry (1750-1806), Massachusetts soldier during and after the American Revolution. He was army commander in chief (1783-84) and the first U.S. secretary of war (1785-95), under Washington.

Knox Co., Ill. (co. seat, Galesburg).
Knox Co., Ind. (co. seat, Vincennes).
Knox Co., Ky. (co. seat, Barbourville).
Knox Co., Me. (co. seat, Rockland).
Knox Co., Mo. (co. seat, Edina).
Knox Co., Neb. (co. seat, Center).
Knox Co., Ohio (co. seat, Mount Vernon).
Knox Co., Tenn. (co. seat, *Knoxville*).
Knox Co., Tex. (co. seat, Benjamin).
Knox, Ind. (co. seat of Starke Co.).
Knox, N.Y. (Albany Co.).
Knoxville, Ga. (co. seat of Crawford Co.).
Knoxville, Ill. (*Knox* Co.).
Knoxville, Iowa (co. seat of Marion Co.).
Knoxville, Tenn. (co. seat of *Knox* Co.).

Few Americans remember the exploits of General Henry Knox, but everyone knows Fort Knox where all the gold is stored. [*New York Public Library*]

KOBUK RIVER. Alaska. Variant form of KOYUK. It flows west into Hotham Inlet.

KODIAK. There are a variety of accounts as to the naming. One is that at the time of discovery (1763), the island was called *Kadyak* by the inhabitants. Another source states that the island was referred to as

kikhtak by the natives, an Innuit (Eskimo) word meaning "island." A variant of the spelling is *kikhtowik*. The spelling *Kadiak* was used until 1901, when the present spelling was adopted.
Kodiak, Alaska. For the island. Earlier, St. Paul.
Kodiak Island, Alaska.
Kodiak Station, Alaska.

KOFA MOUNTAINS, Ariz. From "K of A," property mark for The King of Arizona Mine Company.

KOHALA MOUNTAINS, Hawaii. On Hawaii Island. Of Hawaiian origin, meaning uncertain.

KOKO HEAD, Hawaii. On southeast point of Oahu Island. From Hawaiian, "blood," possibly for an incident.

KOKOLIK RIVER, Alaska. From Eskimo, "bistort," for the edible, flowering plant. It flows northwest into Kasegaluk Lagoon.

KOKOMO, Ind. (co. seat of Howard Co.). For a Miami Indian chief. The name means "black walnut."

KOKOSING RIVER, Ohio. From Algonquian, "place of owls." It flows southeast and east to join Mohican River to form Walhonding River.

KOLOB TERRACE, Utah. For the major star in Mormon cosmography, center of the universe.

KOOCHICHING Co., Minn. (co. seat, International Falls). Origin uncertain, but evidence points to a Cree Indian word meaning "rainy lake," descriptive of the mists from the nearby falls on Rainy River.

KOOTENAI For the Kootenai (or Kutenai) tribe, whose name means "water people."
Kootenai Co., Idaho (co. seat, Coeur d'Alene).
Kootenai Natl. Forest, Mont.
Kootenai River, Idaho.
Kootenai River, Mont.

KOOTENAY A spelling variant of KOOTENAI.
Kootenay Natl. Park, B.C.
Kootenay River, B.C.

KOSCIUSKO, Thaddeus Andrzej Bonawentura (1746-1817), Polish patriot and soldier active in the American cause during the American Revolution. He served with distinction at the Battle of Saratoga (1777) and in later southern campaigns. Active in Polish resistance to Russian dominance, he spent the rest of his life (much of it in exile) fighting for Polish independence. He is now a national hero in Poland.
Kosciusko Co., Ind. (co. seat, Warsaw).
Kosciusko, Miss. (co. seat of Attala Co.).

KOSHKONONG, Lake, Wis. From Ojibway, "closed in by fog," or possibly "hog place" or "place for shaving."

KOSSUTH Co., Iowa (co. seat, Algona). For Lajos (or Louis) Kossuth (1802-1894), Hungarian official, leader in the resistance to Austrian domination, and later dictator, who received enthusiastic acclaim on a visit to the United States. Defeated in 1849, he abdicated and went into exile.

KOTZEBUE SOUND, Alaska. Named by Lt. Otto van Kotzebue (1787-1846), of the Imperial Russian Navy, for himself. He discovered the sound in 1816 while on a voyage around the world (1815-17).

KOUNTZE, Tex. (co. seat of Hardin Co.). For Augusta, Luther, and Barclay Kountze of New York, N.Y., who financed the first railroad there.

KOYUK From Eskimo, "big river," but also probably from the tribal name, for those who lived near the "big river." Many variant spellings exist.
Koyuk Inlet, Alaska. On Norton Bay.
Koyuk River, Alaska. Flows SE into Koyuk Inlet.
Koyukuk River, Alaska. Flows SW into Yukon R.

KRENITZIN ISLANDS, Alaska. In Fox Islands of the Aleutian Islands. For Capt. Lt. Peter Kuzmich Krenitzin, of the Imperial Russian Navy, who explored the area (1768-69).

KUIKUI Cape, Hawaii. On Kahoolawe Island. From Hawaiian, "torch."

KUKPOWRUK RIVER, Alaska. From Eskimo, "a stream." It flows north into Kasegaluk Lagoon.

KUKPUK RIVER, Alaska. Variant form of KOYUK. It flows southwest and northwest into Marryat Inlet.

KULPMONT, Pa. (Northumberland Co.). For Monroe H. Kulp (?-1910), a U.S. representative, land developer, and farmer. Mont, because the town is located on the side of a mountain.

KUMUKAHI, Cape, Hawaii. On east coast of Hawaii Island. From Hawaiian, "first time."

KUPARUK RIVER, Alaska. Probably a variation of KOYUK. It flows north into Gwydyr Bay.

KUPREANOF ISLAND, Alaska. In Alexander Archipelago. For Capt. Ivan Andreevich Kupreanov, governor of Russian America (1836-40).

KUSKOKWIM From Eskimo, meaning unknown, but last syllable means "river."
Kuskokwim Bay, Alaska. Inlet on Bering Sea.
Kuskokwim Mountains, Alaska.
Kuskokwim River, Alaska. Flows SW into the bay.

KUTZTOWN, Pa. (Berks Co.). For George Kutz, founder.

KUYAHOORA LAKE, N.Y. Probably of Indian origin, meaning unknown, possibly "washing place," descriptive of a place to bathe.

KUZITRIN RIVER, Alaska. From Eskimo, meaning unknown. It flows west into Imuruk Basin.

KVICHAK BAY, Alaska. Of Eskimo origin, meaning unknown.

L

LAAU POINT, Hawaii. Westernmost point on Molokai Island. From Hawaiian, "wood."

LA BELLE, Lac, Mich. From French, "the beautiful lake."

LABELLE Co., Que. (co. seat, Mont Laurier). For Antoine LaBelle (1833-1891), Roman Catholic priest and colonizer.

LABETTE Co., Kan. (co. seat, Oswego). For a creek, which was named La Bette, a misspelling of French *la bête*, "the beast," itself probably an attempted translation of an Indian name. An earlier name was Dorn County.

LA CANADA-FLINTRIDGE, Calif. (Los Angeles Co.). A combination of Spanish *La Canada*, "the valley," and *Flintridge*, which was named for Frank Putnam Flint (1862-1929), U.S. senator (1905-11).

LACHINE, Que. (Île-de-Montréal Co.). From French, "China"; allegedly named by La Salle's men, in ironic reference to La Salle's dream of finding the westward route to China (1669).

LA CHUTE, Que. (co. seat of Argenteuil Co.). From French, "the fall," for the falls in the North River.

LACKAWANNA From a Delaware Indian word meaning "the stream that forks." The river was named first.
Lackawanna Co., Pa. (co. seat, Scranton).

Lackawanna, N.Y. (Erie Co.). For the Lackawanna Steel Company, which built a steel plant in this area at the beginning of the twentieth century, in turn for the Indian word.
Lackawanna River, Pa.

LACKAWAXEN From Delaware Indian, "fork," for the confluence of the Lackawaxen and Delaware rivers.
Lackawaxen, Pa. (Pike Co.).
Lackawaxen River, Pa. Flows E into Delaware R.

LACON, Ill. (co. seat of Marshall Co.). For Laconia, Greece.

LACONIA, N.H. (co. seat of Belknap Co.). A pseudo-Latin name for the many lakes in the area (*lake* or *lak* plus *-onia*), but ultimately derived from Laconia, Greece. The name is the 19th-century revival of the name applied to New Hampshire in 1629 by Ferdinando Gorges, an original grantee. It was chosen because the charter provided for lands extending "back to the great lakes and rivers of Canada."

LAC QUI PARLE From French, "talking lake," probably a translation of a Siouan word; origin uncertain, but possible for echoes reflected from surrounding cliffs.
Lac Qui Parle Co., Minn. (co. seat, Madison).
Lac qui Parle Lake, Minn.
Lac qui Parle River, Minn.

LA CRESCENT, Minn. (Houston Co.). The result of confusion between lacrosse, the Indian game, and French *la croix*, "the cross." Settlers chose *crescent* in allusion to the Crusaders who fought the Saracens with a standard, bearing a cross and crescent raised aloft.

LA CRESCENTA–MONTROSE, Calif. (Los Angeles Co.). A combination of Spanish *La Crescenta*, "crescent," and *Montrose*, descriptive or promotional.

LA CROIX, Lake, Minn.-Ont. From French, "the cross," descriptive of shape.

LA CROSSE From the French name for a game (now, in English, *lacrosse*) played by Indians, which they called *baggataway*. It was named by early French explorers who watched the game played on the site and saw a resemblance between the stick used and a bishop's "cross" (crozier).
La Crosse Co., Wis. (co. seat, *La Crosse*).
La Crosse, Kan. (co. seat of Rush Co.). For *La Crosse*, Wis. In this instance, the name also denotes a cross, that is, a point of intersection of two roads.
La Crosse, Wis. (co. seat of *La Crosse* Co.).

LACY-LAKEVIEW, Tex. (McLennan Co.). For two interurban stops.

LADD PEAK, Wyo. For William S. Ladd, a president of the American Alpine Club.

LADERA HEIGHTS, Calif. (Los Angeles Co.). From Spanish *ladera*, "hillside"; descriptive and promotional.

LADYSMITH, Wis. (co. seat of Rusk Co.). For a Lady Smith, bride of a business official. (She never visited the town.)

LAFAYETTE See also FAYETTE and FAYETTEVILLE.

LA FAYETTE, Ga. (co. seat of Walker Co.). A variant form of LAFAYETTE.

LAFAYETTE, Marquis de (1757-1834), French statesman and soldier. He entered the King's Musketeers in 1771, but his enthusiasm and imagination were stirred by accounts of the American insurgents, and, with a desire to avenge France's defeat in the Seven Years' War, he withdrew from active service in the French army, purchased a vessel, and sailed to America. He agreed to serve without compensation in return for a commission and the right to return to France if called by king or family. Congress voted him a rank of major general in July, 1777, but gave him no active command. In August of that year he met George Washington in Philadelphia — the beginning of an historic friendship. Lafayette joined Washington's staff as a volunteer. He was slightly wounded in the leg during the Battle of Brandywine, and on December 1, 1777, Congress voted him command of the division of Virginia light troops. After a winter at Valley Forge, Lafayette was placed in command of the proposed "irruption into Canada," a fantastic scheme of capturing Canada in the dead of winter with a handful of troops — a plan that failed, leaving Lafayette chagrined and disappointed. In 1778 France made an alliance with the Americans. Later, Lafayette helped defeat Cornwallis at Yorktown. Upon returning to France, he was enthusiastically received, and there he was helpful in aiding American agents in seeking supplies and loans. He made a triumphant return to the

Congress honored the descendents of the Marquis de Lafayette by making them honorary American citizens. American volunteers serving in France during World War I again honored him by forming the Lafayette Escadrille. [*New York Public Library*]

United States in 1784. In 1790 he was the most popular figure in France but from 1792 to 1797 he was exiled as a result of the French Revolution, and his fortune was drastically reduced. In 1794 the U.S. Congress voted him emoluments as brigadier general, which he had refused to accept during the American Revolution, although the amount was only a fraction of his own expenditures while aiding the American cause. In 1824, President Monroe invited him to visit the United States again; here he met demonstrations of "frenzied enthusiasm without precedent or parallel in United States history." His grave in France is covered with earth from Bunker Hill.

Lafayette Co., Ark. (co. seat, Lewisville).
Lafayette Co., Fla. (co. seat, Mayo).
Lafayette Parish, La. (parish seat, *Lafayette*).
Lafayette Co., Miss. (co. seat, Oxford).
Lafayette Co., Mo. (co. seat, Lexington).
Lafayette Co., Wis. (co. seat, Darlington).
Lafayette, Ala. (co. seat of Chambers Co.).
Lafayette, Calif. (Contra Costa Co.).
Lafayette, Colo. (Boulder Co.).
Lafayette, Ind. (co. seat of Tippecanoe Co.).
Lafayette, La. (parish seat of *Lafayette* Parish). Earlier, Vermilionville.
Lafayette, Tenn. (co. seat of Macon Co.).
Lafayette, Mount, N.H., in the Franconia Mtns.
Southwest Lafayette, La. (*Lafayette* Parish).
West Lafayette, Ind. (Tippecanoe Co.).

LA FERIA, Tex. (Cameron Co.). From Spanish, "the fairgrounds"; probably promotional.

LA FOLLETTE, Tenn. (Campbell Co.). For Harvey M. La Follette, former president of the La Follette Iron and Coal Company.

LAFOURCHE From French *la fourche*, "the fork."
Lafourche Parish, La. (parish seat, Thibodaux).
Lafourche, Bayou, La. Flows SE into the Gulf of Mexico.
Lafourche, Bayou, La. Flows SE into Boeuf R.

LA GARITA From Spanish, "the sentry box."
La Garita, Colo. (Saguache Co.).

La Garita Creek, Colo. Flows into San Luis Creek.
La Garita Mountains, Colo.

LAGO, Mount, Wash. From Spanish, "lake," but reason for naming is not known.

LA GRANDE, Ore. (co. seat of Union Co.). From French, "the grand one," probably suggested by GRANDE RONDE VALLEY.

LA GRANGE From French, "the barn," but also reminiscent to early settlers of a home in France, especially of the country home of the Marquis de Layette. The name is popular here probably because of both euphonic reasons and its French derivation. See also LAGRANGE.
La Grange, Ga. (co. seat of Troup Co.). For Lafayette's home.
La Grange, Ill. (Cook Co.).
La Grange, Ky. (co. seat of Oldham Co.).
La Grange, Me. (Penobscot Co.).
La Grange, N.Y. (Dutchess Co.).
La Grange, N.C. (Lenoir Co.).
La Grange, Tex. (co. seat of Fayette Co.). For *La Grange*, Tenn.
La Grange Highlands, Ill. (Cook Co.). Promotional.
La Grange Park, Ill. (Cook Co.). Promotional.

LAGRANGE A variant form of LA GRANGE.
Lagrange Co., Ind. (co. seat, *Lagrange*).
Lagrange, Ind. (co. seat of *Lagrange* Co.).

LAGUNA From Spanish, "lake" or "pond."
Laguna Creek, Ariz. Flows NE into Chinle Wash R.
Laguna Dam, Ariz.-Calif.
Laguna Beach, Calif. (Orange Co.).
Laguna Hills, Calif. (Orange Co.).
South Laguna, Calif. (Orange Co.).

LAGUNA DEL PERRO (lake), N. Mex. From Spanish, "dog lake," probably translated from Indian.

LAGUNA MADRE, Tex. From Spanish, "mother lagoon," with connotation of "most important."

LAGUNA NIGUEL, Calif. (Orange Co.). A combination of Spanish *laguna*, "lake," and *niguel*, which is thought to be of Indian origin, *niguile* or *nahill*, transliterated into Spanish; meaning unknown.

LA HABRA, Calif. (Orange Co.). From Spanish, "gorge" or "pass through the mountains."

LAHONTAN RESERVOIR, Nev., in Carson River. For the prehistoric lake that covered much of northwestern Nevada, which was named for Baron de Lahontan, French explorer.

LA JUNTA, Colo. (co. seat of Otero Co.). From Spanish, "junction," here in reference to a railway junction.

LAKE See also the particular name; for example, for Lake Michigan, see MICHIGAN.

LAKE Descriptive, near to or including a lake.
Lake Co., Calif. (co. seat, *Lakeport*). Includes Clear Lake.
Lake Co., Colo. (co. seat, Leadville). Includes Turquoise Lake.
Lake Co., Fla. (co. seat, Tauveres). Includes a number of lakes.
Lake Co., Ill. (co. seat, Waukegan). On L. Michigan.
Lake Co., Ind. (co. seat, Crown Point). On L. Michigan.
Lake Co., Mich. (co. seat, Baldwin). Near L. Michigan.
Lake Co., Minn. (co. seat, Two Harbors). On L. Superior.
Lake Co., Mont. (co. seat, Polson). Includes most of Flathead Lake.
Lake Co., Ohio (co. seat Painesville). On L. Erie.
Lake Co., Ore. (co. seat, *Lakeview*). Includes part of *Goose Lake* and several others.
Lake Co., S. Dak. (co. seat, Madison). Includes several small lakes.
Lake Co., Tenn. (co. seat, Tiptonville). Includes Reelfoot Lake.

LAKE ANDES, S. Dak. (co. seat of Charles Mix Co.). For a nearby lake, which was named for one Handy, operator of a woodyard on the Missouri River and supplier of firewood to the steamboats in the mid 1800s. It was known first as Handy's Lake, then Andy's Lake, and finally a more elegant Lake Andes.

LAKE ARROWHEAD, Calif. (San Bernardino Co.). For the shape of the small lake on which it is situated.

LAKE BLUFF, Ill. (Lake Co.) Adjacent to Lake Michigan and on a bluff about seventy-five feet above the lake. Earlier names were Dulanty, Oak Hill, and Rockland.

LAKE BUTLER, Fla. (co. seat of Union Co.). For Robert Butler, surveyor general of Florida, who received the surrender of East Florida for the United States from the Spaniards. Captain Butler was commander of a small detachment sent by General Jackson in 1835 to fight the Seminoles under the command of Bendoris. At the lake that now bears Butler's name, both commanders were killed, although Butler's forces were victorious.

LAKE CHARLES, La. (parish seat of Calcasieu Parish). For the nearby lake, in turn for Charles Salier, who in 1803 erected a home on the lakefront and on the site of the present city. Also called Charlie's Lake and Charles Town.

LAKE CITY Descriptive.
Lake City, Ark. (co. seat of Craighead Co.).
Lake City, Colo. (co. seat of Hinsdale Co.).
Lake City, Fla. (co. seat of Columbia Co.). For the many lakes nearby.
Lake City, Mich. (co. seat of Missaukee Co.). Near L. Missaukee.
Lake City, Minn. (Wabasha Co.). On a wide stretch of the Mississippi R.
Lake City, S.C. (Florence Co.). For the lagoon of Lynch's R., on which it was built. There is no actual lake there.

LAKE ELMO, Minn. (Washington Co.). For a lake, which was named for the title character in the novel *St. Elmo*, written by Augusta Jane Wilson (1928).

LAKE FOREST, Ill. (Lake Co.). Descriptive and promotional; on Lake Michigan.

LAKE GENEVA, Wis. (Walworth Co.). For GENEVA, N.Y.

LAKE GEORGE, N.Y. (co. seat of Warren Co.). For George II (1683-1760), king of England (1727-60).

LAKEHURST, N.J. (Ocean Co.). Means "a woods by the lake." Lake Horican is in the town.

LAKE JACKSON, Tex. (Brazoria Co.). For the Jackson brothers who owned a plantation on which the man-made lake and

Lake Placid, New York, was host to the 1932 Winter Olympics. It has the only bobsled run in North America. [*Photo by Lionel Green. Frederic Lewis*]

townsite are located. It is a residential city built by Dow Chemical Company.

LAKELAND Descriptive.
Lakeland, Fla. (Polk Co.). For the twelve lakes within the city limits.
Lakeland, Ga. (Lanier Co.). For an 11,000-acre lake, one mile west of the city.

LAKE MILLS, Wis. (Jefferson Co.). For a sawmill and gristmill there.

LAKEMORE, Ohio (Summit Co.). Promotional, from "more lake."

LAKE OF THE WOODS Descriptive.
Lake of the Woods Co., Minn. (co. seat, Baudette).
Lake of the Woods (lake), Minn.-Man.-Ont.

LAKE ORION Name chosen because it "was short, handy to write, and altogether lovely." It has no particular meaning, but was probably influenced by Huron, Oregon,

and particularly the constellation.
Lake Orion, Mich. (Oakland Co.).
Lake Orion Heights, Mich. (Oakland Co.).

LAKE OSWEGO, Ore. (Clackamas Co.). also known as Oswego Lake. The city is on the lake of the same name; both took their name from *Oswego*, a nearby town, which was named for *Oswego*, N.Y. See OSWEGO.

LAKE PARK, Fla. (Palm Beach Co.). Descriptive and promotional.

LAKE PLACID, N.Y. (Essex Co.). Promotional.

LAKE PLEASANT, N.Y. (co. seat of Hamilton Co.). For its quality, a pleasant place.

LAKEPORT, Calif. (co. seat of Lake Co.). Descriptive; on Clear Lake.

LAKE PROVIDENCE, La. (parish seat of East Carroll Parish). Formerly known as

Providence, the city fronts Lake Providence, once a channel of the Mississippi River. The origin of the name is uncertain, but one version is that river boatmen thanked "Providence" for helping them elude the pirates who preyed on them; another is that the area had plentiful game and fish for the first settlers, provided by "Providence."

LAKE SAINT JOHN For Father Jean de Quen, discoverer of the lake and a missionary.
Lake Saint John Co., Que. (co. seats, Saint Joseph d'Alma and Roberval). For the lake.
Lake Saint John (lake), Que.

LAKESIDE, Calif. (San Diego Co.). Descriptive; near Hunzicker Lake.

LAKESIDE PARK, Ky. (Kenton Co.). Descriptive and promotional.

LAKE SUCCESS, N.Y. (Nassau Co.). Promotional. From Indian *sucsat*, meaning unknown.

LAKEVIEW Descriptive.
Lakeview, Mich. (Montcalm Co.). On Tamarack L.
Lake View, N.Y. (Nassau Co.).
Lakeview, Ore. (co. seat of Lake Co.).
Lakeview, Tex. (Hall Co.).

LAKE VILLAGE, Ark. (co. seat of Chicot Co.). Descriptive; on Lake Chicot.

LAKEVILLE, Mass. (Plymouth Co.), town. For the many lakes in the town.

LAKEVILLE, Minn. (Dakota Co.). Descriptive.

LAKEWOOD Descriptive.
Lakewood, Calif. (Los Angeles Co.).
Lakewood, Colo. (Jefferson Co.).
Lakewood, N.Y. (Chautauqua Co.).
Lakewood, Ohio (Cuyahoga Co.). Earlier, East Rockport.

LAKE WORTH VILLAGE, Tex. (Tarrant Co.). This town is served by the Fort Worth Post Office, and is probably so named for that reason. See FORT WORTH.

LAKE ZURICH, Ill. (Lake Co.). For the lake in Switzerland.

LAKIN, Kan. (co. seat of Kearny Co.). For David L. Lakin, an official of the Santa Fe railroad.

LAKOTA, N. Dak. (co. seat of Nelson Co.). For the Teton Sioux tribe of the Dakotas. The meaning of the name is disputed, but usually accepted as "allies," although "land of plenty" or "plenty of heads taken" may also be considered. See also DAKOTA.

LA MALBAIE From French, "the bad bay."
La Malbaie, Que. (co. seat of Charlevoix Co.). For its location at the foot of a bay where the Malbaie R empties into the St. Lawrence R. Also called Murray Bay.
Malbaie River, Que. Named by Samuel Champlain because he had been unable to anchor his ship in it. Flows SE into St. Lawrence R.

LAMAR, Lucius Quintus Cincinnatus (1825-1893), Mississippi soldier and statesman who served in the Confederate diplomatic service. He was a U.S. representative (1857-60; 1873-77), U.S. senator (1877-85), secretary of the interior (1885-88) under Cleveland, and a justice of the U.S. Supreme Court (1888-93).
Lamar Co., Ala. (co. seat, Vernon).
Lamar Co., Ga. (co. seat, Barnesville).
Lamar Co., Miss. (co. seat, Purvis).
Lamar, Colo. (co. seat of Prowers Co.).

LAMAR, Mirabeau Buonaparte (1798-1859), Republic of Texas statesman, and its president (1838-41).
Lamar Co., Tex. (co. seat, Paris).
Lamar, Mo. (co. seat of Barton Co.).

LA MARQUE, Tex. (Galveston Co.). For La Marque, France. Earlier names were Highland and Buttermilk Station.

LAMB Co., Tex. (co. seat, Olton). For George A. Lamb, a Republic of Texas army officer killed at San Jacinto in 1836.

LAMBERTVILLE, Mich. (Monroe Co.). For John Lambert, founder.

LAMBTON Co., Ont. (co. seat, Sarnia). For John George Lambton, 1st Earl of Durham and governor in chief of British North America (1838).

LA MESA, Calif. (San Diego Co.). From Spanish, "the mesa" (flat-topped hill) or "the table."

LAMESA, Tex. (co. seat of Dawson Co.). A variant form of LA MESA.

LAMINE RIVER, Mo. From French, place of "the mine." It flows northeast and north into Blackwater River.

LA MIRADA From Spanish, "the glance" or "the gaze."
East La Mirada, Calif. (Los Angeles Co.).
La Mirada, Calif. (Los Angeles Co.).

LAMOILLE A corruption of French *la mouette*, "the seagull," the name given to the river by Champlain.
Lamoille Co., Vt. (co. seat, Hyde Park).
Lamoille River, Vt.

LA MOINE RIVER, Ill. From French, "the monk," apparently so named by Catholics who were trying to convert the Indians. The stream is also called Crooked Creek, descriptive, and some maps show it as Lamine River. It flows southeast into the Illinois River.

LAMONI, Iowa (Decatur Co.). For a good king in the sacred church literature of the Reorganized Church of Jesus Christ of Latter Day Saints.

LAMONT, Calif. (Kern Co.). For a place in Scotland once home of the MacFaddens, landowners.

LA MOTTE, Lake, Wis. From French, "the clod."

LA MOURE, Judson (1839-1918), pioneer, entrepreneur, and legislator.
La Moure Co., N.Dak. (co. seat, *La Moure*).
La Moure, N.Dak. (co. seat of *La Moure* Co.).

LAMPASAS From Spanish, "water lily"; descriptive.
Lampasas Co., Tex. (co. seat, *Lampasas*).
Lampasas, Tex. (co. seat of *Lampasas* Co.).
Lampasas River, Tex. Flows SE and E into Leon R.

LAMPREY RIVER, N.H. For the elongated fish. It meanders east into Great Bay.

LANARK Co., Ont. (co. seat, Perth). For Lanark, Lanarkshire, Scotland.

LANCASTER For Lancaster, Lancashire, England.
Lancaster Co., Neb. (co. seat, Lincoln).

Lancaster Co., Pa. (co. seat, *Lancaster*).
Lancaster Co., S.C. (co. seat, *Lancaster*).
Lancaster Co., Va. (co. seat, *Lancaster*).
Lancaster, Ky. (co. seat of Garrard Co.).
Lancaster, Mass. (Worcester Co.), town. John Prescott, founder, was born in *Lancaster*, England.
Lancaster, Mo. (co. seat of Schuyler Co.).
Lancaster, N.H. (co. seat of Coos Co.), town. For *Lancaster*, Mass.
Lancaster, Ohio (co. seat of Fairfield Co.). Earlier, New Lancaster, for *Lancaster*, Pa.
Lancaster, Pa. (co. seat of *Lancaster* Co.). Earlier, Hickory Town.
Lancaster, S.C. (co. seat of *Lancaster* Co.).
Lancaster, Tex. (Dallas Co.). For *Lancaster*, Ky.
Lancaster, Va. (co. seat of *Lancaster* Co.).
Lancaster, Wis. (co. seat of Grant Co.). For *Lancaster*, Pa.

LANCASTER, Calif. (Los Angeles Co.). Probably for a railroad official, whose first name has been lost. Some propose the town was named for Lancaster, Pa., by early settlers, but dates of the settlement do not substantiate this.

LANDER, Frederick William (1822-1862), railroad surveyor, road builder, and later a general in the Union army. He surveyed the Oregon Trail (1857).
Lander Co., Nev. (co. seat, Austin).
Lander, Wyo. (co. seat of Fremont Co.).
Lander Mountain, Wyo.
Lander Peak, Wyo.

LANE Co., Kan. (co. seat, Dighton). For James Henry Lane (1814-1866), U.S. representative from Indiana (1853-55), leader in the free-state movement in Kansas and its first U.S. senator (1861-66). He was also an officer in the Mexican War and a general in the Civil War.

LANE Co., Ore. (co. seat, Eugene). For Joseph Lane (1801-1881), Indiana legislator, general in the Mexican War, the first territorial governor of Oregon (1845-49) and first U.S. senator (1859-61) from the state of Oregon. He was candidate for vice-president of the United States on the Democratic ticket in 1860.

LANESBOROUGH, Mass. (Berkshire Co.). For the Countess or Earl of Lanesborough, or both, whose seat was at Lanesborough, Ireland.

LANETT, Ala. (Chambers Co.). For Lafayette Lanier (1845-1910) and one Barnett, cotton manufacturers. An earlier name was Bluffton.

LANGDON, N.Dak. (co. seat of Cavalier Co.). For R. B. Langdon, surveyor of the site and an employee of the Great Northern railroad. He presented the village with a bell for its new school.

LANGLADE Co., Wis. (co. seat, Antigo). For Charles Michael de Langlade (1729-1800), an Indian leader against the British during the French and Indian Wars. He supported the British cause during the American Revolution. Later he settled in the Green Bay area of what is now Wisconsin; he has been called the "founder of Wisconsin."

LANIER Co., Ga. (co. seat, Lakeland). For Sidney Lanier (1842-1881), important post-Civil War Southern poet.

LANSDALE, Pa. (Montgomery Co.). For Philip Lansdale Fox, a railroad surveyor.

L'ANSE From French, "the bay," for Keweenaw Bay.
L'Anse, Mich. (co. seat of Baraga Co.).
L'Anse Bay, Mich. Inlet at S end of Keweenaw Bay.

LANSFORD, Pa. (Carbon Co.). For Asa Lansford Foster, pioneer, coal operator, and mining engineer.

LANSING, John (1754-1829), jurist, a hero in the American Revolution, and a prominent legislator of New York State, serving as speaker of the lower house in 1786. Appointed a justice of the supreme court of New York, he rose to chief justice and later held the position of chancellor of New York (1801-14). A village in New York was named for him. Although it no longer has even a post office, the name was spread westward, seemingly always by settlers from the New York area.
East Lansing, Mich. (Ingham Co.).
Lansing, Ill. (Cook Co.).
Lansing, Iowa (Allamakee Co.).
Lansing, Kan. (Leavenworth Co.). For *Lansing*, Mich.
Lansing, Mich. (Ingham Co.), state capital.
Lansing, Minn. (Mower Co.).
Lansing, Ohio (Belmont Co.).

LANTANA, Fla. (Palm Beach Co.). For the flower.

LA PALMA, Calif. (Orange Co.). From Spanish, "the palms."

LAPEER Local spelling of French *la pierre*, "the stone," or "flint," a translation probably of the Indian name for the Flint River.
Lapeer Co., Mich. (co. seat, *Lapeer*).
Lapeer, Mich. (co. seat of *Lapeer* Co.).
Lapeer Heights, Mich. (*Lapeer* Co.).

LA PLATA From Spanish, "silver." For the silver mines in the area.
La Plata Co., Colo. (co. seat, Durango). Gold and other minerals are also mined there.
La Plata, Md. (co. seat of Charles Co.).

LA PLATTE RIVER, Vt. From French, "the flat," for the slow-moving, shallow stream. It flows southwest and northwest into Lake Champlain.

LA PORTE From French, "entrance," "door," or "port." In this case it is for an opening to an area farther on.
La Porte Co., Ind. (co. seat, *La Porte*).
La Porte, Ind. (co. seat of *La Porte* Co.).
La Porte, Tex. (Harris Co.). Referred to as "the gateway to the sea."

LAPORTE, Pa. (co. seat of Sullivan Co.). For John Laporte (1798-1862), legislator and U.S. representative (1833-37).

LA PUENTE, Calif. (Los Angeles Co.). From Spanish, "the bridge"; descriptive.

LARAMIE, Jacques (?-c. 1818), French-Canadian trapper. He was recognized as honest in his trade and was respected in the territory where he worked. Although generally friendly with Indians, he was killed by Arapahoes near the river that bears his name. The name is also spelled *LaRamie* or *LaRamee*.
Fort Laramie Natl. Monument, Wyo.
Laramie Co., Wyo. (co. seat, Cheyenne).
Laramie, Wyo. (co. seat of Albany Co.). For the river.

Laramie Mountains, Colo., in the Rocky Mtns.

Laramie Peak, Wyo.

Laramie Plains, Wyo. For the river.

Laramie Range, Wyo. For the river.

Laramie River, Colo.-Wyo. Flows generally NE to the North Platte R.

LAREDO, Tex. (co. seat of Webb Co.). For Laredo, Spain.

LARIMER Co., Colo. (co. seat, Ft. Collins). For William Larimer, an early settler.

LARKSPUR, Calif. (Marin Co.). For the flower.

LARKSVILLE, Pa. (Luzerne Co.). For Peggy Lark, original owner of the townsite. An earlier name was Blindtown.

LARNED, Kan. (co. seat of Pawnee Co.). For Fort Larned, which was named for Benjamin F. Larned, U.S. Army paymaster-general.

Robert Cavelier, sieur de LaSalle, established France's claim to the entire Mississippi River basin, including its tributaries. [*New York Public Library*]

LARTO LAKE, La. Anglicized folk spelling of the French family name Lartault.

LARUE Co., Ky. (co. seat, Hodgenville). For an early settler, John Larue.

LA SAL From Spanish, "the salt."

La Sal; Utah. (San Juan Co.).

La Sal Mountains, Utah.

LA SALLE, Robert Cavelier, Sieur de (1643-1687), French adventurer and explorer. He claimed the territory west of the Mississippi River for France, naming it Louisiana in honor of Louis XIV. In 1682 he led his expedition down the headwaters of the Mississippi to the river itself and then down to the Gulf of Mexico. On a second expedition, his men mutinied and murdered him.

La Salle Co., Ill. (co. seat, Ottawa).

La Salle Parish, La. (parish seat, Jena).

La Salle Co., Tex. (co. seat, Cotulla).

La Salle, Ill. (*La Salle* Co.).

LAS ANIMAS Co., Colo. (co. seat, Trinidad). From Spanish, "the souls," first applied to a river. See PICKETWIRE RIVER.

LAS CRUCES, N.Mex. (co. seat of Dona Ana Co.). From Spanish, "the crosses." There is a burial ground with crosses there. Opinions differ as to how they got there.

LASSEN, Peter (1793-1895), respected early settler. The name of the county was probably taken from that of the peak, apparently the first feature to which Lassen's name was attached.

Lassen Co., Calif. (co. seat, Susanville).

Lassen Peak, Calif., in the Cascade Mtns., known locally as Mount *Lassen*. Earlier, San Jose Peak.

Lassen Volcanic Natl. Park, Calif.

Lassen Natl. Forest, Calif.

L'ASSOMPTION From French, "The Assumption," for the holy day.

L'Assomption Co., Que. (co. seat, *L'Assomption*).

L'Assomption, Que. (co. seat of *L'Assomption* Co.). Earlier, St. Pierre du Portage de L'Assomption.

L'Assomption River, Que. Flows into St. Lawrence R.

LAS VEGAS A shortened form of Spanish *Nuestra Señora de los Dolores de Las Vegas*, "Our Lady of Sorrows of the Meadows."

East Las Vegas, Nev. (Clark Co.).

Las Vegas, N.Mex. (co. seat of San Miguel Co.).

Las Vegas, Nev. (co. seat of Clark Co.).

North Las Vegas, Nev. (Clark Co.).

LATAH Co., Idaho (co. seat, Moscow). A combination of two Nez Percé words: *lakah*, "place of the pines," and *tah-ol*, "pestle."

LATHROP, Mich. (Delta Co.). For Azel Lathrop, an agent for the Chicago and Northwestern railroad.

LATHRUP VILLAGE, Mich. (Oakland Co.). For Louise Lathrup, founder.

LATIMER Co., Okla. (co. seat, Wilburton). For James S. Latimer, active in creating the Oklahoma state constitution before statehood.

LATIMERS BROOK, Conn. Locally believed to have been named for a General Latimer of the American Revolution. An earlier name was Latimore. It flows south into Niantic River.

LATIR PEAK, N.Mex. Origin uncertain; claimed to be a French surname, but also possibly from Spanish, "to howl."

LATROBE, Pa. (Westmoreland Co.). For Benjamin Henry Latrobe, Jr. (1806-1878), civil engineer and a mayor of Baltimore. His father was known as the "father of architecture in the United States."

Las Vegas, Nevada, is the epitome of frenetic show business. The combination of posh hotels, top stars, gorgeous showgirls, and round-the-clock gambling make it unique through all the world. [*Frederic Lewis*]

LA TUQUE, Que. (Champlain Co.). For a rock on a river bank thought to resemble a *tuque*, the knitted cap worn by fur traders.

LAUDERDALE, Col. James (?-1814), a soldier killed at the Battle of New Orleans.
Lauderdale Co., Ala. (co. seat, Florence).
Lauderdale Co., Miss. (co. seat, Meridian).
Lauderdale Co., Tenn. (co. seat, Ripley).

LAUGHING FISH POINT, Mich. Extends into Lake Superior. For the shape of the point; probably translated from Indian.

LAUGHLIN PEAK, N.Mex. For a local settler.

LAUREL. For laurel trees.
Laurel Co., Ky. (co. seat, London)
Laurel, Miss. (co. seat of Jones Co.).
Laurel, Md. (Prince Georges Co.).
Laurel, Mont. (Yellowstone Co.).
Laurel Hill, Pa.
Laurel Hill Creek, Pa. Flows SSW into Youghiogheny R.
West Laurel, Md. (Prince Georges Co.).

LAURENCE HARBOR, N.J. (Middlesex Co.). For Laurence Lamb, a wealthy New York businessman who lived in the area during the summer.

LAURENS Co., Ga. (co. seat, Dublin). For John Laurens (1753-1782), heroic soldier in the American Revolution, whose exploits earned him the honor of receiving the sword of General Cornwallis when the latter surrendered at Yorktown, Va. Laurens was later killed in a battle with Indians.

LAURENS, Henry (1724-1792), diplomat and patriot in the American cause during the American Revolution, who served as president of the Continental Congress. He was captured by the British while he was on his way to Holland as minister and was later exchanged for General Cornwallis. His remains were cremated, the first white cremation on record in America.
Laurens Co., S.C. (co. seat, *Laurens*).
Laurens, S.C. (co. seat of *Laurens* Co.).

LAURINBURG, N.C. (co. seat of Scotland Co.). For the McLaurin family, early Scots settlers.

LAURIUM, Mich. (Houghton Co.). For the Laurium Mining Company, which was named for Laurium, Greece, a mining city.

LAUZON, Que. (Levis Co.). For John De Lauzon (1584-1666), governor of New France (1651-1656). He was granted the seigniory of Lauzon in 1656.

LAVACA Originally from French *la vache*, "cow," or *les vaches*, plural, La Salle's name for the area because of the presence of buffaloes, which to him resembled cows. The Spanish write it as *La Baca*. The spelling was changed when the county was created.
Lavaca Co., Tex. (co. seat, Hallettsville). For the river.
Lavaca Bay, Tex. An arm of Matagorda Bay.
Lavaca River, Tex. Flows SE into the bay.

LAVA For the volcanic material.
Lava Flow, N.Mex. Bed of lava.
Lava, Mount, Wyo.
Lava Beds Natl. Monument, Calif.

LAVAL, Que. (Montreal and Jesus Islands Co.). Either for a former resident, who kept a boardinghouse for railroad workers; or the Laval de Montigny, François Xavier de (1623-1708), Jesuit trained cleric and the first bishop of Québec (1658-88). He exercised great political power during his tenure and founded the Séminaire de Québec (1663), which is now Laval University.

Francois Xavier de Laval was not only the first but the most powerful and influential bishop Quebec has known. Laval University in the city of Quebec bears his name. [*New York Public Library*]

The town was created in 1965 by merging Lavel des Rapides, Laval Quest, Laval sur le Lac, plus several other towns and cities.

LAVALE, Md. (Allegany Co.). Named by a local citizen for his birthplace, a farm in Pennsylvania.

LA VERNE, Calif. (Los Angeles Co.). For a ranch, whose owner mistakenly believed that *verne* meant "green," using the name because his plot had more grass than surrounding areas. Another version is that Verne was the first name of a promoter, but no documentation exists. An earlier name was Lordsburg.

LA VISTA, Neb. (Douglas Co.). From Spanish, "the view"; promotional.

LAWNDALE, Calif. (Los Angeles Co.). Descriptive and promotional.

LAWRENCE, Abbott (1792-1855), founder of the town. He was a prominent Boston merchant who helped launch the textile industry in New England with the factory he built at this location.
Lawrence, Mass. (Essex Co.).
Lawrence Brook, Mass.-N.H.

LAWRENCE, James (1781-1813), New Jersey naval commander who fought in Tripoli (1801-05) and in the War of 1812. In command of the *Chesapeake*, he engaged the British frigate *Shannon* off Boston on June 1, 1813. Mortally wounded, he is said to have uttered the famous words, "Don't give up the ship!"
Lawrence Co., Ala. (co. seat, Moulton).
Lawrence Co., Ark. (co. seats, Bowhatan and Walnut Ridge).
Lawrence Co., Ill. (co. seat, *Lawrenceville*).
Lawrence Co., Ind. (co. seat, Bedford).
Lawrence Co., Ky. (co. seat, Louisa).
Lawrence Co., Miss. (co. seat, Monticello).
Lawrence Co., Mo. (co. seat, Mount Vernon).
Lawrence Co., Ohio (co. seat, Ironton).
Lawrence Co., Pa. (co. seat, New Castle).
Lawrence Co., Tenn. (co. seat, *Lawrenceburg*).
Lawrence, Ind. (Marion Co.).
Lawrenceburg, Ind. (co. seat of Dearborn Co.).
Lawrenceburg, Ky. (co. seat of Anderson Co.).
Lawrenceburg, Tenn. (co. seat of *Lawrence* Co.).
Lawrenceville, Ga. (co. seat of Gwinnett Co.).
Lawrenceville, Ill. (co. seat of *Lawrence* Co.).
Lawrenceville, Va. (co. seat of Brunswick Co.).

LAWRENCE, Kan. (co. seat of Douglas Co.). For Amos A. Lawrence, treasurer of the New England Emigrant Aid Society, active in the area. An earlier name was Wakarusa.

LAWRENCE Co., S.Dak. (co. seat, Deadwood). For John Lawrence, Dakota Territory legislator, road builder, and first treasurer of the county.

LAWSON HEIGHTS, Pa. (Westmoreland Co.). For Henry W. Lawson (1874-1953), whose house overlooked Latrobe, the neighboring town.

LAWTON, Okla. (co. seat of Comanche Co.). For Henry Ware Lawton (1843-1899), career soldier, awarded the Congressional Medal of Honor for distinguished gallantry as an officer of the Union army in the Civil War. He was leader of American forces in the Philippine Islands during the Spanish-American War. Fighting against the Philippine insurrectionists, he was killed in action.

LAY LAKE, Ala. For a local citizen.

LAYTON, Utah (Davis Co.). For Christopher Layton, innkeeper. He operated the Prairie House, which accommodated the stage office and provided food.

LEA Co., N.Mex. (co. seat, Lovington). For Joseph C. Lea (?-1904), "father of Roswell" and founder of the New Mexico Military Institute there.

LEAD For the mineral, mined nearby.
Lead, S.Dak. (Lawrence Co.).
Lead Mountain, Me.
Leadville, Colo. (co. seat of Lake Co.).

LEADBETTER POINT, Wash. On Pacific Coast. For Danville Leadbetter, an officer assigned to the United States Coast Survey of 1852.

LEAF Reason for name unknown, but probably translated from an Indian name or for an incident concerning leaves.

Leaf Bay, Que. Inlet on Ungava Bay.

Leaf Passage, Que. Waterway between *Leaf* R. and *Leaf* Bay.

Leaf River, Ill. Flows E into Rock R.

Leaf River, Miss. Flows SE and E to join Chickasawhay R. to form Piscagoula R.

Leaf River, Que. Flows NE into *Leaf* Passage.

LEAKE, Walter (1762-1825), legislator, jurist, U.S. senator (1817-20), and governor of Mississippi (1822-25).

Leake Co., Miss. (co. seat, Carthage).

Leakesville, Miss. (co. seat of Greene Co.).

LEAKEY, Tex. (co. seat of Real Co.). For John Leakey (1824-1900), sawmill operator and rancher who founded the city.

LEAMINGTON, Ont. (Essex Co.). Probably for Leamington (or Royal Leamington Spa), Warwick, England.

LEAVENWORTH, Henry (1783-1834), career army officer and general who fought in the War of 1812 and later against the Indians.

Fort Leavenworth, Kan. (*Leavenworth* Co.).

Leavenworth Co., Kan. (co. seat, *Leavenworth*). For the fort.

Leavenworth, Kan. (co. seat of *Leavenworth* Co.). A pro slavery town established as New Town. For advertising and land speculation purposes, the name was changed to Leavenworth to take advantage of the name of the nearby fort, which had been built (1827) to protect westward travelers on the Santa Fe Trail.

LEAWOOD, Kan. (Johnson Co.). For Oscar G. Lee, realtor and local official, with a change in spelling.

LEBANON From Semitic *laban*, "to be white," probably for the chalk cliffs of the Lebanon Mountains east of the Mediterranean Sea, although they are also snow-capped. The name in the United States usually has Biblical connotations of the "cedars of Lebanon."

Lebanon Co., Pa. (co. seat, *Lebanon*).

Lebanon, Conn. (New London Co.), town.

Lebanon, Ill. (St. Clair Co.).

Lebanon, Ind. (co. seat of Boone Co.).

Lebanon, Ky. (co. seat of Marion Co.).

Lebanon, Me. (York Co.), town.

Lebanon, Mo. (co. seat of Laciede Co.). For *Lebanon*, Tenn.

Lebanon, N.H., (Grafton Co.), town.

Lebanon, Ohio (co. seat of Warren Co.).

Lebanon, Ore. (Linn Co.).

Lebanon, Pa. (co. seat of *Lebanon* Co., Earlier, Steitztown.

Lebanon, Tenn. (co. seat of Wilson Co.).

Lebanon, Va. (co. seat of Russell Co.).

Lebanon South, Pa. (*Lebanon* Co.).

New Lebanon, N.Y. (Columbia Co.). For *Lebanon*, Conn.

New Lebanon, Ohio (Montgomery Co.).

South Lebanon, Ohio (Warren Co.).

LE CENTER, Minn. (co. seat of Le Sueur Co.). For its location at the geographical center of the county. An earlier name was Le Sueur Center; the French article was retained. See also CENTER.

LE CLAIRE, Iowa (Scott Co.). For Antoine Le Claire, Indian interpreter who owned the townsite.

LEDYARD, Conn. (New London Co.), town. For Col. William Ledyard (1738-1781), killed in the American Revolution at Fort Griswold while trying to defend the New London area against Benedict Arnold's troops. He was said to have remarked just before his death, "If today I must lose honor or life, you, who know me, can tell which it will be."

LEE Co., Iowa (co. seats, Fort Madison and Keokuk). For an official of the New York Land Company, which had extensive landholdings in the area.

LEE, Henry, called "Lighthorse Harry" (1756-1818), Virginia soldier and statesman who distinguished himself during the American Revolution at the battles of Guilford Court House (1781), Eutaw Springs (1781), and Yorktown (1781). He was a member of the Continental Congress (1785-88), governor (1792-1801). He commanded the troops that suppressed the Whiskey Rebellion (1794). It was his eulogy of Washington (1799) that characterized the late President as "first in war, first in peace, and first in the hearts of his countrymen." He was the brother of Richard Henry Lee and the father of Robert E. Lee.

Lee Co., Va. (co. seat, Jonesville).

Leesburg, Va. (co. seat of Loudoun Co.).

Confederate General Robert E. Lee was possibly the most brilliant military strategist of his era. In 1865, shortly after his surrender at Appomattox, he was photographed by Matthew Brady. [*Valentine Museum. New York Public Library*]

LEE, Mass. (Berkshire Co.), town and village. For Gen. Charles Lee (1731-1782), a soldier of fortune whose reputation as an officer in the Continental Army deteriorated after the town was named (1777). He quarreled constantly with Washington and was eventually dismissed. Documents discovered in 1858 indicated that his friendship with the English General Howe may have involved the passing of vital military information. See also FORT LEE.

LEE, Richard Henry (1732-1794), Virginia statesman and a prominent figure during the American Revolution. He was a member of the Continental Congress (1774-79; 1784-89; president 1784-85), a signer of the Declaration of Independence (1776), a leader of the opposition to the adoption of the Constitution, and U.S. senator (1789-92). He was the brother of Henry ("Lighthouse Harry") Lee and the uncle of Robert E. Lee.
Lee Co., Ga. (co. seat, *Leesburg*).

Lee Co., Ill. (co. seat, Dixon).
Leesburg, Ga. (co. seat of *Lee* Co.).

LEE, Robert Edward (1807-1870), career soldier, commander in chief of the Confederate armies during the Civil War. Lee was not only a military genius whose tactics and strategy became textbook examples for later generations, but a man whose integrity and gentlemanly qualities impressed friend and foe alike. A graduate of West Point (1829), he served in the Mexican War and led the detachment that suppressed John Brown's raid at Harpers Ferry (1859). After the Civil War, he was president of Washington College (1865-70), which after his death became Washington and Lee University.
Lee Co., Ala. (co. seat, Opelika).
Lee Co., Ark. (co. seat Marianna).
Lee Co., Fla. (co. seat, Fort Myers).
Lee Co., Ky. (co. seat, Beattyville).
Lee Co., Miss. (co. seat Tupelo).
Lee Co., N.Y. (co. seat, Sanford).
Lee Co., S.C. (co. seat, Bishopville).
Lee Co., Tex. (co. seat, Giddings).
Leesville, La. (parish seat of Vernon Parish).

LEECH LAKE, Minn. From Ojibway, "leech," because a large leech was seen in the lake. The French called the lake *La Sangsue*, "the bloodsucker."

LEEDS, Ala. (Jefferson and St. Clair Cos.). For Leeds, Yorkshire, England. The name was suggested by the importance of the iron industry in both places.

LEEDS Co., Ont. (co. seat, Brockville). For Francis Godolphin Osborne, 5th Duke of Leeds and secretary of state for the Home Department in the British Government.

LEELANAU Coined by H.R. Schoolcraft, supposedly for an Indian maid and meaning "delight of life."
Leelanau Co., Mich. (co. seat, Leland).
Leelanau Lake, Mich.

LEESVILLE LAKE, Ohio. For a village, in turn for a local citizen.

LE FLORE, Greenwood (1800-1865), leader of a prominent Choctaw family of French ancestry, landowner, and legislator. Later the family migrated to Oklahoma.

LeFlore Co., Miss. (co. seat, Greenwood).
Le Flore Co., Okla. (co. seat, Poteau).

LEHI, Utah (Utah Co.). Taken from the Book of Mormon.

LEHIGH A corruption of the Algonquian word *lechauweking*, "where there are forks." The river was named first.
Lehigh Co., Pa. (co. seat, Allentown).
Lehigh River, Pa. Flows into the Delaware R.
Lehighton, Pa. (Carbon Co.).

LEHMAN CAVES NATL. MONUMENT, Nev. Limestone caves in the Snake Range. For Abner Lehman, a rancher who discovered the caves.

LE HOMME DIEU, Lake, Minn. From French, "Man of God"; named by Glendy King, early settler and landholder, for a pious friend.

LEICESTER, Mass. (Worcester Co.), town and village. For Leicester, Leicestershire, England.

LEIDY, Joseph, a paleontologist, anatomist, and member of the Hayden survey.
Leidy Mountain, Wyo.
Leidy Peak, Utah.

LEIGH MONUMENT PEAK, Wyo. For Gilvert Leigh, an English-born ranchman who was killed on the mountain.

LEITCHFIELD, Ky. (co. seat of Grayson Co.). For David Leitch, an officer in the American Revolution.

LELAND, Mich. (co. seat of Leelanau Co.). From the nautical term *lee* (direction in which the wind blows) plus *land.*

LELAND, Miss. (Washington Co.). Either for Lela, a daughter of an early settler, or for Lee's Landing, a spot in the town where steamboats used to stop.

LELEWEI POINT, Hawaii. On east coast of Hawaii Island. From Hawaiian, "bone alter."

LE MARS, Iowa (co. seat of Plymouth Co.). From the initial letters of the surnames of the women present during a visit to the new townsite with an official of the new Iowa Falls and Sioux City railroad.

LEMEI ROCK (peak), Wash. From Chinook, meaning uncertain, possibly "rock."

LEMHI Co., Idaho (co. seat, Salmon). For a character in the Book of Mormon.

LEMMON, Mount, Ariz. in Santa Catalina Mountains. For J.G. Lemmon, a botanist who climbed the peak in 1882.

LEMON FAIR RIVER, Vt. Origin uncertain; probably folk etymologized from French, either from *les monts verts*, "the green mountains," or from *le mont*, "the mountain," plus a personal name, possibly that of an early settler. It flows north into Otter Creek.

LEMON GROVE, Calif. (San Diego Co.). Descriptive; in a citrus-growing region.

LEMONT, Ill. (Cook Co.). From French, "the mount"; descriptive.

LEMONWEIR RIVER, Wis. A *weir* is a fishing-place; thus, probably, "Lemon's fishing place." It flows southeast into Wisconsin River.

LEMOORE, Calif. (Kings Co.). For Dr. Lovern Lee Moore, founder of the Lower Kings River (irrigation) Ditch Company.

LEMOYNE, Pa. (Cumberland Co.). For a Dr. Lemoyne, a prominent local physician.

LENA, Mount, Utah. From a woman's forename.

LENAWEE Co., Mich. (co. seat, Adrian). Origin uncertain: It may have been coined by H.R. Schoolcraft. Some authorities on Indian languages derive it from Shawnee *lenawai*, "man," but this derivation is doubtful.

LENEXA, Kan. (Johnson Co.). For Lenagsee, a Shawnee Indian princess.

LENNOX AND ADDINGTON Co., Ont. (co. seat, Napanee). Originally two counties: *Lennox*, for Charles Lennox, Duke of Richmond, and *Addington*, for Henry Addington, Viscount Sidmouth. They were united in 1860 for the purpose of representation in the Legislative Assembly of Upper Canada.

LENOIR, William (1751-1839), soldier and general, a hero of the American Revolution, wounded at the Battle of Kings Mountain in 1780.
Lenoir Co., N.C. (co. seat, Kinston).
Lenoir, N.C. (co. seat of Caldwell Co.).

LENOX (or Lennox). Probably for one of several Charles Lennoxes, Dukes of Richmond.
Lennox, Calif. (Los Angeles Co.). For the original home of early settlers, *Lenox*, Mass.
Lenox, Mass. (Berkshire Co.), town.
New Lenox, Ill. (Will Co.).

LENWOOD, Calif. (San Bernardino Co.). For *Ellen Woods*, whose husband, Frank Woods, planned the town.

LEOLA, S.Dak. (co. seat of McPherson Co.). For Leola Haynes, daughter of a pioneer family.

LEOMINSTER, Mass. (Worcester Co.). For Leominster, Herefordshire, England.

LEON For a Martin de Leon.
Leon Co., Tex. (co. seat, Centerville).
Leon River, Tex.

LEON Co., Fla. (co. seat, Tallahassee). For Juan Ponce de León (1460?-1521), Spanish colonial governor, adventurer, and explorer. He discovered Florida while in search of the "fountain of youth."

LEON, Iowa (co. seat of Decatur Co.). For Leon, Mexico; probably named by soldiers returning from the Mexican War.

LEON, N.Y. (Cattaraugas Co.). For León, Spain, an ancient city near the Portuguese border.

Ironically, Ponce de Leon's quest for the Fountain of Youth ended instead in death. Wounded by hostile Indians in Florida, he died of his injuries on the island of Cuba. [*New York Public Library*]

LEONARDTOWN, Md. (co. seat of St. Mary's Co.). For Leonard Calvert (1606-1647), first colonial governor of Maryland (1634-47). He was the son of George Calvert, 1st Lord Baltimore, and brother of Cecil Calvert, 2nd Lord Baltimore.

LEONA RIVER, Tex. From Spanish, "lioness," because it is believed that one was killed on the bank of the river. It flows southeast and east into Atascosa River.

LEON PEAK, Colo. From Spanish, "lion."

LEOTI, Kan. (co. seat of Wichita Co.). Probably for Leoti Kibbe, wife of an early settler. Also claimed to be the name of a white girl captured by the Indians or from Indian, "prairie flower."

LEROUX WASH RIVER, Ariz. For Antoine Leroux, a guide. It flows southwest into Little Colorado River.

LES SAULES, Que. (Quebec Co.). From French, "the willows." An earlier name was Ste. Monique de Saules.

LESLIE Co., Ky. (co. seat, Hyden). For Preston Hopkins Leslie (1819-1907), Kentucky jurist, legislator, and governor (1871-75).

LESTER MOUNTAIN, Wyo. For Lester Faler, a pioneer.

LE SUEUR, Pierre Charles (1657-1702?), French-Canadian fur trader and explorer of the upper Mississippi River and its tributaries.
Le Sueur Co., Minn. (co. seat Le Center).
Le Sueur, Minn. (*Le Sueur* Co.).

LETCHER Co., Ky. (co. seat, Whitesburg). For Robert Perkins Letcher (1788-1861), Kentucky statesman. He was a U.S. representative (1823-35), governor (1840-44), and minister to Mexico (1849-52).

LEVELLAND, Tex. (co. seat of Hockley Co.). Descriptive; on the plain called Llana Estacado.

LEVEL PARK-OAK PARK, Mich. (Calhoun Co.). Promotional and somewhat descriptive, from two formerly separate communities.

LEVIS For François Gaston, Duke of Levis (1720-1787), French soldier who saw active service in various parts of the world. He was

sent to Canada (1756) as second in command to Montcalm, succeeded to his command (1759), defeated the British at Ste. Foy, and was commander in chief of the French forces in Canada (1759-60).
Levis Co., Que. (co. seat, Saint Romuald).
Levis, Que. (*Levis* Co.).

LEVISA FORK RIVER, Ky.-Va. A variant form of Louisa, possibly because of a misspelling. See LOUISA, Ky. It flows north-west to join Tug Fork River to form Big Sandy River.

LEVITT, William, developer and builder of model suburban communities.
Levittown, N.J. (Burlington Co.).
Levittown, N.Y. (Nassau Co.).
Levittown, Pa. (Bucks Co.).

LEVY Co., Fla. (co. seat, Bronson). For David Levy (1810-1886), West Indian-born Florida statesman and businessman. He was a U.S. senator (1845-51) and a member of the Confederate Congress (1861-65). He later changed his name to D.L. Yulee.

LEWES, Del. (Sussex Co.). For Lewes, Sussex, England.

LEWIS, Meriwether (1774-1809), explorer, governor, neighbor of Thomas Jefferson in Albemarle County, Va., and subordinate to William Clark in Wayne's campaign against the Indians in the Northwest Territory. Jefferson, as President, offered him the post of private secretary in 1801, and he spent two years at the White House before the Lewis and Clark Expedition. The expedition was planned to search for a land route to the

Levittown, Long Island, is a good example of the almost instant community. The builder, avoiding such clichés as "Fairhaven" and "Parkview," simply named it after himself. [*Photo by Flying Camera, Inc. Frederic Lewis*]

Pacific and as a journey of discovery of the far western Indians, but the purchase of the Louisiana Territory made it possible for them also to explore this territory. Lewis was territorial governor of Louisiana (1806-09). In 1809, for some reason, some of his bills to the government for his services had been repudiated. He therefore left St. Louis, intending to go by way of New Orleans and the ocean to Washington. At Chickasaw Bluffs, now Memphis, he changed his plans and went overland, accompanied by two servants. He died in an inn in central Tennessee on the night of October 11. Jefferson later assumed it was suicide. His family and the local people believed it was murder, and there was some evidence to support this belief. There was no money on the body, and his watch was later recovered in New Orleans. In 1848 the state of Tennessee erected a monument to him in the county that now bears his name. See also LEWIS AND CLARK EXPEDITION.
Lewis Co., Idaho (co. seat, Nezperce).
Lewis Co., Ky. (co. seat, Vanceburg).
Lewis Co., Mo. (co. seat, Monticello).
Lewis Co., Tenn. (co. seat, Hohenwald).
Lewis Co., Wash. (co. seat, Chehalis).
Lewis Range, Mont.
Lewiston, Idaho (co. seat of Nez Perce Co.).
Lewiston Orchards, Idaho (Nez Perce Co.). Also called Orchard.
Lewistown, Mont. (co. seat of Fergus Co.).
Meriwether Lewis Natl. Monument, Tenn.

LEWIS, Morgan (1754-1844), New York soldier and statesman who fought in both the American Revolution and the War of 1812. He was also governor of New York (1804-07).
Lewis Co., N.Y. (co. seat, Lowville).
Lewis, N.Y. (Essex Co.).
Lewiston, N.Y. (Niagara Co.).

LEWIS Co., W.Va. (co. seat, Weston). For Charles Lewis (?-1774), a soldier killed during the American Revolution.

LEWIS AND CLARK EXPEDITION (1804-06). Meriwether Lewis and William Clark were sent by President Jefferson after the acquisition of the Louisiana Territory on the "pretext of exploring," although they were actually searching for a passage through the continent of North America.

Meriwether LEWIS, Jefferson's private secretary, commanded the expedition and associated William CLARK in the leadership. They assembled in St. Louis in late 1803 and started up the Missouri River in the spring, sailing to west central North Dakota. The party consisted of twenty-six soldiers; George Drouillard and Toussaint Charbonneau, interpreters; Clark's Negro servant, York; and Sacajawea (Bird Woman), Charbonneau's wife, and her infant son. On November 7, 1805, they reached the Pacific Ocean, by the following route: they ascended the Mission and its Jefferson fork to the mountains, crossed to the Snake, then went down the Snake to the Columbia and down the Columbia to the sea. The winter was passed in a shelter named Fort Clatsop near present-day Astoria. Both the Missouri and Yellowstone rivers were descended by different groups on the return trip, and they were reunited at the junction of these rivers. The expedition ended on September 23, 1806 in St. Louis. Its results were important additions to the existing body of geographic and scientific knowledge, and it also created an enticement to trade and settlement.

Lewis and Clark Co., Mont. (co. seat, Helena).
Lewis and Clark Cavern, Mont.
Lewis and Clark Lake, Neb.-S.Dak.
Lewis and Clark Natl. Forest, Mont.
Lewis and Clark River, Ore. Formerly Netul R., as reported by Lewis and Clark.

LEWISBURG, Pa. (co. seat of Union Co.). For Lewis Derr (or Ludwig Derr, the name he preferred), landowner, mill operator, and founder. An earlier name was Derrstown.

LEWISBURG, W.Va. (co. seat of Greenbrier Co.). For Gen. Andrew Lewis 1720?-1781), early surveyor, builder of forts, and commander of the troops that defeated Chief Cornstalk at the Battle of Point Pleasant.

LEWIS CREEK, Vt. For a local settler. It flows west into Lake Champlain.

LEWIS RIVER, Wash. For A. Lee Lewis, homesteader. It flows southwest into Columbia River.

LEWISTON, Idaho. For Meriwether LEWIS.

LEWISTOWN, Ill. (co. seat of Fulton Co.). For Lewis Ross, son of the founder.

LEWISTOWN, Mont. For Meriwether LEWIS.

LEWISTOWN, Pa. (co. seat of Mifflin Co.). For William Lewis, an ironmaster.

LEWISVILLE, Ark. (co. seat of Lafayette Co.). For Lewis Battle Fort (?-1870), an early settler.

LEWISVILLE, Tex. (Denton Co.). For B.W. Lewis, an early settler.

LEXINGTON For Laxton, Nottinghamshire, England. All other names derive from that of the town in Massachusetts, where, on April 19, 1775, after Paul Revere had spread the alarm, colonial irregulars harassed British troops sent to seize American arms at Concord.
Lexington Co., S.C. (co. seat, *Lexington*).
Lexington, Ga. (co. seat of Oglethorpe Co.).

Liberty is a precious American commodity. To preserve it the Boy Scouts are even pressed into service as this World War I poster shows. [*Poster by J. C. Legendecker. New York Public Library*]

Lexington, Ky. (co. seat of Fayette Co.).
Lexington, Mass. (Middlesex Co.), town. Another possibility is that it was named for Robert Sutton, Lord Lexington (1661-1723), a soldier and diplomat.
Lexington, Miss. (co. seat of Holmes Co.).
Lexington, Mo. (co. seat of Lafayette Co.).
Lexington, Neb. (co. seat of Dawson Co.).
Lexington, N.C. (co. seat of Davidson Co.).
Lexington, Ohio (Richland Co.).
Lexington, Va. (co. seat of Rockbridge Co.).
Lexington, S.C. (co. seat of *Lexington* Co.).
Lexington, Tenn. (co. seat of Henderson Co.).
New Lexington, Ohio (co. seat of Perry Co.).

LIBBY, Mont. (co. seat of Lincoln Co.). For Libby Davis, daughter of an early settler.

LIBERAL, Kan. (co. seat of Seward Co.). So named, it is said, because L.E. Keefer, a landowner and postmaster, was liberal in his policy of allowing anyone to use water from his well at no cost in an area where water was scarce.

LIBERTY Patriotic name.
Liberty Co., Fla. (co. seat, Bristol).
Liberty Co., Ga. (co. seat, Hinesville).
Liberty Co., Mont. (co. seat, Chester).
Liberty Co., Tex. (co. seat, *Liberty*).
Liberty, Ind. (co. seat of Union Co.).
Liberty, Ky. (co. seat of Casey Co.).
Liberty, Miss. (co. seat of Amite Co.).
Liberty, Mo. (co. seat of Clay Co.).
Liberty, N.Y. (Sullivan Co.), town.
Liberty, S.C. (Pickens Co.). Named by a Christian congregation who heard during one of their meetings that peace had been declared between the United States and Great Britain in the American Revolution.
Liberty, Tex. (co. seat of *Liberty* Co.).
Liberty, Mount, N.H.

LIBERTYVILLE, Ill. (Lake Co.). Patriotic name suggested by a nearby settlement named Independence Grove. In fact, Libertyville was named Independence Grove (1836-37), until the other place was found to have priority.

LICKING For the salt licks.
Licking Co., Ohio (co. seat, Newark).
Licking Creek, Pa. Flows W into Mill Creek.
Licking River, Ky. Flows NW into Ohio R.

Patriotic posters often provide interesting combinations. The scantily clad young lady (1919 version) catches the attention while the "honor role" lists names of almost every known ethnic group. [*Poster by Howard Chandler Christy. New York Public Library*]

LIGHTHOUSE. For a lighthouse on the point.
Lighthouse Point, Fla.
Lighthouse Point, Mich.

LIGONIER, Jean-Louis, 1st Earl of (1680-1770), British soldier of Huguenot descent. He served as military counselor to George II of England, for which he was decorated as Field Knight of the Order of Bath.
Ligonier, Ind. (Nbole Co.). For *Ligonier*, Pa.
Ligonier, Pa. (Westmoreland Co.).

LIHUE, Hawaii (co. seat of Kauai Co.). From Hawaiian, "cold chill."

LILLINGTON, N.C. (co. seat of Harnett Co.). For Alexander Lillington (1725-1786), American Revolutionary patriot.

LILLINONAH, Lake, Conn. For Lillinonah, daughter of Waramaug, a chief of the New Milford Indians; she lived in the 18th century.

LIMA, Ohio (co. seat of Allen Co.). For Lima, Peru.

LIMESTONE. For places where limestone exists in quantity.
Limestone Co., Ala. (co. seat, Athens).
Limestone Co., Tex. (co. seat, Groesbeck).
Limestone, Me. (Arrostook Co.), town.
Limestone Butte, S.Dak.

LINCOLN, Abraham (1809-1865), sixteenth President of the United States (1861-65), born in Kentucky but a resident of Illinois. One of the greatest of American Presidents, Lincoln was charged with the task of preserving the Union during the Civil War, with which his administration coincided almost exactly: he took office little over a month before the fall of Fort Sumter and died five days after Lee's surrender at Appomattox. Despite political cross fire from radical abolitionists on the one hand and Southern sympathizers on the other, and hampered by the mediocre quality of his generals during the early years of the war, he persevered and eventually achieved success. His Emancipation Proclamation (1863) abolished slavery in the Confederate states and his memorable Gettysburg Address (1863) stated his belief "that government of the people, by the people, for the people shall not perish from the earth." His early career included membership in the House of Representatives (1847-49) and his famous debates with Stephen A. Douglas in his unsuccessful campaign for the Senate (1858). He was shot at Ford's Theater in Washington by John Wilkes Booth, a fanatical actor with strong Confederate sympathies, and died the following day.

Lincoln Co., Ark. (co. seat, Star City).
Lincoln Co., Colo. (co. seat, Hugo).
Lincoln Co., Idaho (co. seat, Shoshone).
Lincoln Co., Ill. (co. seat, Franklin).
Lincoln Co., Kan. (co. seat, *Lincoln*).
Lincoln Parish, La. (parish seat, Ruston).
Lincoln Co., Minn. (co. seat, Ivanhoe).
Lincoln Co., Mont. (co. seat, Libby).
Lincoln Co., Miss. (co. seat, Troy).
Lincoln Co., Neb. (co. seat, North Platte).

Lincoln Co., Nev. (co. seat, Pioche).
Lincoln Co., N.Mex. (co. seat, Carrizozo).
Lincoln Co., Okla. (co. seat, Chandler).
Lincoln Co., Ore. (co. seat, Newport).
Lincoln Co., S.Dak. (co. seat, Canton).
Lincoln Co., Wash. (co. seat, Davenport).
Lincoln Co., W.Va. (co. seat, Hamlin).
Lincoln Co., Wis. (co. seat, Merrill).
Lincoln Co., Wyo. (co. seat, Kemmerer).
Lincoln, Ill. (co. seat of Logan Co.).
Lincoln, Kan. (co. seat of Lincoln Co.).
Lincoln, Mass. (Franklin Co.).
Lincoln, Neb. (co. seat of Lancaster Co.),
   state capital.
Lincoln, N.H. (Grafton Co.), town.
Lincoln, Ohio (Richland Co.).
Lincoln, Pa. (co. seat of Franklin Co.).
Lincoln, R.I. (Providence Co.), town.
Lincoln, Vt. (Addison Co.), town.
Lincoln Creek, Neb.
Lincoln, Mount, Colo., in the Rocky Mtns.
Lincoln, Mount, N.H., in the White Mtns.
Lincoln Mountain, Vt.
Lincoln Natl. Forest, N.Mex.

Abraham Lincoln had less than a week to recover from the strain of leading the Union through its only Civil War. He was assassinated five days after Lee's surrender at Appomattox. This commemorative envelope illustrates the nation's grief for its lost leader. [New York Public Library]

Lincoln Center, Kan. (co. seat of Lincoln
   Co.).
Lincoln City, Ore. (Lincoln Co.).
Lincoln Heights, Ohio (Hamilton Co.).
Lincoln Park, Colo. (Fremont Co.).
Lincoln Park, Mich. (Wayne Co.).
Lincoln Park, N.Y. (Ulster Co.).
Lincolnshire, Ill. (Cook Co.).
Lincolnton, Mont. (Franklin Co.).
Lincoln Village, Calif. (San Joaquin Co.).
Lincolnville, Me. (Waldo Co.), town.
Lincolnville, Mo. (Franklin Co.).
Lincolnwood, Ill. (Cook Co.). Earlier, Tessville.

LINCOLN, Benjamin (1733-1810), Massachusetts soldier and statesman who commanded American forces in the South (1778-79). He was captured at Charleston (1779) and later exchanged. He was secretary of war (1781-84) under the Continental

Disagreements between presidents and the press have existed since Jefferson's time. This period cartoon shows Abraham Lincoln concocting a noxious mixture to stupify the press and the public. [New York Public Library]

Congress, commander of the troops that put down Shays's Rebellion (1787), and lieutenant governor of Massachusetts (1788).
Lincoln Co., Ga. (co. seat, *Lincolnton*).
Lincoln Co., Ky. (co. seat, Stanford).
Lincoln Co., Mo. (co. seat, Troy).
Lincoln Co., N.C. (co. seat, *Lincolnton*).
Lincoln Co., Tenn. (co. seat, Fayetteville).
Lincolnton, Ga. (co. seat of *Lincoln* Co.).
Lincolnton, N.C. (co. seat of *Lincoln* Co.).

LINCOLN, Calif. (Placer Co.). For C. Lincoln Wilson, of the California Central railroad.

LINCOLN, Enoch (1788-1829), U.S. representative (from Massachusetts, 1818-21; from Maine, 1821-26), and governor of Maine (1827-29).
Lincoln Co., Me. (co. seat, Wiscasset).
Lincoln, Me. (Penobscot Co.), town and village.

LINCOLN For Lincoln, Lincolnshire, England.
Lincoln Co., Ont. (co. seat, Saint Catharines).
Lincoln, Mass. (Middlesex Co.), town.

LINDA, Calif. (Yuba Co.). Named by John Rose for the steamer *Linda*. The name means "beautiful" in Spanish.

LINDEN Ultimately from Linden, Germany, from which many immigrants came. The name is also associated with the linden tree, which settlers often managed to bring with them, as the Blancke family did in New Jersey. Some of the names spreading westward echo eastern names.
Linden, Ala. (co. seat of Marengo Co.).
Linden, N.J. (Union Co.).
Linden, Tenn. (co. seat of Perry Co.).
Linden, Tex. (co. seat of Cass Co.).
Lindenhurst, N.Y. (Suffolk Co.). Earlier, Breslau, for the first settlers' home in Germany. The linden trees growing in the area were planted by these settlers.
Lindenwold, N.J. (Camden Co.).

LINDSAY, Calif. (Tulare Co.). For the maiden name of the wife of Captain A. J. Hutchinson, founder.

LINDSAY, Okla. (Garvin Co.). For Lewis Lindsay (1863-1930), a rancher.

LINDSBORG, Kan. (McPherson Co.). Formed from three Swedish names of early settlers, Lindgren, Lindell, and Linde, plus *-borg*, "town" or "castle."

LINN, Lewis Fields (1795-1843), physician and soldier. He was elected to the Missouri senate (1827), served as U.S. senator (1833-43), and died in office.
Linn Co., Iowa (co. seat, Cedar Rapids).
Linn Co., Kan. (co. seat, Mound City).
Linn Co., Mo. (co. seat, *Linneus*).
Linn Co., Ore. (co. seat, Albany).
Linneus, Mo. (co. seat of *Linn* Co.). A Latinized form of *Linn*.
West Linn, Ore. (Clackamas Co.).

LINNAEUS, Mount, Utah. For Carolus Linnaeus (1707-1778), Harvard botanist.

LINTON, Ind. (Greene Co.). For William C. Linton, after he had made a political speech there. An earlier name was New Jerusalem.

LINTON, N.Dak. (co. seat of Emmons Co.). For George W. Lynn (1863-1933), homesteader, lawyer, and a founder. He refused to have the town named for him, but another citizen suggested *Lin* plus *ton*.

LION PEAK, Utah. Subjectively named for its resemblance to the animal.

LIPSCOMB, Abner S. (1789-1858), Alabama legislator and jurist who later served as secretary of state for the Republic of Texas.
Lipscomb Co., Tex. (co. seat, *Lipscomb*).
Lipscomb, Tex. (co. seat of *Lipscomb* Co.).

LIPSCOMB, Ala. (Jefferson Co.). Probably for James and H. Powell Lipscomb, who were lawyers in the area.

LISBON For the capital of Portugal.
Lisbon, Conn. (New London Co.), town.
Lisbon, Me. (Androscoggin Co.), town.
Lisbon, N.Dak. (co. seat of Ransom Co.).
Lisbon, Ohio (co. seat of Columbiana Co.).
Lisbon Falls, Me. (Androscoggin Co.).

LISBURNE, Cape, Alaska. Extends into the Arctic Ocean. Named by Captain Cook in 1778, probably for the English Earl Lisburne, but the name is also spelled Lisbon.

LISLE, Ill. (Du Page Co.). For S. Lisle Smith, attorney.

LISLE, N.Y. (Broome Co.). Named for Lisle (Lille), France, the location of one of the estates of Lafayette, who is reported to have visited friends in the American town. An earlier name was Mudlick, for the deer which were attracted to a salty substance in the mud.

L'ISLET Co., Que. (co. seat, St. Jean Port Joli). For the seigniory of L'Islet St. Jean, named for a rocky island in the St. Lawrence River.

LITCHFIELD For the cathedral town of Lichfield, Staffordshire, England.
Litchfield Co., Conn. (co. seat, *Litchfield*).
Litchfield, Conn. (co. seat of *Litchfield* Co.), town.

LITCHFIELD, Ill. (Montgomery Co.). For E. B. Litchfield, a founder.

LITCHFIELD, Minn. (co. seat of Meeker Co.). For members of a family who contributed to the construction and financing of the St. Paul and Pacific railroad into the area.

LITITZ, Pa. (Lancaster Co.). For the barony of Lititz in Moravia (Czechoslovakia), where the Moravian Church was first organized. The Moravian Church, a Reformed Church, was begun in the early 1400s. Members pledged themselves to accept the Bible as the only rule of faith and practice.

LITTLE Descriptive of size, usually comparatively. Entries not found here may be found in other parts of the book. For example, for Little Tennessee River, see TENNESSEE.
Little Lake, La. Inlet on Gulf of Mexico.
Little Mountain, Wyo.
Little Peak, Wyo.
Little River, Ala. Flows into Chattooga R.
Little River, Okla. Flows SE into Red R.
Little River, Conn. Flows S into Shertucket R.
Little River, Ga. Flows E into Clark Hill Reservoir.
Little River, Ky. Flows SW and NW into Cumberland R.
Little River, Mass. Flows E into Westfield R.
Little River, N.C. Flows S into Pee Dee R.
Little River, Okla. Flows SE into Canadian R.
Little River, Tex. Flows SE and E into Brazos R.

Little River, Va. Flows W and NW into New R.
Little Belt Mountains, Mont. See BIG BELT MOUNTAINS.
Little Black River, Alaska. Flows NNW into Grass and Sucker Rivers.
Little Black River, Que.-Me. Flows SE into Big Black R.
Little Blue River, Neb. Flows SE into Big Blue R.
Little Cedar River, Mich. Flows S. into Menominee R. See also CEDAR.
Little Chazy River, N.Y. See CHAZY.
Little Colorado River, N.Mex.-Ariz. Flows NW into Colorado R. See COLORADO.
Little Dry Creek, Mont. Glows into Big Dry Creek.
Little Egg. See EGG.
Little Fork River, Minn. Flows NW into Rainy R.
Little Muddy River, Ill. Flows S into Big Muddy R.
Little Sandy River, Ky. Flows NE into Ohio R. Named for comparison in size with BIG SANDY River, Ky.-W.Va.
Little Snake River, Colo. Flows into Yampa R.
Little Valley, N.Y. (Cattaraugas Co.).

LITTLE CANADA, Minn. (Ramsey Co.). For CANADA.

LITTLE CHUTE, Wis. (Outagmie Co.). For falls known as *la petite chute*, partly translated from French.

LITTLE FALLS For falls or rapids on a nearby river or creek.
Little Falls, Minn. (co. seat of Morrison Co.). On the Mississippi R.
Little Falls, N.J. (Passaic Co.). On the Passaic R.
Little Falls, N.Y. (Herkimer Co.). On the Mohawk R.

LITTLEFIELD, Tex. (Lamb Co.). For Maj. George W. Littlefield (1842-1920), veteran of the Civil War, founder of the American National Bank of Austin, and owner of the townsite.

LITTLE KONIUJI ISLAND, Alaska. In the Shumagin Islands. From Aleut *kunuliuk*, "crested auk."

LITTLE RIVER Co., Ark. (co. seat, Ashdown). For a small river.

LITTLE ROCK From French *Petite Roche*, or *Rochelle*, "little rock," to distinguish the place from *Grande Roche*, a promontory farther upstream on the Arkansas River; named by Bernard de la Harpe, a French explorer who set up a trading post near the smaller promontory. Formerly the site of a large Indian village, it was known by earlier settlers as Arkopolis.
Little Rock, Ark. (co. seat of Pulaski Co.), state capital.
North Little Rock, Ark. (Pulaski Co.). Earlier, De Cantillion, Hunterville, and Argenta.
Southwest Little Rock, Ark. (Pulaski Co.).

LITTLE SHAWMUT, Ala. (Chambers Co.). For SHAWMUT, Ala. of which it is a suburb.

LITTLE SILVER, N.J. (Monmouth Co.). For the Portsmouth, R.I. estate of Joseph and Peter Parker (the town's first settlers), called "Silverton."

LITTLE SUGAR RIVER, N.H. For its size and for the sugar maple. It flows northwest into Connecticut River.

LITTLETON For Richard S. Little (1829-1899), civil engineer, homesteader, and town founder.
Littleton, Colo. (co. seat of Araphoe Co.).
Littleton Southeast, Colo. (Araphoe Co.).

LITTLETON Probably descriptive.
Littleton, Mass. (Middlesex Co.), town.
Littleton Common, Mass. (Middlesex Co.).

LITTLETON, N.H. (Grafton Co.), town and village. For Col. Moses Little, Massachusetts, "Surveyor of the King's Woods," and head of a group that owned the land on which the town was formed.

LITTLE VALLEY, N.Y. (co. seat of Cattaraugus Co.). Descriptive; possibly a translation of a Seneca name, *oda squawateh*, "small stone beside a large one," but the connotation is uncertain. It was also known as *Squeaugheta*.

LIVE OAK For the live oak trees, *Quercus virginiana* and *Q. chrysolepis*, indigenous to the southern and western United States, respectively.

Live Oak, Fla. (co. seat of Suwannee Co.).
Live Oak, Tex. (Bexar Co.).
Live Oak Co., Tex. (co. seat, George West).
Live Oak, Calif. (Santa Cruz Co.).

LIVERMORE, Calif. (Alameda Co.). For Robert Livermore (1799-1858), English sailor and first white settler here.

LIVERMORE, Mount, Tex. For William R. Livermore, officer in the U.S. Army and chief of engineers (1898).

LIVERMORE FALLS, Me. (Androscoggin Co.), town. For Elijah Livermore, one of the first settlers.

LIVERPOOL For Liverpool, Lancashire, England.
East Liverpool, Ohio (Columbiana Co.). Earlier Fawcetts Town, for Thomas Fawcett, founder, and Liverpool.
East Liverpool North, Ohio (Columbiana Co.).
Liverpool, N.S. (co. seat of Queens Co.). Earlier Ogumkiqueok and Port Rossignol.

LIVINGSTON, Calif. (Merced Co.). For David Livingstone, the famous explorer of Africa.

LIVINGSTON, Edward (1764-1836), New York representative (1795-1801) and mayor of New York City (1801-03). He later served on Andrew Jackson's staff at the Battle of New Orleans and served as both U.S. representative (1822-29) and senator (1829-31) from Louisiana and as secretary of state (1831-33) under Jackson.
Livingston Co., Ill. (co. seat, Pontiac).
Livingston Co., Mich. (co. seat, Howell).
Livingston Co., Mo. (co. seat, Chillicothe).
Livingston, Ala. (co. seat of Sumter Co.).
Livingston, Tenn. (co. seat of Overton Co.).
Livingston, Tex. (co. seat of Polk Co.). Either for *Livingston*, Tenn. or for *Livingston*, Ala.

LIVINGSTON, Mont. (co. seat of Park Co.). For Crawford Livingston, an official of the Northern Pacific Railroad.

LIVINGSTON, N.J. (Essex Co.). For William Livingston (1723-1790), governor of New Jersey during the American Revolution, representative of New Jersey in the first and second Continental Congresses, a signer of the Constitution, commander of New Jersey troops in 1776, and governor of the state (1776-90).

LIVINGSTON, Robert R. (1746-1813), New York patriot and statesman. He was a member of the Continental Congress (1775-77; 1779-81; 1784-85), secretary for foreign affairs (1781-83), chancellor of New York (1777-1801), and minister to France (1801-04).
Livingston Co., Ky. (co. seat, Smithland).
Livingston Parish, La. (parish seat, *Livingston*).
Livingston Co., N.Y. (co. seat, Geneseo).
Livingston, La. (parish seat of *Livingston* Parish).
Livingston, N.Y. (Columbia Co.), town.

LIVONIA, Mich. (Wayne Co.). For a Livonia in New York, which was named for Livonia, Estonia, now a province of Russia.

LIZARD. For the reptile.
Lizard Creek, Iowa. Flows SE into Des Moines R. For the lizards present at the time of naming.
Lizard Head (peak), Colo. For its shape.
Lizard Head Peak, Wyo. For its shape.

LLANO From Spanish, "plain."
Llano Co. Tex. (co. seat, *Llano*).
Llano. Tex. (co. seat of *Llano* Co.).
Llano River, Tex.
Llano Estacado, N.Mex.-Tex. From Spanish, "staked," either for yucca stalks resembling stakes or for actual stakes used to show travelers the trail.

LLOYDMINSTER, Sask. For the Rev. E. G. Lloyd, Anglican bishop of Saskatchewan, under whose leadership the town was founded (1903) by the "Barr Colonists," a group of about 200 emigrants from London, England, originally recruited by Rev. I. M. Barr.

LOA, Utah (co. seat of Wayne Co.). For Mauna Loa, second highest mountain in the Hawaiian Islands and an active volcano. The name in Hawaiian carries the connotation of "high, large, and powerful." It was suggested by Franklin W. Young, a missionary for the Church of Latter-Day Saints who had visited the Hawaiian Islands.

LOBSTER LAKE, Me. So named because it is supposed to resemble the shape of a Maine lobster.

LOCHLOOSA LAKE, Fla. From Choctaw, "black terrapin," with Scottish spelling influence.

LOCHSA RIVER, Idaho. From Nez Percé Indian, meaning uncertain, but possibly connoting "rough water." It flows southwest to join Selaway River to flow into South Branch Clearwater River.

LOCKE, N.Y. (Cayuga Co.). For John Locke, an early settler.

LOCKHART, Tex. (co. seat of Caldwell Co.). For Byrd Lockhart, surveyor of the first roads from Gonzales to nearby towns. He also served as an officer in the Texas army. The land on which the town was built was given to Lockhart by the Mexican government for his services.

LOCK HAVEN, Pa. (co. seat of Clinton Co.). For the locks on the Pennsylvania Canal and the harbor, or "haven."

LOCKLAND, Ohio (Hamilton Co.). Descriptive of a "landlocked" city.

LOCKPORT For locks on a canal.
Lockport, Ill. (Will Co.). On the Illinois and Michigan Canal.
Lockport, N.Y. (co. seat of Niagara Co.). On the Erie Canal (part of the New York State Barge Canal System).

LOCUST For the tree.
Locust Creek, Iowa-Mo. Flows S into Grand R.
Locust Fork River, Ala. Joins Mulberry Fork R. to form Black Warrior R.
Locust Grove, N.Y. (Nassau Co.).

LODGEPOLE CREEK, Wyo.-Neb.-Colo. For the tepee poles left on the banks of the stream when Indians fled. It flows east and southeast into South Platte River.

LODI For the Bridge of Lodi, in northern Italy, site of Napoleon's victory over the Austrians in 1796.
Lodi, Calif. (San Joaquin Co.).
Lodi, N.J. (Bergen Co.).

LOGAN Co., Ark. (co. seats, Booneville and Paris). For James Logan, an early settler.

LOGAN, Benjamin (c. 1743-1802), Virginia soldier, patriot, and Indian fighter, associated with Kentucky. He was active in the West during the American Revolution.
Logan Co., Ky. (co. seat, Russellville).
Logan Co., Ohio (co. seat, Bellefontaine).
Logan, Iowa (co. seat of Harrison Co.).
Logan, Ohio (co. seat of Hocking Co.).

LOGAN Co., III. (co. seat, Lincoln). For John Logan, father of John Alexander LOGAN.

LOGAN, John (1725-1780), Cayuga Indian chief who figures in the battle of Point Pleasant (1774). Chief Logan was tutored by James Logan, William Penn's secretary and later a representative and chief justice of the Pennsylvania colony.
Logan Co., W.Va. (co. seat, *Logan*).
Logan, W.Va. (co. seat of *Logan* Co.).

LOGAN, John Alexander (1826-1886), Illinois legislator, U.S. representative (1859-61; 1867-71) and senator (1871-77; 1879-85; 1885-86), Union general during the Civil War, and candidate on the Republican ticket for vice-president (1884).
Logan Co., Colo. (co. seat, Sterling).
Logan Co., Kan. (co. seat, Oakley).
Logan Co., Neb. (co. seat, Stapleton).
Logan Co., N.Dak. (co. seat, Napoleon).
Logan Co., Okla. (co. seat, Guthrie).

LOGAN, Mount, Wash. From a personal name, but for whom is uncertain; may have been named for John Alexander LOGAN.

LOGAN, Utah (co. seat of Cache Co.). For a river, in turn probably named for a trapper who was smothered in a landslide when a fur cache collapsed. Another story is that it was named for an ox.

LOGAN MARTIN LAKE, Ala. For a local settler.

LOGANSPORT, Ind. (co. seat of Cass Co.). For Capt. John Logan (1786-1812), whose Shawnee Indian name was Spemica Lawba. His mother was the sister of Tecumseh. His English name was taken from that of Gen. Benjamin LOGAN, in whose household he lived and whom he followed as a young officer in the American forces. He was killed in action during the War of 1812 and is buried at Defiance, Ohio.

LOLA, Mount, Calif. For Lola Montez, actress who entertained miners in the 1850s. She had already achieved fame by precipitating the 1848 revolution in Munich, from which she escaped to the United States and a career in the West.

LOLO Origin in dispute; possibly from an Indian pronunciation of a name such as Lawrence or Lewis, both names of trappers and explorers in Western areas; or from Nez Percé, "muddy water," which does not seem applicable; or from Chinook, "carrying" or "backpacking."
Lolo, Mont. (Missoula Co.), town.
Lolo Natl. Forest, Mont.
Lolo Pass, Idaho-Mont.

LOMA LINDA, Calif. (San Bernardino Co.). From Spanish, "pretty hill."

LOMBARD, III. (Du Page Co.). For Josiah L. Lombard, landowner.

LOMITA, Calif. (Los Angeles Co.). From Spanish, diminutive of *loma*, "hill."

LOMPOC For a valley and ranch, from a Chumash Indian word of uncertain meaning, but which has been interpreted as "where the waters break through."
Lompoc, Calif. (Santa Barbara Co.).
Lompoc North, Calif. (Santa Barbara Co.).
Lompoc Northwest, Calif. (Santa Barbara Co.).

LONDON For London, principal city of England and capital of the United Kingdom.
London, Ky. (co. seat of Laurel Co.). Named after a heated polemic in which Scots and Irishmen proposed Edinburgh and Dublin.
London, Ohio (co. seat of Madison Co.).
London, Ont. (co. seat of Middlesex Co.).
Londontowne, Md. (Anne Arundel Co.).
New London Co., Conn. (co. seat, Norwich).
New London, Conn. (*New London* Co.).
New London, Mo. (co. seat of Raills Co.).
New London, Wis. (Outagamie and Waupaca Cos.). For *New London*, Conn.

LONDONDERRY, N.H. (Rockingham Co.), town. For the county or city of Londonderry (also called Derry), Ireland. See also DERRY.

LONE Descriptive.
Lone Peak, Nev.
Lone Oak, Ky. (McCracken Co.).

LONG Descriptive.
Long Island, Me. in Atlantic Ocean.
Long Island, N.H. in L. Winnipesaukee.
Long Island, N.Y. Surrounded by *Long Island* Sound on N, Atlantic Ocean on S, East R. on W. and the Narrows (strait) on E.
Long Island, Wis. in L. Superior.
Long Lake, Me.
Long Lake, Mich.
Long Lake, N.Dak.
Long Lake, N.Y.
Long Lake, Wis.
Long Mountain, N.H.
Long Pond, Mass.
Long Pond, Me.
Long Branch, Ont. (York Co.). For the famous *Long* Island resort.
Long Island Sound, N.Y. Between *Long* Island, N.Y., and the state of R.I.

LONG Co., Ga. (co. seat, Ludowici). For Crawford Williamson Long (1815-1868), prominent Georgia surgeon.

LONG, Stephen H. (1784-1864), leader of an expedition into the area in 1820.
Longmont, Colo. (Boulder Co.). For the peak.
Longs Peak, Colo. Highest peak in Rocky Mtn. Natl. Park.

LONG BEACH Descriptive.
Long Beach, Calif. (Los Angeles Co.). On the Pacific coast.
Long Beach, Inc. (La Porte Co.). On L. Michigan.
Long Beach, Miss. (Harrison Co.). On Mississippi Sound.
Long Beach, N.J. An island reef, between Little Egg Harbor and the Atlantic Ocean.
Long Beach, N.Y. (Nassau Co.). On the Atlantic shore of Long Island.
Long Beach, N.J. An island reef, between Little Egg Harbor and the Atlantic Ocean.

LONG BRANCH For the longest branch of the Shrewsbury River, which runs through the town.
Long Branch, N.J. (Monmouth Co.).
West Long Branch, N.J. (Monmouth Co.).

LONGMEADOW Descriptive.
East Longmeadow, Mass. (Hampden Co.), town.
Longmeadow, Mass. (Hampden Co.), town.

LONG PRAIRIE For the surrounding flat land, or prairie.
Long Prairie, Minn. (co. seat of Todd Co.).
Long Prairie River, Minn. Flows generally NW to the Crow Wing R.

LONGUEUIL, Que. (co. seat of Chambly Co.). For Charles Le Moyne, founder, seignior of Longueuil and Châteauguay.

LONGVIEW Descriptive and promotional.
Longview, N.C. (Catawba Co.).
Longview, Tex. (co. seat of Gregg Co.).

LONGWOOD, Fla. (Seminole Co.). Promotional.

LONOKE Variant spelling of *lone oak*.
Lonoke Co., Ark. (co. seat, *Lonoke*).
Lonoke, Ark. (co. seat of *Lonoke* Co.).

LOOGOOTEE, Ind. (Martin Co.). From a combination of Lowe, a railroad man, and Gootee, owner of the townsite.

LOOKING GLASS RIVER, Mich. Descriptive of the reflecting qualities of the water; may have been translated from an Indian name. It flows west into Grand River.

LOOKOUT For its observational function or superb view.
Lookout, Cape, N.C. For the lighthouse.
Lookout Mountain, Alaska. In Alaska Range.
Lookout Mountain, N.Mex.
Lookout Mountain, N.Dak.
Lookout Mountain, Ore.
Lookout Pass, Idaho-Mont. In Bitterroot Range.
Lookout Peak, Utah.
Lookout Point, Mich. Extends in Saginaw Bay.

LOON For the water fowl.
Loon Lake, Me.
Loon Lake Mountains (peak), N.Y.

LORAIN For the province of Lorraine in France.
Lorain Co., Ohio (co. seat, Elyria).
Lorain, Ohio (*Lorain* Co.). Supposedly named by a man who had traveled in France. An earlier name was Charleston.

LORDSBURG, N.Mex. (co. seat of Hidalgo Co.). For Delbert Lord, a railroad engineer.

L'ORIGNAL, Ont. (co. seat of Prescott and Russell Cos.). For Pointe a l'Orignal, a nearby river crossing for deer. *Orignal* means "elk" in Canada and "moose" elsewhere.

LORRETTEVILLE, Que. (co. seat of Quebec Co.). For the village of Loretto, Italy.

LOS ALAMITOS, Calif. (Orange Co.). From Spanish, "little poplars (or cottonwoods)"; descriptive.

LOS ALAMOS From Spanish, "poplars" or "cottonwoods."
Los Alamos Co., N.Mex. (co. seat, *Los Alamos*).
Los Alamos, N.Mex. (co. seat of *Los Alamos* Co.).

LOS ALTOS From Spanish, "the heights"; descriptive.
Los Altos, Calif. (Santa Clara Co.).
Los Altos Hills, Calif. (Santa Clara Co.).

LOS ANGELES For the *porciuncula* ("little portion") of land in Assisi given to Saint Francis of Assisi by Our Lady of the Angels, upon which is built the mother church of the Franciscan order. The river and valley were named by the Franciscan monk Father Juan Crespi, who accompanied the Gaspar de Portola expedition, on August 2, 1769, the day of the feast of Porciuncula. When a town was founded, it was named *El Pueblo de la Reina de los Angeles de la Porciuncula* and later shortened.
East Los Angeles, Calif. (*Los Angeles* Co.).
Los Angeles Co., Calif. (co. seat, *Los Angeles*).
Los Angeles, Calif. (co. seat of *Los Angeles* Co.).

LOS BANOS, Calif. (Merced Co.). From Spanish, "the baths."

LOS GATOS, Calif. (Santa Clara Co.). From Spanish, "cats" or "wildcats."

LOS LUNAS, N.Mex. (Valencia Co.). For the Luna family, important in the early history of New Mexico.

LOS PADRES NATL. FOREST, Calif. From Spanish, "the fathers," for the Franciscan fathers who founded missions in the area.

LOS PINOS RIVER, Colo.-N.Mex. From Spanish, "the pines." It flows south into San Juan River.

LOST Descriptive of features which were probably discovered, then "lost," then rediscovered.
Lost Lake, Minn.
Lost River, W.Va. So named because it disappears underground and reappears as Cacapon R.
Lost Land Lake, Wis. Exact reason for naming unknown.
Lost Trail Pass. Mont.-Idaho.

LOST CHANCE CREEK, Utah. Reason for naming unknown, but probably derogatory for missed possibilities. It flows southeast and east to join Muddy Creek to form Dirty Devil Creek.

LOTBINIERE Co., Que. (co. seat, Ste. Croix). For the seigniory granted by Intendant Talon to Louis Theandre Chantier de Lotbiniere.

LOTTS CREEK, Ga. Probably for an early settler. It flows southeast into Canoochee River.

LOUDON, John Campbell, 4th Earl of (1705-1782), British soldier and commander in chief of British forces during the early years of the French and Indian Wars. After a notable lack of success he was recalled in 1757. See also FORT LOUDON.
Loudon Co., Tenn. (co. seat, *Loudon*). Earlier, Christiana.
Loudon Co., Va. (co. seat, Leesburg).
Loudon, Tenn. (co. seat of *Loudon* Co.).

LOUDONVILLE, Ohio (Ashland Co.). Named by James Loudon Priest, a farmer, for his mother, Nancy Loudon.

LOUIS XVI (1754-1793), king of France (1774-92), the ruling monarch while Benjamin Franklin was a representative to France. Several places in the United States were named for him in recognition of his aid to the American Revolution.
Louisburg, N.C. (co. seat of Franklin Co.).
Louisville, Ga. (co. seat of Jefferson Co.).
Louisville, Ky. (co. seat of Jefferson Co.). Though it is believed by some to have been named for Louis XIV, the fact that Louis XVI was king at the time of settlement seems to make that belief infeasible.

LOUISA, Ky. (co. seat of Lawrence Co.). The origin is unresolved: several young women by the name of Louisa lived in the area, but the dates of their lives do not correspond to the date of the founding of the village. It is possible that it was named for Louisa County, Va. Another version states that it was named for the Levisa River, on which it is located, in turn perhaps from French *le visse*, "picture" or "design," or *la visse*, "direction."

LOUISA, queen of Denmark (1724-1751), youngest daughter of George II of England. She married Frederick V of Denmark.

Louisa Co., Iowa (co. seat, Wapello). For *Louisa* Co., Va. A local romantic legend is that the Iowa county was named for a Louisa Massey (or Marcy or Masey), who avenged the death of her brother by killing his murderer.

Louisa Co., Va. (co. seat, *Louisa*).

Louisa, Va. (co. seat of *Louisa* Co.).

LOUISIANA Named (1682) for Louis XIV (1638-1715), king of France (1643-1715), by the French explorer Robert Cavelier, Sieur de La Salle (1643-1687), who, having explored from the Great Lakes to the mouth of the Mississippi River, claimed the great river, its tributaries, and all the lands they drained for France. All lands east of the Mississippi were ceded to Great Britain at the close of the French and Indian Wars. Thomas Jefferson purchased Louisiana from Napoleon in 1803. This vast area, encompassing all or part of the thirteen future states, extended as far west as Wyoming.

Louisiana, State of. 18th State of the Union. Settled: 1699. Territory: 1803. Admitted: 1812. Cap.: Baton Rouge. Motto: *Union, Justice, and Confidence*. Nickname: Pelican State. Flower: Magnolia. Bird: Eastern Brown Pelican. Tree: Bald Cypress. Song: "Give Me Louisiana."

When the French were driven from Acadia (Nova Scotia) by their new British masters, many of these "Cajuns" journeyed down the Mississippi to Louisiana where they established their parishes along its many bayous. [*Photo by George Baker, 1886. Library of Congress*]

LOUISVILLE, Ill. (co. seat of Clay Co.). For the Lewis family, early settlers.

LOUISVILLE, Miss. (co. seat of Winston Co.). For Louis Winston, a distinguished Mississippi citizen. See also WINSTON Co.

LOUISVILLE, Ohio (Stark Co.). Originally Lewisville, for Lewis, son of Henry Lautzenheiser, early settler and landowner. The name was changed because another town in Ohio had prior claim.

LOUISVILLE, Que. (co. seat of Maskinonge Co.). For Princess Louise, wife of the Marquis of Lorne.

LOUP From French *loup*, "wolf," a translation from Pawnee *skidi*, "Wolf," for the tribe. The valley was named first, since the Wolf tribe lived there.
Loup Co., Neb. (co. seat, Taylor).
Loup River, Neb.
Loup Valley, Neb.
Loup City, Neb. (co. seat of Sherman Co.).
Middle Loup River, Neb.
North Loup River, Neb.

LOVE Co., Okla. (co. seat, Marietta). For a prominent Chickasaw family.

LOVELAND, Colo. (Larimer Co.). For W. A. H. Loveland, president of the Colorado Central Railroad.

LOVELAND, Ohio (Hamilton Co.). For James Loveland, first store owner.

LOVELOCK, Nev. (co. seat of Pershing Co.). For George Lovelock, an early settler and landowner.

LOVES PARK, Ill. (Winnebago Co.). For Malcolm Love, landowner.

LOVEWELL MOUNTAIN, N.H. For Capt. John Lovewell, hero in a battle with Indians.

LOVEWELL RESERVOIR, Kan. On White Rock Creek. For a town, in turn for Thomas Lovewell, landowner.

LOVING Co., Tex. (co. seat, Mentone). For Oliver Loving, a rancher.

LOVINGSTON, Va. (co. seat of Nelson Co.). For an early family of pioneers and landowners.

LOVINGTON, N.Mex. (co. seat of Lea Co.). For R. Florence Love, an early settler who served as state legislator.

LOWELL, Francis Cabot (1775-1817), cotton manufacturer. He had formed the Boston Manufacturing Company at Waltham, Mass., and was planning to build a cotton mill at Lowell at the time of his death. His associates carried out his plans, and Lowell became a principal cotton center.
Lowell, Ind. (Lake Co.). For *Lowell*, Mass.
Lowell, Mass. (Middlesex Co.).
Lowell, Mich. (Kent Co.). For *Lowell*, Mass.
Lowell, N.C. (Gaston Co.). Named by Neal Dumont for his hometown, *Lowell*, Mass. Dumont laid out much of the town, and there was much hope that Lowell, N.C. would develop as a manufacturing center like Lowell, Mass.

LOWNDES, William Jones (1782-1822), South Carolina Legislator and U.S. representative (1811-22).
Lowndes Co., Ala. (co. seat, Hayneville).
Lowndes Co., Ga. (co. seat, Valdosta).
Lowndes Co., Miss. (co. seat, Columbus).

LOWVILLE, N.Y. (co. seat of Lewis Co.). For Nicholas Low (1739-1826), a land proprietor.

LOYALHANNA CREEK, Pa. Folk etymologized from Algonquian, "middle river." It flows northwest to join Conemaugh River to form Kiskiminetas River.

LOYALSOCK CREEK, Pa. From Algonquian, "middle mouth." It flows southwest to Susquehanna River.

LUBBOCK, Thomas S., Texas settler, active in organizing the Texas Rangers and a signer of the Texas Declaration of Independence.
Lubbock Co., Tex. (co. seat. *Lubbock*).
Lubbock, Tex. (co. seat of *Lubbock* Co.).

LUCE Co., Mich. (co. seat, Newberry). For Cyrus Gray Luce (1824-1905), Michigan legislator and governor (1887-96).

LUCEDALE, Miss. (George Co.). For Greg Luce, a sawmill owner and lumber manufacturer who founded the town.

LUCERNE, Lake, Wis. For the Lake in Switzerland.

LUDINGTON, Mich. (co. seat of Mason Co.). For James Ludington, a timber investor and landowner.

LUDLAM BAY. N.J. For an early settler. Inlet on Atlantic Ocean.

LUDLOW, Ky. (Kenton Co.). For Israel Ludlow, a prominent pioneer.

LUDLOW, Mass. (Hampden Co.), town. Probably for Ludlow, Shropshire, England.

LUFKIN, Tex. (co. seat of Angelina Co.). For E.P. Lufkin, a surveyor, son-in-law of an official of the Houston, East and West Texas railroad. The road was originally planned to go through Homer, but town officials put some of the railroad workers in jail because they were drunk. Lufkin, the surveyor, said that the railroad would not go through a place where his men were put in jail. He rerouted it through Lufkin and the town flourished, while Homer died.

LULING, La. (St. Charles Parish). For T.A. Luling, a local plantation owner.

LULING, Tex. (Caldwell Co.). For Mrs. J.H. Luling Pierce, the wife of a former railroad president. It has also been said to be named for a Chinese railroad gang cook, Loo Ling, but this has not been substantiated.

LUMBER The name seems to be the result of folk-etymologizing an Indian word, but the meaning is unknown.
Lumber River, N.C. Sometimes called Lumbee River. Flows generally SE to the Little Pee Dee R.
Lumberton, N.C. (co. seat of Robeson Co.). For the river.

LUMPKIN, Wilson (1783-1870). Georgia legislator, U.S. representative (1815-17; 1827-31), U.S. senator (1837-41), and governor (1831-35).
Lumpkin Co., Ga. (co. seat, Dahlonega).
Lumpkin, Ga. (co. seat of Stewart Co.).

LUNA Co., N.Mex. (co. seat, Deming). For the descendants of Diego de Luna, specifically for Don Salomon Luna, leader of the Republican party in the state.

LUNENBURG For Lüneburg, a city and duchy in Germany. Duke of Lüneburg was one of the titles of the British house of Hanover.

Lunenburg Co., N.S. (co. town, *Lunenburg*).
Lunenburg Co., Va. (co. seat, *Lunenburg*).
Lunenburg, Mass. (Worcester Co.), town. From one of the titles of George I of England, who was Elector of Brunswick-Luneburg in the province of Hanover, Prussia.
Lunenburg, N.S. (co. town of *Lunenburg* Co.).
Lunenburg, Va. (co. seat of *Lunenburg* Co.).

LURAY, Va. (co. seat of Page Co.). Origin uncertain, but may be a form of *Lewis Ray*, or a form of *Lorraine*, or from Luray, France, and possibly others.

LUTHERVILLE, Md. (Baltimore Co.). For Martin Luther (1483-1546), leader of the German Reformation. He became an Augustinian friar in 1505, and after his ordination as a priest earned a doctorate in theology, later becoming a professor at the university of Wittenberg. Luther found the then current practices of the Catholic Church to be in conflict with the Gospel and openly criticized the Church in his writings. Upon his calling for reform, he was excommunicated in 1521. His teachings, however, spread throughout Germany and neighboring countries, sometimes resulting in the formation of churches separated from the Pope. The Lutheran Church is named for him.

LUVERNE, Ala. (co. seat of Crenshaw Co.). For Luverne Legrand, wife of a land-company owner.

LUVERNE, Minn. (co. seat of Rock Co.). For Eva Luverne Hawes, daughter of the first settler.

LUZERNE, Anne Cesar, Chevalier de la (1741-1791), French diplomat. He was minister to the United States (1779-84) and a party to the negotiations that terminated the American Revolution.
Luzerne Co., Pa. (co. seat, Wilkes-Barre).
Luzerne, Pa. (*Luzerne* Co.). Earlier, Hartseph.

LYCOMING From Delaware Indian, "sandy or gravel-bed creek."
Lycoming Co., Pa. (co. seat, Williamsport).
Lycoming Creek, Pa.

LYMAN Co., S.Dak. (co. seat, Kennebec). For W. P. Lyman, first settler in Yankton County and a member of the territorial legislature.

LYMAN LAKE, Wis. For a local settler.

LYNN For Lyme Regis, Dorsetshire, England.
East Lyme, Conn. (New London Co.), town.
Old Lyme, Conn. (New London Co.), town.

LYNCHBURG, Tenn. (co. seat of Moore Co.). So named by Thomas Roundtree for the "famous beech tree" that was used for lynching early offenders.

LYNCHES RIVER, N.C.-S.C. For the Lynch family. It flows southeast into Pee Dee River.

LYNDHURST, N.J. (Bergen Co.). For John Singleton Copley, Lord Lyndhurst (1772-1863), lord chancellor of England from 1827.

LYNDON, Josias (1704-1778), governor of Rhode Island, known for his defense of colonial interests against the encroachments of British sovereignty.
Lyndon, Kan. (co. seat of Osage Co.). For *Lyndon*, Vt., former home of one of the founders.
Lyndon, Vt. (Caledonia Co.), town.

LYNN For Lynn Regis, or King's Lynn, Norfolk, England, where the Reverend Samuel Whiting, first minister of Lynn, had been curate.
Lynn, Mass. (Essex Co.).

Lynnfield, Mass. (Essex Co.), town.

LYNN Co., Tex. (co. seat, Tahoka). For a soldier killed at the Alamo (1836),

LYNWOOD, Calif. (Los Angeles Co.). For Lynn Wood Sessions, wife of a dairy owner.

LYON Co., Ky. (co. seat, Eddyville). For Chittenden Lyon (1787-1842). Kentucky legislator and U.S. representative.

LYON, Nathaniel (1818-1861), Union commander in the Civil War and a veteran of the Seminole and Mexican Wars, whose vigorous military campaigns helped preserve Missouri for the Union at a time when it seemed likely to join the Confederacy. He was killed at the Battle of Wilson's Creek, Mo.
Lyon Co., Iowa (co. seat, Rock Rapids).
Lyon Co., Kan. (co. seat, Emporia).
Lyon Co., Minn. (co. seat, Marshall).
Lyon Co., Nev. (co. seat, Yerington). Also said to have been named for Robert Lyon, an officer in a pioneer army.

LYON MOUNTAIN, N.Y. For a local settler.

LYONS Anglicized name of the French city Lyon. Industrial center and third largest city in France.
Lyons, Ga. (co. seat of Toombs Co.).
Lyons, N.Y. (co. seat of Wayne Co.).

LYONS, Ill. (Cook Co.). For a local community member.

LYONS, Kan. (co. seat of Rice Co.). For Truman J. Lyons.

MAALAEA BAY, Hawaii. On west coast of Maui Island. Of Hawaiian origin, meaning unknown, although it has been translated as "beginning of ocherous earth."

MACATAWA, Lake, Mich. From Ottawa, "black," for the dark color of the water.

MACCLENNY, Fla. (co. seat of Baker Co.). For H. C. Macclenny, founder.

MACEDONIA, Ohio (Summit Co.). For the ancient country in southeastern Europe.

MACHIAS From Algonquian, "bad little falls."
Big Machias Lake, Me.
Machias, Me. (co. seat of Washington Co.).
Machias, N.Y. (Cattaraugus Co.). For *Machias*, Me.
Machias Bay, Me.
Miachias Falls, Me.
Machias Lakes, Me.
Machias River, Me. (Aroostook Co.).
Machias River, Me. (Washington Co.).

MACHIPONGO, Va. (Northampton Co.). For the Machapunga tribe, of Algonquian linguistic stock. The name is believed to mean "bad dust."

MACKINAC From Ojibway *Michilimackinak*, "island of the large turtle"; also simplified in English to MACKINAW.

Machinac Co., Mich. (co. seat, St. Ignace).
Mackinac Island, Mich.
Mackinac, Straits of, Mich.

MACINTYRE, Mount, N.Y. Possibly for a speculator in iron.

MACKENZIE, Sir Alexander (1755-1820), fur trader and explorer. He was the first white man to cross Canada overland to the Pacific (1793). He discovered and explored the river in 1789.
Mackenzie Bay, N.W.T.-Yukon. Inlet on Beaufort Sea.
Mackenzie River, N.W.T. Flows NNW into *Mackenzie* Bay.

MACKENZIE, Hon. Alexander (1822-1892), a Scottish-born Ontario statesman. He was prime minister of Canada (1873-78).
Mackenzie, Ont.
Mackenzie Mountain, Ont.

MACKINAW Variant form of MACKINAC.
Mackinaw, Ill. (Tazewell Co.).
Mackinaw River, Ill. Flows W and SW into Illinois R.
Mackinaw City, Mich. (Cheboygan and Emmet Cos.).

MACOMB, Gen. Alexander (1782-1841), commander of the North Country area during the War of 1812 and later commander in chief of the army.

Macomb Co., Mich. (co. seat, Mount Clemens).
Macomb, Ill. (co. seat of McDonough Co.).

MACON, Nathaniel (1757-1837), politician and American Revolutionary patriot. He served as U.S. representative (1791-1815) and senator (1815-28) from North Carolina.
Macon Co., Ala. (co. seat, Tuskegee).
Macon Co., Ga. (co. seat, Oglethorpe).
Macon Co., Ill. (co. seat, Decatur).
Macon Co., Mo. (co. seat, *Macon*).
Macon Co., N.C. (co. seat, Franklin).
Macon Co., Tenn. (co. seat, Lafayette).
Macon Ga. (co. seat of Bibb Co.).
Macon, Miss. (co. seat of Noxubee Co.).
Macon, Mo. (co. seat of *Macon* Co.).

MACOUPIN From Algonquian, "potato."
Macoupin Co., Ill. (co. seat, Carlinville).
Macoupin Creek, Ill.

MAD Probably for an incident causing anger or for the turbulence of the water flow.
Mad River, Calif. Flows NW into Pacific Ocean.
Mad River, Conn. Flows S and W into Nagatuck R.
Mad River, N.H. Flows SW into Pemigewasset R.
Mad River, Ohio. Flows S and SW into Great Miami R.

MADAGASCAL POND, Me. From Abnaki, "meadows at the mouth (of a stream)." The name may also be related to *Madagascar*, from Abnaki, "bad meat," influenced in spelling by the island off the African coast.

MADAWASKA From an Indian word meaning "having its outlet among the reeds." The town is located at the mouth of a river of the same name.
Little Madawaska River, Me.
Madawaska, Me. (Aroostook Co.), town and village.
Madawaska Lake, Me.

MADAWASKA Co., N.B. (co. town, Edmundston). From the Indian word *madaoueska*, "land of porcupines."

MADEIRA, Ohio (Hamilton Co.). For John Madeira, an early treasurer of the Marietta and Cincinnati railroad.

MADELINE ISLAND, Wis. In the Apostle Islands. For the Indian wife of a fur trader.

MADERA From Spanish, "lumber," because the town was centered in a lumbering area.
Madera Co., Calif. (co. seat, *Madera*).
Madera, Calif. (co. seat, of *Madera* Co.).

MADILL, Okla. (co. seat of Marshall Co.). For George A. Madill, an official of the Frisco railroad.

MADISON, James (1751-1836), fourth President of the United States (1809-17), from Virginia. He was a principal figure in the framing of the Constitution and, with Alexander Hamilton and John Jay, author of *The Federalist* (1787-88), a series of essays defending and commenting on the Constitution. He was U.S. representative (1789-97), secretary of state (1801-09) under Jefferson, and rector of the University of Virginia (1826-36). His wife, Dolly (or Dolley) Madison, won renown as a Washington hostess. See also FORT MADISON
Madison Co., Ala. (co. seat, Huntsville).
Madison Co., Ark. (co. seat, Huntsville).
Madison Co., Fla. (co. seat, *Madison*).
Madison Co., Ga. (co. seat, Danielsville).
Madison Co., Idaho (co. seat, Rexburg).
Madison Co., Ill. (co. seat, Edwardsville).
Madison Co., Ind. (co. seat, Anderson).
Madison Co., Iowa (co. seat, Winterset).
Madison Co., Ky. (co. seat, Richmond).
Madison Parish, La. (parish seat, Tallulah).
Madison Co., Miss. (co. seat, Canton).
Madison Co., Mo. (co. seat, Fredericktown).
Madison Co., Mont. (co. seat, Virginia City).
Madison Co., Neb. (co. seat, *Madison*).
Madison Co., N.Y. (co. seat, Wampsville).
Madison Co., N.C. (co. seat, Marshall).
Madison Co., Ohio (co. seat, London).
Madison Co., Tenn. (co. seat, Jackson).
Madison Co., Tex. (co. seat, *Madisonville*).
Madison Co., Va. (co. seat, *Madison*).
Madison, Ala. (*Madison* Co.).

James Madison was one of eight Virginians to be elected to the presidency. In addition to his other accomplishments, he and his famous wife, Dolly, were noted for their lavish entertaining [*New York Public Library*]

Madison, Conn. (New Haven Co.).
Madison, Fla. (co. seat of *Madison* Co.).
Madison, Ga. (co. seat of Morgan Co.).
Madison, Ill. (*Madison* Co.).
Madison, Ind. (co. seat of Jefferson Co.).
Madison, Me. (Somerset Co.), town and village.
Madison, Minn. (co. seat of Lac Qui Parle Co.). For *Madison*, Wis.
Madison, Neb. (co. seat of *Madison* Co.).
Madison, N.J. (Morris Co.).
Madison, S.Dak. (co. seat of Lake Co.). For *Madison*, Wis.
Madison, Va. (co. seat of *Madison* Co.).
Madison, W.Va. (co. seat of Boone Co.). Also said, with justification, to be named for Madison Peyton, coal mine owner and developer, for whom Peytona was also named.
Madison, Wis. (co. seat of Dane Co.), state capital.
Madison, Mount, N.H. In Presidential Range.

Madison River, Mont. Flows NW and N to join Gallatin and Jefferson rivers to form Missouri R.
Madison Range, Mont. Named by Lewis and Clark.
Madison Heights, Mich. (Oakland Co.).
Madisonville, Ky. (co. seat of Hopkins Co.).
Madisonville, Tenn. (co. seat of Monroe Co.). Or for James Madison Grunway, a state legislator from Monroe Co.
Madisonville, Tex. (co. seat of *Madison* Co.).

MADRAS, Ore. (co. seat of Jefferson Co.). An accidental name, suggested by the imprint on a bolt of cloth made in Madras, India.

MADRID From Spanish, "small wood," but place names in the United States are derived from that of the capital of Spain.
Madrid, N.Y. (St. Lawrence Co.), town.
New Madrid Co., Mo. (co. seat, *New Madrid*).
New Madrid, Mo. (co. seat of *New Madrid* Co.).

MAD RIVER, Vt. Folk etymologized form of *madi*, from Abnaki *madi tegon*, "bad river." It flows generally northeast into Winooski River.

MAGAZINE MOUNTAIN, Ark. Probably from French, "storehouse."

MAGEE, Miss. (Simpson Co.). For the Magee family, early settlers.

MAGNA, Utah (Salt Lake Co.). For the Magna Smelters.

MAGNOLIA For the tree, genus *Magnolia*, which grows especially in the southern part of the United States.
Magnolia, Ark. (co. seat of Columbia Co.).
Magnolia, Miss. (co. seat of Pike Co.).
Magnolia, N.J. (Camden Co.).

MAGOFFIN Co., Ky. (co. seat, Salyersville). For Beriah Magoffin, legislator and governor (1859-62).

MAGOG, Que. (Stanstead Co.). Shortened form of *Memphremagog*, which is from Indian *Mamhrobaqak*, "beautiful water."

MAHANOY Variant of MAHONING.
Mahanoy Creek, Pa. Flows W into Susquehanna R.
Mahanoy City, Pa. (Schuykill Co.).

MAHASKA Co., Iowa (co. seat, Oskaloosa). For an Indian chief, whose name in Iowa means "white cloud."

MAHKEENAC, Lake, Mass. From Indian, "home of Mahicans," for the Mahican tribe of Algonquian linguistic stock. *Mahican* means "wolf."

MAHNOMEN From Ojibway, "wild rice," which grows in the region called Wild Rice Lakes, as it does along Wild Rice River.
Mahnomen Co., Minn. (co. seat, *Mahnomen*).
Mahnomen, Minn. (co. seat of *Mahnomen* Co.).

MAHONING From Delaware Indian *mahanoi* or *m'hoani*, "salt lick", a saline deposit where deer congregate. See also MAHANOY
Mahoning Co., Ohio (co. seat, Youngstown).
Mahoning Creek, Pa. Flows generally E.

MAHOPAC From an Indian word meaning "great lake."
Mahopac, N.Y. (Putnam Co.).
Mahopac, Lake, N.Y.

MAHTOMEDI, Minn. (Washington Co.). Either a Dakota or Siouan name, meaning "bear lake," although how the name occurred is unknown.

MAHWAH, N.J. (Bergen Co.). Meaning uncertain. It is an Indian word that possibly means "beautiful," "a field," or "a meeting place."

MAIDEN CREEK, Pa. Direct translation from Indian *ontelaunee*, "little maiden" or "little daughter," probably for an incident. It flows generally southwest into Schuykill River.

MAIDEN PEAK, Ore. Origin in dispute: near but separate from Bachelor Butte and Three Sisters; its shape, either for a breast or for a reclining woman. The first is more probable.

MAIDSTONE For Maidstone, Kent, England. The town was named first.
Maidstone, Vt. (Essex Co.), town.
Maidstone Lake, Vt.

MAINE For the French province of Maine, north of the Loire valley in France. The source and reason for the name are unknown, but before 1500 French explorers were referring to the area west of the Kennebec River as "Maine" and the area to the east as "Acadie" (see ACADIA). In 1622 the Council of New England granted the "Province of Maine" to Sir Ferdinando Gorges and Capt. John Mason.
Maine, State of: 23rd state of the Union. Settled: 1624. Part of Massachusetts until 1820. Admitted: 1820. Cap: Augusta. Motto: *Dirigo* (I Guide). Nickname: Pine Tree State. Flower: Pine Cone and

Maine is known for its rocky coast, its lobsters, and, most of all, for its great north woods. [*Woodcut by Friz Ormant. Courtesy of Robert and Joyce O'Brien*]

Tassel. Bird: Chickadee. Tree: Eastern White Pine. Song: "State of Maine Song."

MAIN STREAM, Me.. So named because it is the main stream of Sebasticook River.

MAJOR Co., Okla. (co. seat, Fairview). For John C. Major, active in obtaining statehood for Oklahoma.

MAKAHA POINT, Hawaii. On west coast of Kauai Island. From Hawaiian, "fierce."

MAKAHUENA POINT, Hawaii. South point of Kauai Island. From Hawaiian, "eyes overflowing heat."

MAKANALUA PENINSULA, Hawaii. On Molokai Island. From Hawaiian, "double gift."

MAKAPUU POINT, Hawaii. On southeast coast of Oahu Island. From Hawaiian, "taboo area."

MAKAWELI RIVER, Hawaii. From Hawaiian, "frightening places." It flows generally southwest on Kauai Island into the Pacific Ocean.

MALAD For the river, derived from French *riviere aux malades*, "a river of the sick ones," in reference to a place where trappers became sick.
Malad River, Idaho-Utah.
Malad City, Idaho (co. seat of Oneida Co.).

MALARTIC, Que. (Abitibi Co.). For the first local gold mine.

MALASPINA GLACIER, Alaska. Extends thirty miles to the Gulf of Alaska. For Capt. Don Alessandro Malaspina, Italian explorer for the Spanish government. He explored the Alaskan coast in 1791.

MALBAIE See   LA MALBAIE

MALDEN, Mass. (Middlesex Co.). For Maldon, Essex, England, in honor of Joseph Hills, speaker of the Massachusetts House of Deputies (1647) and a native of the English town.

MALHEUR From French. After French trappers were attacked by Indians and lost all their furs, they named the river running through the county *Malheur,* "bad hour," or "misfortune," river.
Malheur Co., Ore. (co. seat Vale).
Malheur Lake, Ore.
Malheur Natl. Wildlife Reservation, Ore.
Malheur River, Ore.

MALLETTS BAY, Vt. Inlet on Lake Champlain. For a local settler.

MALLYS FALLS POND, Vt. Said to have been named for Mally, wife of "Indian Joe," who arrived with the first white settlers. The legend is that he pushed her over the falls.

MALONE, N.Y. (co. seat of Franklin Co.). For Edmund Malone (1741-1812), outstanding Shakespearean scholar and critic, who was a friend of the founder. Earlier names were Harison and Ezraville.

MALTA, Mont. (co. seat of Phillips Co.). For Malta Island, in the Mediterranean Sea.

MALVERN For Malvern, Worcestershire, England.
Malvern, Ark. (co. seat of Hot Springs Co.). For a Malvern, Va., home of a railroad official; probably ultimately for the English town.
Malvern, Pa. (Chester Co.).
Malverne, N.Y. (Nassau Co.).

MAMARONECK, N.Y. (Westchester Co.). For a local Indian chief.

MAMMOTH CAVE NATL. PARK, Ky. Preservation and recreational area surrounding and including the cavern and its chambers. So named for the great size of the cave.

MAMOU, La. (Evangeline Co.). From French *mamou,* "prairie."

MANASSAS From a Biblical name of uncertain meaning. The name was taken from a Manassas Gap, also known as Manasseh's.
Manassas, Va. (co. seat of Prince William Co.).

MANISTEE From Ojibway, "sound of winds" in the wood.
Manistee Co., Mich. (co. seat, *Manistee*).
Manistee, Mich. (co. seat of *Manistee* Co.).

MANATEE For the manatee, or sea cow, found in the waterways of the area.
Little Manatee River, Fla.
Manatee Co., Fla. (co. seat, Bradenton).
Manatee River, Fla.

MANCHAUG POND, Mass. From Nipmuc, "island of rushes."

MANCHESTER For Manchester, England, a major industrial center in Lancashire.
Manchester, Conn. (Hartford Co.), town. There were several textile mills here in the 1820s.
Manchester, Mass. (Essex Co.), town.
Manchester, N.H. (Hillsborough Co.). The name was suggested by Samuel Blodgett (1724-1807), a local merchant who was impressed by the canals he saw in the English city and built one in New Hampshire. Earlier, Old Derryfield.
Manchester, Tenn. (co. seat of Coffee Co.). So named in hopes that the town would become a manufacturing center.
Manchester, Vt. (Bennington Co.), town.
North Manchester, Ind. (Wabash Co.). So named because there was former-ly another Manchester in the state, and postal officials insisted upon a change in names.

MANCHESTER, Iowa (co. seat of Delaware Co.). Believed to have been a form of the name of William Chesterman, partner of the town's founder, with perhaps also a suggestion of Manchester, England.

MANCOS From Spanish, "the crippled ones," reason for naming uncertain.
Mancos, Colo. (Montezuma Co.).
Mancos River, Colo.-N.Mex. Flows SW and W into Juan R. Earlier, San Lazaro.

MANDAN, N.Dak. (co. seat of Morton Co.). For the Dakota Indian tribe Mantani, "those who live along the bank of the river." Earlier names were Morton and Lincoln.

MANGUM, Okla. (co. seat of Greer Co.). For A. S. Mangum, owner of the townsite.

MANHASSET, N.Y. (Nassau Co.). For the Manhassett Indians, a tribe on Shelter Island, Suffolk County.

MANHATTAN For the tribe of Indians living in the New York area at the time of arrival of the Dutch.
Manhattan, Kan. (co. seat of Riley Co.). For *Manhattan*, N.Y.
Manhattan, N.Y. (New York Co.), a borough of New York City.
Manhattan Beach, Calif. (Los Angeles Co.). For *Manhattan*, N.Y.
Manhattan Island, N.Y., in New York Bay, coextensive with the borough.

MANHEIM, Pa. (Lancaster Co.). For Mannheim, Germany.

MANILA, Utah (co. seat of Daggett Co.). So named to commemorate the naval victory over the Spanish in Manila Bay, May 1, 1898.

MANISTEE From an Ojibway word, probably "crooked river," though authorities differ; some give "lost river" or "red river."
Little Manistee River, Mich.
Manistee Co., Mich. (co. seat, *Manistee*).
Manistee, Mich. (co. seat of *Manistee* Co.).
Maniskee Lake, Mich.
Manistee River, Mich.

MANISTIQUE From Ojibway, *monistique*, "red" or "reddish orange," for the color of the soil. It may be a variant of Manistee.
Manistique, Mich. (co. seat of Schoolcraft Co.).
Manistique Lake, Mich.
Manistique River, Mich.
South *Manistique* Lake, Mich.

MANITOBA Origin in dispute, but probably derived from either Cree *manito-wapow* or Ojibway *manitou-bau*, both of which mean "the strait of the manito or spirit," referring to Manitu Straight or "narrows" of Lake Manitoba. An early name for Lake Manitoba was Lake of the Prairie, which may have come from Assiniboine *minne*, "water," plus Sioux *toba*, "prairie."

Manitoba, Canadian province. Settled: 1670. Entered confederation: 1870. Cap: Winnipeg. Flower: Prairie Crocus.
Manitoba Lake, Man.

MANITOU From an Algonquian word for "spirit," applied to features where spirits or a spirit dwelled.
Manitou Island, Mich. In L. Superior.
Manitoulin District, Ont. (district seat, Gore Bay). For the island.
Manitoulin Island, Ont. In L. Huron. According to Indian tradition, the island was the dwelling place of both *gitchi-manitou,* "the good spirit," and *Matchi-manitou,* "the evil spirit."
Manitou Springs, Colo. (El Paso Co.). For a hill so named by Indians. Earlier, La Fon.
North Manitou Island, Mich. In L. Michigan.
South Manitou Island, Mich. In L. Michigan.

MANITOWOC From an Indian Indian name meaning "land of the spirit," possibly with a connotation of evil.
Manitowoc Co., Wis. (co. seat, *Manitowoc*).
Manitowoc, Wis. (co. seat of *Manitowoc* Co.).

MANIWAKI, Que. (co. seat of Gatineau Co.). From Algonquian, "Mary's land." The town was originally an Algonquian mission, Notre Dame de Desert.

MANKATO From Siouan, "blue earth." See also BLUE EARTH Co., Minn.
Mankato, Kan. (co. seat of Jewell Co.). For *Mankato,* Minn.
Mankato, Minn. (co. seat of Blue Earth Co.).
North Mankato, Minn. (Nicollet Co.). Across the Minnesota R. from *Mankato,* Minn.

MANNING, N.Dak. (co. seat of Dunn Co.). For Dan Manning, an early settler and promoter of the area.

MANNING, S.C. (co. seat of Clarendon Co.). For the Manning family, landowners and state officeholders.

MANNINGTON, W. Va. For James Mannings, a railway official.

MANSFIELD, Conn. (Tolland Co.), town. For Maj. Moses Mansfield, an early settler.

MANSFIELD, Ohio (co. seat of Richland Co.). For Jared Mansfield, surveyor general of the United States, directed by President Jefferson to inspect the territory.

MANSFIELD, Tex. (Tarrant Co.). A combination of the names of two early settlers, R. S. Mann and Julian Field.

MANSFIELD, William Murray, Lord (1705-1773), eminent English jurist. He was a Tory member of Parliament and was appointed chief justice of the king's bench (1756). He was created 1st Earl of Mansfield in 1776.
Mansfield, La. (parish seat of De Soto Parish). Lord Mansfield was greatly admired by Thomas Abbington, who named the village for him.
Mansfield, Mass. (Bristol Co.), town and village. Named by the loyalist governor Thomas Hutchinson (1711-1780) for his friend Lord Mansfield.

MANTECA, Calif. (San Joaquin Co.). From Spanish, "butter," for a local creamery.

MANTENO, Ill. (Kankakee Co.). For a daughter of Francois BOURBONNAIS, Jr.

MANTEO, N.C. (co. seat of Dare Co.). For an Indian, probably a chief, taken to England (1584) by Philip Amadas and Arthur Barlowe. He is said to have been the first Indian baptized as a Christian in the area.

MANTI, Utah (co. seat of Sanpete Co.). For a city in the Book of Mormon; named by Brigham Young.

MANTORVILLE, Minn. (co. seat of Dodge Co.). For the Mantor brothers, early settlers. Peter Mantor, the eldest, was the founder.

MANTUA, Va. (Fairfax Co.). For Mantua, Italy.

MANVILLE, N.J. (Somerset Co.). For the Johns-Manville Corporation, a leading asbestos products company.

MANY, La. (parish seat of Sabine Parish). For Colonel Many, commander of nearby Fort Jessup, a "trigger point" from which the Mexican War was launched.

MAPLE For the trees.
Maple River, Iowa. Flows SSW into Little Sioux R.
Maple River, Mich. Flows into Grand R.
Maple River, N.Dak. Flows S and NE into Sheyenne R.
Maple River, N.Dak.-S.Dak. Flows S into Elm R.
Maple Grove, Minn. (Hennepin Co.).
Maple Heights, Ohio (Cuyahoga Co.). Promotional.
Maplewood, Minn. (Ramsey Co.). Promotional.

MAQUOKETA From Algonquian, "bear river."
Maquoketa, Iowa (co. seat of Jackson Co.). Earlier, Goodnenow's Mills and Springfield.
Maquoketa River, Iowa.

MARAIS DES CYGNES RIVER, Kan.-Mo. From French, "marsh of the swans." It flows southeast and east to join Little Osage River to form Osage River.

MARATHON For the site of the famous battle in Greece (490 B.C.).

MARBLE For the occurrence of the rock or rock resembling marble.
Marblehead, Mass. (Essex Co.), town. The first settlers here mistook deposits of gray granite for marble.
Marble Hill, Mo. (co. seat of Bollinger Co.).

MARCUS BAKER, Mount, Alaska. In Chugach Mountains. For Marcus Baker (1849-1903), cartographer with the U.S. Coast and Geodetic Survey and the U.S. Geological Survey.

MARCY, Mount, N.Y. For William Learned Marcy (1786-1857), attorney, soldier in the War of 1812, U.S. senator (1831-33), governor of New York (1833-39), secretary of war under Polk (1845-49), and secretary of state under Pierce (1853-57). He instituted a geological survey of the Adirondack region (1837).

MARENGO For a battlefield in northern Italy where Napoleon defeated the Austrians on June 14, 1800.
Marengo Co., Ala. (co. seat, Linden).
Marengo, Ill. (McHenry Co.).
Marengo, Iowa (co. seat of Iowa Co.).
Marengo River, Wis. Flows into Bad R.

MARFA, Tex. (co. seat of Presidio Co.). Named by an engineer's wife for a heroine in a Russian novel.

MARGATE For Margate, Kent, England.
Margate, Fla. (Broward Co.).
Margate City, N.J. (Atlantic Co.).

MARIAN, Lake, Fla. For a local settler.

MARIANA ISLANDS, U.S.A. Trust Territory. For Maria of Austria, wife of Philip IV, king of Spain (1621-65).

MARIANNA, Ark. (co. seat of Lee Co.). For Mary and Anna, daughters of a woman who owned the land selected for the townsite.

MARIANNA, Fla. (co. seat of Jackson Co.). For Mary and Anna, daughters of Robert Beveridge, the original landowner.

MARIAS For Maria Wood, cousin of Meriwether Lewis. The river seems to have been named first, in 1804 by Captain Lewis.
Marias, Mont. (Liberty Co.).
Marias Pass, Mont.
Marias River, Mont. Flows SE into Missouri River.

MARICOPA Co., Ariz. (co. seat, Phoenix). From a tribal name of the Yuman linguistic stock. The meaning is uncertain. It may be a variant of Spanish *mariposa*, "butterfly"; the tribe claimed a meaning, "people."

MARIEMONT, Ohio (Hamilton Co.). Named by Mrs. Mary Hopkins Emery, realtor, for her Rhode Island estate. It is pronounced "Marry-mont."

MARIES From French *marias*, "swamp." *Maries* Co., Mo. (co. seat, Vienna). For the river.
Maries River, Mo.

MARIETTA, Ga. (co. seat of Cobb Co.). Believed to have been for the wife of Thomas Willis Cobb, for whom the county was named.

MARIETTA, Ohio (co. seat of Washington Co.). For Marie Antoinette (1755-1793), queen of France, wife of Louis XVI. The name was chosen by Gen. Rufus Putnam and a group of officers in recognition of her assistance during the American Revolution. She was executed during the French Revolution.

MARIETTA, Okla. (co. seat of Love Co.). For a Marietta in Pennsylvania.

MARIN Co., Calif. (co. seat, San Rafael). Origin is debatable: some claim that it was named for *Bahia de Nuestra Senora del Rosario la Marinera*; others believe it to be the name of a mythical Indian, transliterated as Marin. Both names are related to *mariner*.

MARINA, Calif. (Monterey Co.). From Spanish, "small boat harbor"; a developer's name in this instance.

MARINE CITY, Mich. (St. Clair Co.). For its position at the mouth of the Belle River.

MARINETTE For Marguerite Chevallier, a successful fur trader, who was also known as *Marinette*, a combined form of *Marie Antoinette*, the queen of France executed during the French Revolution.
Marinette Co., Wis. (co. seat, *Marinette*).
Marinette, Wis. (co. seat of *Marinette* Co.).

MARION, Francis (c.1732-1795), South Carolina soldier and legislator who earned the nickname "The Swamp Fox" for his

Francis Marion, "The Swamp Fox", earned his nickname during the American Revolution with his cunning tactics and daring raids against British troops in the swamps of the Carolinas. [*New York Public Library*]

elusive tactics and harassment of British forces during the American Revolution. He distinguished himself at the Battle of Eutaw Springs (1781).
East Marion-Clinchfield, N.C. (McDowell Co.). Clinchfield, probably for the Clinchfield railroad that passed nearby.
Francis Marion Natl. Forest, S.C.
Marion Co., Ala. (co. seat, Hamilton).
Marion Co., Ark. (co. seat, Yellville).
Marion Co., Fla. (co. seat, Ocala).
Marion Co., Ga. (co. seat, Buena Vista).
Marion Co., Ill. (co. seat, Salem).
Marion Co., Ind. (co. seat, Indianapolis).
Marion Co., Iowa (co. seat, Knoxville).
Marion Co., Kan. (co. seat, *Marion*). For Marion Co., Ohio.
Marion Co., Ky. (co. seat, Lebanon).
Marion Co., Miss. (co. seat, Columbia).
Marion Co., Mo. (co. seat, Palmyra).
Marion Co., Ohio (co. seat, *Marion*).
Marion Co., Ore. (co. seat, Salem).
Marion Co., S.C. (co. seat, *Marion*).
Marion Co., Tenn. (co. seat, Jasper).
Marion Co., Tex. (co. seat, Jefferson).
Marion Co., W.Va. (co. seat, Fairmont).

Marion, Ala. (co. seat of Perry Co.).
Marion, Ark. (co. seat of Crittenden Co.).
Marion, Ill. (co. seat of Williamson Co.).
Marion, Ind. (co. seat of Grant Co.).
Marion, Iowa (Linn Co.).
Marion, Kan. (co. seat of *Marion* Co.). For
   the county.
Marion, Ky. (co. seat of Crittendon Co.).
Marion, Mass. (Plymouth Co.).
Marion, N.C. (co. seat of McDowell Co.).
Marion, Ohio (co. seat of *Marion* Co.).
Marion, S.C.)co. seat of *Marion* Co.).
Marion, Va. (co. seat of Smyth Co.).
Marion, Lake, S.C.
West Marion, N.C. (McDowell Co.).

MARIPOSA From Spanish, "butterfly."
They were apparently very abundant there.
Mariposa Co., Calif. (co. seat, *Mari-
   posa*).
Mariposa, Calif. (co. seat of *Mariposa* Co.).

MARKED TREE, Ark. (Poinsett Co.). The
tree indicated a point where travelers could
save some ten miles of travel by transferring
from St. Francis River to Little River. Indians
had first used the marked tree; later, whites
also used it as a landmark.

MARKHAM, Ill. (Cook Co.). For Charles H.
Markham, president of the Illinois Central
railroad.

MARKHAM, Ont. (York Co.). For William
Markham (1720-1806), Bishop of Chester
and later Archbishop of York.

MARKLEEVILLE, Calif. (co. seat of Alpine
Co.). For Jacob J. Marklee, a settler who
was killed in a quarrel over land.

MARKS, Miss. (co. seat of Quitman Co.).
For Leopold Marks, a native of Germany
who established a mercantile business here.
He later bought several thousand acres of
land in the area. An earlier name was
Riverside.

MARKSVILLE, La. (parish seat of
Avoyelles Parish). For Mark Elishe, who was
traveling through central Louisiana when his
wagon broke down. He set up a trading post
on the spot.

MARLBORO For John Churchill, Duke of
MARLBOROUGH.
Marlboro Co., S.C. (co. seat, Bennettsville).
Upper Marlboro, Md. (co. seat of Prince
   Georges Co.).

MARLBOROUGH, Conn. (Hartford Co.),
town. For John Churchill, 1st Duke of
Marlborough (1650-1722), British soldier.
He was a supporter of William of Orange and
commander of the British army in the War of
the Spanish Succession.

MARLBOROUGH, Mass. (Middlesex Co.).
Probably for Marlborough, Wiltshire,
England.

MARLIN, Tex. (co. seat of Falls Co.). For
John, James, and W. M. Marlin, early
settlers. An earlier name was Fort Marlin.

MARLINTON, W.Va. (co. seat .of
Pocahontas Co.). Probably for Jacob Marlin,
an early settler.

MARLOW, Okla. (Stephens Co.). For the
Marlow brothers, outlaws and gunmen
whose bloody antics made the town
notorious.

MAROON PEAK, Colo. Descriptive of the
color.

MARQUETTE, Jacques (1637-1675),
French missionary and explorer known as
Pere Marquette, who was active in the area
of the upper Mississippi River and its
tributaries.
Marquette Co., Mich (co. seat, *Marquette*).
Marquette Co., Wis. (co. seat, Montello).
Marquette, Mich. (co. seat, OF *Marquette*
   Co.). Earlier, Worcester.
Marquette Island, Mich., in L. Huron.
Marquette Natl. Forest, Mich.
Marquette *Heights*, Ill. (Bureau Co.).
   Promotional.

MARSEILLES, Ill. (La Salle Co.). For
Marseilles, France.

MARSH. Descriptive.
Marsh Creek, Mich. Flows S into Manistique
   River.

Marsh Peak, Utah, in the Uinta Mtns.
Marsh Stream, Me. Flows E into Penobscot River.

MARSHALL, John (1755-1835), early statesman, secretary of state (1800-01) under John Adams. He served as fourth chief justice of the Supreme Court (1801-35) and is often called the greatest and most influential of the chief justices.
Marshall Co., Ala. (co. seat, Guntersville).
Marshall Co., Ill. (co. seat, Lacon).
Marshall Co., Ind. (co. seat, Plymouth).
Marshall Co., Iowa (co. seat, *Marshalltown*).
Marshall Co., Ky. (co. seat, Benton).
Marshall Co., Miss. (co. seat, Holly Springs).
Marshall Co., Tenn. (co. seat, Lewisburg).
Marshall Co., W.Va. (co. seat, Moundsville).
Marshall, Ark. (co. seat of Searcy Co.).
Marshall, Ill. (co. seat of Clark Co.).
Marshall, Mich. (co. seat of Calhoun Co.).
Marshall, Mo. (co. seat of Saline Co.).
Marshall, N.C. (co. seat of Madison Co.).
Marshall, Tex. (co. seat of Harrison Co.).
Marshalltown, Iowa (co. seat of *Marshall* Co.). For *Marshall,* Mich.; named by Harry Anson, founder.

MARSHALL Co., Kan. (co. seat, Marysville). For Frank J. Marshall, local businessman and legislator. The county seat was named in honor of his wife, Mary.

MARSHALL Co., Okla. (co. seat, Madill). For the mother of George A. Hendshaw; her maiden name was Marshall.

MARSHALL Co., S.Dak. (co. seat, Britton). For an early homesteader, Marshall Vincent.

MARSHALL, William Rainey (1825-1896), businessman, banker, cattle breeder, general in the Indian uprising (1862-65), and governor (1866-70).
Marshall Co., Minn. (co. seat, Warren).
Marshall, Minn. (co. seat of Lyon Co.).

MARSHALL ISLANDS, U.S.A. Trust Territory of Pacific Islands, under supervision of United Nations. For an English Captain Marshall, who explored the islands after convoying convicts to Australia in 1788.

MARSHFIELD Probably descriptive.
Marshfield, Mass. (Plymouth Co.), town.
Marshfield, Wis. (Wood Co.). Either for *Marshfield,* Mass. or for Samuel Marsh, uncle of John J. Marsh, a founder.
Marshfield Compact, Mass. (Plymouth Co.).

MARTHA'S VINEYARD (island), Mass. Named by Gabriel Archer in 1602 for a woman's name, reason unknown, plus *Vineyard,* for the vines growing on the island.

MARTIN Co., Fla. (co. seat, Stuart). For John W. Martin, governor (1925-29).

MARTIN, John Preston (1811-1862), Kentucky statesman. He was a U.S. representative (1845-47) and senator (1855-59).
Martin Co., Ind. (co. seat, Shoals).
Martin Co., Ky. (co. seat, Inez).

MARTIN, Lake, Ala. On Tallapoosa River. For a local settler.

MARTIN Co., Minn. (co. seat, Fairmont). Either for Henry Martin (1829-1908), a Connecticut land speculator who owned extensive holdings in the area, or for Morgan Lewis Martin (1805-1887), Minnesota Territory legislator and jurist.

MARTIN Co., N.C. (co. seat, Williamston). For Josiah Martin (1737-1786), the last colonial governor of North Carolina. The name was reinforced by the popularity of North Carolina governor Alexander Martin, who served two terms (1782-85; 1789-92), and possibly also by Saint Martin.

MARTIN, S.Dak. (co. seat of Bennett Co.). For Eben Martin, U.S. representative (1908-12).

MARTIN, Tenn. (Weakley Co.). For a local resident, William Martin.

MARTIN Co., Tex. (co. seat, Stanton). For Wyly Martin, active for Texas statehood.

MARTIN CREEK, Pa. For the flocks of martins once found there. It flows south into Tunkahannock Creek.

MARTINEZ, Calif. (co. seat of Contra Costa Co.). For Ignacio Martinez (1774-?), Spanish commander at San Francisco (1822-27).

MARTINSBURG, W.Va. (co. seat of Berkeley Co.). For Thomas Bryan Martin, landowner and local official.

MARTINS FERRY, Ohio (Belmont Co.). For Ebenezer Martin's father, who had maintained a ferry where the town was founded. An earlier name was Martinville.

MARTINSVILLE, Ind. (co. seat of Morgan Co.). Probably for John Martin, the eldest of the commissioners appointed to form the county. He never lived in it.

MARTINSVILLE, Va. (co. seat of Henry Co.). For Gen. Joseph Martin (1740-1808), Indian agent and representative of Virginia in many border disputes. He served in the Virginia legislature (1791-99) and was commissioned a brigadier general in the Virginia militia (1793).

MARVIN CREEK, Pa. For Seth Marvin, early pioneer. It flows northeast into Potato Creek.

MARVINE, Mount, Utah. For A. R. Marvine, geologist.

MARYLAND For Henrietta Maria (1609-1699), wife of Charles I of England. She was the daughter of Henry IV of France and his wife, Marie de Medici, and the mother of Charles II and James II of England. It has been suggested, but not documented, that the Catholic founders of the colony of Maryland were not averse to its being considered "the land of (the Virgin) Mary."
Maryland, State of. Seventh state of the
   Union. Settled: 1634. One of the original
   13 colonies. Ratified Constitution: 1778.

Cap: Annapolis. Motto: *Scuto Bonae Voluntatis Tuae Coronasti Nos* (With the Shield of Thy Goodwill Thou Hast Covered Us). Flower: Black-eyed Susan. Bird: Baltimore Oriole. Tree: White Oak. Song: "Maryland, My Maryland."

MARY MOUNTAIN, Wyo. In Yellowstone Natl. Park. For Mary Clark, member of a tourist party in 1873.

MARYS PEAK, Ore. Conflicting claims exist for the naming of the peak: either for a Mary Wimple, sister of an early settler, or for Mary Lloyd, daughter of an early settler.

MARY'S RIVER, Ill. For a local settler. It flows generally southwest into the Mississippi River.

MARYSVILLE, Calif. (co. seat of Yuba Co.). For Mary Murphy Covillaus (1831-1867), wife of the principal landowner.

MARYSVILLE, Kan. (co. seat of Marshall Co.). For Mary Marshall, wife of Frank J. Marshall. See also MARSHALL Co., Kan.

MARYSVILLE, Mich. (St. Clair Co.). For Mary, name of the wife and the daughter of Myron Williams, a sawmill operator.

MARYSVILLE, Ohio (co. seat of Union Co.). For Mary, daughter of Samuel Culbertson, the original proprietor. (He lived in Zanesville, outside of Union County.)

MARYVILLE, Tenn. (co. seat of Blount Co.). For Mary Grainger Blount, wife of William Blount, governor of the Territory of the United States South of the Ohio. See also GRAINGER Co., Tenn.

MASCOMA Of Algonquian origin, meaning uncertain; it has been translated as "salmon fishing," "much grass," and "red rocks."
Mascoma Lake, N.H.
Mascoma River, N.H. Flows S and W into
   Connecticut R.

MASCOUTAH, Ill. (Saint Clair Co.). From Algonquian, "prairie."

MASHAPAUG POND, Conn. From Narraganset, "a large pond," descriptive.

MASON, George (1725-1792), Virginia statesman and author of the Virginia Declaration of Rights (1776), which served as the model for the American Bill of Rights. He was a member of the Constitutional Convention (1787).
Mason Co., Ill. (co. seat, Havana). For Mason Co., Ky.
Mason Co., Ky. (co. seat, Maysville).
Mason Co., W.Va. (co. seat, Point Pleasant).
Mason City, Ill. (Mason Co.).

MASON, George or G. T., an army officer. He was charged (1849) with the responsibility of choosing locations for forts along the Rio Grande. One of the places was named Fort Mason, near the town that bears his name.
Mason Co., Tex. (co. seat, Mason).
Mason, Tex. (co. seat of Mason Co.).

MASON, Lake, Wis. For a local dweller.

MASON, Stevens Thompson (1811-1843), secretary of Michigan Territory (1831-35) and first governor of the state of Michigan (1835-40). He was active in furthering education in the state.
Mason Co., Mich. (co. seat, Ludington).
Mason, Mich. (co. seat of Ingham Co.).

MASON Co., Wash. (co. seat, Shelton). For Charles H. Mason (?-1859), Washington Territory official and acting governor. An earlier name was Sawamish County.

MASON AND DIXON LINE A boundary line run by Charles Mason and Jeremiah Dixon, English mathematicians and surveyors, to establish the southern border of Pennsylvania and marked for nearly 250 miles between Pennsylvania and Maryland (1763-67). It was extended in 1784 by David Rittenhouse to settle a boundary controversy between Virginia and Pennsylvania. The Line was later used to distinguish between slaveholding states and free ones.

MASON CITY, Iowa (co. seat of Cerro Gordo Co.). So named by members of the local Masonic lodge, and also because the area has a large brick and tile industry. An earlier name was Masonville.

MASSABESIC LAKE, N.H. From Abnaki, "near the large brook."

MASSAC Co., Ill. (co. seat, Metropolis). For a French minister, Massiac. An earlier name was Fort Ascension.

MASSACHUSETTS From the Indian name for a group of hills (the present Blue Hills) near what is now Massachusetts Bay. The name massa, "great," and chuset or wachusett, "hill," in combination means "great hill" or "great mountain place." The bay was named by the Pilgrims, and later the colony became known as the Massachusetts Bay Colony.

When English astronomers Charles Mason and Jeremiah Dixon surveyed the Mason-Dixon line establishing the boundary between Pennsylvania and Maryland, they could not have known that this line would become a symbol of the division of the North and the South [New York Public Library]

Although not all of the New England coast is as rocky as some suppose, Rafe's Chasm, near Gloucester, Massachusetts, seems to confirm the common belief. [*New York Public Library*]

Massachusetts, Commonwealth of. Sixth state of the Union. Settled: 1620. One of the original 13 colonies. Ratified Constitution: 1788. Motto: *Ense Petit Placidam Sub Libertate Quietem* (By the Sword She Seeks Peace, but Peace Only Under Liberty). Nickname: Bay State. Flower: Mayflower. Bird: Chickadee. Tree: American Elm. Song: "Massachusetts" (unofficial).
Massachusetts Bay, Mass.

MASSAPEQUA For the Masapequa or Masapeaque Indians.
East Massapequa, N.Y. (Nassau Co.).
Massapequa, N.Y. (Nassau Co.).
Massapequa Park, N.Y. (Nassau Co.).

MASSENA, N.Y. (St. Lawrence Co.). For Andre Massena (1758-1817), a French soldier who distinguished himself in battle while serving under Napoleon and was named Marshall of the Empire (1804). The town was named by the first white settler, who emigrated from Quebec.

MASSILLON, Ohio (Stark Co.). For the French author Jean Baptiste Massillon, whose works were favorites with the founder's wife.

MASTIC BEACH, N.Y. (Suffolk Co.). A variant of MYSTIC.

MATADOR, Tex. (co. seat of Motley Co.). For a Matador Ranch.

MATAGORDA From Spanish, "thicket" or "rough area." The island was probably named first.
Matagorda Co., Tex. (co. seat, Bay City). For *Matagorda* Bay.
Matagorda Bay, Tex.
Matagorda Island, Tex.
Matagorda Peninsula, Tex.

MATANE From Micmac, "beaver pond." The river was named first.
Matane Co., Que. (co. seats, *Matane* and Amqui).
Matane, Que. (a co. seat of *Matane* Co.).
Matane River, Que. Flows into St. Lawrence River.

MATANZAS From Spanish, "slaughters," for the defeat of the French Huguenots by Spanish forces led by Menendez in 1565.
Matanzas Inlet, Fla.
Matanzas River, Fla. Flows into the Atlantic Ocean.
Fort Matanzas Natl. Monument, Fla.

MATAPOISETT (or Mattapoisett). From Algonquian, "resting place."
Mattapoisett, Mass. (Plymouth Co.).
Matapoisett River, Mass. Flows S into Buzzards Bay.

MATAWAN, N.J. (Monmouth Co.). From Algonquian, "where two rivers come together."

MATHER PEAK, Wyo. For Kirtley Mather, a member of the United States Geological Survey.

MATHEWS, Thomas American Revolutionary general and patriot.
Mathews Co., Va. (co. seat, *Mathews*).
Mathews, Va. (co. seat of *Mathews* Co.).

MATHIS, Tex. (San Patricio Co.). For Thomas Henry Mathis (1834-1899), landowner, developer, shipowner, and businessman.

MATINICUS From Abnaki, "far-out island." The spelling is influenced by Latin.
Matinicus Islands, Me.
Matinicus Isle, Me.

MATOAKA See POCAHONTAS.

MATTABESSET RIVER, Conn. From Wangunk, "the resting place," for the end of a portage. It flows southeast into Connecticut River.

MATTAMISCONTIS LAKE, Me. From Abnaki, "plenty of alewives," for the herring-like fish.

MATTAMUSKEET LAKE, N.C. From Algonquian, meaning uncertain, but probably refers to the swampy area.

MATTAPOISETT See MATAPOISETT.

MATTAPONI RIVER, Va. From a tribal name, meaning uncertain, said by one informant to mean "bad breath." It has many tributaries, formed from parts of *Mattaponi*: Matta, Pini, Mat, Ta, Po, and Ni rivers. It flows southeast to join Pamunkey River to form York River.

MATTAWAMKEAG LAKE, Me. From Algonquian, with different meanings among the Abnaki, Malecite, and Micmac dialects, but probably generally referring to "a sand bar."

MATTERHORN, Mount, Nev. For the peak in Switzerland.

MATTESON, Ill. (Cook Co.). For Joel A. Matteson, governor (1853-57).

MATTOON, Ill. (Coles Co.). For William Mattoon, a railroad engineer and landowner.

MATTYDALE, N.Y. (Onondaga Co.), town. For Francis Victor Matty, Albany alderman and politician.

MAUCH CHUNK, Pa. See   JIM THORPE.

MAUI Co., Hawaii (co. seat, Wailuku). Of Hawaiian origin, possibly from the name of a Polynesian demi-god.

MAUMEE From the Indian tribal name, a variant of *Miami*. The name if derived from Ojibway *omaumeeg*, "people who live on the peninsula."
Maumee, Ohio (Lucas Co.).
Maumee River, Ohio-Ind.

MAUNA KEA (Peak), Hawaii. Highest peak on Hawaii Island. From Hawaiian, "white mountain," descriptive.

MAUNA LOA (volcanic mountain), Hawaii. On Hawaii Island. From Hawaiian, "long mountain," descriptive.

MAUNALUA BAY, Hawaii. On southeast coast of Oahu Island. From Hawaiian, "two mountains."

MAUREPAS, Lake, La. For Frederic Phillipeaux, Count of Maurepas, French political figure of the early eighteenth century.

MAURICE RIVER, N.J. For the *Prince Maurice*, a ship destroyed by the Indians, in turn named for Maurice, governor of the United Dutch provinces, Count of Nassau, and Prince of Orange. It flows south into Delaware Bay.

MAURY Co., Tenn. (co. seat, Columbia). For Abram Maury (1801-1848), editor, state legislator, and U.S. representative (1835-39).

MAUSTON, Wis. (co. seat of Juneau Co.). For M. M. Maughs, a mill owner.

MAVERICK Co., Tex. (co. seat, Eagle Pass). Fro Samuel Augustus Maverick (1803-1870), Republic of Texas patriot and legislator.

MAY, Cornelis Jacobsen, Dutch explorer who in 1612-14 explored the Atlantic coast of North America from Long Island to Cape May. He was later director-general of the Dutch West Indies Company's colony of New Netherlands.
Cape May Co., N.J. (co. seat, *Cape May* Court House).
Cape May Court House, N.J. (co. seat of *Cape May* Co.).
May, Cape, N.J.

MAYERSVILLE, Miss. (co. seat of Issaquena Co.). For David Meyers, landowner, with a change in spelling.

MAYES Co., Okla. (co. seat, Pryor). Named by the Oklahoma constitutional convention (1907) for Chief Samuel Houston Mayes (1845-1927), principal leader of the Cherokee Nation. He was also a prominent merchant and rancher.

MAYFIELD Possibly for Mayfield, Derby, England, but the pleasant associations of the month of May may have had some influence.
Mayfield, Ohio (Cuyahoga Co.).
Mayfield Heights, Ohio (Cuyahoga Co.).

MAYFIELD, George, a settler who according to tradition was kidnapped and held captive in the area. He escaped but was killed or drowned while trying to swim across the stream that also bears his name.
Mayfield, Ky. (co. seat of Graves Co.).
Mayfield Creek, Ky.

MAYNARD, Mass. (Middlesex Co.), town. For Amory Maynard (1804-1890), a textile manufacturer whose mill, the first of its kind in the area, led to the formation of the American Woolen Company.

MAYNARDVILLE, Tenn. (co. seat of Union Co.). For Horace Maynard (1814-1882), U.S. representative (1857-63; 1866-75),

ambassador to Turkey (1875-80), and lawyer. He was postmaster general (1880-81) under Hayes.

MAYO, Fla. (co. seat of Lafayette Co.). Named by James C. Ramsey for county Mayo, Ireland, his ancestors' home. The town was established by William Thomas Dees, son-in-law of Ramsey.

MAYODAN, N.C. (Rockingham Co.). For the Mayo and Dan rivers.

MAYS LANDING, N.J. (co. seat of Atlantic Co.). For George Mays, ship's chandler. Earlier names were The Forks and Great Egg Harbor.

MAYSVILLE, Ky. (co. seat of Mason Co.). For John May, founder.

MAYSVILLE, Mo. (co. seat of De Kalb Co.). Either for the month of May, when the town was established, or for Maysville, Ky., former home of early settlers. The coincidence of the names probably was an influence.

MAYVILLE, N.Y. (Chautauqua Co.). Named for May Busti, daughter of Paul Busti, agent and lawyer for the Holland Land Company.

MAYVILLE, N.Dak. (Traill Co.). For the daughter of Alvin Arnold, an early settler. She was the first white child born at the trading post there.

MAYVILLE, Wis. (Dodge Co.). For the May family, early settlers.

MAYWOOD, Ill. (Cook Co.). For May, the daughter of W. T. Nichols, an owner of the site.

MAZAMA, Mount Ore., the extinct volcano in which CRATER LAKE is located. From Spanish, "mountain goat," from which the Mazamas, a mountain-climbing club, took their name.

McADOO, Pa. (Schuylkill Co.). For William McAdoo (1853-1930) U.S. representative from New Jersey (1883-91), assistant secretary of the navy (1893-97), police commissioner of New York City (1904-05), and chief city magistrate from 1910.

McALESTER, Okla. (co. seat of Pittsburg Co.). For John J. McAlester, a prominent citizen and state official.

McALLEN, Tex. (Hidalgo Co.). For John McAllen, a Scotsman who owned and donated a large portion of land to the railroad. He also built a depot so that the railroad would stop near a hotel that he owned.

McARTHUR, Ohio (co. seat of Vinton Co.). For Duncan McArthur (1772-1839), governor (1830-32) U.S. representative (1823-25), and officer in the War of 1812.

McCAMEY, Tex. (Upton Co.). For George B. McCamey (1882-1960), a successful oil-well driller who became president of Cordova Union Oil Company. He also established the Bedford Stock Farm in Texas.

McCLAIN Co., Okla. (co. seat, Purcell). For Charles M. McClain, active in obtaining statehood for Oklahoma.

McCLINTOCK PEAK, Wyo. For Frank, ten-year-old son of Henry McClintock. They both climbed the peak in 1931.

McCLURE LAKE, Calif. For Nathaniel F. McClure, an army officer stationed in Yosemite Natl. Park in 1894 to 1895.

McCLUSKY, N.Dak. (co. seat of Sheridan Co.). For William H. McClusky, an early settler, landowner, and founder.

McCOLL, S.C. (Marlboro Co.). For D. D. McColl, first president of the Cape Fear and Yadkin Valley railroad.

McCOMB, Miss. (Pike Co.). For Henry Simpson McComb, an official of the Jackson and Northern railroad (now the Illinois Central-Gulf). A claim is also made for Jennings McComb; see JENNINGS, La.

McCONE Co., Mont. (co. seat, Circle). For George McCone, a founder of the county.

McCONNELLSBURG, Pa. (co. seat of Fulton Co.). For Daniel McConnell, Sr., tavern keeper and founder.

McCONNELSVILLE, Ohio (co. seat of Morgan Co.). For Robert McConnell (?-1843), a land developer.

McCOOK, Neb. (co. seat of Red Willow Co.). For Alexander McDowell McCook (1831-1903), general in the Union army during the Civil War. He represented the United States at the coronation of Nicholas II, czar of Russia (1895) and was a commissioner on the committee that investigated the conduct of the Spanish-American War (1898).

McCOOK Co., S.Dak. (co. seat, Salem). For Edwin S. McCook (?-1873), Union general and official of the Dakota Territory, who was killed in a political dispute.

McCORMICK, Cyrus Hall (1809-1884), inventor of the mowing machine and other farm implements.
McCormick Co., S.C. (co. seat, *McCormick*).
McCormick, S.C. (co. seat of *McCormick* Co.).

McCRACKEN Co., Ky. (co. seat, Paducah). For Virgil McCracken (?-1813), a soldier killed at the Battle of River Basin, Mich.

McCREARY Co., Ky. (co. seat, Whitley City). For James Bennett McCreary (1838-1918), Kentucky statesman. He was governor (1875-79; 1911-15), U.S. representative (1885-97), and senator (1903-09).

McCULLOCH Co., Tex. (co. seat, Brady). For Benjamin McCulloch (1811-1862), Republic of Texas patriot and soldier. He was a general in the Confederate army, killed at the Battle of Elkhorn Tavern, Ark., also known as Pea Ridge.

McCURTAIN Co., Okla. (co. seat, Idabel). For a prominent family of Choctaw chiefs.

McDONALD, Lake, Mich. For a local settler.

McDONALD Co., Mo. (co. seat, Pineville). For Alexander McDonald, a soldier in the American Revolution.

McDONALD, Ohio (Trumbull Co.). For Thomas G. McDonald, first superintendent at the Youngstown area plants for the Carnegie-Illinois Steel Company, which developed the town.

McDONOUGH, Commodore Thomas (1783-1825), naval hero. He served in the war with Tripoli and as commander of a squadron on Lake Champlain in the War of 1812. In this position, he was a hero of the Battle of Plattsburgh, which stopped British plans to control the Great Lakes and helped force the British retreat into Canada. He was often decorated for bravery. Under his command were the vessels *Constitution, Constellation, Philadelphia,* and *Enterprise.*
McDonough Co., Ill. (co. seat, Macomb).
McDonough, Ga. (co. seat of Henry Co.).
McDonough, N.Y. (Chanango Co.).

McDOWELL Co., N.C. (co. seat, Marion). For Joseph McDowell (1756-1801), a leader at the Battle of Kings Mountain, legislator, and U.S. representative (1797-99).

McDOWELL Co., W.Va. (co. seat, Welch). For James McDowell (1796-1851), U.S. representative from Virginia (1846-51), and governor (1842-46).

McDUFFIE Co., Ga. (co. seat, Thomson). For George McDuffie (1790-1851), U.S. representative from South Carolina (1821-34), U.S. senator (1842-46), and governor (1834-36).

McELMO CREEK, Colo.-Utah. For an early settler. It flows west into San Juan River.

McFARLAND, Calif. (Kern Co.). For J. B. McFarland (1861-?), large landowner and a founder.

McGEHEE, Ark. (Desha Co.). For Abner McGehee, an early settler.

McGREGOR, Tex. (McLennan Co.). For G. C. McGregor, a leading citizen and landowner.

McGUIRE, Mount, Idaho. For Don Macguire, mining engineer and geologist, with a change in spelling.

McHENRY Co., N.Dak. (co. seat, Towner). For James McHenry, an early settler.

McHENRY, William (1774-1839), Indian fighter in frontier wars. He was an important leader in the Black Hawk War of 1832, fought in this area.
McHenry Co., Ill. (co. seat, Woodstock).
McHenry, Ill. (*McHenry* Co.).

McINTOSH Co., Ga. (co. seat, Darien). Either for the McIntosh family, who were among the first settlers and numbered among them many famous men, including Capt. John McIntosh, Gen. Lachlian McIntosh, and Col. John McIntosh; or for William McIntosh (1775-1825), Creek leader who fought in the Seminole War (1817-18) and then became a Brigadier General in the U.S. Army. He was killed as a traitor by the Creeks.

McINTOSH Co., N.Dak. (co. seat, Ashley). For John J. McIntosh, a state legislator, or for E. H. McIntosh, a territorial legislator.

McINTOSH Co., Okla. (co. seat, Enfaula). For a prominent Creek family.

McINTOSH, S.Dak. (co. seat of Corson Co.). For the McIntosh brothers, railway officials and engineers.

McKAY CREEK, Ore. For William C. McKay (1824-1893), a physician. It flows into Umatilla River.

McKEAN Co., Pa. (co. seat, Smethport). For Thomas McKean (1734-1817). Pennsylvania statesman and jurist. He was a member of the Continental Congress (1774-83) and a signer of the Declaration of Independence (1776) and the Articles of Confederation (1781). He was chief justice of Pennsylvania (1777-99) and governor (1799-1808).

McKEE, Ky. (co. seat of Jackson Co.). For George R. McKee, a jurist.

McKEE CREEK, Ill. For a McKee, sent by the U.S. Government to survey land for homesteaders who were veterans of the War of 1812. He died about 1820 near Versailles, Ill. It flows east and southeast into Illinois River.

McKEESPORT, Pa. (Allegheny Co.) For David McKee, a North Country Irishman who, at the end of the French and Indian Wars, was allowed to settle at the mouth of the Youghiogheny River in Pennsylvania by permission of Iroquois Queen Aliquippa. He was granted exclusive ferriage rights by the colonial government over the Youghiogheny River and Monongahela River at their confluence.

McKEES ROCKS, Pa. (Allegheny Co.). For Alexander McKee, an Indian agent at Pittsburgh until 1776. Suspected of treason during the American Revolution, he escaped before his trial and, through his influence with the Indians, aided the British.

McKENZIE Co., N.Dak. (co. seat, Watford City). For Alexander McKenzie (1856-1922), a local official.

McKENZIE LAKE, Wis. For an early settler or explorer.

McKENZIE RIVER, Ore. Rises in the Cascades and flows west into the Willamette River. For Donald McKenzie (?-1851), an Indian trader who worked for Astor's Fur Company.

McKINLEY, William (1843-1901), twenty-fifth President of the United States (1897-1901), from Ohio. After service during the Civil War, he was a U.S. representative (1877-83; 1885-91) and governor (1892-96). Shot in Buffalo, N.Y. (September 6, 1901) by Leon Czolgosz, he died on September 14

and was succeeded by his vice-president, Theodore Roosevelt. See also FORT McKINLEY

McKinley Co., N.Mex. (co. seat, Gallup).
McKinley, Mount, Alaska, in the Alaska Range. Highest peak in North America. Named in 1896 by a prospector for McKinley, then a presidential nominee.
Mount McKinley Natl. Park, Alaska.

McKINNEY, Collin (1766-1861), an early settler in Texas and one of the five who drew up the declaration of separation of Texas from Mexico.
McKinney, Tex. (co. seat of Collin Co.).
McKinney Mountain, Tex.

McKINNEY, Lake, Kan. For J.R. McKinney, a pioneer in beet cultivation.

McLEAN Co., Ill. (co. seat, Bloomington). For John McLean (1791-1830), Illinois legislator and U.S. senator (1824-25; 1829-30).

McLEAN Co., Ky. (co. seat, Calhoun). For Alney McLean (1779-1841), officer in the War of 1812, U.S. representative (1815-17; 1819-21), and jurist.

McLEAN Co., N.Dak. (co. seat, Washburn). For John A. McLean, mayor of Bismarck when the county was named.

McLEANSBORO, Ill. (co. seat of Hamilton Co.). For William McLean, the first settler.

McLENNAN Co., Tex. (co. seat, Waco). For Neil McLennan, an early resident.

McLEOD Co., Minn. (co. seat, Glencoe). For Martin McLeod (1813-1860), a fur trader for Chouteau and Company, who came to the Northwest in 1836. He was a territorial legislator and a founder of Glencoe.

McLOUGHLIN, Mount, Ore. For John McLoughlin (1784-1857), an official of the Hudson's Bay Company, merchant, and landowner. He aided settlers in the Columbia River area and has been called the "Father of Oregon."

McMECHEN, W. Va. For a family of early settlers and landowners.

McMILLAN, Lake, N.Mex. For a local dweller.

McMINN, Joseph (1758-1824), a member of the territorial legislature (1794) and of the convention of 1796 to frame the constitution of Tennessee. He also served as governor (1817-21).
McMinn Co., Tenn. (co. seat, Athens).
McMinnville, Ore. (co. seat of Yamhill Co.). For *McMinnville*, Tenn.; named by an early settler who had been born there.
McMinnville, Tenn. (co. seat of Warren Co.).

McMULLEN Co., Tex. (co. seat, Tilden). For John McMullen, an early settler.

McNAIRY Co., Tenn. (co. seat, Selmer). For John McNairy, a jurist.

McNARY, Ore. (Umatilla Co.). For McNary Dam on the Columbia River, which was named for Charles Linza McNary (1874-1944), attorney, professor of law at Willamette University, jurist, and U.S. senator (1918-44).

McPHERSON, James Birdseye (1828-1864), heroic commander of the Union Army of the Tennessee during the Civil War. He was killed at the Battle of Atlanta.
McPherson Co., Kan. (co. seat, *McPherson*).
McPherson Co., Neb. (co. seat, Tryon).
McPherson Co., S.Dak. (co. seat, Leola).
McPherson, Kan. (co. seat of *McPherson* Co.).

McRAE, Ga. (co. seat of Telfair Co.). For Daniel Murphy McRae, who donated land for the townsite.

MEAD, Lake, Ariz.-Nev. On Colorado River. For Dr. Elwood Mead, a reclamation commissioner. The lake has a capacity of 10 trillion gallons of water, making it one of the world's largest man-made lakes.

MEADE, George Gordon (1815-1872), career soldier, born in Spain, and a Union general during the Civil War. He fought in the Seven Days Battle, at second Bull Run, Antietam, Fredericksburg, and Chancellorsville and commanded the army that defeated Lee at Gettysburg.
Meade Co., Kan. (co. seat, *Meade*).
Meade Co., S.Dak. (co. seat, Sturgis).
Meade, Kan. (co. seat of *Meade* Co.).

MEADE Co., Ky. (co. seat, Brandenburg). For James Meade (?-1813), an officer killed at the Battle of River Basin, Mich.

MEADOW Descriptive.
Meadow River, W.Va. Flows NW into Gauley R. So named because it heads in a flat section known as Little Meadows.
Meadow Valley Creek, Nev. Flows S to join Clover Creek, to form *Meadow Valley* Wash.
Meadow Valley Wash, Nev. Flows into L. Mead.

MEADVILLE, Miss. (co. seat of Franklin Co.). For Cowles Mead (1776-1844), attorney, Georgia representative to Congress (1805), secretary of Mississippi Territory (1806-07), and Mississippi state legislator.

MEADVILLE, Pa. (co. seat of Crawford Co.). For its founder, David Mead, pioneer, American Revolutionary soldier, general, and commander of militia in western Pennsylvania. He defended Erie in 1813 when Oliver Hazard Perry was building his fleet.

MEAGHER Co., Mont. (co. seat, White Sulphur Springs). For Thomas Francis Meagher (1823-1867), an Irish revolutionary who was tried for sedition and banished to Tasmania. He escaped to New York City, where he engaged in politics and law, was named a brigadier general in the Civil War, and led the "Irish Brigade." He migrated to Montana Territory and was its secretary and acting governor (1864-67).

MECHANIC For the large number of workers in its factories, foundries, or machine shops.

Mechanicsburg, Pa. (Cumberland Co.). Earlier, Drytown, because of water shortages.
Mechanicville, N.Y. (Saratoga Co.).

MECKLENBURG For Charlotte Sophia, Princess of Mecklenburg-Strelitz (1744-1818), wife of George III of England.
Mecklenburg Co., N.C. (co. seat, Charlotte).
Mecklenburg Co., Va. (co. seat, Boydton).

MECOSTA Co., Mich. (co. seat, Big Rapids). For the Potawatomi chief who accepted the Washington Treaty of 1836. His name means "bear cub."

MEDDYBEMPS LAKE, Me. From Passamaquoddy-Abnaki, "plenty of alewives." The form is rendered in English folk spelling.

MEDFIELD, Mass. (Norfolk Co.), town. Possibly descriptive (*med*-is an old form of *mid*-).

MEDFORD For an English place name, "the middle ford."
Medford, Mass. (Middlesex Co.).
Medford, N.Y. (Suffolk Co.).
Medford, Okla. (co. seat of Grant Co.).
Medford, Ore. (co. seat of Jackson Co.).
Medford, Wis. (co. seat of Taylor Co.). For *Medford*, Mass.
Medford Lakes, N.J. (Burlington Co.).
Medford West, Ore. (Jackson Co.).
South Medford, Ore. (Jackson Co.).

MEDIA, Pa. (co. seat of Delaware Co.). For its central location; Latin *media*, "middle." An earlier name was Providence.

MEDICINE For areas used by Indians for medicinal and ritual purposes.
Medicine Creek, Iowa-Mo. Flows S into Grand R.
Medicine Creek, Neb. Flows SE into Republican R. A misinterpretation of Dakota *ble wakan wakpala*, properly translated as "mysterious lake creek," but which was translated as "medicine creek."

Medicine Creek, S.Dak. Flows E and N into Missouri R. Translated from Sioux, "place to make medicine."
Medicine Lake, Mont. The Indians found medicinal plants on the shores.
Medicine Mountain, Wyo. For the "medicine wheel" found on the summit, a circle used by the Indians to worship the sun.
Medicine Hat, Alta. From an old Indian legend about the headdress of a medicine man.
Medicine Lake, Mont. (Sheridan Co.). For the lake.
Medicine Lodge, Kan. (co. seat of Barber Co.). For an Indian lodge on the *Medicine Lodge* R. Several Indian tribes agreed to peace treaties with the Federal governments here (1867).
Medicine Lodge River, Kan.-Okla. Flows into Salt Fork of Arkansas R. The waters were believed to have curative powers.

MEDICINE BOW So named because Indians came to the mountains to obtain wood for their bows and to hold ceremonial, or "medicinal," rituals and dances. The mountains appear to have been named first.
Medicine Bow, Wyo. (Carbon Co.).
Medicine Bow Mountains, Wyo-Colo.
Medicine Bow Natl. Forest, Wyo.
Medicine Bow Peak, Wyo.
Medicine Bow River, Wyo. Flows N into Seminoe Reservoir.

MEDINA For the city of Hejaz, Saudi Arabia, to which Mohammed (570?-632), the founder of Islam, made his famous *hegira* (flight) from Mecca in 622.
Medina Co., Ohio (co. seat, *Medina*). Earlier, Mecca.
Medina, N.Y. (Orleans Co.).
Medina, Ohio (co. seat of *Medina* Co.).

MEDINA For the river. Perhaps for a member of Alonzo de Leon's expedition in 1689. One source states that he was Pedro Medina, a Spanish scholar and engineer; another, that he was Nicolas de Medina, a sergeant major in the expedition.
Medina Co., Tex. (co. seat, Hondo). For the river.
Medina Lake, Tex.
Medina River, Tex.

MEDINA MOUNTAIN, Wyo. For Joe Medina, a sheepman.

MEDOMAC RIVER, Me. From Abnaki, "place of many alewives," for the herring-like fish. It flows into Pemaquid Pond.

MEDORA, N.Dak. (co. seat of Billings Co.). For Marquise Medora von Hoffman, American wife of Antoine de Vallombrosa, Marquis de Mores, who attempted to establish a cattle business there but failed.

MEDORA LAKE, Mich. From a woman's name, possibly from Byron's poem "The Costair."

MEDWAY, Mass. (Norfolk Co.), town and village. So named because it was formed from part of Medfield.

MEEKER, Colo. (co. seat of Rio Bianco Co.). For Nathan C. Meeker (1817-1879), newspaper publisher and Indian agent, killed by Ute Indians in a massacre at White River Indian Agency, known as the Thornburg Battle, for Maj. T. T. Thornburg, commander. It is also known as the Meeker Massacre.

MEEKER Co., Minn. (co. seat, Litchfield). For Bradley B. Meeker (1813-1873), a landowner and jurist.

MEEK MOUNTAIN, Wyo. For Joseph L. Meek, trapper.

MEGANTIC From abnaki *Namesokanjik*, "where they preserve fish."
Megantic Co., Que. (co. seat, Inverness).
Megantic, Que. (co. seat of Frontenac Co.).
   Also called *Lac-Megantic*.
Megantic, Lake, Que.
Megantic Mountain, Que.

MEGUNTICOOK MOUNTAIN, Me. From Algonquian, "big mountain harbor."

MEHERRIN RIVER, Va.-N.C. For the Indian tribe of Iroquoian linguistic stock, meaning of name unknown. It flows generally southeast into Chowan River.

MEIERS CRAG (peak), Wyo. For M. Meier, one of the first to ascend the crag.

MEIGS, Return Jonathan (1764-1824), Ohio soldier, statesman, and jurist. He was U.S. senator (1808-10), governor (1810-14), and postmaster general (1814-23) under Madison and Monroe.
Meigs Co., Ohio (co. seat, Pomeroy).
Meigs Co., Tenn. (co. seat, Decatur).

MEINERS OAKS-MIRA MONTE, Calif. (Ventura Co.). A combination of *Meiners Oaks*, for Carl Meiners, landowner and Spanish *mira*, "Look, behold!," and *monte*, "woods" or "bush."

MELBOURNE, Ark. (co. seat of Izard Co.). So named because a local citizen found the name in an atlas where it was defined as "Mill Stream." Earlier names were Mill Creek and Richardson's Cross Roads.

MELBOURNE, Fla. (Brevard Co.). Named by an Australian for his native city.

MELDRUM MOUNTAIN, Wyo. In Yellowstone Natl. Park. For John W. Meldrum, a jurist and commissioner.

MELLETTE Co., S.Dak. (co. seat, White River). For Arthur C. Mellette (1842-1896), an official in Dakota Territory affairs and first governor of South Dakota (1889-93).

MELOZITNA RIVER, Alaska. Of Indian origin, meaning unknown. It flows southwest into Yukon River.

MELROSE For Melrose, Roxburghshire, Scotland, site of Melrose Abbey, depicted in Sir Walter Scott's *Lay of the Last Minstrel*, or for the Abbey itself.
Melrose, Mass. (Middlesex Co.).
Melrose Park, Fla. (Broward Co.).
Melrose Park, Ill. (Cook Co.).

MELVINDALE, Mich. (Wayne Co.). For Melvin Wilkinson, a founder.

MEMPHIS For the ancient capital of Lower Egypt, noted for its beautiful site and surrounding rich land.

Memphis, Mo. (co. seat of Scotland Co.). For *Memphis*, Tenn.

Memphis, Tenn. (co. seat of Shelby Co.).

Memphis, Tex. (co. seat of Hall Co.).

West Memphis, Ark. (Crittenden Co.). Across the Mississippi R. from *Memphis*, Tenn. Earlier, Hopefield.

MENA, Ark. (co. seat of Polk Co.). A shortened form of *Wilhelmina*; named by a railroad investor, Geojan, from Holland.

MENANDS, N.Y. (Albany Co.) For Louis Menand, whose property was the first stop on the Albany and Northern railroad north of Albany.

MENARD Co., Ill. (co. seat, Petersburg). For Pierre Menard (1766-1844), jurist, legislator, and first lieutenant governor of Illinois.

MENARD, Michel Branaman (1805-1856), Republic of Texas patriot and legislator, called the "father of Galveston." He was a nephew of Pierre Menard (see   MENARD Co., Ill.).

Menard Co., Tex. (co. seat, *Menard*).

Menard, Tex. (co. seat of *Menard* Co.).

MENASHA, Wis. (Winnebago Co.). From an Algonquian word of uncertain meaning, variously translated as "island" and "thorn"; the former is more probable.

MENDENHALL, Miss. (co. seat of Simpson Co.). For Thomas L. Mendenhall (1830-1895), prominent attorney clerk of the circuit court, probate clerk, and member of the Mississippi constitutional convention of 1890. He was also a merchant and land-owner.

MENDHAM, N.J. (Morris Co.). Believed to be for a town in Suffolk, England.

MENDOCINO Early records indicate that Cabo (Cape) Mendocino was named for Antonio de Mendoza (c. 1485-1552), viceroy of New Spain (Mexico, 1535-49) and of Peru (1551-52). He sent out the famous Coronado expedition (1540-42) into what is now Colorado and New Mexico. Another claim is made for Lorenzo Suarez de Mendoza, viceroy of New Spain (1580-83). The name is an adjectival form indicating only someone from Mendoza, a Spanish city. All names derive from the cape, which was named first.

Mendocino Co., Calif. (co. seat, Ukiah).

Mendocino, Calif. (*Mendocino* Co).

Mendocino, Cape, Calif.

Mendocino Canyon Natl. Forest, Calif.

MENDON, Mass. (Worcester Co.), town. For Mendham, Suffolk, England.

MENDOTA From Siouan, probably connoting the coming together of two streams.

Mendota, Calif. (Fresno Co.). Possibly for *Mendota*, Ill.

Mendota, Ill. (La Salle Co.). Through transliterations and transfers, the Siouan word has come to mean here the junction of two railways.

Mendota, Lake, Wis.

Mendota Heights, Minn. (Ramsey Co.). At the confluence of the Minnesota and Mississippi rivers.

MENIFEE Co., Ky. (co. seat, Frenchburg). For Richard Hickman Menefee (1809-1841), attorney and legislator.

MENLO PARK, Calif. (San Mateo Co.). For Menlough, county, Galway, Ireland.

MENOMIN, Lake, Wis. On Red Cedar River. A shortened form of MENOMINEE.

MENOMINEE For an Indian tribe of Algonquian linguistic stock living in the area along the Menominee River and also in the lake region where wild rice grows. The name means "wild rice people."

Menominee Co., Mich. (co. seat, *Menominee*).

Menominee, Ill. (Jo Daviess Co.).

Menominee, Mich. (co. seat of *Menominee* Co.). Earlier, Bleeker.

Menominee Range, Mich.-Wis.

Menominee River, Mich.-Wis. Flows into Green Bay.

MENOMONEE A variant spelling of
MENOMINEE
Menomonee Falls, Wis. (Waukesha Co.).
For falls on the river.
Monomonee River, Wis. Flows SE to the
Milwaukee R.

MENOMONIE, Wis. (co. seat of Dunn Co.).
A variant spelling of   MENOMINEE.

MENTASTA MOUNTAINS, Alaska. Of
Indian origin, meaning unknown.

MENTONE, Tex. (co. seat of Loving Co.).
For Menton (also spelled *Mentone*), France;
named by a French surveyor.

MENTOR Possibly for Hiram Mentor, an
early settler. It has also been suggested that
Mentor, counselor of Telemachus (son of
Odysseus), was the source.
Mentor, Ohio (Lake Co.).
Mentor-on-the-Lake, Ohio (Lake Co.). On
L. Erie.

MENUNKETESUCK From Western
Niantic, "strong-flowing stream."
Menunketesuck Island, Conn.
Menunketesuck River, Conn. Flows SSE into
Long Island Sound.

MEQUON, Wis. (Ozaukee Co.). From
Ojibway *miquan*, "ladle," for the shape of a
bend in a stream at this point. A doubtful
claim is made for *mequin*, "feather."

MERAMEC RIVER, Mo. From an Indian
tribal name, meaning "cat fish." It flows
into Mississippi River.

MERCED From Spanish, "mercy." The
river was named by members of the ex-
pedition of Juan Bautista de Anza in 1774
and 1775 for *Neustra Senora de la Merced*,
"Our Lady of Mercy," shortly after her feast
day.
Merced Co., Calif. (co. seat, *Merced*).
Merced, Calif. (co. seat of *Merced* Co.).
Merced River, Calif.
Merced River, Calif.

MERCEDES, Tex. (Hidalgo Co.). For
Mercedes Diaz, wife of Mexican President
Porfirio Diaz. He held office from 1877 to
1880 and 1884 to 1911. The people at this
time thought that, by their naming the town
for his wife, his efforts to prevent Mexican
raids might increase.

MERCER, Gen. Hugh (1721-1777), Virginia
physician and soldier who served with
General Braddock during the French and
Indian Wars. He was killed in the American
Revolution at the Battle of Princeton.
Mercer Co., Ill. (co. seat, Aledo).
Mercer Co., Ky. (co. seat, Harrodsburg).
Mercer Co., Mo. (co. seat, Princeton).
Mercer Co., N.J. (co. seat, Trenton).
Princeton, where Mercer was killed, is in
this county.
Mercer Co., Ohio (co. seat, Celina).
Mercer Co., Pa. (co. seat, *Mercer*).
Mercer Co., W.Va. (co. seat, Princeton).
Mercer, Pa. (co. seat, of *Mercer* Co.).

MERCER Co., N.Dak. (co. seat, Stanton).
For William H. H. Mercer, an early settler.

MEREDITH, Lake, Colo. For a local settler.

MEREDITH, N.H. (Belknap Co., town. For
Sir William Meredith (?-1790), member of
Parliament, lord of the admiralty, and friend
of Gov. Benning Wentworth. Meredith
supported the demands of the colonies not
to be taxed without representation, stating of
the imposts, in a parliamentary speech, "If I
were an American, I would not submit to
them."

MEREDITH, N.Y. (Delaware Co.), town.
For Reese Meredith, a Philadelphia merchant who bought a large amount of land in
the area.

MERIDEN, Conn. (New Haven Co.). For a
town in England.

MERIDIAN A representation of a circle on
the earth's surface passing through the
poles and any given place. The term is used
by surveyors and has resulted in some place
names.
Meridian, Idaho (Ada Co.).

Meridian, Miss. (Co. seat of Lauderdale Co.). Named mistakenly because the namers believed that *meridian* meant "junction."

Meridian, Tex. (co. seat of Bosque Co.).

Meridian Butte, Ariz. Lies exactly on the 110th meridian.

MERION, Pa. (Montgomery Co.). For Merionethshire, a county in Wales.

MERIWETHER Co., Ga. (co. seat, Greenville). For David Meriwether (1755-1823), a general in the American Revolution who distinguished himself for gallantry under Washington at Trenton, Brandywine, and Monmouth. He was frequently employed by the Federal government in treaty negotiations with the Indians and was a distinguished local citizen who supported churches and schools.

MERRIAM, Kan. (Johnson Co.). Probably for G. F. Merriam, a local official, but a claim is also made for an official of the Santa Fe railroad.

MERRICK For the Merikoke (or Merickoke) Indian tribe, folk etymologized to its present form.

Merrick, N.Y. (Nassau Co.).

Merrick Brook, Conn. Flows S into Shetucket R.

MERRICK Co., Neb. (co. seat, Central City). For Elvira Merrick De Puy, wife of Rep. Henry W. De Puy.

MERRILL, Wis. (Co. seat of Lincoln Co.). For S. S. Merrill, a railway official.

MERRIMAC, Mass. (Essex Co.), town. A variant spelling of MERRIMACK

MERRIMACK From Algonquian, variously translated as "sturgeon," "catfish," "deep place," or "swift water."

Merrimack Co., N.H. (co. seat, Concord).

Merrimack, N.H. (Hillsborough Co.), town.

Merrimack River, Mass.-N.H.

MERRYMEETING LAKE, N.H. Probably either named by early explorers who saw in its contour a resemblance to some other water sheet (such as Merry Meeting Bay, off Maine coast), or translated from an Indian name, origin and meaning unknown.

MERTZON, Tex. (co. seat of Irion Co.). For M. L. Mertz, Orient (now Santa Fe) railroad treasurer.

The Mesa Fachada of New Mexico lies in the distance with the ruins of the Pueblo Una Vida in the foreground. [*New York Public Library*]

The great Mesabi Range in northern Minnesota is one of the greatest sources of iron ore in North America. The Hull Rust Iron Mine is near Hibbing. [*Photo by Frank E. Gunnell. Courtesy of Frederic Lewis*]

MERWIN, Lake, Wash. For a local settler.

MESA From 'Spanish, "table." As a geographic term, it is applied to a high, flat tableland with sharply eroded sides.
Mesa Co., Colo. (co. seat, Grand Junction).
Mesa, Ariz. (Maricopa Co.).
Mesa Peak, Colo.
Mesa de Maya, Colo.
Mesa Verde Natl. Park, Colo.

MESABI RANGE, Minn. From Ojibway, "giant," for a legendary giant who supposedly lived in the hills.

MESHOPPEN CREEK, Pa. From Algonquian, "glass beads." It flows southwest into Tunkahannock Creek.

MESQUITE, Tex. (Dallas Co.). For a creek, which was named for the plant *Prosopis glandulosa*, or mesquite, found in the area.

METAIRIE, La. (Jefferson Parish). From French *metairie*, which designates a farm leased by the owner on a share and share alike basis. Many of the farms in this area were leased on such a basis.

METCALFE Co., Ky. (co. seat, Edmonton). For Thomas Metcalfe (1780-1855), Kentucky legislator and U.S. senator.

METEDECONK RIVER, N.J. From Algonquian *metu*, "medicine man," plus *saconk*, "outlet of stream." It flows southeast into Barnegat Bay.

METHOW RIVER, Wash. From an Indian tribal name, meaning unknown. It flows south into Colorado River.

METHUEN, Mass. (Essex Co.), town. For Lord Paul Methuen (1672-1757), diplomat and lord of the admiralty (1714-17). He was a friend of Massachusetts Governor Dummer, who named the town.

METINIC ISLAND, Me. From Abnaki, "island at a distance."

METONGO, Lake Wis. Of Indian origin, meaning unknown.

METROPOLIS, Ill. (co. seat of Massac Co.). From Greek, "great city." It was formed by the merging of two communities.

METTAWEE RIVER, Vt.-N.Y. Possibly from Narraganset, "black earth," or from Natick, "popular trees." It flows northwest into Lake Champlain.

METUCHEN, N.J. (Middlesex Co.). From *Matochshoning*, the Indian name for the area, for a chief who lived there in the 1600s.

MEXIA, Tex. (Limestone Co.). For Jose Antonio Mexia, a general in the Mexican army.

MEXICO From Aztec, "place of the war god." *Mexitel*, also known as Huitzilopochti, was war god of the Aztecs. The suffix -co refers to a place, in this case the temple of Mexitl from which the surrounding city of Mexico takes its name. Mexico became the capital of New Spain (Nueva Espana), and gradually the name of the capital was used to designate this area of Spanish America. Although Texas achieved independence from Mexico in 1836, it was not until the end of the Mexican War (1846-48) that the United States annexed the vast tract of Mexican territory that was to become California, Arizona, New Mexico, Nevada, Utah, and portions of Colorado.

New Mexico, State of. 47th state of the Union. Settled: 1605. Territory: 1850. Admitted: 1912. Capital: Santa Fe. Motto: *Crescit Eundo* (It Grows as It

New Mexico in old Spanish missions. One of the finest is Acoma's Museum Mission Church. Its four to eight foot thick walls keep out summer heat and winter cold. [*Santa Fe Railway*]

Goes). Nickname: Land of Enchantment. Flower: Yucca. Bird: Road Runner. Tree: Pinon. Song: "O, Fair Mexico."

Mexico, Me. (Oxford Co.), town and village. So named in honor of Mexico's stuggle to throw off foreign rule in the second decade of the 1800s.

Mexico, Mo. (co. seat of Audrain Co.). For the country.

Mexico, Gulf of. On SE coast of North America, bounded by United States, Mexico, and Cuba. Connects with Atlantic Ocean through Straits of Florida, and with Caribbean Sea through Strait of Yucattan.

MIAMI For an Algonquin tribe, formerly in Wisconsin and Illinois, later in northwestern Ohio. They were driven by settlers west into Indiana, Kansas, and Oklahoma. Origin of the name is uncertain: Probably from Ojibway *oumaumeg*, "people of the peninsula," or from Delaware *we-mi-a-mik*, "all friends." Another version is the Ottawa word for "mother."

Miami Co., Ind. (co. seat, Peru).
Miami Co., Kan. (co. seat, Paola).
Miami Co., Ohio (co. seat, Troy).
Miami Co., Tex. (co. seat, *Miami*).
Miami, Ariz. (Gila Co.). For the Miami Copper Company, which was named for *Miami*, Ohio.
Miami, Okla. (co. seat of Ottawa Co.).
Miami, Tex. (co. seat of *Miami* Co.).
Miami River (Great and Little), Ohio. Flows into the Ohio R.
Miamisburg, Ohio (Montgomery Co.).
New Miami, Ohio (Butler Co.).

MIAMI From *Mayaimi*, an Indian name previously applied to a local tribe and also to a large body of water, possibly Lake Okeechobee.

Miami, Fla. (co. seat of Dade Co.).
Miami Canal, Fla.
Miami Beach, Fla. (Dade Co.).
Miami Shores, Fla. (Dade Co.).
Miami Springs, Fla. (Dade Co.).
North Miami, Fla. (Dade Co.).
North Miami Beach, Fla. (Dade Co.).
South Miami, Fla. (Dade Co.).
West Miami, Fla. (Dade Co.).

MIANUS RIVER, Conn. For Mayanno, a Paugusett Indian chief killed in 1683. It flows south into Long Island Sound.

MICHELSON, Albert Abraham (1852-1931), American scientist.

Michelson, Mount, Alaska. In Cnugach Mtns.

Michelson, Mount, Alaska. In Romanzof Mtns.

MICHIGAMME From Ojibway, "big lake," variant of MICHIGAN.

MICHIGAN From an Indian word of uncertain origin. One theory claims derivation from *mitchisawgyegan*, a combination of Indian words meaning "great lake" (presumably Lake Michigan). Another suggests *mishi-maikin-nac*, "swimming turtle," an Indian term used to describe the profile of the northern tip of the southern peninsula of Michigan and a nearby island (Mackinac). Thus, it is unclear which was named first, the lake or the land area.

Michigan, State of. 26th state of the Union. Settled: 1668. Territory: 1805. Admitted: 1837. Cap: Lansing. Motto: *Si Quaeriz Peninsulam Amoenam Circumspice*. (If You Seek a Pleasant Peninsula, Look About You). Nickname: Wolverine State. Flower: Apple Blossom. Bird: Robin. Tree: White Pine. Song: "Michigan, My Michigan" (unofficial).

Michigan Island, Wis. One of the Apostle Islands in L. Superior.

Michigan, Lake, Mich.-Ind.-Ill.-Wis. One of the Great Lakes.

Michigan River, Colo. Flows NW into North Platte R.

Michigan City, Ind. (La Porte Co.). For the state.

MIDDLE Descriptive of a midpoint between two important trade, geographic, political, or other locations.

Middle Creek, Pa. Flows E into Susquehanna R.

Middle Creek, Pa. Flows E into Lackawaxen R.

Middle Lake, Calif. Between Upper and Lower Lakes.

Middle River, Iowa. Flows into Des Moines R.

Middle Island Creek, W.Va. Flows NW and SW into Ohio R.

Middlebourne, W.Va. (co. seat of Tyler Co.). Between two points, but which two is uncertain.

Middleburg, Pa. (co. seat of Snyder Co.). In the central part of the county; it is also located on *Middle* Creek.

Middleburg Heights, Ohio (Cuyahoga Co.).

Middlebury, Conn. (New Haven Co.), town. Created from parts of Waterbury, Woodbury, and Southbury.

Middlebury, Vt. (co. seat of Addison Co.), town. There were three land grants made in the area in one year (1761) and this was the second, hence "middle."

Middlebury River, Vt. Flows W into Otter Creek.

Middlefield, Conn. (Middlesex Co.), town.

Middleport, Ohio (Meigs Co.).

Middle River, Md. (Baltimore Co.).

Middlesborough, Ky. (Bell Co.). .

Middleton, Mass. (Essex Co.), town. Formed from the corners of several adjoining towns.

Middleton, Wis. (Dane Co.).

Middletown, Conn. (co. seat of *Middlesex* Co.). Midway between Hartford and Saybrook.

Middletown, N.J. (Monmouth Co.).

Middletown, Ohio (Butler Co.).

Middletown, Pa. (Dauphin Co.). Between Lancaster and Carlisle, Pa.

MIDDLEBOROUGH, Mass. (Middlesex Co.), town and village. For Middlesborough, Yorkshire, England.

MIDDLESEX For an ancient county in England, most of which became part of Greater London in 1965.

Middlesex Co., Conn. (co. seat, Middletown).

Middlesex Co., Mass. (co. seat, Cambridge).

Middlesex Co., N.J. (co. seat, New Brunswick).

Middlesex Co., Ont. (co. seat, London).

Middlesex Co., Va. (co. seat, Saluda).

Middlesex, N.J. (*Middlesex* Co.).

MIDDLE SISTER. See THREE SISTERS.

MIDDLETON ISLAND, Alaska. In Gulf of Alaska. Named by Capt. George Vancouver in 1794 for Sir Charles Middleton, comptroller of the British Navy.

MIDLAND Descriptive of a central location.

Midland Co., Mich. (co. seat, *Midland*).

Midland Co., Tex. (co. seat, *Midland*). Midpoint on the railway between Fort Worth and El Paso.

Midland, Mich. (co. seat of *Midland* Co.).

Midland, Ont. (Simcoe Co.). Originally named Midland Harbor by the Midland railway.

Midland, Pa. (Beaver Co.). Between Pittsburgh and the Shenango Valley district.

Midland, Tex. (co. seat of *Midland* Co.).

Midland Park, N.J. (Bergen Co.).

MIDLOTHIAN, III. (Cook Co.). From the title of a novel by Sir Walter Scott.

MIDVALE, Utah (Salt Lake Co.). So named because it was halfway between the mines in Cottonwood Canyon and the smelter.

MIDWAY ISLANDS, U.S.A. For their position between North America and Asia. An administrative area and possession, annexed in 1876. The islands were the site of naval victory over Japan in 1942.

MIDWEST CITY, Okla. (Oklahoma Co.). A municipality adjoining Oklahoma City; party promotional.

MIFFLIN, Thomas (1744-1800), first governor of Pennsylvania (1790-99). He had been president of the supreme executive council under the Constitution of 1776 for two years, a member of the Pennsylvania Assembly, president of the Continental Congress at the close of the American Revolution, a major general in the Revolutionary army, and one of the writers of the Constitution. He was president of the convention that drew up the Pennsylvania state constitution in 1790.

Mifflin Co., Pa. (co. seat, Lewistown).

Mifflinburg, Pa. (Union Co.).

Mifflintown, Pa. (co. seat of Juniata Co.).
West Mifflin, Pa. (Allegheny Co.).

MILACA, Minn. (co. seat of Mille Lacs Co.). A shortened and changed form of MILLE LACS.

MILAKOKIA LAKE, Mich. From an Indian word, meaning unknown.

MILAM Co., Tex. (co. seat, Cameron). For Benjamin Rush Milam (?-1836), Republic of Texas army officer killed at the Battle of San Antonio.

MILAN For the city and province in Italy. The name achieved popularity during the period when places in the United States were named for famous cities of the world.
Milan, Ill. (Rock Island Co.).
Milan, Mich. (Washtenaw and Monroe Cos.).
Milan, Mo. (co. seat of Sullivan Co.).
Milan, N.H. (Coos Co.).
Milan, Tenn. (Gibson Co.).

MILBANK, S.Dak. (co. seat of Grant Co.). For Jeremiah Milbank, a railway official.

MILES CITY, Mont. Named for Gen. Nelson Appleton Miles (1839-1925), who led successful campaigns against Indian tribes. He also led campaigns in Cuba and Puerto Rico during the Spanish-American War. An earlier name was Milestown.

MILES MOUNTAIN, Vt. For a local explorer or settler.

MILES RIVER, Mass. For a local settler. It flows northeast into Ipswich River.

MILFORD For a mill by a river crossing.
Milford, Mass. (Worcester Co.), town and village.
Milford, Mich. (Oakland Co.).

MILFORD For Milford, Hampshire, England.
Milford, Conn. (New Haven Co.).
New Milford, Conn. (Litchfield Co.), town and village.
West Milford, N.J. (Passaic Co.). For *Milford*, Conn.

Milford, N.H. (Hillsborough Co.), town and village.
Milford, Ohio (Clermont Co.). For an Eastern town.
Milford, Pa. (co. seat of Pike Co.). Probably for a mill at the ford of Saw Creek, though some say for Milford Haven, Wales, others for Milford, Conn.

MILFORD, Del. (Kent and Sussex Cos.). For a ford located near a mill.

MILK RIVER, Mont.-Alta. For the milky appearance of the water. It flows generally east into Missouri River.

MILL For a mill or mills in the area.
Mill Brook, Vt.
Mill Creek, Ind. Flows SSW and NW into Eel R.
Mill Creek, Mich. Flows SE into Black R.
Mill Creek, Pa.
Mill River, Conn. Flows S into Long Island Sound.
Mill River, Mass. Flows SE to the Connecticut R.
Mill River, Mass.-R.I. Flows S to Narrangansett Bay.
Mill River, Vt. Flows NW into Otter Creek.
Millbury, Mass. (Worcester Co.), town and village.
Mill Creek Reservoir, Pa.
Milltown, N.J. (Middlesex Co.).
Millvale, Pa. (Allegheny Co.).
Mill Valley, Calif. (Marin Co.).
Millville, N.J. (Cumberland Co.).

MILLARD, Neb. (Douglas Co.). For Ezra Millard (1833-1886), founder.

MILLARD Co., Utah (co. seat, Fillmore). From the first name of President Millard FILLMORE.

MILLBRAE, Calif. (San Mateo Co.). For Daius O. Mills, banker and landowner; *brae*, Scottish, "hill slope."

MILLBURN, N.J. (Essex Co.). For Samuel Campbell's first "mill on the burn."

MILLEDGEVILLE, Ga. (co. seat of Baldwin Co.). For John Milledge (1757-1818),

Georgia statesman, a hero in the American Revolution. He was a state legislator, U.S. representative, governor (1802-06), and U.S. senator (1806-09).

MILLE LACS From French, "thousand lakes."
Mille Lacs Co., Minn. (co. seat, Milaca).
Mille Lacs Lake, Minn.

MILLEN, Ga. (co. seat of Jenkins Co.). For John Millen (1804-1843), attorney, state legislator, and U.S. representative (1843).

MILLER Co. Ark. (co. seat, Texarkana). For Gen. James Miller (1776-1851), first territorial governor of Arkansas (1819-25).

MILLER Co., Ga. (co. seat, Colquitt). For Andrew Jackson Miller (1806-1856), Georgia legislator and jurist.

MILLER Co., Mo. (co. seat, Tuscumbia). For John Miller, fourth governor of Missouri (1825-32).

MILLER, S.Dak. (co. seat of Hand Co.). For Henry Miller, first settler and founder.

MILLER BROOK, Vt. For a local settler. It flows south into Winooski River.

MILLER PEAK, Alaska, in Glacier Bay Natl. Monument. For Ben C. Miller (1898-1953), first official in charge of the monument.

MILLERS RIVER, Mass. For an early settler or explorer. It flows generally west into Connecticut River.

MILLERTON LAKE, Calif. On San Joaquin River. For Albert S. Miller, an army officer commanding a post in the area in 1851.

MILLERSBURG, Ohio (co. seat of Holmes Co.). For Daniel Miller, founder.

MILLERSVILLE, Pa. (Lancaster Co.). For John Miller, an early settler and founder.

MILLINOCKETT From an Indian word meaning "dotted with many islands."

East Millinocket, Me. (Penobscot Co.), town and village.
Millinocket, Me. (Penobscot Co.), town and village.
Millinocket Lake, Me. (Penobscot Co.).
Millinockett Lake, Me. (Piscataquis Co.).

MILLS Co., Iowa (co. seat, Glenwood). For Frederick D. Mills (?-1847), an army officer killed during the Mexican War.

MILLS Co., Tex. (co. seat, Goldthwaite). For John T. Mills, Republic of Texas jurist.

MILLSTONE RIVER, N.J. For stones suitable for mill operations. It flows northwest and north into Raritan River.

MILLTOWN, N.J. See MILL.

MILLVALE, Pa. See MILL.

MILL VALLEY, Calif. See MILL.

MILLVILLE, N.J. See MILL.

MILO, Me. (Piscataguis Co.), town. For the ancient Greek Olympic athlete, Milo of Crotona.

MILPITAS, Calif. (Santa Calara Co.). From Aztec *milli*, "land sown with seed," and , "in."

MILTON A form of *mill town*.
Milton, Pa. (Northumberland Co.). Earlier, Mill Town.
Milton, Wis. (Rock Co.). For *Milton*, Pa. or possibly for John Milton, the poet.

MILTON, Fla. (co. seat of Santa Rosa Co.). Origin in dispute: for John Milton (1807-1865), lawyer, Indian fighter, legislator, and governor (1861-65); or a form of *mill town*; or for Milton Amos, an early settler.

MILTON, Mass. (Norfolk Co.), town. Possibly for one of several Miltons in England, or for the poet John Milton (1608-1674). It may also have been suggested by a mill on the Neponsit River.

MILTON, Ont. (co. seat of Halton Co.). For Martin Mills, an early settler. The original settlement was called Milltown.

MILTON, Vt. (Chittenden Co.), town. Possibly for the English poet, but more likely for William Wentworth, Viscount Milton (1748-1833), an associate of William Pitt and a relative of Gov. John Wentworth of New Hampshire.

MILTON-FREEWATER, Ore. (Umatilla Co.). *Milton,* probably a shortened form of *Milltown;* Freewater was a rival community in which the founders offered free irrigation water to obtain settlers.

MILWAUKEE From Algonquian, probably "a good spot or place."
Milwaukee Co., Wis. (co. seat, *Milwaukee*).

Milwaulkee is noted for its German settlers and its beer industry as shown in this 1936 photograph of the Schlitz Brewery. [*New York Public Library*]

Milwaukee, Wis. (co. seat of *Milwaukee* Co.).
West Milwaukee, Wis. (Milwaukee Co.).

MILWAUKIE, Ore. (Clackamas Co.). For MILWAUKEE, Wis. (a misspelling).

MIMBRES From Spanish, "willows." The river was named first.
Mimbres, N.Mex. (grant Co.).
Mimbres Lake, N.Mex.
Mimbres Mountains, N.Mex.
Mimbres Peak, N.Mex.
Mimbres River, N.Mex.

MIMICO Said to have been derived from Missisauga Indian, "place of the wild pigeon," because American passenger pigeons fed in fields near Mimico Creek.
Mimico, Ont. (York Co.).
Mimico Creek, Ont. Flows into Humber Bay.

MINDEN For Minden, Germany.
Minden, La (parish seat of Webster Parish). Named by its founder, C. H. Veeder, a German-American.
Minden, Neb. (co. seat of Kearney Co.).
Minden, Nev. (co. seat of Douglas Co.)., The founder was born in Minden, Germany.
Minden, Ont. (co. seat of Haliburton Co.).

MINEOLA, N.Y. (co. seat of Nassau Co.). From Algonquian *meniolagamika*, "pleasant or palisaded village."

MINEOLA, Tex. (Wood Co.). Supposedly named by Maj. Ira H. Evans, who laid out the town, with a combination of his daughter's name, Ola, and that of her close friend, Minnie Patton, whose father was also a close friend of Major Evans. Also, Major Evans had been a resident of Mineola, N.Y., which provided the original impetus.

MINER Co., S.Dak. (co. seat, Howard). For Nelson Miner (1827-1879) and Ephraim Miner (1833-?), members of the Dakota Territory legislature when the county was formed.

MINERAL For mineral deposits or mining activity.
Mineral Co., Colo. (co. seat, Creede).
Mineral Co., Mont. (co. seat, Superior)
Miheral Co., Nev. (co. seat, Hawthorne).
Mineral Co., W.Va. (co. seat, Keyser).
Mineral Lake, Wis.
Mineral Mountains, Utah.

MINERAL WELLS, Tex. (Palo Pinto Co.). For the mineral water found in a well dug by Judge J. A. Lunch. Later, other wells were dug and the place became famous for water that had curative powers. An earlier name was Millsap Valley.

MINERSVILLE, Pa. (Schuykill Co.). For the many coal miners in area.

MINERVA, N.Y. (Essex Co.). For the Roman goddess associated with wisdom and art.

MINERVA, Ohio (Stark Co.). For Minerva Ann Thomas (or Taylor), niece of John Whitacre, one of the founders. It has also been suggested that the name is for Minerva, goddess of wisdom.

MINGO For an Indian tribe of Iroquoian linguistic stock variously located in the Ohio River valley. The name derives from Algonquian *Mingwe*, "stealthy" or "treacherous."
Mingo Co., W.Va. (co. seat, Williamson).
Mingo Junction, Ohio (Jefferson Co.).

MINIDOKA Co., Idaho (co. seat, Rupert). From Shoshonean, "broad expanse," descriptive of the Snake River plain in this area.

MINNEAPOLIS From *Minnehaha* and Greek *polis*, city. Minnehaha is the heroine of Longfellow's *Hiawatha*; but the name in Siouan means "waterfall."
Minneapolis, Kan. (co. seat of Ottawa Co.).
Minneapolis, Minn. (co. seat of Hennepin Co.).

MINNEDOSA From a combination of Siouan *minne*, "water," plus *duza*, "rapid."
Minnedosa, Man.
Minnedosa River, Man. Flows into Assiniboine R.

MINNEHAHA From Siouan, "waterfall."
Minnehah Co., S.Dak. (co. seat, Sioux Falls).
Minnehaha Falls, Minn.

MINNESOTA From a Dakota Indian term first applied to the river. While scholars agree that *minne* means "water," there is difference of opinion concerning *sota*. Most agree that *sota* refers to the reflection of the sky upon the water but disagree as to whether *Minnesota* means "water reflecting cloudy skies." By tradition Minnesotans have looked on the bright side and referred to their state as "the land of the sky-blue water," and since Minnesota is so dotted with lakes it might be best defined as "the waters reflect the weather."

The business center of Minneapolis was already bustling by 1875. [*New York Public Library*]

A Minnesota farm is shown in the late 1800s. Already the Iron Horse is intruding on the pastoral serenity. [*New York Public Library*]

Minnesota, State of. 32nd state of the Union. Settled: 1805. Territory: 1849. Admitted: 1858. Cap: St. Paul. Motto: *L'Etoile du Nord* (Star of the North). Nicknames: North Star State; Gopher State. Flower: Showy Lady's Slipper. Bird: Loon. Tree: Red (Norway) Pine. Song: "Hail! Minnesota."

Minnesota River, Minn. Flows into the Mississippi R.

Minnesota Experimental City, Minn. (Aitkin Co.). A planned urban-rural city, founded in 1973 by Athelstan Spilhaus, a scientist.

MINNESUING LAKE, Wis. From Indian, possibly "water queen."

MINNETONKA Coined by Gov. Alexander Ramsey from Siouan *minne*, "water," and *tonka*, "big."

Minnetonka, Minn. (Hennepin Co.). For the lake.

Minnetonka, Lake, Minn.

MINNETRISTA, Minn. (Hennepin Co.). From Siouan *minne*, "water," and *trista*, "twisted" or "crooked," for the zigzag outline of the lakes in the area.

MINNEWASKA, Lake Minn. From Siouan, "good water." It has also been called White Bear Lake and Lake Whipple.

MINNEWAUKAN, N.Dak. (co. seat of Benson Co.). For a nearby lake. The name is Siouan, *mini-waukon-chante*, "water-spirit-bad," or Devil's Lake in translation. Other interpretations are "the heart of enchanted water" and "spirit water."

MINNIE MAUDE CREEK, Utah. Believed locally to have been named for Minnie and Maude Hall, two sisters who lived with their father near the stream. It flows east into Green River.

MINOT, N.Dak. (co. seat of Ward Co.). For Henry D. Minot (1859-1890), a director of the Great Northern railroad.

MIO, Mich. (co. seat of Oscoda Co.). Believed to be the family name of Maria Deyarmond, an early settler. She was known as Aunt Mioe, and her home became synonymous with the site of the town. It was named by John Randall, a druggist, surveyor, newspaper owner and publisher, sawmill proprietor, and operator of the telephone company, as well as a town benefactor.

MIRA LOMA, Calif. (Riverside Co.). From Spanish *mira*, "Look, behold!," and *loma*, usually "bare hills."

MIRAMAR, Fla. (Broward Co.). From Spanish *mira*, "Look, behold!" and *mar*, "sea."

MISHAUM POINT, Mass. Extends into Buzzards Bay. From Narraganset, meaning uncertain, possibly "great neck," "great landing place for canoes," or "big ferry."

MISHAWAKA, Ind. (St. Joseph Co.). From Potawatomi, variously interpreted as "swift water," "thick woods," or "place of dead trees." The place is near rapids in the Miami River; there was also at one time a thick growth of oaks in the area.

MISQUAH HILLS, Minn. From Ojibway, "red" descriptive of the color of rocks.

MISSAUKEE For an Ottawa chief.
Missaukee Co., Mich. (co. seat, Lake City).
Missaukee Lake, Mich.

MISSION For a mission church or group of buildings, especially one built in the South-west by Franciscan missionaries to serve the Indians.
Mission, Kan. (Johnson Co.).
Mission, Tex. (Hidalgo Co.).
Mission Hills, Kan. (Johnson Co.). For the Shawnee Indian Mission.
Mission Viejo, Calif. (Los Angeles Co.). *Viejo* from Spanish, "old."

MISSISQUOI From Abnaki, meaning uncertain, possibly "big woman," "big rattlesnake," "much flint," or "great grassy meadows," the last being most acceptable.
Missisquoi Co., Que. (co. seat, Bedrord Co.).
Missisquoi Bay, Vt.-Que.
Missisquoi River, Vt.-Que. Flows into L. Champlain.

MISSISSINEWA RIVER, Ohio-Ind. From Indian, "river of big stones." It flows north-west into Wabash River.

MISSISSIPPI The word *mississippi*, "great water," common to several Indian languages. It is derived from *meeche* or *mescha*, "great," and *cebe*, "river" or "water." The territory and state were named for the river.
Mississippi, State of. 20th state of the Union. Settled: 1699. Territory: 1802. Admitted: 1817. Cap: Jackson, Motto: *Virtute et Armis* (By Valor and Arms).

The mighty Mississippi, nicknamed "Ole Man River" and "The Father of Waters," drains the entire central heartland of the United States and once was the only NorthSouth "road" into the interior. This continued into the heyday of the great side-wheelers. [*New York Public Library*]

"The Mighty Mo", the Missouri River, was the route of the Lewis and Clark expedition. Later, it became central to the growth of the beaver trade. *"Fur Traders Descending the Missouri"*, *painting by George Caleb Bingham.* [Courtesy of the Metropolitan Museum of Art. Morris K. kesup Fund, 1933]

Nickname: Magnolia State. Flower: Magnolia. Bird: Mockingbird. Tree: Magnolia. Song: "Go, Mississippi."

Mississippi River. Flows from Lake Itaska in NW Minnesota to the Gulf of Mexico, SE Louisiana. Except for its source and its mouth, it forms the boundary of the following states: Minnesota, Iowa, Missouri, Arkansas, Louisiana to the west; Wisconsin, Illinois, Kentucky, Tennessee, Mississippi to the east. Principal tributaries (N to S): Minnesota, St. Croix, Wisconsin, Des Moines, Illinois, Missouri, Ohio, Arkansas, Yazoo, and Red rivers.

Mississippi Co., Ark. (co. seats, Blytheville and Osceola).

Mississippi Co., Mo. (co. seat, Charleston).

Mississippi City, Miss. (Harrison Co.).

Mississippi Delta, Louisiana.

MISSOULA From Flathead Indian "feared water," or with the connotation of "dread."

Missoula Co., Mont. (co. seat, *Missoula*).

Missoula, Mont. (co. seat of *Missoula* Co.).

Missoula South, Mont. (*Missoula* Co.).

Missoula West, Mont. (*Missoula* Co.).

MISSOURI For an Indian tribe who inhabited an area near the mouth of the river. The original name for the river was *Pekitanoul* or *Pokitanou*, "muddy water." How the name *Missouri* came to be used in connection with it is unknown. The territory and state were named for the river.

Missouri, State of. 24th state of the Union. Settled: 1735. Territory: 1812. Admitted: 1821. Cap: Jefferson City. Motto: *Populi Suprema Lex Esto* (Let the Welfare of the People Be the Supreme Law). Nickname: Show-Me State. Flower: Hawthorn. Bird: Bluebird. Tree: Dogwood. Song: "Missouri Waltz."

Little Missouri River, Ark. Flows SE into Quachita R.

Little Missouri River, Wyo.-S.Dak.-N.Dak. Flows NE into *Missouri* R.

Missouri River. From the confluence of the Jefferson, Madison, and Gallatin rivers SE to the Mississippi R. It flows through Montana, North Dakota, and South Dakota, part way between Nebraska and Iowa, part way between Kansas and Missouri, and across Missouri.

Missouri City, Tex. (Fort Bend Co.). For the state.

Missouri Valley, Iowa (Harrison Co.).

MISTASSINI From Cree Indian, "great stone," referring to an enormous rock in Mistassini Lake.
Mistassini, Que. (Lake St. John Co.).
Mistassini Lake, Que.
Mistassini River, Que. Flows S into L. St. John.

MISTEGUARY CREEK, Mich. Of Indian origin, meaning uncertain. It flows north into Saginaw River.

MITCHELL, Elisha (1793-1857), a professor at the University of North Carolina. He was killed while exploring the mountain peak that now bears his name.
Mitchell Co., N.C. (co. seat, Bakersville).
Mitchell, Mount, N.C. (Yancey Co.). Highest peak east of the Mississippi.

MITCHELL Co., Ga. (co. seat, Camilla). For Gen. Henry Mitchell.

MITCHELL, Ind. (Lawrence Co.). For O. M. Mitchell, chief surveyor for the Ohio and Mississippi railroad, who platted the town.

MITCHELL Co., Iowa (co. seat, Osage). Named by Irish settlers for John Mitchell, an Irish patriot who never visited America. There is also a possibility that the name came from that of a surveyor of the county.

MITCHELL Co., Kan. (co. seat, Beloit). For William D. Mitchell (?-1865), a Union officer killed at the Battle of Monroe's Cross Roads, N.C.

MITCHELL, Lake, Mich. For William Mitchell, sawmill operator.

MITCHELL, Mount, N.C. Highest peak east of the Mississippi River. For Elisha Mitchell (1793-1857), a professor at the University of North Carolna who fell to his death while trying to measure the height of the peak.

MITCHELL, Mount, Ore. For Roy Mitchell, killed while fighting a forest fire.

MITCHELL, S.Dak. (co. seat of Davison Co.). For Alexander Mitchell, president of the Chicago, Milwaukee and St. Paul railroad.

MITCHELL Co., Tex. (co. seat, Colorado City). For Asa and Eli Mitchell, early settlers.

MITCHELL LAKE, Ala. On Coosa River. For a local settler.

MITCHELL PEAK, Wyo. For Finis Mitchell, mountaineer and early settler.

MOAB, Utah (co. seat of Grand Co.). Biblical, for the kingdom of Moab (II Kings).

MOBERLY, Mo. (Randolph Co.). For an early settler.

MOBILE A Gallicized form of an Indian word of unknown origin, applied to a tribe related to the Choctaws who lived in southern Alabama. Their principal town (various *Mabila, Mavilla, Mavila,* or *Mauvila*), bore the same name. A possible origin is Choctaw *moeil*, "to paddle"; the tribe called themselves *Moila*.
Mobile Co., Ala. (co. seat, *Mobile*).
Mobile Ala. (co. seat of *Mobile* Co.).
Mobile Bay, Ala.
Mobile River, Ala.

MOBRIDGE, S.Dak. (Walworth Co.). From *Mo.* (for MISSOURI) plus *bridge*, because its location at the east end of a bridge across the Missouri River.

MOCKSVILLE, N.C. (co. seat of Davie Co.). For the Mock family, landowners.

MODESTO From Spanish, "modest," for the modesty of William C. Ralston, railroad official and financier, in declining to have the town named for him.
Modesto, Calif. (co. seat of Stanislaus Co.).
South Modesto, Calif. (Stanislaus Co.).
West Modesto, Calif. (Stanislaus Co.).

MODOC For an Indian tribe of the Lutuamian division of the Shapwailutan linguistic stock, located in southern Oregon and northern California. The name, derived from *moatokni*, means "southerners."
Modoc Co., Calif. (co. seat, Alturas).
Modoc Natl. Forest, Calif.

MOFFATT Co., Colo. (co. seat, Craig). For David Halliday Moffat (1839-1911), an official of the Rio Grande railroad.

MOGADORE, Ohio (Summit Co.). Supposedly for the Moroccan city of Mogador, with an *e* added, because the name appeared in a book popular at the time.

MOHALL, N.Dak. (co. seat of Renville Co.). For M. O. Hall, founder and early official.

MOHAVE For a tribe of the Yuman linguistic stock, located on both the California and Arizona sides of the Colorado River. The name means "three mountains" and refers to the Needles. See also MOJAVE.
Mohave Co., Ariz. (co. seat, Kingman).
Mohave Mountains, Ariz.-Calif.
Mohave, Lake, Ariz.-Nev.

MOHAWK For the Iroquois tribal name given to them by their enemies, the Algonquins. It means "cannibals," and refers to the custom of eating the bodies of captured enemies.
Lake Mohawk, N.J. (Sussex Co.).
Mohawk, N.Y. (Herkimer Co.).
Mohawk Mountains, Ariz.
Mohawk River, N.H.
Mohawk River, N.Y.

MOJAVE A variant spelling of MOHAVE.
Mojave, Calif. (Kern Co.).
Mojave Desert, Calif.
Mojave River, Calif.

MOHICAN From the Algonquian tribal name *Mohegan.* The form Mohican has spread in popularity as a result of J. F. Cooper's novel, *The Last of the Mohicans.*
Mohican, Cape, Alaska. On Nunivak Island.
Mohican River, Ohio. Flows S to join Kokosing R. to form the Wahonding R.

MOKAPU PENINSULA, Hawaii. On east coast of Oahu Island. From Hawaiian, "taboo area."

MOKELUMNE From Miwok Indian, probably a tribal name.
Mokelumne Peak, Calif.
Mokelumne River, Calif. Flows SW into San Joaquin R.

MOKIO POINT, Hawaii. On northwest coast of Molokai Island. Of Hawaiian origin, meaning uncertain.

MOLINE From Spanish *molino,* "mill."
East Moline, Ill. (Rock Island Co.).
Moline, Ill. (Rock Island Co.).
Moline Acres, Mo. (independent city in St. Louis Co.). Named by the developer for advertising and euphonious purposes.

MOLUNKUS From Abnaki, "a stream between high banks." The river was named first.
Molunkus Lake, Me.
Molunkus Stream, Me. Flows SE into Mettawamkeag R.

MOMENCE, Ill. (Kankakee Co.). Probably for Isidore Momence, an Indian who was awarded land under the Treaty of Tippecanoe (1832).

MONADNOCK From Abnaki, "at the most prominent island-mountain," used for a lookout.
Monadnock Mountain, N.H.
Monadnock Mountain, Vt.

MONAHANS, Tex. (co. seat of Ward Co.). For John Thomas Monahan, who lived on the site long enough to dig a well and then moved on. Earlier names were Trueheart and Monahan's Wells.

MONCKS CORNER, S.C. (co. seat of Berkeley Co.). For Thomas Monck (?-1747), a merchant in Charleston and landowner.

MONCTON, N.B. (Westmorland Co.). For Robert Monckton (1726-1782), British general sent to Nova Scotia in 1752. He became lieutenant governor of Annapolis Royal (1754), commanded the expedition against Fort Beausejour (1755), winning an easy victory, and became lieutenant governor of Nova Scotia (1756-61). The spelling was changed to *Moncton* in 1860 by the European and North American railway.

MONESSEN, Pa. (Westmoreland Co.). Formed by combining the first syllable of *Monongahela* with *Essen*, the name of the greatest steel town in Germany.

MONHEGAN ISLAND, Me. From Algonquian, "island in the sea."

MONIDA PASS, Mont.-Idaho. From the names of the two states it connects, *Montana* and *Idaho*.

MONITEAU Co., Mo. (co. seat, California). Probably a French transliteration of an Algonquian word, "spirit."

MONITOR Subjectively named for the peak's resemblance to the battleship *Monitor.*
Monitor Peak, Nev.
Monitor Range, Nev. For the peak.

MONMOUTH For Monmouthshire, a county in England.
Monmouth Co., N.J. (co. seat, Freehold).
Monmouth, Ill. (co. seat of Warren Co.). For the Battle of Monmouth, N.J. (1778), between the British under Sir Henry Clinton and the Americans under Washington.
Monmouth, Ore. (Polk Co.). For *Monmouth*, Ill.

MONO Probably a Spanish transliteration of a Shoshonean tribal name and an English shortened form of *monache* or *monachi*, "fly people."
Mono Co., Calif. (co. seat, Bridgeport).
Mono Lake, Calif.

MONOMONAC, Lake, Mass.-N.H. From Nipmuc, "at the deep place" or "deep black mire."

MONOMOY From Wampanoag, meaning uncertain, possibly "lookout" or "deep water."
Monomoy Island, Mass.
Monomoy Point, Mass.

MONONA Said to be the name of a legendary Indian girl who leaped into the Mississippi River when she believed that her lover had been killed. Another version is that the name is that of an Indian divinity. Still another is that it is Ottawa for "beautiful land."
Monona Co., Iowa (co. seat, Onawa).
Monona, Wis. (Dane Co.). Probably for *Monona*, a small village in Iowa.
Monona Lake, Wis. One of the FOUR LAKES.

MONONGAHELA From Indian *menaungehilla*, "river with the sliding banks," or "high banks that break off and fall down."
Monongahela, Pa. (Washington Co.). For the river.
Monongahela Natl. Forest, W.Va.
Monongahela River, Pa. Flows generally SW and joins the Allegheny R. to form the Ohio R.

MONONGALIA Co., W.Va. (co. seat, Morgantown). A variant spelling of MONONGAHELA.

MONROE, James (1758-1831), fifth President of the United States (1817-25), from Virginia. His administration, known as "the era of good feeling," saw the promulgation of the Monroe Doctrine (1823), which warned European powers against interference in the affairs of nations of the Western Hemisphere. He was a U.S. senator (1790-94), minister to France (1794-96), governor of Virginia (1799-1802; 1811), minister to England (1803-07), and secretary of state (1811-17) and secretary of war (1814-15) under Madison.
Monroe Co., Ala. (co. seat, *Monroeville*).
Monroe Co., Ark. (co. seat, Clarendon).
Monroe Co., Fla. (co. seat, Key West).
Monroe Co., Ga. (co. seat, Forsyth).
Monroe Co., Ill. (co. seat, Waterloo).
Monroe Co., Ind. (co. seat, Bloomington).
Monroe Co., Iowa (co. seat, Albia).
Monroe Co., Ky. (co. seat, Thompkinsville).
Monroe Co., Mich. (co. seat, *Monroe*).
Monroe Co., Miss. (co. seat, Aberdeen).
Monroe Co., Mo. (co. seat, Paris).
Monroe Co., N.Y. (co. seat, Rochester).
Monroe Co., Ohio (co. seat, Woodsfield).

Monroe Co., Pa. (co. seat, Stroudsburg).
Monroe Co., Tenn. (co. seat, Madisonville).
Monroe Co., W.Va. (co. seat, Union).
Monroe Co., Wis. (co. seat, Sparta).
Monroe, Conn. (Fairfield Co.), town.
Monroe, Ga. (co. seat of Walton Co.).
Monroe, La. (parish seat of Ouachita Parish). For the James Monroe, first steamboat to sail up the Ouchita R. Earlier, Fort Miro.
Monroe, Mich. (co. seat of Monroe Co.).
Monroe, Ohio (Butler Co.).
Monroe, N.Y. (Orange Co.).
Monroe, N.C. (co. seat of Union Co.).
Monroe, Wis. (co. seat of Green Co.).
Monroe, Lake, Fla.
Monroe Reservoir, Ind.
Monroeville, Ala. (co. seat of Monroe Co.).
Monroeville, Pa. (Allegheny Co.).
South Monroe, Mich. (Monroe Co.).
West Monroe, La. (Ouachita Parish).

MONROVIA, Calif. (Los Angeles Co.). For William Newton Monroe (1841-1935), founder. He was a major in the Union army, railroad contractor, and land developer.

MONSEY, N.Y. (Rockland Co.). From an Indian tribal name, also known as Muncie. See MUNCIE, Ind.

MONSON, Mass. (Hampden Co.), town. For Sir John Monson (1693-1748), president of the British Board of Trade and friend of Governor Pownall of Massachusetts.

MONTAGUE Named by Capt. James Cook in 1778 in honor of John Montagu, Earl of Sandwich, with a slight change in spelling.
Montague Island, Alaska.
Montague Strait, Alaska.

MONTAGUE, Daniel (1798-1876), surveyor and veteran of the Mexican War.
Montague Co., Tex. (co. seat, Montague).
Montague, Tex. (co. seat of Montague Co.).

MONTAGUE, Mass. (Franklin Co.), town. For Capt. William Montague (1720-1757), a naval officer in King George's War who fought in the Battle of Cape Breton (1745).

MONTANA From Latin montana, "mountainous regions." When the Montana Territory was organized in 1864 from a portion of the old Nebraska Territory, the name was suggested by Rep. James M. Ashley of Ohio, chairman of the Congressional Committee on Territories.
Montana, State of. 41st state of the Union. Settled: 1809. Territory: 1864. Admitted: 1889. Cap: Helena. Motto: Oro y Plata (Gold and Silver). Nickname: Treasure State. Flower: Bitterroot. Bird: Meadowlark. Tree: Ponderosa Pine Song: "Montana."

MONTAUK POINT, N.Y. Eastern point of Long Island. Of Indian origin, meaning uncertain, but may refer to a point or observation place.

MONTCALM Co., Mich. (co. seat, Stanton). For Louis Joseph de Saint-Veran Montcalm (1712-1759), commander of French troops in Canada. He was killed at the Battle of Montreal.

MONTCALM Co., Que. (co. seat, Ste. Julienne). For Louis Joseph, Marquis of Montcalm de Saint-Verain (1712-1759), French soldier who distinguished himself as commander in chief of French forces in Canada against the British. Both he and his British counterpart, Gen. James Wolfe, were mortally wounded on the Plains of Abraham (Sept. 13, 1759), the battle which resulted in the fall of Quebec to the British.

MONTCLAIR Descriptive and promotional; from French, "clear (view of the) mountains."
Montclair, Calif. (San Bernadino Co.).
Montclair, N.J. (Essex Co.).

MONTEBELLO, Calif. (Los Angeles Co.). From Italian, "beautiful mountain." An earlier name was Newmark.

MONTELLO, Wis. (co. seat of Marquette Co.). Either from a name in a novel read by one of the founders, or from French mont de l'eau, "hill by the water."

MONTEREY, Gaspar de Zuniga y Azevedo, Count of (1540?-1606), Spanish colonial administrator, viceroy of Mexico (1595-1603), who sent out exploring expeditions. The bay was named by Sebastian Vizcaino, who landed in 1603.
Monterey Co., Calif. (co. seat, Salinas).
Monterey, Calif. (*Monterey* Co.).
Monterey Bay, Calif.
Monterey Park, Calif. (Los Angeles Co.).

MONTEREY, Va. (co. seat of Highland Co.). Formerly Highland, the name was changed to commemorate General Zachary Taylor's victory (1846) at the Battle of Monterrey, Mexico.

MONTESANO, Wash. (co. seat of Grays Harbor Co.). From Italian, "mount-healthful." Originally the name Mount Zion was proposed by a religious enthusiast, but this similar sounding name was adopted instead.

MONTE SERENO, Calif. (Santa Clara Co.). For El Sereno, a near by mountain; from Spanish, "peaceful mountain."

MONTEVALLO, Ala. (Shelby Co.). A pseudo-Italian combination, apparently intended to mean "mountain valley."

MONTEVIDEO, Minn. (co. seat of Chippewa Co.). For Montevideo, Uruguay. The mayor of the South American city presented a flag of his country to this city in 1905.

MONTE VISTA, Colo. (Rio Grande Co.). From Spanish, "mountain view," descriptive.

MONTEZUMA (?-1520), Aztec Indian chief (1479-1520), ruler of Mexico and half-mythical leader. He was killed by the forces of Hernando Cortez.
Montezuma Co., (co. seat *Cortez*).
Montezuma, Ga. (Macon Co.).
Montezuma, Iowa (co. seat of Poweshiek Co.).
Montezuma Peak, Utah.
Montezuma River, Utah.
Montezuma Castle Natl. Monument, Ariz.

MONTGOMERY, Richard (1783-1775), American Revolutionary general, born in Ireland and a resident of New York. Second in command to Gen. Philip Schuyler during the Canadian campaign, he was killed at the Battle of Quebec.
Montgomery Co., Ala (co. seat, *Montgomery*).
Montgomery Co., Ark. (co. seat, Mount Ida).
Montgomery Co., Ga. (co. seat, Mt. Vernon).
Montgomery Co., Ill. (co. seat, Hillsboro).
Montgomery Co., Ind. (co. seat, Crawfordsville).
Montgomery Co., Iowa (co. seat, Red Oak).
Montgomery Co., Kan. (co. seat, Independence).
Montgomery Co., Ky. (co. seat, Mt. Sterling).
Montgomery Co., Md. (co. seat, Rockville).
Montgomery Co., Miss. (co. seat, Winona).
Montgomery Co., Mo. (co. seat, *Montgomery City*).
Montgomery Co., N.Y. (co. seat, Fonda).
Montgomery Co., N.C. (co. seat, Troy).
Montgomery Co., Ohio (co. seat, Dayton).
Montgomery Co., Pa. (co. seat, Norristown).
Montgomery Co., Tex. (co. seat, Conroe).
Montgomery Co., Va. (co. seat, Christiansburg).
Montgomery, Ala. (co. seat of *Montgomery* Co.), state capital.
Montgomery, Ill. (Kane Co.).
Montgomery, Ohio (Hamilton Co.).
Montgomery City, Mo. (co. seat of *Montgomery* Co.).

MONTGOMERY Co., Tenn. (co. seat, Clarksville). For John Montgomery (1748-1794), explorer of the Cumberland area. He was appointed an officer by Gov. Patrick Henry, served with Gen. George Rogers Clark, and was killed by Indians while he and his companions were hunting for their winter supply of food.

MONTGOMERY, W.Va. (Fayette and Kanawha Cos.). For James Montgomery, an early settler and landowner.

MONTICELLO From Italian, "little hill," from the name of the home of Thomas Jefferson in Albermarle County, Va.
Monticello, Ark. (co. seat of Drew Co.).
Monticello, Fla. (co. seat of Jefferson Co.).
Monticello, Ga. (co. seat of Jasper Co.).
Monticello, Ill. (co. seat of Piatt Co.).
Monticello, Iowa (Jones Co.).
Monticello, Ind. (co. seat of White Co.).
Monticello, Ky. (co. seat of Wayne Co.).
Monticello, Miss. (co. seat of Lawrence Co.).
Monticello, Mo. (co. seat of Lewis Co.).
Monticello, N.Y. (co. seat of Sullivan Co.).
Monticello, Utah (co. seat of San Juan Co.).

MONT-JOLI, Que. (Rimouski Co.). From French, "pretty hill," for its location.

MONT-LAURIER, Que. (co. seat of Labelle Co.). For a mountain, in turn for Sir Wilfrid Laurier (1841-1919), attorney and statesman. He was elected to the provincial legislature (1871), and taken into the cabinet of Alexander Mackenzie as Minister of Inland Revenue (1877). He was prominent as a Liberal working for alliance with Catholics, and became prime minister of Canada (1896-1911).

MONTMAGNY, Charles Jacques Huault de (c. 1583-1653), governor of New France (1636-48), succeeded Champlain.
Montmagny Co., Que. (co. seat, *Montgomagny*).
Montmagny, Que. (co. seat of *Montmagny* Co.).

MONTMORENCY Co., Mich. (co. seat, Atlanta). For Lord Raymond de Montmorency (1806-1889), a French officer.

MONTMORENCY, Que. (Quebec Co.). For the Duke of Montmorency, viceroy of New France (1619-24).

MONTOUR, Madame, an early Pennsylvania settler. Born of French-Canadian and Indian stock, she was adopted at age ten by an Iroquois tribe. Later she used her Indian background as an Indian interpreter, and was known for her influence in Indian affairs in Pennsylvania and New York.
Montour Co., Pa. (co. seat, Danville).
Montoursville, Pa. (Lycoming Co.).

MONTPELIER For the French city, Montpelier, in gratitude for French assistance during the American Revolution.
Montpelier, Idaho (Bear Lake Co.). For *Montpelier*, Vt.
Montpelier, Ohio (Williams Co.). For *Montpelier*, Vt.
Montpelier, Vt. (co. seat of Washington Co.), state capital.

MONTREAL From French, "Mount Royal." The insular mountain was discovered and named by Jacques Cartier on Oct. 2, 1535. The name presumably stems from the solitary isolation and majesty of the mountain, or is in honor of Francis I (Francois I) of France, or both. The island from which the mountain rose was henceforth also known by this name. On May 17, 1642, Paul de Chomeday de Maisonneuve established the settlement of Ville-Marle de Montreal, for Saint Mary, the mother of Jesus. When the city fell to the British in 1760, the name was shortened to Montreal. See also MOUNT ROYAL.
Montreal, Que. (co. seat of *Montreal* and Jesus Islands Co.). For the mountain and island.
Montreal Island, Que.
Montreal River, Wis.-Mich. Flows NW into L. Superior. For the Montreal Mine.
Montreal and Jesus Islands Co., Que. (co. seat, *Montreal*). Formed from two islands, *Montreal* Island and Jesus Island.
Montreal East, Que. (*Montreal and Jesus Island* Co).
Montreal North, Que. (Montreal and Jesus *Islands* Co.).
Montreal West, Que. (*Montreal and Jesus Islands* Co.).

MONTROSE For *The Legend of Montrose*, a novel by Sir Walter Scott, because of the similarity of the surrounding country, but also for the romantic mind of the namer; also possibly in allusion to Montrose, Scotland.
Montrose Co., Colo. (co. seat, *Montrose*).
Montrose, Colo. (co. seat of *Montrose* Co.).

Montreal, "the greatest French city outside of France", is named for the famous insular mountain, viewed here from across the St. Lawrence River. [*Line engraving by Pierre Canot after Thomas Patton. New York Historical Society*]

MONTROSE, Pa. (co. seat of Susquehanna Co.). Named by Robert H. Rose, an early settler and owner of vast acreage, by combining French *mont*, "hill," and his own name, *Rose*. The name also echoes Montrose, Scotland.

MONTVILLE, Conn. (New London Co.), town. From French, "mountain village." It was named in 1788 when enthusiasm for French culture was widespread in America.

MONUMENT Subjectively named for its shape.
Monument Hill, Colo.
Monument Peak, Colo.

MOODY Co., S.Dak. (co. seat, Flandreau). For Gideon Curtis Moody (1832-1906), Dakota Territory legislator and land developer. He served in the Union army during the Civil War as an officer and was one of the first two U.S. senators from South Dakota.

MOOERS, N.Y. (Clinton Co.), town. For Maj. Gen. Benjamin Mooers, an early settler.

MOORE Co., N.C. (co. seat, Carthage). For Alfred Moore (1755-1810), American Revolutionary officer and later a justice of the U.S. Supreme Court.

MOORE, Okla. (Cleveland Co.). For Al Moore, a conductor on the Santa Fe railroad.

MOORE Co., Tenn. (co. seat, Lynchburg). For William Moore, Tennessee general in the War of 1812 and later a legislator.

MOORE Co., Tex. (co. seat, Dumas). For Edwin Ward Moore, a naval officer for the Republic of Texas.

MOOREFIELD For Conrad Moore, owner of the townsite.
Moorefield, W.Va. (co. seat of Hardy Co.).
Moorefield River, W.Va.

MOORE HAVEN, Fla. (co. seat of Glades Co.). For James A. Moore, founder.

MOORES Said to have been named for a widow named Moore who lived near the stream.
Moores Creek, N.C.
Moores Creek Natl. Military Park, N.C. Commemorates the Revolutionary War battle fought at Moores Creek Bridge on Feb. 27, 1776.

MOORESVILLE, Ind. (Morgan Co.). For Samuel Moore (1799-1899), merchant and founder.

MOORESVILLE, N.C. (Iredell Co.). For John Franklin Moore (1818-1900), founder and retail merchant.

MOORHEAD, Minn. (co. seat of Clay Co.). For William G. Moorhead, a director of the Northern Pacific railroad.

MOORPARK, Calif. (Ventura Co.). For an apricot of English variety grown in the area.

MOOSE For the animal.
Moose Brook, Mass. Flows S into Ware R.
Moose Hill, Me.-Que.
Moose Lake, Wis.
Moose Pond, Me.
Moose River, N.Y. Flows W into Black R.
Moose River, Vt. Flows S and SW into Passumpsic R.
Moosehead Lake, Me. Translated from Abnaki *mozodup nebes*, "moosehead lake."
Mooseleuk Stream, Me. Flows NE into Arrostook R. From Abanki, "place of moose."
Mooselookmeguntic Lake, Me. From Abnaki, meaning uncertain, but refers to a moose's feeding place.
Moosepayechick Island, Me. From Abnaki, "moose's head."
Moosetookmeguntic Stream, Me. From Abnaki, "moose's river through marshy place."
Moosilauk, Mount, N.H. Of Abnaki origin, meaning uncertain, possibly "a good moose place" or "place of ferns."

MOOSUP For an Algonquian chief.
Moosup, Conn. (Windham Co.).
Moosup River, Conn.-R.I.

MOPANG From Malecite, "solitary place."
Mopang Lakes, Me.
Mopang Stream, Me. Flows SE into Machias River.

MORA From personal and family names of early settlers, such as Mora Pineda and Garcia de la Mora.
Mora Co., N.Mex. (co. seat, *Mora*).
Mora, N.Mex. (co. seat of *Mora* Co.).
Mora River, N.Mex.

MORA, Minn. (co. seat of Kanabec Co.). Named by Myron R. Kent for Mora, Sweden.

MORADA, Calif. (San Joaquin Co.). Probably a Spanish family name.

MORAGA, Calif. (Contra Costa Co.). For Jose Joaquin de la Santissima Trinidad Moraga (1793-1855), soldier and landowner, son of Gabriel Moraga, a wellknown military leader and the original landowner.

MORAINE, Ohio (Montgomery Co.). Descriptive of an area where a ridge, mound, or irregular mass of boulders had been left on the ground by a glacier.

MORAVIA, N.Y. (Cayuga Co.). Name chosen at a meeting to name the town, for no particular reason other than it "sounded well."

MOREAU For a French trader who lived near the mouth of the river.
Moreau Peak, S.Dak. For the river.
Moreau River, S.Dak. Forms from North and South Forks, and flows E into Missouri River.

MOREHEAD, Ky. (co. seat of Rowan Co.). For James Turner Morehead (1797-1854), attorney, state legislator, governor (1834-36), and U.S. senator (1841-47).

MOREHEAD CITY, N.C. (Carteret Co.). For John Motley Morehead (1796-1866), who was elected governor of North Carolina in 1840 and 1842, served in the state legislature, and was president of the national Whig convention in 1848.

MOREHOUSE Parish, La. (parish seat, Bastrop). For Abraham Morehouue (?-1813), colonizer and promoter. He was the first representative of the Ouachita area in the territorial legislature (1805), following the creation of the Territory of Orleans. Morehouse Parish was formerly a part of Ouachita Parish.

MORELAND HILLS, Ohio (Cuyahoga Co.). For George Morr, one of the founders.

MOREY, Lake, Vt. For Captain Samuel Morey, a steamboat builder and pilot.

MORGAN For Jedediah Morgan Grant, Utah legislator and prominent churchman of the Latter-Day Saints.
Morgan Co., Utah (co. seat, Morgan).
Morgan, Utah (co. seat of Morgan Co.).

MORGAN, Christopher Anthony (1825?-1866), colonel in the U.S. Army and inspector general of the Department of Missouri.
Fort Morgan, Colo. (co. seat of Morgan Co.).
Morgan Co., Colo. (co. seat, Fort Morgan).

MORGAN, Daniel (1736-1802), Virginia soldier and frontiersman who fought against Pontiac (1763) and in Lord Dunmore's War (1774). A general in the American Revolution, he fought heroically at Quebec (1775), where he was captured. He fought at Saratoga (1780) led the victorious American forces at Cowpers (1781) and commanded the forces that suppressed the Whiskey Rebellion (1794). He was a member of the U.S. House of Representatives (1797-99).
Morgan Co., Ala. (co. seat, Decatur).
Morgan Co., Ga. (co. seat, Madison).
Morgan Co., Ill. (co. seat, Jacksonville).
Morgan Co., Ind. (co. seat, Martinsville).
Morgan Co., Ky. (co. seat, West Liberty).
Morgan Co., Mo. (co. seat, Versailles).

The giant Virginian, Daniel Morgan, was a soldier much of his life. In some accounts he is reported to have held off dozens of British soldiers at the battle of Quebec before he was finally captured. [*New York Public Library*]

Morgan Co., Ohio (co. seat, McConnelsville).
Morgan Co., Tenn. (co. seat, Wartburg).
Morgan Co., W.Va. (co. seat, Berkeley Springs).
Morgan, Ga. (co. seat of Calhoun Co.).
Morganfield, Ky. (co. seat of Union Co.).
Morganton, N.C. (co. seat of Burke Co.).
Morgantown, Ky. (co. seat of Butler Co.).

MORGAN HILL, Calif. (Santa Clara Co.). For Morgan Hill (?-1914), who married the daughter of a landowner, Daniel Murphy.

MORGANTOWN, W.Va. (co. seat of Monongalia Co.). For Zackquill Morgan, an army officer and son of a prominent citizen.

MORIAH For the mountain on which Abraham was commanded to sacrifice Isaac (Genesis 22:2).
Moriah, N.Y. (Essex Co.), town.
Moriah, Mount, Ore.

MORO, Ore. (co. seat of Sherman Co.). Probably for a Moro in Illinois, but also possibly for a family named Moore, which was connected with the townsite.

MORO CREEK, Ark. Probably from the French personal name Moreau, possibly for a local settler. It flows south into Ouachita River.

MORRILL Co., Neb. (co. seat, Bridgeport). For Charles Henry Morrill, Civil War veteran and a regent of the University of Nebraska.

MORRIS, Ill. (co. seat of Grunday Co.). For Isaac P. Morris, a village official.

MORRIS Co., Kan. (co. seat, Council Grove). For Thomas Morris (1766-1844), outspoken opponent of slavery and a U.S. senator from Ohio.

MORRIS, Lewis (1671-1746), colonial statesman associated with the colonies of New York and New Jersey. He was chief justice of the supreme court of the colony of New York (1715-33) and governor of the colony of New Jersey (1738-46). He was the father of Robert Hunter Morris and grandfather of Lewis, Richard, and Gouverneur Morris.
Morris Co., N.J. (co. seat, Morristown).
Morristown, N.J. (co. seat of Morris Co.).
Morristown Natl. Historical Park, N.J.

MORRIS, Minn. (co. seat of Stevens Co.). For Charles A. Morris (1827-1903), a railway official.

MORRIS, Robert Hunter (1734?-1806), patriot, financier, and a signer of the Declaration of Independence; son of Lewis Morris. He helped to finance the American Revolution and later (1789) became the second U.S. senator from Pennsylvania.
Morrisville, Pa. (Bucks Co.).
Mount Morris, Mich. (Genesee Co.). For Mount Morris, N.Y.
Mount Morris, N.Y. (Livingston Co.).

MORRIS Co., Tex. (co. seat, Daingerfield). For W. W. Morris, thrown off a stagecoach because he was unruly and drunk. He remained in the area and founded a settlement called Morristown.

MORRISON, Ill. (co. seat of Whiteside Co.). For Charles Morrison, a friend of the owner of the townsite.

MORRISON Co., Minn. (co. seat, Little Falls). For William (1785-1866) and Allen (1803-1877) Morrison, active as fur traders and officials in the area.

MORRISTOWN, Tenn. (co. seat of Hamblon Co.). For the Morris brothers, Gideon, Daniel, and Absalom, early settlers who received land grants here.

MORRISTOWN, Vt. (Lamoille Co.), town. Originally Morsetown, for Moses Morse, a grantee in the area.

MORRISVILLE, Pa. For Robert Hunter MORRIS.

MORRO BAY, Calif. (San Luis Obispo Co.). From Spanish morro, "corwn-shaped rock or hill."

MORROW Co., Ohio (co. seat, Mount Gilead). For Jeremiah Morrow (1771-1852), Ohio legislator, U.S. senator, and governor (1822-36).

MORROW Co., Ore. (co. seat, Heppner). For Jackson L. Morrow (1827-1899), merchant and veteran of Indian wars. He was a member of the first state legislature.

MORTON, Marcus, governor of Massachusetts (1840-43).
Morton Grove, Ill. (Tazewell Co.).
Morton Village, Ill. (Tazewell Co.).

MORTON, Miss. (Scott Co.). Named by Col. Caleb W. Taylor, the town's first settler, in honor of his wife, Elizabeth Morton Taylor.

MORTON, Oliver Hazard Perry Throck (1823-1877), Indiana governor (1861-67) and U.S. senator (1867-77).
Morton Co., Kan. (co. seat, Richfield).
Morton Co., N.Dak. (co. seat, Mandan).

MORTON, Pa. (Delaware Co.). For John Morton (c.1724-1777), member of the Pennsylvania provincial assembly from the 1750s to the 1770s, delegate to the Stamp Act Congress and to the Continental Congress (1774-77), and a signer of the Declaration of Independence.

MORTON, Tex. (co. seat of Cochran Co.). For Morton J. Smith, land developer and promoter.

MOSCA PEAK, N.Mex. From Spanish, "fly."

MOSCOW, Idaho (co. seat of Latah Co.). For the capital of Russia. Such names appear often in the United States, probably because they are exotic. Harassed postmasters looking for names different from others in the state often arbitrarily recommended the most far away names they could remember.

MOSHANNON From Algonquian, "moose stream."
Moshannon, Pa. (Centre Co.).
Moshannon Creek, Pa. Flows NE into Susquehanna R.

MOSQUERO, N.Mex. (co. seat of Harding Co.) From Spanish, "flytrap" or "flypaper," used here to mean "swarm of flies (or fleas or mosquitoes)."

MOSQUITO RESERVOIR. Ohio. For the insect.

MOSS POINT, Miss. (Jackson Co.). For primeval moss-laden live-oak trees flourishing in the area.

MOTLEY Co., Tex. (co. seat, Matador). For Junius William Motley (1812-1836), a Republic of Texas physician killed at the Battle of San Jacinto.

MOTT, N.Dak. (co. seat of Hettinger Co.). For C. W. Mott, an official of the Northern Pacific railroad and also a surveyor of the area.

MOULTON, Ala. (co. seat of Lawrence Co.). For Lt. Michael Moulton (?-1813), killed at the Battle of Horseshoe Bend.

MOULTONBORO BAY, N.H. Inlet on Lake Winnipesaukee. For the town, in turn for Col. Jonathan Moulton, early settler.

MOULTRIE, William (1731-1805), American Revolutionary general and later governor of South Carolina (1785-87; 1792-94).
Moultrie Co., Ill. (co. seat, Sullivan).
Moultrie, Ga. (co. seat of Colquitt Co.).
Moultrie, Lake, S.C.

MOUND For an Indian mound or mounds in the area.
Mound, Minn. (Hennepin Co.).
Mound City, Ill. (co. seat of Pulaski Co.).
Mound City, Kan. (co. seat of Linn Co.).
Mound City, S.Dak. (co. seat of Campbell Co.).
Mound City Group Natl. Monument, Ohio.
Mounds View, Minn. (Ramsey Co.). Descriptive of a view from a mound, or a view of mounds.
Moundsville, W.Va. (co. seat of Marshall Co.). For Mammoth Mound, believed to have been built by prehistoric Indians.

MOUNT Generic for "mountain." See the second part of the name (e.g., for Mount McKinely, see MCKINLEY.

MOUNTAIN For location in mountainous country.
Mountain Creek, Pa. Flows NE into Susquehanna R.
Mountain Lake, Mich.
Mountain City, Tenn. (co. seat of Johnson Co.).
Mountain Fork River, Ark. Flows S into Little R.
Mountain Home, Ark. (co. seat of Baxter Co.). Named by slaves of O. L. Dodd, who boasted that they had a mountain home apart from the plantation in Augusta.
Mountain Home, Idaho (co. seat of Elmore Co.). For a stagecoach stop, a "home station" at the base of a mountain.

Mountain Island Lake, N.C.
Mountainside, N.J. (Union Co.).
Mountain View, Ark. (co. seat of Stone Co.).
Mountain View, Calif. (Santa Clara Co.).

MOUNT AIRY, N.C. (Surry Co.). For a home in the town, near the Blue Ridge Mountains.

MOUNT AYR, Iowa (Co. seat of Ringghold Co.). For Ayr, Scotland, and *Mount* because the place is the highest point between the Missouri and Mississippi rivers in this area.

MOUNT CARMEL For a mountain in Palestine. The name in Hebrew means "cultivated land,"
Mount Carmel, Ill. (co. seat of Wabash Co.).
Mount Carmel, Pa. (Norhumberland Co.).

MOUNT CARROLL, Ill. See CARROLL.

MOUNT CLEMENS, Mich. (co. seat of Macomb Co.). For Christian Clemens (1768-1844), pioneer settler and founder. He served as county judge, as commander of the militia, and in other official positions.

MOUNT EIELSON, Alaska. For Carl Ben Eielson, a pioneer in aviation in Alaska and northern Canada, who was killed in a plane crash. An earlier name was Copper Mountain.

MOUNT EPHRAIM, N.J. (Camden Co.). For Ephraim Albertson, landowner.

MOUNT GAY, W.Va. (Logan Co.). For Moses Mounts and Harry Gay. The Gay family were owners of a coal company important in the area. Mounts was a prominent citizen.

MOUNT GILEAD, Ohio (co. seat of Morrow Co.). Biblical, for a mountain and place in Jordan. The name in Hebrew means "hard, rough country."

MOUNT HEALTHY, Ohio (Hamilton Co.). Descriptive and promotional.

MOUNT HOLLY, N.J. (co. seat of Burlington Co.). Descriptive, for holly on a mountain. An earlier name was Bridgetown, for the seven bridges across Rancocas Creek.

MOUNT HOPE BAY, Mass.-R.I. Arm of Narragansett Bay. Folk etymologized name from Narraganset, *montop*, meaning uncertain, possibly "this island is sufficiently fortified."

MOUNT IDA, Ark. (co. seat of Montgomery Co.). Classical, for a mountain near ancient Troy.

MOUNT JOY, Pa. (Lancaster Co.). For a ship that helped terminate the siege of County Londonderry, Ireland in 1689 by the armies of King James II. Many of the early settlers were from Londonderry.

MOUNT KISCO, N.Y. (Westchester Co.). From Indian *chisqua*, "wetlands."

MOUNT LAGUNA, Calif. (San Diego Co.). For a nearby lake and mountain. *Laguna* means "lake" in Spanish.

MOUNT LEBANON, Pa. See LEBANON.

MOUNT MORRIS, Ill. (Ogle Co.). For a Methodist Episcopal minister named Morris.

MOUNT OLIVER, Pa. (Allegheny Co.). The town was built on a hill, and is believed to be named for Oliver Ormsby, who owned several acres of land in the area.

MOUNT OLIVET Biblical, for the mountain, also called Mount of Olives, near Jersualem.
Mount Olive, N.C. (Wayne Co.).
Mount Olivet, Ky. (co. seat of Robertson Co.).

MOUNT OLYMPUS, Utah (Salt Lake Co.). For Mount Olympus in Greece.

MOUNT PLEASANT Usually descriptive or promotional.
Mount Pleasant, Iowa (co. seat of Henry Co.).

Mount Pleasant, Mich. (co. seat of Isabella Co.). Founded and named by David Ward, a lumberman who donated a five-acre square for a county court house, because it was a pleasant place to him.

Mount Pleasant, Pa. (Westmoreland Co.).

Mount Pleasant, R.I. (Providence Co.).

Mount Pleasant, S.C. (Charlston Co.).

Mount Pleasant, Tenn. (Maury Co.).

Mount Pleasant, Tex. (co. seat of Titus Co.).

MOUNT PROSPECT, Ill. (Cook Co.). Promotional and pseudo-descriptive.

MOUNTRAIL Co., N.Dak. (co. seat, Stanley). For Joseph Mountraille, a mailman.

MOUNT RAINIER, Md. (Prince Georges Co.). Named by army officers from Seattle, Wash., who bought a 100-acre tract of land which they named for the peak in Washington.

MOUNT ROYAL Name applied to the hill, from which MONTREAL was derived.

Mount Royal (peak), Que.

Mount Royal, Que. (Montreal and Jesus Islands Co.).

MOUNT STERLING, Ill. (co. seat of Brown Co.). A good, or "sterling," place for habitation.

MOUNT STERLING, Ky. (co. seat of Montgomery Co.). Formerly known as Little Mountain Town from the Indian mound on the site, it was changed to Mount Sterling for Stirling, Scotland.

MOUNT VERNON For George Washington's estate on the Potomac River, which was named for Edward Vernon, admiral in the British navy, by Lawrence Washington, half-brother of George. George Washington, for whom the place is chiefly remembered, lived at Mount Vernon from 1747 until his death in 1799. The name is

Mount Vernon, George Washington's beautiful Virginia estate on the banks of the Potomac River, is shown here in a line engraving by Samuel Seymour after William Birch. [*The I. N. Stokes Collection of American Historical Prints. New York Historical Society*]

usually associated with the house which is situated on a rise, or mount, above the river. Wherever the name occurs in the United States, a hill or mountain is in evidence.
Mount Vernon, Ga. (co. seat of Montgomery Co.).
Mount Vernon, Ill. (co. seat of Jefferson Co.).
Mount Vernon, Ind. (co. seat of Posey Co.). Earlier, McFadden's Landing, for Andrew McFadden, founder.
Mount Vernon, Iowa (Linn Co.).
Mount Vernon, (Co. seat of Rockcastle Co.).
Mount Vernon, Me. (Kennebec Co.), town.
Mount Vernon, Mo. (co. seat of Lawrence Co.).
Mount Vernon, N.Y. (Westchester Co.).
Mount Vernon, Ohio (co. seat of Knox Co.).
Mount Vernon, Tex. (co. seat of Franklin Co.).
Mount Vernon, Wash. (co. seat of Skagit Co.).

MOUSAM RIVER, Me. From Abnaki, either "grandfather," or "a snare." It flows southeast into the Atlantic Ocean.

MOWER Co., Minn. (co. seat, Austin). For John E. Mower (1815-1879), a lumberman and legislator.

MOXIE Origin uncertain, possibly from Indian, "dark water," with an Anglicized spelling.
Moxie Lake, Me.
Moxie Mountain, Me.

MUCKALEE CREEK, Ga. Of Muskogean origin, meaning uncertain. It flows generally southeast into Kinchafoonee Creek.

MUD Descriptive.
Mud Buttes, S.Dak. So named because of the gumbo soil which became muddy when wet.
Mud Creek, Okla. Flows SE into Red R.
Mud Creek, S.Dak. Flows W and SW into James R.
Mud Lake, Me. One of the Fish River lakes.
Mud Lake, Minn.
Mud Lake, Nev. In a marshy area.
Mud River, Ky. Flows NNW into Green R.
Mud Run River, Pa. Flows into Lehigh R.

MUDDY Descriptive.
Muddy Brook, Mass. Flows S into Ware R.
Muddy Creek, Ill. Flows S into Little Wabash River.
Muddy Creek, Mo. Flows NE into Lamine R.
Muddy Creek, Utah. Flows SE into Lost Chance Creek.
Muddy River, Conn. Flows SSW into Quinnipiac R.
Muddy Boggy Creek, Okla. Flows SE to join Clear Boggy Creek.

MUHLENBERG Co., Ky. (co. seat, Greenville). For John Peter Gabriel Muhlenberg (1746-1807), general in the American Revolution, legislator, and U.S. representative from Pennsylvania.

MUIR, John, (1838-1914), geologist, explorer, naturalist, and author, born in Scotland. He was the discoverer of a glacier in Alaska that is named for him. He visited the Arctic regions of North America on the Steamer *Corwin* in search of the DeLong expedition. Muir labored many years in the cause of forest preservation and the establishment of national reservations and parks.
Muir Glacier, Alaska. In Glacier Bay Natl. Monument.
Muir Woods, Natl. Monument, Calif.

MUKUNTUWEAP CANYON, Utah, in Zion Natl. Park. From Ute, said to mean "straight canyon."

MULBERRY For the tree or berry.
Mulberry, Calif. (Butte Co.).
Mulberry, Fla. (Polk Co.).
Mulberry Creek, Ga. Flows SW into Chattahoochee R. Probably translated from Indian.
Mulberry River, Ark. Flows SW into Arkansas R.
Mulberry Fork River, Ala. Flows into Alabama R.

MULCHATNA RIVER, Alaska. From an Eskimo word, meaning unknown. It flows southwest into Nushagak River.

MULESHOE, Tex. (co. seat of Bailey Co.). For a nearby ranch.

MULLEN, Neb. (co. seat of Hooker Co.). For a contractor and local businessman.

MULLENS, W.Va. For A. J. Mullins, an early settler. The spelling change occurred in transcribing the name.

MULLET LAKE, Wis. For the fish.

MULLICA RIVER, N.J. For Eric Mullica, Swedish settler. It flows southeast into Great Bay.

MULLINS, S.C. (Marion Co.). For Col. William Sidney Mullins (1824-1878), a member of the state legislature, president of the Wilmington and Manchester railroad, lawyer, and planter.

MULTNOMAH For a tribe of the Clackamas division of the Chinooks. They lived on Sauvies Island in the Columbia River. The name has been said to be a corruption of Indian words meaning "down river," or to be that of an Indian maiden who leaped over a cliff into the Columbia to save her people from a plague. The falls, having appeared while the Indians prayed, were believed by them to be her soul.
Multnomah Co., Ore. (co. seat, Portland).
Multnomah Falls, Ore. On a cliff beside the Columbia R.

MULVANE, Kan. (Sumner Co.). For John R. Mulvane, an official of the Atchison, Topeka and Santa Fe railroad.

MUNCIE, Ind. (co. seat of Delaware Co.). For the subdivision of the Delaware tribe also known as Minsis or Monsey. The name has been interpreted to mean "at the place where the stones are gathered together," or "people of the stony country."

MUNCY From the Indian tribal name, also spelled Muncie. See MUNCIE, Ind.
Muncy, Pa. (Lycoming Co.).
Muncy Creek, Pa. Flows SW into Susquehanna R.

MUNDELEIN, Ill. (Lake Co.). For Cardinal George William Mundelein (1872-1939), Archbishop of Chicago. An earlier name was Area.

MUNFORDVILLE, Ky. (co. seat of Hart Co.). For Richard I. Munford, an early settler and founder.

MUNGER MOUNTAIN, Wyo. For a miner named Munger.

MUNHALL, Pa. (Allegheny Co.). For Capt. John Munhall, who gave the Pittsburgh, Virginia and Charleston railroad the right of way through his land on the condition that he choose the location for the station.

MUNISING, Mich. (co. seat of Alger Co.). From Algonquian *minissing*, "island in a lake."

MUNROE FALLS, Ohio (Summit Co.). Named in 1817 for Edmond Munroe, a wealthy Boston merchant who bought the mills and surrounding land.

MUNSTER, Ind. (Lake Co.). For Jacob Munster, an early settler.

MUNSUNGAN LAKE, Me. From Abnaki, "humped-up island," reason for naming not clear.

MUNUSCONG From Algonquian, "the place of reeds."
Munuscong Lake, Ont.-Mich.
Munuscong River, Mich. Flows SE and NE into the lake.

MURDO, S.Dak. (co. seat of Jones Co.). For Murdo McKenzie, a cattleman.

MURFREESBORO For Hardy Murfree (1752-1809), officer in the American Revolution and land speculator with large holdings in the Middle Tennessee area.
Murfreesboro, Ark. (co. seat of Pike Co.). For *Murfreesboro,* Tenn. Earlier, Zebulon, for Zebulon Montgomery PIKE.
Murfreesboro, Tenn. (co. seat of Rutherford Co.).

MURFREESBORO, N.C. (Hertford Co.). For William Murfee, a leader in the American cause during the American Revolution and landowner.

MURPHY, Idaho (co. seat of Owyhee Co.). For Pat Murphy, a mining engineer.

MURPHY, N.C. (co. seat of Cherokee Co.). For Archibald Debow Murphey (1758-1862), a prominent North Carolinian.

MURPHYSBORO, Ill. (co. seat of Jackson Co.). For William C. Murphy, a commissioner when the town was selected for the county seat.

MURRAY Co., Ga. (co. seat, Chatsworth). For Thomas W. Murray (1790-1832), a legislator.

MURRAY, Ky. (co. seat of Calloway Co.). For John L. Murray (1806-1842), attorney, state legislator, and U.S. representative (1837-39).

MURRAY, Lake, S.C. For a local settler.

MURRAY Co., Minn. (co. seat, Slayton). For William Pitt Murray (1825-1910), a legislator.

MURRAY, William Henry, known as "Alfalfa Bill" (1869-1956), legislator and governor (1931-35).
Murray Co., Okla. (co. seat, Sulphur).
Murray, Lake, Okla.

MURRAY, Utah (Salt Lake Co.). For Eli H. Murray, Utah Territory governor.

MUSCATATUCK RIVER, Ind. From Indian, "pond river," descriptive. It flows into East Fork of White River.

MUSCATINE A variant name for the Mascouten tribe of the Potawatomis. The meaning of the name is uncertain, but believed locally to be "burning island."
Muscatine Co., Iowa (co. seat, *Muscatine*).
Muscatine, Iowa (co. seat of *Muscatine* Co.).
Muscatine Island, Iowa, in the Mississippi R.

MUSCLE SHOALS, Ala. (Colbert Co.). A translation of the Cherokee name, *dagunahi*, or "mussel place." It was also called *chustanaluy*, "shoals place," from *ustanalahi*, "place of rocks across a stream." The shoals themselves, in the Tennessee River, have been submerged by dams.

MUSCOGEE Co., Ga. (co. seat, Columbus). A variant spelling of MUSKOGEE.

MUSCONETCONG RIVER, N.J. Of Algonquian origin, meaning unclear, but probably referring to a swift stream. It flows southwest into Delaware River.

MUSINIA PEAK, Utah, on the Wasatch Plateau. From Ute, "white mountain."

MUSKEGET From Wampanoag, "grassy place."
Muskeget Channel, Mass. Water passage between Martha's Vineyard and Nantucket Island.
Muskeget Island, Mass. in the channel.

MUSKEGO, Wis. (Waukesha Co.). From Algonquian, "at the swamp," for the Muskegoe Indian tribe.

MUSKEGON From Ojibway, "swampy."
Muskegon Co., Mich. (co. seat, *Muskegon*).
Muskegon, Mich. (co. seat of *Muskegon* Co.).
Muskegon Lake, Mich.
Muskegon River, Mich.
Muskegon Heights, Mich. (*Muskegon* Co.).
North Muskegon, Mich. (*Muskegon* Co.).

MUSKINGUM From Algonquian. The meaning is uncertain, but some translate it as "by the river."
Muskingum Co., Ohio (co. seat, Zanesville).
Muskingum River, Ohio. Flows generally S to the Ohio River.

MUSKOGEE For a Shawnee tribe of Muskhogean linguistic stock.
Muskogee Co., Okla. (co. seat, *Muskogee*).
Muskogee, Okla. (co. seat of *Muskogee* Co.).

MUSKOKA Probably a corruption of an Indian chief's name, *Misquuckkey*, which appears on two treaties for the surrender of the land (1815).
Muskoka District, Ont. (district seat, Bracebridge).
Muskoka, Lake, Ont.

MUSQUACOOK From Abnaki, probably "muskrat place."
Musquacook Mountain, Me.
Musquacook Lakes, Me.

MUSSELSHELL For the abundance of mussels that occur in certain portions of the bed of the river.
Musselshell Co., Mont. (co. seat, Roundup).
Musselshell River, Mont.

MUSSER LAKE, Wis. For an early settler.

MUSTANG, Okla. (Canadian Co.). For the wild ponies that formerly roamed the area.

MYAKKA RIVER, Fla. From a Timucuan town name, perhaps a variant of MIAMI. It flows southwest and southeast into Charlotte Harbor.

MYERSTOWN, Pa. (Lebanon Co.). For Isaac Meier (1730-1770), an early settler.

MYRTLE BEACH, S.C. (Horry Co.). For the myrtle bushes that abound in the area.

MYRTLE CREEK, Ore. (Douglas Co.). For the myrtle groves in the area; the species is the *umbelluria californica*, an evergreen tree.

MYRTLE POINT, Ore. (Coos Co.). For the myrtle trees, and also as a different name from Myrtle Creek, Ore.

MYSTIC From Algonquian, "great tidal river."
Mystic, Conn. (New London Co.).
West Mystic, Conn. (New London Co.).

N

NACHES RIVER, Wash. An Indian word, exact origin and meaning unknown, although possibly from *nahchess*, "plenty of water.", It flows southeast into Yakima River.

NACIMIENTO RESERVOIR, Calif. From Spanish, "birth" or "nativity," connoting in this case the "source of the stream," for the river on which the reservoir now appears.

NACOGDOCHES For an Indian tribe of Caddoan linguistic stock, a member of the Hasianai Confederacy. See also NAT-CHITOCHES.
Nacogdoches Co., Tex. (co. seat, *Nacogdoches*).
Nacogdoches, Tex. (co. seat of *Nacogdoches* Co.).

NAGAI ISLAND, Alaska. In Shumagin Islands. Of Eskimo origin, meaning unknown.

NAHANT From Algonquian, "at the point" or "twin islands." Nahantum was a local Indian chief.
Nahant, Mass. (Essex Co.), town.
Nahant Bay, Mass.

NAHMAKANTA LAKE, Me. From Abnaki, "plenty of fish."

NAHUNTA, Ga. (co. seat of Brantley Co.). Possibly from a Tuscacora Indian word of uncertain meaning; it has been interpreted both as "black creek" and as "tall trees."

NAKALELE POINT, Hawaii. On northwest coast of Maui Island. From Haraiian, "rustling."

NAKNEK LAKE, Alaska. On Alaska Peninsula. Of Eskimo origin, meaning unknown.

NAMEKAGON From Ojibway, "place for sturgeon."
Namekagon Lake, Wis.
Namekagon River, Wis. Flows into St. Croix River.

NAMES HILL, Wyo. So named because emigrants carved their names on the cliff or left messages for others who followed.

NAMPA, Idaho (Canyon Co.). For a Shoshoni chief. The name is questionably translated as "big foot."

NANCE Co., Neb. (co. seat, Fullerton). For Albinus Nance (1848-1911), legislator and governor (1879-83).

NANSEMOND Co., Va. (co. seat, Suffolk). From the Indian word *neunschimend*, "whence we fled" or "whence we were driven off."

NANTAHALA From Cherokee, "Place of the Middle Sun." Literally, it means "middle-sun," for an area where only the noonday sun can shine on, as in a canyon where perpendicular walls keep out all sunlight except the noon sun. The gorge was named first, and was the subject of many Cherokee legends.
Nantahala, N.C. (Swain Co.).
Nantahala Gorge, N.C. and Gorge in *Nantahala* R.
Nantahala Lake, N.C. In *Nantahala* R.
Nantahala Mountain Range, N.C.-Ga.
Nantahala Natl. Forest, N.C.
Nantahala River, N.C. Flows NW and N into Little Tennessee R.
Nantahala Balds, N.C. Meadow areas in the *Nantahala* Mtn. Range.

NANTICOKE For an Indian tribe of Algonquian linguistic stock originally located on the Eastern Shore of Maryland and Delaware, later in Pennsylvania and central New York, and finally in Ohio and Indiana. The name comes from *nentego*, a variant of Delaware Indian *unechtigo* or *unlachtigo*, "tidewater people."
Nanticoke, Pa. (Luzerne Co.).
Nanticoke River, Del.-Md. Flows into Chesapeake Bay.

NANTUCKET From an Indian word of uncertain meaning. An early map marks the island as *Natocko*, which may mean "far away." Others suggest the root *Nantuck*, "the sandy, sterile soil tempted no one."
Nantucket Co., Mass. (co. seat, *Nantucket*).
Nantucket, Mass. (co. seat of *Nantucket* Co.), town.
Nantucket Harbor, Mass.
Nantucket Island, Mass., in the Atlantic.
Nantucket Sound, Mass. Roughly bounded by Martha's Vineyard and Nantucket Island.

NANUALELE POINT, Hawaii. On east coast of Maui Island. From Hawaiian, "the altar heaps."

NANUET, (Rockland Co.). For a local Indian chief.

NAPA There are several theories: for an Indian tribe found there at the time of settlement, probably from northern Patwin territory, the name meaning "house", or it is from an Indian word of uncertain origin, "grizzly bear." A third explanation is that it is from Suisan Indian, "near mother," "near home," or "motherland."
Napa Co., Calif. (co. seat, *Napa*).
Napa, Calif. (co. seat of *Napa* Co.).

NAPATREE POINT, R.I. Although frequently believed to be of Algonquian origin, it is apparently not an Indian name, for early references were made to Naps and to Tree Point; the latter is descriptive, the former perhaps a nickname.

NAPERVILLE, Ill. (Du Page Co.). For Capt. Joseph Naper, founder.

NAPIERVILLE For Napier Christie, son of Gen. Gabriel Christie, who purchased the seigniory of Lery in 1766.
Napierville Co., Que. (co. seat, *Napierville*).
Napierville, Que. (co. seat of *Napierville* Co.).

NAPLES, Fla. (co. seat of Collier Co.). For the city in Italy, probably because of the Mediterranean-like climate and landscape.

NAPOLEON For Napoleon Bonaparte (1769-1821), emperor of France (1804-14).
Napoleon, Ohio (co. seat of Henry Co.).
Napoleonville, La. (parish seat of Assumption Parish). Named by a soldier who had served in Napoleon's army.

NAPOLEON, N.Dak. (co. seat of Logan Co.). For Napoleon Goodsill (1841-1887), president of the Napoleon Townsite Company.

NAPPANEE, Ind. (Elkart Co.). For Napanee, Ont., Canada, a name of uncertain meaning. One version is that it is a Missisauga word meaning "flour," but this seems to be after the fact, since the first gristmill in the rural parts of Ontario was built at Napanee. An Ojibway dictionary lists *nah-pah-nah*, "flour." The spelling was changed in the United States.

Natchez-under-the-Hill, Mississippi, was celebrated as a rough and tumble river town by such writers as Bret Harte and Mark Twain. [*New York Public Library*]

NARBERTH, Pa. (Montgomery Co.). For a town in Pembrokeshire, Wales.

NARRAGANSETT For the predominant Algonquian tribe; from *nanhiggonsick*, either "back and forth" or "people of the point."
Narragansett, R.I. (Washington Co.)., town.
Naragansett Bay, R.I.
Narragansett Pier, R.I. (Washington Co.).

NARRAGUAGUS RIVER, Me. Believed to be from Abnaki, "above the bog." It rises from two branches and flows southeast into Pleasant Bay, an inlet on the Atlantic Ocean.

NASH, Francis (c. 1720-1777), heroic young officer in the American Revolution. He died of wounds received at the Battle of Germantown, Pa. He had been clerk of the Superior Court of Orange County, Tenn., a member of the Asembly (1771; 1773-75), and a member of the provincial congress (1775).
Nash Co., N.C. (co. seat, *Nashville*).
Nashville, Ark. (co. seat of Howard Co.). For *Nashville*, Tenn.
Nashville, Ga. (co. seat of Berrien Co.).
Nashville, Ill. (co. seat of Washington Co.).
Nashville, Ind. (co. seat of Brown Co.).
Nashville, N.C. (co. seat of *Nash* Co.).
Nashville, Tenn. (co. seat of Davidson Co.), state capital.

NASH, Okla. (Grant Co.). For the first postmaster, Clark L. Nash. An earlier name was Nashville.

NASHAWENA ISLAND, Mass. One of the Elizabeth Islands. From Wampanoag, "lies between."

NASH LAKE, Me. For Amaziah Nash, early settler.

NASH STREAM, N.H. For a local settler. It flows south into Upper Ammonoosuc River.

NASHUA For a local Indian tribe, the Nashaways. Their name means "beautiful river with a pebbly bottom."
Nashua, N.H. (co. seat of Hillsborough Co.).
Nashua River, Mass.-N.H.

NASHVILLE For Francis NASH

NASSAU For a duchy in Germany associated with the House of Orange. See WILLIAMSBURG
Nassau Co., Fla. (co. seat, Fernandina Beach).
Nassau Co., N.Y. (co. seat, Mineola).

NATALBANY RIVER, La. The first part is from Choctaw nita, "bear," for the animal, but remainder is uncertain. It flows south into Lake Maurepas.

NATANES PLATEAU, Ariz. From Apache, "chief."

NATCHAUG RIVER, Conn. From Nipmuc, "between rivers." It flows southwest to join Willimantic River to form Shetucket River.

NATCHEZ Probably from a Caddoan name or word, thought to mean "woods" or "timber." The name is important in American history. Meriwether Lewis was killed on the Natchez Trace (trail) near Hohenwald, Tenn., and the trail itself has become a legend. It connected Nashville, Tenn. and Natchez, Miss.
Natchez, Miss. (co. seat of Adams Co.).
Natchez Trace, Tenn.-Miss.

NATCHITOCHES For an Indian tribe, from Caddoan word translated variously as "chinquapin eaters," "chestnut eaters," "pawpaw eaters." or "pawpaws." See also NACOGDOCHES
Natchitoches Parish, La. (parish seat, Natchitoches).
Natchitoches, La. (parish seat of Natchitoches Parish).

NATICK, Mass. (Middlesex Co.), town. For a local Indian tribe, whose name meant "a place of hills," "a clear place," or "my land." Natick was founded by John Eliot, missionary and author of an Indian Bible.

NATIONAL CITY, Calif. (San Diego Co.). From Spanish nacion, "nation," in celebration of Mexican independence.

NATIONAL PARK, N.J. (Gloucester Co.). So named because it was the site of the Battle of Fort Mercer (October 22, 1777), a significant defeat for British forces in the American Revolution.

NATRONA Co., Wyo. (co. seat, Casper). For the mineral natron, a sodium carbonate, found in the area.

The White Man has tended to lump all Indians together. But they differ in their life styles and specialties, from the totem poles of the Pacific northwest to the excellent social organization of the Iroquois, the learning of the Cherokee, the fierceness of the Apache, the headdress of the Sioux, and the artistic talent of the Navajo represented here by one of their famous blankets. [Santa Fe Railway]

Nebraska is noted for many things. Two of its well-known nineteenth century phenomena are included in the unusual title of this engraving: "The Union Pacific Railroad of America: A prairie on Fire in Nebraska." [*New York Public Library*]

NATURAL BRIDGES NATL. MONUMENT, Utah. Descriptive. Local names for the monument include Caroline, Edwin, and Augusta, but these are not recognized by the U.S. Board of Geographic Names.

NAUGATUCK From Algonquian, "lone tree," in reference to a landmark tree at a nearby river.
Naugatuck, Conn. (New Haven Co.).
Naugatuck River, Conn.
Naugatuck River (East Branch and West Branch), Conn.

NAVAJO For an Indian tribe of Athapascan linguistic stock located principally in northern New Mexico and Arizona; meaning unknown. They were called by other tribes "those with reed knives," "bastards," "wild coyotes," and "those who live on the border of the Utes."

Navajo Co., Ariz. (co. seat, Holbrook).
Navajo Indian Reservation, Ariz.-Utah.
Navajo Indian Reservation, N.Mex.
Navajo Mountain, Utah.
Navajo Natl. Monument, Ariz.
Navajo Peak, Colo.
Navajo Reservoir, N.Mex.-Colo.
Navajo River, Colo.

NAVARRO Co., Tex. (co. seat, Corsicana). For Juan Jose Antonio Navarro (1795-1870), Republic of Texas patriot active in promoting statehood.

NAVASOTA Probably from the Indian name *nabototo,* "muddy water."
Navasota, Tex. (Grimes Co.). For the river.
Navasota River, Tex.

NAVIDAD RIVER, Tex. From Spanish, "Nativity Day," either for Christmas Day or for the day the river was discovered by Spanish explorers. It flows generally southeast into Lavaca River.

NAVY YARD, Wash. (Kitsap Co.). So named because it is a naval personnel community.

NAWAKWA LAKE, Mich. Of Indian origin, meaning uncertain.

NAWILIWILI BAY, Hawaii. On southeast coast of Kauai Island. From Hawaiian, "the wiliwili tree."

NAZARETH, Pa. (Northampton Co.). For the home of Christ in Galilee.

NEBRASKA From an Indian word, "flat or spreading water," applied to both the Platte and Nebraska rivers. The Omaha Indian name is *Niubthatka;* the Oto is *Nebrathka.* The territory was named for the river.
Nebraska, State of. 37th state of the Union. Settled: 1847. Territory: 1854. Admitted: 1867. Cap: Lincoln. Motto: Equality Before the Law. Nickname: Cornhusker State. Flower: Goldenrod. Bird: Western Meadow Lark. Tree: American Elm.
Nebraska Natl. Forest, Neb.
Nebraska River, Neb.
Nebraska City, Neb. (co. seat of Otoe Co.). For the state.

NECHES RIVER, Tex. Named by Spaniards for the Neche Indian tribe. It flows southeast into Sabine Lake.

NEDERLAND, Tex. (Jefferson Co.). For the Netherlands; named by Dutch immigrants.

NED LAKE, Mich. For a local settler.

NEEBISH ISLAND, Mich. in St. Mary's River. From Ojibway, "tea," probably for the color of the water. It has also been translated as "where the water boils," for the rapids in the river, "bad water," and, locally, "grand foliage."

NEEDHAM, Mass. (Norfolk Co.), town. For Needham, Norfolk, England.

NEEDLE MOUNTAIN, Wyo. Descriptive of the sharp peaks.

NEEDLES, Calif. (San Bernardino Co.). For nearby sharp mountain peaks or pinnacles.

NEENAH, Wis. (Winnebago Co.). From Winnebago, "water" or "running water."

NEGAUNEE, Mich. (Marquette Co.). From Ojibway, "pioneer."

NEGRITO CREEK, N.Mex. From Spanish, "little black." It flows northwest into San Francisco River.

NEHALEM RIVER, Ore. For the Indian tribe. It flows north into the Pacific Ocean.

NEILLSVILLE, Wis. (co. seat of Clark Co.). For James O'Neill, a local millowner or logger, or both.

NELIGH, Neb. (co. seat of Antelope Co.). For John D. Neligh, an early settler and owner of the townsite.

NELLIS, Nev. (Clark Co.). For the Nellis Air Force Base, which was named for Lt. William H. Nellis of Searchlight, Nev., the first soldier in the Las Vegas area to lose his life in World War II.

NELSON, Neb. (co. seat of Nuckolls Co.). For C. Nelson Wheeler, owner of the townsite.

NELSON Co., N.Dak. (co. seat, Lakota). For N.E. Nelson, a legislator.

NELSON, Thomas (1738-1789), Virginia statesman, member of the Continental Congress, signer of the Declaration of Independence, and governor (1781).
Nelson Co., Ky. (co. seat, Bardstown).
Nelson Co., Va. (co. seat, Lovingston).

NELSON LAKE, Wis. For a local settler.

NELSONVILLE, Ohio (Athens Co.). For Daniel Nelson, founder.

NEMAHA From Oto Indian, "muddy water."
Nemaha Co., Kan. (co. seat, Seneca).
Nemaha, Neb. (co. seat, Auburn).
Nemaha River, (Big and Little), Neb.

NEMASKET RIVER, Mass. From Wampanoag, either "at the fishing place" or "grassy place." It flows north into Winnetuxet River.

NENANA RIVER, Alaska. From an Indian word, origin and meaning unknown. It flows north into Tanana River.

NEODESHA, Kan. (Wilson Co.). Probably a coinage, but locally believed to mean "meeting of the waters," for the confluence of two rivers at the site.

NEOSHO From Osage, "cold, clear water" or "main river."
Neosho Co., Kan. (co. seat, Erie). For the river.
Neosho, Mo. (co. seat of Newton Co.).
Neosho River, Kan.-Okla. Flows into the Arkansas R.

NEPAUG From Wangunk, "fresh pond."
Nepaug, Conn. (Litchfield Co.).
Nepaug Reservoir, Conn.
Nepaug River, Conn.

NEPHI, Utah (co. seat of Juab Co.). For a prophet in the Book of Mormon.

NEPONSET RIVER, Mass. From Natick, meaning uncertain, but may refer to "falls." It flows northeast into Boston Bay.

NEPTUNE For the ancient Roman god of the sea.
Neptune, N.J. (Monmouth Co.).
Neptune City, N.J. (Monmouth Co.).

NERKA, Lake, Alaska. So named because the lake is a great spawning ground of the red or blue-back salmon (Nerka).

NESCONSET, N.Y. (Suffolk Co.). For Nassiconset, the Sachem of the Nissequogues. His name meant "at the second crossing over," the reference being to a river.

NESCOPECK From Algonquian, "black, deep, and still water." The river was named first.
Nescopeck, Pa. (Luzerne Co.).
Nescopeck Creek, Pa. Flows into Susquehanna R.

NESHAMINY CREEK, Pa. From Algonquian, "double stream." It flows southeast into Delaware River.

NESHANNOCK Variant of NESHAMINY
Neshannock Creek, Pa. Flows SW into Shenango R.
Neshannock Falls, Pa. In the creek.

NESHOBA Co., Miss. (co. seat, Philadelphia). From Choctaw, probably "wolf," but debatable.

NESHOBE RIVER, Vt. From Natick, "full of water." It flows southwest into Otter Creek.

NESQUEHONING, Pa. (Carbon Co.). From Algonquian, "at the black lick."

NESS, Noah V. (? 1864), a soldier in the Kansas Cavalry, who died at Abbeyville, Miss. of wounds received in action.
Ness Co., Kan. (co. seat, *Ness City.*).
Ness City, Kan. (co. seat of *Ness* Co.).

NETCONG, N.J. (Morris Co.). From the last two syllables of Algonquian *Musconetcong,* "rapid stream."

NET LAKE, Minn. For the Net Indians, a subtribe of the Ojibways. The name is connected with a mythical battle and pursuit in which the enemies disappeared as though "caught in a net."

NET RIVER, Mich. For the nets which were used to catch fish. It flows south into Paint River.

NEUFCHATEL, Que. (Quebec Co.). For the village in France.

NEUSE RIVER, N.C. From an Indian tribal name *Neusick,* possibly Algonquian, but this is disputed. Meaning of the name is unknown. It flows southeast into Pamlico Sound.

NEVADA A shortened form of *Sierra Nevada*, a mountain range in western Nevada along the California border, named for the range in southern Spain; from Spanish *sierra*, "mountain range," and *nevada*, "snow-covered."

Nevada, State of. 36th state of the Union. Settled: 1850. Territory: 1859. Admitted: 1864. Cap: Carson City. Motto: All for Our Country. Nickname: Silver State. Flower: Sagebrush. Bird: Mountain Bluebird. Tree: Single-leaf Pinon. Song: "Home Means Nevada."

Nevada Co., Ark. (co. seat, Prescott).

Nevada Co., Calif. (co. seat, Nevada City).

Nevada Co., Calif. (co. seat, *Nevada City*).

Nevada, Iowa (co. seat of Story Co.). For the Sierra; named by Joseph M. Thrift, a forty-niner.

Nevada, Mo. (co. seat of Vernon Co.).

Nevada City, Calif. (co. seat of *Nevada* Co.). For the Sierra.

NEVERSINK A folk etymologized form of an Algonquian word, possibly *navesink*, "at the point."

Neversink Reservoir, N.Y.

Neversink River, N.Y. Flows S into Delaware R.

NEW Names that do not appear in this part of the book may be found under the basic name. For example, for New Buffalo, Mich., see BUFFALO

NEWARK Ultimately for Newark, Nottinghamshire, England.

Newark, Calif. (Alameda Co.). For Newark, N.J.

Newark, Del. (New Castle Co.).

Newark, N.J. (Essex Co.).

Newark, N.J. (Wayne Co.). Either for a Lord Newark who owned much of the territory or for *Newark*, N.J., because James Bartle, a prominent citizen, liked that city.

Newark, Ohio (co. seat of Licking Co.). For Newark, N.J.

The Nottinghamshire borough of Newark was noted for its now ruined twelfth century castle where the infamous King John died. [*New York Public Library*]

NEWAYGO Co., Mich. (co. seat, White Cloud). Probably for an Objiway Indian chief who signed the Treaty of Saginaw in 1819. The meaning of the name is unknown.

NEW BEDFORD, Mass. (co. seat of Bristol Co.). For Bedford, Bedfordshire, England.

NEWBERG, Ore. (Yamhill Co.). Origin is in some doubt; probably named by an immigrant and early settler for Neuberg, Austria, although a claim is made for a place in Germany, so far not identified.

NEW BERN, N.C. (co. seat of Craven Co.). For Bern, Switzerland.

NEWBERRY Origin is uncertain: one theory is that it came from a family of the name, but others state that it came from "new berry," for the abundance of fruit grown in the area. Probably the first is correct.
Newberry Co., S.C. (co. seat, *Newberry*).
Newberry, S.C. (co. seat of *Newberry* Co.).

NEWBERRY, Mich. (co. seat of Luce Co.). For Thomas H. Newberry, a Detroit industrialist.

NEW BLOOMFIELD, Pa. (co. seat of Perry Co.). Traditionally believed to have been named for an Irishman, Benjamin Bloomfield, a British army officer stationed at one time in Newfoundland. He was knighted in 1815 and became an Irish peer in 1825. The name may just as plausibly be descriptive, for it was surveyed when a field of clover was in full bloom.

NEW BRAUNFELS, Tex. (co. seat of Comal Co.). Named by the founder, Prince Carl of Solms, for his native home in Germany, Braunfels on the Lahn River.

NEW BRUNSWICK See BRUNSWICK

NEWBURGH, N.Y. (Orange Co.). Named either by settlers from the Palatinate in the lower Rhine valley for their ruler, Frederick of Neuburg, or by Scottish settlers for a village in Scotland named Newburgh.

NEWBURGH HEIGHTS, Ohio (Cuyahoga Co.). Probably for NEWBURGH, N.Y.; the present name has the ubiquitous promotional element *heights.*

NEWBURYPORT, Mass. (Essex Co.). Either for Newbury, Berkshire, England, or as the port for Newbury, Conn.

NEW CARLISLE, Que. (co. seat of Bonaventure Co.). For a town in Northumberland, England.

NEW CASSEL, N.Y. (Nassau Co.). For the village of Cassel in Germany.

NEW CASTLE For Newcastle (or Newcastle-upon-Tyne), Northumberland, England, which in turn was named for William Cavendish, Duke of Newcastle (1592-1676), English statesman and writer. Also spelled *Newcastle.*
New Castle Co., Del. (co. seat, Wilmington).
New Castle, Del. (*New Castle* Co.).
New Castle, Ind. (co. seat of Henry Co.).
New Castle, Ky. (co. seat of Henry Co.).
Newcastle, N.B. (co. seat of Northumberland Co.).
New Castle, Pa. (co. seat of Lawrence Co.).
New Castle, Va. (co. seat of Craig Co.).
Newcastle, Wy. (co. seat of Weston Co.).

NEW CITY, N.Y. (co. seat of Rockland Co.). So named to designate a recent residential area.

NEWCOMERSTOWN, Ohio (Tuscarawas Co.). For a woman known as "The Newcomer." She was the second wife of Chief Eagle Feather, who was found murdered one morning. "The Newcomer" had fled from the place, but was soon captured and executed. The name commemorates the place where she was captured.

NEW ENGLAND Northeastern section of the United States, comprising the states of Connecticut, Maine, Massachusetts, New Hampshire, Rhode Island, and Vermont. For England, native country of many settlers in the area. The name was first used by John

The history of Newfoundland may predate that of the rest of America. There is some evidence that it is the "Vinland" discovered by Leif Ericsson in 1000 A.D. But it may have been used even earlier by Bristol fishermen as a base for fishing the Grand Banks. Many would have sought shelter in St. John's Harbor. [*National Film Board of Canada*]

Smith in his voyage of 1614 and in his book, *A Description of New England* (1616). The name was confirmed by James 1 in a charter of 1620. Such a name had commendatory quality and was also of political value in maintaining nationalistic claims; a New Netherlands, New Spain, and New France had already been established. Only *New England* remains as a place name today.

NEWENHAM, Cape, Alaska. Extends into Bering Sea. Named on July 16, 1778 by an officer in Capt. James Cook's expedition. Probably originally New Enham, for a village in Hampshire, England.

NEWFANE, Vt. (co. seat of Windham Co.). For Thomas or Francis Fane. Thomas Fane (?-1589) participated in Wyatt's Rebellion (1554) against Queen Mary and was committed to the Tower but later pardoned. He was knighted in 1573. Francis, Earl of Westmorland (?-1628), was his eldest son.

NEWFOUND LAKE, N.H. Descriptive.

NEWFOUNDLAND Originally used to describe any of the coasts beyond the Atlantic visited by European fishermen. It was formerly called Brasil, but English records refer to the New Founde Launde as early as 1502.

Newfoundland, Canadian province. Settled: 1610. Colony: 1934. Entered confederation: 1949. Cap: St. John's. Flower: Pitcher-Plant.

Newfoundland, Island of, Nfld. In the Atlantic Ocean.

NEWHALL, Calif. (Los Angeles Co.). For Henry M. Newhall of San Francisco (1825-1882), landowner.

NEW HAMPSHIRE See HAMPSHIRE

NEW HAVEN Descriptive: a new "harbor." See also HAVEN

New Haven Co., Conn. (co. seat, New Haven).

New Haven, Conn. (co. seat of *New Haven* Co.). Earlier, Quinnipiac.

New Haven, Ind. (Allen Co.). For *New Haven,* Conn.

New Haven River, Vt. Flows NW then SW into Otter Creek.

NEW HOLSTEIN, Wis. (Calumet Co.). For the Holstein region of Schleswig-Holstein, Germany; named by German settlers.

NEW HOPE, Minn. (Hennepin Co.). For the pioneers' hope for a better life in a new place.

NEWINGTON, Conn. (Hartford Co.). For an English town.

NEW JERSEY See JERSEY

NEWKIRK, Okla. (co. seat of Kay Co.). Originally Kirk, for a master mechanic Kirk of the Santa Fe railroad. The name was changed to Newkirk when the railway station was moved to another location.

NEWLAND, N.C. (co. seat of Avery Co.). For William Calhoun Newland (1860-1938), lieutenant governor (1909-13).

NEW LISKEARD, Ont. (Timiskaming Co.). For the town in Cornwall, England.

NEWMAN, Calif. (Stanislaus Co.). For Simon Newman (1846-1912), storekeeper and one of principal founders.

NEWMARKET, N.H. (Rockingham Co.), town and village. For Newmarket, Suffolk, England.

NEW MARTINSVILLE, W.Va. (co. seat of Wetzel Co.). For Presley Martin, the founder, with *New* added because there was another such name in the state.

NEW MEXICO See MEXICO

NEW MILFORD, N.J. (Bergen Co.). For a new mill that was located on the Hackensack River.

NEWNAN, Ga. (co. seat of Coweta Co.). For Daniel Newnan (c.1780-1851), an officer in the U.S. Infantry, commander of the Georgia Volunteers during the War of 1812, and major general in the state militia (1817). He was Georgia secretary of state (1825-27) and U.S. representative (1831-33).

NEWNANS LAKE, Fla. For a soldier who fought in the area during the Seminole War (1836-42). The former county seat of Alachua County was Newnansville, also for him, but now is a ghost town.

NEW ORLEANS See ORLEANS

NEW PALTZ, N.Y. (Ulster Co.). Named for Pfalz, the Rhenish Palatinate in Germany. The original settlers in the American town were Dutch who had briefly sought refuge in Pfalz.

NEWPORT Descriptive, but also possibly recalling Newport, Monmouthshire, England.

Newport Co., R.I. (co. seat, *Newport*).

Newport, Ark. (co. seat of Jackson Co.). On the White R.

Newport, Ind. (co. seat of Vermillion Co.).

Newport, Minn. (Washington Co.).

Newport, Ore. (Lincoln Co.). For *Newport,* R.I.

Newport, R.I. (co. seat of *Newport* Co.).

Newport, Tenn. (co. seat of Cocke Co.).

Newport, Vt. (co. seat of Orleans Co.).

Newport, Wash. (co. seat of Pend Oreille Co.). On the Pend Oreille R.

Newport East, R.I. (*Newport* Co.).

NEWPORT, N.H. (co. seat of Sullivan Co.). town and village. Either for Richard Newport (1587-1651), a member of Parliament, or for his son, Francis Newport, Earl of Bradford (1619-1708), also a member of Parliament.

NEWPORT BEACH, Calif. (Orange Co.). For the steamer *Newport,* used in the first lumber business.

NEWPORT NEWS, Va. (independent city in Isle of Wight Co.). For Christopher Newport and William Newce, the latter name changed by folk etymology to *News.* It was known in 1619 as Newportes Newce.

NEW PRAGUE, Minn. (Scott Co.). For Prague, Czechoslovakia; named by settlers from Bohemia.

NEW PROVIDENCE, N.J. (Union Co.). So named because a church gallery plunged into a congregation seated below; no one was injured, but the congregation changed the name from Turkey to the present form to celebrate their escape from disaster.

NEW RICHMOND, Wis. (St. Croix Co.). For Richmond Day, town surveyor, with *New* added to avoid duplication of names in the state. The choice was probably influenced by eastern places named Richmond.

NEW RIVER Descriptive of rivers "newly" discovered or formed.
New River, Calif. A flash flood caused an overflow in what was before a dry river bed.
New River, Fla. Flows SW into Santa Fe R. Named by early explorers.
New River, N.C. Flows SE into Onslow Bay. Rains turned a lake into a "new" river.
New River, N.C.-Va.-W.Va. Flows NE into Gauley R. Named by early explorers for being "new," but also possibly for a man named New.
New River, S.C. Flows SSE into Atlantic Ocean. So named because it was newly discovered.
North New River Canal, Fla.
South New River Canal, Fla.

NEW ROADS, La. (parish seat of Pointe Coupee Parish). For the new road from False River to the Mississippi River, built in the early 1800s.

NEW SCOTLAND, N.Y. (Albany Co.), town. Named by early Scottish settlers for their native land.

NEWTON Descriptive: *Newton* was the original name for a part of Cambridge, Mass. that later separated to become an independent city.
Newton, Kan. (co. seat of Harvey Co.). For Newton, Mass., where stockholders of the local railroad lived.
Newton, Mass. (Middlesex Co.).

NEWTON CO., Ark. (co. seat, Jasper). For Thomas Willoughby Newton (1804-1853), Arkansas legislator and U.S. representative (1847).

NEWTON, John, a soldier in the American Revolution who, with William Jasper, saved several colonial patriots from execution by surprising and capturing the British soldiers who guarded them. Both served under Gen. Francis Marion.
Newton Co., Ga. (co. seat, Covington).
Newton Co., Ind. (co. seat, Kentland).
Newton Co., Mo. (co. seat, Neosho).
Newton Co., Tex. (co. seat, *Newton*).
Newton, Ill. (co. seat of Jasper Co.).
Newton, Iowa (co. seat of Jasper Co.).
Newton, Tex. (co. seat of *Newton* Co.).

NEWTON Co., Miss. (co. seat, Decatur). For Isaac Newton (1642-1727), famed English mathematician, discoverer of the law of gravity.

NEWTON, Miss. (Newton Co.). For Newton Dolittle, son of Roger Dolittle, who donated the land for the town.

NEWTON, N.J. (co. seat of Sussex Co.). Descriptive: originally New Town.

NEWTON, N.C. (co. seat of Catawba Co.). For Issac Newton Wilson, son of a state assemblyman.

NEWTON FALLS, Ohio (Trumbull Co.). A variant of *Newtown,* for Newtown, Conn., former home of early settlers.

NEWTOWN, Conn. (Fairfield Co.), town. Descriptive.

NEW ULM, Minn. (co. seat of Brown Co.). For Ulm, Germany; named by German settlers.

NEW WATERFORD, N.S. For Waterford, Ireland.

NEW YORK See YORK

NEZ PERCE. From *Nez Perce,* the French name for an Indian tribe that called itself *Chopunnish.* The French term, literally, "pierced nose," might be more meaningfully translated as "mashed" or "flattened nose." Also *Nezperce.*
Nez Perce Co., Idaho. (co. seat, Lewiston).
Nezperce, Idaho (co. seat of Lewis Co.).
Nez Perce Mountain, Wyo.
Nez Perce Natl. Forest, Idaho.

NEZPIQUE, Bayou, La. From French, "nose picked," meaning tatooed, probably in reference to facial tatoos of Indians. It flows south into Grand Lake.

NIAGARA For the Indian town of Ongniaahra belonging to a so-called neutral tribe of Iroquoian linguistic stock, located near the mouth of the Niagara River. The name, rendered by the French explorers as *Ongiara* and *Niagara,* originally meant "bisected bottom lands," "at the neck," or "across the neck."
Niagara Co., N.Y. (co. seat, Lockport).
Niagara Falls, N.Y.-Ont., on the *Niagara* R.
Niagara River, N.Y.-Ont.
Niagara Falls, N.Y. (*Niagara* Co.).
Niagara Falls, Ont. (Welland Co.).

NIANGUA RIVER, Mo. Of Indian origin, meaning uncertain. It flows north into Lake of the Ozarks.

NIANTIC From the name of a local Indian tribe, meaning "at the point of land on a tidal river."

Niantic, Conn. (New London Co.).
Niantic River, Conn.

NICATOUS LAKE, Me. From Abnaki, "the small fork," in reference to a stream.

NICHOLAS, George (1754-1799), an officer in the American Revolution and legislator. He served in the Virginia House of Delegates, later moved to Kentucky, where he helped draft the state constitution, and became the first attorney general of Kentucky.
Nicholas Co., Ky. (co. seat, Carlisle).
Nicholasville, Ky. (co. seat of Jessamine Co.).

NICHOLAS Co., W.Va. (co. seat, Summersville). For Wilson Cary Nicholas (1761-1820), Virginia statesman and governor (1814-16).

NICHOLS HILL, Okla. (Oklahoma Co.). For G.A. Nichols, developer.

NICOLET, Jean (1598-1642), French explorer and companion to Champlain.
Nicolet Co., Que. (co. seat, Becancour).
Nicolet, Lake, Mich.
Nicolet Natl. Forest, Wis.

NICOLLET Co., Minn. (co. seat, St. Peter). For Joseph Nicolas Nicollet (1786-1843), French explorer who mapped areas of Minnesota and North and South Dakota. His reputation now rests on his *Map of the Hydrographical Basin of the Upper Mississippi River.* His journals describe and name places he visited, and also provide details concerning Indian tribes and their local history.

NICOMA PARK, Okla. (Oklahoma Co.). A blend of *Nichols* and *Oklahoma;* named by G.A. Nichols, builder and developer.

NIIHAU ISLAND, Hawaii. From Hawaiian, possibly "bound with hau bark."

NILES, Hezekiah (1777-1830), publisher at Wilmington, Del. and Baltimore, Md. He wrote several books on American government, including *Principles and Acts of the*

Revolution, and edited *The Niles' Weekly Register,* which was devoted chiefly to discussion of politics. The latter is regarded as one of the most valuable sources for the study of American history of the period.
Niles, Mich. (Berrien Co.).
Niles, Ohio (Trumbull Co.).

NILES, Ill. (Cook Co.). For a Niles in New York.

NIMROD LAKE, Ark. On Fourche la Fave River. Biblical; from Hebrew, "great hunter."

NINE MILE Descriptive of distance. Also spelled *Ninemile.*
Ninemile Peak, Nev.
Nine Mile Point, Mich. Extends into L. Huron.

NINNESCAH RIVER, Kan.-Okla. From Sioux, "river-salt." Formed by a junction of North and South forks, it flows southeast into Arkansas River.

NIOBRARA From an Omaha-Poca Indian word for the river, *ni obthantha ko,* "spreading water river."
Niobrara Co., Wyo. (co. seat, Lusk).
Niobrara River, Wyo.-Neb. Flows generally E⁻ to the Missouri R.

NIPISSING From Algonquian, "little water" to distinguish Nipissing Lake from the "big water" of Georgian Bay. The Nipissing Indians, of Algonquian linguistic stock, lived in the vicinity of Lake Nipissing.
Nipissing District, Ont. (district seat, North Bay).
Nipissing, Lake, Ont.

NIPOMO, Calif. (San Luis Obispo Co.). Believed to come from a Chumash Indian word; meaning unknown.

NIPPLE Descriptive.
Nipple Mesa, Wyo.
Nipple Top Mountain, N.Y.

NISHNABOTNA From an Indian word, origin and meaning unknown.
East Nishnabotna River, Iowa. Flows into *Nishnabotna* R.
Nishnabotna River, Iowa-Mo. Flows into Missouri R.
West Nishnabotna River, Iowa. Flows into Nishnabotna R.

NISKAYUNA, N.Y. (Schenectady Co.). From Iroquoian; the probable meaning is "cornfields-big."

NISQUALLY RIVER, Wash. From an Indian tribal name. Fed by Nisqually Glacier, it flows northwest into Puget Sound.

NITRO, W.Va. (Putnam and Kanawha Cos.) So named because an explosive plant was erected there by the U.S. Government during World War I.

NITTANY MOUNTAIN, Pa. Probably originally an Indian name, meaning uncertain. It is now a nickname of the Pennsylvania State University football team, the Nittany Lions.

NIXON RIVER, S.Dak. Probably for a local settler. It flows east and southeast into James River. Also known as Snake River.

NO. 4 MOUNTAIN, Me. Reason for name uncertain, but probably for a series of points, either for directional purposes or for identification.

NOATAK RIVER, Alaska. From Eskimo, probably "new land." It flows southwest into Kotzebue Sound.

NOBLE Co., Ind. (co. seat, Albion). For James Noble (1785-1831), Indiana legislator and U.S. senator (1816-31).

NOBLE Co., Ohio (co. seat, Caldwell). For John Noble, an early settler.

NOBLE Co., Okla. (co. seat, Perry). For John Willock Noble (1831-1912), a Union general during the Civil War and secretary of the interior (1889-93) under Benjamin Harrison.

NOBLES Co., Minn. (co. seat, Worthington). For William H. Nobles (1816-

1876), a native of New York State. A machinist and blacksmith by trade, he later served in the Minnesota Territory legislature.

NOBLESVILLE, Ind. (co. seat of Hamilton Co.). For Lavinia Noble, financee of Josiah Polk, founder.

NOBSKA POINT, Mass. From Wampanoag, "rocks."

NOCONA, Tex. (Montague Co.). For Pete Nocona, a chief of the Comanche Indians. He captured and married Cynthia Ann Parker, and their son, Quanah, is said to have been the last of the "Great Chiefs." See QUANAH Tex.

NODAWAY From Indian, meaning unknown.
Nodaway Co., Mo. (co. seat, Maryville).
Nodaway River, Mo.-Iowa.

NOGALES, Ariz. (co. seat of Santa Cruz Co.). From Spanish, "walnuts"; so named because two walnut trees stood on the site.

NOHILI POINT, Hawaii. On west coast of Kauai Island. From Hawaiian, "tedious" or "slow."

NOKOMIS For a character in Longfellow's poem "Hiawatha." It is said to mean "grandmother" in Ojibway.
Nokomis, Ill. (Montgomery Co.).
Nokomis Flowage (lake), Wis.

NOLAN Co., Tex. (co. seat, Sweetwater). For Philip Nolan (1771-1801), an American agitator in Spanish-held Texas, killed by Spanish soldiers.

NOLICHUCKY RIVER, N.C.-Tenn. From Cherokee, "place of spruce trees." It flows northwest and west into French Broad River.

NOLIN RIVER, Ky. According to legend, Benjamin Lynn, a hunter and Indian scout, went hunting with some friends, probably in the summer of 1779. They agreed to meet at the river. The party returned, but no Lynn, hence the name. It flows west and southwest into Green River.

NOLLESEMIC LAKE, Me. Probably from Abnaki, "resting place," as after a long portage or march. The origin is disputed, however.

NO MANS LAND (island), Mass. Off the coast of Martha's Vineyard, it is an isolated place fit for "no man, not even a refugee." From Indian *Cappoquidnet,* "island of refuge."

NONNEWAUG RIVER, Conn. From Mahican, "dry bed," for a stream that dries during summer months. It flows south to join Weekeepemme River to form Pomperaug River.

NO POINT, Point, Conn. Apparently humorous, for land extending into Long Island Sound that was first thought to be a point, then thought not to be, and finally established as one.

NOQUEBAY, Lake, Wis. From a French spelling of an Ojibway word, "place of the bear totem people."

NORANDA, Que. (Temiscamingue Co.). For the Noranda Mines Ltd., which in turn was from a contraction of *North Canada.*

NORCO, Calif. (Riverside Co.) From North Corona Land Company.

NORFOLK For the county of Norfolk, England.
Norfolk Co., Mass. (co. seat, Dedham).
Norfolk Co., Ont. (co. seat, Simcoe).
Norfolk Co., Va. In 1963 *Norfolk* Co. and the city of *South Norfolk* merged to form the city of Chesapeake.
Norfolk, Mass. (*Norfolk* Co.), town.
Norfolk, Va. (independent city).
Norfolk Lake, Ark.

NORFOLK, Neb. (Madison Co.). A contraction of *North Fork,* as being on that branch of the Elkhorn River. The original name submitted was *Nor'fork,* but was changed by postal officials.

NORMAL, Ill. (McLean Co.). For the normal school (teachers' college) once located there.

NORMAN, Lake, N.C. For Norman A. Cocke (1884-?), attorney, who became associated with the Duke Power Company and served it in many capacities. He became a director of the company (1927) and a trustee of Duke University.

NORMAN Co., Minn. (co. seat, Ada). For either Norman Wolfred Kittson, a prominent early citizen, or for the many Norwegians living in the area when the county was formed. The latter were known locally as Normans (Norsemen).

NORMAN, Okla. (co. seat of Cleveland Co.). For Abner Norman, a surveyor for the Santa Fe railroad. An earlier name was Norman Switch.

NORMANDY For the province in northwestern France.
Normandy, Mo. (St. Louis Co.).
Normandy Park, Wash. (King Co.).

NORRIDGE, Ill. (Cook Co.). Combination of the names of two nearby residential areas, *Norwood* and Park *Ridge.*

NORRIS LAKE, Tenn. On Clinch River. For George William Norris (1861-1944), teacher, attorney, jurist, and statesman. He was a U.S. representative (1903-13) and senator (1913-43) from Nebraska. He was a great champion of public power and was instrumental in promoting the Tennessee Valley Authority as a means for obtaining this power.

NORRIS MOUNTAIN, Wyo., in Yellowstone Natl. Park. For Philatus W. Norris, superintendent of Yellowstone Natl. Park (1877-82).

NORRISTOWN, Pa. (co. seat of Montgomery Co.). For Isaac Norris (1671-1736), a commonwealth official and legislator. He was a justice of Philadelphia County and mayor of Philadelphia.

NORTH Directional. Names that do not appear in this part of the book may be found under the basic name. For example, for North Chicago, Ill., see CHICAGO

North Bay, Me. N part of Moosehead L.
North Bay, Wis. On L. Michigan.
North Lake, Me.
North Point, Mich. Extends into L. Huron.
North Pond, Mass.
North River, Mass. Flows into Deerfield R.
North River, Mass. Flows into Massachusetts Bay.
North River, N.H. Flows SE into Lamprey R.
North River, Wash. Flows NW and SW into Willapa Bay. The Indian name was *Nicomanchie,* "shadowy waters."
North River, W.Va. Flows NE into Lacapon R.
North Fork River, Ill. Flows S into Embarrass R.

NORTHAMPTON For Northampton or Northamptonshire, England, or for one of the Earls of Northampton.
Northampton Co., N.C. (co. seat, Jackson). For James Compton, Earl of Northampton (1687-1754).
Northampton Co., Pa. (co. seat, Easton).
Northampton Co., Va. (co. seat, Eastville). Possibly for Spencer Compton, 2nd Earl of Northampton (1601-1643), an English partisan of Charles I in the struggle with Parliament. He commanded the Royalist forces at Hopton Heath, where he was killed.
Northampton, Mass. (co. seat of Hampshire Co.). Or for its location at the time of settlement (1654) as the town farthest north on the Connecticut R.
Northampton, Pa. (*Northampton* Co.).

NORTH BAY, Ont. (Nipissing Co.). Descriptive; a settlement in the north bay of Lake Nipissing.

NORTH BEND, Ore. (Coos Co.). Descriptive of the bend in Coos Bay.

NORTHBOROUGH, Mass. (Worcester Co.), town. So named because it had previously been the north precinct of Westborough.

NORTHBRIDGE, Mass. (Worcester Co.), town and village. So named because it was formed from the northern part of Uxbridge.

NORTHBROOK, Ill. (Cook Co.). Promotional; a northwestern residential suburb of Chicago.

NORTH CAROLINA See CAROLINE

NORTH COLLEGE HILL, Ohio (Hamilton Co.). Promotional; a northern residential suburb of Cincinnati.

NORTH DAKOTA. See DAKOTA

NORTHEAST POND, Me.-N.H. Descriptive.

NORTHFIELD Descriptive.
Northfield, Ill. (Cook Co.). For *Northfield*, Mass.
Northfield, Mass. (Franklin Co.), town. The most northerly town in Massachusetts.
Northfield, Ohio (Summit Co.).
Northfield, Vt. (Washington Co.).

NORTHFIELD, Minn. (Rice Co.). For John W. North (1815-1890), a founder. He was an attorney, a territorial legislator, a presiding officer at the constitutional conventions of both Minnesota and Nevada, a founder of the University of Minnesota, surveyor general of Nevada, and a supreme court judge in Nevada. It is believed that the town was also named for Ira Stratton Field (1813-1892), a Vermont legislator who moved there and became a blacksmith and farmer. He and North were close friends.

NORTHGLENN, Colo. (Adams Co.). Descriptive, for its location north of Denver, and promotional.

NORTH HAVEN ISLAND, Me. So named because it is a place of rest or shelter, north of Vinalhaven Island.

NORTH ISLAND, Calif. (San Diego Co.). Promotional.

NORTHRIDGE, Ohio (Montgomery Co.). Descriptive.

NORTH SISTER See THREE SISTERS

NORTH TRUCHAS PEAK, N.Mex. *Truchas* is Spanish for "trout."

NORTHUMBERLAND For the county of Northumberland in England.
Northumberland, N.B. (co. seat, Newcastle).
Northumberland, Ont. (co. seat, Cobourg).
Northumberland Co., Va. (Co. seat, Heathsville).

NORTH VALLEY, N.Mex. (Bernalillo Co.). Promotional and descriptive.

NORTHVILLE, Mich. (Wayne Co.). So named for its location in the northern part of Plymouth township.

NORTHWEST TERRITORIES Descriptive of location in Canada.
Northwest Territories, Canada. Settled: 1820. Gained territorial status: 1905. Cap: Yellowknife.

NORTHWOOD Descriptive.
Northwood, Iowa (co. seat of Worth Co.).
Northwood, Ohio (Lucas Co.).
Northwood Lake, N.H.

NORTHWOODS, Mo. (independent city in St. Louis Co.). So named for its location in the northern part of the county.

NORTON For a local settler.
Norton, Vt. (Essex Co.), town.
Norton Lake, Vt.

NORTON Possibly for one of several Nortons in England. Since this was originally the north part of Taunton, it may also be descriptive.
Norton, Mass. (Bristol Co.), town.
Norton Reservoir, Mass.

NORTON, Sir Fletcher, speaker of the House of Commons in England. The sound was named first.
Norton Bay, Alaska. Inlet of *Norton* Sound.
Norton Sound, Alaska.

NORTON, Orloff (?-1864), a Kansas army officer killed during a skirmish at Cane Hill, Ark.
Norton Co., Kan. (co. seat, *Norton*).
Norton, Kan. (co. seat of *Norton* Co.).

NORWALK Possibly from a Siwanay Indian word meaning "at the point of land," but it is also said to have come from "north walk" because the land originally purchased from the Indians was supposed to extend a day's walk northward from the sea.
Norwalk, Conn. (Fairfield Co.).
Norwalk River, Conn.

NORWALK, Calif. (Los Angeles Co.). A contraction, of *North Walk*, a trail from Anaheim Landing.

NORWAY For the country in Europe.
Norway, Me. (Oxford Co.). Or by a spelling error (possibly intended to be *Norwich* or *Norage*).
Norway, Mich. (Dickinson Co.).

NORWELL, Mass. (Plymouth Co.), town. For Henry Norwell (?-1903), a summer resident and member of the firm of Shepard Norwell and Company of Boston.

NORWICH For Norwich, Norfolk, England.
North Norwich, N.Y. (Chenango Co.), town. For *Norwich*, Conn. Many settlers in this area came from Connecticut.
Norwich, Conn. (co. seat of New London Co.).
Norwich, N.Y. (Chenango Co.). Named by James Glover, an early settler, for *Norwich*, Conn., his original home.

NORWOOD, Mass. (Norfolk Co.), town. Said to have been so named (1872) by a man who liked it because it "looked well in print, had a pleasing sound, was easy to write, and had no *i* to dot or *t* to cross."

NORWOOD A shortened form of *north woods*.
Norwood, N.J. (Bergen Co.).
Norwood, Ohio (Hamilton Co.).

NOTCH MOUNTAIN, Wyo. Descriptive.

NOTTELY LAKE, Ga. A Tennessee Valley Authority lake. For a river, in turn probably from Cherokee *naduhli*, a town's name, meaning uncertain.

NOTTOWAY From an Indian tribe in Virginia related to the Iroquois. This name, given them by their neighbors, means "rattlesnake" in the sense of "untrustworthy enemy." Their own name, *Cheroenhaka*, is believed to mean "fork of a stream," perhaps to signify a favorite living area.
Nottoway Co., Va. (co. seat, *Nottoway*).
Nottoway, Va. (co. seat of *Nottoway* Co.).
Nottoway River, Va. Flows into the Chowan River.

NOVA SCOTIA From Latin, "New Scotland." Granted by King James I to Sir William Alexander in 1621, the province took its name from Alexander's Latin charter.
Nova Scotia, Canadian province. Settled: 1604. Colony: 1784. Entered confederation: 1867, one of the four original provinces. Cap: Halifax. Flower: Trailing Arbutus.

NOVATO, Calif. (Marin Co.). Supposedly for an Indian chief baptized in the name of an obscure saint.

NOVI, Mich. (Oakland Co.). Origin is in dispute: it may be a spelling of *No. VI*, the place being the sixth stopping point out of Detroit, or from Latin *novi*, "new."

NOWATA From Delaware Indian, "welcome."
Nowata Co., Okla. (co. seat, *Nowata*).
Nowata, Okla. (co. seat of *Nowata* Co.).

NOWITNA RIVER, Alaska. From Indian, meaning unknown. It flows northeast into the Yukon River.

NOXON Probably for an early settler.
Noxon, Mont. (Sanders Co.).
Noxon Reservoir, Mont. On Clark Ford R.

NOXUBEE From Choctaw, "stinking water."
Noxubee Co., Miss. (co. seat, Macon).
Noxubee River, Miss.

Nova Scotia was originally the "Acadia" of Longfellow's "Evangeline". It came entirely under British control after years of assaults on the fortress of Louisbourg on Cape Breton Island, a few miles from this Atlantic beach. [*Canadian Consulate, New York*]

NUBANUSIT LAKE, N.H. From Pennacook, meaning uncertain.

NUCKOLLS Co., Neb. (co. seat, Nelson). For Stephen Friel Nuckolls (1825-1879), a prominent pioneer and legislator.

NUECES From Spanish, "pecans," for the trees there.
Nueces Co., Tex. (co. seat, Corpus Christi).
Neuces Neuces River, Tex.

NULHEGAN From Abanki, "log trap," "deadfall," or may apply to a trap used for fish.
Black Branch Nulhegan River, Vt. Flows S into *Nulhegan* R.
East Branch Nulhegan River, Vt. Flows S into *Nulhegan* R.
North Branch Nulhegan River, Vt. Flows

SEE into *Nulhegan* R.
Nulhegan River, Vt. Flows E and SE into Connecticut R.

NUMBER 4, SEE NO. 4 MOUNTAIN.

NUNIVAK ISLAND, Alaska, in Bering Sea. From Eskimo, meaning unknown, possibly descriptive for a large island.

NUSHAGAK From an Eskimo word, meaning unknown.
Nushagak Bay, Alaska. Extends into Bristol Bay.
Nushagak River, Alaska. Flows into the bay.

NUTLEY, N.J. (Essex Co.). Either for property owned by the Satterwaite family called "Old Nutley Manor House," after a Nutley vicarage in Uxbridge, East Sussex,

England, or because chestnut trees abounded in the area.

NUTZOTIN MOUNTAINS, Alaska. For the Indian tribe.

NUUANI PALI LOOKOUT, Hawaii. On southwest coast of Oahu Island. From Hawaiian, "cool cliff."

NYACK, N.Y. (Rockland Co.). From Algonquian, "point land."

NYE Co., Nev. (co. seat, Tonopah). For James Warren Nye (1814-1876), New York statesman who became the first and only governor of the Nevada Territory (1861-64). He was a U.S. senator from Nevada (1864-73).

NYLON PEAK, Wyo. For the nylon rope once used in climbing it. Also called Mount St. Michel.

NYSSA, Ore. (Malheur Co.). Origin not clear: possibly classical Greek, for a water nymph who, according to myth, had a hand in the upbringing of Bacchus. Immigrants from Greece worked on the railroads in the area and the town is on the Snake River, which might account for the name. However, it has also been said to be an Indian word.

NYSTROM MOUNTAIN, Wyo. Named by F.M. Endlich, a member of the Hayden Survey, for his fiancee's family.

O

OAHE From Sioux, "place of the big building," in reference to a council hall nearby.
Oahe Dam, S.Dak. On Missouri R.
Oahe Reservoir, S.Dak-N.Dak.

OAK For an oak tree or trees.
Oak Brook, Ill. (Du Page Co.). Named by Paul Butler, founder, for the oak trees and brooks on his property.
Oak Creek, S.Dak. Flows SE into Missouri R.
Oak Creek, Wis. (Milwaukee Co.).
Oak Hill, Me.
Oak Island, Wis. One of the Apostle Islands in L. Superior.
Oakdale, Calif. (Stanislaus Co.).
Oakdale, La. (Allen Co.).
Oakdale, Minn. (Washington Co.).
Oakdale, N.Y. (Suffolk Co.). Probably named by the Long Island railroad.
Oak Forest, Ill. (Cook Co.).
Oak Grove, La. (parish seat of West Carroll Parish).
Oak Harbor, Ohio (Ottawa Co.).
Oak Harbor, Wash. (Island Co.).
Oak Hill, W.Va. (Fayette Co.).
Oakland Co., Mich. (co. seat, Pontiac).
Oakland, Calif. (co. seat of Alameda Co.).
Oakland, Me. (Kennebec Co.), town.
Oakland, Md. (co. seat of Garrett Co.).
Oakland, N.J. (Bergen Co.).
Oakland City, Ind. (Gibson Co.).
Oakland Park, Fla. (Broward Co.).
Oak Lawn, Ill. (Cook Co.).

Oakmont, Pa. (Allegheny Co.).
Oak Orchard Creek, N.Y. Flows into L. Ontario.
Oak Park, Ill. (Cook Co.).
Oak Park, Mich. (Oakland Co.).
Oakridge, Ore. (Lane Co.).
Oak Ridge, Tenn. (Anderson Co.).
Oak View, Calif. (Ventura Co.).
Oakwood City, Ohio (Montgomery Co.).
Oakwood Village, Ohio (Lorain Co.).

OAKLEY, Kan. (co. seat of Logan Co.). Named for Eliza Oakley Gardner Hoag by her son, a surveyor.

OBED RIVER, Tenn. Probably from a personal name, short for Obediah. It flows northeast into Emory River.

OBERLIN, Jean Frederic (1740-1826), Alsatian clergyman, teacher, and philantrhropist in Alsace and Lorraine.
Oberlin, Kan. (co. seat of Decatur, Co.). For *Oberlin*, Ohio.
Oberlin, La. (parish seat of Allen Parish).
Oberlin, Ohio (Lorain Co.).

OBEY RIVER, East Fork, Tenn. Reason for the name is unknown. It flows northeast and northwest into Cumberland River.

OBION Either from Indian, "many forks or branches," as of a river, or possibly a personal name.

Obion Tenn. (co. seat, Union City). For the river.
Obion River, Tenn.

O'BRIEN Co., Iowa (co. seat, Primghar). For William S. O'Brien (1803-1864), a leader of the Irish rebellion of 1848.

OBSERVATION For the view.
Observation Peak, Calif.
Observation Point (peak), Wyo.

OCALA, Fla. (co. seat of Marion Co.). From a Timucua Indian name of unknown meaning, first mentioned in the chronicles of the De Soto expedition in 1539.

OCAPILCO CREEK, Ga. From Creek Indian, "big swamp river." It flows southeast into Withlacoochee River.

OCEAN For a location on or near an ocean or other large body of water.
Ocean Co., N.J. (co. seat, Toms River). On the Atlantic Coast.
Ocean Cape, Alaska. Extends into the Gulf of Alaska.
Oceana Co., Mich. (co. seat, Hart). Latin, feminine form of *oceanus;* on Lake Michigan.
Ocean City, N.J. (Cape May Co.).
Oceano, Calif. (San Luis Obispo Co.). From Spanish, "ocean."
Oceanside, Calif. (San Diego Co.). On the Pacific Coast.
Oceanside, N.Y. (Nassau Co.).
Ocean Springs, Miss. (Jackson Co.). On the Gulf of Mexico.

OCHEYEDAN From Sioux, "mourning," for a place to mourn a dead relative. The name supposedly stems from a war in the area between Indian tribes in which two boys were killed.
Ocheyedan River, Minn. Flows SE into Little Sioux R.
Ocheyedan Mound (peak), Iowa.

OCHILTREE Co., Tex. (co. seat, Perryton). For William Beck Ochiltree (1811-1867), Republic of Texas official and Texas state legislator.

OCHLOCKONEE From Hitchiti, "yellow water," descriptive of the river. It was recorded as *Guacuca* by De Soto in 1540.
Ochiockonee, Ga. (Thomas Co.).
Ochlockonee River, Ga.-Fla. Flows SSW into Apalachee Bay.

OCILLA, Ga. (co. seat of Irwin Co.). From Timucua Indian *aucilla,* meaning unknown.

OCMULGEE. Variant form of OKMULGEE.
Ocmulgee Natl. Monument, Ga. On the river. Contains Indian mounds and remains.
Ocmulgee River, Ga. Formed by juncture of Alcovy, South, and Yellow rivers, flows SE to join Ocoinee R. to form Altamaha R.

OCOEE, Fla. (Orange Co.). From Cherokee, "apricot-vine place."

OCONEE For an Indian tribe of Muskhogean linquistic stock; meaning of the name uncertain.
Oconee Co., Ga. (co. seat, Watkinsville).
Oconee Co., S.C. (co. seat, Walhalla). Founders thought the name meant "beautiful springs," for the many springs in the area.
Oconee Natl. Forest, Ga.
Oconee River, Ga.. Flows generally SE to join the Ocmulgee R. and form the Altamaha R.

OCONOMOWOC, Wis. (Waukesha Co.). Probably from Algonquian, "beaver dam." Other interpretations include "waterfall," "falls," and "river of lakes."

OCONTO From Menominee, "place of the pike fish."
Oconto Co., Wis. (co. seat, *Oconto*).
Oconto Falls, Wis. (*Oconto Co.*). For falls on the *Oconto* R.
Oconto River, Wis.

OCRACOKE From Algonquian, meaning uncertain. It has been translated as "bend" or "curve," for the shape of the island, which, however, does not seem to bend, and as "enclosed place" or "fort," perhaps for a village.
Ocracoke, N.C. (Hyde Co.). On the island.

Ocracoke Inlet, N.C. Connects Pamilico Sound and the Atlantic Ocean.
Ocracoke Island, N.C.

OCTORARO CREEK, Pa.-Md. Of Indian origin, probably Iroquoian, but with an English spelling that obscures the derivation. Possible meanings include "where the water is shallow and deep," "rushing waters," "covered water," and "the sound of running water." It flows generally southwest into the Susquehanna River.

ODESSA, Tex. (co. seat of Ector Co.). Probably for Odessa, Russia; named by Russian railroad laborers who believed that the area resembled their homeland, a wheat-producing region. The principal product of the area today, however, is oil.

ODYSSEY PEAK, Wyo. From an article entitled "Wind River Odyssey" (1949), which described the region.

OELWEIN, Iowa (Fayette Co.). For the Oelwein family, early settlers.

O'FALLON, Ill. (Saint Clair Co.). For John O'Fallon, prominent citizen of St. Louis, Mo., who was also a merchant on the east bank of the Mississippi.

O'FALLON, Mo. (St. Charles Co.). For John O'Fallon, a surgeon in the Continental Army. The apostrophe is dropped in local usage.

OGALLALA, Neb. (co. seat of Keith Co.). For a Teton tribe of Siouan linguistic stock. The name means "to scatter one's own."

OGDEN, Peter Skene, a brigade leader of the Hudson's Bay Company, which sent an expedition into the Utah area in the mid 1820s.
North Ogden, Utah (Weber Co.).
Ogden, Utah (co. seat of Weber Co.).
Ogden Peak, Utah.
Ogden River, Utah. Flows W into Weber River
South Ogden, Utah (Weber Co.).

OGDENSBURG, N.Y. (St. Lawrence Co.). For Col. Samuel Ogden (1746-1810), a local land speculator of considerable wealth.

OGEECHEE RIVER, Ga. From Muskogee, "river of the Yuchis," for the Indian tribe that lived along the river banks. The tribe was sometimes called the "untamed," which is also descriptive of the whitewater of the river. It flows southeast into the Atlantic Ocean.

OGEMAW Co., Mich. (co. seat, West Branch). Probably for an Indian chief; meaning of the name is uncertain.

OGLE CO., Ill. (co. seat, Oregon). For Joseph Ogle, first Methodist layman in Illinois and captain of early settlers who organized for Indian raids. He lived in St. Clair County, near St. Louis, and probably never visited the county named for him.

OGLESBY, Ill. (La Salle Co.). For Richard James Oglesby (1824-1899), a soldier in the Mexican and Civil Wars. He was elected to the state senate (1860), and served as governor of Illinois (1865-69; 1872-73; 1885-89) and as U.S. senator (1873-79).

OGLETHORPE, James Edward (1696-1785), English humanitarian who proposed that Georgia be settled by prisoners. He became the first governor of Georgia under the charter granted him.
Oglethorpe Co., Ga. (co. seat, Lexington).
Oglethorpe, Ga. (co. seat of Macon Co.).
Oglethorpe, Mount, Ga.

OGONTZ, Pa. (Montgomery Co.). For a missionary Indian chief.

OHIO Named by French explorers after similar words in several Indian languages. In the Iroquoian tongue it is *oheo,* "beautiful," or *ohion-hiio,* "beautiful river"; in Wyandot, *o, he, zuh,* "great, grand, fair to look upon." The French called it *La Belle Riviere,* "the beautiful river." The territory and state were named for the river.
Ohio, State of. 17th state of the Union. Settled: 1788. Territory: 1799. Admitted: 1803. Cap: Columbus. Motto: With God, All Things Are Possible. Nickname Buckeye State. Flower: Scarlet Carnation. Bird: Cardinal. Tree: Ohio Buckeye.

Ohio Co., Ind. (co. seat, Rising Sun).
Ohio Co., Ky. (co. seat, Hartford).
Ohio Co., W. Va. (co. seat, Wheeling).
Ohio River. Flows from the junction of the Allegheny and Monongahela at Pittsburgh, Pa., W to the Mississippi at Cairo, Ill., forming the boundary between Ohio (N) and West Virginia (S) and between Ohio, Indiana, and Illinois (N) and Kentucky (S).

OHOOPEE RIVER, Ga. Probably of Indian origin, but the name has undergone some fancy Anglicization. It flows southeast into Altamaha River.

OIL For oil deposits or oil industries in an area.
Oil Creek, Pa.
Oil City, Pa. (Venango Co.). On *Oil* Creek.
Oildale, Calif. (Kern Co.).

OJAI, Calif. (Ventura Co.). From Chumash Indian *ahwai,* "moon."

OJIBWAY See   CHIPPEWA

OKALOOSA Co., Fla. (co. seat, Crestview). From Choctaw, "black water," also translated "pleasant place" and "backwater." Compare   OSKALOOSA

OKANAGAN A variant spelling, especially in Canada, of OKANOGAN.
Okanagan Lake, B.C.
Okanagan Landing, B.C.

OKANOGAN For an Indian tribe in the Northwest, primarily in the area now known as Washington and British Columbia. The meaning of the name is uncertain; it may be "meeting place," probably in reference to a place or headquarters on the *Okanogan* (in Canada, *Okanagan*) River. The tribe called itself *Isonkuaili,* "our people." See also OKANAGAN .
Okanogan Co., Wash. (co. seat, *Okanogan*). For the river.
Okanogan, Wash. (co. seat of *Okanogan* Co.). For the river.
Okanogan Natl. Forest, Wash.
Okanogan River, B.C.-Wash. Flows S into the Columbia R.

OKAUCHEE LAKE, Wis. (Waukesha Co.). From Algonquian, "pipe stem."

OKEECHOBEE From Hitchiti (Muskhogan), "big water."
Okeechobee Co., Fla.. (co. seat, *Okeechobee*).
Okeechobee, Fla. (co. seat of *Okeechobee* Co.).
Okeechobee, Lake, Fla. Third largest lake wholly within the U.S.
Okeechobee Waterway, Fla. Links the canals, rivers, and lakes of the *Okeechobee* area.

OKEFENOKEE From Hitchiti (Muskhogean) *oke,* "water," and *finoki,* "trembling," for the quaking nature of the soil. The area is known locally as the Land of Trembling Earth.
Okefenokee Natl. Wildlife Refuge, Fla.
Okefenokee Swamp, Ga.-Fla.

OKEMAH, Okla. (co. seat of Okfuskee Co.). For a Kickapoo Indian noted for his honesty, integrity, and uprightness. The meaning of his name is "high man" or "chief." He was a friend of the founders.

OKEMO MOUNTAIN, Vt. Origin disputed: either from Chippewa, "chieftan," or from Abnaki, "louse."

OKEMOS, Mich. (Ingham Co.). For an Ojibway chief, perhaps the one for whom OGEMAW Co., Mich., was named.

OKFUSKEE Co., Okla. (co. seat, Okemah). For a small community in Cleburne County, Ala., probably transferred by the Creek Indians; from Creek, "point between streams" or "promontory."

OKIES THORN (peak), Wyo. For Leigh Ortenburger, who attended Oklahoma University and wrote *A Climber's Guide to the Teton Range. Thorn* is descriptive of the peak's shape.

OKLAHOMA Suggested by Rev. Allen Wright, chief of the Choctaws, at the establishment of the Indian Territory (1866) under the Choctaw-Chickasaw Treaty. From

390

The first house in Oklahoma City, then in "The Indian Territory," was commenced on April 22, 1889. The sketch above shows the city as it existed on February 22, 1890 — only ten months later [*Lithograph by A.E. Down after T.M. Fowler. New York Historical Society*]

Choctaw, "red people," a combination of *okla*, "people," and *humma* or *homma*, "red". When it became an organized territory in 1890, Col. Elias C. Boudinot, a Cherokee, suggested it be named the Territory of Oklahoma.

Oklahoma, State of 46th state of the Union. Settled: 1889. Territory: 1890. Admitted: 1907. Cap: Oklahoma City. Motto: *Labor Omnia Vincit* (Labor Conquers All Things). Nickname: Sooner State. Flower: Mistletoe. Bird: Scissor-tailed Flycatcher. Tree: Redbud. Song: "Oklahoma."

Oklahoma Co., Okla. (co. seat, Oklahoma City).

Oklahoma City, (co. seat of Oklahoma Co.), state capital.

OKLAWAHA RIVER, Fla. From Seminole-Creek, "muddy." It flows north and east into St. Johns River.

OKMULGEE For an Indian tribe of Muskhogean linguistic stock, from Hitchiti, "where water boils up," probably in reference to the large Indian Springs in Butts County, Ga. The name was transferred to the county and city in Oklahoma. See also *Ocmulgee.*

Okmulgee Co., Okla. (co. seat *Okmulgee*).

Okmulgee, Okla. (co. seat of *Okmulgee* Co.).

OKOBOJO CREEK, S.Dak. From Sioux, "planting in spaces," an agricultural reference. It flows southwest into the Missouri River.

OKOLONA From a Choctaw word of uncertain meaning. The first element, *oka*, means "water."

Okolona, Ky. (Jefferson Co.). Earlier, Lone Oak.

Okolona, Miss. (co. seat of Chickasaw Co.).

OKTIBBEHA, Co., Miss. (co. seat, Starkville). From Choctaw, locally believed to mean "pure water."

OLALLIE BUTTE, Ore. From Chinook, "berries."

OLATHE, Kan. (co. seat of Johnson Co.). From Shawnee, probably "beautiful." John

Barton, town organizer, said that the name he wanted was Shawnee *wessee,* "meadow beautiful"; but whenever he asked the Indians for such a word, he got the answer *olathe.*

OLD Names that do not appear in this part of the book may be found under the basic name. For example, for Old Saybrook, Conn., see SAYBROOK.

OLD BALDY Affectionate and descriptive name for a peak with sparse vegetation.
Old Baldy, Wash.
Old Baldy, Wyo.

OLD BRIDGE, N.J. (Middlesex Co.). For a bridge existing either in ruins or in memory.

OLD FAITHFUL, Wyo., in Yellowstone Natl. Park. The famous geyser that erupts every sixty-five minutes; named by Gen. H. D. Washburn, explorer, in 1870.

OLD FORGE, Pa (Lackawanna Co.) For a forge existing either in ruins or in memory.

OLDHAM Co., Ky. (co. seat, La Grange). For William Oldham (?-1791), an officer in the American Revolution, killed in a battle with Indians.

OLDHAM Co., Tex. (co. seat, Vega). For Williamson Simpson Oldham (1813-1868), Arkansas jurist who became a Republic of Texas patriot. He was also active in the Confederate secession movement.

OLD HICKORY From the nickname of Andrew JACKSON
Old Hickory, Tenn. (Cumberland Co.).
Old Hickory Lake, Tenn. In Cumberland R.

OLD LODGE CREEK, S.Dak. For Joe Old Lodge, a Sioux indian. It flows north into White River.

OLD LOGAN CREEK, Neb. For an early settler named Logan, with *Old* attached as a sentimental reference. It flows southeast into Elkhorn River.

A street in Olympia, Washington Territory, during the late 1800s. [*New York Public Library*]

OLDMAN'S CREEK, N.J. From Swedish *Aldermans Kijlen,* an early name for the creek. The name is folk etymologized and may actually refer to an old man who lived near the stream. It flows northwest into Delaware River.

OLD ORCHARD BEACH, Me. (York Co.), town and village. The town is on Orchard Bay and was named for a nearby orchard.

OLD SPECK MOUNTAIN, Me. For the speckled appearance of the mountain during autumn.

OLD STREAM, Me. Named in remembrance of the first stream down which logs were floated. It flows south into Machias River.

OLD TOWN, Me. (Penobscot Co.). For an Indian "old town" on the site.

OLEAN, N.Y. (Cattaraugus Co.). For Olean Shepard, first white child born in the town.

OLENTANGY RIVER, Ohio. From Algonquian, "place where paint is found," for the red pigment found along the banks. It flows northwest and south into Scioto River.

OLIVEHURST, Calif. (Yuba Co.). For olive orchards in the vicinity.

OLIVER Co., N.Dak. (co. seat, Center). For Harry S. Oliver, a Dakota Territory legislator.

OLIVET, S.Dak. (co. seat of Hutchinson Co.). For an Olivet in Michigan, original home of the platters, A.C. Jones and W.W. White. The name is Biblical, for the Mount of Olives near Jerusalem.

OLIVETTE, Mo. (St. Louis Co.). For the Olive Street road, near which it is located.

OLIVIA, Minn. (co. seat of Renville Co.). Latinized form of Olive, for a female railroad station agent whose surname is not known.

OLMSTED Co., Minn. (co. seat, Rochester). For David Olmsted (1822-1861), a pioneer settler who became the first mayor of St. Paul, or possibly for S. Baldwin Olmstead, a member of the territorial council when the county was formed.

OLNEY, Ill. (co. seat of Richland Co.). For Nathan Olney, a banker and friend of Judge Aaron Shaw, who was a circuit court judge with Abraham Lincoln.

OLNEY, Tex. (Young Co.). For Richard Olney (1835-1917), Massachusetts statesman. He was U.S. attorney general (1893-95) and secretary of state (1895-97) under Cleveland.

OLTON, Tex. (co. seat of Lamb Co.). For Olton Powell, son of Josie V. Powell, the first postmistress.

OLYMPIA, Wash (co. seat of Thurston Co.), state capital. Origin is disputed, but certainly it was influenced by the Olympic Mountains nearby and by the classical Mount Olympus.

Mount Olympus in Thessaly (Greece) was the legendary home of Zeus, Hera, Apollo, Aphrodite and the rest of the Greek "Olympian" gods and godesses.
[Drawn by L.H. Fischer. New York Public Library]

Omaha, Nebraska, grew prosperous as the eastern terminus of the Union Pacific Railway and was briefly capital of the state. The sketch by Frederick Whymper shows the capitol on the left, the terminus and the Missouri River in the distance. [*New York Public Library*]

OLYMPIC. For the classical Mount Olympus, home of the Greek gods. See OLYMPUS
Olympic Mountains, Wash.
Olympic Natl. Forest, Wash.
Olympic Natl. Park.
Olympic Peninsula, Wash. Bounded by Puget Sound. Juan de Fuca Strait, and the Pacific Ocean.

OLYMPUS, Mount, Wash. In Olympic Mountains. Named in 1778 by John Meares, a captain in the British navy, for the classical Mount Olympus in Greece, because the mountain appeared to be worthy of the gods. The name then spread to other places in the area; see OLYMPIC

OLYPHANT, Pa. (Lackawanna Co.). For George Talbot Olyphant, president of the Delaware and Hudson Canal Company. His business interests contributed greatly to the development and prosperity of the Lackawanna region in Pennsylvania.

OMAHA For the Omaha or Maha tribe of Siouan linguistic stock. The tribe lived in what is now northeastern Nebraska, on the Missouri River, and were there when the first white settlers came. The name has been translated as "those going against the wind or current" or "those who live upstream beyond others." It is Anglicized from the ancient tribal name, but there is a French version, "aux maha, of the Maha." It may be a variant of NEMAHA.
Omaha, Neb. (co. seat of Douglas Co.).
Omaha Indian Reservation, Neb.

OMAK From an Indian word, exact origin and meaning unknown.
Omak, Wash. (Okanogan Co.).
Omak Lake, Wash.

OMPOMPANOOSUC RIVER, Vt. From Abnaki, "marsh." It flows south into the Connecticut River.

ONALASKA, Wis. (La Crosse Co.). From Aleut *ilulaq*, "living together happily." The name occurs often in Alaska, usually as *Unalaska*. In this case it was taken from a name that occurred in a poem by Thomas Campbell, "Pleasures of Hope."

ONAWA From Algonquian *onaiweh*, "awake!" The name was inspired by a section of Longfellow's "Song of Hiawatha."

394

Onawa, Iowa (co. seat of Monona Co.).
Onawa Lake, Me.

ONEIDA For an Indian tribe of Iroquoian
linguistic stock, one of the Five Nations of
the Iroquois. They lived in central New York
but moved west during the Iroquois wars.
Their name means "stone people," perhaps
in praise of their bravery.
Oneida Co., Idaho (co. seat, Malad City).
  For *Oneida* Co., N.Y.
Oneida Co., N.Y. (co. seat, Utica).
Oneida Co., Wis. (co. seat, Rhinelander).
Oneida Lake, N.Y.
Oneida River, N.Y.

O'NEILL, Neb. (co. seat of Holt Co.). For
John O'Neill (1834-1878), Irish leader in the
United States, who colonized the area. He
was wounded during the Civil War, was a
leader of the Fenian movement, and
commanded a force that captured Port Erie,
Canada (1866).

ONEONTA From Iroquoian, "stony place"
or "hills."
Oneonta, Ala. (co. seat of Blount Co.).

Oneonta, N.Y. (Otsego Co.). Earlier,
Milfordville.

ONIDA, S.Dak. (co. seat of Sully Co.). A
variant spelling of ONEIDA County, N.Y., for
which it was named by settlers from New
York.

ONONDAGA One of the Five Nations of the
Iroquois, generally located in the county
now bearing their name, which means "hill
people."
Onondaga Co., N.Y. (co. seat, Syracuse).
Onondaga Indian Reservation, N.Y.

ONOTA LAKE, Mass. From Mahican,
meaning uncertain; possibilities include
"blue," "deep," or "he dwells at a
waterstream."

ONSLOW Co., N.C. (co. seat,
Jacksonville). For Arthur Onslow (1691-
1768), speaker of the House of Commons in
England (1728-61).

ONTARIO Of Iroquoian origin, but

Currier and Ives did not limit themselves solely to scenes within the United States. This Canadian
winter scene shows skaters on a frozen Ontario pond. [*Courtesy of Robert and Joyce O'Brien*]

derivation in dispute: from *ontare*, "lake," plus *io*, "beautiful"; or from *Entouhonorons*, a name Champlain used to designate the Lake of the Seneca or Iroquois.

Ontario, Canadian province. Settled 1648. Entered confederation: 1867, one of the four original provinces. Cap: Toronto. Flower: White Trillium.

Ontario Co., N.Y. (co. seat, Canandaigua).

Ontario Co., Ont. (co. seat, Whitby).

Ontario, Calif. (San Bernardino Co.). For *Ontario*, Canada; named by settlers from that province.

Ontario, Ohio (Richland Co.). Probably for *Ontario*, Canada.

Ontario, Ore. (Malheur Co.). For *Ontario*, Canada.

Ontario, Lake, N.Y.-Ont. One of the Great Lakes.

ONTONAGON From Ojibway *onagan*, "dish" or "bowl," but the etymology presents linguistic problems. Other interpretations include "a place for finding game," "lost my bowl," which seems impossible, "hunting river," and "in God's hand."

Ontonagon Co., Mich. (co. seat, *Ontonagon*).

Ontongon, Mich. (co. seat of *Ontonagaon* Co.). For the river. The city was founded by James K. Paul, who managed to locate and carry away the famous Chippewa (or Ojibway) copper boulder that is now in the Smithsonian Institution.

Ontonagon River, Mich. Flows into L. Superior.

OOLOGAH RESERVOIR, Okla. In Verdigris River. For a Cherokee chief, whose name means "dark cloud."

OOSTANAULA RIVER, Ga. From Cherokee, "place of rocks across stream," for a shallow place or a ford. Formed by the confluence of Conesauga and Coosawattee rivers. It flows southwest to join Etowah river to form Coosa river.

OPA CLIFFS, Calif. (Santa Cruz Co.). For the nearby cliffs.

OPA-LOCKA, Fla. (Dade Co.). From Seminole, "swamp-big."

OPELIKA, Ala. (co. seat of Lee Co.). For the Indian village *Opillaka* or *Oppilako*, from Creek, "large swamp." An earlier name was Opelikan.

OPELOUSAS, La. (parish seat of St. Landry Parish). For a small Indian tribe. The name in Choctaw means either "black hair" or "black legs," the latter perhaps metaphorical for "leggings."

OPEN DOOR PEAK, Wyo. Metaphoric, for what looks like an open door on the peak.

OPPORTUNITY, Wash. (Spokane Co.). Promotional.

OQUAWKA, Ill. (co. seat of Henderson Co.). From Sac, "yellow banks," or it may have been an Indian personal name.

OQUIRRH MOUNTAINS, Utah. From Gosiute Indian, "wooded" or "cave" mountains.

ORADELL For *Ora*tam, an Indian chief of the Delaware tribe, and for *Del*ford, the former name of the area.

Oradell, N.J. (Bergen Co.).

Oradell Reservoir, N.J.

ORANGE For the European ruling family of Orange-Nassau. Through a curious turn of events the name came to America in two waves. When the Dutch were establishing New Netherlands (New York, New Jersey, and Delaware), they honored their ruling house by using the names *Orange* and *Nassau* with great frequency. Later, when William, Prince of Orange, ascended the English throne (1689) as William III, the names *Orange* and *Nassau* assumed an English context. Within the former Dutch domains, however, it is safe to assume that any such usage refers to a Dutch origin with, in later namings, perhaps a nod to William. Elsewhere, unless there are obvious indications of a Dutch transplant, the context is English. See also NASSAU and WILLIAM AND MARY

East Orange, N.J. (Essex Co.).
Orange Co., Ind. (co. seat, Paoli). For *Orange* Co., N.C.
Orange Co., N.Y. (co. seat, Goshen).
Orange Co., N.C. (co. seat, Hillsboro).
Orange Co., Vt. (co. seat, Chelsea). Probably a hybrid owing much to the New York (Dutch) influence.
Orange Co., Va. (co. seat, *Orange*).
Orange, Conn. (New Haven Co.), town.
Orange, Mass. (Franklin Co.), town and village.
Orange, N.J. (Essex Co.).
Orange, Va. (co. seat of *Orange* Co.).
Orangeburg Co., S.C. (co. seat, *Orangeburg*).
Orangeburg, S.C. (co. seat of *Orangeburg* Co.).
Orange City, Iowa. (co. seat of Sioux Co.). Named by Hollanders for the House of Orange-Nassau.
South Orange, N.J. (Essex Co.).
West Orange, N.J. (Essex Co.).

ORANGE For orange groves.
Orange Co., Calif. (co. seat, Santa Ana).
Orange Co., Fla. (co. seat, Orlando).
Orange Co., Tex. (co. seat, *Orange*).
Orange, Calif. (*Orange* Co.).
Orange, Tex. (co. seat of *Orange* Co.).
Orange Lake, Calif.
Orange Cove, Calif. (Fresno Co.).
Orange Park, Fla. (Clay Co.).
Orangevale, Calif. (Sacramento Co.).
West Orange, Tex. (*Orange* Co.).

ORANGE CLIFFS, Utah. Descriptive of their color.

ORANGEVILLE, Ont. (co. seat of Dufferin Co.). For Orange Lawrence, owner of the townsite in 1844. An earlier name was The Mills because of the saw mill and flour mill erected there.

ORCHARD For orchards that were in the area.
Orchard Mesa, Colo. (Mesa Co.).
Orchard Park, N.Y. (Erie Co.).

ORCHARD LAKE, Minn. For an early settler.

ORCUTT, Calif. (Santa Barbara Co.). For W. W. Orcutt, a geologist for the Union Oil Company.

ORD, Edward O. C. (1820?-1883), soldier. He rose to the rank of general during the Civil War, fought in the Indian Wars, and was commander of the Department of Texas.
Ord, Neb. (co. seat of Valley Co.). Ord was commanding a unit nearby when the place was named.
Ord Mountain, Tex.

ORDWAY, Colo. (co. seat of Crowley Co.). For George N. Ordway (1844?-1911), merchant, developer, and alderman.

OREGON The origin of the name is obscure, but there are several possible roots: Shoshonean *oyer-un-gon*, "a place of plenty"; Shoshonean *ogwa*, "river," and *pe-on* "of the west," referring to what is now called the Columbia River; an unknown Indian source (possibly Siouan), *ouragon* or *ourigan*, referring to a great western river and which is similar to the French word *ouragan*, "hurricane." The name *Oregon* was first used by Jonathan Carver in his *Travels through the Interior Parts of North America* [1778].
Oregon, State of. 33rd state of the Union. Settled: 1811. Territory: 1848. Admitted: 1859. Cap: Salem. Motto: The Union. Nickname: Beaver State. Flower: Oregon Grape. Bird: Western Meadowlark. Tree: Douglas Fir. Song: "Oregon, My Oregon."
Oregon Co., Mo. (co. seat Alton).
Oregon, Ill. (co. seat of Ogle Co.).
Oregon, Mo. (co. seat of Holt Co.).
Oregon, Ohio (Lucas Co.).
Oregon, Wis. (Dane Co.).
Oregon Butte, Wash.
Oregon City, Ore. (co. seat of Clackamas Co.).
Oregon Trail. Westward trail over which thousands of emigrants traveled, from Independence, Mo. to Oregon. It followed the North Platte River, Sweetwater River, the South Pass over the Tetons, the Snake

Portland, Oregon, has changed since 1895 but some things remain constant. Mount Hood still looms in the distance. [*New York Public Library*]

and Umatilla rivers, and the Columbia, ending at Astoria or in the Willamette valley in Oregon.
Oregon Caves Natl. Monument, Ore.

OREGON INLET, N.C. Water passage between Pamlico Sound and the Atlantic Ocean. For the *Oregon*, the first ship to pass through after a hurricane formed the inlet in 1846.

OREM, Utah (Utah Co.). For Walter C. Orem (1873-1951), president of the Salt Lake and Utah Electric interurban railroad and local property owner, although he never resided in the city that bears his name.

ORGAN PIPE CACTUS NATL. MONUMENT, Ariz. For the organ pipe cactus.

ORILLIA, Ont. (Simcoe Co.). Probably from Spanish *orilla*, "shore" or "edge"; named by Sir Peregrine Maitland, lieutenant governor of Canada who had served in Spain.

ORINDA, Calif. (Contra Costa Co.). Of Latin origin, possibly for the poet Katharine Fowler Philips, who was known as "Orinda."

ORLAND, Calif. (Glenn Co.). For Orland, England.

ORLANDO, Fla. (co. seat of Orange Co.). For Orlando Reeves (?-1835), killed by Indians, or possibly for the character in Shakespear's *As You Like It*.

ORLAND PARK, Ill. (Cook Co.). Probably for an Orland in Maine, ultimately for Orland, England.

ORLEANS For Orleans, Loiret, France.
New Orleans, La. (parish seat of *Orleans* Parish).
Orleans Parish, La. (parish seat, *New Orleans*).
Orleans Co., N.Y. (co. seat, Albion).
Orleans Co., Vt. (co. seat, Newport).

ORLEANS, Mass. (Barnstable Co.), town. Named in honor of the visit of Louis Philippe, Duke of Orleans (1773-1850), to the United States in 1797. He was later king of France (1830-48), known as the "bourgeois monarch," his reign being marked by a prospering middle class and an increasingly miserable working class.

ORMSBY Co., Nev. (co. seat, Carson City). For Maj. William J. Ormsby (?-1860), a soldier killed by Indians at Pyramid Lake.

OROFINO, Idaho (co. seat of Clearwater Co.). From Spanish *oro fino*, "fine ore," for the quality of gold found there, which was said to require quicksilver to collect it.

ORONO Probably for a Penobscot chief who helped the colonists during the American Revolution.
Orono, Me. (Penobscot Co.), town and village.
Orono, Minn. (Hennepin Co.). For *Orono*, Me. Earlier, Stillwater.

OROSI, Calif. (Tulare Co.). From Spanish *oro*, "gold," for the golden poppies that grow wild in California.

OROVILLE From Spanish *oro*, "gold." The town was settled as a gold-mining camp.

Earlier, Ophir City.
Oroville Calif. (co. seat of Butte Co.).
Oroville Dam, Calif.
South Oroville, Calif. (Butte Co.).

ORRINGTON, Me. (Penobscot Co.), town. Possibly from a misspelling of *Orangetown*, which had been proposed as its name. It has also been suggested that an agent of the General Court happened to spot the name in a book and liked the sound.

ORRVILLE, Ohio (Wayne Co.). For Smith Orr (1797-1865), landowner and early developer of the town, who started the first sawmill to provide lumber for the railroad and the building of homes. He served as justice of the peace and in 1846 was elected to serve as associate judge of the court of common pleas, remaining in office until 1853, when the position was abolished by the state constitution.

The War of 1812 was over but the news did not travel to New Orleans fast enough to prevent the bloody battle of 1815 in which Gen. Andrew Jackson defeated the British forces. [*Engraving by Joseph Yeager after West. New York Historical Society*]

ORTIZ MOUNTAINS, N.Mex. Claimed for two families of the same name who lived in the area.

ORTONVILLE, Minn. (co. seat of Big Stone Co.). For Cornelius Knute Orton (1846-1890), founder, merchant, and banker.

OSAGE For an Indian tribe of Siouan linguistic stock from the area near the Osage River. By a series of treaties (1808-65) they were moved into what is now Oklahoma. The name is a corruption of their name in their own language, *Wazhazhe*, the meaning of which is unknown.

Osage Co., Kan. (co. seat, Lyndon).

Osage Co., Mo. (co. seat Linn).

Osage Co., Okla. (co. seat, Pawhuska).

Osage, Iowa (co. seat of Mitchell Co.). Or Possibly for Orrin Sage, a banker of Ware, Mass., who made large investments in the county.

Osage River, Mo. Flows into the Missouri R.

Osage City, Kan. (*Osage* Co.).

Osage Fork River, Mo. Flows into Gascondale R.

OSAWATOMIE, Kan. (Miami Co.). From the names of the Osage and Potawatomi Indian tribes.

OSBORNE, Vincent B. (?-1865), a Kansas soldier who died of wounds received during the Civil War.

Osborne Co., Kan. (co. seat, *Osborne*).

Osborne, Kan. (co. seat of *Osborne* Co.).

OSBORN MOUNTAIN, Wyo. For Robert L. Osborn, early settler.

OSCEOLA (c. 1804-1838), Seminole warrior and one of the most resourceful of their leaders during the early years of the Second Seminole War (1835-42). He was captured, in violation of a flag of truce, and imprisoned in 1837. His name, also spelled *Ashi Vaholo* (or Yahola), means "black drink hallower."

Osceola Co., Fla. (co. seat, Kissimmee).

Osceola Co., Iowa (co. seat, Sibley).

Osceola Co., Mich. (co. seat, Reed City).

Osceola, Ark. (a co. seat of Mississippi Co.).

Osceola, Iowa (co. seat of Clarke Co.).

Osceola, Mo. (co. seat of St. Clair Co.).

Osceola, Neb. (co. seat of Polk Co.).

Osceola, Mount, N.H.

Osceola Natl. Forest, Fla.

OSCODA Coined by Henry R. Schoolcraft, apparently as he sensed the sounds, from *ossin*, "stone," and *muskoda*, "prairie"; hence, descriptive. Although a combination of Algonquian words, it is not itself an Indian word.

Oscoda Co., Mich. (co. seat, Mio).

Oscoda-Au-Sable, Mich. (Iosco Co.). *Au-Sable*, from French, "of the sand," descriptive of the "sandy" river for which the town was named.

OSGOOD MOUNTAINS, Nev. For a local settler.

OSHAWA From a Senecan Indian word meaning "the carrying place" or "the portage."

Oshawa, Minn. (Nicollet Co.).

Oshawa, Ont. (Ontario Co.). Earlier, Skea's Corner for Edward Skea, a local storekeeper.

OSHKOSH (1759-1858), Menominee chief and leader of a band by this name.

Oshkosh, Neb. (co. seat of Garden Co.). For *Oshkosh*, Wis.

Oshkosh, Wis. (co. seat of Winnebago Co.).

OSKALOOSA From Choctaw, "black water," possibly akin to OKLOOSA, but the shortened form has not been explained satisfactorily. Conflicting opinions occur concerning this name although Oskaloosa was definitely one of the wives of Osceola, apparently Mahaska, or White Cloud, the Iowa chief, also had a wife named Oskaloosa.

Oskaloosa, Iowa (co. seat of Mahaska Co.).

Oskaloosa, Kan. (co. seat of Jefferson Co.). For *Oskaloosa*, Iowa.

OSSABAW ISLAND, Ga. One of the Golden Isles. From Guale Indian, probably "place of holly bushes."

OSSEO, Minn. (Hennepin Co.). From Longfellow's "Hiawatha," in which Osseo is called "son of the Evening Star."

OSSINING, N.Y. (Westchester Co.). From Ojibway *ossinee*, "stones." Earlier names were Hunter's Landing and Sing Sing.

OSSIPEE From Abnaki, "beyond the water" or "water on the other side," or possibly "river of the pines."
Ossipee, N.H. (co. seat of Carroll Co.).
Ossipee Lake, N.H.
Ossipee Mountains, N.H.

OSWAYO CREEK, Pa.-N.Y. From Iroquian, "pine forest." It has also been translated as "place of flies," but the former seems more correct. It flows generally northwest into Allegheny River.

OSWEGATCHIE RIVER, N.Y. From an Iroquoian word, meaning uncertain, but probably "black water," although "around the hill" has also been suggested. It flows northwest and northeast into St. Lawrence River.

OSWEGO From Iroquoian *osh-we-ge*, "the outpouring," in reference to the mouth of the Oswego River; also translated "the place where the valley widens." The name was transferred westward by former residents of Oswego, N.Y.
Lake Oswego, Ore. (Clackamas Co.).
Oswego Co., N.Y. (co. seat, *Oswego*).
Oswego, Kan. (co. seat of Labette Co.). For *Oswego*, N.Y.
Oswego, N.Y. (co. seat of *Oswego* Co.).
Oswego Lake, N.Y.
Oswego River, N.Y. Flows generally NW into L. Ontario.

OTAY-CASTLE PARK, Calif. (San Diego Co.). Combination of *Otay*, from Indian *otai*, "brushy," and *Castle Park*, probably promotional.

OTERO, Miguel Antonio (1859-1944), member of a prominent Spanish family that settled in the New Mexico area in the early 1800s. He served as territorial governor (1896-1906).
Otero Co., N.Mex. (co. seat, Alamogordo).
Otero, Colo. (co. seat, La Junta).

OTHELLO, Wash. (Adams Co.). For the tragic hero in the Shakespearean play of that name.

OTIS, Harrison Gray (1765-1848), noted Federalist, speaker of the Massachusetts House of Representatives, U.S. senator, and a leader of the Hartford Convention.
Otis, Mass. (Berkshire Co.).
Otis Reservoir, Mass.

OTISCO LAKE, N.Y. From Ostickney Indian, "waters dried away," because the lake had once been much larger.

OTOE Co., Neb. (co. seat, Nebraska City). For an Indian tribe of Siouan linguistic stock; meaning uncertain, but said to be "lechers," either as "lovers" or in the pejorative sense.

OTSEGO From Iroquoian, "rock site," or "place of the rock."
Otsego Co., Mich. (co. seat, Gaylord).
Otsego Co., N.Y. (co. seat, Cooperstown).
Otsego, Mich. (Allegan Co.).
Otsego Lake, Mich.
Otsego Lake, N.Y.

OTSELIO, N.Y. For an Iroquoian word meaning "plum creek."
Otselio, N.Y. (Chenango Co.).
Otselio River, N.Y. Flows SW into Tioughnioga R.

OTTAUQUECHEE RIVER, Vt. Of Indian origin, meaning uncertain, possibly "cat tails" or "swift current." It flows east into the Connecticut River.

OTTAWA For a tribe of Algonquian linguistic stock whose earliest known location was along the northern shore of Georgian Bay, Ont., where, except for a brief interruption (1649-70), some of them remain to this day. The tribal name is derived from *adawe*, "to trade," from the fact that they were noted intertribal traders and barterers. In the 1600s a southern branch was centered in Michigan but ranged as far west as Wisconsin and east to western Pennsylvania, remaining until, after defeats during the late 1700s and early

1800s, many were pushed west. They settled in Kansas (1831) and later in what is now Oklahoma (1867).

Ottawa Co., Kan. (co. seat, Minneapolis).

Ottawa Co., Mich. (co. seat, Grand Haven).

Ottawa Co., Ohio (co. seat, Port Clinton).

Ottawa Co., Okla. (co. seat, Miami).

Ottawa, Ill. (co. seat of La Salle Co.).

Ottawa, Kan. (co. seat of Franklin Co.).

Ottawa, Ohio (co. seat of Putnam Co.).

Ottawa, Ont. (co. town of Carleton Co.), national capital of Canada. Earlier, Bytown, for Col. John By (1779-1836) of the Royal Engineers, who selected the site for his headquarters while constructing the Rideau Canal.

Ottawa Islands, N.W.T. In Hudson Bay.

Ottawa River, Ohio. Flows generally N to the Auglaize R.

Ottawa River, Ont. Flows generally SE to the St. Lawrence R.

Ottawa Hills, Ohio (Lucas Co.).

OTTER For the animal.

Otter Creek, N.Y. Flows W into Black R.

Otter Creek, Utah. Flows SSW into East Fork Sevier R.

Otter Creek, Vt. Flows N into L. Champlain.

Otter Island, Wis. One of the Apostle Islands in L. Superior.

Otter River, Mass.

Otter River, Mich. Flows NE into Sturgeon R.

Little Otter Creek, Vt. Flows NW into L. Champlain.

OTTER TAIL Co., Minn. (co. seat, Fergus Falls). From an Ojibway word, in reference to the shape of the lake.

Otter Tail Lake, Minn.

Otter Tail River, Minn. Flows generally W to join the Bois de Sioux R. to form the Red R. of the North.

The Houses of Parliament in Ottowa bear a striking resemblance to those in London. Here they are seen with the changing of the guard. [*National Film Board of Canada*]

OTTO, N.Y. (Cattaraugus Co.). For Jacob Otto, an agent of the Holland Land Company.

OTTUMWA, Iowa (co. seat of Wapello Co.). Origin and meaning are not certain. It is said to mean "rapids," which does not seem appropriate here, or "place of the lone chief."

OUACHITA For an Indian tribe, a member of the Natchitoches Confederacy. The meaning is not clear; "big hunt," "country of large buffaloes," "sparkling water," or "large hunting grounds" are possible translations. The tribe belongs to the Caddoan linguistic stock and originally lived in north western Louisiana. It has been suggested that *Ouachita* and WICHITA have the same derivation.
Ouachita Co., Ark. (co. seat, Canden).
Ouachita Parish, La. (parish seat, Monroe).
Ouachita, Lake, Ark.
Ouachita Mountains, Okla.-Ark.
Ouachita Natl. Forest, Ark.-Okla.
Ouachita River, Ark.-La. Flows generally SE to the Red R.

OURAY (1820-1880), Ute Indian chief. His name has been said to be the Ute attempt at saying *Willie,* a name given him by a white family to which he was attached as a boy. Another, and probably more reliable source gives the meaning as "the arrow." He was chief of the Uncompahgre Utes, and his relations with the U.S. government began with a treaty made in 1863, when he signed his name *U-ray* or *Arrow.* He also signed a treaty in 1868 *U-re,* and later that year *Ou-ray.* He had great faith in the white people and was instrumental in calming the attack on the whites by the Utes, which took place in 1879. When he died he was residing in a comfortable, well-furnished house on a farm, which he owned and had built.
Ouray Co., Colo. (co. seat, *Ouray*).
Ouray, Colo. (co. seat of *Ouray* Co.).
Ouray Peak, Colo.

OUTAGAMIE Co., Wis. (co. seat, Appleton). From Ojibway *O-dug-am-eeg,* "dwellers on the other side," in reference to the Fox Indians.

OUTREMONT, Que. (Ile-de-Montreal Co.). From French *outre mont,* "beyond the mount," in reference to the home of the Le-Bouthillier family, which was "beyond" Mount Royal.

OVAL PEAK, Wash. Descriptive of shape.

OVERLAND Descriptive.
Overland, Mo. (St. Louis Co.).
Overland Trail. Emigrant and transportation trail from St. Louis, Mo., to California.
Overland Park, Kan. (Johnson Co.). For the view; promotional.

OVERLOOK-PAGE MANOR, Ohio (Montgomery Co.). *Overlook* is descriptive; *Page* is from *Page,* for the Page Shopping Center.

OVERTON Co., Tenn. (co. seat, Livingston). For John Overton, a jurist and founder of Memphis.

OVID, N.Y. (co. seat of Seneca Co.). For Ovid, (43 B.C.-17-18 A.D.), Roman author of the *Metamorphoses.*

OWASCO LAKE, N.Y. From Iroquoian, "at the bridge."

OWASSO, Okla. (Tulsa Co.). From Cherokee, "end of the trail," because it was the end of the railroad at that time.

OWATONNA, Minn. (co. seat of Steele Co.). From Siouan, "straight," for the Owatonna River, now translated to Straight River.

OWEGO From Iroquoian, "the place that widens," for the widening of the stream.
Owego, N.Y. (co. seat of Tioga Co.).
Owego River, N.Y. Flows S into Susquehanna R.

OWEN, Abraham (?-1811), an officer killed at the Battle of Tippecanoe.
Owen Co., Ind. (co. seat, Spencer).
Owen Co. seat, *Owenton*).
Owensboro, Ky. (co. seat of Daviess Co.).

Earlier, Rossboro, for David Ross, a large landowner.
Owenton, Ky. (co. seat of *Owen* Co.).

OWEN, Lake, Wis. For a local settler.

OWEN, Mont., Col. For an early explorer or settler.

OWENS, Richard, a member of the third expedition (1845-46) of John C. Fremont.
Owens Lake, Calif. S basin of *Owens* R.
Owens River, Calif. Flows generally south into *Owens* L.
Owens Valley, Calif. Between the Sierra Nevada and the White and Inyo Mtns.

OWEN SOUND For Capt. William Fitz-William Owen, British naval officer who chartered the settlement in 1815.
Owen Sound, Ont. Inlet on Georgian Bay.
Owen Sound, Ont. (co. seat of Grey Co.).

OWINGSVILLE, Ky. (co. seat of Bath Co.). For Col. Thomas Dye Owings, owner and operator of Old State Furnace.

OWOSSO, Mich. (Shiawassee Co.). For Chief Wassa or Wosso of the Shiawassee band of the Ojibways. He signed both the Saginaw Treaty (1819) and the Treaty of Detroit (1837). It is believed that he was buried in the Indian burying ground located on the Shiawassee River, between 502 and 506 West Williams Street, Owosso.

OWSLEY Co., Ky. (co. seat, Booneville). For William Owsley, a jurist.

OWYHEE An early spelling of *Hawaii*, so named because two Hawaiians were killed by Indians near what is now the Owyhee River.
Owyhee Co., Idaho (co. seat, Murphy).
Owyhee, Nev. (Elko Co.).
Owyhee Reservoir, Ore.
Owyhee River, Ore. Flows generally NE to the Snake R. Earlier, Sandwich R., for the Sandwich Islands, now Hawaii Islands.

OX CREEK, N.Dak. So named because a dead ox was found in the area. An earlier name was Dead Ox Creek. It flows southwest and west into Souris River.

OXFORD For Oxford University (and for Oxford, the county borough). Oxfordshire, England. In America the name is often used for university or college seats. Occasionally, as did the original name, it may denote a wagon crossing or ford for oxen.
Oxford Co., Me. (co. seat, South Paris). For Oxford, Mass.
Oxford Co., Ont. (co. seat, Woodstock).
Oxford. Ala. (Calhoun Co.).
Oxford, Conn. (New Haven Co.)., town.
Oxford, Ga. (Newton Co.).
Oxford, Mass. (Worcester Co.), town and village.
Oxford, Mich. (Oakland Co.).
Oxford, Miss. (co. seat of Lafayette Co.).
Oxford, N.C. (co. seat of Granville Co.). For a plantation, "Oxford."
Oxford, N.S. (Cumberland Co.).
Oxford, Ohio (Butler Co.).
Oxford, Pa. (Chester Co.).
Oxford, Mount, Colo.

OXNARD, Calif. (Ventura Co.). For Henry T. Oxnard, part owner of a beet-sugar refinery.

OXON HILL, Md. (Prince Co.). Probably for a place in England.

OZARK Anglicized phonetic spelling of French *aux arcs* or *aux Arks*, "in the country of the Arkansas Indians." See ARKANSAS
Ozard Co., Mo. (co. seat, Gainesville).
Ozark, Ala. (co. seat of Dale Co.).
Ozark, Ark. (co. seat of Franklin Co.).
Ozard, Mo. (co. seat of Christian Co.).
Ozard Mountains, Mo.-Ark.-Okla. Also called Boston Mtns.
Ozards, Lake of the. Formed on the Osage R. behind Bagnell Dam.
Ozark Nat. Forest, Ark.
Ozark Plateau, Ark.-Mo.

OZAUKEE Co., Wis. (co. seat, Port Washington). For the Sac (or Sauk) tribe. The name means either "people of the outlet" (also the Ojibway name for the tribe) or "yellow earth."

OZETTE LAKE, Wash. Probably a French form of the Indian name *Hoselth*, meaning unknown.

OZONA, Tex. (co. seat of Crockett Co.). A form of *ozone*, for what was believed to be invigorating air, fresh and clean.

P

PABST PEAK Wyo. So named because climbers drank a bottle of Pabst beer at the top.

PACHAUG POND, Conn. From Mohegan, "fork of the river."

PACIFIC. Associated with, or named for, the Pacific Ocean.
Pacific Co., Wash. (co. seat, South Bend).
Pacific, Mo. So named because it was to be the point of origin for a railroad to the Pacific coast.
Pacifica, Calif. (San Mateo Co.). On the *Pacific* Ocean.
Pacific Grove, Calif. (Monterey Co.).
Pacific Ocean. So named (1520) by Ferdinand Magellan, because of the calmness of its waters during his voyage.
Pacific Palisades, Hawaii (Honolulu Co.). Descriptive of its location on the *Pacific* Ocean and of the line of bold cliffs along the shore.

PACK MONADNOCK, N.H. Two mountain peaks in proximity with combined name. There are many versions of how the name occurred. *Pack* may have originated because the sway between the peaks resembles a cantle and pommel of a pack saddle, or because an exploring group had to camp or "pack" there, or perhaps for Thomas Packer, a proprietor. *Monadnock* is probably from an indian word which, in Abnaki, means "at the mountain which sticks up like an island," and in Natick means "at the most prominent island," for peaks surrounded by a peneplain. Another theory is that the name is a corruption of *Petty Monadnock*. An earlier name was Squachs Menadnaks, "squash mountains," for the "squash" color of the pine and spruce forest.

PACOLET For an indian tribe that lived along the banks of the river.
Pacolet River, S.C.
Pacolet Mills, S.C. (Spartanburg Co.).

PADEN CITY, W.Va. For Obdiah Paden, an early settler and landowner.

PADRE ISLAND, Tex. For Padre Nicolas Baille, who was given a grant to the island by the king of Spain.

PADUCAH For a Chickasaw chief; also a tribal name.
Paducah, Ky. (co. seat of McCracken Co.).
Paducah, Tex. (co. seat of Cottle Co.). For *Paducah*, Ky.

PAGE Co., Iowa (co. seat, Clarinda). For John Page (?-1846), killed during the Mexican War.

PAGE Co., Va. (co. seat, Luray). For John Page (1743-1808), Virginia soldier and statesman who fought in both the French and Indian Wars and the American Revolution. He was U.S. Representative (1789-97) and governor of Virginia (1802-05). He was grandfather of the explorer Thomas Jefferson Page and great-grandfather of the novelist-statesman Thomas Nelson Page.

PAGEDALE, Mo. (St. Louis Co.). For Page Avenue, which is located in a valley (hence *dale*). For whom the avenue was named is not known.

PAINE, Edward (?-1841), first settler and a delegate to the Ohio constitutional convention (1802-03). He had been a general in the American Revolution, general of the New York militia, and New York legislator before moving to Ohio.
Painesville, Ohio (co. seat of Lake Co.).
Painesville Southwest, Ohio (Lake Co.).

PAINT For the presence of pigments or paintings; often translated from an Indian name.
Paint Creek, Ohio. Flows SSE and E into Scioto R. For the presence of pigment.
Paint River, Mich. Flows SE into Bruie R. For minerals found along the river banks used for painting purposes.
Painted Desert, Ariz. For the color created by desert dust, a pink or blue haze.
Paint Rock, Tex. (co. seat of Concho Co.). For Indian paintings on a bluff near the town.
Paint Rock (mountain), Wash. For the color of minerals.
Paint Rock River, Tenn. Flows S into Wheeler L. For prehistoric paintings found on a cliff.
Paintsville, Ky. (co. seat of Johnson Co.).

PAGOSA From Ute, "health" or "having medicinal qualities."
Pagosa Peak, Colo.
Pagosa Springs, Colo. (co. seat of Archuleta Co.).

PAHOKEE, Fla. (Palm Beach Co.). From Muskogean, "grass-water," a term applied to the Everglades by the Indians.

PAILOLO CHANNEL, Hawaii. Water passage between Moiokal and Maui Islands. From Hawaiian, meaning uncertain, possibly "lift-shifting."

PAIUTE Co., Utah. See PIUTE

PAJARITO PEAK, N.Mex. From Spanish, "little bird."

PALACIOS From Spanish, "palaces."
Palacios, Tex. (Matagorda Co.). For the bay.
Palacios Bay, Tex.

PALAOA POINT, Hawaii. On southwest coast of Lanai Island. From Hawaiian, "whale," probably from an incident involving a whale.

PALATINE, Ill. (Cook Co.). For the Rhenish Palatinate, Germany. The term *palatine* was used to designate high officials.

PALATKA, Fla. (co. seat of Putnam Co.). Believed to be from Seminole-Creek *pilotaikita*, "a ferry," composed of *pilo*, "boat," and *taikita*, "ford."

PALESTINE For the region on the Mediterranean, because of its Biblical associations.
East Palestine, Ohio (Columbiana Co.). *East* was added to avoid confusion with another place of the same name.
Palestine, Tex. (co. seat of Anderson Co.).

PALISADE (or Palisades). Descriptive, for a line of bold cliffs.
Middle Palisade Peak, Calif. in Kings Canyon Natl. Park.
North Palisade Peak, Calif. In Kings Canyon Natl. Park.
Palisades, N.Y.-N.J. Line of cliffs along W bank of Hudson R.
Palisades Reservoir, Idaho-Wyo. In Snake River.
Palisades Reservoir, N.J. (Bergen Co.).

PALM BAY, Fla. (Brevard Co.). Descriptive.

PALM BEACH Descriptive.
Palm Beach Co., Fla. (co. seat, *West Palm Beach*).
Palm Beach, Fla. (*Palm Beach* Co.).
West Palm Beach, Fla. (co. seat of *Palm Beach* Co.).
West Palm Beach Canal, Fla.

PALMDALE Descriptive.
Palmdale, Calif. (Los Angeles Co.).
Palmdale East, Calif. (Los Angeles Co.).

PALM DESERT, Calif. (Riverside Co.). Descriptive and promotional.

PALMER RIVER, Mass. For a local settler. It flows south into Warren River.

PALMERTON, Pa. (Carbon Co.). For Stephen Searles Palmer of New York, the first president of the New Jersey Zinc Company.

PALMETTO, Fla. (Manatee Co.). For a small native palm tree with fan-like foliage.

PALM SPRINGS Descriptive.
Palm Springs, Calif. (Riverside Co.). Earlier, Aqua Caliente, from Spanish, "hot water."
Palm Springs, Fla. (Palm Beach Co.).

PALMYRA For a city in ancient Syria, now in ruins. *Palmyra* means "Palm City."
Palmyra, Mo. (co. seat of Marion Co.).
Palmyra, N.J. (Burlington Co.).
Palmyra, N.Y. (Wayne Co.), town and village.
Palmyra, Pa. (Lebanon Co.). Settled by John Palm, who came from Germany.
Palmyra, Va. (co. seat of Fluvanna Co.).

PALO ALTO From Spanish *palo*, "tree," and *alto*, "high" or "tall."
East Palo Alto, Calif. (Santa Clara Co.).
Palo Alto Co., Iowa (co. seat, Em-metsburg). For a small town in Texas, scene of a battle (1846) during the Mexican War.
Palo Alto, Calif. (Santa Clara Co.).

PALO DURO From Spanish, "hard wood."
Palo Duro Creek, Tex. Flows generally E into Prairie Dog Town Fork of Red R.
Palo Duro Creek, Tex.-Okla. Flows NE into Beaver R.

PALO PINTO From Spanish, "painted tree," but the connotation is not clear.
Palo Pinto Co., Tex. (co. seat, *Palo Pinto*).
Palo Pinto, Tex. (co. seat of *Palo Pinto* Co.).

PALOS HEIGHTS, Ill. (Cook Co.). For Palos, Spain, where Columbus began his historic voyage. An earlier name was Trenton, but another town of the name existed, so Medanchon A. Powell suggested the name be changed to *Palos*, because an ancestor of his had sailed from there.

PALOS VERDES From Spanish, "green trees."
Palos Verdes Estates, Calif. (Los Angeles Co.). Promotional.
Palos Verdes Peninsula, Calif. (Los Angeles Co.).

PALOUSE From an Indian tribal name transliterated into French, "grassy expanse," descriptive of the area.
Palouse Falls, Wash.
Palouse River, Idaho-Wash. Flows generally W and SW into Snake R.

PAMLICO For an Indian tribe of Algonquian linguistic stock, destroyed by the Tuscarora Indians in the early 1700s.
Pamlico Co., N.C. (co. seat, Bayboro).
Pamlico River, N.C. Flows generally SE to *Pamlico* Sound.
Pamlico Sound, N.C. Formed by a barrier reef between the Atlantic Ocean and the E coast of North Carolina.

PAMPA, Tex. (co. seat of Gray Co.). Descriptive; the prairie grass was similar to that of the pampas of South America.

PAMUNKEY RIVER, Va. For the Pamunkey Indians, a Powhatan subtribe, located along this river. (The name was also formerly applied to what is now the York River.) It is derived from Algonquian *pam*, "sloping," and *anki*, "uplands." The river flows from the junction of the North and South Anna rivers to its junction with the Mattaponi River to form the York River.

PANA, Ill. (Christian Co.). Origin uncertain, but probably the name of a Cahokia chief. Many translations have been suggested, including "partridge" and "slave," but none has been documented.

PANAMA CITY, Fla. (co. seat of Bay Co.). So named by a developer who observed that the place was on a straight line between Panama City, Canal Zone, and Chicago.

PANAMINT RANGE, Calif. For a subtribe of Shoshonean Indians; meaning of the name is unknown.

PANCAKE RANGE, Nev. Descriptive, for flat rock formations.

PANGUITCH, Utah (co. seat of Garfield Co.). From Ute, "the place where fish can be found."

PANHANDLE, Tex. (co. seat of Carson Co.). In the narrow part of the state that projects northward from the rest.

PANOLA From Choctaw, "cotton."
Panola Co., Miss. (co. seats, Batesville and Sardis).
Panola Co., Tex. (co. seat, Carthage).

PANTHER For the animal, known as "panther" in the east, but usually as "mountain lion" elsewhere.
Panther Mountain, N.Y.
Panther Peak, N.Y.

PAOLA, Kan. (co. seat of Miami Co.). For Baptiste Peoria, a local Indian linguist and interpreter, with a change in spelling and pronunciation.

PAOLI, Pasquale di (1725-1807), Corsican leader of a successful revolt against the Genoese between 1755 and 1768.
Paoli, Ind. (co. seat of Orange Co.). The name was taken from that of a local tavern that carried the patriot's name.
Paoli, Pa. (Chester Co.). For an old tavern that bore his portrait.

PAPILLION, Neb. (co. seat of Sarpey Co.). From French *papillon*, "butterfly." A small stream was named first. The early French explorers found many species of butterflies in the area.

PAPINEAU, Louis Joseph (1786-1871), patriot leader who aroused mixed emotions among his countrymen. He owned the Petite Nation seigniory, where the county and village are located today.
Papineau Co., Que. (co. seat, Papineauville).
Papineauville, Que. (co. seat of *Papineau* Co.).

PAPOOSE PEAK, Wyo. From the Indian term for a baby. Indians once considered the area around the mountain as a good hunting ground. Also called Indian Peak.

PARADISE Descriptive or hopeful.
Paradise, Calif. (Butte Co.).
Paradise, Nev. (Nye Co.). For the valley.
Paradise Valley, Nev. Caused an early prospector to say, "What a paradise!"
Paradise Butte, Calif. (Butte Co.). Another story is that this name is a misspelling of *Paradice*, recorded in 1900, for the "Pair o' Dice" saloon in the town.
Paradise Valley, Ariz. (Maricopa Co.). Promotional.

PARADOX LAKE, N.Y. Named for a contradictory incident, but details unknown.

PARAGOULD, Ark. (co. seat of Greene Co.). A combination of John *Para*more and Jay *Gould*, railroad magnates whose trains served the town.

PARAMOUNT, Calif. (Los Angeles Co.). For Paramount Pictures, the motion picture company.

PARAMUS, N.J. (Bergen Co.). From Algonquian, "turkey river," the Indian name for the Saddle River.

PARIA RIVER, Utah-Ariz. From Piute, "elk water." It flows southeast into Colorado River.

PARIS For Paris, France; so named in the United States to commemorate aid received during the American Revolution.
Paris, Ark. (co. seat of Logan Co.).
Paris, Idaho (co. seat of Bear Lake Co.).
Paris, Ill. (co. seat of Edgar Co.). For *Paris*, Ky.

Paris, Ky. (co. seat of Bourbon Co.).
Paris, Mo. (co. seat of Monroe Co.). For *Paris*, Ky.
Paris, Tenn. (co. seat of Henry Co.).
Paris, Tex. (co. seat of Lamar Co.).

PARIS For Afton Paris, a leader in separating Maine form Massachusetts, or for Paris, France.
Paris, Me. (Oxford Co.), town.
South Paris, Me. (co. seat of Oxford Co.).

PARIS, Ont. (Brant Co.). So named because of extensive plaster of Paris beds in the locality.

PARK Descriptive.
Park Co., Colo. (co. seat, Fairplay). Location of the large mountain valley known as the "South Park."
Park Co., Mont. (co. seat, Livingston), Adjacent to Yellowstone Natl. Park.
Park Co., Wyo. (co. seat, Cody). Adjacent to Yellowstone Natl. Park.
Park, Kan. (Gove Co.). Earlier, Buffalo Park; the name was changed to avoid confusion with other places named Buffalo.
Park.River, N.D.

PARKE Co., Ind. (co. seat, Rockville). For Benjamin Parke (1777-1835), legislator and jurist.

PARKER, S. Dak. (co. seat of Turner Co.). Probably for Kimball Parker, a railroad official.

PARKER Co., Tex. (co. seat, Weatherford). For Isaac Parker (1793-1883), Republic of Texas patriot and legislator.

PARKER DAM, Ariz.-Calif. In the Colorado River. For Gen. Eli Parker, a commissioner of Indian affairs.

PARKER PEAK, Wyo., in Yellowstone Natl. Park. For Samuel Parker, a minister.

PARKER POND, Me. For Scarborough Parker, an early settler.

PARKER RIVER, Mass. For Rev. Thomas Parker, leader of a colonizing group in the 1630s. It flows east into the Atlantic Ocean.

PARKERSBURG, W. Va. (co. seat of Wood Co.). For Alexander Parker, who had owned land at the townsite.

PARK FALLS, Wis. (Price Co.). For the region's resemblance to a park.

PARK FOREST, Ill. (Cook and Will Cos.). Promotional; named by the developers, American Community Builders.

PARK HILLS, Ky. (Kenton Co.). Promotional and descriptive of a park-like region.

PARK RAPIDS, Minn. (co. seat of Hubbard Co.). For rapids and the pastoral appearance of the area.

PARK RIDGE Descriptive and promotional.
Park Ridge, Ill. (Cook Co.).
Park Ridge, N.J. (Bergen Co.).

PARKWAY-SACRAMENTO SOUTH, Calif. (Sacramento Co.). Combination of *Parkway*, probably promotional, and *Sacramento South*, for SACRAMENTO

PARMA For the city in Italy.
Parma, Ohio (Cuyahoga Co.).
Parma Heights, Ohio (Cuyahoga Co.). Promotional.

PARMER Co., Tex. (co. seat, Farwell). For Martin Parmer (1778-1850), Republic of Texas patriot, legislator, and jurist.

PAROWAN, Utah. (co. seat of Iron Co.). From *Paragoon*, the name of an Indian tribe, "the marsh people."

PARRIS ISLAND, S.C. (Beaufort Co.). For Alexander Parris, for many years the public treasurer of South Carolina (early 18th century).

PARRY, Sir William Edward (1790-1855), British Arctic explorer and hydrographer who made five explorations of the Canadian Arctic from 1818 to 1827, including an unsuccessful attempt to reach the North Pole (1827).

Parry Island, N.W.T. The southernmost group of the Queen Elizabeth Islands; includes Bathurst, Byam Martin, Cornwallis, Devon and Melville Islands.

Parry Sound, Ont.

Parry Sound District, Ont. (district seat, *Parry Sound*).

Parry Sound, Ont. (district seat of *Parry Sound* District). For the landlocked sound on which it is located.

PARSIPPANY, Lake, N.J. From an Indian tribal name.

PARSONS, Kan. (Labette Co.). For Levi Parsons, an official of the Missouri Pacific railroad.

PARSONS, W.Va. (co. seat of Tucker Co.). For Ward Parsons, landowner.

PASADENA Believed to be from Ojibway *pa sa de na*, "crown of the valley".

Pasadena, Calif. (Los Angeles Co.)

Pasadena, Tex. (Harris Co.). For *Pasadena*, Calif.

South Pasadena, Calif. (Los Angeles Co.).

PASCAGOULA For an Indian tribe, probably of Muskhogean linguistic stock with close connections with the Siouan Biloxi. They lived along the river that bears their name. It means "bread people."

Pascagoula, Miss. (co. seat of Jackson Co.). For the river.

Pascagoula River, Miss.

PASCO Locally believed to be for a place in Latin America, but possibly for a family name.

Pasco, Wash. (co. seat of Franklin Co.).

Pasco West, Wash. (Franklin Co.).

PASCO Co., Fla. (co. seat, Dade City). For Samuel Pasco (1834-1917), Florida statesman, born in England. He was a U.S. senator (1887-99) and a member of the Panama Canal Commission (1899-1904).

Pasadena, California, is famous as the home of the Rose Bowl where two leading football teams play each New Year's Day. But the Tournament of Roses also includes a colorful parade. In 1923 this float, from Glendale, won first prize. [*New York Public Library*]

PASCOAG From Algonquian, "forking place," a description of a river at this spot. *Pascoag*, R.I. (Providence Co.). *Pascoag* Reservoir, R.I.

PASQUE ISLAND, Mass. In the Elizabeth Islands. Of Indian origin, possibly from Wampanoag, "split" or "barren place."

PASQUOTANK Co., N.C. (co. seat, Elizabeth City). For a subtribe of the Weapemeoc Indians of Algonquian linguistic stock, who inhabited the north shore of Albemarle Sound. The name probably means "tidal divided river."

PASSACONAWAY, Mount, N.H. From Pennacook, "bear cub."

PASSADUMKEAG MOUNTAIN, Me. From Abnaki, "rapids over sandy places," for a small stream nearby.

PASSAIC From a Delaware Indian term, *passaic* or *passajeek*, variously translated as "peace" or "valley." *Passaic*, N.J. (co. seat, Paterson). For the river. *Passaic*, N.J. (*Passaic* Co.). Earlier, Acquackanonk Landing. *Passaic* River, N.J. Flows into Newark Bay.

PASSAMAQUODDY BAY, Me. From Malecite, "location of plenty of pollack," in reference to the fish.

PASS CHRISTIAN, Miss. (Harrison Co.). Named by Christian and Marianne L'Andier as Marianne found the outer pass seaward and Christian the inner pass leading inshore.

PASS CREEK, S.Dak. Translated from Sioux, "travelling creek," in reference to a place for travellers to stop. It flows north into White River.

PASSUMPSIC RIVER, Vt. From Abnaki, "riffling flow." It flows south into the Connecticut River.

PASTOL BAY, Alaska. For an early trader in the area.

PASTORA PEAK, Ariz. For the good pasture land.

PATCHOGUE Probably for an Indian tribe whose name may have been derived from Algonquian *Pachaug*, "turning place." *East Patchogue*, N.Y. (Suffolk Co.). *Patchogue*, N.Y. (Suffolk Co.).

PATERSON, William (1745-1806), attorney and legislator. He was a delegate to the provincial congress (1775-76), a state legislator (1776-77), and a delegate to the Continental Congress (1780). He also served as a U.S. senator (1789-90), governor (1790-93), and associate justice of the U.S. Supreme Court (1793-1806). *East Paterson*, N.J. (Bergen Co.). *Paterson*, N.J. (co. seat of Passaic Co.). *West Paterson*, N.J. (Passaic Co.).

PATHFINDER RESERVOIR, Wyo. In North Platte River. For John C. FREMONT known as "The Pathfinder."

PATOKA RIVER, Ind. For an Indian chief. It flows west into Wabash River.

PATRICK Co. Va. (co. seat, Stuart). For Patrick HENRY.

PATSALIGA CREEK, Ala. From Creek Indian *pachi*, "pigeon," plus *laiki*, "roost." It flows south into Conecuh River.

PATTERSON, Calif. (Stanislaus Co.). For John D. Patterson, the original land-owner.

PATUXENT From an Indian phrase meaning "at the little rapids or falls in a stream." It became the name of a tribe that lived near the river and that was associated with the Toag (or Doag or Taux) Indians. *Lexington Park-Patuxent River*, Md. (St. Marys Co.). *Patuxent* River, Md. Flows into Chesapeake Bay.

PAUL BUNYAN STATE FOREST, Minn. For Paul Bunyan, legendary lumberjack, an American folk hero.

PAULDING, John (1758-1818), remembered as one of the captors (1780) of John Andre, British spy, during the American Revolution.
Paulding Co., Ga. (co. seat, Dallas).
Paulding Co., Ohio (co. seat, *Paulding*).
Paulding, Miss (a co. seat of Jasper Co.).
Paulding, Ohio (co. seat of *Paulding* Co.).

PAULINS KILL RIVER, N.J. From a personal name, probably that of a local settler, plus Dutch *kill*, "stream." It flows southwest into Delaware River.

PAULINS PEAK, Ore. For the famous Snake Indian chief who led raids against Oregon settlers during the 1860s.

PAULSBORO, N.J. (Gloucester Co.). For Philip Paul, a colonist who arrived in the area in 1685.

PAUL STREAM, Vt. For an early settler or explorer. It flows southeast and northeast into the Connecticut River.

PAULS VALLEY, Okla. (co. seat of Garvin Co.). For Smith Paul (1809-1893), a farmer and the first white settler in the area..He came west with Chickasaws by whom he had been raised.

PAUNSAUGUNT PLATEAU, Utah. From Ute. "home of the beaver."

PAVLOF VOLCANO, Alaska. From Russian, "Paul," probably for SAINT PAUL.

PAWCATUCK From Algonquian, "open divided stream."
Pawcatuck, Conn. (New London Co.).
Pawcatuck River, Conn.-R.I. Flows generally SE, forming the boundary between the two states, then into Long Island Sound.

PAWHUSKA, Okla. (co. seat of Osage Co.). From the name of an Osage chief, *Paw-Hiu-Skah*, "white hair."

PAWLING, N.Y. (Dutchess Co.). For Catherine Pawling, who inherited the land from her father, Henry Beekman, the owner of the original patent.

PAWNEE For an Indian tribe of Caddoan linguistic stock. The name may mean "horn," for the shape in which the Pawnees wore their hair lock; the Osages called them *Pa-in*, "long-haired"; they called themselves "civilized people."
North Pawnee Creek, Colo. Flows SE into South Platte R.
Pawnee Co., Kan (co. seat, Larned).
Pawnee Co., Neb. (co. seat, *Pawnee City*).
Pawnee Co., Okla. (co. seat, *Pawnee*).
Pawnee, Okla. (co. seat of *Pawnee* Co.).
Pawnee River, Kan. Flows E into Arkansas River.
Pawnee Rock, Kan. Landmark of a battle between the Comanches and the Pawnees.
Pawnee City, Neb. (co. seat of *Pawnee* Co.).
South Pawnee Creek, Colo.

PAW PAW For a North American tree, *Asimina triloba*, which bears a papaya-like fruit.
Paw Paw, Mich. (co. seat of Van Buren Co.). For the river.
Paw Paw River, Mich. Flows generally SW to the St. Joseph R.
Paw Paw Lake, Mich. (Berrien Co.). On a small lake of the same name.

PAWTUCKAWAY POND, N.H. From Abnaki, meaning uncertain; it has been translated "river falls" and "clear, open, shallow river."

PAWTUCKET, R.I. (Providence Co.). From Algonquian, "at the falls in the river," first applied to a spot near North Providence on the Blackstone River.

PAXTON, Ill. (co. seat of Ford Co.). For Sir Joseph Paxton (1801-1865), English architect who planned to organize a colony and settle in Illinois. The name was given so that he might be influenced to settle there; the plan did not work but the name remained. In the *Atlas of Ford County*, the name is erroneously listed as Sir Richard Paxton.

PAYETTE, Francis, commander of the Hudson's Bay Company outpost, Fort Boise. *Payette* Co., Idaho (co. seat, *Payette*).
Payette, Idaho (co. seat of *Payette* Co.).
Payette Natl. Forest, Idaho.
Payette River, Idaho. Flows S and W into Snake R.

PAYNE Co., Okla. (co. seat, Stillwater). For David L. Payne (1836-1884), active in the Oklahoma Boomer movement.

PAYSON, Utah (Utah Co.). For an early settler, a Mr. Pace.

PEABODY, Mass. (Essex Co.). For George Peabody (1795-1869), a prosperous financier and benefactor of various educational causes. An earlier name was South Danvers.

PEACE DALE, R.I. (Washington Co.). Named by a resident of the town for his wife Mary Peace. *Dale* is for the many dales in Westmoreland, England, where she was sent during the revolution.

PEACE RIVER, Fla. Translated from Spanish *rio de pas*, "river of peace." The name also has French and Indian variations. A Seminole Indian name was *Tolopchopco*, "river of long peas," a mistranslation of the Spanish form, and Indian folk etymologized. It flows south into Charlotte Harbor.

PEACH Co., Ga. (co. seat, Fort Valley). For peach trees and the quality of the peaches grown there.

PEAKED MOUNTAIN, Me. Descriptive of a sharp pinnacle.

PEALE, Mount, Utah. For A. C. Peale, geologist.

PEARISBURG, Va. (co. seat of Giles Co.): For George Pearis, who donated land for the townsite.

PEA RIVER, Ala. For the wild pea, *Pisum satium*. It flows generally south into Choctawhatchee River.

PEARL For the discovery of pearls.
Pearl Harbor, Hawaii. Inlet on Oahu Island where the Japanese Air Force attacked the United States fleet on Dec. 7, 1941, which marked the beginning of U.S. involvement in World War II.
Pearl Peak, Nev. Reason for naming uncertain; it is near Ruby L. in Ruby Valley.
Pearl, Miss. (Rankin Co.). For the river, which borders the town.
Pearl River, La.-Miss. Flows generally S. to Mississippi Sound.
Pearl City, Hawaii (Honolulu Co.).
Pearl River Co., Miss. (co. seat, Poplarville). For the river.
Pearl River, N.Y. (Rockland Co.). For a nearby stream that contained mussels with pink pearls.

PEARLAND, Tex. (Brazoria Co.). For the abundance of pear orchards.

PEAR RIDGE, Tex. (Jefferson Co.). Descriptive and promotional.

PEARSALL, Tex. (co. seat of Frio Co.). For Thomas W. Pearsall, vice-president of the International and Great Northern railroad, or for Nathan G. Pearsall (1856-?), manager of the East Louisiana railroad, or for John W. Pearsall, a conductor for the International and Great Northern. Although Thomas W. Pearsall never visited the area, he seems to have been important enough at the time (1880) to hold chief claim.

PEASE RIVER, Tex. For E.M. Pease, a governor of Texas. It flows east into Red River.

PECATONICA RIVER, Wis.-Ill. From Algonquian, "muddy," descriptive. It flows southeast and northeast into Rock River.

PECKERWOOD LAKE, Ark. For the bird.

PECONIC BAY, N.Y. From Algonquian, "open field," a variant of PEQUANNOCK.

PECOS Origin and meaning uncertain. It is believed to be the name of an Indian tribe

When we remember Pearl Harbor we often think of the sinking of the battleship *Arizona*. But, in addition, the surprise Japanese air attack on December.7, 1941, sank eighteen ships, destroyed one hundred and seventy-four planes and caused over 3500 casualties. It also brought the United States into World War II. [*Photo by Lawrence D. Thornton. Courtesy of Frederic Lewis, Inc.*]

now lost or unidentified and to be a Spanish translation of a Keresan word, "watering place."

Pecos Co., Tex. (co. seat, Fort Stockton).

Pecos, Tex. (co. seat of Reeves Co.).

Pecos River, N. Mex.-Tex. Flows generally SE to the Rio Grande.

PEDDOCKS ISLAND, Mass. In Boston Bay. For Leonard Peddock, who was possibly granted the island in the 1620s. His name occurs as early as 1622 in a New England Council letter.

PEDERNALES RIVER, Tex. From Spanish, "flintrocks." It flows east into Lake Travis.

PEDESTAL PEAK, Wyo. Descriptive, for what look like pedestals on the peak.

PEE DEE For the Pedee tribe, of Siouan linguistic stock, located somewhere along the middle course of the Pee Dee River; meaning of name is unknown, but is possibly from Catawba *piri*, "something good" or "pleasant."

Little Pee Dee River, NC.-S.C. Flows SE into *Pee Dee* R.

Pee Dee River, N.C.-S.C. Flows generally SSE into Winyah Bay.

PEEKSKILL, N.Y. (Westchester Co.). For Jan Peeck (fl. 1640-60), Dutch trader from New Amsterdam who established an Indian trading post on the upper reaches of *Peeck's Kill*, "Peeck's Creek," near the present city.

PEEL, Sir Robert (1788-1850), prominent English statesman.

Peel Co., Ont. (co. town, Brampton).
Peel Sound, N.W.T.

PEKIN, Ill (co. seat of Tazewell Co.). For Peking, China.

PELHAM, N.H. (Hillsborough Co.), town. For Henry Pelham (1695?-1754), prime minister of Great Britain (1743-54). He was a relative of Gov. Benning Wentworth of New Hampshire.

PELHAM MANOR, N.Y. (Westchester Co.). For John Pell, who originally owned the townsite.

PELICAN For the waterfowl.
Pelican Lake, Minn. Translated from Ojibway.
Pelican Lake, Wis.
Pelican Point, La. Extends into Chandeleur Sound.

PELLA, Iowa (Marion Co.). For the ancient city of Palestine, city of refuge; named by Dutch immigrants who were escaping intolerance at home.

PELL CITY, Ala. (a co. seat of St. Clair Co.). For George II. Pell, industrialist and founder.

PELONCILLO MOUNTAINS, Ariz.-N.Mex. From Spanish, "sugar loaf," descriptive of the shape of one of the peaks.

PEMADUMCOOK LAKE, Me. From Malecite, "place of long sand bar."

PEMAQUID From Micmac, "extended land area," for the peninsula which ends at Pemaquid Point.
Pemaquid Point, Me.
Pemaquid Pond, Me. Inlet on Atlantic Ocean.

PEMBINA From Ojibway *anepeminan*, "summer berry," known also as "cranberry." The berry bushes grow along the river, hence called the Red River of the North.
Pembina Co., N.Dak. (co. seat, Cavalier).
Pembina Mountains, Man.

Pembina River, Alta. Flows NE to the Athabaska R.
Pembina River, N.Dak.-Man. Flows generally SE to the Red River of the North.

PEMBROKE Possibly for one of the several Earls of Pembroke. See also PEMBROKE, N.H.
Pembroke, Mass. (Plymouth Co.), town.
North Pembroke, Mass. (Plymouth Co.).

PEMBROKE, Ga. (co. seat of Bryan Co.). For Pembroke Williams, a lawyer.

PEMBROKE, N.H. (Merrimack Co.), town. For Henry Herbert, 9th Earl of Pembroke (1689-1750). He was a soldier and lord chief justice of England, and was related by marriage to New Hampshire Gov. Benning Wentworth.

PEMBROKE, Ont. (co. seat of Renfrew Co.). For the Honorable Sidney Herbert (1810-1861), secretary of the Admirality, and a son of the 11th Earl of Pembroke.

PEMIGEWASSET RIVER, N.H. From Abnaki, "place of long rapids." It flows south to join Winnipesaukee River to form Merrimack River.

PEMISCOT Co., Mo. (co. seat, Caruthersville). From an Indian name of uncertain origin and meaning, perhaps Fox, "at the long place."

PEMMICAN PINNACLE (peak), Wyo. For the food made by Indians and trappers. Dried meat was ground between stones and mixed with dried berries and buffalo tallow, then stored in stomach pouches or rawhide bags.

PENACOOK LAKE, N.H. From Pennacook, "at the foothills."

PEN ARGYL, Pa. (Northampton Co.). From Celtic *pen*, "mountain," and *argyl*, from a Greek word meaning "slate rock." There is much slate in the area.

PENCOYD, Pa. (Montgomery Co.). For the Pencoyd Farm in the area, which was originally owned by John Roberts, the leader of a group of Welsh settlers. The farm got its name from Roberts' family estate in Lyn, Caernavonshire, Wales.

PENDER, Neb. (co. seat of Thurston Co.). For John Pender, a railroad official.

PENDER Co., N.C. (co. seat, Burgaw). For Gen. William Dorsey Pender (1834-1863), Confederate soldier from North Carolina, active with the Army of Northern Virginia. He was killed at the Battle of Gettysburg.

PENDERGRAFT PEAK, Wyo. For O. A. Pendergraft, a game warden.

PENDLETON For Camp Pendleton, which was named for Marine Maj. Gen. Joseph H. Pendleton. He fought in the war in Central America in the 1920s and also was instrumental in the placement of Marine Corps units based on the West Coast.
Pendleton North, Calif. (San Diego Co.).
Pendleton South, Calif. (San Diego Co.).

PENDLETON, Edmund (1721-1803), Virginia statesman and jurist and a leading patriotic figure before and during the American Revolution. He was a member of the Continental Congress (1774-75), was active in the establishment of the state of Virginia, and was president of the Virginia supreme court of appeals (1779-1803).
Pendleton Co., Ky. (co. seat, Falmouth).
Pendleton Co., W.Va. (co. seat, Franklin).

PENDLETON, Ore. (co. seat of Umatilla Co.). For George Hunt Pendleton (1825-1889), politician and diplomat. He was U.S. representative from Ohio (1857-65) and the candidate for vice-president of the United States on the Democratic ticket in 1864. As U.S. senator (1879-85), he made an important contribution to civil-service reform, to the extent that he lost Democratic party support in Ohio. He served as minister to Germany (1885-88).

PENDLETON, S.C. (Anderson Co.). For Henry Pendleton (1750-1788), a local judge.

PEND OREILLE. From the French name for Kalispel Indians who wore pendants from their ears, translated "ear pendants." See also CALISPELL PEAK.
Pend Oreille Co., Wash. (co. seat, Newport).
Pend Oreille Lake, Idaho.
Pend Oreille River, Idaho-Wash. Flows NW into Columbia R.

PENETANGUISHENE, Ont. (Simcoe Co.). From an Indian name signifying "white rolling sands."

PENIKESE ISLAND, Mass. In Buzzards Bay. Of Wampanoag origin, meaning unknown, but believed to be a variant of PASQUE. Another theory is that the name refers to a Chief Penakeson.

PENN CREEK, Pa. For PENNSYLVANIA and William Penn. It flows east and south into Susquehanna River.

RENNELL, Mount, Utah. For a local settler.

PENNINGTON Co., Minn. (co. seat, Thief River Falls). For Edmund Pennington, a railroad president.

PENNINGTON Co., S. Dak. (co. seat, Rapid City). For John L. Pennington, a Dakota Territory governor.

PENNSAUKEN, N.J. (Camden Co.). From Delaware Indian, "tobacco pouch." The Indians had met in this region to trade tobacco.

PENNSYLVANIA For Admiral Sir William Penn (1621-1670), father of William Penn (1644-1718), founder of Pennsylvania; named by Charles II of England. There is a double meaning to the name since, as Penn himself acknowledged, *penn* is a Welsh word meaning "head" or "headland" and, when combined with *sylvania*, a Latinized word for "woodlands," the meaning is "head woodlands" or, more clearly, "high woodlands." The name is generally

In 1682 William Penn sailed up the Delaware River and first saw the land granted to him by Charles Ii, the colony of Pennsylvania. That same year he made his first treaty with the Indians, as shown here. His dealings with the Indians were so just that Pennsylvania was free of Indian attack. [*New York Public Library*]

assumed to mean "Penn's woods."

Pennsylvania, State of. Second state of the Union. Settled: 1682. One of the 13 original colonies. Ratified Constitution: 1787. Cap: Harrisburg. Motto: Virtue, Liberty and Independence. Nickname: Keystone State. Flower: Mountain Laurel. Bird: Ruffed Grouse. Tree: Eastern Hemlock.

PENN YAN, N.Y. (co. seat of Yates Co.). Formerly hyphenated, a compromise name between settlers from Pennsylvania and those who were Yankees from the New England area.

PENOBSCOT From an Indian word, *penobskeag*, "rocky place" or "river of rocks."
Penobscot Co., Me. (co. seat, Bangor).
Penobscot Bay, Me.
Penobscot Lake, Me.
Penobscot River, Me.

PENSACOLA, Fla. (co. seat of Escambia Co.). From Choctaw *panshi*, "hair," and *Okla*, "people": long-haired people.

PENTAGON MOUNTAIN, Mont. For its five sided shape.

PEORIA For a tribe of the Illinois nation anglicized from French *peouarea*, which was taken from an Illinois word possibly meaning "carriers," or "ones who are carrying packs." Authorities differ on the point, and the meaning of the name is debatable.
East Peoria, Ill (*Peoria* Co.).
Peoria Co., Ill. (co. seat, *Peoria*).
Peoria, Ariz. (Maricopa Co.). For *Peoria*, Ill.
Peoria, Ill. (co. seat of *Peoria* Co.).
Peoria Lake, a wide stretch of the Illinois R.
Peoria Heights, Ill. (*Peoria* Co.).
West Peoria, Ill. (*Peoria* Co.).

PEPACTON RESERVOIR, N.Y. Of Algonquian origin, possibly from *popocus*, "place for partridges."

PEPIN. Named by French explorers either for a member of the expedition or for the French king Pepin le Bref. The lake was named first.
Pepin Co., Wis. (co. seat, Durand).
Pepin Lake, Minn.-Wis., in the course of the Mississippi R.

PEPPERELL, Mass. (Middlesex Co.), town. For Sir William Pepperell (1696-1759), a New Englander who participated in the capture of Fort Louisbourg (1745) in King George's War. He was the first native-born American to be made a baron.

PEPPER PIKE, Ohio (Cuyahoga Co.). For the Pepper family, farmers who lived along the Woodland Pike.

PEQUANNOCK From Algonquian, "land made clear for cultivation."
Pequannock, N.J. (Morris Co.). For the river.
Pequannock River, N.J.

PEQUEA CREEK, Pa. Variant of PIQUA, for the Shawnee subtribe. It flows west and south into Susquehanna River.

PEQUEST RIVER, N.J. Probably of Algonquian origin, but has been somewhat folk etymologized. Possible translations include "open land" and, from Pequannock, "land naturally clear and open." It flows southwest into Delaware River.

PEQUOP MOUNTAINS, Nev. Meaning unknown, but probably from a tribal name.

PERCE From French, "pierced." The town takes its name from the island, which was so named because it is pierced by a central arch sixty feet high.
Perce, Que. (co. seat of Gaspe Co.).
Perce Rock Island, Que. A bird sanctuary in Gaspe Bay.

PERCH. For the fish, probably translated from an Indian name.

Perch Lake, Mich.
Perch River, Mich. Rises in *Perch* L., flows N into Sturgeon R.

PERCHE CREEK, Mo. From Osage *paci*, "hilltop"; it then took on the French form *roche percee*, "pierced rock," which was anglicized into *Perche*, pronounced with two syllables. It flows south into Missouri River.

PERDIDO RIVER, Ala.-Fla. From Spanish, "lost." It flows south into Perdido Bay.

PERE MARQUETTE RIVER, Mich. From French, "Father Marquette," for Jacques MARQUETTE, French missionary and explorer. It flows northwest and west into Lake Michigan.

PERINTON, N.Y. (Monroe Co.). For Glover Perin, first settler.

PERKASIE, Pa. (Bucks Co.). For the Manor of Perkasie, a land grant from the time of William Penn.

PERKINS, Mount, Ariz. Probably for a local settler or explorer.

PERKINS Co., Neb. (co. seat, Grant). For Charles E. Perkins (1807-1907), a railroad president. Locally it is also said to be for Joseph Perkins, an early resident.

PERKINS Co., S.Dak. (co. seat, Bison). For Henry E. Perkins, a state senator who helped pass the act that established the county.

PERKIOMEN CREEK, Pa. From Algonquian, "place of cranberries." It flows south into Schuylkill River.

PERQUIMANS For an Indian tribe, a subdivision of the Weapemeocs, probably of Algonquian linguistic stock.
Perquimans Co., N.C. (co. seat, Hertford).
Perquimans River, N.C. Flows from *Perquimans* Co. to Albermarle Sound.

PERRIS, Calif. (Riverside Co.). For Fred T. Perris, an engineer and one of the founders.

PERRY, Fla. (co. seat of Taylor Co.). For Gen. Edward A. Perry (1831-1889), governor (1885-89).

PERRY, Iowa (Dallas Co.). For a Colonel Perry, an official of the Des Moines and Fort Dodge railroad.

PERRY, Okla. (co. seat of Noble Co.). For J.A. Perry, one of the township location commissioners.

PERRY, Oliver Hazard (1785-1819), Rhode Island naval officer who built and manned an American fleet on Lake Erie during the War of 1812. During the naval battle of Lake Erie (Sept. 10, 1813), despite the loss of his flagship, the *Lawrence*, he decisively defeated the British fleet and sent back the message, "We have met the enemy and they are ours."
Perry Co., Ala. (co. seat, Marion).
Perry Co., Ark. (co. seat, *Perryville*).
Perry Co., Ill. (co. seat, Pinckneyville).
Perry Co., Ind. (co. seat, Cannelton).
Perry Co., Ky. (co. seat, Hazard).
Perry Co., Miss. (co. seat, New Augusta).
Perry Co., Mo. (co. seat, *Perryville*).
Perry Co., Ohio (co. seat, New Lexington).
Perry Co., Pa. (co. seat, New Bloomfield).
Perry Co., Tenn. (co. seat, Linden).
Perry, Ga. (co. seat of Houston Co.).
Perry, N.Y. (Wyoming Co.).
Perrysburg, Ohio (Wood Co.).
Perry's Victory and International Peace Memorial Natl. Monument, Ohio.
Perryville, Ark. (co. seat of *Perry* Co.).
Perryville, Mo. (co. seat of *Perry* Co.).

PERRY GO PLACE, Wis. (Dane Co.). For T. Perrigoue, who signed himself as T. Perrygo in the territorial census book of 1836. A French-Canadian fur trader or voyageur, he was an early settler in the area.

PERRY RESERVOIR, Kan. For John D. Perry, a banker and an official of the Union Pacific railroad.

PERRY STREAM, N.H. For a local settler. It flows south into Lake Francis.

PERRYTON, Tex. (co. seat of Ochiltree Co.). For George M. Perry, an early realtor and land developer.

PERSHING Co., Nev. (co. seat, Lovelock). For John Joseph Pershing (1860-1948), Missouri soldier who saw duty in the Far East and in Mexico. He was commander in chief of American forces during World War I (1917-19) and chief of staff (1921-24).

PERSIMMON For the tree.
Persimmon Creek, Okla. Flows NE into Canadian R.
Persimmon Gap, Tex.

PERSON Co., N.C. (co. seat, Roxboro). For Thomas Person (1733-1800), patriot and general in the American Revolution.

PERTH For Perth, Perthshire, Scotland.
Perth Co., Ont. (co. seat, Stratford).
Perth, Ont. (co. seat of Lanark Co.).

PERTH AMBOY, N.J. (Middlesex Co.). For an Earl of Perth, a Scottish earl who in 1685 permitted the immigration of nearly two hundred oppressed Scots to Middlesex County, N.J. See also AMBOY.

PERU For Peru, South America.
Peru, Ill. (La Salle Co.).
Peru, Ind. (co. seat of Miami Co.). So named in expression of sympathy in the struggle of that country for independence from Spain.
Peru, Me. (Oxford Co.).
Peru, N.Y. (Clinton Co.), town. So named because the Adirondack Mtns. resembled those in Peru.

PESHTIGO From Algonquian, meaning unknown. It has been variously translated as "snapping turtle" or "wild goose," but these seem untenable.
Peshtigo, Wis. (Marinette Co.).
Peshtigo River, Wis. Flows SE into Green Bay.

PETALUMA, Calif. (Sonoma Co.). Believed to be from Miwok Indian *peta*, "flat,"·and *luma*, "back." It could also have been named for the Petaluma Indians, whose name appears in records of 1819 and earlier.

PETAWAWA, Ont. (Renfrew Co.). For a small local tributary of the Ottawa River, which in turn is from a corruption of Indian *pitwewe*, "where one hears the noise of the waters."

PETENWELL FLOWAGE, Wis. On Wisconsin River. According to legend the name is for Peter Wells, who figured prominently in a romance with an Indian girl.

PETERBOROUGH For the Honorable Peter Robinson (1785-1838), New Brunswick soldier and colonizer who sent settlers to the area in 1825. He served in the Executive and Legal Councils (1827-36). *Peterborough* Co., Ont. (co. seat, *Peter-borough*).
Peterborough, Ont. (co. seat of *Peter-borough* Co.).

PETERBOROUGH, N.H. (Hillsborough Co.), town. Probably for Charles Mordaunt, 3rd Earl of Peterborough (1658-1735), a naval hero in the wars with France and Spain, first lord of the treasury, and a friend of many prominent writers. It has also been suggested that it began as "Peter's Borough" because Peter Prescott, the proprietors' clerk, owned land in the area. St. Petersburgh, Russia has also been proposed as the source.

PETERSBURG, III. (co. seat of Menard Co.). For Peter Lukins, who owned 160 acres of land where the city is now located.

PETERSBURG, Ind. (co. seat of Pike Co.). For Peter Brenton, an early settler.

PETERSBURG, W.V. (co. seat of Grant Co.). Origin in dispute, but obviously from someone named Peter or Peters or Peterson. There is a claim for Jacob Peterson, an early settler and storekeeper.

PETIT BOIS ISLAND, Miss. In Gulf of Mexico. From French, "little woods."

PETIT JEAN CREEK, Ark. From French, "Little John," for a settler. It flows east into Arkansas River.

PETOSKEY, Mich. (co. seat of Emmet Co.). For an Ojibway chief, Ignatius *Petoseg* (1787-1886), son of Antoine Carre from Paris, France, who married an Indian princess and became leader of a tribe under the name Chief Neeitooshing, "early dawn." *Petosega* was transliterated into *Petoskey*. Since Petosega was born in the early morning, his name has been translated as "the rising sun." It is also said to be Algonquian, "between two swamps," or, by another source, to mean "the sun, moon, or stars."

PETRIFIED FOREST NATL. MONUMENT, Ariz. So named because of the petrified flora found in the area.

PETROLEUM Co., Mont. (co. seat, Winnett). For petroleum deposits.

PETTIS Co., Mo. (co. seat, Sedalia). For Spencer Darwin Pettis (1802-1831), a U.S. representative from Missouri killed in a duel with Thomas Biddle.

PEWAUKEE From Algonquian, "swampy place."
Pewaukee, Wis. (Waukesha Co.). For the lake.
Pewaukee, Lake, Wis.
Pewaukee West, Wis. (Waukesha Co.).

PHARR, Tex. (Hidalgo Co.). For Henry Pharr, sugar cane planter and early settler.

PHELPS Co., Mo. (co. seat, Rolla). For John S. Phelps (1814-1886), state legislator, U.S. representative (1845-63), colonel in the Union army, military governor of Arkansas, and governor of Missouri (1877-81).

PHELPS Co., Neb. (co. seat, Holdrege). For William Phelps, an early settler and former Mississippi steamboat captain.

PHELPS LAKE, N.C. For Josiah Phelps, an explorer.

PHELPS MOUNTAIN, N.J. For Orson "Old Mountain" Phelps (1817-1905), a legendary Adirondack mountaineer and guide.

PHENIX CITY, Ala. (co. seat of Russell Co.). Variant of PHOENIX. So named as a new city with a new and hopeful future when it absorbed the former county seat. An earlier name was Browneville.

PHILADELPHIA For an ancient city of Lydia, in western Asia Minor, seat of one of the "Seven Churches." Mentioned in the Bible, it probably suggested to William Penn the Greek noun *philadelphia*, "brotherly love," which he applied to his "great towne" in Pennsylvania as "the city of brotherly love." The name of the city in Lydia actually meant "the city of Philadelphus," for Attalus II, who had a descriptive name or nickname Philadelphus, "brother-loving."
New Philadelphia, Ohio (co. seat of Tuscarawas Co.).
Philadelphia Co., Pa. (co. seat, *Philadelphia*).

In Philadelphia the Liberty Bell was run in July, 1776, in celebration of the signing of the Declaration of Independence. It bears the inscription: "Proclaim Liberty throughout all the Land unto all the Inhabitants Thereof." (Leviticus 25:10). [*Pennsylvania Railroad Poster. New York Public Library*]

Philadelphia, Miss. (co. seat of Neshoba Co.). For *Philadelphia*, Pa.
Philadelphia, Pa. (co. seat of *Philadelphia* Co.).

PHILIP, S.Dak. (co. seat of Haakon Co.). For Philip James Scott, cattleman and owner of a buffalo herd.

PHILIPPI, W.Va.(co. seat of Barbour Co.). From the first name of Philip Pendleton BARBOUR. The spelling seems to have been influenced by *Philippi*, in ancient Macedonia.

PHILIPSBURG, Mont. (co. seat of Granite Co.). For Philip Deidesheimer, first superintendent of the St. Louis Gold and Silver Mining Company.

PHILIP SMITH MOUNTAINS, Alaska. For Philip Sidney Smith (1877-1949), chief Alaska geologist of the Geological Survey (1925-46).

PHILLIPS Co., Ark. (co. seat, Helena). For Sylvanus Phillips (1766-1830), who explored the area along the Arkansas River in the latter part of the 1700s.

PHILLIPS Co., Colo. (co. seat, Holyoke). For R. O. Phillips, an official in a land company.

PHILLIPS Co., Mont.(co. seat, Malta). For Benjamin D. Phillips, a local landowner and prominent citizen.

PHILLIPS, Tex. (Hutchinson Co.). For Frank Phillips (1873-1950), owner and founder of Phillips Petroleum Company, which located in this area.

PHILLIPS William A., a Union officer in the Civil War and a prominent resident.
Phillips Co., Kan. (co. seat, *Phillipsburg*).
Phillipsburg, Kan. (co. seat of *Phillips* Co.).

PHILLIPS, Wis. (co. seat of Price Co.). For Elijah B. Phillips, an official of the Wisconsin Central railroad.

PHILLIPS BROOK, N.H. For a local settler. It flows south into Upper Ammonoosuc River.

PHILPOTT LAKE, Va. For the nearby town, which was named for an early settler.

PHOENIX For a mythological bird that is supposed to rise from the ashes of its funeral pyre and live again; thus, a symbol of immortality or an expression of hope for the future. See also PHENIX.
Phoenix, Ariz. (co. seat of Maricopa Co.), state capital. Built on the remains of an Indian city.
Phoenix, Ill. (Cook Co.).
Phoenix Mountains, Ariz.
Phoenixville, Pa. (Chester Co.). For the Phoenix Iron Works.

PHOENIX, N.Y. (Oswego Co.). For Daniel Phoenix, owner of the townsite.

PHOTO PASS, Wyo. So named by a mountain club because of the scenic area.

PIATT Co., Ill. (co. seat, Monticello). For James A. Piatt, Sr. (1789-1838), early settler, schoolteacher, and pioneer businessman.

The phoenix, sacred in Egyptian mythology as a symbol of death and resurrection, was believed to have lived 500 years before cremating itself. It then rose triumphant from its own ashes. The woodcut is from a 1602 edition of Pliny. [*Culver Pictures, Inc.*]

PICAYUNE, Miss. (Pearl River Co.). For the New Orleans newspaper, *Picayune*, of which a local woman had been editor.

PICEANCE CREEK, Colo. Probably of Indian origin, meaning uncertain. In Spanish *picea* means "silver fir." It flows northwest and north into White River.

PICKAWAY Co., Ohio (co. seat, Circleville). A folk etymological form of PIQUA.

PICKENS, Andrew (1739-1817), Pennsylvania soldier and Indian fighter, later associated with South Carolina. He fought in the American Revolution, chiefly in the South, where he distinguished himself at the battles of Cowpens and Eutaw Springs. He was a U.S. representative from South Carolina (1793-95).
Pickens Co., Ala. (co. seat, Carrollton).
Pickens Co., Ga. (co. seat, Jasper).
Pickens Co., S.C. (co. seat, *Pickens*]).
Pickens, S.C. (co. seat of *Pickens* Co.).

PICKEREL LAKE, Wis. For the fish.

PICKETT Co., Tenn. (co. seat, Byrdstown). For H. L. Pickett, a legislator instrumental in forming the county.

PICKWICK LAKE, Tenn.-Miss.-Ala. A Tennessee Valley Authority reservoir on Tennessee River. Named by the first postmaster of Pickwick for Charles Dickens' novel *Pickwick Papers*.

PICO PEAK, Vt. From Spanish, "peak."

PICO RIVERA, Calif. (Los Angeles Co.). Incorporation of two towns, *Pico*, named for Pio Pico, governor of Mexican California, and *Rivera*, descriptive.

PICTON, Ont. (co. seat of Prince Edward Co.). For Sir Thomas Picton, a general in the Napoleonic wars.

PICTOU From the French transliteration of Micmac *piktook*, "bubbling water."
Pictou Co., N.S. (co. seat, *Pictou*).
Pictou, N.S. (co. seat of *Pictou* Co.).

PICTURE ROCK PASS, Ore. For the designs found on the rocks nearby.

PIEDMONT From French, "foot-of-the-mountains."
Piedmont, Ala. (Calhoun Co.).
Piedmont, Calif. (Alameda Co.).
Piedmont Lake, Ohio.

PIEDRA RIVER, Colo. From Spanish, "stone." It flows generally southwest into Navajo Reservoir.

PIEDRAS BLANCAS POINT, Calif. On the Pacific Ocean. From Spanish, "white rocks."

PIERCE, Franklin (1804-1869), fourteenth president of the United States (1853-57), from New Hampshire. He was both soldier (brigadier general, 1847) and statesman, and his regime saw the acceleration of events leading up to the Civil War. He had been a U.S. representative (1833-37) and U.S. senator (1837-42).
Pierce Co., Ga. (co. seat, Blackshear).
Pierce Co., Neb. (co. seat, *Pierce*].
Pierce Co., Wash. (co. seat, Tacoma).
Pierce Co., Wis. (co. seat, Ellsworth).
Pierce, Neb. (co. seat of *Pierce* Co.).

PIERCE Co., N.Dak. (co. seat, Rugby). For Gilbert Ashville Pierce (1839-1901), legislator, statesman, and editor. He was a Union officer during the Civil War, governor of Dakota Territory (1884-87), and U.S. senator from North Dakota (1889-91).

PIERCE PONDS, Me. For a local settler.

PIERRE, Bayou, Miss. Origin of name uncertain, but claimed to be for a Frenchman named Pierre who climbed a tree to survey the beautiful river. It flows into the Mississippi River.

PIERRE, S.Dak. (co. seat of Hughes Co.), state capital. For Fort Pierre, a former fort and town across the Missouri at this point, which was named for Pierre Choteau, Jr., a French fur trader.

PIGEON For the bird.
Pigeon Creek, Ala. Flows SE into Sepulga R.
Pigeon Creek, Ind. Flows SE and SW into Ohio R.
Pigeon River, Ind.-Mich. Flows NW into St. Joseph R. For the flocks of wild pigeons found by early explorers and settlers along the banks of the stream.
Pigeon River, Minn.-Ont. Flows SE and E into L. Superior. Translated from Chippewa, for the homing-pigeon.
Pigeon River, N.C.-Tenn. Flows NW into French Broad R.

PIGGOTT, Ark. (a co. seat of Clay Co.). For an early settler.

PIGG RIVER, Va. For John Pigg, an early settler. It flows east and northeast into Roanoke River.

PIKE For the fish.
Pike Lake, Wis.
Pike River, Wis. Flows SE into Menominee River.

PIKE, Zebulon Montgomery (1779-1813), a U.S. Army officer, leader of Jefferson's expedition to the Southwest, and discoverer of Pikes Peak. He was killed during the War of 1812 at the Battle of Lundy's Lane, near Toronto, Ont. See also ZEBULON, Ga.
Pike Co., Ala. (co. seat, Troy).
Pike Co., Ark. (co. seat, Murfressboro).
Pike Co., Ga. (co. seat, Zebulon).
Pike Co., Ill. (co. seat, Pittsfield).
Pike Co., Ind. (co. seat, Petersburg).
Pike Co., Ky. (co. seat, *Pikeville*).
Pike Co., Mo. (co. seat, Bowling Green).
Pike Co., Miss. (co. seat, Magnolia).
Pike Co., Ohio (co. seat, Waverly).
Pike Co., Pa. (co. seat, Milford).
Pike Natl. Forest, Colo. For *Pikes* Peak.
Pikes Peak, Colo., in the Front Range of the Rocky Mtns.
Pikeville, Ky. (co. seat of *Pike* Co.).
Pikeville, Ky. (co. seat of Bledsoe Co.).

PILOT For a landmark.
Pilot Butte, Wyo.
Pilot Knob, Colo.
Pilot Peak, Wyo.

PIMA Co., Ariz. (co. seat, Tucson). For a tribe of Piman linguistic stock (part of the Uto-Aztecan family) located in the Gila and Salt river valleys, Arizona. The word *pima*, misapplied to the tribe by early missionaries, means "no" in the dialect of the Nevome, a related Mexican tribe.

PINAL Co., Ariz. (co. seat, Florence). Probably for the Pinal tribe of the Apaches, or for an Apache chief. In Apache, the name means "deer." In Spanish, *pinal* means "pine," or possibly here "the Apaches who live in the pines," since pine groves are on the nearby mountains.

PINCKNEYVILLE, Ill. (co. seat of Perry Co.). For Charles Coatsworth Pinckney (1746-1825), statesman and soldier. He was the Federalist candidate for President in 1808 and 1812, unsuccessful both times.

PINE Usually descriptive of an area where pine trees or other conifers grow.
Big Pine Mountain, Calif.
Pine Co., Minn. (co. seat, *Pine City*).
Pine Creek, Nev.
Pine Creek, Pa.
Pine Island, Fla.
Pine Mountain, Ky.-Va., in the Appalachian Mtns.
Pine River, Mich. (Alcona and Iosco Cos.).
Pine River, Mich. (Wexford, Manistee, Lake, and Osceola Cos.).
Pine River, Mich. (Mackinac and Chippewa Cos.).
Pine River, Mich. (Mecosta, Isabella, Montcalm, Gratiot, and Midland Cos.).
Pine River, Wis.
Pine Bluff, Ark. (co. seat of Jefferson Co.). Pines on a bluff of the Arkansas R. Earlier, Mount Maria.
Pine City, Minn. (co. seat of *Pine* Co.).
Pinedale, Wyo. (co. seat of Sublette Co.).
Pine Flat Reservoir, Calif.
Pine Forest Range, Nev.
Pine Hill, N.J. (Camden Co.).
Pinehurst, Mass. (Middlesex Co.).

Pine Lawn, Mo. (St. Louis Co.).
Pine Plains, N.Y. (Dutchess Co.).
Pine Ridge, S.Dak. (Shannon Co.).
Pine Ridge Indian Reservation Area, S.Dak.
Pine River Pond, N.H.

Pineville, Ky. (co. seat of Bell Co.).
Pineville, La. (Rapides Parish).
Pineville, Mo. (co. seat of McDonald Co.). For *Pineville*, Ky.
Pineville, W.Va. (co. seat of Wyoming Co.).
Piney Point Village, Tex. (Harris Co.).
Piney River, Mo. Flows N into Gasconade R.

PINELLAS A corruption of Spanish *pinta pinal*, "point of pines."
Pinellas Co., Fla. (co. seat, Clearwater).
Pinellas Park, Fla. (*Pinellas* Co.).

PINGORA, Wyo. A peak named by climbers from Shoshonean, "difficult peak" or "impossible peak."

PINKHAM NOTCH, N.H. Mountain pass. in Presidential Range. For Daniel Pinkham, who held a grant in Coos County.

PINNACLE Descriptive, for the shape of mountains or peaks, often when standing alone.
Pinnacle, (mount), N.Y.
Pinnacle Mountain, Wyo.
Pinnacles Natl. Monument, Calif.

PINNOCCHIO PINNACLE, Wyo. For the resemblance of its profile to that of the fictional character.

PINOLE, Calif. (Contra Costa Co.). From Aztec *pinolli*, "parched or toasted grain or seeds," a staple food of the Indians.

PINOS, Mount, Calif. From Spanish, "pines."

PINTALLA CREEK, Ala. Probably from Creek Indian *opil*, "swamp," plus *lalo*, "fish" or "fish swamp." It may also be interpreted, with variations in form, as "Big Swamp" creek. It flows generally northwest into Alabama River.

PINYON PEAK, Wyo. For the pinyon pine growing on the mountain.

PIOCHE, Nev. (co. seat of Lincoln Co.). For F.L.A. Pioche, a San Francisco banker who invested in the area.

PIPE ORGAN RIDGE, Wyo. Descriptive of the fluted shapes of the columns and ridge wall.

PIPER BROOK, Conn. For the occupational specialists who made "pipes" barrels of a specific size, used in colonial times for storing and shipping liquid and solid products. It flows northeast into Connecticut River.

PIPE SPRING NATL. MONUMENT, Ariz. Established as an example of how settlers survived and protected themselves. The spring was so named because a sharpshooter bet that he could shoot the bottom out of a tobacco pipe.

PIPESTONE For the red stone quarried by the Indians to make peace pipes.
Pipestone Co., Minn. (co. seat, *Pipestone*).
Pipestone, Minn. (co. seat of *Pipestone* Co.).
Pipestone Indian Reservation, Minn.
Pipestone Natl. Monument, Minn.

PIQUA Apparently the name of a Shawnee subtribe, of Algonquian linguistic stock, in which Tecumseh was born and gained fame. It was known as the "bear" tribe, but the name has also been translated as "ashes," in reference to a myth that the first man of the tribe came from the ashes of a fire. The spelling is a French transliteration.
Piqua, Kan. (Wooson Co.). For *Piqua*, Ohio.
Piqua, Ohio (Miami Co.). Earlier, Washington.

PISCATAQUA RIVER, Me.-N.H. From Abnaki, "at the fork of the river" or "place where river divides." Many variant forms exist. It flows into the Atlantic Ocean.

PISCATAQUIS Variant form of PISCATAQUA.
Piscataquis Co., Me. (co. seat, Dover-Foxcroft).
Piscataquis River, Me. Flows into the Penobscot R.

PISCATAQUOG RIVER, N.H. Variant of PISCATAQUA. It flows crookedly east into Merrimack River.

PISCATAWAY, N.J. (Middlesex Co.). From an Indian word meaning "divided river."

PISGAH Biblical; for Mount Pisgah, from which Moses viewed the Promised Land (Deuteronomy 34:1).
Pisgah, N.C. (Randolph Co.).
Pisgah, Mount, N.Y.
Pisgah, Mount, Pa.
Pisgah, Mount, Vt.
Pisgah, Mount, Wyo.
Pisgah Natl. Forest, N.C.

PISMO BEACH, Calif. (San Luis Obispo Co.). Probably from Chumash Indian, "tar" or "mustard," for the plant that grows on the mountains in the area, although influenced by Spanish spelling and word form. It is also said to be a Spanish word meaning "place of fish," but this is unlikely.

PITCHER, N.Y. (Chenango Co.), town. For Nathaniel Pitcher, who served as lieutenant governor of New York in the 1820s.

PITKIN Co., Colo. (co. seat, Aspen). For Frederick Walker Pitkin (1837-1886), governor (1879-83).

PITMAN, N.J. (Gloucester Co.). For Rev. Charles Pitman, a prominent Methodist camp-meeting leader.

PIT RIVER, Calif. For the Indian pits found in the area by explorers. It flows southwest into Shasta Lake.

PITT, William (the Elder), 1st Earl of Chatham (1708-1778), English statesman. He was recognized as the English head of government and prosecuted the war against the French until they surrendered their American possessions. Known as "the Great Commoner," he defended the American colonies before the American Revolution.
East Pittsburgh, Pa. (Allegheny Co.).
Pitt Co., N.C. (co. seat, Greenville).
Pittsburg Co., Okla. (co. seat, McAlester). For Pittsburgh, Pa.
Pittsburg, Calif. (Contra Costa Co.). For *Pittsburgh*, Pa.

Pittsburg, Kan. (Crawford Co.). For *Pittsburgh*, Pa.
Pittsburgh, Pa. (Allegheny Co.). From Fort Pitt, which was named for William Pitt.
Pittsfield, Ill. (co. seat of Pike Co.). For *Pittsfield*, Mass.
Pittsfield, Mass. (co. seat of Berkshire Co.).
Pittsfield, N.H. (Merrimack Co.), town.
Pittston, Pa. (Luzerne Co.).
Pittsylvania Co., Va. (co. seat, Chatham). With *-sylvania*, to mean "Pitt's Woods."
West Pittsburg, Calif. (Contra Costa Co.).
West Pittston, Pa. (Luzerne Co.).

PITTSBORO, Miss. (co. seat of Calhoun Co.). For an early settler named Pitt.

PITTSBURG, Tex. (co. seat of Camp Co.). For W. W. Pitts, pioneer.

PITTSFIELD, Me. (Somerset Co.), town and village. For William Pitts, a landholder from Boston.

PIUTE Co., Utah. (co. seat, Junction). For a sub-tribe of the Ute Indians of Shoshonean linguistic stock. The name means "water Ute." See UTE.

PLACENTIA, Calif. (Orange Co.). Probably for a town in Newfoundland. *Placentia* was the ancient name of Piacenza, a city in northern Italy.

PLACER From a word of Spanish origin designating surface gravel in which gold particles are found and also a place where gold is found.
Placer Co., Calif. (co. seat, Auburn).
Placerville, Calif. (co. seat of El Dorado Co.).

PLACID, Lake, N.Y. See LAKE PLACID.

PLAIN Suggests openness and a flat farming area or a prairie.
North Plainfield, N.J. (Somerset Co.).
Plainedge, N.Y. (Nassau Co.).
Plainfield, Conn. (Hartford Co.), town and village.
Plainfield, Ill. (Will Co.). Earlier, Walker's Grove.
Plainfield, Ind. (Hendricks Co.).

Plainfield, N.J. (Union Co.).
Plains, Pa. (Luzerne Co.). Earlier, Jacob's Plains.
Plains, Tex. (co. seat of Yoakum Co.). On the Llano Estacado.
Plainview, N.Y. (Nassau Co.).
Plainview, Tex. (co. seat of Hale Co.).
Plainville, Conn. (Hartford Co.), town. Earlier, Great Plain.
Plainville, Kan. (Rooks Co.).
Plainville, Mass. (Norfolk Co.).

PLAINWELL, Mich. (Allegan Co.). For two early settlers named Samuel C. Wells and Henry Wellever, the latter a tavern keeper, and also for the prairie or plain.

PLAISTOW, N.H. (Rockingham Co.), town. Probably for Plaistow, Essex, on the outskirts of London, England.

PLANKINTON, S.Dak. (co. seat of Aurora Co.). For John H. Plankinton, meat distributor and railroad official.

PLANO From Spanish, "flat" (land) or "plain."
Plano, Ill. (Kendall Co.).
Plano, Tex. (Collin Co.).

PLAQUEMINE A French rendering of Illinois Indian *piakimin*, "persimmon," for the many such trees in the area. The term came through the Mobile Indian dialect.
Plaquemine, La. (parish seat of Iberville Parish).
Plaquemines Parish, La. (parish seat, Pointe a la Hache).

PLATEAU CREEK, Colo. Descriptive. Flows northwest and west into Colorado River.

PLATTE From French, "flat" or, when applied to a body of water, "shallow."
Little Platte River, Mo. Flows S and SW into *Platte* R.
North Platte, Neb. (co. seat of Lincoln Co.). For its location on the *North Platte* R.
North Platte River, Colo.-Wyo.-Neb. Flows N and S to join *South Platte* R. to form *Platte* R.

The Platte (French for "shallow") River is well named. In some places it is a mile wide and only three inches deep at times. A typical prairie river, it meanders over the major portion of its 300 mile length. [*New York Public Library*]

Platte Co., Mo. (co. seat, *Platte City*). For the *Platte* R. in Iowa and Missouri.
Platte Co., Neb. (co. seat, Columbus). For the *Platte* R. in Nebraska.
Platte Co., Wyo. (co. seat, Wheatland). For the *North Platte* R.
Platte River, Iowa-Mo.
Platte River, Neb. Formed by the junction of the *North Platte* and *South Platte* Rivers, flows generally E into the Missouri R.
Platte River, Wis. Flows SSW into Mississippi R.
Platte City, Mo. (co. seat of *Platte* Co.).
Platteville, Wis. (Grant Co.). For the *Platte* R. in Wisconsin.
Plattsmouth, Neb. (co. seat of Cass Co.). For its location at the mouth of the *Platte* R.
South Platte River, Colo.-Neb. Flows NE and E to join *North Platte* R. to form *Platte* R.

PLATTE LAKE, Mich. For F. B. Van Platten, early settler.

PLATT NATL. PARK, Okla. For Orville Hitchcock Platt (1827-1905), attorney, Connecticut state senator, and U.S. senator from Connecticut (1879-1905).

PLATTSBURG For Zephaniah Platt, landowner, fur trader, and "a man of uncompromising integrity."
Plattsburg, Mo. (co. seat of Clinton Co.). For *Plattsburg*, N.Y.
Plattsburg, N.Y. (co. seat of Clinton Co.).

PLAYAS LAKE, N.Mex. From Spanish, "beaches," for the dry sandy area.

PLEASANT Descriptive and usually promotional.
Pleasant Bay, Mass.
Pleasant Lake, Me.
Pleasant Lake, N.H.
Pleasant, Mount, Va.
Pleasant Pond, Me.
Pleasant River, Me. Flows into Piscataquis R.
Pleasant River, Me. Flows SE into the Atlantic Ocean.
Pleasant Grove, Ala. (Jefferson Co.).
Pleasant Grove, Utah (Utah Co.). An earlier name, Battle Creek, commemorated a battle between whites and Indians.
Pleasant Hill, Calif. (Contra Costa Co.).
Pleasant Hill, Mo. (Cass Co.).
Pleasant Hills, Pa. (Allegheny Co.).
Pleasanton, Calif. (Alameda Co.).
Pleasanton, Tex. (Atascosa Co.).
Pleasant Ridge, Mich. (Oakland Co.). Also for Ridge Road.
Pleasantville, N.J. (Atlantic Co.).
Pleasantville, N.Y. (Westchester Co.).

PLEASANTON, Calif. (Alameda Co.). For Alfred Pleasonton, a general in the Mexican War.

PLEASANTS Co., W.Va. (co. seat, St. Marys). For James Pleasants (1769-1836), Virginia representative (1811-19), senator (1819-22), and governor (1822-25).

PLEASURE RIDGE PARK, Ky. (Jefferson Co.). Promotional.

PLENTYCOOS PEAK, Wyo. For a Crow Indian chief. *Plentycoos* means "many coups."

PLENTYWOOD, Mont. (co. seat of Sheridan Co.). For the availability of much timber.

PLESSISVILLE, Que. (Megantic Co.). For Joseph Octave Plessis, a priest who was cure of Quebec (1792) and bishop of Quebec (1806-25). He played an important part in the organization of the Catholic Church in Canada.

PLOVER RIVER, Wis. For the waterbird. It flows generally southwest into Wisconsin River.

PLUM For wild plum trees.
Plum, Pa. (Allegheny Co.).
Plum Creek, Neb. Flows into Niobrara R.
Plum Island, Mass.
Plum Island, N.Y. in Long Island Sound.
Plum Lake, Wis.
Plum River, Ill. Flows SW into Mississippi R.

PLUM, Pa. (Allegheny Co.). For a creek where numerous wild plum trees grew along the banks.

PLUMAS Co., Calif. (co. seat, Quincy). From Spanish, "feathers," for the FEATHER River, also once known as *Rio de las Plumas*.

PLYMOUTH For Plymouth, Devonshire, England, from which the *Mayflower* sailed for America.
Plymouth Co., Iowa (co. seat Le Mars). For *Plymouth*, Mass.
Plymouth Co., Mass. (co. seat *Plymouth*).
Plymouth, Conn. (Litchfield Co.), town.
Plymouth, Ind. (co. seat of Marshall Co.).
Plymouth, Mass. (co. seat of *Plymouth* Co.), town and village.
Plymouth, Mich. (Wayne Co.). Named by descendants of the Pilgrims of 1620.
Plymouth, Minn. (Hennepin Co.). For *Plymouth*, Mass.
Plymouth, N.Y. (Grafton Co.), town and village.
Plymouth, N.C. (co. seat of Washington Co.).

Plymouth, the oldest town in New England and landing place of the Pilgrim Fathers, is pictured here as seen from the harbor. The colony of New Plymouth, founded by the Pilgrims in 1620, was governed under the Mayflower Compact until 1691, when it became part of the Massachusetts Bay Colony. [*New York Public Library*]

Plymouth, Pa. (Luzerne Co.). For *Plymouth*, Conn.

Plymouth, Wis. (Sheboygan Co.). For *Plymouth*, Mass.

Plymouth Bay, Mass., on the Atlantic Ocean.

Plymouth Rock, Mass. A national monument, supposedly the rock on which the first pilgrims stepped when they landed in 1620.

Plymouth Colony, Mass. (1620-1691), the first permanent British colony in New England, settled by the *Mayflower* Pilgrims, later absorbed by the Massachusetts Bay Colony.

POCAHONTAS An Indian maid, daughter of a Powhatan chief named Powhatan. She interceded with her father to save the life of John Smith, who explored the present Virginia area in 1608. Later she married

Pocahontas, daughter of the great chief, Powhatan, is renowned for having saved the life of Captain John Smith. Later she converted to Christianity and took the name Rebecca. She married John Rolfe and sailed with him to England where she quickly died of smallpox. [*New York Public Library*]

John Rolfe, visited England, and died there in 1617. The name itself means either "radiance" or "playful." After she achieved puberty, and according to the rituals of her tribe, she received a second name, *Matoaka*, "plays with others."

Pocahontas Co., Iowa (co. seat, *Pocahontas*).

Pocahontas Co., W.Va. (co. seat, Marlinton).

Pocahontas, Ark. (co. seat of Randolph Co.). Many of the settlers came from Virginia.

Pocahontas, Iowa (co. seat of *Pocahontas* Co.).

POCATELLO, Idaho (co. seat of Bannock Co.). For a Bannock Indian chief. His name means "the wayward."

POCOMOKE From an Indian word meaning "dark water."

Pocomoke River, Md.

Pocomoke Sound, Md.

Pocomoke City, Md. (Worcester Co.).

POCONO From Algonquian, "stream between mountains," also with the connotation of a "gap between mountains." The stream was named first.

Pocono Creek, Pa. Flows SE into Brodhead Creek.

Pocono Lake, Pa.

Pocono Mountains, Pa.

Pocono Manor, Pa. (Monroe Co.).

Pocono Pines, Pa. (Monroe Co.).

Pocono Summit, Pa. (Monroe Co.).

POCOTOPAUG, Lake, Conn. From Wangunk, "twin ponds."

POCWOCK STREAM, Me. Probably from Algonquian, "shallow stream." It flows southeast into St. John River.

POGE, Cape, Mass. Extends into Nantucket Sound. Despite its being a geographical cape, it seems to be a folk etymologized form of an Indian word, such as *Capipissoke* or *Capesseck*, with the root meaning "obstruction" or "dammed-up."

POGROMNI VOLCANO, Alaska. On Unimak Island. From Russian, "desolation."

POHUE BAY, Hawaii. On southwest coast of Hawaii Island. From Hawaiian, "gourd."

POINSETT, Joel Roberts (1779-1851), South Carolina statesman. He was a state legislator, a U.S. representative (1821-25), first U.S. minister to Mexico (1825-30), and secretary of war (1837-41) under Van Buren.
Poinsett Co., Ark. (co. seat, Harrisburg).
Poinsett, Lake, S.Dak. Named by John C. Fremont.

POINTE A LA HACHE, La. (parish seat of Plaquemines Parish). From French, "ax point," descriptive of the shape of the terrain.

POINTE AU FER ISLAND, La. In Gulf of Mexico. From French, "iron point."

POINTE-AUX-TREMBLES, Que. (Montreal and Jesus Islands Co.). Named in 1674 by early settlers because of the trembling leaves of the aspen trees.

POINTE-CLAIRE, Que. (Montreal and Jesus Islands Co.). From French "clear point," for the clear view which may be had from there.

POINTE COUPEE Parish, La. (parish seat, New Roads). From French *pointe coupee,* "cut-off point," descriptive of a place where the Mississippi River cut a new channel.

POINT MUGU, Calif. (Ventura Co.). Believed to be from Chumash *muwu,* "beach."

POINT PLEASANT Subjectively descriptive of a rather nice place.
Point Pleasant, N.J. (Ocean Co.).
Point Pleasant, W.Va. (co. seat of Mason Co.). At the junction of the Kanawha and Ohio Rivers. At this site Gen. Andrew Lewis pre-pared his troops for battle with the Shawnees (1774) and lost his life in action.

POKEGAMA LAKE, Wis. From Algonquian, "lake with bay extensions" or "arms extending out of bay."

POKE-O-MOONSHINE MOUNTAIN, N.Y. Folk etymologized form of an Indian word, possibly from Algonquian, "where the rocks are smoothly broken off." It has also been translated as "pond clear as moonlight."

POLAND, Ohio (Mahoning Co.). Probably for George Poland, an early settler.

POLK, James Knox (1795-1849), eleventh President of the United States (1845-49), from Tennessee. Although a firm believer in states' rights, Polk was an expansionist who supported the annexation of Texas (1845) and vigorously waged the Mexican War (1845-48), which pushed the American frontier to the Pacific. He also resolved the Oregon boundary dispute with England (1846). Thus, under his regime, the United States added not only Texas but all of the area west of the Rocky Mountains except the small strip in southern Arizona and New Mexico later included in the Gadsden Purchase (1853). He had been a member of the U.S. House of Representatives (1825-39; speaker 1835-39) and governor of Tennessee (1839-41).
Polk Co., Ark. (co. seat, Mena).
Polk Co., Fla. (co. seat, Bartow).
Polk Co., Ga. (co. seat, Cedartown).
Polk Co., Iowa (co. seat, Des Moines).
Polk Co., Minn. (co. seat, Crookston).
Polk Co., Mo. (co. seat, Bolivar).
Polk Co., Neb. (co. seat, Osceola).
Polk Co., Ore. (co. seat, Dallas).
Polk Co., Tenn. (co. seat, Benton).
Polk Co., Tex. (co. seat, Livingston).
Polk Co., Wis. (co. seat, Balsam Lake).
Polk Pa. (Venango Co.).

POLK Co., N.C. (co. seat, Columbus). For William Polk (1758-1834), an officer in the American Revolution.

James Knox Polk presided over the acquisition of the largest tract of land since the Louisiana Purchase, including Texas and eight other western states. Despite his enemies' slogan — "James Knox Polk of Tennessee, the biggest damned fool that you ever did see" — he was one of America's ablest presidents. [*New York Public Library*]

POLLUX PEAK, Wyo. In Yellowstone Natl. Park. Mythogical; for Pollux, one of the twin sons of Leda and a brother of Helen of Troy.

POLO, Ill. (Ogle Co.). For Marco Polo (1254?-1324), medieval traveler.

POLSON, Mont. (co. seat of Lake Co.). For David Polson (1826-1902), who migrated to California during the gold rush of 1849. He later settled as a rancher in the vicinity of the city that bears his name.

POMEROY, Ohio (co seat of Megis Co.). For Samuel Wyllis Pomeroy, the original proprietor.

POMFRET, Conn. (Windham Co.), town. For Pontefract, Yorkshire, England. The name means "broken bridge." The spelling may have been influenced by the way the English name is often pronounced.

POMME DE TERRE From French, "potato," for the edible tuber found along the river.
Pomme de Terre Reservoir, Mo.
Pomme de Terre River, Minn. Refers here to a turnip, *Psoralea esculenta*, a delicacy to the Indians.
Pomme de Terre River, Mo. Flows N into Osage R.

POMONA, Calif. (Los Angeles Co.). For the Greek goddess of fruit trees; named by Solomon Gates, nurseryman.

POMPANO BEACH. For the fish (*trachinotus*) found in warm seas, especially along the coasts of the South Atlantic states.
Pompano Beach, Fla. (Broward Co.).
Pompano Beach Highlands, Fla. (Broward Co.).

POMPERAUG RIVER, Conn. From Paugasett Indian, meaning uncertain, but was the name of a sachem. It flows south into Housatonic River.

POMPTON LAKES, N.J. (Passaic Co.). For several man-made lakes in the area.

PONAGANSET From Narraganset, meaning uncertain, possibly "oyster processing place" or "waiting place at the cove."
Ponaganset Reservoir, R.I.
Ponaganset River, R.I. Flows SE into Scituate Reservoir.

PONCA For an Indian tribe of Siouan linguistic stock. The meaning of the name has been lost. This tribe was located on the banks of the Missouri where the Niobrara River joins it.
Ponca, Neb. (co. seat of Dixon Co.).
Ponca Creek, Neb.-S.Dak.
Ponca City, Okla. (Kay Co.). Earlier, New Ponca.

PONCHATULA, La. (Tangipahoa Parish). From Choctaw, "falling hair." The Indians had given this name to a nearby stream, probably because of the abundance of Spanish moss in the vicinity.

POND Descriptive.
Pond River, Ky. Flows NNW into Green R.
Pond Creek, Okla. (co. seat of Grant Co.). Earlier, Round Pond.

PONDERA Co., Mont. (co. seat, Conrad). There are two theories of derivation: one is that it is from French *pend d'oreille*, for the pendants worn on the ears by the Indians. To avoid confusion with Pend Oreille Lake in Idaho, the name was changed in Montana to *Pondera*, and was taken for the name of the county. According to the other theory, which is less probable, the name comes from a French trader's description of the brown prairies as *pain dore*, "browned toast."

PONGO A shortened form of MACHIPONGO.
Pongo Lake, N.C.
Pongo River, N.C. flows into Pamlico R.

PONOKA, Alta. From Cree Indian, "black elk."

PONTCHARTRAIN, Lake, La. For Louis, Comte de Pontchartrain (1643-1727), a French political figure and explorer.

PONTIAC (fl. mid 1700s) a famous Ottawa chief who fought against the British during the French and Indian Wars. In 1763 he unsuccessfully led his forces against the British-held fort of Detroit. Pontiac would not recognize the English sovereign, but was willing to call him "uncle," to the Indians almost a derogatory appellation. Pontiac was assassinated by a Kashkaskia Indian, probably bribed by the British, in the late 1760s, an event that caused further conflict between the Ottawa and Illinois tribes.
Pontiac Co., Que. (co. seat, Cambell's Bay).
Pontiac, Ill. (co. seat of Livingston Co.).
Pontiac, Mich. (co. seat of Oakland Co.).

PONTOOK RESERVOIR, N.H. In Androscoggin River. From Algonquian, "at the waterfalls."

PONTOOSUC LAKE, Mass. From Algonquian, "falls in the stream."

PONTOTOC From Chickasaw, "cattails growing on the prairie."
Pontotoc Co., Miss (co. seat, *Pontotoc*).
Pontotoc Co., Okla. (co. seat, Ada).
Pontotoc, Miss. (co. seat of *Pontotoc* Co.).

POPE Co., Ark. (co. seat, Russellville). For John Pope (1770-1845), Kentucky legislator. He was a U.S. representative (1837-43), senator (1807-13), and governor of Arkansas Territory (1829-35).

POPE Co., Minn. (co. seat, Glenwood). For John Pope (1822-1892), career soldier. He served in the Mexican War and as a general in the Union army during the Civil War, and was commander of the Northwest Department. Later he was a railroad surveyor. He explored the upper Mississippi area in 1859.

POPE, Nathaniel (1784-1850), delegate to congress (1816-19), secretary of Illinois Territory, and judge for the district of Illinois.
Pope Co., Ill. (co. seat, Golconda).
Pope Creek, Ill.

Facts about the death of Chief Pontiac are obscure. He was supposedly assassinated by a member of the Kaskaskia tribe as shown here. [*New York Public Library*]

POPLAR For the tree.
Poplar River, Sask.-Mont. Flows S into Missouri R.
Popular Bluff Mo. (co. seat of Butler Co.).
Poplarville, Miss. (co. seat of Pearl River Co.).

POPOO GULCH, Hawaii. From Hawaiian, "hollow." It flows northwest across Hawaii Island into the Pacific Ocean. Also spelled *Poopoo*.

POPPLE RIVER, Wis. A variant of POPLAR. It flows generally northeast into Pine River.

POQUONOCK BRIDGE, Conn. (New London Co.). From Algonquian, "small farm" or "field."

POQUOSON, Va. (York Co.). From Algonquian, "swamp" or "overflowed land."

PORCUPINE For the animal.
Porcupine Mountains, Mich.
Porcupine River, Yukon-Alaska. Flows W into Yukon R.

PORTAGE For the portage of canoes or other craft between one watercourse and another.
Portage Co., Ohio (co. seat, Ravenna). Between the Cuyahoga and Mahoning rivers.
Portage Co., Wis. (co. seat, Stevens Point). Between the Fox and Wisconsin rivers.
Portage, Ind. (Porter Co.).
Portage, Mich. (Kalamazoo Co.). For the *Portage* R.
Portage, Pa. (Cambria Co.). For the Portage railroad, the only railroad which transported boats over the Allegheny Mtns. from 1832 to 1852.
Portage Creek, Pa. Flows NW into Allegheny R.
Portage Lake, Me.
Portage Lake, Mich. (Houton Co.).
Portage Lake, Mich. (Manistee Co.).
Portage River, Mich.
Portage River, Ohio.
Portoge La Prarie, Man.

PORTALES, N.Mex. (co. seat of Roosevelt Co.). From Spanish, "gates," "entrances," or "porches." The town was named for Portales Springs, a trailside watering place. The caves at the springs resemble entrances, or porches, of adobe houses.

PORT ALFRED, Que. (Chicoutimi Co.). For J. E. Alfred Dubuc, industrialist and town founder.

PORT ALLEN, La. (parish seat of West Baton Rouge Parish). For Henry Watkins Allen (1822-1866), Confederate general (1860-64) and Louisiana governor (1864-65).

PORT ANGELES, Wash. (co. seat of Clallam Co.). The Spanish explorer Francisco Eliza named the place *Porto de Neustra Senora de los Angeles* in 1791. The shortened name was given by George Vancouver in 1792.

PORT ARTHUR, Tex. (Jefferson Co.). For Arthur Edward Stillwell, a promoter of the town and of railroad service for it.

PORT CHESTER, N.Y. (Westchester Co.). So named because it is a port on Long Island Sound; *Chester*, for the town and county in England. An earlier name was Saw Pit.

PORT COLBORNE, Ont. (Welland Co.). For Sir John Colborne, 1st Baron Seaton (1778-1863), British general who became lieutenant governor of Upper Canada (1830) and governor general (1832).

PORT COQUITLAM See COQUITIAM.

PORT CREDIT, Ont. See CREDIT.

PORTE DES MORTS STRAIT, Wis. Water passage from Lake Michigan to Green Bay, between Washington Island and the mainland. From French, "death's gate."

PORTER, David (1780-1843), naval hero of the War of 1812 and diplomat.
Porter Co., Ind. (co. seat, Valparaiso).
Porter, Ind. (*Porter* Co.).

PORTERVILLE For Royal Porter Putnam, landowner and founder.
East Porterville, Calif. (Tulare Co.).
Porterville, Calif. (Tulare Co.).
Porterville Northwest, Calif. (Tulare Co.).
Porterville West, Calif. (Tulare Co.).

PORT GIBSON, Miss. (co. seat of Claiborne Co.). For Samuel Gibson, who held a Spanish land grant of 800 acres on the Mississippi River.

PORT HOOD, N.S. (co. seat of Inverness Co.). For Admiral Hook, commander-in-chief of the North American Station who played an important part in the American Revolution.

PORT HUENEME, Calif. (Ventura Co.). From the name of a Chumash village, *Wene me* or *Wene mu*, "place where one sleeps (rests)," because it was a halfway point between two other Chumash villages.

PORT HURON, Mich. See HURON.

PORT ISABEL, Tex. (Cameron Co.). Originally located on the Santa Ysabel grant and known as El Fronton de Santa Ysabel, it was later changed to the English version, Point Isabel, and finally, where the water was deepened, changed again to Port Isabel.

PORT JERVIS, N.Y. (Orange Co.). For John P. Jervis, engineer and general superintendent in the construction of the Delaware and Hudson Canal.

PORTLAND For Portland, Dorsetshire, England.
Portland, Conn. (Middlesex Co.), town. The name was suggested by the presence of stone quarries at both sites.
Portland, Me. (co. seat of Cumberland Co.). Earlier, Falmouth.
Portland, N.Y. (Chautauqua Co.). The name was drawn from a hat.
Portland, Ore. (co. seat of Multnomah Co.). Settled by New Englanders, who decided by flipping a coin between *Portland* (for *Portland*, Me.) and Boston (for Boston, Mass.).
South Portland, Me. (Cumberland Co.).

PORTLAND, Ind. (co. seat of Jay Co.). So named because of commercial interests that need a land port for a railroad.

PORTLAND, Mich. (Ionia Co.). For the excellent landing area, on a branch of the Grand River.

PORTLAND, Tex. (San Patricio Co.). Descriptive, designating land adjoining a port, on an arm of the Gulf of Mexico.

PORTLAND, Tex. (San Patricio Co.). For its location on a harbor.

PORT LAVACA, Tex. (co. seat of Calhoun Co.) Believed to be a derivation from French *les vaches*, "the cows," so named by the French explorer La Salle for the abundance of buffalo in the area.

PORTLOCK HARBOR, Alaska. On west coast of Chichagof Island. For Capt. Nathaniel Portlock, who explored the area (1786-87) with Capt. George Dixon.

PORT MOODY, B.C. Named by Capt. Richards, of the survey ship *Plumper*, for Col. Richard Clement Moody (1813-1887), Barbados-born royal engineer who was commissioner of lands and works in British Columbia (1858-63). He surveyed much of the land and laid out settlements in southwestern British Columbia. He later became a major-general.

PORT NECHES, Tex. (Jefferson Co.). For the nearby Neches River, from the Spanish plural form of *Neche*, an Indian tribe. The name appears also in North Dakota; in the Ojibway language it apparently means "friend."

PORTNEUF Co., Que. (co. seat, Cap Sante). Named *Port* by the first settlers, for its location on the north shore of the St. Lawrence River. Later the Sieur de Neuf, seignior of the land, added his name.

PORTOLA VALLEY, Calif. (San Mateo Co.). For Gaspar de Portola, Spanish explorer.

PORT ORCHARD, Wash. (co. seat of Kitsap Co.). Named by George Vancouver for H.M. Orchard, a ship's clerk.

PORT ROYAL Named in 1562 by Jean Ribaut, Huguenot colonizer, "calling the noble entrance a royal sound and the land to starboard Port Royal."
Port Royal, S.C. (Beaufort Co.).
Port Royal Island, S.C.
Port Royal Sound, S.C.

PORTSMOUTH For Portsmouth, Hampshire, England. The name means "the mouth of the port, or harbor," and is used thus in the United States also.
Portsmouth, N.H. (Rockingham Co.). At the mouth of the Piscataqua R.
Portsmouth, Ohio (co. seat of Scioto Co.). On the Scioto R., where it joins the Ohio River.
Portsmouth, R.I., (Newport Co.), town. On Aquidneck Island near the head of the Sakonnet R.
Portsmouth, Va. (city of Chesapeake.). On the Elizabeth R.
West Portsmouth, Ohio (Scioto Co.).

PORT SULPHUR, La. See SULPHUR.

PORT TOWNSEND, Wash. (co. seat of Jefferson Co.). Named by George Vancouver for the Marquis of Townshend; the name was later simplified in spelling.

PORTVILLE, N.Y. (Cattaraugas Co.). Descriptive; lumber was shipped down the Allegheny and Ohio Rivers from here.

PORT WASHINGTON For George WASHINGTON.
Port Washington, N.Y. (Nassau Co.).
Port Washington, Wis. (co. seat of Ozaukee Co.).
Port Washington North, N.Y. (Nassau Co.).

POSEN, Ill. (Cook Co.). For Poznan, Poland, origin of early settlers, in the German and anglicized form.

POSEY Co., Ind (co. seat, Mount Vernon). For Thomas Posey (1750-1818), officer in the American Revolution, Louisiana legislator and U.S. senator (1812-13), and Indiana territorial governor (1813-16).

POSSUM KINGDOM LAKE, Tex. Lake and dam in Brazos River. For the presence of many opossums.

POST, Tex. (co. seat of Garza Co.). For C. W. Post (?-1912), cereal manufacturer and founder.

POTAGANNISSING BAY, Mich. From Ojibway, "at the gaps," for entrances to islands and bodies of water in the area.

POTATO CREEK, Pa. From Algonquian *nunundah*, "potato," for the tuberous plant. The name dates from 1832, but has been criticized by those who believe it a "barbarous" name for such a beautiful valley; they prefer the more euphonious Indian name *Nunundah*. It flows generally northwest into Marvin Creek.

POTEAU From French, "post," for a trading area.
Poteau, Okla. (co. seat of Le Flore Co.).
Poteau River, Ark.-Okla. Flows into Arkansas R.

POTEET, Tex. (Atascosa Co.). For Francis Marion Poteet (1833-1907), who at one time owned a store and a blacksmith shop in the area.

POTHOLES RESERVOIR, Wash. Descriptive of holes in the area.

POTOMAC From an Indian word meaning "where goods are brought in." This became the name of the river, where Indians were known to do trading. It may be a mixture of Iroquoian, Delaware, and Powhatan forms. The name was first recorded by John Smith in 1608 as *Patawomeck,* which he took to be the name of a tribe.
North Potomac, Md. (Montgomery Co.).
Potomac River, W.Va.-Va.-Md. Flows into Chesapeake Bay.
Potomac Valley, Md. (Montgomery Co.).

POTOSI, Mo. (co. seat of Washington Co.). Probably for Potosi, Bolivia, a silver-mining center, and from the name of mines and cities in other countries in Mexico and Central and South America.

POTSDAM, N.Y. (St. Lawrence Co.). For Potsdam, a city in eastern Germany.

POTTAWATOMIE For an Indian tribe of Algonquian linguistic stock, originally located on the southern peninsula of Michigan. The name means "people of the place of the fire." They moved to Wisconsin, Ohio, and southern Michigan, but after 1795 retreated west to Illinois and Iowa. In the 1840s many of them moved to Kansas and later Oklahoma. There are still scattered groups in the various states they inhabited.
Pottawatomie Co., Kan. (co. seat, Westmoreland).
Pottawatomie Co., Okla. (co. seat, Shawnee).

POTTAWATTAMIE Co., Iowa (co. seat, Council Bluffs). A spelling variant of POTTAWATAMIE.

POTTER Co., Pa. (co. seat, Coudersport). For Gen. James Potter (1729-1789), Irish-born Pennsylvania soldier and frontiersman. He fought in the American Revolution and was wounded at the Battle of Princeton (1777).

POTTER Co., S.Dak. (co. seat, Gettysburg). For Joel A. Potter, legislator.

POTTER Co., Tex. (co. seat, Amarillo). For Robert Potter (1800-1842), North Carolina legislator and U.S. representative (1829-31), Texas patriot, and Republic of Texas official . . . He was killed in a battle between the Moderators and Regulators, two Texas rival political groups.

POTTER MOUNTAIN, Ore. For a local settler or explorer.

POTTSTOWN, Pa. (Montgomery Co.). For John Potts, one of the leading ironmasters of his time. He owned nearly a thousand acres of land in this area and in 1754 laid out the town.

POTTSVILLE, Pa. (co. seat of Schuylkill Co.). For John Pott, iron founder and furnace owner. He was also proprietor of the White Horse Tavern.

POUGHKEEPSIE, N.Y. (co. seat of Dutchess Co.). From an Algonquian term of uncertain meaning, although certainly referring to water. In 1680 a creek was known as *Pacaksing*. In 1683 a waterfall was called *Pooghkepesingh*. The name may then mean "waterfall," or perhaps "pool at the base of the fall"; an early definition was given as "safe harbor."

POULTNEY For William Pulteney, Earl of Bath (1684-1764), Whig politician and brilliant orator.
Poultney, Vt. (Rutland Co.), town.
Poultney River, N.Y.-Vt.

POWAY, Calif. (San Diego Co.). Believed to be from Spanish, "it is finished" or "the end of the valley."

POWDER For the river banks lined with dark gray powdery sand much like gunpowder.
Powder River, Mont.-Wyo. Flows into the Yellowstone R.
Powder River, Ore.
Powder River Co., Mont. (co. seat, Broadus). For the river.
Powder River Pass, Wyo. (Sheridan Co.). For the river.

POWELL, Ambrose, who carved his name on a tree near the river, but is otherwise unknown now.
Powell Mountain, Va.-Tenn.
Powell River, Va.-Tenn. Flows SW into Norris Reservoir.

POWELL, John Wesley (1834-1902). First head of the U.S. Bureau of Reclamation and early conservationist. He was also director of the U.S. Geological Survey and the first to explore the Colorado River Basin.
Powell Co., Mont. (co. seat, Deer Lodge).
Powell, Wyo. (Park Co.).
Powell, Lake, Utah

POWELL Co., Ky. (co. seat, Stanton). For Lazarus Whitehead Powell (1812-1867), Kentucky legislator, U.S. representative, senator, and governor of Kentucky (1851-55).

POWER Co., Idaho (co. seat, American Falls). For the American Falls Canal and Power Company.

POWESHIEK Co., Iowa (co. seat, Montezuma). For a Fox chief, properly *Pawishika*, "he who shakes (something off himself)." This is a masculine proper name in the bear clan, the ruling clan of the Foxes. He was the chief during the Black Hawk War (1832), and it was he, rather than Keokuk, who weakened the fighting power of the Black Hawks. With the Foxes, he crossed the Mississippi to the vicinity of Davenport, Iowa. They were joined later by Keokuk. On behalf of his tribe he signed the Treaty of Fort Armstrong at Rock Island, Ill.

POWHATAN (c. 1550-1618), chief of the Powhatan tribe, of Algonquian stock, whose Indian name was Wahunsonacock. A formidable chieftain who controlled most of what is now eastern Virginia, Powhatan maintained an uneasy truce with the Jamestown colonists, but relations improved after his daughter, Pocahontas, married a colonist, John Rolfe. The name *powhatan* is said to mean "falls in a current of water" or "at the falls."
Powhatan Co., Va. (co. seat, *Powhatan*).
Powhatan, Ark. (co. seat of Lawrence Co.).
Powhatan, Va. (co. seat of *Powhatan* Co.).

POYGAN, Lake, Wis. From Algonquian, "pipe," for tobacco.

PRAIRIE Descriptive of surrounding countryside.
Prairie Co., Ark. (co. seats, Des Arc and De Valls Bluff).
Prairie Co., Mont. (co. seat, Terry).
Prairie Lake, Wis.
Prairie Du Chien, Wis. (co. seat of Crawford Co.). From French, "Dog, or Dog's Prairie," named for an Indian chief.
Prairie View, Tex. (Waller Co.).
Prairie Village, Kan. (Johnson Co.).

PRAIRIE DOG CREEK, Kan.-Neb. For the animal. It flows generally northeast into Harlan County Reservoir.

PRATT, Caleb (?-1861), a Union officer killed at the battle of Wilson's Creek, Mo., on August 10, 1861, during the Civil War.
Pratt Co., Kan. (co. seat, *Pratt*).
Pratt, Kan. (co. seat of *Pratt* Co.).

PRATTVILLE, Ala. (co. seat of Autauga Co.). For Daniel Pratt (1799-1873), landowner and founder. He built the first cotton gin in Alabama and also the first dam to provide power for industrial purposes. He was a pioneer in the development of coal and iron mines in the South.

PREBLE Co., Ohio (co. seat, Eaton). For Edward Preble (1761-1807), naval officer. He was commander of the *Constitution*, which bombarded Tripoli in 1804.

PREMONT, Tex. (Jim Wells Co.). For Charles Premont (1867-1941), ranch foreman on the site where the town was established.

PRENTISS, Sergeant Smith (1808-1850), Mississippi legislator and U.S. representative (1838-39).
Prentiss Co., Miss. (co. seat, Booneville).
Prentiss, Miss. (co. seat of Jefferson Davis Co.).

The prairies, or the Great Plains, occupy most of the United States between the Mississippi and the Rocky Mountains as well as the so-called Canadian "Prairie Provinces" — Manitoba, Saskatchewan, and Alberta. [*New York Public Library*]

PRESCOTT, Ariz. (co. seat of Yavapal Co.). For William Hickling Prescott (1796-1859), noted historian of the Aztecs.

PRESCOTT, Ark. (co. seat of Navada Co.). For a judge who presided during early settlement days.

PRESCOTT, Robert (1725-1815), lieutenant governor of Canada (1796) and governor general (1797-1807). He served under Gen. Jeffrey Amherst during the French and Indian War and during the American Revolution.
Prescott Co., Ont. (co. seat, L'Original).
Prescott, Ont. (Grenville Co.). Earlier, Johnstown.

PRESIDENTIAL RANGE, N.H. So named because many of the peaks are named for presidents of the United States.

PRESIDIO Co., Tex. (co. seat, Maria). From Spanish, "garrisoned fortress."

PRESQUE ISLE From French, "almost an island"; that is, a peninsula.
Presque Isle Co., Mich. (co. seat, Rogers City).
Presque Isle, Me. (Aroostook Co.).
Presque Isle Peninsula, Pa., on L. Erie.
Presque Isle Point, Mich.
Presque Isle River, Mich. Flows into L. Superior.

PRESQUILE RIVER, Me.-N.B. A contraction of PRESQUE ISLE. It flows southeast into St. John River. Also called *Prestile*.

PRESTON For Preston, Lancashire, England.
Preston, Conn. (New London Co.), town.
Preston, Ont. (Waterloo Co.).

PRESTON, Idaho (co. seat of Franklin Co.). For William B. Preston, leader of the Mormons in the area.

PRESTON, James Patton (1774-1843), Virginia soldier and statesman who fought in the War of 1812 and served as governor (1816-19).

Preston Co., W.Va. (co. seat, Kingwood).
Preston, Ga. (co. seat of Webster Co.).

PRESTON, Minn. (co. seat of Floyd Co.). For Col. John Preston, state treasurer of Virginia, who held a 100,000-acre grant in the Big Sandy Valley of Kentucky.

PRETTY Descriptive; subjectively named as pleasing to the sight.
Pretty Butte, N.Dak.
Pretty Rock Butte, N.Dak.

PREWITT RESERVOIR, Colo. For a local settler.

PRICE, William, an early settler in Utah.
Price, Utah (co. seat of Carbon Co.). For the river.
Price, River, Utah.

PRICE Co., Wis. (co. seat, Phillips). For William T. Price (1824-1886), Wisconsin legislator and U.S. representative.

PRIEST For Father Roothaan, a Jesuit, even though he probably never set foot in the United States. As general of the Society of Jesus, he resided in Rome, Italy.
Priest Lake, Idaho.
Priest River, Idaho.
Prist Lake, Idaho (Bonner Co.).

PRIEST BROOK, Conn.-Mass. For Joe Priest. It flows into Millers River.

PRIESTLY LAKE, Me. For a local dweller.

PRIMGHAR, Iowa (co. seat of O'Brien Co.). Formed from the initials of the names of eight men active in platting the town:
Pumphrey, the treasurer, drives the first nail,
Roberts, the donor, is quick on his trail,
Inman dips slyly his first letter in,
McCormack adds M, which makes the full Prim.
Green, thinking of groceries, gives them the G,
Hayes drops them an H, without asking a fee,

Albright, the joker, with his jokes all
at par,
Rerick brings up the rear and crowns
all "Primghar."

PRINCE Co., P.E.I. (co. seat, Summerside). Named by Capt. Samuel Holland
as an expression of loyalty to the royal
family.

PRINCE EDWARD See EDWARD.

PRINCE FERDERICK, Md. (co. seat of
Calvert Co.). For Frederick, son of George I
(1660-1727) of England. Frederick died
before his father.

PRINCE GEORGE For George of Den-
mark, (1653-1708), husband of Queen Anne
of England.
Prince George Co., Va. (co. seat, *Prince
George*].
Prince George, Va. (co. seat of *Prince
George* Co.).

PRINCE GEORGES Co., Md. (co. seat,
Upper Marlboro). For PRINCE GEORGE of
Denmark.

PRINCE OF WALES For the Prince of
Wales of England.
Prince of Wales Archipelago, Alaska. In the
Alexander Archipelago. Named in 1793
by Capt. George Vancouver.
Prince of Wales, Cape, Alaska. Named in
1778 by Capt. James Cook.
Prince of Wales Island, Alaska. Largest
island in the Alexander Archipelago.
Earliest recorded in 1825, in a treaty
between Russia and Great Britain.

PRINCESS ANNE, Md. (co. seat of
Somerset Co.). For Princess Anne (1665-
1714), daughter of James II and later Queen
Anne of England (1702-14).

PRINCETON In colonial times, for the
reigning royal family.
Princeton, Ill. (co. seat of Bureau Co.). For
Princeton, N.J.
Princeton, Mo. (co. seat of Mercer Co.). For
Princeton, N.J., where Gen. Hugh MER-
CER, for whom the county was

named, was mortally wounded during the
American Revolution.
Princeton, N.J. (Mercer Co.). Earlier,
Prince's Town (now Kingston), N.J.
Princeton, W.Va. (co. seat of Mercer Co.).
For *Princeton*, N.J.
Princeton, Mount, Colo. For Princeton
University in *Princeton*, N.J.
Princeton North, N.J. (Mercer Co.).

PRINCETON, Ind. (co. seat of Gibson Co.).
For a Captain Prince, one of the county
commissioners when the site was named.

PRINCETON, Ky. (co. seat of Caldwell
Co.). For William Prince (1752-?), who
donated the land for the site. An earlier
name was Prince's Place.

PRINCETON, Minn. (Millie Lacs Co.). For
John S. Prince (1821-1894), fur trader,
insurance agent, banker, member of the
Minnesota constituional convention (1857),
twice mayor of St. Paul, and civic leader.

PRINCE WILLIAM Co., Va. (co. seat,
Manassas). For William Augustus, Duke of
CUMBERLAND

PRINE, Barney, a whiskey dealer and seller
of blacksmith equipment.
Prineville, Ore. (co. seat of Crook Co.).
Prineville Reservoir, Ore.

PROCTOR, Minn. (St. Louis Co.). For
James Proctor Knott (1830-1911), U.S.
representative from Kentucky (1867-71;
1877-83) and governor of Kentucky (1883-
87). He was also dean of the law school at
Centre College. He made a humorous
speech about Duluth, Minn., and a segment
of the city honored him by using his middle
name for the town's name.

PROMONTORY BUTTE, Ariz. Descriptive.

PROSPECT For gold prospectors.
Prospect Peak, Nev.
Prospectors Mountain, Wyo.

PROSPECT For a fine view.
Prospect, Conn. (New Haven Co.), town.
Prospect, Mount, N.H.
Prospect Heights, Ill. (Cook Co.). A developer's name; promotional.
Prospect Park, N.J. (Passaic Co.).
Prospect Park, Pa. (Delaware Co.).

PROSSER, Wash. (co. seat of Benton Co.). For William Ferrand Prosser (1834-1911), an early settler and landowner.

PROVIDENCE For divine providence.
East Providence, R.I. (*Providence* Co.).
North Providence, R.I. (*Providence* Co.).
Providence Co., R.I. (co. seat, *Providence*).
Providence, Ky. (Webster Co.).
Providence, R.I. (co. seat, *Providence* Co.), state capital. Named by Roger Williams, "for God's merciful providence to me in my distress."

PROVINCE For the "provinces," an early name for the American colonies.
Province Lake, N.H.

Provincetown, Mass. (Barnstable Co.), town and village. As residents of the "Province Town," inhabitants were exempt from taxation.

PROVO, Utah (co. seat of Utah Co.). For Etienne Provot, a French-Canadian trapper and explorer.

PROWERS Co., Colo. (co. seat, Lamar). For John Wesley Prowers (1839-1884), who married Amanche, daughter of a Cheyenne chief and worked with Indian agent Col. William Bent. Prowers was on the first board of commissioners for the county and also a member of the state General Assembly. A rancher, he introduced Hereford stock to the county.

PRUDENCE ISLAND, R.I. in Narragansett Bay. An early Puritan name, for the virtue.

PRYOR CREEK, Okla. (co. seat of Mayes Co.). For Nathaniel Pryor (c. 1785-1831), a scout in the Lewis and Clark Expedition and

Providence, Rhode Island, is the capital of the first colony to grant widespread religious liberty. This was the view of the city from Prospect Hill in 1872. [*New York Public Library*]

a great grandson of Nicketti, daughter of Powhatan and sister of Pocahontas. He kept a trading establishment near here.

PTARMIGAN MOUNTAIN, Wyo. For the Ptarmigan birds.

PUCKAWAY, Lake, Wis. On Fox River. Probably from an Indian personal name.

PUEBLO From Spanish, "town."
Pueblo Co., Colo. (co. seat, *Pueblo*).
Pueblo, Colo. (co. seat of *Pueblo* Co.).
Pueblo Colorado Wash (river), Ariz.

PUEO POINT, Hawaii. On east coast of Nihau Island. From Hawaiian, "owl."

PUERCO From Spanish, "dirty" or "pig."
Puerco River, N.Mex. Flows generally S into the Rio Grande R.
Puerco River, N.Mex.-Ariz. Flows SW into Little Colorado R.

PUGET SOUND, Wash. For Peter Puget, an officer in the expeditionary group led by Capt. George Vancouver in 1792.

PULASKI, Count Casimir (1748?-1779), Polish soldier who distinguished himself in support of the American cause during the American Revolution. He was killed at the siege of Savannah.
Fort Pulaski Natl. Monument, Ga.
Fort Pulaski Co., Ark. (co. seat, Little Rock).
Pulaski Co., Ga. (co. seat, Hawkinsville).
Pulaski Co., Ill. (co. seat, Mound City)
Pulaski Co., Ind. (co. seat, Winamac).
Pulaski Co., Ky. (co. seat, Somerset).
Pulaski Co., Mo. (co. seat, Waynesville).
Pulaski Co., Va. (co. seat, *Pulaski*).
Pulaski, Tenn. (co. seat of Giles Co.).
Pulaski, Va. (co. seat of *Pulaski* Co.).

PULLMAN, Wash. (Whitman Co.). For George Mortimer Pullman (1831-1897), inventor and railroad car manufacturer, famous for the Pullman sleeping car. The town was named for him in hope of making him a benefactor to the town.

PUMPKIN CREEK, Neb. Probably for the vegetable, but reason unknown. It flows east into North Platte River.

PUNTA GORDA, Fla. (co. seat of Charlotte Co.). From Spanish, "wide point," for a point of land extending into Charlotte Bay.

PUNXSUTAWNEY, Pa. (Jefferson Co.). From Algonquian *ponsetunik,* "town of the ponkies," or "gnats." The place was so named by its early settlers because of the large number of gnats.

PURCELL, Okla. (co. seat of McClain Co.). For E. B. Purcell, a director of the Santa Fe railroad.

PURCELL MOUNTAIN, Alaska. For J. L. Purcell, a U.S. Navy ensign who was a member of expeditions to the area (1884-85).

PURGATOIRE RIVER, Colo. Originally from Spanish, *Las Animas,* "lost souls (in purgatory)," the name was changed to El Purgatoria and then to the present French form. It is also known as Picketwire, a folk etymologized form from the local pronunciation. It flows northeast into Arkansas River.

PURVIS, Miss. (co. seat of Lamar Co.). For Thomas Melvin Purves (1820-?), who granted the Southern railroad the right of way through the town. The railroad officials misspelled the name.

PUSHAW LAKE, Me. For the Pushaw family, early English settlers.

PUSHMATAHA Co., Okla. (co. seat, Antlers). For the Pushmataha district of the Choctaw Nation, which was named for Pushmataha, noted Choctaw chief who served with Andrew Jackson. The name may mean "ready to be a sapling," that is, now grown to a young man. It is also interpreted as "qualified sapling," indicating a rank to which he belonged.

PUTNAM, Israel (1718-1790), Massachusetts general who served with the

British during the French and Indian Wars (1754-63) and against them during the American Revolution. He was the American commander at Bunker Hill.

Putnam Co., Fla. (co. seat, Palatka).
Putnam Co., Ga. (co. seat, Eatonton).
Putnam Co., Ill. (co. seat, Hennepin).
Putnam Co., Ind. (co. seat, Greencastle).
Putnam Co., Mo. (co. seat, Unionville).
Putnam Co., N.Y. (co. seat, Carmel)
Putnam Co., Ohio (co. seat, Ottawa).
Putnam Co., Tenn. (co. seat, Cookeville).
Putnam Co., W.Va. (co. seat, Winfield).
Putnam, Conn. (co. seat of Windham Co.), town and village.

PUU WAAWAA (mountain), Hawaii. On Hawaii Island. From Hawaiian, "hill-wrinkled."

PUYALLUP From the Indian tribal name, meaning "generous people."
Puyallup, Wash. (Pierce Co.).
Puyallup River, Wash. Flows NW into Puget Sound.

PYLON PEAK, Wyo. Descriptive, for the pylon-like peaks.

PYMATUNING From Delaware Indian, "the place where the crooked-mouthed one lives," descriptive of the creek.
Pymatuning Creek, Pa.
Pymatuning Reservoir, Ohio-Pa.

PYRAMID LAKE, Nev. Named in 1844 by J. C. Fremont for the rock that extended out of the lake and seemed to resemble "the great pyramid of Cheops."

Q

QUABBIN RESERVOIR, Mass. From Nipmuc, meaning uncertain, possibly "it twists and turns about," "crooked streams," or from the name of a chieftain.

QUABOAG From Nipmuc, "pond-before."
Quaboag Pond, Mass.
Quaboag River, Mass.

QUADDICK RESERVOIR, Conn. Of Indian origin, meaning uncertain, but in different dialects has been translated as "bend of river" or "marsh."

QUADRANT MOUNTAIN, Wyo., in Yellowstone Natl. Park. Descriptive of shape, similar to that of a segment of a sphere.

QUAKER For settlements of Quakers.
Quakertown, Pa. (Bucks Co.).
Quakertown North, Mich. (Oakland Co.). Earlier, Quaker Valley Farms.

QUANAH, Tex. (co. seat of Hardeman Co.). For the "Last Great Comanche Chief," Quanah Parker, son of Cynthia Ann Parker, who was captured (1836) at Parker's Fort. Parker was famous for his ability to lead and yet be able to negotiate with the colonists in the best interests of his people. He was instrumental in early peace treaties signed by the Comanches. Supposedly his name meant "fragrance" or "perfume," associated with the wild prairies on which he grew up.

QUANTICO, Va. (Prince William Co.). From Algonquian, possibly "long reach-at."

QUASSAPAUG LAKE, Conn. From Quinnipiac, "gravel in the pond," descriptive.

QUARTZ For the mineral.
Quartz Mountain, Ore.
Quartz Mountains, Wash.
Quartz Hill, Calif. (Los Angeles Co.).
Quartz Mountain Pass, Ore.

QUAY Co., N.Mex. (co. seat, Tucumcari). For Matthew S. Quay (1833-1904), U.S. senator from Pennsylvania (1887-99; 1901-04). He was active in establishing the area.

QUEBEC From Algonquian, "where the river narrows", referring to the site of Quebec City. The name first appeared on Levasseur's map of 1601 and was spelled *Quebecq*.
Quebec, Canadian province. Settled: 1608. Entered confederation: 1867, one of the four original provinces. Cap: *Quebec City*. Flower: White Garden Lily.
Quebec Co., Que. (co. seat, Loretteville).
Quebec City, Que. (*Quebec* Co.), provincial capital.
Quebec West, Que. (*Quebec* Co.).

QUEEN ANNES Co., Md. (co. seat, Centreville). For Queen Anne of England.

QUEENS For Charlotte Sophia, Princess of Mecklenburg-Strelitz (1744-1818), wife of George III of England. See also CHARLOTTE
Queens Co., N.B. (co. seat, Gagetown).
Queens Co., N.S. (co. seat, Liverpool).
Queens Co., P.E.I. (co. seat, Charlotte-town).

QUEENS Co., N.Y. (co. seat, Jamaica), conterminous with the Borough of Queens, New York City. For Catharine of Braganza (1638-1705), wife of Charles II of England.

QUEETS RIVER, Wash. For the Quaitso Indian tribe. Flows southwest into the Pacific Ocean.

QUINAULT RIVER, Wash. From the French form for the Kwinaithl Indian tribe. It flows southwest into the Pacific Ocean.

QUINCY For John Quincy ADAMS.
Quincy, Calif. (co. seat of Plumas Co.). For *Quincy,* Ill.
Quincy, Fla. (co. seat of Gadsden Co.).
Quincy, Ill. (co. seat of Adams Co.).
Quincy, Wash. (Grant Co.). For *Quincy,* Ill.

Quincy Adams, Mount, Alaska. In Glacier Natl. Monument.

QUINCY, Mass. (Norfolk Co.). For Col. John Quincy (1689-1767), a local resident and member of the Massachusetts House of Representatives. Earlier names were Mount Wollaston, Merry Mount (unofficial), and Braintree.

QUINEBAUG RIVER, Conn. From Nipmuc, "long pond." It flows south and southwest into Shetucket River.

QUINNIPIAC RIVER, Conn. From Algonquian, "route change," for the change in directions. It flows south into Long Island Sound.

QUINN RIVER, Nov. For a local settler; often confused with *Queen*. It disappears into a sink in Black Rock Desert.

QUINSIGAMOND, Lake, Mass. From Nipmuc, probably "place to catch pickerel." "Enclosed place at the long brook" has also been suggested as a possible meaning.

The fortified city of Quebec, founded in 1608 (one year later than Jamestown, Virginia), has played a major role in the history of North America. The British victory on the Plains of Abraham near the city drove the French from the mainland of North America. When American troops failed to take Quebec during the Revolution Canada was preserved as a separate dominion. [*New York Public Library*]

QUINTET MOUNTAIN, Wyo. For five climbers who climbed the five peaks.

QUITMAN, John Anthony (1799-1858), Georgia legislator and state official and a major-general in the U.S. Army. He also served as the tenth and sixteenth governor of Mississippi (1835-36; 1850-51) and U.S. representative (1855-58).

Quitman Co., Ga. (co. seat, Georgetown).
Quitman Co., Miss. (co. seat, Marks).
Quitman, Ga. (co. seat of Brooks Co.).
Quitman, Miss (co. seat of Clarke Co.).
Quitman, Tex. (co. seat of Wood Co.).

QUIVER, Mount, Wyo. So named because the climbers were supposedly so frightened that they "quivered."

RABBIT For the animal.
Rabbit Butte, S.Dak. For its resemblance to a rabbit, probably to its ears.
Rabbit Creek, S.Dak. Flows SE into Moreau R. Either for presence of many rabbits, or for *Rabbit* Butte.

RABUN Co., Ga. (co. seat, Clayton). For William Rabun (1771-1819), governor of Georgia (1817-19).

RACCOON For the animal.
Middle Raccoon River, Iowa. Flows into *Raccoon* R.
Raccon Creek, N.J. Flows NW into Delaware R.
Raccoon Creek, Ohio. Flows generally S into Ohio R.
Raccoon Creek, Ohio. Flows into Licking R.
Raccoon Creek, Pa. Flows N into Ohio R.
Raccoon River, Iowa. Flows S and SE into Des Moines R.
South Raccoon River, Iowa. Flows into *Raccoon* R.

RACE POINT, Mass. Extreme point on Cape Cod. For the tidal movement, called a "race."

RACINE From French, "root," translated from the Potawatomi *ot-chee-beek*.

The name was taken from that of the Root River, which had so many roots growing out of its banks that boats had difficulty navigating it.
Racine Co., Wis. (co. seat, *Racine*).
Racine, Wis. (co. seat of *Racine* Co.).

RACQUETTE RIVER, N.Y. Probably from French, "snowshoe," for the shape of a meadow at the mouth. However, the name also has the forms of Racket, Ragged, and Raquette, plus several Indian ones, mostly meaning "rapid river," descriptive of the river. It also creates a racket as it flows, so the French form may be a fancified folk etymologized one. The lake from which the river rises has a Mohawk name, *killograw,* "rayed like the sun," but somehow in translation became Ragged Lake. The river itself is called *Tanawadeh,* "swift water," in Iroquioian. It flows generally north into St. Lawrence River.

RADCLIFF, Ky. (Hardin Co.). Probably for a Major Radcliffe from nearby Camp Knox (now Fort Knox), who helped an early settler obtain a building to move to the townsite. Development did not begin until the middle of the 1900s.

RADISSON, Wis. (Sawyer Co.). For a French explorer, Pierre Esprit Radisson.

RAEFORD, N.C. (co. seat of Hoke Co.). Formed from the surnames of two founders, Mac*Rae* and Willi*ford.*

RAGGED Descriptive of rough terrain.
Ragged Island, Me. In Casco Bay. Also famous as "Elm Island" of stories of Elijah Kellogg.
Ragged Island, Me. In the Matinicus isle group. From Abnaki *Raggertask,* "Island rocks." It was folk etymologized to *Ragged Ass,* which was changed by the U.S. Board of Geographic Names to its present form.
Ragged Lake, Me. Either for the surrounding terrain or the shape of the lake.

RAHWAY Named by an Indian chief, Rawhawhack, perhaps for himself, or from *na-wak-wa,* "in the middle of the woods" or "a winding through the woods."
Rahway, N.J. (Union Co.). For the river.
Rahway River, N.J. Flows generally S and E to Arthur Kill.

RAID PEAK, Wyo. So named because cowboys raided sheepherders in the area around the mountain.

RAINBOW Descriptive.
Rainbow Lake, Wis. Probably for the sighting of a rainbow in connection with some incident.
Rainbow Bridge Natl. Monument, Utah. A natural bridge. Translated from Ute *barahaini,* "rainbow."

RAINIER, Peter, an admiral in the British navy. The mountain was named in 1792 by his friend, Capt. George Vancouver.
Mount Rainier Natl. Park, Wash.
Rainier, Mount, Wash.

RAINS Co., Tex. (co. seat, Emory). For Emory Rains (1800-1878), Republic of Texas legislator and surveyor.

RAINY Adaptation of an Indian word meaning "it rains all the time," in reference to the mist surrounding the waterfall where the lake empties into the river. The French called it *La Pluie,* "The Rain."
Rainy Lake, Minn.-Ont.

Rainy River, Minn.-Ont. Forms the international boundary; flows from *Rainy* L. to Lake of the Woods.
Rainy River District, Ont. (district seat, Fort Frances).

RAINY RIVER, Mich. Probably a translation from an Indian name resulting from an incident related to rain. It flows northwest into Black Lake.

RAISIN RIVER, Mich. From French, "grapes." It flows northeast and southeast into Lake Erie.

RALEIGH, Sir Walter (1552?-1618), English naval commander, courtier, soldier, colonizer, and author. At times a favorite of Queen Elizabeth 1, he obtained a patent to take possession of lands in the queen's name. Through his efforts the colony of Virginia, named for Elizabeth, the "Virgin Queen," was established, with himself as first lord proprietor (1584-1603), although he never saw the place. Out of favor with the queen, he organized expeditions to Orinoco and Guiana. James 1, who succeeded Elizabeth, disliked Raleigh and imprisoned him in the Tower of London for thirteen years (1603-1616). Released to form an expedition to find gold in Orinoco, he met misfortune in his efforts and was beheaded on the orders of James 1.
Fort Raleigh Natl. Historic Site, on Roanoke Island, N.C.
Raleigh Co., W.Va. (co. seat, Beckley).
Raleigh, Miss. (co. seat of Smith Co.).
Raleigh, N.C. (co. seat of Wake Co.), state capital.
Raleigh Bay, N.C., on the Atlantic Ocean.

RALLS Co., Mo. (co. seat, New London). For Daniel Ralls (?-1820), a legislator who died the year the county was formed.

RALSTON, Neb. (Douglas Co.). For a Mr. Ralston, an early settler and businessman.

RAMAPO RIVER, N.Y.-N.J. From Delaware Indian, meaning in dispute, but pertaining to streams or ponds in sequence, one after another. It flows southwest to join Pequannock River to form Pompton River.

RAMONA, Calif. (San Diego Co.). For Helen Hunt Jackson's play *Ramona.*

RAMSEY, Alexander (1815-1903), the first governor of Minnesota Territory and the second governor after the state was admitted. He was a U.S. senator (1863-75) and secretary of war under Hayes (1879-81).
Ramsey Co., Minn. (co. seat, St. Paul).
Ramsey Co., N.Dak. (co. seat, Devils Lake).

RAMSEY, N.J. (Bergen Co.). Either for Peter Ramsey (?-1854), a local landowner, or for a Ramsey who owned a tavern in the area in the 1700s.

RANCHO CORDOVA, Calif. (Sacramento Co.). For the Cordova vineyards in the vicinity.

RANCHO RINCONDA, Calif. (Santa Clara Co.). Believed to be from Spanish *rincon,* which designates a small portion of land, or *rinconada,* which means an inside corner on a plot of land. The names seem to have been used interchangeably.

RANCHO SANTA CLARITA, Calif. (Los Angeles Co.). Promotional.

RANCOCAS CREEK, N.J. From an Indian tribal name, meaning unknown. It flows northwest into Delaware River.

RANDALL Co., Tex. (co. seat, Canyon). For Horace Randal (1833-1864), a general in the Confederate army, killed at Saline, Ark. His name was misspelled through a clerical error.

RANDALLSTOWN, Md. (Baltimore Co.). Founded (early 1700s) by Thomas Randall and his brother Christopher Randall, Jr.

RANDOLPH, Edmund Jennings (1753-1813), Virginia soldier and statesman who served during the American Revolution as aide-de-camp to General Washington (1775). He was a member of the Continental Congress (1779-82), governor (1786-88), member of the Constitutional Convention (1787), first attorney general of the United States (1789) under Washington, and secretary of state (1794-95) under Washington.
Randolph Co., Ill. (co. seat, Chester). Or possibly for Beverly Randolph, governor of Virginia (1788-91).
Randolph Co., W.Va. (co. seat, Elkins).

RANDOLPH, John (1773-1833), Virginia statesman. He served as U.S. representative (1799-1813; 1815-17; 1819-25; 1827-29) and U.S. senator (1825-27). In 1830 Jackson appointed him U.S. minister to Russia.
Randolph Co., Ala. (co. seat, Wedowee).
Randolph Co., Ark. (co. seat, Pocahontas).
Randolph Co., Ga. (co. seat, Cuthbert).
Randolph Co., Mo. (co. seat, Huntsville).

RANDOLPH, Peyton (c.1721-1775), Virginia statesman and leader in the American Revolution. He was speaker of the Virginia House of Burgesses, chairman of the Virginia Committee of Correspondence, and first president of the Continental Congress. He was known for his moderation as well as his patriotism.
Randolph Co., Ind. (co. seat, Winchester). For *Randolph* Co., N.C.
Randolph Co., N.C. (co. seat, Asheboro).
Randolph, Mass. (Norfolk Co.), town.

RANDOLPH, Tex. (Fannin Co.). For an official of the Cotton Belt railroad.

RANDOLPH, Utah (co. seat of Rich Co.). For Randolph Stewart, a leader in the Mormon Church (Church of Latter-Day Saints).

RANDOLPH PEAK, Wyo. For an early settler and character named Randolph.

RANGELEY, James, Sr., one of the purchasers of the township in 1815.
Rangeley, Me. (Franklin Co.).
Rangeley Lake, Me.

RANGER, Tex. (Eastland Co.). For the Texas Rangers, who at one time camped here to protect the builders of the Texas and Pacific railroad.

RANKIN Co., Miss. (co. seat, Brandon). For Christopher Rankin (1788-1826), Mississippi legislator and U.S. representative (1817-26).

RANKIN, Tex. (co. seat of Upton Co.). For F.E. Rankin, (1856-1916), donor of land for the townsite.

RANSOM Co., N.Dak. (co. seat, Lisbon). For a fort, which was named for Thomas E. G. Ransom (1834-1864), a Union general killed during the Civil War.

RANTOUL, Ill. (Champaign Co.). For Robert Rantoul, a railroad official.

RAPID. Descriptive.
Rapid Creek, S.Dak.
Rapid River, Mich. Flows SE into Little Bay de Noc.
Rapid River, Minn. Formed from North and South Forks, flows NE into Rainy R.
Rapid City, S.Dak. (co. seat of Pennington Co.). For *Rapid* Creek.

RAPIDAN RIVER, Va. Probably a shortened form of RAPPAHANNOCK, , although one source says that it is a combined form of *Rapid Anne.* It meanders east into Rappahannock River.

RAPIDES Parish, La. (parish seat, Alexandria). From French, "rapids"; for rapids on the Red River.

RAPPAHANNOCK From an Indian word meaning "stream that ebbs and rises" or "river of quick-rising water."
Rappahannock Co., Va. (co. seat, Washington).
Rappahannock River, Va. Flows into Chesapeake Bay.

RARITAN Of Delaware Indian origin, from a tribal name, meaning uncertain. Possible translations include "forked river" and "stream-overflows."
Raritan, N.J. (Somerset Co.).
Raritan Bay, N.J. Inlet of Atlantic Ocean.
Raritan River, N.J. Flows into *Raritan* Bay.

RATON From Spanish, "mouse," in this area used to mean a certain breed of ground squirrel or rock squirrel.
Raton, N.Mex. (co. seat of Colfax Co.).
Raton Pass, Colo.-N.Mex.

RAT RIVER, Wis. Probably for the muskrat. It flows southeast into Peshtigo River.

RATTLESNAKE. For rattlesnakes found in the area.
North Rattlesnake Butte, Colo.
Rattlesnake Butte, S.Dak. (Corson Co.).
Rattlesnake Butte, S.Dak. (Ziebach Co.).
Rattlesnake Creek, Ore. Flows NW into Owyhee R.
Rattlesnake Mountains, Wyo.

RAVALLI Co., Mont. (co. seat, Hamilton). For Father Anthony Ravalli (1812-1884), a Jesuit missionary to the Flathead Indians (Salish-Kootenai Tribes) at St. Mary's Mission, Stevensville, Mont., the first white settlement in Montana.

RAVENA, N.Y. (Albany Co.). Variant of RAVENNA.

RAVENNA, Ohio (co. seat of Portage Co.). For Ravenna, Italy.

RAVENSWOOD, W.Va. Origin uncertain; perhaps from a surname, or for the Lord of Ravenswood, a character in Sir Walter Scott's novel *The Bride of Lammermoor.*

RAWLINS, John Aaron (1831-1869), aide to General Grant and later a general in the Union army during the Civil War. He was secretary of war (1869) under Grant.
Rawlins Co., Kan. (co. seat, Atwood).
Rawlins, Wyo. (co. seat of Carbon Co.). Rawlins camped near here in 1867.

RAY Co., Mo. (co. seat, Richmond). For John Ray, a legislator when the county was named.

RAYMOND, Miss. (a co. seat of Hinds Co.). For Raymond Robinson, who donated land for the townsite.

RAYMOND, N.H. (Rockingham Co.), town. For Capt. William Raymond of Beverly, Mass., a soldier who fought in a Canadian expedition in the early 1700s.

RAYMONDVILLE, Tex. (co. seat of Willacy Co.). For E.B. Raymond, manager of the King Ranch.

RAYNHAM, Mass. (Bristol Co.), town and village. For a town in England.

RAYNOLDS PEAK, Wyo. For W.F. Raynolds, a leader in an expedition to the area in 1859 to 1860.

RAYSTOWN BRANCH RIVER, Pa. For John Wray, trader. It flows east and northeast into Juniata River.

RAYTOWN, Mo. (independent city in St. Louis Co.). Probably for the founder, but a claim has also been made for John Ray (see RAY Co., Mo.).

READING   For Reading, Berkshire, England.
North Reading, Mass. (Middlesex Co.), town.
Reading, Mass. (Middlesex Co.), town.
Reading, Ohio (Hamilton Co.). An early citizen was born in Reading, England.
Reading, Pa. (co. seat of Berks Co.). Named by Thomas and Richard Penn, sons of William Penn, for the native city of the Penn family.

REAGAN Co., Tex. (co. seat, Big Lake). For John Henninger Reagan (1818-1905), Indian fighter, statesman in the Confederacy, U.S. representative (1857-61; 1875-87), and U.S. senator (1887-91) from Texas.

REAL Co., Tex. (co. seat, Leakey). For Julius Real (1860-1944), a jurist and legislator.

RECAPTURE CREEK, Utah. So named to commemorate an incident involving the recapturing of escaped outlaws. It flows south into San Juan River.

RECHESNOI, Mount, Alaska. On Umnak Island. From Russian, "peak" or "point of land."

RED   Descriptive, often for the color of soil.
Red Hill, Hawaii. Volcanic mountain on Maui Island.
Red Lake, S.Dak.
Hed Mountain, Calif.
Red Mountains, Wyo., in Yellowstone Natl. Park. For the porphyry.

RED BANK   For the color of the soil. Also spelled *Redbank.*
Red Bank, N.J. (Monmouth Co.).
Redbank Creek, Pa. Flows SW and W into Allegheny R.

RED CEDAR. For the tree.
Red Cedar Lake, Wis.
Red Cedar River, Mich. Flows N and W into Grand R.
Red Cedar River, Wis. Flows S from *Red Cedar* L. into Chippewa R.

RED CLOUD, Neb. (co. seat of Webster Co.). For Red Cloud (1821-1909), chief of the Teton Indians.

REDCLOUD PEAK, Colo. A subjective, descriptive name.

REDDING, Calif. (co. seat of Shasta Co.). Named in 1872 for B.B. Redding, land agent for the railroad when the town was laid out. In 1874, the town name was changed by legislative act to Reading, for P.B. Reading, a local pioneer, but the pronunciation remained *Redding.* The railroad, however, did not change its station name, and in 1880 the legislature changed the name back to Redding. Because of the greater fame of P.B. Reading, however, the name is often still credited to him.

REDDING, Conn. (Fairfield Co.). For John Reed, principal settler. An earlier name was Reading, but the spelling and pronunciation were changed because of popular dislike of John Reed.

REDFIELD, S.Dak. (co. seat of Spink Co.). For J.B. Redfield, a railroad official.

RED HOOK, N.Y. (Dutchess Co.). Origin in doubt: so named because it was originally covered with red cranberries and shaped like a hook, or possibly for the Red Brick Tavern.

RED LAKE. A translation of Ojibway, "red," for the reddish color of the lake.
Red Lake Co., Minn. (co. seat, *Red Lake Falls*). For the river, which was named for the lake.
Red Lake (*lake*), *Minn.*
Red Lake River (Upper and Lower), Minn.
Red Lake Falls, Minn. (co. seat of *Red Lake* Co.).

RED LION, Pa. (York Co.). For the old Red Lion tavern, which had the picture of a lion painted on a swining sign out front.

RED LODGE, Mont. (co. seat of Carbon Co.). Origin in dispute; either for the color of the lodges of the Crow Indians, who once inhabited the area, or for the "red men" who lived there.

RED OAK. For the tree.
Red Oak, Iowa (co. seat of Montgomery Co.).
Red Oaks Mill, N.Y. (Dutchess Co.).

REDONDO BEACH, Calif. (Los Angeles Co.). From Spanish, "round"; descriptive.

REDOUBT VOLCANO, Alaska, in Aleutian Range. Translated from Russian *sopka redutskaya.*

RED RIVER For its color.
Little Red River, Ark. Flows SE into White R.
Red River Parish, La. (parish seat, Coushatta).
Red River Co., Tex. (co. seat, Clarksville).
Red River. Flows from Mexico and Texas through Arkansas and across Louisiana into the Gulf of Mexico through the Atchafalaya R. and into the Mississippi R. through Old R.
Red River, Ky. Flows WSW into Cumberland R.

RED RIVER OF THE NORTH, N.Dak.-Minn. Man. Flows generally N to Lake Winnipeg. Named for the red berries (cranberries) that grow along its banks in North Dakota. See also PEMBINA.

RED ROCK. Descriptive.
Red Rock Creek, Okla. Flows E into Arkansas R.
Red Rock River, Mont. Flows NW and NE into Beaverhead R.

RED SPRINGS, N.C. (Robeson Co.). For mineral springs with rust-covered sediment caused by iron and sulfur deposits.

REDSTONE CREEK, S.Dak. For the color of the stone. It flows south and southwest into James River. Also known as Rock Creek.

RED WILLOW The creek was named first, by mistranslation of a Dakota word, "Red Dogwood Creek," for the dogwood trees that grow there.
Red Willow Co., Neb. (co. seat, McCook).
Red Willow Creek, Neb. Flows generally SE.

REDWOOD. Translated from a Dakota phrase, *chan sha ayapl,* "wood-red-on the river," for the red bark taken from a shrub. The bark was dried and mixed with tobacco to provide the Indians with a more pleasant material for smoking.
Redwood Co., Minn. (co. seat, *Redwood Falls*). For the river.
Redwood River, Minn. Flows generally E to the Minnesota R.
Redwood Falls, Minn. (co. seat of *Redwood* Co.). For the falls at the site of the city.

REDWOOD CITY, Calif. (co. seat of San Mateo Co.). So named because it was the center of the original stands of redwood trees, *Sequoia sempervirens.* An earlier name was Embarcadero.

REED CITY, Mich. (co. seat of Osceola Co.). For one of its founders, James M. Reed.

REEDLEY, Calif. (Fresno Co.). For Thomas L. Reed, generous donor to the city and a veteran of Sherman's "March to the Sea."

REEDS BAY, N.J. For a local settler.

REEDSBURG, Wis. (Sauk Co.). For David C. Reed, founder.

REEDSPORT, Ore. (Douglas Co.). For Alfred W. Reed, an early settler.

REEDY RIVER, S.C. Descriptive of the canebrakes along the banks. It flows southeast into Saluda River.

REELFOOT LAKE, Tenn. For a Chickasaw chief. Formed by earthquakes in 1811 and 1812, when the land area sank below the level of Mississippi River.

REESE RIVER, Nev. For John Reese, a guide. It flows north into Humboldt River.

REEVES Co., Tex. (co. seat, Pecos). For George R. Reeves (1826-1882), Tennessee-born Texas statesman and soldier. He fought in the Civil War, was a U.S. representative (1855-61), and was speaker of the Texas House (1881-82).

REFUGIO. From Spanish, "refuge," in reference to the mission established there, our Lady of Refuge, which honored the Virgin Mary.
Refugio Co., Tex. (co. seat, *Refugio*).
Refugio, Tex. (co. seat of *Refugio* Co.).

REGINA, Sask., provincial capital. From Latin, "queen," for VICTORIA, Queen of England. The city was named in 1882 by Victoria's daughter, Princess Louise, wife of the Marquis of Lorne, governor general of Canada. An earlier name was Waskana.

REHOBOTH. From the name of the well dug by Isaac, son of Abraham (Genesis 26:22), because "the Lord hath made room for us." The Hebrew word means "enlargement."
Rehoboth, Mass. (Bristol Co.), town.
Rehoboth Bay, Del. Landlocked bay.
Rehoboth Beach, Del. (Sussex Co.).

REISTERSTOWN, Md. (Baltimore Co.). For John Reister, a German immigrant who bought twenty acres of land here in 1758. The settlement that later developed consisted mostly of his own family.

REMMEL MOUNTAIN, Wash. Probably for an early explorer or settler.

RENFREW. Named by early Scottish settlers for Renfrew and Renfrewshire, Scotland.
Renfrew Co., Ont. (co. seat Pembroke).
Renfrew, Ont. (*Renfrew* Co.).

RENO, Jesse Lee (1823-1862), Virginia-born Union general killed at the Battle of South Mountain during the Antietam campaign of the Civil War. He had previously served as an ordinance officer during various Western surveys, including those in the Utah Territory.
Reno Co., Kan. (co. seat, Hutchinson).
Reno, Nev. (co. seat of Washoe Co.).

RENOVO, Pa. (Clinton Co.). From Latin, "I renew"; so named because of the railroad repair shops located there.

RENSSELAER, Ind. (co. seat of Jasper Co.). For the Van Rensselaer family of New York State.

RENSSELAER, Kiliaen Van (1595-1644), Dutch businessman and entrepreneur. He was one of the early "patroons" of the Dutch New Netherlands (New York) territories and a founder of the Dutch West India Company.
Rensselaer Co., N.Y. (co. seat, Troy).
Rensselaer, N.Y. (*Rensselaer* Co.).

RENSSELAERVILLE, N.Y. (Albany Co.), town. For Stephen Van Rensselaer (1764-1839), eighth patroon, huge landowner, Federalist assemblyman, state senator, and lieutenant governor of New York (1789-1801). He commanded the northern tier of the state in the War of 1812, but was defeated and resigned his command. He served as a U.S. representative (1822-29) and was the founder of Rensselaer Polytechnic institute.

RENVILLE Co., Minn. (co. seat, Olivia). For Joseph Renville (1779?-1846), of French and Indian descent. He obtained a commission in the British Army and led a group of Sioux against frontier settlements during the War of 1812. In the later years of his life he became a fur trader.

RENVILLE Co., N.Dak. (co. seat, Mohall). For Gabriel Renville, an early settler. He was a guide, trapper, and trader.

REPUBLIC Co., Kan. (co. seat, Belleville). For the REPUBLICAN RIVER.

REPUBLICAN RIVER, Neb.-Kan. For the valley that was the home of the Pawnee Republic, a division of the Pawnee Tribe. It flows generally southeast to join the Smoky Hill River to form the Kansas River.

RESCUE LAKE, Vt. Named by S.A. Giffin, former principal of Black River Academy, who felt that Ludlow Lake, its former name, was too commonplace for such a beautiful body of water. He invented, with some fellow campers, a romantic story in which a little girl was lost in the woods nearby and after some bizarre and complicated experiences was rescued, hence the name for the lake. The story is now a part of the lore of the area.

RESERVE, La. (St. John the Baptist Parish). So named because a local settler "reserved" the plantation for himself after he was refused lodging there one night and vowed to buy it some day, which he later did.

RESERVE, N.Mex. (co. seat of Catron Co.). For a forest reserve established here.

RESTIGOUCHE From Micmac Indian *lust-a-gooch,* variously translated as "five-fingered river," "river branching like a hand," "big river," "broad river," and "river of the long war."
Restigouche Co., N.B. (co. town, Dalhousie).
Restigouche River, N.B. Forms part of the boundary with Quebec and flows into Chaleur Bay.

REVERE, Mass. (Suffolk Co.). For Paul Revere (1735-1818), patriot, printer, and silversmith. He gained immortality for his ride from Boston to Lexington on the night of April 18, 1775, to warn Samuel Adams and John Hancock of advancing British troops, the subject of a poem by Longfellow. An earlier name was Rumney Marsh.

REXBURG, Idaho (co. seat of Madison Co.). For Thomas E. Ricks, a Mormon leader. The spelling is a phonetic scribal rendering.

REYNOLDS Co., Mo. (co. seat, Centerville). For Thomas Reynolds (1796-1844), legislator and governor (1840-44).

REYNOLDSBURG, Ohio (Franklin Co.). Probably for Jeremiah N. Reynolds, an early settler.

RHEA Co., Tenn. (co. seat, Dayton). For John Rhea (1753-1832), American Revolutionary soldier, legislator, and U.S. representative (1803-15; 1817-23).

RHINELANDER, Wis. (co. seat of Oneida Co.). For F.W. Rhinelander, president of the Milwaukee, Lakeshore and Western railroad.

RHODE ISLAND Derivation is uncertain, for there are two contending theories. The island (now called Aquidneck Island) may have been the one sighted by the Italian explorer Giovanni di Verrazano in 1524, which he said was about the size of the island of Rhodes in the Dodecanese Islands off the west coast of Asia Minor. Certainly the island was seen by the Dutch explorer Adriaen Block, who named it *Roodt Eylandt,* "red island." Early English settlers used the Indian name, Aquidneck Island, until 1644, when it was changed to the "Isle of Rhodes." The colony was called "Rhode Island and Providence Plantations."
Rhode Island, State of. 13th state of the Union. Settled: 1636. One of the original 13 colonies. Ratified Constitution: 1790. Motto: Hope. Nickname: Little Rhody. Flower: Violet. Bird: Rhode Island Red. Tree: Red Maple. Song: "Rhode Island."
Rhode Island Sound, R.I.

RHODES PEAK, Idaho. For a local settler.

RIALTO, Calif. (San Bernardino Co.). Believed locally to have been named for the Rialto Bridge in Venice, Italy. It is also said to be a contraction of Spanish *rio,* "river," and *alto,* "high."

RIB Translated from an Indian word descriptive of the shape of the mountains.
Big Rib River, Wis. Flows SE into Wisconsin R. For the mtns.
Rib Mountains, Wis.

RICE Co., Kan. (co. seat, Lyons). For Samuel A. Rice (1828-1864), Union general in the Civil War. He died of wounds received in action.

RICE Co., Minn. (co. seat, Faribault). For Henry Mower Rice (1817-1894), official in a fur-trading company, territorial delegate, and U.S. senator (1853-63).

RICE HILL, Vt. For a local dweller.

RICE LAKE, Wis. (Barron Co.). For wild rice growing along the Red Cedar River.

RICH Co., Utah (co. seat, Randolph). For Charles Coulson Rich, a Mormon apostle.

RICHARDSON Co., Neb. (co. seat, Falls City). For William A. Richardson (1811-1875), Illinois legislator, U.S. representative (1847-56; 1861-63), and U.S. senator (1863-65). He was governor (1858) of Nebraska Territory.

RICHARDSON, Tex. (Dallas Co.). Origin uncertain: for E.H. Richardson, the contractor who built the Houston and Texas Central railroad, or for the surveyor who laid it out, or for a George Richardson, also said to have had something to do with the railroad.

RICHARDSON LAKES, Me. For the Richardson family, early settlers.

RICHELIEU, Armand Jean du Plessis, Duke of (1585-1642), French statesman and cardinal. He was appointed cardinal (1622)

and chief minister (1624-42) to Louis XIII, and actually directed domestic and foreign policies in France. He was known as *Eminence Rouge,* "Red Eminence," for the color of his habit.
Richelieu Co., Que. (co. seat, Sorel).
Richelieu, Que. (Rouville Co.).
Richelieu River, Que., a main tributary of the St. Lawrence R. Flows N into St. Lawrence R.

RICHFIELD For a fertile area.
Richfield, Kan. (co. seat of Morton Co.).
Richfield, Minn. (Hennepin Co.). Earlier, Richland.
Richfield, Utah (co. seat of Sevier Co.). For a bounteous first harvest from the rich, red soil.

RICHIBUCTO, N.B. (co. seat of Kent Co.). Of Indian origin, probably Micmac, meaning uncertain.

RICHLAND Descriptive of the quality of the soil.
North Richland Hills, Tex. (Tarrant Co.).
Richland Co., Ill. (co. seat, Olney). For *Richland* Co., Ohio.
Richland Parish, La. (parish seat, Rayville).
Richland Co., Mont. (co. seat, Sidney).
Richland Co., Ohio (co. seat, Mansfield).
Richland Co., S.C. (co. seat, Columbia).
Richland Co., Wis. (co. seat, *Richland Center*).
Richland, Wash. (Benton Co.). Formerly a small farming center, now mostly housing employees of Hanford Atomic Products Operation.
Richland Balsam (peak), N.C. Also for the balsam tree.
Richland Center, Wis. (co. seat of *Richland* Co.).
Richland Hills, Tex. (Tarrant Co.). Also promotional.

RICHLAND Co., N.Dak. (co. seat, Wahpeton). For Morgan T. Rich, settler and landholder, founder of Wahpeton.

RICHMOND For Richmond, Surrey, England.

New Richmond, Ohio (Clermont Co.). Probably for Richmond, Va.

Richmond Co., Va. (co. seat, Warsaw).

Richmond, B.C.

Richmond, Calif. (Contra Costa Co.). For *Richmond,* Va.

Richmond, Ind. (co. seat of Wayne Co.). For *Richmond,* Va.

Richmond, Ky. (co. seat of Madison Co.). For *Richmond,* Va.

Richmond, Mo. (co. seat of Ray Co.). For *Richmond,* Va.

Richmond, Tex. (co. seat of Fort Bend Co.). For *Richmond,* Va.

Richmond, Va. (co. seat of Henrico Co.), state capital.

Richmond Heights, Mo. (St. Louis Co.). For *Richmond,* Va.; promotional.

RICHMOND, Charles Lennox, 1st Duke of (1672-1723), natural son of Charles II and Louise de Keroualle, Duchess of Portsmouth (1649-1734).

Richmond Co., Ga. (co. seat, Augusta).

Richmond Co., N.Y. Conterminous with the Borough of *Richmond* (Staten Island), New York City.

Richmond Co., N.C. (co. seat, Rockingham).

RICHMOND, Charles Lennox, 4th Duke of (1764-1819), son of Lord George Henry Lennox and Louisa, daughter of the 4th Marquess of Lothian. He was a major general and governor-in-chief of Canada (1818-1819).

Richmond Co., N.S. (co. seat, Arichat).

Richmond Co., Que. (co. seat, *Richmond*).

Richmond, Ont. (Carleton Co.).

Richmond, Que. (co. seat of *Richmond* Co.).

Richmond Pond, Mass. Another theory is that it is from French *riche mont,* "rich or fertile mountain."

RICHMOND, Mich. (Mecosta Co.). For Susan Richmond, mother of an early settler.

RICHMOND, R.I. (Washington Co.), town. Probably for Edward Richmond, attorney general of Rhode Island (1677-80).

RICHMOND HEIGHTS, Ohio (Cuyahoga Co.). For the Richmond family, especially Elihu Richmond (1770-?), early settler and landowner, plus the promotional *heights.* Earlier names were Euclid and Claribel.

RICHMOND ISLAND, Me. Origin uncertain. George Richmond, entrepreneur, lived in the area in 1636, but apparently had no connection with the island. Another possibility is that it is named for the Duke of Richmond, on the council of Plymouth. However, in the island's history the names of Richman and Richmond seem to be confused, for an earlier name was Richman's Island.

RICH MOUNTAIN, Okla. Probably for an early resident in the area.

RICHWOOD, W.Va. (Nicholas Co.). For the land and timber.

RIDGECREST, Calif. (Kern Co.). Descriptive and promotional.

RIDGEFIELD. Descriptive.

Ridgefield, Conn. (Fairfield Co.), town and village.

Ridgefield, N.J. (Bergen Co.).

Ridgefield Park, N.J. (Bergen Co.). Also promotional.

RIDGELAND, S.C. (co. seat of Jasper Co.). Descriptive.

RIDGEWOOD, N.J. (Bergen Co.). For wooded, hilly terrain.

RIDGWAY, Pa. (co. seat of Elk Co.). For Jacob Ridgway, owner of the townsite.

RIFLE RIVER, Mich. Probably for an incident which is now forgotten. It flows south and southeast into Saginaw Bay.

RIGBY, Idaho (co. seat of Jefferson Co.). For William F. Rigby, a prominent leader of the Mormons in the area.

RILEY Co., Kan. (co. seat, Manhattan). For Fort Riley, which was named for Gen. Bennett Riley (1787-1853), professional soldier and Indian fighter. He served as territorial governor of California in 1848.

RIMOUSKI. From a Micmac indian term which probably means "where there are moose," although "abode of dogs" has also been suggested.
Rimouski Co., Que. (co. seat, *Rimouski*).
Rimouski, Que. (co. seat of *Rimouski* Co.).

RINGGOLD, Samuel (?-1846), professional soldier and Indian fighter. He died of wounds received in action during the Mexican War.
Ringgold Co., Iowa (co. seat, Mount Ayr).
Ringgold, Ga. (Catoosa Co.).

RINGWOOD, N.J. (Passaic Co.). For the Ringwood Company, the first large-scale producer of iron in America.

RIO ARRIBA Co., N.Mex. (co. seat, Tierra Amarilla). From Spanish, "upper river."

RIO BLANCO Co., Colo. (co. seat, Meeker). From Spanish, "white river," for the whitecaps of the rapids; probably translated from the Ute name.

RIO DELL, Calif. (Humboldt Co.). *Rio* is from Spanish, "river"; for a river valley.

RIO FELIX, N.Mex. From Spanish, "happy river." It flows generally east into Pecos River.

RIO GRANDE. From Spanish, "great river." The river was named first.
Rio Grande Co., Colo. (co. seat, Del Norte).
Rio Grande Natl. Forest, Colo.
Rio Grande River, Colo.-N.Mex.-Tex. Flows SE and S into Gulf of Mexico. Forms an international boundary between the United States and Mexico. In Mexico, it is called *Rio Bravo del Norte.*
Rio Grande City, Tex. (co. seat of Starr Co.).
Rio Grande Pyramid (peak), Colo.

RIO HONDO, N.Mex. From Spanish, "deep river." It flows east into Pecos River.

RIO LINDA, Calif. (Sacramento Co.). From Spanish, "pretty river."

RIO PENASCO, N.Mex. From Spanish, "cliff river." It flows east into Pecos River.

RIO VISTA, Calif. (Solano Co.). From Spanish, "river view."

RIPLEY, Eleazar Wheelock (1782-1839), soldier and legislator. After serving in the Massachusetts legislature (1807-09; 1811-12; speaker 1811), he served as a general in the War of 1812, being cited for bravery on the Canadian front, and as a frontier Indian fighter. He moved to Louisiana and served that state as a U.S. representative (1835-39).
Ripley Co., Ind. (co. seat, Versailles).
Ripley Co., Mo. (co. seat, Doniphan).
Ripley, Miss. (co. seat of Tippah Co.).
Ripley, N.Y. (Chautauqua Co.), town.
Ripley, Ohio (Brown Co.).
Ripley, Tenn. (co. seat of Lauderdale Co.).

RIPLEY, W.Va. (co. seat of Jackson Co.). For Harry Ripley, a minister who drowned in a nearby stream.

RIPON. For Ripon, Yorkshire, England.
Ripon, Calif. (San Joaquin Co.). For *Ripon,* Wis.
Ripon, Wis. (Fond du Lac Co.).

RIPPOWAM RIVER, N.Y.-Conn. From Sinanoy Indian, "cliff of rocks." It flows south into Long Island Sound.

RISING SUN, Ind. (co. seat of Ohio Co.). For its site, which is favorable for watching the sunrise.

RISON, Ark. (co. seat of Cleveland Co.). For William R. Rison, a Confederate veteran of the Civil War.

RITA BLANCA CREEK, N.Mex.-Tex. From Spanish, "white Rita," but reason for naming is uncertain. Rising from two branches, it flows intermittently southeast into Canadian River.

RITCHIE Co., W.Va. (co. seat, Harrisville). For Thomas Ritchie (1778-1854), newspaper publisher.

Rivers have always been central to American life. They provided transportation, nutrition and recreation. This was true not only of the great arteries such as the St. Lawrence, the Hudson, and the Columbia but to lesser streams as well. The Black River, near Elyria, Ohio, recalls bygone and less hurried times. [*New York Public Library*]

RITTER, Mount, Calif. For Karl Ritter (1779-1859), geographer.

RITTMAN, Ohio (Wayne Co.). For Frederick B. Rittman, treasurer of the Atlantic and Great Western railroad, now the Erie-Lackawanna railroad.

RITZVILLE, Wash. (co. seat of Adams Co.). For Philip Ritz, a homesteader.

RIVERBANK, Calif. (Stanislaus Co.). Descriptive.

RIVERDALE For a site in a river valley.
Riverdale, Ga. (Clayton Co.).
Riverdale, Ill. (Cook Co.). Named by Frederick C. Schmidt in 1848 for choice

property at the intersection of an Indian trail and the Calumet R.
Riverdale, Md. (Prince Georges Co.).
Riverdale, Utah (Weber Co.).
Riverdale Heights, Md. (Prince Georges Co.).

RIVER FALLS, Wis. (Pierce and St. Croix Cos.). For the falls on the Kinnickinnic River.

RIVER FOREST, Ill. (Cook Co.). Descriptive of the "forest" along the Des Plaines River.

RIVER GROVE, Ill. (Cook Co.). For its location on the bank of the Des Plaines River.

RIVERHEAD, N.Y. (co. seat of Suffolk Co.). For its site at the head of navigation on the Peconic River, an arm of Peconic Bay.

RIVER OAKS, Tex. (Tarrant Co.). Descriptive. An earlier name was Castleberry.

RIVER ROUGE, Mich. (Wayne Co.). *Rouge* is from French, "red," for the color of the river's banks. It is on the Detroit and Rouge rivers.

RIVERSIDE For a site beside a river.
North Riverside, Ill. (Cook Co.). Earlier, Frog Pond; in a swampy area.
Riverside Co., Calif. (co. seat, *Riverside*).
Riverside, Calif. (co. seat of *Riverside* Co.).
Riverside, Ill. (Cook Co.). On the Calumet R.
Riverside, N.J. (Burlington Co.). On the Delaware R.
Riverside Mountains, Calif.
Riverside Reservoir, Colo.

RIVERTON From "River town."
Riverton, N.J. (Burlington Co.).
Riverton, Utah (Salt Lake Co.). On the Jordan R.
Riverton, Wyo. (Fremont Co.). On the Wind River.

RIVERVIEW Descriptive.
Riverview, Mich. (Wayne Co.). Overlooks the Detroit R.
Riverview, Mo. (St. Louis Co.). Near the Mississippi R.

RIVIERA BEACH For the French coastal district.
Riviera Beach, Fla. (Palm Beach Co.).
Riviera Beach, Md. (Anne Arundel Co.).

RIVIERE-DU-LOUP From French, "river of the wolf," for timber-wolves in the vicinity.
Riviere-du-Loup Co., Que. (co. seat, *Riviere-du-Loup*).
Riviere-du-Loup, Que. (co. seat of *Riviere-du-Loup* Co.).

RIVIERE-DU-MOULIN, Que. (Chicoutimi Co.). From French, "river of the mill," for the small mill built on the nearby river in 1750.

ROAN CREEK, Colo. For a roan horse, perhaps because of the color of the area. It flows southeast into Colorado River.

ROANE Co., Tenn. (co. seat, Kingston). For Archibald Roane (1759-1818), American Revolutionary soldier, Tennessee jurist, and governor (1801-03).

ROANE Co., W.Va. (co. seat, Spencer). For Spencer Roane (1762-1822), Virginia statesman and jurist, son-in-law of Patrick Henry. He served on the Virginia supreme court of appeals (1794-1822).

Three years after its founding, the Roanoke Island colony had vanished without a trace. The first English child born in America, Virginia Dare, vanished with it. While rumors persist, it is unlikely that she lived long enough to develop quite so well as the artist imagines. [*New York Public Library*]

ROANOKE From an Indian word spelled *Roanoak* by the first English settlers. The Indians applied it to an island, meaning "place where white shells are found" or perhaps "shells which are used for money."

Roanoke Co., Va. (co. seat, Salem).

Roanoke, Ala. (Randolph Co.). For *Roanoke*, Va.

Roanoke, Va. (independent city in *Roanoke* Co.). Earlier, Big Lick.

Roanoke Island, N.C., in Croatan Sound. Site of the first attempt to establish a permanent English settlement in North America. After failure in 1585, a new settlement was established in 1587, but when a supply ship returned in 1591 it had disappeared.

Roanoke River, Va.-N.C. Flows into Albemarle Sound. For the island.

Roanoke Rapids, N.C. (Halifax Co.). For the nearby rapids of the *Roanoke* R.

Roanoke Rapids Lake, N.C.

ROARING BROOK, Conn. Believed locally to be a translation of the Indian tribal name *Nayaug*, "noisy river," although it has also been translated as "at the point." It flows southwest into the Connecticut River.

ROARING FORK RIVER, Colo. Descriptive. Flows northwest into Colorado River.

ROBBINS, Ill. (Cook Co.). For Eugene Robbins, landowner and real-estate salesman.

ROBBINSDALE, Minn. (Hennepin Co.). For Andrew B. Robbins, founder.

ROBBINSVILLE, N.C. (co. seat of Graham Co.). For a local family named Robbins.

ROBERT LEE, Tex. (co. seat of Coke Co.). For Robert E. LEE, Confederate general.

ROBERTS Co., S.D. (co. seat, Sisseton). For S.G. Roberts, publisher and a member of the legislature when the county was established.

ROBERTS Co., Tex. (co. seat, Miami). For both John S. Roberts (1796-1871), a veteran of the War of 1812 who served with Andrew Jackson at the Battle of New Orleans and a signer of the Texas Declaration of Independence, and Oran Milo Roberts, Texas jurist and governor (1879-83).

ROBERTS MOUNTAIN, Wyo. For John Roberts, a minister.

ROBERTSON Co., Ky. (co. seat, Mount Olivet). For George Robertson (1790-1874), jurist, educator, and U.S. representative (1817-21).

ROBERTSON Co., Tenn. (co. seat, Springfield). For James Robertson (1742-1814), career soldier and a general in the American Revolution. Active in support of statehood for Tennessee, he has been called "Father of Tennessee." He served in the North Carolina assembly and the Tennessee legislature. He founded Nashville, Tennessee, as a fort on the Cumberland River, which he named Fort Nashborough. See also NASH.

ROBERTSON Co., Tex. (co. seat, Franklin). For Sterling Clark Robertson (1775-1842), career soldier who rose to the rank of general and fought at the Battle of New Orleans (1815). After moving to Texas as a colonizer, he became active in promoting the independence of the territory. He signed the Texas Declaration of independence and served as a legislator.

ROBERVAL, Que. (co. seat of West Lake St. John Co.). For Jean Francois de la Roque, Sieur de Roberval (1500-1560), who led the first French colonizing expedition to North America (1542).

ROBESON Co., N.C. (co. seat, Lumberton). For Thomas Robeson (1740-1785), an officer in the American Revolution.

ROBINSON, Ill. (co. seat of Crawford Co.). For John McCracken Robinson (1794-1843), U.S. senator (1830-41). He was elected an associate justice of the state supreme court (1843) and served until his death two months later.

ROBINSON, Lake, S.C. For a local settler.

ROBINSON, Tex. (McLennan Co.). For John Robinson, first settler. An earlier name was Hague.

ROBSTOWN, Tex. (Nueces Co.). For Robert Driscoll, Jr., son of a local rancher.

ROBY, Tex. (co. seat of Fisher Co.). For D.C. and M.L.Roby, settlers from Mississippi who donated the land for the townsite.

ROCHELLE. For La Rochelle, France, a seaport on the Atlantic.
New Rochelle, N.Y. (Westchester Co.).
Rochelle, Ill. (Ogle Co.).
Rochelle Park, N.J. (Bergen Co.). When the name of the town was changed in 1929, this name was chosen as it was the name of the railroad station at the time.

ROCHESTER, Nathaniel (1752-1831), an army colonel who owned much of the land on which Rochester, N.Y., was platted.
East Rochester, N.Y. (Monroe Co.).
Rochester, Ind. (co. seat of Fulton Co.). For *Rochester,* N.Y.
Rochester, Mich. (Oakland Co.). For *Rochester,* N.Y.
Rochester, Minn. (co. seat of Olmsted Co.). For *Rochester,* N.Y.
Rochester, N.Y. (co. seat of Monroe Co.).
Rochester, Pa. (Beaver Co.). Earlier, Logan Town, for James Logan, a Mingo chief.

ROCHESTER, N.H. (Strafford Co.). For Laurence Hyde, 1st Earl of Rochester (1641-1711). Gov. Samuel Shute, who named the town, was his friend. Hyde was a diplomat, member of Parliament, and lord high treasurer of England.

ROCK. Usually for a prominent rock or for the prevalence of rocks in the area.
Rock Co., Minn. (co. seat, Luverne).
Rock Co., Neb. (co. seat, Bassett).
Rock Co., Wis. (co. seat, Janesville).
Rock Creek, D.C.-Md.
Rock Creek, Ill.-Wis.
Rock Creek, Pa.
Rock Creek, S.Dak.
Rock Creek, Utah.
Rock Creek, Wash.
Rock River, Iowa-Minn. Flows generally S to the Big Sioux R.

Rock River, Vt. (Windham Co.).
Rock River, Vt.-Que.
Rock River, Wis.-Ill. Flows generally SW to the Mississippi R.
Rock Creek Butte, Ore.

ROCKAWAY. From the name of an Algonquian tribe whose principal place of residence was what is now Rockaway Beach, New Jersey. It means "sand place."
East Rockaway, N.Y. (Nassau Co.).
Rockaway, N.J. (Morris Co.).
Rockaway River, N.J. Flows S and E into Passaic R.

ROCKBRIDGE Co., Va. (co. seat, Lexington). For the Natural Bridge of Virginia.

ROCKCASTLE. For the castle-like rock formations along the banks of the river.
Rockcastle Co., Ky. (co. seat, Mount Vernon). For the river.
Rockcastle River, Ky. Flows SSW into Cumberland R.

ROCKCHUCK PEAK, Wyo. For "hardy" animals that live under rocks there, probably a kind of marmot related to the woodchuck.

ROCKDALE Co., Ga. (co. seat, Conyers). For stone outcroppings near Stone Mountain, Ga.

ROCKDALE, Tex. (Milam Co.). For a large rock in a depression just north of the townsite.

ROCK FALLS, Ill. (Whiteside Co.). For falls on the Rock River.

ROCKFORD. For a rocky ford on a river.
New Rockford, N.Dak. (co. seat of Eddy Co.). So named because *Rockford* resembled another name in the state; on the James R.
Rockford, Ala. (co. seat of Coosa Co.).
Rockford, Ill. (co. seat of Winnebago Co.). On the Rock R.

ROCK HILL, Mo. (Independent city in St. Louis Co.). Descriptive and promotional.

ROCK HILL, S.C. (York Co.). For a small flint-rock (quartz) hill in the area.

ROCKINGHAM, Charles Watson-Wentworth, Marquis of (1730-1782), British statesman, prime minister (1765-66; 1782), who opposed a severe policy toward the American colonies and was largely responsible for the repeal of the Stamp Act.
Rockingham Co., N.H. (co. seat, Exeter).
Rockingham Co., N.C. (co. seat, Wentworth).
Rockingham Co., Va. (co. seat, Harrisonburg).
Rockingham, N.C. (co. seat of Richmond Co.).

ROCK ISLAND For an island in the Mississippi River near the mouth of Rock River.
Rock Island Co., Ill. (co. seat, *Rock Island*).
Rock Island, Ill. (co. seat of *Rock Island* Co.).

ROCKLAND, Me. (co. seat of Knox Co.). For nearby limestone deposits. An earlier name was East Thomaston.

ROCKLAND Co., N.Y. (co. seat, New City). Descriptive of the rugged area and also influenced by the Palisades on the Hudson River.

ROCKLIN, Calif. (Placdr Co.). *Lin,* from Celtic, "spring." Descriptive.

ROCKPORT For rock formations near a river port or seaport.
Rockport, Ind. (co. seat of Spencer Co.). For the overhanging rock, "Lady Washington Rock," on the Ohio R.
Rockport, Mass. (Essex Co.). Also for the local granite industry.
Rockport, Mo. (co. seat of Atchison Co.).
Rockport, Tex. (co. seat of Aransas Co.). Earlier, Rocky Point.

ROCK RAPIDS, Iowa (co. seat of Lyon Co.). For rapids in the Rock River.

ROCK SPRINGS Descriptive. Also spelled *Rocksprings.*
Rocksprings, Tex. (co. seat of Edwards Co.).
Rock Springs, Wyo. (Sweetwater Co.).

ROCKVILLE Descriptive.
Rockville, Conn. (co. seat of Tolland Co.).
Rockville, Ind. (co. seat of Parke Co.).
Rockville, Md. (co. seat of Montgomery Co.).
Rockville Centre, N.Y. (Nassau Co.).

ROCKWALL For geological formations that resemble walls.
Rockwall Co., Tex. (co. seat *Rockwall*).
Rockwall, Tex. (co. seat of *Rockwall* Co.).

ROCKWELL CITY, Iowa (co. seat of Calhoun Co.). For J. M. Rockwell, land developer, manufacturer, hotel owner, and founder.

ROCKWOOD Descriptive.
Rockwood, Mich. (Wayne Co.).
Rockwood, Tenn. (Roane Co.). For limestone deposits.

ROCKY Descriptive.
Rocky Island, Wis. One of the Apostle Islands.
Rocky Lake, Me.
Rocky Mountain, Me.
Rocky River, N.C. Flows SE and E into Pee Dee R.
Rocky River, N.C. Flows SW into Deep R.
Rocky River, S.C. Flows S into Savannah R.
Rocky Comfort Creek, Ga. Flows SSE into Ogeechee R. Translated from Indian.
Rocky Ford, Colo. (Otero Co.). For a crossing on the Arkansas R.
Rocky Fork Lake, Ohio.
Rocky Fork River, Ohio.
Rocky Hill, Conn. (Hartford Co.), town.
Rocky Peak Ridge, N.Y.
Rocky River, Ohio (Cuyahoga Co.).

ROCKY MOUNT Descriptive.
Rocky Mount, N.C. (Nash and Edgecombe Cos.). For a rocky mound in the Tar R.
Rocky Mount, Va. (co. seat of Franklin Co.). On or near a rock bluff.

ROCKY MOUNTAINS Part of a vast range that extends from Alaska to the tip of South America. In the North American area, the range has been called Missouri, Mexican, Shining, Snowy, Stony, Montagnes

Rocheuses, and probably many other names recorded and not recorded, originally from an Indian name.

RODEO, Calif. (Contra Costa Co.). Originally, a cattle exhibit at a market or fair. The Mexican connotation was a round-up; the present-day American meaning is a cowboy contest.

ROELAND PARK, Kan. (Johnson Co.). For John Roe, who came to the United States from Ireland in the 1860s and through savings as a bookkeeper and farm worker bought hundreds of acres of land in the area. His mansion was a landmark until destroyed to make way for the Roe Avenue cloverleaf.

ROESSLEVILLE, N.Y. (Albany Co.). For the Roessle family, large landowners.

ROGER MILLS Co., Okla. (co. seat, Cheyenne). For Roger Q. Mills (1832-1911), Confederate army officer, U.S. representative (1873-92), and U.S. senator (1892-99).

ROGERS, Ark. (Benton Co.). For C. W. Rogers, president of the St. Louis and San Francisco railroad.

ROGERS, Mount Va. Highest point in Virginia. For William Barton Rogers, geologist.

ROGERS Co., Okla. (co. seat, Claremore). For Clement V. Rogers, a member of the Oklahoma constitutional convention. He was father of the humorist Will Rogers.

ROGERS CITY, Mich. (co. seat of Presque Isle Co.). For William Evans Rogers (1846-1913), railroad promoter, landowner, and founder. He was active in the organization of Presque Isle County.

ROGERS LAKE, Calif. Possibly for John Rogers, leader of an expedition that had difficulty escaping out of Death Valley.

ROGERSVILLE, Tenn. (co. seat of Hawkins Co). For Joseph P. Rogers (1764-1833), founder. He bought land from the heirs of David Crockett, Sr., and became the first postmaster.

ROGUE For "rogues," or troublemakers.
Rogue Island, Me. In Englishman Bay. Or possibly named by Champlain for St. Roch. Also called Roque Island.
Rogue River, Ore. Flows into Pacific Ocean. Translated from French *les coquins*, "the rogues."

ROHNERT PARK, Calif. (Sonoma Co.). For the Rohnert family, original developers of the town.

ROHNERVILLE, Calif. (Humboldt Co.). For Henry Rohner, a settler from Switzerland and storekeeper.

ROHUNTA, Lake, Mass. Formed from the name of Rodney Hunt, whose power company built the dam that formed the lake.

ROLETTE Co., N.Dak. (co. seat, Rolla). For Joseph Rolette (1820-1871), fur trader, public official, and legislator.

ROLLA, Mo. (co. seat of Phelps Co.). Origin debatable, but possibly for a name borrowed from Richard B. Sheridan's translation of Kotzebue's play *Pizarro*, which had the subtitle "The Death of Rolla." The melodrama was widely popular in the early 1800s. Other theories include the name of a mangy dog, Rollo, and an attempt at a phonetic spelling of Raleigh, N.C., the state from which many of the early settlers came.

ROLLA, N.Dak. (co. seat of Rolette Co.). Origin uncertain: one theory is that it is a contraction of *Rolette*; another, a transfer from ROLLA, Mo., by early settlers; or it may be for Rolla, the brother of Arthur Noyes, a railway attorney.

ROLLING FORK, Miss. (co. seat of Sharkey Co.). For a nearby creek that forks in the middle of the city.

ROLLING FORK RIVER, Ky. Descriptive of the flow of water. It flows west and northwest into Salt River.

ROLLING HILLS ESTATES, Calif. (Los Angeles Co.). For hills on the Palos Verdes Peninsula; promotional.

ROLLING MEADOWS, Ill. (Cook Co.). Promotional and descriptive.

ROLLING THUNDER MOUNTAIN, Wyo. Descriptive and metaphoric.

ROMANZOF, Cape, Alaska. For Count Nicholas Romanzof, chancellor of the Russian Empire and a patron of science.

ROME For the capital of Italy. In the United States, the connotation of the name is classical, not modern. Sometimes it indicates only a hilly site reminiscentf of the Seven Hills of Rome, or some great defense against an enemy, or simply that a place was named during the nineteenth-century period when classical names were popular. *Rome*, Ga. (co. seat of Floyd Co.). *Rome*, N.Y. (co. seat of Oneida Co.).

ROMEO, Mich. (Macomb Co.). Named "just to be different," but probably influenced by the hero of Shakespeare's *Romeo* and *Juliet.*

ROMEOVILLE, Ill. (Will Co.). For the hero of Shakespeare's *Romeo* and *Juliet*

ROMNEY, W.Va. (co. seat of Greenbrier Co.). For Romney, Kent, England.

RONDOUT RESERVOIR, N.Y. Folk etymologized form from Dutch, "redoubt," for a fortification.

RONKINKOMA, N.Y. (Suffolk Co.). From Algonquian; earlier *-oma* was written *-amuck*, "fishing place"; the rest of the word is of uncertain meaning.

ROOKS Co., Kan. (co. seat, Stockton). For John C. Rooks (?-1862), a soldier who died of wounds received at the Battle of Prairie Grove, Ark.

Rome was just one of the classical names chosen to grace midwestern New York State. Others included Ithaca, Syracuse, and Utica. The engraving shows the Fontana di Trevi as it looked in 1845. [*New York Public Library*]

ROOSEVELT, Franklin Delano (1882-1945), thirty-second President of the United States (1933-45), from New York, the first president to be re-elected for a third term. He had been an attorney, New York senator (1910-13), assistant secretary of the navy (1913-20), and governor of New York (1929-33).
Roosevelt, N.Y. (Nassau Co.).
Roosevelt Park, Mich. (Muskegon Co.).

ROOSEVELT, Theodore (1858-1919), twenty-sixth President of the United States (1901-09), from New York. He served with his Rough Riders during the Spanish-American War and was governor of New York (1899-1900) and vice-president of the United States (1901). He succeeded to the Presidency upon the assassination of McKinley. During his administration, he began construction of the Panama Canal, won the Nobel Peace Prize (1906) for his mediation in the Russo-Japanese War, and was active in the conservation of American natural resources. Dissatisfied with the administration of his successor, William Howard Taft, he ran unsuccessfully for President (1912) as the Candidate of the Bull Moose party. See also THEODORE ROOSEVELT.
Roosevelt Co., Mont. (co. seat, Wolf Point).
Roosevelt Co., N.Mex. (co. seat, Portales).

ROOT RIVER, Minn. Translated from either Dakota *hutkan*, or French *racine*, both meaning "root" or "snag." Formed by North and South branches, it flows east into the Mississippi River.

ROOT RIVER, Wis. A translation of Potawatomi *ot-chee-beek*, "root." It flows generally SE into L. Michigan.

ROSAMOND LAKE, Calif. For the daughter of a Southern Pacific railroad official.

ROSCOMMON For county Roscommon, Ireland; named by Irish settlers.
Roscommon Co., Mich. (co. seat, *Roscommon*).
Roscommon, Mich. (co. seat of *Roscommon* Co.).

ROSEAU From French, "reed," which is also a translation of an Ojibway word that refers to the coarse grass growing along the Roseau River. The town and county were named for the river.
Roseau Co., Minn. (co. seat, *Roseau*).
Roseau, Minn. (co. seat of *Roseau* Co.).
Roseau River, Minn. Flows generally NW into the Red River of the North in Canada.

ROSEBUD Co., Mont. (co. seat, Forsyth). For a Rosebud Creek, descriptive of the flowers, probably wild roses.

ROSEBURG, Ore. (co. seat of Douglas Co.). For Aaron Rose (1813-1899), a tavern owner and prominent citizen.

ROSEDALE, Md. (Baltimore Co.). For wild roses.

ROSEDALE, Miss. (a co. seat of Bolivar Co.). For a nearby plantation owned by Lafayette Jones. An earlier name was Floreyville, for the Radical leader H. T. Florey.

ROSE HILL, Va. (Lee Co.). Descriptive.

ROSELAND, Calif. (Sonoma Co.). Promotional.

ROSELAND, N.J. (Essex Co.). First named Roslyn (origin unknown), it became Roseland through mispronunciation.

ROSELLE, Ill (Du Page Co.). For Rosell Hough (1827-1898), prominent Chicago citizen and leader.

ROSELLE For John C. Rose, developer.
Roselle, N.J. (Union Co.).
Roselle Park, N.J. (Union Co.).

ROSEMEAD, Calif. (Los Angeles Co.). For Leonard J. Rose (1827-1899). The name is a combination of his name and *meadow*, for his horse farm, later shortened to *mead*.

ROSENBERG, Tex. (Fort Bend Co.). For Henry Rosenberg, president of the Gulf, Colorado and Santa Fe railroad (1874-77).

ROSE PEAK, Ariz., in Blue Range. For the wild roses found on the peak.

ROSEVILLE, Calif. (Placer Co.). For the roses found there when settlers decided to name the town, or possibly for the pleasant qualities of the sound.

ROSEVILLE, Mich. (Macomb Co.). For William C. Rose, first postmaster.

ROSEVILLE, Minn. (Ramsey Co.). For George Rose, an early settler of what is now Roseville township.

ROSS, Calif. (Marin Co.). For James Ross, landowner.

ROSS, Co., Ohio (co. seat, Chillicothe). For James Ross (1762-1847), U.S. senator from Pennsylvania (1794-1803).

ROSS BARNET RESERVOIR, Miss. On Pearl River. For Ross Barnet, governor of Mississippi (1960-64).

ROSSFORD, Ohio (Wood Co.). For Edward Ford (1843-1920) and the maiden name of his wife, Carrie Ross Ford. Ford was the founder of the Edward Ford Plate Glass Company, later merged into the Libbey-Owens-Ford Glass Company.

ROSS LAKE, Wash. For a local settler.

ROSWELL, N.Mex. (co. seat of Chaves Co.). For Roswell Smith, father of a founder.

ROTHSCHILD, Wis. (Marathon Co.). For the Rothschild family of financiers, but the claim of relationship may have been spurious.

ROTTERDAM, N.Y. (Schenectady Co.). For Rotterdam, Netherlands.

ROUGH RIVER, Ky. So named because of the difficulty in crossing and navigating it. It flows generally southwest into Green River.

ROUND Descriptive. Hundreds of features are so named; included here are some prominent examples.

Round Lake, Mich.
Round Lake, Minn.
Round Lake, N.Dak.
Round Lake, Wis. (Price Co.).
Round Lake, Wis. (Sawyer Co.).
Round Mountain, Me.
Round Mountain, N.J.
Round Mountain, Vt.
Round Mountains, Calif.
Round Pond, Me.
Round Hill Point, Mass. Extends into Buzzards Bay.
Round Lake Beach, Ill. (Lake Co.). For a small lake nearby.
Round Lake Park, Ill. (Lake Co.). For a nearby lake.
Round Top (mountain), Mass.

ROUND ROCK, Tex. (Williamson Co.). For a round rock by a creek where travelers rested.

ROUNDUP, Mont. (co. seat of Musselshell Co.). For the old-time cattle roundups held in the area.

ROUTT, John Long (1826-1907), state official, mayor of Denver, and governor of Colorado (1876-79; 1891-93).
Routt Co., Colo. (co. seat, Steamboat Springs).
Routt Natl. Forest, Colo.

ROUVILLE Co., Que. (co. seat, Marieville). For Jean Baptiste Hertel, Sieur de Rouville, who was granted a tract of land along the Richelieu River.

ROUYN, Que. (Temiscamingue Co.). For an officer of the Royal Roussillon Regiment in Montcalm's army.

ROWAN Co., Ky. (co. seat, Morehead). For John Rowan (1773-1843), statesman. He was U.S. senator from Kentucky (1825-31).

ROWAN Co., N.C. (co. seat, Salisbury). For Matthew Rowan (?-1760), local officeholder, legislator, and acting governor when the county was established (1763).

ROWLETT, Tex. (Dallas Co.). For George Rowlett, an early settler.

ROWLEY, Mass. (Essex Co.), town. For Rowley Regis, Staffordshire, England.

ROWLEY BAY, Wis. Inlet on Lake Michigan. For Peter Rowley, early settler.

ROXBORO, N.C. (co. seat of Person Co.). For Roxburghshire (or Roxburgh county), Scotland.

ROY, Utah (Weber Co.). For the deceased son of the Baptist minister, Rev. David Pebbles.

ROYAL OAK, Mich. (Oakland Co.). Named by Lewis Cass for the Royal Oak in Scotland in which, according to legend, "Bonnie Prince Charlie" (Charles Edward Stuart), the Pretender to the English throne, hid from his pursurers.

ROYAL RIVER, Me. For William Royal, early inhabitant. It flows generally southeast into Casco Bay.

ROYERSFORD, Pa. (Chester Co.). For a ford at the end of a road that separated the farms of David and Benjamin Royer, two brothers who were local farmers.

RUBIDOUX, Calif. (Riverside Co.). For Louis Robidoux, a pioneer and landowner.

RUBY For the stone.
Ruby Lake, Nev. One of a cluster of features in the area named for precious stones.
Ruby Range, Mont.
Ruby Valley, Nev.

RUGBY, N.Dak. (co. seat of Pierce Co.). For Rugby, Warwickshire, England; named by English railroad investors.

RUMFORD, Me. (Oxford Co.), town and village. For Benjamin Thompson, Count Rumford (1753-1814), one of the town proprietors.

RUMP MOUNTAIN, Me. For its shape.

RUM RIVER, Minn. From Sioux *waken*, "spirit," which is rendered by a pun into the present name. It flows generally south from Mille Lacs Lake into the Mississippi River.

RUMSON, N.J. (Monmouth Co.). From Algonquian, a shortened form of *Navaarumsunk*, meaning uncertain.

RUNNELS Co., Tex. (co. seat Ballinger). For Hiram G. Runnels (1796-1857), lawyer and governor of Mississippi, later a member of the Texas legislature.

RUNNEMEDE, N.J. (Camden Co.). For Runnymede, or Runnemede, a meadow near London, England, where King John signed the Magna Carta in 1215.

RUPERT, Idaho (co. seat of Minidoka Co.). For a personal name, said to be that of an engineer who platted the town.

RUSH For the rushes growing along the banks or shores.
Rush Creek, Colo. Rises in two branches, flows SE and S into Arkansas R.
Rush Creek, Neb. Flows E and N into North Platte R.
Rush Lake, Minn. For bulrushes.
Rush Lake, Wis.

RUSH, Benjamin (1746-1813), Philadelphia physician and one of the signers of the Declaration of Independence (1776).
Rush Co., Ind. (co. seat, *Rushville*).
Rushville, Ind. (co. seat of *Rush* Co.).

RUSH Co., Kan. (co. seat, La Crosse). For Alexander Rush (?-1864), killed in action at Jenkins Ferry, Ark.

RUSHFORD, N.Y. (Allegany Co.). For a ford, and either for patches of rushes along streams or for Dr. Benjamin RUSH of Philadelphia.

RUSHMORE, Mount, Natl. Memorial, S.Dak. For Carlos E. Rushmore, an attorney from New York who was representing investors in the Etta Mine. The peak has become famous for the sculptures of the heads of Presidents Washington, Jefferson, Lincoln, and Theodore Roosevelt chiseled into the face of the mountain by Gutzon Borglum and later by his son.

RUSHVILLE, Ill. (co. seat of Schuyler Co.). For Richard Rush (1780-1859), statesman and diplomat. He served as attorney general of the United States (1814-17) under Madison and Monroe and temporary secretary of state (1817) under Monroe and was then appointed minister to England, serving until 1825, when he was recalled to be secretary of the treasury (1825-29) under John Quincy Adams. He was a candidate for the vice-presidency in 1828 and in 1836 was appointed a commissioner by Jackson to obtain a legacy for the founding of the Smithsonian Institution, which he readily accomplished. After serving as minister to France (1847-51), he retired from political activity.

RUSHVILLE, Neb. (co. seat of Sheridan Co.). For Rush Creek, a stream near the town. The creek is supposed to have been named for the rushes that grow along its banks, but it may also have been the translation of an Indian name.

RUSK, Thomas Jefferson (1803-1857), Republic of Texas statesman, signer of the Texas Declaration of Independence, jurist, and U.S. senator (1846-57).
Rusk Co., Tex. (co. seat, Henderson).
Rusk, Tex. (co. seat of Cherokee Co.).

RUSK Co., Wis. (co. seat, Ladysmith). For Jeremiah McLain Rusk (1830-1893), statesman, U.S. representative, and general in the Union army in the Civil War. He was secretary of agriculture under Benjamin Harrison and governor of Wisconsin (1882-89).

RUSK, Wyo. (co. seat of Niobrara Co.). For Frank Rusk, a rancher.

RUSSELL For a man named Russell who died on the mountain in Piscataquis County.
Russell Mountain, Me. (Piscataquis Co.).
Russell Mountain, Me. (Somerset Co.). For the mtn. in Piscataquis Co.
Russell Stream, Me. Flows SE into West Branch Penobscot R.

RUSSELL Co., Ala. (co. seat, Phenix). For Gilbert Christian Russell, professional soldier.

RUSSELL, Avra P. (?-1862), a Union army officer who died of wounds received at Prairie Grove, Ark.
Russell Co., Kan. (co. seat, *Russell*).
Russell, Kan. (co. seat of *Russell* Co.).

RUSSELL Co., Ont. (co. seat, L'Original). For the Hon. Peter Russell (1733-1808), administrator of the government of Upper Canada (1796-99).

RUSSELL, William (1758-1825), Virginia soldier and statesman who fought in the American Revolution and at the Battle of Tippecanoe (1811). He served in the legislatures of both Virginia and Kentucky.
Russell Co., Ky. (co. seat, Jamestown).
Russell Co., Va. (co. seat, Lebanon).
Russellville, Ky. (co. seat, of Logan Co.).

RUSSELL CAVE NATL. MONUMENT, Ala. For an early white settler and landowner. The cave was inhabited from about 7,000 B.C. to relatively recent times.

RUSSELLVILLE, Ala. (co. seat of Franklin Co.). For Maj. William Russell, a scout for Gen. Andrew Jackson.

RUSSELLVILLE, Ark. (co. seat of Pope Co.). For Thomas Russell, an early Pope County citizen and physician.

RUSSIAN RIVER, Calif. Commemorates the Russian colony; may have been translated from Spanish *Rio Ruso*, "Russian River." It flows south then southwest into the Pacific Ocean.

RUSTBURG, Va. (co. seat of Campbell Co.). For Jeremiah Rust, landowner who donated land for the site.

RUSTON, La. (parish seat of Lincoln Parish). For Robert E. Russ, landowner.

RUTHERFORD, Griffith (1731-1800), American Revolutionary hero and general. He served as president of the Tennessee legislative council in 1796.

Rutherford Co., N.C. (co. seat, *Rutherfordton*).
Rutherford Co., Tenn. (co. seat, Murfreesboro).
Rutherfordton, N.C. (co. seat of *Rutherford* Co.).

RUTLAND For Rutlandshire (or Rutland county), England.
Rutland Co., Vt. (co. seat, *Rutland*).
Rutland, Mass. (Worchester Co.).
Rutland, Vt. (co. seat of *Rutland* Co.).

RYAN, Okla. (co. seat of Jefferson Co.). For a personal name, probably that of an early settler, but no other information is available.

RYAN PEAK, Idaho. For Mike Ryan, early settler.

RYDAL, Pa. (Montgomery Co.). For Rydal, Westmorland, England, in the Lake District.

RYE For Rye, Sussex, England.
Rye, N.Y. (Rickingham Co.). town.
Rye, N.Y. (Westchester Co.).

RYEGATE, Mont. (co. seat of Golden Valley Co.). For a field of rye, but probably also reminiscent of Eastern names, especially a Ryegate in Connecticut.

RYE PATCH RESERVOIR, Nev., dam and lake in Humboldt River. For the fields of rye grain formerly grown in the area.

SABAO From Algonquian, "passage," in reference to the chain of lakes, through which a canoe could pass.
Lower Sabao Lake, Me.
Sabao Mountain, Me.
Upper Sabao Lake, Me.

SABBATIA An Abnaki rendering of the name of St. Jean Baptiste, an Abnaki who aided Benedict Arnold's Continentals during their invasion of Quebec in 1775. Also rendered as *Sabbatus*.
Sabbatia Lake, Mass.
Sabbatus Pond, Me.

SABINE From the French form of Spanish *sabinas*, "red cedars," for the trees along the Sabine River.
Sabine Parish, La. (parish seat, Many).
Sabine Co., Tex. (co. seat, Hemphill).
Sabine Lake, La.-Tex.
Sabine Natl. Forest, Tex.
Sabine Pass, La.-Tex. Waterway.
Sabine River, Tex.-La. Flows into the Gulf of Mexico.
Sabine-Neches Waterway, Tex. Deep-water channels through Sabine Pass to the Gulf of Mexico.

SABLE, Cape, Fla. From French, or possibly from an obsolete Spanish word, "sand," descriptive.

SAC For an Indian tribal name, meaning "outlet." The name is also spelled *Sauk*.

Little Sac River, Mo. Flows NW into *Sac* R.
Sac Co., Iowa (co. seat, *Sac City*).
Sac River, Mo. Flows NW into *Sac* R.
Sac City, Iowa (co. seat of *Sac* Co.)

SACAJAWEA PEAK, Ore., in the Wallowa Mountains. For Sacajawea, or "bird wom-

Sacajawea, the Shoshone "Bird Woman," befriended the members of the Lewis and Clark expedition and led them over the Rockies to the Pacific. [*New York Public Library*]

an," the Shoshoni woman who traveled with the Lewis and Clark Expedition, serving as a guide and interpreter. See also SAKAKAWEA.

SACANDAGA From Iroquoian, "drowned land," in the sense of "swampy."
Sacandaga Reservoir, N.Y.
Sacandaga River, N.Y. Formed from East and West branches, flows E into the Hudson R.
Sacandaga Park, N.Y. (Fulton Co.).

SACO From an Indian word, "the outlet of the river." The village is on the lower part of the Saco River.
Saco, Me. (York Co.).
Saco River, Me.-N.H.

SACRAMENTO From Spanish, "holy sacrament." The city and county are named for the river.
North Sacramento, Calif. (*Sacramento* Co.).
Sacramento Co., Calif. (co. seat, *Sacramento*).
Sacramento, Calif. (co. seat of *Sacramento* Co.). State capital. Earlier, New Helvetia; founded by John A. Sutter.
Sacramento Mountains, N.Mex.
Sacramento Pass, Nev.

Sacramenta River, Calif. Flows generally S to San Francisco Bay.
Sacramento Valley, Calif.
South Sacramento-Fruitridge, Calif. (*Sacramento* Co.). *Fruitridge*, descriptive.
West Sacramento, Calif. (*Sacramento* Co.).

SADDLE Descriptive of shape.
Saddle Buttes, N.Dak.
Saddle Mountain, Colo.
Saddle Mountain, Wyo.

SADDLEBACK Descriptive of shape.
Saddleback Mountain, Me. (Aroostook Co.).
Saddleback Mountain, Me. (Franklin Co.).
Saddleback Mountain, N.Y.

SADDLE RIVER, N.J. Origin unknown; probably refers to an incident. It flows south into Passaic River.

SAFETY HARBOR, Fla. (Pinellas Co.). Descriptive of a place of security.

SAFFORD, Ariz. (co. seat of Graham Co.). For Anson P. K. Safford, governor of Arizona Territory (1869-77).

SAGADAHOC Co., Me. (co. seat, Bath). From an Indian word, "land of the mouth" or "mouth of the river." The county is situ-

The Sacramento Valley of California, besides being the site of the state capital, has a long and varied history. It was the terminus of one of the major pioneer routes to the west and was made famous by the fabulous gold rush of the Forty-Niners. Lassens Peak is in the background. [*New York Public Library*]

ated where the Androscoggin and Kennebec rivers join and meet the sea.

SAGAVANIRKTOK RIVER, Alaska. From Eskimo, "strong current." It flows north into Beaufort Sea.

SAGINAW From Ojibway, "the place of the Sacs."
Saginaw Co., Mich. (co. seat, *Saginaw*).
Saginaw, Mich. (co. seat of *Saginaw*).
Saginaw Bay, Mich., on L. Huron.
Saginaw River, Mich.

SAGUACHE From Ute, "blue earth." The creek was named first.
Saguache Co., Colo. (co. seat, *Saguache*).
Saguache, Colo. (co. seat of *Saguache* Co.).
Saguache Creek, Colo. Flows generally SE to San Luis Creek and finally into San Luis Lake.

SAGUARO NATL. MOMUMENT, Ariz. From Mexican-Spanish *saguaro*, a giant cactus (*Carnegiea gigantea*). Its blossom is the Arizona state flower.

ST. ALBANS For St. Albans, Hertfordshire, England, which was named for Saint Alban, first English martyr, beheaded by Roman soldiers at Verulam (c.300 A.D.) during the persecution by Diocletian. A small church was built on the supposed place of martyrdom and existed until King Offa of Mercia founded a Benedictine Abbey there in 793. Formerly a Roman village, the city developed around the abbey. In 1213 King John of England held an assembly at St. Albans to redress wrongs perpetrated by the clergy. From this meeting eventually came the Magna Carta (1217) and the future House of Commons. In this, St. Albans is looked upon also as a symbol of freedom and the rights of the common people. All places with this name in the United States derive ultimately from the city in England.
St. Albans, Me. (Somerset Co.), town.
St. Albans, Vt. (co. seat of Franklin Co.), town and village. Another possibility is for the Duke of St. Albans (1670-1726), son of Charles II.
St. Albans, W.Va. (Kanawha Co.).

ST. ALBERT, Alta. For Father Albert Lacombe (1827-1916), a missionary.

ST. ANDREWS, N.B. (co. seat of Charlotte Co.). Named by a French priest who set the Cross of St. Andrew on the site. See also SAN ANDREAS.

ST. ANDREWS, S.C. (Charleston Co.). For St. Andrews Episcopal Church in Paris, which was named for Saint Andrew.

ST. ANNE For Saint Anne, mother of the Virgin Mary.
St. Ann, Mo. (St. Louis Co.).
Ste. Anne de Bellevue, Que. (co. seat of Gaspe-Ouest Co.). Earlier, Bellevue, from French, "fine view."

The shrine at Sainte-Anne-de-Beaupre, twenty miles east of the city of Quebec, has attracted millions of pilgrims over the past three centuries. [*National Film Board of Canada*]

ST. ANTHONY For Saint Anthony (or Antony) of Padua (1195-1231), theologian. He entered the Franciscan order at Coimbra, Portugal, changing his name from Fernando to Anthony. He served as an evangelist in Italy and France and became famous as lecturer. See also SAN ANTONIO.
St. Anthony, Idaho (co. seat of Fremont Co.). For *St. Anthony*, Minn.

St. Anthony, Minnesota, is just across the Mississippi River from Minneapolis. St. Anthony's Falls were a prominent feature in 1872. [*New York Public Library*]

St. Anthony, Minn. (Hennepin Co.). Anthony was the patron saint of Louis Hennepin.

ST. AUGUSTINE, Fla. (co. seat of St. Johns Co.). For the saint's day, August 28, 1565, when land was first sighted by the Spaniards. See also SAN AUGUSTINE.

ST. BARBARA See SANTA BARBARA.

ST. BENEDICT See SAN BENITO.

ST. BERNARD See SAN BERNARDINO.

ST. BERNARD Parish, La. (parish seat, Chalmette). For Don Bernardo de Galvez (1746-1786), Spanish colonial governor who supplied American forces against the British during the American Revolution. He led forces that captured the British settlements in West Florida, for which he was rewarded with the title of viscount and rank of major general. He died while serving as viceroy of Mexico. See also SAN BERNARDINO.

ST. CATHERINE, Lake, Vt. So named by Jesuits for one of the saints. They also named it Lake St. Augustine, which is still used locally.

ST. CATHERINES, Ont. (co. seat of Lincoln Co.). For Catherine Askin Hamilton (?-1796), wife of the Honorable Robert Hamilton, founder of Queenston, and mother of George Hamilton, founder of Hamilton.

ST. CATHERINES ISLAND, Ga. Named Santa Catalina by Spanish missionaries in 1566, probably for Catherine of Siena, patroness against pestilence and headache. The saint's day is on April 29th or 30th, and the islands were visited by the Spanish in April.

ST. CHARLES For Saint Carlo (or Charles) Borromeo (1538-1584), Italian cardinal and reformer who founded the order of the Oblates of Saint Ambrose (1578). See also SAN CARLOS.
St. Charles Parish, La. (parish seat, Hahnville).
St. Charles Co., Mo. (co. seat, *St. Charles*).
St. Charles, Ill. (Kane Co.).
St. Charles, Mo. (co. seat of *St. Charles* Co.).
St. Charles River, Colo. Flows NE into Arkansas R.

ST. CHARLES, Ill. (Kane Co.). For Charlestown, N.H. The name was changed to the inspirational form to avoid confusion with Charleston, Ill.

ST. CLAIR, Gen. Arthur (1736-1818), Scottish-born American soldier, associated with Pennsylvania. He participated in the Quebec campaign during the French and Indian Wars and, during the American Revolution, saw action at the battles of Trenton and Princeton (1777). He was a member of the Continental Congress (1785-87; president, 1787) and governor of the Northwest Territory (1787-1805).

St. Clair Co., Ala. (co. seats, Ashville and Pell City).

St. Clair Co., Ill. (co. seat, Belleville).

St. Clair Co., Mich. (co. seat, Port Huron).

St. Clair Co., Mo. (co. seat, Osceola).

St. Clair, Mich. (St. Clair Co.). For the lake, which had originally been named for Saint Clare by La Salle, but was changed to honor Arthur St. Clair.

St. Clair, Mo. (Franklin Co.).

St. Clair, Pa. (Schuylkill Co.).

St. Clair Lake, Mich.

St. Clair River, stream forming the international boundary between Michigan and Ontario, flows between Lake Huron and St. Clair Lake.

St. Clair Shores, Mich. (Macomb Co.). For the lake.

St. Clairsville, Ohio (co. seat of Belmont Co.).

ST. CLARE See SANTA CLARA.

ST. CLOUD For Saint Cloud, or Chlodoald (524-560), grandson of King Clovis I of France and son of King Chlodomer of Orleans. He became a monk in order to escape being murdered by his uncles after the death of his father. After living for some years in solitude in Provence, he returned to Paris, where he planned and supervised the building of the abbey at St. Cloud, a few

St. Augustine, Florida, the oldest city in the United States, also boasts the oldest house, built in the late sixteenth century. [New York Public Library]

477

miles from Paris. Since *clou* in French means "nail," he is the patron of nailsmiths.

St. Cloud, Fla. (Osceola Co.).

St. Cloud, Minn. (co. seat of Stearns Co.). Named by the founder, John L. Wilson, after reading a biography of Napoleon. He noted "that the Empress Josephine spent much of her time at the magnificent palace at St. Cloud."

ST. CROIX From French, "holy cross." In Wisconsin, the names are most likely for an explorer named St. Croix who drowned in the river, although other claims refer to signs of the cross or streams crossing at right angles to form a cross. The features in Maine take their name from that of the river, which was named by the French explorer Jacques Cartier, who saw it on Holy Cross Day, Sept. 14, 1535.

St. Croix Co., Wis. (co. seat, Hudson).

St. Croix. Flowage, Wis.

St. Croix Island, Me.

St. Croix River, Me.-N.B. Flows S and E into Passamaquoddy Bay, forming international border.

St. Croix River, Minn.-Wis. Flows generally S to the Mississippi R.

St. Croix River Natl. Forest, Wis.

St. Croix Stream, Me. Flows E and NW into Aroostook R.

Upper St. Croix Lake, Wis.

STE. AGATHE-DES-MONTS, Que. (Terrebonne Co.). For the patron church in Rome of the first settlers, who were Irish.

STE. ANNE DES MONTS See ST. ANNE.

STE. CROIX, Que. (co. seat of Lotbiniere Co.). Named by Jesuit Father Jerome Lalemant, who took possession of the seigniory on behalf of the Ursuline Order of the feast-day of the Exaltation of the Cross; thus he named it Ste. Croix, from French, "holy cross."

STE. FOY, Que. (Quebec Co.). For a village in France.

STE. GENEVIEVE. For Saint Genevieve (422-512), French nun. Born into a shepherd's family she became a nun at fifteen. After the death of her parents she moved to Paris and apparently did not live in a regular religious community. It is said that her prayers caused Attila the Hun to turn away

from Paris (451). Although she led a life of penance, charity, and prayer, she had strong influence with rulers and through her efforts the Church of Saint Denis was built. She is the patroness of Paris.

Ste. Genevieve Co., Mo. (co. seat, *Ste. Genevieve*).

Ste. Genevieve, Mo. (co. seat of *Ste. Genevieve* Co.).

Ste. Genevieve de Batiscan, Que. (co. seat of Champlain Co.). For its location on the Batiscan R.

ST. ELIAS For Elias, also known as Elijah, the Thesbite, Hebrew prophet of the 9th century B.C., who flourished during the reign of Achab (876-54 B.C.). It is prophesied that he will appear with Christ at the end of time. He is patron against drought and earthquakes. The saint's day is July 20th.

St. Elias, Cape, Alaska. On Kayak Island. Named in 1741 by Vitus Bering.

St. Elias, Mount, Alaska-Yukon border. In *St. Elias* Mtns.

St. Elias Mountains, Alaska-Yukon border.

STE. MARIE, Que. (Beauce Co.). Named in 1737 for Marie Claire Fleury de la Gorgendiere, wife of the seignior.

STE. THÉRÈSE, Que. (Terrebonne Co.). For Therese, granddaughter of the first seignior.

ST. EUSTACHE, Que. (Deux Montagnes Co.). For Eustache Lambert, seignior of Mille Isles.

ST. FRANCIS For Saint Francis of Sales (1567-1622). French bishop and theologian.

St. Francis Co., Ark. (co. seat, Forrest City).

St. Francis, Wis. (Milwaukee Co.).

St. Francis Natl. Forest, Ark.

St. Francis River, Mo. Flows into the Mississippi R.

St. Francisville, La. (parish seat of West Feliciana Parish). For the St. Francis monastery, built around 1785, which burned.

ST. FRANCIS, Kan. (co. seat of Cheyenne Co.). Said to be named for Frances Emerson, wife of one of the founders. The reasons for the change in spelling is not known, but was probably influenced by that of the saint.

ST. FRANCOIS French form of SAINT FRAN-
CIS.

St. Francois Co., Mo. (co. seat, Farmington).

St. Francois Mountains, Mo.

ST. FRANÇOIS DU LAC, Que. (co. seat of Yamaska Co.). Probably for François de Lauzon, son of Jean Lauzon, who owned the seigniory in the area.

ST. FROID LAKE, Me., one of Fish River lakes. For Sefroi Nadeau, early settler. The spelling form occurred from a confusion of the French sound and an English spelling.

ST. GEORGE For Saint George (?-c.303 A.D.). Christian martyr and patron saint of England. Legends exist about his conquest of the dragon, which represented the devil, and his rescue of the king's daughter Sabra, who represented the Church.

St. George, Me. (Knox Co.).

St. George, N.Y. (co. seat of Richmond Co.).

St. George, Cape, Fla. On *St. George* Island.

St. George Island, Fla.

St. George Lake, Me. For the river.

St. George, Point, Calif. On Pacific Coast. Named by Capt. George Vancouver.

St. George River, Me.

ST. GEORGE, S.C. (co. seat of Dorchester Co.). Named by and for James George (1789-1887), first settler, who leased his land to the railroad that was built through the area. Earlier names were George's Turn-out, George's Station, and St. George's, which became St. George, obviously influenced by the name of the legendary saint.

ST. GEORGE, Utah (co. seat of Washington Co.). For Saint George, in honor of George Albert Smith, an aide to Brigham Young, the Mormon leader.

ST. GEORGES For Georges Payette, reverend.

St. Georges, Que. (Beauce Co.).

St. Georges West, Que. (Beauce Co.).

ST. HELEN, Lake, Mich. Probably for ST. HELENA.

ST. HELENA For Saint Helena (c.250-330), mother of Constantine the Great. Born of poor parents in Drepanum, Bithynia, Asia Minor, she married Constantine Chlorus and was later repudiated by him. When her son Constantine succeeded to the throne, she returned to court as Matron and was converted to Christianity by him. The remainder of her life was given to piety and charity. She is patroness of dyers, needlers, and nailsmiths.

St. Helena Parish, La. (parish seat, Greensburg).

St. Helena, Calif. (Napa Co.).

St. Helena Island, S.C. Named by Francis Gordillo, who discovered it on the saint's day, Aug. 18, 1820.

ST. HELENS, Alleyne Fitzherbert, Baron (1753-1839), British ambassador to Spain (1790-94).

St. Helens, Ore. (co. seat of Columbia Co.). For the mountain.

St. Helens, Mount, Wash., in the Cascade Mtns. Named by Capt. George Vancouver.

ST. HYACINTHE For Hyacinthe Simon Delorme, who in 1753 purchased the seigniory granted five years earlier to Pierre François de Rigaud, Sieur de Vaudreuil.

St. Hyacinthe Co., Que. (co. seat, *St. Hyacinthe*).

St. Hyacinthe, Que. (co. seat of *St. Hyacinthe* Co.).

ST. IGNACE, Mich. (co. seat of Mackinac Co.). For Saint Ignace (or Inigo or Ignatuis) of Loyola (1491-1556), founder of the Society of Jesus, commonly known now as Jesuits. Born in Loyola Castle, Spain, he led a secular life, including that of a soldier, before his conversion. While recuperating from wounds received at Pamplona (1521), he began a course of study that led to his acceptance of the Catholic Church. His ability eventually brought him to the head of an order which he changed into the Society. His innovations included dispensing with the monastic dress and exempting his clerics from common devotional exercises and from choir singing of their offices. He instilled in his followers the spirit of educating the young.

ST. JAMES For James (?-A.D.), one of the Apostles. He was present at the Transfiguration and at the Prayer of the Lord in the

Garden of Olives. He carried the nickname "Son of Thunder," for his fiery temper and speaking ability. Herod had him imprisoned and then beheaded.

St. James Parish, La. (parish seat, Convent).

St. James, Minn. (co. seat of Watonwan Co.). Named by a railroad official, perhaps influenced by St. Paul, Minn., from which he had just traveled.

St. James, N.Y. (Suffolk Co.).

ST. JAMES, Mo. (Phelps Co.). Probably for Thomas James, founder.

ST. JEAN Probably for Jean Fréderic Phelypeaux, Comte de Pontchartrain, the French Minister of Marine when Fort St. Jean was built (1748), from which the present town and county take their name.

St. Jean Co., Que. (co. seat, *St. Jean*).

St. Jean, Que. (co. seat of *St. Jean* Co.).

St. Jean Port Joli, Que. (co. seat of L'Islet Co.). *-Joli*, from French, "pretty," for its port on the St. Lawrence R.

ST. JOE For ST. JOSEPH. The river was named first, in 1844 by the Jesuit missionary De Smet.

St. Joe, Idaho (Benewah Co.).

St. Joe Natl. Forest, Idaho.

St. Joe River, Idaho. Flows W into Coeur d'Alene L. Earlier, St. Joseph R.

ST. JOHN, Kan. (co. seat of Stafford Co.). For John Pierce St. John (1833-1916), American prohibitionist. He fought in the Indian wars in Oregon and served in the Union army (1862-65), after which he moved to Missouri and became a lawyer. He was governor of Kansas (1879-83), and Prohibition candidate for President (1884). In 1912 and 1914 he toured Kansas speaking for women's suffrage.

ST. JOHN (The Baptist). (c.5 B.C.-30 A.D.), Hebrew prophet who described himself as "the voice of one crying in the wilderness," announcing the imminent coming of the Messiah. He recognized Jesus as the Messiah and baptized him in the Jordan River. He was later executed by Herod. Saint's day is June 24.

Fort St. John, B.C.

St. John Co., N.B. (co. seat, *St. John*).

St. John, N.B. (co. seat of *St. John* Co.).

St. John Pond, Me.

St. John River, Me./N.B. Flows into Bay of Fundy. Named by Samuel de Champlain, who sailed into its mouth on the saint's day, 1604.

St. Johns Co., Fla. (co. seat, St. Augustine). For the river.

St. John's, Nfld. Provincial capital. Named by John Cabot, who entered its harbor on the saint's day, 1497.

St. Johns River, Fla. Flows N and E to the Atlantic Ocean at Jacksonville.

St. John the Baptist Parish, La. (parish seat, Edgard).

ST. JOHN MOUNTAIN, Wyo. For Orestes St. John, geologist with the Hayden survey of 1877.

ST. JOHNS, Ariz. (co. seat of Apache Co.). Origin uncertain. It may have been named for Señora Maria San Juan Baca de Padilla, the first woman settler. Another possible source is the feast of San Juan (Saint John), June 24. It may also have been named directly for the Apostle.

ST. JOHNS, Mich. (co. seat of Clinton Co.). Several theories are available: for John Swegles, a land speculator who was also auditor general of Michigan; Johnsville was suggested at a naming meeting, along with Sweglesville and others, but a church elder persuaded the group to name it St. Johns; a box of goods arrived with the name St. Johns marked on it, and a founder nailed one such marking on a tree and proclaimed the place St. Johns; named for Jonesville, N.Y., a station on the New York Central railroad; or for the St. Johns Land Company, which included John Swegles among its directors.

ST. JOHNSBURY, Vt. (co. seat of Caledonia Co.). Name suggested by Col. Ethan Allen as a tribute to Michel Guillaume Jean de Crèvecœur (1735-1813), an officer in the French army in Canada, where he was wounded. He became a naturalized colonist and farmer in Orange County, N.Y. His home was destroyed during the American Revolution. He later served as French consul in New York. His *Letters from an American Farmer* (1782) were justly celebrated when published. Crèvecœur suggested adding -bury to the name to differentiate it from other places named St. John.

ST. JOSEPH For Joseph, husband of the Virgin Mary. According to biblical accounts, he was a carpenter in Nazareth when he married Mary. The Apocrypha account claims that he was ninety and Mary fourteen and that he also had been married before to Meicha and had two daughters and four sons, the "sisters and brothers of Christ." Nothing is known concerning his death. He is patron of artisans and of the dying. See also SAN JOSE and ST. JOE.
St. Joseph Co., Ind. (co. seat, South Bend).
St. Joseph Co., Mich. (co. seat, Centerville).
St. Joseph, La. (parish seat of Tensas Parish).
St. Joseph, Mich. (co. seat of Berrien Co.).
St. Joseph, Mo. (co. seat of Buchanan Co.).
St. Joseph Island, Ont., in L. Huron.
St. Joseph Island, Tex., between Aransas Bay and the Gulf of Mexico.
St. Joseph, Lake, La.
St. Joseph, Lake, Ont.
St. Joseph Point, Fla.
St. Joseph River, Mich.-Ind. Flows W and SW to L. Michigan.
St. Joseph River, Mich.-Ohio. Flows generally SW to join the St. Marys R. to form the Maumee R.
St. Joseph d'Alma, Que. (co. seat of Lake St. John East Co.).
St. Joseph de Beauce, Que. (Beauce Co.).
St. Joseph de Grantham, Que. (St. Hyacinthe Co.).
St. Joseph de Sorel, Que. (Richelieu Co.).

ST. LAMBERT, Que. (Chambly Co.). For Lambert Closse, a soldier who came to Montreal with Maisonneuve, its founder and governor.

ST. LANDRY Parish, La. (parish seat, Opelousas). For Saint Landry (or Landri or Landericus) (?-656), bishop of Paris (650-656). He gave away all his possessions to help the poor and sick during the famine of 651.

ST. LAURENT French form of ST. LAWRENCE.
St. Laurent, Man.
St. Laurent, Que. (Montreal and Jesus Islands Co.).

ST. LAWRENCE For Saint Lawrence (?-258), a martyr of Rome. He has become the most celebrated of those persecuted and executed by Valerian. Reportedly, he was born in Spain and came to Rome as a deacon of the Roman Catholic Church. When Valerian put to death Pope Sixtus II and most of the clergy of the Church, Lawrence (or Laurentius) appeared before him with the poor of the city, whereupon it is said he was sentenced to death by being broiled over a slow fire. See also ST. LAURENT.
St. Lawrence Co., N.Y. (co. seat, Canton). For the river.
St. Lawrence, Gulf of. Arm of the Atlantic; outlet of the St. Lawrence R.
St. Lawrence Island, Alaska, in Bering Sea. Discovered (1728) by Vitus Bering on the saint's day, August 10.
St. Lawrence River. Flows generally NE from L. Ontario to the Gulf of St. Lawrence. It was named (1535) by Jacques Cartier on the saint's day, August 10. He applied the name to a harbor, but it spread to the gulf and river and finally the county. The river also forms part of the boundary between Canada and the United States.

ST. LIBOIRE, Que. (co. seat of Bagot Co.). For Abbé Liboire Girouard, a parish priest.

ST. LOUIS For Louis IX of France (1214-1270), who participated in the Sixth Crusade (1248-54) and, with the Treaty of Paris (1259), adjusted English claims on the French mainland. He was canonized in 1297.
East St. Louis, Ill. (Saint Clair Co.). Across the Mississippi R. from St. Louis, Mo.
St. Louis Co., Minn. (co. seat, Duluth). For the river.
St. Louis Co., Mo. (co. seat, Clayton).
St. Louis, Mich. (Gratiot Co.). For St. Louis, Mo.
St. Louis, Mo. (independent city in St. Louis Co.).
St. Louis River, Minn. Rising in St. Louis Co., it flows generally SE to L. Superior at Duluth.
St. Louis Park, Minn. (Hennepin Co.).

ST. LUCIE For Saint Lucy (c.283-303), Sicilian martyr. Born of an aristocratic Greek family at Syracuse, she was educated as a Christian and was allowed to take the vow

The pious St. Louis, Louis IX of France, was instrumental in the founding of many of the most famous French cathedrals, including Amiens, Chartres and the Sainte-Chapelle in Paris. He also founded the Sorbonne, one of the world's great universities. [*New York Public Library*]

of virginity and to dispose of her worldly possessions. Denounced for her belief, she was tortured and then killed, it is reported, by having her throat pierced by a sword. She is patroness against sore eyes, sore throat, and epidemic diseases. See also SANTA LUCIA.

St. Lucie Co., Fla. (co. seat, Fort Pierce).
St. Lucie Canal, Fla.

ST. MARIES, Idaho (co. seat of Benewah Co.). From the Catholic mission established there, for the Virgin Mary. See ST. MARY.

ST. MARKS RIVER, Fla. For Saint Mark. Believed to have had the name of John Marcus, he was one of the Apostles and the inspired writer of one of the Gospels. Little is known of his life, except as noted in the Scriptures, and even then the identification is not always clear. He may have been converted by Saint Peter, and he was a companion of Saint Paul but soon became dis-

pleased with Paul's conversions. He is said to have been the founder and first bishop of the Church of Alexandria.

ST. MARTIN For Saint Martin (c.315-399). Born in Sabaria, Pannonia, Hungary, the son of a Roman tribune, he was baptized as a Christian at the age of twenty, at which time he was a soldier in the imperial cavalry in Gaul. Leaving the army, he began service for Saint Hillary. He was elected Bishop of Tours in 371. A soldier-priest, he destroyed pagan temples and opposed Arianism. He died at Claudes and was entombed at Tours.

St. Martin Island, Mich.
St. Martin Parish, La. (parish seat, *St. Martinville*).
St. Martinville, La. (parish seat of *St. Martin* Co.).

ST. MARY (or St. Marys). For the Virgin Mary, the mother of Jesus Christ. See also ST. MARIES.

St. Mary Parish, La. (parish seat, Franklin).
St. Marys Co., Md. (co. seat, Leonardtown).
St. Marys, Ohio (Auglaize Co.). Earlier, Girty's Town.
St. Marys, Ont. (Perth Co.), town. In honor of Bishop Strachan's daughter, the wife of T. M. Jones of the Canada Company. Earlier, Little Falls.
St. Marys, Pa. (Elk Co.).
St. Marys, W.Va. (co. seat of Pleasants Co.). A landowner had a vision of Mary.
St. Marys River, Fla.-Ga.
St. Marys River, Ind.-Ohio. Flows NW to join St. Joseph R. to form Maumee R.
St. Marys River, Minn.

ST. MATTHEWS For Saint Matthew, an Apostle of Christ, a former tax collector. He is author of the first canonical gospel. He first preached in Palestine and later was reported in Ethiopia. Nothing certain is known about his death. He is patron of tax collectors and bankers.

St. Matthews, S.C. (co. seat of Calhoun Co.).
St. Matthews, Ky. (Jefferson Co.). For the St. Matthews Episcopal Church, which was named for the saint.

ST. MAURICE Probably for Maurice Poulin, Sieur de la Fontaine, who was granted a seigniory north of Trois-Rivières in 1668.

St. Maurice Co., Que. (co. seat, Yamachi-che). For the river.

St. Maurice River, Que. Flows SE to St. Lawrence R.

ST. MICHAEL See SAN MIGUEL.

ST. PASCAL, Que. (co. seat of Kamouraska Co.). For Pascal Tache, seignior of Kamouraska.

ST. PATRICK See SAN PATRICIO.

ST. PAUL For the Apostle Paul (?-67 A.D.). Originally a Jew of Tarsus, his conversion to Christianity was inspired by a vision. He then became an apostle to the Gentiles, journeyed to many places and founded many churches. It was to these churches that he addressed his famous "Pauline epistles," which now make up a large part of the New Testament canon. He is supposed to have been martyred at Rome.

North St. Paul, Minn. (Ramsey Co.).

St. Paul, Minn. (co. seat of Ramsey Co.), state capital. Named in 1841 by Father Lucian Galtier for Saint Paul, "the apostle of nations." A small chapel was the first so named, but it was extended to the town and then the city. Earlier, St. Paul Landing.

St. Paul Park, Minn. (Washington Co.). Promotional.

South St. Paul, Minn. (Dakota Co.).

West St. Paul, Minn. (Ramsey Co.).

ST. PAUL, Neb. (co. seat of Howard Co.). Name suggested by Phineas W. Hitchcock, in honor of the founders, J. N. and N. J. Paul.

ST. PETER For Saint Peter, called Simon Peter (?-c.67 A.D.), disciple of Jesus, and an Apostle. He established Jerusalem as headquarters for preaching and proselytizing, and is probably an author of two epistles of the New Testament. He died as a martyr in Rome during the persecution of Nero. See SAN PEDRO, SAN SIMON, and ST. SIMONS.

ST. PETER, Minn. (co. seat of Nicollet Co.). For the St. Peter River, former name of the Minnesota River. It was probably named for the saint in honor of Pierre (Peter) Charles Le Sueur.

ST. PETERSBURG Named by Peter Demons, president of a local railroad, for the city in Russia, his former home.

St. Petersburg, Fla. (Pinellas Co.).

St. Petersburg Beach, Fla. (Pinellas Co.).

ST. RAPHAEL, Que. (co. seat of Bellechasse Co.). For Rev. François-Raphael Paquet, parish priest (1860-38) of a nearby town.

ST. RAYMOND, Que. (Portneuf Co.). For St. Raymond Nonnat, whose anniversary is celebrated on August 31st, the day the first parish priest was chosen.

ST. REGIS For a Jesuit missionary.

St. Regis River, N.Y. Flows NW then NE into St. Lawrence R.

St. Regis Falls, N.Y. (Franklin Co.).

ST. ROSE OF LIMA See SANTA ROSA.

ST. ROSE OF VITERBO See SANTA ROSA (de Viterbo).

ST. SIMONS For Simon Peter, one of the twelve apostles. See ST. PETER.

Little St. Simons Island, Ga.

St. Simons, Ga. (Glynn Co.).

St. Simons Island, Ga.

ST. TAMMANY Parish, La. (parish seat, Covington). From Delaware Indian *Tamanend*, "friendly" or "affable," the name of a celebrated Delaware chief who lived in the 1600s. Those who admired him claimed him as their "patron saint" during the American Revolution. The parish named for him was inhabited by Indians only until late in the 1700s.

ST. THOMAS, Ont. (co. seat of Elgin Co.). For Col. Thomas Talbot (1771-1853), British soldier and colonizer in Canada. He received a grant of several thousand acres of land in Canada from the British Government and founded the Talbot settlement, of which St. Thomas was the capital.

ST. VINCENT ISLAND, Fla. For the Spanish Franciscan mission of Cape San Vicente, which was probably named for Saint Vincent of Saragossa (?-304), a Spanish martyr and patron of winegrowers.

ST. VITAL, Man. For Rev. Vital Grandin (1829-1902), bishop of St. Albert in Alberta.

SAKAKAWEA, Lake, N.Dak. For Sacajawea. See SACAJAWEA PEAK.

SAKONNET From Narraganset, probably "outlet," but also possibly "where the black goose lives."
Sakonnet, R.I. (Newport Co.).
Sakonnet Point, R.I. Extends into Rhode Island Sound.
Sakonnet River, R.I. Arm of Mount Hope Bay.

SALADO RIVER, N.Mex. From Spanish, "salty." It flows intermittently south and southwest into the Rio Grande River.

SALAMANCA, N.Y. (Cattaraugus Co.). For the Duke of Salamanca, who provided capital for the Atlantic and Great Western railroad in this area. The Duke had gained his wealth from similar investments in European railroads.

SALAMONIE RIVER, Ind. From Algonquian, "bloodroot," for the plant. It flows northwest into Wabash River.

SALCHA RIVER, Alaska. Of Indian origin, meaning unknown. It flows southwest into Tanana River.

SALEM Anglicization of the Hebrew word *shalom*, "peace." The popularity of the word as a place name is due partly to the fact that it also serves as a shortened form of Jeru*salem*, "the City of Peace." Apparently, the first mention of the name occurs on a cuneiform tablet dating from the reign of Ikhnaton, or Amenhotep IV (1375?-1354? B.C.), king of Egypt and the first ruler to profess his belief in one god.
Salem Co., N.J. (co. seat, *Salem*).
Salem, Ark. (co. seat of Fulton Co.).
Salem, Conn. (London Co.), town.
Salem, Ill. (co. seat of Marion Co.).
Salem, Ind. (co. seat of Washington Co.).
Salem, Mass. (co. seat of Essex Co.).
Salem, Mo. (co. seat of Dent Co.).
Salem, N.H. (Rockingham Co.), town.
Salem, N.J. (co. seat of *Salem* Co.).
Salem, Ohio (Columbiana Co.).
Salem, Ore. (co. seat of Marion Co.), state capital.
Salem, S.Dak. (co. seat of McCook Co.). For *Salem*, Mass.
Salem, Va. (co. seat of Roanoke Co.).

Salem, W.Va. (Harrison Co.). For *Salem*, N.J. Earlier, New Salem.
Salem River, N.J., flows generally S to the Delaware R.
Salem Heights, Ore. (Marion Co.).
Salem Maritime Natl. Historic Site, Mass. For *Salem*, Mass.

SALIDA, Colo. (co. seat of Chaffee Co.). From Spanish, "exit," "outlet," or "departure," for an opening from a canyon; named in 1880 by the wife of a Colorado governor.

SALINA, Kan. (co. seat of Saline Co.). Variant of SALINE; named for the Saline River.

SALINAS From Spanish, "salt marshes."
Salinas, Calif. (co. seat of Monterey Co.). For the River.
Salinas River, Calif. Flows NW into Monterey Bay.

SALINE For a source of salt, or for salty water. Salt deposits were important to the early settlers because they not only provided salt for their cattle (salt licks) and their own consumption, but also because salt was used in the preservation of meat.
Saline Co., Ark. (co. seat, Benton).
Saline Co., Ill. (co. seat, Harrisburg).
Saline Co., Kan. (co. seat, Salina). For the river.
Saline Co., Mo. (co. seat, Marshall).
Saline Co., Neb. (co. seat, Wilber).
Saline, Mich. (Washtenaw Co.). For salt springs.
Saline Lake, La.
Saline River, Ark. Flows generally SE to the Ouachita R.
Saline River, Ill. Flows generally SE to the Ohio R.
Saline River, Kan. Flows generally E to the Smoky Hill R.

SALISBURY For Salisbury, Wiltshire, England.
Salisbury, Conn. (Litchfield Co.), town.
Salisbury, Md. (co. seat of Wicomico Co.).
Salisbury, Mass. (Essex Co.). town.
Salisbury, N.C. (co. seat of Rowan Co.). For *Salisbury*, Md.
Salisbury, Vt. (Addison Co.), town.

SALKEHATCHIE From the Indian tribal name interpreted to be *Santee*, plus *Hatchie*, "river"; this "river of the Santees."

Little Salkehatchie River, S.C. Flows SE to join *Salkehatchie* R.

Salkehatchie River, S.C. Flows SE to join *Little Salkehatchie* R. to form Combahee R.

SALLISAW Anglicized spelling of French *salaison*, "salt provisions."

Big Sallisaw Creek, Okla.

Sallisaw, Okla. (co. seat of Sequoyah Co.). For the creek.

SALMON For the fish.

Little Salmon River, N.Y. Flows N to join *Salmon* R.

Salmon, Idaho (co. seat of Lemhi Co.). For the river.

Salmon Brook, Conn. Flows SE into Farmington R.

Salmon Brook, Mass.-N.H. Flows N into Merrimack R.

Salmon Creek, Conn. Flows SE into Housatonic R.

Salmon Natl. Forest, Idaho-Mont.

Salmon Reservoir, N.Y.

Salmon River, Conn. Flows SW into Connecticut R.

Salmon River, N.Y. Flows E into L. Champlain.

Salmon River, N.Y. Flows NW to join *Little Salmon* R. to flow into St. Lawrence R.

Salmon Falls Creek, Idaho-Nev.

Salmon Falls River, Me.-N.H. Flows SSE to form the boundary between the states.

Salmon River Mountains, Idaho.

SALT For all salt licks.

Salt Creek, Ill. Flows into Des Plaines R.

Salt Creek, Ill. Flows WSW into Sangamon R.

Salt Lakes, Tex.

Salt River, Ariz. Flows W into Gila R. For the salty taste.

Salt River, Ky. Flows N and W into Ohio R. For the salt deposits, which caused Shepherdsville, Ky. to become a salt-producing center.

Salt River, Mo. Flows SE and E into Mississippi R.

Salt Fork River, Ill. Flows S and E into Vermilion R.

Salt Fork of Arkansas River, Kan.-Okla. Flows into Arkansas R.

Salt River Range, Wyo.

SALT LAKE See GREAT SALT LAKE.

Salt Lake Co., Utah (co. seat, *Salt Lake City*).

The description of Salt Lake City accompanying this lithograph describes the city as follows: "It covers an area of about 9 square miles and is probably the most beautifully laid out and finest watered city in America. The streets are very wide, with rows of shade trees on each side, and water cool and pure from the mountains capped with Eternal Snows running through nearly every street and garden. Every block is filled up with fruit trees, shrubbery and flowers, making the city look like an immense orchard. The mountains in view vary in distance from 40 to 150 miles. The suburbs of the city reach the shore of the lake. This singular body of water is 55 miles wide by 85 long and is intensely salty. There are four rivers emptying into it without any visible outlet." [*New York Historical Society*]

Salt Lake City, Utah (co. seat of *Salt Lake* Co.), state capital.

South Salt Lake, Utah (*Salt Lake* Co.).

SALTON SEA (lake), Calif. Coined from "salt," for the salt content.

SALTVILLE, Va. (Washington and Smyth Cos.). For its salt deposits.

SALUDA Perhaps from Cherokee *selu*, "corn," for the corn-growing area, with ending *tah*, "river": "corn river." Apparently the river was named first.

Saluda Co., S.C. (co. seat, *Saluda*).

Saluda, N.C. (Polk Co.).

Saluda, S.C. (co. seat of *Saluda* Co.).

Saluda, Va. (co. seat of Middlesex Co.).

Saluda River, S.C. Flows generally SE across the Piedmont to join the Broad R. to form the Congaree R.

SALVADOR, Lake, La. From Spanish, "savior."

SALYERSVILLE, Ky. (co. seat of Magoffin Co.). For Samuel Salyer, a state legislator.

SAMPSON Co., N.C. (co. seat, Clinton). For John Sampson (?-1784), army officer, legislator, and adviser to royal governors.

SAM RAYBURN RESERVOIR, Tex., in Angelina River. For Sam Taliaferro Rayburn (1882-1961), attorney, state legislator, and U.S. representative from Texas (1913-1961), who served as speaker during nine sessions of Congress.

SAMUEL R. McKELVIE NATL. FOREST, Neb. For Samuel R. McKelvie, farmer, rancher, businessman, publisher, and governor of Nebraska (1919-23).

SANAK ISLAND, Alaska. From Aleut, meaning unknown.

SAN ANDREAS, Calif. (co. seat of Calaveras Co.). For Saint Andrew, one of the twelve apostles and patron saint of Scotland. He was crucified as a martyr at Achaia.

SAN ANGELO For Santa Angelo, sister-in-law of Bart J. DeWitt, founder. She was the Mother Superior of the Ursuline Convent in San Antonio. Another source states that the name comes from DeWitt's deceased wife, Carolina Angela, a descendant of one of the Canary Islanders brought from Spain to settle in Texas.

San Angelo, Tex. (co. seat of Tom Green Co.).

San Angelo Reservoir, Tex.

SAN ANSELMO, Calif. (Marin Co.). Probably for a baptized Indian.

SAN ANTONIO For Saint Anthony of Padua, in Spanish San Antonio de Padua. (See ST. ANTHONY.) An earlier name was Villa de Bejar. The accompanying mission, San Antonio de Valero, is more commonly known as The Alamo.

San Antonio, Tex. (co. seat of Bexar Co.).

San Antonio Bay, Tex.

San Antonio Mountain, Tex.

San Antonio Peak, N.Mex.

San Antonio River, Tex.

SAN AUGUSTINE For San Augustine de Ahumade, the presidio, which was named for Saint Augustine (354-430), the great father and doctor of the Catholic Church. For years he led a dissolute life, although he was becoming deeply steeped in his studies, especially rhetoric. His *Confessions* relate the steps that led to his conversion. His philosophy is usually called Christianized Neoplatonism, strongly defended in *The City of God*. He became bishop of Hippo Regius in 395 and held the position until his death.

San Augustine Co., Tex. (co. seat, *San Augustine*).

San Augustine, Tex. (co. seat of *San Augustine* Co.).

SAN BENITO For Saint Benedict (?-c.543). Born of a rich family in Rome, he lived and studied there until he was seventeen, when he left to live in a cave in the Sabine Mountains. He remained an anchorite for three years. Later he founded an order, now called the Benedictine Order. Much of his later life was spent in the monastery at Monte Cassino. He died at his altar after Holy Communion.

San Benito Co., Calif. (co. seat, Hollister).

San Benito, Tex. (Cameron Co.). Direct source was the San Benito Land and Water Company, which furnished water to Magic Valley.

San Benito River, Calif.

SAN BERNARDINO For the Italian monk, known in English as Saint Bernard of Siena (1380-1444), and in Italian as Bernardinus

Even before the Alamo, San Antonio was central to the birth of Texas, first as a republic and then as a state. This is a view of the Military Plaza in the mid-1800s. [*James D. Smillie after Arthur Schott. New York Historical Society*]

degl'Albizzeschi of Siena. He was ordained in 1404, after having served the sick during a plague at Siena, and then lived for twelve years in retirement. Emerging from his self-imposed silence, he became famous as an eloquent preacher, one who could allay the tensions of quarreling parties. Called the greatest monk of his time, he restored the Order of the Friars Minor and was vicar-general of the order (1438-44) until his death.

San Bernardino Co., Calif. (co. seat, *San Bernardino*). For the city.

San Bernardino, Calif. (co. seat of *San Bernardino* Co.). A party from the Gabriel mission nearby named the site on the saint's day, May 20, 1810.

San Bernardino Mountains, Calif.

San Bernardino Natl. Forest, Calif.

SAN BERNARD RIVER, Tex. For SAN BERNARDINO. Flows generally southeast into the Gulf of Mexico.

SAN BLAS, Cape, Fla. Named by Spanish explorers for Saint Blasius, one of the fourteen holy helpers and bishop of Sebaste (?-316). He was patron of wool combers, because he was supposedly martyred by having his flesh torn with woolcombers' irons before he was beheaded.

SANBORN Co., S.Dak. (co. seat, Woonsocket). For George W. Sanborn, a railroad official.

SAN BRUNO, Calif. (San Mateo Co.). Named by Lt. Bruno Hecate, naval officer to the king of Spain, while on a surveying expedition in 1775, for his patron saint, Bruno (c. 1030-1101), founder of the Carthusian Order.

SAN BUENAVENTURA, Calif. (Ventura Co.). For Saint Bonaventura (or Bonaventure), a Franciscan saint of the 1200s.

SAN CARLOS For the river, which was named for Saint Charles Borromeo (1538-

1584). The stream was discovered by the Spanish in 1775 on the saint's day, November 4. See ST. CHARLES.
San Carlos, Ariz. (Gila Co.).
San Carlos Lake, Ariz.
San Carlos River, Ariz.

SAN CARLOS, Calif. (San Mateo Co.). For the ship *San Carlos*, which brought provisions to the colonists in Alta, Calif. It is also believed that it was named for Saint Charles's feast day, November 4, but there is some doubt. The immediate name comes from that of the San Carlos Land Company, which developed the town.

SAN CLEMENTE For Saint Clement, third pope and bishop of Rome.
San Clemente, Calif. (Orange Co.).
San Clemente Canyon, Calif.
San Clemente Island, Calif. Named by Sebastien Vizcaino on the saint's day, Nov. 23, 1602.

SAN CRISTOBAL WASH RIVER, Ariz. For one of the many San Cristobals in Central and South America. It flows northwest into Gila River.

SAND Descriptive.
Sand Creek, Ind. Flows SW and W into East Fork White R.
Sand Creek, Okla. Flows E into Caney R.
Sand Creek, Okla. Flows E into Beaver R.
Sand Creek, S.Dak. Flows SE into James R.
Sand Hills, Neb. For their shape.
Sand Island, Wis. One of the Apostles islands in L. Superior.
Sand Lake, Minn.
Sand Lake, Wis.
Sand Point, Mich. Extends into Saginaw Bay.
Sand Hill River, Minn. Flows W into Red R. For the sand dunes.
Sand Springs, Okla. (Tulsa Co.).

SANDERS Co., Mont. (co. seat, Thompson Falls). For Wilbur Fiske Sanders (1834-1905), Civil War veteran, legislator, and U.S. senator (1890-93).

SANDERSON, Tex. (co. seat of Terrell Co.). Probably for Thomas P. Sanderson, a railroad construction engineer, or possibly for two Sanderson brothers who owned a small ranch near the site.

SANDERSVILLE, Ga. (co. seat of Washington Co.). For an early settler named Sanders, or Saunders, who had a store at a crossroads.

SANDIA From Spanish, "watermelon."
Sandia, N.Mex. (Sandoval and Bernalillo Cos.).
Sandia Peak, N.Mex.

SAN DIEGO For San Diego de Alcala de Henares (Saint Didacus), Spanish Franciscan saint of the 1400s. He was born in Andalusia. Although he was uneducated, he distinguished himself for his knowledge, zeal, humility, and charity. During the plague in Rome in 1450, he attended the sick and continuously prayed for them.
San Diego Co., Calif. (co. seat, *San Diego*).
San Diego, Calif. (co. seat of *San Diego* Co.). Earlier, San Miguel San Diego de Alcala.
San Diego, Tex. (co. seat of Duval Co.).
San Diego Bay, Calif. Although the bay had been discovered earlier, Sebastian Vizcaino and his expedition entered it in November 1602 and named it on November 12, the saint's day, possibly also for his flagship, the *San Diego*.
San Diego River, Calif. Flows generally SW to Mission Bay.

SAN DIMAS, Calif. (Los Angeles Co.). For Saint Dismas, the robber crucified at the side of Christ and made a saint.

SAND LAKE, Alaska. Descriptive.

SANDOVAL Co., N.Mex. (co. seat, Bernalillo). For the Sandoval family, descendants of Juan de Dios Sandoval Martinez, who came to the area in 1692.

SANDPOINT, Idaho (co. seat of Bonner Co.). For a point of sandy land that extends into Pend Oreille Lake.

SAN GABRIEL For Saint Gabriel.
San Gabriel, Calif. (Los Angeles Co.).
San Gabriel Mountains, Calif.
San Gabriel Reservoir, Calif.
San Gabriel River, Calif.
San Gabriel River, Tex.
South San Gabriel, Calif. (Los Angeles Co.).

SANDUSKY. From a Wyandot word, now lost, which seems to have meant "cold water" or "pure water." Though the name ap-

Sandusky, Ohio, was a relatively quiet place in the 1800s, facing Lake Erie and a string of islands stretching out toward the Canadian shore. The view is from St. Paul's Church. [*New York Public Library*]

pears to have a Polish form, no evidence exists that it had such origin.

Sandusky Co., Ohio (co. seat, Fremont). For the river.

Sandusky, Mich. (co. seat of Sanilac Co.).

Sandusky, Ohio (co. seat of Erie Co.).

Sandusky Bay, Ohio, on L. Erie.

Sandusky River, Ohio. Flows W and N into L. Erie.

Upper Sandusky, Ohio (co. seat of Wyandot Co.).

SANDWICH For Sandwich, Kent, England.

Sandwich, Ill. (De Kalb Co.). For *Sandwich*, Mass.

Sandwich, Mass. (Barnstable Co.), town.

Sandwich Dome (peak), N.H.

SANDY. Descriptive.

Little Sandy River, Ky.

Sandy Brook, Mass.-Conn. Flows SE into Farmington R.

Sandy Creek, N.Y. Flows SW into Allegheny R.

Sandy Creek, Wyo. Flows S into Green R.

Sandy River, Me. Flows SE then NE into Kennebec R.

Sandy Stream, Me. Flows S into Carrabassett R.

Sandy Bay Mountain, Me.-Que.

Sandy Hook, Ky. (co. seat of Elliott Co.). For the hook in *Little Sandy* R.

Sandy Hook Bay, N.J.

Sandy Hook Peninsula, N.J. Separates *Sandy Hook* Bay from the Atlantic Ocean.

Sandy Lick Creek, Pa. Flows W into Redbank Creek. Also for the salt licks.

SANDY CITY, Utah (Salt Lake Co.). For Alexander ("Sandy") Kinghorn, the engineer on the first train coming from Salt Lake City in 1871. The place became known as Sandy's Station. The fact that the soil is sandy may also have encouraged the name.

SAN FERNANDO, Calif. (Los Angeles Co.). For Ferdinand III, king of Castile and León.

SANFORD, Fla. (co. seat of Seminole Co.). For Henry Shelton Sanford (1823-1891), founder. A brilliant student, he obtained a degree of Doctor of Laws at the University of Heidelberg and embarked on a career in the diplomatic service, beginning as secretary of the legation in St. Petersburg, Russia. He held the same post in Paris (1849) and later became chargé d'affaires. In 1861, after some years of law practice, he was appointed by President Lincoln as U.S. minister to Belgium.

SANFORD, Me. (York Co.), town and village. For the Sanford family. John Sanford (?-1653) originally owned the land, and his widow passed it on to their children.

SANFORD, Mount, Alaska, in the Wrangell Mountains. Named in 1885 by Lt. H. T. Allen for his ancestors, the Sanford family, and especially for Reuben Sanford, Allen's great-grandfather.

SANFORD, N.C. (co. seat of Lee Co.). Believed to have been named for C. O. Sanford, a railroad official.

SAN FRANCISCO For Saint Francis of Assisi (1182-1226), Italian friar and preacher and founder of the Franciscan order. The Presidio, or fortified area, was founded first. The Mission de los Dolores de San Francisco was established in October 1776, possibly on the 4th, the saint's day. The name had been applied to this general area of California (1769) by an early Spanish sea expedition.

San Francisco Co., Calif. (co. seat, *San Francisco*).

San Francisco, Calif. (co. seat of *San Francisco* Co.). Earlier, Yerba Buena.

San Francisco Bay, Calif.

San Francisco River, Ariz.-N.Mex.

South San Francisco (San Mateo Co.).

San Francisco, founded in 1776, was for many years the only major Pacific port in what is now the United States. This view from Russian Hill in 1862 shows a vital and prosperous community. Many of these buildings were destroyed in the great earthquake and fire of 1906. [*Lithograph by Charles Gifford. New York Historical Society*]

SANGAMON From Ojibway, probably "the outlet." The form indicates transliteration through French. The river was named first by French explorers as Saguimont.
Sangamon Co., Ill. (co. seat, Springfield).
Sangamon River, Ill. Flows generally NW to the Illinois R.

SANGER, Calif. (Fresno Co.). For Joseph Sanger, Jr. (?-1899), secretary-treasurer of the Railroad Yardmasters Association, who was in San Francisco when the town was named. He never had any official capacity with any railway company and never saw the town that bears his name. It is the site of the famous General Grant Tree, a *Sequoia gigantea* over 4,000 years old.

SAN GORGONIO MOUNTAIN, Calif. For Saint Gorgonius, a freedman of Emperor Diocletian, martyred on March 11, 303 A.D. His feast day is uncertain, either March 13th or Sept. 9th. Two other saints of the same name have feast days on Sept. 9th.

SANGRE DE CRISTO MOUNTAINS, N.Mex. From Spanish, "Blood of Christ," believed to have been so named because of the reddish tint on the snow at sundown.

SANILAC Co., Mich. (co. seat, Sandusky). For Sanilac, a Wyandot chief who was a friend of Gov. Lewis Cass of Michigan Territory.

SAN JACINTO Several saints carry the name Hyacinth or Hyacintha, the English translation of *Jacinto* or *Jacinta*. Many place names honor the different saints, and the name is usually bestowed on a site with plenty of water and where water hyacinths grow. The Polish Saint Hyacinth (?-1257) was a Dominican who founded monasteries in central and eastern Europe.
San Jacinto Co., Tex. (co. seat, Coldspring).
San Jacinto, Calif. (Riverside Co.). For the San Jacinto Ranchero, which was probably named for Hyacintha of Mariscotti (1585-1640), a lady of Viterbo, Italy, who became a member of the Order of Saint Francis.
San Jacinto Battlefield, Tex. Scene of battle between Sam Houston's troops and those of Santa Anna. Houston's defeat (April 1836) of Santa Anna assured Texas of independence.

San Jacinto, Mount, Calif.
San Jacinto River, Calif.
San Jacinto River, Tex. Flows generally S to San Jacinto Bay, a part of Galveston Bay.

SAN JOAQUIN Spanish form of *Saint Joachim*. The tradition, as told in the Apocrypha, is that he was the father of the Virgin Mary. Nothing is known about his life. He also is mentioned under other names: Sadoch, Jonachir, Eliacim, Cleopas, and Heli.
San Joaquin Co., Calif. (co. seat, Stockton). For the river.
San Joaquin River, Calif. Flows generally W to the Sacramento R. Named by Gabriel Moraga in the early 1800s for the saint's day, then March 20, the day he first reached the river.
San Joaquin Valley, Calif.

SAN JOSE Spanish form of ST. JOSEPH.
San Jose, Calif. (co. seat of Santa Clara Co.). Named (1768) by Jose de Galvez; Saint Joseph was patron saint of an earlier expedition to California.
San Jose River, N.Mex. Flows SE into Puerco R.
South San Jose Hills, Calif. (Los Angeles Co.).

SAN JUAN See ST. JOHN (the Baptist).
San Juan Co., Colo. (co. seat, Silverton).
San Juan Co., N.Mex. (co. seat, Aztec).
San Juan Co., Utah (co. seat, Monticello). For the river.
San Juan Co., Wash. (co. seat, Friday Harbor).
San Juan, Tex. (Hidalgo Co.). For John Clossner, whom the Mexicans called "San Juan" or "Saint John."
San Juan Channel, Wash., in Puget Sound. Apparently named first by the Spanish explorer Eliza. The name must have been influenced by that of Don Juan, viceroy of Mexico at the time. The *San* may have been prefixed by analogy and also with reference to *Apostolos* Valerianos, the probable true name of the navigator who went by the name of JUAN DE FUCA.
San Juan Creek, Calif.
San Juan Islands, Wash., in Puget Sound. San Juan Island is the largest of the group.
San Juan Mountains, Colo.-N.Mex., in the Rocky Mtns.

San Juan Natl. Forest, Colo.

San Juan River, Colo.-N.Mex.-Utah. Rises in the San Juan Mtns.; flows generally SW to the Colorado R.

SAN JUAN CAPISTRANO, Calif. (Orange Co.). For Saint John Capistrano (1385-1456), a priest who fought against the Turks' first invasion of Vienna.

SAN LEANDRO, Calif. (Alameda Co.). For Saint Leander, sixth-century archbishop of Seville.

SAN LORENZO, Calif. (Alameda Co.). For Saint Lawrence. See ST. LAWRENCE.

SAN LUIS Probably for Saint Louis of Toulouse, though apparently influenced by other places of the same name. See SAN LUIS OBISPO.

San Luis, Colo. (co. seat of Costilla Co.).

San Luis Creek, Colo.

SAN LUIS OBISPO For Saint Louis of Toulouse (1274-1297), son of King Charles II of Naples. He was sent to Spain as a hostage and while there studied under two Franciscans, taking the habit in 1296. Appointed by Boniface VIII, he took charge of the diocese of Toulouse but lived only a few months.

San Luis Obispo Co., Calif. (co. seat, *San Luis Obispo*).

San Luis Obispo, Calif. (co. seat of *San Luis Obispo* Co.). Founded on the site of Father Junipero Serra's Mission of *San Luis Obispo de Tolosa*, "St. Louis Bishop of Toulouse."

San Luis Obispo Bay, Calif.

SAN LUIS REY RIVER, Calif. For ST. LOUIS, king of France. It flows generally west into the Pacific Ocean at the Gulf of Santa Catalina.

SAN MANUEL, Ariz. (Pinal Co.). For the San Manuel Mine of the Magma Copper Company. The mine was named (c. 1925) by Anselino Laguna, probably for a patron saint, but which one is not certain.

SAN MARCOS. For Saint Mark the Evangelist. See ST. MARK'S RIVER.

San Marcos, Calif. (San Diego Co.).

San Marcos, Tex. (co. seat of Hays Co.).

SAN MARINO, Calif. (Los Angeles Co.). For a place in Emmitsburg, Md., which was probably named for the European republic of San Marino.

SAN MATEO. See ST. MATTHEW.

San Mateo Co., Calif. (co. seat, Redwood City).

San Mateo, Calif. (*San Mateo* Co.).

SAN MIGUEL. For Saint Michael. He is known as "the Archangel," the principal angel in the battle with Satan and his followers in Heaven. He is traditionally charged with rescuing souls from Satan's power, defending the people of God, and calling forth the dead to judgment.

San Miguel Co., Colo. (co. seat, Telluride).

San Miguel, N.Mex. (co. seat, Las Vegas).

San Miguel Island, Calif.

San Miguel Peak, N.Mex.

San Miguel River, Colo. Flows NW into Dolores R.

SAN PABLO, Calif. (Contra Costa Co.). For Saint Paul. See ST. PAUL.

SAN PATRICIO. For Saint Patrick. Although he was definitely a historical figure, the dates of his life and the place of his activities are difficult to ascertain. One account is that he was born in Scotland in 383, and at sixteen was carried off in captivity to Ireland. After learning Irish, he escaped to Britain and went to Gaul for his education. In 432 he returned to Ireland and began converting the Irish through his eloquent preaching. His efforts led to the establishment of the Catholic Church in Ireland. He is said to have died on March 17, 493, a date that can be seriously challenged. Another account gives his dates as c.409-493. It is possible that several Patricks have fused into one as far as historical accounts are concerned. He is patron saint of Ireland and of cathedrals in several counties.

San Patricio Co., Tex. (co. seat, Sinton). For the village.

San Patricio, Tex. (*San Patricio* Co.). Founded by James McGloin, an Irish colonist, and named *San Patricio Hibernia*, "Saint Patrick of Ireland," for his patron saint.

SAN PEDRO. Spanish form of ST. PETER.

San Pedro Mountain, N.Mex.

San Pedro River, N.Mex. Flows N into Gila River. Possibly for a Mexican place of the same name.

SANPETE Co., Utah (co. seat, Manti). Origin uncertain, but probably an anglicized form of SAN PITCH.

SAN PITCH RIVER, Utah. From Ute *sampitches*, "homelands," folk etymologized into its present form. It flows generally southwest into Sevier River.

SANPOIL RIVER, Wash. For a sub-tribe of the Spokane Indians. It flows south into Columbia River.

SAN RAFAEL. For Saint Raphael, guardian angel of humanity.
San Rafael, Calif. (co. seat of Marin Co.).
San Rafael Knob, Utah.
San Rafael Mountains, Calif.
San Rafael River, Utah. Flows into Green R.

SAN RAMON, Calif. (Contra Costa Co.). This name did not originally honor a saint, but the *San* was added in keeping with surrounding towns. The *Ramon* was supposedly given to it in honor of a *mayor domo*, "foreman," by the name of Ramon who at one time cared for sheep in the area.

SAN REMO, N.Y. (Suffolk Co.). Probably for San Remo, Italy, on the Riviera.

SAN SABA. From Spanish, short form of *San Sabado*, "Holy Saturday." The river was named first, for the day it was discovered by Spanish explorers.
San Saba Co., Tex. (co. seat, *San Saba*). For the town.
San Saba, Tex. (co. seat of *San Saba* Co.). For the river.
San Saba River, Tex. Flows generally NE to the Colorado R.

SANSBOIS MOUNTAIN, Okla. From French, "without wood."

SAN SIMON CREEK, N.Mex.-Ariz. Probably ultimately for Simon Peter. (See ST. PETER.) The present form of the name was most likely derived through folk etymologizing of different Spanish names. It flows northwest into Gila River.

SANSOM PARK VILLAGE, Tex. (Tarrant Co.). Formed from the promoter's name, with promotional *park* and *village* attached.

SANTA ANA, Calif. (co. seat of Orange Co.). For Saint Anne, mother of the Virgin Mary.

SANTA BARBARA For Saint Barbara, virgin martyr executed by her father because she had professed Christianity. The story is probably mythical, for no definite dates or details of her life have been found. One of the fourteen Holy Helpers, she is protectress against lightning, thunderstorms, fire, and impenitence. She is also patroness of mariners, architects, prisoners, stonemasons, gravediggers, and makers of certain war materials. Each feature and place derives its name from the channel, named on the saint's day, December 4, 1602, by the spanish commander Sebastian Vizcaino.
Santa Barbara Co., Calif. (co. seat, *Santa Barbara*).
Santa Barbara, Calif. (co. seat of *Santa Barbara* Co.).
Santa Barbara Channel, Calif.
Santa Barbara Islands, Calif.

SANTA CATALINA The island was named first, by Sebastian Vizcaino on Nov. 25, 1602, the feast day of Saint Catherine.
Santa Catalina, Gulf of, Calif.
Santa Catalina Island, Calif. In Gulf of *Santa Catalina*.

SANTA CLARA. For Saint Clare of Assisi (1194-1253), founder of the Poor Clares, an order that practiced extreme poverty, lived an ascetic life, and existed solely on alms. Her order was so rigorous that Pope Gregory IX entreated her to relax the rules, but she refused.
Santa Clara Co., Calif. (co. seat, San Jose). For the river.
Santa Clara, Calif. (*Santa Clara* Co.). Founded by Father Junipero Serra along with the Mission of Santa Clara de Asis.
Santa Clara Peak, N.Mex.
Santa Clara River, Calif. Flows generally W into the Pacific Ocean. Named by Juan Crespi, a member of a Spanish expedition that camped there August 9, 1769.

SANTA CRUZ. From Spanish, "Holy Cross."
Santa Cruz Co., Ariz. (co. seat, Nogales).
Santa Cruz Co., Calif. (co. seat, *Santa Cruz*).
Santa Cruz, Calif. (co. seat of *Santa Cruz* Co.). For the island.
Santa Cruz Island, Calif., in the Santa Barbara Islands. Apparently so named be-

cause a priest lost a staff which had the shape of a cross.

Santa Cruz Island, Calif. In the Santa Barbara Islands.

Santa Cruz River, Ariz.-Mexico.

SANTA FE. From Spanish, "Holy Faith."

Santa Fe Co., N.Mex. (co. seat, *Santa Fe*).

Santa Fe, N.Mex. (co. seat of *Santa Fe* Co.), state capital. Founded in 1610, it was the first European settlement west of the Mississippi.

Santa Fe Lake, Fla.

Santa Fe Natl. Forest, N.Mex.

Santa Fe River, Fla. Flows generally W to the Suwannee R.

Santa Fe Trail. Famous overland trail during the 1800s. It began at Independence, Mo. and terminated at Santa Fe, N.Mex.

Santa Fe Springs, Calif. (Los Angeles Co.).

SANTA LUCIA RANGE, Calif. For Saint Lucy; named by Sebastian Vizcaino on the saint's day, Dec. 13, 1602. See ST. LUCIE.

SANTA MARIA. For a saint, probably not the Virgin Mary.

Santa Maria, Calif. (Santa Barbara Co.).

Santa Maria River, Ariz.

Santa Maria South, Calif. (Santa Barbara Co.).

SANTA MONICA. For Saint Monica, mother of Saint Augustine.

Santa Monica, Calif. (Los Angeles Co.).

Santa Monica Bay, Calif.

Santa Monica Mountains, Calif.

SANTANONI PEAK, N.Y. Believed to be an Abnaki corruption of the French *Saint-Antoine*, for ST. ANTHONY.

SANTA PAULA, Calif. (Ventura Co.). Probably for Saint Paula, a Roman matron who became a disciple of Saint Jerome.

SANTA RITA PEAK, Calif. Probably for Saint Rita of Cassis (or Cascia) (?-1457). The saint's day is May 22nd.

SANTA ROSA. For Santa Rosa de Lima, or Saint Rose of Lima (1586-1617). Born in Lima, Peru, of Puerto Rican parents, she became the first American saint. From childhood she gave herself to prayer, virtue, and austerity. Her life was glorified by mystical visions and revelations.

Santa Rosa, Calif. (co. seat of Sonoma Co.).

Named on August 30, the saint's day, by Gen. Mariano Guadalupe Vallejo.

Santa Rosa, N.Mex. (co. seat of Guadalupe Co.).

Santa Rosa Island, Calif.

Santa Rosa Peak, Nev.

Santa Rosa Range, Nev.

SANTA ROSA. For Santa Rosa de Viterbo, or Saint Rose of Viterbo (1235-1252), a virgin saint noted for her piety and poverty. She was canonized in 1457.

Santa Rosa Co., Fla. (co. seat, Milton).

Santa Rosa Island, Fla.

SANTEE, Calif. (San Diego Co.). For Milton Santee, the first postmaster.

SANTEE RIVER, S.C. For the Siouan tribe, meaning unknown, for no words from the language have survived. Formed by the confluence of Congaree and Wateree rivers, it flows southeast into the Atlantic Ocean.

SANTIAM. For the Indian tribe.

North Santiam River, Ore. Flows W to join *South Santiam* R.

Santiam River, Ore. Flows into Willamette R.

South Santiam River, Ore. Flows NW to join *North Santiam* R. to form *Santiam* R.

SAPELO ISLAND, Ga. An anglicized form of Zapala, for the province in Spain.

SAPPA CREEK, Kan.-Neb. From Sioux, "black." Formed by North and South Forks, it flows into Harlan County Reservoir.

SAPPINGTON, Mo. (independent city in St. Louis Co.). For a local citizen.

SAPULPA, Okla. (co. seat of Creek Co.). For a Creek Indian, James Sapulpa. The name means "sweet potato."

SARANAC. Origin unknown, possibly from an Iroquoian word.

Saranac Lakes, N.Y. Consists of three lakes, Upper, Middle, and Lower.

Saranac River, N.Y. Flows NE through the three lakes into L. Champlain.

Saranac Lake, N.Y. (Franklin and Essex Cos.).

SARASOTA. For a Seminole village near the site of the city. The name means "point of rocks."

Sarasota Co., Fla. (co. seat; *Sarasota*).
Sarasota, Fla. (co. seat of *Sarasota* Co.).
Sarasota Bay, Fla.
Sarasota South, Fla. (*Sarasota* Co.).
Sarasota Southeast, Fla. (*Sarasota* Co.).
Sarasota Springs, Fla. (*Sarasota* Co.).

SARATOGA. Possibly a Mohawk name, "springs from the hillside." Another explanation is Mahican, from an Iroquoian term, "beaver place." Another translation "the place of the miraculous water in a rock" is obviously fanciful and invented after the springs were used for health purposes. Matters are further complicated by the fact that Saratoga was originally on the Hudson River.
Saratoga Co., N.Y. (co. seat, Ballston Spa).
Saratoga, Calif. (Santa Clara Co.). For the resemblance of its springs to those at *Saratoga Springs*, N.Y.
Saratoga Lake, N.Y.
Saratoga Springs, N.Y. Famous health resort.

SARDINIA, N.Y. (Erie Co.). Possibly named by General Ezra Nott, a devout Baptist and one of the town's first settlers, for a hymn called "Sardinia."

SARDIS. For the ancient city in Asia Minor, mentioned in the Book of Revelations.
Sardis, Miss. (a co. seat of Panola Co.).
Sardis Lake, Miss.

SARGENT Co., N.Dak. (co. seat, Forman). For H. E. Sargent, a railway official interested in developing the Red River Valley.

SARITA, Tex. (co. seat of Kenedy Co.). For Capt. Mifflin Kenedy's daughter Sarita, or possibly for Sarita Kenedy, daughter of Mrs. John G. Kenedy.

SARNIA, Ont. (co. seat of Lambton Co.). Named in 1835 by Sir John Colborne, lieutenant governor of Upper Canada, and former lieutenant governor of the island of Guernsey, which the Romans had called *Sarnia*.

SARPY Co., Neb. (co. seat, Papillion). For Peter A. Sarpy (1805-1865), an early settler and prominent Nebraska citizen.

SASKATCHEWAN. From Cree *kishiska*, "rapid," plus *djiwan*, "current." The name was first used to describe the river and appeared in fur-trade literature in 1754.
Saskatchewan, Canadian province. Settled: 1774. Entered confederation: 1905. Cap.: Regina. Flower: Prairie Lily.
Saskatchewan River, Sask. Flows E into L. Winnipeg.

SASKATOON, Sask. From Indian, for the name of a local red berry; named in 1882 by John N. Lake of the Temperance Colonization Society of Toronto.

SASSAFRAS MOUNTAIN, S.C. For the tree, *Sassafras albidum*.

SATILLA. Named for Saint Illa, by Spanish expeditionary forces. The river was named first.
Satilla, Ga. (Wayne Co.).
Satilla River, Ga. Flows SE into the Atlantic Ocean.
Satilla Bluff, Ga. (Camden Co.).

SATSOP RIVER, Wash. From a Salish Indian tribal name, believed to mean "on the creek." Formed by three forks, West, Middle, and East, it flows south into Chehalis River.

SATUS CREEK, Wash. Different interpretations exist: from a Yakima word meaning "rich land": or for a Yakima subtribe, whose name is translated as "people or the rye prairie" by the Bureau of American Ethnology. It flows northeast into Yakima River.

SAUGATUCK. From Paugusett, "tidal outlet."
Saugatuck, Conn. (Fairfield Co.), town.
Saugatuck Reservoir, Conn.
Saugatuck River, Conn. Flows SE and S into Long Island Sound.

SAUGERTIES. A folk etymologized form of the town name first recorded in 1663 as *Zager's kiletie*, from Dutch, "Zager's streamlet." Zager was the first Dutch settler on the stream.
Saugerties, N.Y. (Ulster Co.).
Saugerties South, N.Y. (Ulster Co.).

SAUGUS, Mass. (Essex Co.), town. From Algonquian, "small outlet," or it may mean "wet" or "overflowing grassland."

SAUK. A variant form of SAC.
Sauk Co., Wis. (co. seat, Baraboo).
Sauk, Ill. (Cook Co.).

Sauk Lake, Minn. at *Sauk Center.*

Sauk River, Minn. Flows generally E to the Mississippi R.

Sauk River, Wash. Flows NW into Skagit R.

Sauk Center, Minn. (Stearns Co.). On the *Sauk* River, which was named for a small group of Indians who came as refugees from their own tribe to what is now Osakis Lake, the source of the *Sauk* R.

Sauk Rapids, Minn. (Benton Co.). For the rapids on the Mississippi R., just below the mouth of the *Sauk* R.

SAULT STE. MARIE From French, "the rapids of Saint Mary"; so named by early missionaries, including Père Marquette.

Sault Ste. Marie, Mich. (co. seat of Chippewa Co.).

Sault Ste. Marie, Ont. (co. seat of Algoma Co.).

SAUNDERS Co., Neb. (co. seat, Wahoo). For Alvin Saunders (1817-1899), Nebraska Territory governor (1861-67), also active in the territorial legislature.

SAUSALITO, Calif. (Marin Co.). From Spanish, "little grove of willows."

SAVAGE, Minn. (Scott Co.). For Marion Willis Savage (1859-1916), horse trainer and breeder of racers. He constructed an electric railway to connect outlying cities with Minneapolis.

SAVANNA, Ill. (Carroll Co.). A variant spelling of SAVANNAH.

SAVANNAH From the Spanish form of the Carib Indian word, *zabana*, possibly connoting a level grassy plain, often marshy. Others state the name is the Spanish rendering of the Shawnee name for the Savannah River, near which that tribe lived.

Savannah, Ga. (co. seat of Chatham Co.). For the river.

Savannah, Mo. (co. seat of Andrew Co.). For

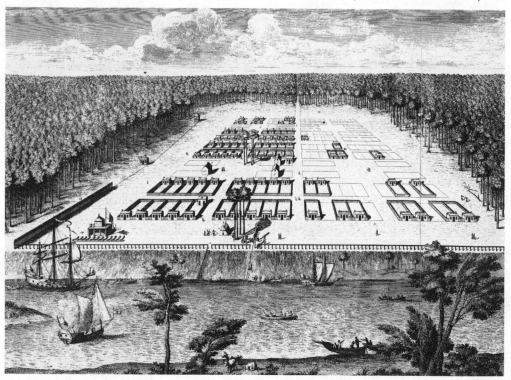

One-year-old Savannah, Georgia, included eighty-four identical houses in four wards and such structures as a guardhouse, tabernacle, and courthouse, store, mill and parsonage. This 1820 map shows the city as it was in 1734. [*New York Public Library*]

the first white child, Savannah Woods, born there; so named because the parents came from *Savannah*, Ga. Or it may have been named out of deference to Samuel Crowley, who also came from *Savannah*.

Savannah, Tenn. (co. seat of Hardin Co.).
Savannah River, Ga.-S.C. Forming most of the Georgia-South Carolina border, flows generally SW to the Atlantic Ocean.

SAWMILL For a lumber mill or sawmill.
Sawmill Bay, Alaska.
Sawmill Lake, Ill.
Sawmill River, Mass. Flows generally W into Connecticut R.
Sawmill River, N.Y. Flows SSW into the Hudson R.

SAWTOOTH RANGE, Idaho. For the resemblance of the peaks to sawteeth.

SAWYER Co., Wis. (co. seat, Hayward). For Philetus Sawyer (1816-1900), U.S. representative (1865-75) and U.S. senator (1881-93).

SAXTONS RIVER Believed to have been named for a Mr. Saxton who drowned in the stream.
Saxtons River, Vt. (Windham Co.), town.
Saxtons River, Vt. Flows SE into Connecticut R.

SAYBROOK Probably for William Fiennes, 1st Viscount Say and Sele (1582-1662), a participant in the Puritan Revolution. He was active in the colonization of America and showed a particular interest in this area of Connecticut.
Saybrook, Conn. (Middlesex Co.).
Old Saybrook, Conn. (Middlesex Co.), town.

SAYERVILLE, N.J. (Middlesex Co.). For James F. Sayer, Jr., founder of Sayer and Fisher Brick Company, which at that time was one of the largest brick manufacturers in the world.

SAYRE, Robert H. (1824-?), a railway developer.
Sayre, Okla. (co. seat of Beckham Co.).
Sayre, Pa. (Bradford Co.). Sayre was superintendent of the Lehigh Valley railroad in 1873.

SAYVILLE, N.Y. (Suffolk Co.). Originally intended to be named Seaville for its location on Long Island's Great South Bay, this town ended up as Sayville because a clerk at the town meeting, when the name was given, misspelled it. After the error was discovered, the post office department prevailed upon the town to keep the name because it was unique.

SCANTIC RIVER, Conn. From Nipmuc, "river branch." It flows west and southwest into the Connecticut River.

SCAPEGOAT MOUNTAIN, Mont. Probably for an incident now forgotten, but involving blame.

SCARBOROUGH, Me. (Cumberland Co.), town. For Scarborough, Yorkshire, England.

SCARSDALE, N.Y. (Westchester Co.). For the Manor of Scarsdale, owned by Caleb Heathcote, who came from a Scarsdale in England.

SCHAUMBURG, Ill. (Du Page Co.). For a local citizen named Schaum, with -*burg* added.

SCHELL, A. J., an army officer who commanded a detachment of troops to protect the mail service. The stream was named first.
Schell Creek, Nev.
Schell Creek Range, Nev.
Schell Creek North Peak, Nev.
Schell Creek South Peak, Nev.

SCHENECTADY For the Mohawk village of *Schaunactada* near the present site of Schenectady or a little south of Albany. The name has been variously defined as "on the other side of the pinelands" or "the other side of the plains."
Schenectady Co., N.Y. (co. seat, *Schenectady*).
Schenectady, N.Y. (co. seat of *Schenectady* Co.).

SCHENEVUS CREEK, N.Y. From Iroquoian, "hoeing of corn," but may also be the name of a local chief. The present spelling was probably influenced by a Dutch form. It flows southwest into Susquehanna River.

SCHENOB BROOK, Conn.-Mass. From Mahican, "mouth of pond." It may be derived from *ashimops*, "water spring at the rocky ledge." It flows north and northeast into Housatonic River.

SCHERERVILLE, Ind. (Lake Co.). For Scherer Wright, founder.

SCHERTZ, Tex. (Guadalupe Co.). For Sebastian Schertz (1822-1890), who donated land for the site. An earlier name was Cutoff.

SCHIESTLER PEAK, Wyo. For Felix Schiestler, early settler.

SCHILLER PARK, Ill. (Cook Co.). For Johann Christoph Friedrich von Schiller (1759-1805), German poet, dramatist, and composer; named by early citizens who formed a singing society, the Schiller Leidentofel.

SCHLEICHER Co., Tex. (co. seat, Eldorado). For Gustave Schleicher (1823-1879), legislator. Confederate army veteran, and U.S. representative (1875-79).

SCHLEY Co., Ga. (co. seat, Ellaville). For William Schley (1758-1858), legislator, jurist, U.S. representative, and governor (1835-37).

SCHOFIELD, Wis. (Marathon Co.). For William Scholfield, a sawmill owner, with a slight change in spelling.

SCHOHARIE From Iroquoian, "driftwood." Variants exist, such as *skoharle, towasschoher, shoary, skohary,* and *schughhorre.* The creek was named first.
Schoharie Co., N.Y. (co. seat, *Schoharie*).
Schoharie, N.Y. (co. seat of *Schoharie* Co.).
Schoharie Creek, N.Y. Flows generally NE
   to the Mohawk R.
Schoharie Reservoir, N.Y.

SCHOODIC Probably from Abnaki, "place of trout," but in Algonquian dialects the same form can also mean "place of fire" (for burned-over land) and "point of land."
Schoodic Lake, Me.
Schoodic Point, Me.

SCHOOLBOOK GLACIER, Wyo. So named because it exhibits all features of a glacier.

SCHOOLCRAFT Co., Mich. (co. seat, Manistique). For Henry Rowe Schoolcraft

(1793-1864), explorer, territorial legislator, author of many books on Indians, and ethnologist. He coined many names that had a superficial resemblance to original Indian words.

SCHOOLEYS MOUNTAIN, N.J. For the Scholey family, specifically for Thomas Scholey, with a change in spelling. He came from England in 1677 to join a colony of the Society of Friends and settled in the area.

SCHRADER CREEK, Pa. For a local settler. It flows northeast into Susquehanna River.

SCHROON Derivation uncertain, but there is strong Dutch spelling influence, which may be the basis of the belief that the name is for Duchess Scharon, of Louis XIV's court. Also claimed from Iroquoian *sknoonapus*, in reference to a lake, possibly meaning "the largest lake."
Schroon Lake, N.Y.
Schroon Mountain, N.Y.
Schroon River, N.Y.

SCHURZ MOUNTAIN, Wyo., in Yellowstone Natl. Park. For Carl Schurz, secretary of the interior (1877-81) under Hayes.

SCHUYLER, Philip John (1733-1804), New York soldier and statesman who served in the French and Indian Wars and the American Revolution. He was a member of the Continental Congress (1775-81) and a U.S. senator (1789-91; 1797-98); Alexander Hamilton was his son-in-law.
Schuyler Co., Ill. (co. seat, Rushville).
Schuyler Co., Mo. (co. seat, Lancaster).
Schuyler Co., N.Y. (co. seat, Watkins Glen).

SCHUYLER, Neb. (co. seat of Colfax Co.). For Schuyler COLFAX (for whom the county was also named).

SCHUYLER FALLS, N.Y. (Clinton Co.), town. For a prominent early settler.

SCHUYLKILL From Dutch *schuy*, "hidden," and *kill*, "stream." The name was first applied to the river.
Schuylkill Co., Pa. (co. seat, Pottsville).
Schuylkill, Pa. (*Schuylkill* Co.).
Schuylkill River, Pa. Flows generally SE to
   the Delaware R.
Schuylkill Haven, Pa. (*Schuylkill* Co.).

SCHWATKA MOUNTAIN, Alaska, in Brooks Range. For Frederick Schwatka, U.S. Army lieutenant, who explored' the Yukon in 1883.

SCIOTO From an Iroquoian word of uncertain meaning, said by some scholars to be Wyandot, "deer."
Scioto Co., Ohio (co. seat, Portsmouth).
Scioto River, Ohio.

SCIPIO PEAK, Utah, in the Canyon Mountains. For Publius Cornelius Scipio, Roman general who defeated Hannibal.

SCITUATE From Algonquian, possibly "cold stream." It may also come from *see*, "salt," *tuck*, "stream," and *et*, "at": "at the salt stream."
North Scituate, Mass. (Plymouth Co.).
Scituate, Mass. (Plymouth Co.), town and village.
Scituate, R.I. (Providence Co.), town.
Scituate Reservoir, R.I.

SCOBEY, Mont. (co. seat of Daniels Co.). For C. R. A. Scobey, Indian fighter and Indian agent.

SCONTICUT POINT, Mass. Extends into Buzzards Bay. From Narraganset, "at the end of the cold stream" or possibly "at the end of the crooked stream."

SCOTCH PLAINS, N.J. (Union Co.). For the Scottish families from Perth Amboy, N.J., who settled here in the 1680s.

SCOTIA, N.Y. (Schenectady Co.). A variant of SCIOTO.

SCOTLAND For Scotland, in the British Isles, the former home of early settlers or their ancestors.
Scotland Co., Mo. (co. seat, Memphis).
Scotland Co., N.C. (co. seat, Laurinburg).
Scotland Neck, N.C. (Halifax Co.). Named by Scotch–Irish settlers from Scotland Landing, Jamestown, Va.
Scotlandville, La. (East Baton Rouge Parish).

SCOTT Co., Ark. (co. seat, Waldron). For Andrew Scott, an early Arkansas Territory jurist.

SCOTT, Charles (?-1813), Kentucky soldier and statesman. Active in the French and Indian Wars, he became a general in the American Revolution and was a prisoner of war (1780-83). He later served as governor of Kentucky (1808-12).

Scott Co., Ill. (co. seat, Winchester). For *Scott* Co., Ky.
Scott Co., Ind. (co. seat, *Scottsburg*).
Scott Co., Ky. (co. seat, Georgetown).
Scott, Ill. (*Scott* Co.).
Scottsburg, Ind. (co. seat of *Scott* Co.).

SCOTT Co., Miss. (co. seat, Forest). For Abram M. Scott (?-1833), governor of Mississippi (1832-33).

SCOTT Co., Mo. (co. seat, Benton). For John Scott (1782-1861), first U.S. representative from Missouri who served in several Congresses.

SCOTT, Winfield (1786-1866), Virginia soldier whose military career extended from the War of 1812 through the Civil War. He became general in chief of the U.S. Army in 1841 and was the military commander during the Mexican War (1846-48). Although a southerner, he was commander of the Union armies at the beginning of the Civil War and it was his strategy, the so-called anaconda policy of encirclement and isolation, that later defeated the Confederacy. He was an unsuccessful Whig candidate for President (1852). See WINFIELD.
Scott Co., Iowa (co. seat, Davenport).
Scott Co., Kan. (co. seat, *Scott City*).
Scott Co., Minn. (co. seat, Shakopee).
Scott Co., Tenn. (co. seat, Huntsville).
Scott Co., Va. (co. seat, Gate City).
Scott City, Kan. (co. seat of *Scott* Co.).
Scottsville, Ky. (co. seat of Allen Co.).

SCOTTDALE, Pa. (Westmoreland Co.). For Col. Thomas Alexander Scott (1823-1881), appointed assistant secretary of war (1861) under Lincoln.

SCOTTS BLUFF (or Scottsbluff). For a prominent bluff on the North Platte River, which was named for Hiram Scott, who died there. He was a member of the Bonneville expedition of 1832.
Scotts Bluff Co., Neb. (co. seat, Gering).
Scottsbluff, Neb. (*Scotts Bluff* Co.).
Scotts Bluff Natl. Monument, Neb.

SCOTTSBORO, Ala. (Jackson Co.). For Robert T. Scott, an early settler.

SCOTTSDALE, Ariz. (Maricopa Co.). For Winfield Scott (1837-1910), an early settler and founder.

The hero of many campaigns, Gen. Winfield Scott scored his greatest successes during the Mexican War culminating with his triumphant entry into Mexico City. His enormous popularity was not quite strong enough to carry him into the White House. In 1852 he was the Whig candidate for president (the last from that party) and lost to Franklin Pierce by some 200,000 votes. [*New York Public Library*]

SCOTTS VALLEY, Calif. (Santa Cruz Co.). For Hiram Daniel Scott, landowner and sailor.

SCRAGGLY LAKE, Me. Descriptive and uncomplimentary of the lake outline and area.

SCRANTON, Pa. (co. seat of Lackawanna Co.). For the Scranton brothers, George Whitfield (1811-1861) and Seldon T., and their cousin, Joseph H. Scranton (1813-1872). They developed the ironworks and founded the enterprises that made the city known. Earlier names were Lackawanna, Harrison, and Scrantonia.

SCREVEN Co., Ga. (co. seat, Sylvania). For James Screven (?-1778), a general in the American Revolution, killed in action. The spelling *Scriven* is sometimes used.

SCURRY Co., Tex. (co. seat, Snyder). For Gen. William Read Scurry (1821-1864), attorney, veteran of the Mexican War, publisher of the *Austin State Gazette*, and Con-

federate army officer, killed at the Battle of Jenkins Ferry.

SEABROOK, N.H. (Rockingham Co.), town. For a small river that flows into the Atlantic Ocean.

SEABROOK, Tex. (Harris Co.). For Seabrook Sydner, an early setter.

SEA CLIFF, N.Y. (Nassau Co.). So named because it is on a cliff overlooking Long Island Sound.

SEAFORD, Del. (Sussex Co.). For Seaford, East Sussex, England; also descriptive of the shallow area in a river.

SEAGOVILLE, Tex. (Dallas Co.). For T. K. Seago, an early settler, first merchant, and first postmaster.

SEAL BEACH, Calif. (Orange Co.). For seals seen offshore.

SEALY, Tex. (Austin Co.). For George Sealy, a landowner and promoter of a railroad through the area.

500

SEARCY, Richard (1796-1832), lawyer, jurist, and legislator.
Searcy Co., Ark. (co. seat, Marshall).
Searcy, Ark. (co. seat of White Co.).

SEARLES For John and Dennis Searles, discoverers of borax, a major industry.
Searles Lake, Calif.
Searles Valley, Calif. (San Bernardino Co.).

SEASIDE Descriptive.
Seaside, Calif. (Monterey Co.).
Seaside, Ore. (Clatsop Co.). Also for a hotel, Seaside House.

SEATTLE From the name of a local Indian chief, whose name was spelled *See-yah* and *Sealth*.
Seattle, Wash. (co. seat of King Co.).
Seattle, Mount, Alaska, in St. Elias Mtns. For *Seattle*, Wash.

SEBAGO LAKE, Me. From Abnaki, "big lake."

SEBASTIAN Co., Ark. (co. seats, Fort Smith and Greenwood). For William King Sebastian (1812-1865), jurist and U.S. senator (1848-61).

SEBASTICOOK. From Penobscot-Abnaki, "almost-through-place."
Sebasticook Lake, Me.
Sebasticook River, Me. Flows SW into Kennebec R.

SEBASTOPOL, Calif. (Sonoma Co.). A variant spelling of *Sevastopol*, a port city and naval base in the southern Crimea.

SEBEC LAKE, Me. From Abnaki, "much water."

SEBOEIS From Abnaki, "small lake."
Seboeis Lake, Me. (Piscataquis Co.).
Seboeis River, Me. Flows S from *Seboeis* L. into Penobscot R.

SEBOOMOOK LAKE, Me. From Abnaki, "near large stream."

SEBRING, George Eugene, owner of a pottery factory in Sebring, Ohio.
Sebring, Fla. (co. seat of Highlands Co.).
Sebring, Ohio (Mahoning Co.).

SECAUCUS, N.J. (Hudson Co.). From an Indian word meaning "snake land."

SECOND CONNECTICUT LAKE, N.H. Lies north of First Connecticut Lake. See also CONNECTICUT.

SECOND LAKE, Me. So named because it is the second of two lakes, although the first one is named Grand Lake.

SEDALIA, Mo. (co. seat of Pettis Co.) . For Sarah Elvira Smith by her father, founder. *Sed* was a pet name for Sarah; the ending *alia* "came as an inspiration." A strangely popular name, it has since appeared in a number of states.

Seattle, Washington, was just a small lumber town in the mid-1800s, as in this view of the town looking west toward Puget Sound. [*Watercolor by Harrison Eastman. New York Historical Society*]

SEDAN, Kan. (co. seat of Chautauqua Co.). For Sedan, France.

SEDANKA ISLAND, Alaska. In Fox Islands. From Aleut, "braided" or "curled."

SEDGWICK, John (1813-1864), a Union general in the Civil War, killed in action at Spottsylvania, Va.
Sedgwick Co., Colo. (co. seat, Julesburg).
Sedgwick Co., Kan. (co. seat, Wichita).
Sedgwick, Kan. (*Sedgwick* and Harvey Cos.).

SEDRO-WOOLLEY, Wash. (Skagit Co.). From the consolidation of two towns in 1898. *Sedro* is a derivative of one of the original town names, Cedro, for the fine cedars in the area, with a Spanish ending, while *-Woolley* was for P. A. Woolley, town founder.

SEEKONK, Mass. (Bristol Co.), town. From Algonquian, probably "at the outlet," or it may be from *seaki*, "black," and *honk*, "goose."

SEGUIN, Tex. (co. seat of Guadalupe Co.). For Juan Seguin (1807-1890), a colonel in the Texas Cavalry at the Battle of San Jacinto.

SELAH, Wash. (Yakima Co.). From a local Indian word, "still water," descriptive of a section of a nearby river.

SELAWIK LAKE, Alaska. For an Eskimo tribal name.

SELBY, S.Dak. (co. seat of Walworth Co.). For a railway official.

SELINSGROVE, Pa. (Snyder Co.). Founded and named by Capt. Anthony Seling or Selin, a veteran of the American Revolution.

SELKIRK, Man. For Thomas Douglas, 5th Earl of Selkirk (1771-1820), who founded the Red River settlement (1815).

SELLERSBURG, Ind. (Clark Co.). For Moses W. Sellers, a proprietor and Baptist minister.

SELMA, Ala. (co. seat of Dallas Co.). From the Ossian poems by James McPherson (1736-1796). In the poems, *selma* is supposed to mean "a high seat or throne," and here it is applied to the high northern bank of the Alabama River. Earlier names were Bienville Bluff, High Soapstone, and Moore's Landing. The present name was chosen by a land company formed (1817) by William Rufus King.

SELMA, Calif. (Fresno Co.). For the daughter of Max Gruenberg, or for Selma Michelson Kingsbury, wife of an official of the Central Pacific railroad.

SELMER, Tenn. (co. seat of McNairy Co.). For SELMA, Ala. The man who submitted the name to the Post Office Department misspelled it.

SELWAY RIVER, Idaho. For the Selway family, early Western settlers. It flows north and West into Clearwater River.

SEMIDI ISLANDS, Alaska. In the Pacific Ocean. From Russian, "seven," for seven islands, although there are actually nine.

SEMINOE For Basil Cimineau Lajeunnesse, a French trapper and guide who married an Indian woman named Cimineau and added her name to his. The spelling of the name was Anglicized.
Seminoe Mountains, Wyo.
Seminoe Reservoir, Wyo. For the mountains.

SEMINOLE For the Muskhogean tribe, who lived in Florida until the conclusion of the Seminole War (1835-42), which concluded when Osceola, the great chief, was captured by treachery on the part of the U.S. Army. Remnants of the tribe moved into the Everglades and descendants still live there. The larger group of survivors were forced to move to Oklahoma. The name is from Creek, "the separate ones." It has also been translated as "runaway," but with a connotation of separateness.
Seminole Co., Fla. (co. seat, Sanford).
Seminole Co., Ga. (co. seat, Donaldsonville).
Seminole Co., Okla. (co. seat, Wewoka).
Seminole, Okla. (*Seminole* Co.).
Seminole, Tex. (co. seat of Gaines Co.).
Seminole, Lake, Fla.-Ga.

SENATOBIA, Miss. (co. seat of Tate Co.). From Choctaw, *sen-ato-ho-ba*, said to be the name of a chief, "White Sycamore."

SENECA For the Senecas, who belonged to the Iroquoian linguistic stock and were one of the Five Nations of the Iroquois. They

The Seminoles of southern Florida are among the few American Indian tribes to live in a wet, semitropical area — in or near the Everglades. Their homes and dress more closely resemble those of the Indians of Central America than those in the United States and Canada. [*Museum of Natural History, New York*]

were located in what is now New York in the area between Seneca Lake and the Genesee River. The name probably means "stony area," although other interpretations have been advanced. Through transliteration and folk etymology, it acquired its classical shape.
Seneca Co., N.Y. (co. seat, Waterloo).
Seneca Co., Ohio (co. seat, Tiffin).
Seneca, Kan. (co. seat of Nemaha Co.).
Seneca Lake, N.Y. The largest of the Finger Lakes.
Seneca Lake, Ohio.
Seneca River, N.Y. Flows generally NE to join the Oneida R. to form the Oswego R.
Seneca Falls, N.Y. (*Seneca* Co.). For falls on the *Seneca* R.

SENECA, S.C. (Oconee Co.). For a Cherokee tribe that lived nearby.

SENTINEL BUTTE, N.Dak. So named because the peak was used as a lookout. The graves of two Indian sentinels are said to be on the top.

SENTINEL PEAK, Ore., in the Wallowa Mountains. Probably so named because it stands somewhat apart from others.

SEPT-ÎLES, Que. (Saguenay Co.) From French, "seven islands," although there are actually only six.

SEPULCHER MOUNTAIN, Wyo., in Yellowstone Natl. Park. For a tomb-like rock on its northwest slopes; the rock has a prominent footstone and a headstone.

SEPULGA RIVER, Ala. Probably from Creek Indian, "pine tree grove." It flows south into Conecuh River.

SEQUATCHIE From Cherokee, "hog river"; also for a Cherokee chief.
Sequatchie Co., Tenn. (co. seat, Dunlap).
Sequatchie River, Tenn.

SEQUOIA NATL. PARK, Calif. Established to preserve, and named for, the giant redwood trees, *Sequoia gigantea*. The tree was named for Sequoya, inventor of the Cherokee alphabet; see SEQUOYA Co., Okla.

SEQUOYAH Co., Okla. (co. seat, Sallisaw). From the name of a district of the Cherokee Nation, which was named for George Guess (c.1773-1843), who invented the Cherokee alphabet. His Indian name is Sequoyah.

SESSIONS MOUNTAIN, Wyo. For Byron Sessions, Mormon pioneer.

SETAUKET From Algonquian, probably "river-mouth-at."
East Setauket, N.Y. (Suffolk Co.).
Setauket, N.Y. (Suffolk Co.).

SEVEN HILLS, Ohio (Cuyahoga Co.). Descriptive and reminiscent of the famous Seven Hills of Rome.

SEVERNA PARK, Md. (Anne Arundel Co.). For the Severn River, on which it is located, in turn for a river in England and Wales.

SEVIER Co., Ark. (co. seat, De Queen). For Ambrose Hundley Sevier (1801-1848), statesman. He was a U.S. senator (1836-48) and minister to Mexico (1848).

SEVIER, John (1745-1815), statesman active in the formation of the state of Tennessee. He served as first governor of Franklin (the first name of the state). When the name was changed, he served as first and third governor of Tennessee (1796-81; 1803-09) and as a U.S. representative (1811-15).
Sevier Co., Tenn. (co. seat, *Sevierville*).
Sevier Co., Utah (co. seat, Richfield).
Sevier Lake, Utah.
Sevier River, Utah.
Sevier Bridge Reservoir, Utah.
Sevierville, Tenn. (co. seat of *Sevier* Co.).

SEWARD, William Henry (1801-1872), statesman. He served as secretary of state (1861-69) under both Lincoln and Andrew Johnson. Although he was governor of New York (1838-42) and also a U.S. senator, he is remembered chiefly for his negotiating the purchase of Alaska (1867).
Seward Co., Kan. (co. seat, Liberal).
Seward Co., Neb. (co. seat, *Seward*).
Seward, Alaska.
Seward, Neb. (co. seat of *Seward* Co.).
Seward Glacier, Alaska.
Seward Mountain, N.Y.
Seward Mountains, Alaska.
Seward Peninsula, Alaska. Extends into Bering Strait.

SEWICKLEY, Pa. (Allegheny Co.). For an Indian tribe. Earlier names were Fifetown, Dogtown, Contention, and Devil's Race Track.

SEYMOUR, Thomas H. (1807-1868), governor of Connecticut (1850-53).
Seymour, Conn. (New Haven Co.), town.
Seymour Point, Conn.

SEYMOUR, Ind. (Jackson Co.). For a civil engineer.

SEYMOUR, Tex. (co. seat of Baylor Co.). For a stream, which was named for Seymour Monday, a famous character in early days, who camped on the stream.

SEYMOUR LAKE, Vt. For Israel Seymour, early settler and landowner.

SEYMOUR POND, Mass. On Cape Cod. For a local settler.

SEYMOURVILLE, La. (Iberville Parish). For Frank Seymour, the first postmaster.

SHACKELFORD Co., Tex. (co. seat, Albany). For John Shackelford (1790-1857), who, though trained as a physician, spent much of his career as a legislator. A veteran of the War of 1812, he organized the Red Rovers, an army that took part in the Texas War of Independence. He was captured by the Mexicans but later released.

SHADEHILL RESERVOIR, S.Dak. On Grant River. Named for the hill, which was named for M. L. Shade, a highway commissioner.

SHADYSIDE, Ohio (Belmont Co.). Probably promotional.

SHAFTER, Calif. (Kern Co.). For Gen. William ("Pecos Bill") Shafter (1835-1906), commander in Cuba during the Spanish-American War.

SHAKER HEIGHTS, Ohio (Cuyahoga Co.). For a former colony of Shakers.

SHAKOPEE, Minn. (co. seat of Scott Co.). From Siouan, "six," a hereditary name of chieftains.

SHALLOW LAKE, Me. Descriptive.

SHAMOKIN, Pa. (Northumberland Co.). For a Shamokin Creek, which was named for an Algonquin village that had once been there. The name is thought to mean "eel place."

SHAMROCK, Tex. (Wheeler Co.). For the national floral emblem of Ireland, usually associated with good luck.

SHANK LAKE, Mich. Descriptive of its long and narrow shape.

SHANNON Co., Mo. (co. seat, Eminence). For George F. Shannon (1785-1836), a member of the Lewis and Clark expedition.

SHANNON Co., S.Dak. For Peter Shannon (1821-?), Dakota Territory jurist. The county is attached to Fall River County for administrative purposes.

SHARKEY Co., Miss. (co. seat, Rolling Fork). For William Lewis Sharkey (1798-1873), jurist and legislator. He served as governor in 1865.

SHARON For the region in Palestine mentioned in the Bible as being rich and fertile.
Sharon, Conn. (Litchfield Co.), town.
Sharon, Mass. (Norfolk Co.), town.
Sharon, N.H. (Hillsborough Co.). For *Sharon*, Conn.

Sharon, Pa. (Mercer Co.).
Sharon, Vt. (Windsor Co.), town.
Sharon Hill, Pa. (Delaware Co.).
Sharon Springs, Kan. (co. seat of Wallace Co.). For *Sharon Springs*, N.Y.
Sharon Springs, N.Y. (Schoharie Co.).
Sharonville, Ohio (Hamilton Co.). For *Sharon*, Pa.
Sharon West, Ohio (Trumbull Co.). For *Sharon*, Pa.

SHARP Co., Ark. (co. seat, Hardy). For Ephraim Sharp, a Union officer in the Civil War.

SHARP, James (?-1861), a settler in Allegheny County, Pa. (1826) who ran a temperance hotel.
Sharpsburg, Pa. (Allegheny Co.).
Sharpsville, Pa. (Mercer Co.).

The village green, such as this one in Sharon, Connecticut, is still a common sight throughout New England where the early settlers were proud folk who avoided places names honoring royalty or noblemen. They preferred their old hometowns — Plymouth, Greenwich, Manchester — or Biblical references such as Sharon, Providence, or Canaan. [*Photo by Mary Lou Estabrook. Courtesy of The Lakeville Journal*]

SHASTA For the tribe, of Hokan linguistic stock, located in northern California and southern Oregon, specifically along the Klamath River and its tributaries. The original meaning is uncertain.
Shasta Co., Calif. (co. seat, Redding).
Shasta Lake, Calif.
Shasta, Mount, Calif.
Shasta Natl. Forest, Calif.

SHAVER CREEK, Pa. For a local settler. It flows southwest into Juniata River.

SHAVERS FORK RIVER, W.Va. For the Shaver family, early settlers. It flows generally northeast to join Blackwater River to form Cheat River.

SHAW, Miss. (Bolivar Co.). For Gus and Thad Shaw, who owned the land where the town was built.

SHAW, Mount, N.H. For an early settler or explorer.

SHAWANGUNK KILL RIVER, N.Y. Of Algonquian origin, although the meaning is in dispute. Some claim that the name was first applied to a fertile lowland, and then spread to the stream and mountains. It may then be a directional name, perhaps "south meadow." H. R. Schoolcraft translated it "white rock," apparently without any reason. Others have translated it variously as "swift current," "mink place," "leek place," "salt," and "pile of rocks." A Dutch influence in the spelling and in *kill*, "stream," is apparent. It flows northeast into Wallkill River.

SHAWANO, a variant form of SHAWNEE.
Shawano Co., Wis. (co. seat, *Shawano*).
Shawano, Wis. (co. seat of *Shawano* Co.).
Shawano Lake, Wis.

SHAWINIGAN, Que. (St. Maurice Co.). From Algonquian, "crest," so named because the portage beside the nearby falls led over a crest of rocks.

SHAWNEE For the tribe of Algonquian linguistic stock. It moved quite often, but apparently inhabited the southern part of what is now the United States, later moving north into the Cumberland River area and into Illinois and Ohio. Traces can be found in other states. The name means "southerner."

Shawnee Co., Kan. (co. seat, Topeka).
Shawnee, Kan. (Johnson Co.).
Shawnee, Okla. (co. seat of Pottawatomie Co.).
Shawnee Natl. Forest, Ill.
Shawneetown, Ill. (co. seat of Gallatin Co.).

SHAWSHEEN RIVER, Mass. Of Algonquian origin, meaning uncertain, possibly derived from *Shoshanim*, the alias name of Sagamore Sam, an Indian chief. It flows generally northeast into Merrimack River.

SHEBOYGAN From Algonquian, of uncertain meaning, probably "reed like," for an object that is tubular. The river was named first.
Sheboygan Co., Wis. (co. seat, *Sheboygan*).
Sheboygan, Wis. (co. seat of *Sheboygan* Co.).
Sheboygan River, Wis. Flows generally E to L. Michigan.
Sheboygan Falls, Wis. (Sheboygan Co.). For falls on the *Sheboygan* R.

SHEENJEK RIVER, Alaska. From Indian, presumably "salmon," It flows south into Porcupine River.

SHEEP For the presence of sheep.
Sheep Butte, N.Dak. For bighorn sheep.
Sheep Mount, S.Dak. For Rocky Mtn. sheep.
Sheep Mountain, Colo.
Sheep Mountain, Wyo. For wild sheep that lived there until 1904
Sheep Peak, Nev. For bighorn sheep.
Sheep Range, Nev.

SHEEPSCOT POND, Me. From Abnaki, "many rocky channels." The form is influenced by folk spelling.

SHEFFIELD For Sheffield, Yorkshire, England.
Sheffield, Ala. (Colbert Co.).
Sheffield Lake, Ohio (Lorain Co.).

SHEFFORD Co., Que. (co. seat, Waterloo). For Shefford, Bedfordshire, England.

SHELBURNE, William, 2nd Earl of (1737-1805), English statesman. He was president of the Board of Trade and was known in the colonies for his opposition to the Stamp Act. Shelburne also opposed New York claims to territory in what is now Vermont.
Shelburne, Vt. (Chittenden Co.).

Shelburne Pond, Vt.
Shelburne Road Section, Vt. (Chittenden Co.).

SHELBY, Isaac (1750-1826). Maryland soldier who defeated the British at the Battle of King's Mountain (1780) and was active elsewhere in the South during the rest of the American Revolution. He also fought at the Battle of the Thames (1813) during the War of 1812. He was governor of Kentucky (1792-96; 1812-16).
Shelby Co., Ala. (co. seat, Columbiana).
Shelby Co., Ill. (co. seat, *Shelbyville*).
Shelby Co., Ind. (co. seat, *Shelbyville*).
Shelby Co., Iowa (co. seat, Harlan).
Shelby Co., Ky. (co. seat, *Shelbyville*).
Shelby Co., Mo. (co. seat, *Shelbyville*).
Shelby Co., Ohio (co. seat, Sidney).
Shelby Co., Tenn. (co. seat, Memphis).
Shelby Co., Tex. (co. seat, Center).
Shelby, N.C. (co. seat of Cleveland Co.).
Shelby, Ohio (Richland Co.).
Shelbyville, Ill. (co. seat of *Shelby* Co.).
Shelbyville, Ind. (co. seat of *Shelby* Co.).
Shelbyville, Ky. (co. seat of *Shelby* Co.).
Shelbyville, Mo. (co. seat of *Shelby* Co.).
Shelbyville, Tenn. (co. seat of Bedford Co.).

SHELBY, Miss. (Bolivar Co.). For the first landowner in the area, Dr. Tom Shelby.

SHELBY, Mont. (co. seat of Toole Co.). For an official of the Great Northern railroad.

SHELDON, Iowa (O'Brien Co.). For Israel Sheldon (1717-1814), a railroad director and financier in New York.

SHELIKOF STRAIT, Alaska. Water passage between Alaska Peninsula and Kodiak Island. For Grigori Ivanovich Shelikov, Russian shipbuilder.

SHELL For the shape of the lake, resembling a shell.
Shell Lake, Wis. (co. seat of Washburn Co.).
Shell Lake, Wis.

SHELLEY, Idaho (Bingham Co.). For John F. Shelley, a Mormon bishop.

SHELLROCK RIVER, Minn.-Iowa. Named in 1843 by Joseph N. Nicollet because the stream had in it "limestone filled with petrifications." It flows generally southeast into Cedar River.

SHELTON, Conn. (Fairfield Co.), town. For Daniel Shelton, an early settler.

SHELTON, Wash. (co. seat of Mason Co.). For David Shelton (1812-1907), a pioneer, legislator, and mayor.

SHENANDOAH From Algonquian, probably *schind-han-dowi*, "spruce stream." It has also been translated as "great plains" and even "beautiful daughter of the stars."
Shenandoah Co., Va. (co. seat, Woodstock). For the river.
Shenandoah, Iowa (Page Co.). For *Shenandoah* Valley, Va.
Shenandoah, Pa. (Schuylkill Co.).
Shenandoah Mountains, Va.-W.Va.
Shenandoah River, Va.-W.Va. Flows generally NE to the Potomac R.
Shenandoah Valley, Va.-W.Va. Part of the Appalachian Valley.
Shenandoah Natl. Park, Va.

SHENANGO RIVER, Pa. From Indian, meaning uncertain, although it is accepted as meaning "beautiful one." It flows generally south to join Mahoning River to form Beaver River.

SHENIPSIT LAKE, Conn. From Mohegan, "great-pool-place."

SHEPAUG RIVER, Conn. From Tunxis, "large pool." It flows south into Housatonic River.

SHEPHERD BROOK MOUNTAIN, Me. Probably for a local settler.

SHERBORN, Mass. (Middlesex Co.), town. For Sherborne, Dorsetshire, England, home of one of the original settlers.

SHERBROOKE, Sir John Coape (1764-1830), governor general of Canada (1816-18).
Sherbrooke Co., Que. (co. seat, *Sherbrooke*).
Sherbrooke, Que. (co. seat of *Sherbrooke* Co.).

SHERBURNE Co., Minn. (co. seat, Elk River). For Moses Sherburne (1808-1868), Minnesota Territory jurist active in the formation of the state.

SHERIDAN, N.Y. (Chautauqua Co.). For Richard B. Sheridan (1751-1816), British dramatist and member of Parliament.

Among his plays were *The Rivals* and *The School for Scandal*. In politics he was known for his support of the French Revolution.

SHERIDAN, Philip Henry (1831-1888), a career military officer. He rose to general during the Civil War and became commander in chief of the Union forces (1864). He later helped defeat Napoleon III at the Mexican border and served again as commander in chief (1883-88). Sheridan established the first postgraduate military institution for officers.
Fort Sheridan, Ill. (Lake Co.).
Sheridan Co., Kan. (co. seat, Hoxie).
Sheridan Co., Mont. (co. seat, Plentywood).
Sheridan Co., Neb. (co. seat, Rushville).
Sheridan Co., N.Dak. (co. seat, McClusky).
Sheridan Co., Wyo. (co. seat, *Sheridan*).
Sheridan, Ark. (co. seat of Grant Co.).
Sheridan, Colo. (Arapahoe Co.).
Sheridan, Wyo. (co. seat of *Sheridan* Co.).
Sheridan, Mount, Wyo., in Yellowstone Natl. Park. Sheridan worked to support the continuation and preservation of the park.

SHERMAN For an early settler or explorer.
Sherman Mountains, Wyo. For *Sherman* Pass.
Sherman Pass, Wash. In Kettle River Range.

SHERMAN, Mount, Colo. For a local settler or explorer.

SHERMAN, N.Y. (Chautauqua Co.). For Roger Sherman (1721-1793), lawyer, merchant, public official, and signer of the Declaration of Independence. Some of the early settlers in this location came from Sherman's native town in Connecticut and he is known to have given financial assistance to the first church built here.

SHERMAN, Sidney (1805-1873), a general in the Republic of Texas army. He also served in the Texas state legislature and organized and headed the first railroad in Texas.
Sherman Co., Tex. (co. seat, Stratford).
Sherman, Tex. (co. seat of Grayson Co.).

SHERMAN, William Tecumseh (1820-1891), career military officer. He rose to general in the Union army during the Civil War and

was the leader of the "march to the sea" through the Southern states. He is also remembered for the statement "War is hell." He became commander in chief of the army (1869).
Sherman Co., Kan. (co. seat, Goodland).
Sherman Co., Neb. (co. seat, Loup City).
Sherman Co., Ore. (co. seat, Moro).
Sherman Reservoir, Neb.

SHERMAN CREEK, Pa. For an early settler who lived in the area prior to 1755. It flows generally northeast into Susquehanna River.

SHERRELWOOD, Colo. (Denver Co.). From a personal name plus *-wood*, promotional.

SHERRILL, N.Y. (Oneida Co.). For the infant son of Congressman James Sherman (1855-1912). Sherman was the congressman who was petitioned to establish a post office in the town. He was later vice-president (1909-12) under Taft.

SHETEK, Lake, Minn. From Ojibway, "pelican."

SHETUCKET RIVER, Conn. From Mohegan, "land between streams." It flows south into Thames River.

SHEYENNE River, N.Dak. A variant spelling of CHEYENNE.

SHIAWASEE From Algonquian, "the water straight ahead."
Shiawassee Co., Mich. (co. seat, Corunna).
Shiawassee River, Mich.

SHILLINGTON, Pa. (Berks Co.). For Samuel Shilling who, in 1860, laid out the town on his farm.

SHILOH For a place where the Israelites set up a tabernacle (Joshua 18:1). The Hebrew word means "place of rest."
Shiloh, Ohio (Richland Co.).
Shiloh Natl. Military Park, Tenn. For a nearby church, in turn for the Biblical city. Commemorates the Battle of Shiloh (April 6-7, 1862), a Union victory which soon led to the capture of Vicksburg, Miss., and the splitting of the Confederacy.

SHINNSTON, W.Va. (Harrison Co.). For Levy Shinn, an early settler and founder.

SHIP ISLAND, Miss. In Gulf of Mexico. For a harbor which accommodated ships.

SHIPPENSBURG, Pa. (Cumberland Co.). For Edward Shippen, founder. He was a grandson of the first mayor of Philadelphia, and was himself elected mayor of Philadelphia (1744).

SHIP ROCK PEAK, N.Mex. Named apparently for the shape by Indians, who also had several myths involving ships associated with the peak.

SHIRLEY, Mass. (Middlesex Co.), town. For Gov. William Shirley (1694-1771), whose chief contribution to Massachusetts was to put its finances on a sound basis.

SHIRLEY MOUNTAINS, Wyo. A granite range named for Shirley, a fur trader and trapper who once frequented the region.

SHISHALDIN VOLCANO, Alaska. On Unimak Island. Transliteration from Russian *sopka shishaldinskaya*.

SHIVELY, Ky. (Jefferson Co.). For Christian William Shively (?-c.1826), an early settler.

SHOAL Descriptive, for shoals on a stream.
Shoal Creek, Ill. Formed from East and West forks, flows S into Kaskaskia R.
Shoal Creek, Mo.
Shoal River, Fla. Flows S and SW into Yellow R.
Shoals, Ind. (co. seat of Martin Co.). For shoals on the East Fork of White R. Earlier, West Shoals.

SHOHOLA CREEK, Pa. From Algonquian *schauwihilla*, "weak" or "faint," probably referring to an incident. It flows northeast into Delaware River.

SHOREVIEW, Minn. (Ramsey Co.). Descriptive and promotional.

SHOREWOOD Descriptive and promotional.
Shorewood, Minn. (Hennepin Co.).
Shorewood, Wis. (Milwaukee Co.).

SHOSHONE For the Shoshoni, or Shoshone, one of the major tribes of the northern Rocky Mountain region. Their language is called Shoshonean.
Shoshone Co., Idaho (co. seat, Wallace).
Shoshone, Idaho (co. seat of Lincoln Co.).
Shoshone Falls, Idaho, on the Snake R.

Shoshone Lake, Wyo.
Shoshone Mountains, Nev.
Shoshone Natl. Forest, Wyo.
Shoshone Peak, Nev.
Shoshone Plateau, Wyo. Contains remains of a petrified forest.
Shoshone River, Wyo.
Shoshone Cavern Natl. Monument, Wyo.

SHREVE, Henry Miller, a steamboat captain and superintendent of western river improvement, who arrived in the area in 1833 to supervise the clearing of log jams in the Red River. Choosing the bluffs as a campsite for his crew, he recognized the strategic importance of the area and joined a group to form a town, first known as Shreve Town.
North Shreveport, La. (Caddo Parish).
Shreveport, La. (parish seat of Caddo Parish).

SHREWSBURY For Shrewsbury, Shropshire, England. Possibly also for Charles Talbot, Duke of Shrewsbury (1660-1718), one of those who invited William of Orange to take the English throne.
New Shrewsbury, N.J. (Monmouth Co.).
Shrewsbury, Mo. (St. Louis Co.).
Shrewsbury, N.J. (Monmouth Co.). Shrewsbury, England, was the birthplace of many of the earliest settlers.

SHUKSAN, Mount, Wash. Of Indian origin, meaning unknown.

SHUYAK ISLAND, Alaska. From Indian, meaning unknown.

SIBLEY, Henry Hastings (1811-1891), pioneer, fur company official, and general officer. He led a militia in suppressing an Indian revolt at Morton, Minn., and supervised the hanging of about 300 Indians. He served as first governor of the state of Minnesota (1858-60).
Sibley Co., Minn. (co. seat, Gaylord).
Sibley, Iowa (co. seat of Osceola Co.).
Sibley Peak, Wyo. For its resemblance in shape to a Civil War army tent invented by Sibley. The shape has now been destroyed by highway construction.

SIDELING HILL CREEK, Pa.-Md. Descriptive, referring to a particular area in which the stream flows beside a hill in a unique way. It flows south into Potomac River.

SIDNEY, Mont. (co. seat of Richland Co.). For Sidney Walters, son of an early settler.

SIDNEY, Neb. (co. seat of Cheyenne Co.). For Sidney Dillon. See DILLON Co., Mont.

SIDNEY, Sir Philip (1554-1586), English soldier, statesman, and poet, author of *Arcadia*, killed in battle against the Spaniards.
Sidney, Iowa (co. seat of Fremont Co.). For *Sidney*, Ohio.
Sidney, N.Y. (Delaware Co.). Or possibly for William Sidney (1764-1840), English vice–admiral.
Sidney, Ohio (co. seat of Shelby Co.). May also have been influenced by the middle name of Charles Sidney Starrett, who donated the land for the townsite.

SIDNEY LANIER, Lake, Ga. In Chattahoochee River. For Sidney Lanier. See LANIER Co., Ga.

SIERRA From Spanish, "mountain range."
Sierra Co., Calif. (co. seat, Downieville).
Sierra Co., N.Mex. (co. seat, Truth or Consequences).
Sierra Natl. Forest, Calif. In Sierra Nevada Mtns.

SIERRA BLANCA (mountain), Tex. From Spanish, "white mountain," descriptive.

SIERRA DE SAL, Utah. From Spanish, "salt mountains."

SIERRA GRANDE (peak), N.Mex. From Spanish, "great mountain."

SIERRA MADRE From Spanish, "mother range."
Sierra Madre, Calif. (Los Angeles Co.).
Sierra Madre (mountains), Calif.
Sierra Madre (mountains), Wyo.-Colo., in the Rocky Mtns.

SIERRA NEVADA (mountains), Calif. From Spanish, "snow mountains."

SIERRA VISTA, Ariz. (Cochise Co.). From Spanish "mountain view"; promotional and descriptive. Earlier names were Garden Canyon and Fry.

SIGNAL For places from which signals were made.
Signal Cliff, Wyo. Used as signal place by Indians.
Signal Hill, Wyo. Used as a lookout by early Mormon travellers, who signaled when unannounced parties were seen entering the valley.
Signal Mountain, Wyo. When Robert R. Hamilton became lost in the vicinity, friends agreed to use this mountain as a place of signal if he were found.
Signal Peak, Wyo. Indians built signal fires on its summit to call distant bands to hunt or to war.
Signal Mountain, Tenn. (Hamilton Co.).

The great Sierra Nevada range, dividing California from Nevada are both beautiful and treacherous. Donner Lake commemorates the ill-fated Donner party which was trapped in the Sierras during the winter of 1846. The few survivors were later charged with cannibalism. [*New York Public Library*]

SIGNAL HILL, Calif. (Los Angeles Co.). Descriptive; designation originated during wartime.

SIGNOR For Signor Eli, early storekeeper.
Signor Reservoir, Wyo.
Signor Ridge, Wyo.

SIGOURNEY, Iowa (co. seat of Keokuk Co.). For Mrs. Lydia Huntley Sigourney (1791-1865), popular poet of the 1800s.

SILER CITY, N.C. (Chatham Co.). For Samuel Siler (1810-1900), landowner and gristmill operator.

SILETZ RIVER, Ore. For the Indian tribe. It meanders southeast then northeast into the Pacific Ocean.

SILLERY, Que. (Quebec Co.). For Noel Brulart de Sillery, a partner in the Company of New France, whose generosity made possible the establishment of a Jesuit mission here in 1638.

SILOAM SPRINGS, Ark. For the springs made famous by the miracle of a blind man (John 9), supposedly having healing powers.

SILSBEE, Tex. (Hardin Co.). For Nathaniel B. Silsbee, a Boston industrialist and friend of the founder.

SILVER For a silvery appearance.
Silver Lake, Mass.
Silver Lake, Mich.
Silver Lake, Mo.
Silver Lake, Ore. (Harney Co.).
Silver Lake, Ore. (Lake Co.).
Silver Bay, Minn. (Lake Co.). A commercial fisherman thought the rocks along the shore line had the appearance of silver.
Silver Bow Co., Mont. (co. seat, Butte). For a creek, which was named by trappers who saw the sun shining "like a silver bow" on its waters.
Silver Creek, N.Y. (Chautauqua Co.). For a local creek with a sandstone base that gives it a silvery appearance.
Silver Lake, Ohio (Summit Co.). Also promotional.
Silver Spring, Md. (Montgomery Co.).

SILVER For silver mines and mining operations.
Silver River, Mich. Flows N into Huron Bay.

Silver City, N.Mex. (co. seat of Grant Co.). Earlier, San Vicente.
Silver Crown Hills, Wyo. For the gold and silver mining boom of 1885, in reality, holes were "salted"; the fraud was exposed by University of Wyoming Professor Wilbur C. Knight.
Silver King Mountain, Ore.
Silverpeak, Nev. (Esmeralda Co.).
Silver Peak Range, Nev.
Silverton, Colo. (co. seat of San Juan Co.).

SILVERTON, Ohio (Hamilton Co.). Probably the name was originally Silver Town, changed to the present form; descriptive and promotional.

SILVERTON, Ore. (Marion Co.). For a stream probably named for James ("Silver") Smith, an early sawmill operator. An earlier name was Milford.

SILVERTON, Tex. (co. seat of Briscoe Co.). So named by Mrs. T. J. Braidfoot "because she thought it was pretty."

SILVIES RIVER, Ore. For Antoine Sylvaille, a trapper. The spelling has been Anglicized. It flows generally south into Malheur Lake.

SILVIS, Ill. (Rock Island Co.). For Thomas Sharp Silvis (1841-1896), farmer and sheriff of Rock Island County.

SIMCOE From Indian, said to mean "waist-spine," descriptive of the range around the valley of the same name.
Simcoe Mountain, Wash. In *Simcoe* Mtns.
Simcoe Mountains, Wash.
Simcoe Valley, Wash.

SIMCOE, John Graves (1752-1806), British soldier and administrator who served in the American Revolution. He was the first lieutenant governor of Upper Canada (Ontario) (1792-96), and helped open the province to settlement; although he made many enemies.
Simcoe Co., Ont. (co. seat, Barrie).
Simcoe, Ont. (co. seat of Norfolk Co.). Named in 1829.

SIMCOE, Lake, Ont. Named by John Graves Simcoe for his father, Capt. John Simcoe, a British naval officer.

SIMEONOF ISLAND, Alaska. In Shumagin Islands. From Russian, "Simon," a personal name.

SIMI VALLEY, Calif. (Ventura Co.). From Chumash Indian, "valley of the wind," for the winds that usually rise each afternoon from the ocean. The term has also been interpreted as "place" or "village"; the first version is more nearly correct.

SIMMS STREAM, N.H. For a local settler. It flows northwest into Connecticut River.

SIMPSON Co., Ky. (co. seat, Franklin). For James Simpson (?-1812), legislator, killed in action during the War of 1812.

SIMPSON Co., Miss. (co. seat, Mendenhall). For Josiah Simpson, a judge in the Mississippi Territory.

SIMPSONVILLE, S.C. (Greenville Co.). For Peter Simpson, the first known settler on the site.

SIMSBURY, Conn. (Hartford Co.), town and village. Probably for Simondsbury, Dorsetshire, England.

SIMTUSTUS, Lake, Ore. In Crooked River. Of Indian origin, meaning unknown.

SINCLAIR, Lake, Ga. For Benjamin W. Sinclair, a power company executive.

SINISSIPPI LAKE, Wis. From Algonquian, "rock river." The lake is the headwater of Rock River.

SINNEMAHONING CREEK, Pa. From Algonquian, "stony lick." It flows generally south into Susquehanna River.

SINTON, Tex. (co. seat of San Patricio Co.). For David Sinton (1808-1900), an investor in the Coleman Fulton Pasture Company. His only daughter married Charles P. Taft, brother of President Taft. The Coleman Fulton Pasture Company eventually came to be known as the Taft Ranch.

SIOUX For the tribe, sometimes known as the Dakotas. Their earliest place of habitation was generally west of the Mississippi River in what is now southern Minnesota and parts of Iowa. Later the tribe drifted westward. The name comes from Ojibway *nadouessioux*, "snakes" or "enemies," a designation rival tribes applied to each other in various languages. It was transliterated through French.
Big Sioux River, Iowa-S.Dak. Flows S to the Missouri R.

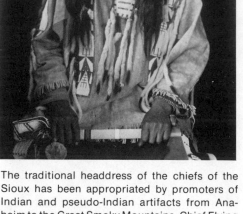

The traditional headdress of the chiefs of the Sioux has been appropriated by promoters of Indian and pseudo-Indian artifacts from Anaheim to the Great Smoky Mountains. Chief Flying Hawk of the Oglalla Sioux poses in his distinctive dress. [*Museum of Natural History, New York*]

Little Sioux River, Iowa.
Sioux Co., Iowa (co. seat, Orange City).
Sioux Co., Neb. (co. seat, Harrison).
Sioux Co., N.Dak. (co. seat, Fort Yates).
Sioux Center, Iowa (*Sioux* Co.). In the exact center of the county.
Sioux City, Iowa (co. seat of Woodbury Co.).
Sioux Falls, S.Dak. (co. seat of Minnehaha Co.). For falls on the *Big Sioux* R.
Sioux Lookout, Ont. (Kenora District).
South Sioux City, Neb. (Dakota Co.).

SIPSEY RIVER, Ala. From Chickasaw-Choctaw, "poplar" or "cottonwood" tree. It flows generally southwest into Tombigbee River.

SISKIYOU A name of doubtful origin for which conflicting meanings have been given. One suggestion is that it is from Cree Indian, "bob-tailed horse"; another that it

comes from French *six cailloux*, "six boul-
ders."
Siskiyou Co., Calif. (co. seat, Yreka).
Siskiyou Mountains, Calif.-Ore. border.

SISQUOC RIVER, Calif. From Chumash,
"quail." It flows northwest into Cuyama
River.

SISTERS See THREE SISTERS.

SITKA From Tlingit Indian, believed to
mean "by the sea" or "on Shi" (native name
of Baranof Island).
Sitka, Alaska. Capital of Alaska until 1900.
Sitka Natl. Monument, Alaska.

SITKINAK ISLAND, Alaska. In Trinity Islands. From Eskimo, meaning unknown.

SIUSLAW RIVER, Ore. From an Indian tribal
name. It flows generally northwest into the
Pacific Ocean.

SIX MILE LAKE, La. Descriptive of its
length.

SIX RIVERS NATL. FOREST, Calif. So
named because it covers the watersheds of
six rivers: Smith, Klamath, Trinity, Mad, Van
Duzen, and Eel.

SIX RUN CREEK, N.C. For the six small
streams, or "runs," that merge with the
Great Coharie Swamp. Shown on some
maps as Six Runs Creek. It flows south to
join Great Coharie Creek to form Black
River.

SIXTY-SIX MOUNTAIN, Wyo. A high mountain ridge, on which sixty-six emigrants
were massacred by Indians in the early
1860s near the Oregon Trail and Nebraska
state line. One man, Ed Stemier, escaped
because Indians were superstitious of his
red hair; he later established a ranch near
the mountain.

SKAGIT For an Indian tribe of Salishan lin-
guistic stock. They lived along the Skagit
and Stillaguamish rivers in Washington.
Meaning of the name is unknown.
Skagit Co., Wash. (co. seat, Mount Vernon).
Skagit Bay, Wash. Inlet on Puget Sound.
Skagit River, Wash. Flows generally SW
from Canada to *Skagit* Bay.

SKAMANIA Co., Wash. (co. seat, Stevenson). From Indian, but of uncertain origin
and meaning. The usual interpretation is

"swift water," which may apply to the Columbia River.

SKANEATELES. From Indian *Skahnegh-
ties*, "very long lake."
Skaneateles, N.Y. (Onondaga Co.). For the
lake.
Skaneateles Lake, N.Y.

SKELETON CREEK, Okla. So named because skeletons of Indians were found on
the bank of the stream. It flows southeast
into Cimarron River.

SKIATOOK, Okla. (Tulsa and Osage Cos.).
For Skiatooka, a prominent Osage Indian.

SKILLET FORK RIVER, Ill. Reason for name
unknown, but probably for an incident. It
flows southeast into Little Wabash River.

SK MOUNTAIN, Wyo. For the "SK" horse
brand of Plunkett, Roche and Company.

SKOKIE, Ill. (Cook Co.). From Potawatomi,
"marsh."

SKOKOMISH RIVER, Wash. From the Indian tribal name; *kaw* means "fresh water,"
and *mish*, "people." It flows southeast and
northeast into Hood Canal.

SKOWHEGAN, Me. (co. seat of Somerset
Co.), town and village. From Algonquian,
"place of the watch," referring to the nearby falls on the Kennebec River where local
Indians watched for and caught salmon. An
earlier name was Milburn.

SKULL LAKE, Ga., in Okefenokee Swamp.
So named because it was used by the
Creeks as a ceremonial and sacrificial area.
Skulls of animals were placed on bushes
and trees.

SKUNK RIVER, Iowa. For the animal. It
flows southeast into Mississippi River.

SKYKOMISH RIVER, Wash. From the tribal
name; *skaikh* means "inland," and *mish*,
"people." It flows west to join Snoqualmie
River to form Snohomish River.

SKYLIGHT, Mount, N.Y. Poetic and descriptive.

SLATINGTON, Pa. (Lehigh Co.). So named
because slate is mined in the area.

SLATON, Tex. (Lubbock Co.). For O. L. Slaton (1867-?), landowner, banker, and developer.

SLAYTON, Minn. (co. seat of Murray Co.). For Charles Slayton (1835-1906), founder. He was active in many business affairs and was a promoter of colonization.

SLEEPY EYE, Minn. (Brown Co.). For "Sleepy Eye" (c.1800-1860), a Sisseton Sioux chief who signed several treaties with the whites in the first half of the 1800s. His name in Siouan was *Ishtakhaba*, supposedly meaning "sleepy eye."

SLICK MOUNTAIN, Wyo. For its appearance: It is solid rock, steep, and appears to be polished.

SLIDE MOUNTAIN, N.Y. For rock slides.

SLIPPERY ROCK Descriptive of rocks in the stream.
Slippery Rock, Pa. (Butler Co.). For the stream.
Slippery Rock Creek, Pa. Flows SW into Connoquenessing Creek.

SLOATSBURG, N.Y. (Rockland Co.). For Jacob Sloat, an early settler.

SLOPE Co., N.Dak. (co. seat, Amidon). Descriptive of the general eastward sloping grade of the county.

SLOW FORK RIVER, Alaska. Descriptive of the flow of the stream. It flows northwest into East Fork of Kuskokwim River.

SMART MOUNTAIN, Me. For a local settler.

SMARTS MOUNTAIN, N.H. For an early explorer or settler in the area.

SMETHPORT, Pa. (co. seat of McKean Co.). For Raymond and Baron Theodore de Smeth, Amsterdam bankers who provided funds for the land speculator John Keating, manager of the Ceres Land Company.

SMITH, J. Nelson (?-1864), a Union officer killed in action.
Smith Co., Kan. (co. seat, *Smith Center*)
Smith Center, Kan. (co. seat of *Smith* Co.). For its location in the center of the county.

SMITH Co., Miss. (co. seat, Raleigh). For a David Smith; other information has been lost.

SMITH, Philip. See PHILIP SMITH MOUNTAINS.

SMITH Co., Tenn. (co. seat, Carthage). For Daniel Smith (1748-1818), soldier in the American Revolution, active in the promotion of statehood for Tennessee. He served as U.S. senator (1798-99; 1805-09).

SMITH Co., Tex. (co. seat, Tyler). For James Smith (1792-1855), Republic of Texas general.

SMITH BAY, Alaska. Inlet on Beaufort Sea. Named in 1837 for Chief Factor Smith, employee of the Hudson's Bay Company.

SMITH CREEK, S.Dak. Probably for an early settler. It flows south and west into Missouri River.

SMITHFIELD, N.C. (co. seat of Johnston Co.). For John Smith, landowner and a founder.

SMITHFIELD, Utah (Cache Co.). For John G. Smith (1808-1888), first Mormon bishop of the district. An earlier name was Summit.

SMITHLAND, Ky. (co. seat of Livingston Co.). For Col. James Smith, a hunter and explorer. He was also known as Scowa, an Indian name given him by his captors. He settled near the confluence of the Cumberland, Tennessee, and Ohio rivers, and was a member of Kentucky's first Constitutional Convention in 1792. An earlier name was Smith's Town.

SMITH RIVER, Ore. For Jedediah Strong Smith (1798-1831), a fur trader killed by Comanche Indians. It flows west into Umpqua River.

SMITHS FALLS, Ont. (Lanark Co.). For the series of falls on the Rideau River, beside which Major Thomas Smyth obtained a land grant after serving in the American Revolution.

SMITHVILLE, Mo. For Humphrey Smith, owner of a sawmill and gristmill, who bought the original site from the Indians.

SMITHVILLE, Tex. (Bastrop Co.). For Frank Smith, an early settler.

SMOKY HILL Descriptive, but reason for the naming is uncertain. It was either because of the haze over the hills along the river, or a translation from a French name for "fork of smoky hill."
North Fork Smoky Hill River, Colo-Kan. Flows ENE to join *South Fork Smoky Hill* R.

Smoky Hill River, Kan. Flows E, SE, and NE to join Republican R.

South Fork Smoky Hill River, Colo-Kan. Flows E. to join *North Fork Smoky Hill* R. to from *Smoky Hill* R.

SMUGGLER'S NOTCH, Vt. So named because according to legend it was used as a place where cattle and other goods were hidden during the United States embargo on goods to Canada in the War of 1812.

SMYRNA For the ancient Greek seaport on the Aegean Sea in Asia Minor. A wealthy urban center, it was an early center of Christianity and was the site of one of the "seven churches of Asia." It is now the Turkish city of Izmir.

New Smyrna Beach, Fla. (Volusia Co.).

Smyrna, Del. (Kent and New Castle Cos.).

Smyrna, Ga. (Cobb Co.).

Smyrna, Tenn. (Rutherford Co.).

SMYTH Co., Va. (co. seat, Marion). For Alexander Smyth (1765-1830), Virginia soldier and legislator who attempted an unsuccessful invasion of Canada during the War of 1812. He was a U.S. representative (1817-25; 1827-30).

SNAKE For the Indian tribe.

Snake Range, Nev.

Snake River, Wyo.-Idaho-Ore.-Wash. Flows into Columbia R.

Snake River Range, Wyo. For the river.

SNAKE For the presence of snakes.

Snake Buttes, N.Dak. For the rattlesnakes.

Snake Creek, S.Dak. Flows SE into Frozeman's Creek. For the rattlesnakes. Also called Plum Creek, for the plum trees.

Snake Mountain, Vt. For the small, green, harmless snakes.

Snake River, Minn. Flows S and E into St. Croix R. From Ojibway *kanabec*, "a snake."

Snake River, Neb. Flows E and NE into Nibrara R. Or so named because the course of the river resembles a snake.

SNEEDVILLE, Tenn. (co. seat of Hancock Co.). For William Henry Sneed (1812-1869), attorney, state legislator, and U.S. representative (1855-57).

SNEFFELS, Mount, Colo. For the Sneffels, the crater mountain in Jules Verne's novel, *Journey to the Center of the Earth*.

SNIPATUIT POND, Mass. From Wampanoag, "at the rocky river" or possibly "palisades."

SNOHOMISH For the Indian tribe, of Salishan linguistic stock. They lived along the Snohomish River in Washington. The meaning of the name is unknown.

Snohomish Co., Wash. (co. seat, Everett).

Snohomish, Wash. (*Snohomish* Co.).

Snohomish River, Wash. Flows NW to Everett Harbor.

SNOQUALMIE From the tribal name, claimed to mean "moon."

Snoqualmie Natl. Forest, Wash.

Snoqualmie Pass, Wash. In Cascade Range.

Snoqualmie River, Wash. Flows NW to join Skykomish R. to form Snohomish R.

SNOW Descriptive, usually applied to mountains whose peaks are habitually covered with snow.

Snow Mountain, Me.

Snow Mountain, N.Y.

Snow Mountain, Ore.

Snow Mountain East, Calif.

Snowcap Mountain, Alaska. In Alaska Range.

Snow King Mountain, Wyo. For the excellent skiing.

Snowmass Mountain, Colo.

Snowy Range, Wyo.

SNOWBANK LAKE, Minn. Translated from Ojibway, probably referring to a wintry condition in which snow was piled in banks.

SNOW HILL, Md. (co. seat of Worcester Co.). Believed to have been named for a city in England, possibly Snowshill, Gloucestershire, in a form easier to pronounce.

SNOW HILL, N.C. (co. seat of Green Co.). For a plantation of that name, which was probably named for a mound covered with either sea salt or white sand.

SNOWSHOE Descriptive of the shape.

Snowshoe Lake, Me.

Snowshoe Peak, Mont.

SNOW WATER LAKE, Nev. So named because it is a dry lake except when fed by melting snow.

SNYDER Co., Pa. (co. seat, Middleburg). For Simon Snyder (1759-1819), Pennsylvania statesman and jurist. He was speaker of the Pennsylvania House of Representatives (1802-07) and governor (1808-17).

SNYDER, Tex. (co. seat of Scurry Co.). For William Henry ("Pete") Snyder (1837-1916), trading-post proprietor, freighter, railroad contractor, and miner. Earlier names were Robbers Roost and Hidetown, the latter named by buffalo hunters.

SOCORRO From Spanish, "aid" or "help"; the city and county commemorate aid in the form of food given by the Piro Indians to members of a Spanish expedition led by Don Juan de Onate in 1598. The Spaniards gave the place the name Nuestra Señora de Socorro de Pilabo.
Socorro Co., N.Mex. (co. seat, *Socorro*).
Socorro, N.Mex. (co. seat of *Socorro* Co.).

SODA LAKE, Calif. For the mineral water in the lake.

SODA SPRINGS, Idaho (co. seat of Caribou Co.). For the taste of the water.

SOLANA BEACH, Calif. (San Diego Co.). *Solana*, from Spanish, "sunny place."

SOLANO Co., Calif. (co. seat, Fairfield). For an Indian chief who had accepted the Christian name of the saint, and for Saint Francis Solano (1549-1610), known as the "apostle of Peru and Wonder Worker of the New World." Born in Spain, he joined the order of Saint Francis and during an outbreak of plague in Grenada proved himself brave and charitable and unstinting in giving aid to others. Coming to Peru in 1589, he devoted the remainder of his life to working among the Indians and the colonists at Lima.

SOLBERG LAKE, Wis. For a local settler.

SOLEDAD, Calif. (Monterey Co.). From Spanish *La Mision de Nuestra Señora de la Soledad*, "The Mission of Our Lady of Solitude."

SOLEDUCK RIVER, Wash. Probably a folk etymologized form of an Indian name, possibly meaning "sparkling water," for the mineral springs. It flows generally northwest then southwest into the Pacific Ocean.

SOLOMON RIVER, Kan. Believed to have been named for Solomon Petit, trade in about 1800. An earlier name was Solomon's Fork. Formed from North and South forks, it flows southeast into Smoky Hill River.

SOLON, Ohio (Cuyahoga Co.). For Solon Bull (c.1800-1850), one of the early settlers.

SOLVAY, N.Y. (Onondaga Co.). For a factory using the Solvay Process for manufacturing sodium bicarbonate.

SOMERS, Conn. (Tolland Co.), town. For Lord John Somers (1651-1716), chancellor, solicitor general, and one of the drafters of the English Bill of Rights, He was a friend, patron and colleague of many writers and philosophers.

SOMERSET For Somerset county (Somersetshire), in England.
Somerset Co., Me. (co. seat, Skowhegan).
Somerset Co., Pa. (co. seat, *Somerset*).
Somerset Ky. (co. seat of Pulaski Co.). For *Somerset*, Pa.
Somerset, Mass. (Bristol Co.), town.
Somerset, Pa. (co. seat of *Somerset* Co.).
Somerset Reservoir, Vt.

SOMERSET, Lord John Berkeley, Duke of.
Somerset Co., N.J. (co. seat, *Somerville*).
Somerville, N.J. (co. seat of *Somerset* Co.). A back formation that substituted *-ville* for *-set*.

SOMERSET Co., Md. (co. seat, Princess Anne). For Edward Somerset (c.1601-1667), Marquis of WORCESTER.

SOMERSWORTH, N.H. (Stafford Co.). Probably coined from "summer" and the common English suffix, *-worth*, by Rev. John Pike who spent his summers preaching there.

SOMERVELL Co., Tex. (co. seat, Glen Rose). For Alexander Somervell (1796-1854), Texas patriot. He fought as an officer in the Texas War of Independence, rising to the rank of general after the war. He served in the Republic's administration and also in its congress.

SOMERVILLE, Mass. (Middlesex Co.). Probably for Capt. Rochard Somers (1778-1804), a naval hero killed in the war with Tripoli.

SOMERVILLE, N.J. For the Duke of SOMER-SET.

SOMERVILLE, Tenn. (co. seat of Fayette Co.). For a Lieutenant Somerville, killed near Chattanooga during the Creek War.

SONOMA For a Wintun Indian "tribelet" that lived in the Sacramento Valley. It was originally *Soninmak*, but has been given a rather typical Spanish ending. The name means "nose," but the reason for it is unknown. A fanciful interpretation is "valley of the moon."
Sonoma Co., Calif. (co. seat, Santa Rosa). The city was named first.
Sonoma, Calif. (*Sonoma* Co.).
Sonoma Peak, Nev.
Sonoma Range, Nev.

SONORA From Spanish, feminine form of *sonoro*, "sonorous," connoting "grand," "great," or "grandiloquent." The ending *-a* was substituted for the usual Spanish *-o* probably out of deference to the custom or belief that places should be given names of feminine gender. Names in the United States were taken from that of Sonora, a state in Mexico.
Sonora, Calif. (co. seat of Tuolumne Co.).
Sonora, Tex. (co. seat of Sutton Co.).
Sonora Pass, Calif., in the Sierra Nevada.
Sonora Peak, Calif.

SOPCHOPPY RIVER, Fla. From Seminole-Creek, "acorn-stem," applied to the red oak tree. The name has been hopelessly folk rendered. An earlier form was Lockchoppee. It flows south into Apalachee Bay.

SOPERTON, Ga. (co. seat of Treutlen Co.). Origin uncertain; believed to have been named either for a construction engineer or for someone with an interest in the railroad that was being built through the area.

SOPRIS, Mount, Colo. For Richard Sopris (?-1893), territorial legislator and mayor of Denver (1878-79).

SOQUEL, Calif. (Santa Cruz Co.). For an Indian village on the townsite. The name translates into "water-in-the-willows."

SOREL, Que. (co. seat of Richelieu Co.). For Pierre de Saurel (or Sorel), local commander, who in 1672 obtained a grant of land around what was then Fort Richelieu, on the site of the present town.

SOUCOOK RIVER, N.H. From Abnaki, "rocky place." It flows south into Merrimack River.

SOUHEGAN RIVER, Mass.-N.H. From Pennacook, meaning uncertain, possibly "watching place." It flows northeast into Merrimack River.

SOULANGES Co., Que. (co. seat, Coteau Landing). Named by Pierre Jacques de Joybert for his seigniory, which he named after a seigniory of the same name that had been his in Champagne, France.

SOURIS RIVER, Sask.-N.Dak.-Man. From French, "mouse," so named because of a mice epidemic at a camp on the river. The river is also known as Mouse River. It flows into Assiniboine River.

SOURLAND MOUNTAIN, N.J. Named by someone who did not like the land; to him it was "sour."

SOUTH Directional. Names that do not appear in this part of the book may be found under the basic name. For example, for South Houston, Tex., see HOUSTON.
South Butte, Idaho.
South Pass, Wyo. The most southern of the important passes in the Continental Divide.
South Mountain, Wyo. For its position south of Laramie Peak.
South Mountain, Pa.-Va.
South Peak, Utah.
South Point, Mich. Extends into L. Huron.
South Pond, Mass.
South River, Iowa. Flows NE into Des Moines R.
South River, Md. Tidal inlet on Chesapeake Bay.
South River, Mass. Flows E. into Deerfield R.
South River, Mass. Flows NE into Massachusetts Bay.
South River, N.C. Flows SSE into Black R.
South River, N.J. Flows NW into Raritan R. Also known as Deep South Run.
South Branch Lake, Me.
Southeast Point, R.I. On Block Island.
South Fork River, Ark. Flows into Little Red R.

South Grand River, Kan.-Mo. Flows SE into Lake of the Ozarks.

SOUTHAMPTON   For   Southampton, Hampshire, England.

Southampton, Mass. (Hampshire Co.), town. Also so named because it was formerly the southern section of the town of Northampton.

Southampton, N.Y. (Suffolk Co.), town. For *Southampton*, Mass.

SOUTHAMPTON Co., Va. (co. seat, Courtland). For Henry Wriothesley, 3rd Earl of Southampton (1573-1624), English statesman, one of the leaders in the formation of the Virginia Company of London, for which he served as councilor (1609) and treasurer (1620-24). He was also councilor for the Plantation of New England (1620). He is remembered as a patron of William Shakespeare; Shakespeare dedicated his *Venus and Adonis* (1593) and *Rape of Lucrece* (1594) to him.

SOUTH BEND   For a southward bend in a river.

South Bend, Ind. (co. seat of St. Joseph Co.). On the most southerly bend of the St. Joseph R.

South Bend, Wash. (co. seat of Pacific Co.). For a bend in the Wallapa R.

SOUTHBOROUGH, Mass. (Worcester Co.), town. So named because it was formed from the south part of Marlborough.

SOUTHBRIDGE, Mass. (Worcester Co.), town and village. So named because it was formed from the south part of Sturbridge.

SOUTH BROADWAY, Wash. (Yakima Co.). Promotional and descriptive of its location south of Yakima.

SOUTHBURY, Conn. (New Haven Co.). So named because it was formed from the south part of Woodbury.

SOUTH CAROLINA   See CAROLINA.

SOUTH DAKOTA. See DAKOTA.

SOUTHERN PINES, N.C. (Moore Co.). For the North Carolina longleaf pines that abound in the area.

SOUTHERN SHOPS, S.C. (Spartanburg Co.). For the company that services and repairs engines and cars for the Southern railway system.

SOUTHFIELD, Mich. (Oakland Co.). Descriptive; in the southern part of the county.

SOUTH FORK COTTONWOOD CREEK, Calif. For its location and the tree. It flows east into Sacramento River.

SOUTH GATE, Calif. (Los Angeles Co.). Descriptive; southern suburb of Los Angeles.

SOUTHGATE, Ky. (Campbell Co.). Probably for Southgate, Middlesex, England.

SOUTHGATE, Mich. (Wayne Co.). So named because it is located south of Detroit.

SOUTH HAVEN, Mich. (Van Buren Co.). So named because it is located south of Grand Haven.

SOUTH HOLLAND, Ill. (Cook Co.). For the province of South Holland, Netherlands; named by early settlers from there.

SOUTHINGTON, Conn. (Hartford Co.), town. So named because it was formed from the south part of Farmington.

SOUTH JORDAN, Utah (Salt Lake Co.). So named because it was located on a south bend of the Jordan River.

SOUTH LYON, Mich. (Oakland Co.). For its location in the southern part of the township, which was named for Lucius Lyon (1800-1851), deputy surveyor general of Michigan Territory, legislator (1832-36), U.S. senator (1836-40), and surveyor general of Ohio, Michigan, and Indiana.

SOUTHPORT, N.C. (co. seat of Brunswick Co.). So named as the southernmost port in the state.

SOUTH RUSSELL, Ohio (Geauga Co.). For Gideon Russell, original settler.

SOUTH SISTER   See THREE SISTERS.

SOUTH STICKNEY, Ill. (Cook Co.). For its location and for a local community member.

SOUTH VALLEY, N.Mex. (Bernalillo Co.). So named because it is located south of Albuquerque.

SOUTHWICK, Mass. (Hampden Co.). Probably for a town in England.

SOUTH YOLLA BOLLY (mountain), Calif. From Wintu Indian *yola boli*, "high snow-covered peak."

SPALDING Co., Ga. (co. seat, Griffin). For Thomas Spalding (1774-1851), U.S. representative (1805-06) and state official.

SPALDING PEAK, Wyo. For Frank S. Spalding, a bishop who led the second ascent of Grand Teton in 1898.

SPANAWAY, Wash. (Pierce Co.). From Indian, meaning unknown. It was first recorded as Spanuch, and was folk-etymologized to its present form.

SPANISH FORK, Utah (Utah Co.). For a river, which was named for the Spanish expedition of Dominguez-Escalanta in 1776. The canyon in which it is located became a Spanish trail in the 1800s.

SPANISH LAKE, Mo. (St. Louis Co.). So named (also called Spanish Pond) because Spanish soldiers camped there in the late 1700s.

SPARKS, Nev. (Washoe Co.). For John Sparks, governor (1903-08) at the time of naming (1905).

SPARTA For the ancient city in Greece, capital of Laconia. Its soldiers were noted for their strict discipline, courage, and austere life. Possibly such symbolic qualities were thought to be transferred to citizens of towns so named.
Sparta, Ga. (co. seat of Hancock Co.).
Sparta, Ill. (Randolph Co.).
Sparta, Mich. (Kent Co.).
Sparta, N.J. (Sussex Co.).
Sparta, N.C. (co. seat of Alleghany Co.).
Sparta, Tenn. (co. seat of White Co.).
Sparta, Wis. (co. seat of Monroe Co.).

SPARTANBURG For the Spartan Regiment of South Carolina militia, which distinguished itself in the American Revolution.
Spartanburg Co., S.C. (co. seat, *Spartanburg*).
Spartanburg, S.C. (co. seat of *Spartanburg* Co.).

SPAVINAW Probably from French, but changes in form have left the meaning uncertain. It is possibly derived from *cepee* plus *vineux*, "young growth," in reference to trees.

Spavinaw Creek, Okla.
Spavinaw Lakes, Okla.

SPEARFISH, S.Dak. (Lawrence Co.). For a creek, apparently one in which the Indians speared fish.

SPEARMAN, Tex. (co. seat of Hansford Co.). For Thomas E. Spearman, a railway official.

SPECIMEN RIDGE, Wyo. in Yellowstone Natl. Park. For the petrified forests and great variety of minerals and semiprecious stones found there.

SPECKLED MOUNTAIN, Me. For its appearance, resulting from the variety of tree colors.

SPECK PINNACLE, Wyo. For Dr. John F. Speck, who led the first ascent of this pinnacle with other Iowa mountaineers in 1948.

SPECTACLE POND, Me. So named because it supposedly resembles the shape of eyeglasses.

SPEEDWAY, Ind. (Marion Co.). For the Indianapolis Speedway, the 500-mile track on which the annual automobile race is held at the end of May.

SPENCER, Iowa (co. seat of Clay Co.). For George E. Spencer, U.S. senator from Alabama (1868-79), who had lived in Iowa.

SPENCER, Mass. (Worcester Co.), town and village. Probably for Lt. Gov. Spencer Phipps (1685-1757), who helped to achieve the status of "district" for the area.

SPENCER, N.C. (Rowan Co.). For Samuel Spencer (?-1906), first president of the Southern Railway Company.

SPENCER, Okla. (Oklahoma Co.). For A. M. Spencer, railroad developer.

SPENCER, Capt. Spier, or Spear (?-1811), a Kentucky officer killed at the Battle of Tippecanoe.
Spencer Co., Ind. (co. seat, Rockport).
Spencer Co., Ky. (co. seat, Taylorsville).
Spencer, Ind. (co. seat of Owen Co.).

SPENCER, Tenn. (co. seat of Van Buren Co.). For the Spencer family, early settlers and landowners.

SPENCER, W.Va. (co. seat of Roane Co.). For Spencer ROANE.

SPENCERPORT, N.Y. (Monroe Co.). For Daniel Spencer, a local farmer.

SPENCER STREAM, Me. For a lumberman. It flows east into Dead Stream.

SPHINX PEAK, Mont. For its resemblance to the Sphinx in Egypt.

SPIDER LAKE, Me. So named because it supposedly resembled the shape of a spider.

SPIDER PEAK, Wyo. Named by D. Dornan for the numerous hairy, brown spiders, as large as a nickel, that he found there.

SPINDALE, N.C. (Rutherford Co.). For the textile industry.

SPINK Co., S.Dak. (co. seat, Redfield). For Solomon Lewis Spink (1831-1881), Dakota Territory secretary. He was also a territorial delegate to Congress (1869-71). In earlier years, he had published a newspaper in Illinois and served as a legislator there.

SPIRIT For the supposed presence of spirits or supernatural beings. Translated from Indian names.
Spirit Lake, Wash.
Spirit Lake, Wis. (Burnett Co.).
Spirit Lake, Wis. (Price and Taylor Cos.).

SPIRIT LAKE, Iowa (co. seat of Dickinson Co.). A translation of Siouan *minni waukon*, "spirit water."

SPOKANE For an Indian tribe of Salishan linguistic stock. They inhabited the area along the Spokane River and its tributaries. The name seems to have as part of its meaning "sun," which has given rise to poetic renderings such as "child of the sun" and "chief of the sun." It may mean "toward the sun," but this too is doubtful.
Spokane Co., Wash. (co. seat, *Spokane*).
Spokane, Wash. (co. seat of *Spokane* Co.).
Spokane Indian Reservation, Wash.
Spokane, Mount, Wash.
Spokane River, Idaho-Wash. Flows generally W to the Columbia R.

SPOONER LAKE, Wis. For John C. Spooner, lawyer and railroad developer.

SPOON RIVER, Ill. From Algonquian, "mussel shell." It flows into Illinois River.

SPOTSWOOD, N.J. (Middlesex Co.). For a town in Scotland; named by James Johnstone, the first white settler, who was a member of the Spotswood clan.

SPOTSYLVANIA For Alexander Spotswood (1676-1740), English statesman and lieutenant governor of the colony of Virginia (1710-22) who actually assumed all the duties of the nominal governor, the Earl of Orkney. An able and vigorous administrator, Spotswood was at first opposed by the independent colonial leaders but eventually achieved harmony. *Spotsylvania* is a combination of *Spotswood* and *sylvania*, "woodlands." While this was a common practice (Pennsylvania, Pittsylvania), there is additional word play in this case since the governor's name was *Spotswood*.
Spotsylvania Co., Va. (co. seat, *Spotsylvania*).
Spotsylvania, Va. (co. seat of *Spotsylvania* Co.).

SPRAGUE, Conn. (New London Co.), town. For William Sprague, founder.

SPRAGUE RIVER, Ore. For F. B. Sprague, an army officer active in the Snake and Piute Indian wars. It flows west into Williamson River.

SPRING For a spring or springs in an area.
Spring Creek, Ga. Flows S into L. Seminole.
Spring Creek, Ill. Flows NE into Iroquois R.
Spring Creek, Colo.-Neb. Flows SE into Frenchman R.
Spring Creek, N.Dak.
Spring Creek, S.Dak.
Spring River, Mo.-Ark. Flows S into Black R.
Spring River, Mo.-Kan. Flows W and S into L. of the Cherokees.
Springboro, Ohio (Warren Co.).
Spring Brook Mountain, Me.
Springdale, Ark. (Washington Co.).
Springdale, Ohio (Hamilton Co.).
Springdale, Pa. (Allegheny Co.).
Springfield, Colo. (co. seat of Baca Co.). For *Springfield*, Mo.
Springfield, Fla. (Bay Co.).
Springfield, Ga. (co. seat of Effingham Co.).
Springfield, Ill. (co. seat of Sangamon Co.), state capital.
Springfield, Ky. (co. seat of Washington Co.).
Springfield, Mich. (Oakland Co.).

Springfield, Minn. (Brown Co.).

Springfield, Mo. (co. seat of Greene Co.).

Springfield, N.J. (Union Co.). For springs that feed the headwaters of the Rahway R.

Springfield, Ohio (co. seat of Clark Co.).

Springfield, Ore. (Lane Co.).

Springfield, Tenn. (co. seat of Robertson Co.).

Springfield, Lake, Ill.

Springfield Place, Mich. (Oakland Co.).

Springhill, La. (Webster Parish).

Spring Lake, Mich. (Ottawa Co.).

Spring Lake, N.J. (Monmouth Co.).

Spring Lake, N.C. (Cumberland Co.). For a spring-fed lake.

Spring Lake Heights, N.J. (Monmouth Co.).

Spring Lake Park, Minn. (Hennepin Co.). Promotional.

Springvale, Me. (York Co.). In the valley of the Mousam R.

Spring Valley, Calif. (San Diego Co.).

Spring Valley, Ill. (Bureau Co.). Also for a coal mine of the same name.

Spring Valley, Minn. (Fillmore Co.).

Spring Valley, N.Y. (Rockland Co.).

Spring Valley, Tex. (Harris Co.).

Springview, Neb. (co. seat of Keya Paha Co.).

Springville, N.Y. (Erie Co.), town.

Springville, Utah (Utah Co.).

SPRINGFIELD See SPRING.

SPRINGFIELD For Springfield, Essex, England, the native town of William Pynchon (1590-1662), founder of the Massachusetts town.

Springfield, Mass. (co. seat of Hampden Co.). Earlier, Agawam.

Springfield, Minn. (Brown Co.). For *Springfield*, Mass.

Springfield, Vt. (Windsor Co.), town and village. For *Springfield*, Mass.

Springfield Reservoir, Mass.

West Springfield, Mass. (Hampden Co.), town.

SPRUCE For the tree.

Spruce Mountain, Nev.

Spruce Mountain, Vt.

Spruce Knob (peak), W.Va.

Sprucemont, Nev. (Elko Co.).

SPURR, Mount, Alaska. In Tordrillo Mountains. For Josiah Edward Spurr (1870-1950), of the U.S. Geological Survey.

SQUAM LAKE, N.H. From Abnaki, "salmon."

SQUANNACOOK RIVER, N.H.-Mass. Probably from Algonquian, meaning uncertain, but also possibly from Natick, "green place." It flows into Nashua River.

SQUAPAN From Abnaki, "bear's den."

Squapan Lake, Me.

Squapan Knob, Me.

SQUARE Descriptive of shape.

Square Butte, N.Dak.

Square Lake, Me. One of the Fish River Lakes. Not square; named from a mistranslation of an Indian word meaning "round."

Square Pond, Me.

Squaretop Mountain, Wyo. It has steep granite walls and a squared summit.

SQUAW From the Indian term for a woman.

Squaw Mountain, Me. According to legend, the wife of a chief died there.

Squaw Mountain, Wyo. For a rock formation's resemblance to a squaw with a blanket over her head.

SQUIRREL LAKE, Wis. For the animal

STAFFORD For Stafford, Staffordshire, England.

Stafford, Conn. (Tolland Co.), town.

Stafford Springs, Conn. (Tolland Co.).

STAFFORD For the county of Staffordshire, England.

Stafford Co., Va. (co. seat, *Stafford*).

Stafford, Va. (co. seat of *Stafford* Co.).

STAFFORD, Lewis (?-1863), Union army officer killed in action.

Stafford Co., Kan. (co. seat, St. John).

Stafford, Kan. (*Stafford* Co.).

STAFFORD, Tex. (Fort Bend Co.). For Col. William M. Stafford, landowner. An earlier name was Stafford's Point.

STAGNER FLATS For Speed Stagner, a Missourian who married a squaw and was adopted into the Shoshone tribe.

Stagner Flats Mountain, Wyo.

Stagner Flats Ridge, Wyo.

STAMFORD For Stamford, Lincolnshire, England.

Stamford, Conn. (Fairfield Co.).

Stamford, Tex. (Jones Co.). For *Stamford*, Conn.

Stamford, Lake, Tex.

STANARDSVILLE, Va. (co. seat of Greene Co.). For Robert Stanards, who donated land for the townsite.

STANDARD PEAK, Wyo. So named because the eleventh standard parallel crosses a shoulder of this mountain.

STANDING STONE CREEK, Pa. For the totem pole that stood on the site of what is now Huntingdon, Pa. It flows southwest into Juniata River at Huntingdon.

STANDISH, Me. (Cumberland Co.), town. For Miles Standish. See DUXBURY.

STANDISH, Mich. (co. seat of Arenac Co.). For John D. Standish, millowner and founder.

STANFORD, Calif. (Santa Clara Co.). For Leland Stanford, Jr. (1868-1884), son of Leland Stanford, Sr. (1824-1893), who subsidized the building of Stanford University nearby.

STANFORD, Ky. (co. seat of Lincoln Co.). A modification of the Indian name, translated "Standing Fort," because it could not be taken.

STANFORD, Mont. (co. seat of Judith Basin Co.). For a Stanfordville in New York.

STANISLAUS For an Indian leader who had been baptized and given the Christian name of Estanislao. His band of Indians was defeated by regular Mexican troops in a battle that took place at the Rio de los Laquisimes. In time the river became known as *Rio Estanislao* and was Anglicized by John C. Fremont to Stanislaus River.
Stanislaus Co., Calif. (co. seat, Modesto).
Stanislaus Natl. Forest, Calif.
Stanislaus Peak, Calif.
Stanislaus River, Calif. Flows generally SW to the San Joaquin R.

STANLEY, D. S. (1829-1902), career army officer. He fought in the Civil War and against the Indians on the frontier, rising to the rank of general. After retirement, he served as director of the U.S. Soldiers' Home for five years.
Stanley Co., S.Dak. (co. seat, Fort Pierre).
Stanley, N.Dak. (co. seat of Mountrail Co.).

Or possibly for King Stanley, an early settler.

STANLY Co. N.C. (co. seat, Albermarle). For John Stanly (1774-1834), North Carolina legislator and U.S. representative (1801-03; 1809-11).

STANSBURY MOUNTAINS, Utah. For Howard Stansbury, government surveyor of the Great Salt Lake (1849-50).

STANSTEAD Co., Que. (co. seat, Ayer's Cliff). For one of the three English villages of the same name.

STANTON, Calif. (Orange Co.). For Philip A. Stanton, assemblyman and landowner.

STANTON, Edwin McMasters (1814-1869), Pennsylvania statesman. He served as U.S. attorney general (1860-61) under Lincoln. Appointed secretary of war during the difficult Civil War years, he continued in office (1862-68) under Andrew Johnson.
Stanton Co., Kan. (co. seat, Johnson).
Stanton Co., Neb. (co. seat, *Stanton*).
Stanton, Ky. (co. seat of Powell Co.).
Stanton, Mich. (co. seat of Montcalm Co.).
Stanton, Neb. (co. seat of *Stanton* Co.). Or possibly for the maiden name of the wife of S. L. Halman, founder.
Stanton, Tex. (co. seat of Martin Co.).

STANTON, N.Dak. (co. seat of Mercer Co.). For the maiden name of the mother of Thomas and James McGrath, early settlers and businessmen.

STAPLES, Minn. (Todd Co.). For Isaac (1816-1898) and Samuel (1805-1887) Staples, lumbermen.

STAPLETON, Neb. (co. seat of Logan Co.). For a Stapleton who was a friend of the founder.

STAR CITY, Ark. (co. seat of Lincoln Co.). So named because it is located in the center of five surrounding hills that resemble the points of a star.

STARK, John (1728-1822), career soldier. An officer in the French and Indian Wars (1755-63), he later became a commander in the American Revolution, rising to the rank of general. Among his major battles were Bunker Hill, Bennington, Trenton, and Princeton, in the latter two of which he was commander of the American forces. See also STARKE Co., Ind.

Stark Co., Ill. (co. seat, Toulon).

Stark Co., Ohio (co. seat, Canton).

Starkville, Miss. (co. seat of Oktibbeha Co.), locally called Stark.

STARK Co., N.Dak. (co. seat, Dickinson). For George Stark, a railway official.

STARKE, Fla. (co. seat of Bradford Co.). For Madison Starke Perry (1814-1865), fourth governor (1857-61), legislator, and plantation owner; or possibly for Thomas Starke, also a landowner.

STARKE Co., Ind. (co. seat, Knox). For John STARK. No reason is known why the spelling was altered.

STARR Co., Tex. (co. seat, Rio Grande City). For James Harper Starr (1809-1890), an official in the Republic of Texas government.

STATE COLLEGE, Pa. (Centre Co.). So named because it is the home of Penn State University.

STATEN ISLAND, N.Y. in New York Bay, forms Richmond borough of New York City and Richmond County. From Dutch, "the states," for the Staaten General, governing body of Netherlands.

STATENVILLE, Ga. (co. seat of Echols Co.). For James W. Staten, the first representative in the Georgia legislature from Clinch County.

STATESBORO, Ga. (co. seat of Bulloch Co.). So named in honor of the fight for states' rights made by Thomas Jefferson.

STATESVILLE, N.C. (co. seat of Iredell Co.). For North Carolina's having become a state (1789). An earlier name was Fourth Creek.

STAUNTON, Ill. (Macoupin Co.). For Hugh Staunton, a local citizen who agreed to pay for the expense of changing the entry in the records if he were allowed to choose the name.

STAUNTON, Va. (co. seat of Augusta Co.). For Lady Staunton, wife of colonial governor William Gooch.

STAYTON, Ore. (Marion Co.). For Drury S. Stayton, founder.

STEAMBOAT SPRINGS, Colo. (co. seat of Routt Co.). So named because the springs on the edge of town sounded like a steamboat.

STEARNS Co., Minn. (co. seat, St. Cloud). For Charles Thomas Stearns (1807-1898), a territorial legislator. In the original bill, the county was to be named Stevens for a governor and Civil War hero (see STEVENS, Isaac Ingalls), but apparently a clerical error was made and was allowed to stand.

STEELE Co., Minn. (co. seat, Owatonna). For Franklin Steele (1813-1880), a prominent landowner and civic leader. He was a member of the first board of regents of the University of Minnesota and had a lifelong interest in the history of Minnesota Territory.

STEELE Co., N.Dak. (co. seat, Finley). For J. A. Steele, president of the Red River Land Company, which purchased the land from the Northern Pacific railroad.

STEELE, N.Dak. (co. seat of Kidder Co.). For Wilbur Fisk Steele (1844-1917), founder. He was a member of the lower house of North Dakota's first legislature, was active in railroad development, and was a leader in the attempt to have the state capital located at Steele.

STEELTON, Pa. (Dauphin Co.). For its steel industry.

STEELVILLE, Mo. (co. seat of Crawford Co.). For James Steel, a landowner.

STEENS MOUNTAIN, Ore. For Maj. Enoch Steen of the U.S. Army, who fought a band of Snake Indians in the area.

STEGER, Ill. (Will and Cook Cos.). For the founder, but other information is not available.

STEILACOOM, Wash. (Pierce Co.). A folk-etymologized form of *Tail-a-koom*, for an Indian chief.

STEINBACH, Man. Named for Steinbach, Ukraine, Russia, by Mennonites who emigrated from there in 1874.

STELLARTON, N.S. (Pictou Co.). For its stellar coal, so called because during combustion it emits sparks resembling stars.

STELLER, George Wilhelm, naturalist with Capt. Vitus Bering's expedition in 1741.
Steller, Mount, Alaska. In the Aleutian Range.
Steller, Mount, Alaska. In the Chugach Mtns.

STEPHENS, Alexander Hamilton (1812-1883), Georgia statesman. He served in many offices including legislator, U.S. representative (1843-59), and governor (1882-83). He was also a vice-president of the Confederacy (1861).
Stephens Co., Ga. (co. seat, Toccoa).
Stephens Co., Tex. (co. seat, Breckenridge).

STEPHENS Co., Okla. (co. seat, Duncan). For John H. Stephens (1847-1924), U.S. representative (1897-1917) from Texas.

STEPHENSON Co., Ill. (co. seat, Freeport). For Benjamin Stephenson (?-1821), an officer in the War of 1812. He held many territorial offices and was a prominent banker in his later years.

STEPHENVILLE, Tex. (co. seat of Erath Co.). For John M. Stephen (1814-1862), donator of the land on which much of the town was built.

STERLING, Samuel, an early settler in Illinois.
Sterling, Colo. (co. seat of Logan Co.). For *Sterling*, Ill.
Sterling, Ill. (Whiteside Co.).

STERLING, N.Y. (Cayuga Co.), town. For William Alexander, Lord Sterling.

STERLING, W. S. (?-1881), a frontiersman in Texas killed by Indians while he was a marshal.
Sterling Co., Tex. (co. seat, *Sterling City*).
Sterling City, Tex. (co. seat of *Sterling* Co.).

STERLING HEIGHTS, Mich. (Macomb Co.). For Azariah W. Sterling, an early settler.

STEUBEN, Baron Friedrich Wilhelm Ludolf Gerhard Augustin von (1730-1794), Prussian soldier who served in the American Revolution and later settled in New York. Named inspector general of the Continental Army (1789), he was chiefly responsible for creating trained soldiers from undisciplined recruits. He served with distinction in the field, particularly in the South.

Baron Friedrich Wilhelm von Steuben was one of many Europeans, such as Count Pulaski and the Marquis de Lafayette, to ally themselves with the American revolutionaries. Von Steuben, a master of logistics and discipline, played a major role at Valley Forge ·in preventing the ill-organized American army from degenerating into a mob. [*New York Public Library*]

Steuben Co., Ind. (co. seat, Angola).
Steuben Co., N.Y. (co. seat, Bath).
Steubenville, Ohio (co. seat of Jefferson Co.)

STEVENS, Isaac Ingalls (1818-1862), career soldier and legislator. He served as an officer in the Mexican War, after which he commanded a team that surveyed a railroad route from St. Paul to Puget Sound. After serving as the first governor of Washington Territory, he became a delegate to Congress. At the outbreak of the Civil War, he accepted a commission as colonel and rose quickly to the rank of major general. He was killed in action at Chantilly, Va. See also STEARNS Co., Minn.
Stevens Co., Minn, (co. seat, Morris).
Stevens Co., Wash. (co. seat, Colville).
Stevens Lake, Wash.
Stevens Pass, Wash.

STEVENS Co., Kan. (co. seat, Hugoton). For Thaddeus Stevens (1792-1868), Pennsylvania legislator and U.S. representative (1849-53; 1859-68) who strongly opposed slavery.

STEVENS BROOK, N.H. For a local settler. It flows southeast into Contoocook River.

STEVENSON, Wash. (co. seat of Skamania Co.). For George H. Stevenson, pioneer and founder.

STEVENSON MOUNTAIN, Wyo., in Yellowstone Natl. Park. For James Stevenson, director of the Hayden surveys in the Tetons.

STEVENS POINT, Wis. (co. seat of Portage Co.). For George Stevens, the first settler.

STEWART Co., Ga. (co. seat, Lumpkin). For Daniel Stewart (1759-1829), a general in the American Revolution.

STEWART Co., Tenn. (co. seat, Dover). For Duncan Stewart.

STEWART MOUNTAIN, Me. For a local settler named Stewart.

STEWART PEAK, Colo. For a local community member.

STEWARTVILLE, Minn. (Olmsted Co.). For Charles N. Stewart, founder and millowner.

STICKNEY, Ill. (Cook Co.). For a local community member.

STIGLER, Okla. (co. seat of Haskell Co.). For Joseph Simeon Stigler (1857-1949), real-estate developer.

STIKINE From Tlingit Indian, "great river."
Stikine Mountains, B.C.-Yukon. Range in the Rocky Mtns.
Stikine River, B.C.-Alaska. Flows W and SW into the Pacific Ocean.

STILL RIVER. Description for sluggishness of river flow.
Still River, Conn. (Litchfield Co.), town.
Still River, Conn. Flows E and N into Housatonic R.

STILLWATER Usually for a stream or body of water.
Stillwater Co., Mont. (co. seat, Columbus). For the river.
Stillwater, Minn. (co. seat of Washington Co.). For the stillness of the water in McKusick's Lake and Lily Lake, and also for a village in Maine from which the founder, John McKusick, came.
Stillwater, Okla. (co. seat of Payne Co.). For the creek.
Stillwater Creek, Okla.
Stillwater Range, Nev.
Stillwater River, Mont. Flows generally NW to the Yellowstone R.

STILWELL, Okla. (co. seat of Adair Co.). For Arthur E. Stilwell, a railway official.

STINKINGWATER PEAK, Wyo. For a nearby river with an unpleasant odor.

STINNETT, Tex. (co. seat of Hutchinson Co.). For A. S. Stinnett, one of the founders.

STOCKPORT, N.Y. (Columbia Co.). Named by James Wild, local mill owner, for his native town in Cheshire, England.

STOCKTON, Kan. (co. seat of Rooks Co.). So named because it began as a "stock town," a center for cattle raising.

STOCKTON, Robert Field (1795-1866), naval officer who claimed California (1847) for the United States. He was a U.S. senator (1851-53), was president of the Delaware and Raritan Canal (1853-56), and was a member of the peace convention at Washington (1861).
Fort Stockton, Tex. (co. seat of Pecos Co.).
Stockton, Calif. (co. seat of Joaquin Co.).
Stockton, Mo. (co. seat of Cedar Co.).
Stockton, N.Y. (Chautauqua Co.).

STOCKTON ISLAND, Wis. One of the Apostle Islands in Lake Superior. For a settler.

STOCKVILLE, Neb. (co. seat of Frontier Co.). For a cattlemen's town in good cattle country.

STODDARD Co., Mo. (co. seat, Bloomfield). For Amos Stoddard (1762-1813), acting governor of Louisiana Territory (1804-05). A veteran of the American Revolution, he served also as an officer in the War of 1812 and died as the result of a wound received in action.

STOKES Co., N.C. (co. seat, Danbury). For John Stokes (1756-1790), a hero of the American Revolution, legislator, and jurist.

STONE Descriptive.

North Stonington, Conn. (New London Co.), town.

Stone Co., Ark. (co. seat, Mountain View).

Stone Mountain, Vt.

Stoneham, Mass. (Middlesex Co), town. Earlier, Charlestown End.

Stonington, Conn. (New London Co.), town.

Stonington, Me. (Hancock Co.). Famous for granite deposits used for public monuments and edifices.

STONE Co., Miss. (co. seat, Wiggins). For John Marshall Stone (1830-1900), Confederate army officer and governor of Mississippi (1890-96).

STONE Co., Mo. (co. seat, Galena). For John W. Stone, an early settler.

STONE CORRAL LAKE, Ore. One of the Warner Valley lakes. For the corral on the edge of the lake.

STONES RIVER For Uriah Stone, one of a party of four men who discovered the river in 1766.

Stones River, Tenn. Formed from two forks, flows NW into Cumberland R.

Stones River Natl. Battlefield, Tenn. Site of a battle (Dec. 31, 1862 to Jan. 2, 1863) when the Union forces led by Gen. William S. Rosecrans forced the Confederates under Gen. Braxton Bragg to retreat.

STONEWALL Co., Tex. (co. seat, Aspermont). For Thomas Jonathan ("Stonewall") Jackson (1824-1863), Confederate army general. He earned the nickname "Stonewall" from his stand at Bull Run (1861). He was elected to the American Hall of Fame (1955).

STONY Descriptive.

Stony Creek, Pa. Flows SW into Susquehanna R.

Stone Mountain, Georgia, not far from Atlanta, was conceived as a memorial to the heroes of the Confederacy. [*Photo by Max Humm. Frederic Lewis*]

Stony Creek, Pa. Flows N. into Conemaugh R.

Stony Island, Mich. In Saginaw Bay.

Stony Island, N.Y. In L. Ontario.

Stony River, Alaska. Flows SW and NW into Kuskokwim R.

Stony Brook, N.Y. (Suffolk Co.).

Stony Point, N.Y. (Rockland Co.).

STOREY Co., Nev. (co. seat, Virginia City). For Edward F. Storey (?-1860), an army officer killed by Indians at Pyramid Lake.

STORM For rough waters on the lake; named by an early trapper, who experienced a severe storm here.

Storm Lake, Iowa.

Storm Lake, Iowa (co. seat of Buena Vista Co.).

STORMONT Co., Ont. (co. seat, Cornwall). For David Murray, Viscount Stormont of Perth, Scotland.

STORY Co., Iowa (co. seat, Nevada). For Joseph Story (1779-1845), Massachusetts legislator, U.S. representative (1808-09), and associate justice of the U.S. Supreme Court.

STOUGHTON, Mass. (Norfolk Co.), town. For William Stoughton (1631-1701), commissioner of the United Colonies (1674-76; 1680-86) and a judge on various courts. He was a major benefactor of Harvard College and acting governor of Massachusetts (1694-1700). He was also the chief justice of the court that tried the Salem witchcraft cases.

STOUGHTON, Wis. (Dane Co.). For Luke Stoughton, founder.

STOW, Mass. (Middlesex Co.), town. Named by Governor Bradstreet for a John Stow who had traveled with him to the New World.

STOW, Ohio (Summit Co.). For Joshua Stow, landowner.

STOWE, Pa. (Allegheny Co.). For the Stowe family, early settlers.

STRAFFORD Earl of Strafford was a title held by the Wentworth family in England. The first Earl was Thomas Wentworth (1593-1641), famous for making many reforms in the Irish government when he was lord deputy for Ireland. Two of his descendants, Benning Wentworth and John Wentworth, became governors of New Hampshire. It is probable, however, that the place names stem directly from William Wentworth, 4th Earl of Strafford, who was a cousin of John Wentworth.

Strafford Co., N.H. (co. seat, Dover).

Strafford, N.H. (*Strafford* Co.), town.

Strafford, Vt. (Orange Co.), town.

STRATFORD For Stratford-on-Avon, Warwickshire, England, Shakespeare's home.

Stratford, Conn. (Fairfield Co.), town.

Stratford, N.J. (Camden Co.).

Stratford, Ont. (co. seat of Perth Co.).

STRATFORD, Tex. (co. seat of Sherman Co.). For a Stratford in Virginia.

STRATHROY, Ont. (Middlesex Co.). For Strathroy, a small Irish seaport, native home of John Stewart Buchanan, who became owner of the site of land in 1832.

STRATTON MEADOWS, Colo. (El Paso Co.). Combination of a personal and promotional name.

STRATTON MOUNTAIN, Vt. For Samuel Stratton, early settler.

STRAWBERRY For wild strawberries.

Strawberry Mountain, Ore.

Strawberry Reservoir, Utah. On *Strawberry* R.

Strawberry River, Ark. Flows SE into Black R.

Strawberry River, Utah. Flows SE and E into Duchesne R.

STREAMWOOD, Ill. (Cook Co.). For the Stream family, plus *-wood*, promotional.

STREATOR, Ill. (La Salle Co.). For W. S. Streator of Cleveland, Ohio. Earlier names were Hardscrabble and Unionville.

STRONG RIVER, Miss. For a settler named Strong. It flows southwest into Pearl River.

STRONGVILLE, Ohio (Cuyahoga Co.). For Caleb Strong (1745-1819), Massachusetts statesman. He was a representative and senator (1776-88) in the state legislature and was named a member of the national convention in Philadelphia (though he did not attend because of illness). He served as U.S. senator (1789-96) and as governor of Massachusetts (1800-07; 1812-16).

Stratford, Connecticut, was one of many American communities that began the tradition of the commuter in the second half of the nineteenth century. It was once a more leisurely experience as shown in this painting by Edward Lamson Henry: "The 9:45 Accommodation." [*Metropolitan Museum of Art*]

STROUD, Okla. (Lincoln Co.). For James W. Stroud, a prominent citizen.

STROUD PEAK, Wyo. For William J. ("Rocky Mountain Bill") Stroud, a Rock Springs man who always wore the same suit and hat, whether conducting business, visiting friends, or climbing mountains.

STROUSS HILL, Wyo. For John Strouss, rancher.

STRUTHERS, Ohio (Mahoning Co.). For John Struthers, an army officer in the Pennsylvania militia who purchased land in the area.

STUART, Fla. (co. seat of Martin Co.). For Samuel C. Stuart, a telegraph operator and station agent for the Florida East Coast railroad.

STUART, Mount, Wash. Probably for an early climber or settler.

STUART, Va. (co. seat of Patrick Co.). For James Ewell Brown ("Jeb") Stuart (1833-1864), famous general of the Confederate army who accompanied Lee in the attack on John Brown at Harpers Ferry. He attained the rank of major general and participated in many battles, including Bull Run and Williamsburg. After the death of "Stonewall" Jackson (1863), Stuart took command of Jackson's corps and completed the brilliant work begun by Jackson. Stuart died from a wound received at Yellow Tavern, near Richmond, Va., when he tried to stop Sheridan from entering Richmond.

STUART ISLAND, Alaska. In Norton Sound. Named by Capt. James Cook in 1778, reason unknown, although Stuart was a common personal name and also that of a Scottish and English ruling family.

STUMP LAKE, N.Dak. So named because oτ the tree stumps in the lake. It is believed that the lake was formed by a geological occurrence in which a forest sank into what is now the lake.

STURBRIDGE, Mass. (Hampden Co.), town. For Stourbridge, Worcestershire, England.

STURGEON For the fish.
Sturgeon Bay, Mich. Inlet on L. Michigan.
Sturgeon Bay, Wis. Arm of Green Bay. Also for its shape.
Sturgeon Point, Mich. Extends into L. Huron.
Sturgeon River, Mich. Flows N into Burt L.

Sturgeon River, Mich. Flows S into Big Bay de Noc.

Sturgeon River, Mich. Flows SE and S into Menominee R.

Sturgeon River, Mich. Flows WNW into Portage L.

Sturgeon River, Minn. Flows into Little Fork of Rainy R.

Sturgeon Bay, Wis. (co. seat of Door Co.). For the bay.

Sturgeon Falls, Ont. (Nippissing Co.).

Sturgeon River Falls, Mich. On the river which flows into Portage L.

STURGIS, Mich. (St. Joseph Co.). For John Sturgis (1787-1872), the first settler.

STURGIS Co., S.Dak. (co. seat of Meade Co.). Either for Samuel D. Sturgis, an army officer who commanded a post there when the town was founded, or for his son, an officer killed (1876) at Little Big Horn.

STURTEVANT, Wis. (Racine Co.) For the B. F. Sturtevant Company.

STUTSMAN Co., N.Dak. (co. seat, Jamestown). For Enos Stutsman, a member of the Dakota Council and a legislator.

STUTTGART, Ark. (Arkansas Co.). For Stuttgart, Germany.

STUTTS CREEK, Mich. For a local dweller. It flows southeast into Manistique River.

STUYVESANT, N.Y. (Columbia Co.), town. For Peter Stuyvesant (1592-1672), Dutch administrator in the United States. He was director general of New Netherland, and served in that position at the time of the Dutch surrender of New Netherland to the English in 1664.

STYX RIVER, Ala. Mythological; for the River of Styx in Greek mythology. It flows generally southeast into Perdido Bay of the Gulf of Mexico.

SUBLETTE, William Lewis (1799-1845), explorer and entrepreneur who was active in the Rocky Mountain region.

Sublette Co., Wyo. (co. seat, Pinedale).

Sublette, Kan. (co. seat of Haskell Co.).

Sublette Peak, Wyo.

SUCCESS, Mount, N.H. A promotional and hopeful name.

SUCKER CREEK, Ore. Probably for some miners from Illinois, known as the "Sucker State." Another possibility is that it is from Spanish *socorro*, "aid." It flows into a tributary of the Illinois River.

SUCKER RIVER, Mich. For the fish. It flows east and north into Lake Superior.

SUDBURY For Sudbury, Suffolk, England.

Sudbury District, Ont. (district seat, *Sudbury*). Named by James Worthington, superintendent of construction for the Canadian Pacific railroad, for his wife's birthplace.

Sudbury, Ont. (district seat of *Sudbury* District).

Sudbury, Mass. (Middlesex Co.), town.

Sudbury Reservoir, Mass.

Sudbury River, Mass.

SUFFERN, N.Y. (Rockland Co.). For John Suffern, one of the original settlers and a member of the first state legislature.

SUFFIELD, Conn. (Hartford Co.), town. Named by the Massachusetts General Court, because of a mistake in state boundaries, for a town in England; the court also recognized the meaning "southfield," because the town was thought to be near the southern border of Massachusetts.

SUFFOLK For Suffolk county, England.

Suffolk Co., Mass. (co. seat, Boston).

Suffolk Co., N.Y. (co. seat, Riverhead).

Suffolk, Va. (co. seat of Nansemond Co.).

SUGAR For maple sugar trees.

Sugar Creek, Ind. Flows SW into Wabash R.

Sugar Creek, Ind. Flows W and SSW into East Fork White R.

Sugar Creek, Ind.-Ill. Flows W and N into Iroquois R.

Sugar Creek, Pa. Flows E into Susquehanna R.

Sugar Island, Me. In Moosehead L.

Sugar Island, Mich. In St. Marys R.

Sugar River, N.H. Flows W into Connecticut R.

Sugar River, Wis. Flows SE into Pecatonica R. Translated from Indian.

Sugarbush Hill, Wis.

Sugar Creek, Mo. (Jackson Co.).

SUGARLAND, Tex. (Fort Bend Co.). For sugar cane grown and processed there.

SUGARLOAF For a conical shape, that of a so-called sugarloaf—a cone of sugar about five inches in diameter, which was the form sugar generally came in from colonial days to the 19th century. Also, *Sugar Loaf*.
Sugarloaf Mountain, Me.
Sugar Loaf (mountain), N.H.
Sugarloaf Peak, Colo.

SUIATTLE RIVER, Wash. Of Indian origin, meaning unknown. It flows northwest into Sauk River.

SUISUN CITY, Calif. (Solano Co.). Possibly for a nearby Indian tribe; meaning unknown.

SULLIVAN, Daniel, a messenger killed while delivering messages from Capt. George Rogers Clark after the capture of Vincennes, Ind. (1779).
Sullivan Co., Ind. (co. seat, *Sullivan*).
Sullivan, Ind. (co. seat of *Sullivan* Co.).

SULLIVAN, Ill. (co. seat of Mouitrie Co.). For Sullivan's Island, at Charleston, S.C., on which Fort Moultrie was located.

SULLIVAN, Gen. John (1740-1795). New Hampshire soldier, statesman, and jurist, active during the American Revolution. He was a member of the Continental Congress (1774, 1775, 1780, 1781) and president of New Hampshire (1786, 1787, 1789).
Sullivan Co., Mo. (co. seat, Milan). For *Sullivan* Co., Tenn.
Sullivan Co., N.H. (co. seat, Newport).
Sullivan Co., N.Y. (co. seat, Monticello).
Sullivan Co., Pa. (co. seat, Laporte).
Sullivan Co., Tenn. (co. seat, Blountville).

SULLY For Fort Sully, which was named for Alfred Sully (1821-1879), a career army officer, famous as an Indian fighter. During the Civil War, he rose to the rank of general and was cited several times for bravery.
Sully Co., S.Dak. (co. seat, Onida).
Sully Butte, S.Dak.

SULPHUR For the mineral (now usually spelled *sulfur*).
Port Sulphur, La. (Plaquemines Parish). For the sulphur industry in the area.
Sulphur, La. (Calcasieu Parish). For vast deposits of sulfur once found in the area.
Sulphur, Okla. (co. seat of Murray Co.). For sulfur springs in the area.

Sulphur Creek, S.Dak.
Sulphur River, Tex.-Ark. Flows E into Red R.
Sulphur Springs, Tex. (co. seat of Hopkins Co.). For sulfur springs there. Earlier, Bright Star.

SUMMER LAKE, Ore. Named by John C. Fremont in 1843 as a contrast between the barrenness of the nearby ridge, which he named Winter, and the lushness of the grass and water of the lake, which he named Summer.

SUMMERS Co., W.Va. (co. seat, Hinton). For George William Summers (1807-1868), Virginia legislator, U.S. representative (1831-45), and jurist.

SUMMERSIDE, P.E.I. (co. seat of Prince Co.). For the home of Daniel Green, who received a grant of land on the present site of the town in 1780. After his death, his son converted the home into an inn and named it Summerside House. The first postmaster put the name on the mailbags to the settlement.

SUMMERSVILLE, W.Va. (co. seat, Hinton). For George William Summers (1807-1868), Virginia legislator, U.S. representative (1831-45), and jurist.

SUMMERVILLE For the pleasant climate.
Summerville, Ga. (co. seat of Chattooga Co.).
Summerville, S.C. (Dorchester Co.).

SUMMIT Descriptive.
Summit Co., Colo. (co. seat, Breckenridge). Part of the county's southeastern border follows the Continental Divide.
Summit Co., Ohio (co. seat, Akron). The highest point on the Ohio Canal is at the county seat, Akron (Greek for "summit").
Summit Co., Utah (co. seat, Coalville). On the divide between the Colorado River basin and that of Great Salt Lake.
Summit, Ill. (Cook Co.). On the divide between the Mississippi valley and the Great Lakes.
Summit, N.J. (Union Co.). On the crest of First Watchung Mtn. Earlier, Turkey Hill, for wild turkeys found there.
Summit Mountain, Nev.
Summit Peak, Colo.
Summit Hill, Pa. (Carbon Co.).

SUMNER Co., Kan. (co. seat, Wellington). For Charles Sumner (1811-1874), lawyer, one of the founders (1848) of the Free-Soil Party, and U.S. senator from Massachusetts (1851-74).

SUMNER, Miss. (a co. seat of Tallahatchie Co.). For Joseph Burton Sumner, first settler, first postmaster, and first mayor.

SUMNER Co., Tenn. (co. seat, Galiatin). For Jethro Sumner (1733-1785), Indian fighter, active in promotion of statehood for Tennessee, and a general during the American Revolution.

SUMTER, Thomas (1734-1832), soldier and statesman, born in Virginia but associated with South Carolina. He fought in the French and Indian Wars and in the American Revolution, where his campaigns against superior British forces earned him the nickname "Gamecock of the Revolution." He was a U.S. representative (1789-93; 1797-1801) and senator (1801-10). See also FORT SUMTER NATL. MONUMENT.

Sumter Co., Ala. (co. seat, Livingston).
Sumter Co., Fla. (co. seat, Bushnell).
Sumter Co., Ga. (co. seat, Americus).
Sumter Co., S.C. (co. seat, *Sumter*).
Sumter, S.C. (co. seat of *Sumter* Co.).
Sumter Natl. Forest, S.C.

SUN, Calif. (Riverside Co.). For the pleasant climate.

SUNAPEE, Lake, N.H. From Pennacook, "rocky pond."

SUNBEAM PEAK, Wyo. So named because it catches the early sunshine.

SUNBURY, Pa. (co. seat of Northumberland Co.). For Sunbury, Middlesex. England. Earlier (Indian), Shamokin.

SUN CITY, Ariz. (Maricopa Co.). For the pleasant climate.

SUNCOOK From Algonquian, "at the rocks."
Suncook, N.H. (Merrimack Co.).
Suncook Lakes, N.H.
Suncook River, N.H.

SUNDANCE For the colorful annual ceremony held by the Indians in worship of the sun.

Sundance, Wyo. (co. seat of Crook Co.). For the mountain.
Sundance Mountain, Wyo. The Sioux held ceremonies annually on the mountain, which was known as the "Temple of the Sioux."
Sundance Pinnacle, Wyo.

SUNFLOWER For the plant, *Helianthus annuus*, common in North America, the state flower of Kansas.
Sunflower Co., Miss. (co. seat, Indianola). For the river.
Sunflower, Mount, Kan.
Sunflower River, Miss. Flows generally S to the Yazoo R.

SUNLIGHT So named because prospectors who were lost in the fog broke through to sunlight at this place.
Sunlight Basin, Wyo.
Sunlight Creek, Wyo.
Sunlight Peak, Wyo.

SUNNYMEAD, Calif. (Riverside Co.). A combination of *sunny* (descriptive) and a Mr. *Mead*, landowner.

SUNNY Descriptive.
Sunnyside, Wash. (Yakima Co.).
Sunnyvale, Calif. (Santa Clara Co.).

SUN PRAIRIE, Wis. (Dane Co.). Named by a caravan that had undergone many days of rainy weather when it came upon a sunny day west of what is now Madison. The prairie itself was also so named.

SUNRISE Descriptive and promotional.
Sunrise Peak, Utah.
Sunrise Peak, Wash.
Sunrise Manor, Nev. (Clark Co.).

SUNSET Descriptive and promotional.
Sunset, Utah (Davis Co.).
Sunset Hills, Mo. (St. Louis Co.).

SUNSET CRATER NATL. MONUMENT, Ariz. So named for the shades of volcanic ash.

SUPERIOR For superior (higher) position or some superior quality.
Superior, Ariz. (Pinal Co.). For the Arizona and Lake Superior Mining Company.
Superior, Mont. (co. seat of Mineral Co.). For *Superior*, Wis.
Superior, Neb. (Nuckolls Co.). For the quality of the soil.

Superior, Wis. (co. seat of Douglas Co.). For the lake.

Superior, Lake, Ont.-Mich.-Wis.-Minn. Largest and farthest north of the Great Lakes.

Superior Natl. Forest, Minn. Covers more than one million acres.

SUR, Point, Calif. Extends into the Pacific Ocean. From Spanish, "south."

SURFSIDE, Fla. (Dade Co.). Descriptive.

SURREY, B.C. So named because it is south of New Westminster, British Columbia, just as Surrey, England, is south of Westminster.

SURRY For the county of Surrey, England.
Surry Co., N.C. (co. seat, Dobson).
Surry Co., Va. (co. seat, *Surry*).
Surry, Va. (co. seat of *Surry* Co.).

SURVEY PEAK, Wyo. Descriptive.

SUSANVILLE For Susan Roop Arnold (1841-1921), daughter of Isaac Roop (1822-1869), founder.
Susanville, Calif. (co. seat of Lassen Co.).
Susanville, Ore. (Grant Co.). For *Susanville*, Calif.

SUSITNA From Tanaina Indian, "sandy river."
Susitna Lake, Alaska.
Susitna River, Alaska. Flows SW into Cook Inlet.

SUSQUEHANNA For the Indian tribe of Iroquoian linguistic stock located along the river of the same name in New York, Pennsylvania, and Maryland. Originally *Sasquesahonock* or *Susquehannock*, the origin of the name is uncertain. It has been suggested that it comes from a combination of *sisku*, "mud," and *hanne*, "river," or a variation on *suckahanne*, "water." The names of places derive from that of the river.
Susquehanna Co., Pa. (co. seat, Montrose).
Susquehanna Flats, Md. Marshy area on the *Susquehanna* R.
Susquehanna River, N.Y.-Pa.-Md. Flows S to Chesapeake Bay.

SUSSEX For the county of Sussex, England.
Sussex Co., Del. (co. seat, Georgetown),
Sussex Co., N.J. (co. seat, Newton).

Sussex Co., Va. (co. seat, *Sussex*).
Sussex, Wis. (Waukesha Co.).
Sussex, Va. (co. seat of *Sussex* Co.).

SUTHERLAND CANAL, Neb. An irrigation canal extending between two parts of South Platte River. For the nearby town, which was named for an official of the Union Pacific railroad.

SUTHERLIN, Ore. (Douglas Co.). For Fenden Sutherlin (1822-1901), land developer and agriculturist.

SUTTER Co., Calif. (co. seat, Yuba City). For John Augustus Sutter (1803-1880), made famous by the discovery of gold (1848) on his property. Although he did not profit from the discovery, he is also remembered as an early developer of the area in which he lived.

SUTTON, Mass. (Worcester Co.), town. Probably for one of several Suttons in England.

SUTTON Co., Tex. (co. seat, Sonora). For John S. Sutton (1821-1862), Confederate army officer from Texas, who died of wounds received in action.

SUTTON, W.Va. (co. seat of Braxton Co.). Said to be for John Davidson Sutton, an early settler.

SUTWIK ISLAND, Alaska. From an Eskimo name, meaning unknown.

SUWANNEE From a Seminole name of uncertain origin and meaning, possibly *sawni*, "echo," or it may be an English rendering of Spanish *San Juan*. The linguistic problems existing in this possibility have not been solved and may never be, since so far no documentary evidence or data have been found.
Suwannee Co., Fla. (co. seat, Live Oak).
Suwannee River, Fla. Flows generally S to the Gulf of Mexico. Stephen Foster made the river famous with his popular song *The Swanee River*.
Suwannee Sound, Fla.

SWAIN Co., N.C. (co. seat, Bryson City). For David L. Swain (1801-1868), governor (1832-35) and educator.

SWAINSBORO, Ga. (co. seat of Emanuel Co.). For the Swain family, pioneer settlers.

The Suwanee (or Swanee) River has always been a great favorite among songwriters since Stephen Foster wrote his memorable tune. This sentimental confection by O. W. Lane was dedicated in 1878 to the popular performer, Sam Lucas. [*New York Public Library*]

SWAMP LAKE, Ore. One of the Warner Valley lakes. Descriptive.

SWAMPSCOTT, Mass. (Essex Co.), town. From Algonquian *muski-ompsk-ut*, "at the red rocks" or "broken waters."

SWAN For the waterfowl.
Swan Creek, S.Dak. Flows S and W into Missouri R.
Swan Lake, Minn. Translated from Ojibway *wabiziwi*, "swan."

SWAN LAKE, Me. For a family named Swan, settlers in the area.

SWAN QUARTER Said to be for an early settler, Samuel F. Swann.
Swan Quarter, N.C. (co. seat of Hyde Co.).
Swan Quarter Natl. Wildlife Refuge, N.C.

SWAN RIVER, Mont. For Emmett Swan, postmaster. It flows north into Flathead Lake.

SWANSEA For Swansea, Glamorganshire, Wales.
Swansea, Ill. (St. Clair Co.). Named by Welsh miners in the mid 1800s.
Swansea, Mass. (Bristol Co.), town. The first minister here came from Wales.

SWANSON LAKE, Neb. For Carl Swanson, who was active in bringing irrgation to the area.

SWANTON Probably from the Mohawk word for "wood," *ohswa* or *ohswenka*. Another possibility is that it was named for Capt. William Swanton, a British officer who fought in the French and Indian Wars.
Swanton, Ohio (Fulton Co.). For *Swanton*, Vt.
Swanton, Vt. (Franklin Co.), town and village.

SWANZEY, N.H. (Cheshire Co.), town. Variant of SWANSEA.

SWARTHMORE, Pa. (Delaware Co.). For Swarthmore Hall, the home of George Fox, founder of the Society of Friends.

SWARTSWOOD For Jacob Swartwout, killed by Indians near the lake.
Little Swartswood Lake, N.J.
Swartswood Lake, N.J. Earlier, New Paterson.

SWARTZ CREEK, Mich. (Genesee Co.). For a small stream; from German *schwartz*, "black."

SWATARA Anglicization of Iroquoian *Swahadowri*, "place of eels."
Little Swatara Creek, Pa. Flows W into *Swatara* Creek.
Swatara Creek, Pa. Flows SW into Susquehanna R.

SWEENY, Tex. (Brazoria Co.). For John Sweeny, who came to Texas (1833) with Stephen Fuller Austin's "Three Hundred" families as a colonist.

SWEET GRASS Co., Mont. (co. seat, Big Timber). For a fragrant grass of the genus *Glyceria*.

SWEET HOME, Ore. (Linn Co.). Sentimental and connotative of security and the end of a journey; possibly influenced by the song *Home Sweet Home*. An earlier name is said to have been Buckhead.

SWEETWATER Descriptive.
Sweetwater Co., Wyo. (co. seat, Green River).
Sweetwater, Fla. (Dade Co.).
Sweetwater, Tenn. (Monroe Co.).
Sweetwater, Tex. (co. seat of Nolan Co.).
Sweetwater River, Wyo.

SWIFT Descriptive of the flow of a stream.
Swift River, Alaska. Flows W and NW into Kuskokwim R.
Swift River, Me. Flows S into Androscoggin R.
Swift Creek Reservoir, Wash. In Lewis R.
Swift Diamond River, N.H. Flows SSE into Magalloway R. *Swift* is in contrast to *dead* of Dead Diamond R.

SWIFT Co., Minn. (co. seat, Benson). For Henry Adoniram Swift (1823-1869), attorney. He held several public offices, including state senator, lieutenant governor, U.S. senator, and governor (1863-64).

SWIFT'S CREEK, Ky. For Jonathan Swift, an English sea captain, who visited the area.

SWISHER Co., Tex. (co. seat, Tulia). For James Gibson Swisher (1795-1864), Texas patriot and a signer of the Texas Declaration of Independence.

SWISSVALE, Pa. (Allegheny Co.). For James Swisshelm, who donated half an acre of land to the Pennsylvania railroad (1854) for a railroad station. Out of gratitude the railroad used the name Swissvale, invented by Jane Gray Swisshelm, James's wife, as the name of the station.

SWITZERLAND Co., Ind. (co. seat, Vevay). For the country in Europe; named by Swiss settlers.

SWOYERSVILLE, Pa. (Luzerne Co.). For John Henry Swoyer, an operator of two large coal breakers in the area.

SYCAMORE, Ill. (co. seat of De Kalb Co.). For the tree, *Platanus occidentalis*, usually found along streams. The name was taken

Founded in 734 B.C., Syracuse was one of the greatest of Greek colonies. Not only was it the major port on the island of Sicily but a cultural center as well. It was also the birthplace of the mathematician, Archimedes. [*New York Public Library*]

from Sycamore Creek, now Kishwaukee River, and was almost certainly a translation of the Indian name *Kishwaukee*.

SYCAN RIVER, Ore. From Klamath Indian *saiga* plus *keni*, "level, grassy," descriptive of the area. It flows west and south into Sprague River.

SYDNEY For Thomas Townshend, Lord Sydney, colonial secretary; named by Joseph F. W. Des Barres, who founded the city as the capital of the colony of Cape Breton in 1785.
North Sydney, N.S. (Cape Breton Co.).
Sydney, N.S. (co. seat of Cape Breton Co.).
Sydney Harbor, N.S. Inlet of the Atlantic Ocean.
Sydney Mines, N.S. (Cape Breton Co.).

SYLACAUGA, Ala. (Talladega Co.). Two possibilities have been suggested: for the Shawnee town of Chalakagay, which had previously occupied the site, or from Creek *suli*, "buzzards," *kagi*, "roost."

SYLVA, N.C. (co. seat of Jackson Co.). For William D. Sylva, a carpenter and builder.

SYLVANIA Poetic name, from Latin *silva* or *sylva*, "woods" or "grove."
Sylvania, Ga. (Screven Co.).
Sylvania, Ohio (Lucas Co.).

SYLVESTER, Ga. (co. seat of Worth Co.). From Latin *sylva*, "wood," and *vester*, "your," to mean "your wood."

SYMMETRY SPIRE, Wyo. Named by climbers in 1929 on its first ascent for its slender and symmetric shape.

SYOSSET, N.Y. (Nassau Co.). Probably of Algonquian origin, meaning uncertain.

SYRACUSE For the city in Sicily, once a colony of Greece, supposedly because the terrains were similar.
North Syracuse, N.Y. (Onondaga Co.).
Syracuse, N.Y. (co. seat of Onondaga Co.).
Syracuse, Kan. (co. seat of Hamilton Co.).

SYSLADOBSIS From Malecite, "rock that resembles dogfish."
Lower Sysladobsis Lake, Me.
Upper Sysladobsis Lake, Me.

T

TABBY MOUNTAIN, Utah. For a famous Ute chief.

TABER, Alta. For Senator Tabor of Colorado, who visited there in 1903; the spelling was changed when the town was incorporated.

TABLE Descriptive of a flat top.
Table Mountain, S.Dak. Also known as Flat Top Butte
Table Mountain, Wyo.
Table Rock Reservoir, Mo.-Ark. On White R.
Table Top Mountain, N.Y.

TABOR, Mount, Vt. For the Biblical Mount Tabor.

TABOR MOUNTAIN, Wyo. For "Buckskin Joe" Tabor, U.S. senator from Colorado.

TACOMA, Wash. (co. seat of Pierce Co.). Probably of Indian origin; meaning uncertain. It may be from Algonquian, "near to heaven," or from an Indian generic term meaning simply "mountain." The name was formerly applied to Mount Rainier.

TACONIC MOUNTAINS, Vt.-Mass.-Conn.-N.Y. Of Algonquian origin, meaning uncertain and in dispute. It may mean "steep ascent" or "small field," or may be from the root *tugk*, "tree," "wood," or "forest."

TADOUSSAC, Que. (co. seat of Saquenay Co.). From Algonquian, "breasts," in reference to the low rounded hills that characterize the locality.

TAFT, Calif. (Kern Co.). For William Howard Taft (1857-1930), the twenty-seventh President of the United States (1909-13) and chief justice of the U.S. Supreme Court (1921-30).

TAFT, Tex. (San Patricio Co.). For Charles Phelps Taft (1843-1929), lawyer, and owner and editor of the *Cincinnati Times Star*. He was the son-in-law of the original land-owners.

TAHLEQUAH, Okla. (co. seat of Cherokee Co.). From Cherokee; meaning uncertain. The name seems to have come from *tallegewi* or *talega*, the name for the Cherokees. It is the same as *Tellico*, a place name in Tennessee. Local tradition says that the meaning is "two are enough," referring either to two beautiful springs, or "two are enough to vote." Tahlequah was selected in September 1839 as national capital of the Cherokee Nation.

TAHOE From Washo, "big water."
Tahoe, Lake, Calif.-Nev.
Tahoe Natl. Forest, Calif.

TAHOKA, Tex. (co. seat of Lynn Co.). For a lake, which was named what is believed to be a word of Spanish-Indian origin, meaning "deep water," "clear water," or "fresh water."

TAHQUAMENON From Ojibway, "dark water," descriptive of the water which contains copper. The river and falls are associated with Longfellow's poem "Hiawatha."
Tahquamenon Falls, Mich. On the river.
Tahquamenon River, Mich. Flows into Whitefish Bay.

TAINTER LAKE, Wis. For a local settler.

TAKOMA A variant of TACOMA.
North Takoma Park, Md. (Montgomery Co.).
Takoma Park, Md. (Montgomery and Prince Georges Cos.).

TAKU From the Indian tribal name, probably meaning "ocean people." The inlet was named first.
Taku Inlet, Alaska.
Taku River, B.C.-Alaska. Flows SW into *Taku* Inlet.

TALBOT Co., Md. (co. seat, Easton). For Grace Talbot, daughter of George Calvert, 1st Baron Baltimore, and sister of Cecilius Calvert, first proprietor of the colony of Maryland.

TALBOT, Matthew (1762-1827), legislator and governor (1819).
Talbot Co., Ga. (co. seat, *Talbotton*).
Talbotton, Ga. (co. seat of *Talbot* Co.).

TALIAFERRO Co., Ga. (co. seat, Crawfordville). For Benjamin Taliaferro (1750-1821), an officer in the American Revolution captured at Charleston; U.S. representative (1799-1802) and jurist.

TALKEETNA MOUNTAINS, Alaska. From Tanaina Indian, "river of plenty," for a river in the area.

TALLADEGA From Cree *talwa*, "town," and *atigi*, "border," the place being on the boundary between the Creeks and the Natchez.

Talladega Co., Ala. (co. seat, *Talledega*).
Talladega, Ala. (co. seat of *Talladega* Co.).
Talladega Natl. Forest, Ala.

TALLAHASSEE, Fla. (co. seat of Leon Co.), state capital. From Creek *talwa*, "town," and *hasi*, "old."

TALLAHATCHIE From Cree *talwa*, "town," and *hachi*, "river": "river town."
Tallahatchie Co., Miss. (co. seats, Charleston and Sumner).
Tallahatchie River, Miss. Flows generally SW to join the Yalobusha R. to form the Yazoo R.

TALLAPOOSA From Indian; meaning uncertain. The most acceptable interpretation is Choctaw *tali*, "rock," and *pushi*, "crushed," for a place where there is sand or crushed stone. The translation "golden water" has also been given. The river was named first, but possibly for an older Indian town on its banks.
Tallapoosa Co., Ala. (co. seat, Dadeville).
Tallapoosa, Ga. (Haralson Co.).
Tallapoosa River, Ga.-Ala. Flows generally SW to join the Coosa River to form the Alabama River.

TALLASSEE, Ala. (Tallapoosa and Elmore Cos.). From Indian *talise*, "beautiful water." The Tallapoosa River divides the town in half.

TALLULAH, La. (parish seat of Madison Parish). From a Cherokee name whose meaning has been lost.

TOLOGA, Okla. (co. seat of Dewey Co.). Probably from Cree "rock place," to indicate a boundary. Locally the name is translated as "beautiful city."

TAMA Either for a Fox chief or for the wife of Chief Poweshiek. The meaning is uncertain, but has been interpreted as "beautiful," "lovely," or "pleasant," or "a bear with a voice that makes the rocks tremble." A member of the Mesquaki Indians, who live nearby, derived it from *tewaime*, associated with the sound of thunder.

Tama Co., Iowa (co. seat, Toledo).

Tama, Iowa (*Tama* Co.). Earlier, Iuka, for a battlefield in Mississippi where local soldiers had died, and Tama City.

TAMAQUA, Pa. (Schuylkill Co.). From Delaware Indian, "beaver."

TAMIAMI CANAL, Fla. Extends east into the Atlantic Ocean at Miami. Formed from *Tampa* plus *Miami*.

TAMPA Probably from Cree *itimpi*, "near it." Another translation suggested is "split wood for fires," but it is also claimed to be named for a Spanish city.

Tampa, Fla. (co. seat of Hillsborough Co.).

Tampa Bay, Fla.

TANANA RIVER, Alaska. For the Tanana Indian tribe, of Athapascan linguistic stock. The name means "mountain river." It flows northwest into Yukon River.

Tampa is one of the older Florida cities. In a state where architects often let their imaginations run riot, there are few sights to compare with some of the exotic early buildings on the campus of the University of Tampa.

[*Photo by O. Johnson. Frederic Lewis*]

TANEY Co., Mo. (co. seat, Forsyth). For Roger Brooke Taney (1777-1864), chief justice of the U.S. Supreme Court (1836-64), who wrote the decision in the Dred Scott Case (1857). He had earlier been U.S. attorney general (1831-33) under Jackson. He failed to obtain confirmation as secretary of the treasury.

TANGIER SOUND, Md. Inlet off Chesapeake Bay. For Tangier, Africa.

TANGIPAHOA For a tribe, probably from Choctaw *tanchapi*, "cornstalk" or "cob," and *ayua*, "gather": "corn gatherers." The tribe has disappeared.

Tangipahoa Parish, La. (parish seat, Amite).

Tangipahoa River, La. Flows generally SE to L. Pontchartrain.

TANK PEAK, Colo. For the presence of water on the peak.

TAOS From either *tuota*, "red willow place," or *tuatah*, "at the village." The form is a Spanish transliteration, for a town of the Tewa Pueblos, of Tanoan linguistic stock, located in what is now Taos County.

Taos Co., N.Mex. (co. seat, *Taos*).

Taos, N.Mex. (co. seat of *Taos* Co.).

TAPMAN MOUNTAIN, Wyo. For a pioneer named Tapman; he made a saddle from a tree stump, to which he bolted a buffalo horn.

TAPPAHANNOCK, Va. (co. seat of Essex Co.). From an Algonqian variant of Rappahannock, "water moving back and forth," in reference to the tides.

TAPPAN From an Indian tribal name meaning "cold stream."

Tappan, N.Y. (Rockland Co.).

Tappan Lake, Ohio. Reservoir on Little Stillwater Creek. Probably a name-transfer from the East, but a claim is also made for M. W. Tappan, a U.S. representative.

TAR For the then principal product of the area, or possibly from an Indian word.

Tar River, N.C. Flows generally SE to Pamlico Sound.
Tarboro, N.C. (Edgecombe Co.). For the river.

TARENTUM, Pa. (Allegheny Co.). For an ancient city in southern Italy, now called Taranto, in Taranto province.

TARGHEE NATL. FOREST, Idaho-Wyo. For Chief Targhee of the Shoshones.

TARKIO Probably from Indian, meaning unknown.
Tarkio, Mo. (Atchinson Co.).
Tarkio River, Iowa-Mo. Flows S into Missouri R.

TARLETON, Lake, N.H. For a settler in the area.

TARPON SPRINGS, Fla. (Pinellas Co.). For the fish found in the warmer waters of the Atlantic Ocean.

TARRANT Co., Tex. (co. seat Fort Worth). For Edward H. Tarrant (1796-1858)., Texas patriot, legislator, and army general.

TARRYALL Origin uncertain, but probably a folk etymologized form of an earlier name, possibly a family name.
Tarryall, Colo. (Park Co.).
Tarryall Creek, Colo. Flows SE into South Platte R.
Tarryall Mountains, Colo.

TARRYTOWN, N.Y. (Westchester Co.). Several theories exist: either from Dutch *tarwe*, "wheat," as there was much wheat grown in the area, or for a local resident named Tarry or Terry, or for the farmers who came to town to "tarry" at the taverns.

TATE Co., Miss. (co. seat, Senatobia). Named by T.S. Tate, an early settler, for his family.

TATMAN MOUNTAIN, Wyo. For J. J. Tatman, rancher, one of the first settlers in Bighorn Basin.

TATOW KNOB (peak), Utah. From an Indian word, meaning unknown.

TATTNAL Co., Ga. (co. seat, Reidsville). For Josiah Tattnall (1764-1803), general in the American Revolution, U.S. senator (1896-99), and governor (1801-02).

TATUM CREEK, Ga. For George J. Tatum, who lived near the head of the creek, but moved to Florida in 1867. It flows southeast into Suwanee River.

TAUM SAUK MOUNTAIN, Mo. Highest peak in Missouri. From Indian, meaning uncertain; *Sauk* is a tribal name.

TAUNTON For Taunton, Somersetshire, England, the family seat of one of the founders, Elizabeth Poole (1589-1654).
Taunton, Mass. (co. seat of Bristol Co.).
Taunton River, Mass.

TAVAPUTS From Ute, meaning uncertain; *tave* may mean "sun."
East Tavaputs Plateau, Utah.
West Tavaputs Plateau, Utah.

TAVARES, Fla. (co. seat of Lake Co.). According to one source, for a Spanish ancestor of Alexander St. Clair Adams, the founder. Locally it is believed to mean "center," for its position in the county. The former is probably correct.

TAWAS Either an abbreviated form of *Ottawas* or from the name of an Ojibway chief.
Tawas City, Mich. (co. seat of Iosco Co.).
Tawas Point, Mich.

TAYLOR For an early explorer or settler.
Taylor Peak, Colo.
Taylor River, Colo. Flows SE and SW to join Tomichi Creek to form Gunnison R.

TAYLOR, Neb. (co. seat of Loup Co.). For Ed Taylor, an early settler.

TAYLOR, Pa. (Lackawanna Co.). For Moses Taylor (1806-1882), a prominent New York merchant and banker who had extensive business interests in the area.

540

TAYLOR Co., Tex. (co. seat, Abilene). Either for three Taylor brothers who died at the Alamo or for Edward Taylor, an early settler in a colony of Tennesseans led by Sterling Clark Robertson.

TAYLOR Co., W.Va. (co. seat, Grafton). For John Taylor (1754-1824), Virginia statesman. He was U.S. senator (1792-94; 1803; 1822-24).

TAYLOR Co., Wis. (co. seat, Medford). For William Robert Taylor (1820-1909), governor (1874-76).

TAYLOR, Zachary (1784-1850), twelfth President of the United States (1849-50), from Virginia. A professional soldier and Indian fighter, Taylor won acclaim during the Mexican War at the battles of Palo Alto (1846), Resaca de la Palma (1846), and Buena Vista (1847). Elected President in 1848, he died after a year in office and was succeeded by his vice-president, Millard Fillmore.
Taylor Co., Fla. (co. seat, Perry).
Taylor Co., Ga. (co. seat, Butler).
Taylor Co., Iowa (co. seat, Bedford).
Taylor Co., Ky. (co. seat, Campbellsville).
Taylor, Mich. (Wayne Co.).
Taylorville, Ill. (co. seat of Christian Co.).
Taylorsville, N.C. (co. seat of Alexander Co.).

TAYLOR MILL, Ky. (Kenton Co.). For the owner of a mill.

TAYLOR MOUNTAIN, Idaho. For Bob Taylor, early day horse grower on Big Hat Creek.

TAYLOR MOUNTAINS, Alaska. For a local prospector.

TAYLORSVILLE, Ky. (co. seat of Spencer Co.). For Richard Taylor, an extensive land-owner.

TAZEWELL, Henry (1753-1799), Virginia statesman, one of the framers of the state constitution, and U.S. senator (1794-99). He was the father of Gov. Littleton
TAZEWELL.

Tazewell Co., Va. (co. seat, *Tazewell*).
Tazewell, Tenn. (co. seat of Claiborne Co.). For *Tazewell*, Va.
Tazewell, Va. (co. seat of *Tazewell* Co.).

TAZEWELL Co., Ill. (co. seat, Pekin). For Littleton Waller Tazewell (1774-1860), legislator, U.S. senator from Virginia (1824-32), and governor of Virginia (1834-36).

TAZLINA From Ahtena Indian, "swift river."
Tazlina Lake, Alaska. For the river.
Tazlina River, Alaska. Flows E from *Tazlina* L. into Copper R.

TEAGUE, Tex. (Freestone Co.). Named by B. F. Yoakum, noted railroad builder, for his mother's family. She was Narcissus Teague before her marriage to Franklin L. Yoakum. An earlier name was Brewer.

TEAL LAKE, Wis. For the teal duck.

TEANECK, N.J. (Bergen Co.). For a local Dutch family name, Teneyck or Ten Eyck.

TECHE, Bayou, La. From a French rendering of *Deutsch*, "German," an earlier German mame for the bayou. It flows southeast into Atchafalaya River.

TECUMSEH (1768-1813), famous Shawnee chief killed in Ontario at the Battle of the Thames between the British and the Americans, the latter under the command of William H. Harrison. Two American colonels, both commanding troops from Kentucky, have been given credit for killing Tecumseh: William Whitley, whose grandson's name is commemorated in Sublette, and Richard M. Johnson. (Ironically, Tecumseh is the county seat of Johnson Co., Neb., although that name comes from another source.) Actually, no one knows who killed him. Tecumseh was a brilliant leader and an eloquent orator; he is known as "the most extraordinary Indian character in United States history." Given the rank of colonel in the British army, he was constantly combating the encroachment of the whites upon Indian territories. The name is Shawnee, "one who springs," probably with the connotation of "panther."

Tecumseh, Mich. (Lenawee Co.).
Tecumseh, Neb. (co. seat of Johnson Co.).
Tecumseh, Okla. (Pottawatamie Co.).
Tecumseh, Ont. (Essex Co.).
Tecumseh, Mount, N.H.

TEEWINOT MOUNTAIN, Wyo. From the Shoshone name that once applied to the entire Teton Range, meaning "many pinnacles." The Shoshones are also claimed to have called the Tetons "Hoary-Headed Fathers."

TEHACHAPI Believed to be from Southern Paiute *tilaci*, "frozen."
Tehachapi, Calif. (Kern Co).
Tehachapi Mountains, Calif.

TEHACHAPI MOUNTAINS, Calif. From Southern Paiute, "frozen," applied at first to a river.

TEHAMA Co., Calif. (co. seat, Red Bluff). Origin and meaning are uncertain. It is almost certainly Indian, though an Arabian origin in *tihama*, "hot lowlands," has been seriously suggested. Tihama does exist as a place name. The Indian term that parallels, coincidentally, may also mean "lowlands," descriptive of this area.

TEKAMAH, Neb. (co. seat of Burt Co.). From an Indian name of uncertain origin, possibly "cottonwood trees" or "field of battle"; another version is that it came from farther west, possibly a variant of TACOMA.

TELFAIR Co., Ga. (co. seat, McRae). For Edward Telfair (1753-1791), a delegate to the Continental Congress, active in forming the Union, and governor of Georgia (1786-87; 1790-93).

TELL CITY, Ind. (Perry Co.). For the legendary hero, William Tell. He was a Swiss patriot and archer who, after refusing to salute the cap that Gessler, the Austrian governor, had set up in the market place, was sentenced to shoot an apple from his son's head. Having successfully completed this feat, he shot Gessler and freed his country from Austrian rule.

TELLER Co., Colo. (co. seat, Cripple Creek). For Henry Moore Teller (1830-1914), statesman. He was U.S. senator (1876-82; 1885-1909) and secretary of the Interior (1882-85) under Arthur.

TELLURIDE, Colo. (co. seat of San Miguel Co.). From the chemical name of a compound of tellurium, which is mined nearby.

TELOS LAKE, Me. Origin uncertain, but probably an early explorer's or hunter's rendering of an Indian word into English, or, in this case, into Greek, "far" or "the end." Another version is that it is from "tealos," (tea-less or without tea), by analogy with the name of a nearby lake, Coffee-los.

TEMBLOR RANGE, Calif. From Spanish, "earthquake."

TEMISCAMINGUE Co., Que. (co. seat, Ville Marie). The French spelling of TIMISKAMING.

TEMISCOUATA From Malecite, "deep lake forming the source of a river."
Temiscouata Co., Que. (co. seats, Riviere du Loop and Notre Dame du Lac). For the lake.
Temiscouata Lake, Que.

TEMPE, Ariz. (Maricopa Co.). For the Vale of Tempe in Greek mythology.

TEMPLE Descriptive of shape, for a supposed resemblance to a temple.
Temple Mountain, Utah.
Temple Peak, Wyo.

TEMPLE, Tex. (Bell Co.). For Maj. B. M. Temple, chief construction engineer for the Gulf, Colorado and Sante Fe railroad (1880-81).

TEMPLE CITY, Calif. (Los Angeles Co.). For Walter P. Temple (?-1938), founder.

TEMPLETON, Mass. (Worcester Co.), town. For John Temple (1731-1798), an American relation of Richard Grenville, Earl Temple (1711-1779). John Temple was surveyor general of Boston customs and was a friend of most of the prominent citizens of that city. He later became lieutenant governor of New Hampshire, emigrating to England (1786) to become Sir John Temple.

TENAFLY, N.J. (Bergen Co.). Named by early Dutch settlers from Dutch *thyne*, or *tuin, vly*, "garden valley."

TENANT MOUNTAIN, N.Y. For the Tenant family, landowners and businessmen.

TEN MILE Descriptive of distance. Also, *Tenmile*.
Tenmile Creek, Pa. North and South forks flow generally SE and NE into Monongehela R. North Fork flows into the Monongehela ten miles SW of Brownsville, site of an important fort in earlier days.
Ten Mile Lake, Minn.

TENNESSEE For an important Cherokee town, *Tanasi* (and other spellings *Tenasee, Tanasee, Tanassee, Tansi*), on the Little Tennessee River in what is now eastern Tennessee. The meaning of the name is unknown. When North Carolina ceded its western lands to the Union in 1784, the area created a formal but unofficial government as the state of Franklin (1784-88) and, after reverting to North Carolina, became officially the Territory South of the Ohio (1790).
Tennesse, State of. 16th state of the Union. Settled: 1757. Territory: (as Territory South of the Ohio) 1790. Admitted: 1796. Cap: Nashville. Motto: Agriculture and Commerce. Nickname: Volunteer State. Flower: Iris. Bird: Mockingbird. Tree. Tulip Poplar. Song: "Tennessee Waltz."
Little Tennessee River, Ga.-N.C.-Tenn. Flows into *Tennessee* R.
Tennessee River, Tenn.-Ala.-Miss.-Tenn.-Ky. Flows generally SW, then N, to the Ohio R.

TENSAS From the Indian tribe Taensa, which lived in the area. The origin and meaning of the name have been lost.
Tensas Parish, La. (parish seat, St. Joseph).

Tennessee has become closely identified with what used to be called "hillbilly music". From Nashville, Recording center, home of the Grand Ole Opry, and "Country and Western Music Capital of the World" to the hamlet of Maynardsville (above), enthusiasm for this music has never waned. [*Photo by Shawn, 1935. New York Public Library*]

Tensas River, La. Flows generally SW to the Ouachita R.

TENSAW RIVER, Ala. Variant of TENSAS. It flows into Mobile Bay.

TEN THOUSAND ISLANDS, Fla. In Gulf of Mexico. An exaggeration, but there are several islands.

TEPEE For the Indian tent.
Tepee Buttes, N.Dak. For a resemblance to tepees.
Tepee Creek, Okla. Flows E into Beaver R. For tepees in the area.

TERLINGUA CREEK, Tex. Originally *Arroya Lates Lingua,* from Spanish, "stream of the tongue fish," the name was changed through error of interpretation to *Teslingua;* as a result of a misreading of the handwritten form, the name then became *Terlingua*. It flows south into the Rio Grande.

TERRACE MOUNTAINS, Utah. So named (1849) by Howard Stansbury because they resembled terraces.

TERREBONNE From French, "good land," for an area in which there is rich land, or it is hoped that there is.

Terrebonne Parish, La. (co. seat, Houma).
Terrebonne Co., Que. (co. seat, *Terrebonne*). Named by Davlier des Landed, who was granted land there in 1673.
Terrebonne, Que. (co. seat of *Terrebonne* Co.).
Terrebonne Bay, La., on the Gulf of Mexico.
Terrebonne, Bayou, La. Flows into *Terrebonne* Bay.

TERRE HAUTE From French, "high land"; situated on a plateau on the east bank of the Wabash River.
Terre Haute, Ind. (co. seat of Vigo Co.).
West Terre Haute, Ind. (Vigo Co.).

TERRELL Co., Ga. (co. seat, Dawson). For William Terrell (1778-1855), legislator and U.S. representative (1817-21).

TERRELL Co., Tex. (co. seat, Sanderson). For Alexander Watkins Terrell (1827-1912), Virginia-born Texas statesman and soldier. He fought during the Civil War and served as minister to Turkey (1893-97).

TERRELL, Tex. (Kaufman Co.). For Robert A. Terrell (1820-1881), Civil War veteran, surveyor, and early settler.

TERRELL HILLS, Tex. (Bexar Co.). For Frederick Terrell, promoter of the area.

TERRY, La. (West Carroll Parish). For the Terry family, a black family who were landowners and in the lumber business.

TERRY, Mont. (co. seat of Prairie Co.). For Alfred Terry, general and Indian fighter.

TERRY Co., Tex. (co. seat, Brownfield). For Benjamin Franklin Terry (1821-1861), an officer in the Confederate army killed in action in Kentucky.

TESHEKPUK LAKE, Alaska. From Eskimo, "big coastal lake."

TETLIN LAKE, Alaska. Probably named for Tetling, a local Indian chief.

TETON From French, "teat." The mountain range was so named by early French fur trappers because the peaks resembled women's breasts. See also GRAND TETON.
Teton Co., Idaho (co. seat, Driggs).
Teton Co., Mont. (co. seat, Choteau).
Teton Co., Wyo. (co. seat, Jackson).
Teton Pass, Wyo.
Teton Range, Wyo.-Idaho, in the Rocky Mtns.
Teton River, Mont. Flows generally E to the Missouri R.
Teton River, Wyo.-Idaho. Flows generally NW to Henrys Fork R.

TEWKSBURY, Mass. (Middlesex Co.), town. For Tewkesbury, Gloucestershire, England.

TEXARKANA For its location at the meeting point of *Texas, Arkansas,* and *Louisiana.*
Texarkana, Ark. (co. seat of Miller Co.).
Texarkana, Tex. (Bowie Co.).
Texarkana, Lake, Tex.

TEXAS From an Indian variation, *texia*, of Spanish *tejas*, "allies," used by various tribes in reference to their mutually protective alliances. The name was recorded as early as 1690 and eventually came to be applied to the area north of the Rio Grande that now includes the state of Texas. Texas won its independence from Mexico in 1836 and became a republic.
Texas, State of. 28th state of the Union. Settled: 1691. Independent Republic: 1836-46. Admitted: 1845. Cap: Austin Motto: Friendship. Nickname: Lone Star State. Flower: Bluebonnet. Bird: Mockingbird. Tree: Pecan. Song: "Texas, Our Texas."
Texas Co., Mo. (co. seat, Houston).
Texas Co., Okla. (co. seat, Guynon).
Texas City, Tex. (Galveston Co.). Promotional, for the state. Earlier, Shoal Point.

TEXOMA, Lake, Tex.-Okla. In Red River. From a combination of *Texas* plus *Oklahoma.*

Texas is so well known for its size, pride, cowboys, longhorns and oil that many forget that the state also had its share of professional hunters, such as this group who posed in 1879. [*New York Public Library*]

THAMES RIVER, Conn. For the Thames River in England. It flows south into Long Island Sound.

THAYER Co., Neb. (co. seat, Hebron). For Gen. John Milton Thayer (1820-1906), Indian fighter, U.S. senator (1867-71), and governor (1887-92).

THE DALLES, Ore. (co. seat of Wasco Co.). From Fench, "flagstones," a transferred meaning since such stones were used to line gutters. The rapids resembled such gutters to the early French explorers.

THEDFORD, Neb. (co. seat of Thomas Co.). For Thedford in Ontario; named by officials of a railroad company.

THEODORE ROOSEVELT See also ROOSEVELT, Theodore.
Theodore Roosevelt Lake, Ariz. Formed by Roosevelt Dam, which was dedicated in 1911 by President Roosevelt.
Theodore Roosevelt Natl. Memorial Park, N.Dak. Commemorates his contributions to conservation of natural resources.

THERMALITO, Calif. (Butte Co.). From Spanish "little heat"; promotional.

THERMOPOLIS, Wyo. (co. seat of Hot Springs Co.). From Greek *therme* and *polis*, "heat-city," for the hot springs.

THETFORD MINES, Que. (Megantic Co.). For the town of Thetford, Norfolk, England.

THE VILLAGE, Okla. (Oklahoma Co.). So named by the developer.

THIBODAUX, La. (parish seat of Lafourche Parish). For Henry Schuyler Thidodaux (1769-1827), founder, member of the territorial legislature, and governor (1824).

THIEF The name originated when a small force of Dakota Indians concealed themselves behind earth works near a waterfall to escape their enemies, the Ojibways; finally discovered, they were killed. The Ojibways gave the nearby stream the name "Secret Earth River," for the hiding place; but through erroneous translation by the French and English fur traders, the name appeared finally as Thief River, a far different connotation from the original.
Thief Lake, Minn.
Thief River, Minn.
Thief River Falls, Minn. (co. seat of Pennington Co.).

THIENSVILLE, Wis. (Ozaukee Co.). For Joachim Heinrich Thien, German settler and founder.

THIMBLE PEAK, Wyo. So named because it sticks up like a thimble among larger peaks.

THOMAS, George Henry (1816-1870), career soldier. He rose to the rank of major general in the U.S. Army during the Civil War and achieved military honors and recognition by Congress for his command of the Army of the Cumberland, which succeeded in forcing Gen. John Bell Hood's army out ot Tennessee.
Fort Thomas, Ky. (Campbell Co.).
Thomas Co., Kan. (co. seat, Colby).
Thomas Co., Neb. (co. seat, Thedford).

THOMAS, Jett (1776-1817), general in the state militia and supervisor of the building of the state capitol at Milledgeville.
Thomas Co., Ga. (co. seat, *Thomasville*).
Thomaston, Ga. (co. seat of Upson Co.).
Thomasville, Ga. (co. seat of *Thomas* Co.).

THOMAS, Lake, Tex. For a local settler.

THOMASTON, Conn. (Litchfield Co.), town. For Seth Thomas (1785-1859), clock manufacturer.

THOMASTON, Me. (Knox Co.), town. For Gen. John Thomas (1724-1776), who held a command at the beginning of the American Revolution.

THOMASVILLE, Ala. (Clarke Co.). For Gen. Samuel Thomas, a New York businessman who was one of the financiers of a new railroad in the area in the late 1880s.

THOMASVILLE, N.C. (Davidson Co.). For John W. Thomas (1800-1875) and Dr. Henry E. Rounsaville, a local resident. Thomas was a state senator and civic and educational leader. He helped establish Union Institute (which later became Duke University).

THOMPSON, Conn. (Windham Co.), town. For Sir Robert Thompson of England, largest property owner in the town, though he did not reside there.

THOMPSON, Lake, S.Dak. For John Thompson, pioneer farmer.

THOMPSON FALLS, Mont. (co. seat of Sanders Co.). For David Thompson, a trader with the Northwest Fur Company during the early 1800s. The falls are on the Clark Fork River.

THOMPSON LAKE, Me. Believed to have been named for a Thompson who drowned in the lake.

THOMPSON PEAK, Calif., in Klamath Mountains. For Packer Thompson, who climbed the peak in the 1870s.

THOMPSON PLACE - TANGLEWILDE, Wash. (Thurston Co.). Developmental name coined by Alvin H. Thompson, realtor.

THOMPSON RIVER, Iowa-Mo. For a settler who lived near the river. It flows south into Grand River.

THOMPSON'S MOUNTAIN, Wyo. For David Thompson, an astronomer and surveyor, who was also a member of William Ashley's fur expeditions of the 1820s.

THOMSON, Ga. (co. seat of McDuffie Co.). For J. Edgar Thomson, a civil engineer who helped survey the right of way for the Georgia railroad.

THORNAPPLE For the tree.
Thornapple River, Mich. Flows NW and N into Grand R.
Thornapple River, Wis. Flows SW into Chippewa R.

THORNTON, Colo. (Adams Co.). For Dan Thornton, governor.

THORNWOOD, N.Y. (Westchester Co.). No known reason for the name; probably for thorny shrubs or trees, or for someone named Thorn.

THOROLD, Ont. (Welland Co.). For Sir John Thorold, British member of Parliament from Lincolnshire, who opposed the war with the American colonies and voted against the constitutional act of 1791.

THOR PEAK, Wyo. For Thor, mythological god of thunder.

THORPE LAKE, N.C. For J.E.S. Thorpe, official of the Nantahala Power and Light Company. Earlier names were Glenville Lake and Thorpe Reservoir.

THOUSAND LAKE MOUNTAIN, Utah. For the many small lakes on its surface.

THOUSAND OAKS, Calif. (Ventura Co.). Descriptive.

THREE FINGERED JACK, (Mountain), Ore. Reason for the name is unknown: possibly descriptive, for the shape of the mountain, or for a trapper named Jack who was so nicknamed.

THREE RIVERS Descriptive of the site.
Three Rivers, Mass. (Hampden Co.). At the confluence of Jabish Brook, Muddy R., and Quaboag R.
Three Rivers, Mich. (St. Joseph Co.). At the confluence of the St. Joseph, Rocky, and Portage rivers.

THREE SISTERS, Ore. Three peaks in the Cascade Mountains: North Sister, Middle Sister, and South Sister. It is said that they were once named Mounts Faith, Hope, and Charity.

THROCKMORTON, William Edward (1795-1843), the father of Gov. J. W. Throckmorton.
Throckmorton Co., Tex. (co. seat, *Throckmorton*).
Throckmorton, Tex. (co. seat of *Throckmorton* Co.).

THUNDER Translated from Indian, probably for incidents in which thunder was heard.
Thunder Bay, Mich. Inlet on L. Huron.
Thunder Bay, Ont. Inlet on L. Superior. Translated from Indian *Animikie Wekwed*, "Thunder Bird Bay," so named by Indians in whose folklore the thunder bird was the cause of thunder.
Thunder Butte, S.Dak. Translated from Sioux.
Thunder Lake, Wis. Or for the mythical thunderbird.
Thunder Bay District, Ont. (district seat, Port Arthur). For *Thunder* Bay, Ont.
Thunder Bay River, Mich. Flows NE and E into *Thunder* Bay.
Thunderbolt, Ga. (Chatham Co.). According to tradition, the Indians believed that a thunderbolt had struck the ground there.
Thunder Butee, S.Dak. (Ziebach Co.).
Thunder Butte River, S.Dak. Flows SE into Moreau R.

THURSTON Co., Neb. (co seat Pender). For John Mellen Thurston (1847-1916), U.S. senator (1895-1901), active in establishing the county.

THURSTON Co., Wash. (co. seat, Olympia). For Samuel Royal Thurston (1816-1851), the first delegate from the Oregon territory (1849-51).

TIBER RESERVOIR, Mont. For the nearby village, in turn probably for a local citizen.

TIBURON, Calif. (Marin Co.). From Spanish, "shark." Probably descriptive (Shark's Point is nearby).

TICONDEROGA, N.Y. (Esex Co.). From Iroquoian, probably "between lakes."

TIERRA AMARILLA, N.Mex. (co. seat of Rio Arriba Co.). From Spanish, "yellow earth," for the color of the land; possibly a translation of a Tewa Indian term.

TIETON RIVER, Wash. Transliteration of an Indian name meaning "roaring water." It flows northeast into Naches River.

TIFFIN, Edward (1766-1829), minister, physician, first governor of Ohio (1803-07), and U.S. senator (1807-09).
Tifflin, Ohio (co. seat of Seneca Co.).
Tifflin River, Ohio.

TIFT, Nelson (1810-1891), legislator, officer in the Confederate army, and U.S. representative (1868-69).
Tift Co., Ga. (co. seat, *Tifton*).
Tifton, Ga. (co. seat of *Tift* Co.).

TIGARD, Ore. (Washington Co.). For Wilson M. Tigard, an early settler and local landowner.

TIGER TOWER, Wyo. A knife-edged ridge named for its difficult faces for climbers.

TILDEN, Samuel J. (1814-1886), statesman, governor of New York, and Democratic candidate for the Presidency in 1876. He received the majority of popular votes, but failed the election by one electoral vote. His opponent was Rutherford B. Hayes.
Fort Tilden, N.Y. (Queens Co.).
Tilden, Tex. (co. seat of McMullen Co.).

TILLAMOOK From Chinook, "people of Nekelim," for the tribe. This tribe, important in Oregon, belonged to the Salishan linguistic stock and lived on the coast, especially on the Nehalem and Salmon rivers.
Tillamook Co., Ore. (co. seat, *Tillamook*).
Tillamook, Ore. (co. seat of *Tillamook* Co.).
Tillamook Head, Ore. High cliff and lighthouse.

TILLERY, Lake, N.C. Reservoir on Pee Dee River. For Paul A. Tillery (1880-1933), official of the Carolina Power and Light Company.

TILLMAN Co., Okla. (co. seat, Frederick). For Benjamin Ryan Tillman (1847-1918), governor of South Carolina (1890-94) and U.S. senator from South Carolina (1895-1918), active in the formation of Oklahoma State.

TILLSONBURG, Ont. (Oxford Co.). For George Tillson, first settler, who emigrated from Massachusetts in 1825.

TILTON, Ill. (Vermilion Co.). For Lucien B. Tilton, who helped finance the forerunner of the Wabash railroad, now part of the Norfolk and Western railroad. He was also a developer of the elevated railway system of Chicago.

TILTON, N.H. (Belknap Co.), town. For Nathaniel Tilton, an early settler, at the suggestion of his grandson, Charles, a wealthy resident.

TIMBER LAKE, S.Dak. (co. seat of Dewey Co.). Origin unknown; for a lake which now is known for the lack of trees on its banks.

TIMBER MOUNTAIN, Tex. Descriptive.

TIMBERWOLF MOUNTAIN, Wash. For the animal.

TIMISKAMING From Indian, "at the place of deep dry water," in reference to the clay flats in the lake which dry up at low water.
Timiskaming District, Ont. (district seat, Haileybury).
Timiskaming, Lake, Ont.

548

TIMMINS, Ont. (Cochrane Co.). For the Timmins brothers, Noah and Henry, who formed an early mining syndicate and developed the Hollinger Mine.

TIMPANOGOS From the Ute tribal name, "rock river people."
Timpanogos, Mount, Utah.
Timpanogos Cave Natl. Monument, Utah. Three cave areas notable for their tinted filigree rock. One stone, "The Great Heart of Timpanogos," resembles the human heart.

TIM'S HILL, Wis. For a local settler named Tim.

TIN CUP So named because a tin cup was needed to get a drink from the springs in the creek.
Tin Cup Creek, Wyo.
Tin Cup Mountain, Wyo.

TINGMERPUK MOUNTAIN, Alaska. In De Long Mountains. From Eskimo, "largest bird" or "eagle."

TINLEY PARK, Ill. (Cook Co.). For the Tinley Brothers, who were prominent Rock Island railroad executives.

TINTIC MOUNTAINS, Utah. For a Gosiute Indian chief.

TIOGA From Iroquoian, "place between two points," or "at the forks," as commonly used. The particular Indian town was situated on the Susquehanna River near Athens, Pa., itself called *Diahoga* or *Tioga*.
Tioga Co., N.Y. (co. seat, Owego).
Tioga Co., Pa. (co. seat, Wellsboro).
Tioga Pass, Calif.
Tioga River, Pa.-N.Y. Flows generally N to join the Cohocton R. to form the Chemung R.

TIONESTA From Iroquoian *tiyohwenoisto*, "it penetrates the island," metaphorical for the rush of the current in the creek upon Hunter Island, where it joins the Allegheny River.
Tionesta, Pa. (co. seat of Forest Co.).
Tionesta Creek, Pa.

TIOUGHNIOGA RIVER, N.Y. From Iroquoian, "fork of river," descriptive of the place where it meets Chenango River. It flows generally southeast into Chenango River.

TIPPAH Co., Miss. (co. seat, Ripley). Either for a tribe or for Tippah, wife of the Chickasaw chief Pontotoc. The name is said to mean "cut-off."

TIPP CITY, Ohio (Miami Co.). See TIP-PECANOE

TIPPECANOE From Potawatomi *quit-te-pe-con-nac*, modification of *kith-tip-pe-ca-numk*, "buffalo fish," which were plentiful in the river now known as the Tippecanoe. The name is partially folk etymologized. William Henry Harrison was governor of Indiana in 1800. During his term he was instructed to win the confidence of the Indians and secure justice for them from the settlers, but also to obtain cession of as much land as possible for the government. He obtained Indian grants of millions of acres in the present states of Illinois and Indiana, but the Indian resentment of invading settlers increased. An Indian confederacy under the Shawnee warrior Tecumseh and his brother, the Prophet, began to develop in 1805. When Harrison, by the treaty of Fort Wayne (1809), secured some 2.5 million acres on the Wabash River, Tecumseh warned him he would oppose occupation. The Indians encamped in force near the point where the Tippecanoe River enters the Wabash. On November 6, 1811, with a force of about 1,000 men, Harrison encamped near the Indian village and was attacked the next morning by the Shawnees. Harrison took possession of their settlement, but his losses were heavy and the Indians were bold again by spring. The victory was considered significant enough to provide a nickname for Harrison and a campaign slogan when he ran for President in 1840 — "Tippecanoe and Tyler, too" (Tyler being the vice-presidential candidate).
Tippecanoe Co., Ind. (co. seat, Lafayette).
Tippecanoe, Ohio. Former name of Tipp City.
Tippecanoe River, Ind. Flows generally SE to the Wabash R.

TIPTON, Jacob (?-1791), killed in a battle with Indians.
Tipton Co., Tenn. (co. seat, Covington).
Tiptonville, Tenn. (co. seat of Lake Co.).

TIPTON, John (1786-1839), veteran of Indian wars and the War of 1812, legislator, and U.S. senator from Indiana (1832-39).
Tipton Co., Ind. (co. seat, *Tipton*).
Tipton, Ind. (co. seat of *Tipton* Co.).
Tipton, Iowa (co. seat of Cedar Co.).

TIPTON, Kan. (Mitchell Co.). For Tipton, Staffordshire, England.

TIPTON, Mo. (Moniteau Co.). For William Tipton Seely, founder.

TIPTON, Mount, Ariz. For a Lieutenant Tipton, member of an exploratory expedition in 1858.

TIPTON, Okla. (Tillman Co.). For John T. Tipton, a railway conductor.

TISBURY GREAT POND, Mass. For Tisbury, Wiltshire, England.

TISHOMINGO (1733?-1837?), the last fullblooded war chief of the Chicasaws. After 1830 he was instrumental in the acquisition of land in the Mexican Territory and, in one instance after this, was arrested and fined by Mississippi courts for seizing and selling the goods of two white traders who had moved into the Territory. His name means "assistant chief" (at this time he was the principal leader next to Ishtehotopa, the Chickasaw king).
Tishomingo Co., Miss. (co. seat, Iuka).
Tishomingo, Okla. (co. seat of Johnston Co.).

TITTABAWASEE RIVER, Mich. From Algonquian, meaning uncertain, interpreted by one authority as "following the line of the shore," for the direction of the flow of the river.

TITUS Co., Tex. (co. seat, Mount Pleasant). For Andrew Jackson Titus (1823-1855). Texas patriot.

TITUSVILLE, Fla. (co. seat of Brevard Co.). For Henry T. Titus, an opponent of John Brown over the introduction of slavery into the Kansas Territory. He was also postmaster of the town.

TITUSVILLE, Pa. (Crawford Co.). For Jonathon Titus, a pioneer and surveyor who built his cabin on the site of the town in 1796.

TIVERTON, R.I. (*Newport* Co.), town. For Tiverton, Devonshire, England.

T LAKE MOUNTAIN, N.Y. For the alphabetical shape of the nearby lake.

TOANA RANGE, Nev. From Indian, "black hill," descriptive.

TOBACCO RIVER, Mich. For the plant. North and South branches flow east into Cedar River.

TOBIN For the Tobin Family, a prominent family in the area.
Tobin, Mount, Nev.
Tobin Range, Nev.

TOCCOA, Ga. (co. seat of Stephens Co.). From Cherokee, "catawba place," for the CATAWBA tribe.

TODD, John Blair Smith (1814-1872), career soldier. He served in the Mexican War, and rose to the rank of general during the Civil War. He was also a delegate from the Dakota Territory and served as governor (1869-71). He was a relative of Mary Todd Lincoln.
Todd Co., Ky. (co. seat, Elkton).
Todd Co., Minn. (co. seat, Long Prairie).

TODDY POND, Me. Said to have been named for the British "toddy," an intoxicating liquor of any kind. British soldiers picked up the word in India.

TOE RIVER, N.C. Origin and meaning uncertain, but probably from Indian, a back formation of *estatoe*, or some similar word. According to legend, Estatoe was an Indian maiden who drowned herself in the river

Toledo was traditionally one of the great royal cities of Castile and later Spain. Although this engraving does not share the fame of El Greco's "View of Toledo", it conveys the craggy magnificence of the city. [*New York Public Library*]

because her lover was killed by her relatives. It flows northwest to join Cane River to form Nolichucky River.

TOGIAK BAY, Alaska. From Eskimo, meaning unknown.

TOGWOTTE PASS, Wyo. Named in 1873 by Capt. William A. Jones for his Indian guide, Togwotee.

TOHICKON CREEK, Pa. From Algonquian, probably "driftwood." It flows east into Delaware River.

TOIYABE From Paiute *toyavi*, "mountain."
Toiyabe Natl. Forest, Nev.
Toiyabe Peak, Nev.
Toiyabe Range, Nev.
Toiyabe Dome (peak), Nev.

TOKLAT RIVER, Alaska. From Tanana Indian, "dish water." It flows northwest into Kantishna River.

TOLEDO For Toledo, Spain.
Toledo, Ill. (co. seat of Cumberland Co.). For *Toledo*, Ohio.
Toledo, Iowa (co. seat of Tama Co.). For *Toledo*, Ohio.
Toledo, Ohio (co. seat of Lucas Co.).
Toledo, Ore. (co. seat of Lincoln Co.). For *Toledo*, Ohio.

TOLLAND For a town in England.
Tolland Co., Conn. (co. seat, Rockville). Abolished as a governmental unit since 1960.
Tolland, Conn. (*Tolland* Co.), town.

TOLLESON, Ariz. (Maricopa Co.). For W. G. Tolleson, founder.

TOLOVANA RIVER, Alaska. From Tanana Indian, meaning unknown. It flows southwest into Tanana River.

TOMAH, Wis. (Monroe Co.). For Thomas Carron, Menominee chief. The name reflects the attempt to represent the French pronunciation of *Thomas*; also, *Tomah* seemed more "Indian."

TOMAHAWK For the hatchetlike shape of the lake.
Tomahawk, Wis. (Lincoln Co.). For the river and lake.
Tomahawk Lake, Wis.
Tomahawk River, Wis. Flows from *Tomahawk* L. to the Wisconsin R.

TOMAH STREAM, Me. From Algonquian; the name has different meanings in the different dialects: in Micmac "pipe rock," in Abnaki "deep," and in Natick, "it is flooded." Another possibility is that it is from the name of an Indian chief. It flows southeast and southwest into Grand Falls Lake.

TOMBALL, Tex. (Harris Co.). For Thomas Henry Ball (1859-1944), U.S. representative (1896-1903) and candidate for governor (1914).

TOMBIGEE From Choctaw *itombi*, "coffin," plus *ikbi*, "makers."
Tombigee Natl. Forest, Miss.
Tombigee River, Miss.-Ala. Flows SE and S to join Alabama R. to form Mobile R.

TOM GREEN Co., Tex. (co. seat, San Angelo). For Gen. Thomas Green (1814-1864), Texas patriot and veteran of the War for Texas independence. He was killed in action while serving in the Confederate army.

TOMICHI CREEK, Colo. From Indian, meaning uncertain. It flows south and west to join Taylor River to form Gunnison River.

TOMPKINS, Daniel D. (1774-1825), statesman. Elected a U.S. representative, he resigned before serving to take a position as associate justice of the New York State Supreme Court (1804-07). He was governor of New York (1807-17) and served as vice-president (1817-25) under Monroe.
Tompkins Co., N.Y. (co. seat, Ithaca).

Tompkins, N.Y. (Delaware Co.).
Tompkinsville, Ky. (co. seat of Monroe Co.).

TOMS RIVER For Thomas Luker, who came from England on the ship *Falcon* (1685) and built the first bridge across the river. He married an Indian chieftain's daughter, Princess Ann, and settled in a wigwam in sight of the bridge.
Toms River, N.J. (co. seat of Ocean Co.). For the river.
Toms River, N.J. Flows into Barnegat Bay.

TONAWANDA From Iroquoian, "swift water," descriptive of rapids on the river.
Tonawanda, N.Y. (Erie Co.).
Tonawanda Creek, N.Y. Flows W into Niagara R.

TONGUE RIVER, Wyo.-Mont. Translated from Cheyenne *itaniho*, "tongue," for a rock in the river.

TONKAWA, Okla. (Kay Co.). For an Indian tribe, probably from Waco *tonkaweya*, "they all stay together." The tribe is also called *kadiko* or *kuikogo*, "man-eating men," or "cannibals."

TONOLOWAY RIVER, Pa.-Md. From Algonquian, "long tail." It flows into the Potomac River.

TONOPAH, Nev. (co. seat of Nye Co.). From Paiute, variously translated as "spring." "greasewood spring," "water bush spring," "little water," and "thorny bush."

TONTO From Spanish, "fool," applied erroneously to Indians in the area.
Tonto Basin, Ariz.
Tonto Creek, Ariz. Flows S into Salt R.
Tonto Natl. Monument, Ariz. Established to preserve an ancient Indian village.

TONZONA RIVER, Alaska. Of Indian origin, meaning unknown. It flows northeast and northwest into Slow Fork River.

TOOELE Probably for Tuilla, an Indian chief, but other possibilities have been suggested: that it designates a place where an abundant growth of bulrushes is found; that it was named for Mat Tooele, an Austrian village; that an Englishman called the place "too'illy," for the many hills, and that this was changed to "too willy," for the many willows.
Tooele Co., Utah (co. seat, *Tooele*).
Tooele, Utah (co. seat of *Tooele* Co.).

TOOLE Co., Mont. (co. seat, Shelby). For Joseph Kemp Toole (1851-1929), delegate (1885-89) and governor (1889-93; 1901-08).

TOOMBS Co., Ga. (co. seat, Lyons). For Gen. Robert Toombs (1810-1885), Georgia statesman who became secretary of state of the Confederacy. He had served as U.S. senator (1853-61).

TOPAGORUK RIVER, Alaska. From Eskimo, "place for tent." It flows north into Admirality Bay.

TOPAZ MOUNTAIN, Utah. For the stones found on the mountain.

TOPEKA, Kan. (co. seat of Shawnee Co.), state capital. From Siouan, "a good place to dig potatoes." It is said that the Indian term designated any edible root, not specifically the potato.

TOPNOTCH PEAK, Wyo. For the distinctive notch at the summit.

TOPPENISH From an Indian tribal name.
Toppenish, Wash. (Yakima Co.).
Toppenish Creek, Wash. Flows into Yakima River.

TOPSHAM, Me. (Sagadahoc Co.), town and village. For Topsham, Devonshire, England.

TOQUIMA RANGE, Nev. For the Indian tribal name, which means "black backs."

TORCH LAKE, Mich. Translated from an Indian name, for torches used to light the area for fishing at night.

Toronto, little more than an outpost and known as York, was little more than a few homes and a blockhouse when this engraving was made. The name was changed in 1834. [*New York Public Library*]

TORONTO From an Indian name of uncertain origin applied to the harbor and recorded as early as 1615. There are several possible definitions drawn from Iroquoian or Huron (a branch of the Iroquoian linguistic stock): Iroquoian *Thorontohen*, "timber in the water"; Iroquoian *Deondo*, "logs floating on the water"; Seneca Iroquoian *Kanitare*, "lake" and *onto*, "to open," in reference to the entrance to the route leading to the heart of the Huron (Wyandot) country; and Huron words of doubtful origin meaning "much" or "many" and variously defined as a place where many met or gathered, or a place that had much game and fish. Until 1793 the site was known informally as Toronto, but in that year Lt. Gov. John Simcoe, in developing the townsite for the future capital of Upper Canada (later Ontario), chose the name York, for Frederick, Duke of York, son of George III. The name reverted to Toronto in 1834.
New Toronto, Ont. (York Co.).
Toronto, Ont., (co. seat of York Co.) provincial capital.
Toronto, Ohio (Jefferson Co.). For *Toronto*, Ont., the home town of a man named Dunspaugh, who was influential in developing the clay industry for which this city is famous. Earlier, Newburg, Sloan's Station.
Toronto Harbor, Ont., on L. Ontario.
Toronto Reservoir, Kan. For Toronto, Ont.

TORRANCE, Calif. (Los Angeles Co.). For Jared S. Torrance, owner of the townsite.

TORRANCE Co., N.Mex. (co. seat, Estancia). For Francis J. Torrance, a railroad promoter.

TORREY, Capt. Robert A., commander at Fort Washakie.
Torrey Creek, Wyo.
Torrey Lake, Wyo.
Torrey Peak, Wyo.

TORREY, John (1796-1873), a botanist.
Torrey, Utah (Wayne Co.).
Torrey Mountain, Mont.
Torrey Pines Park, Calif. (San Diego Co.).
Torreys Peak, Colo.

TORRINGTON For Torrington, Devonshire, England.
Torrington, Conn. (Litchfield Co.). Earlier, Wolcottville, for the Wolcott family, builders of an early woolen mill.
Torrington, Wyo. (co. seat of Goshen Co.). For *Torrington*, Conn.

TOSI For Tosi, a Shoshone medicine man of the late 1800s, who hunted with author Owen Wister.
Tosi Creek, Wyo.
Tosi Peak, Wyo.

TOTOGATIC LAKE, Wis. From Ojibway, "spongy or boggy stream."

TOTOWA, N.J. (Passaic Co.). From an Indian name of uncertain meaning. Dutch scholars translate the Algonquian word *totowa*, or *totua* as it appears in some early records, as "where you begin," suggesting that it was once a frontier town. Other interpretations are: "ground between," "to sink under water," "to dive and reappear," and "a bridge."

TOUCHET RIVER, Wash. From the French form of Indian *toosha*, meaning uncertain, possibly "fire-cured salmon."

TOULON, Ill. (co. seat of Stark Co.). For the French city on the Mediterranean, known chiefly for its naval base and its large arsenal.

TOUTLE RIVER, Wash. From the Indian tribal name, *hullooetell*, meaning unknown.

TOWALAGA RIVER, Ga. From Creek, possibly "place of sumac trees," but the meaning is in dispute. It flows southeast into Ocmulgee River.

TOWANDA From Algonquian, "place of burial."
Towanda, Pa. (co. seat of Bradford Co.).
Towanda Creek, Pa.

TOWER POINT (peak), Ore. Descriptive.

TOWN AND COUNTRY Promotional.
Town and Country, Mo. (St. Louis Co.).
Town and Country, Wash. (Spokane Co.).

TOWNER, Oscar M. (1842-1897), Elk Valley Farm supervisor, landowner, and member of the Dakota Territory legislature. *Towner* Co., N.Dak. (co. seat, Cando). *Towner,* N.Dak. (co. seat of McHenry Co.).

TOWNS Co., Ga. (co. seat, Hiawassee). For George Washington Bonaparte Towns (1801-1854), U.S. representative (1835-36; 1837-39; 1846-47) and governor (1847-51).

TOWNSEND, Mass. (Middlesex Co.), town. For Charles Townshend, 2nd Viscount Townshend (1674-1738), British statesman and diplomat. He was an early Whig and a champion of religious liberty.

TOWNSEND, Mont. (co. seat of Broadwater Co.). For a Northern Pacific railroad official.

TOWSON, Md. (co. seat of Baltimore Co.). For Ezekial and Thomas Towson, earliest settlers and owners of Towson's Tavern. The first recorded mention of Thomas Towson notes that he was paid "the bounty on 113 squirrel skins."

TOYAH Believed to be an Indian word meaning "much water." *Toyah,* Tex. (Reeves Co.). *Toyah* Creek, Tex. Flows NNE into Pecos R. *Toyah* Lake, Tex. On *Toyah* R.

TOZITNA RIVER, Alaska. From Indian, meaning unknown. It flows west and south into the Yukon River.

TRACY, Calif. (San Joaquin Co.). For a railroad official, Lathrop J. Tracy.

TRACY, Minn. (Lyon Co.). For John F. Tracy, president of the Chicago and Northwestern railroad.

TRACY, Que. (Richelieu Co.). For the Marquis of Tracy (1602-1670), lieutenant-general of the French territories in America (1663-67).

TRACY MOUNTAIN, N.Dak. For a local settler.

TRADEWATER RIVER, Ky. So named for its accessibility to trade travel, since it is navigable and forms the borders of several counties. It flows northwest into Ohio River.

TRAFFORD, Lake, Fla. For an early settler of that name.

TRAIL CREEK, Ind. (La Porte Co.). Probably descriptive, suggesting an Indian trail.

TRAILL Co., N.Dak. (co. seat, Hillsboro). For Walter J.S. Traill, a founder of the county.

TRAIL POINT (peak), Utah. For a path near the peak.

TRANSYLVANIA Co., N.C. (co. seat, Brevard). From Latin *trans* plus *sylva,* "beyond the woods." The name may echo that of the province of Transylvania, now in Rumania, but more probably is a literary or promotional name.

TRAP FALLS RESERVOIR, Conn. For the fish traps.

TRAPPER PEAK, Mont. For a trapper who inhabited the slopes.

TRAVERSE From French *lac travers,* translation of Siouan *mdehdakinyan,* "lake lying crosswise." See also GRAND TRAVERSE. *Little Traverse* Bay, Mich., on L. Michigan. *Traverse* Co., Minn. (co. seat, Wheaton). *Traverse,* Lake, S.Dak.-Minn. *Traverse* Point, Mich. Extends into Keneewaw Bay. *Traverse City,* Mich. (co. seat of Grand Traverse Co.).

TRAVIS, William Barret (1809-1836), an officer in the Texas cavalry who fought in the Texas War for independence. *Travis* Co., Tex. (co. seat, Austin). *Travis,* Lake, Tex.

TREASURE Co., Mont. (co. seat, Hysham). For the nickname of Montana, the "Treasure State."

TREASURE ISLAND, Fla. (Pinellas Co.). Probably promotional, influenced by the title of the novel by Robert Lewis Stevenson.

TREGO Co., Kan. (co. seat, Wakeeney). For Edgar P. Trego (?-1863), a Union army officer killed in action at Chickamauga, Tenn.

TREMONTON, Utah (Box Elder Co.). Probably from Spanish *tres* plus *monton,* "three peaks," or possibly for a Tremont in Illinois.

TREMPEALEAU. From French, *la montagne qui trempe a l'eau,* "mountain drenched with water." The county name was taken from a settlement at the foot of the hill; it was probably translated from an Indian name.
Trempealeau Co., Wis. (co. seat, Whitehall).
Trempealeau River, Wis.

TRENT For the Trent River in England.
Trent River, N.C. Flows SE into Neuse R.
Trent River, N.C. Flows N into Bay R.

TRENTON For William Trent, founder of *Trenton,* N.J. The place was the scene of a battle (1776) during the American Revolution in which troops under the command of George Washington defeated the Hessians in an important engagement. The name thus became popular for patriotic reasons.
Trenton, Fla. (co. seat of Gilchrist Co.). For *Trenton,* Tenn.; named by a settler from there.
Trenton, Ga. (co. seat of Dade Co.).
Trenton, Mich. (Wayne Co.). For *Trenton,* N.J.
Trenton, Mo. (co. seat of Grundy Co.). Earlier, Bluff Grove, Lomax's Store.
Trenton, Neb. (co. seat of Hitchcock Co.). For *Trenton,* N.J.
Trenton, N.J. (co. seat of Mercer Co.), state capital. Earlier, Trent's Town.
Trenton, Ohio (Butler Co.). For *Trenton,* N.J.
Trenton, Tenn. (co. seat of Gibson Co.).

TRENTON, N.C. (co. seat of Jones Co.). For a river, which was named for the Trent River in England.

TREUTLEN Co., Ga. (co. seat, Soperton). For John Adam Treutlen (1726-1783), first governor (1777-78).

TRIBUNE, Kan. (co. seat of Greeley Co.). For the *New York Tribune,* edited by Horace Greeley, a supporter of westward expansion, for whom the county was named.

TRIGG Co., Ky. (co. seat, Cadiz). For Stephen Trigg (?-1782), an officer killed in action against Indians at Blue Lakes.

TRIMBLE Co., Ky. (co. seat, Bedford). For Robert Trimble (1777-1828), a U.S. Supreme Court Justice (1826-28).

TRINCHERA PEAK, Colo. From Spanish, "trench," for the shape of the canyon for which the peak was named.

TRINIDAD, Colo. (co. seat of Las Animas Co.). From Spanish, "Trinity" for the Holy Trinity.

TRINITY For a group of three, usually the Holy Trinity, though named for various reasons. See also TRINIDAD.
Trinity Co., Calif. (co. seat, Weaverville). For Trinity Sunday.
Trinity Co., Tex. (co. seat, Groveton).
Trinity, N.Mex. Site of the dropping of the first atomic bomb. It was named by Robert Oppenheimer to commemorate Protestant, Jewish, and Catholic faiths. The inspiration was taken from a poem by John Donne, "Hymn to God, My God, in My Sickness."
Trinity, Tex. (*Trinity* Co.).
Trinity Bay, Nfld.
Trinity Bay, Tex. See GALVESTON Bay.
Trinity, Cape, Que.
Trinity Islands, Alaska. Named by James Cook, in translation of *Trinidad,* as the islands had been named earlier by Spanish explorers. They were called *Ostrovy Troitsy* by Russian colonizers.
Trinity Natl. Forest, Calif.
Trinity Reservoir, Calif.

Trinity River, Calif. Flows into the Klamath River.

Trinity River, Tex. Flows generally SE to Galveston Bay; named by a priest in the de Soto expedition in 1542 or 1543 because the river's three forks came together just above what is now Dallas. The obvious reference here is to the Holy Trinity.

TRIPP Co., S. Dak. (co. seat, Winner). For Bartlett Tripp (1842-1911), statesman, active in promoting South Dakota's statehood. He served as minister to Austria-Hungary and was an educator and a trustee of Yankton College.

TROIS-PISTOLES, Que. (Riviere du Loup Co.). From French, *trois* meaning "three," and *pistole* being a gold coin. It is said that in 1621 one of two sailors seeking fresh water dropped his silver goblet in the water; the other exclaimed, "Well, three *pistoles* lost!" And so they presumably called the river *Trois Pistoles*.

TROIS-RIVIERES, Que. (St. Maurice Co.). So named because it is at the mouth of the St. Maurice River, which has three outlets separated by delta islands.

TROTWOOD, Ohio (Montgomery Co.). Named by the postmaster, a Dickens en-

Troy has fascinated the world ever since Homer composed *The Iliad*. The tale culminates with the Greeks' gift of a gigantic horse which they surreptitiously filled with warriors who opened the gates of the city so that their comrades could utterly destroy it. [*New York Public Library*]

thusiast, for Betsy Trotwood of *David Copperfield.*

TROUP Co., Ga. (co. seat, La Grange). For George Michael Troup (1780-1856), U.S. representative (1816-18; 1829-33), senator (1807-1815), and governor (1823-27).

TROUSDALE Co., Tenn. (co. seat, Hartsville). For William Trousdale (1790-1872), statesman, governor (1849-51), and minister to Brazil (1852-57). He also served in the Indian wars and in the Mexican War, in which he was wounded.

TROUT For the fish.
Trout Creek, Ore. Flows NW into Deshutes River.
Trout Creek, Ore. Flows NW into Alvord L.
Trout Lake, Wis.
Trout Peak, Wyo. For a nearby creek.
Trout River, Vt. Flows N and NW into Missisquoi R.
Trout Creek Hills, Colo.

TROY For the ancient city in Asia Minor, made famous through the poetry of Homer, especially the *Iliad,* from which the name was taken in many cases.
Troy, Ala. (co. seat of Pike Co.).
Troy, Kan. (co. seat of Doniphan Co.).
Troy, Mich. (Oakland Co.). For *Troy,* N.Y.
Troy, Mo. (co. seat of Lincoln Co.).
Troy, N.Y. (co. seat of Rensselaer Co.). The first place so named in the United States.
Troy, Ohio (co. seat of Miami Co.).
Troy Peak, Nev.

TROY, N.C. (co. seat of Montgomery Co.). Either for Robert Troy (?-1807), legislator and a trustee of the University of North Carolina, or for John B. Troy (?-c.1837), a state legislator; also possibly for ancient Troy.

TRUCKEE RIVER, Calif.-Nev. For an Indian guide, said to be a chief. It flows northeast into Pyramid Lake.

TRUMANN Ark. (Poinsett Co.). For an official of the St. Louis and San Francisco railroad.

TRUMBULL, Conn. (Fairfield Co.), town. For Jonathan Trumbull (1710-1785), merchant, member of the General Assembly, and colonial governor (1769-1784), father of Jonathan Trumbull (1740-1809). The only colonial governor to take the colonies' side in the American Revolution, he was an advisor to Washington and supplied materials to the Continental Army. Washington called him "Brother Jonathan," which may have been the origin of that nickname for the United States.

TRUMBULL Co., Ohio (co. seat, Warren). For Jonathan Trumbull (1740-1809), Connecticut statesman, son of Jonathan Trumbull (1710-1785), the colonial governor. He served in the American Revolution as paymaster (1776-80) and aide-de-camp to Washington (1780-83). He was a U.S. representative (1789-95) and senator (1795-96) and governor of Connecticut (1798-1809).

TRURO For a shire town in Cornwall, England.
Truro, Iowa (Madison Co.).
Truro, Ill. (Knox Co.).
Truro, Mass. (Barnstable Co.).
Truro, N.S. (county town of Colchester Co.). Earlier, Cobequid, an Acadian town destroyed by the British.

TRUSSVILLE, Ala. (Jefferson Co.). For Warren Truss (1772-1837), large plantation and slave owner.

TRUTH OR CONSEQUENCES, N.Mex. (co. seat of Sierra Co.). For the popular radio show (later also on television); named when Ralph Edwards, the master of ceremonies, promised to hold an annual program here.

TRYON, Neb. (co. seat of McPherson Co.). Origin debatable: for William Tryon (1725-1788), a colonial governor of North Carolina and later New York, or for a local judge; another theory is that it is the combination of *try* plus *on,* from a resident having said, "Let's keep trying on to have a town."

TSALA APOPKA LAKE, Fla. From Seminole-Creek, "trout eating place."

"If you don't tell the truth, you must take the consequences." The popular radio quiz show specialized in antics for failing to answer impossible questions. The program searched for a community willing to change its name to Truth or Consequences. Hot Springs, New Mexico, agreed in March, 1950. [*Culver Pictures*]

TSCHIDA, Lake, N.Dak. From Arikara Indian, meaning unknown.

TUCANNON RIVER, Wash. From Nez Perce, "bread-root" or "bread-root creek." It flows northwest into Snake River.

TUCKAHOE, N.Y. For a tuber-type vegetable, *Orontium aquaticum,* like the potato. The Indian word was *tuckahog,* first recorded by John Smith as *tuckwhogh.*
Tuckahoe, N.Y. (Westchester Co.).
Tuckahoe River, N.J. Flow S and E into
    Great Egg Harbor.

TUCKASEIGEE RIVER, N.C. From Cherokee *tsiksitsi,* meaning uncertain, possibly "crawling terrapin," for the sluggishness of the flow of water. It flows northwest into Little Tennessee River.

TUCKER Co., W.Va. (co. seat, Parsons). For Henry St. George Tucker (1780-1848), Virginia soldier, statesman, and jurist. He was a U.S. representative (1815-19), president of the Virginia court of appeals (1831-41), and professor of law at the University of Virginia (1841-45).

TUCKERNUCK ISLAND, Mass. In Muskeget Channel. From Wampanoag, "round loaf of bread," for its supposed resemblance in shape.

TUCSON From a Spanish rendering of the Papago Indian name, *Chuk Shon,* for Sentinel Mountain, meaning "black base." *South Tucson,* Ariz. (Pima Co.). *Tucson,* Ariz. (co. seat of Pima Co.).

TUCUMCARI Origin uncertain; possibly from Comanche *tukamukaru,* "to lie in ambush for someone" or "to wait for someone." Others believe the city was named for the mountain, from Comanche, "signal peak," for the messages sent from there.
Tucumcari, N.Mex. (co. seat of Quay Co.).
Tucumcari Mountain, N.Mex.

TUG FORK RIVER, W.Va.-Ky. Probably from Indian, "fork," but conflicting claims exist: that members of an exploring party had to eat "tugs" of buffalo skins while near the river, or that canoes had to be "tugged" on the river. The Indian origin is most probable. It flows northwest to join Levisa River to form Big Sandy River.

TUGIDAK ISLAND, Alaska. In Trinity Islands. From Aleut, either "moon" or "mouth."

TUG MOUNTAIN, Me. Folk etymologized form from Abnaki, "tree."

TUKWULA, Wash. (King Co.). Probably from Indian *tuck-will-la,* "land of hazelnuts," suggested when the post office was being named.

TULARE From Spanish, "rush" or "reed," perhaps originally from Aztec *tullin* or *tollin,* meaning a cattail, bulrush, or similar plant.
Tulare Co., Calif. (co. seat, Visalia).
Tulare, Calif. (*Tulare* Co.). For the lake.
Tulare Lake, Calif.
Tule Lake, Calif.

TULAROSA, N.Mex. (Otero Co.). From Spanish, "reddish reeds or willows."

TULIA, Tex. (co. seat of Swisher Co.). A Latinized form of *tule,* for the species of bulrush, *Scirpus acutas.*

TULLAHOMA, Tenn. (Coffee Co.). From Muskogean, *tulla,* "town," and *-homa,* "red."

TULSA Probably from Creek *talwa,* "town," and *hasi,* "old." The name was apparently transferred from Alabama when the Creeks were forced to move west.
Tulsa Co., Okla. (co. seat, *Tulsa*).
Tulsa, Okla. (co. seat of *Tulsa* Co.). Earlier, Tulsey Town.

TUMACACORI NATL. MONUMENT, Ariz. From Pima Indian, "curved peak." Established to preserve the remains of an historically important Franciscan Mission.

TUMBLEDOWN MOUNTAIN, Me. For rock slides that occur on its sides.

TUMWATER, Wash. (Thurston Co.). Descriptive of the sound of falling water.

TUNICA From a tribe of Tunican linguistic stock located on the lower Yazoo River in Mississippi. Their name means "the people" or "those who are the people."
Tunica Co., Miss. (co. seat, *Tunica*).
Tunica, Miss. (co. seat of *Tunica* Co.).

TUNKHANNOCK From Algonquian, "a small stream," but may also mean "forest." Probably two Algonquian words have been confused.
Tunkhannock, Pa. (co. seat of Wyoming Co.).
Tunkhannock Creek, Pa. Flows SW into Susquehanna R.

TUNK LAKE, Me. From Abnaki, "main stream." According to a folk tale, the name resulted from a battle of "doeboys," a soft bread dumpling, in which the participants threw the doeboys at each other, and when they missed, the dumpling went "tunk" on the wall. The story is a good one, but there are too many places named Tunk in Maine to have had a doeboy battle occur at each one.

TUNNEL HILL, Wyo. So named because waters of a creek are tunnelled under the hill, to irrigate farms beyond it.

TUOLUMNE For a subtribe of the Miwok Indians, themselves of Penutian linguistic stock. They probably lived along the river that now bears their name, although this is not certain. Early mention of the tribe gives the spellings *taulamne, tahualamne,* and *towalumnes,* among others. The Mexicans named the river *Rio de los Towalumnes.* The name *tuleyomi,* from which the modern form derives, has not been translated satisfactorily. The suffix *yomi* means "people," a designation common among Indians.
Tuolumne Co., Calif. (co. seat, Sonora).
Tuolumne Meadows, Calif., in Yosemite Natl. Park.
Tuolumne River, Calif. Rises in Yosemite Natl. Park and flows W to the San Joaquin River.

TUPELO Ultimately from Creek Indian *ito opelwa;* "swamp tree," now recognized scientifically and popularly as any tree of the genus *Nyssa,* especially *N. sylvatica,* "black gum."
Tupelo, Miss. (co. seat of Lee Co.).
Tupelo Natl. Battlefield Site, Miss.

TUPPER For a surveyor who helped lay out the Macomb Purchase lands between 1795 and 1799.
Little Tupper Lake, N.Y.
Tupper Lake, N.Y.
Tupper Lake, N.Y. (St. Lawrence Co.).

TURKEY RIVER, Iowa. For the wild turkey. It flows southeast into the Mississippi River.

TURLOCK, Calif. (Stanislaus Co.). For Turlough, county Mayo, Ireland.

TURNER Co., Ga. (co. seat, Ashburn). For Henry Gray Turner (1839-1904), legislator and jurist.

TURNER Co., S. Dak. (co. seat, Parker). For John W. Turner (1800-1883), an early settler who was active in promoting the community. He was a member of the legislature and a superintendent of public instruction.

TURRET PEAK, Ariz. Descriptive of its shape.

TURTLE For the presence of turtles.
Turtle River, N.Dak. Flows E and NNE into Red River of the North.
Turtle River, S.Dak. Flows E and N into James R.

TURTLE For the resemblance in shape to a turtle's back.
Turtle Mountain, Man.
Turtle Mountains, Man.-N.Dak.

TURTLE CREEK, Pa. (Allegheny Co.). A translation of the Delaware Indian name, *tulpewisipu,* for the stream on which the town is built.

TURTLEFORD, Sask. For a river, which was named for the turtles there.

TUSCALOOSA From Choctaw *tashka,* "warrior," and *lusa,* "black," applied to the river now called the Black Warrior, and apparently also a tribal name for the chief.
Tuscaloosa Co., Ala. (co. seat, *Tuscaloosa*).
Tuscaloosa, Ala. (co. seat of *Tuscaloosa* Co.), former capital (1826-46) of Alabama.

TUSCARAWAS Co., Ohio (co. seat, New Philadelphia). From an Indian word meaning "open mouth."

TUSCARORA From the Iroquoian tribal name, which means "hemp gatherers."
Tuscarora Creek, Pa. Flows NE into Juniata River.
Tuscarora Mountains, Pa.
Tuscarora Mountains, Nev.

TUSCOLA Coined by H.R. SCHOOLCRAFT, probably from Mushogean *tanshka,* "Warrior," plus *-ola.* He said it meant "warrior prairie," but also called it "level lands." Schoolcraft had a fondness for "euphonic" endings.
Tuscola Co., Mich. (co. seat, Caro.).
Tuscola, Ill. (co. seat of Douglas Co.).

TUSCUMBIA For a famous Cherokee chief. The translation is usually given as "warrior killer," as from Choctaw or Chickasaw *taska*, "warrior," and *abi* or *ambi*, "killer," or it may come from a Choctaw combination of *tashka* and *umbachi* or *umba ikbi*, for "warrior rain maker." See also ESCAMBIA.
Tuscumbia, Ala. (co. seat of Colbert Co.). Earlier Coldwater, Big Springs.
Tuscumbia, Mo. (co. seat of Miller Co.). For *Tuscumbia*, Ala.

TUSHAR MOUNTAINS, Utah. Probably a folk derivative of "tusk," descriptive of the shape of the peaks.

TUSKEGEE, Ala. (co. seat of Macon Co.). From Muskhogean, "warrior."

TUSSEY MOUNTAIN, Pa. Origin and meaning of the name unknown.

TUSTIN, Columbus (1826-1883), founder and first postmaster.
Tustin, Calif. (Orange Co.).
Tustin-Foothill, Calif. (Orange Co.).

TUSTUMENA LAKE, Alaska. From Tanaina Indian, meaning unknown.

TUTTLE CREEK RESERVOIR, Kan. For the creek, which was named for a settler in the area.

TUZIGOOT NATL. MONUMENT, Ariz. From Apache, "crooked water," for the shape of a nearby lake. Established in 1939 as a national preservation for Indian pueblos of pre-Columbian times.

TWENTYNINE PALMS Descriptive.
Twentynine Palms, Calif. (San Bernadino Co.).
Twentynine Palms Base, Calif. (San Bernardino Co.).

TWIGGS Co., Ga. (co. seat, Jeffersonville). For John Twiggs, a general in the American Revolution.

TWIN Descriptive, for a pair of similar features.
East Twin River, Wis. Flows S into L. Michigan.
North Twin Lake, Mich.-Wis. The southern twin name is no longer used.
North Twin Mountain, N.H. Lies N of *South Twin* Mtn.
South Twin Mountain, N.H. Lies S of *North Twin* Mtn.
Twin Lakes, Me. Two lakes joined in a Siamese-like fashion.
Twin Lakes, Neb.
Twin Mountains, Tex.
Twin Butte Creek, Kan. Flows E into Beaver Creek. For the two nearby buttes.
Twin Falls Co., Idaho (co. seat, *Twin Falls*). For falls on the Snake R.
Twin Falls, Idaho (co. seat of *Twin Falls* Co.).
Twin Lakes, Calif. (Santa Cruz Co.).
West Twin River, Wis. Flows SE into L. Michigan.

TWINSBURG, Ohio (Summit Co.). For the Wilcox twins, born of early settlers. One became a teacher, the other a minister.

TWITCHELL RESERVOIR, Calif. On Santa Maria River. For a local citizen.

TWO BUTTES Descriptive.
Two Buttes, Colo. (Baca Co.).
Two Buttes (peaks), Colo.
Two Buttes Creek, Colo. Flows NE into Arkansas R.

TWO HARBORS, Minn. (co. seat of Lake Co.). For two bays of Lake Superior.

TWO HEARTED RIVER, Mich. Probably translated from an Indian name for the two branches of the river, North Branch and an unnamed branch. It flows northeast into Lake Superior.

TWO MOUNTAINS For two prominent mountains near the shore of the lake. Also called *Deux Montagnes*.
Two Mountains Co., Que. (co. seat, Ste. Scholastique).
Two Mountains Lake, Que.

TWO RIVER, Wis. (Manitowoc Co.). A translation of French *Deux Rivieres*; descriptive, for East Twin and West Twin rivers.

TWO RIVERS RESERVOIR, N.Mex. Reason for the name is not clear, since only one river exists in the area.

TWO SISTERS LAKE, Wis. Probably so named because two sisters lived on the shore.

TYBEE ISLAND, Ga. Probably from Uchee, "salt," but other possible derivations also exist.

TYGART, David, an early settler in · the area.
Tygart Lake, W.Va. For the river.
Tygart River, W.Va.

TYGARTS CREEK, Ky. For a local settler. It flows generally northeast into Ohio River.

TYHE PEAK, Wyo. For Tyhe, a Shoshone medicine man.

TYLER, John (1747-1813), Virginia statesman and jurist, father of President John Tyler. He was judge of the Virginia general court (1789-1808) and governor (1808-11).

Tyler Co., W.Va. (co. seat, Middlebourne).
Tyler, Tex. (co. seat of Smith Co.).

TYLER Co., Tex. (co. seat, Woodville). For John Tyler (1790-1862), tenth President of the United States (1841-45) succeeding on the death of William Henry Harrison. A Virginian, he was a U.S. :epresentative (1817-21), governor (1825-27), senator (1827-36), and vice-president of the United States (1841). He was the son of the Virginia governor, John Tyler (1747-1813).

TYLERTOWN, Miss. (co. seat of Walthall Co.). For William G. Tyler, sailor, mechanic and blacksmith.

TYNDALL Co., S.Dak. (co. seat of Bon Homme Co.). For John Tyndall (1820-1893), English physicist who lectured in the United States late in the 1800s.

TYNGSBOROUGH, Mass. (Middlesex Co.), town. For Jonathan Tyng (1643-1724), a large landowner in colonial Massachusetts.

TYRONE, Pa. (Blair Co.). For county Tyrone, Northern Ireland.

TYRRELL Co., N.C. (co. seat Columbia). For John Tyrrell (1685-1729), a lord proprietor of North Carolina during the colonial period.

U

UGASHIK. From Eskimo, meaning unknown.
Ugashik Bay, Alaska.
Ugashik River, Alaska. Flows W into *Ugashik* Bay.

UHRICHSVILLE, Ohio (Tuscarawas Co.). For Michael Uhrich (1751-1817), an early settler who owned the first grist mill and sawmill.

UINTA. For a subtribe of the Utes, of Shoshonean linguistic stock, located in northeastern Utah. The name is said to mean "pineland." See also UINTAH.
Uinta Co., Wyo. (co. seat, Evanston).
Uinta Mountains, Utah-Wyo.
Uinta Natl. Forest, Utah.
Uinta River, Utah. Flows generally SW to the Duchesne R.

UINTAH. A variant spelling of UINTA.
Uintah Co., Utah (co. seat, Vernal).
Uintah and Ouray Indian Reservation, Utah.

UKIAH, Calif. (co. seat of Mendocino Co.). Believed to be from Central Pomo Indian *yo*, "south" or "deep," and *kaia*, "valley." Rather than "south valley," the preferred interpretation is "deep valley."

ULYSSES, Kan. (co. seat of Grant Co.). For Ulysses S. GRANT.

UMATILLA. For an Indian tribe that belonged to the Shapwailutan linguistic stock and resided on the Umatilla River and also on the banks of the Columbia, near the mouth of the Umatilla. The meaning of the name is unknown; one authority says that it may mean "water rippling over sand."
Umatilla Co., Ore. (co. seat, Pendleton).
Umatilla Dam, Ore., also known as McNary Dam.
Umatilla Natl. Forest, Wash.
Umatilla River, Ore. Flows W and NW to the Columbia River.

UMAUMA CREEK, Hawaii. On Hawaii Island. From Hawaiian, "chest," "breast," or, figuratively, "heart." It flows east into the Pacific Ocean.

UMBAGOG LAKE, Me.-N.H. From Abnaki, "clear lake," descriptive.

UMBAZOOKSUS LAKE, Me. From Abnaki, "clear but gravelly mouth," for its outlet.

UMNAK ISLAND, Alaska. In Fox Islands. From Aleut, "fish line."

UMPQUA RIVER, Ore. For an Indian tribe in Oregon, meaning and origin unknown. They belonged to the Athapascan linguistic stock. The river flows generally NW into the Pacific Ocean.

UMSAKIS LAKE, Me. From Malecite, "linked together," referring to a chain of lakes.

UNADILLA RIVER, N.Y. From Iroquoian, "meeting." The river flows generally SW to the Susquehanna R.

UNAKA MOUNTAINS, N.C.-Tenn. From Cherokee, "white," for the color of the rocks. The range, part of the Appalachians, includes the Great Smoky Mountains.

UNALASKA ISLAND, Alaska. In Fox Islands. From Aleut, probably a tribal name, since *Unanak* was the name the natives of Fox Islands applied to themselves.

UNCOMPAHGRE. From Ute, "red water canyon."
Uncompahgre Mountains, Colo.
Uncompahgre Natl. Forest, Colo.
Uncompahgre Peak, Colo.
Uncompahgre Plateau, Colo.
Uncompahgre River, Colo. Flows generally NW to the Gunnison River.

UNDERHILL RIDGE, Wyo. Probably for Bob and Marian Underhill. Mrs. Underhill is one of the great women mountain climbers of this generation.

UNGA ISLAND, Alaska, in Shumagin Islands. Shortened form of UNGALIK.

UNGALIK RIVER, Alaska. From an Aleut word, meaning unknown. It flows southwest into Norton Bay.

UNICOI. A variant form of UNAKA.
Unicoi Co., Tenn. (co. seat Erwin).
Unicoi Gap, Ga. A mountain pass.

UNIMAK. Of Aleut origin, meaning unknown.
Unimak Island, Alaska. In Fox Islands.
Unimak Pass, Alaska. Strait between *Unimak* Island and Krenitzin Island.

UNION. Often for the American union of the states, but also for other kinds of union.
Union Co., Ark. (co. seat, El Dorado).

Union Co., Fla. (co. seat, Lake Butler). So named as an expression of unity between political parties in the division of Brandford County, from which this was formed, and in the location of the county seat.
Union Co., Ga. (co. seat, Blairsville).
Union Co., Ill. (co. seat, Jonesboro). For the temporary union of two churches, in a combined meeting of Dunkards and Baptists.
Union Co., Ind. (co. seat, Liberty).
Union Co., Iowa (co. seat Creston).
Union Co., Ky. (co. seat, Morganfield).
Union Parish, La. (parish seat, Farmerville).
Union Co., Miss. (co. seat, New Albany).
Union Co., N.J. (co. seat, Elizabeth). So named (1857) as an expression of belief in the union of the United States during the debate over the division between North and South; also in the hope that citizens of Elizabeth and Newark would settle their differences.
Union Co., N.Mex. (co. seat, Clayton).
Union Co., N.C. (co. seat, Monroe).
Union Co., Ohio (co. seat, Marysville). Formed by the union of four counties.
Union Co., Ore. (co. seat, La Grande).
Union Co., Pa. (co. seat, Lewisburg).
Union Co., S.C. (co. seat, *Union*).
Union Co., S.Dak. (co. seat, Elk Point).
Union Co., Tenn. (co. seat, Maynardville).

The Star-spangled Banner in triumph
SHALL wave,
O'er the land of the free, and the home
of the brave.

"The Union forever! Hurrah, boys, hurrah!" Union has always been an important phrase and concept in the United States. During the Civil War, in the North it became a passion and the name appears in places from coast to coast. [*New York Public Library*]

Union, Me. (Knox Co.), town.
Union, Mo. (co. seat of Franklin Co.).
Union, N.J. (*Union* Co.).
Union, Ohio (Montgomery Co.).
Union, S.C. (co. seat of *Union* Co.).
Union, W.Va. (co. seat of Monroe Co.). Probably so named because it was the site where troops prepared to fight the Indians. In later times, no doubt, it was considered a rallying name for patriotism. The former interpretation is closer to the fact; the latter closer to fantasy, however effective.
Union Lake, N.J.
Union, Lake, Wash.
Union, Mount, Ariz.

Union Peak, Ore.
Union Peak, Wyo.
Union River, Me. Flows into Blue Hill Bay.
Union Beach, N.J. (Monmouth Co.).
Union City, Calif. (Alameda Co.).
Union, City, Ga. (Fulton Co.).
Union City, Ind. (Randolph Co.). For the Union of Indiana and Ohio; situated on the border.
Union City, N.J. (Hudson Co.).
Union City, Pa. (Erie Co.).
Union City, Tenn. (co. seat of Obion Co.).
Uniondale, N.Y. (Nassau Co.).
Union Flat Creek, Idaho-Wash. Flows NW and W into Palouse River.
Union Grove, Wis. (Racine Co.). For a Union school and a grove of oaks.
Union Springs, Ala. (co. seat of Bullock Co.).
Uniontown, Pa. (co. seat of Fayette Co.).
Uniontown,Wash. (Whitman Co.). For a junction of streams.
Unionville, Mo. (co. seat of Putnam Co.).
West Union, Iowa (co. seat of Fayette Co.).
West Union, Ohio (co. seat of Adams Co.).

UNITED STATES. Generally known as the United States of America, seldom, except by South Americans, as the United States of North America, which would be more appropriate. The name probably came into being during the events leading to the Declaration of Independence in 1776. With the granting of statehood to Hawaii in 1959, the republic was extended beyond the North American continental limits and acquired its fiftieth state. Puerto Rico, a Commonwealth, was ceded to the United States in 1898 by Spain. By treaty with the Republic of Panama, the United States holds certain powers over the operation of the Panama Canal and the Canal Zone. Other islands in the Caribbean and in the Pacific are now under the jurisdiction of the United States. The national capital is Washington, in the District of Columbia.

UNIVERSAL CITY, Tex. (Bexar Co.). A promotional name for a new city outside Randolph Air Force Base, the showplace of the U.S. Air Force.

UNIVERSITY. Sometimes a post office convenience for a city or town in which a university or college is located, but also because of pride in the presence of a cultural institution.
University City, Mo. (St. Louis Co.).
Univeristy Heights, Ohio (Cuyahoga Co.). Site of John Carroll U. Earlier, Idlewood.
University Park, Md. (Prince Georges Co.).
University Park-Tortugas, N.Mex. (Dona Ana Co.). *University Park*, for New Mexico State University; *Tortugas*, from Spanish, "turtles," either for the abundance of the animal or for a mountain that looks like a turtle.
University Park, Tex. (Dallas Co.). Site of Southern Methodist U.

UNSOELD NEEDLE (Mountain), Wyo. For Willi Unsoeld, who ascended it in 1952 with a party of climbers.

UNUK RIVER, B.C.-Alaska. Of Indian origin, meaning unknown. It flows southwest into Burroughs Bay.

UPATOIE CREEK, Ga. From Muskogean, meaning uncertain, postulated by some to mean "on the fringe," "furthest out," or "bullfrog." It flows southwest into Chattahoochee River.

UPLAND. Descriptive.
Upland, Calif. (San Bernardino Co.). In the foothills of the San Gabriel Mtns.
Upland, Ind. (Grant Co.). The highest elevation between Chicago, Ill., and Columbus, Ohio.
Upland, Pa. (Delaware Co.).

Utah is internationally known as the home of the Mormons, the Church of Jesus Christ of the Latter-Day Saints. Founded by Joseph Smith in New York, the Mormons moved progressively westward, led by their most famous apostle, Brigham Young, whose Utah home is shown above. [*London Illustrated Times, 1858. New York Public Library*]

UPOLU POINT, Hawaii. Northernmost point of Hawaii Island. For an island in Samoa.

UPPER Either for higher ground, or north from a point, or farther toward a source, regardless of direction. Place names not in this part of the book may be found under the basic name.
Upper Lake, Calif. The most northern of three lakes: Upper, Middle, and Lower.
Upper Arlington, Ohio (Franklin Co.). For the Upper Arlington Company, a development organization. Arlington's name was changed to Marble Cliff, since there existed an Arlington in Ohio. Upper Arlington was acceptable, however, since it was a different name. The city developed north of the original Arlington.

UPSHUR, Abel Parker (1791-1844), jurist, statesman, U.S. secretary of the navy (1841-43), and U.S. secretary of state (1834-44).
Upshur Co., Tex. (co. seat, Gilmer).
Upshur Co., W.Va. (co. seat, Buckhannon].

UPSON Co., Ga. (co. seat, Thomaston). For Stephen Upson (1786-1824), attorney.

UPTON For Upton, Yorkshire, England.
Upton, Me. (Oxford Co.), town.
Upton, Mass. (Worcester Co.), town.

UPTON Co., Tex. (co. seat, Rankin). For John Cunningham Upton (1823-1862), a Confederate officer killed at the Battle of Manassas.

URANIA, La. (La Salle Parish). Named by Henry Hardtner because he thought the place was heavenly compared to his former mill site at a place called Enterprise. Besides being the celestial Muse, Urania was also the Muse of agriculture, appropriate to an area that had been almost completely cleared of timber.

URANIUM PEAK, Colo. For the mineral.

URBANA From Latin *urbanus*, ''citified.'' The addition of -*a* is common in the United States to designate a place.
Urbana, Ill. (co. seat of Champaign Co.).
Urbana, Ohio (co. seat of Champaign Co.).

URBANDALE, Iowa (Polk Co.). Promotional. *Urban*, from Latin, *urbanus*, ''citified,'' and *dale*, descriptive for a valley.

UTAH. From the Indian name *Ute* or *Eutaw*, variously defined as "in the tops of the mountains," "high-up," "the land of the sun," and "the land of plenty." Variant spellings include *Youta, Eutah,* and *Utaw.* See also UTE and UNITA

Utah, State of. 45th state of the Union. Settled: 1847. Territory: 1850. Admitted: 1896. Cap: Salt Lake City. Motto: Industry. Nickname: Beehive State. Flower: Sego Lily. Bird: California Gull. Tree: Blue Spruce. Song: "Utah, We Love Thee."

Utah Co., Utah (co. seat, Provo).

Utah Lake, Utah.

UTE For an important and warlike Indian tribe that belonged to the Shoshonean linguistic stock, a subgroup of the Uto-Azeteccan family. The tribe was mainly located in what is now western Colorado and Utah, although groups also lived in New Mexico, Nevada, and Wyoming. The meaning of the name is unknown. See also UNITA and UTAH.

Southern Ute Indian Reservation, Colo.

Ute Creek, N.Mex.

Ute Mountain Indian Reservation, Colo.

Ute Mountain Indian Reservation, N.Mex.

Ute Pass, Colo.

Ute Peak, Colo.

Ute Peak, N.Mex.

UTICA An ancient city in North Africa, said to have been founded by Phoenicians from Tyre. It became second to Carthage in importance. After the Third Punic War, it became a Roman provincial capital. It was here that Cato the Younger committed suicide in 46 B.C., after being defeated by forces commanded by Caesar.

Utica, Mich. (Macomb Co.). For *Utica*, N.Y.

Utica, N.Y. (a co..seat of Oneida Co.).

UTSAYANTHA, Mount, N.Y. From Iroquoian, "beautiful spring," for the headwaters of the Delaware River.

UTUKOK RIVER, Alaska. From Eskimo, "old." It flows northwest into Kasegaluk Lagoon.

UVALDE, Jose de, a Mexican army officer in the late 1700s. Although for a time he was Mexican governor of Texas, he gained fame for his successful campaigns against the Apaches and other tribes.

Uvalde Co., Tex. (co. seat, *Uvalde*).

Uvalde, Tex. (co. seat of *Uvalde* Co.).

UWHARRIE. From a tribal name, meaning unknown; it was listed as *Heighwaree* in 1701.

Uwharrie, N.C. (Montgomery Co.).

Uwharrie Mountains, N.C.

Uwharrie Natl. Forest, N.C.

Uwharrie River, N.C. Flows S and SW to join Yadkin River to form Pee Dee River.

UXBRIDGE. For Uxbridge, Middlesex, England.

Uxbridge, Mass. (Worcester Co.). Or for Henry Paget, Earl of Uxbridge (1665-1749), a member of the Privy Council.

Uxbridge, Ont. (Ontario Co.).

V

VACAVILLE, Calif. (Solano Co.). For a Spanish family named Vaca, who came to the area in 1841.

VADNAIS HEIGHTS, Minn. (Ramsey Co.). For John Vadnais, who staked a claim in 1846 or earlier.

VAIDEN, Miss. (a co. seat of Carroll Co.). For the Vaiden family and in particular for Dr. Cowles Mead Vaiden, landowner and state legislator.

VALDESE, N.C. (Burke Co.). Named by Waldensian settlers who came to this area to escape religious persecution. They are a Protestant sect that claims to be a pure remnant of the primitive church. They are often called Valdenses.

VAL D'OR, Que. (Abitibi Co.). From French, "valley of gold," for gold deposits in the area.

VALDOSTA, Ga. (co. seat of Lowndes Co.). A contraction of the name of the estate of Gov. George M. Troup, Val d'Aosta, "vale of beauty," after a district in the Alps of northwestern Italy.

VALE, Ore. (co. seat of Malheur Co.). No satisfactory explanation has been given; possibly descriptive.

VALENCIA City and province on the east coast of Spain. In New Mexico, named particularly for Juan de Valencia, an early Spanish settler.

Valencia Co., N.Mex. (co. seat, Los Lunas).
Valencia, N.Mex. (*Valencia* Co.).

VALENTINE, Neb. (co. seat of Cherry Co.). For Edward Kimball Valentine (1843-1916), officer in the Union army, jurist, and a U.S. representative for three terms.

VALLEJO, Calif. (Solano Co.). For Mariano Guadalupe Vallejo, founder.

VALLEY Descriptive.
Valley Co., Idaho (co. seat, Cascade). For the Payette River valley.
Valley Co., Mont. (co. seat, Glasgow). For the Milk and Missouri river valleys.
Valley Co., Neb. (co. seat, Ord). For the Calamus River valley.
Valley Center, Kan. (Sedgwick Co.). For its location in the Arkansas River valley.
Valley City, N.Dak. (co. seat of Barnes Co.). For the Sheyenne River valley.
Valley Park, Mo. (St. Louis Co.).
Valley Station, Ky. (Jefferson Co.).

VALLEY COTTAGE, N.Y. (Rockland Co.). So named because when the New York Central railroad needed a right of way through the area, it was granted by a Mr. Green, a large property owner, on condition they change the name for his "cottage" in the valley. An earlier name was Forrest Glen.

VALLEYFIELD, Que. (Beauharnois Co.). Formerly called Salaberry-de-Valleyfield for Colonel de Salaberry, victor over the Americans at Chateauguay in 1812. *Valleyfield* was added to satisfy the English-speaking community, and was derived from the name of a Scottish papermill.

VALLEY STREAM For various brooks and streams running through the town.
South Valley Stream, N.Y. (Nassau Co.).
Valley Stream, N.Y. (Nassau Co.).

VALPARAISO From Portuguese, "valley of paradise," with influence from the name of the city in Chile.
Valparaiso, Fla. (Okaloosa Co.).
Valparaiso, Ind. (co. seat of Porter Co.).

VAL VERDE Co., Tex. (co. seat, Del Rio). From Spanish, "green valley."

VAN BUREN, Martin (1782-1862), eighth President of the United States (1837-41), whose administration was marred by a severe financial crisis. More politician than statesman, he rose through the New York Democratic party to become senator (1821-28) and governor (1829). He was secretary of state (1829-31) and vice-president (1833-37) under Jackson. Van Buren ran again, unsuccessfully, for President in 1840 and 1848. He is credited with being one of the initiators of modern party politics.
Van Buren Co., Ark. (co. seat, Clinton).
Van Buren Co., Iowa (co. seat, Keosauqua).
Van Buren Co., Mich. (co. seat, Paw Paw).
Van Buren Co., Tenn. (co. seat, Spencer).
Van Buren, Ark. (co. seat of Crawford Co.).
Van Buren, Me. (Aroostook Co.), town and village.
Van Buren, Mo. (co. seat of Carter Co.).
Van Buren, Tenn. (co. seat of Culbertson Co.).

VANCE, N.C. (co. seat, Henderson). For Zebulon Baird Vance (1830-1894), statesman. He served as governor (1862-65; (1870-79), U.S. representative (1858-61), and U.S. senator (1879-94).

VANCEBURG, Ky. (Lewis Co.). For Joseph Vance, an early settler and prospector.

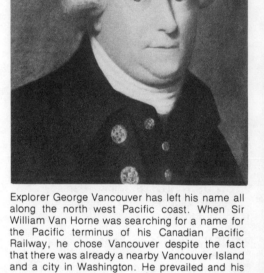

Explorer George Vancouver has left his name all along the north west Pacific coast. When Sir William Van Horne was searching for a name for the Pacific terminus of his Canadian Pacific Railway, he chose Vancouver despite the fact that there was already a nearby Vancouver Island and a city in Washington. He prevailed and his city is now the most famous. [*New York Public Library*]

VANCOUVER, George (1758-1798), British navigator and explorer. He first went to sea at the age of thirteen, sailing under the command of Capt. James Cook. Between 1790 and 1795, in his ship *Discovery,* he explored the western coast of North America and the Australian area and circumnavigated the globe. He and members of his expedition named many features and accurately surveyed for the first time the North American coast above San Francisco, as well as other areas under British control in the Pacific.
Vancouver, B.C. Named by Sir William Cornelius Van Horne, then general manager of the Canadian Pacific railroad. He wanted a name that was recognizably "western," and chose the established name *Vancouver* for the railroad's Western terminus.
Vancouver, Wash. (co. seat of Clark Co.).

Vancouver, Cape, Alaska. On Bering Strait.
Vancouver Island, Alaska.
Vancouver Island, B.C. Largest island on the Pacific coast of North America.
Vancouver, Mount, Alaska.
Vancouver Heights, B.C.
West Vancouver, B.C.

VANDALIA From the Vandals, a Germanic tribe known for its ferocity (hence, *vandal*). In Illinois it is said that the commissioners who named the city naively believed the name to be taken from that of a famous Indian tribe, but the story is probably apocryphal. Euphonic to American ears, the name has achieved a popularity that belies its derivation.
Vandalia, Ill. (co. seat of Fayette Co.).
Vandalia, Mo. (Audrain Co.).
Vandalia, Ohio (Montgomery Co.). For *Vandalia,* Ill., or possibly because vandals once lived in this area, robbing stage coaches, canal boats, or whatever happened to be there.

VANDERBILT MANSION NATL. HISTORICAL SITE, N.Y. Developed by Frederick W. Vanderbilt, grandson of Cornelius Vanderbilt, financial entrepreneur in the 19th century. The site preserves the type of estate established by the tycoons after the Civil War.

VANDERBURGH Co., Ind. (co. seat, Evansville). For Henry Vanderburgh, a judge in the Indiana Territory.

VANDERGRIFT, Pa. (Westmoreland Co.). For J.J. Vandergrift of Pittsburgh, a large stockholder in the Apollo Iron and Steel Company, which was responsible for the original town.

VAN ETTAN LAKE, Mich. For a local settler.

VANETTEN, N.Y. (Chemung Co.). For James B. Van Etten (1811-1856), businessman and member of the New York State Legislature.

VAN HORN, Tex. (co. seat of Culberson Co.). For Col. J.J. Van Horn, who at one time was stationed here to guard against Indians.

VAN WERT, Isaac (?-1828), a captor of John Andre during the American Revolution.
Van Wert Co., Ohio (co. seat, *Van Wert*).
Van Wert, Ohio (co. seat of *Van Wert* Co.).

VAN ZANDT Co., Tex. (co. seat, Canton). For Isaac Van Zandt (1813-1847), Republic of Texas patriot and legislator.

VASSALBOROUGH, Me. (Kennebec Co.), town. For Florentine Vassall, a proprietor of the Plymouth Company, or for William Vassal, one of the first assistants of the Massachusetts Bay Colony.

VASSAR, Mich. (Tuscola Co.). For Matthew Vassar, a founder of Vassar College; named by his niece's husband, a founder.

VAUDREUIL, Pierre de Rigaud, Marquis de (1698-1778), last French governor of Canada (1755-60).
Vaudreuil Co., Que. (co. seat, *Vaudreuil*).
Vaudreuil, Que. (co. seat of *Vaudreuil* Co.).

VEGA, Tex. (co. seat of Oldham Co.). From Spanish, "meadow."

VEGAS CREEK, Nev. (Clark Co.). For a very small stream that ran through Las Vegas many years ago during the rainy season. *Vegas,* from Spanish, "meadows."

VENANGO Co., Pa. (co. seat, Franklin). From an Indian term of uncertain origin, possibly from *innungah,* "a figure carved on a tree."

VENETIAN VILLAGE, Ill. (Lake Co.). Promotional name for a subdivision of Lake Villa; apparently named for Venice, Italy.

VENIAMINOF, Mount, Alaska. In Aleutian Range. For Father Ioann Veniaminov (1797-1879), Bishop of Russian America and author of material on Aleut languages.

VENICE For Venice, Italy.
Venice, Fla. (Sarasota Co.).
Venice, Ill. (Madison Co.). Its streets were often flooded before levees were built on the Mississippi River.
Venice South, Fla. (Sarasota Co.).

VENTURA From Spanish, "fortune," but in this case the name is taken from San Buenaventura.
Ventura Co., Calif. (co. seat, *Ventura*).
Ventura, Calif. (co. seat of *Ventura* Co.).

VERCHERES, Francois Jarret, Sieun de, builder of a fort near the townsite.
Vercheres Co., Que. (co. seat, *Vercheres*).
Vercheres, Que. (co. seat of *Vercheres* Co.).

VERDE RIVER, Ariz. From Spanish, "green," a translation of an Indian equivalent; descriptive. It flows south into Salt River.

VERDI, Giuseppi (1813-1901), Italian operatic composer.
Verdi, Nev. (Washoe Co.). For the peak.
Verdi Peak, Nev. Named by an opera lover.

VERDIGRE CREEK, Neb. An Americanized spelling from the French pronunciation of VERDIGRIS. It flows northeast and north into Niobrara River.

VERDIGRIS RIVER, Kan.-Okla. From French, "green-gray," descriptive. It flows generally southeast into Arkansas River.

VERDUN, Que. (Montreal and Jesus Islands Co.) Named for the French birthplace of its first colonist.

VERMEJO RIVER, Colo. From Spanish, "brown." It flows southeast into Canadian River.

VERMILION. For the color of the soil. See also VERMILLION.
Vermilion Co., Ill. (co. seat, Danville).
Vermilion Parish, La. (parish seat, Abbeville).
Vermilion, Ohio (Erie Co.). For the river in South Dakota.
Vermilion Bay, La.
Vermilion, Lake, Minn.
Vermilion Range, Minn.
Vermilion River, Ill.
Vermilion River, Middle Fork, Ill.-Ind.
Vermilion River, Ohio.
Vermilion River, S.Dak.

Vermont is famed for its maple products — syrup, sugar, and candies. As shown in this early twentieth century photograph, the maple sap is tapped in the early spring, loaded onto sledges, and then boiled down into syrup. [*New York Public Library*]

VERMILLION. A variant spelling of VERMILION.
Vermillion Co., Ind. (co. seat, Newport).
Vermillion, ·S.Dak. (co. seat of Clay Co.).
Vermillion Bluffs, Colo.

VERMONT. From French *mont vert,* "green mountains," applied to areas east of Lake Champlain by Samuel de Champlain in his map of 1612.
Vermont, State of. 14th state of the Union. Settled: 1724. Independent Republic: 1777-91. Admitted: 1791. Cap: Montpelier. Motto: Freedom and Unity. Nickname: Green Mountain State. Flower: Red Clover. Bird: Hermit Thrush. Tree: Sugar Maple. Animal: Morgan Horse. Song: "Hail, Vermont."

VERNAL, Utah (co. seat of Uintah Co.). From the adjective *vernal,* implying youthfulness or growing, hence progress

VERNON For   MOUNT VERNON,   George Washington's home overlooking the Potomac River in Virginia.
North Vernon, Ind. (Jennings Co.).
Vernon Parish, La. (parish seat, Leesville).
Vernon Co., Wis. (co. seat, Viroqua).
Vernon, Ala. (co. seat of Lamar Co.).
Vernon, Conn. (Tolland Co.), town.
Vernon, Ind. (co. seat of Jennings Co.).
Vernon, Tex. (co. seat of Wilbarger Co.).
Vernon Fork Muscatuck River, Ind. Flows SW into Muscatuck R.

VERNON Co., Mo. (co. seat, Nevada). For Miles Vernon (1786-1866), veteran of the Battle of New Orleans and a legislator.

VERO BEACH Believed to be from Latin *veritas,* "truth," but may also be a personal name.
Vero Beach, Fla. (co. seat of Indian River Co.).
Vero Beach, South, Fla. (Indian River Co.).

VERONA For Verona, Italy.
Verona, N.J. (Essex Co.).
Verona, Pa. (Allegheny Co.). Named by local railroad workers for their former home.

VERRET, Lake, La. Probably for Nichols Verret, one of the earliest parish officials. He was granted a tract of land by the French government.

VERSAILLES For the city near Paris, France. It is the site of the palace of Louis XIV.
Versailles, Ind. (co. seat of Ripley Co.).
Versailles, Ky. (co. seat of Woodford Co.).
Versailles, Mo. (co. seat of Morgan Co.).
Versailles, Pa. (Allegheny Co.).

VETA, Mount, Alaska. From Spanish, "vein," for mineral veins.

VEVAY, Ind. (co. seat of Switzerland Co.). For Vevey, Switzerland; named by Swiss settlers. The spelling has been Americanized.

VICKSBURG For Newitt Vick (1766-1819), founder. He owned a plantation where the city is now located.
Vicksburg, Miss. (co. seat of Warren Co.).
Vicksburg Natl. Military Park, Miss.

VICTORIA For Queen Victoria of England (1819-1901). See also REGINA, Sask.
Victoria Co., N.B., (co. seat, Andover).
Victoria Co., N.S. (co. seat, Baddeck).
Victoria Co., Ont. (co. town, Lindsay).
Victoria, B.C. Provincial capital.
Victoriaville, Que. (Arthabaska Co.).

VICTORIA For Manuel Felix Fernandez, called Guadalupe Victoria (1789-1843), first president of the Republic of Mexico.
Victoria Co., Tex. (co. seat, *Victoria*).
Victoria, Tex. (co. seat of *Victoria* Co.).

VICTORVILLE, Calif. (San Bernardino Co.). For J.N. Victor, a railway official.

VIDALIA For Jose Vidal (1755-?), a Spanish army officer who was secretary to Gov. Gayoso de Lemos at Natchez.
Vidalia, Ga. (Toombs Co.).
Vidalia, La. (parish seat of Concordia Parish).

VIDOR, Tex. (Orange Co.). For Charles Vidor, a lumber-mill operator.

VIEJA (peak), Tex. From Spanish, "old."

VIENNA A city and province in Austria. All places so named in the United States derive ultimately from the European city, although places farther west often take their names from Eastern places.
Vienna, Ga. (co. seat of Dooly Co.).
Vienna, Ill. (co. seat of Johnson Co.).
Vienna, Me. (Kennebec Co.), town.
Vienna, Mo. (co. seat of Maries Co.).
Vienna, Va. (Fairfax Co.).
Vienna, W.Va. (Wood Co.). For *Vienna*, Va.

VIGO Co., Ind. (co. seat, Terre Haute). For Joseph Maria Francesco Vigo (1740-1836), fur trader of Italian descent who became a Spanish citizen and joined the Spanish army to come to America. He furnished funds and assistance to George Rogers Clark before and during the American Revolution. He was known also as Col. Francis Vigo.

VILAS Co., Wis. (co. seat, Eagle River). For William Freeman Vilas (1840-1908), a statesman who served in many state and national capacities. including U.S. postmaster general (1885-88) and secretary of the interior (1888-89) under Cleveland. He was also U.S. senator (1891-97).

VILLA A name often given to a subdivision or suburban area where affluent citizens live, or it is hoped will live. It appears in the singular, as a promotional name for a village, whatever the financial worth of the people living there.
Villa Grove, Ill. (Douglas Co.).
Villa Park, Calif. (Orange Co.). From Spanish, "town." The name as a whole may be thought of as "residence park."
Villa Park, Ill. (Du Page Co.).

VILLA RANCHERO, S.Dak. (Pennington Co.). From Spanish, "ranch city"; promotional name for a shopping center just outside the main gate of Ellsworth Air Force Base. Although it is platted with streets and blocks and filed as an unincorporated city, there are no residents in it.

VILLA RICA, Ga. (Carroll Co.). From Spanish, "rich city"; so named because it was a gold-mining town.

VILLE MARIE, Que. (co. seat of Temiscamingue Co.). From French, "city of Mary," so named by the Oblates of Mary Immaculate. An earlier name was St. Vierge.

VILLE PLATTE, La. (parish seat of Evangeline Parish). From French, "flat town."

VINALHAVEN For John Vinal, a Boston merchant who helped settlers. He never lived on the island, but his sons did.
Vinalhaven, Me. (Knox Co.). For the island.
Vinalhaven Island, Me. In Penobscot Bay. Named in the late 18th century.

VINCENNES, Ind. (co. seat of Knox Co.). For Francois Bissot, Sieur de Vincennes (?-1736), a French soldier, fur trader, and explorer, who established a fort at the site. He was burned at the stake by the Chickasaw Indians.

VINE GROVE, Ky. (Hardin Co.). For a grove of vine-covered trees.

VINELAND, N.J. (Cumberland Co.). Named by Charles K. Landis, founder, for the abundance of grapes there.

VINEYARD SOUND, Mass. Between Martha's Vineyard and Elizabeth Islands. Name taken from that of MARTHA'S VINEYARD.

VINITA For Vinnie Ream (1847-1914), sculptor who fashioned the statue of Abraham Lincoln that stands in the Capitol rotunda. Her statue of the Cherokee Sequoyah led to this town being named for her.
Vinita, Okla. (co. seat of Craig Co.).
Vinita Park, Mo. (St. Louis Co.).

VINTON Co., Ohio (co. seat, McArthur). For Samuel Finley Vinton (1792-1862), U.S. representative (1823-37; 1843-51).

VINTON, Plynn, an Ohio congressman who reportedly offered residents fifty dollars if they named the town for him.
Vinton, Iowa (co. seat of Benson Co.).

Vinton, La. (Calcasieu Parish). For *Vinton,* Iowa; named by residents wintering in Louisiana from Iowa.

VIRDEN, Ill. (Macoupin Co.). For John Virden, founder.

VIRGIN From Columbus' name, *Las Virgines,* "the virgins," for the martyred virgins' Saint Ursula and her followers.
Virgin Islands of the United States. A territory of the United States. They were discovered by Columbus in 1493 and named *Las Virgines* by him, and purchased by the United States from Denmark in 1917 as a defensive measure. Some fifty of the islands belong to the United States; the remainder are British administered. The largest islands are St. Croix, St. Thomas, and St. John. Capital: Charlotte Amalie. Flower: Yellow Cedar.
Virgin Passage. A strait in the Caribbean between Culebra Island and St. Thomas Island.

VIRGIN MOUNTAINS, Ariz.-Nev. For Thomas Virgin, a member of an expedition to the area in 1827-28.

VIRGINIA For Elizabeth 1 of England, "the Virgin Queen." Originally the name applied to all territory claimed by the British on the continent of North America. An unsuccessful attempt at colonization was made at Roanoke island (now in North Carolina) in 1584. The first permanent English settlement was at Jamestown (1607).
Virginia, Commonweath of. 10th State of the Union. Settled: 1607. One of the original 13 colonies. Ratified Constitution: 1788. Cap: Richmond. Motto: *Sic Semper Tyrannis* (Thus Always to Tyrants). Nickname: The Old Dominion. Flower: Flowering Dogwood. Bird: Cardinal. Tree: Flowering Dogwood (unofficial). Song: "Carry Me Back to Old Virginny."
West Virginia, State of. 30th state of the Union, established when forty western Virginia counties rejected the state's secession from the Union and applied for admission as a separate state. Settled:

1727. Admitted: 1863. Cap: Charleston. Nickname: Mountain State. Motto: *Montani Semper Liberi* (Mountaineers Are Always Free). Flower: Big Rhododendron. Bird: Cardinal. Tree: Sugar Maple.
Virginia, Ill. (co. seat of Cass Co.).
Virginia, Minn. (St. Louis Co.).
Virginia Falls, N.W.T. On the South Nahanni River.
Virginia Key, Fla. Part of Miami between Biscayne Bay and the Atlantic Ocean.
Virginia Beach, Va. (independent city in Princess Anne Co.).
Virginia City, Mont. (co. seat of Madison Co.).
Virginia Gardens, Fla. (Dade Co.).

Virginia was proudly named for Elizabeth I, "the Virgin Queen", and the powerful monarch of England during one of its periods of greatest expansion. The famous "Dixley Portrait" was completed around 1592. [*New York Public Library*]

VIRGINIA For "Old Virginia" Fenimore, an early miner and local eccentric who was very popular.
Virginia Mountains, Nev.
Virginia City, Nev. (co. seat of Storey Co.).

VIROQUA, Wis. (co. seat of Vernon Co.). The origin and meaning have been lost. There are stories that it is the name of one of a number of Indian maidens.

VISALIA, Calif. (co. seat of Tulare Co.). Apparently a pseudo-Latinized form of *Vise*, for Nathaniel Vise, an early settler.

VISTA, Calif. (San Diego Co.). From Spanish, "view"; often used as both a descriptive and a promotional name.

VOLUSIA Co., Fla. (co. seat, De Land). Origin uncertain, but said to be for Volus, an English settler.

W

WAAS, Mount, Utah. From Ute, for an Indian chief.

WABASH From Miami *wahba*, "white," and *shik-ki*, "color-bright," translated usually as "white water," Some differences exist among authorities, but the above seems most probable and sensible. The river was named first.
Wabash Co., Ill. (co. seat, Mt. Carmel).
Wabash Co., Ind. (co. seat, *Wabash*).
Wabash, Ind. (co. seat of *Wabash* Co.).
Wabash River, Ohio-Ind.-Ill. Flows across Indiana and forms the Illinois-Indiana border, flowing generally SW and S to the Ohio R.

WABASHA From the name of hereditary Sioux chiefs whose bands inhabited the area. Although said to have derived from *Wabash*, there are linguistic changes that mitigate against that origin. Obviously, the present name was influenced by the pronunciation and spelling of *Wabash*. The name of the chiefs has been transliterated as *Wapashaw*, and is said to mean "red leaf," "red hat," or "red battle-standard." The origin of the last, seemingly fanciful etymology, probably is decoration and red uniform given by the British to one of the chiefs.
Wabasha Co., Minn. (co. seat, *Wabasha*).
Wabasha, Minn. (co. seat of *Wabasha* Co.).

WABAUNSEE, Co., Kan. (co. seat, Alma). For a Potawatomi chief. The meaning of the name is uncertain; "dawn of day" seems fanciful and invented, and also related to the influx of poetic and classical names during the mid 1800s. Other suggestions, also not documented or satisfactory, are "he lives through the winter," "daylight," and "boggy day." The chief was quite brave and gave the whites much trouble with his singular exploits. When the county was named, the citizens preferred the name of a difficult Indian chief to that of a proslavery advocate.

WACCAMAW For an Indian tribe, possibly of Siouan linguistic stock.
Waccamaw, Lake, N.C.
Waccamaw River, N.C.-S.C. Rises in *Waccamaw* L., flows SW into Winyaw Bay.

WACHUSETT, Mount, Mass. From Natick, "near the mountain."

WACO, Tex. (co. seat of McLennan Co.). For an Indian tribe of Caddoan linguistic stock. The name may be from *wehico*, a corruption of *Mexico*, approximately the Mexican and Spanish pronunciation. Others derive it from Seminole *wako*, "little blue heron," or *tawakoni*, "river bend among red sand hills."

The Wabash in Indiana is one of the most celebrated of American rivers, along with the Mississippi, the Suwannee, the Rio Grande, and the Red River. It has given rise to such bits of nostalgia as "the Wabash Cannonball" and "On the banks of the Wabash far away." [*New York Public Library*]

WADENA From Ojibway, "a little round hill."
Wadena Co., Minn. (co. seat, *Wadena*).
Wadena, Minn. (co. seat of *Wadena* Co.).

WADESBORO, N.C. (co. seat of Anson Co.). For Thomas Wade, an officer in the American Revolutpon.

WADING RIVER, N.J. So named because it could be waded easily. It flows southeast into Mullica River.

WAGONER. The switch to the area by the Missouri, Kansas and Texas railroad was ordered by a Mr. Wagoner, who became the dispatcher. The town was named first.
Wagoner Co., Okla. (co. seat, *Wagoner*.).
Wagoner, Okla. (co. seat of *Wagoner* Co.).

WAHKIAKUM Co., Wash. (co. seat, Cathlamet). For a Chinook chief. The origin and meaning of the name are unknown.

There was once a tribe of that name, but traces seem to have been lost in the debris of miscellaneous information about Indians.

WAHOO, Neb. (co. seat of Saunders Co.). For a Wahoo Creek, from a Siouan word for the "burning bush," genus *Euonymus*, that grew there and was believed to have medicinal properties.

WAHPETON, N.Dak. (co. seat of Richland Co.). For one of the Indian tribes that lived on the site.

WAH WAH MOUNTAINS, Utah. From Ute, "salty or alkaline seeps."

WAIALUA BAY, Hawaii. Inlet of the Pacific Ocean on Oahu Island. From a Hawaiian word, used in reference to "the presence of two bodies of water in proximity."

WAILUKU From Hawaiian, "destruction-stream," so named because it was the site of a battle in the 1700s.

Wailuku, Hawaii (co. seat of Maui Co.). For the river.

Wailuku River, Hawaii. Flows across Maui Island into Kahului Bay.

WAIMEA RIVER, Hawaii. From Hawaiian, "red water," descriptive. It flows west on Hawaii Island into the Pacific Ocean.

WAINWRIGHT, Alta. For William Wainwright (1840-1914), second vice-president of the Grand Trunk Pacific railway. An earlier name was Denwood.

WAITE PARK, Minn. (Stearns Co.). For Henry Chester Waite (1830-1912), attorney in St. Cloud, farmer, banker, and legislator.

WAITS RIVER, Vt. For Joseph Waite, who killed a deer near the stream during the retreat of Rogers Rangers (1759), when his party was threatened with starvation. It flows southeast into Connecticut River.

WAKE Co., N.C. (co. seat, Raleigh). For Margaret Wake (1733-1819), Gov. William Tryon's wife.

WAKEENEY, Kan. (co. seat of Trego Co.). For Albert E. Warren and James E. Keeney, the founders.

WAKEFIELD, Mass. (Middlesex Co.), town. For Cyrus Wakefield (1811-1873), a local businessman and philanthropist. Earlier names were Reading and South Reading.

WAKEFIELD, Mich. (Gogebic Co.). For George M. Wakefield, a founder.

WAKE FOREST, N.C. (Wake Co.). For a large oak forest called "the forest of wake."

WAKE ISLAND, U.S.A. In the Pacific Ocean, midway between Midway Island and Guam. Origin and meaning of name uncertain.

WAKULLA From Creek, "loon." Other translations exist, including "mystery." *Wakulla* Co., Fla. (co. seat, Crawfordville).

For the river.

Wakulla River, Fla.

Wakulla Springs, Fla. The source of the *Wakulla* R.

WALBRIDGE, Ohio (Wood Co.). For Henry Walbridge, early settler. An earlier name was Owls Nest.

WALCOTT, Lake, Idaho. For the director of the United States Geological Survey when the lake and reservoir were completed (1906).

WALDEN, Colo. (co. seat of Jackson Co.). For Marcus A. Walden, first postmaster.

WALDEN, N.Y. (Orange Co.). For Jacob Treadwell Walden, owner of the Franklin Company, manufacturer of cotton and woolen cloth.

WALDO, Gen Samuel (1695-1759), an officer in the French and Indian Wars, prosperous Boston merchant, and a landowner and promoter of settlement in the area that became Maine.

Waldo Co., Me. (co. seat, Belfast).

Waldoboro, Me. (Lincoln Co.), town.

WALDO LAKE, Ore. For John B. Waldo (?-1907), jurist.

WALHALLA, S.C. (co. seat of Oconee Co.). Named by a member of the German Colonization Society of Charleston for the mythological Valhalla, the hall of Odin, or palace of immortality.

WALHONDING RIVER, Ohio. From Algonquian, "ditch," but believed locally to mean "white woman," in honor of Mary Harris, wife of a chief. Formed by the junction of the Mohican and Kokosing rivers, it flows east to join the Tuscarawas River to form the Muskingum River.

WALK, Lake, Tex. For Sam Walk, manager of the Central Power and Light Company.

WALKER Co., Ala. (co. seat, Jasper). For John Williams Walker (1783-1823), legislator and U.S. senator (1819-22).

WALKER, Joseph R., frontiersman from Tennessee who led an expedition through the area in 1833.
Walker Lake, Nev.
Walker Pass, Calif. Discovered by Walker in 1833; named by John C. Fremont.
Walker River, Calif.-Nev. Formed by the confluence of East and West branches, flows NE and S into *Walker* L.

WALKER Co., Ga. (co. seat, La Fayette). For Freeman Walker (1780-1827), legislator and U.S. senator (1819-21).

WALKER, Mich. (Kent Co.). Probably for an early settler.

WALKER, Minn. (co. seat of Cass Co.). For Thomas Barrow Walker (1840-?), lumberman and mill owner.

WALKER Co., Tex. (co. seat, Huntsville). For Robert James Walker (1801-1869), statesman. He served as U.S. senator from Mississippi, as territorial governor of Kansas, and in other national capacities. He is honored in Texas for having introduced the resolution to annex Texas to the United States. Also claimed as a source is Samuel Hamilton Walker, a Mexican War casualty.

WALKER LAKE, Alaska. For a local settler.

WALKER MOUNTAIN, Wyo. For Ben Walker, who mined at the head of Wolf Creek.

WALKERTON, Ont. (co. seat of Bruce Co.). For Joseph Walker, an Irish miller, who in 1850 settled there and erected the first sawmill.

WALLACE, Idaho (co. seat of Shoshone Co.). For W.R. Wallace, owner of the townsite.

WALLACE Co., Kan. (co. seat, Sharon Springs). For William H. L. Wallace (?-1862), Mexican War soldier and a general of Union volunteers in the Civil War. He died of wounds received at the Battle of Shiloh.

WALLACE, N.C. (Duplin Co.). Named for himself by a Mr. Wallace, a conductor of the Atlantic Coast Line railroad.

WALLACEBURG, Ont. (Kent Co.). Named by Hugh McCallum, the first postmaster, for Sir William Wallace, a champion of Scottish independence.

WALLAGRASS LAKE, Me. Origin uncertain, but may be folk spelling for a word derived from an Algonquian dialect, either from Micmac, "good river," or from Abnaki, "shallow." The latter is more probable in context.

WALLA WALLA. Apparently for a small tribe, which takes its name from the river, "little river." The tribe belonged to the Shapwailutan linguistic stock, closely related to the Nez Perce. Lewis and Clark recorded the name as *Wollah Wollah*. *Walla*, "running water," or something like it, can mean "little running water" when duplicated.
Walla Walla Co., Co., Wash. (co. seat, *Walla Walla*).
Walla Walla, Wash. (co. seat of *Walla Walla* Co.).
Walla Walla River, Wash.-Ore. Flows generally NW to the Columbia R.
Walla Walla East, Wash. (*Walla Walla* Co.).

WALLED LAKE, Mich. (Oakland Co.). For a lake; descriptive of the walled appearance of the shoreline.

WALLENPAUPACK LAKE, Pa. Small stream formerly called Wallenpaupack Creek. From Algonquian, "deep, stagnant water."

WALLER Co., Tex. (co. seat, Hempstead). For Edwin Waller (1800-1881), who took part in the Battle of Velasco (1832). He was a signer of the Texas declaration of independence, postmaster general of the Republic of Texas, first mayor of Austin, a member of the secession convention of 1861, and chief justice of Austin County.

WALLINGFORD, Conn. (New Haven Co.), town. For Wallingford, Berkshire, England.

WALLINGTON, N.J. (Bergen Co.). For George Walling, an early settler who owned most of the tract on which it was built.

WALLKILL RIVER, N.J.-N.Y. From Dutch, probably "Walloon's Creek." (See also Walloon Lake). It flows generally northeast into Roundout Creek.

WALLOOMSAC. From Mahican, "paint rocks."
Walloomsac, N.Y. (Rensselaer Co.).
Walloomsac River, Vt.-N.Y. Flows N and W into Hoosic R.

WALLOPS ISLAND, Va. Named in 1672 for John Wallop, colonizer and settler.

WALLOWA. Probably from Nez Perce, "triangular stakes," for a set of three stakes that were used to support netting for the catching of fish.
Wallowa Co., Ore. (co. seat, Enterprise).
Wallowa Lake, Ore.
Wallowa Mountains, Ore.
Wallowa Natl. Forest, Ore.
Wallowa River, Ore. Flows generally NW to the Grande Ronde R.

WALLUM LAKE, R.I.-Mass. From Nipmuc, "dog."

WALNUT. For walnut trees.
Walnut, Calif. (Los Angeles Co.).
Walnut Creek, Kan. Flows E into Arkansas River.
Walnut River, Kan. Flows SW and S into Arkansas R.
Walnut Canyon Natl. Monument, Ariz. Established in 1915 to preserve the many pre-Columbian Indian cliff dwellings on ledges in the canyon walls.
Walnut Creek, Calif. (Contra Costa Co.).
Walnut Creek West, Calif. (Contra Costa Co.).
Walnut Park, Calif. (Los Angeles Co.).
Walnut Ridge, Ark. (a co. seat of Lawrence Co.).

WALLOON LAKE Mich. From a name found on an old railroad map, originally for a group or colony of Walloons, in reference to the

French-speaking Belgians, who settled on the lake that now bears their name. Also spelled *Walloon*.

WALPOLE, Sir Robert (1676-1745), member of Parliament (1701-42) and first modern prime minister of England. He strongly supported the Hanoverian succession, and his ministry was marked by a great shift in power from Lords to Commons.
Walpole, Mass. (Norfolk Co.), town.
Walpole, N.H. (Cheshire Co.), town.

WALSENBURG, Colo. (co. seat of Huerfano Co.). For Fred Walsen, founder and first mayor.

WALSH Co., N.Dak. (co. seat, Grafton). For George H. Walsh, a legislator and newspaper publisher.

WALT BAILEY PEAK, Wyo. For Albert Walter Bailey, who founded the first classes in mountaineering at Casper College.

WALTERBORO, S.C. (co. seat of Colleton Co.). For the Walter family, landowners and prominent citizens.

WALTER F. GEORGE RESERVOIR, Ga.-Ala. On the Chattahoochee River. For Walter F. George (1878-1957), U.S. senator from Georgia (1922-57).

WALTERS, Okla. (co. seat of Cotton Co.). For William R. Walter (perhaps Walters), or for Walter McKnight, son of the founder. It was named McKnight on the day of drawing for homesteads (August 6, 1901), but postal officials would not accept the name because there was another McKnight in Oklahoma.

WALTHALL, Edward Cary (1831-1898), Confederate general during the Civil War and later U.S. senator (1885-86; 1895-98).
Walthall Co., Miss. (co. seat, Tylertown).
Walthall, Miss. (co. seat of Webster Co.).

WALTHAM, Mass. (Middlesex Co.). For Waltham Abbey, Essex, England. Many of the settlers came from there.

WALTON Co., Fla. (co. seat, De Funiak Springs). For George William Walton, secretary to Andrew Jackson when the latter was governor of the Florida Territory.

WALTON Co., Ga. (co. seat, Monroe). For George Walton (1750-1804), a signer of the Declaration of Independence, an officer during the American Revolution, U.S. senator (1795-96), and governor of Georgia (1799-1804).

WALTON HILLS, Ohio (Cuyahoga Co.). For a local community member, plus *hills*, promotional.

WALWORTH, Reuben Hyde (1788-1867), a jurist of stature in New York State, having been a circuit judge at the age of twenty-three. After serving in the War of 1812 as an officer, he became a U.S. representative (1821-23) and then again a judge. He was known for his fairness and temperance, but he failed to be confirmed as an associate justice of the U.S. Supreme Court.
Walworth Co., Wis. (co. seat, Elkhorn).
Walworth Co., S.Dak. (co. seat, Selby). For
   Walworth Co., Wis.

WAMEGO, Kan. (Pottawatomie Co.). Probably named for a Pottawatomi Indian chief; the name has been variously translated as "running water," "clear of swamp," and "no water in the village." The exact meaning is uncertain.

WAMGUMBAUG LAKE, Conn. From Algonquian, meaning uncertain.

WANAQUE From Algonquian, "place of the sassafras."
Wanaque, N.J. (Passaic Co.).
Wanaque Reservoir, N.J.

WANDO RIVER, S.C. From Indian, meaning unknown. It has been translated as "deer," but the more probable explanation is that it is from a tribal name.

WANSHIP PEAK, Utah. For a Shoshoni chief.

WANTAGH A variant of WYANDANCH.
North Wantagh, N.Y. (Nassau Co.).
Wantagh, N.Y. (Nassau Co.).

WAPAKONETA, Ohio (co. seat of Auglaize Co.). Probably for a Shawnee chief.

WAPATO, Wash. (Yakima Co.). From Indian, origin uncertain; possibly Algonquian, or from a local Indian word meaning "arrowhead" or "wild potato."

WAPELLO (1787-1842), a Fox Indian chief who figured prominently in the signing of several treaties. The name is variously spelled. It has been translated as "light," "dawn," and "he of the morning." It may be just a birth-time designation, for which the last translation would be correct.
Wapello Co., Iowa (co. seat, Ottumwa).
Wapello, Iowa (co. seat of Louisa Co.).

WAPOGASSET LAKE, Wis. From Ojibway, "white pelican."

WAPPAPELLO RESERVOIR, Mo. In Saint Francis River. Probably a variant of WAPELLO

WAPPASENING CREEK, Pa. From Algonquian, "the place of white stones." It flows northwest into Susquehanna River.

WAPPINGER For the Algonquian tribe, actually a Confederacy of small tribes, whose name means "easterners." They lived on the east bank of the Hudson River, from Manhattan Island north to Poughkeepsie.
Wappinger Creek, N.Y. Flows generally SW into the Hudson R.
Wappinger Falls, N.Y. (Dutchess Co.).

WAPSIPINICON RIVER, Minn.-Iowa. Said to be named for legendary Indian lovers, Pinicon, a beautiful Indian maid, and Wapsie, a young Indian brave, who drowned in the river while trying to escape from the maid's father. It flows generally southeast into the Mississippi River.

WARAMAUG, Lake, Conn. From Mahican, "good fishing place."

WAR BONNET RIDGE, Wyo. So named because towers or "feathers" on its wedge-like summit give it the appearance of a war bonnet.

WARD Co., N.Dak. (co. seat, Minot). For J. P. Ward or Mark Ward, or both, members of the Dakota Territory legislature in 1885 when the county was formed and named.

WARD Co. Tex. (co. seat, Monahans). For Thomas William Ward (1807-1872), Indian fighter, Austin, Tex., city official, and consul to Panama. He was also a Texas Republic patriot and was seriously wounded at the Battle of Bexar (1835).

WARD MOUNTAIN, Nev. For B. F. Ward, early settler and founder of the town of Ward.

WARE From a translation of the Indian name for the river, *Nonamoooolr*, "fishing weir."
Ware, Mass. (Hampshire Co.), town and village.
Ware River, Mass. Flows SW to join Quaboag R. to form Chicopee R.

WARE Co., Ga. (co. seat, Waycross). For Nicholas Ware (1769?-1824), attorney and much-esteemed legislator of the Georgia General Assembly. He was also mayor of Augusta and U.S. senator (1821-24).

WAREHAM, Mass. (Plymouth Co.), town. For Wareham, Dorsetshire, England.

WARM SPRINGS Descriptive.
Warm Springs Ore. (Jefferson Co.).
Warm Springs, Va. (co. seat of Bath Co.).
Warm Springs Reservoir, Ore. In Malheur R.
Warm Springs River, Ore. Flows E into Deschutes R.

WARR ACRES, Okla. (Oklahoma Co.). For C. B. Warr (1900-1958), founder.

WARNER VALLEY, Ore. For Capt. William Horace Warner, killed by Indians in 1849. The valley contains many lakes, including Hart, Swamp, Flagstaff, Flook, Stone Carrol, and Guano.

WARREN, Ark. (co. seat of Bradley Co.). For Warren Bradley, black servant of Hugh Bradley, for whom the county was named.

WARREN, Francis E. (1844-1929), governor of Wyoming Territory (1885-86; 1889-90), first governor (1890) of the state of Wyoming, and U.S. senator (1890-93; 1895-1925). He had been awarded the Congressional Medal of Honor for bravery in the Civil War.
Warren, Wyo. (Niobrara Co.).
Warren, Mount, Wyo.
Warren Peaks, Wyo.

WARREN, Joseph (1741-1775), Massachusetts soldier, statesman, and physician, one of the foremost American Revolutionary leaders in New England. He was a member of the Continental Congress (1775), and it was Warren who sent Paul Revere on his famous ride (1775). He was killed at the Battle of Bunker Hill.
Warren Co., Ga. (co. seat, *Warrenton*).
Warren Co., Ill. (co. seat, Monmouth).
Warren Co., Ind. (co. seat, Williamsport).
Warren Co., Iowa (co. seat, Indianola).
Warren Co., Ky. (co. seat, Bowling Green).
Warren Co., Miss. (co. seat, Vicksburg).
Warren Co., Mo. (co. seat, *Warrenton*).
Warren Co., N.J. (co. seat, Belvidere).
Warren Co., N.Y. (co. seat, Lake George).
Warren Co., N.C. (co. seat, *Warrenton*).
Warren Co., Ohio (co. seat, Lebanon).
Warren Co., Pa. (co. seat, *Warren*).
Warren Co., Tenn. (co. seat, McMinnville).
Warren Co., Va. (co. seat, Front Royal).
Warren, Mass. (Worcester Co.), town.
Warren, Mich. (Macomb Co.).
Warren, Ohio (co. seat of Trumbull Co.). Or for Moses Warren, a founder.
Warren, Pa. (co. seat of Warren Co.).
Warrenton, Ga. (co. seat of *Warren* Co.).
Warrenton, Mo. (co. seat of *Warren* Co.).
Warrenton, N.C. (co. seat of *Warren* Co.).
Warrenton, Va. (co. seat of Fauquier Co.).

WARREN, Minn. (co. seat of Marshall Co.). For Charles H. Warren, a local railroad agent.

WARREN, R.I. (Bristol Co.), town. For Admiral Sir Peter Warren (1703-1752). He figured prominently in the French and Indian Wars and commanded the fleet in the British victory at Fort Louisbourg.

WARRENSBURG, Mo. (co. seat of Johnson Co.). For Martin Warren, an early settler and founder.

WARRENSBURG, N.Y. (Warren Co.). For a local tavern owner.

WARRENSVILLE, Ill. (Du Page Co.). For Daniel Warren (1780-1866); named by his son, who was a founder and leading citizen.

WARRENSVILLE HEIGHTS, Ohio (Cuyahog Co.). For the David Warren family. An earlier name (1908) was Warrensville.

WARRENTON. See Joseph WARREN

WARRICK Co., Ind. (co. seat, Boonville). For Jacob Warrick (1773-1811), a distinguished early settler and Indian fighter. He was killed while leading a charge at the Battle of Tippecanoe.

WARRIOR For the BLACK WARRIOR
Warrior, Ala. (Jefferson, Ala.). On a fork of the river.
Warrior Dam, Ala.

WARRIOR RIDGE, Wyo. For its precipitous and unclimbed faces.

WARSAW For the capital city of Poland. Because of association with Thaddeus Kosciusko, aide-de-camp to Washington during the American Revolution, the name apparently has come to symbolize rebellion against oppression (Kosciusko led an unsuccessful rebellion in Poland after he returned to his homeland). It also had an exotic connotation at a time when settlers were giving such names to new places.
Warsaw, Ind. (co. seat of Kosciusko Co.).
Warsaw, Ky. (co. seat of Gallatin Co.).
Warsaw, Mo. (co. seat of Benton Co.).
Warsaw, N.Y. (co. seat of Wyoming Co.).
Warsaw, Va. (co. seat of Richmond Co.).

WARSAW, N.C. (Duplin Co.). For a native of the town who was called "Thaddeus of Warsaw," given that nickname after a novel of the same name.

WARSON WOODS, Mo. (St. Louis Co.). For the Warson Road, which was named for a property owner in the area.

WARTBURG, Tenn. (co. seat of Morgan Co.). For Wartburg, Germany.

WARWICK, N.Y. (Orange Co.). Presumably for Warwick, Warwickshire, England.

WARWICK, Robert Rich, 2nd Earl of (1587-1658), a prominent defender of the Puritan clergy. He was active in the colonization of Massachusetts and Connecticut and played a role in the founding of Rhode Island. He was also known for his defense of religious freedom.
Warwick, R.I. (Kent Co.).
West Warwick, R.I. (Kent Co.), town.

WASATCH From Ute. It has been translated as "mountain pass," but the meaning is uncertain.
Wasatch Co., Utah (co. seat, Heber City).
Wasatch Natl. Forest, Utah.
Wasatch Range, Utah-Idaho. Highest point, Mt. Timpanogos.

WASCO For an Indian tribe of Chinookan linguistic stock. The name means "cup," or a hollow object of the type. They inhabited the area around The Dalles, Ore. One authority says that the name was transferred from a Cayuga word meaning "lake at the floating bridge." This is doubtful, although the name *Wasco* is also found in Illinois.
Wasco Co., Ore. (co. seat, The Dalles).
Wasco, Calif, (Kern Co.). For *Wasco* Co., Ore.

WASECA From Dakota, "rich," in reference to the good soil.
Waseca Co., Minn. (co. seat, *Waseca*).
Waseca, Minn. (co. seat of *Waseca* Co.).

WASHABAUGH Co., S.Dak. For Frank J. Washabaugh (1849-c.1890), noted jurist and legislator. For administrative purposes, the county is attached to Jackson County.

WASHAKIE For a Snake Indian chief (1804-1900). The meaning of the name is uncertain.
Washakie Co., Wyo. (co. seat, Worland).
Washakie Creek, Wyo.
Washakie Lake, Wyo.
Washakie, Mount, Wyo.
Washakie Natl. Forest, Wyo.
Washakie Needles, Wyo.

WASHBURN, Cadwallader Colden (1818-1882), Union general in the Civil War, U.S. representative (1867-71) and governor (1872-73).
Washburn Co., Wis. (co. seat, Shell Lake).
Washburn, N.Dak. (co. seat of McLean Co.). Either for Cadwallader Colden Washburn or for his brother, W.D. Washburn, also a Union general and a businessman and developer.

WASHBURN, Henry Dana, general officer who surveyed the area in 1870.
Washburn, Mount, Wyo., in Yellowstone Natl. Park.
Washburn Range, Wyo.

WASHINGTON, George (1732-1799), first President of the United States (1789-97), from Virginia. The most popular and one of the greatest figures in American history, the "father of our country" made American independence possible as commander in chief of the Continental armies (1775-83) and then served as a prime mover in the establishment of the new nation by serving two terms as President. He was a surveyor in early life and later an officer in the British army in the French and Indian Wars, during which he was commander in chief of the Virginia militia. He was a member of the Virginia House of Burgesses (1759-74) and of the first and second Continental Congresses (1774-75), president of the Constitutional Convention (1787), and again commander in chief of the army (1798-99). The nation's capital bears his name; he is the only American to have a state named for

George Washington was not only first president of the United States but first president of the Society of the Cincinnati, a fraternal order of officers of the Continental Army which brought on attacks from the Republicans and the Tammany societies. The painting, showing Washington wearing the order of the society is by Thomas Sully. [*Metropolitan Museum of Art. Gift of Mrs. George F. Baker, 1954*]

him; and more counties (thirty-one) bear his name than any other. His home, Mount Vernon, has also been honored as a place name.
Washington, State of. 42nd state of the Union. Settled: 1811. Territory: 1853 (formerly part of the Oregon Territory). Admitted: 1889. Cap: Olympia. Motto: *Al-Ki* ("By-and-By" in Chinook). Nickname: Evergreen State. Flower: Coast Rhododendron. Bird: American Goldfinch. Tree: Western Hemlock. Song: "Washington, My Home."
Washington Co., Ala. (co. seat, Chatom).
Washington Co., Ark. (co. seat, Fayetteville).
Washington Co., Colo. (co. seat, Akron).
Washington Co., Fla. (co. seat, Chipley).
Washington Co., Ga. (co. seat, Sandersville).
Washington Co., Idaho (co. seat, Weiser).
Washington Co., Ill. (co. seat, Nashville).
Washington Co., Ind. (co. seat, Salem).
Washington Co., Iowa (co. seat, *Washington*).

Washington Co., Kan. (co. seat, Washington).
Washington Co., Ky. (co. seat, Springfield).
Washington Parish, La. (parish seat, Franklinton).
Washington Co., Me. (co. seat, Machias).
Washington Co., Md. (co. seat, Hagerstown).
Washington Co., Minn. (co. seat, Stillwater).
Washington Co., Miss. (co. seat, Greenville).
Washington Co., Mo. (co. seat, Potosi).
Washington Co., Neb. (co. seat, Blair).
Washington Co., N.Y. (co. seat, Hudson Falls).
Washington Co., N.C. (co. seat, Plymouth).
Washington Co., Ohio (co. seat, Marietta).
Washington Co., Okla. (co. seat, Bartlesville).
Washington Co., Ore. (co. seat, Hillsboro).
Washington Co., Pa. (co. seat, Washington).
Washington Co., R.I. (co. seat, West Kingston).
Washington Co., Tenn. (co. seat, Jonesboro).
Washington Co., Tex. (co. seat, Brenham).
Washington Co., Utah (co. seat, St. George).
Washington Co., Vt. (co. seat, Montpelier).
Washington Co., Va. (co. seat, Abingdon).
Washington Co., Wis. (co. seat, West Bend).
Washington, Conn. (Litchfield Co.), town.
Washington, D.C. Capital of the United States.
Washington Ga.(co. seat of Wilkes Co.). Said to be the first town in the United States named for George Washington.
Washington, Ill. (Tazewell Co.).
Washington, Ind. (co. seat of Daviess Co.).
Washington, Iowa (co. seat of Washington Co.).
Washington, Kan. (co. seat of Washington Co.).
Washington, Me. (Knox Co.), town.
Washington, Mass. (Berkshire Co.), town.
Washington, Mo. (Franklin Co.).
Washington, N.H. (Sullivan Co.), town.
Washington, N.J. (Warren Co.). For a tavern named for George Washington, built (1811) by Col. William McCullough.

Washington, N.C. (co. seat of Beaufort Co.).
Washington, Ohio (Guernsey Co.).
Washington, Pa. (co. seat of Washington Co.).
Washington, Tex. (Washington Co.). Here the Texas declaration of independence was signed in 1836, and the village was the capital of the Republic of Texas in 1842.
Washington, Vt. (Orange Co.), town.
Washington, Va. (co. seat of Rappahannock Co.).
Washington Harbor, Mich. On Isle Royale, in L. Superior.
Washington Island, Wis., in L. Michigan. For the ship George Washington, which anchored there in 1816.
Washington Lake, Wash.
Washington, Mount, N.H., in the White Mtns. Highest peak of the Presidential Range.
Washington Birthplace Natl. Monument, Va.
Washington Court House, Ohio (co. seat of Fayette Co.).
Washington Heights, N.Y. Section of New York City.
Washington North, Pa. (Washington Co.).
Washington Park, Ill. (St. Clair Co.).
Washington Terrace, Utah (Ogden Co.). Promotional.
Washington West, Pa. (Washington Co.).

WASHITA WICHITA and QUACHITA. The origin and meaning of the names are uncertain.
Washita Co., Okla. (co. seat, Cardell).
Washita River, Tex.-Okla. Flows generally E into Lake Texoma.

WASHOE For the Washo or Washiu tribe in northwestern Nevada and adjacent areas of California. Their name has been variously translated as "person," "tall bunch grass," and "rye grass." The first seems most probable.
Washoe Co., Nev. (co. seat, Reno).
Washoe Lake, Nev.
Washoe Range, Nev.

WASHOUGAL, Wash. (Clark Co.). From Indian, probably "rushing water."

WASHTENAW Co., Mich. (co. seat, Ann Arbor). From Ojibway *wash-ten-ong*, "on the river" or "far off." A small stream nearby was named first.

WASKANA CREEK, Sask. From the Cree Indian term meaning "pile of bones," in reference to the piles of buffalo bones near the site of Regina, which was originally called Wascana. The creek flows north to Lost Mountain Lake.

WASSATAQUOIK STREAM, Me. From Abnaki, "clear, shining lake." It flows southeast into Penobscot River.

WASSUK RANGE, Nev. Of Indian origin, meaning unknown.

WATAUGA From a Cherokee word whose meaning has been lost. It has been variously interpreted as "river of plenty," "beautiful water," "river of islands," "I heard," and "foaming at the mouth," among others. Spelled also *Wataga* and *Wautauga*. *Watauga* Co. N.C. (co. seat, Boone).

WATAUGA Cherokee tribal name, meaning unknown.
Watauga Co., N.C. (co. seat, Boone).
Watauga Dam, Tenn. on Watauga R.
Watauga Lake, Tenn.
Watauga River, N.C.-Tenn. Flows into the South Holston R.

WATCHAUG POND, R.I. From Nipmuc, "hill country."

WATERBURY For a nearby stream or body of water.
Waterbury, Conn (New Haven Co.). On the Naugatuck R.
Waterbury, Vt. (Washington Co.), town and village. For *Waterbury*, Conn.
Waterbury Dam, Vt.

WATEREE From a Siouan tribal name, meaning unknown, since its language has not survived. Some have postulated that it refers to the turbulence of the stream.
Wateree Pond, S.C. In *Wateree* R.
Wateree River, S.C. Flows SE to join Congaree R. to form Santee R.

WATERFORD, Conn. (New London Co.)., town. Descriptive; on Long Island Sound.

WATERLOO For a town in central Belgium, famous for the battle at which Gen. Arthur Wellesley, 1st Duke of Wellington, with allied forces, defeated Napoleon's forces on June 18, 1815.
Waterloo Co., Ont. (co. seat, Kitchener).
Waterloo, Ill. (co. seat of Monroe Co.).
Waterloo, Iowa (co. seat of Black Hawk Co.).
Waterloo, N.Y. (a co. seat of Seneca Co.).
Waterloo, Ont. (*Waterloo* Co.).
Waterloo, Que. (co. seat of Shefford Co.).

WATERTON-GLACIER INTERNATL. PEACE PARK, Alta.-Mont. For the many lakes in the Glacier Natl. Park area. Established in 1932 by acts of the British Parliament and U.S. Congress as a gesture of peace and friendship between the two nations.

WATERTOWN For a nearby stream or body of water.
Watertown, Conn. (Litchfield Co.), town. On the Naugatuck R.
Watertown, Fla. (Columbia Co.).
Watertown, Mass. (Middlesex Co.), town. On the Charles R.
Watertown, N.Y. (co. seat of Jefferson Co.). On the Black R., near L. Ontario.
Watertown, S.Dak. (co. seat of Codington Co.). For *Watertown*, N.Y.; on the Big Sioux R.
Watertown, Wis. (Dodge and Jefferson Cos.). For *Watertown*, N.Y.; on the Rock R.

WATER VALLEY, Miss. (a co. seat of Yalobusha Co.). Translation from Choctaw *oke chukna*, "good water."

WATERVILLE For a nearby stream or body of water.
Waterville, Me. (Kennebec Co.). On the Kennebec R.
Waterville, Ohio (Lucas Co.). On the Maumee R.

WATERVLIET, N.Y. (Albany Co.). From Dutch, "flat lands"; named by settlers from Holland.

WATERFORD, N.Y. (Saratoga Co.). For an important colonial fording place over the Mohawk River.

WATFORD CITY, N.Dak. (co. seat of McKenzie Co.). Named by a settler for his former home, Watford, in Ontairo, Canada.

WATKINS GLEN, N.Y. (co. seat of Schuyler Co.). For Samuel Watkins a druggist and early settler. An earlier name was Salubria.

WATKINSVILLE, Ga. (co. seat of Oconee Co.). For Robert Watkins, a state legislator.

WATONGA, Okla. (co. seat of Blaine Co.). For an Arapaho chief, *Watongha,* whose name means "black coyote."

WATONWAN Probably from Dakota, "where fish bait can be found."
Watonwan Co., Minn. (co. seat, St. James). For the river.
Watonwan River, Minn. Flows E to the Blue River.

WATSEKA, III. (co. seat of Iroquois Co.). For a Potawatomi woman, said to have borne the name of a mythical Indian woman, heroine of a battle between the Potawatomi and the Iroquois. The translation "pretty woman" has been given. An earlier name was South Middleport.

WATSONVILLE, Calif. (Santa Cruz Co.). For Judge John H. Watson, landowner.

WATTS BAR LAKE, Tenn. For a local settler plus *bar,* descriptive of a shoal that obstructs navigation in a river.

WATUPPA POND, Mass.-R.I. Probably from Wampanoag, "roots," for use in sewing.

WAUBAY LAKE, S.Dak. From Siouan, "nesting place for wild fowl."

WAUBESA, Lake, Wis. From Ojibway, "swan."

WAUCHULA, Fla. (co. seat of Hardee Co.). Probably from Creek *wiwa,* "water," and *achuli,* "stale," or "place where there is stale water."

WAUCONDA, III. (Lake Co.). From Dakota, "spirit," also used by a number of other tribes. The term is variously spelled in English, as is usual with Indian names.

WAUKEGAN, III. (co. seat of Lake Co.). For a creek at the site, from an Indian word meaning "sheltering place," such as a home or communal building. An earlier name was Little Fort.

WAUKESHA From Potawatomi *wakusheg,* "foxes," for the Fox Indian tribe.
Waukesha Co., Wis. (co. seat, *Waukesha*).
Waukesha, Wis. (co. seat of *Waukesha* Co.). Earlier, Prairieville.

WAUKEWAN, Lake, N.H. From Algonquian, "place of crooked way."

WAUKON, Iowa (co. seat of Allamakee Co.). For a Winnebago chief, Wawkon, "white crow."

WAUPACA From an Indian name. Many meanings have been suggested, the most probable being "place of clear water."
Waupaca Co., Wis. (co. seat, *Waupaca*).
Waupaca, Wis. (co. seat of *Waupaca* Co.).

WAUPUN, Wis. (Fond du Lac Co.). From Algonquian *wabun,* "dawn"; the spelling was changed in recording the name.

WAURIKA, Okla. (co. seat of Jefferson Co.). Probably a coinage of some Indian term, but locally it is believed to mean "pure water."

WAUSAU From Algonquian, probably "far away." An earlier name was Gros Taureau, from French, "big bull."
Wausau, Wis. (co. seat of Marathon Co.).
Wausau West, Wis. (Marathon Co.).

WAUSEON, Ohio (co. seat of Fulton Co.). For a Potawatomi chief, half-brother of Chief Ottokee.

WAUSHARA Co., Wis. (co. seat, Wautoma). From Winnebago, "foxes." The name is that of a chief, but it is also akin to, if not the same as, WAUKESHA.

WAUTOMA, Wis. (co. seat of Waushara Co.). Origin and meaning are uncertain, but possibly from *wau*, "good," plus *Tomah*, for a well-known chief.

WAUWATOSA, Wis. (Milwaukee Co.). From Algonquian *wauwautaesie*, "firefly," reinforced by the name of a legendary Indian chief.

WAVERLY From *Waverly*, title of a novel by Sir Walter Scott (1771-1832), published in 1814, one of the "Waverley Novels." Its popularity led to the name being used occasionally in the United States, mostly for romantic reasons, though euphony played a part.
Waverly, Iowa (co. seat of Bremer Co.). An avid reader mistakenly called the place *Waverly* during a speech in which he was to have named it for William P. Harmon, credited with being the founder.
Waverly, N.Y. (Tioga Co.).
Waverly, Ohio (co. seat of Pike Co.).
Waverly, Tenn. (co. seat of Humphreys Co.).

WAWASEE, Lake, Ind. For an Indian chief.

WAWAYANDA MOUNTAIN, N.J. From Algonquian, "crooked creek."

WAXAHACHIE, Tex. (co. seat of Ellis Co.). From an Indian name, "cow creek."

WAYCROSS, Ga. (co. seat of Ware Co.). For the many trails that crossed at the site. An earlier name was Yankee Town.

WAYLAND, Mass. (Middlesex Co.). Name was chosen from the many that were suggested at a town meeting in 1835, when the town was formed by merging the towns of Sudbury and East Sudbury. The reason for this choice is not known.

WAYNE, Gen. Anthony (1745-1796), Pennsylvania soldier and statesman, nicknamed "Mad Anthony" for his daring during the American Revolution. He distinguished himself at Brandywine (1777), Germantown (1777), Monmouth (1778), Stony Point (1779), and Green Spring (during the Yorktown Campaign, 1781) and thwarted the British occupation of West Point (1780) after Benedict Arnold's treason. After the war he defeated a combined Indian force at Fallen Timbers (1794). He was a U.S. representative from Georgia (1791-92).
Wayne Co., Ga. (co. seat, Jesup).
Wayne Co., Ill. (co. seat, Fairfield).
Wayne Co., Ind. (co. seat, Richmond).
Wayne Co., Iowa (co. seat, Corydon).
Wayne Co., Ky. (co. seat, Monticello).
Wayne Co., Mich. (co. seat, Detroit).
Wayne Co., Miss. (co. seat, *Waynesboro*).
Wayne Co., Mo. (co. seat, Greenville).
Wayne Co., Neb. (co. seat, *Wayne*).
Wayne Co., N.Y. (co. seat, Lyons).
Wayne Co., N.C. (co. seat, Goldsboro).
Wayne Co., Ohio (co. seat, Wooster).
Wayne Co., Pa. (co. seat, Honesdale).
Wayne Co., Tenn. (co. seat, *Waynesboro*).
Wayne Co., W.Va. (co. seat, *Wayne*).
Wayne, Me. (Kennebec Co.), town.
Wayne, Mich. (*Wayne* Co.).
Wayne, Neb. (co. seat of *Wayne* Co.).
Wayne, N.J. (Passaic Co.).
Wayne, W.Va. (co. seat of *Wayne* Co.).
Wayne, Fort, Mich. See FORT WAYNE.
Waynesboro, Ga. (co. seat of Burke Co.).
Waynesboro, Miss. (co. seat of *Wayne* Co.).
Waynesboro, Pa. (Franklin Co.).
Waynesboro, Tenn. (co. seat of *Wayne* Co.).
Waynesboro, Va. (independent city in Augusta Co.).
Waynesburg, Pa. (co. seat of Greene Co.).
Waynesville, Mo. (co. seat of Pulaski Co.).
Waynesville, N.C. (co. seat of Haywood Co.).

WAYNE Co., Utah (co. seat, Loa). Named by Willis Robinson, a delegate to the state constitutional convention, for his deceased son Wayne.

WAYZATA, Minn. (Hennepin Co.). From Siouan, "at the pines, north." (There are no pines near the site now.).

WEAKLEY Co., Tenn. (co. seat, Dresden).For Robert Weakley (1764-1845), U.S. representative.

WEARE, Meshech, a jurist.
Weare, N.H. (Hillsboro Co.).
Weare Reservoir, N.H.

WEATHERFORD, Okla. (Custer Co.). For William J. Weatherford, deputy U.S. marshal for western Oklahoma Territory. His wife was postmistress.

WEATHERFORD, Tex. (co. seat of Parker Co.). For Jefferson Weatherford, instrumental in creating Parker County.

WEAVERVILLE, Calif. (co. seat of Trinity Co.). For George Weaver, an early prospector. According to a local source, there were three men who settled here— James Howe, Daniel Bennett, and John Weaver. As the story goes, these men drew straws to determine the name of the town and Weaver won. All three were miners.

WEBB, Lake, Me. Probably for an early hunter whose relics, one of which recorded the name of Thomas Webb, were found near the lake.

WEBB Co., Tex. (co. seat, Laredo). For James Webb (1792-1856), Republic of Texas legislator and state official.

WEBER Either for John G. Weber (?-1859), a trapper in the Ashley expedition into the area in the mid 1820s, or for another trapper named Weber, a member of the OGDEN party.
Weber Co., Utah (co. seat, Ogden). For the river.
Weber River, Utah. Flows generally NW to join the Ogden R. and then into Great Salt Lake.

WEBSTER, Daniel (1782-1852), Massachusetts statesman. He took part in the famous debates with John C. Calhoun and Henry Clay during the 1830s and 1840s. He was a U.S. senator (1827-41; 1845-50) and secretary of state under Tyler (1841-43) and Fillmore (1850-52).

Webster Co., Ga. (co. seat, Preston).
Webster Co., Iowa (co. seat, Fort Dodge).
Webster Co., Ky. (co. seat, Dixon).
Webster Parish, La. (parish seat, Minden).
Webster Co., Miss. (co. seat, Walthall).
Webster Co., Mo. (co. seat, Marshfield).
Webster Co., Neb. (co. seat, Red Cloud).
Webster Co., W.Va. (co. seat, *Webster Springs*].
Webster, Mass. (Worcester Co.), town and village.
Webster, N.Y. (Monroe Co.).
Webster S.Dak. (co. seat of Day Co.).
Webster, Lake, Mass.
Webster Lake, N.H.
Webster Reservoir, Kan.
Webster City, Iowa (co. seat of Hamilton Co.). Probably for Daniel Webster, but a local tradition is that it was named for a popular stage driver.
Webster Groves, Mo. (St. Louis Co.).
Webster Springs, W.Va. (co. seat of *Webster* Co.).

Daniel Webster's powers as an orator were legendary. In Stephen Vincent Benet's famous story, "The Devil and Daniel Webster," he argued so eloquently with Satan that the contest between the two resulted in a draw. [*New York Public Library*]

WEDOWEE, Ala. (co. seat' of Randolph Co.). For a Creek chief (?-c. 1834). The name is interpreted as possibly meaning "sumac water" or "old water," from Creek *wiwa*, "water," plus *tawa*, "sumac."

WEED, Calif. (Siskiyou Co.). For Abner Weed, local citizen and president of the Weed Lumber Company.

WEEHAWKEN, N.J. (Hudson Co.). From an Algonquian word, variously translated as "maize land," "place of gulls," "rocks that look like trees," "at the end" (of the Palisades), and "field lying along the Hudson." Whatever the original word or words, the name was changed to its present Dutch-sounding form.

WEEKEEPEMEE RIVER, Conn. From Algonquian, meaning unknown. It flows south into Pomperaug River.

WEIR, Lake, Fla. For a local settler.

WEIRTON, W.Va. (Hancock Co.). For the Weirton Steel Company, in turn named for the Weir family, which owned it.

WEISER For Peter Wiser, a member of the Lewis and Clark Expedition. The spelling change has not been accounted for.
Weiser, Idaho (co. seat of Washington Co.).
Weiser River, Idaho.

WELBY, Colo. (Adams Co.). From the surname Welby, but other information is lacking.

WELCH POINT, Conn. For an early settler.

WELCH, W.Va. (co. seat of McDowell Co.). For Isaiah A. Welch, a founder, who served as an officer in the Confederate army.

WELD Co., Colo. (co. seat, Greeley). For Lewis Ledyard Weld, a territorial official.

WELLAND Named by John Graves Simcoe, first lieutenant governor of Upper Canada, for the river in Lincolnshire, England.

Welland Co., Ont. (co. seat, *Welland*).
Welland, Ont. (co. seat of *Welland* Co.).
Welland River, Ont. (*Welland* Co.).

WELLESLEY, Mass. (Norfolk Co.), town. For the estate of Horatio H. Hunnewell (1810-1902), banker and railroad executive. The estate was so called from the maiden name of his wife, Isabelle Pratt Welles.

WELLESLEY ISLAND, N.Y. One of the major Thousand Islands in the St. Lawrence River. For Sir Arthur Wellesley, 1st Duke of WELLINGTON.

WELLFLEET Either for the Wallfleet oyster bed in Blackwater Bay, England, or for the "whale fleet" that operated out of the harbor.
Wellfleet, Mass. (Barnstable Co.). For the harbor.
Wellfleet Harbor, Mass. Inlet of Cape Cod Bay.

WELLINGTON, Arthur Wellesley, 1st Duke of (1769-1852), English general in command of the army that defeated Napoleon's forces at Waterloo.
Wellington, Kan. (co. seat of Sumner Co.). Named by English settlers.
Wellington, Tex. (co. seat of Collingsworth Co.). Named by British cattlemen and promoters.

WELLINGTON, Ohio (Lorain Co.). For William Welling (1782-1826), an early settler. It is also possible that it was named for the Duke of Wellington, but this has not been verified.

WELLS Co., Ind. (co. seat, Bluffton). For William Wells (?-1812), a white man who served with the Indians but returned to the whites and fought against the Indians at the Battle of Tippecanoe (1811). He was killed at Fort Dearborn.

WELLS, Cap. Jonathan, military commander at Deerfield, Mass., during a raid by Indians (1704).
Wells River, Vt. Flows SE into Connecticut River.
Wells River, Vt. (Orange Co.).

WELLS, Me. (York Co.), town. For Wells, Somersetshire, England.

WELLS, Minn. (Faribault Co.). For Mrs. Clark W. Thompson, whose maiden name was Wells. By coincidence, a few years after the village was founded, numerous artesian wells were found in the area.

WELLS Co., N.Dak. (co. seat, Fessenden). For E. P. Wells, Dakota Territory legislator and developer of the James River valley.

WELLSBORO, Pa. (co. seat of Tioga Co.). For Mary Hill Wells, the maiden name of the wife of Benjamin Wistar Morris, founder; or possibly for the Wells family, which was prominent, including in it a U.S. senator.

WELLSBURG, W.Va. (co. seat of Brooke Co.). For Alexander Wells, son-in-law of Charles Prather, for whom Charleston, W.Va., was named.

WELLSTON, Ohio (Jackson Co.). For Harvel Wells, founder.

WELLSVILLE, N.Y. (Allegany Co.). For Gardiner Wells, a farmer who built the first log cabin in the village.

WELLSVILLE, Ohio (Columbia Co.). For William Wells, who developed the plans for the town.

WENAHA BACKCOUNTRY, Wash.-Ore. A wilderness area in the Blue Mountains. From the Indian tribal name, meaning unknown.

WENATCHEE. For an Indian tribe of Salishan linguistic stock located on or near the river that bears their name. The name, a Yakima word, is said to mean "those who live at the river source." They are also known as the Pisquows.
Wenatchee, Wash. (co. seat of Chelan Co.).
Wenatchee Natl. Forest, Wash.
Wenatchee River, Wash. Flows generally SE to the Columbia R.

WENHAM, Mass. (Essex Co.), town. For Little Wenham, England.

WENTWORTH, Lake, N.H. For Benning Wentworth, a former governor of New Hampshire.

WENTWORTH, N.C. (Rockingham Co.). For Charles Wentworth, Marquis of Rockingham (1730-1782), a Whig who, as prime minister in 1765, favored the repeal of the Stamp Act.

WENTWORTH Co., Ont. (co. seat, Hamilton). For Sir John Wentworth (1737-1820), lieutenant governor of Nova Scotia (1792-1808).

WENTZVILLE, Mo. (St. Charles Co.). For a citizen named Wentz plus -*ville*.

WEPAWAUG RIVER, Conn. From Paugusett, "ford." It flows south into Long Island Sound.

WEQUAQUET LAKE, Mass. From Wampanoag, meaning uncertain, possibly "shining place," "torchlight place," or "swampy place." It is believed locally to mean "swan," "orchard," or "fair weather."

WESLACO, Tex. (Hidalgo Co.). Coined from the *W. E. Steward Land* Company, which laid out the town.

WESSERUNSETT. From Abnaki, "bad water place."
Wesserunsett Lake, Me.
Wesserunsett Stream, Me. Flows S into Kennebec R.

WEST. Directional. Names that do not appear in this part of the book may be found under the basic name. For example, for West Elmira, N.Y., see Elmira.
West Creek, Pa. Flows E to join Driftwood Branch.
West Island, Mass. In Buzzards Bay.
West Mountain, Me.
West Mountain, Mass.
West Mountain, Vt.
West Passage, R.I. Arm of Narragansett Bay, between Conanicut Island and the mainland.

West River, Conn. Flows S into Long Island Sound.

West River, Vt. Flows S and SE into Connecticut R.

WEST ALLIS, Wis. (Milwaukee Co.). For a plant of the Allis-Chalmers Company, west of the main plant in Milwaukee.

WEST BEND, Wis. (co. seat of Washington Co.). For a bend in the Milwaukee River.

WESTBOROUGH, Mass., (Worcester Co.), town and village. So named because it was formed from the western part of Marlborough.

WEST BRANCH, Mich. (co. seat of Ogemaw Co.). So named because it is situated on the west branch of the Rifle River.

WESTBROOK, Conn. (Middlesex Co.), town. So named because it was originally the west parish of Saybrook.

WESTBROOK, Me. (Cumberland Co.). For Col. Thomas Westbrook, a soldier in the French and Indian Wars and a prosperous businessman in the town. An earlier name was Saccarappa.

WESTBURY. For one of two Westburys in England.

Old Westbury, N.Y. (Nassau Co.).

South Westbury, N.Y. (Nassau Co.).

Westbury, N.Y. (Nassau Co.).

WEST CANADA. For the trail which leads to CANADA.

West Canada Creek, N.Y. Flows SW and SE into Mohawk R.

West Canada Mountain, N.Y.

WEST CHESTER. For the town and county of Chester in England. Also spelled *Westchester.* See also CHESTER.

Westchester Co., N.Y. (co. seat, White Plains).

Westchester, Ill. (Cook Co.).

West Chester, Pa. (co. seat of Chester Co.).

WESTCLIFFE, Colo. (co. seat of Custer Co.). For Westcliffe-on-the-Sea at the mouth of the Thames River in England; named by an early resident who was born in the town in England.

WESTCONNAUG RESERVOIR, R.I. From Narraganset, possibly "at place of walnut trees."

WEST ELK PEAK, Colo. Directional and for the wild animal.

WESTERLO, N.Y. (Albany Co.). A group of early settlers named this town for the Rev. Eilardus Westerlo, pastor of the Reformed Dutch Church of Albany.

WESTERLY. Descriptive.

Westerly, R.I. (Washington Co.), town. Earlier, Misquamicut.

Westerly Center, R.I. (Washington Co.).

WESTERN SPRINGS, Ill. (Cook Co.). For the mineral springs on the site.

WESTERVILLE, Ohio (Franklin Co.). For the Westervelt family, prominent farmers in the area.

WESTFIELD. The Massachusetts town so named because it was formed from the western part of Springfield.

Westfield, Mass. (Hampden Co.), town.

Westfield, N.Y. (Chautaugua Co.). Named Named by Joseph Tinker, an early merchant in the town, for *Westfield,* Mass., his native town.

Westfield River, Mass. Formed by three branches, flows into the Connecticut R.

WESTFIELD, N.J. (Union Co.). For its location in the area west of Elizabeth.

WESTFORD, Mass. (Middlesex Co.), town. So named because it was originally the western precinct of Chelmsford.

WESTLAKE, La. (Calcasieu Parish). So named because it is located west of Lake Charles.

WESTLAKE, Ohio (Cuyahoga Co.). Probably for its location southwest of Lakewood.

WESTLAND, Mich. (Wayne Co.). For its location west of Detroit.

WESTMINSTER For Westminster, a borough of London, England, or something related to it.

New Westminster, B.C. First capital of British Columbia (1859-66).

Westminister, Calif. (Orange Co.). Named by Presbyterian settlers who followed the rules of the Westminister Assembly (1643-49).

Westminister, Colo. (Adams Co.).

Westminister, Md. (co. seat of Carroll Co.).

Westminister, Mass. (Worcester Co.), town.

Westminister, S.C. (Oconee Co.). Named by Presbyterian settlers for Westminister

Abby, the huge London cathedral where all British sovereigns except Edward V and Edward VIII have been crowned.

Westminster East, Colo. (Adams Co.).

WESTMONT For a western location on high land; promotional.

Westmont, Calif. (Los Angeles Co.).

Westmont, Ill. (Du Page Co.).

Westmont, Pa. (Cambria Co.).

WESTMORELAND For Westmorland, a county in England.

Westmoreland Co., N.B. (co. seat, Dorchester).

Probably so named because it borders Cumberland Co., as does the county in England, and also perhaps for its marshes, recalling its English namesake.

Westminster Abbey is one of the magnificent ornaments of English history, scene of its coronations, and final resting place of many of its most famous citizens. [*Frederic Lewis*]

Westmoreland Co., Pa. (co. seat, Greensburg).

Westmoreland Co., Va. (co. seat, Monttross).

Westmoreland, Kan. (co. seat of Pottawatomie Co.). For *Westmoreland* Co., Pa.

WESTON, Conn. (Fairfield Co.), town. So named because it was formed from the western part of Fairfield.

WESTON, Mass. (Middlesex Co.), town. So named either because it was formed from the western part of Watertown, or for one of two Westons in England.

WESTON, W.Va. (co. seat of Lewis Co.). Apparently for the surname West. Several persons of that name lived in the area, according to early records. Earlier names were Pearson and Flesherville.

WESTON, Wis. (Marathon Co.). For Charles Weston, a sawmill owner in the early 1850s.

WESTON Co., Wyo. (co. seat, Newcastle). For J. B. Weston.

WESTOVER, W.Va. (Monongalia Co.). For its location west of Morgantown and over (across) the Monongahela River.

WEST PLAINS, Mo. (co. seat of Howell Co.). Descriptive.

WEST POINT Descriptive of its western location.
West Point, Ga. (Troup Co.). For its location on the western border of Georgia.
West Point, Miss. (co. seat of Clay Co.). For its location, at the time, in the westernmost part of Lowndes County (now it is centrally located in Clay County).
West Point, Neb. (co. seat of Cuming Co.). For its location west of the Fremont, Elkhorn and Missouri Valley railroad.
West Point, N.Y. (Orange Co.). U.S. military post.
West Point (peak), Alaska.

WESTPORT, Conn. (Fairfield Co.), town. So named because it was founded as a port on Long Island Sound, in the western part of the state. An earlier name was Saugatuck.

WESTPORT, Mass. (Bristol Co.), town. So named because it was created from the western part of Dartmouth and is near the coast.

WESTPORT, N.Y. (Essex Co.), town. For its location on a southwest bay of Lake Champlain.

WESTPORT RIVER, Mass. Directional and descriptive. It flows south into Rhode Island Sound.

WEST TAVAPUTS PLATEAU, Utah. For a Ute chief.

WEST UNIVERSITY PLACE, Tex. (Harris Co.). For its location near Rice University.

WEST VIEW Descriptive and probably promotional.
West View, Ohio (Cuyahoga Co.).
West View, Pa. (Allegheny Co.).

WESTVILLE, Ill. (Vermillion Co.). For Elizabeth Scott West (1824-1917), a housewife.

WESTVILLE, Ind. (La Porte Co.). Probably descriptive and promotional.

WESTVILLE, N.J. (Gloucester Co.). For Thomas West, a real-estate developer.

WEST VIRGINIA See VIRGINIA.

WESTWEGO, La. (Jefferson Parish). Locally it is believed to be from the phrase "West we go!" because the site was on the road to the West; however, -*wego* may be a shortening of OSWEGO.

WESTWOOD Descriptive and probably promotional.
Westwood, Mass. (Norfolk Co.), town.
Westwood, Mich. (Kalkaska Co.).
Westwood, N.J. (Bergen Co.).
Westwood Lakes, Fla. (Dade Co.).

WESTWORTH, Tex. (Tarrant Co.). Descriptive and promotional; a suburb of Fort Worth.

WETASKIWIN, Alta. From a Cree Indian term meaning "the place where peace was made," so named because the Cree and Blackfoot Indians smoked a peace pipe there.

WETHERSFIELD, Conn. (Hartford Co.). For a town in England.

WETUMPKA, Ala. (co. seat of Elmore Co.). From *Wetumka*, a Creek town formerly occupying a nearby site, from *we-wau*, "water" and *tumcau*, "rumbling." The name refers to the effect of the Coosa River flowing over rocks at this point.

WETZEL Co., W.Va. (co. seat, New Martinsville). For Lewis Wetzel, an Indian scout. The name is German, but the spelling has been varied; it is said that the family preferred *Wetzel*.

WEWAHITCHKA, Fla. (co. seat of Gulf Co.). From Creek *wiwa*; "water," plus either *ahichka*, "view," or *ahichkita*, "to obtain." Ther former is more probable, since a lake is nearby. Another version is "water eyes," for the way the lakes look from above.

WEWEANTIC RIVER, Mass. From "crooked river," descriptive. It flows generally southeast into Buzzards Bay.

WEWOKA From Creek, "water-roaring," and probably for an Indian town.
Wewoka, Okla. (co. seat of Seminole Co.).
Wewoka Creek; Okla.

WEXFORD Co., Mich. (co. seat, Cadillac). For county Wexford, Ireland, from which some of the settlers came.

WEYBURN, Sask. Believed to have been named by a Scottish settler, who described the river at this point as a "wee burn."

WEYMOUTH, Mass. (Norfolk Co.), town. For Weymouth, Dorsetshire, England, from which many of the early colonists left for America.

WHARTON, William Harris (1802-1839), Republic of Texas patriot and minister to the United States, killed accidentally.
Wharton Co., Tex. (co. seat, *Wharton*).
Wharton, Tex. (co. seat of *Wharton* Co.).

WHATCOM Co., Wash. (co. seat, Bellingham). Probably from a Nootsack Indian name, but whether for a chief or for something else is not certain.

WHEATLAND Descriptive of land suitable for wheat farming.
Wheatland Co., Mont. (co. seat, Harlowton).
Wheatland, Wyo. (co. seat of Platte Co.). Earlier, Gilchrist, for a rancher.

WHEATON, Ill. (co. seat of Du Page Co.). For the Wheaton family, early settlers.

WHEATON, Minn. (co. seat of Traverse Co.). For Daniel Thompson Wheaton (1845-1910), a railroad official.

WHEAT RIDGE, Colo. (Jefferson Co.). Descriptive, for the rich fields of wheat.

WHEELBARROW PEAK, Nev. Named subjectively for its shape.

WHEELER, Joseph (1836-1906), famous general in the Confederate army. He later held important positions in the U.S. Army, serving as a general and as a negotiator in the Spanish-American War. He was also a U.S. representative from Alabama (1881-82; 1883; 1885-1900) and the author of many books of military and political nature.
Wheeler Co., Ga. (co. seat, Alamo).
Wheeler Lake, Tenn. A Tennessee Valley Authority Lake.

WHEELER Co., Neb. (co. seat, Bartlett). For Daniel H. Wheeler (1834-?), a state official.

WHEELER Co., Ore. (co. seat, Fossil). For Henry H. Wheeler (1826-1911), a stage driver who became a prominent rancher in the area.

WHEELER, Royal Tyler (1810-1864), prominent Texas jurist.
Wheeler Co., Tex. (co. seat, *Wheeler*).
Wheeler, Tex. (co. seat of *Wheeler* Co.).

WHEELER LAKES, Mich. For a local settler.

WHEELER PEAK, Nev. For George M. Wheeler, army officer and surveyor who led an expedition in the area (1869-70).

WHEELERSBURG, Ohio (Scioto Co.). For Maj. Porter Wheeler, early Indian fighter and veteran of the War of 1812.

WHEELING Despite the English form, evidence points to an Indian origin of the name, of uncertain etymology and meaning. *Wie* or *wihl* may translate as "head," for a river or any other prominent place; *-ling* also translates as "head," which has given rise to "place of the head."
Wheeling, Ill. (Cook Co.). For *Wheeling*, W.Va.
Wheeling, W.Va. (co. seat of Ohio Co.).

WHEELOCK, John, a president of Dartmouth College.
Wheelock, Vt. (Caledonia Co.).
Wheelock Mountain, Vt.

WHETSTONE For the stone used for sharpening tools.
Whetstone Brook, Vt. Flows E into Connecticut R.
Whetstone Creek, Wyo. Two versions exist: either the creek was named for the Whetstone Mining Company, or the company was named for the creek because a rock on its bank resembled a whetstone.
Whetstone Mountain, Wyo. For the creek.

WHISKEY For the various stills on the mountain; early settlers thought it was cheaper to make whiskey than to buy it.
Whiskey Creek, Wyo.
Whiskey Gap, Alta.
Whiskey Mountain, Wyo.
Whiskey Peak, Wyo. For *Whiskey* Gap.

WHITBY, Ont. (co. seat of Ontario Co.). For Whitby, Yorkshire, England. Earlier Perry's Corners for Peter Perry, founder.

WHITCOMB MOUNTAIN, N.H. For a local settler or explorer.

WHITE Descriptive of color.
White Butte, N.Dak. (Slope Co.).
White Butte, N.Dak. (Stark Co.).
White Lake, La.
White Lake, Mich.
White Lake, N.Dak.
White Lake, S.Dak. For the whiteness of the water reflecting light.
White Lake, Wis. For the birches.
White Mountains, Alaska. For the white limestone.
White Mountains, N.H. Part of Appalachian chain. Descriptive of how the first explorers saw them, when covered with snow.
White River, Alaska. Flows NE into Yukon R.
White River, Ind. Formed from West and East forks, flows SW into Wabash R. Translated from French.
White Mountain Natl. Forest, N.H.
White Mountain Peak, Calif. For the color of its rock.

WHITE Co., Ark. (co. seat, Searcy). For Hugh Lawson White (1773-1840), Tennessee legislator and U.S. senator (1825-40).

WHITE Co., Ga. (co. seat, Cleveland. Believed to be for David Thomas White (1812-1871), supporter of a bill to create the county.

WHITE Co., Ill. (co. seat, Carmi). For Leonard White, a delegate to the Illinois constitutional convention (1818).

WHITE Co., Ind. (co. seat, Monticello). For Col. Isaac White.

WHITE Co., Tenn. (co. seat, Sparta). For John White (?-1782), an officer in the American Revolution.

WHITE BEAR For an Indian legend in which a white bear was about to spring on

the wife of a young brave, who managed to kill it.
White Bear Lake, Minn.
White Bear Lake, Minn. (Ramsey Co.). For the lake.

WHITE CAP Descriptive, applied to a mountain.
White Cap (mountain), Me. (Franklin Co.). For its baldness.
White Cap (mountain, Me. (Piscataquis Co.). So named because snow remains on its peak late into the year.

WHITE CITY, Utah. (Salt Lake Co.). For the color of salt deposits near Sandy, Utah.

WHITE CLOUD, Mich. (co. seat of Newaygo Co.). For the billowy clouds that were drifting overhead when the townspeople met to choose a name. The name may also have been suggested by an apocyphal legend about an Indian chief, White Cloud, who supposedly rescued a white girl who had been kidnapped.

WHITE DEER CREEK, Pa. For the animal. It flows generally northeast into Susquehanna River.

WHITE EARTH RIVER, N.Dak. Translated from an Indian word for "white clay," descriptive of the color of the sand in the stream. It flows south into Garrison Reservoir on the Missouri River.

WHITEFACE Descriptive of lengthy white rock scars.
Whiteface Mountain, N.Y.
Whiteface Mountain, Vt.

WHITEFISH For the fish, of the family *Coregonidae,* found in American and Canadian lakes.
Whitefish, Mont. (Flathead Co.).
Whitefish Bay, Mich.-Ont., an arm of L. Superior.
Whitefish Point, Mich., on *Whitefish* Bay.
Whitefish Range, in the Rocky Mtns., from British Columbia to *Whitefish,* Mont.
Whitefish River, Mich. Flows into L. Michigan.
Whitefish Bay, Wis. (Milwaukee Co.).

WHITEHALL For Whitehall, site of the principal government offices in London, England. Whitehall Palace, where both Henry VIII and Cromwell died and Charles I was executed, is there.
Whitehall, Mich. (Muskegon Co.).
Whitehall, N.Y. (Washington Co.).
Whitehall, Ohio (Franklin Co.).
Whitehall, Pa. (Allegheny Co.).
Whitehall, Wis. (co. seat of Trempealeu Co.).

WHITE HALL, Ill. (Green Co.). For a long white hall that stood near Seminary Creek.

WHITEHORSE LAKE, Me. Probably named for an incident involving a white horse, but may be a translation from an Indian word.

WHITE LAKE-SEVEN HARBORS, Mich. (Oakland Co.). For a small lake and for seven harbors on Lake Michigan.

WHITEMAN, Mo. (St. Charles Co.). For a local citizen.

WHITE MEADOW LAKE, N.J. (Morris Co.). For a lake near the town.

WHITE OAK For the tree.
White Oak, Md. (Montgomery Co.).
White Oak, Pa. (Allegheny Co.).
White Oak Bayou, Tex. Flows E into Sulphur River.

WHITE OAK RIVER, N.C. Folk etymologized form of *Weetock,* a tribal name. Also called *Weitock* River. Rising in two branches, it flows southeast into the Atlantic Ocean.

WHITE PINE For the trees.
White Pine Co., Nev. (co. seat, Ely).
White Pine Mountains, Nev.

WHITE PLAINS, N.Y. (co. seat of Westchester Co.). A free translation from Weckquaeskeck Indian *quaropas,* "white marshes," for white balsam trees. Early settlers called it "the white plains" before this became a proper name.

WHITE POTATO LAKE, Wis. For the plant, the Irish or white potato.

WHITE RIVER Descriptive: often translated from French, Spanish, or Indian.
White River, Alaska. Flows into the Yukon River.
White River, Ariz.
White River, Colo.-Utah. Earlier (Spanish), Rio Blanco.
White River, Ind. Formed from East and West forks, flows W and SW into Wabash R.
White River, Mich.
White River, Mo.-Ark. Flows generally SE to the Arkansas R.
White River, Neb.-S.Dak. Flows generally NE to the Missouri R.
White River, Nev.
White River, Ore.
White River, Tex.
White River, Vt.
White River, Wash.
White River, Wis.
White River, Ont.
White River, S.Dak. (co. seat of Mellette Co.).
White River Natl. Forest, Colo.
White River Junction, Vt.

WHITE ROCK Descriptive.
White Rock, Alta. For a large white granite boulder on the beach.
White Rock, N.Mex. (Los Alamos Co.).
White Rock Creek, Kan. Flows E into Republican R.
White Rock Mountain, Ark. In Boston Mtns.
White Rock (mountain), Vt.
White Rocks Mountain, Vt.

WHITE SAND LAKE, Wis. Descriptive.

WHITE SANDS NATL. MONUMENT, N. Mex. Descriptive.

WHITE SETTLEMENT, Tex. (Tarrant Co.). So named because it was the only white settlement in the area at the time of founding.

WHITESBORO, N.Y. (Oneida Co.). For an early settler, Judge Hugh White. It is said to have been originally White's Burrow, because Judge White dug into a bank so that the lower story of his house was underground.

WHITESBORO, Tex. (Grayson Co.). For Capt. Ambrose B. White (1811-1885), veteran of the Texas revolution and founder of the town.

WHITESBURG, Ky. (co. seat of Letcher Co.). For C. White, a state legislator.

WHITESIDE Co., Ill. (co. seat, Morrison). For Samuel Whiteside, a soldier in the War of 1812 and a general during the Black Hawk War (1832).

WHITE SULPHUR SPRINGS For mineral springs.
White Sulphur Springs, Mont. (co. seat of Meagher Co.).
White Sulphur Springs, W.Va. (Greenbrier Co.).

WHITE VALLEY RANGE, Utah. Translated from Spanish, *blanco*, probably originally for an explorer.

WHITEVILLE, N.C. (Columbus Co.). For J. B. White, the first state senator from this county.

WHITEWATER Descriptive, of either the water or the sediment.
Whitewater, Wis. (Walworth Co.).
Whitewater River, Ind.-Ohio. Flows generally SE to the Great Miami R.
Whitewater River, Mo. Flows generally SE to the Mississippi R.
Whitewater Baldy (peak), N.Mex.

WHITFIELD Co., Ga. (co. seat, Dalton). For George Whitfield (1714-1770), a prominent clergyman and early social worker.

WHITING, Ind. (Lake Co.). From the surname of a conductor on the Michigan Southern railroad whose train was wrecked when it collided with another at the crossing. The siding built to avoid such collisions was at first called Whiting's Crossing.

WHITINGHAM. For Nathan Whiting, founder of the town.
Whitingham, Vt. (Windham Co.).
Whitingham, Lake, Vt.

WHITINSVILLE, Mass. (Worcester Co.). For Col. Paul Whitin (1767-1831), a blacksmith and founder of P. Whitin and Sons, manufacturers of textile machinery.

WHITLEY, William (1749-1813), soldier and Indian fighter who fought in the War of 1812 and was killed at the Battle of the Thames. It is believed by some that he killed Tecumseh.
Whitley Co., Ind. (co. seat, Columbia City).
Whitley Co., Ky. (co. seat, Williamsburg).
Whitley City, Ky. (co. seat of McCreary Co.). Earlier, Coolidge.

WHITMAN, Mass. (Plymouth Co.), town. For Jared (1784-1878) and Augustus (1821-1880) Whitman, benefactors of the town. An earlier name was South Abington.

WHITMAN Co., Wash. (co. seat, Colfax). For Marcus Whitman (1802-1847), leader of a missionary colony that was massacred. A small town of the same name appears near the place of the massacre in Walla Walla County, as does the Whitman Natl. Monument.

WHITMORE LAKE, Mich. (Washtenaw Co.). For a nearby lake, named for Luke H. Whitmore, an early settler.

WHITNEY, Lake, Tex. On Brazos River. For the nearby town, which was named for a local community member.

WHITNEY, Mount, Calif. In Sequoia Natl. Park. Highest peak in the United States. Named for Joseah Dwight Whitney, geologist and chief of the State Geological Survey (1860-74).

WHITNEY, S.C. (Spartanturg Co.). For a local textile mill.

WHITTIER. John Greenleaf (1807-1892), Quaker poet and reformer.
South Whittier, Calif. (Los Angeles Co.).
West Whittier-Los Nietos, Calif. (Los Angeles Co.). *Los Neitos*, for Manuel Nieto, large landowner and grantee of this track of land.
Whittier, Calif. (Los Angeles Co.). Named by Quaker founders.

WIARTON, Ont. (Bruce Co.). For Wiarton Place, England, the birthplace of Governor General Head of Canada.

WIBAUX, Pierre, a rancher.
Wibaux Co., Mont. (co. seat, *Wibaux*).
Wibaux, Mont. (co. seat of *Wibaux* Co.).

WICHITA. For one of the more important tribes of the Caddoan linguistic stock. The Wichitas lived in what is now Kansas and were visited by Coronado in 1541. In the latter part of the 1700s they had been forced into the Oklahoma area, but they moved north again during the Civil War when they refused to fight on the Confederate side. After the war they moved back to Oklahoma. The name is translated as "man," or as taken from Choctaw *owa chito*, "big hunt," among others. See also WASHITA and QUACHITA.
Wichita Co., Kan. (co. seat, Leoti).
Whichita Co., Tex. (co. seat, *Wichita Falls*).
Wichita, Kan. (co. seat of Sedgwick Co.).
Wichita Mountains, Okla.
Wichita River, Tex. Flows generally NE to the Red R.
Wichita Falls, Tex. (co. seat of *Wichita* Co.).

WICKABOAG POND, Mass. From Natick, "head of pond."

WICKENBURG, Ariz. (Maricopa Co.). For Henry Wickenburg (1820-1905), miner, rancher, and founder.

WICKIUP RESERVOIR, Ore. From Algonquian *wikiyapi*, "dwelling," probably connoting a brush or mat hut in which Indians camped.

WICKLIFFE. For a prominent Kentucky family, particularly Charles A. Wickliffe, a Nelson County lawyer, who was postmaster general (1841-44) under Tyler. He was governor of Kentucky (1839-40) and served

in the state legislature and the U.S. Congress.
Wickliffe, Ky. (co. seat of Ballard Co.).
Wickliffe, Ohio (Lake Co.).

WICOMICO Co., Md. (co. seat, Salisbury). For a subtribe of the Nanticoke Indians, of Algonquian linguistic stock. Their name may derive from *wicko-mekee*, "where houses are being built," but "pleasant place of dwelling" may be more appropriate.

WIGGINS PEAK, Wyo. For Jack Wiggins, who homesteaded what is now Rocking Chair Ranch, named for its brand.

WILBARGER Co., Tex. (co. seat, Vernon). For Josiah Pugh Wilbarger (1801-1845), a surveyor killed by Indians, or the name may commemorate his whole family.

WILBER, Neb. (co. seat of Saline Co.). For C. D. Wilber, who platted the town.

WILBRAHAM, Mass. (Hampden Co.). Either for the town of Wilbraham, England, or for a Viscount Wilbraham who was a Royalist.

WILBURTON, Okla. (co. seat of Latimer Co.). For Elisha Wilbur, a railroad official.

WILCOX Co., Ala. (co. seat, Camden). For Lt. Joseph M. Wilcox, killed (1814) by Indians.

WILCOX Co., Ga. (co. seat, Abbeville). Either for Gen. Mark Wilcox (1800-1850), an early settler, or for his father, John Wilcox.

WILDCAT. For the presence or supposed presence of the animal. The name often occurs because of an incident or for humorous reasons.
Wildcat Creek, Ind. Flows generally W into Wabash R.
Wildcat Mountain, Neb.
Wildcat Peak, Nev.

WILDHORSE. For wildhorses in the area.
Wildhorse Creek, Okla. Flows E into Washita R.
Wild Horse Hill, Neb.

WILD RICE. For the aquatic plant and the grain.
Wild Rice Lake, Wis.
Wild Rice River, Minn. Flows W into Red River of the North. Translated from Ojibway.
Wild River River, N.Dak. Flows into Red River of the North.

WILD RIVER, N.H.-Me. For its turbulence. It flows northeast into Androscoggin River.

WILDWOOD. For the "wild woods" that once covered the area.
North Wildwood, N.J. (Cape May Co.).
Wildwood, N.J. (Cape May Co.).
Wildwood Crest, N.J. (Cape May Co.).

WILKES, John (1725-1797), a member of the British House of Commons who opposed the severity of the English toward the American colonists. Wilkes was an agitator with great persuasive power and eloquence and was often in the midst of controversy.
North Wilkesboro, N.C. (*Wilkes* Co.).
Wilkes Co., Ga. (co. seat, Washington).
Wilkes Co., N.C. (co. seat, *Wilkesboro*).
Wilkes-Barre, Pa. (co. seat of Luzerne Co.). Also for Isaac Barre, another member of Parliament (1761-90) sympathetic to the American colonies.
Wilkesboro, N.C. (co. seat of *Wilkes* Co.).

WILKIN Co., Minn. (co. seat, Breckenridge). For Alexander Wilkin (1820-1864). He served as an officer in the Mexican War and later as an official in the Minnesota Territory. Interested in military operations, he studied warfare in Europe and in the Crimea under battle conditions. An officer in the Union army, he was killed at the Battle of Tupelo.

WILKINSBURG, Pa. (Allegheny Co.). For William Wilkins (1779-1865), Pennsylvania statesman. He began his career as a lawyer in Pittsburgh in 1801 and served as president of the Common Council, a member of the Pennsylvania legislature, a presiding judge, and a Federal district court judge for western Pennsylvania. He was also a U.S. senator (1831-34), minister to Russia, and secretary of war (1844-45) under Tyler.

WILKINSON, James (1757-1825), an officer in the American Revolution. He fought under several generals, including Washington. He was active in the negotiations for the Louisiana Purchase and served as the first governor of the Louisiana Territory. As a general, he commanded troops in the War of 1812.
Wilkinson Co., Ga. (co. seat, Irwinton).
Wilkinson Co., Miss. (co. seat, Woodville).

WILL Co., Ill. (co. seat, Joliet). For Dr. Conrad Will (1779-1835), a physician who first practiced in Pennsylvania, then moved to the Illinois Territory and operated a spa at Salt Springs. After serving as a member of the Illinois constitutional convention (1818), he was elected the first state senator from Jackson County.

WILLACY Co., Tex. (co. seat, Raymondville). For John G. Willacy (1850-1943), Texas legislator.

WILLAMETTE RIVER, Ore. Probably of Indian derivation, with French influence in the transliteration. The meaning is unknown. The river flows generally north to the Columbia River.

WILLAPA. From an Indian tribal name, meaning unknown.
Willapa Bay, Wash. Sheltered harbor on Pacific Coast.
Willapa River, Wash. Flows NW into *Willapa* Bay.

WILLARD, Ohio (Huron Co.). For Daniel Willard, president of the Baltimore and Ohio railroad. He was an outstanding business leader and industrialist.

WILLCOX, Gen. Orlando B. (1823-1907), Arizona territorial official.
Wilcox, Ariz. (Cochise Co.).
Willcox Playa, (basin), Ariz.

WILLET, N.Y. (Cortland Co.). For Marinus Willet, soldier and public official. He fought in the French and Indian Wars and the American Revolution, participating in the battle at Fort Stanwix. He was given land in this area after the Revolution, and later served as mayor of New York City.

WILLIAMS, Ariz. (Coconino Co.). For William Sherley Williams (1787-1849), preacher, hunter, and trapper.

WILLIAMS, Elijah, a descendant of Roger Williams of Rhode Island and the son of Ephraim Williams, who was the head of a pioneer family selected as a model of what a Christian English family might be. Elijah established an iron forge beside the river.
Williams River, Mass.
Williamsville, Mass. (Berkshire Co.).

WILLIAMS, Co., N.Dak. (co. seat, Williston). For Erastus A. Williams, Dakota Territory legislator.

WILLIAMS Co., Ohio (co. seat, Bryan). For David Williams, a captor of Maj. John Andre, British spy in the American Revolution.

WILLIAMSBURG. For William III (1650-1702), king of England with Mary (1689-1702).
Williamsburg Co., S.C. (co. seat, Kingstree).
Williamsburg, Va. (co. seat of James City Co.). The oldest incorporated city in the United States.

WILLIAMSBURG, Ky. (co. seat of Whitley Co.). For Col. William WHITLEY.

WILLIAMS FORK RIVER, Colo. For a local settler. It flows northwest into Yampa River.

WILLIAMS MOUNTAIN, Okla. For Alexander S. Williams, a Choctaw Indian.

WILLIAMSON, Hugh (1735-1819), physician and legislator. He served as surgeon general to North Carolina troops during the American Revolution. Later he became a legislator and U.S representative (1789-93).
Williamson Co., Ill. (co. seat, Marion). For *Williamson* Co., Tenn.
Williamson Co., Tenn. (co. seat, Franklin).

WILLIAMSON Co., Tex. (co. seat, Georgetown). For Robert McAlpin Williamson (1806-1859), Republic of Texas patriot, military officer, and jurist.

Williamsburg, the first incorporated (1722) city in Virginia, was the capital of the colony until after the American Revolution. This early nineteenth century lithograph by Thomas C. Millington is of America's second oldest college, William and Mary. The building in the center is the only one in the Western Hemisphere designed by architect Christopher Wren. [*New York Historical Society*]

WILLIAMSON, W.Va. (co. seat of Mingo Co.). For Wallace J. Williamson, who owned the townsite.

WILLIAMSON RIVER, Ore. For Lt. Robert Stockton Williamson, surveyor for the Pacific Railroad Company. Flows north then southwest into Upper Klamath Lake.

WILLIAMSPORT. Three theories of the origin of the name exist: for Judge William Hepburn, a state senator largely responsible for the establishment of Lycoming County; for William, the son of Michael Ross, who founded the town in 1795; for William Russell, a boatman on the river at this point. There is some documentary evidence for the third.
South Williamsport (Lycoming Co.).
Williamsport, Pa. (co. seat of Lycoming Co.).

WILLIAMS RIVER, Vt. For Parson John Williams and his family, who were captured during the French and Indian raid on Deerfield, Mass., in 1704. After two years of captivity, he and two children were released and returned to Deerfield. His wife and two other children died. It flows southeast into Connecticut River.

WILLIAMSTON, Mich. (Ingham Co.). For O. B. and James M. Williams, early settlers and proprietors.

WILLIAMSTON, N.C. (co. seat of Martin Co.). For Col. William Williams, first county registrar of deeds and civic leader in early government. An earlier name was Skewarkey.

WILLIAMSTOWN, Ky. (co. seat of Grant Co.). For William Arnold, probably the first settler.

WILLIAMSTOWN, Mass. (Berkshire Co.)., town and village. For Col. Ephraim Williams (1714-1755), who left a bequest for a school (Williams College), with the stipulation that the town in which it was located be named Williamstown. He was killed in the French and Indian Wars.

WILLIAMSTOWN, W.Va. (Wood Co.). For Isaac Williams (1737-1820), an early settler and probably founder. He also served as an Indian fighter under Gen. Edward Braddock.

WILLIMANTIC From Nipmuc Indian, "good cedar swamp," also translated as "land of swift-running waters."
Willimantic, Conn. (co. seat of Windham Co.). For the river.
Willimantic Reservoir, Conn.
Willimantic River, Conn.

WILLINGBORO, N.J. (Burlington Co.). For Thomas Olive of Wellingborough, Northhamptonshire, England, an English commissioner.

WILLINGTON, Conn. (Tolland Co.). For Wellington, Shropshire, England.

WILLISTON For Samuel Willis (1784-?), who was willed the property by Philip Valentine, original settler.
East Williston, N.Y. (Nassau Co.).
Williston Park, N.Y. (Nassau Co.).

WILLISTON, N.Dak. (co. seat of Williams Co.). For S. Willis James, a railroad official.

WILLISTON, S.C. (Barnwell Co.). For Robert Wills, a plantation owner.

WILLISTON, Vt. (Chittenden Co.), town. For Samuel Willis, an original grantee.

WILLITS, Calif. (Mendocino Co.). For Hiram Willits, who built the first two-story house in the area.

WILLMAR, Minn. (co. seat of Kandiyohi Co.). For Leon Willmar, a Belgian investor in the St. Paul and Pacific railroad.

WILLOUGHBY Lake, Vt. For a local settler.

WILLOUGHBY, Dr. Westel, of Herkimer, N.Y. He helped to establish the first medical college in the Western Reserve, which later was moved to Columbus, Ohio, the original site being used as a "female seminary."
Willoughby, Ohio (Lake Co.).
Willoughby Hills, Ohio (Lake Co.). Probably promotional.

WILLOW For willow trees.
Willow Creek, Ore.
Willow Creek, Utah.
Willow Reservoir, Wis.
Willow River, Mich. Flows into L. Huron.
Willowbrook, Calif. (Los Angeles Co.).
Willow Grove, Pa. (Montgomery Co.).
Willows, Calif. (co. seat of Glenn Co.).
Willow Springs, Ill. (Cook Co.).

WILLOWICK, Ohio (Lake Co.). A combination of personal names, Willoughby and Wickliff, coined in 1951.

WILLS For the surname of an early settler or explorer.
Wills Creek, Pa. Flows E and S into Potomac River.
Wills Mountain, Pa.-Md.

WILLS CREEK, Ohio. For a settler named Wills. It flows northwest and west into Muskingum River.

WILLS POINT, Tex. (Van Zandt Co.). For William Wills, contractor and early settler, or possibly for F. C. Wills, whose home was supposedly located at a point of timber extending out onto the prairie.

WILMETT, Ill. (Cook Co.). For Archange Ouilmette, Indian wife of Antoine Ouilmette, first white settler on land that is now Chicago. By the treaty of Prairie du Chien, she was granted land in the area.

WILMINGTON, Spencer Compton, Earl of (c. 1673-1743), member of the Privy Council and patron of colonial administrators, who had interests in both the colonies and in England.
East Wilmington, N.C. (New Hanover Co.).

New Wilmington, Pa. (Lawrence Co.). For *Wilmington*, Del.

Wilmington, Del. (co. seat of New Castle Co.).

Wilmington, Ill. (Will Co.). For *Wilmington*, Ohio.

Wilmington, Mass. (Middlesex Co.), town.

Wilmington, N.Y. (Essex Co.). For *Wilmington*, Del.

Wilmington, N.C. (co. seat of New Hanover Co.). Earlier, New Liverpool.

Wilmington, Ohio (co. seat of Clinton Co.).

WILMORE, Ky. (Jessamine Co.). For a local community member.

WILSON Co., Kan. (co. seat, Fredonia). For Hiero T. Wilson (1806-?), army officer and merchant. He was appointed sutler to local army units.

WILSON, Brig. Gen. Louis Picken (1789-1847), legislator and officer in the Mexican War.

Wilson Co., N.C. (co. seat, *Wilson*).

Wilson, N.C. (co. seat of *Wilson* Co.).

WILSON, Mount, Colo. For Allen Davis Wilson (1844-1920), explorer and topographer.

WILSON, Mount, Nev. For Charles Wilson, early settler and community official.

WILSON, Pa. (Allegheny Co.). Probably for E. J. Wilson, a local landowner.

WILSON Co., Tenn. (co. seat, Lebanon). For David Wilson (?-1804), an officer in the American Revolution. He received a land grant of over 10,000 acres for his war service. He was a member of the General Assembly of the Territory South of the Ohio River (1794) and presided over the session at which the state of Tennessee was organized.

WILSON Co., Tex. (co. seat, Floresville). For James Charles Wilson (1816-1861), Republic of Texas patriot and legislator.

WILSON, Woodrow (1856-1924), twenty-eighth President of the United States (1931-21), born in Virginia. He was an attorney, a professor, president of Princeton University (1902-10), and governor of New Jersey (1911-13),. He is the author of several books on American politics and history, and was elected to the Hall of Fame (1950). See also WOODROW WILSON'

Wilson Dam, Ala.

Wilson Lake, Ala. A Tennessee Valley Authority lake on Tennessee R.

WILTON, Conn. (Fairfield Co.), town. For Wilton, Wiltshire, England.

WILTON, Me. (Franklin Co.), town. For a small town in New Hampshire; named by a settler from there.

WILTON MANORS, Fla. (Broward Co.). For the English town, plus *Manors*, promotional.

WINAMAC, Ind. (co. seat, of Pulaski Co.). For a Potawatomie chief.

WINCHENDON, Mass. (Worcester Co.). Named by the royal governor for the town in Buckinghamshire, England, in which he had an heir's interest.

WINCHESTER For Winchester, Hampshire, England.

Winchester, Conn. (Litchfield Co.), town.

Winchester, Ill. (co. seat of Scott Co.).

Winchester, Ind. (co. seat of Randolph Co.).

Winchester, Ky. (co. seat of Clark Co.). For *Winchester*, Va.

Winchester, Tenn. (co. seat of Franklin Co.).

Winchester, Va. (co. seat of Frederick Co.). Earlier, Fredericktown.

WINCHESTER, Mass. (Middlesex Co.), town. For Col. William P. Winchester (1801-1850), a benefactor of the town.

WINCHESTER, Nev. (Clark Co.). Apparently for the Winchester Rifle Company.

WINCHESTER, N.H. (Cheshire Co.), town. For Charles Paulet (1685-1754), Marquis of Winchester and 3rd Duke of Bolton. He was governor of the Isle of Wight and constable of the Tower of London.

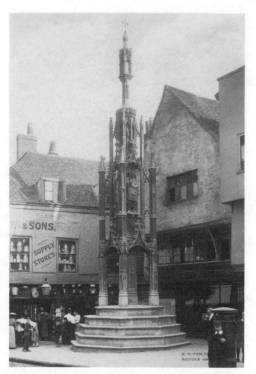

Many Americans can trace their ancestry back to the borough of Winchester in Hampshire. The city is known as the possible site of King Arthur's Camelot, its famous cathedral, and the "City Cross" shown above. [*New York Public Library*]

WINCONISCO CREEK, Pa. From Algonquian, "wet, mess camp." It flows west into Susquehanna River.

WINDBER, Pa. (Somerset Co.). Coined by transposing the two syllables of the surname of E. J. Berwind, the chief stockholder in the Berwind-White Coal Company.

WINDCREST, Tex. (Bexar Co.). Promotional name, to give the impression of height and quality.

WINDER, Ga. (co. seat of Barrow Co.). For John H. Winder, industrial leader and railroad builder. He also managed the Seaboard Coast Line railroad. Earlier names were Snodon and Jug Tavern.

WINDHAM. For Wymondham, Norfolk, England.
Windham Co., Conn. (co. seat, Putnam).
Windham Co., Vt. (co. seat, Newfane). For *Windham* Co., Conn.
Windham, Conn. (*Windham* Co.), town.
Windham, Me. (Cumblerland Co.), town.
Windham, Ohio (Portage Co.).

WINDHAM, N.H. (Rockingham Co.), town. For Charles Wyndham (1710-1763), member of Parliament and secretary of state. He was a friend of Gov. Benning Wentworth and was known for his advocacy of a peaceful settlement of differences with the American colonies.

WINDOM, William (1827-1891), statesman. He served as U.S. senator from Minnesota (1871-81; 1881-83), secretary of the treasury (1881) under Garfield, and U.S. Representative (1859-69). In 1889 he was again appointed secretary of the treasury by Benjamin Harrison and served until his death.
Windom, Minn. (co. seat of Cottonwood Co.).
Windom Peak, Colo.

WIND POINT, Wis. Extends into Lake Michigan. So named because of the strong wind that sweeps across it from the lake.

WIND RIVER. Probably for the strong winds in the area which caused the river to flow "like the wind."
Wind River, Wyo.
Wind River Indian Reservation, Wyo.
Wind River Peak, Wyo.
Wind River Range, Wyo.

WINDSOR. For Windsor, Berkshire, England, or the royal castle there.
East Windsor, Conn. (Hartford Co.), town.
New Windsor, N.Y. (Orange Co.), town.
South Windsor, Conn. (Hartford Co.).
Windsor Co., Vt. (co. seat, Woodstock).
Windsor, Conn. (Hartford Co.), town.
Windsor, Mo. (Henry Go.). Earlier, Bellmont.
Windsor, Nfld.
Windsor, N.C. (Bertie Co.).
Windsor, N.S. (co. seat of Hants Co.).

Windsor, Ont. (co. seat of Essex Co.).
Windsor, Que. (Richmond Co.).
Windsor, Vt. (*Windsor* Co.).
Windsor Height, Iowa (Polk Co.).
   Promotional.
Windsor Locks, Conn. (Hartford Co.), town.
   Also for canal locks.

WINDSOR, N.H. (Windsor Co.). For John
Stuart, Earl of Windsor.

WINDY PEAK, Wyo. So named because it
was believed that all the wind in
southeastern Wyoming was made up there.

WINFIELD. For Winfield SCOTT.
Winfield, Ill. (Du Page Co.).
Winfield. W.Va. (co. seat of Putnam Co.).
Winfield, Kan. (co. seat of Cowley Co.).
Winfield, W.Va. (co. seat of Putnam Co.).

WINGATE, N.C. (union Co.). For Dr.
Washington Martin Wingate (1828-79),
president of Wake Forest College (1856-79).

WING RIVER, Minn. Translated from
Ojibway. It flows into Leaf River.

WINHALL RIVER, Vt. For the township,
which was named for Win and Hall, the
original land grantees. It flows north and
east into West River.

WINIFRED PEAK, Wyo. For Winifred,
daughter of A. C. Tate, who climbed the
mountain in 1919.

WINKLER, Man. For Valentine Winkler
(1864-1920), landowner, prominent
businessman, and legislator.

WINKLER Co., Tex. (co. seat, Kermit). For
Clinton McKamy Winkler (1827-1882),
Republic of Texas legislator, officer in the
Confederate army, and jurist.

WINN, Walter O., a prominent citizen.
Winn Parish, La. (parish seat, *Winnfield*).
Winnfield, La. (parish seat of *Winn* Parish).

WINNEBAGO. For an Indian tribe of Siouan
linguistic stock. They occupied the south
side of Green Bay and areas from Illinois to
South Dakota. In other tribal languages they
were known as "stinkers," or "people who
lived in filthy water." Their own name is
thought to mean "fish eaters."
Winnebago Co., Ill. (co. seat, Rockford).
Winnebago Co., Iowa (co seat, Forest
   City).
Winnebago Co., Wis. (co. seat, Oshkosh).
Winnebago Indian Reservation, Neb.
Winnebago, Lake, Wis.
Winnebago River, Minn.-Iowa. Flows
   into Shellrock R.

WINNEMUCCA. From a hereditary name of
Paiute chiefs. The name apparently means
"chief," but this has been disputed.
Winnemucca, Nev. (co. seat of Humboldt
   Co.).
Winnemucca Lake, Nev.

WINNER, S.Dak. (co. seat of Tripp Co.). So
named because it was the winner in a
contest to establish a town along the right of
way of a railroad.

WINNESHIEK Co., Iowa (co. seat,
Decorah). For a chief of the Winnebago
tribe. There were two chiefs of this name,
but the county was named for the younger
one (1812-1872?), who took part in the
Black Hawk War and moved with his people
through several areas in the Midwest. The
name was probably formed from *Winne* (for
Winnebago) and *shiek*, "leader."

WINNETKA, Ill. (Cook Co.). Meaning
uncertain. Promotional interests indicate
"beautiful place," but no documentation
exists.
Winne may be from Algonquian,
"beautiful,". but -*tka* was apparently added
for euphonious reasons and has no Indian
origin.

WINNETT, Mont. (co. seat of Petroleum
Co.). For Walter John Winnett, rancher,
proprietor, and founder.

WINNETUXET RIVER, Mass. From
Wampanoag, "at the good small river." It
flows generally southwest into Taunton
River.

WINNFIELD, La. For Walter O. WINN.

Winnipeg, capital of Manitoba, is a major rail center and one of the largest cities on the Canadian prairie. The Red River, just south of its junction with huge Lake Winnipeg, is shown in the background. [*Canadian Consulate General, New York*]

WINNIBIOGOSHISH, Lake Minn. From Ojibway, "very dirty water," or "filthy water," probably in reference to its being muddy.

WINNIPEG Derived from Cree Indian, *win*, "dirty," plus *nipi*, "water," an aboriginal name for the Winnipeg River.
Winnipeg, Man., provincial capital. In 1835, Upper Fort Garry, for Nicholas Garry (1782?-1856) of the Hudson's Bay Company, was established on the site of the present city of Winnipeg. It was known as Winnipeg, although it is situated on neither the river nor lake of that name.
Winnepeg, Lake, Man.
Winnipeg River, Minn.-Ont.-Man. Flows from Lake of the Woods into L. *Winnipeg*, Man.

WINNIPESAUKEE Lake, N.H. Largest lake in New Hampshire. From Pennecook, meaning uncertain, if not impossible, for it has been claimed that the name has more than one hundred different recorded spellings. The most favored translation is "good outlet."

WINNISQUAM LAKE, N.H. From Abnaki, "place for salmon fishing."

WINNSBORO, La. (parish seat of Franklin Parish). For John Winn, pioneer settler and state senator through whose efforts Franklin Parish was created. Earlier names were Marion and Winnsborough.

WINNSBORO, S.C. (co. seat of Fairfield Co.). For Richard Winn (1750-1818), merchant and surveyor. He served in the American Revolution and rose to the rank of major general. He was superintendent of Indian affairs for the Creek Nation (1788) and U.S. representative (1793-97; 1803-13).

WINNSBORO, Tex. (Wood Co.). For John E. Winn, an early settler.

WINONA From a Siouan name often given to a first-born daughter, specifically that of a Winnebago woman who was active in the removal of the Winnebagos from Iowa. She was a cousin of the last chief of the tribe, Wahasha. The name was also popularized by H. L. Gordon's poem "Winona" (1881) and was adopted by Americans as a woman's name.
Winona Co., Minn. (co. seat, *Winona*).
Winona, Minn. (co. seat of *Winona* Co.).
Winona Lake, Ind. (Kosciusko Co.).
   Probably for a local resident.

WINONA, Miss. (co. seat of Montgomery Co.). For an Indian maid in the household of a Colonel Moore, an official of the Illinois Central and Gulf railroad.

WINOOSKI From Abnaki *winos*, "onion," and , "land."
Winooski, Vt. (Chittenden Co.).
Winooski River, Vt.

WINSLOW, Ariz. (Navajo Co.). Either for a prospector or for Edward F. Winslow, president of the St. Louis and San Francisco railroad.

WINSLOW, Me. (Kennebec Co.), town and village. For John Winslow (1703-1774), who directed the construction of nearby Fort Halifax.

WINSTED, Conn. (Litchfield Co.). A contraction of the names Winchester and Barkhamsted, on which the village borders.

WINSTON Co., Ala. (co. seat, Double Springs). For John Anthony Winston (1812-1871), governor of Alabama (1854-57). He

was also a merchant and a Confederate army officer.

WINSTON Co., Miss. (co. seat, Louisville). For Louis Winston (?-1824), attorney general (1809-17) of Madison County, Tenn. (Now in Alabama). He served as secretary of the Mississippi constitutional convention (1817) and was elected to the Mississippi supreme court (1821).

WINSTON-SALEM, N.C. (co. seat of Forsyth Co.). Formerly two towns; *Winston*, for Maj. Joseph Winston (1746-1815), an officer in the American Revolution and member of the North Carolina legislature. See also SALEM.

WINTER Promotional; suggestive of a place offering an escape from the cold winters of the North.
West Winter Haven, Fla. (Polk Co.).
Winter Garden, Fla. (Orange Co.).
Winter Haven, Fla. (Polk Co.).
Winter Park, Fla. (Orange Co.).

WINTERS, Tex. (Runnels Co.). For J. N. Winters (1858-1928), owner and operator of a realty company and of the Tarrant County Building and Loan Association.

WINTERSET, Iowa (co. seat of Madison Co.). Apparently descriptive; said to have been named by a group of men who arrived by train on a cold day.

WINTERSVILLE, Ohio (Jefferson Co.). For the Winters family.

WINTHROP, John (1588-1649), first governor of Massachusetts Bay Colony. Winthrop helped to set up the theocratic policies of the colony and was an early advocate of New England unity. He served several non-consecutive terms as governor between 1629 and 1649.
Winthrop, Mass. (Suffolk Co.), town.
Winthrop, Me. (Kennebec Co.), town.

WINTHROP HARBOR, Ill. (Lake Co.). Named by a land developer, but the reason for the choice of *Winthrop* has been lost. The harbor was planned but never materialized.

Wisconsin's Devil's Lake is guarded by the rock formation known as the Devil's Doorway. Artists in 1872 when this engraving was made had difficulty resisting the impulse to include a train whenever they could possibly justify it. [*New York Public Library*]

WINTON, Calif. (Merced Co.). For Edgar Winton, one of the town surveyors.

WINTON, N.C. (co. seat of Hertford Co.). For Benjamin Wynns, owner of the land on which the town was platted. An earlier spelling was Wynnton.

WINYAH BAY, S.C. Inlet on Atlantic Ocean. From an Indian tribal name, meaning unknown.

WIRT Co., W.Va. (co. seat, Elizabeth). For William Wirt (1772-1834), attorney general of the United States (1817-20) under Monroe and candidate for President in 1832.

WISCASSET, Me. (co. seat of Lincoln Co.). From an Indian word meaning "the outlet." It is located at the outlet to a bay.

WISCONSIN Probably from Ojibway *Weeskon-san,* "the gathering of the waters." first applied to the river. *Quisconsin* (probably the same word or a variant), "a grassy place," has also been suggested. Variant spellings include *Misconssin, Misconsing, Mesconsin, Mescousing, Miskous, Misconsin, Ousconching, Ouiskensing, Wiskonsan,* and *Wiskonsin.*
Wisconsin, State of. 30th State of the Union. Settled: 1766. Territory: 1836. Admitted: 1848. Cap: Madison, Motto: Forward. Nickname: Badger State. Flower: Butterfly Violet. Bird: Robin. Tree: Sugar Maple, Song: "On, Wisconsin."
Wisconsin, Lake, Wis.
Wisconsin River, Wis. Flows generally SW to the Mississippi R.
Wisconsin Rapids, Wis. (co. seat of Wood Co.). For rapids on the Wisconsin R.

WISE, Henry A. (1806-1876), Virginia statesman and soldier. He was a U.S. representative (1833-44), governor (1856-

60), and a Confederate major general in the Civil War.

Wise Co., Tex. (co. seat, Decatur).

Wise Co., Va. (co. seat, *Wise*).

Wise, Va. (co. seat of *Wise* Co.).

WISSOTA, Lake, Wis. On Chippewa River. Formed from a combination of *Wis*consin and Minn*esota.*

WISTER, Mount, Wyo. For Owen Wister, author of *The Virginian.*

WISTER LAKE, Okla. On Poteau River. For the nearby town, in turn for a railway official of the Choctaw, Oklahoma and Gulf railroad.

WITHLACOOCHEE RIVER, Ga.-Fla. From Creek, "little river," although it can also be translated as "big river." It flows southeast and south into Suwanee River.

WIXOM LAKE, Mich. For Abijah Wixom, early settler; named by his son.

WOBURN, Mass. (Middlesex Co.), town. For Woburn, Bedfordshire, England.

WOLCOTT, Conn. (New Haven Co.), town. For Oliver Wolcott (1726-1797), legislator, judge, governor (1796-97), and a signer of the Declaration of Independence.

WOLF For the animal.

Wolf Creek, Mich. Flows NE into Thunder Bay R.

Wolf Creek, Tex.-Okla. Flows ENE into North Canadian R.

Wolf Creek, Pa. Flows S into Slippery Rock Creek, S.Dak. Flows E into Turtle R.

Wolf Range, Wyo. Known to old-timers as Panther Range.

Wolf River, Miss.-Tenn. Flows WNW into Mississippi R.

Wolf River, Wis. Flows generally S into L. Polygan.

WOLFE Co., Ky. (co. seat, Campton). For Nathaniel Wolfe (1810-1865), a legislator.

WOLFE, Gen. James (1727-1759), English soldier who fought the French at Fort Louisbourg and gained lasting fame in his

victory over the French General Montcalm at the Plains of Abraham in Quebec. He died of wounds suffered in that engagement.

Wolfe Co., Que. (co. seat, Ham Sud).

Wolfeboro, N.H. (Carroll Co.).

WOLF JAW Descriptive, for a supposed resemblance to the jaws of a wolf.

Lower Wolf Jaw Mountain, N.Y.

Upper Wolf Jaw Mountain, N.Y.

WOLF POINT, Mont. (co. seat of Roosevelt Co.). Probably for the creek which at this point flows into the Missouri R. An old wolf trappers' story claims that trappers once killed a large number of wolves and dragged their carcasses to this point, giving the area its name.

WOLVERINE LAKE, Mich. (Oakland Co.). For the wolverine, Michigan state animal.

WONDER LAKE, Ill. (McHenry Co.). For a lake, a "wonder" because it was man-made, formed by a dam built (1929) across Nippersink Creek.

WOOD Descriptive, usually for wooded areas.

Wood River, Neb. Flows SE and NE into Platte R. For the wood supply.

Wood River, R.I. Flows S and W into Pawcattuck R.

Woodcliff Lake, N.J. (Bergen Co.).

Wood Dale, Ill. (Du Page Co.). Promotional.

Woodhaven, Mich. (Wayne Co.). Probably promotional.

Woodlake, Calif. (Tulare Co.).

Woodland, Calif. (co. seat of Yolo Co.).

Woodlawn, Ohio (Hamilton Co.). An oxymoronic term, as it suggests both trees and their absence.

Woodridge, Ill. (Du Page Co.). Promotional.

Wood-Ridge, N.J. (Bergen Co.). Promotional.

Wood River, Ill. (Madison Co.). For a small stream that has now vanished.

Woodside, Calif. (San Mateo Co.).

Woodville, Miss. (co. seat of Wilkinson Co.). Origin uncertain, but locally believed to be descriptive of the heavily wooded land.

WOOD, George Tyler (1795?-1856), second governor of Texas (1847-49).

Wood Co., Tex. (co. seat, Quitman).
Woodville, Tex. (co. seat of Tyler Co.).

WOOD Co., Ohio (co. seat, Bowling
Green). For Eleazer Derby Wood (1783-
1814), an officer in the War of 1812 under
Gen. William Henry Harrison.

WOOD, Joseph, legislator, jurist, and
mayor of Grand Rpaids.
Wood Co., Wis. (co. seat, Wisconsin
   Rapids).
Wood Lake, Wis.
Wood River, Wis.

WOOD Co., W.Va. (co. seat, Parkersburg).
For James Wood (1747-1813), Virginia
soldier, statesman, and Indian fighter who
served in the American Revolution. He was
governor of Virginia (1796-99).

WOODBINE For a flowering vine, probably
either honeysuckle or Virginia creeper.
Woodbine, Ga. (Camden Co.). A claim is
   also made for a plantation owner
   named Flower Woodbine.
Woodbine, N.J. (Cape May Co.).

WOODBRIDGE, Conn. (New Haven Co.),
town. For Benjamin Woodbridge, the town's
first pastor.

WOODBRIDGE, N.J. (Middlesex Co.). For
Woodbridge, Suffolk, England.

WOODBURN, Ore. (Clackamas Co.).
Probably descriptive; *burn* means
"stream," especially in Scotland.

WOODBURY. Descriptive: "wood town."
Woodbury, Conn. (Litchfield Co.).
Woodbury Heights, N.J. (Glouchester
   Co.). Promtional.

WOODBURY, Levi (1789-1851), New
Hampshire statesman. He was secretary of
the navy (1831-34) under Jackson and
secretary of the treasury (1834-41) under
Jackson and Van Buren. A governor of New
Hampshire (1823-24), he also served as
U.S. senator (1825-31; 1841-45) and
associate justice of the U.S. Supreme Court
(1845-51).

Woodbury Co., Iowa (co seat, Sioux City).
Woodbury, Minn. (Washington Co.).
Woodbury, Tenn. (co. seat of Cannon Co.).

WOODBURY, N.J. (co. seat of Gloucester
Co.). For Henry Wood and his son John,
Quaker farmers who founded the place.
Bury is for their former home, Bury,
England.

WOODFORD, William (1735-1780), Indian
fighter and general during the American
Revolution. He died while a prisoner of the
British.
Woodford Co., Ill. (co. seat, Eureka). For
   Woodford Co., Ky.
Woodford Co., Ky. (co. seat, Versailles).

WOODHULL, Maj. Nathan (1722-1766),
soldier, who was given the land for his
service during the early part of the American
Revolution. He served as brigadier general
of the Suffolk and Queens Militia during the
Battle of Long Island.
Woodhull, N.Y. (Steuben Co.).
Woodhull Lake, N.Y.

WOODRING, Mount, Wyo. For Sam T.
Woodring, first superintendent of Grand
Teton Natl. Park.

WOODROW WILSON, Mount, Wyo. For
Woodrow WILSON

WOODRUFF Co., Ark. (co. seat, Augusta).
For William Edward Woodruff (1795-1885),
publisher. He established the famous
Arkansas Gazette.

WOODRUFF, Lake, Fla. For a local settler.

WOODRUFF, S.C. (Spartanburg Co.). For
Thomas Woodruff, at whose home the first
post office was established.

WOODS Co., Okla. (co. seat, Alva). For
Samuel N. Wood (?-1814), career army
officer. He distinguished himself in the War
of 1812 and was killed in action in Canada.

WOODS CROSS, Utah (Davis Co.).
Shortened form of *Woods Crossing*, for
Daniel Wood, founder, who was with the

group led by Brigham Young that came to Utah in 1848. Young, it is said, crossed the Utah railroad into Davis County without permission.

WOODSFIELD, Ohio (co. seat of Monroe Co.). For Archibald Woods, a founder, who furnished a keg of brandy to the men who cleared the site.

WOODSON Co., Kan. (co. seat, Yates Center). For Daniel Woodson, an official in the territorial administration and also a governor.

WOODSON TERRACE, Mo. (independent city in St. Louis Co.). For a local citizen, plus *Terrace,* promotional.

WOODS RESERVOIR, Tenn. For Col. Lebbeus B. Woods (?-1953), active in the development of the Arnold Engineering Center at Arnold Air Force Station.

WOODSTOCK For Woodstock, Oxfordshire, England. The name first appeared in Maine (1689-90). Other names are transfers, probably also influenced by the later publication of the novel of the same name by Sir Walter Scott.
Woodstock, Conn. (Windham Co.), town.
Woodstock, Ill. (co. seat of McHenry Co.). Named by State legislator Joel Johnson for his former Vermont home.
Woodstock N.C. (co. seat of Carleton Co.).
Woodstock, Va. (co. seat of Shenandoah Co.).
Woodstock, Vt. (co. seat of Windsor Co.), town.

WOODSVILLE, N.H. (co. seat of Grafton Co.). For John L. Woods (1791-1855), a lumberman and sawmill owner.

WOODVILLE, Tex. For George Tyler WOOD

WOODWARD, Brinton W., a railway official.
Woodward Co., Okla. (co. seat, *Woodward*).
Woodward, Okla. (co. seat of *Woodward* Co.).

WOODWAY, Tex. (McLennan Co.). Combination of *Midway* and *Westwood,* named at the time of incorporation of the two towns as one.

WOOLSEY MOUNTAIN, Wyo. For Betty Woolsey's father, whose death occurred tragically just before the first ascent of this peak.

WOONSOCKET From Algonquian, probably "at a steep spot."
Woonsocket, R.I. (Providence Co.).
Woonsocket, S.Dak. (co. seat of Sanborn Co.). For *Woonsocket,* R.I.; named by an early settler from there.

WOOSTER, Ohio (co. seat of Wayne Co.). For David Wooster, a general in the American Revolution.

WORCESTER Either for the town of *Worcester* or for Worcestershire, the county in England in which it is located.
Worcester Co., Mass. (co. seat, *Worcester*).
Worcester, Vt. (Washington Co.).
Worcester Mountains, Vt.

WORCESTER Co., Md. (co. seat, Snow Hill). For Edward Somerset, Earl of Worcester (c. 1601-1667), son-in-law of Lord Baltimore. See also SOMERSET

WORDEN POND, R.I. For a local settler.

WORLAND, Wyo. (co. seat of Washakie Co.). For C.H. ("Dad") Worland, an early settler and owner of the Hole in the Wall saloon.

WORMLEYSBURG, Pa. (Cumberland Co.). For John Wormley, a prominent businessman who laid out the town.

WORTH, William Jenkins (1794-1849), career army officer. He was commander of the eighth U.S. Infantry, rose to general

during the Mexican War, and was cited by Congress for bravery. A noted Indian fighter, he had taken part in the Indian wars of the 1830s and 1840s.
Fort Worth, Tex. (co. seat of Tarrant Co.).
Worth Co., Ga. (co. seat, Sylvester).
Worth Co., Iowa (co. seat, Northwood).
Worth Co., Mo. (co. seat, Grant City).
Worth, Ill. (Cook Co.). Some of the citizens were called to duty (1846) in the Mexican War and probably named the village for their leader.

WORTHINGTON For the mother of Mrs. Mary Dorman Miller of Worthington, Minn., whose husband was an officer in a local company and a founder of the town. The Worthington family lived in Chillicothe, Ohio, and was active in Ohio government, one becoming a governor.
Worthington, Minn. (co. seat of Nobles Co.).
Worthington, Ohio (Franklin Co.).

WRANGELL MOUNTAINS, Alaska. For Admiral Baron Ferdinand Petrovich von Wrangell, of the Imperial Russian Navy.

WRAY, Colo. (co. seat of Uuma Co.). Probably for Miss Wray Newell daughter of the local hotel owner. A claim is also made for a Mr. Wray.

WRENTHAM, Mass. (Norfolk Co.), town. For Wrentham, Suffolk, England.

WRIGHT Co., Iowa (co. seat, Clarion). For Joseph Albert Wright (1810-1867), Indiana statesman, or possibly for Silas WRIGHT. Joseph Wright served as both U.S. representative and U.S. senator. He was also minister to Prussia during the presidency of James Buchanan.

WRIGHT, Silas (1795-1847), New York statesman. He served as both U.S. representative and U.S. senator and he was governor of New York (1844-46). See also WRIGHT Co., Iowa.
Wright Co., Minn. (co. seat, Buffalo).
Wright Co., Mo. (co. seat, Hartville).

WRIGHT BROTHERS NATL. MEMORIAL, N.C. On Boddie Island. For Wilbur (1867-1912) and Orville (1871-1948) Wright, American pioneers in aviation. On Dec. 17, 1903, Orville became the first man to fly a motor-powered airplane. The attempt was made from nearby Kill Devil Hill.

WRIGHTSVILLE, Ga. (Johnson Co.). For John B. Wright, one of the antebellum South's largest slave owners.

WRIGHTSVILLE, Pa. (York Co.). For John Wright, the first established settler. He also served in the state assembly.

WRIGHTSVILLE RESERVOIR, Vt. For a local citizen plus *-ville.*

WUPATKI NATL. MONUMENT, Ariz. From Indian, "red ruins in black cinder," descriptive. Established in 1924 to preserve the remains of Indian pueblos.

WYACONDA RIVER, Iowa. From Siouan, "sacred being" or "spirit." It flows southeast into the Mississippi River.

WYALUSING From Algonquian, "old warrior's home."
Wyalusing, Pa. (Bradford Co.).
Wyalusing Creek, Pa. Flows SW into Tunkhannock Creek.

WYANDANCH, N.Y. (Suffolk Co.). For a friendly local Indian chief in the 1600s.

WYANDOT For a tribe of Iroquoian linguistic stock. Their earliest habitation was in the St. Lawrence Valley and Ontario. An unattached tribe, they were driven westward along with the Eries and Hurons; the latter were often confused with the Wyandots. Eventually they settled in Kansas. The tribe was named "snake" by its enemies, but this is a common name given by opponents. Since members of the tribe lived originally on islands in the St. Lawrence River and on a peninsula, the name is thought to mean "islanders" or "those who live on a peninsula." Also spelled *Wyandotte.*
Wyandot Co., Ohio (co. seat, Upper Sandusky).

The Wyoming Valley in northeastern Pennsylvania became famous in 1778 because of an Indian massacre. It has since been overshadowed by the better known state of Wyoming named by settlers with roots in this area. [*New York Public Library*]

Wyandotte Co., Kan. (co. seat, Kansas City).

Wyandotte, Mich. (Wayne Co.).

WYLIE, Tex. (Collin Co.). For Col. W. D. Wylie, an agent for the Sante Fe railroad.

WYMAN LAKE, Me. For Walter Scott Wyman, who was president of the Central Maine Power Company when the dam, which impounds the lake, was constructed in the Kennebec River.

WYNNE, Ark. (co. seat of Cross Co.). For Jessie Wynne (1838-c.1891), Confederate army officer, prominent businessman, and banker.

WYNOOCHEE RIVER, Wash. From Indian, "shifting." It flows south into Chehalis River.

WYOMING From Delaware Indian *maughwauwame*, "large meadows," applied to a valley in northeastern Pennsylvania. The narrative poem *"Gertrude of Wyoming"* (1809) by the British poet Thomas Campbell (1777-1844), concerning an Indian attack on the Wyoming Valley, became extremely popular and led to the use of the name in various localties. When the Wyoming Territory was organized in 1868 from a portion of the old Nebraska Territory, the name *Wyoming*, suggested by Rep. James M. Ashley of Ohio, was chosen over *Cheyenne*.

Wyoming, State of. 44th state of the Union. Settled: 1834. Territory: 1868. Admitted; 1890. Cap.: Cheyenne. Motto: *Cedant Arma Togae* (Let Arms Yield to the Gown). Nickname: Equality State. Flower: Indian Paint Brush. Bird: Meadowlark. Tree: Plains Cottonwood (Balsam Poplar). Song: "Wyoming State Song."

West Wyoming, Pa. (Luzerne Co.).

Wyoming Co., N.Y. (co. seat, Warsaw).

Wyoming Co., Pa. (co. seat, Tunkhannock).

Wyoming Co., W.Va. (co. seat, Pineville).

Wyoming, Mich. (Kent Co.).

Wyoming's castellated rocks and wide expanses are far different from the small, forested Pennsylvania valley from which it takes its name. The site shown in this 1891 engraving is unknown. [*New York Public Library*]

Wyoming, Ohio (Hamilton Co.).

Wyoming, Pa. (Luzerne Co.).

Wyoming Peak, Wyo.

Wyoming Range, Wyo. Named in 1869 after the creation of Wyoming Territory.

WYOMISSING, Pa. (Berks Co.). From an Indian name meaning "place of flats."

WYSOX, Pa. (Bradford Co.). From Algonquian, "place of grapes."

WYTHE, George (1726-1806), Virginia patriot, statesman, and jurist, member of the House of Burgesses (1754-55; 1758-68) and the Continental Congress (1775-76) and a signer of the Declaration of Independence (1776). He was a leading figure in the revision of the Virginia legal code and served as sole chancellor of the Virginia high court of chancery (1778-1801). Among the principal figures in the establishment of American jurisprudence, he numbered among his students John Marshall and Henry Clay.

Wythe Co., Va. (co. seat, *Wytheville*).

Wytheville, Va. (co. seat of *Wythe* Co.).

XYZ

XENIA, Ohio (co. seat of Greene Co.). From Greek, "hospitality."

YADKIN For an Indian tribe of western North Carolina, probably of Siouan linguistic stock. The meaning of the name is unknown.
Yadkin Co., N.C. (co. seat, *Yadkinville*).
Yadkin River, N.C. Flows from the Blue Ridge Mtns. to the Pee Dee R.
Yadkinville, N.C. (co. seat of *Yadkin* Co.).

YAINAX BUTTE, Ore. From Klamath Indian, "Little hill."

YAKIMA For an Indian tribe belonging to the Shahaptian branch of the Shapwailutan linguistic stock and located along the Yakima River in south central Washington. The name is believed to mean "runaway," but the connotation is unclear.
Yakima Co., Wash. (co. seat, *Yakima*).
Yakima, Wash. (co. seat of *Yakima* Co.).
Yakima Indian Reservation, Wash.
Yakima River, Wash. Flows generally SE to the Columbia R.

YAKOBI ISLAND, Alaska. In Alexander Archipelago. Probably for Gen. Ivan Yakobi, Russian colonial director.

YAKUTAT BAY, Alaska. Inlet off Gulf of Alaska. For the Tlingit Indian subtribe.

YALE For Yale University in New Haven, Conn. The university was named for Elihu Yale (1649-1721), an official of the East India Company and an early benefactor of the school.
Yale Lake, Wash. On Lewis River. For a town in Washington, which was named by officials of the U.S. Post Office Department
Yale, Mount, Colo. In Collegiate Range.

YALOBUSHA From Choctaw, "tadpole-little."
Yalobusha Co., Miss. (co. seats, Coffeeville and Water Valley).
Yalobusha River, Miss. Flows S, W, and SW to join Tallahatchie R. to form Yazoo R.

YAMACHICHE, Que. (co. seat of St. Maurice Co.). From Algonquian, "muddy river," for a river that empties into the St. Lawrence River there.

YAMASKA Co., Que. (co. seat, St. Francois du Lac). An Indian word, also rendered as *Ouamaska* or *Hiamaska,* meaning "where there is grass under water," probably descriptive of the extensive marshes in the area.

YAMHILL For an Indian tribe, of Kalapooian linguistic family. The origin and meaning of the name are unknown. It was first spelled *Yamhela,* but has been folk etymologized. The river was named first.

Yamhill Co., Ore. (co. seat, McMinnville).
Yamhill, Ore. (*Yamhill* Co.).
Yamhill River, Ore. Flows into Willamette R.

YAMPA For the yamp (or yampah) plant, genus *Carum,* with edible roots, also called squawroot.
Yampa Plateau, Utah (Uintah Co.).
Yampa River, Colo. Flows into the Green R.

YAMSAY MOUNTAIN, Ore. From Klamath Indian, "north wind."

YANCEY, Bartlett (1785-1828), North Carolina legislator. He was U.S. representative (1813-17) and presiding officer of the state senate (1817-27).
Yancey Co., N.C. (co. seat, Burnsville).
Yanceyville, N.C. (co. seat of Caswell Co.).

YANKEETOWN, Fla. (Levy Co.). Advertising name that succeeded; contrasted with Crackertown, which did not succeed. Named by Northerners in 1925, after it had already been informally so-called by local residents.

YANKTON For the Indian tribe, of Siouan linguistic stock that inhabited the North Dakota area. The name is from Siouan *ihanktonwan,* "end village," probably a site designation.
Yankton Co., S.Dak. (co. seat, *Yankton*).
Yankton, S.Dak. (co. seat of *Yankton* Co.).

YANTIC RIVER, Conn. From Mohegan, "the tide limit." It flows southeast into Thames River.

YAPHANK, N.Y. (Suffolk Co.). From Algonquian, probably "riverbank."

YARMOUTH For Yarmouth, Norfolk, England.
South Yarmouth, Mass. (Barnstable Co.)
West Yarmouth, Mass. (Barnstable Co.).
Yarmouth Co., N.S. (co. town, *Yarmouth*).
Yarmouth, Me. (Cumberland Co.), town.
Yarmouth, Mass. (Barnstable Co.), town.
Yarmouth, N.S. (co. town of *Yarmouth* Co.).

YATES Co., N.Y. (co. seat, Penn Yan). For Joseph Christopher Yates (1768-1837), governor of New York (1823-24).

YATES CENTER, Kan. (co. seat of Woodson Co.). For Abner Yates, donor of the land for the townsite.

YAVAPAI Co., Ariz. (co. seat, Prescott). For a tribe of Yuman linguistic stock, located in western Arizona. The name has been variously defined as "sun people" (*enyaeva,* "sun"; *pai,* "people"), "hill country" (*yava,* "hill"; Spanish *pais,* "country"), and "crooked-mouth (surly) people." The first meaning seems most probable.

YAZOO For the Indian tribe of Tunican linguistic stock that inhabited the lower part of Yazoo River. The meaning and origin of the name are unknown. The tribe seems to have been absorbed into the Chickasaw and Choctaw tribes.
Yazoo Co., Miss. (co. seat, *Yazoo City*).
Yazoo River, Miss. Formed by juncture of Tallahatchie and Yalobusa rivers; flows generally SW into the Mississippi R.
Yazoo City, Miss. (co. seat of *Yazoo* Co.).

YELL, Archibald (1797-1847), statesman, legislator, Indian fighter, and veteran of the War of 1812. He was U.S. representative from Arkansas (1836-39; 1845-46) and governor (1840-44). He was killed at the battle of Buena Vista in the Mexican War.
Yell Co., Ark. (co. seats, Danville and Dardanelle).
Yellville, Ark. (co. seat of Marion Co.).

YELLOW Descriptive of the color.
Yellow Lake, Wis.
Yellow River, Ala.-Fla. Flows SSW into Blackwater Bay.
Yellow River, Ind. Flows SW and W into Kankakee R. Translated from French and Indian.
Yellow River, Wis. Flows NW into St. Croix R. Translated from French, *riviere jaune,* "yellow river," in turn a translation of an Indian name meaning "yellow" for the yellow sand in the lake and river.
Yellow River, Wis. Flows SSE into Castle

Rock Flowage on Wisconsin R.

Yellow River, Wis. Flows SW into L. Wissota.

Yellow Springs, Ohio (Green Co.).

YELLOW DOG RIVER, Mich. Probably translated from an Indian name and transliterated through French, for an incident involving a dog or for the sighting of one. It flows into Lake Independence.

YELLOW MEDICINE Co., Minn. (co. seat, Granite Falls). Translated from the Siouan name for a medicinal plant identified as *Menispermum canadense,* "moonseed."

YELLOWSTONE From French *Roche Jaune,* "yellow stone," the French translation of Indian *mitsiadazi,* "yellow rock river." The river was named first.

Yellowstone Co., Mont. (co. seat, Billings).

Yellowstone Falls, Wyo. In *Yellowstone* R.

Yellowstone Lake, Wyo.

Yellowstone Natl. Park, Wyo. Largest national park in the world. Contains about three thousand geysers, the most famous being Old Faithful.

Yellowstone River, Wyo.-Mont.-N.Dak. Meanders E and NE into Missouri R.

YENTNA RIVER, Alaska. From Tanaina Indian, meaning unknown. It flows southeast into Susitna River.

YERINGTON, Nev. (co. seat of Lyon Co.). For Henry Marvin Yerington, a railway official.

YOAKUM Co., Tex. (co. seat, Plains). For Henderson King Yoakum (1810-1856), military career officer, veteran of the Mexican War, and author of a book, *History of Texas.*

YOAKUM, Tex. (Lavaca Co.). For Benjamin Franklin Yoakum, founder of the town and promoter of the San Antonio & Aransas Pass railroad.

YOCONA RIVER, Miss. From Choctaw, meaning uncertain, although "far reached" and "land, soil, or earth" have been suggested. It flows west into Tallahatchie River.

YOLO Co., Calif. (co. seat, Woodland). For a subtribe of Patwin Indians, of Wintun linguistic stock. The tribe inhabited the area around Knights Landing, Calif. The original form of the name is *Yodoi,* meaning uncertain, perhaps "place where rushes grow."

YONKERS, N.Y. (Westchester Co.). From the possessive form of *jonkheer,* the title of Adriaen Van der Donck, who purchased the land from the Indians.

YORBA LINDA, Calif. (Orange Co.). Combination of *Yorba,* for Bernardo Yorba, son of Antonio Yorba, both early settlers, plus *Linda,* for Olinda, a nearby town.

YORK For James, Duke of York and Albany (1633-1701), later James II of England (1685-88). When the British acquired the Dutch territories in America (1664), those which later comprised the colonies of New York and New Jersey were granted by Charles II of England to his brother James. The territory west of the Hudson River was briefly called "Albania" after the second of James's titles, the area east of the Hudson, "Yorkshire," after the first. When James granted his western territories (now New Jersey) to Lord Berkeley and Sir George Carteret, Yorkshire became known as New York.

New York, State of. 11th state of the Union. Settled: 1614. One of the original 13 colonies. Ratified Constitution: 1788 Cap: Albany. Motto: *Excelsior* (Ever Upward). Nickname: Empire State. Flower: Rose. Bird: Bluebird. Tree: Sugar Maple.)

New York Co., N.Y. (co. seat, *New York*). Conterminous with the Borough of Manhattan in New York City.

New York, N.Y. (co. seat of *New York* Co.). Divided into five boroughs, each conterminous with a county: Manhattan (New York Co.), Bronx (Bronx Co.), Queens (Queens Co.), Brooklyn (Kings Co.), and Richmond (Richmond Co.) on Staten Island.

New York Pass, Wyo. For New York climbers.

New York Mills, N.Y. (Oneida Co.).

New York is known as the city of skyscrapers although Louis Sullivan perfected the steel skeleton form in Chicago, which still refuses to yield to the eastern metropolis in this area. One of the earliest and most beautiful of the skyscrapers was the Flatiron Building, recorded one evening in 1905 by master photographer Edward Steichen. [*Metropolitan Museum of Art*]

For the cotton mills of the same name in the area, which, at the time of naming, were the largest in the state.
New York State Barge Canal, N.Y. Connects L. Erie with the Hudson R.
York Co., Me. (co. seat, Alfred).
York, Me. (*York* Co.), town and village.
York Factory, Man.
Yorkville, Ill. (co. seat of Kendall Co.).

YORK For York, Yorkshire, England.
York Co., Neb. (co. seat, *York*). Either for *York*, England, or for *York* Co., Pa.
York Co., Pa. (co. seat, *York*).
York Co., S.C. (co. seat, *York*). For *York*, Pa. or *York* Co., Pa.
York, Neb. (co. seat of *York* Co.).
York, Pa. (co. seat of *York* Co.).
York, S.C. (co. seat of *York* Co.).

YORK, Charles, Duke of (1600-1649), the second son of James I of England. He later reigned as Charles I (1625-49).
York Co., Va. (co. seat, *Yorktown*).
York River, Va. Flows from the junction of the Pamunkey and Mattaponi rivers to Chesapeake Bay.
Yorktown, N.Y. (Westchester Co.), town. For *Yorktown*, Va.
Yorktown, Va. (co. seat of *York* Co.). Besieged here during the American Revolution by Washington's forces, the British General Cornwallis surrendered (Oct. 19, 1781), thus effectively ending the war and ensuring American independence. The town was again besieged and taken (May 4, 1862) during the Peninsula Campaign of the Civil War by Union General McClellan.
Yorktown Heights, N.Y. (Westchester Co.). For *Yorktown*, Va.

YORK, Frederick, Duke of (1763-1827), second son of George III of England.l.
East York, Ont. (*York* Co.).
North York, Ont. (*York* Co.).
York Co., Ont. (co. seat, Toronto).
Yorkton, Sask. The earliest settlers came from *York* Co., Ont.

YOSEMITE For the local Indian tribe; the name means "grizzly bear."
Yosemite Falls, Calif.
Yosemite Natl. Park, Calif.
Yosemite Valley, Calif. Valley of the Merced R. Named in 1851 by the first white men to enter the valley.
Yosemite Peak, Wyo. So named because its east face resembles some of the giant formations in *Yosemite* Valley.

YOUGHIOGHENY From Algonquian, "meandering stream," descriptive.
Youghiogheny River, W.Va.-Pa. Flows generally NW into Monongahela R.
Youghiogheny River Reservoir, Pa.-Md.

YOUNGSTOWN, Ohio (co. seat of Mahoning Co.). For an early settler, John Young, who moved on west without knowing that one of the great steelmaking cities of the world would be named for him.

YOUNTS, Harry S., a packer for the Hayden Survey of 1878. He climbed the west spur of Grant Teton that year, and in 1880 he was appointed gamekeeper of Yellowstone Natl. Park, thus becoming the first "ranger."
Younts Creek, Wyo.
Younts Peak, Wyo.

YPSILANTI, Mich. (Washtenaw Co.). For Demetrius Ypsilanti (1793-1832), a leader in the Greek war of independence.

YREKA CITY, Calif. (co. seat of Siskiyou Co.). From *Wy-e-kah,* a Shasta name for Mount Shasta. It may also mean "north mountain," as *wai* means "north" in the Wintu language.

YUBA From a Maidu Indian village and tribal name.
South Yuba, Calif. (Sutter Co.).
Yuba Co., Calif. (co. seat, Marysville).

Yubà River, Calif. Formed from three tributaries, North, Middle, and South; flows generally W into Feather R.
Yuba City, Calif. (co. seat of Sutter Co.).

YUCAIPA, Calif. (San Bernardino Co.). Meaning uncertain because of the numerous variations in spelling, ranging from *Ucipe,* which means "evergreen" in Serrano Indian, to *Yucipa, Ucaipa, Yucypa, Yucape,* and up to present spelling. The *-pa* may be from Shoshonean, "water," with *Yucaipa* connoting "wet land."

YUCCA VALLEY, Calif. For the genus of flowering plants that grow abundantly there.

YUKI RIVER, Alaska. Of Indian origin, meaning unknown. It flows northeast into Yukon River.

YUKON From Indian, "the river" or "big river." The river was named first.

The Yukon is best known as the site of the great Klondike gold strike which was celebrated by the Canadian poet, Robert Service. In the heart of the Klondike region lies Dawson City on the banks of the Yukon River. [*National Film Board of Canada*]

Yukon Territory, Canada. Settled: 1842. Gained territorial status: 1898. Cap: Whitehorse.
Yukon, Okla. (Canadian Co.). For the river.
Yukon River, Yukon-Alaska. Flows NW into Norton Sound on the Bering Sea. Named by John Bell, who explored the area in 1846 for the Hudson Bay's Company.

YUMA For an Indian tribe of Yuman linguistic stock in southern Arizona, principally along the Colorado River. The Yumas controlled a land route from Mexico to California and often exercised control to keep settlers from moving into the area, making it possible for the United States to conquer California with a minimum of resistance. After the Gadsden Purchase, the Yuma territory became a part of the United States. The meaning of the name is uncertain; "sons of the river" has been advanced.
West Yuma, Ariz. (*Yuma* Co.).
Yuma Co., Ariz. (co. seat, *Yuma*).
Yuma Co., Colo. (co. seat, Wray).
Yuma, Ariz. (co. seat of *Yuma* Co.). Earlier, San Dionisio, Colorado City, and Arizona City.
Yuma Desert, Ariz.
Yuma Station, iz. aeezUMA Co.).

ZACHARY, La. (East Baton Rouge Parish). For Earl Zachary, a local farmer.

ZANESVILLE For Ebenezer Zane, a founder. His great-great grandson was Zane Grey, the famous writer of Western stories.
North Zanesville, Ohio (Muskingum Co.).
Zanesville, Ohio (co. seat of Muskingum Co.).

ZAPATA, Antonio, an officer in the Mexican army, also a rancher. He was murdered in 1840.
Zapata Co., Tex. (co. seat, *Zapata*).
Zapata, Tex. (co. seat of *Zapata*).

ZAVALA Co., Tex. (co. seat, Crystal City). For Manuel Lorenzo Justiniano de Zavalo (1789-1836), a governor of the state of Mexico who became a Texas Republic patriot and served as a vice-president. He was a signer of the Texas Declaration of Independence.

ZEBULON, Ga. (co. seat of Pike Co.). For Zebulon Montgomery PIKE.

ZEELAND, Mich. (Ottawa Co.). For the Dutch province of Zeeland; named by early settlers from there.

ZELIENPOPLE, Pa. (Butler Co.). For Zelie Basse, daughter of the founder. The ending *-nople* is a rendering of the Greek word *polis*, "city," which was probably influenced by such great names as Constantinople.

ZEPHYRHILLS, Fla. (Pasco Co.). Descriptive of a gentle breeze and a rolling terrain.

ZIEBACH Co., S.Dak. (co. seat, Dupree). For Frank M. Ziebach (1830-1929), publisher of the *Weekly Dakotian*. He seems to have been a local character as well as a solid citizen. During an Indian outbreak in 1862, he received an appointment as captain and in battle stood fast while other officers sought safety. For this he was given the humorous title of "Squatter Governor." There are other versions of this tall story.

ZION For Mount Zion in Palestine.
Zion, Ill. (Lake Co.).
Zion Natl. Park, Utah. Named by Mormons.

ZIRKEL, Mount, Colo. For an early settler or explorer.

ZOAR, Lake, Conn. On Housatonic River. For the Biblical city; from Hebrew, "little," probably descriptive.

ZUMBRO RIVER, Minn. From French, *Riviere aux Embarras*, "River of Obstacles," for the drifting debris. The present form has resulted from attempts to pronounce the French name. Formed by North and South branches, it flows east into the Mississippi River.

ZUNI For the Zuni Indians, of Zunian linguistic stock, who inhabited the largest of

the pueblos, in western New Mexico.
Zuni Indian Reservation, N.Mex.
Zuni Mountain, N.Mex.
Zuni River, Ariz.-N.Mex.
Zuni Pueblo, N.Mex. (McKinley Co.).

Bibliography

Akrigg, G. P. B. & Helen. *1001 British Columbia Place Names*. Vancouver, 1970.

Allsopp, Frederick William. *Folklore Romantic Arkansas*. New York, 1931.

Anon. *A History of the Origin of the Place Names connected with The Chicago & North Western and the Chicago, St. Paul, Minneapolis & Omaha Railways, including States, Counties, Towns, Villages and Stations*. Chicago, 1908.

Anonymous. "Wyoming Place Names," *Annals of Wyoming,* 14-15 (1942-3), 85-90; 323-4.

Armstrong, George, compiler. *Names and Places in the Old and New Testament and Apocrypha*. Revised by Colonel Sir Charles W. Wilson, and Major Conder. London, 1889.

Balcom, Mary G. *Ghost Towns of Alaska*. Chicago, 1965.

Banner, John C. "Some Old French Place Names in the State of Arkansas," *Arkansas Historical Quarterly,* 19 (1960), 191-206.

Barge, William D., and Norman W. Caldwell, "Illinois Place-Names," *Journal of the Illinois State Historical Society,* XXIX (1936), 189-311.

Beauchamp, William M. *Aboriginal Place Names of New York*. Albany, 1906.

Beidelman, William. *The Story of the Pennsylvania Germans*. Easton, Pa., 1898.

Biographical Directory of the American Congress, 1774-1971. Washington, D.C., 1971.

Bloodworth, Bertha. *Florida Place-Names*. Ann Arbor, 1959.

Carlson, Helen S. *Nevada Place Names: A Geographical Dictionary*. Reno, Nev., 1974.

Carter, Rebecca McCormick. *Some Facts and Fancies About Mississippi Indian Place-Names*. University, Miss., 1963.

Cassidy, Frederic G. *Dane County Place-Names*. Madison, 1968.

Chadbourne, Ava H. *Maine Place Names*. Bangor, 1955.

Cheney, Roberta Carkeek. *Names on the Face of Montana*. Missoula, Mont., 1971.

Corley, Wayne E. *County and Community Names in Kansas,* 1962.

DeArmond, R. N. *Some Names Around Juneau*. Sitka, Alaska, 1957.

Dunlap, A. R., and C. A. Weslager. *Indian Place-Names in Delaware.* Wilmington, Del., 1950.

_____. *Dutch and Swedish Place-Names in Delaware.* Newark, Del., 1956.

Ehrensperger, Edward C. *South Dakota Place Names.* Vermillion, 1941.

Ekwall, Eilert. *The Concise Oxford Dictionary of English Place-Names.* Oxford, 1960.

Espenshade, O. Howry, *Pennsylvania Place Names.* State College, Pa., 1969.

Fairclough, G. Thomas, ed. *Nebraska Place-Names,* by Lilian L. Fitzpatrick, including selections from *The Origin of the Place-Names of Nebraska.* Lincoln, Neb., 1960.

Farquhar, Francis P. "Naming America's Mountains—The Colorado Rockies," *The Alpine Journal,* 319-346.

Field, Thomas P. *A Guide to Kentucky Place Names.* Lexington, Ky., 1961.

Finnie, W. Bruce. *Topographic Terms in the Ohio Valley, 1748-1800.* Publication of the *American Dialect Society,* No. 53 (April, 1970). University, Ala., 1970.

Fitzpatrick, Lilian Linder. *Nebraska Place-Names.* University of Nebraska Studies in Language, Literature, and Criticism, No. 6. Lincoln, Neb., 1925.

Fraser, Robert W. *Forts of the West.* Norman, Okla., 1965.

Fullerton, Ralph O. *Place Names of Tennessee.* Nashville, Tenn., 1974.

Fulmore, Z. T. *The History and Geography of Texas, as told in County Names.* Austin, 1935.

Gannett, Henry. *The Origin of Certain Place Names in the United States.* Washington, D.C., 1971.

Gard, Robert E., and L. G. Sorden. *The Romance of Wisconsin Place Names.* New York, 1968.

Granger, Byrd H. *Arizona Place Names,* a revision and enlargement of the edition of Will C. Barnes. Tucson, 1960.

Gudde, Erwin G. *California Place Names.* Berkeley, 1962.

Hanson, Raus McDill. *Virginia Place Names.* Verona, Va., 1969.

Hastie, Eugene N. *High Points of Iowa History,* 1966.

Hodge, Frederick Webb. *Handbook of American Indians North of Mexico.* Washington, D.C., 1910.

Holweck, F. G. *A Biographical Dictionary of the Saints.* London, 1924.

Huden, John C. *Indian Place Names of New England.* New York, 1962.

Kane, Joseph Nathan, and Gerard L. Alexander. *Nicknames and Sobriquets of U.S. Cities and States.* Metuchen, N.J., 1970.

_____. *The American Counties.* New York, 1962.

Kenny, Hamill, *The Origin and Meaning of the Indian Place Names of Maryland.* Baltimore, 1961.

_____. *West Virginia Place Names.* Piedmont, W. Va., 1945.

Kramer, Fritz L. "Idaho Town Names," *Idaho State Historical Society,* Biennial Report, 23 (1951-52), 14-114.

Laird, Charlton. *Language in America.* Englewood Cliffs, N.J., 1970.

Leigh, Rufus Wood. *Five Hundred Utah Place Names.* Salt Lake City, 1961.

Lindsey, David. *Ohio's Western Reserve: The Story of Its Place Names.* Cleveland, 1955.

Little, Charles E., compiler. *Cyclopedia of Classified Dates.* New York, 1900.

Madison, Virginia, and Hallie Stillwell. *How Come It's Called That? Place Names in the Big Bend Country.* Albuquerque, 1958.

Mardon, Ernest G. *Community Names of Alberta.* Alberta, 1973.

Matthews, C. M. *Place Names of the English-Speaking World.* New York, 1972.

McArthur, Lewis Ankeny. *Oregon Geographic Names.* 3rd ed. Portland, 1952.

Meany, Edmond S. *Origin of Washington Geographic Names.* Seattle, 1968.

Mott, D. C. *Abandoned Towns, Villages and Post Offices of Iowa.* Council Bluffs, Iowa, 1973.

Murley, Olga Chadwell. *Texas Place Names: Voices from the Historic Past in a Goodly Land.* M. A. Thesis. Commerce, Tex., 1966.

Orth, Donald J. *Dictionary of Alaska Place Names.* Geological Survey Professional Paper 567. Washington, D.C., 1967.

Phillips, James W. *Alaska-Yukon Place Names.* Seattle, 1973.

_____. *Washington State Place Names.* Seattle, 1971.

Pearce, T. M., ed. *New Mexico Place Names: A Geographical Dictionary.* Albuquerque, 1965.

Powell, William H. *List of Officers of the Army of the United States from 1779 to 1900.* New York, 1900; Detroit, 1967.

Powell, William H. *The North Carolina Gazetteer.* Chapel Hill 1968.

Pukui, Mary Kawena, and Samuel H. Elbert. *Place Names of Hawaii.* Honolulu, 1966.

Ramsey, Robert L. *Our Storehouse of Missouri Place Names.* Columbia, Mo., 1952.

_____. *The Place Names of Franklin County, Missouri.* Columbia, Mo., 1954.

Rayburn, Alan. "Acadia/The Origin of the Name and its Geographical and Historical Utilization," *The Canadian Cartographer,* 10 (1973), 26-43.

_____. *Geographical Names of Prince Edward Island.* Ottawa, 1973.

Read, William A. *Florida Place-Names of Indian Origin and Seminole Personal Names.* Baton Rouge, 1934.

_____. *Indian Place-Names in Alabama.* Baton Rouge, 1937.

_____. *Louisiana Place-Names of Indian Origin.* Baton Rouge, 1927.

Reader's Digest Association. *These United States.* Pleasantville, N.Y., 1968.

Reaney, P. H. *A Dictionary of British Surnames.* London, 1958.

Romig, Walter. *Michigan Place Names.* Grosse Point, Mich.

Rothrauff, Conrad M., ed., *et al. Names,* Journal of the American Name Society. Potsdam, N.Y. 1953-present.

Rudolph, Robert S. *Wood County Place Names.* Madison, 1970.

Rutherford, Phillip R. *The Dictionary of Maine Place-Names.* Freeport, Me., 1970.

Rydjord, John. *Indian Place-Names.* Norman, Okla., 1968.

_____. *Kansas Place-Names.* Norman, Okla., 1972.

Sealock, Richard B., and Pauline A. Seely. *Bibliography of Place-Name Literature: United States and Canada,* 2nd ed. Chicago, 1967.

Seary, E. R. *Place Names of the Avalon Peninsula of the Islands of Newfoundland.* Toronto, 1971.

Seltzer, Leon E., ed. *The Columbia Lippincott Gazetteer of the World.* New York, 1952, 1962.

Shirk, George. *Oklahoma Place Names.* Norman, Okla.,1965.

Stewart, George R. *American Place-Names.* New York, 1970.

_____. *Names on the Land.* Rev. and enl. Boston, 1958.

Swanton, John R. *Indian Tribes of North America.* Smithsonian Institution, Bureau of American Ethnology, Bulletin 145. Washington, D.C., 1952.

Tarpley, Fred. *Place Names of Northeast Texas.* Commerce, Tex., 1969.

Taylor, Isaac. *Names and Their Histories: A Handbook of Historical Geography and Topographical Nomenclature.* London, 1898.

Texas Almanac. Dallas, Tex., 1970.

Tooker, William Wallace. *The Indian Place-Names on Long Island and Islands Adjacent with Their Probable Significations.* Port Washington, L.I., N.Y., 1962.

Upham, Warren. *Minnesota Geographic Names.* St. Paul, 1969.

Urbank, Mae. *Wyoming Place Names.* Boulder, Colo., 1967.

U.S. Department of Commerce, Coast and Geodetic Survey. *Geographic Names in the Coastal Areas of Alaska.* Philadelphia, Pa., 1939-40.

U.S. Department of Interior. *The National Register of Historical Places, 1969.* Washington, D.C., 1969.

U.S. Georgraphic Board. *Sixth Report of the United States Geographic Board: 1890-1932.* Washington, D.C., 1933.

BIBLIOGRAPHY

U.S. Postal Service. *Directory of Post Offices, 1973, 1974.* Washington, D.C.

Vogel, Virgil J. *Indian Place Names in Illinois.* Springfield, Ill., 1963.

Welch, Richard W. *County Evolution in Michigan, 1790-1897.* Lansing, 1972.

Williams, Cynthia, ed. *Ohio Almanac, 1973.* Lorain, Ohio, 1973.

Williams, Mary Ann Barnes. *Origins of North Dakota Place Names.* Washburn, N.D., 1966.

Wraight, A. J. *The Field Study of Place: Washington, D.C.* Washington, D.C. 1954.

Zelinsky, Wilbur. "Classical Town Names in the United States," *The Geographical Review*, (LVII (1967), 463-495.